CW00537046

Edited by Jonathan Downes
Typeset by Jonathan Downes
Cover and Internal Layout by Jon Downes for Gonzo Multimedia
Using Microsoft Word 2000, Microsoft , Publisher 2000, Adobe Photoshop.

First edition published 2016 by Gonzo Multimedia

c/o Brooks City,
6th Floor New Baltic House
65 Fenchurch Street,
London EC3M 4BE
Fax: +44 (0)191 5121104
Tel: +44 (0) 191 5849144
International Numbers:
Germany: Freephone 08000 825 699
USA: Freephone 18666 747 289

© Gonzo Multimedia MMXVI

All rights reserved. Without limiting the rights under copyright reserved above, no part of this publication
may be reproduced, stored in or introduced into a retrieval system, or transmitted, in any form of by any
means (electronic, mechanical, photocopying, recording or otherwise), without the prior written permission of both the copyright owners and the publishers of this book.

ISBN: 978-1-908728-66-1

For Richard, Felix and Jim

Trial begins 22 June
Any information contact Friends of Oz,
39a Pottery Lane, London W11. 01-229 5887.

Introduction

Back in the day, and this particular day was about twenty years ago, I was friendly with a notorious Irish Republican musical ensemble known as *Athenrye*, and particularly with their guitarist, a guy called Terry Manton. I was very angry about a lot of things at the time, and quite how drinking with various groups of slightly dodgy Hibernians actually made me feel any better I am not sure, but it seemed to have the desired effect.

On one of their albums there is a song about Éamon de Valera. For those of you not in the know, over to those jolly nice people at Wikipedia.

"Éamon de Valera first registered as George de Valero; changed some time before 1901 to Edward de Valera; 14 October 1882 – 29 August 1975) was a prominent politician and statesman in twentieth-century Ireland. His political career spanned over half a century, from 1917 to 1973; he served several terms as head of government and head of state. He also led the introduction of the Constitution of Ireland.

De Valera was a leader in the War of Independence and of the anti-Treaty opposition in the ensuing Irish Civil War (1922–1923). After leaving Sinn Féin in 1926 due to its policy of abstentionism, he founded Fianna Fáil, and was head of government (President of the Executive Council, later Taoiseach) from 1932 to 1948, 1951 to 1954, and 1957 to 1959, when he resigned after being elected as President of Ireland. His political creed evolved from militant republicanism to social and cultural conservatism.

Assessments of de Valera's career have varied; he has often been characterised as

Lucky man of our times

<u>Chorus</u>
He was loved he was hated he was cherished despised
There were rivers of tears when the chieftain he died
But love him or hate him I cannot decide
What to make of old Dev this man of our times."

And it ended up:

"Now Spain had it's Franco and France it's De Gaulle
We had our Dev and god rest his soul"

It has been many years since I bounced up and down in a weird Gaelic moshpit shouting "Tiocfaidh ár lá" and I strongly doubt whether I shall ever do so again. My foray into such things had more to do with my reaction to the way that I perceived that I had been treated by my family over my particularly scabrous divorce, than any genuine political fervour, although I thought then (and think now) that the British history in Ireland has not been our greatest or most honourable hour. However, today I have had that song going round and around my head, ever since I read an email from Tony Palmer telling me that Richard Neville had died at the age of 74, in Byron Bay, New South Wales, the Australian hippy enclave where Gilli Smyth breathed her last only a few days before.

Now I never met Neville. Our acquaintanceship was confined to two emails about five years ago when I was working on the new edition of Tony Palmer's *The Trials of Oz*. I exchanged a few more emails with Jim Anderson, and had no contact whatsoever with Felix Dennis, so I cannot really be called an insider of the *Oz* scene. But Neville came out with one of my favourite quotes from the counterculture: "There is some corner of a foreign field that is forever Woodstock", and was an undeniably major figure in that much maligned social movement.

He seemed to be someone who brought out strong reactions in people. Whilst I was working on *The Trials of Oz* I discovered that people were either terribly fond of the man or disliked him intensely. I never found anyone who was ambivalent towards him. Even after his death, as I sent emails around the usual suspects asking for their memories of him, most people refused to be drawn one way or the other, with those who had been friends with him at various periods of their lives being totally devastated that they had woken up this morning to a planet on which Richard Neville was no longer alive.

Me? I am no better than any of the others. I have no knowledge of him personally, and whereas I found large chunks of *Oz* unreadable, I was impressed by his book *Playpower* and in the passages about him in Tony Palmer's book he struck an undeniably heroic figure against the same sort of establishment malice which had (as alluded to above) turned me against my parents twenty years back.

His book *Hippy Hippy Shake* was entertaining, even though its hedonism left a slightly bitter taste in one's mouth, but I remember being told that the movie that was made from it was so bad that several of the major figures portrayed refused to let it come out. In July 2007, in a piece for *The Guardian*, feminist author Germaine Greer vehemently expressed her displeasure at being depicted, writing, "You used to have to die before assorted hacks started munching your remains and modelling a new version of you out of their own excreta." Greer refused to be involved with the film, just as she declined to read Neville's memoir before it was published (he had offered to change anything she found offensive). She did not want to meet with Emma Booth, who portrays her in the film, and concluded her article with her only advice for the actress: "Get an honest job."

So where is this taking me? I truly don't know, but if there had not been a Richard Neville, there might well not have been a *Gonzo Weekly* magazine. I first read *The Trials of Oz* whilst on holiday with my patients back when I was a Registered Nurse for the Mentally Subnormal [RNMS] nearly thirty years ago, and it was one of the sacred texts, together with *A Series of Shock Slogans and Mindless Token Tantrums* by Penny Rimbaud et al, that set me on the path that I am on now. But when I finally read the *Schoolkid's Oz*, I thought it was puerile bollocks, and was massively underwhelmed.

And I too find it hard to adjust to the fact that I have woken up this morning to a planet on which Richard Neville was no longer alive.

So, if I may:

"He was loved he was hated he was cherished despised
There were rivers of tears when the Oz editor died
But love him or hate him I cannot decide
What to make of old Nev this man of our times."

Hare Bol Mr Neville

GOD SAVE US

ELASTIC OZ BAND

OUTCRY AS OZ EDITORS ARE JAILED

Labour MPs attack 'act of revenge'

Daily Telegraph

FURY OVER OZ JAILINGS

Angry MPs join the wave of protest

The Sun

OZ: OBSCENE! BUT WHY THE FEROCIOUS SENTENCES?

Fury as three editors are jailed

Daily Mirror

Oz sentences — Labour MPs sign protest

Daily Express

MPs condemn OZ gaolings as 'Establishment revenge'

The Guardian

Demonstrations and protests against 'Oz' jail sentences

Shocked MPs protest: It looks like revenge

Apple are donating royalties on this record to the Oz Obscenity Fund

STORM OVER OZ SENTENCES

Daily Mail

In Mitigation

So what was *Oz?* And why was it so important?

OZ was an underground alternative magazine. First published in Sydney, Australia, in 1963, a second version appeared in London, England from 1967 and is better known.

The original Australian *OZ* took the form of a satirical magazine published between 1963 and 1969, while the British incarnation was a "psychedelic hippy" magazine which appeared from 1967 to 1973. Strongly identified as part of the underground press, it was the subject of two celebrated obscenity trials, one in Australia in 1964 and the other in the United Kingdom in 1971. On both occasions the magazine's editors were acquitted on appeal after initially being found guilty and sentenced to harsh jail terms. An earlier, 1963 obscenity charge was dealt with expeditiously when, upon the advice of a solicitor, the three editors pleaded guilty.

The central editor throughout the magazine's life in both Australia and Britain was Richard Neville. Co-editors of the Sydney version were Richard Walsh and Martin Sharp. Co-editors of the London version were Jim Anderson and, later, Felix Dennis.

In early 1966 Neville and Sharp travelled to the UK and in early 1967, with fellow Australian Jim Anderson, they founded the London *OZ*. Contributors included Germaine Greer, artist and filmmaker Philippe Mora, illustrator Stewart Mackinnon, photographer Robert Whitaker, journalist Lillian Roxon, cartoonist Michael Leunig, Angelo Quattrocchi, Barney Bubbles and David Widgery.

With access to new print stocks, including metallic foils, new fluorescent inks and the freedom of layout offered by the offset printing system, Sharp's artistic skills came to the fore and *OZ* quickly won renown as one of the most visually exciting publications of its day. Several editions of *Oz* included dazzling psychedelic wrap-around or pull-out posters by Sharp, London design duo Hapshash and the Coloured Coat and others; these instantly became sought-after collectors' items and now command high prices. Another innovation was the cover of *Oz* No.11, which included a collection of detachable adhesive labels, printed in either red, yellow or green. The all-graphic "Magic Theatre" edition (*OZ* No.16, November 1968), overseen by Sharp and Mora, has been described by British author Jonathon Green as "arguably the greatest achievement of the entire British underground press". During this period Sharp also created the two famous psychedelic album covers for the group Cream, Disraeli Gears and Wheels Of Fire.

Sharp's involvement gradually decreased during 1968-69 and the "Magic Theatre" edition was one of his last major contributions to the magazine. In his place, young Londoner Felix Dennis, who had been selling issues on the street, was eventually brought in as Neville and Anderson's new partner. The magazine regularly enraged the British Establishment with a range of left-field stories including heavy critical coverage of the Vietnam War and the anti-war movement, discussions of drugs, sex and alternative lifestyles, and contentious political stories, such as the magazine's revelations about the torture of citizens under the rule of the military junta in Greece.

In 1970, reacting to criticism that *OZ* had lost touch with youth, the editors put a notice in the magazine inviting "school kids" to edit an issue. The opportunity was taken up by around 20 secondary school students (including Charles Shaar Murray and Deyan Sudjic), who were responsible for *OZ* No.28 (May 1970), generally known as "Schoolkids OZ". This term was widely misunderstood to mean that it was intended for schoolchildren, whereas it was an issue that had been created by them. As Richard Neville said in his opening statement, other issues had been assembled by gay people and members of the Female Liberation Movement. One of the resulting articles was a highly sexualised Rupert Bear parody. It was created by 15-year-old schoolboy Vivian Berger by pasting the head of Rupert onto the lead character of an X-rated satirical cartoon by Robert Crumb.

OZ was one of several 'underground' publications targeted by the Obscene Publications Squad, and their offices had already been raided on several occasions, but the conjunction of schoolchildren, and what some viewed as obscene material, set the scene for the *Oz* obscenity trial of 1971.

The trial was, at the time, the longest obscenity trial in British legal history, and it was the first time that an obscenity charge was combined with the charge of conspiring to corrupt public morals. Defence witnesses included artist Feliks Topolski, comedian Marty Feldman, artist and drugs activist Caroline Coon, DJ John Peel, musician and writer George Melly, legal philosopher Ronald Dworkin and academic Edward de Bono.

At the conclusion of the trial the "OZ Three" were found not guilty on the conspiracy charge, but they were convicted of two lesser offences and sentenced to imprisonment; although Dennis was given a lesser sentence because the judge, Justice Michael Argyle, considered that Dennis was "very much less intelligent" than the others. Shortly after the verdicts were handed down, they were taken to prison and their long hair forcibly cut, an act which caused an even greater stir on top of the already considerable outcry surrounding the trial and verdict.

The best known images of the trial come from the committal hearing, at which Neville, Dennis and Anderson all appeared, wearing rented schoolgirl costumes.

At the appeal trial (where the defendants appeared wearing long wigs) it was found that Justice Argyle had grossly misdirected the jury on numerous occasions and the defence also alleged that Berger, who was called as a prosecution witness, had been harassed and assaulted by police. The convictions were overturned. Years later, Felix Dennis told author Jonathon Green that on the night before the appeal was heard, the *OZ* editors were taken to a secret meeting with the Chief Justice, Lord Widgery, who reportedly said that Argyle had made a "fat mess" of the trial, and informed them that they would be acquitted, but insisted that they had to agree to give up work on *OZ*. Dennis also stated that, in his opinion, MPs Tony Benn and Michael Foot had interceded with Widgery on their behalf.

Despite their supposed undertaking to Lord Widgery, *OZ* continued after the trial, and thanks to the intense public interest the trial generated, its circulation briefly rose to 80,000. However its popularity faded over the next two years and by the time the last issue (*OZ* No.48) was published in November 1973 Oz Publications was £20,000 in debt and the magazine had "no readership worth the name".

We are publishing these magazines in these collected editions, partly as a tribute to the late Richard Neville (1943-2016) and partly because we believe that they constitute a valuable socio-political document reflecting the counterculture of 1967-74. This collection has been made available due to its historical and research importance. It contains explicit language and images that reflect attitudes of the era in which the material was originally published, and that some viewers may find confronting. However, we have taken the decision to blank out a very few images which would be seen as unacceptable in today's society.

Times have changed a lot in the past half century. The magazine's obsession with pornography, for example, has not stood the test of time very well, and some of the typography is so muddy as to be unreadable. Every effort has been made by the present publishers to clean up the typography, but in most cases it proved to be impossible, so we have left it as it was. The *Oz* readers of the late 1960s were unable to read it. Why should the present generation be any different?

Some of the pictures in the original magazine, especially artwork by Martin Sharp, was printed so it could fold out into a poster. We have therefore included these twice - as per the original pages so they can be read easily, and as extrapolations of the original artwork. Richard Neville stipulated in the extract from the notorious *Schoolkid's Oz* reproduced below that the material in these magazines could be used for any purpose, and we are taking him at his word.

Peace and Love

Ronnie Rooster
September 2016

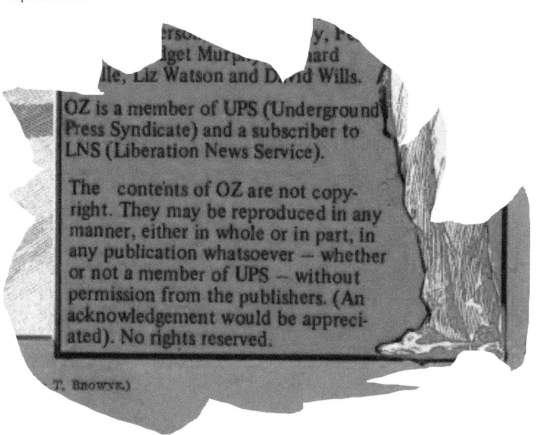

...rso... ...y, ...
...lget Murp... ...ard
...le, Liz Watson and D...id Wills. ...

OZ is a member of UPS (Underground Press Syndicate) and a subscriber to LNS (Liberation News Service).

The contents of OZ are not copyright. They may be reproduced in any manner, either in whole or in part, in any publication whatsoever — whether or not a member of UPS — without permission from the publishers. (An acknowledgement would be appreciated). No rights reserved.

T. Brown.)

LONDON

OZ

2'6

Theological striptease/ turn on, tune in, drop dead/ Why 'New Statesman' editor Paul Johnson is so bloody success- ful /In bed with the...English/Free!... LBJ playmate fold-out/Private Eye?/the Death

of a President/Colin MacInnes & Malcolm X/"Raped Congo
Nuns whipped with Rosary beads"/Yankee Doodles/and so much more in
this first issue of London **OZ**, February 1967...

PANTHER 'a publisher who is steadily producing more and more of the cream of modern fiction' -QUEEN

HENRY MILLER
TROPIC OF CANCER
TROPIC OF CAPRICORN
PLEXUS
NEXUS

JEAN GENET
OUR LADY
OF THE FLOWERS

JOHN BARTH
THE SOT-WEED FACTOR *

JOHN RECHY
CITY OF NIGHT

JAKOV LIND
* SOUL OF WOOD

DORIS LESSING
MARTHA QUEST
A PROPER MARRIAGE
A RIPPLE FROM
THE STORM
* LANDLOCKED

SIMON RAVEN
BROTHER CAIN
DOCTORS WEAR SCARLET
THE RICH PAY LATE
FRIENDS IN LOW
PLACES

WILLIAM EASTLAKE
* CASTLE KEEP

WILLIAM WILSON
* THE L.B.J.
BRIGADE

EDMUND WILSON
* MEMOIRS
OF HECATE COUNTY

CHESTER HIMES
* COTTON COMES TO
HARLEM

B. S. JOHNSON
* ALBERT ANGELO

ANTHONY WARD
* THE RIVER SLEA

* to be published on February 23rd.

COMPLETE LISTS AVAILABLE
FROM PANTHER BOOKS LIMITED 108 Brompton Road, London S.W.3

OZ

[Edi]tor: Richard Neville
[As]sistant Editor: Paul
[...]yson
[De]sign: Jon Goodchild
[Art] Direction: Martin
[...]rp
[Pho]tography: Robert
[...]taker
[Edit]orial Board: Peter
[...]eboer, Martin
[...]ertson
[Con]tributors, Etc:
[...]rew Fisher, Mike
[...]yman, Martin Seymour-
[...]th, Chester, David
[...]nolds, David Widgery,
[...] Munton, Matt Connelly,
[...] Davies, Terry Bunton,
[...]om Hincliffe, and the
[...]y Louise.

[Lon]don OZ' is Published by
[...] Publications Ink Limited,
[...]arendon Road, London,
[...]; phone BAY 0320 or
[...] 8407. Advertising en-
[...]ies should be addressed
[...]ter Ledeboer, 40 Anhalt
[...], SW11

[Lon]don OZ' derives from
[...]— a monthly satirical
[...]azine founded in
[...]ralia in 1963 by Richard
[...]le and Richard Walsh.
[...] (Australia) is still thriv-
[...] with a circulation of
[...]ximately 40,000 and a
[...]heque sent to OZ, 16
[...]er Street, Sydney, with
[...]name and address will
[...]ntee a whole year's
[...]y of this delightful,
[...]y oddity.

Good Vibrations

A gigantic machine has been constructed on the outskirts of the Pentagon. In future American soldiers will not be sent to Vietnam but will be put inside this machine where giant hammers will pound them to a pulp.

The machine will be programmed to take in soldiers at the same rate as the average death rate in the Vietnam war. Thus the machine will in every way be a substitute for the U.S. commitment to Vietnam and—best of all—her soldiers will not have to leave their homeland to die.

To those who have criticised the operation of the machine U.S. Defence Secretary Robert MacNamara says, "Those people sitting there in perfect safety have no right to criticize while our boys are in there dying for us."

On the advice of State Department officials, the Australian Prime Minister, Mr. Harold Holt, has ordered a similar machine to be constructed on the outskirts of Canberra. It will be modified to pulverise at their average Vietnam commitment death rate.

Will Malcolm Muggeridge write for OZ?

[Le]t's hope not. He [al]ready dominates [c]ontemporary [m]edia. Here's your [ch]ance to break [in]to print. Contri-[b]utions are [en]couraged and [wi]ll be paid for. [P]ush hard core [sa]tire, soft core [p]ornography, [ar]ticles, offbeat [ne]ws, *CARTOONS*, [a]nd a stamped [sel]f-addressed en-[ve]lope for return [of] manuscripts — [Lo]ndon OZ, 70 [Cl]arendon Road, [SW].11, London.

OBITUARY—

The novel was pronounced officially dead yesterday evening by a committee of eminent pathologists consisting of Mr. Norman Mailer, Mr. Truman Capote, Mr. Samuel Beckett and Mr. James Joyce. (Mr. Joyce is himself dead, but then so, to one extent or another, was everyone else present, Particularly Mr. Mailer) The committee convened at the Park Lane premises of the Playboy Club for no particular reason. Mr. Mailer put the cause of death down to excessive indulgence in buggery and added that in his opinion nothing could breath life into the inert form but literary necrophilia and even he lacked the energy for that. Mr. Capote dissented, alleging murder for personal profit. Mr. Beckett, asked what did he think was the cause of death, glanced over his shoulder and said "Yes." Asked what did he mean by "Yes," he replied "No." His agent, who was present, fell about the floor laughing and offered world rights to Mr. Beckett's conversation for ten thousand pounds. The corpse, at this point, got up and waltzed out of the door arm-in-arm with Mr. Joyce and two bunnies. None of the four have been seen since, but there are rumours.
Stan Gebler Davies.

Department of malicious gossip

Mr. Michael Randall, who was recently fired for trying to improve the *Daily Mail*, will, as is the custom, receive a considerable sum of money to compensate for the loss of his editorship. This rigmarole is known as a settlement and the point of it is to prevent editors from sueing for wrongful dismissal. On the afternoon of the evening Randall appeared on the Frost Programme, the Frost people inquired if Lord Rothermere would like to appear on the programme to put his side of the case. Rothermere declined to answer before seven in the evening. Randall meanwhile got a phone call from his erstwhile employer. Was he appearing on the Frost show? Would he in that case kindly remember before he said anything displeasing to Lord Rothermere or the *Daily Mail*, that the question of his settlement had not yet been agreed? Mr. Randall hardly said anything on the programme and gossip has it that there will be a transferral of funds in the region of fifty thousand pounds.

THE EXPERIMENT
AT THE NEW
ARTS THEATRE CLUB

SUBSCRIBE TO **OZFAM**

ONLY 30/- FOR 12 ISSUES!

Name:

Address:

I enclose 30/- for 12 Issues:

Signature:

40 Anhalt Road, SW11

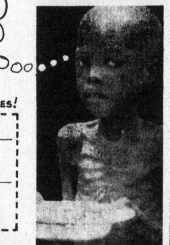

OZ 2

Martin Seymour Smith's 'Teach-in'

OZ talks to Malcolm Muggeridge

The Great Church Confidence Trick

'Wilson in Wonderland' gatefold

Subscribe now or order March OZ from your newsagent

Distributed exclusively in the UK by Moore Harness Ltd., 11 Lever Street. EC1
Printed by
D.G.M. LTD. S.W.7

PhallUSA

from Polly Peachum

Every time a clock strikes the hour (or so it would seem from the vast number of these pictures around) a young man somewhere in the United States is taking off his blue jeans and having his picture taken.

He is taking them off, though sometimes they are left on for novelty, because the last thing the photographer is interested in is his face.

And that's just as well, because where some of these pictures will end up, a man wouldn't even want his chest left on, let alone his face. Why, there are people who have seriously asked to have their navel airbrushed out in case someone recognises it.

A strange thing has been happening to American pornography lately. Until recently, every decent collector prided himself on the wide range of his collection—Xeroxed comic strips, a stack of smudgy photographs and drawings, a carbon copy of a short story or two, all, if nothing else, full, rich and varied, hyperactive and VERY sociable.

Now, suddenly, the togetherness is gone. The action (paralleling a whole trend in underground movies) is non-existent. No second person, let alone third or fourth, in fact, not even a face, arms, legs or too much of a torso is allowed to distract the purity of the viewer's visual experience.

In other words, Pop has finally caught up with *Pornography*. The American collector has turned specialist.

What might be best, but not always quite accurately, be described as still life has completely taken over the field for the moment.

The new pop oriented porno is presented in much the same way. It is not, as in the old days, kept well away from the ladies under lock and key in an old tin box. On the contrary, being respectable still life and a found object, in a sense the pictures are whipped out for ladies at almost any good opportunity and very, very rarely with intent.

(This is partly because most collectors, not surprisingly, have not that much intent for ladies anyway.)

What is surprising, however, is not that these pictorial portfolios exist but that they exist in such numbers and lately to the exclusion of more complex and varied related matter. It is as if all the stamp collectors in the world had suddenly started saving only African stamps and then just those featuring a woodland flower.

Generally speaking, one tends to see them on Sunday afternoons in winter when there is little else to do, often when the original owners are out of town on business or ski-ing and the house has been left in the care of whoever comes to cat-sit, dog-sit or water the indoor plants.

Stored in cardboard boxes or, for starter collections, in manila envelopes, they are usually ten by eight, glossy, not very well lit, invariably over-exposed and always looking as though composition was not on the photographer's mind while he was working. Many, especially those that present both full face and profile, bear an odd and melancholy resemblance to police station mug shots. All that is missing is the number. (In fact, since nature and science often imitate art, they may eventually come to replace, or at least supplement, the fingerprint system.)

All sorts of complicated ethics come into it. Some collectors swear that they would die sooner than take a picture themselves. They see it as decidedly kinky and a form of cheating to boot.

Others, the brisk do-it-yourself types found involved in almost any hobby, carry Polaroids everywhere.

Some think it completely unsporting to expose someone they may have briefly dallied with to the cruel and critical eyes of the collector's world. Others think the exact opposite—that showing pictures of someone they have not dallied with is as unsporting as going fishing and coming home with someone else's catch.

What all the collectors have in common is the bright-eyed eagerness of the schoolboy swapping marbles or baseball cards and it is not surprising to learn that minor variations, like tattoos for in-

stance, carry much the prestige of those lovely cat's eye marbles that always brought in eight ordinary marbles at primary school.

It has been said that to a white man, all Chinese look alike. To the untrained eye then, the pictures—like Andy Warhol's Soup cans, are frankly monotonous with variations that are soon seen to be firmly limited.

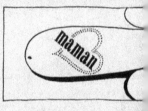

To the connoisseur, however, the man who has trained his eye by going through perhaps a hundred such collections, it is a fascinating world.

The connoisseurs seem to know everything—where each picture came from, what sort of person posed for it and under what circumstances.

Some of the pictures are classics and no collection is considered complete without them. As in other fields, there are stars and superstars. Some of the models are long established, familiar and quickly recognised, professionals. Others are brilliant amateurs.

The professional amateurs (after all, every man has his price) is a recognised classification, as is the obliging friend or acquaintance, who sometimes may never be aware that he has been photographed, let alone near immortalised across the nation, albeit in part only.

Some collectors like these unknowing models best and claim to be able to recognise one immediately.

One of New York's best collections is owned by a top fashion photographer. Someone who does not fully appreciate the finesse of the game might understandably expect him to produce from his particular cardboard box a series of masterpieces in aesthetic tone.

But his collection is as splodged and mottled and scratched and badly printed as any other.

This, he explains impatiently, is just the way he wants it. They should, he says, look amateurish, as if they had been photographed in a moment of feverish preoccupation by one whose mind was not truly on the task.

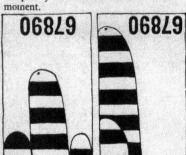

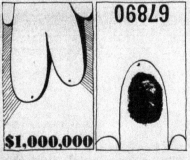

Anything posed, lit, slick or arty, he insists, would be "positively sick" And no one in America ever wants to be accused of that.

With this kind of cinema verité approach, where the medium *is* the message, any picture which shows marks of being a photograph of a photograph of a photograph takes on a special aura, like a chain letter but more so. It puts the whole thing on a national, perhaps even international level.

Collectors like to emphasise how much time and space a well travelled picture might have covered. One soon learns which were taken in Italy by an Illinois friend on holiday; which were part of a classic and, alas, now mostly destroyed by fire, sequence from Mexico; and which are reputedly old Hollywood pictures taken when a now big-name and very happily married male star was a penniless unknown. Anyone who shows scepticism over this last claim is very quickly assured that the original pictures from which these still lifes were taken still circulate from time to time. (No one however seems to have them. Pictures with heads, arms, chests and legs are, in the light of the current fad, passé and not worth keeping.)

But surely, one ventures to ask, faces and the rest provide more excitement and

't that what pornography is about? "Good god," they say indignantly, "we can't do this for excitement!"

It's just a silly fad, a big mad laugh except that, like stamp collectors, you get involved . . ."

that's what's in these days in the unsavoury postcard department. What's out?

Heterosexual pornography. (Well, of course, when it's in all the art galleries, cinemas and paper back book stores already).

The syrupy, biased controversial and previously unpublished account of the tragedy at Dallas; by the self-effacing, establishment licking, contract breaking, money grubbing WILLIAM MANCHESTER is here for the first time ever, brought to you in LONDON OZ . . .

DEATH OF A PRESIDENT

It was on the third day, when He didn't rise again, that Jackie knew for certain the President was dead. During those tense, terrible, tragic hours following the brutal assassination, she had nursed a faint, desperate hope that the days of a Kennedy in the White House were not yet over.

For, as searingly tragic as J.F.K's world-crippling death was (as Jackie was to disclose to me, privately, in an exclusive interview for my epic eulogy, still on tape, remembered and contested), even more shattering was the tragedy of a succession so garishly personified by Lyndon Boofhead Johnson.

She was to recount to me, three years later, in a chic Fifth Avenue salon—manifesting that exquisite, graceful compound of modesty and refined humility that we've come to see photographed so often—she was to recount, clad tastefully in a discreet off-black mini-skirt and obviously still suffering from the grim effects of the previous night's social commitments, she was to recount perceptively, accurately, and in poignant hysterical detail her unforgettable flight back to Washington.

"From the time we left hospital to the time we boarded the Presidential plane, we were still wearing our ensemble splashed by our husband's blood to demonstrate what the masses had done. What piqued us most on the plane was Johnson's effrontery—even during those calamitous moments in mid-air—that he, a mere Vice-President, should presume to contemplate our beloved throne. This is a goal far and away beyond the reach of someone with his looks—even if he

had the money."

Here she wept—movingly, meaningfully, ferociously.

During the flight Johnson begged Jackie to appear in the picture that was to be taken while he took the Oath of Office as President. Magnanimously, she condescended and moved up from the rear of the plane. Now something extraordinary was to happen; something so spellbinding, so sensational that many readers have already heard rumours of it before serialisation of my book. The official photographer's camera failed! There was an embarrassing, agonising delay in the most uncomfortable of circumstances.

It is now known that Johnson took the unprecedented step of contacting the Attorney-General, Robert Kennedy, by telephone from the plane to seek details of the swearing-in ceremony. Details, most of us felt, that could best be ignored. Bobby, quite naturally, greeted Johnson's tactless telephone call with a reaction one would expect from this sensitive college football hero, this old close friend of the late Senator MacCarthy, this sly liberal phone tapper—he said nothing.

What could Bobby do when Johnson, in his ill-bred provincial manner, made maudlin and extravagant gestures of sympathy? He could do—and did—the only thing possible.

He turned his back.

Always, Bobby had worshipped the ground his sister-in-law danced on. It was in the Bethesada Naval Hospital while waiting for the President's autopsy that Jaqueline Kennedy heard of Lee Oswald for the first time. Bobby took her to one side and told her, "They think they've found the man who did it. He says he is a communist." The beautiful black widow responded with her penetrating (Vassar schooled) wisdom, "He didn't even have the satisfaction of being killed for civil rights. It had to be some silly little communist." How unfashionable.

Johnson was a weak and ineffectual Vice-President. So much so, that prior to the fateful Dallas procession, many of the Kennedy entourage refused to ride with him.

Some of Johnson's contemptible defenders point out that Johnson pushed Civil Rights reform through Congress with more vigour and success than his predecessor could have managed. They stress Johnson's achievements in the War on Poverty. But they are wrong. His minor successes here are not due to acumen or energy, they are due to political skulduggery, publicity.

Even now, the Kennedys have not forgotten that dark day in Dallas and they have not forgotten their destiny. And Bobby especially is a dutiful and dapper mourner at his brother's graveside. He has not, and will not, recover from his brother's historic, headline - making murder.

He is crying all the way to the White House.

When you hear an Englishman shouting 'It's going down the drain,' it is odds on that he is referring to the British economy: but, providing he stands somewhere to the left of Enoch Powell, there's a fair chance that he is talking about the New Statesman. This publication has been allegedly seeping down the plug-hole ever since its foundation in 1913. In this it has perhaps followed the fortunes of those whose favourite stamping ground it has been—the British liberal intelligentsia. Notwithstanding the obsequies, its circulation has risen to above 90,000, its readership to 450,000. It is read not only by those of leftish aspect, but also by the far larger section of the populace who, for varying reasons, do not wish to have the Economist, the Spectator, New Society or the Times Literary Supplement as weekly nutriment.

Its editor must therefore be a sanctuary of the British progressive tradition. For many years Kingsley Martin performed this role admirably. Following his retirement the position was assumed by John Freeman, who to the relief of all shortly left to become High Commissioner in New Delhi, an imperial task in keeping with his character. After a short pause, Paul Johnson, at the age of 36, was confirmed as editor. Since his assumption of office the circulation has continued to rise, and standards alleged to have sunk. The make-up has changed: centre pieces have appeared: Levin's voice is heard in the land; Alan Brien holds Private Views.

Johnson himself has the virtues and vices of a pragmatic left-wing journalist. His prose, pleasantly clear and fierce, has been pressed into service in admirable vituperation against American action in Vietnam, mistaken hopes that with the wage freeze Labour Blundered into Socialism, and stern admonitions about the education of, as he would term him, the future Monarch. His early Jesuit training gives his thought a logic, sometimes more acceptable than its premises. While a lot of Catholic writers and pundits have hearkened back to an organic paternalism of medieval design. Johnson prefers to remember the glories of the late eighteenth-century and the high seriousness of the Victorians. There is something about him of a Milner fallen among Fabians. He has little sense of the Labour movement as such beyond its exaltations in the House of Commons.

Personal encounters with him are entertaining. Distant hostility turns out, at closer quarters, to be mere truculence: this can, if all goes well, turn into stiff good cheer.

I WENT TO STONYHURST & THEN TO MAGDALEN. I DID MY MILITARY SERVICE RATHER FOOLISHLY AFTER I WENT TO OXFORD: THE NORMAL THING, INFANTRY, OFFICER CADET SCHOOL, THEN I HAD A YEAR...

...AND A BIT IN GIBRALTAR DEFEN-

ding the rock. I came out of the army and got a job in Paris, working for Realité as a sort of Assistant Executive Editor. That lasted three and a half years, and towards the end of that period I became the New Statesman's Paris correspondent.

Cockburn: And at this time you became interested in socialism?

Johnson: When I was at Oxford I was passionately interested in history, which was what I was reading. When I was up, from 1946 to 1950 Oxford was politically dead, and I took very little interest in politics: it was the same thing in the army. In Paris I met a lot of people on the left bank, where I lived, and we had a great deal of political discussion and I became what I suppose you would broadly call a Bevanite. If one is in a process of intellectual conviction a sudden dramatisation of the forces at work is always influential: I watched the last really big riots in Paris since the war—when General Ridgeway was appointed Nato Commander and there was a whole week of fighting in the streets. It was very horrible. Indeed I was jolly nearly beaten up myself. I was already beginning to be intellectually convinced, to be left wing broadly speaking, and there is no doubt that this was assisted

by what I saw. I never found Marxism in the least appealing, though. You see, I had an orthodox Catholic background, taught by the Jesuits, and once you've been through that particular dogmatic mill and survived it with your mental independence more or less intact, you are not likely to fall for another system which is vaguely similar and which is equally based on a dogmatic view of life. So I've never been a doctrinaire.

Cockburn: Not what Wilson would call a doctrinaire socialist . . .

Johnson: No, not at all, I'm more a pragmatist like him.

Cockburn: On this question of Catholicism, did you lapse or have you always been a Catholic?

Johnson: Well, I've always been very fond of the Catholic Church. It fascinates me, but of course it's very wrong-headed in many ways. And I think the Vatican is an absurd set-up. I think Hilaire Belloc said what could you expect of an organisation run by a lot of Italian clergymen. But one tries to kick them into doing the right thing.

Cockburn: What do you imagine the purpose of the New Statesman to be?

Johnson: Broadly speaking what it was when it was founded. It was started in 1913 by the Webbs and George Bernard Shaw as a sort of Fabian

socialist influence paper, aime[d] primarily at a small elite [of] people, cabinet ministers, leade[rs] of the opposition, M.P.s, seni[or] civil servants, a certain numb[er] of enlightened businessmen, [to] influence them along progressi[ve] lines. Of course, as the Labo[ur] Party gradually established itse[lf] as the chief progressive party [in] the country, it has tended to ai[m] more at that and it has bee[n] loosely associated with th[e] Labour Party, but it has nev[er] been a party magazine. It [is] written by intellectuals, for i[n]tellectuals, trying to influen[ce] people in authority.

Cockburn: Do you feel there [is] a limit to the criticisms you c[an] make of the government, a poi[nt] beyond which you might lo[se] whatever influence you m[ay] think you have on them?

Johnson: This is precisely t[he] tricky thing. We have to achie[ve] the right balance between givi[ng] broad support and, on the oth[er] hand, criticising what one thin[ks] is wrong. It's a razor-edged cl[iff] that one is on, and I don't mai[n]tain I've always got the balan[ce] right.

Cockburn: This kind of suppo[rt] came out most strongly in th[e] piece you wrote after the wa[ge] freeze, called How Labour Blu[n]dered into Socialism . . .

Johnson: Now that was quite i[n]teresting. A lot of peop[le] thought I had been put up [to] this by the government, and [in] particular by Dick Crossm[an.] Quite untrue. I was in Irela[nd] when the bill went throu[gh.] When I got back it seemed [to] me that people had misund[er]stood what could become [the] purpose of this particular poli[cy.] The government had put [the] whole thing through in [a] muddle, rather against th[eir] wishes, and hadn't realised th[at] it could contain the seeds [of] quite an important socialist [de]velopment, which I've alwa[ys] been in favour of, namely [a] social wages policy.

ALEXANDER COCKBURN TALKS TO PAUL JOHNSON

Cockburn: Blunders apart, [do] you think the government p[re]sents any prospect of adva[nce] to socialism?

Johnson: I think this governm[ent] will go where it is kicked. A[nd] we intend to do a great deal [of] kicking. The most fundame[ntal] point is the government's c[on]tinued determination to uph[old] sterling as a world currency. [As] long as they do that, pressu[re] from the city, from internatio[nal] bankers and so forth, are bou[nd] to prevail. I don't think [the] government has a long-te[rm]

ure as a socialist instrument
long as sterling is sacrosanct.
ckburn: But do you really
nk the government will ever
e the guts to do anything
ut sterling, or, on another
nt, to dissociate themselves
e strongly from the Ameri-
s over Vietnam?

nson: They are all tied up
ether, you see. So long as
sacrifice everything to de-
d sterling, you are not in a
tion to have an independent
ign policy.

kburn: You recently said the
nam war was the foulest in
ory. . . .

son: I think it has become
The range and odiousness of
weapons now being deployed
so horrible, used day by day,
great extent on a civilian
lation which has had over
ty years of war. The spec-
of the largest and strongest
r in history hurling itself
all the resources of scien-
technology on this small
ry, is so repulsive as to be
st beyond description. And
ntally, I don't think criti-
of the government for its
ion is useless: it's arguable
if there had not been such
re from the left, we would
ore firmly committed to
ican policy than we now
for all I know, British
would be at present
g in Vietnam.

burn: But you don't always
to have been so against
ry presences. In 1963 you
Statesman readers: "A
h military presence is the
sian Federation's only pro-
against the totalitarian,
alist powers of China and
esia . . . British military
tion offers the best chance
gradual development of
e of the law." Would you
the same sentiments

n: I don't think I would
The fact is, one makes
es and misjudgments. I
back a few years ago over
at I had written in the
and I roughly calculated
had been right 40%,
30% and the other 30%
guable. Any editor who
maintain that he's always
ght is either a fool or a
But I would be prepared
e about those points you
I'm not against a British
presence overseas in all
tances. I don't have any
repugnance about that,
d the people want us
and provided we can
.

rn: On another front, a
people were rather sur-
by your lengthy article
the Royal Family on
to do about Prince
s education—the sug-
ourse seemed almost at
parallel your own—why
write the piece?

Johnson: I thought that it was
very important that anyone who
runs the monarchy should have
a proper education. They've
always been terribly badly educated in the past. I worked it
out on balance that he would get
the best education at somewhere
like Oxford or Cambridge. If
he went to one of the provincial
universities he would be looked
on as such a freak that the whole
experiment would be a failure.
Oxford and Cambridge are much
more used to absorbing curious
characters. Anyway, I think it
was good journalism to raise the
point just before his eighteenth
birthday. It did arouse a lot of
interest, and one hopes that these
things are influential: I've no
doubt it was read in certain
quarters. As a matter of fact the
Statesman has always taken a
great interest in the Royal
Family. We keep a close eye on
these people, and articles we
publish on them always arouse
enormous interest in our readers.
We accept the fact that the
monarchy is going to be with us
for quite some time, and that
being the case, we think it is
only right that the monarch
should be properly advised to do
the right thing.

Cockburn: The Statesman seems
to have gone in for a jauntier,
more personal style recently. Is
this part of a general policy?

Johnson: This kind of impression
arises from the fact that I started
the Centrepiece column. This
was an attempt to revive the
short essay form in which people
like Jack Priestley can expound
their views: secondly it allows a
kind of personalised view of
events, underlying trends in our
society.

Cockburn: But when you have
Levin and Alan Brian bickering
in the pages of the same paper,
don't you think that is getting a
little incestuous?

Johnson: I think it's something
that has got to be done with
great skill and not very often.
This business of over-personalis-
ation is very bad and silly.

Cockburn: People often talk in
very differing terms about the
front and back half of the paper.
Do you see a contradiction between the two?

Johnson: It's awfully difficult to
tell. Most people, to judge from
the surveys, read between 80%
and 90% of the paper. You
can't really say people buy it
for the front or the back. This
is an old myth.

Cockburn: Did your literary
editor, Karl Miller's, resignation
have anything to do with different plans of yours, as far
as the back half is concerned?

Johnson: I'm interested in improving the back half. It has a
great deal of very skilful and
erudite academic reviewing, but
I'm interested in improving the
back half, seeing it appeal more
broadly to people. Indeed, by
the time this interview appears,
you will, I hope, see the beginnings of changes.

Cockburn: Now you are the
father figure of the Statesman,
discoursing weekly in the diary
and other pieces, what kind of
image of yourself do you imagine
the readers are getting?

Johnson: God knows. That's not
for me to say. Writing a weekly
diary is an exercise in egotism.
It's bound to be. If you don't
reveal a certain amount of yourself then the thing is dull. And
if you do reveal bits of yourself,
then to some extent you hold
yourself up to ridicule. I get a
lot of that.

Cockburn: Yes, you recently described how you had a tussle
with the police after some Suez
demonstration and then went
along to the Ritz and had a
button sewn on by a waiter.
Did it surprise you that people
thought this funny?

Johnson: It was meant to be
funny. I knew they'd think it
was funny. It was true. I
thought it was quite comic,
though I'm bound to say I
thought it was a perfectly sensible thing to do, because in
those days the Ritz gave you a
jolly good tea for 4s. 6d., a good
Socialist tea.

Cockburn: Again, you've attacked
the Beatles, Francis Bacon, got
quite worked up, indeed . . .

Johnson: I just write the diary in
the way I would ordinarily write
a diary. I think the whole of
the pop music thing is deplorable
and I said so, and I got into
frightful trouble for saying so.
I still get a lot of trouble from
it. As for Francis Bacon, I like
him and think he's an extremely
nice man and very talented. I
just happen not to like his paintings, along with a lot of other
people.

Cockburn: You thought you
were going to be prime minister
when you were twelve. Were
there any other transitional
ambitions, before the climax, as
editor of the New Statesman?

Johnson: At one time I wanted
to be a don. At another I
wanted to be an art critic. In
fact I wouldn't mind ending my
days as an art critic, it's always
seemed a marvellous occupation . . .

Cockburn: Voicing opposition to
Francis Bacon, no doubt.

Johnson: Not necessarily, but
putting a different point of view,
maybe, to the one generally held
today. I think it's possible I
might still go into politics. I
don't know. I can't see myself
editing the Statesman indefi-
nitely, and I don't think anyone
would want me to do so. After
one's been doing it a maximum
of ten years, one ought to go,
provided one has trained a good
successor.

Cockburn: So you're safe till
1974 . . .

Johnson: I don't want to lay
down any deadlines, otherwise
continued on page 17

(Paint it Black)

One of the more endearing sides of Cassius Clay's nature is that he abhors violence. He has told Uncle Sam in no uncertain way that he is not prepared to go and slug it out with the Vietcong.

It's something Cassius has in common with nearly all of us. Some of us think it would be better to stop raining napalm on Uncle Ho's venerable head. Others just think throwing bottles at the referee gives soccer a bad name. But we are against violence. Just ask any of us.

Of course it doesn't stop us enjoying a bit on the side. (Okay, Mrs. Whitehouse, you can start taking notes here.)

We sit slate-eyed in front of the television set while a steady stream of clean-jawed heroes marches off to blow somebody's brains out.

Sit through "Thunderball" with a stop-watch and you'll find sex outstripping violence three to one.

Books are going the same way too. The market researchers say sex we can take or leave, but violence runs to six editions with paperback publishers clamouring for the rights and no one accepts a penny under £50,000 for the film.

None of this worries me much. (Okay, Mrs. Whitehouse, you can put that notebook away.) If we all want to get our twilight kicks from an endless stream of thudding fantasies, who am I to argue?

What does bother me is the way violence is becoming a journalistic formula for instant excitement.

Take the perfectly ordinary situation which develops at 3.15 every Tuesday and Thursday afternoon in a large meeting hall in Westminster.

Two middle-aged gentlemen, their silver hair gleaming, sit on opposite sides of a largish table and argue. They do this in a way that would leave Emily Post speechless with admiration.

Each calls the other The Right Honourable Gentleman. Failing this, they call each other the Prime Minister and the Leader of the Opposition. Sometimes they are rude to each other.

One says the other is a bully. And he is told no one would be so cowardly as to bully him.

But it is all done with unfailing restraint, and the nearest hint of violence is an occasional bellow from the extras in the stalls.

How is all this reported to you? Have a look at some quotes:

"**He** (Mr. Wilson) **diverted attention by attacking the Tory leader Mr. Edward Heath with what even many of his own supporters thought was needless savagery.**" (Daily Express 4.11.66.)

Hot dog! The bleeding and insensible body of Mr. Heath was presumably dragged from the Chamber by his sorrowing supporters, amid cries of "Shame" from horrified Labour benches.

But the Tories were not to be outdone. According to the same paper eight days later Mr. Enoch Powell "**lashed out at government by intimidation.**" The issue of individual liberty "**came to the boil**". But the Attorney-General, who had been "**under fire**", sharply defended the record of his party.

The idea of Mr. Powell, an amiable and peaceful man if ever there was one, lashing out at anybody is nothing short of preposterous.

The list could go on. In recent months I can recall sundry Members of Parliament being whipped, lashed, hammered, clobbered, battered, slammed and, on one celebrated occasion, cut to pieces.

It goes without saying that the carnage extends well beyond Westminster. The impending earthquake around Manchester, discovered by the headline writer of the Daily Sketch, went unreported elsewhere. "**Granada-land to be split in biggest ITV shake-up,**" he thundered.

Others? How about: "**Consumers attack the decimal £.**" What with, one wonders. Or: "**Union chiefs hit out in pay rules storm.**" The thought of Mr. Clive Jenkins and his cohorts flailing along through a blizzard of bound copies of the Prices and Incomes Bill is a delightful one, also from the fertile pens of the Daily Sketch. "**UNO slaps on oil ban,**" said the Daily Express. Just like sticking on labels, really.

These headlines were, of course, sandwiched between the usual rapes, murders, and bashings which are part and parcel of every newspaper. (I have not yet seen a headline to beat one which appeared in an overseas afternoon newspaper, a veritable tour de force of sex, sadism, race, religion and politics. "**Raped Congo nuns whipped with Rosary beads.**")

But the point about the political and other headlines is that in an essentially non-violent situation they had to draw on violent images to sound exciting. It's a pretty miserable reflection on the lot of us that we can't record a Tory censure motion without having to drag out the metaphorical machine guns and make it sound like second billing to the St. Valentine's Day massacre.

This isn't an argument for the kind of headline The Times specialises in—"**Mild earthquake in Chile, no many dead**". Nor is it an argument for the weary, defeated headline writer of the Guardian who once labelled a Victor Zorza story: "**Another reshuffle in Khazakastan**".

I suppose what I have to come round to is some newspaper equivalent of the peacemakers' slogan "Make love, not war". If only we could get a bit of sex into those stories to replace the violence we might be able to save the Sun, Sketch, Mail, Standard, Guardian and Times from whatever dreadful fate awaits them at the moment.

So let's take a straightforward account of a parliamentary debate as it might be reported now. "Mr. Heath," it might begin, "last night lashed the government for its failure to make Chatham House grammar school a national shrine. In a hard-hitting attack on the Home Secretary, Mr. Heath hammered away at Mr. Jenkins' alleged neglect in allowing escaped prisoners to use it as a staging post on the way to Europe. A bedraggled Mr. Jenkins was forced to admit that this was true, but he struck back by declaring that it had also been used for hash parties by Pakistani tax-evaders during Henry Brooke's spell at the Home Office."

by Nigel Stone

Under my new system it might be something like this. "Women Cabinet ministers swooned last night after a breathtaking speech by the Leader of Opposition, Edward "call me Casanova" Heath. His handsome grey hair glowed in the soft light of the House of Commons, the 49-year-old bachelor huskily wooed his audience with a seductive plea for the creation of a national shrine at Chatham House grammar school. Heath's lithe figure at the dispatch box seemed to dominate the Chamber as he dealt gracefully with the Home Secretary, Mr. Roy Jenkins. The rugged Mr. Jenkins himself had Tory backbenchers sighing as he replied smoothly to Mr. Heath's points, reminding the Opposition Leader that Chatham House had been used, etc., etc."

Well, at least it's an idea.

PRIVATE EYE

1/6

Bloody Ingrams can pose for the next one himself!

PRIVATE EYE
SWALLOWS
ITS
WORDS
amazing
picture

Gerald Scarfe

eyewash (I–wosh)n. lotion for the eyes;
(sl) humbug; pretence; flattery.

Penguin English Dictionary.

A Genuine Apology 29 April 66
PRIVATE EYE & MR ELKAN ALLAN

In the issue of Private Eye dated November
26th. 1965 we published an anonymous article
about Mr. Elkan Allan, the television producer
and scriptwriter.
We now realise that this article was based
on misinformation and went a long way past
our intention to poke fun. We now see that it
was unfair, malicious and damaging to Mr.

Gnome

Dear Readers,

the 'persons' I hire to produce
this rubbish have become so obsessed with so-
called 'serious' journalism, that they constantly delude themselves that they "Do Good"with
their witless exposes. In doing so, they, in
typically self contradictory fashion, have
adopted the intolerant totalitarian manner
for which I am justly famous. Gnomism
flourishes and I get no credit for it. I am
getting out of hand.

Yours very 'seriously',

Lord Gnome,

pp.OZ.

MISS
SAGBUM !
TREAD SOFTLY
FOR YOU TREAD
ON MY JOKE

Sales of PE Things have been slow. In
an effort to redress the imbalance between
income and expenditure - the readibility
gap - PE's Editorial Board and sundry Ad
'mins' took to the bawds last Sunday evening at the Royal Court. Having assured
themselves that all proceeds would be
equally divided between both North and
South - London members of the board, a
reading of the Best of PE took place. The
half minute's silence which followed,
appeared to baffle a small audience.

Berating them for their indifference to
theatrical artifice, the first speaker, (a
dandified person evidently mimicking Lord
Mountbatten,) sat down abruptly to cries of
"Go bag your head," from the front stalls.

No, I wouldn't say our approach
was entirely negative.

A second speaker then volunteered to
"keep the ball rolling" with an unillustrated
explanation of past cartoons. Confronted
by escalating audience apathy, he
apologised, "Much funnier when you actually
see them." The audience expressed some
disbelief.

At this, a portly young man in a rather
tweedy hat announced he would "liven things
up" and shouted, "Piss,bum,poop, old
droopy tits," into the mike. Rather ostent-
atiously a scrawny matron left the hall.
She was later identified as a Madame
Barrie Humphries. "That's the first
funny thing you've said all night", said
someone in the third row. Whereupon the
young man sat down (or rather wrinkled the
crease behind his fat knees a little more ,it
amounts to the same thing) evidently
embarrassed.

2 Sept. 66
MR. PERCY CLARK. An apology.

We apologise to Mr. Clark for any incon-

A large brooding person now began to
outline PE's committment to social purposes
and its editor's aim to influence contemporary events. In the midst of this speech, a
gent in row five farted loudly. At which the
entire cast descended upon him to effect a
citizen's arrest, charging him with both
pla giarism and infringement of copyright.
In the ensuing fracas the'performance'
ended with spirited audience participation.

4 March 66
"Private Eye" wishes to apologise to Mr.
McGrath and to Mr. Stonehouse for any
embarrassment or injury to their reputations
which they may have suffered as a result of
any inaccuracy in this article.

Henry Masterman, gardening correspondent
for the Daily Telegraph. His name a house-
hold word you say? The only man within the
context of that hysterically right wing organ
who appears to have maintained an oasis of
political impartiality? If that is the case
then no one can begrudge him his success.

Yes, Masterman does live in a modest semi-
detached house in suburban Acton with a "wife"
and three children. But, although he bought
this house fifteen years ago, Masterman has so
far not shown himself ready to tell Private Eye
where the money came from. His failure to
send this information unsolicited to Private Eye
in anticipation of this article can be nothing else
than a straight forward admission of guilt.

Even so, having said all that, Masterman
would still seem to be a person that any
reasonable man, whatever his political outlook, would appreciate as a next door neighbour.
We can report however, in all fairness, that
Henry Masterman is a swine. And is as two
faced as the insane fascist rag he writes for and
that I and all other reasonable men use to wipe
our bumholes with — and proof.

Unlike Masterman we can back up our statements. First. His dog. Why does Masterman keep a dog that constantly barks to the annoyance of his neighbours? This is no malicious fantasy on our part. We have found the dog barking on every occasion that we have entered Masterman's premises for the purpose of observing the dog. This is particularly true late at night, a time when all honest men are asleep.

And his compost heap. One realises that Masterman must use one in the course of normal gardening activities. But need it be so large? Might not this one be used for more sinister purposes? When confronted in the street by our members of the Private Eye staff and cross-examined about the compost heap, Masterman's six year old child seemed both evasive and frightened. Masterman's way of life is liberal and tolerant to a dangerous extreme. *delete* Although these undeniable facts show Masterman's cleverly worded gardening articles to be a fraud, nevertheless in all fairness we must admit that he is probably married to the woman who poses as his wife. But as our close surveillance of his house has shown, this doesn't stop another completely different woman from visiting Masterman once a week at an unusual hour. Subsequent enquiries produced the prevaricating and ambiguous reply from close associates of both parties that the woman was Masterman's mother. Does this seem likely when Masterman is reputedly Anglo-Saxon and his "mother" has red hair? More than that, since Masterman's "wife" has occasionally been present at these sinister Sunday lunches, it would seem that the "wife" too is implicated. The coincidences mount up but the beer halls of Munich once looked as innocent.

Even the three young children living with Masterman and his associate/"wife" do not escape the corrupting hands of this monster. Masterman has been seen by our correspondent with a *towel eagerly wiping* the hot, wet and barely naked body of the youngest of these unfortunates. The eldest can be seen bringing other uniformed youths back to the Masterman *sties* and there has been as many as *eight young* *men* in the house at the one time. Yet the authorities still do not move.

delete I do this myself.

Words by
Barry Humphries *check political affiliations of Boy Scouts.*

THE EYEING OF THE PRIVATES

In the Conqueror's reign, the court jester earned himself a fee simply by performing his celebrated simultaneous leap, whistle and fart, each Pancake Tuesday. The custom survives. Each Tuesday fortnight, certain of Her Majesty's simples earn themselves a fee of 1/6 (and multiples thereof) as they perform a similar act, now known as the Eyeing of the Privates.

The ramifications of the revived custom are best explained by self styled 'editor' Ingrams – the Corporal in charge of Private Eye. "We see our job as taking the mickey, the moses and in some (integrated) cases the rastus out of everyone. Well, that is, everyone who is Someone. Establishments are defined by their critics, assured of an eminence from which to be tippled, ah, toppled. Hence our own particular licence is really licensed I suppose. Establishments relish cock and old balls. And in this respect, I think we can rightly claim to have courted favour assiduously.

Yet I suppose we started as a sort of New Satirical Express, cataloguing Pop of the Top People. Once upon a time, you know, it was trendy to have been attacked by us. Lately, of course, we're more whipping boys. But then we've all heard of the kiss of the lash, dear.

But we've never equivocated. We've always taken a point of view. Look Back in Anger gave us that point of view and for six long years we've done little else. That we have been boring repetitive is of course another issue. In fact, often was the next issue.

Now the public are a little satired of it all. But I think I'm confident in saying our share-cropping of the Fourth Estate has meant something. To a discerning populace, due to our efforts, Disestablishmentarianism has added up to something new, Anti-Disestablishmentarianism."

O'Booze

WHAT KIND OF MAN IS PITMAN?

In a frank, outspoken attack, Lunchtime O'Booze, Britain's most fearless columnist, answers this question in his own inimitable way:

Robert Pitman

IN
MY
OPINION
IS A SHIT

So much for satire!

RODNEY BENNETT-ENGLAND
A CORRECTION

11 Nov. 66

We apologise to Mr. Bennett-England for any inconvenience he may have suffered as a result of this article.

BARRY McKENZIE

Drawings by
Nicholas Garland

Much of what makes 'Private Eye' boring and ineffectual is parabled in the dogged tussle for power waged these last eighteen months between the present editor, Richard Ingrams and immediate editor emeritus, John Wells. Wells is an ex-Eton master who relishes his strong personal connections with minor royalty and really wants to be a celebrity - unlike Ingrams, despite his former period of facile punditry on swinging London. Typically 'Old Pal', Wells tried to stifle 'P.E.'s' farts at Meg because, as he put it, she couldn't answer back.

Ingrams loathed Son of Bumhole and Wells covered himself by writing bitter gossip about it. He was billed once in 'P.E.' as 'Literary Influence' and was later relegated to mere 'Contributor' after a putsch by Ingramites on the Board. Wells took to writing idiotic T.V.criticism for the Daily Mail and is currently the best of a bad lot on the 'Late Show'. He also pens two columns of 'Afterthought' for the 'Spectator' which is mostly belated gossip about media and the posh parties he attends and delivered in a prose style for which he has at least had the humility to apologise.

'Private Eye' still reeks of this old guard bumhole element who are eternally adolescent and self-consciously upper class...the sort of inept and arrogant T.V. debators which public schools now manufacture instead of Major Generals.

The William Rushtons and Christopher Bookers who are responsible for the Blue Records, the Dirty Book and 'P.E.' things. ...all the classic revue satire stuff that bright young aristos have been titillating each other with for years. Rushton, for example, was once employed on the I.T.V.extravaganza, 'Stars and Garters' as resident dirty comic and was so awful - even by I.T.V.standards - that he was fired. 'P.E.' retaliated with an ill-written diatribe against the show's Elkan Allen who had despised Rushton and dubbed him 'Ginger Judas''. They were compelled to retract and publish their usual licking apology. Rushton, incidentally, is currently in Australia posing as the brains of Greek Street satire and frantically marketing other people's stale 'P.E.' jokes (much to the irritation of Ingrams, who likes to save them for Oxbridge debates). Rushton's new found employer is Sir Frank Packer, unenlightened monopolist, whose vast press, radio and T.V. media grind out a philosophy somewhat to the right of Robert Pitman's.

So much for satirical conviction.

Not that anti-bumhole paranoic, Ingrams, is concerned much with satire anyway. He often rejects cartoon contributions for being 'too satirical'', requesting "whimsy" instead. He is not above staging office tantrums in front of visitors to embarrass Tony Rushton, amiable business manager, into raising his £30 weekly salary.

ILLUSTRATED
LONDON
NEWS

IT'S ALL GREEK ST.

A huge, somewhat scarred figure, he sallies forth from his rose-covered weekender, astride an imposing iron bicycle to tilt mightily at the treadmills of Fleet Street. The Ray Gunter of satire, Ingrams sees himself as the Messiah of 'Private Eye', is tautly religious about its continuation but in practice has proved all Exodus and no Revelations. His persistent vision is to print the sort of hard reportage of political malfeasance that distinguishes 'Der Spiegel' and 'Le Canard Enchaine'. With rare exceptions (e.g. Hanratty) he has, of course, failed.

His attempt to politicise 'P.E.' resulted in the recruitment of Claude Cockburn and Paul Foot - both bitterly resented and boldly resisted by the bumhole boys.

Cockburn's 'This Week' is hardly the coruscating, witty moulder of society's opinion that Ingrams hoped it would be. The envisaged Thunderer role emerges as rather the sound of one hand clapping: largely because the ruined Limerick mansion Cockburn writes from is not Cliveden and he is no Nancy Astor.

Ingram's second appointment was more hopeful. Paul Foot, Mandrake of the Sunday Telegraph, and source of all those contemptuous stories about laughable editor McLauchlin (now retired) was brought in as effective political editor. Ingrained aristocrat and past President of the Oxford Union, he fitted-in to Greek Street well. A journalist and author of a heavy-handed Penguin on race relations, he introduced relatively well-informed and irreverent but principled information on a number of occasions.

Never popular at the "Telegraph", Foot is soon to move permanently to 'Private Eye' where he will double the back page output.

Apart from the odd useful piece of information that slips through, Ingrams has never really had the staff or sources able to yield anything more than personal slanders. 'Colour Section' and 'London Illustrated News' lack real facts and compensate for this ignorance with a peculiar, literary cannibal style.

Occasional bitter feeds are sent by disgruntled Transport House research staff, fired P.R. men and barroom world correspondents. Often 'P.E's' political

THE ONLY MAGAZINE WHICH DOES NOT CONTAIN BORING ARTICLES BY COLIN MACINNES

correspondents. Often 'P.E's' political expose's consist of bitches at G. Kauffman by those of Wilson's aides who are jealous of him.

However, the days of its wild political irreverences are numbered. It is said that a gentleman's agreement has been reached between 'P.E.' and establishment celebrities, the quid pro quo being milder satire for a less sensitive response to libel.

Most of the brilliant and able undergrad generation have abandoned 'Private Eye'. Miller and Cook are busily sustaining their reputations for being rich and clever without doing much except boosting each other on T.V. guest appearances.

Final estrangement between Miller and 'P.E.' came when the mag vomited some drivel about pooves (Ingrams is still obsessed by homosexuality) allegedly written by Dr. Jonathan Miller. The good doctor responded with an angry, hurt letter (now pinned on the office walls) hoping they would "rot in hell" - a quote subsequently reproduced on the cover of Penguin Private Eye.

Cook still sweats over archetypal Cook comedy and is a staunch supporter of the mag although caught up in his self indulgent success spiral. Hence the sad 'Wrong Box', tedious guest appearances on the late R.S.G. and drab visual gags on telly. His country mansion and Chrissy presents glamourise the colour supplements, likewise his fashionable wife: "it would be fun to give a party with a roast sucking pig for an American friend"; ho, ho, her in the "Sunday Times'.

* * * *

Some argue that 'Private Eye' is still the most agreeable thing in print, despite its petty nihilism, stubborn inaccuracies and the self indulgencies of its staff. It is just these factors, however, which have prevented 'P.E.' from achieving any importance.

Even if it doesn't want to, it has become part of the paraphernalia of swinging London; entrapped as an artifact of glossy society which longs to be attacked in this painless gossipy way by its own class and in its own terms of amusing titter and bicker.

It is not surprising that 'P.E.' is subsidised from the pocket money of such outspoken, anti-establishment, radical intellectuals as Jane Asher, Lady Bonham-Carter, Bob Monkhouse, Anthony Blond, Peter Sellers, Joyce Grenfell........

So controversy between Cook and Frost becomes staple of colour supplement public quarrel; Mrs. Cook becomes an ikon of contemp kitch; Ingrams appears as both evidence and anti-image of London's brilliance; Greek Street continues to market tasteless, embroidered gimmicks.... all as significant as an empty cellophane bag.

'P.E.' is Andrex pretending to be Kleenex; Tampax pretending to be Durex.

THEOLOGICAL STRIPTEASE

-Kit Mouat

no terms save those of an essentially mixed-up society can the strip-tease form entertainment make sense. But today there is another kind of "stripping" which is gaining popularity, and that is the intellectual stripping of modernist Christians who are discarding their theological veils one by one. "The Fall of Man," "the Devil," "God the Father," the Virgin Birth," "Hell" and even the "Incarnation" lie crumpled at the performers' feet, while they clutch desperately at the remaining flimsies of "Ultimate Reality" and "Unique Christian Love." Sometimes it seems that the it may be developed so that these, too, be tossed aside—if only to attract a more sophisticated audience; but when this does happen, it is hushed-up as much as possible. Generally the fear of complete exposure is as acute as ever it was.

Malcolm Muggeridge is the Gipsy Rose Lee of these strippers, fluttering his eyelids—now towards the Roman Catholics and now at the Anglicans, pretending to drop a veil, then clutching it all the closer to him as he croons:

"It's edu-edu-cation
That's ruining the nation . . ."

and drawing larger and larger crowds. His fans include Mary Whitehouse, but only since he started having his veils made of red flannel. And then there is his special performance when the stage is lit only by "glow worms," shining with an intrinsic light" while he is caught in all-encompassing radiance. the dust in a sun-beam." Some people might suggest, unkindly perhaps, that he is getting just a little beyond it now, and must surely be able to afford a comfortable retirement from his rather pitiful intellectual antics. There are plenty to carry on with his work.

Several highly paid stars (John Robinson, for one) actually perform in church, although they do the show in reverse, arriving part-exposed at the door, humming,

"God is superfluous . . .
God is dispensable . . .
God is intolerable . . ."

and then picking up the veils one by one as they go down the aisle, ready to recite

"I believe
in God the Father Almighty,
Maker of Heaven and Earth . . ."

with their delighted audience. Others have their own groups such as the "Christian Humanists," the "Christian Agnostics" and the "Secular Christians": but top of the pops are probably the lively little company of "Cambridge Theologians." Most of the performers are men, strangely enough, but Monica Furlong is an exception. Some years ago she admitted that stripping (or "being a Christian," as she put it) was "intellectually more exhausting" than it had been for years. There is no doubt at all about that; it is exhausting, even for the audience, if they take it all as seriously as they should. Monica gives a very sexy performance, one has to admit, but she has not yet dropped the last veil, which seems to be made of very old Irish linen. The idols of these modern strippers are of course Tillich, Bonhöfer and Barth, who play much the same sort of role as do Nijinsky and Pavlova in the hearts of balletomanes.

So far very few complaints have been made about "Stripping on the Telly." It says something for the tolerance of our age that these performances are allowed to come right into our homes. In such a way the Man in the Street (and his wife) can be made to feel part of the sleazy

underworld of the mind; they can watch others doing what they secretly long to do themselves, but without being tempted to go too far. If any viewers are disturbed it will be, I suppose, those Spaniards and Italians and Latin Americans to whom all the veils are sacred. Dropping even a few of them (in their view) is to risk a most unnatural sort of revelation. Billy Graham is especially intolerant; but then he hasn't yet got used to the mini-skirt. Fortunately no one really takes him very seriously. They just let him have Earl's Court, the freedom of the radio, TV and the press, and then leave him to get on with it.

Inevitably some criticism comes from the old-time strippers, who, in their own "Quaker" and "Unitarian" clubs, reached their peak of stripping hundreds of years ago. They simply cannot see what all the fuss is about, and are justifiably a little peeved that these modern performers should be so highly paid for what is really so terribly old-fashioned.

The Education Act of 1944 laid down that once a day (and at another period during the week), the children shall put on these absurdly out of date veils, and, although they are not expected to go through the strip routine themselves,

some teachers have actually been performing striptease in front of their classes! First they throw off "Adam and Eve" and then "Eternal Damnation," and, if they are only amateurs, before they know where they are, they have dropped the lot.

Other RI teachers demonstrate a special ritual movement (quite obscene) by which the God-veil is ripped and torn but never finally discarded. It is no wonder that the public is worried about an increase in immorality. Few teachers, however, are

continued on page 17

RAAStus: W1 in W.2.
Colin MacInnes

'Defense' needs money. Send to Michael Abdul Malik, Leith Mansions, Grantully Road, W9.

RAAS, in England, is the nearest thing we have to the American Black Muslims. It is not in fact very near, since the social-racial contexts are so different. Although we are a racist society here, white racism is diluted and polite, so that black opposition to it, however militant, is correspondingly mild.

The letters *RAAS* purport to stand for Racial Action Adjustment Society, but in reality (on an analogy with, say, Ian Fleming's *SPECTRE*) the title is chosen to give four letters that spell out an exceedingly rude West Indian word—it denotes, in fact, a saturated menstrual cloth.

The President of *RAAS* is a Trinidadian called Michael Abdul Malik, or Michael X, formerly Michael de Freitas. He is a converted and practising Muslim (I mean religiously, as well as being a "Muslim"), a poet, a former hustler in his unregenerate days, and an impressive man, if rather unorganised.

I have long believed that only Negroes will help Negroes, and that white allies harm as much as they help. As Stokeley Carmichael points out—to my mind, accurately —whites should convert whites, not hinder blacks by trying to back them. I was thus sympathetic to Michael's endeavours; though in contradiction to my own belief, joined his organisation as an associate member (only blacks can be full members). This involved my suggesting a task I could take on to further the movement's objectives.

Before describing this, a word about black racialism, or racialism in reverse. Here one must judge not so much by theory, as by practice. I know Michael is not a racialist, and that his shoulders are entirely chipless. Nor can I discover that his members are. In this, I admit, they differ from the American Muslims. But

apart from personal inclination, the English situation does not encourage black racialism for three reasons. First, because Negroes are one-fiftieth, not one-tenth of the population as in America, too small a minority for racial aggression. Next, because the aloof, wet cotton-wool style of white English racialism has—with few exceptions—none of the neurotic violence found in the US, which makes the call there to Black Power meaningful. Lastly, neither West Indians, nor Africans, nor Pakistanis have any experience, historically, of being bullied by a white

majority, and this gives them a greater assurance in relation to whites. (It is significant, incidentally, that Stokeley himself is a Trinidadian.)

Liberals, of course, deem all exclusive racial organisations tainted. But it seems to me they only say this when the organisation is black. What liberal objects to the multiplicity of Jewish bodies, with not a Gentile on their committees, which succour their own race? Does any liberal resent Cypriot, Maltese or, for that matter, Australian self-help organisations? No, such are thought to be both practical and patriotic. But not any

body founded by Negroes for helping one another: *this*, says the liberal, is racialism.

The real reason the liberal doesn't like the idea of a group like *RAAS* is that it doesn't want him. Well, let him console himself with CARD, or other excellent multi-racial bodies striving, so they say, for the same ends. And perhaps he is to some extent right: the battle against racialism can be fought on many fronts, in many ways, and let he who is concerned with this choose the one he thinks the most effective.

So once an associate member of *RAAS*, I suggested to Michael we undertake the defence of coloured men and women accused in criminal cases. I have direct and visual experience of the brutality and perjury that arises when coloured persons are arrested, and of their hostile treatment in the courts. I am not saying this doesn't happen to whites too—indeed it does—but coloured people are especially vulnerable. First, because of racialist attitudes of the authorities, and next, because they have less knowledge than whites of how to handle an arrest and its consequences, and usually less chance of practical help and advice from friends.

He accepted the idea, and we went into business. The first two problems were lawyers and money. Anyone with experience of courts will know that a solid defence is half the battle. The scared Barbadian fisherman in the dock, speaking a scarcely comprehensible dialect and having failed to muster witnesses and solid citizens who can stand surety for him, is greatly helped by preliminary advice in the cells (to which only lawyers have access), and the presence in court of a sharp expert who is not intimidated by its atmosphere of doom.

This brings us first to the matter of legal aid. Many think this, like the National Health Service, is a free and automatic privilege. Not a bit of it. It is granted at the magistrate's discretion, and often refused. Of course, if legal aid *is* granted, the financial problem—and that of legal defence—are both looked after. But since most coloured people haven't the faintest idea how to go about getting legal aid, it is important to have a lawyer in court to apply for it on his behalf. And until it is (or isn't) granted, this lawyer, naturally, has to be paid. Then if legal aid is refused, he has to be paid a great deal more to carry the case to its conclusion.

Most criminal lawyers are willing—subject to this initial payment—to take on legal aid cases since, though these are not generously paid, they cover costs and keep the office busy. We had to find, and did, solicitors who would accept the rather odd cases we sent them, and be prepared to charge as little as possible for the first appearance (to ask for legal aid) and for subsequent efforts if legal aid was not granted.

I say "odd" cases because we made it a principle that guilt or innocence were of no interest to us. To try to decide this would be speculation anyway, and we

ved the excellent
ple of the British courts
nnocent until proved
." Of course, this
ple, in practice, is not
olute as is thought—
to name one of dozens
stances, should the
t-proved-guilty person
t into a dock, and not
d to sit by his lawyer,
America? Additionally,
roposed Criminal
e Bill, with its
ring with juries, seems
end to undermine this
t principle even
r.

several cases, we had
es and successes—some
se " successes " being
t convictions, but with
ces much less severe,
ere sure, than if the
d had not been
ded at all. We were
ble to arrange sureties
il when the defendant
't supply these—
h our sureties, despite
impeccable
tability (and sometimes
Caucasian skins) were
refused by the
trates. Meanwhile we
ut of our own pockets
than we could afford,
an up bills about which
licitors were, on the
, patient.

this time, a rather
ional immoral earnings
ame up about which a
many other West
s were concerned,
ng the accused to be
nt. They raised funds
s defence (which the
subsequently suggested
ntended to bribe the
s). The persons
ed with this case—
ich the accused was
ally sentenced to four
—heard of our
yours, we got together,
committee came into
which we called
nse ".

in two minds about this
since sad experience
ght me that individual
of one or two persons
n more effective than
f a quarrelsome group.
er, there seemed
feeling among the
ed community of W.11
mething should be
and we soon had nine
ttee men with a whole
ul paraphernalia of
an, secretary, treasurer
forth. After several
l rows, we settled
with an office,
ne (operating day and

night so that victims could
call from the station on
arrest), a part-paid secretary,
and we have hitherto handled
about a dozen case.
Sceptics will say—what is the
use of all this? At best it
is a drop in the ocean of
coloured woe . . . and why
only operate in London
W.11, and why only defend
coloured persons, and what if
the accused has a white wife,
and so on?

In moments of anguish and
fatigue I agree with these
strictures. We seem to be
using up a lot of our own
precious time (all the
committee members have
other active occupations),
subsidising solicitors, losing a
lot of cases—and no' doubt
raising false hopes in the
process. Nor is our initiative
greeted with approval by
much of the coloured
community. Murmurs are
heard that we are making
money somehow out of this,
or playing politics, or
antagonising the law and
making things worse.
My only reply to this is that
if we can establish that
coloured cases will be
defended, maybe official
attitudes to coloured accused
will gradually alter. I was
once accused of something
with eleven others, all
coloured. One of these and
myself, having a bit of
money, got lawyers and were
acquitted. All the rest were
convicted on an identical
charge. I have not forgotten
this.
As to the argument that if we
are " Defense " we should
defend anybody—a point that
was put to me in a court
canteen by an intellectual
detective who follows, he
said, my writing with
professional interest—okay,
okay, we will; and in fact, in
one case we have defended a
white. But the need for
support of coloured peoples
seems to me greater and
anyway, the organisation is
coloured, so why should it not
defend its own? As Michael
X, in his poetic manner, put
it, " Islam teaches me the
whole world is my family, but
the coloured man is more,
he is my brother."
Then what about me, the
only white face on the
committee? Isn't this
inconsistent? Highly so, and
as soon as I can I'm going

continued on page 17

The Land of Cockaigne

As I sink deeper into the irredeemable state of over-twenty-five-ism, I find that failing even faster than my virility is my never-plentiful fund of tolerance for the antics of adolescents, and *a fortiori*, for those of the ageing worshippers of adolescence. Unlike Mr. Muggeridge, I have no objection to an increasing sexual permissiveness, nor do I look back to some Eden of public purity; but the bitter bile of contempt which he spews forth smells sweet to me.

Consider, for example, the matter of drugs. Very few who have actually used such mild stimulants as hashish or amphetamines can put much faith in the ravings of the old men who run society concerning the dangers of drugs, the consequent decadence of ' swinging London ' and so on (perhaps the most absurd recent example of this kind of thing was the exhortations of the ridiculous Lord Radcliffe, than whom none is more Established, printed some months ago in the *Spectator*). It is a commonplace that alcohol is a physically more debilitating drug than either of the two mentioned; the unstable personality can be pushed over the edge of disintegration by the excess use of any of them: would Dylan Thomas have suffered any more if he had gobbled pills, or even made like a sewing-machine with a syringe?

The sincerity of our masters when they address themselves to the problem of drugs (or even just alcohol) must be questioned when they so deliberately confuse the use of ' big ' drugs and ' little ' drugs; when they use any and every means to cloud the issues, even threatening to prosecute a silly little clergyman who demonstrated how very easy it is to buy hash.

But having said all this, having made our bow to human rights, freedom of the individual, common sense, and all that, what of the under-twenty-fivers who increasingly flock to ' turn-on ', reverently passing their joint from hand to hand, slobbering over the sodden end of a crudely confected bundle of tobacco mixed with the sacred substance?

I do not know what the under-twenty-fivers of ten or twenty years ago were like; nor do I underestimate the roseate glow which youth sheds over the most squalid scenes. But can the mumbling morons, mouthing the incoherencies of talentless poetasters, conversing in the out-dated hand-me-down slang of the casualties of the race war, can these be the best that ' consciousness-expanding ' drugs can do?

More pathetic even than these, however, are the over-twenty-fivers who throw themselves so eagerly into the ranks of Youth—the Adrian Mitchells who can't write poetry, but do know how to invent doggerel to exploit the amorphous emotions of an amorphous protest; the Julie Felixes who can't play the guitar but who know how to pounce upon the gropings towards music and song of children struck deaf by Radio Luxembourg and its relatives all over the world; and, most absurd, the greying men who, having read about the Provo riots in Amsterdam, but being themselves neither young nor beautiful, have invented an ersatz provo movement in London, and babble about white bicycles in Trafalgar Square.

But they are worse than pathetic, these inferior talents who batten upon the gullibility of a lettered but semi-literate horde of children, who are the product of a generation of elders themselves beset and besotted by the combined efforts of the pulpit Freudians and the parlour Marxists. These modern Dukes of Plaza Toro posture before their adoring audience, and annually march them up to Trafalgar Square, only to march them down again; the children raising their little standards of revolt regularly have them dashed into the ground by those whom they idolise.

And so they turn to the liberation of ineffectual drugs, and sometimes seek refuge from their still apparent inadequacies in more powerful varieties; or sometimes they accept the fantasy world of those of their elders who lust after their youth. They become pop-singers, or pop-painters, or even pop-philosophers; and to disguise their deficiencies subscribe to what is now called (poor Isherwood!) ' camp '—the glorification of inability to discriminate.

No wonder Mr. Muggeridge would like to be able to say, God . . . help us! . . . But God is dead, of an overdose.

Sebastian Scragg

Darling...

I'd love to write the straight - talking McCarthy-Brophy rundown on the most intimate activities of the English male, but I can't for the simple reason that I've never been to bed with one. It's true that I have no lack of standards of comparison. I regard your request as a compliment to my energy and enterprise, not to mention the catholicity of my taste; under normal circumstances I should have plunged into exhaustive field work, but I can't even do that, because I have taken a vow never to go to bed with, or indeed have sexual traffic anywhere with, an Englishman.

Those who know how passionately I hold my convictions of complete lack of possessiveness and prejudice in sexual affairs would be aghast at this uncharacteristic and illiberal action, which was not so much freely taken by me, as forced upon me by the circumstances.

In Cambridge, where I live, there are (reputedly) eight men to every woman. It seems the ideal spot for a devoted practitioner of the arts of love, for nearly all the men are in the full flower of their potency, being between the ages of eighteen and twenty-two. When I arrived I was elated at the vastness of the opportunity for proselytising.

For six months after I arrived there, the only sex I experienced directly, apart from endlessly repeated discussions in which I found it necessary to explain that there had been improvements upon *coitus interruptus* as a contraceptive method, or about venereal disease of the order, " Sweetie, those are lice. You are not so much diseased as dirty," was the sight, one by one, of three, grubby, scrawny men in their forties, who derived some wan satisfaction from exposing to me their genitals, pallid and bluish in the frosty air.

In those six months I altered my image violently and constantly, but no real change in my fortunes resulted. I settled down to being bottom-wiper and information service about contraception and venereal disease and matters of the heart generally, and transferred my sexual hopes to the metropolis.

I was sick to the gills of the usual sights provided for my delectation at undergraduate parties, where the girls arrived blazing in spangled mininesses and shinned up the gilded youths like natives up a coconut palm, glueing themselves on by their lip-slicker and moon-drops, while the boys signalled optically to their mates, and waited only for the girls to drop off to ask them for a cigarette. (The same girls who hie them southwards in summer and feed the egos of the lazier and vainer Latin Lovers.)

One evening I went down to stay with a smooth young architect whom I was ready to love distractedly, in his witty little flat near the Fulham Road. He Michael Cained all over the kitchen in his cunning barbecue apron, lit candles and plumped cushions, burnt incense and selected records, and never even looked at me. In desperation I thought of stripping all'improvviso, but rejected it on several counts (principally my sensible St. Michael smalls). Eventually it was bed-time. He carefully prepared the spare bed, ran the bath, warmed the towels, lent me his bubble bath and other manly cosmetics packaged in leather and gun-metal, and said good night. When I was warm in bed, scrubbed shiny and sleepy, he suddenly slid in beside me. " Ciao," he said, and lay there, all friendly and casual like. I fell asleep. I took care never to see him again.

He is not always an architect. Sometimes he is a lawyer or a fledgling lawyer, or a baby stockbroker, or an accountant or in advertising. He is always *very nice*. He has an ideal of nice, gentle, restful, *uncomplicated* sex. He is legion.

My resolution to bed me an Englishman continued bloody but unbroken. I went into the country to sample the gentry. I lolled and played tennis and rode a bit and went to the races with clear - eyed heavy - limbed young gentlemen with a desperate tendency to down one's earhole the malicious gossip heard where, generally on theme of the *parven* the designing female seeks to marry into death duties class. At a party given by one su others such, I noticed th an oddly early hour guests began to melt while the liquor lasted, I was suddenly *tête à* with my host and it was eleven o'clock. I was Victim of a Plot. beamed gormlessly began to remove his school shoes and blaring some subtleties while about being snug.

How the plot can been expected to th without some attemp gain my complicity I c imagine. I grasped opportunity presented b bare feet and struck iron-jawed, across the l through the hedge and a the cricket ground separated the house wh was guest from his. would-be ravisher thumping after me, plunged wildly on whil nettles stung me all up i my wild silk. On the a pitch, gleaming ready i moonlight for the mor play, he sprang. We thr about desperately for a and I bawled reproach him for his lack of loya

continued on page 18

In bed with the English

STRIP

continued from page 13

...guilty of deliberately exposing themselves completely; those who are (or who dare to advise the children not to touch the veils at all) find that they are barred from promotion. Most people think this absolutely right and fair—especially the professional stripper who, naturally, want to continue to lay down the rules as to how far stripping can decently go.

One recognises that for some people theological strip-tease is all part of growing up, like reading Penthouse or Woman's Own. All the same, they can't help being impatient for the time when Stripping Veils will take their place in museums alongside the stays, chastity belts, and bustles of previous ages, and Strip-Tease will be as out of fashion as cock-fighting and the Lancers.

A suggestion was made recently by Dr. J. M. Allegro that scrolls should take the place of veils. He tells the story of how, soon after the war, he found that stripping could be particularly effectively performed with an accompaniment of Hebrew, which he took the trouble to learn. It is quite possible that his ideas may prove a considerable embarrassment and challenge to the groups, although the stars have a powerful backing of half-believers, and will, no doubt, be as ready as the Beatles to extend their repertoires in order to retain their popularity. They have already switched some of their bookings this year from the church to the **non**-church, and they may even go so far as to suggest that "**NSS**" stands for "Church of England" rather than for the National Secular Society, which (like most things they say) would make appropriate **non**-sense. It is, however, exceedingly unlikely that any of the strippers will go so far as to risk endangering their undoubted privileges as "Christian" clergymen, parents, authoritarians, newspaper columnists, or radio and TV stars. Theological striptease is here to stay.

JOHNSON

continued from page 7

...people might hold me to them. Of course I'm getting a bit old for politics really, by present day standards, and I'm not sure I'd make a good M.P. Unless you're a strong extrovert with a good dash of personal vanity, it's a difficult life to enjoy.

Cockburn: So it looks like out to pasture as an art critic.
Johnson: Yes, though, on the other hand, if one feels one can do it, it would be rather a dereliction of duty if one didn't try ministerial office, if one felt one had some particular contribution to make.
Cockburn: What would you regard as your great virtue?

Johnson: Well, I think I'm very conscientious and responsible-minded, probably overmuch, because I worry too much about things.
Cockburn: And your vice?
Johnson: I'm impatient, terribly impatient.
Cockburn: Yes, I asked someone who had met you once, what

question she would like to ask you, and she said Ask him why he's so bloody unpleasant. Do you feel you have this effect on people?
Johnson: Well, I think I do on people I meet very briefly, occasionally: but much less so than I used to. I'm now much more humble-minded, more benevolent.

RAAS

continued from page 15

...hand over my job (Press Officer) to a wise young Caribbean, African or Pakistani. But I was in from the start, they asked me to stay, and there for the present I still am.

...hat there are elements of vanity in my presence (the white pet of the dark committee) is undeniable, but in my interfering way I think coloured citizens have to be prodded into organising themselves if they're going to get any sort of a deal in this country. Most of the immigrants still don't realise that they'll lay their bones here, and dream of an eventual return to sunny skies. Few of them see their children will grow up to whom Africa and the West Indies will be no more than a hazy legend.

Thus, while white immigrant groups in England are close-knit mafia, the coloured communities remain largely disunited. The result is that, despite individual courage, they are easy to exploit as a minority group.

MEET THE STARS

FACE TO FACE

EVERY WEEK IN

Melody Maker

9d

EVERY THURSDAY
Make sure of your copy by placing a regular order!

continued from page 16

the cricket club and lost a fifteen guinea earring. Then I was up again and running across the out-field and through the rose-garden. The last I saw of him. he was remorsefully smoothing and patting the ravaged wicket.

There seemed to be nothing for it but the wilds of Bohemia, where everything comes right for Shakespeare, at any rate. Things were generally much more promising after I had ferreted out the fuckers from the drunks who can't and the drugged who don't want to, and, of course, your classic pederasts. The first conquest brought brink of so greasy a pallet presided over by underpants of so implacably tertiary a colour that I excused myself hurriedly and left. I have tried to overcome my bourgeois aversion for old grime, but there the English have me defeated.

The second sally put me in a curious situation which has been paralleled many times since. Hardly had we arrived in the bedsitter than he was divesting himself of a yellow gray interlock and insisting that I pass my fingers lightly over his moonscape back barely touching the skin. An hour later, stiff in both arms and still fully dressed, I slipped downstairs and hopped gratefully on the 49.

Other variants of this situation can be indicated thus:

"Would you mind leaving your boots on?" (On one occasion, "Would you mind leaving your hat on?")

"Sorry, I can only make it with flat-chested girls."

"What are you kinky for?" (Standard answer, "Lord Mountbatten.")

"Let's pretend you're dead."
"I adore squeezing blackheads."

"What a *super* scar!"

To save myself from further midnight flits along the clanging pavements, I took the vow and I've never regretted. Nor, I imagine, have the English.

Ask me about Italians, Persians, Arabs, West Indians, Jews from anywhere, Irishmen, Welshmen, Africans, men from anywhere else but England and you've got yourself an article, but about the English lover, as you see, I know nothing.

How LBJ lost an election/gained a friend/and won.

On Saturday, August 28th, 1948, a Democratic Primary Election took place in Texas. (For the winner this meant automatic victory in the November election into the Senate.)

On Wednesday, September 1st, the Texan Election Bureau announced that a Mr. Coke Stevenson had beaten Lyndon B. Johnson in the Primary by 100 votes. Yet on Thursday, September 2nd, at midday, LBJ proclaimed that he was the true victor and exhorted his followers to 'do their duty'. Appropriately enough, on Friday, September 3rd, Jim Wells County, the centre of the Texan's camp, filed an amended return which gave Johnson just enough votes to win. Mr. Coke Stevenson immediately assigned two former F.B.I. men to visit Jim Wells County and check the week late votes. Here's what they found:

● All the late votes were in green ink.
● Some of the late votes had been cast by late members of the electoral roll.
● The 'voters' just happened to stroll into the polling booth in alphabetical order.

When Johnson was told about Stevenson's investigations, he got an injunction from the State Court House in Austin forbidding Jim Wells County to change the returns.

Then, on September 13, with the shadow of the November elections growing imminent, the State Democratic election committee had to decide whose name was to appear on the ballot boxes. By a vote of 29 to 28, LBJ won.

Stevenson then attempted to fight the Texan's 'victory' before the State Democratic Convention, but his followers were barred from the door. Undaunted, Stevenson went to the Federal District Court and argued that his civil rights had been violated when he was deprived of an honest and fair election count. After a full hearing during which both sides produced their evidence, the Federal Court judge, T. W. Davidson, ruled in favour of Stevenson and issued an order restraining the Secretary of State from placing the LBJ brand on the ballot boxes.

The Federal Court then sent its own investigators to Jim Wells County to have a look at Mr. Johnson's votes. This was making things a bit too uncomfortable for the Texan. In a last-ditch fight to stop the Federal investigation, LBJ's legal advisors again resorted to the State court system, but this time the Texas Supreme Court refused to interfere with the Federal action.

LBJ seemed doomed.

However, the Federal investigators in Jim Wells County found that they were going to have a difficult time trying to secure the voting list in question. It appeared that one of the two copies of the list had been 'stolen' and that the remaining copy was tucked away in a sealed ballot box. To get at that box would require a day or so more time, time that was not to be made available. For now, when things never looked more hopeless for the

Texan, the reins of his fortune were placed in the sure hands of Abe Fortas. (The Honourable Abe Fortas is now a Justice of the Supreme Court of the United States—how he got there is yet another sordid story.) It was Abe Fortas who carried LBJ's battle to the Supreme Court of the United States where what had appeared to be the Alamo of Byrdland was turned into an irresistible victory.

The Supreme Court held that the Federal Court's Order had to be set aside as unwarranted interference in state election procedures. Thus, the Federal investigation was brought to a grinding halt on the eve of the opening of the ballot box containing the revealing votes.

In a final, dogged effort, Stevenson appealed to the United States Senate to refuse to seat Johnson. The Senate responded by sending its own investigating committee to Jim Wells County in order to look at the mysterious Pandora's box. But, strangely enough, the Senate investigators never saw proof because the ballot boxes had been accidentally 'burned' by a well intentioned janitor.

And so, in 1948, 'Landslide' Lyndon became a Senator of the United States. Fifteen years later he was able to side-step yet another election to become President.

(Condensed from Underground Press Syndicate report by Irving Shushick)

Following the tradition set by rival fat glossies, OZ each month unfolds a sumptuously satirical Playmate and adds a special bonus of a monthly calendar.

Our hack cartoonist spotted the lovely Lyndon—President of the United States—deep in the heart of no-one. 'I keep telling folks they can go off the way with LBJ,' sighs our dimpled anti-yellow rose of Texas— 'but none of them are game to.'

After brooding over this month's erotic exposé, randy OZ readers will certainly seek him out (we warned him) and plug his alluring credibility gap.

'Oh, it won't be that easy,' giggled gorgeous Lyndon, 'it's so wide and getting even wider all the time—I'm such a naughty fibber.'

Tall (6 ft. 4 in.), gaunt and temptingly body scarred, LBJ's favourite hobby is genocide. 'Women and children first' he grimaced coquettishly.

Although our shimmering, sensuous, sun-tanned Texan is a relatively new arrival on the international power scene, his political maidenhead was first shattered some eighteen years ago in the most bizarre election of all time—even for Texas.

Following the tradition set by rival fat glossies, OZ each month unfolds a sumptuously special Playmate and adds a special bonus of a monthly calendar.

Our hack cartoonist spotted the lovely Lyndon—President of the United States—deep in the heart of no-one. 'I keep telling folks they can go all the way with L.B.J.' sighs our dimpled anti-yellow rose of Texas—'but none of them are game to'.

After brooding over this month's erotic exposé, randy OZ readers will certainly seek him out (we warned him) and plug his alluring credibility gap.

'Oh, it won't be that easy,' giggled gorgeous Lyndon, 'it's so wide and getting even wider all the time—I'm such a naughty fibber.'

Tall (6 ft. 4 in.), gaunt and temptingly body scarred, LBJ's favourite hobby is genocide 'Women and children first' he grimaced coquettishly.

Although our shimmering, sensuous, sun-tanned Texan is a relatively new arrival on the international power scene, his political maidenhead was first shattered some eighteen years ago in the most bizarre election of all time—even for Texas.

PLAMATE OF THE MONTH

LONDON TWO AND SIX

OZ

SHUT THAT GUY UP!

TOM JONES   MARK LANE   BRITISH BREAST   30s a GRAIN   WHITEHALL TOAD   PETER PORTER

BITE SIZED OZ! MONSTER POSTERS!

MARK LANE: "RUSH TO JUDGEMENT"

SHUT THAT GUY UP!

What really happened at the BBC's Lime Grove studios on January 29? Ostensibly, a much fan-fared impartial investigation into the death of Kennedy which pitted Mark Lane, author of 'Rush to Judgement' against two Warren Commission lawyers, Arlen Spector and David Belin and two of the Warren Report's influential defenders, Lord Devlin and Professor Bickel. What actually appeared on TV screens outraged an undisclosed number of viewers; prompting them to jam BBC switchboards. The strict format of the programme seemed loaded against Lane, to say nothing of compere Kenneth Harris's compulsive partiality. What didn't appear on camera is even more fascinating. Here Mark Lane recounts his negotiations with the BBC, reveals how rehearsals with other protagonists were underway 12 days before he arrived and discloses astonishing occurrences behind-the-scenes.

PLEASE LIFT PAGE

If you were watching BBC-2 for almost five hours on January 29 you should have been informed that the distortion was not caused by a faulty television set in your home. It originated at BBC's Lime Grove studio. It was, in fact, planned that way.

ON January 17 I drove to a college in Philadelphia with the anticipation of a debate with Arlen Spector, one of the most inventive of the Warren Commission's lawyers. Mr Spector had been, I was informed, a young Democrat, given an assignment as an assistant district attorney by the Democratic District Attorney of Philadelphia. His employer permitted him to serve as a Commission lawyer, an extra-curricular bit of activity that enhanced both his reputation and his finances. Mr Spector returned from the Washington crusade. He changed his political party, announced his candidacy for the office of District Attorney, and the prestige that his work for President Johnson's Commission brought enabled him to defeat his former friend and supporter. On the very afternoon of my arrival in Philadelphia the leading newspaper announced that Mr Spector would be the Republican candidate for Mayor. You may well imagine my desire to meet so famous a person in public debate in his own city. But, alas, it was not to be. Mr Spector's office announced that he must retire early that night the debate was set for 7:30 pm) for he was required to catch an early plane for London the next day in order to debate with me —twelve days later. (In the interim I flew to California, appeared on radio and television programmes there and debated another Warren Commission lawyer at the University of California at Los Angeles before flying to London.)

However, as the reader will discover, perhaps to his amusement, and as I discovered, much to my regret, my absence from London was apparently an error for I missed the BBC rehearsals for the extemporaneous debate programme. In retrospect I must add that I am not now sure that my mere presence in London would have ensured my knowledge of the rehearsal schedule or an invitation to the preparations.

It seemed just a bit odd to me that so astute a politician as Mr Spector would refuse to debate with me in America (the major networks and leading universities had sought to arrange such debates on many occasions but Mr Spector was adamant in his rejection of every such invitation) and so quickly agree to escape across the ocean for the encounter. One less naïve would have had a clue that the BBC had somehow made the confrontation most attractive to the Commission's representatives. I confess to having speculated about the matter with myself for a moment or two. I concluded that the suites at the Connaught, the expense account, the trip to London for the lawyers and presumably their wives or associates, and perhaps even a fee might have tipped the balance. No—it could not be my assurances regarding the programme's format. My own genuine admiration for the English respect for fair play ruled out that consideration.

The format was, of course, soon to become the question of the day. This being so let me trace my contact with it from the outset. The film's director, Emile de Antonio (who having now been identified to you I must henceforth refer to as D, for I have only known him so, and I should forget who it is I write about if I call him anyone else), bore the burden of the original negotiation with the BBC officials.

He told me that the BBC had agreed to show the film on January 29, that there would be an intermission, and that it would be followed by a general discussion in which it was hoped that I would participate. I agreed at once. BBC insisted that I sign a document in which I agreed not to appear on any other radio or television programme to be broadcast in England prior to January 29. This effort at the creation of a very small monopoly hardly seemed appropriate, but as it was the condition for the showing of the film, and as I did not plan to be in London much before that date anyway, I executed the document and it was submitted to the BBC. Subsequently, the BBC officials signed the contract purchasing the film for one showing.

My first direct contact with a BBC staffer came when I was in Los Angeles. A call came from London. A very correct and polite English voice informed me that it was owned by one Peter Pagnamenta who was the assistant director of the programme which had been named "The Death of Kennedy". He called to find out when I would arrive and to be sure that I understood the approach that the director had taken to the programme. I would arrive on the 28th I said, and I should like to hear the director's approach. He explained that the film would be shown. It would constitute the opening statement of "your case" as he put it. Then the Commission lawyers would be permitted to make comments. Didn't I think it fair that they should speak next? I did, indeed. And then you will rebut and the debate will proceed. It all sounded fine, I said, but weren't there to be two other participants? Oh yes. Lord Devlin, you know who he is? I did. Well he and a Professor Bickel will speak later in the programme. In other words, I said, you will have four Commission supporters present the Commission's case and I alone will speak for the critics? In a sense you might say that, he replied, but Lord Devlin and Professor Bickel are not Commission personnel. I let that one pass not saying that they had been more effective for the Commission even if more ignorant of the facts. I said I would like to make a suggestion. Perhaps you might invite Professor Hugh Trevor-Roper—you know who he is? Among his credentials to qualify as a participant was the fact that he has read the 26 volumes, and his writings on the subject seemed to demonstrate that he was almost the only person in England to have bothered to examine the evidence. Certainly Lord Devlin gave no sign of such an acquaintance with the facts. The answer was that Professor Trevor-Roper was not to be a participant. And now that that's out of the way, what hotel would you like to stay at. I couldn't care less. Any will do. Well, then we'll make a reservation for you at the X hotel, and if there is any change we'll have a message waiting for you when you arrive at the airport. Please cable Dick Francis the time of your arrival and contact Paul Fox after you're settled in your hotel in London. The cable was sent.—Arrive January 28th 7:00 AM.

And that was the first and last word regarding the format of the programme before my 7,000 mile journey from Los Angeles to London in reliance upon that conservation.

Aarrived at 7:00 AM. It was raining. I was tired from the trip from New York to Los Angeles, a busy schedule on the west coast, the flight to London from Los Angeles, and the thought of flying back to New York in three days for two days there before flying back to Paris. But this was an important programme and well worth the effort. By worth the effort, I meant not that it would be worth it financially, for since I was not paid a farthing for the programme, and in fact was compelled to cancel speaking engagements for it which were to have paid handsomely, the programme was, in that sense, to be worse than a total loss. But the chance to meet the imaginative creator of the single bullet theory in an open, no holds barred encounter, before some seven million viewers, with the knowledge that it would be fully reported in my own country, was worth any sacrifice of time or money or effort. Still, I was tired. I cleared Immigration quickly with a greeting from the clerk. He said he'd be watching the programme. Customs, too, was fast and pleasant. There was no message waiting. I called the X hotel to find that there was no reservation. Since D had told me that the Commission lawyers, Mr Spector who you have already met, and Mr Belin from Iowa, were to stay in rather luxurious quarters at the Connaught, I called there as well. No reservation for me. I called the BBC. A gentleman, obviously a night-time receptionist hoping the morning would pass without the kind of problem I was about to present, answered. He said he had no authority. Of course Mr Fox was not in and wouldn't be for hours and, sir, no one is in, except me and I know nothing about hotels, perhaps you might call back in a couple of hours. Two hours passed rather slowly in the drafty terminal building. It was almost nine and I had left New York the evening before and hadn't yet been to sleep. In due course a responsible and concerned young lady at the BBC was located and a reservation made at a hotel. I was too tired to care that the hotel was undergoing noisy renovation and that the lobby resembled a bombed out village or that the room was dark and musty.

Before I left the States, D had told me that the BBC had constructed a most elaborate model of Dealey Plaza and that it was hoped, by the BBC, that instead of aerial photographs of the area which appeared in our film, live, on camera, shots of the model might be substituted. D agreed to the substitution upon my agreement that the model was accurate. I took a shower, shaved, and called Paul Fox. The operator at the BBC cut me off. I called again. He was not in but would call back. He never did. I called Peter Pagnamenta. He was at a meeting and his office would switch me to the meeting room. We were cut off again. I called back. Mr Pagnamenta will call you in a minute. He didn't. I called back in fifteen minutes and reached him. I said that I would like to see the model. He said, sorry about the renovation at the hotel; hope it hasn't disturbed you. I said that it is quite all right, thinking that if he knew about it why didn't he book a room at some other hotel. I would like to see the model. He said, how would tomorrow do. Not too well, I said, for if any changes have to be made you may need some time and tomorrow is the day of the programme. Well, let's see what time might be convenient for us for you to arrive. He said he'd call back. The phone rang and it was Per Hanghoj, a journalist for the Danish afternoon newspaper Ekstrabladet.

I said, how would you like to see the BBC model and meet some BBC officials? He said he'd like to and we took a taxicab to the BBC Lime Grove studio. There we met Mr Pagnamenta who permitted us to see the model. It was breath-taking in detail.

And in each crucial respect it was inaccurate.

One of the participants, Mr Bickel, in an effort to prove that no shots could have come from behind the wooden fence, the area from which some of the shots originated, had written in an American publication (Commentary, October 1966) "people were milling about this area and looking down on it from the railroad bridge over the underpass, and no one saw an armed man". Mr Bickel's argument obviously rests upon the allegation that one can observe the area behind the wooden fence from the railroad bridge which is above it. His abysmal ignorance of the geography of the area can probably be explained by his failure to visit the location. The railroad bridge is the same height as the base of the five foot wooden fences, not above it, and the fence area is heavily landscaped with bushes and trees so dense that it is absolutely impossible to see anyone behind the fence from the bridge. Yet the BBC model seemed almost designed to accommodate Mr Bickel's false impression, although I felt quite certain that slovenly supervision, not mischievousness, was responsible for the model which placed the bridge above the fence and removed all of the bushes and most of the trees from the area thus giving the model witnesses a view which the real witnesses could never secure.

In its Report the Commission had said that a mos important witness, S. M. Holland, was living proo that no shots came from behind the fence since he ran to th area behind the fence from the railroad bridge "immediately" after the shots were fired. In our film Holland answered tha incorrect conclusion by stating that it took him two or two and half minutes to get to the fence since the area between him an that destination was "a sea of cars". He said, they were s tightly packed, bumper to bumper, that he had to climb ove them. Again the BBC model accomodated the Commission rather than the facts. There was no sea of cars, just a few scattered models that would not have prevented Holland from speeding to the fence.

Mr Pagnamenta resisted my suggestions for change in the model. I suggested that we compare th model to photographs. We don't have any photographs here the studio, was the reply. How could you construct a detaile model without photographs, I asked, but interrupting myself said, never mind, I have some at the hotel and I'll fetch the now. But before I left to get them I observed the remainder the set. On the far left, appearing almost as if it were in a hol was a small table, at which I was told I would sit during th programme. A larger table, raised, as is a judge's bench, was the middle, and it was this that created the hole in the groun impression for my table. To the right was another larger tab for two, and still further along, the set for our imparti moderator, Kenneth Harris.

Why the elevated table, I asked? For the two judg or assessors, as we call them, was the reply. A who might they be? As I told you before, Lord Devlin a Professor Bickel. I thought that they were participants in t debate. Well, they will participate as judges, that is they w give their verdict at the end of the programme, and as to t debate, it will not really be a debate. That is you will be giv a chance to speak when you are personally attacked. When, r if? You make it sound as if it is already set. Surely I didn't co all this way to defend myself. I came to discuss the facts su rounding the death of the President. Isn't that the name of yo programme? Well, you had better talk with Mr Fox about th was the answer.

Mr Hanghoj and I were ushered into a small dow stairs room to await Mr Fox. In time he appear with Kenneth Harris. We were offered a drink as is the custo at the BBC. I accepted. My scotch arrived at once with ice a water as all Americans presumably like it, although I saic would prefer it straight. Mr Harris' gin arrived just after began to depart.

Mr Fox seemed deeply perturbed. I understand y have some problems, he said. I explained them The model was not accurate. How can two Warren Commiss sycophants be judges. Lord Devlin has served as the alm official salesman for the Warren Report in England for m than two years. He endorsed the Report before the evidence published, and since the publication of the 26 volumes he betrayed no trace of having examined them. Bickel, on a sma scale, has tried to serve the establishment in his own countr much the same way. How can you suggest that they be judg Mr Fox said, after all we are showing your two hour film there is no need for everyone on the panel to agree with yo submitted that he had not understood my point. If he desi he could have a dozen Warren Commission spokesmen on programme, and I would not object. What I objected to was BBC establishing two such spokesmen as judges. Mr Fox, r

by the impartial moderator, said that we can hardly be
~~ted~~ to withdraw the invitation to Lord Devlin. I did not
~~t~~ or hope that would be done. Just take off their black
~~and~~ make them mere mortals as were the rest of us.
~~ot~~ be done, said Mr Fox. Well, then, I said, introduce them
~~rly~~. That is let the audience know that they have written
~~report~~ of the Commission's central conclusion that Oswald
~~the~~ lone assassin. Surely, said Mr Fox, you don't doubt the
~~ity~~ of two such important men in public life. Surely you
~~see~~ that they can be swayed by the evidence if it proves that
~~previously~~ held position was wrong. Their integrity was
~~want~~ to the discussion—their prejudice central, I offered.
~~Harris~~ resolved the problem by stating that he would
~~duce~~ them as two men who have supported the Com-
~~n's~~ view. He added that if I wanted to discuss my objec-
~~to~~ them on the air, I would be given every opportunity
~~so~~. I said that I would do so.

Vhen we approached the crux of the matter—my
role in the debate. It was set, it could not be changed.
~~d~~ only respond to personal attacks, said Harris and Fox in
~~voice~~ and several times. I doubt that the audience cares
for hearing personal attacks made or defended against,
**I think, perhaps they would like to hear about the
of the President—that is why they will turn to the
amme called The Death of Kennedy. If you want to
other programme, called Mark Lane Attacked and
ded, I will come back for it, but I do not suppose
nyone will care to watch it!**

The format is set. The format is set. It cannot be
changed. It cannot be changed. The film will be
~~ted~~ in four segments, the Commission lawyers will attack
~~ortion~~ and if, in doing so, they make any personal attacks
~~you~~, you will be permitted some time to respond. In
~~n~~, as we have agreed, you will be given ample time to
~~ut~~ what you consider to be weaknesses in the programme's
~~and~~ with its choice of assessors.

In four segments, I asked? We worked for two years
to make that film. We drove from New York to
~~and~~ back because we could not afford the air fare. My
~~cooked~~ dinner for us all in Texas because we could not
~~to~~ eat in resturants. We have sacrificed to make that film.
~~its~~ world premiere. And you intend to chop it up into
~~pieces~~. Let it be seen as it was made, and then let your
~~say~~ what they will. The film has an integrity and an
~~of~~ its own. Do not destroy that.

Ir Fox said that in the contract, that Mr de Antonio
signed, we have the right to show the film in four
~~ts~~ and that we intend to do it that way.

Icalled D. He said that the BBC had told him that
the film would be shown with just one intermission.

Iwrung but one concession from the BBC. **Harris
and Fox both agreed, both gave solemn
~~commitments~~, that I would be given ample time at the
~~of~~ the programme to dissent from the format, to
~~my~~ objection to the judges, to explain that the
~~uld~~ not possibly present the case against the Report
~~ly~~ those portions which were, for want of a better
~~filmic~~, and that, in my view, the BBC formula
~~d~~ a genuine exchange of the facts.** We shook hands

and were about to depart when Mr Hanghoj, as journalists will
do, asked a few questions of Mr Harris.

Q: Don't you write for the Observer?
Harris: Yes, I do.
Q: What is the Observer's position on the assassination?
Harris: We don't have one.
Q: You don't have one?
Harris: No.
Q: Don't you think that the subject is sufficiently important
   for you to think about it and take a position?
Harris: Well, we did do that when the Report came out.
Q: Yes?
Harris: Well, we supported the Commission.
Q: Have you taken another position since then?
Harris: No, we haven't.
Q: Then the Observer's position is in support of the Warren
   Commission?
Harris: Well, you might say that.
Q: Wouldn't you say that?
Harris: Yes, I suppose so.
Q: You will be the moderator tonight?
Harris: Yes.

We arrived back at the studio one hour and a half
before air time. The parties were well separated.
I was placed in a small cubicle, lavishly furnished with food,
liquor, and excellent wine. Some doors away were Spector and
Belin and the visiting BBC brass, all of whom, we were told in
whispers, had arrived for the programme—the longest live
studio production in British history.

Just before air time I asked what was to be done
about make-up. A veteran of three to four hundred
appearances in America, I had expected that matter to be disposed of in a dressing room long before then. It will be taken
care of in the studio. Make-up was applied to some but not to
me. Of serious concern was the fact that there was but one set
of the 26 volumes and these were given to Belin and Spector
and placed far out of my reach. As the programme began it
became clear that Harris was working from a script and that
both Belin and Spector had copies of the script. I had none and,
in fact, I thought that the spontaneous programme which had
been described to me would preclude the use of one.

Ishall not offer an account of the programme here.
The English press was fair in its reportage, more fair
than the American press has been on this subject. The Times
reported on its front page that the BBC switchboard was
jammed with viewers complaining that the programme was
unfair. The Daily Mirror said, "Chairman Kenneth Harris
officiously and for me, embarrassingly clumsily silenced Mr Lane
whenever he tried to cross verbal swords with the rival lawyers
. . ." The Daily Sketch said that Harris conducted the programme "far too brusquely". The Daily Express headlined its
story, "Viewers Protest 'Unfair' During TV Marathon" and
added "Harris did appear to behave pompously". In a story
headed "Verdict on Harris" the Londoner's Diary in the
Evening Standard evidently found him, Harris, guilty of being
"nervous", "too abrupt", and "fairly childish". On the facts,
the Times pointed out that many witnesses did insist that the
shots came from behind a fence on a grassy knoll, and the
Guardian, an original supporter of the Commission, did a
complete turn about "Mark Lane seems now to have won his
case, or Oswald's case." And, "Now it seems clear to almost
everyone but the Warren Commission that it was indeed a rush
to judgment." Could one bullet have hit both the President and
Governor Connally? If not, there were at least two assassins.
Said the Daily Mirror, "It just doesn't seem possible."

The next day The Times ran a fairly lengthy and scrupulously fair and accurate story presenting some of my objections and the BBC reply. By combining that reply with the Kenneth Harris statement to the Standard the day before the definitive establishment position can be ascertained. But before that some more facts.

After the witnesses in the film said that they heard shots come from behind the fence, and saw a puff of smoke come from that location as well, Cliff Michelmore, not waiting for the Belin-Spector response, said for the BBC, the whole of Dealey Plaza is bowl shaped and that the area behind the fence is criss-crossed with steam pipes thereby accounting for the "smoke". Ignorance, Mr Bickel's only excuse, cannot be brought forward in defence of that false allegation since the BBC had sent Mr Michelmore to Dallas to look about. I know not what passes for a bowl in England but there would be little room for so flat a bowl to accommodate enough porridge for a very young child in my country. **The area behind the fence is not criss-crossed with steam pipes.** There is but one pipe anywhere in the entire area and it runs in a straight line from the overpass and not behind the fence. Does Mr Michelmore really think that a man who spent 42 years working that section of the railroad yards, as in the case of Mr Holland, would state that he saw smoke, that he knows that it came from a weapon, and be totally unaware of the presence of steam pipes that the clever Mr Michelmore found in his first trip there? I mention Mr Michelmore's criss-crossed pipes because it was unfortunately typical of several false statements that he made—all of which conformed to the Commission's case, if not to the facts.

But, of course, you saw all this and I should tell you of the programme that BBC did not transmit. While the film was playing, the debate in the studio flourished, only to die under Mr Harris' heavy hand when the live broadcast, so to speak, commenced. An example. During an early segment of the programme Mr Harris began questioning Mr Belin, asking him in effect if he had been engaged in any correspondence with me regarding the making of the film. Mr Belin, it seems, wished to become a movie star and, unable to make it on his own, felt that we should provide a camera, film, a crew and an opportunity for him to speak in our film for a minimum of thirty minutes. Mr Belin was well prepared for the leading questions put to him. He had the correspondence in question spread out before him even before the first question was asked which, I must confess, raised some question in my normally unsuspicious mind regarding the possibility that the area had been explored before the programme began. I quickly put that evil thought aside but it recurred in a more persistent form shortly thereafter when, for a moment, Mr Harris forgot what he was about and departed from the script. Mr Harris, perhaps to establish his own identity, asked Mr Spector about a glaring inconsistency that the BBC had tracked down in the Warren Report. The FBI agent, Frazier, had testified that an examination of the President's shirt did not prove that a shot came from the rear but only that it was "possible" that a shot came from the rear. In the Report the word "possible" was escalated into "probable". Despite Mr Harris' sheepish grin regarding this discovery, it must be said that he appeared to have been fishing in shark water and to have hooked a baby minnow. Spector had no answer at first for this misdemeanour. Then Belin handed him the wrong page of the volume, after I had volunteered the correct one, and there the word "probable" did appear but in another context. Spector read probable with his booming district attorney voice and thus the matter was settled. That is almost settled. I asked if I might comment upon that for just a moment. The answer from Mr Harris, who had now regained his composure and commitment, was a stern no. The matter *was* settled. But it was not forgotten. Soon a portion of the film was shown.

This generally would herald an immediate peri‹ relaxation, but when the cameras in the studio off the tension began to build. Spector scowled and raise‹ voice so that it registered in menacing terms. His anger directed at a crumbling Harris. Why did you ask that ques We never went over that. If you do that again—well ‹ better not. I'm not fooling now. And then the prosec‹ attorney gestured towards me while still addressing H And you'd better shut that guy up too—I'm telling you I had spoken but a few words, mostly they were, "May something now?" Harris apologized. He promised to d from the pre-arrangement no further. I left my little tabl‹ casually approached Mr Harris. Sir, I said, I have the fe‹ that I have missed something by not arriving a week ago. you been having rehearsals in my absence? Mr Harris sai‹ they had gone over the general area of the questions wit Commission lawyers, yes we have. I suggested that it app that even some specifics had been agreed upon, based Mr Spector's anger regarding one question and Mr H agreement to stray never again. Mr Harris replied tha Spector only meant that if he was not prepared for a sp question then he would be placed in the embarrassing po of having to fumble for papers and, added Mr Harris, Mr Sp was certainly more than half right about that. But, I sai‹ never even discussed general areas with me. No answer. ‹ asked Mr Harris if I might have a copy of the script. H‹ that there were but three, his, Belin's and Spector's. Of c‹ I could not doubt his word, but in my own country we mimeograph just three copies of a document, we use c‹ paper, and it was that which prevented me from fully acc‹ his answer. During the next four hours I made fifteen, them, fifteen, requests to four different BBC representativ‹ a copy of the script.

At about eleven o'clock I found Mr Fox and tol‹ that he had made a solemn commitment to n‹ day before. That it had been agreed that at the outset ‹ programme I might register a dissent from the progra‹ format and choice of judges. Mr Fox said that I would be a‹ have time at 11:30. While that did not meet my definition programme's outset, I agreed. Closer to midnight than ‹ Mr Harris said I could have a few minutes. I began by ‹ that the BBC had rendered a disservice to the truth whe Harris stopped me and then picked up his phone to co‹ with the powers that be at the BBC. Silence. More on c‹ silence. Then Mr Harris spoke. I could almost have sympa with him had he appeared torn between his commitment word of honour and the word from above. But that c‹ evidently did not confront him. He said, you may not d‹ that subject at all. I then began to discuss the single theory. At this moment, Spector, who invented the whole left his seat and charged over to Harris telling him quite l‹ and now on camera, that I should not be allowed to trifl‹ *his* theory. (It had made him a district attorney and a can‹ for the mayoralty and was not to be fooled with.) Mr ‹ supinely yielded once again saying that I could only c‹ subjects that came up in the second part of the progran‹ asked him to tell me what to talk about and promised to c‹ any subject he wished to hear when he informed me th‹ time was up.

During a studio intermission it had b‹ plain that Prof. Bickel had a surprise in He was going to depart somewhat from his prev‹ published position and say that he was not quite sa‹ with the single bullet theory and that if the single theory failed there were two assassins. Spector wa‹ The fixed jury was no longer under control. Spector den‹ an opportunity to answer Prof. Bickel who had hardly u‹ word for almost five hours. Harris approached Bickel an‹ if he would mind if Spector answered him when he re‹

his verdict. They must have wild court scenes in Philadelphia, I kept on thinking. Bickel was a bit put out. Harris was insistent—at last showing the stern stuff he was made of. Bickel reluctantly yielded.

After Bickel spoke briefly, Harris, as if the thought just struck him, turned to Spector and said, sir, would you like to comment on that. Well, as long as he was asked, Spector was willing. It did occur to me during this exchange that this was the very subject that I was prevented from discussing because it was not in the 'second part of the programme', whatever that meant. Surely, now that it had been introduced twice more, I would not be denied my first comment on the subject. Waiting until Spector concluded I addressed a rather brief request to our chairman. May I comment upon that? The reply was no.

The evening ended on an unmistakably light note. Lord Devlin summed up. He wanted us to let President Kennedy's soul rest in peace. Anyway, suppose there was another assassin, no one has proved that he was a subversive, and if he wasn't subversive what difference does it make? I was about to ask Lord Devlin for a definition of the word "subversive" that does not include one who kills his own President, but I decided not to.

The BBC officials invited me to wine and dine in my cubicle below. I was somehow neither hungry nor thirsty, just anxious to say a few words. Reporters from two London daily papers were there. They asked for an interview. I agreed. A young BBC officialette approached. He said no rooms were available for a press conference. It was not much before one on the morning and I found it difficult to believe that they could not scare up one empty room. Oh, it's not that, the young man replied, but we cannot permit you to talk with the press here. I said that the BBC had made a room available to me and that I wished to utilize it for a conference. Cannot be done. Against the rules. The reporters were incredulous. We began to pack our belongings for a trip back to my hotel for the conference when the BBC relented and permitted it to take place here. I said that the programme had been rigged by the BBC to protect the Warren Commission lawyers from debate. I added that we never ran into that sort of trouble in countries, France as one example, whose economies are not entirely dependent upon the United States. The Socialist government indeed. Lenin must be twirling in his tomb.

I left BBC's Lime Grove studio to find a few citizens waiting outside. One offered his hand and his sympathy and said that the BBC does not speak for the English people, not this disgraceful night it doesn't, he added. Others agreed.

At my hotel a delegation of three, sent by twenty who had watched the programme, expressed similar views but in stronger language.

At Oxford University the next day the students made their views known also.

Mr Harris told the Evening Standard, "I don't think Mark Lane has any grounds for complaint. He was here for one purpose, and one purpose only. As it was stated

weeks ago, he was invited to attend so that if anybody made charges against him personally—for example he was just interested in making money out of the whole business or that he was a Communist—he could answer the charges against him." Mr Harris added that if he permitted me to debate with Spector or Belin "I should have had trouble with the two lawyers. They only came on the basis of this agreement." Mr Harris added that if he allowed me to enter the debate the two Commission lawyers "would have walked off". I have never refused a debate on equal grounds with Commission personnel. One must wonder what the two lawyers know about their own case which would cause them to walk away rather than debate.

BBC told the Evening Standard, "We arranged a viewing session for a number of representatives from foreign TV networks, and they *all* made a point of saying how impressed they were by Mr Harris' handling of the programme." That statement appears to be untrue. I spoke with just one representative, Klaus Toksvig, of Danish TV. He told me that the BBC programme was extremely unfair. Perhaps the representative of the Austin, Texas, TV station took another view.

The BBC spokesman concluded, "We arranged a press conference for Mr Lane after the programme ended."

As I prepared to leave London a BBC programme announced that Barrow and Southampton had tied 2-2. I just knew that I couldn't be sure unless I read it in the Times the next morning.

Mark Lane.
Nykobing, Danmark.
9 February, 1967.

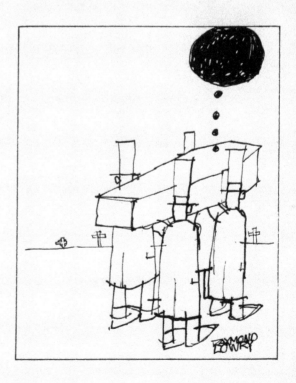

Editor: Richard Neville
Business Manager: Peter Ledeboer
Deputy Editor: Paul Lawson
Design: Jon Goodchild
Photography: Harry Youlden
Art Direction: Martin Sharp
Contributors, Etc: Andrew Fisher, David Reynolds, Dr. Herod Peron
Advertising: Ian Stocks, & Louise.

'London **OZ**' is Published by OZ Publications Ink Limited, 70 Clarendon Road, London, W.11; phone BAY 0320 or BAT 8407. Advertising enquiries should be addressed to Peter Ledeboer, 40 Anhalt Road, SW11

'London **OZ**' derives from 'OZ'— a monthly satirical magazine founded in Australia in 1963 by Richard Neville and Richard Walsh. 'OZ' (Australia) is still thriving with a circulation of approximately 40,000 and a £1 cheque sent to **OZ**, 16 Hunter Street, Sydney, with your name and address will guarantee a whole year's supply of this delightful, cheeky oddity.

Letters are welcome. Address them to the Editor, OZ, 70 Clarendon Rd, London W11

Owing to the last minute arrival of Mark Lane's expose, some of the promised features have been dropped. Better luck next time.

Please quote:
L1/DH/RC/TD
PRIVATE & CONFIDENTIAL
London Oz.

Dear Sir,

We thank you for your letter of January 23rd and for the copy of the publication London Oz. We regret to advise you however, that after due consideration we would prefer not to accept (an Oz) advertisement for insertion in our columns.

Yours faithfully,
Office Manager*i*
Advertising Dept
The Times
London EC4

February 9

Dear Sir,

It's a pleasure to have your support. Remind me one day to tell you about *Private Eye* and the assassination. Not that they were involved in planning it, but they played an interesting role in joining with the establishment to lead the attack upon critics of the Warren Commission. They apologised (Wells did) and a year later agreed to run a favourable article or interview. They never did. Wells apologised again and said that Bernard Levin was very close to the publication and he was in love with the Report, PE could do nothing.
Good luck with *Oz*. I'm framing the drawing of LBJ.

Sincerely,

Mark Lane
Denmark

January 24

Dear Sirs,

Haveing just purchased your first issue of 'London OZ', I was, to say the least, somewhat amused by the article 'In Bed With The **English**',
The poor woman that wrote it must be pretty ugly, or a raving **Nympho**; trying too hard, As an Englishman I must say, The english, **If he is** good, is the best lover in the World, And if your poor frustrated writer wishes proof of this statement, I invite her to spend a night or two with me, and if I cannot, in her oppinion, back up my statement with actions, in other words, give her complete sexual satisfaction, she can write an article on the one Englishman She **has** had, and really run the Englishman down and even use my name.
This is not just a proposition to your writer for a cheap thrill, It is an Englishman trying to stand up for his fellow countrymen, and to prove his statement, Which your writer hasn't done. I gathered from her article, that she has not in ever really been to bed with an English Man, and I would like to add, That until She has, She should shut up. A personal reply from your writer would be very much appreciated, (If she has the nerve.)

Yours faithfully,

Rod C B Lake Esq
40, Penywern Road
Earls Court
London SW5

(Our author accepts Mr Lake's invitation, although reserving her right to refuse consummation upon inspection. Results will be published next issue.)

January 31

Dear Sir,

At last, I said to myself as I ran all the way home, a real adult-type satirical magazine in London—the kind you can still read after you've come down from the university. Maybe even a good hard-hitting serious article or two thrown in, the sort they wouldn't dare to print elsewhere.
And, by God, there it all was: a brief but thought-provoking article on RAAS; a very funny, informed metaphorical post-mortem on the Death of God; an entertaining hopped-up Fourth Leader on violence in the news media; even a peep behind the scenes of that ever-popular soap opera for liberals, the *New Statesman*.
But what an almighty effort to dig it all out! What endless pages of whiz-bang topography! What plethoric paraphernalia for optical exhaustion! And what dizzying condensed, allusive, learned, convoluted, acrobatic prose! By the time I got to your catty little exposé of *Private Eye*, I was too exhausted to decide whether it was the ultimate send-up, or simply the sort of internecine battle which rages

---

THE NEW LONDON SPY

A DISCREET GUIDE TO THE CITY'S PLEASURES
EDITED BY HUNTER DAVIES
30s.net

BLOND

between the Pilgrim Free Holiness Apostolic Anabaptists and the Reformed Immersive Holiness Faith Healers. Or then again, maybe your PR boys have determined that this is the stuff it takes to sell satire in London. If it's commercial I won't knock it.
I did finally get all the way through, even the tiny little IT reprints, but I've had to go to bed and send for my oculist.

Yours sincerely,

John Whiting
London Correspondent
Pacifica Radio
7 Gledhow Gardens
London SW5

JONATHAN CAPE LIMITED
THIRTY BEDFORD SQUARE
LONDON W.C 1

Peter Ledeboer, Esq.,
40 Anhalt Road,
London. S.W.11.   8th February, 1967.

Dear Sir,

Thank you for your letter of February 8th. We consider that OZ is extremely immature, amateur and completely lacking in taste, and therefore we are not likely to take advertising space with you now or in the future.

Yours Faithfully,

Jean Maxfield

JEAN MAXFIELD.
Publicity Department.

Printed by
Sharptone Litho Ltd.,
83 Bellenden Road, S.E.15

Distributed by
Moore Harness Ltd.,
11 Lever Street, E.C.1

WELL... THE RUBY CAME FROM THE CZARINA'S NECKLINE AND THE GOLD FROM THE CZAR'S TEETH

Peter Clarke

DAY BY DREARY DAY

The Lord Chancellor decided today to abolish all appeals from the Court of *The Sunday Times*. It was thought that once the court had given its decision in any case, further consideration of the matter would be a waste of column inches. Justice Frost dissented.

The Russian offer of a peace treaty has alarmed the British Government. Troop movements have commenced throughout the country. Cabinet is reported as seeing the situation as similar to the Munich crisis. "It is too late to appease Britain now", said a spokesman.

Once upon a time the Kennedy family commissioned a book to "tell the truth about November 22, 1963".

It was to sensationalise Johnson's indelicate behaviour following the assassination and to boost Robert Kennedy's Presidential chances. The tenor of the book was discussed in Washington circles. The Wall Street Journal reported that the Kennedy family feared the wrath of President Johnson because of passages in it.

It has become known that an accommodation between the Kennedys and Johnson was arranged. Johnson was to stand aside after his final term and offer no opposition to Robert Kennedy's ambitions. All that the Kennedys were required to do was to stop the book. Their contract with Manchester gave them absolute right to do so. However, Robert, who drew up the contract, was never much of a lawyer. The contract dealt solely with hard cover sales. Not included were book clubs, paper back rights and serialisation rights which Manchester was industriously flogging.

Johnson demanded that the Kennedy family should keep its part of the bargain. In the face of that insistence the Kennedys felt constrained to proceed with legal action although well aware of the dangers.

The book, of little real literary interest and historic significance, has yet played its part in history. Designed as a weapon to be used to assist Robert Kennedy in his private and personal war with Lyndon Johnson it resulted in harming them both; Johnson far less.

Extensive investigations have conclusively established the link between newspapers and narcotics. There can be no doubt. The newspaper is a dangerous drug.

Yet millions of doses of this depraving substance are allowed to fall into the hands of men, women and even children, every day. With strict medical supervision, this hallocinogen undoubtedly can benefit man. But to-day's indiscriminate traffic on the streets where the addict can attain his daily trip, without fuss, for as little as 4d. from a street corner pusher (impregnated on 60 sq. ft. of absorbent paper) is causing deep concern in government and medical circles.

Users apparently think nothing of fixing in full view .Hence it is hard to avoid noticing the characteristic symptoms of addiction. Examining the effect on a typical patient, we find, only minutes after purchase, a contraction of neck, arm, and leg muscles. Worry lines appear on the forehead. The eyes fix opaquely in a set expression as the visually overstimulated imagination begins to colour the mind with every possible form of death and disaster. The heartbeat accelerates rapidly as endless visions unroll of all that is unnatural to the consciousness, from incest and rape to economic disasters and world starvation.

The more disturbing addict moves in even more dangerous realms—with a morning and evening fix daily and often up to three on Sunday. Sometimes 'supplemented' even further in very extreme cases. This massive overdosing produces comas

and a total inability to communicate thoughts or feelings in any way connected with everyday life.

Rehabilitation methods are in their infancy. No antidote is yet known. But with at least 15,000,000 heads on our hands, action is essential.

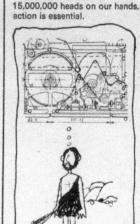

Can the foetus feel pain ? This is the question that many of our young people are asking today Our special reporter went down into the womb to find out. He found Sir Francis sitting in a swivel chair wearing his smoking jacket and mending a tooth. "Only the bombing gives me trouble", he said. "If the Americans agree to stop that then I shall be willing to come out and start negotiating." Here is the spirit that made Britain great. The answer is plain—we must learn to grit our teeth and bear it.

BRITISH BREASTS

here is no doubt about it, the bosom is being driven out of England. One glance at our women's magazines, at the narrow-chested models hanging dresses made of riveted metal plates on their naked bodies, and any lass with boobs knows that fashion has passed her by. Imagine the soft roundness of a breast oozing between those metal plates, or butting into the severity of a prickly lamé mini-dress. The buttock went long ago, and the hip followed it, but surely we should make a stand about the bosom. Paris cannot be blamed for this. The little dress in Paris is knitted, and fits like a second skin of jersey or angora over the round eminences; be they large or be they small, suffice it that they be round and full.

The mini-pull is an impossibility in England, because its whole appeal is derived from the contrast between the straightness and skimpiness of its line and the pushing rotundity of the bosom beneath. It would need a full-scale revolution in the British bra industry which knows only two shapes, the bump and the pouch, and neither of those will do.

For a long time, the breast has been sorely neglected in England. There are advertisements in a certain kind of magazine for treatments to enlarge the bust, but nothing at

l about keeping the bust one already has smooth-skinned
nd firm and pretty. It is regarded as a sexy thing, all night, if
ou like that sort of thing, but not a beautiful thing. But if it
omes to that, I dare say connoisseurship in bodies, of the
nd practised by a Parisian with a few minutes to spend
a café, has lapsed rather, perhaps as a result of the
epredations of two wars upon the British physique.
ne attitude of the British manufacturer towards the great
ritish breast is downright unsympathetic. As far as he is
oncerned it is either under-developed or over-developed
d never just right. Either he connives with the scrawny
deceive, or he battles with the blousy to support the
eight without cutting the shoulders.
atins are aware of the bosom as a thing of infinite variety
nd positive caprice), capable of piquancy and poignancy
luxury and velvet surfeit. Basically it is to be seen and
ressed, and clothes must suggest that. The *soutien-
orge* or *reggipetto* must not be obtrusive, but must be
tractive, seen or unseen. It does not insist upon con-
olling, moulding and supporting. Advertisement stresses
uch more that the bra must be light, flattering, easy to
ear. The breast is not regarded as an encumbrance (the
ke about Grandma catching her tits in the mangle is
glish). Women's magazines carry almost as much
vice on the care of the breast as they do for the face. It
supposed that the breast is beautiful, for its owner has
lashed it morning and night with cold water to stimulate
e circulation and keep it firm, and massages it with skin
ods and hormone creams. It is assumed that her husband/
ver has paid it the requisite attention. Above all, it is
portant. It has an identity, and somewhere there is the
rment that suits it.
e British manufacturer is convinced, possibly rightly,
at the British breast is either meagre and knobby or big
d floppy. It has either to be built up by gay deceivers
d 'foam' and cushions, or hoisted as far up and out as
will go.
t us consider the case of the girl whose breast is neither
ant and scrawny nor droopy nor super-droopy. Let's
ppose she is a slender-backed, round bosomed 34C,
easuring 37" around. She has enough muscle tone to do
thout a brassiere (the very name indicates the anti-
thetic nature of the object) and probably would, expect
at variations of temperature cause the odd eyebrow to
oot up, and sweaters are a bit rough on the old erogenous
sue. She doesn't much like the bobbing about caused by
atively energetic movement either.
e takes her pretty bosom to the corsetiere, who has a
ined *(ho-ho)* fitter, and bares her chest to the same.
is lady, who usually belongs to the surgical category
rself, plants a cold, splayed hand over one warm and
mulous breast, and oracularly pronounces a model for
dom. Where two pretty hemispheres went in, two
ngular prisms come out. Her own lineaments are
med into a massive contraption of cotton or nylon
hich is worse because it scratches) and elastic, hooked
tly across the back, and hoisted up to a dizzy angle on
collarbone.
e saleslady alais fitter explains that fashionable breasts
meant to look like two little Matterhorns in the vertical
ne, and Miss 34C believes her. Half bras aren't made in
size anyway, because C cups need all the support they
get. It is axiomatic that C sizes sag. All Miss 34C knows
at when she twists round to do up her zipper, one of the
tterhorns sticks in her eye. For added freedom of move-
nt Madam may have elastic straps which let the right
amids zoom about. Uncomfortable and self-conscious
er new piercing bosom hoist aloft by block and tackle,
takes the Underground home, and slightly injures a
oolboy who falls against one of her pyramids.
she decides to avoid the fitters in future and shops
und instead. One salesgirl declares categorically that
ording to the firm's special graded chart Miss 34C is
ly a 38 medium, only in that shop you are not allowed
y them on. There the bras are called after an archangel.
discovers that she may change her block and tackle,
the more popular pre-formed bra. It is usually made in
an, or the Empire, and is called Lovable or Adorable or

something of the sort. The idea is that it has a shape of its
own, hewn out of polystyrene or polythene, that will not
alter no matter what goes inside it. That of course is its
great advantage, for the only way of telling whether it be
full or empty is to give it a sharp knock, when it is empty
it will dint, and if it is full you'll get a reaction. It costs less
than other bras and is probably more comfortable, because
it has less seaming. Nevertheless, Miss 34C couldn't find
one that suited her, because the pretty ones had no room
for her bosom in them, and the big ones were pretty much
like the block and tackle she already had. She thought they
were clammy as well.
She resolved to pretend she was a B cup, and ventured
into the fascinatingly naughty world of the half-bra. Most
half-bras exist to create cleavage where none existed,
therefore they have semi-circular armatures which are
joined in the middle. The massive junction is disguised by
a coy bow or a heart of a flower. Thus the bosom is
presented as a kind of joggly pudding in the middle of the
chest. The rigid armature rubs ulcers on the rib cage, and
the ends of it keep piercing the binding and stabbing into
the tit, or appearing at the neckline. The effect in a sweater
is distressing, because the actual shape of the pudding is
more or less amorphous.
She found that it was tacitly assumed that most girls who
affect half-bras are really flatchested, and that the sizes are
not those of the actual bosom, but of the bosom that the
buyer would like to think she had. Inside the meagre B cup
she found that all the room was already taken up by a little
cushion, so that even when she asked for a 36 and thought
she could take it in at the sides, her breasts sprang out, or
else the seaming at the top was so tight that it divided the
breasts into a top and bottom bulge, which made it look
as if she had four. Many were cunningly built up with foam
(it never says what the foam is made of—rubber is not
mentioned in the lingerie business these days) so that her
bosom had to escape round the edges.
Nowhere could she find a brassiere which would perform
the simple task of housing her peach of a bosom. Her body
stocking flattened it. The rude bras she tried on in strange
little shops in Soho were ugly, or distorting, or uncomfortable. The salesladies convinced her that it was her
fault that the stock lines didn't suit her, and upbraided her
for her narrow back, and positively sneered at the intrac-
tible firmness and roundness of her breasts.
One day she went to Paris and she never came back. She
got a job as a brassiere model.

Germaine

THE LONDON OZ

BEAUTIFUL ☆
BREASTS COMPETITION.
ENTER NOW

Was Prince Philip right when he lashed out at
sagging British breasts? Have they lost prominence since the War? London OZ means to show
the Duke he's blind. Help us put the British breast
back where it belongs. You could win £20 and
have your bust immortalised over a double page
OZ pin-up. (INTERNATIONAL COMPEDITORS ARE ALSO WELCOME.)
Send in two photos of your breasts: (1) Profile; (2) full face; no other part of the body need be
included. Send your name (or pseudonym) plus a
self-addressed envelope to: London OZ Competition, 70 Clarendon Road, London, W11.
Some correspondence might be entered into.
P.S. IF YOU HAVE NO SUITABLE PHOTOGRAPHER PLEASE
RING OUR PHOTOGRAPHER, BOB WHITAKER - FLA 8878 FOR
A FREE APPOINTMENT.

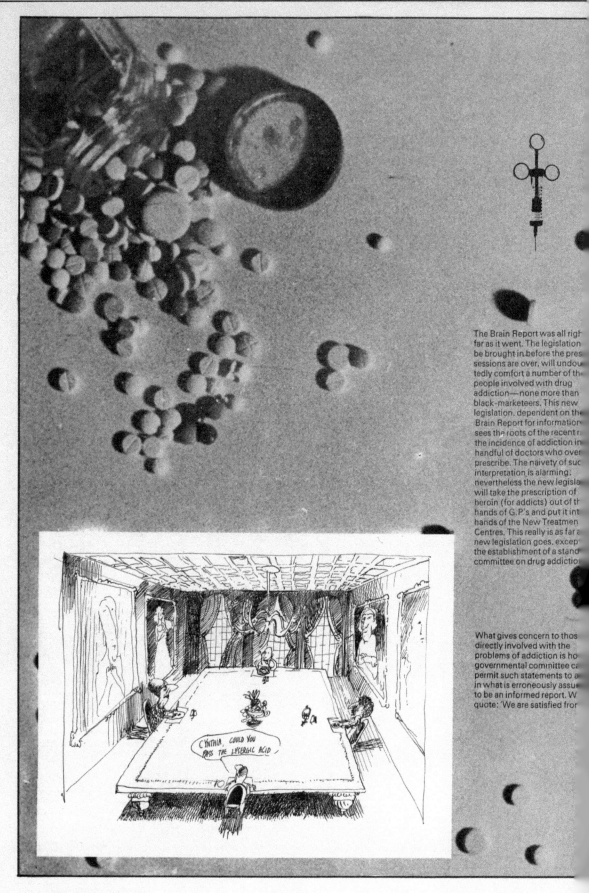

The Brain Report was all righ
far as it went. The legislation
be brought in before the pres
sessions are over, will undou
tedly comfort a number of th
people involved with drug
addiction—none more than
black-marketeers. This new
legislation, dependent on the
Brain Report for information
sees the roots of the recent r
the incidence of addiction in
handful of doctors who over
prescribe. The naivety of suc
interpretation is alarming:
nevertheless the new legisla
will take the prescription of
heroin (for addicts) out of th
hands of G.P.'s and put it int
hands of the New Treatmen
Centres. This really is as far a
new legislation goes, excep
the establishment of a stand
committee on drug addictio

What gives concern to thos
directly involved with the
problems of addiction is ho
governmental committee ca
permit such statements to a
in what is erroneously assu
to be an informed report. W
quote: 'We are satisfied fror

enquiries of the Home Office, the Metropolitan Police and our witnesses that there is at present no evidence of any significant traffic, organized or otherwise, in dangerous drugs that have been stolen or smuggled into this country'. **(Brain Report '65)**

The Brain Report is quite right in assuming that a number of so-called junkies, as yet unregistered, obtain their first supplies from registered addicts. Piccadilly Circus, will, until the new legislation is introduced, provide an open source of NHS heroin. The most well-known method (not for the shy) is to stand outside Boots, or if tired, to sit on the baskets situated just to the left of the entrance. Most of the young junkies are willing to sell and are easily identified by their ability to sleep in an upright position.

One of the most amenable pushers is a blonde well-built American girl of 22 who collects her heroin every evening

between 6 and 7. 'I think your English Health Service is wonderful!' The usual routine is to follow her until she stands by the left-luggage lockers in Piccadilly Tube after 6 p.m. After a brief conversation she will sell heroin at 3/4d. a jack or £1 a grain. This has been the standard price for some time; such heroin is good unadulterated NHS heroin.

Precisely how many heroin users purchase supplies in this way is difficult to assess, but on one Friday evening 34 non-registered junkies were seen to

purchase or to attempt to purchase heroin within a period of two hours. If this were the only, or even the chief, source of supply, the innane mumblings of Sergeant Arthur Kilner of Scotland Yard's Dangerous Drugs' department, who said on January 29th, 1967, that the National Health Service was

fulfilling the role of Mafia in other countries by supplying drug addicts with their needs' might be worthy of some attention; and the new prescription control might have some chance of dealing with illicit trafficking. Unhappily, though this may be the most obvious, it is already perhaps one of the more insignificant sources of supplies.

Trafficking in amphetamines has long been widespread in the West End; it is virtually impossible to find a teenager dancing in a West End club who hasn't pilled up beforehand; blues (drynamil) sell at 1/3d. each, and can be purchased by the 1,000, but are normally bought in 5's, 10's, 20's, 50's and 100's.

Although technically 'mild stimulants', when taken in overdoses the comedown is unpleasant, and when taken in overdoses continuously a much more intense and powerful drug is often sought in order to avoid this very unpleasant comedown. Pushers of pills are often young and unintelligent, frequently blocking themselves before they try to block anyone else. Two such pushers are Paul and Cliff; both are 21. Both own their own 66 Zephyrs; their sole source of income is their drug pushing. Their joint income is between £200 and £400 per week, of

which they pass a third to their boss, whom they refer to as Big Syd. They work with two West Indians, whom they employ full-time as a protective measure and with whom they share a 20-guinea-a-week set of rooms in Chelmsford.

Starting their work at the Marquee club they sell to a market of 13-year-old mods; after a meal they move into the clubs around **Greek Street;** then to a stand just outside **Tiffany's** at about 1 in the morning. When necessary they work a pitch in the **Lyons' Cafes** around Trafalgar Square; if on Sunday morning they have

any pills remaining, they move into **Chelsea** where apparently tired debs are always a ready market. In conversation with one reporter as to the origin of the amphetamine, they said that some of their pills were knocked off, but most came as a regular supply through London docks— they weren't sure where, but 'Big Syd looks after that end'. In one week-end they never sell less than 3,000 pills and some-times in excess of 6,000, undercutting other pushers by selling at 1/– each. The only other market they have is for hash which, for a good roll, they sell at about 3/– to 5/– a joint. It is this sort of trading that began exploiting the market for a stimulant drug lying open in the all-night clubs in Soho. But this has been taken over by another, more threatening kind of trading.

Chris is one such pusher, 5' 8" tall and about 35 years old. He prefers the cafes and standing around to entering the clubs. He carries with him (and offered me) amphetamines, barbiturates, heroin, cocaine, methadryne; the barbiturates were all tuinal, a combination of seconal and sodium amytal; the heroin was

powdered, which is significant, because the heroin obtained by registered drug addicts is in pill form; but again this does not lend any weight to any suggestion that there is any organized traffic.

One ex-junky obtained all his heroin from his own pushing of heroin; he worked for Ken Collins (now serving time) who he claimed to be boss of most men whose names were linked, perhaps erroneously, with the distribution of drugs in Soho— Big Syd, Big Dave (a front), Jimmy McIntyre, Sigi and Babe: the heroin that this boy pushed was again in powdered form, was collected through the East India dock and was of Italian origin (on analysis); he sold regularly to about 100 non-registered heroin users and alone sold about 500 grains a week— again at £1 per grain; but sees the price already rising sometimes up to £5 per grain. When these prices are too high, Notting Hill and Kilburn are resorted to, or the numerous cafes in the Back Lane area of the East End have always been an excellent source.

While drugs of most kinds can be purchased easily in the majority of clubs, a certain score can be marked up on **The Duke of York** (not very fashionable with mods), now taken over from **Finches** as the 'in' scene; pot is available, but also police (who seem to spend their time searching the young drifters for this relatively innocuous intoxicant).

Tiles, Oxford Street—often has more pushers than dancers.

The Angel, Islington, is good for heroin and cocaine at £1 to £1 10s. per grain, and pot, but it is a bit out of the way. (L.S.D. 30/– a trip—Czech manufacture).

Marquee has pills a-plenty; but for anything at all—heroin (£1 to £3 per grain), coke, meths (5/– an ampule), amphetamines, barbiturates—the **Casino,** Wardour Mews is the place to go, and maybe you can brush shoulders with many of those directly involved with trading. Prices are rising, but that's the price we have to pay for organized drug trafficking, so buy now!

Drugs were purchased by one American Sociologist in each of the clubs named above in one evening.

MARCH 67/LONDON OZ 13

Metamorphoses

Jocelyn Brouha,
Wykhamist Accounts Executive,
deviser of award-winning bra
                              campaigns
and originator of the slogan 'Tat for Tit',
is reconstituted as page 257
of the Penguin Edition
of the Annotated Elinor Glyn.

Christopher Columbus,
for turning back at landfall
Hispaniola,
in reward for not discovering America
is elected Pope Urban XIX
and publishes the first
bull on contraception
'De temporibus tutis'.

Martin Seymour-Smith
by a costive diet of integrity,
a perilous run of rule-breaking
and through extravagant
over exposure to the demands of
                              friendship
is turned into a Soho pub clock
and forced to show
closing time for ever.

by Peter Porter

Simon Puer
while chatting up a critic
at the Festival Hall bar
sees himself fade
to a smile on the face
of Alexander Goehr.

En route to the Out Patients Dept.,
a scorching article
on five elder poets in his pocket
under his favourite pseudonym,
Ian Hamilton
is side-tracked to Madame Tussaud's
and melted down
for their new tableau
'The Suicide of Hart Crane'.

Playing the first of the '48
on his Bermondsey gas pipe
didgeree-du, Wolfe Morris
becomes 'The Wanderer's Pozzie'
motel at Surfer's Paradise
on the Gold coast near Brisbane,
Queensland, Australia.

No fearful indignation lacerates the heart of Malcolm Muggeridge, so far as I can see, but then, he is not exiled like poor Swift, buried in the provincial hell of Dublin, but indulged, heard and forgotten as fast as the Epilogue. A pity, because he has more to say than all the mumbling prelates and incompetent satirists in England—and a great band of them there are too. He is the most irritating man in England and the least loved after Harold Wilson.

He is not above farting while on the phone to eminent people, or using what is called filthy language by way of emphasis, or to comment on the character of other eminent people, and is vain enough to keep a particularly unfortunate bust of himself stored amongst his books. These and other things I discovered last week after trudging through a mile-and-a-half of mud, carrying a decrepit and uncertain tape-recorder to his house in Sussex through the most sodden landscape I have ever seen.

I asked him questions from the viewpoint of a world-improver, an attitude he has long since given up, and he was pleasant enough to keep his amusement reasonably well hidden. Why, I began, do you so strenuously object to the twentieth century?

The whole essence of my view of life, he said, is that I intensely dislike the way the world is going. Putting it in its simplest terms, the world is going in the direction of what is called the American way of life. This is what everyone wants and what the whole world is going to have, even the communist countries.

'What's wrong with giving people cars and television and too much food?"

It's not the higher standard of living itself. It's the method whereby it is achieved and sustained that makes people's lives spiritually less rich, the method being primarily to subordinate everything to production, to accept this mysterious thing the gross national product as a sort of deity and then to build up this terrible structure of advertising and mass communication to ensure that the pot is kept boiling."

True, but might it not free people from the nasty business of having to work all day?"

Oh I approve of that, but it might not. It depends how they use it. There is a great fallacy of our time, that if you can raise the standard of life or even the standard of education, you automatically enrich people's lives. Not so. The most barren and wretched place in the world I've ever visited is California, which also happens to have the highest standard of life and education. Yet all the reformers and people like that at their international conferences always assume that if only you could give say, Africa, the standard of life prevailing in California, it would be a great thing.

Technology doesn't make it easier to read books, listen to music, look at paintings?

Depends whether you use it for that purpose. It makes it easier to print things, but what are you printing? When I see what's put on a typical bookstall in America or, for that matter, here, I wish printing had never been invented.

But that's only filling empty minds with rubbish which would in any case be filled with rubbish, or remain empty. Surely in the last century minds were filled with rubbish too?

It's possibly true. My feelings about this century has nothing to do with other centuries. I'm not saying the middle ages were marvellous or the nineteenth century was marvellous, simply that I see in the world a certain way of life which is increasingly held up and accepted by my fellows as the aim and object of living, and it is obnoxious. There never was a golden

age or ever could be. I take the Christian view that man is bound at all times to make a mess-up of things. He is bound to be unhappy because he is a creature who can conceive perfection but is intrinsically imperfect. *His comfort* lies in relation to circumstances which are greater than the circumstances of his life. Insofar as he can look beyond the circumstances of his life, there is his comfort, his joy, his greatness. He tries to *understand.* Pascal says the greatness of man is a simple thing: he is so made that he tries to understand.

That reminds me of Shaw recommending

LITTLE MALCOLM AND HIS STRUGGLE AGAINST THE 20TH CENTURY

INTER-VIEWED BY STAN GEBLER DAVIES.

SHARP

that evolution proceed to the point that m achieve supreme ecstasy by walking arour thinking about mathematics.

I don't object to that.

Isn't it a rather impractical proposal f the great mass of mankind?

Certainly, and therefore was typical Shaw. But what is not impractical is to s that, whatever sort of mess-up human bein make, and I'm quite sure will always contin to make, and however ignoble many of th pursuits may be (war, affluence) *still* the will be in them this passion to understand, a that will never desert them and can never destroyed.

You wrote an article in 'Playboy' th December that the twentieth century has d tinguished itself by producing not a sing work of art of lasting value. Not even fro Joyce or Yeats or Proust or Stravinsky Shostakovich or Britten?

The point, really, was that in the twe tieth century human genius had gone in what is called science rather than into imagi ative pursuits such as writing or architectu Neither Proust nor Joyce are writers I wo be quite as adulatory towards as is the pres fashion, but neither they nor Joyce are rea *twentieth* century. The twentieth century D. H. Lawrence, Dylan Thomas (a most min tenth-rate poet), T. S. Eliot, Ezra Pound. I do know enough about music to pronoun about it, but I suspect, for instance, Britter not as good as Beethoven. I have a *feeli* that it might be so.

I will agree with you *he continued benigr possibly feeling he had been a little unki* since you are, a nice young-man, that t sentence was an exaggerated sentence, bu contains a truth in it and that is that it is v difficult to think of any artistic achievement this century that you could put in a major cla There's no novel written that you could ev think of in the same breath *(sic)* as s Tolstoy.

We had got tired of literature, so tal about sex. Muggeridge is not supposed approve of sex, and yet he had written: "Th is nothing serious under the sun except lo of one's fellow mortals and of God. All ridiculous save ecstasy" *without exclud* sexual ecstasy, which is the most most of are capable of. He said sexual ecstasy v ecstasy in his sense of the word only whe was accompanied by great love. "All mystics are unanimous on the point that m can find ecstasy only through escape fr the self. Love produces ecstasy, but sex d not if it is the pursuit of personal physi satisfaction." *I wanted to know why he approved of the famous set of experime done by Masters and Johnson with g penises and what-have-you in the interest those who found sex less than it is descri in D. H. Lawrence and 'Playboy'. What the harm of it if it helped people amus th selves? The trouble with it, he said, apart f the fact it was ludicrous and absurd, was there were no sexual problems you co solve with science.* "It's absurd to regard sexual act as something that can be perfec physically. The scientific interest in it is less morbid than the pornographic inte in it. I strongly suspect all of society is mov in the direction of masturbation and literature in the direction of what they ca in the Weimar Republic, 'one-han literature'."

The exploiting classes undoubte used religion to keep people quiet, and it a blasphemy and corruption of religion, b think today they're more inclined to use and it's a great and wicked corruption of If you stupify people's minds with erotic

won't question things. An idiot mind,
bling over a Playmate in the middle of
yboy' is much less 'likely to worry about
t's happening in Vietnam than otherwise.

Maybe, I said, having ambitions myself
contribute to 'Playboy', but aren't they
cently employed?

No, said Muggeridge, this sort of thing
them off from a satisfactory fulfilment of
To me it's pathetic. It's a debasement of
that is utterly abhorrent.

Do you mind being called a puritan?

In the sense that the word is used
ratively, which is of someone who avoids
vement in sensuality for reasons of pru-
e. Now that I'm old, I want to avoid
vement in sensuality because I consider
thereby one's mind is released for other
its.

Have you wasted time on sensuality?

No, I don't think it's wasted because I
think that's a thing any mortal man can
really decide about—what is wasted and
s not. I have a very strong feeling that if
ver understand all of this we shall see
nothing is wasted. All forms of human
rience contribute to fulfilling whatever
e here for.

Have you any programme at all for the
vement of humanity?

None. All collective schemes for the
ment of man have been disastrous.

Have you then just settled down to
at folly and occasionally fling ink pellets
n who still imagine there is something
done to improve things?

That is a just criticism, and I think at
I have been guilty of that, but I'd like to
it doesn't represent the whole effort one's
, I don't think, either, that my ridiculing,
was necessary, was any more negative,
ame a great maestro, than Swift's.
nly no writer could be more conscious
am that I haven't done as much as I
have.

I agreed, and mentioned that I could not
ny great difference in potential, reading
ork, enjoying his language and intelli-
, between himself, Shaw and Voltaire.
credit (I cannot stand the English habit
pocisy), neither could he. When I
sted that, possibly, he too was a victim
twentieth century he dislikes so much,
reed it was possible, since this is not
e to encourage dedication to an art
is one to encourage journalists, witness
n efforts. Shaw, he mentioned, was no
journalist than he, with the difference
haw had chosen the stage to parade his
ns and make his money. He preferred
ion. Muggeridge and I disagreed over
but not, I think, over Muggeridge,
I consider a great journalist and the
man I have met. He may have taken
tachment to the point that he does not
to the idea of our all being incinerated
ow, but then there is nothing he or
ther sane man can do to stave off
ation, if we are going to be incinerated,
se sane men are not put in charge of
ments or bombs.

Muggeridge's greatest usefulness is
n this credulous age, when we will
in anything except God and selfless-
e can take our minds for a while off
lious and futile business of trying to
e humanity, and have us spend some
me improving our own spiritual condi-
He would not have anyone cease
ng wickedness, but he would advise
cease trying to impose "good" on
ty in the form of politically or culturally
s systems. Virtue institutionalised is
t purely wicked, and revolutions have
f revolving.

THE CLUB AT THE COURT

OPEN FROM 6pm to MIDNIGHT and LATER

TO ENGLISH STAGE SOCIETY MEMBERS ONLY

SUBSCRIPTION One Guinea

Food, Drink, Dancing, Plays, Films,
Ballet, Jazz, Folk, Opera, Palmistry,
+ PEOPLE

SLOANE SQUARE S.W.3   SLO 2273

£50

EXTRA
FOREIGN
CASH
FOR
YOU

1001 prizes to be won in INTERGUIDE '67.
Don t go down The Spain Drain, dad, without
INTERGUIDE '67 – 128 pages of photos, facts
and maps. Order NOW – 10s cheque or P.O.
Available only from L-B Editions. Box)O3(

PSYLOSIS

will be a triennial magazine purporting
to be for the sixth form mentality.
The first edition will be out soon.
2s 6d to: Psylosis
    Stuarts
    Radley College
    Abingdon
    Berks
will ensure swift delivery of this new
departure in sixth form creativity.

Glory
hole
BOUTIQUE

324a King's Road S.W.3

Telephone FLAxman 0296

You are invited to become a member of

C.M.C.

Facilities include:-
Substantial discounts on clothes, etc.
FREE use of Accommodation address, same
day forwarding service.
FREE use of PEN PAL register.
FREE use of HOLIDAY register.
Members only - CMCN (Naturists)

Send for detailed Brochure (8d in stamps please)
   to: Dept O1
     C.M.C.
14 Alexandra Road, Clacton-on-Sea, Essex.

Are you a member of any political,
social or religious organisation?
London OZ invites members or
executives of such groups to contribute a 300 to 500 word justification of its existence.
Start from the assumption that your
organisation is tedious, redundant,
anachronistic and crackpot.
Send copy to:
London OZ 'Groups'
70 Clarendon Road W.11

OZ NEEDS AN OFFICE.
Suitable areas are Covent Garden,
Holborn, Soho, Chelsea, Pimlico,
Marylebone and the Hilton.
Space required approx. 500 sq. ft.
Contact Peter Ledeboer at BAT 8407.

U S E T A X I T R U C K S
For light removals. Dormobiles with helpful
working drivers. HAM 1466 or HAM 6351.
Please quote this advert.   O2

T R A N S P O R T
FOR ALL   PROBLEMS

REMOVALS, DELIVERIES, ETC.
DORMOBILES WITH HELPFUL,
WORKING DRIVERS.

TAXIMOVES GULliver 8923

ALICE PAUL

Elphinstone Gibb's creations designed,made
and sold at 12 Abingdon Road W.8

Open Mondays, Tuesdays, Wednesdays
    & Fridays   9 am to 6 pm
    Thursdays   9 am to 7 pm
    Saturdays   9 am to 1 pm

Telephone WEStern 4466

PROTEST!

B A D G E S - U N I Q U E O F F E R

Medical Aid for Vietnam.................1/-
Hands off Vietnam......................1/-
Rhodesia; One Man – One Vote..........1/-
No Wage Freeze........................ 1/-
Y.C.L. Symbol......................... 1/-
Teachers: No To Wage Freeze...........1/-
Make Love Not War..................... 1/-
Against Racialism..................... 1/-
Votes at 18........................... 1/-
Peace and Socialism 6d
Cut the Arms Bill......................6d
YCND.................................. 6d
C.N.D. Symbol..........................6d
Remember Hiroshima.....................6d
Movement for Colonial Freedom..........6d
Peace In Vietnam.......................6d
Anti-Apartheid........................ 6d

Send cash/cheque/P.O.(Plus Post) to:
Y.C.L. 16 King Street, London W.C.2

As his lips came close to mine, I felt as if our breaths had turned to fire...

N-NO-OO-O!

And this time, besides his gentleness, I felt the stunning passion of his kiss... and my heart beat wildly...

His lips were a sweet whisper against mine...

And this time when his kiss told me the truth -- I believed it...

...after all...!

DEAREST!

At that moment I felt that life could offer no greater happiness than that which filled my soul!

And, with his second kiss, I knew my dream had at last come true!

And I saw the mysterious sea draw our lips together as if by a magnet no human could resist...

DARLING -- DARLING -- I LOVE YOU --! DO YOU LOVE ME --?

But he wouldn't wait... and crushed my answer against his mouth...

HOW CAN I TELL HIM THAT ALL I WANT IS A GOOD SCREW?

A WORK OF ART

Sin whispers and is dark and secret. It is wicked, but it has an underground thrill. It comes at night, insinuating intimately. I have an iron cot, with a moveable side that goes up and down. I can reach my hand through the bars and stroke the flamboyant birds trailing over the wallpaper. At night, though, in the homely silence when the nightblinds are drawn, but the world is awake outside, I make my own patterns.

This is the sin. This is the most forbidden thing. I would die of shame to admit it.

I pick my nose. I pick it under the covers like a thief with stolen loot, wrestling absorbedly and guiltily, and put it onto the wall below the line of the cot, where it can't be seen. I am making a great pattern, each one spaced so. I am glad, like a diligent workman when I get a big wieldy one. The pattern is rounding out. It is a great circle, designed like heavenly bodies, none to collide or unbalance the mystical whole. Nobody knows. And when my little sister picks her nose I shame her out of it. I call her a pig in terrible outrage and make her get a cloth and wipe it off. Kiki! Kiki!' I say in disgust, watching her virtuously. All the time my pattern grows.

But soon we are to leave the hotel, and fear strikes me like an underground tremor. I go cold at the thought of discovery. But I cannot believe they will find me out. How can they know what material covers the wall so beautifully in that great design?

One day I come in and see their hanging faces. Ah. The Day. The Storm. I sidle around.

'Did you do that?' the enormous hard horselike face of the landlady says.

'No.'

'What is it?' Grief, wrath, and outrage in her voice. Her huge impotent body. The thing is done. What can she do? I don't know.'

'What is it?'

'I don't know.'

'Betty,' my mother says, looking me in the eye – to show the dire eternal consequences of an untruth – 'Did you do that on the wall?'

'No.' I say. I lower my head. I am dying of shame. I am scarlet with revealed intimacies. My privacy violated. But even in my shame I have a soft exhultant joy. I did it ill. I did it!

And there is nothing they can do! It is on the wall and they cannot undo the deed.

They could make me wash it off.

But I won't admit I did it.

Sin! Sin! Terrible, shameful and sweet. Such tender ardent work despoiled and despised! The sin of its conception. I trembled guiltily on my legs, my lying eyes were slits.

But I walked out into the sun. I went to the dandelion place. 'I am good, I am good.' The dandelions said Yes. All was yellow sun. The day. The bright yellowness. The dandlions said I was good. I was good. Day and night were apart. My day was like the sun. A yellow dandelion. It is twenty years ago. But I still cannot walk by that old hotel. I feel a vague guilt, even forgetting. I see the huge tone outraged face peering at me through the menacing lace curtains.

Elizabeth Smart.

DAVID WIDGERY

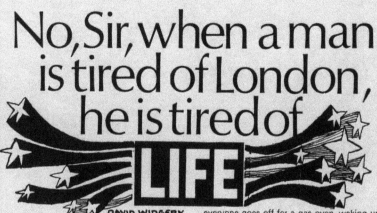

Living in London is like trying to set up home on the pendulum of a clock telling the wrong time. London life is about as exciting as the Eurovision Song Contest . . . as regards significant living experience the average glass of water has got more to get your teeth into. The objects are all right still; St Pancras Library is still running its legendary book amnesty, the old men still fly kites in Hyde Park on Sundays, gold top milk is good as is Benoir Bulka's game pate, there are still some bookstands where you can't buy International Times, there's a shop in Old Compton St. where you can change your name to Mick Jagger by deed of poll. There are still *things* to stay around for: Penguin Classics, Dinky Toys, The British Medical Journal, the 11 o'clock news on the Third, jumping up and down on tightly coiled copies of the 'Observer' on Sundays, Cadbury's Fruit and Nut advertisements.

But on the whole the place is horrible and this is due to the people. There are far too many Australians. The Incredible Love Generation is completely wrapped up with glittering their beautiful eyes at each other to show how great the cold unpleasant Round House really is—spend far too much time getting high and getting nowhere. The tender sexy warm new things don't even notice the vast pyramid of crap we are heaping on ourselves in aid of self liberation or adult movies or something. God help the new thing if it's IT and the Friday night strobes . . . they make me think of the oesophagus of a man who has lived all his life on 10c. hamburgers and pasteurised milk.

The rich old hippies are substantially worse though. There's always been an overfed, overblown appendix of society who lapse into semi-permanent excess. But this lot expect you to take boutique society as an art form as well and between one pull of the forelock and the next, we are supposed to draw brief inspiration from their antics. The incredible pace of Sybilla society is really about as interesting as an 'Evening Standard' lunchtime leader. It's the 'who's for tennis' people now gossiping about their trips but still with the servant problem and the bad-tempered sports car and their mothers' drugs. They're all as dead as Tara Browne. The women have hearts as hard as pecan crunch bars and gossip in the clubs like a seaside sales conference. They are like an Autumn Tints Coach Tour, all yellow and falling down. All their parties are the same one, built out of the same pieces of Meccano. Inside them the same handy units, pretty boys punching their stomachs and eating floor polish, everywhere the Stones and pointless flared-up eyes. The pecan girl is high now, hears nougat voices on the roof; it's only the hat burglars stealing overcoats. Then if it's an upper class of party someone overdoses, a 'head' from Golden Beach . . . kicks in the record player and

everyone goes off for a gas oven, waking up in different rooms to the same formica morning. *This* is the Wipeout Gang operating their Insanity Factory.

What's worse—the Factory is the people sent by 'Time' and 'Life' to look for it. American boys trying to grow out of their haircut, always reading the menu from outside and telling the identical story about a panty raid or a trip or something that was broken up by the House Sister. There are wistfu, girls in almanacks and gaberdine hair who walk around Old Compton Street in threes wanting to be picked up. They are as sexy as Chapter 3 of The Group and as unhappy as doctored cats (who are very happy). Everyone is cheated. French men shaking their fists at Dollys from the outside. Italian ladies being fiddled on the change. Americans from places like Ohio in Renta Cars picking up bleached boys outside of Piccadilly Underground station,who when they come through want money for their prescriptions. Danish girls secretly being sold herbal cigarettes. London's a big hoax, luv. We have got acclimatised to the lies, but you ought to be bitter about them. Bitter like the old 'Confidential' headlines, "Rubirosa was fizzle in bed Latin Beauty says".

In fact, once upon a time there was a swinging Britain—before this Golden Book of Reptiles. The time when London was really zinging was when the Bulge Babies were in school, reading 'Tit Bits' in the back of the class with NHS specs and Sellotape. 'Chalky' taught us long division and to keep our bowels open and our traps shut. We played Dan Dare on the building sites where no one dared to build, with the Mekon as green as a processed pea. Rock Around the Clock was banned throughout Warwickshire. Time and Life's London Bureau didn't notice us then, in the High Street billiards saloons with our duck's arse haircut and Warner Bros. hip talk, always planning world trips on unmuffled Harley Davidsons. On Saturdays watching the birds go past with layers of bouncy petticoats meant to show like that and bouffant sticky hair and everyone looking like a Giles cartoon. The old man remembering El Alamein, when really he spent his war singing dirty songs in the shelters and making lighters in the Spitfire factories and fortunes on vacuum cleaner spares. Thank the Lord for the lads flogging left-handed nylons on bomb sites and smashing up cinema seats for Bill Haley and bunching sports cars on the bikes and ripping the roofs off. This was real, in the abrasive world where people travel in second-class trains to Slough and put cash in the Coop Xmas Box and buy Batchelors records and don't even know about the Psychedelic Revolution.

It hasn't stopped because some American journalist has discovered debs kneecaps. So Wipeout Gang you better start to build bigger and better Borstals, you're going to need them.

free Membership of 250 Clubs

By taking advantage of this once only special offer you can belong to over 250 leading London and Provincial clubs completely FREE for 2 months by joining The Clubman's Club.

Also you may then continue your membership, if you wish to and only if you are completely satisfied, at only 6 guineas a year.

Simply fill in the application form and the Banker's Order which is dated for 1st May 1967, and return it to us. We will then make you a full member of the Clubman's Club and send you your membership card.

If you do not wish to continue your membership, simply return your membership card and cancel your Banker's Order before 1st May 1967, and so you will not have to pay one penny.

Members of the Clubman's Club are members of all the clubs on our list and as you will see they are the leading clubs in every major town. So don't let this opportunity slip, but join now.

London Clubs to which you will belong:

Astor	Gargoyle	Mazurka	Spanish Garden
Beak	Georgian	Monument	Swallow
Blenheim	Golden	Mountview	Toby Gym
Candlelight	Horseshoe	Theatre	Town House
Casino de Paris	Golden Nugget	Nell Gwynne	Trojan
Chalet Suisse	Hampstead	New Manhattan	Tropicana
Charlie	Theatre Club	Northwick Park	(Croydon)
Chesters	Knightsbridge	'100' Club	Vanity Fair
Churchills	Studio	Raymond	Victoria
Concorde	Living Room	Revuebar	Sporting
Court	Maddox	Renaissance	Windmill
Cromwell	Madingley	Ricky Renée's	Saloon
Sporting	Mandrake	Ronnie Scott	Wine Centre
Establishment	Marquee	Shanghai	Winstons

You will also belong to the leading clubs in:

Aberdeen, Abersoch, Ayr, Battle, Bedford, Birmingham, Blackburn, Blackpool, Bognor Regis, Boston, Bournemouth, Bridlington, Brighouse, Brighton, Bristol, Burnley, Buxton, Cardiff, Carlisle, Castle Bromwich, Castleford, Cheltenham, Chester, Chesterfield, Chichester, Chorley, Colchester, Coventry, Darlington, Derby, Doncaster, Dublin, Durham, Eastbourne, Edinburgh, Falmouth, Glasgow, Gloucester, Great Malvern, Great Yarmouth, Harrogate, Hastings, Herne Bay, Huddersfield, Hull, Ipswich, Jarrow, Kingsbridge, Lavant, Leeds, Leicester, Lincoln, Littlehampton, Liverpool, Lowestoft, Ludlow, Luton, Macclesfield, Malton, Manchester, March, Margate, Market Harborough, Marple, Middlesbrough, Newcastle, Northampton, Norwich, Nottingham, Paignton, Peacehaven, Penarth, Peterborough, Plymouth, Portsmouth, Port Talbot, Preston, Reading, Redcar, Salford, Salisbury, St Anne's-on-Sea, St Leonard's-on-Sea, Saundersfoot, Scunthorpe, Seaford, Skegness, Southampton, Southport, Southsea, Stockport, Stockton-on-Tees, Stoke-on-Trent, Sunderland, Swansea, Taunton, Teignmouth, Tewkesbury, Torquay, Usk, Walsall, Wakefield, Warwick, Westerham, Weston-super-Mare, Whalley, Whitley Bay, Widnes, Wigan, Winchester, Winsford, Windsor, Woking, Wokingham, Wolverhampton, Worthing, York.

- -

Clubman's Club

35 Albemarle Street Mayfair London, W1 Hyde Park 5933

I hereby apply for membership of **The Clubman's Club** until 1st May 1967 completely free. I agree for myself and my guests to conform with the rules of each club visited. I understand that if I return my membership card before 1st May 1967, my application will be cancelled.

Name_____

Address_____

_____

Occupation_____

Signature_____(I am over 18 years of age) OZ .43

Banker's Order

To_____Bank Ltd. Branch_____

Address_____

Please pay to the order of **The Clubman's Club**, Lloyds Bank Ltd. Golders Green (30-93-50) the sum of 6 guineas on 1st May 1967, and thereafter on the same date each year being my annual subscription to **The Clubman's Club**.

Signed_____

Address_____

"Ho, ho!" he cried, in ecstasies... "Toad as usual comes out on top."

London OZ's spectacular Playmate of the Month: Toad Wilson of Whitehall. Toad's twice the size of last month's inaugural Playmate of LBJ – but then he's twice as conceited.

"As he tramped along gaily, he thought of his adventures and his escapes, and how when things seemed at their worst he had always managed to find a way out; and his pride and conceit began to swell within him. Ho, ho!" he said to himself as he marched along with his chin in the air, "what a clever Toad I am! There is surely no animal equal to me for cleverness in the whole world!"

"I am, unfortunately, born into a Toad family, but immediately I became Head Toad I am able to abandon its tiresome principles."

"I am the only Toad bold enough to use old-fashioned Weasel economics to save managers and hurt working Toads."

Toad began to giggle, and from giggling he took to laughing, and he laughed till he had to sit under a hedge.

Now he thought about the famous forest market – and how once an important Weasel tried to lead all the river people to it but went astray.

"But I'll do it," laughed Toad, "or if I fail I'll tell everyone that the Frogs stopped us."

"Ho, ho!" he cried, in ecstasies of self admiration. "Toad again! Toad, as usual comes out on top."

"And what about the grown-up animals?" laughed Toad.

"I stop telling on the naughty eagle, and he gives us food. I invite the clumsy bear to dinner and he wants to be my best friend."

"Ho! ho! I am the Toad, the handsome, the popular, the successful Toad!" He got so puffed up with conceit that he made up a song as he walked, in praise of himself, and sang it at the top of his voice, though there was no one to hear it but him. It was perhaps the most conceited song that any animal ever composed.

'The world has held great Heroes, As history books have showed; But never a name to avoid all blame Like that of Wilson Toad!

'The clever men at Oxford Know all there is to be knowed. But none of them know half as much As intelligent Wilson Toad!

'At number 10, the Cabinet sat, Abuse in torrents flowed But who un-ruffled, simply re-shuffled? Why! The dexterous Wilson Toad!

'Oh, when the Government's ratings slump, And Party morale's down There's a jolly handy scapegoat In bumbling Badger Brown.

'The Queen and her Ladies-in-Waiting Sat at the window and sewed She cried, "Look! Who's that fat little man?" They answered, "Wilson Toad!"'

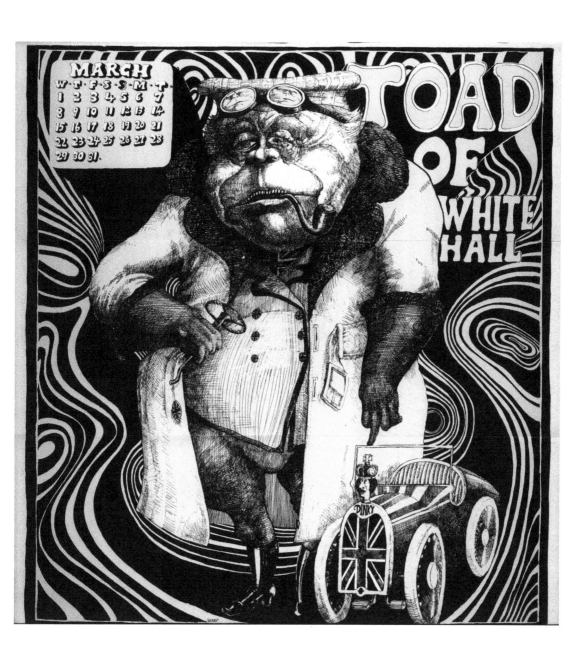

OZ's cut-out image seekers

Is it a bird? Is it a plane? Both! It's birdman BILLY FURY, the Barnes Wallis of Beat, in his all-British-wing wing entry for the Daily Mail's Man Powered Flight contest.

Nature boy: "Where have all the poppies gone?" Sniffed by DONOVAN, every ozz.

When is a spade not a spade? When it's Uncle TOM JONES rolling his fans down Old Man River.

CLIFF'S new film with the Shadows, aptly renamed the Holy Spirits, is a remake of 'The Bells of St. Mary's'. At curtain fall CLIFF gets the girl—the Singing Nun.

"We meet again." VERA LYNN, "Sweetheart of the Forces," whose comeback record flopped. EMI's Promotion cocked up, failing to arrange a Third World War to coincide with release.

Posthumous Pop—A memorial to BUDDY HOLLY, JIM REEVES and all the other Hereafter Hitmakers still heard, (but not seen), on the Pye (in the sky) label.

FARMAN-SMITH-CASTLE

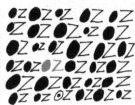

Editor: Richard Neville
Deputy Editor: Paul Lawson
Business Manager: Peter Ledeboer
Design: Jon Goodchild
Photography: Robert Whitaker
Art: Martin Sharp
Contributors, Etc.: Andrew Fisher, David Reynolds, & Louise
Advertising: Ian Stocks
Enquiries should be addressed to 40 Anhalt Road, SW11
London OZ is published by OZ Publications Ink Limited, 40 Anhalt Road, London, SW11
Phone: REG 0427, BAY 0320 or BAT 8407.
Contributions: are welcome and should be addressed to: The Editor, 70 Clarendon Road, W11, enclosing s.a.e.

Printer:
Sharptone Litho Ltd
83 Bellenden Road, SE15
Distributed by:
Moore Harness Ltd
11 Lever Street, EC1
CLE 4882
OZtralia is obtainable from 16 Hunter Street, Sydney.
Enclose £1 for 12 quivering issues.

Beautiful Breast competition. There's still time to send profile and full face photos of a handsome set and win £20.

Meanwhile, entries pour in. So far received: 1 pair of male bottoms, 1 rubber falsie, 2 sets of breasts (our semi-finalists printed below) and 7 giggling phone calls. The winning breasts will be spread over a double page in OZ 4.

Best way to fight the tiresome square backlash is to support IT's defence appeal. Cheques to Freedom of Speech Benefit, 102 Southampton Row, WC1. Similar support should be offered to Calder and Boyars Ltd, publishers of *Last Exit to Brooklyn*—despite a petulant indictment of his publishing methods on page 11, penned by a well known Calder author.

This OZ blazes away at politicians in an irresponsible fit of bad temper. It includes three 'Instant Protest' post-cards to send to your favourite hypocrites. Post early for Christmas. (We'll publish any replies).

We care, dear reader, we care for your warts, spots, unsightly blemishes, superfluous hairs, embarrassing odours . . . for the young executive on his way down, the flops, the failures, the losers; hence Ugliness and Failure p 00 to p 00.

Our *In Bed with the English* girl, Germaine, has not yet filed a report of her rendevouz with challenger Rod C B Lake. Like a detailed and hilarious *In Bed with the Americans* it appears next issue.

letters

Dear Sir,

Your correspondent on Swinging London, as we call it, has got it all wrong. He represents what one might call the third reaction to the phenomenon: one which could be described as coming from the miss-outs; except that patently, having contributed to your magazine, he is not himself a miss-out.

Sure, Time–Life did a massive injustice to the UK scene when they coined that phrase Swinging London - it imposed on the city an image which simply didn't fit. If the scene is nothing but Sibylla's, strobes, and The Incredible Love Generation, then, yes he's right, London is about as exciting as the Eurovision Song Contest. More to the point, if this were in fact true, then you could get the same sort of excitement in Paris, Brussels, Amsterdam, Copenhagen, Bradford and I suppose even Sydney, NSW. The fact that remains is that Paris, Brussels, etc., are *not* the same, and that's not just because they were built by a different set of architects. The atmosphere in London at this time is different; the cultural environment here is unique. *Not only* can you get pot at ▓▓▓▓▓ (as you have been able to do these ten years), *but also* . . .

(1) David Bailey, in his 20s, is earning more than Cecil Beaton ever did as a photographer.
(2) Peter Watkins, in his 20s, is making better films than Cecil B. de Mille ever made. And these films are being shown to the public at a modest profit.
(3) Mary Quant, to take an archetypal example, and four hundred other original dress designers and fashion buyers and clothes retailers, are making more money each than Balenciaga ever did in the rag trade. And they are selling attractive clothes to everyone who can wear them for pocket money prices. Which is more than you could ever say for Balenciaga, Dior, Chanel, etc.
(4) Clive Rees, in his 20s, directs television commercials for multi-million pound spending advertisers, and owns one of the top ten television commercial production companies in London. Rosser Reeves was 50 before anybody knew who he was, and David Ogilvy's advertising ideas were formulated before the war.
(5) Ken Loach, in his 20s, directed three television plays which made more impact on this country in any sense than the sum total of every movie made before 1950.
(7) Michael Peacock, in his 30s, is responsible for the entire programme output of BBC1. Say what you will about BBC1 (and I notice that you already have) Peacock has done more good for the Corp in three or four years than John Reith did in twenty.
(8) Ronan O'Rahilly, in his 20s, has changed the face of British broadcasting for ever, and runs a million-pound business into the bargain.

(9) Etcetera.
The fact that people like yourself have managed to get London Oz, not to mention Aussie Oz, under way, goes to demonstrate that for the first time anywhere young people, in the prime of their talents, have had a proper chance to make their impressions on culture, business and commerce while they are still young, and before they are battered into conformity by their elders. Sibylla's, and all the rest, are just by-products of this environment, and don't matter two hoots. What does matter is that business, social, and leisure services and products are being provided more and more by young people and less and less by old people. The young are getting richer and the old are getting older. That's as it should be, and unless you recognise it your magazine is going to have a problem. Because you're either on the side of the swingers or you're dead.

Sincerely,

Rod Allen
Television Mail
31 George Street
London W7

Dear Sir,

I would enter your Beautiful Breasts Competition except that the current taste for an overblown, cleft shelf of bulging, fat bubbies makes girls like me with swinging, separated breasts surmounted with ripe, red tits feel unfashionable. Too many men (and women) think a double handful with a droopy, pale, insignificant dug is desirable.

A few years of being torturously strapped down in the sort of contraption Germaine describes ruins both the natural elasticity and bounce of the breasts and deadens the nipples' reaction to stimulation. I, too, am tired of dykey salesladies who maliciously shove my soft boobs into hard, unnatural shapes—probably because nobody wants to play with their own ugly, uninteresting protruberances. I bet you find your competition winner wears a bra only because prudish people around are frightened by their sexual reaction to shapely nipples on free-moving breasts. If she *is* one of those pneumatically swollen types, I shall lose faith in the honesty

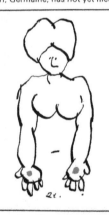

SEMI FINALISTS

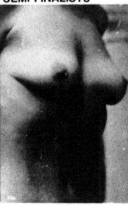

e way, now you have
d truthful beauty contests,
just cling to stimulating,
ul and soft tits. How about
male beauty contest (not
es Atlas poovy nonsense)
e most palpably pro-
ive prick—according to
nsion, colouring and
euverability?

up the good work.

da Breustom (Mrs)
on SW19

Mr. Competition Editor,

what about us British
? Don't you think our nice
bottoms ought to be
ortalised over a double
of OZ''? We do. Equal
for males!

ay here's my entry for
you come to your sense
n a comp. for us.

sincerely,

n NW8

ir,

'm Muggeridge is tired,
red of our masters. He is
our slaves. He is tired
am tired of him. His
ine pieces are skilful, and
entertaining.

ng about his experiences
sh espionage, writing
he chose to inform, he was
ine treat. But so often his
sm decries journalism.
ten we buy magazines to
n sneering at us for doing
ve seen him on television.
radox is only possible
e he does not mount a
sed campaign, he does
ate. He does not expose;
os. His criticisms can not
ued to any result, his
na is not seriously
o be effected. This is
g. His speciality is the
sive application of mud,
ers caking as he scrabbles
next clawful. It is like
cting an ode, or the
stroking of a cat.
-you is the strong basic
II left to him. The
actoriness of God is
d by MM's contempt
ists. Our capitalism
im; their socialism he
thinkable. There is much,

---

indeed, that he finds
unthinkable; in general,
anything not obviously
shameful.

His acidulation, his wit, his
pitilessness might enrich us if
we could get a book out of him.
Writing a good book is harder
than going on television and
poking borak at everything in
sight, but if you write a good
book people take more notice.
Muggeridge may not live much
longer; I guess his digestive
system is a perpetual rack, and
if there is any sincerity behind
all that babbling despair we
must be prepared for his
suicide.

We cannot afford to let him
fritter his talent away in pieces
and glimpses. A 12-month ban
by all the mass media might
cork him enough to produce
something worthwhile. A vicious
long pamphlet, with well-
supported argument, on the evil
of universal literacy, might well
suit for subject.

The public display of this man's
sharp mind has become so
standard a performance that it is
now a ceremony. By the end of
each article, by the end of
each programme, Muggeridge's
target is nicely caked with dried
mud. Its essence thoroughly
disguised by his potter's hand,
we are given a last look at in
the round, now a distorted
artifact. See, says MM, see you
mortals, your idol is but a hunk of
clay. And by that time it is. But by
that time little Malcolm has been
working so hard in the barnyard,
a close look reveals that he
himself has feet of shit.

Contrariness can only get you so
far, and that backwards.
Muggeridge is too old and too
bright to be our court jester. That
aimless, confidence-ridden
Kenneth Tynan once made the
irrelevant plea that *Private Eye*
should have a *point of view*.
It would be good to see
Muggeridge at least trying to
find one. It would be good to see
him exercising his intellect
instead of merely flexing it.

They gave him a part in the BBC
Alice. He took an unpaid ad in
the *New Statesman* to write
about it. He said Lewis Carroll
was a sick pervert, Peter Cook's
Mad Hatter was 'too nice',
Miller's competence as a director

---

is doubtful. Alice 'had no idea
what acting meant', but he liked
the movie. Maybe he's getting
soft. It may be too late. Do you
think perhaps he is soft?
The black Dalek's heart and the
puppets' jaw-twitch just a
masquerade, like playing the
Gryphon? This is really a man, a
human being, in love with life?
It is time he levelled with us.
For your own sake, man, stop
cheating. Do something you can
be proud of.

Yours sincerely

Chester, Hampstead NW3

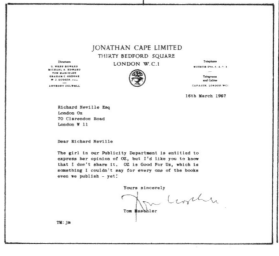

Dear Sir,

My biggest criticism is of OZ's
self-consciousness. To print
letters from businesses which
refuse to advertise OZ or
whatever shows a threadbare
awareness of protocol and
besides seems rather arrogant
and narrow-minded. If a
particular quarter does not like
OZ then surely that is their
privilege—and you are abusing
that privilege; by printing these
letters it is apparent that you
feel in some way hurt and your
criticism of the opinion
motivating the refusal to
advertise is implicit. I don't
think you can fight narrow-
mindedness from a similar
position.

The drugs article in March OZ
I thought very good, with one

---

exception. What about some
editorial responsibility, both for
your own protection and others?
Subtle editing could I think
have neutralised the tone of the
article—but perhaps I mistake
your intention: maybe you
condone the drug scene. (I
don't object, I might add, to the
right to take drugs if you feel
too weak to deal with life as
it is.)

Yours sincerely,

Peter Leech,
27 de Crespigny Park
London SE5

Dear Sir,

Colin MacInnes's misinter-
pretation of a West Indian four-
letter word in February OZ
points up the pitfalls of being
a PRO to a group from a
different environment with
unfamiliar idiom.

I would not venture to suggest
the usage of the word 'Raas' in
the vulgar currency of the other
West Indian islands outside of
Jamaica where 'Raas' is the
local corruption of the English,
or British, 'Your a̓rse', hence
'You Raas', and is interpreted
similarly regardless of gender.
MacInnes's interpretation is
applicable only in the adjectival
form 'Raas-Cloth' which is
humorously said to be the most
authentic and identifiable
password among Jamaicans
abroad.

Yours sincerely,

P Alexander
4 Grenville Road
London N19

After six months of wedded bliss,
my wife and I, to celebrate
the kiss
which ratified the union a
computer bound,
gratefully pilgrimaged to
Kingston, and found
gay students in a one-room flat,
picking fated names from
a bowler hat.

...ty school bus, painted like a flourescent Easter egg in orange, chartreuse, cerise, puce, green, blue and, yes, black, was parked outside the solitary mountain cabin, which made it an easy guess that Ken Kesey, the novelist, turned psychedelic Hotspur, was inside. So, of course, was Neal Cassady, the Tristram Shandy of the Beat Generation, prototype hero of Jack Kerouac's *On The Road*, who had sworn off allegiance to Kerouac when the beat scene became menopausal and signed up as the driver of Kesey's fun & games bus, which is rumoured to run on LSD. Except for these notorious luminaries, the new hippie subculture, convened in the lowlands of California's High Sierras during an early spring weekend last month, seemed a little like an Apalachin Mafia gathering without Joe Bananas.

Where was Allen Ginsberg, father goddam to generations of the underground? In New York, reading his poetry to freshmen. And where was Timothy Leary, self styled guru to tens or is it hundreds of thousands of turned on people? Off to preach the gospel of Lysergic Acid Diethylamide to nice ladies in drip dry dresses.

The absence of the elder statesmen of America's synthetic gypsy movement meant something. It meant that leaders of the booming psychedelic bohemia in the seminal city of San Francisco were their own men, and strangely serious men indeed for hippies. Ginsberg and Leary may be Pied Pipers but they are largely playing old tunes. The young men who make the new scene accept Ginsberg as a revered observer from the older generation; Leary they abide as an Elmer Gantry on their side, to be used for proselytizing squares only.

The mountain symposium has been called for the extraordinary purpose of discussing the political future of the hippies. Hippies are many things, but most prominently the bearded and beaded inhabitants of San Francisco's Haight Ashbury area, a little psychedelic city state edging Golden Gate Park. There, in a daily street fair atmosphere, upwards of 15,000 unbonded girls and boys interact in a tribal, love seeking, free swinging, acid based type of society where, if you are a hippie and have a dime, you can put it in a parking meter and lie down in the street for an hour's suntan (30 minutes for a nickel) and most drivers will be careful not to run you over.

Speaking, sometimes all at once, inside the Sierra cabin were many voices of conscience and vision of Haight Ashbury—belonging to men who, except for their Raggedy Andy hair, paisley shirts and pre mod western levi jackets, sounded for all the world like Young Republicans.

They talked about reducing government controls, the sanctity of the individual, the need for equality among men. They talked, very seriously, about the kind of society they wanted to live in, and the fact that if they go out and make it for themselves, because nobody, least of all the government, was going to do it for them.

The utopian sentiments of the hippies were not to be put down lightly. Hippies have a clear vision of the ideal community—where everyone is turned on and beautiful and loving and happy and floating free. But it is a vision that, despite the Alice in Wonderland phraseology hippies usually employ to describe it, necessarily embodies a radical political philosphy; communal life, drastic restriction of private property, rejection of violence, creativity before consumption, freedom before authority, de-emphasis of government and traditional forms of leadership.

This is all very solemn talk about people who like to skip rope and wear bright colours, but after spending some time with these fun and fey individuals you realize that, in a very unexpected way, they are as serious about what they're doing as the John Birch Society. It is not improbable, that after a few more mountain seminars by those purposeful young men wearing beards, that Haight Ashbury may spawn the first utopian collectivist community since Brook Farm.

Despite a disturbing tendency to quietism, all hippies *ipso facto* have a political posture—one of unremitting opposition to the Establishment which insists of branding them as criminals because they take LSD and marijuana, and hating them, anyway, because they enjoy sleeping nine in a room and three to a bed, seem to have free sex and guiltless minds, and can raise healthy children in dirty clothes.

The hippie choice of weapons is to love the Establishment to death rather than protest it or blow it up (hippies possess a confounding disconcern about traditional political methods or issues). But they are decidedly and forever outside the Consensus on which US society places such a premium, and since the hippie scene is so much the scene of those people under 25 that Time magazine warns will soon constitute half the US population, this is a significant political fact.

Kesey a state visit were seven members of The Diggers, a radical organization even by Haight Ashbury standards, which exists to give things away, free. The Diggers started out giving out free food, free clothes, free lodging and free legal advice, and hope eventually to create a totally free co-operative community. They had come to ask Kesey to get serious and attend the weekend meeting on the state of the nation of the hippies.

The dialogue had hardly begun, however, before Kesey loaded all comers into the bus and pushed off into the dark to search for a nocturnal ice cream store. The bus, which may be the closest modern man has yet come to aping the self sufficiency of Captain Nemo's submarine, has its own power supply and is equipped with instruments for a full rock band, microphones, loudspeakers, spotlights and comfortable seats all round. The Pranksters are presently installing microphones every three feet on the bus walls so everybody can broadcast to everybody else all at once.

At the helm was the Intrepid Traveller, Ken Babbs, who is auxiliary chief of the Merry Pranksters when Kesey is out of town, or incommunicado, or in jail, all three of which he has recently been. Babbs, who is said to be the model for the heroes of both Kesey novels, *One Flew Over the Cuckoo's Nest* and *Sometime a Great Notion*, picked up a microphone to address the guests in the rear of the bus, like the driver of a London Monuments tour: "We are being followed by a police car. Will someone watch and tell me when he turns on his red light."

The law was not unexpected of course because any cop who sees Kesey's bus just about *has* to follow it, would probably end up with some form of professional DT's if he didn't. It is part of the game; the cop was now playing on their terms, and Kesey and his Pranksters were delighted In fact, a discernible wave of disappointment swept across the bus when the cop gave up chasing this particular UFO and turned onto another road.

That US society finds it so difficult to take such rascally looking types seriously is no doubt the indication of a deep rooted hang up. But to comprehend the psychosis of America in the Computer Age, you have to know what's with the hippies.

Games people play, Merry Prankster Division

Let us go, then, on a trip. You can't miss the Tripmaster: the thick-necked lad in the blue and white striped pants with the red belt and the golden eagle buckle, a watershed of wasted pro-mises in his pale blue eyes, one front tooth capped in patriotic red, white and blue, his hair downy, flaxen, straddling the incredibly wide divide of his forehead like two small toupees pasted on sideways. Ken Kesey, Heir Apparent Number One to the grand American tradition of blowing one's artistic talent to do some other thing, was sitting in a surprisingly comfortable chair inside the bus with the psychedelic crust, puffing absentmindedly on a harmonica.

The bus itself was ambulatory at about 50 miles an hour, jogging along a back road in sylvan Marin county, four loudspeakers turned all the way up, broadcasting both inside and outside Carl Orff's Carmina Burana and filled with two dozen people simultaneously smoking marijuana and look-ing for an open ice cream store. It was the Thursday night before the Summit Meeting weekend and Kesey, along with some 15 members of the turned on yes men and women who call him "Chief" and whom he calls the "Merry Pranksters" in return, was demonstrating a "game" to a delegation of visiting hippie firemen.

Crossing North over the Golden Gate Bridge from San Francisco to Marin County to pay down the nation's highways, high on LSD watching and waiting for the cops to blow their minds.

At least, the Kesey posture has the advant-age of being intellectually consistent with the point of view of his novels. In *One Flew Over the Cuckoo's Nest*, he uses the setting of an insane asylum as a metaphor for what he considers to be the basic insanity, or at least the fundamentally bizarre illogic, of American Society. Since the world forces you into a game that is both mad and unfair, you are better off inventing your own game. Then at least you have a chance of winning.

At least that's what Kesey thinks.

When the Hell's Angels, California's guerrilla force of rockers, rumbled by, Kesey welcomed them with LSD. "We're in the same business. You break people's homes, I break people's heads," he told them. The Angels seem to like the whole acid thing, because today they are a fairly constant act in the Haight Ashbury show, while Kesey has abdicated his role as Scoutmaster to the fledgling acid heads and exiled himself across the Bay. This self imposed Elba came about when Kesey sensed that the hippie community had soured on him. He had committed the one mortal sin in the hippie ethic: *telling* people what to do. "Get into a responsibilit, bag," he urged some 400 friends attending a private Halloween party. This sudden social conscience may have had something to do with beating a jail sentence on a compounded marijuana charge, but when Kesey obtained his freedom with instructions from the judge to "preach an anti-LSD warning to teenagers", it was a little too much for the Haight Ashbury set. Kesey, after all, was the man who had turned on the Hell's Angels. At 31, Ken Kesey is a hippie has been.

The games he plays are very important to Kesey. In many ways his intellectual rebellion has come full circle; he has long ago rejected the structured nature of society, the foolscap rings of success, conformity and acceptance of "normal" people must regularly jump through. To the liberated intellect, no doubt, these requirements constitute the most sordid type of game. But, once rejecting all the norms of society, the artist is free to create his own structures—and along with any new set of rules, however personal, there is necessarily, the shell to the tortoise, a new set of games. In Kesey's case at least, the games are usually fun. Running round the outside of an insane society, the healthiest thing you can do is laugh.

It helps to look at this sort of complicated if not confused intellectual proposition in bas relief, as if you were looking at the simple pictures on Wedgewood china. Stand Successful Author Ken Kesey off against, say, Successful Author Truman Capote. Capote, as long as his name is accepted by the system, is free to be as mad as he can. So he tosses the biggest, most vulgar Ball in a long history of vulgar balls, and achieves the perfect idiot synthesis of the upper middle and lower royal classes. Kesey, who cares as much about the system as he does about the Eddie Kantor Memorial Forest, invents his own game. He purchases a pre '40s International Harvester school bus, paints it psychedelic, fills it with undistin-guished though lovable individuals in varying stages of eccentricity, and drives brazenly

rock group, to his acid tests and, the vinegar on the chips, the light show atmospheric technique of projecting slides and wild colours on the walls during rock dances. This combination he called "trips". Trip is the word for an LSD experience, but in Kesey's lexicon it also meant kicks, which were achieved by rapidly changing the audience's sensory environment what seemed like approximately ten million times during an evening by manipulating bright coloured lights, tape recorders, slide projectors, weird sound machines, and whatever else may be found in the electronic sink, while the participants danced under stroboscopic lights to a wild rock band or just played around on the floor.

It was a fulgorous, electronically orgiastic thing (the most advanced tests had closed circuit television sets on the dance floor so you could see what you were doing), which made psychedelics very "fun" indeed. and the hippies came in droves. Almost every hippie in San Francisco went to at least one Acid Test, and it is not exceeding the bounds of reasonable speculation to say that Kesey may have turned on at least 10,000 people to LSD during the 24 presentations of the Acid Tests. (During these Tests the Merry Pranksters painted everything including themselves in fluorescent tones and bright colours became the permanent thing in psychedelic dress.)

Turning so many unsuspecting people onto LSD at once could be dangerous, as the Pranksters discovered on a 1965 psychedelic road show when they staged the fated Watts Acid Test. Many of the leading citizens of Watts came to the show, which was all very fine except that whoever put the LSD in the free punch that was passed around put too much in by a factor of about four. This served to make for a very wild Acid Test, and one or two participants "freaked out" and had a very hard time of it for the next few days.

scouting somebody else's act, a Swami's at that, who was turning on the hippies at the Avalon ballroom by leading them in an hourlong Hindu chant without stopping much for breath. The Avalon is one of the two great drafty ballrooms where San Francisco hippies, hippie hangers on, and young hippies to be congregate each weekend to participate in the psychedelic rock and light shows that are now as much a part of San Francisco as cable cars and a lot noisier.

This dance was a benefit for the new Swami, recently installed in a Haight-Ashbury storefront, with a fair passage sign from Allen Ginsberg whom he had bumped into in India. The hippies were turning out just to see what the Swami's *shtick* was, but Dr. Leary had a different purpose. He has a vested, professional interest in turning people on, and here was this Swami, trying to do it with just a chant, like it was natural childbirth or something.

The word professional is not used lightly. There is a large group of professionals making it by servicing and stimulating the hippie world—in the spirit of Haight Ashbury we should refer to these men as merchant princes—and Timothy Leary is pretender to the throne.

Dr. Leary claims to have launched the first indigenous religion in America. That may very well be, though as a religious leader he is Aimee Semple MacPherson in drag. Dr. Leary who identifies himself as "prophet", recently played San Francisco in his LSD road show where he sold $4 seats to lots of squares, but few hippies (Dr. Leary's pitch is to the straight world), showed a technicolour movie billed as simulating an LSD experience (it was big on close ups of enlarged blood vessels), burned incense, dressed like a holy man in white pyjamas, and told everybody to "turn on, tune in, and drop out".

In case you are inclined to make light of this philosophic advice you should not laugh out loud. Because Dr. Leary is serious about his work, he cannot be dismissed as a cross between Father Divine and Nietzsche, no matter how tempting the analogy. He has made a substantial historic contribution to the psychedelic scene, although his arrest records may figure more prominently than his philosophy in future hippie records.

Acid Tests—From Unitarians to...

Kesey is now a self-sufficient but lonely figure—if you can be lonely with dozens of Merry Pranksters running around your house all day. If he ever gets maudlin, which is doubtful, he can look back fondly on his hippie memories, which are definitely in the wow! category, because Ken Kesey did for acid roughly what Johnny Appleseed did for trees, and probably more.

He did it through a unique and short-lived American institution called the Acid Test. A lot of things happened at an Acid Test, but the main thing was that, in the Haight Ashbury vernacular, everyone in the audience got zonked out of their minds on LSD. LSD in cake. LSD in coffee. LSD in the community punch. Most people were generally surprised because they didn't know they were getting any LSD until it was too late. Later, when word got around that this sort of thing was happening at Acid Tests, Kesey sometimes didn't give out LSD on purpose, just so people wouldn't know whether they did or did not have LSD. Another game.

The Acid Tests began calmly enough. In the early versions Kesey merely gave a heart to heart psychedelic talk and handed LSD around like the Eucharist, which first happened at a Unitarian conference in Big Sur in August of 1965. He repeated this ritual several times, at private gatherings in his home, in La Honda, on college campuses, and once at a Vietnam Day Committee rally at Berkeley. Then Kesey added the Grateful Dead, a pioneer San Francisco

After the California legislature played Prohibition and outlawed LSD on October 6, 1966, Kesey wound up the Acid Test syndrome with what was billed as a huge "Trips Festival" in San Francisco. People who regularly turn on say the Trips Festival was a bore: it embodied all the Acid Test elements except acid, and happily for the coffers of Intrepid Trips Inc., attracted a huge crowd of newspapermen, narcotics agents and other squares, but very few hippies. The Merry Pranksters slyly passed out plain sugar cubes for the benefit of the undercover agents.

Suddenly San Francisco, which for a grown up city gets excited very easily, was talking about almost nothing but "trips" and LSD. Hippies, like overnight, had become fashionable.

If you are inclined to give thanks for this sort of thing, they go to the bad boy wonder of psychedelphia, disappearing there over the horizon in his way ward bus.

Dr. Leary—Pretender to the Hippie Throne

The suit was Brooks Brothers '59 and the paisley tie J. Press contemporary, but the bone carved Egyptian mandala hanging round his neck, unless it was made in occupied Japan, had to be at least 2,000 years old. Dr. Timothy Leary, BA University of Alabama, PhD. University of California LSD Cuernavaca and rusticated Harvard College, was dressed up for a night on the town, but as his devotees say of this tireless proselytizer of the psychedelic cause, it was work, work, work. Tonight Leary was

when the reds got *their* chance the country would know just what was coming off. It was back to the old drawing board after that article, but Alpert and Dr. Leary made their main contribution to the incredibly swift spread of LSD through the US in 1964 by the simple act of publishing a formula for LSD, all that was needed for any housewife with a B-plus in high school chemistry and an inclination for black market activity. Dr. Leary's religious crusade has been a bust, convert wise, not so salutary financially either so he announced recently he was dropping out himself to contemplate his navel under the influence. It would be easier to take Dr. Leary seriously if he could overcome his penchant for treating LSD as a patent snake bite medicine.

An enlightening example of this panacea philosophy is found back among the truss ads in the September 1966 issue of Playboy. In the midst of a lengthy interview, when, as happens in Playboy, the subject got around to sex. Dr. Leary was all answers: "An LSD session that does not involve an utimate merging with a person of the opposite sex isn't really complete," he said, a facet of the drug he neglected to mention to the Methodist ladies he was attempting to turn on in Stockton, California. But this time, Dr. Leary was out to turn on the Playboy audience.

The following selection from the interview is reprinted in its entirety. Italics are Playboy's.

Playboy: We've heard that some women who ordinarily have difficulty achieving orgasm find themselves capable of multiple orgasm under LSD. Isn't that true?

Leary: In a carefully prepared, loving LSD session, a woman will inevitably have several hundred orgasms.

Playboy: Several *hundred?*

: Yes several hundred.

After recovering from that intelligence, the Playboy interviewer, phrasing the question as diplomatically as possible, asked Dr. Leary if he got much, being such a handsome LSD turn on figure. Dr. Leary allowed that women were always falling over him, but responded with the decorum of Pope Paul being translated from the Latin: "Any charismatic person who is conscious of his own mythic potency awakens this basic hunger in women and pays reverence to it at the level that is harmonious and appropriate at the time."

Dr. Leary also said that LSD is a "specific *cure* for homosexuality."

The final measurement of the tilt of Dr. Leary's windmill, his no doubt earnest claim to be the prophet of his generation, must be made by weighing such recorded conversations against his frequent and urgent pleas to young people to "drop out of politics, protest, petitions and pickets" and join his new "religion" where as he said recently:

"You have to be out of your mind to pray."
Perhaps, and quite probably so.

Will the Real Frodo Baggins Please Stand Up?

Except for the obvious fact that he wasn't covered with fur, you would have said to yourself that for sure there was old Frodo Baggins, crossing Haight Street. Frodo Baggins is the hero of J. R. Tolkien's classic trilogy, *Lord of the Rings*, absolutely the favourite book of every hippie, about a race of little people called Hobbits who live somewhere in prehistory in a place called Middle Earth. Hobbits are hedonistic, happy little fellows who love beauty and pretty colours.

Hobbits have their own scene and resent intrusion, pass the time eating three or four meals a day and smoke burning leaves of herb in pipes of clay. You can see why hippies would like Hobbits.

The hustling heroic looking fellow with the mistaken identity was Emmett Grogan, king-pin of the Diggers and the closest thing the hippies of Haight-Ashbury have to a real live hero. Grogan, 23 with blond unruly hair and a fair freckled Irish face, has the aquiline nose of a leader, but he would prefer to say that he "just presents alternatives." He is in and out of jail 17 times a week, sometimes busted for smashing a cop in the nose (Grogan has a very intolerant attitude towards policemen), sometimes bailing out a friend, and sometimes, like Monopoly, just visiting. The alternatives he presents are rather disturbing to the hippie bourgoisie since he thinks they have no business charging hippies money for their daily needs and should have the decency to give things away free like the Diggers do, or at least charge the squares and help out the hippies.

Grogan has a very clear view of what freedom means in society: "Why can't I stand on the corner and wait for nobody? Why can't everyone?" and an even clearer view of the social position of the hippie merchants: "They just want to expand their sales, they don't care what happens to people here: they're nothing but goddamn shopkeepers with beards."

Everyone is a little afraid of Grogan in Haihgt-Ashbury including the cops. A one man crusade for purity of purpose, he is the conscience of the hippie community. He is also a bit of a daredevil and a madman, and could easily pass for McMurphy, the roguish hero of Kesey's novel set in an insane asylum. There is a bit of J. P. Donleavy's *Ginger Man* in him too.

A few weeks ago, collecting supplies for the Diggers daily feed, Grogan went into a San Francisco wholesale butcher and asked for soup bones and meat scraps. "No free food here, we work for what we eat," said the head butcher, a tattooed bulgar named Louie, who was in the ice box flanked by seven assistant butchers. "You're a fascist pig and a coward," replied Grogan, whom Louie immediately smashed in the skull with the blunt side of a carving knife. That turned out to be a mistake, because the seven assistant butchers didn't like Louie too much, and all jumped him. While all those white coats were grunting and toiling in the sawdust, a bleeding Grogan crawled out with four cardboard boxes full of meat.

Since, something like Eve, he bit into the psychedelic mushroom while lounging beside a swimming pool at Cuernavaca, he has been hounded by the consequences of his act. Since Dr. Leary discovered LSD, he has been booted out of Harvard for experimenting a little too widely with it among the undergraduate population, asked to leave several foreign countries for roughly the same reasons, and is now comfortably, if temporarily ensconced in a turned on billionaire friend's estate near Poughkeepsie, New York while awaiting judicial determination of a 30 year prison sentence for transporting a ½oz. of marijuana across the Rio Grande without paying the Texas marijuana tax, which has not been enforced since the time of the Lone Ranger.

If he were asked to contribute to the "L" volume of the World Book Encyclopaedia, Dr. Leary would no doubt sum up his work as having "turned on American culture", though his actual accomplishments are somewhat more prosaic. Together with Richard Alpert, who was to Dr. Leary what Bill Moyers was to President Johnson, Leary wrote an article in May 1962, in surprise, *The Bulletin of Atomic Scientists*. The article warned that in event of war the Russians were likely to douse all our reservoirs with LSD in order to make people so complacent that they wouldn't particularly care about being invaded, and as a civil defence precaution we ought to do it ourselves first—you know, douse our own reservoirs douse our own reservoirs—so that

Ashbury, the Diggers happened. "Everybody was trying to figure how to react to the curfew. The SDS (Students for Democratic Society) came down and said ignore it, go to jail. The merchants put up chicken posters saying "for your own safety, get off the street." Somehow, none of those ideas seemed right. If you had something to do on the streets, you should do it and tell the cops to go screw off. If you didn't you might as well be inside."

Something to do, to Grogan was to eat if you were hungry, so at 8 p.m. at the curfew witching hour, he and an actor friend named Billy Landau set up a delicious free dinner in the park, right under the cop's noses, and the hippies came and ate and have been chowing down, free, every night since. The Haight-Ashbury has never been quite the same.

A Psychedelic "Grapes of Wrath"

Every bohemian community has its inevitable coterie of visionairies who claim to know what it is all about. But the Diggers are, somehow, different. They are bent on creating a wholly cooperative subculture and so far, they are not just hallucinating, they are doing it.

Free clothes (used) are there for whomever wants them. Free meals are served every day. Next, Grogan plans to open a smart mod clothing store off Haight Street and give the clothes away free too (the hippie merchants accused him of trying to undercut our prices"). He wants to start digger farms where partici-pants will raise their own produce. He wants to give away free acid, to eliminate junky stuff and end profiteering. He wants cooperative living to forestall inevitable rent exploitation when the Haight-Ashbury becomes chic.

Not since Brook Farm, not since the Catholic Workers, has any group in this dreadful co-optive consumer society been so serious about a utopian community.

If Grogan succeeds or fails in Haight–Ashbury it will not be as important as the fact that he has tried. For he is at least providing the real possibility of what he calls alternatives in the down the rabbit hole culture of the hippies.

Grogan is very hung up on freedom. "Do your thing, be what you are, and nothing will ever bother you", he says. His heroes are the Mad Bomber of New York who blissfully blew up all kinds of things around Manhattan over 30 years ago because he just liked to blow things up, and poet Gary Snyder, whom he considers "the most important person in Haight-Ashbury" because instead of siting sitting around sniffing incense and talking about it, he went off to Japan and became a Zen master. "He did it, man."

This is an interesting activist ethic, but it remains doubtful just what the hippies will do. Not that many certainly will join Grogan's utopia because utopias after all have a size limit.

The New Left has been flirting with the hippies lately, even to the extent of singing "The Yellow Submarine" at a Berkeley protest rally, but it looks from here like a largely unrequited love.

The hip merchants will of course go on making money.

And the youngsters will continue to come to Haight-Ashbury and do—what?

That was the question put to the hippie leaders at their summit Meeting. They resolved their goals, but not the means, and the loud noise you heard from outside was probably Emmett Grogan pounding the table with his shoe.

The crisis of the hippie ethic is precisely this: it is all right to turn on, but it is not enough to drop out. Grogan sees the issue in the gap

between the raw radical political philosophy of Jerry Rubin and Mario Savio and psychede-lic love philosophy." He himself is not interested in the war in Vietnam, but on the other hand he does not want to spend his days like Ferdinand sniffing pretty flowers. That is why he is so furious at the hip merchants. "They created the myth of this utopia; now they aren't going to do anything about it."

Grogan takes the evils of society very personally, and he gets very angry, almost physically sick, when a pregnant 15-year-old hippie's baby starves in her stomach, a disaster which is not untypical in Haight-Ashbury, and which Grogan sees being repeated ten-fold this summer when upwards of 200,000 migrant teenagers and college kids come as psychedelic "Grapes of Wrath", to utopia in search of the heralded turn on. The danger in the hippie movement is more than overcrowded streets and possible hunger riots this summer. If more and more youngsters begin to share the hippie posture of unrelenting quietism, the future of activist, serious politics is bound to be affected. The hippies have shown that it can be pleasant to drop out of the arduous task of attempting to steer a difficult, unrewarding society. But when that is done, you leave the driving to the Hell's Angels.

is was a typical day in Dogpatch for rogan who has had his share of knocks. A rooklyn boy, he ran away from home at 15 nd spent the next six years in Europe, working s a busboy in the Alps, and later, studying lm making Italy under Antonioni. Grogan had naturally forgotten to register for the draft, so when he returned to the United States he was n the Army four days later. That didn't last long however, because the first thing Grogan had to do was clean the barracks. His idea of cleaning the barracks was to throw all the guns out the window, plus a few of the rusty beds, and artistically displeasing foot lockers. Then he began painting the remaining bed frames yellow. "I threw everything out, everything that was not esthetically pleasing," he told the sergeant.

Two days later Grogan was in the psychiatric ward of Letterman Hospital in San Francisco where he stayed for six months before the authorities decided they couldn't quite afford to keep him. That was shortly after an Army doctor, learning of his film training, ordered Grogan to the photo lab for "work therapy". "It was a beautiful, tremendously equipped lab," Grogan recalls, and since it wasn't used very much, he took a print of his own big blond face and proceeded to make 5,000 prints. When the doctors caught up with him, he had some 4,700 ten by twelve glossies of Emmett Grogan neatly stacked on the floor, and all lab machines: driers, enlargers, de-velopers were going like mad, and water was running over on the floor. "What did you do that for?" a doctor screamed.

Grogan shrugged, "I'm crazy," he said.

He was released a little later, and acted for a while with the San Francisco Mime Troupe, the city's original and brilliant radical theatre ensemble. Then last autumn, when the negro Riots broke out in San Francisco and the National Guard put a curfew on Haight-

Last exit to Brewer St.

A recent letter to *The Guardian* from publisher John Calder put ironic and sad smiles on veteran faces of London's literary scene. Calder proposed setting up an English literary prize whose value and kudos would make it an English equivalent of the *Prix Goncourt*, and asked all those interested to write in and offer help.

Such a prize would obviously benefit the book trade, though it would probably do little for the author's profession. It would almost inevitably heap additional emoluments on an already widely acknowledged author, and become something of an Oscar. The intrigues over French literary prizes are scarcely the pleasantest feature of French literary life.

But the pros and cons of the idea aren't our main concern, which is the equally significant question of whether Calder himself takes his own idea seriously.

One remembers Calder's previous project for a West End arts centre, complete with art-gallery, coffee-bar, social centre for creative people, and so on.

Then there was the silly business of bringing a nude into an Edinburgh literary conference, which brought Calder plenty of free publicity as trailblazer and challenger of tabus, the Peter Brook of the publishing world.

There was the 'mock trial' of 'Sir Byril Slack' at a Better Books literary soiree, while the *Last Exit to Brooklyn* case was on the cards. Overtly, it was a 'satirical' manifesto on behalf of freedom, although its underlying purpose was, obviously, to quicken the book's suddenly accelerated sale. It was one of Calder's less successful gimmicks; about 15 spectators turned up, four of Calder's employees and four Better Books staff, leaving about seven paying customers, but no press. Calder then broke the show off halfway through, hinting that his

time was far too valuable to give a mere 7 people their money's worth. Actually their response was one of relief, since they didn't see what was so witty about alternating the reading of choice passages from the book under promotion with John Calder, pretending to be a dimwitted 'Sir Byril', crumbling under the trenchant questioning of the enlightened. Things didn't quite turn out like that, did they?

They might even have done so if Calder had spent more time preparing his case and less on a footling sales gimmick.

Publicity-hunting is part of a publisher's job, and Calder's taste for it can't be held against him. But he might be better-advised to take more paid publicity rather than concoct plausible schemes which involve well-intentioned people.

What's more serious is that Calder's 'image-making' is successful enough to attract manuscripts from young, artistically promising authors, whose work deserves, and needs, efficient promotion.

My criticism is that Calder's tactics do a great deal for Calder and very little for just those authors of his, who, lacking reputations, need help.

This remark may surprise, in view of the fact that Calder's lists contain many avant-garde works. His primary lines are (1) the French nouveau-roman (Robbe-Grillet, Duras, etc), (2) drug and beatnik literature (Burroughs, Trocchi), and (3) obscure European classics. However enterprising the list may seem at first, one soon realises that Calder has simply taken over talked-about books from foreign catalogues, that is to say, already proven successes. Importation has its risks, but, so far as the adoption of young, experimental, unknown authors is involved, Hutchinson, Methuen or Anthony Blond have equally impressive lists. What facilitates Calder's image-

making is the limited range he adopts because his firm is, in the best and the worst senses of the word, an amateur outfit. It's amateur in the best sense, in that he doesn't need to make money, only to cover his costs (for he is amply equipped with income connected with the family estate in Scotland). He can afford to indulge his own taste, and only his own taste. He doesn't need steady sellers or best sellers. He can flourish on what other publishers find a loss. But the Calder outfit is also amateur in the worst sense. Thus Calder's co-director, Marion Boyars, advanced the (surprisingly) low sales of *Last Exit to Brooklyn* as evidence that its exploitation avoided salacious appeal, no doubt —but an explanation of its poor sales performance is required.

And they're to hand. Calder and Boyars' advertising is exceptionally restricted; few of their books are given any paid advertising at all. Their salesmanship is often peculiar (one major Hampstead bookshop won't allow any Calder representative on the premises). Distribution arrangements are gruellingly casual (one large bookshop a mile from Calder's offices had to write 3 letters and make 10 phone-calls over 9 weeks before Calder's met an urgent order for a just-published book).

Production arrangements are even dicier. Some sort of nadir was attained when Raymond Durgnat's *Eros in the Cinema*, a topical book, was announced every year for three years running, and finally appeared with such incredible production howlers as a two-page photo appearing on page 196 and 199 and type which changed size in the middle of a line. Eighty-eight photographs looked as if blocks had been cut out of soggy blotting-paper; and the book was grossly overpriced (at £1 when 10/- would have been appropriate). Marguerite Duras was so vexed by similar publication

delays that she decided to take her work elsewhere. And the literary editor of one national magazine facetiously suggested a feature on *Books That Have Been Sitting Under Calder's Arse for Ten Years Without Getting Published*. Calder and Boyars are probably the only publishing firm which omits such standard procedures as sending authors a biographical questionnaire, or submitting blurbs for discussion. (The blurb for *Eros* consists entirely of such flatulent banalities as: 'It is, as its title suggests, concerned with eroticism...'). Calder's lack of interest in his authors is summed up by his remark to an author requesting a payment which was already a month overdue: 'I'm much too busy to bother about that this week, I'll sign a cheque for you when I have time.' At this point *dilettantism* comes very near contempt for his authors.

All these samples of inefficiency and insouciance have a common source. Calder's interest is not in sales, but in being a publisher, not in his authors but in his own image.

What this means to his authors is obvious. It means less promotion, fewer copies sold, a smaller impact and reward, than if the book had been sent to a less pretentious firm. And authors who are more concerned with advancing their own fortunes than with gratifying Calder's narcissism would be well advised to hitch their wagons to a better organised publisher.

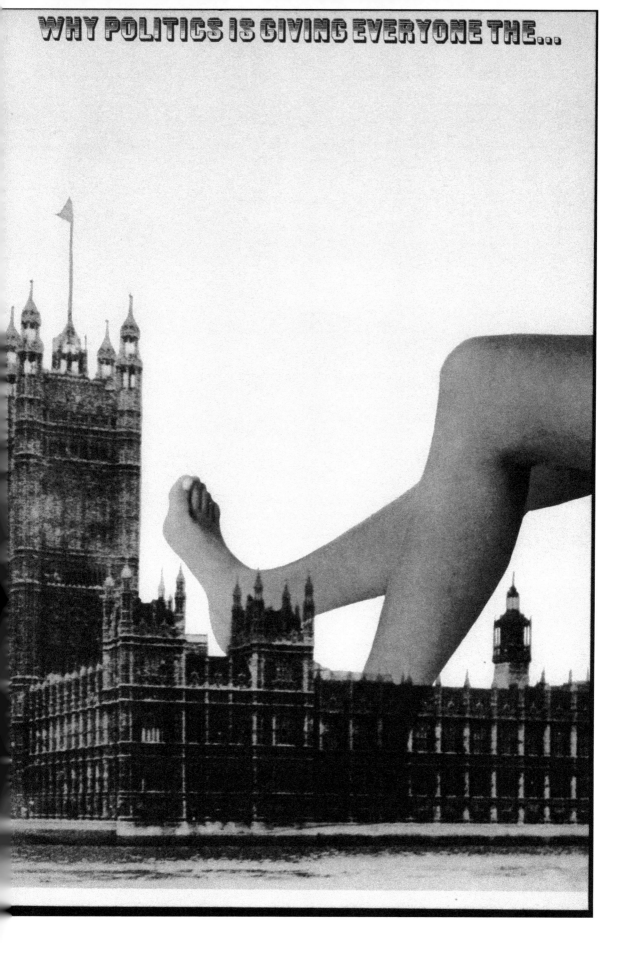

An address to politicians

"Complacency, pride and dead imagination these are the corruptions of politics. Most of them are moral prostitutes, randy for power, and theirs, perhaps, is the world's oldest profession. Humanity has paid over and over again in blood and suffering for its politicians."
J. H. Plumb.
Politicians and Corruption/The Spectator, 17.3.67.

"120 of the 180 (L.S.E.) demonstrators polled said they belonged to no political society."
'Insight/'Sunday Times'
19 March 67

"At a time when the Government seem to be enforcing middle-aged respectability on the motor cyclist, where does the rocker find excitement?"
Brian Priestley.
Rocker's Ambition is to Fly a Spitfire/The Times, 17.3.67.

"The new movement is slowly, carelessly, constructing an alternative society. It is international, inter-racial, equisexual, with ease."
Tom McGrath.
Editorial/International Times.

"In a general way, it would seem 'direct'— if not revolutionary—action is approved of since thinking must not become 'apoliticized'. The purpose of provos is to put 'a spoke in the wheel of (material) progress' and to evolve from 'creative beatniks' to persons 'dangerous to the state'."
Colin McInnes
New Society

"Despite a disturbing tendency to quietism, all hippies *ipso facto* have a political posture—one of unremitting opposition to the Establishment which insists on branding them criminals because they take LSD and marijuana, and hating them anyway, because they enjoy sleeping nine to a room and three to a bed, seem to have free sex and guiltless minds, and can raise healthy children in dirty clothes."
Warren Hinckle
Hippies/Ramparts, March 1967.

First to you who are currently successful: you who made it mouthing phony, ill-written, unutterably boring, lying, arse-licking speeches. Lend an unctuous ear—it may prove expedient.

And you out of office need not look so pious. Sincerity, sensitivity or honesty did not cost you election. Had you possessed any of these qualities you would never have stood. Only the scum of a society could bother to fashion a career so ruthlessly opportunist, so intellectually parasitic, so spiritually unrewarding.

Platitudes. This indignation doesn't bruise your egotism, this rage prompts no self-assessment, nor costs you votes. Philosophers, poets, authors, dramatists, artists and tele-pundits have interminably exposed the vileness of your methods, the sordidness of your ambitions. The masses, whom you despise, hold your profession beneath contempt.

And still you survive.

You think that Parliament is the greatest institution in the world. Parliament! Parliament; bloated with fat pompous, dying alcholics who babble on with:here, here honourable member, procedural motions, precious amendments, last ditch filibustering; farts who can't free their daughters to abort legally without dragging in the corpse of an anachronistic God, irrelevancies of hypothetical foetal discomfort, the population explosion and the burdens of motherhood . . . Parliament; the gulch parting promise from achievement.

"We're not all fat alcholics!" We hear you bleat; you academically brilliant whiz kids who stormed provincial rostrums thumping your chests righteously against corruption and ignorance, randy and hell-bent on steam cleaning the House. Where are you now?
You, Ben Whitaker, who once leapt around Hampstead canvassing 'revolutionary' reforms (shouting, Abolish Public Schools! Abolish House of Lords! Protest U.S. Vietnam policy!), now as silent as fear. You, Tony Greenwood, once the dapper hero of Aldermaston, co-founder of the radical 'Voice of the Union', now a gutless sycophant. You, Stephen Swingler, who once lead the rabid ginger group 'Victory for Socialism', now seen on telly exhorting people to drive carefully. And you, Richard Marsh, and you, Andrew · Faulds, and you, Raymond Fletcher . . . and all the others who betrayed ideals at the crack of a Whip. Where are you now? Lost in that gap between action and words. Words, words, the fetid words of politicians, becoming more incomprehensible as we grow younger. Words, words . . . a vocabulary of bullshit, a syntax of cynicism, a language of grandiose inconsequence.

You waffle in abstract generalities about peace, love, freedom, yet you're bewildered by your daughter's hatred. Do you know she's been fucking since she was 16, like everyone else? She doesn't give a stuff about the Magna Carta or your duty to the party machine. Your son is on pot. He can't follow the quibbling legalisms of the '54 Geneva Accords but he knows that thousands of Vietnamese kids are frying to death and you sit at breakfast dribbling marmalade, droning on about Britain's new role.

Oh yes, you smugly remind us, upper class Oxbridge intellectuals ARE busy joining Conservative clubs or publishing seedy left wing journals or praying that the young libs won't buckle to filthy compromises. They accept your frailities as the rules of politics, and channel their rancour into arbitrary dialectics. They are tomorrow's political con-men momentarily dazzled by copy-written credos.

And there are the sad cells of anarchists, Marxists, pacifists and humanists who think they understand how power works. Scribbling notes to their M.P.'s; revelling in the impossible prospect of affecting the legislative machinery.

You'll ban the pirate radios—not for the public benefit—but because the wrong people are getting a rake off. You'll pounce on a bawdy book because it offends your wretched concept of what life's all about, then crawl into the lobby bar to swap army jokes.

You humbug: setting up a Monopolies Commission to grovel before Lord Thomson. Socialising economic planning to victimise the workers. Promising disarmament and launching the Polaris.

All your life you've known there are too many slums, that families were being chucked into the gutters. You saw the statistics—200,000 homeless families in London alone. You know the British home building rate is an index of despair, a barometer of bumbling. But you have a cosy fireplace. You didn't care—until the public conscience was pricked by a sexy Cathy in distress. Then you were there on late night panels preening with mock concern, boasting instead of apologising.

Practically everyone under thirty smokes pot and you disapprove out of prejudice (lamenting the lost Excise). Yet you countenance coffee which screws nervous systems, Coke which dissolves teeth, alcohol which erodes livers, and tobacco which causes cancer.

At your most liberal you will distastefully offer a mildly tolerant homosexual bill burdened with primitive amendments. You limit the age of consent to 21 though we reach puberty 7 years earlier (in case you hadn't noticed).

This maxim guides your exercise of power: Authority should adopt or change a moral position only when self interest makes this necessary. That is, when positive disapproval of authority's existing position outweighs the combined effect of indifference and positive approval. It has nothing to do with ethics, morals or absolutes.

You will jump at anything to further your chances. This Labour Government is built on the wreckage of one politician's sex life—whose only crime (in your eyes) was being caught.

Whenever it becomes known a Minister is screwing his secretary, The Right Honourable opposition telephone their scruples to the news-desks. (Last year the 'Evening Standard' averaged ten calls a day over one top minister's indiscretion.) It matters not that his liason is harmless and human, only that its disclosure could weaken his party and so further the chances of the informer's.

That's politics.

Such a filthy game, that it is, after all, best left to politicians.

Have you ever tried to listen to BBC radio? Can anyone be really serious about suggesting it as an alternative to Pirate Radio. And the third. Put aside those who like classical music. They must be catered for even if it does mean Boulez for breakfast. What about the rest? Early

Assyrian earthworms for lunch, shorthand fantasies for dinner and the Gay Sparkling stock exchange as a nightcap.

The light and home. Most people who tune to the radio do so for background. Few have time to listen attentively during the day. In the evening they either want background or watch telly. So what do we get during the day. Soap operas, educational talks and fearsome music. By night quizzes, soap operas and more fearsome music. That music— they must be joking. "Music to remember", "Gems from Musical Comedy", "Strings by Starlight", "Family Favourites" etc etc.

This is where that argument about putting musicians out of work breaks down. No one hesitated to retire the horse when they found out about steam. The BBC makes people remember all that forgettable music simply because having a monopoly they play nothing else. Live. The orchestration often sounds like the harmonic variations of a vibrating jelly. Here is an artificially created class of anachronistic artisans producing something people would avoid if they could. Talk about the monarchy.

Just suppose that in fifteen years time or whenever it's going

be, the BBC does-set up a pop
...tion. Can you imagine it; the
...nd breaks down and whimpers.
... dead touch of "live"
...formance again. By those
...ple. Not the pop groups
...mselves. Or suppose they
...rted commercial radio. Who
...uld apply for and get the
...nses. Not the delightful,
...ginal, experienced pirates that
...ryone knows and likes so
...ch. The sump oil
...nufacturers, the newspaper
...bines, the fertilizer cartels
...ld all move in and take over.
... wouldn't be able to hear
...thing for the ads and good
...e.

... it's balls to say that pirates
...re record sales. Most people
... buy records because they've
...rd them on the air. Los
...eles with 28 FM stations and
...M stations, most playing
...100, 24 hours a day buys
...e records than London.
...don's population is three
...es that of Los Angeles.

DRUGS

... end the gratuitous savagery
...ncomprehending Magistrates.
...l servitude for smoking pot?
... not, as with alcohol, make
...d L.S.D. freely available to a
...ified age group. The
...rence between these
...cinogens and hard-core
...-up drugs like cocaine,
...in and morphine needs to be
...hasised. Unlike alcohol and
...cco, no evidence has been
...ced to demonstrate the
...gnant effects of L.S.D. and
... (For every acid-soaked
...naniac, there are hundreds of
...ken driving fatalities.)

...sometimes suggested that
...ance towards harmless
...ulants lower one's threshold
...sistance to the compulsive
...ctives. There is no evidence
...his. Any social pressure to
...duate" would almost
...pear if the Law recognised
...ichotomy.

...t are the benefits of pot and
....? Timothy Leary's
...gerated, though lucid
...rsement of acid has been well
...cised. An OZ correspondent
...lived under a pot cloud for
...onths regards cannabis as
...d, clean smoke". She writes:

...our first puff, muscles relax,
...on dissolves and suddenly the
...d is benign. While your body
... a deep breath, your mind
... another dimension:
...ption sharpens and you
...ver a tremendous capacity
...oncentration and details.

Dear Mr Short,

How dare you take away the pirate stations without giving us a real
substitute. I cannot bear the BBC and will go out of my mind if I have
to listen to it.

Yours Faithfully, _____

I am......years old. All
Most of my friends listen only to Pirates and hate the BBC.
Some
None

Unless you stop harrassing the pirates I will vote against your government.

I'm not old enough to vote, but will bear the grudge until I am.

"I know no method to secure the repeal of bad or obnoxious laws so effective as
their stringent execution."
Ulysses S Grant

Dear Mr St John Stevas,

I demand you ensure stringent execution of the present Abortion Law,
which you are so determined ought not be reformed.
Send all abortionists (back street and Harley St.), every women who has ever had
an illegal abortion and the police who tolerate the present system, to gaol now.
Begin with me and my friends.

Yours Faithfully. _____

I am......years old. All
Most of my friends have had at least one illegal abortion.
Some
None

Dear Mr. Jenkins,

Either produce clear and undisputed evidence that pot and/or L.S.D.
are more harmful than alcohol or stop interfering with personal liberty.
As it stands now, the drugs law, like Prohibition, is widely abused
and is thus a bad one.

Yours Faithfully, _____

I am......years old

All
Most of my friends smoke pot and/or take L.S.D.
Some
None
Those that do have been in my opinion harmed
                                    unharmed.

I will vote against your Government unless you adopt a more enlightened
attitude and stop putting me and my friends in fear of gaol.

affix stamp here

The Right Hon Edward Short
Postmaster General
House of Commons
Westminster
London W1

affix stamp here

The Right Hon Norman St John Stevas
House of Commons
Westminster
London W1

affix stamp here

The Right Hon Roy Jenkins
Home Office
Whitehall
SW1

Your sense of hearing changes from mono to stereo, you look mundane objects with child-li freshness, everything smells li frankincense. Everything you tastes like a Cordon Bleu speciality and your appetite, which you thought had gone way of your laughter, become chef's delight.

The months I spent as a depraved pot-head in Tangier were the healthiest of my life put on a stone in weight, slep like the heroine of an Ovaltine and ate like a farm-hand. My consumption of normal cigarettes dropped from forty odd to half a dozen. My cough (notorious on three continent shakes, frustrations and gene neuroses quietened down; I w contented for the first time i years. Most of the other foreigners felt the same way-many did their best creative v in the lotus-eating atmosphe claiming that marijuana (obtained with a minimum of worry and expense) heighten their imagination and clarifie their senses.

The local Arabs and Berbers seemed to have started smok as children without being noticeably stunted. The anti-social and erotic effects with which marijuana is popularly (and hopefully) endowed we very rare. The only aggressive Moroccans were backsliders who had been slyly tipping th vitriolic indigenous wines. Ev with them the routine seeme be I'll kill (and/or rape) you! . . . but tomorrow.

ABORTIO

Reason is the life of t law, so why not abort on demand? When custom runs counter t law then the law is a b one, and bad laws are worst form of tyrann A skilful abortion carr with it less risk than childbirth. It is only dangerous under the sordid back street conditions the presen law encourages. A law based on beliefs now accepted by only a sm section of the popula Opposition to reform stemmed mainly fron the Royal College of

naecologists and
tholic lobbyists, the
rmer are afraid of
sing income, the latter
losing their souls.
eological bickering is
elevant to a bill which
als, not with the
mber of angels that
uld dance on the head
a pin, but with human
ings, whose freedom of
oice is being denied.
nority groups are
titled to minority
ws, but not to impose
em on the rest of us.
course if orals were
iciently distributed
rtion would become
outdated and
neccessary as
ckets.

IETNAM

e Right Honorable Anthony
nwood, Minister of Housing
Local Government.

he Labour Party Conference, 1954:
the Labour Movement we rose to
er because we were on the side
he 'have-nots' of this country. We
t never lose our community of
rest and our identity with the
e-nots' of the world. We have got
onvince the masses of Asia that
are on their side in their struggle
that their struggle against
oitation and foreign domination
actly the same struggle that we
carried on in this country.''
s still, of course, on the side of the
-nots. Formerly, he embraced
e who have-not wealth: today,
immoderately, he aligns with those
have-not conscience.

e Right Honorable Richard
sman, Leader of the House.

se of Commons, 1953:

as delighted to hear Mr. Attlee
what we all know is true, that
hi Minh leads the real national
ement in Indo-China. Do not let us
ypocritical about it. It is time to tell
rench and the Americans that
are fighting an unjust war in
-China. If the French had done the
thing, Indo-China today would
d alongside Indonesia and Burma.
hi Minh and his rebels are not
munists by nature but by
ulsion. They are driven to be
munists in order to get national
ation. If we accept the Chinese
lution we must accept the
-Chinese Revolution, and tell our
ds not to waste millions of dollars
eserving a few square miles
d Saigon.''

●The Right Honorable Barbara Castle,
Minister of Transport.

House of Commons, 1953:
''The foreign policy of the United States
of America is to destroy communism.
That is a policy which does two things.
First it says that the nationalist
movements in Asia are all Moscow-
inspired, Kremlin-financed, part of a
great Russian plot. It fails completely to
understand what is happening in Asia,
the revolution which is taking place over
large parts of the earth's surface —
which, as hon. members on this side
of the House have shown quite clearly,
springs from the natural needs and
indigenous demands of the peoples
themselves.''

●The Right Honorable Jennie Lee,
''Minister for The Arts.''

House of Commons, 1953:
''There are liberal Americans who are
anxious to see Indo-China liberated
from what they call old-fashioned
colonialism.
We cannot talk to those Americans,
when at the same time, we approach
Washington with a begging-bowl held
out, because money talks louder than
words. I am grieved and shamed when
I hear that the contribution which our
country can make to international
affairs is lost because of the clatter
of the dollars falling into the
begging bowl.''

● The Right Honorable Harold Wilson,
Prime Minister.

Mayday 1954:
''We must not join or in any way
encourage an anti-communist crusade
in Asia under the leadership of the
Americans or anyone else . . .''.
''I believe at the moment the danger to

BEEN HERE LONG ?

a negotiated settlement in Asia is
provided by a lunatic fringe in the
American Senate. Asia, like other parts
of the world, is in revolution, and what
we have to learn today in this country
is to march on the side of the peoples
in that revolution and not on the side
of their oppressors.''

Well, once in power, Harold and his
colleagues soon stopped worrying
about Vietnam and learnt to love
the dollar.

Researched by Ken Coates

LON DON LO OK

100,000 VERY AWARE

READERS KNOW THIS

IS WHERE THE

TRENDS START

Theatre
Films
Galleries
Salerooms
Antiques
Books
Music and Ballet
Good Eating
Night Out
Property

EACH WEEK

O!

in praise of ugliness

Colin MacInnes

Somerset Maugham tells us that his mother and father were known in Paris as Beauty and the Beast. Dr Maugham senior, whose patients were the Anglo-American colony of the day, was apparently of quite sensational ugliness, whereas photographs confirm that his mother was exquisitely pretty. Why then, young Somerset wondered, had his mother never deserted Dr Maugham, or even taken lovers? After his father's death, he asked her this. She answered: 'Because in all our married life, he never humiliated me.'

In the Louvre, there is a painting an old man with a hideously pocked and bulbous nose looking down at a boy whose young face promises a resounding masculine beauty in the future. Far from being repelled by the old monster, the boy is looking up at him with confident affection.

Picasso, whose rare statements about his art are gnomic, yet always worthy of close attention, once answered the perpetual philistine question as to why his pictures are so ugly. They are not, he replied. All necessary destruction in order to create *seems* ugly, because of a pre-conceived public notion as to what is beautiful. All creation *is* ugly. The act of birth itself, the greatest beauty in our world, does not seem specially 'beautiful' until the child is washed and laid in its elegant cradle.

Francis Bacon is generally believed to be an artist who portrays, in terms of anguished satire, the horror of our age. Yet he has more than once assured me that his object is to create true beauty—the beauty, that is, of our particular times. I am sure he is right about this, and that his intentions have been largely misunderstood. (He was not very pleased, nevertheless, when I once compared his art to that of Fragonard).

The French understand this better than we do. For their term *belle-laide*, no equivalent exists on our language. A *belle-laide* is an ugly person whose ugliness is so striking, so expressive, and so touching that it at once seems beautiful. Bogart and Peggy Ashcroft are perfect examples.

We can see this at work in our own day among pop groups. A decade or so ago, the heroes of pop song were conventionally beautiful: Whitfield, Vaughan or, from America, Ray or Laine. Then lo and behold, dozens of boys and girls who were objectively ugly, seemed dazzlingly beautiful.

From these examples, I think we can deduce two principles:
1. In physical beauty, there are no absolutes. Beauty is indeed in the eye of the beholder, and if the social conventions of the beholder alter, so does his sense of what is beautiful.

2. True beauty or ugliness depend as much on the inner moral quality of the person as on the outward features bestowed on his flesh by nature. Thus, Dr Maugham and the bottle-nosed Florentine, though hideous, were seen as beautiful.

The confusions that arise from the first of these two principles are the easier to explain. As a key to doing so, we might compare a painting by Giorgione to one by Rembrandt. Both will be masterpieces by men of genius, and the purely aesthetic beauty of both will be undeniable.

But whereas Giorgione, perhaps because he was a southerner and a Venetian, adheres, in portraying human persons, to a classic, conventional style of beauty, the figures in almost all of Rembrandt's paintings are, objectively considered, hideous—including even his splendid self. Yet do they not seem, paradoxically, to be overwhelmingly beautiful—even more so, indeed, than those of Giorgione, lovely as these are?

And is this not because Giorgione, fettered (or inspired) by the Renaissance rediscovery of classic Graeco-Roman beauty, could not re-invent a new Venetian beauty of his own day? Whereas Rembrandt, unfettered (or unhelped) by any equivalent Dutch tradition, had to start from scratch with an ugly girl like Hendrikje Stoffels and make her look absolutely ravishing?

When we come to consider the moral reality underlying beauty, and which can create the feeling of it despite exterior ugliness, the definition is more complex. Negatively, we can all think of 'handsome' men or 'pretty' women whom we all know to be bastards or bitches, so that their physical beauty, however scintillating, seems like some monstrous fraud; and once we have got over our bedazzlement, their splendour fills with fear and horror. Equally, there are ugly people whom we know just *are* damn ugly, inside and out. Hermann Goring is a good example.

But positively, who can discern, in an objectively ugly man or woman, the inner spiritual quality that makes them in fact seem beautiful? The key to the answer may be in the reply of Mrs Maugham to her son, and the upward gaze of confidence by the young Florentine to his ugly old preceptor: each spectator of the ugly person was himself an innocent, a pure person.

Sometimes, the two factors creating beauty in ugliness coincide in a single person. That is to say, the person, though ugly, will seem beautiful because his epoch has grown to see his face as such, and also because his inner spiritual qualities have become so apparent as to transcend completely his physical lack of beauty.

I saw *Chimes at Midnight* the other day, and was immediately struck—as I suppose everyone else was—by the way Gielgud acted everyone right off the screen: even Orson Welles, and the handsome young actors and actresses surrounding him. Was this merely due to his greater experience or even talent? Not entirely.

No one could call Sir John a beauty. He's bald, has a big nose, and a somewhat ungainly figure. And yet always try to transcend them, this battered old mask seems beautiful. And because the moment he opens his objectively ugly mouth the words that soar out are of such stunning beauty as to make all his colleagues seem mumbling amateurs, one is instantly aware of the intellectual and spiritual depths within him.

Some artists, unlike Bacon or Picasso, get bogged down in mere ugliness when they attempt to transform this into beauty. Such an artist, it seems to me, is Gerald Scarfe. He makes his sitters ugly, which is entirely correct, since almost all of us are, yet fails to provide the alchemy by which this ugliness then becomes beautiful. This is because his drawing is feeble and his imaginative faculty mediocre, so that his drawings remain merely sensational and rather vulgar. Yet even Giles, whose figures are invariably hideous, achieves real beauty of a sort by his authentic poetic and ironic gifts.

The perfect master of beauty-from-ugliness in our era seems to me to be Soutine. His subjects are almost always revolting. His paintings, because of his tragic sense and immense pictorial skill, are startlingly beautiful.

To conclude, let us consider the features of James Baldwin. He told me he was known as 'frog-face' in his youth, and was much mocked for this. Once a nice teacher (white, liberal and female) took him to the movies—his very first visit, and only after the fierce disapproval of his terrifying pastor daddy had been overcome. They entered in mid-film, and the first thing he saw was a close-up of Bette Davis. 'She's a frog-face too,' he thought, 'and yet the world thinks she's beautiful. Then perhaps I am too, despite what the kids say.'

He is indeed—and I think his is the most beautiful face I have yet seen. And that may be because our times are etched on his features, and the light that shines through them is the same one we may recognize when we read what he has written.

THE DREAMLAND EXPRESS

IS COMING

pq

Do you publish a scrappy, drab, badly printed magazine? Printquick helps frustrated editors, impatient subs hamstrung production men. Printquick will produce your magazine (club journal, student paper, house mag) quickly, efficiently, imaginatively and cheaply. Ring 228 8407 for a full quote.

print quick

TEMPS–TEMPS–TEMPS–TEMPS
s/t 11/-
d/t 10/- **TEMPS**
c/t 9/-up RING or CALL AT
MATHIS EMPLOYMENT
21-22 Poland Street, W.1
Telephone: REG 0424-5-6

BE THERE!
WORLD CUP
MEXICO
1970

TICKETS-TRAVEL-ACCOMMODATION

Ensure your place on this 3-week
holiday of a lifetime, TODAY.
Through our exclusive

World Cup Travel Savings Plan

for as little as £1 a week with 3
years to pay!
Tickets are limited, so do send now
for full details of this unique offer.

Please send me ...... brochures for my friends
and family giving full details of the
"World Cup Travel Savings Plan".

NAME ....

ADDRESS ....
.... OZ

To AIR SPORT TRAVEL LTD.,
Kent House, 87 Regent Street, London, W.I.

MAGNIFICENT FAILURES

Hitler's Art teacher—politics was Hitler's second choice.

Zhivago overcoats.

The Plan to relieve Dien Bien Phu.

Princess Margaret's marriage.

The Great Society.

Bob Dylan—pale imitation of Donovan.

'Wrong Way' Corrigan—who set out to fly to Labrador, arrived in Los Angeles 27 hours later. Thus, either the first man to circumnavigate the globe in a Curtis biplane at Mach 1.5, or else the only aviator ever to be blown backwards across the USA.

The LSE's late porter—attempted to quell a scuffle in a passageway.

Marlowe—after centuries of valiant effort he has still failed to prove that he is Shakespeare.

The American who designed the Confederate 'Chain' Cannon, Two cannons were placed parallel on either side of the main street of a beseiged Virginian town facing the enemy. Their cannon balls were linked by a chain, so that when the cannons were fired simultaneously the entire invading army would be mown down. However, once in flight, the device whiplashed and gracefully boomeranged to massacre the defenders.

The Brabazon Flying Boat and the TSR-2—first deliveries were made dead on schedule, to the Imperial War Museum.

Bert Russell and J-P. Sartre's War Crimes Trial of LBJ.

The Yoko Ono Film Protest Rally—4 of a promised 500 eventuated to picket the British Censorship Board Offices.

Walter Craig, President of the Americian Bar Association—appointed by the Warren Commission to 'defend' Oswald. Craig attended 2 of the 51 sessions and only spoke once, but not on behalf of Oswald.

Jean Rook, Fashion Editor of the Sun, who for more than two years has been predicting the imminent demise of the mini-skirt.

The hippie London Underground Movement— failed to stay underground.

The first two issues of C

Leslie Parkes—soldier.

Any British boxer.

Fonthill Abbey— cost Beckford a millior pounds and fell down.

The *International Time.* bid for *The Spectator*

The Monkees—unable to suppress the information that they didn't play their own instruments on their hit records, now face the leak that they didn't sing either.

The Irish Famine 1846–1849—a heaven sent chance of solving once and for all England's Irish Problem. It is one of the great historical failures of the 19thC that only 1½ million died and that a million were allowed to escape to America.

THE ABERFAN TIPMASTER

Woodrow Wilson, Clemenceau, Lloyd George etc.—foolishly ignored the territorial claims advanced at the Versailles Peace Treaty Conference by a young Indo-Chinese named . . . Ho Chi Minh.

The French Army at Agincourt—at a cost of 36 head, English Archers slaughtered 12,000 French knights in armour.

Captain Cook—who discovered Australia, but lacked the foresight to forget about it, as William Dampier had done before him.

The Beach Battle Cabinet, The Royal Navy, 300 Royal Marine Commandos, The Army, 4 RAF rescue launches, a 'Flying Squad' of 00 men and 50 pumps, the Coastguard, ten Fire Brigades in the West Country, the fishing fleets of Cornwall, 24 1,000 lb. bombs, and 250,000 ons of detergent.

Sir Walter Raleigh—spent most of life in the Tower writing unrecognized sonnets until beheaded by James I.

Erasmus—tried to argue there was no real quarrel round the Reformation.

Wat Tyler, Pugachev, Munzer, Jack Cade, James Connoly who turned out not to be Fidel Castros of their times.

Richard Lester—A Funny Thing Didn't Happen On The Way To The Forum.

Winston Churchill—born of syphilitic father, suffered from obesity, his war strategy disastrous, author of the most catastrophic budget of the twentieth century, inadvertent creator of Australian mythology at Gallipoli, only man England could find to meet Hitler on his own terms.

Bonar Law—the Unknown Prime Minister. His one joke, used strenuously throughout his life, was to tap his pipe on the mantlepiece and shout 'come in'.

Harold—failed to repel Norman Invaders: his only claim to fame, the famous arrow-in eye canard, has lately been questioned.

Cyril Connelly—a special prize for failing to make a success out of being a self-confessed failure.

Gordon of Khartoum—practised unnatural vices and died by mistake.

Donald Macrae—such a failure that even his obscurity has remained unnoticed.

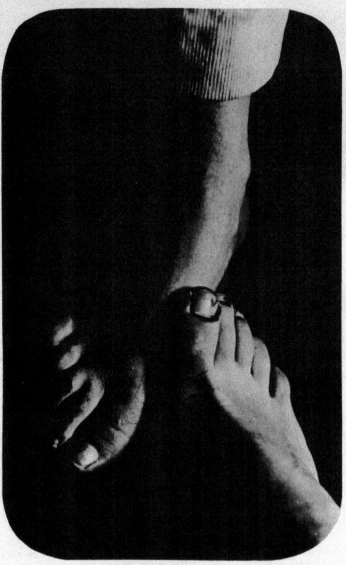

they may be in in some groups but

DATELINE 67

can't supply dirty toenails on demand. What we do promise for your £1 is four dates computer matched to your personality and tastes.

Because DATELINE 67 has a clientele of thousands, superior coding and a carefully designed questionnaire. You have a 95% chance of meeting a suitable partner through the DATELINE 67 service.

Rush the form below with £1 to receive your questionnaire. And two weeks after the end of the month when we get it back you will receive the names, addresses and telephone numbers of the four people the computer has selected as most suitable for you.

DATELINE 67

| POST TO:
Box D/T 1 .
40 Anhalt Road
LONDON SW 11. | Please rush me a pre-paid questionnaire. I enclose £1 and understand that the form will be re-run or my money will be refunded if the four dates are not satisfactory. | NAME....................
(Block Letters)
ADDRESS.................
....
....
....
PHONE NO............... |

The Scottish Match King

David Davidson is 67 and comes from Aberdeen. He hasn't seen his 9 children for a while, nor his wife since the war. "I was in the Navy, had this woman. Thought I was a real fly man. All the time me wife was flyin' me."

David sells matches at Waterloo station and makes about six or seven bob a night. He sings a lot and laughs a lot and people often stop to talk to him.
Is he happy?
"I don't give a fuck. All my mates are dead." From the war?
"The drink. Got one leg in meself. An' the other one's slipping. Here, let me tell you a joke. Three bairns, one, two, three," he counts with his fingers, "didnae come to school on Monday. Tuesday, the teacher says, where was ye? We couldnae come to school because our father got burned. Was he burnt badly, says the teacher. They don't fuck about when they cremate you, miss." He throws his head back and laughs Falstaff like and someone passing, a little shamefaced, bobs to put a sixpence on his handkerchief.
"See, it hasn't been a bad night," he says.

A Man of Leisure

Mick LeBeau "just like the King of France" is 35.
He couldn't quite remember where he came from, but it sounds as though it was somewhere in Ireland.
Mick says he does "fuck all".
But the ladies who run the tea stall at Waterloo says he bothers them all night and would we mind taking him away from there.
Mick says he would like a sixpence.
The ladies say don't give him one or he'll bother you too.
Mick laughs, smiles for the camera and puts out his hand.
Is he happy?
"No. Not since I was dead."
How long ago was that?
"A long time ago," says Mick and puts out his hand to the cameraman, "he hasn't given me my sixpence yet."
The cameraman gives Mick a two shilling piece and he laughs a lot, then calls us close.
"Would you like a little drink?"
A gent in a bowler hat and the tea ladies disapprove.

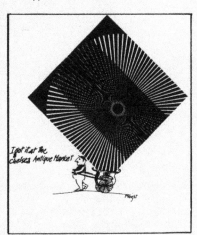

I got it at the Chelsea Antique Market

IS THERE A CHINK IN YOUR INTELLECTUAL ARMOUR?

SUBSCRIBE to OZ 30/- for 12

I enclose 30/- for 12 OZ.
Name.................
Address...............
....

OZ Subscriptions 40 Anhalt road London SW11.
Full time students receive 9/- reduction. Rush 21/- & NUS No.

FRISCO SPEAKS

FOREVER, FELLOW-BLOWN-MINDS... YOUR SUPER-COOL GURU OF INNER-SPACE REPORTS FROM NIRVANA.... A WARNING ABOUT THAT BANANA SCENE.... ITS A HOAX, MAN, I ATE 37 LAST WEEKEND A JUST GOT VERY SICK, MAN, VERY SICK.....VERY UNCOOL.. BUT BLOWN-MINDS YOU'LL BE PLEASED TO HEAR I'M INVESTIGATING THE "MESSAGES" OF OTHER POP SONGS AND AT PRESENT... .(NOW)... IM CONCENTRATING MY CONCENTRATION UPON STRAWBERRIES AND EIDLEWEISS SOOOO..... KEEP IN TOUCH

STOP PRESS FELLOW BLOWN-MINDS I HAVE JUST CONSULTED "I CHING" ABOUT WE ALL KNOW WHAT, DON'T WE. AND CAN NOW COFIDENTLY REPORT DIRECT FROM THE LAP OF BUDDHA: "P'I" STANDSTILL (STAGNATION) - THINGS CANNOT REMAIN UNITED, HENCE THERE FOLLOWS The HEXAGRAM OF THE STANDSTILL!! THE JUDGEMENT! EVIL PEOPLE DO NOT FURTHER The PERSEVERANCE OF THE SUPERIOR MAN. THE GREAT DEPARTS The SMALL APPROACHES.. UPPER and LOWER DO NOT UNITE. AND IN The WORLD STATES GO DOWN IN RUIN - WHEN RIBBON GRASS IS PULLED UP, THE SOD COMES WITH IT !! SO NOW YOU KNOW YOU KNOW YOU KNOW.. THAT'S THE SCENE FROM NIRVANA... FREAKOUT FOREVER-er..er FRISCO. xxx

An ugly side of some beautiful people

"She wasn't in that case both‹ by a tiresome social conscienc 'No. I don't bother about the millions being killed in Vietna do you?' " LADY MARY GAY‹ CURZON. Family motto: Let Curzon hold, what Curzon he‹ NOVA, April.

On Valentine Day, George Hamilton sent Lynda Johnson rose. "You are my Valentine to and every day of the year," sa card accompanying the first ro from the actor. Next day along came 364 more red roses. Lyn Bird described George's gestu "a wild, gay, romantic thing to Hollywood gossip Sheilagh Graham figured the current romantic odds: "I have 10 dol that says YES she quite obvio adores him. At the other end the bet is his press agent who wagering 100 dollars that the marriage will not come off." Shortly after, Hamilton annou that his draft board had reclas him as 1A. "I'll go anywhere," he said, "r country needs me." TIME and NEWSWEEK.

"When Jean (Shrimpton) announced to me she was go to do the film, I felt a sense of loss," Terence Stamp said, "Obviously she had come und the influence of the director P Watkins, *he* was beginning to Svengali her and I regarded th *my own* responsibility, a role I always assumed in my relation ships with women." THE PEOPLE, Aug. 14, 1966.

free Membership of 250 Clubs

By taking advantage of this once only special offer you can belong to over 250 leading London and Provincial clubs completely FREE for 2 months by joining The Clubman's Club.

Also you may then continue your membership, if you wish to and only if you are completely satisfied, at only 6 guineas a year.

Simply fill in the application form and the Banker's Order which is dated for 1st June 1967, and return it to us. We will then make you a full member of the Clubman's Club and send you your membership card.

If you do not wish to continue your membership, simply return your membership card and cancel your Banker's Order before 1st June 1967, and so you will not have to pay one penny.

Members of the Clubman's Club are members of all the clubs on our list and as you will see they are the leading clubs in every major town. So don't let this opportunity slip, but join now.

London Clubs to which you will belong:

Astor
Beak
Blenheim
Candlelight
Casino de Paris
Chalet Suisse
Charlie
Chesters
Churchills
Concorde
Court
Cromwell
 Sporting
Establishment

Gargoyle
Georgian
Golden
 Horseshoe
Golden Nugget
Hampstead
 Theatre Club
Knightsbridge
 Studio
Living Room
Maddox
Madingley
Mandrake
Marquee

Mazurka
Monument
Mountview
 Theatre
Nell Gwynne
New Manhattan
Northwick Park
'100' Club
Raymond
Revuebar
Renaissance
Ricky Renée's
Ronnie Scott
Shanghai

Spanish Garden
Swallow
Toby Gym
Town House
Trojan
 (Croydon)
Vanity Fair
Victoria
 Sporting
Windmill
 Saloon
Wine Centre
Winstons

You will also belong to the leading clubs in:

Aberdeen, Abersoch, Ayr, Battle, Bedford, Birmingham, Blackburn, Blackpool, Bognor Regis, Boston, Bournemouth, Bridlington, Brighouse, Brighton, Bristol, Burnley, Buxton, Cardiff, Carlisle, Castle Bromwich, Castleford, Cheltenham, Chester, Chesterfield, Chichester, Chorley, Colchester, Coventry, Darlington, Derby, Doncaster, Dublin, Durham, Eastbourne, Edinburgh, Falmouth, Glasgow, Gloucester, Great Malvern, Great Yarmouth, Harrogate, Hastings, Herne Bay, Huddersfield, Hull, Ipswich, Jarrow, Kingsbridge, Lavant, Leeds, Leicester, Lincoln, Littlehampton, Liverpool, Lowestoft, Ludlow, Luton, Macclesfield, Malton, Manchester, March, Margate, Market Harborough, Marple, Middlesbrough, Newcastle, Northampton, Norwich, Nottingham, Paignton, Peacehaven, Penarth, Peterborough, Plymouth, Portsmouth, Port Talbot, Preston, Reading, Redcar, Salford, Salisbury, St Anne's-on-Sea, St Leonard's-on-Sea, Saundersfoot, Scunthorpe, Seaford, Skegness, Southampton, Southport, Southsea, Stockport, Stockton-on-Tees, Stoke-on-Trent, Sunderland, Swansea, Taunton, Teignmouth, Tewkesbury, Torquay, Usk, Walsall, Wakefield, Warwick, Westerham, Weston-super-Mare, Whalley, Whitley Bay, Widnes, Wigan, Winchester, Winsford, Windsor, Woking, Wokingham, Wolverhampton, Worthing, York.

Clubman's Club

35 Albemarle Street Mayfair London, W1 Hyde Park 5933

I hereby apply for membership of **The Clubman's Club** until 1st June 1967 **completely free.** I agree for myself and my guests to conform with the rules of each club visited. I understand that if I return my membership card before 1st June 1967, my application will be cancelled.

Name_____
Address_____
_____
_____
Occupation _____
Signature_____(I am over 18 years of age) OZ.44
Banker's Order
To_____ Bank Ltd. Branch_____
Address_____

Please pay to the order of **The Clubman's Club,** Lloyds Bank Ltd., Golders Green (30-93-50) the sum of 6 guineas on 1st June 1967, and thereafter on the same date each year being my annual subscription to **The Clubman's Club.**

Signed_____
Address_____

?WAY OUT

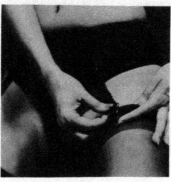

Lonely? GET LISTED

TERRIFIC DEMAND!

COUPLES (ADULTS ONLY)

GIRLS guys

Advertiser". Filled with intimate ad's. from ladies, men, couples, groups. (LADIES ADVERTISE FREE) Sold to discreet adults only.

TO International Personal Advertiser, Westbourne Park Mews, Westbourne Gds. London, W.2

PLEASE FIND ENCLOSED 7/6 FOR MY POST PAID COPY OF YOUR MAGAZINE. I AM OVER THE AGE OF 21.

Name (Block capitals) ....

Address ....

Open from 6pm till MIDNIGHT
and later to ENGLISH STAGE
SOCIETY MEMBERS only.
SUBSCRIPTION: 1 guinea

food, drink, coffee, jazz, folk
palmistry, plays, films
                    +people
ROYAL COURT THEATRE
SLOANE SQUARE SW3 SLO2273

FRESH NUDES TO LOOK AT

Under the blankets, behind the screens, beyond
visual range lie images of fact and fancy about
women; researchers in non-verbal communication
an t comparative mores may find that the
photographic studies of the female nude produced
by Jean Straker form a useful visual authority
or fresh enquiry.
For details of membership, Illustrated booklet and
specimen studies, send £1 ($5.00 by air) to
ACADEMY OF VISUAL ART
Studio House, 12 Soho Square, London, W.I. England

You are invited to become a member of

C.M.C.

Facilities include:-
Substantial discounts on clothes, etc.
FREE use of Accommodation address, same
day forwarding service.
FREE use of PEN PAL register.
FREE use of HOLIDAY register.
Members only - CMCN (Naturists)

Send for detailed Brochure (8d in stamps please)
to: Dept O1
          C.M.C.
14 Alexandra Road, Clacton-on-Sea, Essex.

COME
UNDERWATER..

DREAMING IN A DANDY FASHIONS SUIT.
161 Kings Road. London, S.W.3
Telephone: FLA 6851

'MR MADAM' tells the bizarre and intimate story of Kenneth Marlowe—a female impersonator and active homosexual. In his autobiography, he writes about his shocking Hollywood life and its world of love-hungry homosexuals, sexual degenerates and unique orgies with complete and detailed honesty. MR MADAM is by far the most candid and startling homosexual autobiography ever written. Order your copy. 42s POST FREE, direct from the Luxor Press now.

LUXOR PRESS 50 Alexandra Rd., London SW19

glory **g**hole

BOUTIQUE

324a King's Road S.W.3

Telephone FLAxman 0296

IF YOUR HEART'S IN LEATHER
HEARTEL FASHIONS
HAVE THE ANSWER. SEND 5s
NOW TO:
HEARTEL FASHIONS
131, ALBERT ROAD. N.22

CONFIDENTIAL ADVICE on the Pill for all
women everywhere. Write Step One Ltd.
(O) 93, Regent St. W.1. (S.A.E.) or
telephone 01-622-7815.

HOLD THAT,
WOMAN!

NEW FROM GERMANY-
                    SECURA LONGTIME
the contraceptive sheath designed to
increase your happiness. You naturally expect security from a contraceptive. SECURA LONGTIME gives you
much more; by means of a special
treatment it prevents premature emiss-
ion and gives you literally a LONG
TIME, so increasing your chances of
perfect harmony with your partner.

Be happier with SECURA LONGTIME;
try a sample pack of two for 7/6
                    six for £1

C.J.P. distributors

30 BAKER STREET LONDON W.I.
MAIL ORDERS ONLY.
S.A.E. for further products.

BOOKS FOR KINKS
          & KICKS
EXCITING & EROTIC
Send for comprehensive list POST-FREE
          DANJAC: 50 Parsons Green Lane SW6
Phone REN 2871   evenings REN 3911

use taxi · trucks
For light removals. Dormobiles with
helpful working drivers. HAM 1466 or
HAM 6351. Please quote this advert.

SILVER RINGS..

TURKISH trick rings......... from 19s
FRIENDSHIP-sick rings...... from 26s
SEMIPRECIOUS STONES......from 75s
VICTORIANA barrels.........from 84s
                    gold
Also   Hand made & to order. Mod:
WED or ENGAGE 10% 'off for two'

32 St Martins Lane WC2   (COV 1742)
          ADMIRAL'S EYE DESIGNCRAFT.

FOR ALL **transport** PROBLEMS
          REMOVALS, DELIVERIES, ETC.
          DORMOBILES WITH HELPFUL
          WORKING DRIVERS.

taximoves GULLIVER 8923

PREGNANCY TEST. £2. Inquiries: Bell
Jenkins Laboratories Ltd; Charlotte St;
Portsmouth. (23366)

WANT to see a really good Rag Mag?
One which has succeeded in hitting out
at the old stodgy ideals? Then get a copy
of PLINTH, published by Ealing Technic
College Rag in support of the Muscular
Dystrophy Society of Great Britain and a
local Kidney Machine Fund. It can be
obtained from the Student's Union, 2s 6
post paid, or from many of the students
at the College. It's a real collector's
piece.

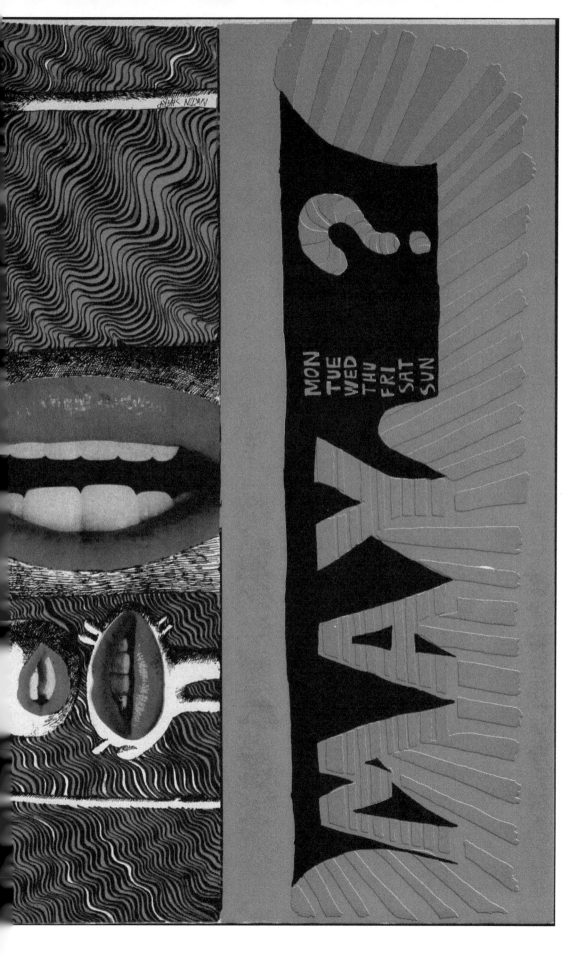

MARTIN SHARP

MAY

MON
TUE
WED
THU
FRI
SAT
SUN

I'm not the only 90 year old student who subscribes to OZ

e same
minority
suade
ers that
rity.
only
ak for the
er 25, but
sion.

Issue:
our
n

Since she
else.'
nder 30
ething
would
nd so on,
hampions
om realise
youth,
all blacks;
frogen
Vietnam;
of capital
nt. still
to 'do
have a
sexual
for illegal

content
, and will
or
You
n from
ower and,
)
v of
g; I wish

under-
male
half-men

write to
ngratulate
ontents of
the
nearest
I have
in. This
ry that
ll be the
w cultural
natives.

e and
London
g wrong
re asked
s
unique,
rich
ow in
es, 'you're

gers he
selves . . .

---

even a month later they are looking a little shopsoiled. Michael Peacock and the BBC's Great Leap Backward . . . now resigned and crawling for the Yorkshire contract. Peter Watkins, now sitting in the wreckage of Privilege, shoddily written and plank acted, David Bailey, whose G Passion made one long for a Barclays commercial. Certainly they are young. But there doesn't seem to me to be a qualitative difference between 'being battered into conformity by their elders' and being battered into conformity, trendy and youthful as it is, by Peacock and O'Rahilly. Intellectually they are as full of promise as a cigarette butt, though I don't doubt that their bank managers are happy men. For judged on an intellectual level, Mr Allen's thesis is little more than the Playboy Philosophy meeting Swinging London; of interest primarily to bank managers and their spiritual allies.

What's really frightening is the success with which the Trendy False Consciousness has managed to admire the pop products for precisely their banality, predictability and secondhandedness. Attached to society by their lead, the iconoclasts caper about celebrating their own submission and defeat. It's all signature and no painting. You can't see the prick for the codpiece.

The new trendies, impressarios, producers and 10%ers may be younger and richer these days. They may conceivably be rationalising and manufacturing things and ideas which are pretty, funny or cheap. But they are still cultural and economic exploiters, in the precise technical sense of that word. They should be treated as that, not as some recherche art form.

Yours, cheesed, tired & revolutionary.
David Widgery,
15 Queen Alexandra Mansions,
Judd St WC1

Sir,

Your recent issue contains a personal attack on myself and a general one on this firm. It is impossible ever to reply effectively to a personal attack, especially when anonymous, because protesting merely spreads the libel, but like most low-level scurrility, it should tell your readers more about the writer than the subject. Such nastiness usually goes with a self-recognised lack of talent.

More serious is the inference that our firm is unprofessional and inefficient. The article is full of every kind of malicious misinformation, but the source of some items can be checked. Mr Durgnat knows very well the reasons why **Eros in the**

Cinema was held up, reasons that involved the censoriousness of printers and the disappearance of one large printing firm in a series of mergers and takeovers. The other allegations are either based on misinformation or pure fantasy.

As for the 'large bookshop' a mile from our office, this turns out to be a new and extremely small bookshop, not yet even recognised by the Booksellers Association, that for some time we did not supply as they would not pay their bills. We have in fact one of the best international sales distributions of any publisher, and our authors know it.

Yours etc
John Calder
Calder and Boyars Ltd/
Publishers
18 Brewer St
London

Dear Sir,

Why did the author of the recent attack on Calder & Boyars not reveal his identity? Hit and run isn't done!

As a publisher I can say that advertising books does not sell them — it only inflates authors' vanity and causes them to complain when it falls off. Publishing foreign writers who are unknown here is more hazardous and expensive than to publish new English authors. It's a well-known fact that many scribes are paranoiac and that most of us publishers are megalomaniac.

Yours narcissistically,
Peter Owen
Peter Owen Ltd/Publishers
12 Kendrick Mews
London SW7

Dear Sir,

I am not one to balls ache about what other people do, let alone print. However, I find it intensely boring that out of the eight photographs of dimensions over one inch square in the last issue of your excellently printed magazine, six were non-consequential pictures of tits and bums.

Why don't you stop shitting about, so to speak? If you want to be different, print something to contravene the Obscene Publications Act. If you haven't got the spunk, print beautiful photographs not infantile pictorial stupidity.

Yours most sincerely,
A. de Gris.
14 Wood Mews
London W.1.

Students get older every day so rush 21s for 12 OZ before YOU pass out

40 ANHALT ROAD SW11

GLOBE FISH.

London OZ is published by
OZ Publications Ink Limited,
40 Anhalt Road, London, SW11
Phone: REG 0427, BAT 8407.
Editor: Richard Neville
Deputy Editor: Paul Lawson
Business Manager: Peter
Ledeboer
Advertising: Ian Stocks
Design: Jon Goodchild
Art: Martin Sharp
Staff: Andrew Fisher, Robert
Whittaker, David Reynolds
Louise

Contributions: are welcome
and should be addressed to:
The Editor, enclosing s.a.e. *

Printer:
Sharptone Litho Ltd
83 Bellenden Road, SE15
Distributed by:
Moore Harness Ltd
11 Lever Street, EC1
CLE 4882
OZtralia is obtainable from
16 Hunter Street, Sydney.
Enclose £1 for 12 quivering issues.

Dear Sir,

I have before me a copy of
OZ3, which I foolishly bought
yesterday. You know, you've
got a fucking nerve, charging
2/6 for—what? A banal attack
on politicians, a few platitudes
on drugs, commercial radio and
abortion, a piece of cloying
'Winn-ism' by Colin MacInnes,
a few scraps of rather flat
'humour' and some infantile
artwork by semi-literates
(psychedelic is mis-spelt on
the cover, and tongue on the
fold-out.)

The only worthwhile thing in
the magazine is the article
reprinted from 'Ramparts'. I
think you could add OZ3 to
your list of failures, if it were
not so tired and phony.

Yours faithfully,
Michael North,
42 Littlejohn Rd.,
St. Mary Cray,
Orpington.

P.S. Is it really necessary to
devote a full page to an attack
on John Calder. Is he that
important?

Dear Sir,

I'm afraid you make the same
mistake as every other minority
group – you try to persuade
yourself and your readers that
you speak for the majority.
True, in your case you only
usually pretend to speak for the
majority of people under 25, but
this is still a great delusion.

For example in the last issue:
'The masses . . . hold your
profession (politics) in
contempt.' '. . . fucking since she
was 16 like everyone else.'
'practically everyone under 30
smokes pot.' '. . . something
(B.B.C. music) people would
avoid if they could.' – and so on.
When will the various champions
of liberalism and freedom realise
that 99 per cent of the youth,
like their parents, hate all blacks;
would like to see a hydrogen
bomb dropped on N. Vietnam;
want to see the return of capital
and corporal punishment, still
rely on political parties to 'do
something for us'; still have a
pretty ancient code of sexual
'morals'; have no time for illegal
drugs, etc., etc.

On the whole they are content
with things as they are, and will
do whatever the State or
convention demands. You
really must climb down from
your intellectual ivory tower and.
admit that you (and me)
represent a tiny minority of
misfits. One other thing: I wish
you would have more
consideration for your under-
sexed readers. Your female
contributors make us half-men
feel pretty useless.

Yours faithfully,
Victor Coughtrey

Dear Sir,

I have been wanting to write to
you for some time to congratulate
you on the excellent contents of
the first two issues of the
London OZ. This is the nearest
thing to real satire that I have
seen come out of Britain. This
proves my private theory that
Britain's expatriates will be the
initiators of any real new cultural
change rather than the natives.

Yours sincerely,
Rajat Neogy.
Editor, *Transition*
Uganda

Dear Sir,

Rod Allen's attack on me and
panegeric of swinging London
epitomises what is going wrong
with the trendies. We are asked
to accept that London's
cultural environment is unique,
because the young get rich
quick. If you do not throw in
your lot with the trendies, 'you're
for dead'.

The procession of swingers he
evokes speak for themselves . . .

even a month later they are
looking a little shopsoiled.
Michael Peacock and the BBC's
Great Leap Backward . . . now
resigned and crawling for the
Yorkshire contract. Peter
Watkins, now sitting in the
wreckage of Privilege, shoddily
written and plank acted. David
Bailey, whose G Passion made
one long for a Barclays
commercial. Certainly they are
young. But there doesn't seem
to me to be a qualitative
difference between 'being
battered into conformity by
their elders' and being battered
into conformity, trendy and
youthful as it is, by Peacock and
O'Rahilly. Intellectually they are
as full of promise as a cigarette
butt. though I don't doubt that
their bank managers are happy
men. For judged on an
intellectual level, Mr Allen's
thesis is little more than the
Playboy Philosophy meeting
Swinging London: of interest
primarily to bank managers and
their spiritual allies.

What's really frightening is the
success with which the Trendy
False Consciousness has
managed to admire the pop
products for precisely their
banality, predictability and
secondhandedness. Attached to
society by their lead, the
iconoclasts caper about
celebrating their own
submission and defeat. It's all
signature and no painting. You
can't see the prick for the
codpiece.

The new trendies, impressarios,
producers and 10%ers may be
younger and richer these days.
They may conceivably be
rationalising and manufacturing
things and ideas which are
pretty, funny or cheap. But they
are still cultural and economic
exploiters, in the precise
technical sense of that word.
They should be treated as that,
not as some recherche art form.

Yours, cheesed, tired &
revolutionary,
David Widgery,
15 Queen Alexandra Mansions,
Judd St WC1

Sir,

Your recent issue contains a
personal attack on myself and a
general one on this firm. It is
impossible ever to reply
effectively to a personal attack,
especially when anonymous,
because protesting merely
spreads the libel, but like most
low-level scurrility, it should tell
your readers more about the
writer than the subject. Such
nastiness usually goes with a
self-recognised lack of talent.
More serious is the inference
that our firm is unprofessional
and inefficient. The article is full
of every kind of malicious
misinformation, but the source of
some items can be checked.
Mr Durgnat knows very well
the reasons why **Eros in the**

Cinema was held up, reasons
that involved the censoriousness
of printers and the disappearance
of one large printing firm in a
series of mergers and takeovers.
The other allegations are either
based on misinformation or pure
fantasy.

As for the 'large bookshop' a
mile from our office, this turns
out to be a new and extremely
small bookshop, not yet even
recognised by the Booksellers
Association, that for some time
we did not supply as they
would not pay their bills.
We have in fact one of the best
international sales distributions
of any publisher, and our authors
know it.

Yours etc
John Calder
Calder and Boyars Ltd/
Publishers
18 Brewer St
London

Dear Sir,

Why did the author of the recent
attack on Calder & Boyars not
reveal his identity? Hit and run
isn't done!

As a publisher I can say that
advertising books does not sell
them – it only inflates authors'
vanity and causes them to
complain when it falls off.
Publishing foreign writers who
are unknown here is more
hazardous and expensive than to
publish new English authors.
It's a well-known fact that
many scribes are paranoiac and
that most of us publishers
are megalomaniac.

Yours narcissistically,
Peter Owen
Peter Owen Ltd/Publishers
12 Kendrick Mews
London SW7

Dear Sir,

I am not one to ball's ache
about what other people do,
let alone print. However, I find
it intensely boring that out of
the eight photographs of
dimensions over one inch
square in the last issue of your
excellently printed magazine,
six were non-consequential
pictures of tits and bums.
Why don't you stop shitting
about, so to speak? If you want
to be different, print something
to contravene the Obscene
Publications Act. If you
haven't got the spunk, print
beautiful photographs not
infantile pictorial stupidity.

Yours most sincerely,
A. de Gris,
14 Wood Mews
London W.1.

Hysteria About Abortion

WITH just a month to go before report stage in the Commons, the campaign in favour of the Medical Termination of Pregnancy Bill is showing signs of hysteria.

Mr. St. John-Stevas, the Bill's chief critic, is receiving scores of identical printed postcards daily. Each is headed by a dictum of Ulysses Grant, who became President of the United States in 1869: "I know no method to secure the repeal of bad or obnoxious laws so effective as their stringent execution."

I reproduce the rest of one card, allegedly from a girl of 16 whose signature I have blacked out.

What the source of this peculiar method is, and whether the signatures are genuine, Mr. St. John-Stevas has no idea.

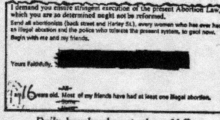

I demand you ensure stringent execution of the present Abortion Law, which you are so determined nught not be reformed.
Send all abortionists (back street and Harley St.), every woman who has ever had an illegal abortion and the police who tolerate the present system, to gaol now.
Begin with me and my friends.

Yours Faithfully,

16 years old. Most of my friends have had at least one illegal abortion.

Daily bombardment of an M P

Mr Norman St John-Stevas
House of Commons
Westminster
SW1

Dear Sir ....

As you will be inundated next week with postcards urging you to reconsider your stand on the projected abortion law, we thought you might care to know what it was all about.

Forewarned *is* forearmed, but we trust you will give these protests serious consideration.

Yours sincerely,
Paul Lawson
Deputy Editor

April 25

(EXTRACT FROM THE SUNDAY TELEGRAPH, MAY 5th)

Extract from Rod C B Lake's letter of January 24:

❝And if your poor frustrated writer wishes proof of this statement, I invite her to spend a night or two with me, and if I cannot, in her oppinion, back up my statement with actions, in other words, give her complete sexual satisfaction, she can write an article on the one Englishman She has had, and really run the Englishman down and even use my name.❞

Mr Rod C B Lake turned out to be a tall, fair-haired man, with a clear steady gaze.

His hair is combed up into a quiff and his even features are twisted by the ghost of an ironic smile. He has a virgin girl friend he is not yet ready to marry, who is slightly uneasy about the consequence of his challenge to Germaine. His early sexual training (which began when he was 'only' 14) was with women in their late thirties and consequently, as he disarmingly confesses, he is not much good at wooing. But awfully good when it comes to the point. 'Dead kinky,' he murmured.

Despite his inviolate steady, he never sleeps alone on the nights his air-steward flatmate works. Asked if he felt any affection for the other women who satisfy his gargantuan sexual needs, he replied that there had been one who satisfied him. 'Only she never came back after the first time,' because of the 'things' he made her do.

To our correspondent he offered complete satisfaction after half an hour. Indeed, she would 'ejaculate' *(sic)*, twice, he assured her, 'before he even put it in.' Where? was the question she did not ask. Moreover, he would carry on for at least two hours, 'before even coming.' This he appeared to believe was the ultimate in sexual bliss.

When Miss Greer pointed out that his only motive for unleashing such virtuosity was his own patriotism, which could hardly constitute motivation for her, he readily agreed, but hoped that the attractiveness of the prospect would induce her to break an oath taken after mature consideration and with complete fervour. It didn't.

OXFORD LOCAL EXAMINATIONS

---

transport PROBLEMS

REMOVALS, DELIVERIES, ETC. DORMOBILES WITH HELPFUL WORKING DRIVERS.

taximoves
GULLIVER 8923

Continued page 8

Three department store corsetry assistants have written to complain about Mrs Brenda Breustom's scornful reference to 'dikey salesladies'. (OZ 3).

'It is the customers', they write, 'who make the advances'. It's gratifying that some people took Mrs Breustom seriously. Many readers wrongly suspect that such bizarre letters are editorial inventions.

Even more bizarre are the ones we reject (eg: [i.] The first entry into Mrs Breustom's proposed prick competition. [ii.] A follow-up to Larry's bottom photo —one that had been savagely scoured by the lash).

OZ is as bored with British Breasts (?) as readers must be. There is no winner, so no prize. A special honorary award, however, to the 'IT' girl, Susie, who's splashed in gold on page two.

John Calder, Peter Fryer, Peter Watkins and others will be pontificating on censorship in a public forum organised by the National Secular Society at the Caxton Hall, June 23.

Now that London's 'Speakeasy' club seems destined for frenzied fashionability, the attitude of management to patrons has degenerated from reluctant courtesy to belligerent contempt—a pretty typical syndrome of success. Bibas boutique is renowned for the coolness of its staff. Though of course, wages at Bibas are low, the hours long (from 9 am to 8 pm on Saturdays with two short breaks) and staff suffer the caprice of bizzkid employer Stephen Fitz-Simon. (He recently dismissed 5 girls unjustly, accepting three of them back only when pressured by angry parents.) Business is good.

For possessing cannabis resin, Mr John Hopkins has been sentenced to 9 months gaol. Such outrageous injustice underlines the urgency of law reform. Those readers who completed last issue's pot post-card to Mr Jenkins may soon be invited to take further action. Watch 'The Times'. Meanwhile, come to the benefit for Absent Friends, July 8, Saturday, Roundhouse from 8 pm to 8 am.

MAILORDER FROM J.L.T.Y & CO.

49 KENSINGTON PK. ROAD
LONDON W.II.

Love Life-Marijke Koger
18x23-Red & Black

Book a Trip-Marijke Koger
18x23-Green & Black

Love Bob Dylan-Marijke Koger
18x23-Red on Saffron

'Stomach Dancer' by Aubrey Beardsley
18x23-Black on White

Peacock Train' by Aubrey Beardsley
18x23-Black on White

'Danger Marihuana'
18x23- Black, Red, Yellow

The Lord's Prayer
18x23 Gold&Black

Friday? Good ! by Jacob & The Coloured Coat
18x23-Silver on Black

All posters 7/6 each.
Cheques & P.O.s to
J.L.T.Y. & Co.
49 Kensington Park Road
LONDON W.II.
Add 1/6 Postage to all
orders up to 12.

WHOLESALE
ENQUIRIES FOR POSTERS
AND BUTTON BADGES
INVITED.

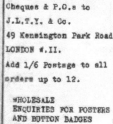

BUY THESE AND OTHER TRIPPY GOODIES AT THE HEAD SHOP
202 KENSINGTON PK. ROAD LONDON W11

SGT NASSER'S LONELY HEARTBREAK BAND

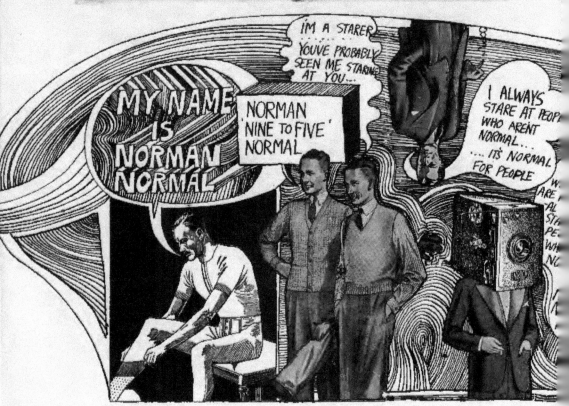

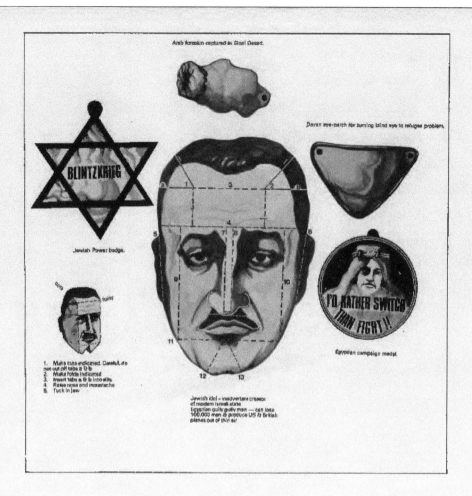

Paul Lawson/Bernard Alum

smalls

OZ ADVERTISING: SMALLS: 1s. per word.
1/6d. semi display. 2/6d. box no.
DISPLAY: £65 page. £35 half page. £2-10s. column inch.

GENTS! A black leather swimbrief, 3' sides, for your hols. this summer? 90s. Details s.a.e. Larry Knight, 4 Hamilton Close, London, N.W.8.

SHORTCOMINGS?

Prolong the pleasure of intercourse with Suifan's 'Kwang Tze' Solution. This Chinese preparation is specially beneficial to men who suffer from premature ejaculation, and is Guaranteed to end mutual frustration and bring satisfaction to both partners. The Suifan's 'Kwang Tze' Solution is completely safe and reliable, as stated in Government Certificate supplied with each bottle.

Special Offer:
To prove our claim we will send you by return—and in complete confidence—a bottle of the 'Kwang Tze' Solution for only 2 Gns.

Order Direct from Sole Distributors:
Blacks International,
Suite A,
24, Cranbourn Street,
Leicester Square,
London, W.C.2.
Please Cross Cheques & P.O. & Payable to: Blacks International.

BOOKS FOR KINKS AND KICKS. Candid, Exciting, and Erotic.
Send S.A.E. for comprehensive lists.
"Danjac" 50, Parsons Green Lane, S.W.6.
Telephone REN 2871. Evenings REN 3911.

DUREX GOSSAMER. 7/6 per doz. Post Free.
Tit-Bits, 709, Fulham Road, S.W.6.

PREGNANCY TEST. £2. Inquiries: Bell Jenkins Laboratories; Charlotte Street; Portsmouth (23366)

come underwater

DREAMING IN A DANDY FASHIONS
SUIT. 161, Kings Road London, S.W.3.
Telephone FLA 6851

CONFIDENTIAL ADVICE on the Pill for all women everywhere. Write Step One Ltd (O) 93, Regent St. W.1. (SAE) or telephone 01-622-7815

'You are invited to become a member of'

C.M.C.

Facilities include:—
Substantial discount on clothes, etc
FREE use of accomodation address, same day forwarding service
FREE use of PEN PAL register
FREE use of HOLIDAY register
Members only—CMCN (Naturists)
Send for detailed Brochure (8d in stamps please) to Dept 03, C.M.C., 14 Alexandra Road, Clacton-on-Sea, Essex

For light removals Dormobiles with helpful working drivers HAM 1466 or HAM 6351
Please quote this advert

Continued from page 4

Be at the be-in, Hyde Park Serpentine, Sunday, July 16. Bring along gifts and goodies to give to friends. Leave behind ambitions to star in a BBC documentary. Many at Alexandra Palace drifted about aimlessly until spotted by TV teams—then they freaked out sensationally, self-consciously.

Expatriate Americans have formed a committee to urge US withdrawal from Vietnam. Poets, pop singers, jazzmen, comedians, actors et all are hurling themselves into its inaugural manifestation, 'Angry Arts Week' at the Roundhouse from June 27 to July 2. Non Americans welcome.

The greedy hypocrisy of W H Smith's is so notorious as to be non newsy. Yet every so often a work of real merit is banned by these ruthlessly commercial quakers. A recent victim is the first novel by Clement Biddle-Wood, 'Welcome to the Club' (Weidenfield & Nicholson) which was supposedly suppressed for an overuse of dirty words. In fact it is a coyly restrained work which illuminates the pitfalls of contrived intergrationism befalling the quaker army officer hero. It is sad that mass appreciation of 'Welcome to the Club' is hampered by Smith's impetuous ban.

WAY OUT

THE MONTHLY ADVERTISER FOR THE SEXUALLY AWARE

300 PERSONAL AD'S

TO WAY OUT 29 WESTBOURNE PARK MEWS,

LONDON, W.2

PLEASE FIND ENCLOSED 7/6 FOR MY POST PAID COPY OF YOUR
MAGAZINE. I AM OVER THE AGE OF 21.

Name (Block capitals) ....

Address ....

NORMAL IS SUCH A NICE WORD

IT'S NICE AND NORMAL TO WANT TO BE NORMAL

WOULD'NT YOU LIKE TO BE NORMAL TOO?

NORMAL

VERY NORMAL

NORMAL

SENSIBLY NORMAL

WHY CANT WE ALL BE NORMAL

NORMAL I AM WE ARE

MARTIN SHARP.

Kensington Post

Hamlet: 'I say, we will have no more marriages.' Ophelia: 'but dahling, mommy's already sent out the invitations.'

On May 13, Katie took Mike McInnerny ✱ as her lawful wedded husband and gave birth to the first hippie wedding. You were all invited to the gay outdoor nuptials; incense, exotic garlands, fifes and drums, the fuzz and mums.

'We married', says Mike, 'on an impulse'. Previously they had lived together, separated, met again then decided to trip up the aisle. 'It was about the only thing left we hadn't tried'. Marriage as kicks, as a happening, as a rave. If you must capitulate, that's the spirit. But must you?

Now that even Women's Magazines are timidly suggesting that marriage is outdated, it is odd that the exuberent avant garde should still channel their love through the Registry Office. Old fashioned cynics regard marriage as merely a public declaration of a private intention and squares share the philosophy of the Andrew Sisters that love and marriage go together like a horse and carriage.

Others denigrate the roll of love and hold marriage to be function of the intellectual will, a convenient contractual arrangement, a device necessary for the rearing of children. Marriage is more than this. Marriage is a masochistic ritual, an unhappy, anachronistic hoax. Most are disastrous.

Add to the sombre statistics of divorce the number of dead partnerships rotting under a facade deemed essential for social or breeding purposes—the spiritual divorcees. Look around you. Look at your wedded contemporaries. A phoney bliss croaking under the strain of compulsory cohabitation, their partnership rendered impotent by a future robbed of mystery, a love affair wet-blanketed by the gnawing responsibilities of permanent contractual obligations.

Remember your parents? Look at them in family album wedding photos. Look at them now . . . incessant bickering, relentless incompatability, conflicting desperate pleas for loyalty—the drab legacy of 30 years of togetherness.

Some marriages work brilliantly, of course. For a while. But who needs it? How many enhance the original relationship?

Society should encourage pre-marital cohabitation. Parents should assist newly unmarrieds to set up house, avoid pregnancies and take on responsibilities. Living in sin could be more than a chic prelude to marriage—why not a serious rehearsal for long term living together? Relationships can be worked out fully and abandoned painlessly when bankrupt. There is a current craze to simplify divorce, a short term measure. Instead, marriages should be made more difficult or left to evolve into redundancy. Certainly human liasons can be intellectually and emotionally fruitful and it is not suggested they should depend on the compatability of crotches. However, 'marriages'—legal and/or spiritual— are less likely to degenerate into frightening sagas of destruction if the participants are practised. The only problem of casual cohabitation is children. Means of support can be worked out.

The legal machinery used need not be complicated. The legislature is able to draft far more intricate bills to deal with tax avoidance. At the moment the law, typically, penalises unmarried mothers by making the maximum support they can get from their fathers about 30/- per week. Compare that with incentive destroying alimony awards.

Perhaps a modified Kibbutz system could be applied to groups of people sharing accommodation. It might be more interesting than the domestic vegetable patch. (Removing the stigma from illegitimacy, incidentally, would remove pressure for abortions.)

While many affect to despise the institution of marriage, most are resigned to its inevitability. If not for themselves, for their friends. We urge all readers to accept *Punch's* classic advice to those on the verge—

don't.

It is better to burn than to marry.

GUIDE TO LIVING IN SIN

Item 1. *Tax.* Claim your lover as a dependent.

Item 2. *National Assistance.* 'Cohabitation' qualifies you for the same extra benefits as if you were married. Be sure to press for your rightful increment.

Item 3. *Travel.* Honesty is often a handicap. P&O Shipping won't offer double cabins to unmarried couples. If, on the other hand, they accepted a 'married' booking and then discover you are unmarried, your names will be left on the passenger lists as Mr & Mrs. The P&O booking clerk said this attitude is common to most shipping lines. Was it illegal to sell sinful double berths? 'Er, I don't know. Probably. The Government might get us for encouraging immorality.'
British Railways are quite happy to supply double sleepers. 'We don't ask for wedding certificates. If you both use the same surname, who are we to argue?'

Item 4. *Accommodation.* Avoid Irish boarding houses. One we contacted' had no objection so long as the couple had been living together a long time. He wasn't sympathetic to the suggestion that 'newly unmarrieds' pretend they were married. 'It still doesn't alter the facts', he said grumpily.
Flat sharing agencies are reluctant to register unmarried couples. One had had some on his books for over six months. 'People don't want to know', he said. Apparently this was due partly to moral prejudice and partly to the inconvenience of 'mixed' dwellings.

Item 5. *Credit Accounts.* No problems. Even square old Derry & Toms, for instance, suggested that one of the partners have an authority to operate on the other one's account.

Item 6. *Contraception.* Family planning clinics are quite reasonable. If they are too overcrowded to assist unmarrieds, they advise clinics which do. One we contacted agreed to fit a coil to an unmarried OZ girl as long as she'd had one child. For the pill, see your friendly, non-Catholic, family doctor.

Item 7. *Education for your Bastard.* Middle class boarding schools are cautious but willing to accept illegitimate children. One advised that illegitimacy ought not to be recorded on the application but 'raised discreetly with the head during a personal interview'. Eton regarded the question as irrelevant to consideration of an application.

Item 8. *Holidays.* Keep away from Butlins. 'If you were unmarried you wouldn't get a chalet between you'. Their representative agreed that some unmarrieds might bluff their way through. Well, why not if you were honest? 'Use your common sense'. What did that mean? Use your common sense, it might be your outlook on life, but not other people's'.

Item 9. *Marriage Guidance.* The Marriage Guidance people counsel married couples, unmarried couples, single people, anyone. There's no pressure to bear on unmarrieds to sanctify their union.

Item 10. *Marriage.* For the British the nearest thing to a 'quickie' Mexican divorce may be in Iceland. If possible, get married there and you will be in a stronger position to reap the benefits. For your divorce to be recognised in England one of you will need to be a resident there at the time of it (three weeks is enough). Of course, you don't have to be a resident to get married there.
The grounds for divorce in Iceland are many and sensible and include mutual incompatability and general breakdown of marriage.
Formalities are speedy. Icelandic Steamship Co. run a special excursion in August and September for £49.10 return, enabling you to stay for up to one month.

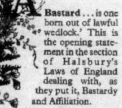

A Bastard ... is one born out of lawful wedlock.' This is the opening statement in the section of Halsbury's Laws of England dealing with, as they put it, Bastardy and Affiliation.

You, an intelligent, emancipated woman, may decide to have a child without marrying the father. There are any number of good reasons for doing this. Maybe you hate him now, possibly you think your lives would be happier apart or perhaps you simply can't remember who he was. Of course you have rejected the idea of an abortion as it's against the law. You may consider you have enough money either to bring the child up or at least to care for him until you find someone you do feel like marrying. Everyone, including the oldies, may approve. But it's useless because as Lord Halsbury says:

'The child of an unmarried woman is always born a **Bastard**.'

And it's no good saying you had a husband once but he died because his Lordship adds:

'The child, too, of a widow is a **Bastard** if he is born so long after the husband's death that he cannot by any possibility be the issue of the husband.' If you want to go on sleeping around make sure you do it while he's still alive.

So you decide to get married. But there are pitfalls. If marriage takes place between 'parties who are within the prohibited degrees of relationship contained in the Table of Kindred and Affinity set out in the Marriage Act 1949 then the marriage is invalid and any child a **Bastard**.'

As a check list we reproduce for you the Table itself. Cut it out and keep it with you for reference:

But don't marry anyone in the Table or you will produce **Bastards**.

Be careful about the time you get married. It must be done between the hours of 8 am and 6 pm or all your children will be **Bastards**. If a clergyman is reckless enough to solemnize your marriage after the rush hour he will make himself liable to imprisonment for **fourteen years**!

Suppose you and your friend have a child. It will of course be a **Bastard**. Some day you may want to legitimise it by getting married. It's all right if neither of you were married before. But if the father was married to someone else and then got a divorce to marry you, the child is, and very properly so, punished for the father's wickedness and will remain a **Bastard**.

If you yourself are a **Bastard** you are not regarded as a child of your parents for the purposes of inheriting, taking title, etc. However, don't try and marry your sister because even though a familyless **Bastard** you must observe the dreaded Table of Kindred and Affinity.

In a fit of anger you may decide to try and prove one of your children is a little **Bastard** and so take advantage of the law's fearsome disapproval. It may make him behave better. Remember, then, that Halsbury says you can, in court, 'compel your wife's **paramour** to answer questions as to adultery.' If she hasn't got one (and who can afford the birdseed these days) you're out of luck.

Men! Imagine that you've managed to work it all out and marry someone you fancy. You are not in the clear yet because the law's restraining hand will lie groping in the marriage bed . . .

THERE ARE A NUMBER OF THINGS YOU CAN'T DO TO YOUR WIFE

A wife may present a petition for divorce on the ground that her husband has since the celebration of the marriage been guilty of sodomy or bestiality. Sodomy with the petitioner herself is within the section.' *(Halsbury Vol 12 P281)*

Sodomy is defined by the law as doing it up the anus and bestiality as doing it with animals. Some immortal is on record as being divorced for having it off with chooks. Anyway they're both out. Getting that Labrador will be a waste of time.

As Lord Hanworth (Master of the Rolls) once said when talking about sodomy 'in its very essence every person must realise that such an act is against nature.' The law is clear. We must not go against nature. Up with nature. But don't get caught.

In Statham v Statham* it was said: '. . . solicitations to sodomy or other beastly acts were in themselves cruelty (i.e. grounds for divorce) unless they proceeded at the invitation of or with the consent of the wife.'

So beastly acts are out too.

Watch carefully the books you buy. They should always be in English. In Statham v Statham evidence was given of the husband's awful nature. He had '. . . books containing accounts of depraved vice. Three of the books were in **German** and one in **French**.' The brain reels with lust at the thought.

Needless to say, all forms of beating are regarded as cruelty. Put aside all your whips and Devices, sado-masochism is out.

The list goes on. In Lawson v Lawson (1955) a divorce was obtained on the grounds of persistent cruelty in that the husband *(inter alia)* '. . . had insisted on the wife masturbating him against her wish.'

Masturbation is forbidden.

In Bampton v Bampton which was decided in the far-off days of 1959, part of the proof of cruelty was held to be '. . . that the wife was a consenting party to some disgusting sexual perversions which had taken place between them, the husband using the wife's mouth.'

Eliminate fellatio from your repertoire.

A hint of things to come is contained in the words of counsel as he questioned the wife in a more recent case in 1963. The husband was accused of cruelty: '. . . Well now, take the most horrible, much the most horrible of all I should have thought, one I can refer to by saying to you the 'swallowing'. . .'

Even swallowing is out.

A final thought. You and your wife may be sick of each other. You may feel that to go on living together would create tension unhappiness and lead to bad health and disastrously affect your respective careers. In other words your marriage has broken down and there's no point in going on. That, note, is not grounds for divorce. You will have to go on until one

Kindred and affinity, Part 1 *Prohibited degrees of relationship*	Brother's daughter Sister's daughter Father Son
Mother	Father's father
Daughter	Mother's father
Father's mother	Son's son
Mother's mother	Daughter's son
Son's daughter	Brother
Daughter's daughter	Husband's father
Sister	Husband's son
Wife's mother	Mother's husband
Wife's daughter	Daughter's husband
Father's wife	Father's mother's husband
Son's wife	Mother's mother's husband
Father's father's wife	Husband's father's father
Mother's father's wife	Husband's mother's father
Wife's father's mother	Husband's son's son
Wife's mother's mother	Husband's daughter's son
Wife's son's daughter	Son's daughter's husband
Wife's daughter's daughter	Daughter's daughter's husband
Son's son's wife	Father's brother
Daughter's son's wife	Mother's brother
Father's sister	Brother's son
Mother's sister	Sister's son

You probably didn't realize so many people were forbidden to you. However we have found loopholes. Life is not as dull as it seems.

Some suggestions for this month:
Why not propose to . . .
Your great grandmother   Your cousin!
Your great grandson   Your grandniece

Continued page 17

The thunderous organ music drowning, my head and my heart and my body in its long white dress going under. This was the sound of my sacrificial drums. My Woman's Own moment. I could not think of the staggering vows I was uttering before the grey faced man in the lace robes, and I don't remember the man at my side, and I don't remember where my mother was crying. Only that she was crying. 🖐 Afterwards came the champagne; wet kisses; flash bulbs; pretty pink telegrams. The rain in the London night. And the first night together was not the first night together at all. But it was the first time alone together for months. The incessant drone of planes invaded the privacy of sex and sleep and sorrow. 🖐 Honeymoon. A riotous sally into guiltless sensuality. Extraordinary to make love without feeling guilt. There is a heavy responsibility on somebody's shoulders for the stunted growth of my early sexuality. My husband was the first and the only man that I had been to bed with, yet the feelings of shame imbued in me by the haunting puritan shadows of childhood, served to disort and disturb the clarity of emotion about sex to a fearsome degree. Marriage was an assuagement of this guilt. 🖐 That was six years ago. Now I sometimes feel that the most awful thing is that I really don't like him very much. In the end, when you get to the core of another human being, you have to face the fact that whatever you do to unite the surfaces, at the bottom you are two separate entities that will never merge. I've undertaken to live with this man for the rest of my life, and now what do I see? A deep covering layer of charm, which often succeeds in charming me. Areas of sensitivity that take me by surprise. A baby smooth scented cheek, bright eye, well shot cuff of expensive silk that beguiles me for the instant. With admiration I observe the intellectual demolition of lesser men. But the ponderous words cover a cold guiltless mind. And isn't the sensitivity part of possessiveness?   Can a man's brain make you like him, in the way that his body can make you dislike? 🖐 And now I can lie here and think of how great my life is, because I can ski in the snow time and swim in the sun. Because I have a car and a hi fi and a maid and a gracious fucking neutral drawing room that I wanted painted bright white all over and jammed with ridiculous things and screaming colours and screaming ridiculous music and people. 🖐 How did I get this house and it isn't me? How do I find myself in consort with gliding gilded people that I can't talk to or think with? The night stretches hopeless with fury and remorse. 🖐 Beat my heels on the feather bed and spit on the remote controlled upholstered tenway television. 🖐 Bury my toes in the Persian rug as my feet race to the strawberry laden fridge. Fling the silver wrapped unsalted Normandy butter at the monster cat who is only a monster now because of castration. And I didn't want him castrated I wanted him to roam wild and free and what if he does come home with torn ears and a full belly? But who are you fooling baby in your cream silk night attire when you should be rolling on a naked floor in any old shirt without pants and who does it hurt if there's no lace ever ever on your underclothes and the doors of Helena Rubenstein are shut in your face? 🖐 Do I go? Must I stay? Somebody somebody please know the difference between right and wrong. I'm splitting up. I'm disintegrating. One leg goes one way one heart beat the other. The parting in my hair goes through my body. You didn't know that did you, onlookers? You thought ah ha another licentious trollope indulging her mind and her ha ha body. The cat may be away but you have ever stopped to think what it can be like for the mouse. Mice get bored. Mice get lonely. Mice get lost in a whirlpool of emptiness. 🖐 It isn't that I hate him. Of course I don't. Sometimes I think about not liking him. But it isn't even that. That would be simple. But it isn't simple. It's the two separate identities bit. I try to find honesty. Not the honesty that says yes I've been talking and talking and learning about and being with some one I might love instead of saying yes I've been to the cinema with Lucy from next door. But the honesty to recognise where the cheat is. The strength to make the decision to reject it. What is **right?** 🖐 There is right for my children. It must be right for them to be with their mother. 🖐 There is right for my husband. Here is where I stumble I stagger the soles of my feet are bleeding with the paces I take over this thorny terrible ground. It is easy when I hate him for something. But how can I hate him? He isn't there for three quarters of my life. And he is not hatable for the remaining quarter. He is entertaining, expensive, mannered, indifferent, tough, intelligent, unwarm, possessive, protective, infuriating, wildly generous, thoughtlessly mean, and perhaps for one tenth of the quarter, hateable. 🖐 Try to leave a man when you don't hate him. Hit him. Scratch out his eyes and his soul. 🖐 Try to calmly pack your bags and walk from the house you built together with the children you built together and say tata I think there's something better somewhere else. And what he says is, what? 🖐 And what do you see when you look around you? You see the packed bags and you see the ravaged lives that wither in loneliness and unpaid bills. 🖐 So you try to tot up what matters. What matters most for you all. It matters to me that my children live in light and warmth and learning. That they are forced to accept no one's values but their own. 🖐 It matters to me that my husband is well fed, and well bed, but you can live a lie in every corner of the house except the bed.

Why did Svetlana's Old Man Marry anyway?

POLLY TOYNBEE

HERE was a time, a golden generation, when the family was set free, when marriage was optional and all children were equally legitimate, when divorce was easy and given on demand, and abortions were legal, unlimited and free, when contraceptives were issued by the state and free-love was welcomed and encouraged for all. It was the time to be alive, this age of uninhibited private lives, free from the hypocrisy and inconsistencies of current attitudes on sex.

In Russia, after the revolution there was a whole generation of people who were allowed to choose their instincts themselves – a generation when all restrictive sex laws were stripped off like the seven veils.

But the family has always been an instrument of the state. It imposes sexual inhibition so as to organise men's lives into communities, trying to make society stable by an unnatural means. So, in 1936 Russian policy changed, to suit new political ends. The state wanted stability, not mobility as in 1917, and it adopted a more violently puritanical outlook than before, and it now has the most rigid laws in Europe. What happened to the brave new freedoms that the revolution brought?

The rest of Europe felt comforted and complaisant when Russia clamped down in 1936, and backpeddling hurriedly reverted to all the old bourgeois cant about the sanctity of marriage, and the wickedness of sex. I'm sure they gloated with satisfaction and told each other that free-love doesn't work, and virtue will out, and all that, but Russia's retraction was purely political, not social. After the revolution the state needed a flexible and mobile population, so as to get labour to areas where it was needed most. In a time when the country was in such desperate need the government demanded that every comrade should be prepared to put his country and communism before all personal ties. Everyone was to dedicate his life to the state, and to do this, had to be released from all other conflicting

responsibilities. The state was justifying itself for tearing husbands away from their families, for making women work and for bringing up children in collective nurseries. Free-love was only a political expedient, not an end in itself. Strelnikov in *Doctor Zhivago*, the tough political leader, leaves his wife and child, changes his name, denounces family life in favour of service to the state, and even bombs the town where he knows his family is living. The family was disrupted to make good revolutionaries, not for sexual freedom.

Then the state softened up, and began to use bourgeois techniques for stabilizing the country. In 1936 a *Pravda* editorial said that 'free love and disorder in sexual life' had 'nothing in common with social principles or with the ethics and rules of conduct of a soviet citizen,' and that they were bourgeois concepts. Looking round at the British bourgeosie I dont' see free love as one of its maxims, just the old attitudes, 'Nice girls don't' and the like, but there it is. *Pravda* had forgotten what bourgeois meant, and the state wanted its citizens pushed back into family pigeon-holes.

And now the government pumps out endless propaganda about chastity, and continence and married bliss. The generation of the revolution, the free-love-makers, are strapped back in their strait-jackets. Women are forced to have children they don't want through lack of contraception and abortion, and unmarried mothers are offered no sympathy. Divorce is less easy and all marriages have to be registered. It's all just like Britain, but worse. Sex is progeny, not for pleasure and love-making is outlawed, and all the bourgeois Billy Holiday girls, both sides of the iron curtain, sing plaintively to their lovers,
*'Just wish you'd make it proper
To call my old man Poppa'*,
because nice girls don't any more.

Russia's tyrannical puritanism isn't a case for England and the rest of Europe to pat itself on the back and criticise the lack of freedom under communist rule. It seems to me that Britain's triple think on sex is far more damaging and disreputable than Russia's consistent restriction.

It isn't a question of making a law that there shall be no marriage, but of allowing all people to live with whom they like, as they like, letting people choose for themselves how best to run their lives, and of

giving them the new opportunities for choice that contraception, abortion and divorce should offer. In fact the family survived, as the key unit in society, throughout a generation in Russia, without needing the added pressure of the law and social custom. In the cities a great many people did make use of the new laws, and many marriages were dissolved. The revolution itself had caused rifts in families that couldn't be accommodated. Women, many of whom had been forced into arranged marriages, under feudal law, were free to divorce their husbands without even telling them. Contraception, although it was freely available, was resisted strongly, and free and unlimited abortion was used instead. So the law benefited many and released them from burdens they didn't want. Yet most people went on getting married and having children, and especially in the country, things changed very little, but there was nothing forcing families to stay together. I would have thought that pressure and compulsion makes most people feel claustrophobic and resentful. Where both partners know that the other is there because he wants to be, not because he has to be, a relationship is bound to be more successful, and perhaps, in a way, more permanent.

"I PAINT WHAT I SEE, MAN"

SNAKE & SNAKES

a lovely game for courting couples

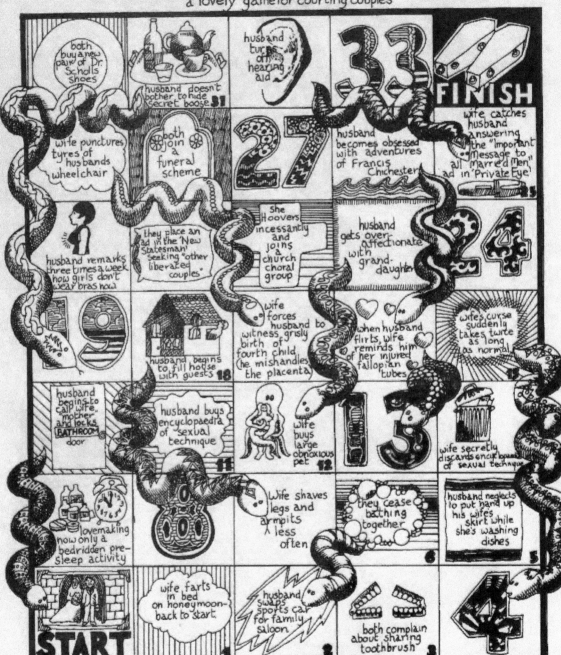

Candy is dandy
Liquor is quicker
Penguins are pink
But don't tell the
Vicar

by the author of **Last Exit to Brewer St.**

The split between Penguin's founder-proprietor Sir Allen Lane and whizzkid chief editor Anthony Godwin has been explained in various ways, of which the most popular are

1. The new colour covers were too jolly and disturbed the old guard, which still clings to the puritanical functionalism of the '30s;

2. Godwin wanted Penguin Books pushed through Boots, Woolworths and all sorts of infra dig outlets as well as through the bookshops to whom the veterans wanted to stay loyal.

3. Godwin and Sir Allen got on each other's nerves.

It's also been suggested that many sub-editors and writers will go if Godwin goes, and none of the above reasons justifies what's either a mass walkout or a mass purge. Maybe we should take our speculations for a little walk

in another, political, direction.

Interviewed on radio not long ago, Sir Allen explained that when he began Penguins, paperbacks generally were a gaudy lot that you slipped under the cushions when the vicar came to tea. Penguins were to be paperbacks that you'd have no need to hide.

Penguin Specials soon became discreetly left, but it wasn't an offensive thing to be, what with Hitler, the Beveridge Report, the Attlee administration, and it still isn't, if you follow the literary-ethical tone of the *New Statesman*. You can be left without shocking the vicar. After all, 'whoever governs, the Whigs rule.' And merely thinking in terms of entertaining the vicar to tea is sufficient to attach Sir Allen to the Whig tradition.

Over the last few years, though, Penguin Specials have taken a sharper radical edge. It's only escaped comment because English literary journals prefer not to review anything so vulgar as a paperback, and because where politics are concerned they're as innocent as the water-babies.

But, or so rumours run, Sir Allen has been disturbed by the lifting of establishmentarian eyebrows at the number of Penguin Specials which are not only to the left of Mr Heath, but actually to the left of Mr Wilson. Some sort of crisis was reached over the Penguin Special on the Trade Unions, compiled as it was by editors of the *New Left Review*.

Within the book trade, there have been rumours about other pressures. In particular, the Penguin West African series was thought by some civil servants, and their old boy network, as too outspoken in its criticisms of the way the West is shouldering the white man's burden. The book of Siné cartoons is said to have brought strong pressures to bear from our Roman Catholic brethren. (However, there's no evidence to implicate your friend and mine, Norman St. John Stevas, the maiden auntie of the swinging Tories and the patron saint of back street abortionists). At any rate, this book, it's said, won't be reprinted by Penguins, and copies may actually be withdrawn from bookshops. After all, it's just the sort of book a timid Whig would slip under the cushions when the priest comes to tea.

Such pressures have, reputedly, been accumulating for some time. But, so the theory runs,

there could be a more pressing consideration to clinch Sir Allen's resolution that Godwin must go. One day Penguin Books may be sold. Maybe one or two British publishers could, just about, afford to buy it. But the price would shoot skyhigh if American concerns were in there pitching. And what American publisher would want to pay x-million dollars for a set-up which is notoriously packed with pinkos?

It's significant that Penguins have proved liveliest in just these spheres which one knows (from how he built up Better Books) are Godwin's. One may have reservations about the extent to which the English Literature section is near-monopolised by what one of the Sundays called 'the hidden network of the Leavisites'. But nobody's perfect. And Penguin's dreariest and most confused sectors are those whose editors operate outside Godwin's area of competence. The Psychology series is a cranky collection of, mainly, umpteen volumes by Eysenck and, in default of anything solid and central on psychoanalysis, just those vague, irrelevant titles one would expect from an editor who's trying to be representative but would much rather not have to be. Red-hot subjects like **Homosexuality** get assigned to Anthony Storr, who's also the telly's most reassuring consultant psychologist and operates with a synthesis of Freudian and Jungian ideas; as a master of tact, he's almost the only challenging writer the series has. The History series has emitted a few respectable classics, but kept its 1930-era Whig skirts well clear of the challenging breakthrough in the writing of social history. Increasingly Penguins seem uncertain as to where popularisation ends and the specialised textbook begins. The *Penguin Survey of the Social Sciences 1965* is even more unreadably abstruse than anything in *The British Journal of Sociology*. One isn't surprised that Penguin's competitors have steadily been creeping up on them, snatching popular titles which Penguins neglected.

How Penguins will manage after the purge of the Godwinites is a gloomy thought. Even gloomier is the thought that the almighty dollar has, simply by its **potentiality** taken over another of the few fields in which a genuinely English political tradition was still reaching the mass public.

Continued from page **13**

happen without any sort of agreement between you because that would be collusion. You will have to face the expense, trouble, waste of time and humiliation of going to court to prove:

1. Adultery
2. 3-year desertion
3. One of you is incurably insane. (Not surprising!)
4. An unnatural offence
5. Cruelty – and here you may be in luck because at one time or another the courts have held that any of the following may, under certain circumstances, amount to cruelty ——

Coitus Interruptus
Sulking
Abstinence of one party. Needless to say, the other party wanted it.
Meanness. Shiftlessness,
Nagging
Lesbianism
Communicating V.D.
Humiliating abuse in public.

On the other hand, if you're two of the most decent people that anyone's ever met and none of these things apply to you – you've goofed. You're stuck **together.**

LET HIM DIE

And De Gaulle presents himself at the Gates, where God is waiting to receive him. 'Where do you want to go from here?' 'Where there are no Americans,' answers Charles. And is admitted to Paradise beside Charlemagne, who has been waiting for centuries.

Nobody wants him alive. Wilson wishes him dead because De Gaulle stands between him and history. The French workers want him buried because he stands between them and decent wages. The Americans, because unlike the Russians he doesn't talk reason. The Chinese because he is the Mao of the bourgeoisie. His prime minister because he wants to replace him before the Left gets the upper hand. His wife, because he is seventy-six, and there's talk about a protege of his in the Ministry of Aviation whose career is rising abnormally quickly.

The King is dying a slow political death. Listen to Mitterand, Mephistopheles of the Left, talking about Gaullism: 'You had a spontaneous consensus of opinion in 1958, a surprise consensus of opinion in 1962, a resigned consensus of opinion in 1965, a consensus with a discount in 1967, and now you are forcing the concensus...''

The 'forced consensus' is the small *coup d'etat* which dismisses parliament from now until October by invoking Article 38 of the Constitution. A constitution made by the King, for the King, against the country.

The country he wants to save from the apocalypse of nuclear war which he believes is inevitable. Living in the foggy twilight of his declining years, the History of France as his bible. Machiavelli his abacus, lending a near-deaf ear to the under-privileged millions, shutting his eyes to the dirty work of his courtiers, alone he rules — in the name of French Civilisation. Not that of Voltaire but that of Louis XIV; and like that other general, Napoleon, abusing the French for the glory of France.

Louis XIV made the aristocrats his lackeys. Daily they attended his ritual meal at Versailles. De Gaulle's Versailles are his twice-a-year press conferences. He emerges from the curtain (red except for the last, which was golden for colour televison) and talks of the 'State of the World'.

He is brave, they say. He is taking a stand against the Americans in Vietnam. The G.I.s murder God's children and God's trees and De Gaulle says he would rather they didn't but he wouldn't like to get involved. The Americans pillage Vietnam. He proclaims they are not in the right — but they are still old friends. And the Bertrand Russell War Crimes Tribunal had to go to Sweden because De Gaulle didn't want to offend his old friends who err; and doesn't want to upset the Russians who are fighting to the last Vietnamese.

But in foreign embassies mousy officials discuss the latest Viet Cong body count, and

casualties of illiterate marines, praising De Gaulle between lunches with hopeful Canadian emissaries and dinners with South Korean diplomats.

He is a great statesman, they say. He doesn't want England to join the self-righteous six — getting fat on American crumbs and cashing in on the repentance of the once socialist Eastern republics. To share the bones of the carcass of the so-called underdeveloped calls for great skill; high politics are involved. De Gaulle's mysticism works better than the verger Wilson's pragmatism.

Summer fat, glossy families go in pilgrimage to Colombey les deux Eglises and buy souvenir leaves from the trees round his villa, for half-a-crown each. The king is adored. The King wants more children for France. Contraceptives are illegal in France. Five hundred thousand back-street abortions are performed each year in France. She who has the money goes to Switzerland — following Voltaire's road to freedom.

Since '59, the year of his resurrection, De Gaulle has been building a pyramidal structure, called the fifth republic, and organised in this way: first comes Pompidou, whose best political sentence is 'De Gaulle makes the decisions, I decide the price of milk.' He is a devout servant to his master, passably stupid; and previously served the Rothschild family. His greatest achievement is to have organized, on behalf of Madame de Gaulle, a philanthropic society for disabled children. Under him are a dozen puppet ministers representing the three hundred families, the Catholic Church and the local squires. Then the army purged of rebellious generals during the Algerian affair, and now, fortunately, politically castrated. Next, the prefects who rule every district of France with almost unlimited power. Under them, the civil servants who make sure everything works smoothly between the political power (ministers and prefects) and the masters of the economy (private capital). The police, a strong arm of paid assassins (Metro Charonne, Feb. 8th, 1962 — nine Parisians shot by police during peaceful demonstration) have a place of their own, a privileged one. After them comes the bourgeosie, wealthy, arrogant, ignorant, catholic and reactionary. Then shop and restaurant owners absorbing the most enterprising of the lower classes and the less capable of the bourgeosie. Finally, in order, the concierges, unpaid police informers, planted in every building; whores, all with the yellow card which entitles them to their profession — and the workers. Intellectuals have a special status, they are generally bribed into the administration or the teaching profession; otherwise they join the parties of the left and live in a condition of virtual exile.

The King's priorities are: '(1) The *force de frappe* — a tiny atom bomb which allows the French the right to be destroyed in their own right and not only because of criminal American foolishness. (2) The French lan-guage, which must be preserved against contamination and spread throughout the world to the greater glory of 'La France Eternelle'. (3) French food and wine, which consumed daily, lull you into a condition of revolting animality, keep the family together (mealtimes) and the poor in their place (cheap wine).

This is the Kingdom of Charles the Tall, where the dogs are asked to piss in the gutter so as not to dirty the pavements where the clochards drink and sleep. Where the girls have Etruscan noses and perfumed cunts, where they dress to show they are respectable, and undress only to make their respectability pay. Where the good go to mass on Sunday

and ask God to give them more money. Where villages are run by absentee land-lords and administered by the priest and the gendarme. Where television after a stupefying dinner has taken the place of the once ritual fucking. The fields are rich, the peasants poor. Kids dream of England but can't leave the family until they're twenty-one. The police are hated but can arrest you simply for having less than ten francs in your pocket or for not having your identity card on you.

But the Kingdom is rich and strong and free. Charles the Tall, having blackmailed the French Communists into accepting starvation wages in exchange for a meaningless friend-ship with Mother Russia, having thrown out the American soldier but kept open the door

QUICKLY

to dollar infiltration — like any African general — he launches his first atomic submarine at Cherbourg.

One fine spring day in 1963, his puritanical, shadowy wife, crossing Les Halles in her state car, going from the Elysee to the Galeries Lafayette, noticed on the pavements ladies of easy virtue. She was very upset by the spectacle, and asked Charles to do something about it. Charles called the Paris Prefect and he cleaned up the streets. Now Algerians and others, tongue-tied by language and cock-tied by taboos, linger in front of narrow all-glass doors, looking into expressionistic corridors and up staircases where the girls are lined up, all breasts, high heels and lipstick.

It's still the Paris of the 'thirties, a post-Hemingway cardboard naughtiness loved by foreign girls (English, American, Swedish) who study French at the Alliance and feel happily sordid, what with wine before and bidet after (to wash the baby in? No, to wash it out, Madam).

Charles, like all good kings, is also romantic — when the time calls for it. On his way to Mururoa, the Pacific island where his scientists concoct the French deterrent, he stopped off at Tahiti, and talked to the natives. He told the French Pacific islands were like sleeping beauties, waiting to be awakened by the good technological prince, riding a mushroom cloud and spelling death in French.

And yet miserable and corrupt underdeveloped leaders, who receive third-hand thanks from Russia and fertilizers from the States (or vice versa) look up to him as a symbol of Freedom; forgetting Algeria, forgetting Djibuti, pretending not to know what Castro did and how — or what Che Guevara is doing and why.

Let him die — let him die quickly, and the quicker the better. Let him die so that Mendes France can take over. So that Sartre, and not he will be the best example of what the French can be. So that he will not again insult the people's intelligence at his press conferences. Let him die, firstly and mostly because we want the France of the French revolution, not the France of Napoleon. Because we admire France of the Commune and not the France of the Roi Soleil; because the country which gave freedom to the bourgeosie has become the country where the bourgeoisie is God — and De Gaulle its prophet.

Angelo Quattrocchi

Photo: David Larcher **Changes**: to be published by Peter Whitehead/Lorimer Films

In common with Steve McQueen, Lee Marvin, Dean Martin,
'and a lot of other cats', Norman goes on UFO hunts.
Recently in a field near London, Norman says he was sure *they* were there,
but for some reason would not show themselves.
'Maybe they didn't want to frighten us.'
He prayed for a sign. Suddenly, behind him, he heard thud thud thud. It was the
sign—a cow shitting. 'And that just goes to show what a weird sense of humour
they have,' says Norman, 'they're *so* human.' Norman is a mystic. Like a lot of
other cats.
Transcendentalism is in (Even Cliff Richard is joining the C of E.) Sadly, Camus'
man, who 'without negating it, does nothing for the eternal, because his courage
has taught him he can live without appeal, and his reasoning informed
him of his limits', seems extinct.
Perhaps it is because the drug experience has created a whole new
area of awe. Certainly the passing of the joint could hardly be less sacramental
and the Dark Night of the Soul might well have been a bad trip. Or maybe it's
the inevitable reaction to the 'cool' of the times, a response to the force feed
of fact knowledge, an antithesis to the credibility gap which withholds
our trust from the institutions that pattern our daily lives.
Or it may be as simple as W. S. Gilbert thought, 'You must lie upon the daisies
and discourse in novel phrases of your complicated state of mind. The meaning
doesn't matter if it's only idle chatter of a transcendental kind.
And everyone will say
As you walk your mystic way,
If this young man expresses himself in terms deep for me,
Why what a very singularly deep young man this deep young man must be.'
Whatever the causes, the field of contemporary mysticism is fecund. In the
following pages four parts of the scene catch our eye; The Process one of the
psychiatry oriented religion substitutes; Ying and Yang, a classic Eastern
philosophy, like so many others pioneering the West; Ken Andrew suggests there's
more to Astrology than the astrologists think; finally there's a set of Tarot cards
for you to be your own diviner.
Today's mystics seem muddled, yet reason shakes them hardly at all (and they
don't believe in verbal communication.) It is faith itself they want to believe in,
the very *act* of believing they affirm.
In this age of irony, probably not a bad thing.
As Dr. Alex Comfort puts it, 'We've forgotten how to use magic and our
subconscious. We don't know how to cope with our emotions whereas the
aborigines have a very complex emotional technology.'
'Stonehenge started off as magic—for instance— and ended up with science.
We start up with fact and what do we end up with? Nothing but the moon
that is no use to anyone.'
'What we need is religion rather than religions—the gods are only shorthand
for the gods inside your head—and more contact with ourselves.'

JEHOVAH CHRIST LUCIFER

REVELATIONS EVERY SUNDAY 11.00/230 JEHOVAH 200/330 CHRIST 430/600 LUCIFER

THE PROCESS

The Process, a sub-species of Scientology, is one of the latest of the innumerable mystic quasi-religions.

After an abortive attempt at Utopia in Nassau, the organisation now maintains properties in Wigmore St and Balfour Place, Mayfair, owns a yacht in Greece, and something of a mystics Club Meditteranée in Xtul, Mexico.

It first made headlines last year when family lawyers flew out to Xtul to rescue one or two rich adherents, and no doubt their inheritances as well, family lawyers being what they are.

Subsequently, *Mind Benders of Mayfair* appeared in the Sunday Telegraph. Litigation continues.

A year later, The Process seems a little more benign than formerly. However, as the founders, the De Grimstons, are still centrally involved, information about the origins and rather disturbing early days still seems pertinent to the present. Hence our double-barrelled approach.

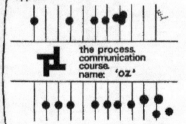

the process. communication course. name: 'OZ'

Buried deep in the well ordered streets of Mayfair there is a house of bearded anarchists, intensely debating the immediate destruction of the grey forces (unprocessed humanity), as they chuck wholewheat bread to their skulking Alsatians and sip black coffee to the tune of one and threepence and American Soul.

Do the cool grey ancient streets know they shelter such a turmoil of rebellious youth?

Difficult for them to escape this knowledge. *The Sunday Telegraph* calls them the 'Mindbenders of Mayfair'. They call themselves 'the Process'.[1] Radio London's pop palm is heavily greased to spread the word over the air. The King's Road is all a-flutter with hairy Process hands thrusting magazine and pamphlet at the Saturday shopper. Marianne Faithfull tells all (all?) in the May issue.

Walk through this red brick area of established wealth, up the smug stone steps, and press a beckoning silver tit marked 'rec' (receive, reclaim, recoup, recluse . . . ?).

Heavy. P-emblazoned door swings open on to close-carpeted luxury. Beards lurk in the gloom. A battery of eyes glitter as you cross the threshold. Two eyes and a beard behind a monstrous typewriter smacking of the latest word in secretarial electronics, gleam as you fumble for your coins (all twenty-one of them religiously checked): entrance fee for a new life.

Everyone coslly on Christian name terms.

Follow the leader up sweeping flights of stairs. Spotlights. Mahogany. The hush of deep pile carpets — white walls streaking up on every side. Large blobs of abstract paintings and the discreet gurgle of a chromium-plated loo. Slim hipped figures flit through quietly opened doors. Secret.

This door opens — the Communication Course: Man's Relationship to Man. First step in the Process plan for widening the scope of your tiny grey life.

A surgery. The ceiling high enough for all manner of thoughts and gems to mingle above our heads.

Slippery cold parquet floor. Bare. Full of sprawling bodies, yet still bare.

The jumbling bodies are taken in hand. Christopher in charge. Christopher Fripp. old Wykehamist (in common with Robert de Grimston Moor, founder of the Process). ex-chartered accountant — kicking the post-Victorian traces. Power in his blue eyes, bristling beard. The strings are jerked and the puppets move into action. (Meglomaniac?)

Perhaps we want this domination. Otherwise we'd be playing hopscotch in the wet streets outside these curtainless

Notes

1. Mr and Mrs Robert de Grimston, or rather Bob and Mary Ann, as they prefer to be called upon introduction, are the innovators of a hybrid psychological treatment, which they have named 'The Process'. 'The Process' was supposedly designed to help people suffering from debilitating neuroses, which prevented them from achieving their full potential. It has been in existence for some two & a half years and has gradually evolved into a quasi-religion, and for the faithful, a way of life.

Mr de Grimston fills the necessary and sacrificial role of a Messiah; his wife appears, with some conviction, as the Queen of the Night, with hints of a Prussian Mary Poppins. 'We do not practise tolerance here', she said.

The de Grimstons claim that their movement, 'is the last hope for mankind', and Bob asserts that his 'message is as valid as that of Jesus Christ.' Unlike the followers of Jesus Christ, the de Grimston's disciples have to pay substantial sums of money in order to receive and fully comprehend the message. An introductory four evenings (2-3 hours) would cost £2.10s. A further 48 evenings, which comprise a 'communication course' (mainly mingling with the initiated) will cost £30. After, or during, the 'communication course', it is advised that the 'Process' course of individual therapy sessions should be started. The discovery of the individual's problems, neuroses, blocks, are aimed at in these sessions. In 'Process' language they are termed goals (by Adler and out of Hubbard). It is considered necessary to undergo at least sixty hours of therapy (at a cost of about £250) in order to discover the patient's chronic, i.e. ever present, goal, and to reach the ultimate goal in the downward progression. This always is an equivalent of death — to be unconscious, to be incapable, to want death. Naturally, having reached rock-bottom, further sessions are recommended. In order that the 'patient' can start travelling hopefully; upwards. By this time, the 'Patient' will be in a state of emotional dependence on his 'therapist' and open to suggestions of all kinds. In qualified practice this state is always induced, in order that the patient should gain insight into his problems. It is called a transference. It is always terminated by the psychiatrist, at some stage of treatment, otherwise the patient will remain in a state of dependancy, unable to act of his own will.

Neither of the de Grimstons (or other 'Process' therapists) have any recognized medical or sociological training and qualifications. Their techniques, methods and much of their jargon is derived from L. Ron Hubbard, an American living in England. Hubbard is the founder of a cult known as 'Scientology', and once was a writer of science fiction. This cult, which has thousands of members over the world, has been somewhat discredited. It has been outlawed in certain parts of Australia.

Bob and Mary Ann met at the Hubbard Institute of Scientology in Fitzroy Street. They were both training to be Scientologist

windows. Splattering canvas. Walking the dog. Making love.

Schoolroom chairs are put face to face. Grown children put body to body. 'Communicate', says the beard.

A babel of voices. And the sound rises and settles in layers, like Neapolitan ice cream, starting at the ornate ceiling, working down to the top of the unwashed heads. Into the brain. Did you know there are layers of sound, generated by you, pressing down on your skull? You with the typist's glasses and painter's hands — you, with the suburban mouth and cuban heels — you, spotty, with the schoolgirl hysteria bubbling below the surface of your hippy gear?

Here we are. Slumped in solid concentration over one another. Eyeball to eyeball, knee to knee. Exercise one in Communication. Exercises to help us overcome our aggressions, repressions, hostilities, withdrawals, to help us become controlled and intense and aware — and who knows what this newfound, now heightened, awareness might lead to?[2] The gods they say. And who can resist that?

You can reach God. *The* God. Or rather, for those who might bridle under the implications of the term: a singular deity. You can reach *Him* in three expensive months with the Process.

You must communicate. Thirty times. Under the roof of No. 2 Balfour Place. At a guinea for three hours of exercise, lecture and knees up (which is a sort of raucous fling to unheard music intended to release all possible inhibitions — it succeeded in totally inhibiting me, quite a feat since dancing is usually a release).

Lectures come after the coffee break, when participants repair to the underground coffee bar to trip over cowering black dogs and indulge in some free for all questioning over beige coffee slurping in transparent cups. Don't imagine though that you'll get much precision out of any ruthless interrogation of the inmates. There will be nervous plucking of downy baby beards and noises in the throat, but in the end they will slide away into the peaceful harbour of their own reality — matching trousers, matching dogs, matching minds. Intellectual argument is airily dispensed with because it is not on their side.

So. Communication, coffee, lectures: we're back upstairs in our luxury cell. It's silence and concentration again. But not by ourselves any more (how delicious to swim so guiltlessly in self-analysis for so long with so many). *No.* Now we sit round in these shitty uncomfortable chairs and gaze into the ever-moving mud-brown eyes of Christopher de Payer. Founder member of the Process — caught by ex-scientologists Bob and Mary de Grimston Moor (they've dropped the Moor now — for the sake of

I BRING YOU WAR, WAR AS YOU HAVE NEVER KNOWN IT, KILLING AS YOU HAVE NEVER SEEN IT, DESTRUCTION AS YOU HAVE NEVER FELT IT, DEVASTATION AS YOU HAVE NEVER IMAGINED IT

their simpler disciples?) in pre-Nassau, pre-Mexico days.

The Communication Course lectures serve as a tintillation for your eventual entry to the Advanced Course.

It all begins with the subconscious: that seven-eighths of your mind that seethes[3] below your consciousness. Want to cross the road in peace? Yeah. Oh no you don't — you really want to destroy yourself — see that lorry belting down the road at the same time as you are crossing it, with the driver tripping out on LSD — he runs you over there; you lie in a crumpled heap but you wanted it man — that's why you crossed the road in the first place . . .

When you've swallowed all that, after thirty communication classes, five 'Circles' (we'll get to them in a minute) and I don't know how many Sessions, then . . then . . you are ready for God.

However, along the way you must be prepared to get some grounding in the facts about that dual charmer Jehovah/Lucifer. He's an elevated Being to whom the Process owe their mission to destroy the world. Jehovah is the white side. Lucifer the black. Hitler is a good example of a Luciferian figure, but he was okay because he wasn't grey and killed the Jews who were and who wanted to be killed anyway. Subconsciously. Of course. Process example of a conveniently mass subconscious drive for destruction.

Through this great mess of heightened awareness that the Process moves in & breathes like oxygen, they have found themselves a direct link with Jehovah. You might wonder about the sense of purposelessness amidst all this grooving intensity — that's basically because Jehovah has not yet told them exactly what to do to get their mission over to the masses.

The faction is divided — more than once it seems — first of all there's the desire to tell humanity about this divine revelation, then there's this anti-grey masses scene which means no one is actually very keen on mingling with the 'greys' in order to put across the message. Thus a Process magazine is born. A lovely, remote way of making the word Process known — just pay your thousands and have it printed on glossy paper, without actually having to touch the outsiders yourself. Then you sit and wait for the right ones to come pouring in: all those Gurdjieff initiated meditating hippies whose subconscious draws them to pinstripe hiphuggers and clingyknit black polo shirts.

'auditors': in the jargon of this movement an auditor corresponds to a therapist. Bob and Mary Ann were attracted to each other, found that they had much in common and married. They left the Hubbard Institute after a few months and decided to seek, then spread, the 'Truth' together. Their personalities and temperaments are fantastically complementary. It is doubtful if one of them would have any impact operating alone. They are like a uniquely united Tweedle brothers, facing the world together, with their strange assortment of weapons.

Robert de Grimston

Robert de Grimston is thirty years old. He is over six foot tall, powerfully built, has medium-pale blue eyes, very well cut blonde hair and sports an equally well cut beard. Despite his height and girth, his physical presence is not aggressive. He is a sharp dresser (pale blue leather pants) and at a meeting in the Oxford town hall, an exuberant young man sitting at the back, hailed him as 'the Christ of Carnaby Street . . . by heaven.' He was educated at Winchester, but shows few traces of the academic proficiency nurtured in most of its sons. He joined the army on a short-term commission and spent some of this time in Malaya. When he left the army he did some preliminary architectural training at the Regent Street polytechnic. He has always been interested in psychology — and its applied techniques — and found his main influence in the work of Adler.

His wife, Mary Ann, is thirty-six years old. She wears little make-up, except to colour her long fingernails silver, sometimes she draws her wiry-looking copper coloured hair into a bun. She dresses in pale colours, oatmeal sweaters and skirts, consciously restrained and if Mrs Dale's Diary was a television serial, Jenny Dale, the ex-actress, would be clothed in much the same way. She has an aggressive personality and the ability to project it forcefully. She appears to be the tough one of the team and certainly possesses the courage to carry out her convictions. Mary Ann received little formal education. She was brought up by foster-parents just outside Glasgow. She missed a lot of schooling, as she was required to nurse her foster-mother, who died when Mary Ann was 13½. Her foster-father re-married almost immediately and Mary Ann was wanted no longer. For a time she was passed from one family to another but was never offered a permanent home. While she was still in her 'teens she came to London and found work as a waitress. She wanted to broaden her knowledge and displayed considerable initiative by taking various courses in pseudo-sciences. She found these advertised in magazines: they included — numerology, hypnosis, palmistry, spiritualism, occultism, yoga, reading the future in tea-cups, modelling in Mayfair, anatomy and physiology in Bayswater. Finally she became interested in 'Scientology', but did not completely agree with some aspects in it. This led to the forming of the 'Process' with her husband. She also found time to become a partner in a dry cleaning firm, and said she had 'acquired a few shares — here and there.'

2. There are two, equally important, aims to be achieved in the 'Process'. They are:
(a) the need to convert, through 'Process' therapy.
(b) the need to convert, by using religious and metaphysical methods.
These two aims must function interdependently in order to be efficacious. The religious side of the 'Process' is culled from a hotch-potch of religions and incorporates the concepts

There is a feeling of unrest in Balfour Place today. Expand, expand the message goes . . . publish the magazine, put up circulation get more *into* the Process, more money, use that money & Hugh's inheritance money, & entrance fee money & magazine money & lecture money to buy that £25,000 boat in Greece so the twenty or so chosen ones can hold hands and cross the seas in comfort between the £120 weekly London residence, the Grecian hang-out and Mexico.

But Jehovah hasn't been too explicit lately. The last message — save the world — was abandoned after Nassau because this rotten grey world is anti-salvation Process style. So now the Light and the Truth is that Jehovah's cycle of rejection by humanity is over. Now he goes up, and unless you go with him (synonymous with becoming a member of the Process) you've goofed completely because they'll be there wielding their hatchets.

The communication scene is fine. It's groovy to sit around knocking knees with a lot of people whose minds are tuned in to what your mind is tuned in to, whose bodies are nice and skinny and who have a few Redding/Dylan/Hendrix records about the place.

The second stage in the Process, the Circle meditation is, I am told by my dedicatedly meditative friends, kid's stuff compared to the real thing. This I can appreciate as the circle more resembles after-dinner junked-up telepathic games that the deep psychological trance induced by solitary meditation. But then games are amusing. And if you can afford your fun at 10/6 a time and you like to vibrate a little, this could replace the telly in your life.

Lights out. The communicating arena turns into an unlit temple of concentration. Chairs form a shadowy circle; linked hands conduct the indefinable currents; yellow-haired babyfaced Johnny takes control and silence covers the jiggling dances of a dozen subconscious minds.

Don't feel guilty the first time around when experienced circlers start spewing out their lurid hallucinations:

Well, first of all, Johnny. I get these two lions, weaving backwards and forwards in front of a great gaping hole, like a cave, menacing . . .

What did this mean to you Ken? They were a threat, right?

Yeh. Well I got them coming very strongly from Ian's direction. I guess it has something to do with the feelings of hostility (favourite word) that I pick up from Ian.

Ian, does this have any reality for you?

Pulls fluffy beard and looks knowing: Yeh, this is real to me, Johnny. I had a couple of strong aggressions take over about half-way through.

"Therefore do I now prophesy, I no longer command. Instead I prophesy, and My prophecy upon this wasted earth and upon the corrupt creation that squats upon its ruined surface is: "Thou shalt kill".

But don't worry if you didn't get any quivering tarmac roads or broken eggs or orange-striped end of the world kaleidoscopes for the group to interpret for you. They'll come out and hit you the next time round.

Once you get the name of the game.

Then there's psychometry.

Johnny baby cools the meditation with a deep belly 'thanks' to the deep-breathing deeply sensitive deeply relaxed circle of bodies that he has so manfully welded into one beautiful unit of awareness. Flips us around

a bit so that not everyone is sitting next to the same person (in the cause of purity, celibacy, singlemindedness?), and directs the exchange of personal objects: rings, watches, medallions . . . anything that has been soaking up your body heat long enough to transmit your intimate vibrations. Wow!

Like you give him that jelly baby you keep slung between your breasts and he says I get this feeling of sweet heat from you, doll . . .

After five Circles you can have a Session, if you dare.

These are conducted in an atmosphere of hushed secrecy by those sinister members of the Process whose bosoms swell with the comforting knowledge of their cosy bi-monthly chats with Jehovah.

Sit with this impressive Being, 'Therapist' is the god-given title, in a pitch dark room. Don't think. Don't speak. Any verbal communication is out. Your subconscious takes over and spills all the necessary beans about the murky workings of your inner self in its own inimitable language.

Your therapist will give you the answers straight from below the belt. Interpret them as you will. After all, you might as well be given some pleasure for that money you've spilt into the Process coffers. But if you find that idea unnerving, just don't hang around long enough for them to make you believe they can do a Session on you when you're not there. It's more than spooky to feel you are having your subconscious burgled while your body is quietly bopping somewhere miles away.

So. Until Session time, the scene remains pleasantly, harmlessly, self-indulgent. The process is a tingling little womb waiting for all those battered, bleeding rich bodies who want to crawl back, out of the cold grey world.

Let them move on, to Lucifer, subconscious manipulation, and a violently destructive God, then — because of their lack of direction and proper psychiatric training — the Process 'therapists' are floundering in waters too deep for them. There is a serious danger of their damaging the psyches of the more vulnerable of their followers, beyond repair. **Danaë**

of free-will, reincarnation, pre-destination A Deity, a possible trinity, Buddism, Hinduism, spiritualism, *et alia*. They believe that man, rather than being made in the image of God, has the same identity as God. To them, God is a TOTALITY, a Being both good and evil. (Apparently a composite of Himself and Satan.) De Grimston states that 'mankind is heading for destruction', and he was 'sent to instruct'. When he was questioned as to whether he believed himself to be the Son of God, he did not at first reply; a few minutes later he agreed with his wife that the description of 'Evangelist' would be more suitable; and less restricting.

There appears to be an immense plasticity in the religious area of the 'Process', perhaps in order to embrace all-comers. There will be something familiar and useful for everybody: like Macy's bargain basement.

Confusingly enough, the plasticity and apparent tolerance disappear in practice. A sort of Victorian teacher-pupil form of authoritarianism is displayed. Followers are scarcely allowed to question current 'Process' procedures, let alone deviate from them. The de Grimstones have a very stern interpretation of the concept of free will. It does not stop at the accepted Christian, or Behaviourist understanding which is the belief that each individual is granted the freedom of choice between good and evil. The 'Process' understanding of this is really non-existent as their approach is basically Calvinistic and incorporates Calvin's ideas on pre-destination. The 'Process' believes that the individual is totally responsible for his own (usually miserable) condition. They believe that the individual is totally responsible for his subconscious motivations and actions. These beliefs are extended to a point where they alleged, at a public meeting, that a child born with a hereditary disease (e.g. congenital syphilis) had chosen to be born in this condition and that it was the responsibility of the child. This is clearly regressive thinking and can become a form of extremism leading to the abuse and persecution of the individual; particularly the innocent and vulnerable. For instance Mary Ann said that, 'all the Jews in Hitler's Germany walked into the gas ovens because they chose to do so.'

The *raison d'etre* given for the 'Process' is that it can cure the individual of his necessarily self-inflicted neuroses and disabilities. It can also provide him with a hitherto unsuspected religious awareness. The de Grimstones claim that nobody can achieve the state of physical and spiritual well-being aimed at, without doing a course of 'Process' sessions. This proposition activates the aim to convert through therapy, and of course brings in money. The de Grimstons appear to be supremely confident of their ability to achieve success with everyone they treat. 'Process' sessions are a much more gruelling ordeal than those usually endured by patients treated by a qualified psychiatrist or analyst. Since none of the 'Process' therapists have medical training, they cannot possibly assess the true psychological state of a person, which all too often may appear deceptively rational and balanced. Only a specialist training can detect the signs which show that an apparently

MEANWHILE . . . LIFE CONTINUES AS NORMAL

UNTIL

... In which the
Grey Forces suffer
a temporary setback...

jolly man may be a manic depressive, who can be plunged into self-destruction if subjected to the wrong pressures. A 'Process' patient is allowed to book his block of six sessions in the way he wants to. He is even allowed to book a six-hour session, to run consecutively. Mary Ann said, 'We let the patient go at the speed he chooses.' When questioned several times on the advisability on this undoubted 'blitzkrieg' upon the psyche, the de Grimstons gave repeated assurances that they had never had a case they were unable to handle. When asked what they would do if a deeply disturbed patient came to them for help (e.g. schizoid, melancholic, psychotic, paranoic) they stated most firmly that this situation had never arisen, but that when it did they would know what to do.

2. When dredging the subconscious, highly unpleasant and unsuspected aspects of the personality will surface, and cause intense pain to the patient. Few people can digest too much disgust and disenchantment — en bloc — without being damaged, sometimes crippled.

The techniques used by a 'Process' therapist, or a Scientologist, are curiously analogous to those of brainwashing. Brainwashing is achieved through a series of intellectual, emotional, environmental and occasionally, haphazard machinations.

The questions start off beguilingly enough at the beginning but soon enough the guilt which exists already in each human is played upon, and maintained, new, sometimes utterly false guilt is induced, through group pressures, and believed in confusion, all past values are destroyed, the future holds nothing without conformation, and worry is a waking and dozing condition.

The following questions and answers are taken from the notebook of a very young boy, during his first few months at the 'Process'. Luckily, he has an extremely resilient personality, even for youth; it is a sort of 'supaball' radiation that he emanates. He is wilful, but aware of it. He is frivolous, which naturally implies that he is an extremely serious person. He has an orderly but extremely curious brain, a strong sense of humour. Most important of all he likes people and is kind by nature.

Q. What would happen if you rejected the Process?
A. To be out of control
to be schizoid
to be completely emotional
to fail
to be quite schizoid
to sink.

Q. What would happen if you accepted the Process
A. To possess me
To be totally committed
To be warm
I'd know
To be safe
To be strong
To be untouchable

The questions above, and those which follow pose two utterly false sorts of possibilities — for this boy here — but this sort of Through the Looking Glass alternative is commonplace.

Q. Not to accept Mary Ann?
A. To be a black hideous being
To be quite dead.
To go down to hell.
To be the devil.
To be crucified.
To have my heart cut out.
To throw away my body.
To destroy Christ.

Q. To accept Mary Ann?
A. To communicate her light
To understand Christ.
To comprehend all.
To have chosen.
To project love.
To show up the devil.

SIX QUESTION PROBLEM CYCLE
Sylvia (a girl he had been in love with)
Q. What have I done to her?
A. Burnt her as a witch
Given her my guilt.
Made her my excuse.
Made her my God.
Left her alone.
Destroyed her friends.
Killed her parents.
Q. What I have failed to do
Worship her
Give her reality.
Have sex.
Stay uncommitted.

Got engaged.
Be faithful.
Q. What Sylvia could do to me
A. Be a Mary Anne to me
Take Mary Anne's place in my life.
Give me life.
Smell my house out.
Be a torment.
Suggest escapes.
Send me right up.
Say No.
Q. What Sylvia could fail in
A. Be real
Be with me.
Stop me going to sleep.
Be alive.
Be warm.
Be burnt.
Be destructive.
Exist.
Q. What Sylvia could make me do
A. Be extreme
Worship Mary Anne.
Run away from the 'Process'.
Have sex.
Make or break.
Q. What Sylvia could prevent
A. Getting stuck into the 'Process'
Being explosive.
Being in fear.
Being la-de-da.
Q. What are you here to achieve?
A. To be total
To be a therapist.
To be out of control.
To destroy myself.
To love.
To be an evangelist.

Q. How are you trying to be total?
A. By feeling every feeling
By embracing past lives.
By compassion.
By giving everything.
Q. Criterion of Progress? Show?
A. I'd be worth slandering
I'd go fascist.
I'd stop being schizoid.
I'd make sense.
I'd understand.
I'd be clearcut.
I'd be el Cordobes.
I'd be Hitler.
It should be clear that the 'Process' and Scientology, from which it stems, possess all the characteristics found in an authoritarian regime. They demand complete dedication and unswerving obedience from their followers. They punish deviators by ostracism, ridicule and expulsion. They are positively anti-intellectual, though many of their theories appear to be gained from the written word, this is seldom acknowledged. They use a fabricated jargon to bolster their dogmas and to weaken the accepted meaning of the language: it also helps to preserve a sense of mystery and exclusiveness. They KNOW that they alone are 'The Truth'. Their techniques bear an uncanny resemblance to the highly sophisticated and effective brainwashing methods used in China today: robbing the individual of his freedom in all things and reducing him to a near zombie-like state of subjection.

Henrietta Morses

ROBERT DE GRIMSTON

Yin and Yang

is a dialectical method of classifying all things, a means of grouping into two antagonistic yet complementary categories everything in the Universe and the Universe itself.

Yin and Yang,
Negative and Positive forces,
are as indispensable to each other as man to woman. They are the two fundamental and opposite factors that create and destroy in an endless cycle, all that exists. The Yin-Yang theory is a revolutionary theory, in which Yin represents the reactionary force and Yang the inevitably following revolutionary forces.

Out of the infinite pure expansion, out of the ecstasy of the Universe and the human body,
out of every atom or plant or orgone Yin and Yang are produced infinitely. Yin is dark, cold, wet, negatively charged (the electron) feminine and at the violet end of the spectrum. Yang is bright, hot dry, positively charged (the proton), and masculine. Yang is Red.

All things and phenomena are composed of Yin and Yang in different proportions; nothing can ever be completely Yin or completely Yang, all is relative.

Yin produces Yang,
Yang in the extreme produces Yin.
Thus a very Yang hot, dry sunshiny day will produce a very Yin cool electric hailstorm. A living thing which is Yin will produce Yang. Thus if a person is sick, cold, tired, inactive, negative in outlook he becomes well by producing heat (Yang) in the form of fever that activates a new revolution in the wheel of life.

When a living thing fails to do this it dies.
Direct experience of infinite pure expansion occurs in sex and eating. Like charges attract,
unlike repel.
Orgasm occurs when the positive and negative charges of man and woman unite and the cycle of death and rebirth is made. If a man is excessively Yang he will become
cruel and destructive
and have difficulty achieving a truly refreshing orgasm. His excess of Yang can turn into excess of Yin and he may become impotent, and

unhappy, losing his appetite for sex, food and oxygen. A woman who becomes too Yin cannot be readily loved.
She is cold,
anti-social, and suspicious.
Perhaps she will be very mystical.
Eating presents the opportunity for man and woman to affect the Yin-Yang nature of their mindbodies. Cereal foods, the staple diet of all vital civilizations, do not produce disruptive imbalances towards Yin or Yang. They encourage the continuous rejuvenation of the total being, that process by which the cells and corpuscles and nerve-endings are forever dying

and being reborn.
Animal foods are Yang.
They can produce a dependency in their user as they displace the functions of the user's body. Thus eating a lot of meat provides the Yang qualities of heat and activity but may lead to a weakening of the heart and other organs that would otherwise do the job.
Sugar, fruits, and alcohol are Yin foods. They inhibit the flow of nervous energy as well as the renewal of cell-tissue. They are often addictive and the user feels he can't go on without them.
Money and political power are Yin and are the weapons of a

Yin society. Imperialism occurs when a nation has become too weak to keep itself and must prey on other nations for raw materials and labour to maintain its own existence. A dependency is established and the imperial nation as a whole becomes more and more Yin as it allows its social work functions to be taken up by another nation, its colony. When cancer strikes an organism it manifests as large mutated cancer cells parasitic on the body's healthy cells. Eventually either the healthy cells purge themselves of the cancerous influence or become themselves cancer cells.
At a certain point there aren't enough healthy cells to feed the cancer cells and the body dies.
Either Yin Imperialism will devour the rest of the human social organism or a very strong Yang force will be produced to initiate a new cycle. There has been no true revolution in Western Society for a long time. This necessary rejuvenating process has been delayed by Industrial, Technological, Atomic, Police, and other 'revolutions'.
The extent of Western Yin is serious. World Yang is preparing for global intercourse that must succeed or be faced with an even greater frigid Yin reaction.
IMMUNITY to what **REICH** calls the Emotional Plague (Yin cancer) is temporarily obtained with LSD.
Permanent immunity requires that continuous conscious application of Ying-Yang judgment in place of suicidal subconscious compulsive judgment; by stretching or dancing when one is bored or tired instead of eating pep pills and sweets, by moving in contact with other bodies when it is cold instead of eating meat,
in short by staying in a permanent state of revolution.
Without revolution there can only be reaction, fear, stagnation and the weak vampirizing the strong on every level.
The bigger the difficulty the bigger the happiness.

Craig Sams

TwinkleTwinkle

by courtesy of the
Vlastivedne Museum
Czechoslovakia

Although it has been quite impossible to actually prove one single tenet, Astrology is a branch of the occult sciences hard to entirely dismiss.

With the decline of religion and the hegemony of science, our time seems to demand a form of knowledge or teaching which claims infallibility through faith, as Christianity has done previously, and which has sufficient content to be not too easy to grasp lest naivete be implied. The new discipline ought neither be too provable scientifically at the cost of its mystery and infinite possibility.

Astrology seems to be satisfying this urge to the spiritual in us, a real human need often misunderstood or dismissed as neurosis, totem, or leftover from a primitive past. Rank scepticism seems to have given way to rabid reading of Astra Nova.

There have been sufficient 'co-incidences' to suggest that Astrology works though not necessarily the astrology of the daily Your Stars column.

Initially, any sort of prognostication, any determination of the future depends on the notion of an entirely rational universe which sufficient evidence will expose in its entirety. But this presumes that what there is to be known will be an extension of what we already know, and will take place on the terms and level which we currently accept.

Which has almost never been so. The war so terrible as to produce a lasting peace has recurred with depressing regularity in history. The second premise necessary to astrology

hinges round the idea of the solar system as an orderly system which interacting forces or streams of energy hold together and in which each body in the system has a mutual effect on each other. Of course, Newton thought so. Though the principle of gravity he posited is not now thought so explanatory. But there is a strong possibility that the nature of the energy, for instance, which the moon exerts on the earth is electro-magnetic in character. Thus the overlapping of the magnetic fields creates the tides.

Our difficulty comes when the principle is applied to human beings. It is necessary to understand man as a smaller cosmos repeating on a small scale the same system of energies contained in the solar system, the receiving and communicating apparatus being the nervous system, which in its turn alerts and connects up with the glands system. The glands, of course, containing the energies which when released produce the various manifestations of characteristics which make up a person.

If one makes a spiral, taking the Solar plexus as starting point, the distance of the various glands from each other, following the path of the spiral, tallies very closely with that of the corresponding planets from the sun, apparently obeying Bodes' Law, which states that each planet is twice as far from the sun as the preceding one.

Therefore, the Moon corresponds with the thymus which has to do with early growth, maternal instinct. Venus is equivalent to the flesh covering the body and certain harmonious emotions corresponding with the parathyroids.

Mercury, which has to do with movement, muscle control, speed of reaction corresponds with the thyroids. Mars to do with fight and flight corresponds with the adrenal glands.

Jupiter corresponds to the Posterior pituitary, indicating emotional stability, expansive outgoing emotions and the muscular structure. Saturn corresponds to the Anterior pituitary gland, which controls the bone structure and is connected with the depth of thought and emotion.

Uranus which takes 84 years to make a complete orbit of the star system must be considered the last planet to have a relevance to human life as a whole, corresponding with a human life span. Which would seem to apply to the Gonads, the glands containing the most highly evolved energy normally produced by a human being and possessing all that is necessary for a new life.

For a more complete understanding of the real implications of Astrology it helps to think of the solar system as a highly involved series of spirals interwoven and moving through space with the sun as the spindle.

The solar system then takes on the aspect of a poly-phase transformer, the paths of the planets forming ever widening coils which transform different manifestations of energy at over increasing speeds, which akin to electricity, act on the glands and thus determine our actions.

It is in the slight preponderance of the sensitivity of one gland over another that the basis of the idea of different types of man lies.

Thus there are basically six types, corresponding to Saturn, Jupiter, Mars, Venus, Mercury and the Moon.

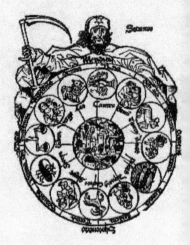

Rodney Collin in *Theory of Eternal Life*, borrowing the ideagram invented by Gurjieff, suggested a plan by which each type led or modified the previous one, which also had an opposite of maximum attraction and repulsion.

There is some doubt that people really are distinctive types; however, the theory has the advantage that it ties in exactly with the tenets of traditional astrology. The only question left is that of the Zodiacal signs. These are defined by virtue of the fact that there are groups of stars which form an almost exact circle around the solar system and which, it is supposed, feed energies of differing character into the solar system via the sun, which does the same for the planets.

The above suggests a way in which astrology may work, but to really be able to predict a person's future one would have to know many other things besides the day they were born, hereditary conditions, climatic and social surroundings and childhood to name a few.

Further reading: *A New Model Universe.* Ouspensky.

Ken Andrew.

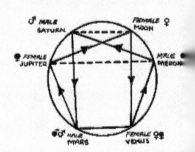

Egypt Tarot predicted an Israeli victory. Avoid your disaster...

Results depend on the clearness of the questions. For instance "Will I be happy?" is a very wide and general question. Better still is to ask, for instance, "How will the picnic tomorrow be for me?"

An important point that needs to be stated clearly in the questions is the Time factor. Is the question short term or long term? Ask the question as clearly as possible. If necessary ask the question more than once, changing the time element from shorter to longer term.

Do not limit yourself to the meanings given on the outline. They are general, and under the special circumstances of a divination, may be altered. Say what comes to you.

It is better to learn the meanings of the cards than write the meanings on them. Better for yourself; more impressive for the seeker. By learning the meanings of three cards a day, you learn the whole pack in a week.

Method

The 22 cards are shuffled and the seeker asks the cards the question while shuffling (they need not say the question aloud if they do not want to). The seeker cuts asking the question again as he or she does so. The interpreter puts out the first four cards like this:

```
        A
    D   B
        C
```

The numbers at the top of the cards are now added together. If the total comes to more than 21, for instance 33, the two figures in the total are added together, i.e. 3+3=6. This number gives the number of the card which is to be placed in the centre of the star. If it already appears in the star, it has to be visualised as being in both places at once.

Make a special note of the fact that the Joker or Fool, which is un-numbered, is for the purposes of the draw No. 22.

The Reading

The centre card is the most important and sets the tone of the whole answer. Card A is directly related to it and affects it. Card B is more remote or possibly happens later in time. Card C follows B. Card D follows C.

It is now the duty of the interpreter to examine the meanings of the five cards in the cross in accordance with the list of meanings given in this book and to inform the seeker what the cards foretell. It is therefore essential for the interpreter to study the meanings of the Major Arcana very thoroughly and in particular the way in which the presence of one card next to another influences or modifies the meaning of the two combined. For example, if Temperance is followed by the Hanged Man the two cards together mean that the seeker will be faced by some indecision in the matter which is in his mind and that this indecision has been caused by the hypocrisy or double-dealing of some other person. Death followed by the Hanged Man signifies that someone known to the seeker will die with unpleasant consequences for the seeker; for example, the seeker might be expecting to inherit a large sum of money under the will of the deceased, whereas he would, in fact, inherit little or nothing, or there might be some unpleasant condition attached to his inheritance by the legator.

(b) Your Dearest Wish

The seeker should shuffle and cut the pack with his right hand, and the interpreter will then turn up a card which represents the fate of the seeker's wish. Then place from the right two cards on either side of it—

```
    E   D   A   C   B
```

These flanking cards will represent the factors affecting the achievement or end of your wish.

B and C represent factors of influence by people, possibly relations, associates or friends.

D and E are events or material influences which work on the wish.

B and E taken together represent influences further away in time from the wish. If the wish appears likely to be granted, then these outside cards will indicate the factors controlling how long it will be before the wish is successful. If the wish appears to be lost, then the outside cards can again help to gauge the time element as to whether there is a chance of it being granted at some time in the future.

D and C taken together represent the significance of the wish to the person who asks. In cases where it is not

clear whether the wish card is positive or negative, these two cards on either side will determine the result by an assessment of the elements involved. They can also often be a give-away to the nature of the wish itself—will it bring happiness or satisfaction?

Card Numbers

The wish fulfilled: 1, 2, 3, 4, 5, 6, 11, 19, 21.

The wish not granted: 9, 12, 13, 15, 16, 18; and Inverted 4, 6, 7, 8, 11, 15, 16, 21; and the Fool either way.

Fulfilled, but delayed: Inverted 3, 10, 19.

Delayed and uncertain: 7, 8, 10, 14, 17, 20.

Unlikely, but just possible subject to having long delay: Inverted, 9, 13, 17, 20.

(c) Seeing the Year Ahead

1. Take out the cards representing the 12 astrological signs of the Zodiac.
2. Shuffle them and lay them face downwards on the table.
3. Ask the seeker to shuffle the remainder of the cards and to cut them to the left with his right hand. Then to replace the bottom stack on the top.
4. Deal the remaining ten cards face down on to end of the astrological signs of the Zodiac, starting from the right. Two cards will remain unpaired.
5. Turn up the Zodiac pack and sort into chronological order starting with the month ahead on the right, the others ranging to the left.
   Read the significance of each month according to the meaning of its sister card bearing in mind its normal value when placed alongside each month.
6. Place on one side the two single cards. When you have finished reading the ten other months collect up the ten astrological cards and shuffle them.
7. Repeat the request to the seeker to shuffle and cut.
8. Deal five cards on each of the two remaining months (as they will be the most significant in the year ahead).
9. Set out the cards in a line with the card of the month on the right. Read across the line starting from the right.

(d) Asking a Private Question

1. Before beginning, be sure that the seeker has formulated his question. Explain to him that all questions come under four major headings:
   (a) Work, business, etc.
   (b) Love, marriage or pleasure.
   (c) Trouble, loss, scandal, quarrels, etc.
   (d) Money, goods or such purely material matters.
   Be careful that the seeker does not tell you his question or its nature before you begin.
2. Make your mind as passive as possible while you are shuffling and lay out the cards. Do not try to guess, go by what the cards suggest to you.
3. Shuffle the cards.
4. Hand them to the seeker and ask him to think of the question attentively that he wishes to put to the cards, and cut the cards with his left hand. He should then restore the cards, i.e. put the previous bottom stack uppermost.
5. Cut the pack with the left hand and place the top half to the left.
6. Cut each of these packs to the left.
7. Find the birth card. If in the right-hand pack the question refers to work, enterprise, ideas, etc. If in the next, marriage, love or pleasure. If in the third to trouble, loss, scandal, quarrels, etc., and if in the left-hand pack to money, foods, purely material matters.
8. Tell the seeker what he has come for, i.e. from the position of his astrological birth card, declare the general nature of the question. If wrong, abandon the divination. Do not resume the attempt within two hours.
9. If right, spread out the pack containing the birth card arranging the cards in a half circle, make a consequential story of these cards.
10. For additional information pair the cards on either side of the birth card.

The order of the 12 signs of the Zodiac is:

1.	Aries	4	The Emperor
2.	Taurus	5	The Pope
3.	Gemini	6	The Lovers
4.	Cancer	7	The Chariot
5.	Leo	11	Force
6.	Virgo	9	The Hermit
7.	Libra	8	Justice
8.	Scorpio	13	Death
9.	Sagittarius	14	Temperance
10.	Capricorn	15	The Devil
11.	Aquarius	17	The Star
12.	Pisces	18	The Moon

MEN IT CAN BE DONE

Now available --- MAGNAPHALL --- a sound and successful method of improving virility and increasing the size of the male organ. A method which is absolutely SAFE , involves no drugs or apparatus and is GUARANTEED. MAGNAPHALL has helped thousands of men, all over the world. There is no longer a need for any man to envy the sexual vigour or proportions of others. You don't have to believe us -- we can send you such PROOF as will convince even the most skeptical.

For full details of how MAGNAPHALL works and positive proof of it's success, in strict confidence and with no obligation, write to:-

RAVENSDALE PRODUCTS LTD.
PERSONAL DEPARTMENT,
SPRINGFIELD ROAD,
LONDON. N.15.

PERSONAL

FOR YOU
From C.J.P. Distributors

The latest and most modern of contraceptives in the world. Unique, they are for males, but designed to assist and encourage female pleasure for married people. Packed in an attractive box of five, each one different and patented, they sell for 105/- in the west end of London - where they can be obtained only sporadically.

Now available at 50/- per box (5)
**********NEW**********from C.J.P. Distributors

SEX a problem? Get HARMONY

You naturally expect security from a contraceptive, SECURA LONGTIME is a first-class product on which you can rely completely, and SECURA LONGTIME also gives you literally 'a long time'. By means of a special inner layer it lengthens the time before you, as a man, reach your climax (and your partner benefits as well, of course.)

Trial Pack of 6 at 20/-
           12at 35/-
From C.J.P. Distributors, 97 Westbourne Park Villas, London W.2
Write for our FREE illustrated catalogue of BIZARRE and EXOTIC products.

2'6

SPECIAL SURPRISE ISSUE!

THE TRUTH ABOUT THE GREAT ALF CONSPIRACY!

2'6

OZ

SPECIAL SURPRISE ISSUE!

Suddenly its Alfs! This bizarre cult of grey, short-haired nine-to-fivers is sweeping the country. They work as Accountants, Executives, Journalists, Bank Managers, Doctors, Lawyers, Salesmen, Dentists, Insurance Clerks, Civil Servants... In fact, most people are Alfs these days. They are becoming a public menace... a threat to world peace... a social embarrassment.

AIMS OF THE EVIL ALF MOVEMENT

1. To make Britain a fit place for their children to live.
2. Full employment.
3. Democracy.
4. To bring back the industrial revolution.

LITTLE KNOWN FACTS ABOUT ALFS

1. Alfs kill more people in automobiles in this country than any other ethnic group.
2. They are clannish. Observe buses, trains, places of public amusement. And remember, Alfs usually only employ other Alfs and often under conditions so appalling as to prevent them ever becoming non-Alfs.
3. Despite their overall stupidity they are SMART in business.
4. Alfs love to sing and dance. They can easily be pacified by humming a ragtime tune.
5. The captain of the Torrey Canyon was an Alf.
6. Few Alfs admit they are Alfs. That's why they are so difficult to help.
7. They sometimes try and change their names so they can'pass' - Ringo Starr, Lord Avon, John Le Carre, Engelbert Humperdink, George Weidenfield.
8. They are trying to marry your daughters.

GAMES ALFS PLAY

1. Coitus Interruptus.
2. Engagements.
3. Drowning.
4. Malnutrition.
5. Praying.

an Alf symbol

Your Favourite Pub - EVENING STANDARD AWARD - LONDON'S BEST PUB 1961

GREAT ALF ACHIEVEMENTS

A popular Alf recreation

The crucifixion, War, Custard, The World Cup, Electrification of the London Manchester Railway, The Fox trot, Not buying any of Vincent Van Gogh's paintings during his lifetime, The Process, I.Q. tests, 'Our World' Georgette Heyer, The Kama Sutra, Life Insurance, The local, The condom, Post Office Savings accounts, Cathy McGowan, North Sea Gas.

Great Alf Reunions

1. The Queen with the Duchess of Windsor.
2. The Pope with the Archbishop of Canterbury.
3. St. Francis Chichester with his wife.

NOTORIOUS ALFS

A typical Alf Underground publication

The chief accountant at British Railways, Hughie Green, C.P. Snow, Mr. Gannex, Ken Dodd, Chapman Pincher, Barry Humphries, David Wynne Morgan Mr. Marks and Mr. Spencer, your neighbours and thousands of others too obvious to mention. But Alfs weren't all born yesterday - they abound throughout history:

Historic Alf Apologists

Winston Churchill: "The maxim of the British people is 'Business as usual'".
St. Paul: "Let all things be done decently and in order".
Robert Kennedy: "I basically agree with both positions".
Sarah Flower Adams: "Nearer, my God, to thee".
George I: "I hate all boets and bainters".
George V: (Last words) "How is the Empire".
E.M. Forster: "Ulysses is a dogged attempt to cover the universe with mud".
Mao Tse Tung: "Be united, alert, earnest and lively".
Grantland Rice:
"When the One Great Scorer, comes,
To write against your name,
He marks - not what you won or lost -
But how you played the game".

ARE YOU AN ALF?

Even Alfs read OZ. Check these questions to make sure you're not an Alf.
1. Despite this country's present economic difficulties and the precarious state of sterling we shall soon be back on our feet.
   ☐ True or false ?
2. London swings.
   ☐ True or false ?
3. The sun will never set on the British Hovercraft.
   ☐ True or false ?
4. God is on our side.
   ☐ True or false ?

NOTE: If you attempted any of these questions then you are an Alf

Clay Alfs on a Wimpy trip. Here they are maintaining 'Wimpy-burgers' - curious slabs of gristle and grease pre-cooked, re-heated then consumed between two chunks of unfresh bun. Colourless, tasteless, odourful and "deliciously addictive", the Wimpy constitutes a classic square meal. (Alfs maintain that the number of deaths from an overdose is negligible).

The rush-hour shove-in. Conceived originally as a 'happening', the Alf shove-in is now a twice daily ritual. Sombre, colourfully dressed in colourless garb, often clutching newspapers and mysterious brown paper parcels, Alfs jostle and surge playfully into passing trains. There is an overwhelming smell of deodorant - used by Alfs to disguise the telltale reek of perspiration and unbathed skin tissues.

Communalism is inherent in Alf philosophy. It sometimes extends to their sex life. A pioneer Alf, Billy Butlin, has opened nine seaside holiday camps which absorb "over one million" Alfs annually. It is here that they HAVE FUN and manifest their basic drive - hedonism.

Some Alf do-gooders, called "entrepreneurs" or "business-men" have started shops which stock basic Alf gear and quaint accessories which are given away to needy Alfs at "bargain prices".

THE FINAL SOLUTION

Although you are drastically outnumbered it's still not too late. You can:
(a) Turn them on - This is only a temporary palliative. An Alf will always turn himself off eventually.
(b) Export them to Tasmania - This is permanent, inexpensive (£10 per Alf courtesy of Australian Immigration Dept. - less bulk reductions) and humane. Alfs love Tasmania - they are the only inhabitants.

This makes Alfs randy

an Alf Happening

As Cleopatra, Sarah Bernhardt stabbed the slave who bore to her the tidings of Mark Antony's defeat at Actium; she stormed, raved, wrecked some of the scenery in her frenzy and finally, as the curtain fell, dropped in a shuddering convulsive heap.
As the applause died, a middle-aged British matron was heard to say to her neighbour:
'How different, how very different from the home life of our own dear Queen.'

AN ALF REFUTATION

FORWARDE

A s for "SQVARENESS" that is a charge unusual: WHAT MAKETH THE AN ALF? Yet my accusers have bent me on with this 'ttone when I bootth no all intoll towards them SO if you life wlooke on the whole courtß of my argument I shall ITEM by ITEM werte myselfe of eache patt – so compareding a REFVTATION and CONCLVSION &ß the 'all which hath beene objected to me for a sinne.

REFVTATION. ITEM – That I visiteth not places of marriage that might be knowne as extra-ordinarii such as night-CLVBS and othe' divers manner of MEETING HOVSES. YET once did I visite and then to make much use of the facilities of a TVRKISH BATH in Paddington. Is such a place so marvaile unto a vigourous vigorous vapouralt (And I'll be not extra-ordinary that sundry oligochaeta; yet in my pique by gather of the wer' had not prompted my hasty departure)

ITEM – That I am wont to wear a BOWLER HAT, YET while much dispute may be moved as to whether my owne HAT or the LONG HAIR of my accuser be the better production from the element; there can only but be little doubte as to which one be the easier to raise on the greeting of a lady.

ITEM – That I am in the right of the land, married YET serveth not my lauthall cauße as well for COPVLATION and the MENDING of house as the male of him who causeth me to LAND as the record of thee unfeigly duties I quote I warrant the far better)

ITEM – That I eat not out in places of cullynary varietie and specialitie, YET the eating house to which on the thirde Saturday of eache severall moneth I accompanie mine dulcty AUNT, in the manner of all similar places called LYONS, hath varietie borne to extremitie in the choice availeble to menne of greatealf and quease religious stomacks betweene BEEF and PORK sausages.

ITEM The LAST. That I thinketh not YET mayst assurers to the above will be rebußal enough to thee the laßt ittem.

CONCLVSION. What I am 'SQVARE-NESS', is but a PIG in the unproud fantasie of him who hath not dainte cointenant – in short amoth I see daylie in the faces of them that refuse to purchase the ENCYCLOPÆDIAS that I would selle them.

PLANT A FLOWER CHILD

Other Scenes & Oz

This is a special issue produced for John Wilcock of 'Other Scenes'; edited by John Wilcock and Richard Neville.

London OZ is published by OZ Publications Ink Limited, 40 Anhalt Road, London, SW11 Phone: BAT 8407, or, in emergencies, BAY 4623

Editor: Richard Neville
Deputy Editor: Paul Lawson
Business Manager: Peter Ledeboer
Design: Jon Goodchild
Photography: Robert Whitaker
Art: Martin Sharp
Staff: Andrew Fisher, Ian Stocks Newman, David Reynolds Louise

Contributions: are welcome and should be addressed to: The Editor, enclosing s.a.e.

Printer:
Sharptone Litho Ltd
83 Bellenden Road, SE15
Distributed by:
Moore Harness Ltd
11 Lever Street, EC1
CLE 4882

CORRESPONDENCE

Dear Sir,

Thank you for your generous four-page spread on us in your last issue. The two articles were as clear, lucid, comprehensible, intelligent, devoid of contradiction and confusion,' and as close to the truth as the bent minds of the two female weirdies you hired to write them.

Let's sum up our position for you.

The Process combines the worst aspects of both Nazi Germany and Communist China. Our methods bear a striking resemblance to the techniques of brainwashing and we incorporate all the components of an authoritarian, Nazi, Communist, brainwashing organisation in the business. Members of The Process are both anarchist and fascist, dangerous megalomaniacs and brainwashed zombies (on alternate days?)

We are rabidly anti-intellectual and punish all deviators with ostracism, ridicule - particularly ridicule, nothing more ridiculous than someone deviating from The Process - and expulsion of course, what else would we do with such trash? We can never make up our minds whether we are desperately keen to lure everyone into The Process or primarily concerned with keeping everyone out.

The Process is wholeheartedly anti-Semitic, hence all the Swastikas (ignore the hammers and sickles), excluding, of course, all our Jewish members, of which our Fuehrer is one. Jehovah gets faintly bothered about this from time to time, but not to worry.

As a result of all this The Process makes countless enemies, draws persecution, condemnation and legal action against itself from every side, sustains frequent attacks by the press in many parts of the world, which of course makes it the safest, cushiest niche in town, just the thing for people too scared to be part of the establishment.

One thing surprises us. Your two sleazy would-be exposers managed to invent so much other rubbish about us, but no sex? no orgies? no perversions? not one sex maniac amongst the lot of us? Or would this make us too acceptable to your readers?

Yours sympathetically,
The Process
2 Balfour Place
London W1

Dear Sir,

I congratulate you on your 'Process' expose. I inadvertantly went to 2 Balfour Place and experienced several bearded loons with large alsation dogs.

I was approached by one bearded fellow who tried to explain his reasons for living. I didn't realise he was a religious pervert, and said an individual could find meaning in worship of an abstract superbeing, inferring God. I wondered why he left hastily until another bearded fellow announced they were a religious organisation. I then fell in, the other poor sod didn't want to get involved in an argument. They believed they were on the outside of a brainwashed society, but this fellow was the most brainwashed creep I had ever seen (apart from the pope).

You can acquire 'The Process' from an easy start. Communication lessons (3 gns andhour) learning how to talk. This is a racket preying on the insecure with inferiority complexes. Most religions do (mystic). It's a good money earned. The Process believe in 'truth', why don't they speak it? They want money to live at Xtul, their chosen paradise. Process are the most hypocritical group on the 'god will come' scene. The bloke even called me 'blocked', adding 'sweetie' after, so as to communicate his feeling.

Yours faithfully,
J N Warne
60 Repton Road
Orpington, Kent.

Dear Sir,

Surely Auden is the first of the modern hippies - he said twenty five years ago that we "must" love one another or die" and, I beleive, his house in Austria is surrounded in flowers. Also, doesn't Gandi come into it somewhere (plus, of course, all the religious figures who have preached love).

But, what really, is the flower-power craze all about, apart from being an excuse to act mad and have a good time (which you can do without subscribing to any half-formulated philosophies from America); there are no manifestoes or even clear declarations and aims to argue about. Of course, it is the drug aspect of the "movement" that gets all the publicity in the daily papers, but again, we get no flowery spokesman to rattle his beads in reply. If people want to escape from an ugly world and attain a level of consciousness in which mundane conformity, policemen and politics do not exist, then good luck to them. However, you don't get change in the world if you attempt to escape from it all the time:

It's not wrong to live for the moment, but transitory experiences at Alexandra Palace or Hyde Park have no lasting significance. If the sincere among the flower people want to establish a loving, beautiful society, then light shows and wierd dancing will not help. Let's have a clear statement of aims and some constructive alternatives to the existing set-up, or else the hippies will die out; and they will leave nothing to mark their existence (the Beat Generation left some literature), except a few plastic flowers.

Yours faithfully,
John Whiteman

The following were members of the Underground Press Syndicate as of June 1967 :
ART AND ARTISTS: c/o Marie Amaya, 16 Buckingham Palace Rd,
 London SW1, England
AVATAR: 145 Columbia Street, Cambridge, Mass. 02139
BERKELEY BARB:2886 Telegraph Ave. Calif. 94705
CANADIAN FREE PRESS: Student Co-op Argyle House, 53 Argyle,
 Ottowa, Ontario, Canada
CONNECTIONS: 714 Conklin Place, Madison, Wisconsin
CROCODILE: P.O. Box 12488, Univ. Station, Gainesville, Fla. 32601
COMMUNICATIONS COMPANY: 26 Bond St., New York
COMMUNICATIONS COMPANY: 406 du Boce Ave. San Francisco
THE EAGLE: The American University, Massachusetts & Nebraska
 Aves., Washington, D.C. 20016
THE EAST VILLAGE OTHER: 105 Second Ave., New York, N.Y.10003
THE FIFTH ESTATE: 923 Plum St., Detroit, Michigan 48201
GRAFITI: P.O. Box 8326, Philadelphia., 19101
GUERILLA: Artists Workshop Press, 4825-27 John Lodge,
 Detroit, Michigan 48201
HELIX: 4526 Roosevelt Way N. E., Seattle, Wash 98105
THE ILLUSTRATED PAPER: c/o Philip Bianchi, P.O. Box 541,
 Mendocino, Calif. 95400
THE INTERNATIONAL TIMES: 102 Southampton Row,
 London WC2, England
INNER SPACE: Box 212, Chelsea Station, New York, N.Y. 10011
THE LOS ANGELES FREE PRESS: 938 No. Fairfax,
 Los Angeles, Calif. 90046
John Wilcock's OTHER SCENES, Box 8, Village P.O.,
 New York 10014 NY.
THE PAPER: P.O. Box 367, East Lansing, Michigan 48823
PEACE BRAIN: 3430 N Blaine P1.(Apt.2) Chicago, Ill. 60657
PEACE NEWS: 5 Caledonian Rd., Kings Cross, London, England
PUNCH: c/o Paperbook Center, 568 Main St., Worcester, Mass. 01608
PROMETHEAN: c/o Dave Oved, 560 Grover Cleveland Hgwy.
 Eggertsville, N.Y. 14226
MODERN UTOPIAN: Tufts Univ. PO Box 44, Medford, Mass. 02153
MAVERICK PRESS: PO Box 792, San Francisco, Calif. 94101
NOTES FROM UNDERGROUND: PO Box 536, Dallas, Tex. 75222
THE RAG: c/o Thorne Dreyer, 2506 Nueces, Austin, Texas
SEER: 1824 S.W. Market St., Portland, Oregon 97201
SOUNDS ON CAMPUS: Box 211, Village Station, N.YN.Y. 10014
SPOKANE'S NATURAL: Mandala Print Shop, 522 S.Cannon,
 Spokane, Wash.99204
SANITY: 3237 St. Lawrence Blvd., Montreal 18, p. Quebec, Canada
SATYRDAY: Box 12, 340 8 athurst St. Toronto, Ontario, Canada
SAN FRANCISCO ORACLE: 1642 Haight St., San Francisco 94117
ORACLE OF SOUTHERN CALIFORNIA: 840 N. Fairfax L.A., Calif.

This issue is sponsored jointly by John Wilcock's 'Other Scenes', a fortnightly newsletter published in New York City, and Oz magazine, published monthly in England and Australia. In the style of the fast-growing "underground press" in the United States, this will hopefully demonstrate the need (and the audience) for a truly international 'paper' devoted to the creative, avant garde community. Distribution of this issue is not only in England but throughout Europe and the United States. John Wilcock's 'Other Scenes' appears 20 times each year from wherever its publisher happens to be. Mailing address is P.O. Box 8, Village Station, New York 10014, U.S.A. Subscriptions from September 1967 through December 1968 cost three guineas or $10, payable either to the New York address listed or via Oz magazine in London.

OTHER
scenes

The British distribution rights to Andy Warhol's twin-screen movie, "The Chelsea Girls", are held by Louis Scher who left his California home for a year and set up shop in London anticipating a long and profitable run for the four-hour film. A friendly lunch with British film censor Trevelyan however convinced him that in view of the current furore over drugs "Chelsea Girls" wouldn't even get an "X" certificate. So now the plan is, hopefully, to screen the film at the London film festival in October in an effort to make it "respectable" enough for a release afterwards.

In actual fact the film is more notable for its technical experimentation (two vignettes shown simultaneously, side by side; acid-trip sequences shot under rotating colour gels) than its theme. The more perceptive U.S. critics have spotted this; the others being still hung up on the kind of orthodox moviemaking that has had its day. All the indications are that we are heading into an era when total environments will be commonplace - film as moving tapestry on four walls and ceiling; strobe lights and coloured spots strategically placed; "instant newspapers" projected in homes; wall-sized television bringing live coverage at all times.

That some people deplore such a future is irrelevant because (a) it will never be obligatory to watch, and (b) there will always be more filmless oases than environments. But two things make this prediction a certainty: the technological possibility and the profit potential. One sure thing about this society is that if there is money to be made, somebody will do it.

One of the factors that most of the "underground" movie visionaries have in common is that the people who put them down invariably spend hours arguing about whether or not they really have anything to offer. It should be self-evident by now that an artist who can provoke lengthy discussions about his work has obviously proved his capacity to <u>involve</u> an audience which, by any standards, is a measure of art.

2

The British are so trusting. Where else in the world would the government ask people to voluntarily pay a license fee for having a radio or television set -- with virtually no way of enforcing the law against those who don't comply? Does the GPO have the right, for example, of coming to anybody's door and demanding to search the house for a TV set or radio? Surely not without a warrant. And can a warrant be issued to search <u>anybody's</u> home just on suspicion that there might be such an unlicensed set? So it boils down to citizens' honesty in reporting such sets themselves (i. e. by getting a license).

A similar situation is the naive law which prohibits a British subject from taking more than £50 abroad when going on vacation.

3 4

Apart from the sheer arrogance of a government that not only heavily taxes your income but then proceeds to tell you where and how you can spend it, there's the idiocy of a people who do what they're told on the grounds that "respect" for the law is more important than individual liberty.

To start with, the law is totally unfair penalising, as it does, the poor compared with the rich who can find a score of ways to <u>legally</u> evade it. Secondly, it's a stupid law that is totally unenforceable against anybody who makes the slightest attempt to avoid it. The post office can't check the contents of every letter that leaves the country any more than the customs officials can search everybody's pockets.

So once again what are we left with but a people who willingly subscribe to restrictions on their freedom voluntarily -- kept in check by a cynical government that knows honesty is the best police.

5

The majesty of the law, as a matter of fact, is little more than a joke to people who give any thought to these matters. Do you have respect for a law that allows fishermen to be arrested and jailed for fishing for their livelihood?

Well, you see these happened to be Polish fishermen and they were trawling off the waters of Northumberland within the so-called "12-mile limit". What kind of crazy humanity is it that states that a citizen of the world can't go into the world's seas and catch fish?

Of course we all know the dumb arguments about national rights and that every country behaves in the same way about its so-called territory. But it is exactly this type of greed and acquisitiveness - whether individual or national - that causes most of the violence in men and always has.

6

And then we come to the matter of the courts. Anybody who has ever spent any time in one knows what a colossal waste of time they are: the petty tyranny of court officials; the endless, pointless arguments of lawyers; the irrelevant pomposity of magistrates and judges giving lectures to unlucky victims of a system that, once again, is loaded against the poor.

7

London's transport system is one of the best in the world but is there no solution to the endless lines that must form every night outside the ticket booths of underground stations? As often as not the ticket dispensing machines either don't work or take only specific coinage and it's too much to expect that people always carry the exact change. There is a solution, as it happens, and it's an obvious one: make all public transport free with buses stopping ANYWHERE to pick up somebody who wants to get on and both buses and subway trains running all night.

Here we have three ideas that only sound radical but actually make a lot of sense. It is unlikely that the money saved by abolishing ticket collectors, guards, machines, checkers, printers etc. would compensate for the loss of passenger revenue but it would certainly make life a lot simpler and any deficit could be made up by a transport tax on the more affluent car owners and the stores that benefit so much from the mass of subway passengers.

There is also, at this stage of history, no reason at all why transport should cease at the ridiculous hour of 11:30 P.M. For the London Transport Authority to maintain that there is no need for buses and subways to run later because nothing is open later is begging the question: if transport started to run all night, things would stay open all night. In any case, the present system is discriminatory - if you have a car or can afford to travel by taxi, you can get home at late as you like.

8

Gerson Legman, in a still-to-be-published diatribe called The Fake Revolt ("the gangsters of the new freedom are already mopping up your kids with narcotic drugs and drivelling pretenses of fake revolt" says the atom bomb is "nothing but the Marquis de Sade on a government grant". From the safe distance of Valbonne, France, he writes: "The Fake Revolt movement is, very simply, a trick of the money and power organization and its dead-end culture whereby all real revolt, emotion and art are siphoned off into degenerate static and snowblitz which are no danger at all to the status quo."

9 12

Recent visitors to the badly organized Dialectics of Liberation Conference - Stokeley Carmichael, Allen Ginsberg, Emmett Grogan - have demonstrated that American is exporting not only murder, napalm, death and colonialism, but a more constructive type of social revolution. But it seems significant that all the aforementioned find themselves increasingly caught in the trap of becoming more and more famous while repeatedly avowing they merely represent popular viewpoints and seek no attention for themselves. The cult of personality is too deeply ingrained in the culture for people not to worship at its shrine but apparently one of the best ways to cultivate it is to turn one's back.... To be released soon: an LP record of the thoughts of Mao Tse Tung, recently recorded in London (seriously).... How do London shops get away with charging customers for an adequate paper bag to carry away their groceries?.... Most overrated shrink in England: Ronald David Laing whose unintelligible, second-rate corruptions of the original Tim Leary message have created a cult of believers apparently unfamiliar with the original.

12½-20

Most of the production staff of the recent (mainly positive) ITV show about pot turned on in the course of the show's preparation. Even the young lady researcher - who reported that it didn't do anything to her although she appeared to be ideologically converted.... The people who invented the hoola-hoop, WHAM-O Corp. of San Gabriel, Calif., recently reintroduced the gimmick in "a few test areas" to see if they could chalk up some more sales. But, according to one of the partners, "the trouble is that today's teen-age dancing has far surpassed the body movement of the hoops". . . Philip Morris and other major U.S. tobacco companies have been promoting a special deal so that Americans at home can send cigarettes to servicemen in Viet Nam tax free ($10.61 for 100 packets). It has helped the Saigon black market no end.... Most British restaurants offer you a choice of coffee "black or white?" and seem quite unable to cope with any variations on this theme.... The N.Y. Times quoting a recent sociological study on hippies' homelife came to the conclusion that hippies' kids tend to ignore their parents rather than fight with them. "How can you rebel sexually against a mother who will be happy to fit you for a diaphragm at the age of fourteen?" one asked.... The Indian government has been reading the 1,100 year old Hindu love manual, the Kama Sutra, and thinks it has discovered a contraceptive drug therein named the Palash flower. Research continues.... "It was noted, with considerable irony, that on the anniversary of the assassination Bobby (Kennedy) visited his brother's grave and then returned for another visit because photographers had not been present the first time" (Ralph de Toledano in "RFK: The Man Who Would Be President" recently published in America by Putnam).... What could be stupider than the recent deportation from Britain of the two Australian members of the Bee Gees voucher to stay here permanently but there is already a two year waiting list. What is the advantage of a waiting list that prevents British subjects from working in any of the countries of the so called Commonwealth?

21-30

WHY doesn't Civil Defense tell you about germ warfare? This is one of the new type provo stickers to be seen in London Underground stations. Suggested new slogans for sticking anywhere: KEEP AWAY FROM THIS CORNER; WARNING - DANGEROUS FUMES IN THIS VICINITY and OUT OF ORDER (for parking meters, phones and subway ticket machines).... Should U.S. athletes be boycotted at next year's Mexico Olympics as has been suggested? Yes, all OFFICIAL representatives of the United States should be boycotted, spurned, humiliated, spat upon and rejected (according to taste) until Official America ends the murderous, inhumane war in Viet Nam. This includes athletes, diplomats, congressmen and all military types.... When it comes time to build some kind of new, loving society on the ruins of the present Establishment the names Kingsley Amis, John Braine, Simon Raven and Bernard Levin should all be remembered with disfavor. These self-righteous champions of human liberty (masquerading as literary lions) all signed the letter to the Times expressing "respect and good will" for LBJ and his G.I. murderers.... Amnesty International (Turnagain Lane, Farringdon St., E.C. 4) is one of the most humane things in the world you can join. Currently it is running a postcard campaign to get prisoners out of jails into which they were tossed for their political views. Kit with full info costs £2.10s.... New from the enterprising Panther Books: Rolling Stones File (5s.), a documented semi-transcript of the recent trial.... Sheffield University Union of Students have produced an imaginative magazine, Arrows with a dazzlingly psychedelic cover.... "Hippies may be on the way to solving a problem that is almost certainly going to hit straight society one of these days: how to live, without working. The hippies are the first sizeable group in the US to work out in their sub-culture a way of coping with the cybernetic revolution. This is not a small thing to be doing. I think the effort, like the hippies themselves, should be viewed with sympathy", writes Charles McCabe in the SF Chronicle.... Living Screen, a process being used at Las Vegas' Tropicana Hotel is a three dimensional screen made of elasticed strips closely fitting together so that when a man is shown full sized on film he can step through his image onto the stage.... Soccer is being introduced into American television in a special version that allows longer intermissions for fourteen minutes of commercials.

31

Michael X. (photo by Horace Ove)

case 3003/66

Case no 3003/66 in the European Court of Human Rights is listed as STRAKER v. UNITED KINGDOM. It is an attempt to recover some 500 negatives of female nudes seized by the police from Jean Straker's Academy of Visual Arts in Soho-square which have been declared by the courts to be obscene. He's a pioneer photographer in the field of female nudity who's been challenging the whole moral attitude of authority for years, standing his ground and defending himself in the courts as a litigant in person. He tells his own story in this exclusive letter to Other Scenes & OZ.

You asked me to tell you something about my involvement. It's a long tale, but it goes something like this:- I make pictures of female nudes to help people find themselves: they're not the sort of chick snaps that you take in ten seconds with a polaroid; nor are they the bunny cheesecake that gulls the girlie mags. They're a kind of mainstream flow from the psyche to the id - and they're an attempt to search for, discover and trigger whatever it is that makes sense in each one of us.

Unfortunately the scene here sends the police with warrants to grab my negs and prints and cart them off to prison; eight detectives the other day charged through my studios and workrooms creating the kind of chaos that would make to think they were the FBI looking for the CIA. One of them, a kind of sub-leader, was Detective Sgt. Terence Beale, a soft-eyed pious, innocent sweetie who gained for himself some notoriety last year when he prosecuted the Robert Fraser Gallery for hanging the Jim Dine Graffiti in sight of the passers-by in Duke Street. He told the magistrate that pictures of the male and female genital organs offended him - and that this was an offence under the Vagrancy Act of 1834.

A while later he showed me a reproduction of one of the offending pictures which Jim Dine labelled with the word 'cunt'. I said this was an accurate anatomical description of the particular organ drawn, with a respectable Latin etymological antecedent in "cunnus", and Terence admitted he was learning. But a few weeks later he turned up again with seven chums and he said he thought my photographs were both indecent and obscene.

NON-CRIMINAL

Now, as most lawyers know, I been through all this jazz before; apart from a few thousand motorists, and a few hundred barrow boys, I must be the most prosecuted non-criminal in town.

The whole business is a bit negative, because the words they use have got perverted by a kind of case law process that collects up every bit of legal nonsense and makes it sacrosanct.

According to the Lord Chief Justice, my Danae study - the seduction of the virgin princess by Zeus, the king of the gods - is indecent. This is what he said in the Divisional Court:-

"In the present case there is no question in issue as to whether this photograph is obscene; the only question is whether it was indecent, and the Court, having seen the photograph and read the summing up is quite satisfied that looked at objectively it is indecent."

At the Freedom of Vision Teach-in on Censorship in the Arts, which we ran last year at Hampstead Old Town Hall, I displayed a large reproduction of this study. Charles Prebble made following point from the hall:

"I've racked my brains as to how on earth I could ever explain, for instance, this Danae picture - which I have in my collection - to a child."

And it was Ronald Clark who answered with these words:

"May I ask at the risk of offending some people's feelings a little, perhaps, how they would explain to their children the birth of Christ?"

ETERNAL THEME

So what did I say? I said that the theme was one which poets and writers had drooled over for two thousand years; that Rembrandt and Titian and Tintoretto had painted it, that Horace had used it as a basis for satire, that it was the same eternal theme that for ever fascinated man - the creation of new life. Then someone said:

"I think that children may have to ask questions?" And I answered:

"Well, this is education, isn't it? I use the theme to show graphically, literally, without evasion, how a woman's body looks when exposed to penetration. There's no teasing here, no titillation - it's a frank, artistic statement. I show two girls, one on guard, the other lying down, her pubic anatomy defined in detail; I show, imaginatively, in the background, a flash of light, a thunderbolt, a ray of sunshine - however you wish to interpret it. I should say you can use this picture to explain to any child not only the mechanics, but also the poetry of sexual congress."

The voice came again:

"Would you be prepared to give the explanation you've just given to a fourteen year old boy?"
And I answered:

"There's my fourteen year old son over there." So that's how I defended the picture, - but I can't give you a copy to print, because if you printed it in Other Scenes & OZ you couldn't send the paper through the post.

The Lord Chief Justice put it this way:

"It is an attractive point put forward by Mr. Straker that just as 'obscenity' must be tested by the effect on the people to whom it may be published, so must questions of indecency relate to the people to whom they are published. Mr. Straker prides himself on being very careful in his distribution, as he puts it, in only sending photographs to people who, he is quite satisfied, will not find them indecent. It is, as I said, an attractive way of saying it, but unfortunately the Post Office Act of 1953 does not so provide."

ABUSE BY JUDGES

Now I regard such attempts on the part of judges and justices to arrogate to themselves the right to say that a photographic study of a female pubis is indecent as an abuse of words and authority, and a denial of a fundamental human right - the right to look- and a dangerous denial too, for by making it impossible for people to educate themselves, men and women were growing up to be ignorant and stupid.
Peter Watkins made the point at the National Secular Society's forum on censorship at Caxton Hall the other day, when he said:

case 3003/66

"It was as though authority regarded the bulk of the public as porridge-minded, grey painted, woolly, fluffy nits, who have nothing up here.'

The type of censorship that worried him was that subtle, eroding, pulling away of knowledge, pulling away of stimulation.

Ian Fraser came to see me a few weeks ago. He told me that often after he had married a couple they ask him for advice on sex. He was amazed how green some of them were. In his book, Sex as Gift, published for the Scottish Council of Churches, he says:

"Basic information about physical parts and functions should be given, as a right, to those whose lives it affects. In a survey of sexual attitudes and habits in certain colleges in the USA the source of knowledge which was said to give the most help was pornographic photographs. People wanted to know what happened, and how it happened. Knowledge of differences of male and female make-up must also be provided."

And just the other day, on another level, Dr. Dalzell-Ward, of the Central Council for Health Education told the 25th general assembly of the International Union against Venereal Diseases and Treponematoses in Munich:

"The aim of health education should be the promotion of psychological and sexual maturity rather than the avoidance of venereal disease and illegitimate pregnancy. One would lead to the other."

blue films by the yard

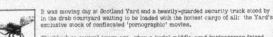

DIRTY MINDS

What Reginald Ethelbert Seaton, Chairman of Inner London Quarter Sessions Appeals Committee said was that some of my pictures were of women alone and some of women in association with other women, committing severe acts of a lesbian character. He thought that some undergraduate might possibly, as a medical student, choose some of my pictures and take them back to his university, where they might fall into the hands of persons who had no idea that such gymnastics were performed 'between the sexes' - and it "might well be that people would become depraved and corrupted by the fact that they had seen these photographs - not because they were interested in the opposite sex but because they were dirty minded young persons."

And then came the judgment: He said to me:

"You are a pioneer, are you not? .....the painful pioneer.....If you are going to be a pioneer and if you think the law is wrong it has painful consequences."

The pain was a fine of £150 - just one month after the United Kingdom

Government had accepted the compulsory jurisdiction of the European Court on Human Rights in regard to the provisions of the European Convention on Human Rights, of which Article 10 says:-

"Everyone has the right to freedom of expression. This right shall include freedom to hold opinions and to receive and impart information and ideas without interference by public authority and regardless of frontiers."

So you see, there's a kind of social malaise here causing psychologically immature people to fill beds in mental homes because the law takes upon itself the right to stop people getting educated. I know that young people - like the Oxford University students who got away with pubic hair in Oxymoron - are discovering their own psychological and sexual maturity; but it's the moronic adults who worry me. I am told that in Japan, sex is no problem. Why not print my Danae study in your Tokyo issue?

Good luck. Jean.

It was moving day at Scotland Yard and a heavily-guarded security truck stood by in the drab courtyard waiting to be loaded with the hottest cargo of all: the Yard's exclusive stock of confiscated 'pornographic' movies.

Flashback to several years ago, when a jovial middle-aged businessman friend of mine, whom I had originally met, bowler-hatted and umbrella stomping, at a lunchtime trad, jazz session in a City pub, asked me if I would care to make my flat available for a "film show". What kind of films? Nudge, nudge, whisper, whisper, ha ha ha. Of course, I'd be delighted. My friend would bring along a dozen or so well-heeled, dirty-minded business acquaintances who would contribute £5 each plus a share of the cost of a crate of whiskey and beer, for the pleasure of seeing a film show organised by - guess who? - Scotland Yard.

I was legitimately inquisitive and asked for details - it couldn't have been simpler. A detective inspector (friend of my chubby jazz-loving City acquaintance) together with a detective sergeant shared a duty roster supervising the "Black Library" at Scotland Yard, and paid a rake-off to their reliefs which allowed them to take their pick of the best films in the library, remove them from the premises and return them to Scotland Yard before the next detail came on duty.

GUARDIANS OF MORALS

Which is how I met Detective Inspector X and Detective Sergeant Y. My sitting room was full of tweedy, prosperous, shiny-faced, amiable, embarrassed businessmen drinking whiskey and beer and watching my friend and I pinning a bedsheet over the window curtains to act as a screen. In came the two guardians of our country's public morals, the inspector carrying a pile of film-reels, the sergeant carrying a movie projector. The sergeant set up the apparatus, while the inspector and my chubby chum discussed the menu (so to speak). At last the films rolled. While the sergeant attended the projector, the inspector delivered a running commentary on the extraordinary scenes of sexual athleticism being depicted on the improvised screen - not so much a commentary on the action as on the cast.

It went something like this: "That's Harry so-and-so" (describing a naked gentleman doing indescribable things to a double-jointed young woman decently clothed in suspender belt and stockings), "he's up for three at the Scrubs". Turning to the sergeant, "What was the name of the bird he's rogering, Bill? Oh yes, Norma, doing a stretch at Holloway Ladies' College right now. Mind you, they got hitched while the case was waiting to come to trial, thought being married might soften the Judge's stony heart. "Not at all, His Lordship was even more appalled by the idea that the sanctity of the marriage oath could be perverted by such vile and abominable conduct".

During this monologue the screen continues to show us its extraordinary panorama of fellatio, pedicatio, irrumatio, cunnilinctus and other forms of human contact which the Romans never imagined.

The main characters in these films had been given nicknames by the custodians of their art: one was known as The Walrus because of the luxuriance of the moustache which was his sole covering as he performed his weird rituals ('On the Moors, that one, five years'); another's sobriquet was Santa Claus because he serviced a succession of youthful angels while clad (basically) in that costume... These titles were written on the reels containing the films which were presumably stacked in alphabetical order on the shelves at Scotland Yard: Ape Man, Birching Betty, Chain Gang ... and so on down to the Ss (Santa Claus) and W (the Walrus).

VICARIOUS SEX

After the tired businessmen, surfeited with vicarious sex, had been seen off the premises and the loot counted out (a cut for my friend the entrepreneur, a cut for the sergeant, the rest into the inspector's bulging trouser pocket) the Constabulary set out on the second part of the evening's entertainment, which consisted of touring the more "bohemian" Chelsea pubs, chatting up the birds, and inducing one or more of them to return for a private viewing of some of the more astonishing films - the principle being that the combined effect of large whiskies (courtesy of the tired businessmen) and the disorientation produced by the sight of such incredible goings-on on the screen would arouse

n the breasts of these busty blondes or tousled redheads some flicker of
sexual interest in the charms of the burly sergeant and the saturnine
inspector.

As far as I can remember, they were remarkably successful and sooner or
later a mildly protesting female in a state of shock after being sub mitted to the
film programme would be dragged towards the spare bedroom for a practical
demonstration that the constabulary, contrary to slanderous allegations, are
not entirely reliant on their truncheons when performing the act of love.

All this merrymaking had to come to a stop in time for Inspector X and
Sergeant Y to stow away their gear in the Inspector's car and make it back to
the Yard before their suborned colleagues were relieved by a less sophisticated
team.

I often wonder what happened to those two enterprising policemen. I'm sure
they went far.

Simon Watson-Taylor

In Memoriam Rene Magritte

What does LONDON need most?

A little anger. Everybody is so godamned polite about everything all the time.
They're told to line up and they line up. They're told to obey orders and they
obey orders. It's so unnecessarily docile.

Why shouldn't they be?

Well they shouldn't be all the time. Don't accept rules just because they're
there. Who made the rules and why? Do they make sense? Those are the
questions that people should ask themselves before meekly obeying everything.
Freedom comes by taking it -- always has -- not be patiently waiting until
somebody offers it to you. American Negroes are the latest to find that out
but it's an age-old lesson.

**You're not suggesting that Londoners get out into the streets and start shooting
policemen?**

No, of course not, because Londoners aren't oppressed to the degree that
American Negroes are. But they ought to get out into the streets and protest.

What specifically?

Well, they can protest Wilson's fawning acceptance of Johnson's murderous
war in Viet Nam. They could protest some of the damned silly regulations
that the British have to endure such as being told that they can't go a house
or a telephone until the government sees fit to give them one; or being told
how much money they can take out of the country. They could protest some of
the social issues concerning discrimination, such as the restriction on coloured
West Indians - who are Britons after all...

But there aren't enough jobs for the people here already.

That isn't the point - there aren't enough jobs for anybody anywhere looked at
in that light. The restriction on West Indians is a discriminatory one -
because they're coloured and most Britains are white supremacists.

How about some more personal issues that people could protest?

Well how about just the freedom to be. To stand on the sidewalk and look at
something without being arrested for loitering. To play a guitar in the park
without getting a music license, things like that.

If people were willing to fight for simple issues like this - in other words call
the officials' bluff and go to court about it - they'd soon achieve a climate where
it was easier to have this freedom without being harrassed or arrested for

such simple, harmless things. The trouble with the English is that too many
of them are busybodies and killjoys who immediately get officious if they see
somebody doing something that they wouldn't or daren't do themselves.

**Surely such protests would also result in more repressive measures from the
authorities like in America?**

Possibly, but I doubt it. I think protest and social action always get a results
of some kind even if it's only to make more people aware of the possibilities.
The vast majority of people in a society would like their lives to be better --
and even for other people's lives to be better -- but it's just never occurred
to them they could do anything about changing them. Look how many people
are affected by the wiping out of pirate radio, for example, but most people
don't see it as a matter of principle at all -- just as the disappearance of a
few pop stations.

Why is it a matter of principle?

Why? Because what right has a bunch of politicians to arrogantly say that
you must ask their permission before you can communicate with people? What
the pirate radio stations should do -- and what the government is afraid of --
is criticize the way the politicians are doing (or not doing) their jobs. If you
have a communications system and you use it politically, to get social justice,
you have a potent weapon that can never be silenced.

Aren't there more important issues?

All issues of freedom are important. In my view Vietnam is the main priority
in the world today and if only Britain would raise its voice against America's
murderous policy the war might come to an end a lot sooner. Too many
Britains think Viet Nam is irrelevant. Of course, it's quite a cynical
attitude that the British government has adopted -- help America and America
will help you, the rights or wrongs of the case hardly enter into it. What
Britain refuses to realise is that a so-called Socialist government should be
on the side of the humane Americans who want to stop the war, not giving
moral support to the military/business establishment in America that considers
it more important to murder poor Asians 8,000 miles away than to cater to
the needs of poor Americans in their own country. One gutsy statement by
Wilson to the effect that Her Majesty's Government felt Vietnam to be an
unjust war might change America's posture overnight. And, incidentally,
restore Britain's prestige as a nation that believed in principles over profit.

The King & his Coca Cola Court

Richard Neville

Nepal is an exotic kingdom sandwiched impudently between India and China. Buddha was born there. You can get high there - on cannabis, opium and Everest. It is tiny, sedentary, backward - although, with the help of generous financial investment from Russia and America, Nepal is hurtling headlong into the 14th Century.

Hippies were dropping out in Kathmandu long before Haight-Ashbury exploded in 'Time'. See them strolling high through the cobbled labyrinthes, crashing mini cymbols at nightly native concerts, spinning copper prayer wheels at the brooding monkey temple. Hippies happen in Kathmandu because it represents the opposite of L.B.J's Great Society. It's ancient, aesthetic, spiritual, tribal and, as the tourist brochure puts it, 'the most beautiful place on earth'.

And yet there is one striking parallel with U.S. policy which the hippies, being apolitical, have probably not noticed. The suppression of its peoples by a non-elected but officially blessed autocrat. Nepal is ruled by His Majesty King Mahendra Bir Bikram Sha Deva and is considered by himself - and some of his subjects - to be the reincarnation of a Hindu God. He governs his people with a blend of ruthlessness, ineptitude and insanity which is so often the trade-mark of mortal instruments of divine wisdom.

To make his autocracy more palatable to the purveyors of international Aid, he claims to have invented a brand new form of democracy called the panchayat system. The 'panchayat' (as opposed to 'parliament') is simply a state advisory body with most of its 69 members elected by the King - little more than institutionalised sycophancy.

Because King Mahendra is known to confer favours impulsively, members conspire to organize "accidental" confrontations with him. Indeed, accidental confrontations are the most his 'cabinet' can ever hope for. The King rarely grants audiences to anyone - except crazed Hindu Fakirs with recurring Majesterial visions.

Because it is a "partyless democracy", the function of the panchayat assembly is to presumably imitate only the theatre of parliament. Despite Mahendra's claims of originality, its administrative mechanism has been lifted directly from the Code Napoleon.

Some years ago in a stunt to provide his national daily, 'The Rising Nepal' with some pin-up photos, King Mahendra set out on a white horse to fraternise with some of his 9½ million odd subjects. What was never mentioned in the glowing descriptions of Mahendra's grandiose goodwill gesture was the fact that he took the entire Nepalese domestic army with him. Some of the villages are still recovering from the economic catastrophy of this tour (e.g. villagers were made to sell rice to his troops at ⅓ the accepted price).

Last year some Nepalese teenagers paraded harmlessly outside the U.S. Embassy to protest Vietnam. Police swooped in and arrested all those involved. A resident British lawyer later revealed that the demonstrators were beaten by police so sadistically that "bones projected through flesh". They were then sentenced to twenty years in gaol. At the end of this time it will be King Mahendra's perogative to decide whether or not the luckless demonstrators are to be executed.

The British Council once organised the staging of 'Macbeth' in a local hall. King Mahendra intervened personally to ban the production on the grounds that Shakespeare depicts the murder of a King - an insult to Mahendra's conception of omniscient monarchy.

These are just some of the facts of how monarchism operates in Nepal. Below is some of the fiction. These are extracts from a special issue of 'The Rising Nepal', the national daily, celebrating King Mahendra's birthday.

(A few weeks later the nation celebrated the Diamond Jubilee of King Mahendra's father. The fact that he has been dead for some years did not dampen official enthusiasm).

The editorial:

A RED-LETTER DAY

"Every country or nation has a number of red-letter days in a year and so Nepal or the Nepalese also have theirs. The most important and significant of them for the celebration of which, all the Nepalese in every nook and corner, whether in the hills and dales, high hills and the Terai, the midlands of the valleys and foothills within the country or anywhere in the world - join their hand amidst various functions in the massive demonstration of their love and loyalty - is June Eleven the suspicious day on which His Majesty the King was born. To-day June eleven which comes once every year is being celebrated with added rejoicing and jubilant enthusiasm by all the Nepalese wherever they may be or whatever they may be doing. For His Majesty is not only just a King to them but their saviour, deliverer, benefactor and above all leader. He has done so much to assure them a bright present and a brighter future that moved deeply by feelings of gratitude, they are offering prayers in temples in Vibars, and Gompas for the long and glorious life of His Majesty the King."

The newspaper also included a lengthy poem by King Mahendra plus a photograph, taken at night, of him actually composing the poem in the palace gardens, wearing spats. It is called "Rara, a Nymph of Paradise, Every Wave with a Precious Bead" which is about his wife. She, incidentally, is extraordinarily ugly, even for a Queen, and has never been known to smile in public.

An extract from the poem:

> And hold in trance
> And those who chance
> To cast a glance
> On your expense
> Fleetingly for only once?
>
> "Likely a lovely maiden
> Of elegant proportion,
> Where did you learn
> To drop those long-limbed eyes
> And tantalize

Here's a typical extract from one of many eulogies to Mahendra; this one titled 'King Mahendra: Politician, Poet and Philosopher".

> Speaking of His Majesty's idealism, one is inevitably reminded of his poetry. It is poetry drenched in the air, water, and soil of Nepal. Its cadence is the voice of the Nepalese; its lilt is the dance of the Nepalese.
>
> We must never forget that King Mahendra's poetry is at its best only a reflection of the white-hot brilliance of his life. His whole life has been aglow with the fire and faith of the bursting romantic—the romantic of not mere passion for womanly beauty, the beauty of the flowery and the fields, of the streams
>
> and the mountains, but the romantic ablaze with the fire of revolutionary fervour, the statesman who wants the world changed better to suit his heart's pattern— a world without feuds, a world without selfishness where poetic harmony rules over the jarring notes of mutual suspicion and spative.

From a poem titled 'Forty Seven Lines - written in a mood of adoration.

> That Man may celebrate with festivity and mirth
> This blessed blessed day of King Mahendra's birth!
>
> Blow, Zephyr! blow, blow, gently blue—
> Not too fast nor too slow, blow or gently flow!
>
> Blessed with the fullsome fragrance, of flowers frail fragile
> Flowers for the sense so essentially sensuous
> There is another fragrance, of mind alert and agile
> Such is the mind of Mahendra, so essentially righteous!
> Ah! such is the fragrance of Mahendra, our poet-philosopher-king
> The propounder of Panchayat, thus peace and plenty to bring!
>
> Blow, Zephyr! blow, laden with Mahendra's high renown
> Broadcast all around the majesty of the Nepalese Crown!

For all his white-hot brilliance and fullsome flagrance, King Mahendra Bir Bikram Shah Deva, has human appetites. His land is poor. Coca Cola is unavailable. However, the King is not deprived. Every month a crate of this precious liquid is flown in for the Palace. The empty bottles later reach the villagers who fill them with a vile, sugary, scarlet liquid and palm them off to tourists. No wonder the U.S. Government has classified Nepal, for the benefit of its Aid personal, as a 'hardship area'.

And it's not exactly a ball for Mahendra's subjects.

Nepal's King Mahendra Bir Bikram Sha Deva

The original of Peter Sellers' kingly caricature in 'The Mouse that Roared' - a film banned in Nepal

Ray Leong

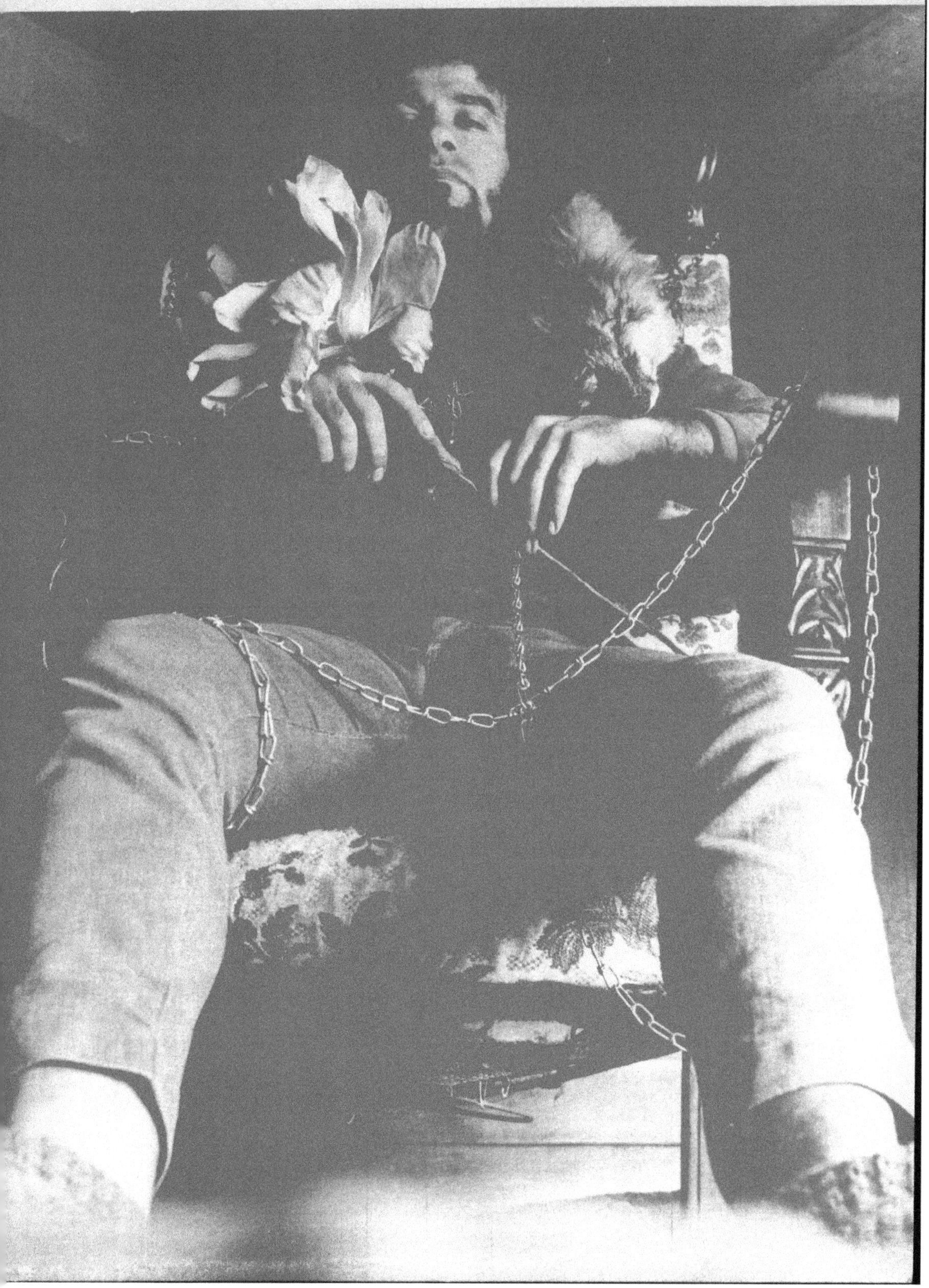

dope sheet

All drugs are dangerous, just like everything else, & just like everything else (almost), the danger lies n ot quite so much in the drugs as in how they are used. Even so, the drug scene – – dealing, being flamboyant & furtive simult- aneously, trying to be HiP, distrusting cops, &c – – is far more dangerous than the drugs themselves. But since we will take drugs, it behooves us to minimize the risks. The traditional & best way to do this is through knowledge. If you know what you're doing & doing it right, it probably won't hurt you.

What acid does is restore the balance of your senses. This can be pretty confusing. Suddenly you can feel & hear & smell & taste as well as you've always been able to see, as well as evolution designed you to, as well as any nat- ural animal. Your brain, used to handling mainly visual data, is suddenly flooded with information from senses it has always up to now pretty much ignored. You change in a flash from a set of eyes mounted in a flesh & blood transport ation device to a Whole Man, which is pretty upsetting at first.

You should direct your trips, most especially your early trips, with this in mind. Although acid has no value in & of itself will not make you good or holy or wise or anything else except high it can be used (& to take it all is to use it) in a valuable way. It can be an educational tool. You can learn something from it.

Arrange to take your trip with someone else (also on acid) who is wiser &/or more experienced than you someone you trust, who should be able to answer whatever questions you may be able to ask, who knows what's happening & what to do about it if something has to be done – – whom you like well enough to share the intimate experience of acid with. A guru.

Avoid crowds until you're used to acid. Crowds can overwhelm you & even set up paranoid reactions in you. Avoid most restaurants & coffeehouses. Avoid people who are not on the trip. All these things can wait until you're at home with acid & know how it works with you. In the yoga of acid you must eventually experience all of there things & more, but that's the third phase of your course, & comes a long time after your earliest trips.

Bathe beforehand, otherwise you're likely to be acutley aware that you haven't. Don't eat for at least four hours beforehand, otherwise you're likely to be acutely aware of the digestive process. Spend at least an hour beforehand relaxing your mind & body & spirit, becoming calm & peaceful, otherwise you're likely to have a troubled trip.

Provide your tripplace with things to touch, to feel, to smell, to taste, to hear, & eventually to do. Things for your expanded senses to experience.

Now comes the most important hour of the trip, the hour before you become high. This hour determines the shape & nature of the trip. I like to consult the I Ching at this time. Cast the oracle & spend that time reading & med- itating on what it says. For me this determines the intellectual & spiritual content of the experience. You should certainly do something analogous to this. Determine the course of your trip while you can, because once you're high you'll be too busy.

When the acid first takes effect, lean back, consciously relax, & let it happen. Do not be afraid.

While you are high use your sense. Give them real workout. Learn yoga & their language. You & the guru you have chosen to travel with can teach you to be real again, undoing The System's years of teaching you to be unreal, un- aware, unconscious, useful only to The System. In this way you can become free, & freedom is what all of this – – acid, Haight/Ashbury, dropping out, the whole bit – – – is all about. Otherwise acid isn't worth breaking the law for.

That's where it's at. Be with a beautiful person in a beautiful place doing beautiful things & being beautiful, & you will have a beautiful trip. Instead of thinking about yourself, be. Be what you are, what the moment dictates, exper- iencing yourself & the world without your intellect

Rest a few days, at least, between trips. It takes an average of three days for your blood chemistry to recover from a trip, & until it does, acid won't have any effect. And you need the rest. Acid trips are more work than most jobs.

Finally, in as tranquil a mood as you can muster, drop the acid. It's good if you can do this with a certain amount of ritual, since the psychedelic experience really is a religious experience. (Any experience that restores you to wholeness is religious, no matter what metaphysic you espouse. Whatever makes you whole again is a true sacrament.)

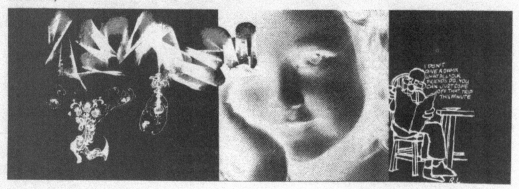

As one of its side effects, acid stimulates the production of adrenaline, to which it is very similar. Fear is what usually stimulates adrenaline production, part of the mechanism by which the animal we are copes with & escapes danger. Now, what makes you human is your forebrain, those enormous frontal lobes, evolution's latest improvement on the original model-T brain that dogs & cats & monkeys have. Your hindbrain, however, is still that same old model-T animal thing, & what it does for you is keep your body running & your basic instincts/emotions going so as to leave your forebrain free for thinking. The hindbrain is an idiot. It equates increased adrenaline secretion with fear, but the equation is circular: fear = adrenaline, thus adrenaline = fear.

What acid does is stimulate adrenaline secretion & keep it stimulated for upwards of eight long hours (usually, in cases of fright, the secretion continues for only a few minutes). This can reduce you to gibbering terror unless you remember (it's easy to remember) that it isn't fear you feel but chemistry. Some people do get horribly frightened, despite the objective fact that there is neither anything to be afraid of nor any real fear. They suffer from an abstract, backwards fear. This is not necessary. Don't do it.

Your mind is yours, & you can do with is just about what you wish. You can remove the fear from the adrenaline simply by knowing that there is no fear & willing yourself to be calm. This leaves you with all that adrenaline floating about in your bloodstream, adding a prolonged adrenaline high to the effects of the acid. Adrenaline minus fear produces euphoria, which is a gas, baby.

Acid is a consciousness-expanding drug & should be used as such. A standard hip error is to devote trips to introspection, which is logically foolish & guaranteed to generate bad trips, at least in the early stages of the acid curriculum. Self-knowledge is even more important than you think it is, but introspection is the last step in the last step in the process of knowing yourself. (Here follows a digression from "A Handbook for Unicorns.")

"The way to know yourself is to know everybody else. You are different. A Martian couldn't tell you & anybody else apart.

"All men are more alike than different. They all have the same long evolution & genetic organization & physical structure, the same neural circuitry, the same kind of brain, the same chemistry, the same needs & desires, the same sensory equipment. We all have more experience in common than otherwise. The same language (way of thinking), the same general childhood history, the same kind of education. We've done the same things, read the same things, heard said eaten touched felt endured suffered craved enjoyed known all the same things, all of us. The differences are almost insignificant, no other race could easily detect them, & they startle us because similarities are invisible.

"Introspection – – delving into your own minute infinity – – is at best a vague adventure. How can you tell what all this subjective & symbolic data means? How can you tell what all this subjective & symbolic data means? How do you know what's real & what's just a subconscious smokescreen? How can you tell when you're fooling yourself?

"But if you first study everbody else & learn the elements of commonality, the billion things all men share alike, introspection becomes practical, because you have established standards for determining reality.

"Otherwise introspection is a solitary vice, a masturbation, a fearsome & unsatisfactory substitute for a real thing. Real people insist on real things."

Acid is only acid, but a full course of trips properly taken will make you a better & freer, more real & loving human being. This seems to take something like five years, but results are visible from the very beginning. (What causes the improvement is not the acid but the trips.)

The least beautiful aspect of acid is the business of acid: dealing. I don't know why, but the acid business is the dirtiest of all the drug industries. There are a spate of honourable dealers, but by & large there more burns short counts, adulterations & frauds in the acid trade than in any other (except, possibly, the methedrine trade, which is notoriously immoral & unethical).

Most acid hereabouts is cut with methedrine. Dealers lie outrageously about dosages, claiming 1000 micrograms for a tab that has less than 250. Other drugs, notably methedrine but sometimes worse are sold as acid. Thousand dollar deals in which somebody runs off with the money are commonplace. It's a dirty business.

The standard dose, worked out the hard way by Timothy Leary & friends, is about 250 micrograms & no matter what the dealer tells you (unless you know him will to be honest, ethical & generally right about such things), that's about how much there is in the usual tab or cap.

If you're having a bad trip, there are several things you can do about it. First of all, stop panicking, relax, breathe slowly & deeply. Will yourself to be calm. Find out what's wrong & correct it if you can, & take care to avoid that next time. Learn from your bad trips, or else stop taking acid.

If you feel you have to teminate the trip, vitamin B3 will bring you down safely. Take five tablets, & if that hasn't worked in 30 minutes, take five more.

Remember, you are under the influence of a drug that will wear off. No bad trips are permanent. (No good ones are, either.) You can get out of a bad trip simply by waiting until you come down, if there's no other way available.

Don't take a bad trip seriously (except to learn from it). It may be distressing, but it is not real. It will go away. You will not go mad or any other such newspaper-bullshit thing. Bad trips are produced by misunderstandings & misinterpretations, not by truths or by anything true. Do not take any serious action on the basis of a bad trip.

It's useless to take more acid after you've become high, because it won't work. You can get the same effect from a saccharine tablet. Don't exceed the standard dosage until you've learned to handle the standard dosage.

Speed kills. It really does. Methedrine, amphetemine &c can & will rot your teeth, freeze your mind & kill your body. The life expectancy of the average speed-freek, from first shot to the morgue, is less than five years. What a drag.

Don't become a dealer. It's habit-forming, messy, unpleasant, dangerous & a drag.

Don't do anything to your body that your body can't veto. No needles. Consider the psychological & symbolic implications of sticking a needle into yourself. Do you really want to do that?

Don't let dope be the only thing you do, or the most important thing in your life. That's the quick way to be bored with having fun, which is a drag.

Be cool.

Chester Anderson

DAVID PHILLIPS & MICHAEL GRAY TALK TO EX RADIO LONDON D.J. JOHN PEEL.

If you take a walk
I'll tax your feet.

The decibel level dropped suddenly in large blocks of flats; housewives stopped frying their Quicky-Snak Cod Pieces; afternoon teenyboppers rose in mid-jerk, and supermarkets fell silent. Only Promethian chords of 'We Shall Overcome' lumbered across the aether from Radio Caroline - but growing fainter and sadder and further away.
The kind of experimental and avante-garde pop music that Peel had been free to play will be particularly hit. We await the over-whelming boredom of Radio 1, putting out an up-tempo "musical accompaniment" to damp and falling Autumn leaves.

Peel does see the Marine Offences Act as a restriction of a basic liberty. He believes that pirates allowed artist and listener an unprecedented release from the demands and limits which The Establishment placed on Pop.

The farmers and the businessmen,
they all did decide.

"I can see some of the arguments for the Bill - I don't know how justified they are - the electronic things, that it interferes with other people's signals and stuff like this. The logical thing for them to do, of course, would have been for them to license the pirate stations and bring them on shore. This is probably entirely naive but the way I look at it, one of the main reasons they closed down the pirates was sour grapes - the fact that they, the Lord Thompsons and such who already control the mass communications media, hadn't thought of it first and therefore it wasn't being run by the people who were safe and on their side. I don't think it matters which party is in office. I don't know whether the Conservative Party, if they get in, will introduce commercial radio as such, but if they do I'm sure it'll be controlled by the people who control everything anyway. I don't know who they are, but there's this great faceless mass of people who seem to watch over everything."

"This new Marine Offences Bill is one of the most terrifying things I've ever read in my entire life and the majority of people don't seem to realise exactly how far-reaching the thing is. I was down at Tiles the other day and the d-j on stage said something about Radio Caroline - and under the Bill he could go to gaol for that. And if you have a Radio Caroline sticker on your car you can go to gaol for that too."

And then the kerosene
Is strapped across their shoulders.

"The majority of people who've been hired for this new thing, Radio 1 - I don't know who they all are, but of the pirate disc-jockeyes - they seem to hire the safe and the pliable ones. You're going to get The Northern Dance Orchestra rendering "See Emily Play" and Harold Smart Swings and stuff like this. I think when it starts off people are going to say 'No'. We've been led to believe we're going to get some thing reasonably like the pirates - whether they were good or bad doesn't really matter here - but that's what's expected; and when it doesn't come along people are going to be very angry."

Please don't wake me
No don't shake me
Leave me where I am
I'm only sleeping.

"But of course British people only seem to be angry for a very short period of time and then they settle back and accept whatever it is that's being thrown at them with great vacant stares on their faces. This is the way that people have become conditioned to react. They get aroused about something and they never stay roused. England's so absurd you can't get angry with it yourself. People seem to be getting progressively more illogical. It's beyond apathy: it's reached some ecstatic new state where there aren't words to describe it.

"In America - which is far from being the ideal country - I worked just outside Los Angeles for a time, and you could pick up something like fifty radio stations; so that regardless of how bizarre your tastes were there'd be something somewhere to accommodate you. That is just not heard of here - and I think people should be angry.

"Mind you, I also worked for KLF, this Gordon McClendon station, and he runs this enormous anti-everything movement on the station. If a song mentions the word Mind that's a Drugs Song and if you mention Skirt well then that's a Sex Song, so the poor guy found himself with an almost entirely instrumental station. I think even 'Tequila' is banned out there (KLF is in Oklahoma) as 'conducive to a permissive attitude to alcoholism'."

The country music station plays soft
But there's nothing, really nothing to turn off.

"And this is more or less the situation here. The BBC is a great quivering mass creeping into the 1940s and out of the 1920s.

"You know I sent them a tape initially and word drifted back to me that they thought my programme was 'conducive to a permissive attitude to drug-taking.' Anyway, later on I went down there and talked with this person - who actually turned out to be quite aware of the things that were going on and it looks as though possibly I might be getting on there after all. The programme I'll be doing is supposed to be the anchor programme of the new service and this bloke wants me to get back to playing the sort of experimental records I was playing on Radio London. He can't start off right away by doing it because the BBC won't let him; so we'll have to build up to it gradually.

"But at the BBC it's so different. There are great crowds of people all around you - girls to put on the records, officials to watch them doing it, producers, programme controllers, shop stewards and all the rest. You need a studio the size of the Festival Hall. The nice thing about Radio London was that you could just sit there on your own out in this rusty boat and play the kind of music you wanted to (well I could anyhow) and people could just let their imaginations run riot. I have this great hang-up about being shy."

Hey, you've got to hide your love away.

"I learnt a lot from the letters I got on the Perfumed Garden. You know, they weren't the 'Dear John, I think you're fab, please send a pic' sort. Basically the music makes the programme and I was fortunate to have the freedom to choose what I wanted to play on London. It wasn't a question of converting people to one particular set of beliefs, either the listeners or other disc-jockeys, but of expanding them and increasing possibilities. This is why it was so valuable, despite the fact that there were some pretty distasteful people involved in Pirate Radio. And the insidious thing about the non-pirate 'professional' d-js is their incredible ignorance. They know very little about the music they're playing and so their picture of what their audience wants is no more than a myth."

Ezra Pound and T.S. Eliot fighting in the captain's tower
While calypso-singers laugh at them and fishermen hold flowers.

Maybe Big L meant lots of money for its American backers, but you could always find a record you actually liked. And when the pirates scratched their armpits, at least you know that it didn't come from the library of Special Effects.
The unofficial censorship that the BBC bureaucracy exerts as corporate scoutmaster will continue its sad-eyed vigilance against the Drug Peril-Sex Peril-Red Conspiracy. Victor Sylvester will creep up on us unawares and bring back Aspidistra Power. Down Your Way the Everready Batteries are going to last a whole lot longer.

"The more the bureaucracy is 'dehumanised', the more completely it suddeeds in eliminating from official business love, hatred, and all purely personal, irrational, and emotional elements which escape calculation." (Max Weber).

NOTHING
is
happening
Mr
Jones...

No one went wild when H. Wilson became our leader. I assume, probably justifiably, that you didn't either. But I entertained hopes, small modest, self-effacing ones. Marginal changes here and there, things would not surely be worse than they had been in the previous wasted years; if no improvement was registered once again the government would be composed of rogues and villains with no attachment to principle. But our new leaders said they were Socialists, and Socialists are good men as we all know.

But nothing got better and everything worse, our new leaders were indeed rogues and villains and not socialists at all. All this was very disillusioning.

We observed from a distance that the nation, according to many reputable newspapers, was undergoing some form of crisis. Fat men with bald heads marched into important offices in Whitehall. Thin men made speeches deploring the deterioration in the quality of our national fibre. Better fibre means perhaps the ability to offer more relevant and purposive help to our allies in their efforts to eliminate unwashed peasants hiding in smelly swamps in various parts of the world. All we have been able to provide so far, however, have been encouraging noises which sounded like so much slobbering on a pair of fat Texan buttocks.

If these people who came to power under the banner of Socialism have in fact proved to be imposters who are they? Agents of the Comintern? the CIA? hirelings of a worldwide Jewish conspiracy? No, I fear, humble Englishmen just like me or even perhaps you. But with a difference - humble Englishmen whose principal aim is the preservation of a number of large smug corporations run by men with names like Chambers, Robens and Beeching. When the Corporation proves inadequate in size a larger one is produced and a new captain of industry is constructed: Lord Melchett and the National Steel Corporation go together like Love and Marriage.

Thus these humble men, with a little help from their friends, have constructed a large edifice known as the National Interest. Is it a small, domed building? A Hyde Park Bog, perhaps with a dash of Albert Memorial? British it may be but it is not the stuff of which Socialism is made.

For there is such a thing as Socialism and it does involve a rather different order of priorities to those of that humble man in number ten. It amounts to more than attacks on small drafty tramp steamers marooned around the British coast crammed with embittered colonials, North Americans and elderly Liverpool Teenagers. OH GOD! the irony of Caroline "exposing" the PRIVATE life of Wilson, as if sweaty fumblings with an elderly secretary could be any more boring than the exposure of his public parts.

What's Socialism? It's NOT succumbing to a grubby Racialist, John Hanson in Rhodesia; and flogging vast quantities of consumer durables to the Union of South Africa; and wining and dining villainous old gangsters from obscure Kingdoms and Sheikdoms in Arabia; and slamming on a pay freeze that differs only from its Tory predecessor in the amount of wool that has been pushed over the eyes of the worker, the supposed Labour Party Folk Hero.

It is in fact the elimination of fat smug corporations. The effects of this kind of action would be considerable and might even enable us to live without the wads of dollars that MAKE life with LBJ the fun it is.

But under this So-called Socialist government it isn't happening.

Indeed, nothing is happening. We are all asleep. Public consciousness was asphyxiated with the second endorsement of Wilson just fifteen months ago and now we dream....in our dream comes nothing but wraiths in the night, the return of the vanquished and almost vanished Tories. No one really wants them, but no one really minds them. They are after all there. Stupid yes, but certainly no more so than their opponents; hypocritical yes, and almost as efficiently, immoral but in the correctly uninteresting way. Turn over in your sleep and there they are.....

Nigel Rourtain

13

Letter from a Greek Prison

As you know, this sad land is censored by the hot-eyed colonels who recently captured it, but I smuggle this random comment from the inside of the slam because they shouldn't escape without having this view of their black deeds exposed. The operating methods of Greek fuzz have always been vile — violent nerve-shattering two-month "interrogations" in the station, mysterious disappearances in the night, sick old junkies hanged by the thumbs, smashed balls — all the insane trappings of the police state.

Once I lived half a year in a pretrial prison and saw maybe 200 accused go to court without a single not-guilty decision. They have it as they want it, apparently even the judges and juries are terrified. Foreigners inhale it too, the favourite tactic being to take a "confession" written in Greek, which said tourist can't read, then fill it up with fuzzy fantasies and trick or beat a signature out of the man who then gets convicted of half the unsolved crimes in the country and doesn't even know what they are.

Especially dangerous for heads here, as Athens is full of multilingual stooges, often bearded and hip-sounding, who seduce tourists to push or score or turn on, then bring a fuzz-trap to the rendezvous. Courts not particular here, any old piece of evidence will do the job. Greek prisons must have the highest percentage of foreigners of any country in the world. I suppose these dirty fuzz aren't any sicker than anybody else's cops but here they're given more freedom to act out their psychosis by the military-monarchy-church-businessman syndrome which rules the place and protects its interests by holding the numbed masses in tightest fear and ignorance.

Same old story but worse here, as this has always been one of the world's most selfish oligarchies, although in places like Dubuque, El Paso and the Pentagon it's known as one of the lucky democracies American military aid has saved from the dirty Reds. Fuck the ghost of John Foster Dulles. The rifles marching around these prison walls are American and if the CIA didn't trigger this coup then at least it's grateful, for the election it prevented would have been won by the Papandreou family which threatened to do such dirty commie tricks as build some schools, make the obscene-rich pay taxes, castrate the massive police force throw the king out of politics and build a couple of factories. Sad, sad affair, the demise of the people's choice, the death of the Left and the Center, too.

NAILED TO THE CROSS

An old lifer cornered me in the toilet the other day and whispered, "Papandreou went forward carrying the cross and the fascists nailed him too it. Tell that to the good people in your country if you can find any." So I found you and I tell you.

So now we have the military apparatus on top of the police apparatus, operating their own courts and prosecuting for thought-crimes, a true 20th century witch-hunt. This enormous medieval slam is loaded with the results of this new menace. A student bows before a public picture of the king and says. "We're lucky to have such a fine king," but the court reads his mind, says he was being sarcastic and pays five years upon his young soul. Another spends the night at his brother's house without the permission of the government gets three years, his brother disappears into exile. Those stories are endless, each sicker than the last, the latest chapter of Kafka.

Behind much of this is a system of false witnesses for this is a land where families quarrel and don't speak for generations, a bitter hung-up mentality full of mystical fuck-hatreds, the home of revenge and duplicity and this new dictatorship brings out the rat in everybody. The military, like the fuzz, don't care; they need victims and when they don't exist they'll create them.

So it becomes a completely schizophrenic nation where almost nobody is speaking or behaving as he wishes, a country of madmen whose appearance is the only real and constant concern, words mean absolutely nothing, truth is death and therefore it is dead. Martial music and strident speeches rip out of the loudspeakers, military genius everywhere, including such gems as "We're saving you from Communism, Fascism and Nazism", whatever that means, and "Karl Marx was a stupid pig". Wow.

And these prisons are a long stepdown from Sing Sing. They're rat-infested and dark, totally without heat in the bitter winters, twenty-five crowded into stone rooms, hardly any food or medical care, no schools sports workshops or libraries. Nothing. The all-consuming question is the simple one of survival and by no means all can answer it.

PRISONS ARE SEXY

as to what happens here, have explained that aspect elsewhere but I tell you that prisons are among the sexiest places on earth, beginning with the goonie-con relationship. Often ask the uniformed performers why they want to spend their lives pushing helpless men around and locking them in cells and if I get an intelligent reply they sort of say, "Because it takes a MAN to do it", so I say, "If this makes you a MAN, then we must be less than men so what are we, WOMEN or something?", and they can't follow it, but what it really makes us is eunuchs, less than men because we are castrated, and the power they hold over us, the contempt they have for us, the self-esteem they derive from our plight is essentially due to the fact that they are heterosexual pricks and we do not. This difference manifests itself in all phases of the dance and dialogue. It can be resisted, but at great cost.

What is actually demanded is that you repent your big crime, and that you quite literally fall into some sort of love with your keepers. This is why narcotics visions have so much friction in all prisons and why they're so despised. They can never repent their deeds because they know very well they've done nothing wrong (except some junkies who feel they've sinned against themselves) and thus they can only feel contempt or pity for their keepers which drives said keepers straight up the wall.

And the whole concept of "rehabilitation" is just as phony here as it is everywhere, for the qualities everybody's schoolteacher said we were supposed to have — courage, conviction, creativity etc. — are the same qualities which will get you completely burned in here. What they want to turn out of here are a bunch of walking zombies, too down and terrified to do anything but obey even the dumbest orders for the rest of their petty lives, a servile army of the spiritually lobotomized. Anyway I've been denied parole three times and

it's clear I'm never going to get it, which is encouraging. Let's fill all the dungeons in the world up with dirt and grow sacred mushrooms in them.

ARROGANT COLONELS

So these arrogant colonels are shamelessly determined to convert all the people into miniature reflections of their one-minded selves, to "purify" Greece as they say. This means to eliminate whatever they cannot understand, which is everything that doesn't think their simple thoughts and fall in love with their brass and bearing, and it's clear that nothing here can stop them. They can only be toppled from outside, by a big drop in tourist support (already happening) and the frequent smashing of their embassy windows, which wounds them deeply.

People can play the tourist here if they wish, but they play it at their deadly peril and every coin dropped here helps to perpetuate this black jazz. I've seen the blood they spill, plenty of it, it's red and it runs.

Which brings up to the talking butterfly which once made it into this cave and told me it is aerodynamically capable of flying as straight and efficiently as an arrow, but it makes it around zit-flut-flit because it feels like it, which seems to be one of the more important things learned in this long walk into strange.

Time here in its mysterious vortex stretches folds and snaps like the turned-on mind that it is, but the final realization is that eternity plus or minus a few years still equals eternity, so nothing is finally altered. It is truly possible to dance everywhere, even in the far reaches of Lost. Your news from the outer world, your talk of the vast turn-on and the worldwide defiance of of the forces of destruction gives proof that the countless casualties paying the price in faceless prisons are being revenged in the only way we care about: we continue to exist, and we multiply.

With love, peace and music.

(Name Withheld)

15

JAGGER SAGA

R.COBB

EVERYTHING Say Kelm writes (144) about New York newspapermen is doubly true about the Fleet Street veterans who, if anything, can be more ingeniously vicious than their Manhattan counterparts. The latest example of this is what one might have called the Mick Jagger Saga had it not broadened subsequently into The Drug Story.

As you might remember, it was a newspaper that began it – he smutty-minded, holier-than-thou News of the World (everybody's purveyor of the week's dirt, disguised-as-crime) which ran allegedly libellous accusations against Jagger's drug habits and then, when all went with a libel suit, sent a police posse out to a party the Rolling Stones were giving in a private house.

Leaving aside the suggestion that the newspaper might have blamed the hash that it's still undeniable that a newspaper went much further than merely reporting was subsequently found – a suggestion that can never be proved for certain – the news; it actually created the news it then reported. This is a venerable practise among the less-(principled) papers and tends to be copied by All the papers if only in self-defence.

"FOLLOW MICK JAGGER"

Let us speculate on what happened next. In a dozen news rooms an editor gave his instructions: Follow Mick Jagger.

Now a reporter sent out on a story, like most mortals in any job, is determined to come up with something. To start with he wouldn't keep his job for long if he didn't and, by no means secondly, he had to justify all those exorbitant expenses.

The stringer in Dublin who sees Jagger turn up at a party won't be paid much for reporting his item. But there's a lot more space to be gained in the Daily Mirror by pretending that Jagger and his girl were thrown out of the party and so, not very mysteriously, that's what the story becomes. Makes no difference that no decent people know (and the quotes) are altered to fit, with a bit of drama now and for Dublin readers (and libel) no celebrities are offered to it.

FLEET ST.

[signature] Tomp

Less than 24 hours later Mick Jagger and his girl arrive back home at London airport and, what do you know? All kinds of trouble with taxi drivers, some who harass the moral as always that they wouldn't have such such in hair cars, newspapers run their second (sensation) story in as many days and nobody minds that they might be their fiance in the paper. If they adopted certain moralistic postures and were quoted as such for all their friends to read.

"SO-CALLED POLLS"

Much the same type of thing seems to be happening. Most of these mysterious public opinion polls" that have been printed in such papers as the Daily Mail and Daily Telegraph in the past few weeks. Teenagers, it now appears from these so-called polls, don't really want pot legalized at all. In fact, he teenagers interviewed are apparently so busy helping old people to repaint their homes, planting potatoes on local allotments and assisting pensioners across the street, when they have no time for such skullduggery at all. Which is probably why, when asked their reasons for participating in such soundly helpful practises they reply

(To quote "actual phrases"): "it's something to do"; "it's better than laying about".

"I fills in the time".

These are the answers, mark you, of kids who DON'T smoke pot or drop acid and, if we're to believe 'the propaganda, don't even want other teenagers to have the right to do so. So much for the argument that soft drugs are responsible for kids' lack of drive and sense of purpose these days.

The fact of the matter is that we all rely on polls to bolster our own beliefs and prejudices. But most polls are nonsense, the real evidence known to be rigged even by the people who prepare it. Teenagers could be asked whether they smoke pot either by people of their own kind, in relaxed surroundings, or they could be cross-questioned in their own homes with members of their family present by people by bowler-hatted, briefcase-carrying representatives of the Daily Telegraph. It is not hard to tell which way the Telegraph poll was compiled in neither probe.

It is possible that its data for the Daily Telegraph poll was compiled in neither ways, but certainly the latter method is the more likely.

—J.W.

In Manhattan newspaper (and weekly magazine shops you'll find veterans who spit on their work and automatically say that the important veterans who spit on their work and face of today's newspaper is to provide the wrapper for a smelly flounder tomorrow. The movie-portraits are for real, chemists no one is more snottily, and superficially cynical about both reality and writing than the old-time news alcoholic, security-obsessed news paper grandad whom you'll run into on the overnight rewrite desk of a metropolitan paper. The idea that they might be front-runners, standing and interpreting reality as it broke before their eyes would have been a joke in the majority of these put-down experts who envied the stars on the world stage that they covered but never perceived that they themselves were in the position to make history and not merely record it.

But underneath the cocked fedora and the rest of the so-called glamor crest you could find a man who thought of himself as a failure by the worldly standards drummed in to his being by his work, money achievement and status.

LAING

Much has been written on the oligarchic aspects or organisations but next to nothing on the same features of "non-organisations". What follows is a comment on the non-organisation centering around R.D. Laing and on what happens in the social transformation of his ideas. Laing's work which is a moving protest on the alienating characteristics of institutionalised socialisation seems to have provided little resistance to the emergence of those very same tendencies in the resocialisation of his cult of followers.

Laing probably realises this only too well. "We are born into a world where alienation awaits us. We are potentially men, but in an alienated state, and this state is not simply a natural system. Alienation as our present destiny is achieved only by outrageous violence perpetrated by human beings on human beings". And then, "Sometimes it seems that it is not possible to do more than reflect the decay around and within us, than sing sad and bitter songs of disillusion and defeat".

The disillusion and defeat that I feel about the Laing movement (but not with him or his words) stems from a dilemma facing any liberating movement; The dilemma as Gene Debs the American socialist put it, "If you are looking for a Moses to lead you out of the capitalist wilderness, you will stay right where youare. I would not lead you into the promised land ... because if I can lead you in, others can lead you out.

The point is that when men are dependent on leadership for their liberation they're caught before they even start. The paradox is that in order to become independent through the action of a movement you have to be independent to begin with.

This is highly relevant to-day when for argument's sake we can say there are two opposed models of revolutionary or underground movement. We can characterise this duality as it exists in the present world in several ways; Marxists versus anarchists, activists versus dropouts, Leninists versus acid heads, guerrillas versus diggers, material versus spiritual, external versus internal, etc., This dichotomy also parallels that between the affluent societies and the "Third World".

What Laing is trying to do is have afoot in both camps. And this is the importance of his message. Whether he will end up with the best or the worst of two worlds is another question. One side is for freedom and the other side is for movement. Do you have to choose one or the other or can you have both?

The concern for individual freedom which was once the monopoly of anarchist theory has now become subject to the efforts of an existentialist anti-psychiatry (R.D. Laing, David Cooper and Frank Atkin in this country) and in a different sort of way, the acid head. Liberation - in the individual-psychological sense which was Laing's first concern - involved the study of the obstacles in interpersonal relationships which resulted in the diffusion and disintegration of one's wholeness resulting in the label "schizophrenia". Like the acid merchants this was a concern with "freeing the mind", but unlike them it was also a critique of alienated society - not so much a sick or hung up society but one of which you, whether you like it or not, are a part. And if you don't get it before it gets you, brother, then you're cooked. But how can you get it before it gets you when you are born into it?
In many ways Laing has moved on from a study of the individual in small groups and is now dealing with the question of society itself, with emphasis on what is to be done right now rather than a passive study of what has been going on. This transformation from the analytic critique to the prescriptive formula and the outwinding from the individual to the social system cannot be said to be a success so far. The reasons for this lie in the metaphysical nature of his concepts and their metamorphosis into a group culture.

The concepts of alienation, identity and self, for example, are not only inherently ambiguous but find their concrete application in a bewildering multitude of different states. If we try to pin

down exactly what someone means when they use a concept like alienation we find it almost impossible because the term has a sneaky way of eluding any fixed categories. For instance, it is common practice to describe alienation in terms of powerlessness isolation, meaninglessness and self-estrangement. But when we try to think of some concrete particular situation in which any or all of these things are NOT present we find we can't. This is because alienation is as multidimensional as the whole spectrum of any possible human experience.

Another, puzzling thing has been the literal acceptance of Laing's descriptions as though they were theories. Theories, I would submit, are propositions which have a general reference, are empirically grounded and contain implicit or explicit causal connections which can be tested. In contrast to this Laing's network of statements are, at their precise best, mapping strategies which only occasionally embody a suggestion of where to look for connections.

The real bite comes when we examine what happens to these ideas when they become part of a group ethos. I think it fair to suggest that Laing's work has become alienated over and against him. While he is an advocate of internal and external prescriptions for revolution (let us say an "acid-marxist") he has become a leader, if only passively. Now while leaders by definition only exist in conjunction with followers the tragedy of this particular dialectic is that followers seem to need and generate leaders. Charisma for example, would seem to be as much a property of prophets as a property of those who project it onto the prophet and the phenomenon of power is also the phenomenon of compliance.

What we should try to understand are the conditions which have led to and perpetrate this state of affairs. Why is it that a brilliant set of speculations on "schizophrenia" has achieved the social configuration of a messianic movement? And what is more a movement that is retreating hot foot into irrationality and a mystification almost as great as that it condemns.

Part of the answere, in psychological terms at least, can be found in Laing's work itself. It starts off from the notion of the social origin of the self (you are what certain significant other people think you are) and the postulated effect of one sort of limitation on personal development. Somewhere there is a "real you", a non-alienated you, awaiting its existential birth, but the others in your life are frantically determining what you shall become instead. The emergence of this true self only occurs in a situation we shall call freedom. But the catch is not only that you are fighting a losing battle in a war with others who have completely lost themselves in the same process, but that in a very meaningful way you need them and are dependent on them.

To understand the implications of all this for the particular context in which the Laingians exist one can start first of all by taking is issue with the way a group, their group, mangles ideas. One example is their theme of "phenomenonology" - a general obscurantism which serves to control the group in the same way as Marx discussed ideaology. In this case, however, the control is initiated by the controlled. For our purposes, phenomenology is the direct and spontaneous subjective experience of "a totality" in an anti-analytical way.

To begin with a totality is defined and selected by one's prior experience which determines the parts and their patterning from an infinatude of possible totalities.

Secondly this process of selection and definition is dependent on an intervening grid of concepts which the Laingians like anybody else (must) allow to stand between them and their field.

Now the important point is that the Laingians delude themselves into thinking that they take this intervention into account by their talk of meta-levels of perception of on-going processes since each meta-level involves its own intervening concepts. They allow for this intervention only in the formal sense of not denying its general existence.

Michael Tausig

17

UNDERGROUND TELEVISION

The next art form scheduled for liberation is television. Long a slave of film, this workhorse medium is beginning to find its wings.

"As collage replaced oil paint, the cathode tube will replace the canvas." These are the words of Nam June Paik, a Korean artist living in New York who has become the prophet of The New Television.

Paik uses direct electronic manipulation to produce distorted television images, some surrealistic and some abstract. He may adjust the interior mechanism of the set so that it shows a garbled but pleasing picture. Or he may use a powerful electro-magnet to interefer with the cathode ray beam of the television tube, making "crazed" electrons line up in op-art-like force-field patterns across the picture tube.

Potentially, the main instrument of The New Television is the videotape recorder. This is an instrument with which the artist can work and rework his material, instantly replaying what he has done, collecting images from various visual sources (commercial television, film, magazines) or producing his own live. Unlike film it allows him to be free from censorship. He can put anything he wants on tape. There's no Kodak Labs to return blank film if they disapprove. Making a videotape can be as private as writing a poem or painting a picture.

Television is like film, but it is not film. Film is light moderated by shadow, and the texture is of thousands of tiny grains. Television is florescent light, and the texture is of hundreds of horizontal lines. The quality of the image is different. The quality of the television image is of immediacy, and never of immediacy, and never of spectacle (film); of flow, and never of stability (film). With its electric presence, it is the medium of our time.

Few artists are using television at present. It is more expensive to work with than film right now. Presumably it can be dangerous without some electronic knowledge. But many artists are making plans for using television, and the cost of videotape recorders is coming down in a hurry. An equipment salesmen here on the West Coast told me there may be a $100 recorder by 1975.

Meanwhile a sort of highclub in New York has already started using videotape for "underground television." People pay $1.75 to see a private hour videotape. Some of this is described as looking like a "psychedelic 'Today Show' ".

Sheldon Renan

author of the forthcoming
"An Introduction to the American Underground Film"
(Dutton Paperback, $1.95)

Hmm four in the morning and it's my birthday, thirty-one or fifteenth same thing. Number one squaw has folded her tent and silently stolen away leaving the aura of a vanishing Hitchcock flavoring under my thumb. We had some fresh orange juice at the air terminal, and costume changes, and Dinner under the clock at The Big A (Alvaro's) with a Medicine bag with a comb in it and my oldest friend who filmed it all. I powdered her nose. and then the Hilton to bring the new day in. She's a crazy tearaway heiress on her way to being a boss woman. It's down to me.

Surrealist pillow 1500 words and PAUL BUTTERFIELD BLUES BAND cooking taking me back to Chicago and Muddy Waters sipping an Old Fitz and coke. "Those kids over there sing from the heart" he says about this scene here. Small world. I'm going home I was born there. Lenny lives. All the spirits are out. THINK.

Those American cats that blew in last month weren't kidding about there being about twenty people in this own and papa's got a brand new bag. To bridge the gap between acting and expression. Whatever happened to strolling players actors are getting so hung up with the career thing they've forgotten what it's all about. They're playing parts or something dumb. Even the best ones are off playing that stale eight-note staccato bebop for a price. Pawns n other peoples' fantasys. Godard has some very hip things to say about that scene. And when I'm really cookin' out here in life almost in anguish and tongue firmly in cheek I scream "where are the cameras NOW?"

Movies are like five years behind fashion and pop and here I am a cinema child trying to freak out. And hese young musician image beautiful people are going to replace actors, because they're the true expressionists. Coltrane lives. It's not easy. Gonna carry a   camera fast draw one and everybody works.

TAKE YOUR COAT OFF   AND STAY FOR A   WHILE

reakout

ook at that stupid girl.
ng a good Christian mean. Let
st stone. It is now time for the
e third eyes floating around.
ws on the box They got their
olutionized mayhem. They
my neighbor next door has a gazebo
't Brian Jones too much man? And
Keith Richard and the backing voices on
aying light years and back. Bird is a pop

FLIGHT 505. What does
he that is without sin jail the
moment of truth. and all of
Joe and Mike.   It's all bad
Biafran race riot stateside cultural
won't give Mick any privacy.
meditation room in his back yard.
the Baghdad. And Michael Cooper
"We Love You". Jimi Hendricks
star.. And big bob, and the flower children singing

the subway and Huntington losing three tanners in the phone box. What's happening in China today

Paisley Doctor robert. JobtimeHigh and Dry. Carruthers M15, must get that together, Scots Dumfries fany of disguises. Africa Brass. Nelson Algren in the neon wilderness. "the punks just squawkin' cause his knees are aking" applies to this scene. Lucy in the skies with Diamonds and the burning of the midnight lamp, the moving ger writes the singer not the song, the songer not the sing. Breakfast at the Maze. Oxygen at Harrods Senior Service

saw a film today in one of those moseleums called the a.b.c. and even the kids were bored. and the scene anges. simone and marike and apple juice capes. brian and suki back from marbella, olympic recording, and henetta may be pregnant walkin' blues. daddy walsh with two godparents for his new ariel ring a ding ding purple tangersnowflake eleven and the jolly giant. if i only had one hour for every second boy, would i cook. who wants yester-'s papers? just take it or leave it, it's just my liiiife   own up

and christine had the word, looking as beautiful talking about the new toppling. groucho marz. caramel the ment you start playing the game that's the moment you have to be one step ahead of the game and it's called being n.   who's been sleeping here. are you experienced?   claire de loon.
And isn't Richard Harris too much. Ian keeps burning just keeping up the beat. ABRACADABRA, and the eet sensation of getting it together with the help of my friend stargazers. Implosion

                              Ben Carruthers

smalls

OZ ADVERTISING: SMALLS. 1s. per word.
1/6d. semi display. 2/6d. box no.
DISPLAY: £65 page. £35 half page. £2-10s. column inch.

SHORTCOMINGS?

Prolong the pleasure of intercourse with Suifan's 'Kwang Tze' Solution. This Chinese preparation is specially beneficial to men who suffer from premature ejaculation, and is Guaranteed to end mutual frustration and bring satisfaction to both partners. The Suifan's 'Kwang Tze' Solution is completely safe and reliable, as stated in Government Certificate supplied with each bottle.

Special Offer:
To prove our claim we will send you by return—and in complete confidence—a bottle of the 'Kwang Tze' Solution for only 2 Gns.

Order Direct from Sole Distributors:
Blacks International,
Suite A,
24, Cranbourn Street,
Leicester Square,
London, W.C.2.
Please Cross Cheques & P.O. & Payable to: Blacks International.

BOOKS FOR KINKS AND KICKS. Candid, Exciting, and Erotic.
Send S.A.E. for comprehensive lists.
"Danjac" 50, Parsons Green Lane, S.W.6.
Telephone REN 2871. Evenings REN 3911.

DUREX GOSSAMER. 7/6 per doz. Post Free.
Tit-Bits, 709, Fulham Road, S.W.6.

PREGNANCY TEST. £2. Inquiries: Bell Jenkins Laboratories; Charlotte Street;. Portsmouth (23366)

FOR ALL **transport** PROBLEMS
REMOVALS, DELIVERIES, ETC.
DORMOBILES WITH HELPFUL WORKING DRIVERS.

taximoves GULLIVER 8923

APARTMENT IN GREENWICH VILLAGE
Available on part-time sublease. Ideal for airline pilot/steward making frequent trips accro across Atlantic. Or will swap for few months each year for similar accomodation in London. Write Wilcook, 26 Perry Street, New York 10014

SILVER RINGS..
TURKISH TRICK RINGS.............from 19s
FRIENDSHIP SICK RINGS...........from 26s
SEMIPRECIOUS STONES.............from 75s
VICTORIANA BARRELS..............from 84s

Also/ Hand made & to order MOD
WEDDING OR ENGAGE RINGS 10% 'off for two'

ADMIRAL'S EYE DESIGNCRAFT
32 ST. MARTIN'S LANE WC2 (COV 1742)

Uninhibited performers wanted for 'The Troupe', new improvisation ensemble. Workshop sessions beginning soon. Contact Neil Hornick, 101 Constantine Road, N.W.3.

For light removals Dormobiles with helpful working drivers HAM 1466 or HAM 6351 Please quote this advert

come Underwater
DREAMING IN A DANDY FASHIONS
SUIT. 161, Kings Road London, S.W.3.
Telephone FLA 6851

CONFIDENTIAL ADVICE on the Pill for all women everywhere. Write Step One Ltd (O) 93, Regent St. W.1. (SAE) or telephone 01-622-7815

'You are invited to become a member of'

C.M.C.
Facilities include:—
Substantial discount on clothes, etc
FREE use of accomodation address, same day forwarding service
FREE use of PEN PAL register
FREE use of HOLIDAY register
Members only—CMCN (Naturists)
Send for detailed Brochure (8d in stamps please) to Dept 03, C.M.C., 14 Alexandra Road, Clacton-on-Sea. Essex

'XTRAORDINARILY TALL beautiful, Anglophilic flowergirl sought by ancient nondescript (30's, salubrious, undeteriorated, non-indolent. Intentions : occasional scene-making. BOX F1.

'MOSLEY - Right or Wrong?'. 300 questions answered. 3/6 (including postage) 15 Garston Lane, WATFORD, HERTS.

You've heard all about it.
NOW HERE IT IS :
Super Art Tattoo the rage of the Continent & USA. Card contains a dozen multi-coloured, assorted, waterproof tattoos. (They remove with nail polish remover). Available only from :
ART TATTOO DEPARTMENT (LO)
88-90 Hatton Garden, London, E.C.1.

Turn on/Tune in/drop us a fiver for a hot line to infinity/ journey through the incredible landscapes of your mind/ kaleidoscopic moving changing image on which your mind projects its own patterns/ stun yourself & astonish friends

This light machine is designed for easy operation and personal adaption/ works in rooms of all sizes – with full instructions.
SEND CHEQUE/POSTAL ORDER FOR 5gns plus 5/- post & packaging with full postal address to:
ISETCO   13 Miranda Road LONDON N.19.

---

by RAYMOND DURGNAT 45s

FILMS & FEELINGS
by RAYMOND DURGNAT 45s

FILMS & FEELINGS
by RAYMOND DURGNAT 45s

FILMS & FEELINGS
by RAYMOND DURGNAT 45s

FILMS AND FEELINGS
by Raymond Durgnat

Not the least difficulty faced by a writer on the cinema is that the medium he confronts is a hybrid of theatrical, visual and literary forms. All too often those who understand aesthetic theory dismiss the different tastes of most cinemagoers, and those who understand their tastes have themselves little taste for aesthetic theory. Through close attention to details of style and content alike in films which range from Cocteau's 'Orphée' to Westerns like 'Ride Lonesome', Mr Durgnat attempts to establish a common 'sphere of experience' from which to approach some of the aesthetic problems posed by cinema as an art-form. With 30 photographs. 45s

FABER & FABER LTD
24 Russell Square WC1

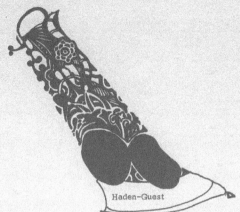

Haden-Guest

"So I'm back in business" says Maurice Girodias "Getting my Dirty Books out again at last - ".

He raises the spectre of a smile. Girodias has the wan, suffering look of a baroque saint, and seems elegantly weary as a diplomat who has spent a lifetime arguing at the Geneva Disarmament Conference. He is the greatest pornographer in the world, the single most dedicated provider of sexual delicatessen for the Anglo-Saxon mental meat-market. He is now to be canonised in the first big-budget Dirty Movie.

"Girodias" says Mel Fishman "was the First Man on the Underground". Fishman is a Californian with a satyr beard, and is planning to make the first mass-audience blue film. The script is by Stephen Schneck, a not-so-underground novelist, and is being called The Olympia Reader, and it was Girodias' Olympia Press in Paris - when Paris was still The City of Light. Remember? - which brought the waiting world Jean Genet, Henry Miller, Burroughs' Naked Lunch, Nabokov's Lolita, Donleavy's The Ginger Man, Candy, a homosexual number by Jean Cocteau, and a great quantity of delicious, untalented, hard-core porn.

"And now we are republishing. In New York" says Girodias, who is holed up at the Chelsea Hotel (favourite holing-up place for the more Established Avant-Garde, ever since Thomas Wolfe raved there, Brendan Behan had DT's there, and Dylan Thomas went into a coma there. Now Arthur Miller lives there. Which isn't the same thing, really). "First I bring out The Travellers Companion " - and these were the green covers, as internationally recognisable an image as a Coke top - "No, I never liked that green colour myself ... Perhaps they should shoot this film in green? Then in October I bring out the Ophelia Series. This will be cheaper, in every sense of the word. In Paris we had many series that started with the letter 'O'. It is the most significant letter in pornography.

"The first book will be Stradella" - and this, I recall from pubertal reading, is a good meaty stretch of thrashing thighs - "I own the rights on all my books, but always there is trouble with writers. The moment their book does well, they see that they can make more money on the straight market. All except Bill Burroughs. Having been through that junkie thing, he doesn't seem to mind ...

"But Nabokov! He pretends that when he sent me Lolita, he did not know that I was a publisher of what he calls 'obscene novelettes'. I had already brought out Sam Beckett's Watt. And, anyway, people attack me for publishing obscenity for obscenity's sake. So what. I admit it? What's wrong with that? What

are these analytical standards? Isn't this the worst form of hypocrisy?" Certainly Girodias is an ambiguous figure. Half hustler, and half freedom-fighter; impelled by a drive to make money - "Why is publishing pornography different from other publishing? They think they can treat me like a convicted criminal. It's a business" - but impelled by an equally urgent drive to extend the frontiers of taste, and, in fact, time and time again losing all his loot through acts of wilful defiance - ("Maurice Girodias" an unusually tedious Parisian poet intoned at me once "Will Always Go Too Far").

Girodias is now forty-eight. While he was operating in Paris, it seemed as if the heady mood of the thirties still hung over that moribund capital. The French Law disapproves of headiness, in any form. They busted him. Girodias started a club, a multi-layer cake of a place, including bars, sitaround places, an avant-garde theatre - it was, in fact, a fun palace, such as Joan Littlewood and John Calder never seem to get around to starting - but the theatre put on a production of De Sade. So that was busted too.

So he moves to Denmark. And the Danish Police, who have never taken it into their Viking minds to bother about the printed word before, bust his printing-press. So he hires a barge and send it across to England, loaded to the gunwales with sex books. Unprecedentedly, the barge sinks. Finally, he comes over to set up in London ("The Permissive Society", if you have been following the press), and he meets some beautiful people, publishers with thick, soft suits, and great affluent smiles, like the cat that got the cream ... They set up to acquire his rights - "And now" says the most fatly affluent, amiably ... "Now we want to drop the Dirty Books Image ¦.".

So now New York, and hoping for the best. Girodias sits in Fishman's suite in the London Hilton, and sips a Pouilly Fuisse moodily - "A recent vintage. But good" - while Mike Wilson, who has been working on Science Fiction with Stanley Kubrick, plays some sitar, Fishman sends down for some hamburgers, and explains about the movie ... which is to be, well, partly biographical, but, interleaved, With fantasies. And frank, all so frank, no nonsense - The public is ready for Real Blue Movies, of a studio excellence, isn't it? Girodias looks a bit puzzled, and makes a telephone call to a lady in Paris. "The film" explains Fishman "Will be screened at selected cinemas, like the Plaza in New York, or even better, the Rivoli ... "And there will be special times, like in the theatre, except there will be effects impossible to duplicate in the theatre. Will it be illegal? "No, of course not ... and kids? Kids shouldn't be up that late anyway." Girodias is still puzzled, but quiescent. Blue Movies aren't really his scene. His scene is Dirty Books. He telephones New York ...

THE PORNBOOKER

Anthony Burgess

Rosetalk

Hippie language is, in terms of the English-speaking community and even beyond, pretty well universal. There are, however and inevitably, local variants. The following are some of the latest in-terms or endoglosses used in London, S.W.1.

arc, to	To ascend the psychodelic curve (NB: psychedelic is a false spelling) that culminates in the definitive vision.
boncum	Originally bum-come but, by assimilation, transformed into a form that comes off the tongue more easily. To attain an orgasm (both sexes) that does not involve the grosser forms of coition. As noun: such an orgasm.
brell	The quiet note of jubilation sounded in gentle orgasm.
chrom	Colour content of a psychodelic vision.
death, the	Police or other repressive forces of the community.
droll	Not funny but frightening - like the utterances of the enemy.
dustbowl	A pipe used for smoking marijuana.
dwellsell	A cell where several hippies live but where also supplies may be obtained.
epileap	To achieve the destination of a trip.
for cough	Clearly enunciated, with the accompanying indication of something harmless - like a beer or cigarette, this can be used as a gentle rebuke to the enquiring fuzz.
fistular	Used with some such term as group or force, is signifies the police. Evidently a compound of fist and the ular of constabulary, ular also being the Malay word for snake. And the whole word connotes a disease.
greenland	The psychodelic visionary world. Also just THE LAND.
hotpot	A Liverpool importation. Marijuana that is in danger of confiscation.
itching	In need of marijuana.
jug	The head (presumably as a receptable for the wine of visions).
knowledge, have	A Biblical revival, and none the worse for that. To indulge in pre-coital sex. Best used in the expression of a gentle wish: "I'd like to have knowledge of you".
lippy	A reefer.
long trail	A trip embarked on in solitude.
long lie	The sexual act when deliberate techniques of prolongation are used.
lubber	The female breast.
mist	Pot when alight.
notch	For beginners, a unit of psychodelic experience.
notchy	The night (from the Russian?)
ochre	Marijuana
presentation	A trip (perhaps an attempt to translate the German hippies' Vorstellung).
roseboys, rosegirls	British flower-children. Thus, ROSEGARDEN: a place of meeting.
tramlined	Hooked on hard drugs.
U-tube	The brain as a thoroughfare for trips. (Perhaps from Underground and its popular synonym tube).
way-yay-hay	A rosegirl's cry of jubilation (this seems to be derived from Pitman's Shorthand Manual).

"We're citizens of a new enlightened age
We're all revolutionararies nowdays"   (Coulmier   Marat/Sade)

We believe a lot of lies. We like to put myths between ourselves and what could be. So we convince ourselves that
David Frost has no talent and that Katherine Whitehorne is a
raving nymph and that the queen loves her Corgis more than
Prince Phillip. The myths exist as obituaries of our achievement. Thus a lot of people, who for a long time thought that
a revolution would be a good idea are announcing that the
Hippies have the modern state on its knees. The world's
turned on; the lockstepped chessgames of the USA's iron and
steel insanity is defeated by our heads; its the psychedelic
storming of the Winter Palace; Dictatorship of the Chemical
Provotariate. The grownup revolutionaries have seized on
Flower Power like they used to get worked up about CND in the
days that the better educated debs patronised the Aldermaston
Marches. Now it's UFO between Finishing School and Merchant
Banker.

Which is a pity. Because at the moment the hippies in England
represent about as powerful challenge to the power of the state
as the people who put foreign coins in their gas meters. Alice
Bacon's hairdresser is nearer to the counsels of state. For
without a fundamental change in the economic system which at
present controls our societies every dimension, the hippies will
be forced to live like jackals; first to bowdlerise their own
experience to make it intelligible, then, very soon, to make it
commercial. Hippies without radical social forms like the
Diggers and the Communes are unable to float off the surface of
the society from which it derives its meaning.

What happens instead is that hippies confuse alienation from
society with influence over it, ending in formal demonstrations
of their own impotence. Thus the first Love In in the Golden
Gate Park was in 10 months debased to the Ally Pally "Love In"
(£1 a Head) making two crooks, £5,000, and a lot of people very
unlovely. Leary begins as the Johny Appleseed of the Mind and,
like Davy Crockett, ends up in Disneyland with blue rinse coach
tours block booking for the Reincarnation of the Buddha at $4.50.
The Dialectics of Liberation end as a cultural bay of pigs; a
high cultural massage leaving the demystifiers clambering about
in a complicated scaffold of language and assumptions which
had become a new orthodoxy. Its recommendations as soggy as
cornflakes in hot milk; as respectable as G Plan. So even the
things we control, a fairly pathetic list to begin with, the
boutiques, head shops, clubs and light shops are forced to
become pushy and ugly. Punchups at UFO, turnstiles at the
Love In's, the mini cooper people now in transfers and beads
but still the frantic pleasures of a ruling minority, the who's-for-
tennis crowd in drag.

For that majority of the population - those on the receiving end
of the News of the World and the Palladium - even the chance to
drop out isn't there. Pleasure is not just free time which may
be spent either with Billy Cotton or William Blake, Reveille or
International Times. For two centuries the working people of
this country have been systematically deprived of the self
conciousness and awareness for the Flower Peoples sort of power.
Far from wanting to change this, heads celebrate it, "LSD users
are not the ghetto people but the middle class who want to immerse
themselves in their own abundance, see more of it, not escape it

in the manner of the black junky". At best the head gives a
maddening lucidity from the richness of the drug experience, at
worst an emotional client state ruled by whatever banana boss
holds its keys. Pot could certainly be legalised tomorrow and
apart from a few narcotic squad men getting transfered to traffic
duty, we would proceed untouched into the Stagnant Seventies an
and the Awful Eighties. For that great rump of the British
people who remain turned on to mild and bitter, life would be
still submerged in Pink Stamps, HP on the tele and the Greyhound
Standard ... The men John Gerassi talked to in NW Brazil die
of old age at 26 and chew cocoa leaves not for visions but to
block out the agony of their bellies.

We choose between life as style, style as value, value as fact;
the ethic of the strutting Beautiful Person attacking the modern
state where it likes, not where it hurts. The alarm bells ring
for nobody but ourselves; if you eat health foods, you must
expect to look like a banana.

There's more ways to blow H. Wilson's mind than STP in the
Sanitogen. The tactics of the urban guerilla in an over ripe
welfare capitalism cannot be the same as a Fidelista in the
Sierra Meistra ... But the point of doing the thing is to transform
the values and aims of a society. The old folk's homes in the
college aren't going to do this any more; the radical intelligensia are too absorbed in the perfect simulation of Youth, trying to
swallow time like Capt. Hook's crocodile; Progress Westminster style has all the pace of a tractor going uphill with the
handbrake on. At least the Young see that what we are offered
as social change from above is just a little more rouge on a
very old whore's face. The Old Left is, in David Mercer's
words, like a kipper, two faced and gutless, if the hippies
don't want to go that way, the this-sidedness of psychedelics
must flower a thousand Communications Companies and
Underground Press and Hippy Teleprinters, more Diggers (who
are English anyhow) and King Street Communes, Free Schools,
and youthplay in Happenings and Gatherings, take flowers to
strikers and throw them at fuzz. As the corporate land of
Wilson nudges itself into a liberal fascism with Labour Capital
and Gnome joined in a National Interest; so the need to
eradicate dissent will grow and the Underground; strikers and
psychedelics; dropouts and demonstrators will bear the weight
of the dissent. As the New Britain subsides into its white-
between-the-mind, wet-between-the-legs crematorium, Albion
Arise.

David Widgery

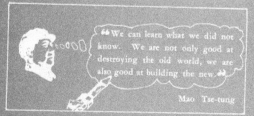

**We can learn what we did not
know. We are not only good at
destroying the old world, we are
also good at building the new.**

Mao Tse-tung

SNaREaRt

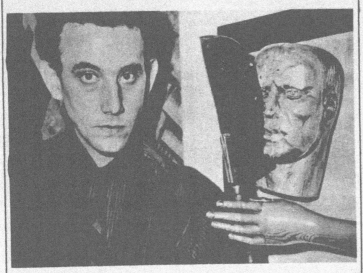

Snare-picture: objects found in chance positions, in order or disorder (on tables, in boxes, drawers, etc.) are fixed ("snared") as they are. Only the plane is changed: since the result is called a picture, what was horizontal becomes vertical. Example: remains of a meal are fixed to the table at which the meal was consumed, and the table hung on the wall.

Snare-picture squared (snare-picture of a snare-picture): the tools used to fix the objects in a snare-picture are themselves snared along with the objects at a certain "snared" moment.

In the "Grocery Store" at the Galerie Koepcke in Copenhagen in October 1961, groceries were recognized as individual works of art without being incorporated into an assemblage. They were stamped "Caution, Work of Art" and bore my certifying signature. Nothing else about them was changed, and the price was the current market price of each article.

Once the creation of objects through the imagination is accepted (at first the imagination was totally rejected), the false snare-picture enters. It consists of imagining and composing a situation in which the details appear to be a chance situation, so that the result cannot be distinguished optically from a real snare-picture. Example: a baby-pen with scattered objects and toys that a baby might have left in disorder, except that the pen was never used by a baby.

Working with chance situations implies the acceptance of chance as a collaborator after the initial result has been achieved, of transformations due to time, weather, corrosion, dirt, etc. Example: the rats who devoured the organic matter on two of my snare-pictures at Galleria Schwarz in Milan have been accepted as collaborators. Taboos have as their objective the preservation of traditions and forms,

an objective that I reject: at the Galerie Koepcke «Grocery Store», sandwich rolls, in which garbage and junk were mixed during the kneading, were baked and sold as «taboo catalogues.»

When the supporting element of a snare-picture represents something (if it is a realist painting, for instance) a relationship is automatically established between the snared objects and the supporting element. This relationship destroys the false perspective of the representation: a deliberate choice of added objects interprets, profanes and changes the meaning of the supporting element. Example of a dé-trompe-l'oeil: a romantic view of the Alps—a valley with a stream flowing toward the spectator—is augmented by bathtub faucets and a shower.

Chance and creation merge, the difference between the snare-picture and the false snare-picture gradually disappear, when the real snare-picture is multiplied by false ones. In the «art multiplier,» a chance situation is fixed to a mirror, and the same situation is reflected onto another mirror joined to the first by hinges. In addition, the objects are reflected and multiplied in proportion to the angle at which the mirrors are set.

Everything is a snare-picture, anybody can choose a chance situation and make a picture out of it. To demonstrate this, I accepted an invitation to exhibit at the Danish «Salon de Mai» in 1962 on the condition that Addi Koepcke be allowed to choose

and fix situations in my name. The copied certificate of guarantee was printed for the occasion.

The foregoing principles can be applied to the other arts. A conversation, snared on tape, between four persons, reproduced as was, became the play «Yes, Mamma, We'll Do It,» first performed at the Municipal Theater in Ulm, Germany, in 1962. This true snare-play became a false snare-play when it was acted out on the stage; but it became a true snare-play in the second part of the play when the actors listened to themselves speaking their roles in the first part and commented spontaneously.

During the group manifestation Dylaby (dynamic labyrinth) at the Stedelijk Museum in Amsterdam in September 1962, I transformed two rooms of the museum. In one, converted into a dark labyrinth, the spectators were exposed to sensory experiences (warm and humid surfaces, varied textures, sounds and odors) as they had to develop their senses to appreciate the environment. In the other room, a principle of the snare-picture (changing of plane) was applied to a whole room containing an exhibition of fin de siecle painting and sculpture. The real floor was «hung» with paintings, so that it was transformed into a wall; sculpture «stood» on one of the real walls, transforming a real wall into the floor; and the other walls shifted their position in relation to the new «floor.»

In March 1963, a composite photograph of my room. composed of 55 individual shots, was exhibited as a snare-picture at the Comparaisons exhibition in Paris.

In the Dorotheanum (Non-Profit Suicide Institute), at Dorothea Loehr's gallery in Frankfurt-am-Main in October 1963, different facilities for suicide were offered in eleven rooms. (No one profited by the opportunities offered.)

In March 1964 at the Allen Stone Gallery in New York, I exhibited 31 «Variations on a Meal,» extending the variations-on-a-theme principle of hard-edge art to include the collaboration of chance. Thirty-one identically set tables were transformed through the agency of the invited guests. The results were exhibited.

The «word traps» made together with Robert Filliou were an attempt to visualize proverbs and sayings. Example: «Raining cats and dogs,» in which toy cats and dogs were fixed to the top of an open umbrella.

The exhibition of my hotel room. These principles developed in an unmethodical fashion, and are much less precise categories than they might seem as outlined above.

Daniel Spörri

PICASSO'S PLAY AT ST. TROPEZ

The man described by Life magazine as "Europe's most admired young artist", Hean-Jacques Lebel has a remarkable capacity for upsetting the squares. A few years ago he was run out of Italy after a painting of his on show at the Milan Gallery was found to contain the words "Fuck the Pope"; last year his Happening near Marseilles caused consternation as an immense rubber penis arose out of the harbor accompanied by almost-nude swimmers.

This summer J-J turned his attention to St. Tropez, a once swinging Riviera resort now noted for gorgeous chicks sporting bare midriffs, exorbitant prices and a strangely bourgeois set of local morals.

Lebel had thoughtfully obtained the consent of Pablo Picasso to interpret the latter's only play, "Desire Caught by the Tail" and ambitiously planned to present this in a tent behind the Papagayo on the least visited side of St. Tropez's lovely harbor. The Papagayo's owner, a thoughtful looking man who wandered around dressed in kimono and smoking a foot long pipe, was only too anxious to host the performance, but the mayor had other ideas.

Irked by a story in Paris' conservative Le Figaro to the effect that the play would include nudes, anarchistic viewpoints and a stripper actually pissing on stage, the mayor refused permission to the company who then proceeded to erect the tent at a crossroads about three miles from town in the neighboring village of Gassin.

" We thought it would be nice to bring all the tourists a piece of genuine art to liven their vacation and we get sent away" complained J-J in aggrieved tones.

His disappointment was somewhat alleviated a few days later by the appearance at a Papagayo press conference of Le Figaro's female correspondant, author of the original story which had provoked all the tourble. Quite genially Lebel called her "a whore" and suggested that she might be happier if she returned to her supposed trade in the streets. The correspondent, not surprisingly, left in a huff and wrote another angry story about the production.

Two weeks before the show opened the cast and miscellaneous staff were frantically dividing their time between the Papagayo, the tent, an old villa in which some of the cast were billeted and the elegant, barely finished $50,000 mansion of J-J's mother about 15 miles out of town. Here total nudity swiftly became routine and the succession of guests (including a novice correspondent from Time and staid reviewers from Le Monde) were stunned to be greeted by assorted nudists covered with art tattoos.

Living in the spacious, unfurnished house was al fresco style with foam rubber mattresses on the floor, canvas beach chairs and continual indoor picnics of yoghurt, red wine, bread and cheese.

By the time the show opened the chaos, far from resolving itself had become institutionalized. The play itself - a surrealistic fantasy featuring such characters as The Thin Anguish, Big Foot, the Onion and Taylor Mead portraying a vulgar dog - was a prescient allegory of the artist's dilemma, but this was almost dwarfed by the subsequent happening.

In this, bare-breated waitresses served wine to the audience, a car was driven into the tent and spray painted, girls changed clothes on stage in front of psychedelic films, two actors pulled down their pants and displayed their asses, a violin was dramatically smashed and a seemingly endless plastic tube slowly inflated and snaked back and forth between the seats.

At last report the event was fulfilling what seems to be the inevitable Lebel predestination: mysterious assailants had put two rifle bullets through the portable generator and the mayor of Gassin had forthwith prohibited future happenings.

Said J-J: "We are planning to move events to the beach".

marſhall mᶜ₵Ɯɑn's

wun ied kirgdom

Printing is a ditto device.

All media are extensions of some human ɩ psychic or physical.

Art is anything you can get away with.

We now live in a global village – a simultaneous happening.

There is absolutely no inevitability as long as ther willingness to contemplate what is happening.

McLuhan has complained, fairly, about the literati's hostile or ostrich attitudes to the new "electric" media (aural and audio-visual). The following criticisms of his Understanding Media are meant as contributions to a sort-out, not a put-down.

But a sort-out is needed. In Madison Avenue and Greenwich Village, and, increasingly, Bloomsbury, McLuhan is semi-canonised, and oracle. His current charisma recalls that accorded such fallen idols as Arnold Toynbee and Colin Wilson. This sort-out is a pre-emptive move against the coming backlash.

It's already ominous that it's this, McLuhan's third, and worst, book which has found such favour. Read McLuhan, but read his first, The Gutenberg Galaxy, first. Innumerable sentences in the recent book are only explained adequately in the first, and the study of the impact of printing on thinking is better researched than his trigger happy (shoot-first-and-ask-questions-afterwards) notions on the electric media.

These, necessarily brief, samples, indicate some major reservations.

1. "The medium is the message" isn't a new message. Henry James asked what would become of the ghost story with the invention of electric light (Answer: it became the horror film. But more people still believe in ghosts than understand relativity). Some of us know we're media fans (film lovers, pop fans, bibliophiles, etc) . Of course we're also content lovers (no film lover finds all films equally interesting) . Content is still half the story.

2. Alas, that's what McLuhan tries to deny. In trying to stress that the medium's form is a message, proceeding, constantly, whatever its content, he throws the baby out with the bathwater, repetitively dismissing and deriding content-analysis. This leaves him totally helpless to explain why you prefer one movie to another, or a good film to a banal TV show, or the rise of pirate radio, or why the masses shy off everything the schoolroom teaches. He says "radio has this effect" when what he means is "radio could have had this effect if used at maximum pitch and if no other variables were involved" which is like saying "radio didn't have this effect", and the "because" involves principles which McLuhan's hop, skip and jump style might have been designed to distract your own thinking from.

His remarks on the movie Marty (p. 293) afford a useful touchstone. He attributes its success to the fact that the public was conditioned by TV, and that Marty was like TV, because (a) its photography was "low definition" and (b) it sacrificed "hot" stars for "cool" realism, TV-style. (a) is wrong: Marty is as well-photographed as any other movie. And films that fit (b) regularly flop (e.g. such follow-ups to Marty as The Bachelor Party and Take A Giant Step). Indeed, Marty itself flopped, until it got its Oscars, when the producers re-released it with a publicity campaign costing as much as the movie, whereupon it succeeded, because its Oscars gave it glamour as "the film that dignifies "ordinary people" ".

McLuhan's terms are bankrupt before this next problem. Here are six post-Marty, Marty-style, movies. Why, of two "Osborne" movies, was Look Back In Anger a hit (in G.B.) and The Entertainer a flop? Why, of two "Sillitoes", was Saturday Night and Sunday Morning a hit and The Loneliness of The Long-Distance Runner a flop? (Incidentally, all four movies are directed by the same man; the first two both have stars, the last two didn't). Why, of two "abortion" stories, was The L-Shaped Room a hit and The Pumpkin Eater a flop? Why was A Taste of Honey a hit and This Sporting Life a flop? All these problems can be explained, in detail, satisfyingly, in, and only in, terms of the content analysis which McLuhan so brusquely assigns to the scrapheap (note too, how he edits his evidence; not cynically, he just doesn't know enough. But who does! ?).

3. McLuhan oversimplifies the media. He's right about print splitting word-sound from word-sight, brilliantly so. But most of the poetry in our anthologies was written to be read aloud (not just listened to) and poetry is still a vocal medium (even more than an aural one!). So is much prose (e.g. Dickens' novels were often read aloud in the Victorian family circle). Even eye-prose retains strong vocal associations (and not simply in dialogue). The "typewriter" poems of which McLuhan makes so much are a very minor genre; Mallarme and Lewis Carroll wrote them before typewriters, and most poets still work by mouth, ear and pen.

McLuhan really ought to stop talking about "magazines" as a medium and distinguish between (say) a poem in Encounter, a Reader's Digest inspirational feature, and, discussions of abstruse philosophical or knotty legal points, all of which are matters of content, and affect the thinking-styles of those who read them. Apply such principles to all media and McLuhan's generalisations read like a Martian's-eye-view of earth.

4. McLuhan's style is dazzling because it's confusing and puzzling because it's vague. He calls Western literacy visual in that (a) you read it with your eyes and (b) you may accompany it with images in your mind's eye. This is also to say that it's non-visual, in that what you see (print) becomes transparent to what you only think you see, i.e. print is what we always thought it was, avisual and conceptual. Instead of suggesting, as he does, that reading makes us visual, he should have said that it makes us "visual", i.e. starers, but visually unobservant. More important, though: the content of printing (concepts) makes us abstract-minded and therefore unobservant.

The content of movies is never, as McLuhan says, novels; it's usually theatre, and the content of theatre is spoken word, mime (gesture, physiognomy). McLuhan oddly omits the theatre from his media, which is extraordinary, and significant, since it's the medium which most clearly displays what the content of media really is. He slides round it with a weird formulation (p. 8), that the content of a medium is another medium; but this, if true, would be a vicious circle, and leave all media with no content. The content of all media (including the content of all their forms) is whatever associations are triggered off in the spectator by the form-content alloy. All media work by association (as McLuhan notes), e.g. music can be tactile, muscular, intellectual, emotional, in different proportions, depending on both the content, and the spectator's responsiveness.

5. McLuhan's tunnel-vision blinkers him in other contexts, as when he tries to trace big spiritual shifts to, and only to, changes in me dia forms. He writes as if the only difference between movie and TV were that the former's visual image is sharp and clear (high definition), and therefore makes you a passive spectator, while the latter is poor and grey (low definition) and therefore involves you as a participant.

But let's start from the beginning. The major distinction between movies and TV is that you watch movies on a big screen which dominates you, in a dark hall which conceals you, among a big crowd which includes mostly strangers. But you watch TV on a tiny screen which you dominate, by full or twi-light which doesn't conceal you, in your old familiar sitting-room, with a small group of friends. The moviegoer is cut off from the real world, he's dominated by the image, he's all but unobserved, but the sounds of crowd-excitement can reach and infect him. So he can get carried away, lose self-consciousness, identify with the hero, etc. (However if the film's boring he's furious, he has no alternative distractions, he's come all this way, and paid so much, specifically for this).

The TV-watcher isn't dominated, isn't unobserved, hasn't got away from it all, so completely, has alternative distractions, and doesn't much mind half-boredom. Hence movies tend to exaggeration, excitement and climaxes. TV tends to a quieter, more even style, keyed down to the commonsense of your sitting-room and friends. Also, it's always there, to be looked at or not or half-looked at. That's why the content of TV is nearer newspaper-content than movies, which correspond to a "night out".

Placing the me dia in their contexts takes care of all McLuhan's points, except for the absurdities, as when he says (p. 312) that you can't use TV as background, as you do radio. Most British working-class families do, getting on with the ironing and the chat, glancing at the box if a remark or image interests them, looking away again, or half-attending; just as I'm writing this to the accompaniment of The Avengers.

This account also shows that McLuhan has got things the wrong way round. Movies in moviehouses involve you, TV leaves you more detached and contemplative, sympathetic. Movie is swimming, TV is sitting by a porthole. Definition is nothing to do with it, as McLuhan could have seen if he'd thought about home movies or TV screenings in cinemas, when the movies become less participational (though still hot!) and TV shows move (e.g. Cassius Clay fights), though still cool. Nor does this contrast prove anything about the relative power of the media. Maybe TV lingers in your mind more insidiously because (a) it lacks, the discontinuity between the movie's fantasy darkness and the real world, or because (b) it has more newspaper-fact content or (c) because you see more of it. On the other hand, you remember movies longer and clearer, the moments stand out and don't merge in a general, even-tempered grey.

Maybe, after all, modern coolth comes not from the TV image, but from (a) the audience's increasing exposure to all the audiovisual media, i.e. their gradual loss of impact, i.e., their approaching the "contemplative" distance, the non-actuality, of prose; (b) affluence ousting economic anxieties and replacing them by a habit of boredom; and (c) a greater sophistication about life anyway, so that we're all in the habit of withholding judgement until we've processed a great deal more information than the old "who's the baddie?" or "who started it?".

6. On the media's side-effects McLuhan is as unreliable as he's stimulating. He implies (p.178) that print taught people to visualise distant goals. But all (illiterate) primitives believe in an after-life and Christ taught, orally, 14 centuries before the Gutenberg Galaxy. Maybe printing encouraged introversion, which is another matter entirely. I suspect that many of the effects McLuhan attributes to print can be attributed to mercantilism and the trading mentality. Among them: distant goals ("if I take this cargo from here where it's cheap to there where it's dear...."), abstractions (laws of supply and demand, ideas of profit and utility as divorced from the physical commodity), calculation (profit-margins), rationality, ("it's not the magic it's the value"), etc.

Beware of McLuhan's wild-swipe analogies. "By electricity" (i.e. TV, radio) "we everywhere resume person-to-person relationships as if on the smallest village scale." (cf. Chaps 30, 31). Thus McLuhan, when it suits his need for startling statements, forgets that for him the medium is the message.

For a TV presence is very different from "flesh impact" (as in theatre) and even more different from the long, committed, mutual relationships of the village scale. TV speed produces quick, shallow, relationships, informal perhaps but restless, all the symptoms of alienation, the lonely crowd. The village scale produces good neighbourliness in some socio-economic contexts (e.g. the growing, thriving American West), hereditary feuds and suspicion in others (e.g. French or Sicilian peasants). Indeed the comparison isn't so much between TV and village, as between village and city. The lonely crowd antedates TV. It comes with the city, it takes different forms with different cities. Electric speed is nothing compared with seeing 500 faces a minute as you walk down Oxford St.

Two more examples out of three hundred. McLuhan attributes to TV everything from (p. 321) the disappearance of assembly lines (have they!!?) to (p. 325) the egghead paperback explosion. Peering at TV images, he says, gave people the idea of reading slowly, and therefore understanding more difficult texts. Not a word about the possibility that more people now have better education and more liesure, and so read more, and therefore more easily, and need, and tackle maturer stuff. The idea that until TV no-one thought of reading slowly is crazy; the trouble with semi-literates is either they can't read quickly, they're so busy making out the words they can't follow the thought, or that they try and understand each word before they've got to the end of the sentence, or both, which your super-literate rarely does; he usually carries on until he's got a drift, and then works back. (Reading is far more "mosaic" than McLuhan realises).

Again, McLuhan suggests (p. 327) that TV (being fuzzy) has promoted a love of fuzzy textures in real life, and tactile-sensuous pleasures. Alternatively: Maybe people always relished them, but can indulge them now because (a) tactile things tend to be expensive and need affluence, and (b) sensuous pleasures need a decline in puritanism (which favours abstraction against the senses). In the '50s Americans still relished steak, ice-cream and chromium-plate - simple-mindedly brash flavours, which went with a liking for smooth, plasticized surfaces. Now everything is smooth and plastic and the rough is a blessed relief. It's perhaps puritanical afterglow that leads the Americans back to brick-and-homespun rather than on to, say, the Jewish key of spices and furs. But TV's nothing to do with it. The masses have always been sensuous, one way or another, and middle-class changes can be plotted against the puritan-trading syndrome.

7. By omitting both content and context, and thinking only of one medium "versus" another, McLuhan closes more avenues than he opens. He closes, for example, the avenue of function. The (sociology based) Himmelweit Report on TV spoke of "functional equivalence": if TV hit the comicbook hard it would be because it performs a similar function better. Not for McLuhan, who because he derides content can't understand function (since a main function of a medium is to put you in touch with the mental experiences triggered off by the content). So why does McLuhan think TV hit the comic? Out comes the same old line: both have low-definition images.

McLuhan, like the hi-fi maniacs who listen to sound, but never music, scarcely focuses on anything except the media's quality of definition!

8. McLuhan is concerned with how the me dia-forms influence our thinking, whether un-, pre-, or just plain conscious. But his account of thinking has some bad gaps. He attributes modern forgetfulness about names to our "visual" culture - not to the speed and informality with which the electric age showers us with information which we get into the habit of forgetting. Nor does the fact that the TV image is produced by a scanner-dot mean we perceive it differently from a photographic print. The fact that we see print with our eyes means we don't think about what we're seeing. McLuhan mashes up (a) how an image is produced (b) our perceptual

processes (c) our interpretation of our perceptions and (d) what we think about. Certainly these processes influence each other. But since McLuhan never clearly separates them, he comes up with simple one-for-one correspondences between the physical form the media and their effects on our souls.

He assumes that audience involvement depends on information-density. But the satisfactions of empathy and identification, of the mind's own selectivity, aren't reducible to information-density. While taking the odd titbit from gestalt (or Freudian) psychology, McLuhan clings, basically, to the exploded, Lockean assumption whereby the mind takes the form of the outer stimulus. The mind is a strip of blank film recording whatever form impinges on it. The mind is the slave of form because it can't refer back to any content (experience). No modern psychologist of any school goes as far as McLuhan in making the mind a passive "camera" of sense-pictures.

The wayward butterfly of McLuhan's thought alights briefly on points that, excavated (by corny old logic) could have been goldmines. He remarks that the ear is more emotional than the eye, and loses himself in a tangle of generalisations about radio being "tribal". What's interesting is that in the animal the ear is an alarm-signal for the eye. What's behind you may be nearer than what's in your field of vision, so the ear is more "jumpy". And that's why musical rhythms make you jump (tap your feet). Visual rhythms don't, and the eye is more closely linked to precise information (look before you jump). Hence music has always been more abstract than the visual arts. It can be more abstract because it's more urgent. Abstract painting is a late, sophisticated development (schizophrenic in requiring both formal sensitivity and a cut-off of extroversion?). Abstract painting is best when you've just taken mescalin. Decorative patterns (as one finds in primitives) are best when one lets one's eyes mover over them slowly (children look at things this way; decoration fascinates them). This also happens to be movement of reading, but it precedes reading. What makes the Western adult so "illiterate" about pattern is nothing to do with reading. It's his habit of merely noting what a thing is, which he does because he lives in a world of utility and cause. He can't stroke things for pattern (tactility) with his eye: he has a slightly better grasp of form; but all he really looks at is identity. The trouble with literate people is that they don't bring the eye-movements of literacy into the world around!

9. McLuhan (shrewdly) distinguishes American or Anglo-Saxon from "European" types of sensibility, and keeps implying the Anglo-Saxons are more literate than the Europeans. But the English and the Americans are less literate than the Scandinavians, Germans, French and Dutch, though more so than the Italians and Spanish, so what happens to the "Europeans"?

If he didn't skim around so fast, McLuhan would have had to call to his aid more conventional social factors: e.g. puritanism, mercantilism, the shifting of commodities other than information, even that dreaded Marxist notion, social class.

Marx saw how technology (the means of producing wealth) interacted with the social process, and with human relationships, and with human consciousness. After all, consciousness is an artefact, determined like other artefacts by all these factors working together.

In other words: technology, as a part of the whole social process, produces the industrial revolution which produces modern capitalism; and improved methods of producing and transmitting everything include improved methods of producing and transmitting information. The cowboys beat the Red Indians not because the cowboys had the telegraph and the Indians only had smoke signals; but because the cowboys had the telegraph + maps + the Winchester 73 + wagontrains + more men + more money, etc.

But McLuhan won't have this. He reduces the history of society to the history of communications and the history of communications to the history of communicating information. What led to the downfall of the Roman Empire? Shortage of papyrus (p. 101). What causes today's civil wars? The press (p. 21). And so on and so forth (Of course at other times he allows non-informational processes a certain autonomy; and such contradictions would be more obvious if his style were less wayward).

No wonder McLuhan dazzles his readers with a sense of being in the presence of a mind which is subtle, agile and amazing. He's straining to make information format, responsible, all by itself, for everything he can think of; foresight (print), Hitler (radio), psychoanalysis (photography), the switch from jobs to roles (TV).

Why has his last, scrappiest, book, been uncritically accepted, where his first was, and it's a pity, ignored here, bar a tiny circle of aficionados? First, Understanding Media is impressively full of nuggets of interesting information; It's a great, incoherent, machine of miscellaneous stimuli (and worth reading for that alone). Second, the sense of strain exuded by his prose strikes the impressionable as the surprises of brilliance (and the Gutenberg Galaxy often is brilliant. Third, the electric media now fascinate us all, so wild guesses about them are welcome, and McLuhan reads more flip than square, which balm is in Gilead. Fourth, what men of letters want to do is bask in the hammock of endless speculation, without commitment, without conviction. And you can endlessly weave strands of McLuhanesque speculation because it's an unverifiable metaphysic.

It can blend perceptual subtlety ("How sensitive we are!")with intellectual complexity ("how clever we are!") with, as epoques rise and fall apocalyptic overtones ("how profound we are!"). You don't have to bother to define your terms or organise your thoughts for your thinking isn't old-hat linear, it's electric-age "mosaic" or "iconic". (Actually only the lines are spokes: McLuhan's "pepperpot" style conceals a relentless, obsessive "linearity"; every point leads directly to his central concern, media-formats).

These marginal muddles are a pity, because his main point is true as it's neglected. The forms of messages do influence our mind's workings, on all levels. The medium is much of the message, it is a major link in the chain of civilisation.

Maybe McLuhan's Messianic style was the best way of attracting due attention to his hypotheses. But now it's time for testing them, and I'm not at all sure that McLuhan, then, will have transformed our thinking about the media at all. A man can fly a 1,000 kites and never get anything else off the ground.

WHO IS MARSHALL McLUHAN

He looks like this.

He reads like this.

UNDERSTANDING MEDIA:
The Extensions of Man
Marshall McLuhan

UNDERSTANDING MEDIA is the essential McLuhan. Over 250,000 copies sold in the United States. Now for the first time in paperback in England and the Commonwealth.

UNDERSTANDING MEDIA:
The Extensions of Man 10/6 from your bookseller or newsdealer.

SPHERE

Release
603·8654

IF YOU ARE ARRESTED

you are advised:

To insist on telephoning the number on the front of this card for assistance.

To make no statements.

Not to discuss the matter with which you are charged.

To request that any property taken from you is packaged and sealed in your presence.

To be polite to police officers.

acts arising out of

JUDGES' RULES AND ADMINISTRATIVE DIRECTIONS TO THE POLICE *(Jan. '64)*

You are entitled to telephone your friends or your solicitor. *(7(a))*

You need never make any statement unless you wish to do so. *(II)*

You should not be harassed by the police to make a statement. *(e)*

Reasonable arrangements should be made for your comfort and refreshment. *(3)*

dear Sir,

A few weeks ago i visited london. i found your magazin at betterbooks. i bought it, not knowing, that over here i would be offered a half an hour broadcast about the hippie-movement. since the offer i am trieing very hard to get information, in london and in san francisco, as there is none in germany. i liked your magazin; if i could get more information about the question how much politics, social structure etc. mean to the hippies, i could put down all the scepticism from the left, which regards the hippies as a reactionary group, a group which never brings to fall the political systems of the western world, but which never them even stronger, by being a undangerous and accepted outcast. more then once it was mentioned in your magazin, that this would not be so, that the hippies would know perfectly well, that without a radical political philosophy, there would only be a chance for a few thousand, for a few years to live quite freely - and not even that.

The feature will be broadcasted in october. i have to get informations very fast - i i hope, that you will help me.

love cornelia vogel
6 frankfurt — main
beethovenstrasse 3a
Germany

Can anyone assist Miss Vogel?

TINA DATE, beautiful singer of songs (You saw her on Dee Time) is forming a new group. Interested musicians write to Danne Hughes Management, 51 Hanover Gate Mansions, Park Road NW1. Bookings : Spencer Davis Management, Royalty House, Dean St., W1.

OZ writers Andrew Fisher and Michael Newman have made a comedy film 'The Adventures of X' on a BFI grant. The Evening Standard and Guardian critics raved after the NFT screening. Hire it for club screening, happenings. Recommend it to distributors, TV stations. X is a man who believes all the mailorder ads he reads and gets what he deserves. 16mm, black & white, sound, about 27 min. Get it from the British Film Institute, Distribution Department, Lower Marsh, S.E.1.

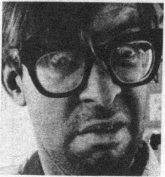

X is maddened by delusions of power.

The International Times

COPS POPS JEWS QUEERS
MAPS   REAL   NEWS
DREAMS & MAGIC

You can get it anywhere (almost)

OZ
free back copies

Subscribe now to OZ and you'll be sent 2 free copies of past issues — including the OZ with the famous golden cover.

Name:

Address:

Country

I enclose 30/- for 12 OZ (US - $4; student rate - 21/-) plus two free back issues. Send to OZ Subscriptions, 40 Anhalt Road, London, SW11.

OTHER SCENES & OZ 25¢

6

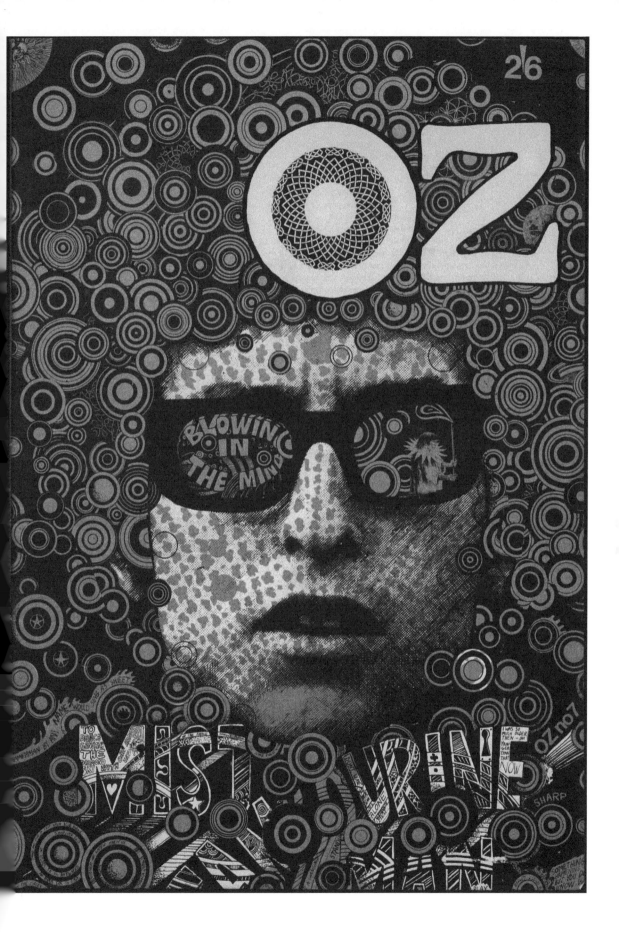

by Angello Quattrochi

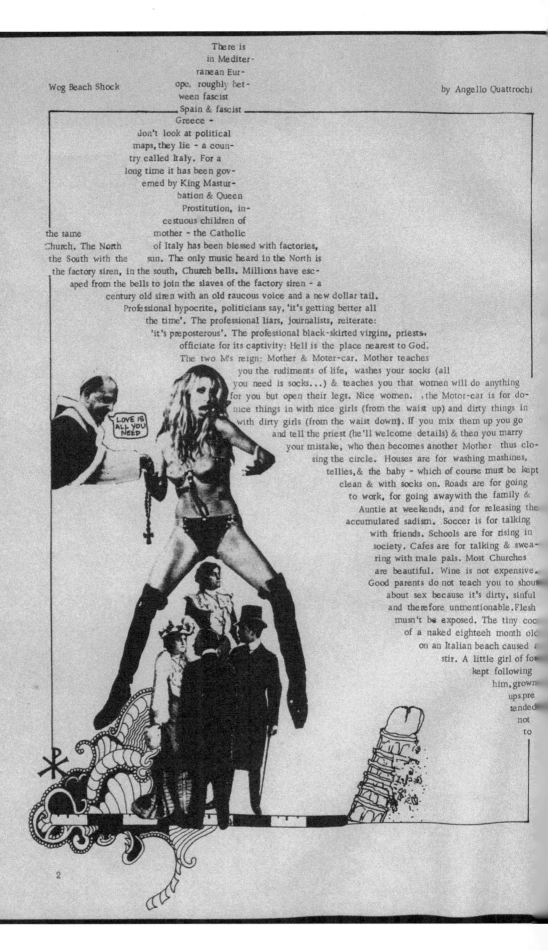

There is
in Mediter-
ranean Eur-
ope, roughly bet-
ween fascist
Spain & fascist
Greece -
don't look at political
maps, they lie - a coun-
try called Italy. For a
long time it has been governed by King Mastur-
bation & Queen
Prostitution, in-
cestuous children of
the same   mother - the Catholic
Church. The North   of Italy has been blessed with factories,
the South with the   sun. The only music heard in the North is
the factory siren, in the south, Church bells. Millions have escaped from the bells to join the slaves of the factory siren - a
century old siren with an old raucous voice and a new dollar tail.
Professional hypocrite, politicians say, 'it's getting better all
the time'. The professional liars, journalists, reiterate:
'it's preposterous'. The professional black-skirted virgins, priests,
officiate for its captivity: Hell is the place nearest to God.
The two M's reign: Mother & Moter-car. Mother teaches
you the rudiments of life, washes your socks (all
you need is socks...) & teaches you that women will do anything
for you but open their legs. Nice women. the Motor-car is for do-
nice things in with nice girls (from the waist up) and dirty things in
with dirty girls (from the waist down). If you mix them up you go
and tell the priest (he'll welcome details) & then you marry
your mistake, who then becomes another Mother thus closing the circle. Houses are for washing mashines,
tellies, & the baby - which of course must be kept
clean & with socks on. Roads are for going
to work, for going awaywith the family &
Auntie at weekends, and for releasing the
accumulated sadism. Soccer is for talking
with friends. Schools are for rising in
society. Cafes are for talking & swea-
ring with male pals. Most Churches
are beautiful. Wine is not expensive.
Good parents do not teach you to shout
about sex because it's dirty, sinful
and therefore unmentionable. Flesh
musn't be exposed. The tiny coc
of a naked eighteeh month old
on an Italian beach caused a
stir. A little girl of fou
kept following
him, grown
ups pre
tended
not
to

LOVE IS
ALL YOU
NEED

2

see,
some
called
their chil-
dren, mortally
embarassed. The
preeious father of
aneamic doll-like two
year old girl, suffered.
Young people muttered their disapproval in audible words
- old women stared hard. It
was a middle-class lake shore.
Confronted with such scandal they
were squirming with embarrasment
but the management did'nt intervene.
In a rather working class swimming
pool the reaction was more straightforward - the lifeguard in charge asked
us to cover the baby because there were girls   around.
In their teens boys are encouraged to take cold   showers
to do physical jerks; and in the confessionals
are told that theyhave sinned because they wet the bed with
white stuff. The feeling of guilt attached to all bodily matters
is inoculated before puberty & is re-inforced with moral pressures during adolescence. God does not want you to fuck, alright, but not only that, he doesn't even wish you to have an erection: Girls store their
private capital, a stale cunt - boys learn their first lessons with whores. The girl says 'If you want that, go with a
pro.' The pro says 'I do what your girl doesn't.' They put bromide in soldiers' soups, leave on statues' pricks andi

continued P.22

I'm out here a thousand miles from my home
Walkin' a road other men have gone down
I'm seein' your world of people and things
Hear paupers and peasants and princes and kings

Hey Hey Woody Guthrie I wrote you a song
'Bout a funny ol' world that's a-comin' along
Seems sick an' its hungry its tired an' its torn
It looks like its a-dyin' an' its hardly bin born

Hey Woody Guthrie but I know that you know
All the things that I'm a-sayin' an' a many times more
I'm a-singin' you the song but I can't sing enough
'Cos there's not many men done the things that you done

Here's to Cisco an' Sonny an' Leadbelly too
An' to all the good people that traveled with you
Here's to the hearts and the hands of the men
That come with the dust and are gone with the wind

I'm a-leavin' tomorrow but I could leave today
Somewhere, down the road, someday...
The very last thing that I'd want to do
Is to say I bin hittin' some hard travelin' too.

(Bob Dylan, 1961)
Courtesy of Duchess Music Ltd

4

What's so good about Dylan?

Dylan's lyrics are not poems, they are parts of songs. This is not to assert that Dylan is not a poet but simply to remember that he is certainly a pop singer. The medium he has chosen involves more than language – and therefore a number of limits are placed on the selection and organisation of language within his work.

I don't think there are any other pop artists who experience the same difficulties; the other writer–singers labour under strains of a different quality. They are inevitably less aware than Dylan of the tension between linguistic, musical and dramatic expression because – unlike Dylan – they lack the necessary sureness of touch in one or more of those directions.

Jagger is usually worth watching and his records communicate the ethos of the sexual sneer; but the words of a Jagger song are mere dilettante junkie–ism, scratched inarticulacy on its own prison wall, with methedrine as a deified scapegoat.

Paul Simon – record, stage or paper – belongs to part of Americana which assumes that an indiscriminate eagerness plus Doe–Eyed sensitivity = creative intelligence. The latter has not yet revealed itself on his SON OF

'SEPTEMBER IN THE RAIN' LP's.

Lennon–McCartney compositions, the Beatles records, are, at best, artistically disciplined, cameos, cave–paintings in the primeval pop–world. And like cave–paintings they do not need their authors to explain, accompany or complete them. This is a notable achievement – although the self reliant is not always the valuable and The Beatles' writing seems to me to attain a standard that is fairly placed by being called Noel Cowardish. Nevertheless, Lennon–McCartney's compositions do not need blood–transfusions from Beatle performances in order to lend for themselves.

Dylan, on the other hand, is about 60% singer, musician and performer. This is one of the obstacles in the way of the attempt to isolate his lyrics. And though Dylan has often said "I am my words" this is merely to invite further difficulty; for an analysis on these grounds tends to suffer also in assuming the form of a Great Message Hunt.

I am not against messages. A writer without message is without real interest – contrary to a public opinion which distrusts preaching and gives that label to anything

served up without choc–bars. Literature is inseparable from the moral life of man and cannot afford to give the public what it wants; the creative writer must offer as humble as possible what he believes the public needs. And as the Establishment knows, and as the Harold Robbinses prove by their passivity (for Mr. Robbins is one of humanity's drop–outs), "giving the public what it wants" is the easiest way to control what it wants.

Dylan is one of those who seek honestly to speak out against this, against the de–humanising of society. To Message Hunt through Dylan's lyrics is to pursue the preconception of a cohesive whole or something single: a philosophy of life that is without contradiction. Dylan does not claim to offer this. He is still searching both for his essential beliefs and an appropriate form in which to express them. What I think he does offer is the artistic re–creation of the experience of life within chaos. The 1960s. And the virtue lies not in the immediacy but in the honesty. Dylan's work possesses that individual integrity which belongs to the artist who can be said to "represent the age" and this characteristic is essentially different from the ability to put

BANK OF ENGLAND

EZRA POUND

They're selling postcards of the hanging
They're painting the passports brown
The beauty-parlour is filled with sailors
The circus is in town
Here' comes the blind commissioner
They've got him in a trance
One hand is tied to the tight-rope walker
The other is in his pants
And the riot squad they're restless
They need somewhere to go
As Lady 'n' I look out tonight
From Desolation Row

Cinderella she seems so easy
'It takes one to know one', she smiles,
And puts her hands in her back pockets
Bette Davis style
And in comes Romeo he's moaning
You Belong To Me I Believe
And someone says you're in the wrong place my friend
You better leave
And the only sound that's left
After the ambulances go
Is Cinderella sweeping up
On Desolation Row.

Now the moon is almost hidden
The stars are beginning to hide
The fortune-telling lady
Has even taken all her things inside
All except for Cain and Abel
And the hunch-back of Notre Dame
Everybody is making love
Or else expecting rain
And the Good Samaritan he's dressing
He's getting ready for the show
He's going to the carnival tonight
On Desolation Row

Ophelia she's 'neath the window
For her I feel so afraid
On her twenty-second birthday
She already is an old maid
To her, death is quite romantic

She wears an iron vest
Her profession's her religion
Her sin is her lifelessness
And though her eyes are fixed upon
Noah's great rainbow
She spends her time peeking in
To Desolation Row

Einstein disguised as Robin Hood
With his memories in a trunk
Passed this way an hour ago
With his friend a jealous monk
Now he looked so immaculately frightful
As he bummed a cigarette
And he went off sniffing drainpipes
And reciting the alphabet.
You would not think to look at him
But he was famous long ago
For playing the electric violin
On Desolation Row

Dr. Filth he keeps his world
Inside of a leather cup
But all his sexless patients
They are trying to blow it up
Now his nurse, some local loser,
She's in charge of the cyanide hole,
And she also keeps the cards that read
Have Mercy On His Soul
They all play on the penny whistle
You can hear them blow
If you lean your head out far enough
From Desolation Row

Across the street they've nailed the curtains
They're getting ready for the feast -
The Phantom of the Opera
In a perfect image of a priest
They are spoonfeeding Casanova
To get him to feel more assured
Then they'll kill him with self-confidence
After poisoning him with words
And the Phantom's shouting to skinny girls
Get Outa Here If You Don't Know

Casanova is just being punished
For going to Desolation Row

At midnight all the agents
And the superhuman crew
Go out and round up everyone
That knows more than they do
Then they bring them to the factory
Where the heart-attack machine
Is strapped across their shoulders
And then the kerosene
Is brought down from the castles
By insurance men who go
Check to see that nobody is escaping
To Desolation Row

Praise be to Nero's Neptune
The Titanic sails at dawn
Everybody is shouting
Which Side Are You On?
And Ezra Pound and T. S. Eliot
Fighting in the captain's tower
While calypso singers laugh at them
And fishermen hold flowers
Between the windows of the sea
Where lovely mermaids flow
And nobody has to think too much
About Desolation Row

Yes I received your letter yesterday
(About the time the door-knob broke)
When you asked me how I was doing
Was that some kind of joke?
All these people that you mention
Yes I know them they're quite lame
I had to re-arrange their faces
And give them all another name.
right now I can't read too good
Don't send me no more letters no -
Not unless you mail them
From Desolation Row.

(Bob Dylan, 1965)
© Blossom Music/ Leeds Music Ltd.

together a few common denominators as Amis did in the 195Os and as the Beatle-writers do today. Dylan' is a personal perception - the perception of an intelligent acquisitive mind. The focus is sensitive, the expression disciplined and therefore the product is art. At this point it is no longer useful to compare Bob Dylan with other pop stars; it may later be constructive instead to measure him against other poets. If Dylan is influenced by early Presley he is also influenced by Whitman; and though he is saying more than Simon-Garfunkel, Lennon or P.F. Sloan, he may be saying less than Yevtushenko, S. T. Coleridge or Stephen Wycherley.

So what is Dylan saying?

ONG TO WOODY, the first of the two lyrics printed here, expresses the desire for an innocent drop-out, but also, as with Mr. Tambourine Man, the concern to find a new allegiance:

"Hey Mr. Tambourine Man play a song for me -
In the jingle-jangle morning I'll come following you. "

- and the allegiance declared here is to the inner world. The intention is to come upon self-discovery (I doubt if one can 'come upon it' with quite that facility), to free the mind in the hope that its isolation will bring independent thought. I am not concerned to argue the pros and cons of whether this

works in general, or whether, if it does, the independent thinking is likely to be redirected towards "dropping back in" in any socially constructive way. It is enough to say that it has w is enough to say that it has worked for Dylan. Drugs have not dulled the finer edges nor restricted his ability to perceive and remain articulate. "People should not know more than they can creatively digest, " wrote Neitzche. That Dylan has the capacity for this creative assimilation - it is abundantly clear in his work - is what gives him his authority.

The allegiance sought in SONG TO WOODY is the "hard travelin'" ethos represented by Guthrie. In that sense it is, too, the world of the American West to which

6

emingway and his "Lost
eneration" looked for fulfilment -
nd failed to discover. Hemingway
ould only find instead the
asturbation-habit of attending
panish bullfights. Guthrie, on
e other hand, lived a life of
ard Travelin' and the intensity
d compassion of Dylan's lyric
confirmed by a reading of the
uthrie autobiography 'Bound for
ory'. The lines:

ere's to the hearts and the hands
the men
at come with the dust and are
ne with the wind

thfully reflect Guthrie's ethnic
nsibility but communicate
so (they flow naturally from
at undramatic statement of a
rsonal admiration which makes
 second line of this fourth
nza so effective) Dylan's
dge of involvement with
thrie's America. That line in
 opening verse acts, in
rospect, as confirmation:

 seein' your world of people
d'things

onfirmation that, as the rhythmic
ance of the lyric insists, Dylan
 an incisive grasp of that world
 (as part of that reality) of
romantic implications. One
es too that the awareness of
 latter is evidence also that
an can see the Guthrie World
he context of others. Guthrie's
d Travelers shared a landscape
ust, wind and poverty, seen
oot and rattled through in
-crowded box-cars. And
wind and dust are evoked in
construction of the song.
s and syllables take the form
list: the suggestion is one
stless movement within a
ordained pattern of repetition.
felicity of Dylan's intimations
xperience within and outside
e ethos described is focused
e combination of the general
nse personalised:

eavin' tomorrow but I could
 today

Somewhere, down the road,
someday .....

and the personal response
generalised:

Hey Hey Woody Guthrie I wrote
you a song
Bout a funny ol' world that's
a-comin' along
Seems sick an' its hungry its
tired an' its torn
It looks like its a-dyin' an'
its hardly bin born.

And there, most economically,
is the rhythmic and onomatopoeic
repetition. Also evoked, one
notes, is the acquired fortitude
of mild amusement which is the
necessary survival-kit of the
hard traveler. 'Hey Hey Woody
Guthrie I wrote you a song'
pinpoints this with a deceptive
ease. That Dylan can render
this with such felicitous
poignancy is sufficient indication
that neither the intention nor the
effect is one of ill-considered
sentimentalism. And although
in 'God On Our Side' he lingers
over the line:

The country I come from is
called the Mid-West

and the romantic vision of
dying on a freight train occurs
in his version of 'Man of
Constant Sorrow' and again in
'It Takes A Lot To Laugh It
Takes A Train To Cry', the last
two lines of 'Song to Woody' are
of at least equal significance:

The very last thing that I'd want
to do
Is to say I bin hittin' some hard
travelin' too.

With those lines - deriving as
they do a particular strength from
the clipped reluctant flirtation
of the cadence - we are given
a greater understanding of the
spirit of the lyric as it is
stated in the title. To say
he'd been hittin' some hard
travelin' too is, emphatically,
not the last thing he'd want to be
able to do. 'Song to Woody',

---

most pungently, includes in its
pledge of involvement a plea for
that involvement. And it
expresses the same inner drive of
desire which we find directed
elsewhere in 'Mr. Tambourine
Man' and again in, say, 'Pledging
My Time'. In the one the desire
is for the freedom to make a
reality out of dancing:

beneath the diamond sky with
one hand waving free
Silhouetted by the sea

and in the other the desire is to
achieve an unknown fulfilment in
a personal relationship. Strange
that Dylan is so often dismissed
as a professional protest-merchant.

When we ask what this rather crude
label means, of course, there
is no answer - except from those
agents of the existing order who
disapprove of people who sing for
a living and who resent their having
opinions. (The most offensive
lapel-badge of all, in their eyes, is
the one that reminds them in
moderate type that BOB DYLAN IS
A RATE-PAYER). The label
Protest-Merchant, then, is hardly a
critical term.

ylan is, patently,
a critic of society;
I hope we all are.
But Dylan's
criticism, as it is
presented in his
writing, seems to
me to be characterised by a
personal insight unusually
abrasive in quality. Some of his
earlier criticism appeared then,
and appears more so in
retrospect, obvious and, to that
extent, naive. 'Blowin In The
Wind' and 'Masters of War' are
not memorable pieces of
writing. It is not simply the
cliches that mar them but also
the assumption that thier incl-
usion is necessary for the emphasised
communication of his theme. The
implication is that the listener
needs to be spoonfed.

In his more recent work, however, Dylan has learnt to trust his public. The criticism of human values in society, though sometimes harsh and sometimes rendered as an ingenuous reproach, is always offered in a form dictated by his art, not by an anxiety based on lack of trust.

I should like to put a case for judging Dylan's 'Desolation Row' to be a distinguished and brilliantly sustained critique of modern American society.

Desolation Row is a Cannery Row, the logical consequence, in one way at least, of the society surrounding it. Dylan is writing from within Desolation Row and though part of his pessimism is the product of his living there

When you asked me how I was doing
Was that some kind of joke?

the intention is not to repeat the theme of, say, North Country Blues, which was basically a chronicle of a community's suffering in the face of encroaching poverty. Dylan's despondence in 'Desolation Row' is his reaction to what he sees around him. And what he sees is life regimented by false values, lived out with dishonesty; norms which produce a denial of humanity being acted upon by man. Dylan explores this unreal society, recognises it as pernicious in its denial of essential human truths and insists upon the urgency of the need to assert and re-establish these.

He communicates his conviction of society's perversity, in the first place, by a sustained reversal of norms within the logic of the poem: the beauty-parlour is filled with sailors and it is the riot squad that is restless. Casanova, the dominating lover, is being spoon-fed; Romeo is moaning. And the determined use of a

barrage of folk-heroes, in careful disarray, participants in and agents of this world of sick disorder, emphasises his theme. There is Bette Davis, Cain and Abel, the hunchback of Notre Dame, the Good **Samaritan, Ophelia,** Noah, Einstein, Robin Hood, the Phantom of the Opera, Casanova, Romeo, Nero, Neptune, Ezra Pound and T.S. Eliot – not to mention Dr. Filth. There is Cinderella too, but she is the exception. She is, with Dylan, on Desolation Row; she is victim, not agent, and therefore she is less of a victim. But though she can afford to be more honest – "to live outside the law you must be honest" is a line from a later song – the real "sweeping up" must be done outside: across the street, where they've nailed the curtains.

The other general character-istic of the poem is the recurring intimation of imminent disaster.

The commissioner, who is blind, is tied (by one hand) to the tight-rope walker; and:

All except for Cain and Abel
And the hunchback of Notre Dame
Everybody is making love
Or else expecting rain.

Now the moon is almost hidden
The stars are beginning to hide
The fortune-telling lady
Has even taken all her things
inside .....

But it is the single line:
'The Titanic sails at dawn'
which is most strikingly evocative of catastrophe. It summarises with the conciseness of the true artist the theme and colouring of the whole poem. It is the Titanic which epitomises present-day American society as Dylan interprets it; for the Titanic was the ship of the future, the proof of man's progress and civilisation, the unsinkable ship which, on her

maiden voyage, sank. And when she began to sink the majority of her passengers refused to believe it could happen; the palm court orchestra played on and the people in the ship's ballroom continued to dance.

 he different kinds of denial – the various ways in which the "dancing" continues, as Dylan sees it – are presented with an incision which incorporates Dylan's essential sanity within an impressionistic evocation of escalating malaise. They're selling postcards of the hanging at the beginning of the song; but by the middle some local loser is in charge of the cyanide hole:

And she also keeps the cards that read
Have Mercy On His Soul.

The first two stanzas present a general picture, establishing the nature of the poem being offered and laying the foundations of its "Wasteland" connotations. The only specific criticism made is that contained in the observation that:

the riot squad they're restless
They need somewhere to go.....

That the society has riot-quelling machinery out on the streets is a denial of its democratic basis; and that this arrangement is taken for granted – accepted as normal – is indicative of the malaise which a corrupted system of government inculcates in the process of rendering its citizens morally, as well as politically, impotent.

In the third stanza – again with a striking economy of language – Dylan questions the essential quality and effectiveness of modern humanitarian liberalism in the context of the society he sees:

And the Good Samaritan he's dressin

He's getting ready for the show .....

When we meet the Good Samaritan preparing for his carnival the stars have already begun to hide. The darkness is already closing in, and it is not the sort of darkness which should encourage dressing for dinner. Like everybody's making love it is an inappropriate response. It exposes that lethal unawareness against which Dylan is concerned to speak out.

This is why, in the final stanza, Dylan demands of his correspondent that she submit herself to the experience of being on Desolation Row - the one place where it remains possible to possess, or re-discover, an honesty of response. There is, after all, nothing Desolation Row can offer in the way of compromising or deluding alternative. Consequently the letter received from outside communicates nothing beyond what Dylan knows already of that . outside society. His receiving it, therefore, is of no importance to him at all:

Yes I received your letter yesterday
(About the time the door-knob broke) ..

That pay-off line is beautiful, as Dylan's put-downs usually are.

In this final stanza of 'Desolation Row'. The real emphasis is on the hope that the girl from outside will come to the Row, to be redeemed, as it were:

Don't send me no more letters no -
Not unless you mail them from
Desolation Row.

This blindness which is under attack (it is a society of commissioners with which Dylan is dealing) is examined in terms of a kind of cause and effect in stanzas eight and nine. Stanza eight is an indictment of the tightly-organised human betrayal which the American educational system represents. It is portrayed as essentially a nightmarish machinery for bringing the potential

enemies of the status quo - the potential saviours, the independant thinkers - into line:

At midnight all the agents
And the superhuman crew
Go out and round up everyone
That knows more than they do

Mockingly, Dylan shows that the system's "education" consists in the maintenance of ignorance. Moreover, that "crew", in the context, asserts in combination with the opening phrase "At midnight.." the telling connotative suggestion of collective vandalism, political purges and press-gangs. The over-riding element of violence, then, is evoked in those first two lines of the verse. We are forewarned of the "heart-attack machine", the kerosene and the near-impossibility of escape.

The consequent powerlessness of the individual, in the face of all this, is a conclusion urged upon us also by the link with Kafka's vision of life contained in the remainder of the stanza: the kerosene is

brought down from the castles
By insurance men who go
Check to see that nobody is
escaping
To Desolation Row.

Stanza nine deals with the result of this extermination of individuality and returns us to the element of urgency which Dylan finds consonant with his analysis.

Everybody is shouting
Which Side Are You On?

Perhaps the palm-court orchestra is playing it. And 'Which Side Are You On?', one remembers, is the song used by the Chorus in Duberman's play 'In White America'

So we have Dylan's America, presented with a power of conviction for which his artistry is responsible. What we have in 'Desolation Row' is far removed from the blanket, grating assemblage of accusation which pop-protesters like Mr. Barry McGuire will always assume to be adequate and worthy of attention. Neither is it a product of the easy occupation of preaching to the converted: Dylan

does not preach - he offers his comment, throws out the hint but with the poet's virility. And even for those who are, in a general sense, "converted" to the view that American society is nauseously uncivilised, Dylan's analysis is of a quality likely to make its expression in the poem a means of enhancing the reader's awareness. That is its value.

Where I think Dylan is immature in his judgement is in contending as he does in that ninth stanza that Eliot and Pound have sold out to the non-human values. Eliot in

continued on page 27

COCK UP SPANIELS

David Widgery

The Observer and Sunday Times are weekly installments in the collapse of the liberal British intellectual. Each Sunday we receive a new failure of nerve and intelligence, a further retreat from the wintry Moscow of their imagination, a new capitulation to the fantasies of consumerism. These papers are written by intellectuals for intellectuals and are a moving tribute to the total integration of both to the values and purposes of the Establishment. Whereas every European capitalist country has, in some form, a self aware, antagonistic intelligensia, with serious historical and social recourses, our spaniels have cut with the grain and are indistinguishable from it. The papers conviviality with its readers depends on their shared interest in personalities, commodities, clothes and cars, anything rather than ideas, because the profound bluff philistinesm of our spaniel intellectuals finds the very idea of a belief difficult and degrading. The absence of ideas does not of course prevent a great deal of pompous reflection by the graduates of some of our finest universities.

Cyril Connelly once had a little mag in Bloomsbury and has never quite got over it, Muggeridge can be found grinding in what's left of the two thoughts he has every year, Maurice Richardson moved his home so he could receive BBC2 and Kathrine Whithorne cares deeply about Hornblower, and social work and I can't imagine why people don't jolly well realise it. The heavies are still thought of as part of the social purpose of the magazine. Like Crash Courses in Philosophy, and Wall Charts on Modern Literature, no one reads them but they give the paper tone. Nowdays Totynbee Connely and Mortimer are harder to find in the index and among the tea rose by post adverts, but their tone of magnificient authority is still there:

Both papers care a lot about politics and war reporting. They run long editorials about Poverty and Race and Hunger when these topics are occasionally uncovered by events. While their politics, especially the Observers editorial line on Rhodesia and Africa and ST and defence may tend to radical, where it counts they accept throughout the logic of Wilsonism, modernisation, efficiency, growthism and the Freeze That Will Hurt (i.e. hurt the working class and the social programmes). The message, refracted 50 ways is a dense infatuation with the present, which is a sensible scheme for the million or so people who read these papers, who also own 67% or so of capital wealth and 82% of personal wealth, who take the lions share of the public social services and the elephant Share of occupational welfare and tax allowances. Both papers editorial on Greece, Detroit and Vietnam have been hurt and rather angry that everyone is so irrational. But its rationality is seen when the Sundays come to deal with the extremists who plot all these undesirable outbreaks. The ST systematically witchhunts. Examples: the 63 Greek Visit, the Society for Anglo Chinese Understanding, The Amalgamated Engineering Union, the National Union of Students, the National Union of Seamen in all of which cases the ST has carried partisan material before an election of meeting which names and smears left wingers. The Observer has not the reporters to manage this very often but does its bit with Grankshaw scissors and paste Kremlinology (which reached lower depths of vulgarity in his obituary of Deustcher) and its purchase of the Svetlana memoirs at a price which one can only hope will bankrupt the paper. The Sunday Times can report with extreme efficiency and technical ability on any given conflict, but this news is so skillfully handled by these great agencies of misinformation, that it becomes, not the basis for radical action but a palliative to it. The full colour coverage of the Vietnam and Israel Wars submerge us in a cluster of facts and opinion, probe and analysis but they manage to leave the reader distanced and academic, unable to relate human action to this world of powers and maps and diagrams which might as easily be Montgomery's Desert War.

But the central feebleness of their thought comes out in the photojournalism sired by Antony Sampson out of Lord Snowden whose prose aims at the complete replication of static reality (i.e. the ST on Cambridge and London Airport) or its Observererersion which consists of sending out John Gale, Colin McGlashin or Michael Braun to talk to Girls or Negroes or Debs. Not much writing is required for this instamix articles but what we get is the belief, shared by Aitken, that we are living in the time of a social revolution, a "new classness equalitarianism" (the O has applied this word to yatching, comprehensive schools, Birmingham and new universities). So Forget those dole ques that grow, the class rooms that fill, the houses that rot and the old lady who has just delightedly pulled a comic book out of the dustbin across the street.   In this land where all that matters is static, the revolutions must be in North Sea Gas, the struggle is one to turn a tank the right way round again, the discoveries" a delicious new toilet soap we've found, we keep the strawberry next to the bidet" The only change they dare hope for is change in late night telly; J. Millers Monitor "will break through the cliches of telly thinking and presentation and the defences of all but the most conventional viewer": David Frost will "express a new-style 1960-ish non-U youth leader, reclaimed from the verge of deliquency".

And all that it ever demonstrates is the wretchedness of their moral imagination, the fact that they have sold out without even being aware of the transaction. What's left is a pantomine of ruling class chic; the pert vulgarity and idiot condescension of Briefing and Hers. John Crosby, like DeeTime without guests, determined to laugh his way out of anything serious. The fashion pages which aren't about clothes any longer but beautiful nervous costumes to tide them over the blackness of the present. The supplement dream world not for people but for consumers who want to look like a director, smell like a man and have electrified teeth. It's a picture book world designed for evasion, and consists of what Hoggart called "anti life value full of a corrupt brightness, of improper appeals and moral evasions". The nervous twitches of the prose are the hectic verbless sentences, the oral phrases and the eternal use of the Observer We as if to prove there is some kind of umbellicus between the fashion staff and Life. The language attempts a flawed ambiguity which distances itself from its own excesses (as in the Atticus bad pun titles) and this in turn reflects an uncertain unstated relationship with its audience, uncertain because it has no basis in common intellectual ideas of values but rather in styles and behaviour. It is in the gossip feature that the Observer is being most honest; conversational, chi chi, object infested. It is culture of a decaying class consisting not of ideas, but ideas about ideas, ouvres rather than reviews, but gossip better than both. It differs from the Guardians Miscellany and the Observer's Colour Section only in the degree of self deceit. Its a culture entirely appropriate to its audience whose real problems are about au pairs, water proof leg make up, young children on aeroplanes and what to say at the next publishers'party. Not an antagonism to consumer values but a celebration of them. For there is no problem so serious that it can't be solved with a new negligee and "any girl who gets by on a pettycoat and a warm pair of pajamas deserves to sleep alone".

Its a world of spaniel words and spaniel ideas, some are friendly, some are even intelligent but they are all happiest when they are rolling on their backs.

MICHAEL X
& THE FLOWER CHILDREN

Because black people in this country and in America comprise such a small percentage of the population; how can you possibly expect a victory by force?

Malik: Don't you realise that the struggle is international and of the 3000,000,000 people in the world, only a small percentage are of non coloured races, like white? You are outnumbered by 2 to 1 at least.

But there are different battle-fronts, aren't there? Australia doesn't let any coloured people in, so you could never help the aborigines. And in America the whites could go out and shoot every black person they wanted to.

Malik: One of the strange things about the black man in the white western world is that he lives in the cities. Now he has proven that he can control the city because in Watts, which was the first experiment in this kind of thing, it took just 20 men to flatten it. By the time they reached Detroit, they were that efficient that the numbers had been cut down ...it took only 11 men to stop Detroit. It would take no more than 6 men in London to halt London completely. Obviously we can win.

But for how long could the 11 men halt Detroit and the 6 men halt London?

Malik: But it is not the point of holding something. It is stopping a machine that has gone insane; and if you can halt the machine for just a while there is a great

possibility that the thinkers insider of there will start thinking of what they are doing, because if you halt...if 6 men can stop 14 million from moving in the London area then surely you have to sit and think and not allow the machine to get out of control, beserk. The system is driving us as a people completely insane. I recognise the type of insanity that they are trying to throw at me. I too am being dehumanised and I resent that.

But there are whites who have already begun to think and begun to act and you won't work with them. Recently the chance of an alternative political party in America was jeopardised because even the extreme radical whites weren't able to work with the black militants. The blacks were unco-operative. There was a break up of this potential party. Don't you think it would have been tactically wiser to have joined forces with the radical whites and to have co-operated in establishing an alternative political party?

Malik: To begin with the party that calls itself 'radical white', is no such thing - it will be just a pack of other vicious white men: that's what they really are because they will sit and intellectualise about a lot of nonsense but they will do nothing about it when it comes to actually working.

Let's take for example the hippie element. They will do something positive about the system, like they will not pay attention to it - they intend to ignore it, depriving the politicians and so on of themselves as little pawns which the politicians call voters, and in this they have negated the very actions of these politicians. Now our arguments against the society and the system as a whole is one wherein there is no other answer but to destroy the system, there is no nature of a compromise, there is no compromise position that I can ever come to with the existant system. I could not use their structure. For example I could not use their machinery of the electorate and have one of us elected who will become Prime Minister or an M.P. or something - this doesn't mean anything because then we will have to operate with the same system and we too will be oppressors. What it is we would like to see done with the system is the total destruction of it, wherein a new sense of values will be established, wherein human beings will be the important thing that the system will be set up to protect. The present system is set to protect material things, property. This we think is one of the key bits of insanity in the present machine that is being run. Where it has gone mad. And this we will change. So I couldn't possibly join up with these type of people nor could I possibly think of ever running for an election. This is not the kind of thing we are at - I don't want to be Prime Minister of anywhere.

Although you say you can't work with white people, you seem to share hippie sentiments. Do you think you will ever co-operate with them?

Malik: We try to talk now which is very important- we cannot talk to anybody else in the community. We go through the motions of talk but we don't hear each other, whereas the hippies and ourselves have a pretty reasonable understanding. We listen to each other which doesn't mean we have to act on what each one says. For example, in the present issue of the Los Angeles Free press, you will see that Rap Brown is talking to the hippies in America. Take the present issue of IT and you will see that I am talking to the hippies here in England - so we are on a talking relationship, both in America and here and that's not coincidence.

You once said that amongst a sea of white faces in a riot, you wouldn't recognise any individual white faces. Would you see the hippies?

Malik: Well, man, if we can't see them we're going to going to hear them - they've taken precautions about that. They've put bells about their bloody necks.

You say that black or white men are essentially different. That they have a different frame of reference. That's what racists like Mike Hoare and Governor Wallace say. How would you differ from them?

Malik: I can understand hippies because they talk and they make themselves very clear - people like Mike Hoare and other racists also make their positions plain - now the vast majority of the white people in the world, I find, never make their positions plain. They say one thing and they do another. This makes it very difficult for me to understand such people, because basically I recognize and like the honest ones. I like those who say what they mean and do what they mean and what they say - so people like Mike Hoare, I understand him; it's not a matter of a cat I'd want to have breakfast with in the morning.

I do believe that the black peoples and the white peoples are basically quite different. Like we have had different types of experience all our lives, things that you know, I don't know. Simple things, like talking about this electoral system I don't know anything about that because I have never been there. I have no idea of what it is like to be white and free, just like you have no idea of what it is like to be black and be a slave. You may look in on it but you don't really know the feelings inside of it. I'm sure you have no idea of what your girlfriend feels like when she is pregnant. She may tell you, but you can never really feel that. This is something which is private only to her, and there is really no way she can get that feeling into you. I can give you as much as a look in as I can, as much as my pride and my ego and my sufferings, my pain and my joys and everything else will allow me to show you me.

I want to show you me, I want desperately to show all of me, because no doubt you might be able to communicate with the cat, whoever he is and he must exist, who can do something to change this nonsense that is happening, that fellow exists, he must live somewhere and I wish he could find out. I think they keep the news from him, whoever they are, they must, because if he knew and he was a just man he wouldn't allow what is happening now to happen.

He wouldn't allow us to be going completely along a path which is really to our own destruction - and his - because we have been driven so far now that the language we talk is "if we can't live in them fine houses now then noone is going to live in them". I think this is a very just statement, I think this is very very just and a great lot of our people think it is very very just. One can intellectualise their way in and out of that, they can say I'm right and they can say I am wrong, and they can argue it anyway they want. I'm not interested in that. I'm just telling you what I'm saying. So you can see what I am at and from there we can begin, you know, sorting that out.

A lot of white people are becoming involved with your problems even if sometimes only superficially.

15

like journalists out for a story. Certainly the white people in Watts and the people who rode freedom buses, they might have done the wrong thing but they were involved in the problem, black against white. I just wonder if black people ever get involved in other problems outside the race one. Say, the incredible oppression of the working classes in this country, the white working classes.

Malik: What you said clears up so much about what it is the National Press ignores about us. Like recently the hippies have set up a body called 'Release' designed to defend themselves when they get themselves arrested. Now before they had set that up, the facilities that they used for this purpose were our facilities which is a life organisation called 'Defense'.

Now you may have heard of something called the London Free School, which John Hopkins dreamt up a long time ago - I worked very hard with him and we did some very nice things in the Notting Hill area. Our mob has been working at all manner of strange things for people for centuries but no one seems to have known about it or otherwise you couldn't have asked such a question. We have worked in all manner of strange things, like we acted non violently before violently which is doing something for people, because that in itself is what has kept the human race alive. Otherwise we should have exterminated every white man a long time ago.

Stokey Carmichael

Michael X (Malik)

Surely if we all fucked each other the race problem would cease after a few generations?

Malik: I think this is a very wild and silly fantasy because Mr. Wilson certainly doesn't want his son to go fuck that pigmy girl I know down in the Congo, that isn't the kind of thing he will want done to his son and his son most certainly doesn't what that chick. And I don't want Princess Anne or Queen Elizabeth, you know, they just don't turn me on. There will always be white people and there will always be black people and there will always be yellow people. And all other manner of strange shades, greys, and yellows and browns and in betweens; they will always exist. That type of argument doesn't really mean anything to me. Whether it is we can do things by being exactly what I am, a big nigger, that's what I am, a black man. Whether it is I can remain a black man and at the same time relate to you, who is the white man. Whether we would be able to establish a talking relationship, a working relationship and a loving relationship between ourselves. Now this is important. But I don't want you to become me to do so: I want you to be you but a good you not the evil you, and I don't want to be the evil me in order to relate with you. But if I have to become the white man in order to relate to you then I am becoming the evil me, because the white man is evil. I want to be just me, and let us relate to each other, see what we can give to each other, and then in that there will be no tensions.

Notes from his pre-trial, Sept.29.

The press went to Reading and reported most of the words but none of the drama of the proceedings.

Because the prosecution had no complete record of Malik's contentious utterances, witnesses present at the Rainbow Hall speech were called to recall the bits they remembered or had noted at the time. Thus the record of the speech pieced together by the prosecution was a series of sensationalised statements plucked out of context and divorced from narrative logic.

Most of Malik's alleged speech was reproduced in the dailies. One quote was conspicuous by its absence:

Malik (to reporters): "You bastards follow me wherever I go and you write lies about me. Buy the paper tomorrow and you will see the lies they have written."

During the trial a negro rose from the gallery, walked to the dock and handed Malik a note. Spying this, a young ginger-headed policeman hurried to the dock and ordered Malik to surrender it. "Oh go away little boy", said Malik.

Further insults followed until the policeman left empty handed.

A clean cut, chiseled faced, self satisfied reporter from the Express, Brian Park, was the first to give evidence of Malik's speech. He was questioned at the end.

Malik: Do you understand black people when they talk.

Park: Yes, just as I hope they understand me.

Malik: Are you mamma-guy?

Park: I beg your pardon. I do not understand you.

After a fruitless quarrel between the Court and the defendent, Malik sighed: "We are not speeking the same language. We are on a different wave length".

Magistrate: No. We are speaking basic English.

Most of the proceedings were unforgettably boring. This was because the witnesses were duplicating each other's testimony and their depositions were recorded by an antique, non electric, non sound proof typewriter.

Prosecutor: Were you at Rainbow Hall on July 24?

Witness: Yes.

Typewriter: Ratatatatatatatat , .

Prosecutor: Did you take notes?

Witness: Yes.

Typewriter: Ratatatatatatat.

Prosecutor: Have you those notes with you now?

Witness: Yes.

Typewriter: Ratatatatatatat.

Etc.

During the trial a black member of the gallery lit a cigarette. A policeman swept over and ordered him to remove it. The black man stared angrily back at the policeman, cigarette jutting defiantly. No one moved. Suddenly another black man jumped up and extracted the cigarette. The policeman retreated and the two black brothers bickered furiously.

Occasionally the proceedings were interrupted by Malik's emotional outbursts ... "I cannot speak a language I cannot understand.....I will desperately try and communicate.....I am not going to play your game..."

The two magistrates, Clerk of the Court, witnesses and policemen all fidgeted uncomfortably and uncomprehendingly during those ejaculations. Once, one of them responded bewilderdly: "But we are not playing a game."

"WOULDN'T YOU LIKE TO BE ONE OF THE BEAUTIFUL PEOPLE...

THANKS

by A Haden-Guest/Keith Morris

DO YOU WANT MORE OUT OF YOUR SEX LIFE?

We have an extensive range of items designed to increase the intensity of sexual pleasure. Many of these have never before been available in this country. If there is something that you a that you may heard of, but can't get - try us!..

Room 3

Pellen Personal Products LTD.

47 Muswell Hill Broadway, London N.10

MEN IT CAN BE DONE

Now available --- MAGNAPHALL --- a sound and successful method of improving virility and increasing the size of the male organ. A method which is absolutely SAFE , involves no drugs or apparatus and is GUARANTEED MAGNAPHALL has helped thousands of men, all over the world. There is no longer a need for any man to envy the sexual vigour or proportions of others. You don't have to believe us -- we can send you such PROOF as will convince even the most skeptical.

For full details of how MAGNAPHALL works and positive proof of it's success, in strict confidence and with no obligation, write to:-

RAVENSDALE PRODUCTS LTD.
PERSONAL DEPARTMENT,
SPRINGFIELD ROAD,
LONDON. N.15.

JOIN THE BADGE SCENE

Wholesale enquiries invited

Send us your slogan ideas - 25 free badges for each one used!

KISS ME

IF IT MOVES FOND

I'm a Genius

UNITE all QUEER

LSD not LBJ

SMILE IF YOU HAD SEX LAST NIGHT

All badges 1½" diameter
Dayglow colours
1/6 each, 6 for 8/-,
12 for 15/-
plus 6d postage
Free catalogue available
New titles regurlarly.

BADGE & NOVELTY CO. (LONDON) 21 FITZROY ST. LONDON W1

smalls

OZ ADVERTISING WORKS BRILLIANTLY
Smalls: 1s. per word, 1/8 semi-display, 2/6
box no. Display: £65 per page, £35 half page,
£20 ¼ page, £2/10/- column inch. Book through
Paul Lawson, 12 Crescent Mansions, Elgin Crescent.
PAR 1042.

SHORTCOMINGS?

Prolong the pleasure of intercourse with Suifan's
'Kwang Tze' Solution. This Chinese preparation
is specially beneficial to men who suffer from premature ejaculation and is guaranteed to end mutual
frustration and bring satisfaction to both partners.
The Suifan's 'Kwang Tze' Solution is
completely safe and reliable, as stated in Government certificate supplied with each bottle.

Special Offer

To prove our claim we will send you by return-
and in complete confidence- a bottle of the

'Kwang Tze' Solution for only 2 Gns.

Order Direct from Sole Distributors

Blacks International,
Suite A,
24 Cranbourne St.,
Leicester Square,
London W.C.2.
Please Cross Cheques & P.O. & make payable
to Blacks International.

TURN ON / TUNE IN / DROP US A FIVER FOR A HOT
LINE TO INFINITY / JOURNEY THROUGH THE
INCREDIBLE LANDSCAPES OF YOUR MIND /
KALEIDOSCOPIC MOVING CHANGING IMAGE ON
WHICH YOUR MIND PROJECTS ITS OWN PATTERNS/
STUN YOURSELF & ASTONISH YOUR FRIENDS

This light machine is designed for easy operation and
personal adaption / works in rooms of all sizes - with
full instructions/ Send cheque, postal order for 5Gns. +
5/- post and packaging with full postal address to
ISETCO 13 Miranda Rd. LONDON N.19.

SILVER RINGS..

TURKISH TRICK RINGS .... from 19s.

FRIENDSHIP SICK RINGS.............. from 26s.
SEMIPRECIOUS STONES.............. from 75s.
VICTORIANA BARRELS................ from 84s.

Also Gold Hand made & to order MOD wedding or
engagement rings 10% 'off for two'

ADMIRAL'S EYE DESIGNCRAFT
32 St. Martin's Lane W.C.2. COV 1742.

A JACK FOR EVERY JILL OR JOE
5/- Each introduction, no extra charge whatever.
Write INTROBOUTIQUE
709 Fulham Rd. S.W.6.
736 2871

DUREX GOSSAMER 7/6 per doz.
POST FREE.

Tit-Bits, 709 Fulham Rd., S.W.6.

PREGNANCY TEST £2. Inquiries: BELL JENKINS
LABORATORIES.
Charlotte St. Portsmouth (23366)

FOR LIGHT REMOVALS DORMOBILES WITH HELP-
FUL WORKING DRIVERS. HAM 1466 or HAM 6351.
Please quote this advertisement.

come underwater

Dreaming in a DANDIE FASHIONS SUIT.
161 Kings Rd. LONDON S.W.3.
FLA 6851

PSYCHEDELIC FLOWER MOTIFS FOR YOUR CAR
or anything needing FLOWER POWER.
Send 20/- for large assorted pack.
SOLIDIA
370 Hornsey Rd.,
LONDON N.19.

Money back if not chuffed.

Coitus (Form -fitting............. 15/-doz.
Durex Fetherflite............... 15/-doz.
Durex Gossamer................. 15/-doz.
Crest Naturae................. 10/-doz.
Silver Tex.................... 8/-doz.
Fifteen assorted.............. 14/-doz.

Booklet Free, Return Post, Double Packed, plain
wrapper.
SUREX LTD. 8 Edward St. Blackpool.

THE MONTHLY ADVERTISER FOR THE SEXUALLY AWARE / WAY OUT / 2nd PERSONAL ADS
29 Westbourne Pk Mews, London W.2.

You are invited to become a member of

C.M.C.

SUBSTANTIAL DISCOUNT ON CLOTHES ETC.
FREE USE OF ACCOMODATION ADDRESS, SAME
DAY FORWARDING SERVICE.
FREE USE OF PEN PAL REGISTER,
FREE USE OF HOLIDAY REGISTER,
Members only CMCN Naturists
Send for detailed brochure (8d. in stamps please)
to Dept O
CMC 14 Alexandra Road,
Clacton-on-sea, ESSEX,

You've heard all about it.
NOW HERE IT IS !
Super Art Tattoo the rage of the Continent & USA.
Card contains a dozen multi-coloured, assorted,
waterproof tattoos. (They remove with nail polish
remover). Available only from :
ART TATTOO DEPARTMENT (LO)
88-90 Hatton Garden, London, E.C.1.

FOR ALL **transport** PROBLEMS

REMOVALS, DELIVERIES, ETC.
DORMOBILES WITH HELPFUL
WORKING DRIVERS.

taximoves GULIVER 8923

Young unattached girl or man who doesn't know where he
where he she is going/or who does know and doesn't
like it) invited to join team living in freedom and
for freedom.
BOX 71. OZ 38a Palace Gardens Terrace, LONDON W.8

SLEEKS
Young men's skintight stretch nylon underjeans,
shorts, 30s. Details s.a.e. LARRY KNIGHT
4 Hamilton Close, London N.W.8.

CONFIDENTIAL ADVICE ON THE PILL FOR ALL
WOMEN EVERYWHERE. WRITE STEP ONE LTD.
(O) 38 Regent St. W.1. s.a.e. or telephone
01-622-7915.

SUBSCRIBE

Newsweek is available in 166 lands on six
continents. OZ is hard to find almost everywhere.
That's why Nancy Stick took out a subscription.
She lives in Addis Ababa.
But even if you live as close as Stoke Poges, a
subscription makes sense. It's the only
way you can ever be sure of your monthly copy of
OZ.
& if you subscribe now, you'll receive immediately
two back issues free.
So clip out the form below and mail it with your
cheque or P.O. for 30/- or $4 to OZ Subscription
right now.

I enclose 30/- or $4 for 12 issues of OZ

Name...

Address..

OZ Subscription 38a Palace Gardens Terrace.
London W.8.
*I enclose 9/- for 4 back issues.

OZ wants an experienced space salesman - 25%+
commission on graduated scale. PAR 1042.

Ray Durgnat wrote 'Marshall McLuhan's
One Eyed Kingdom' in OZ 6. His latest book
'Films and Feelings' published by Faber & Faber
is in bookstores now.

continued from Page 3

black veils on cinema projectors. Inhibitions breed frustrations, frustrations breed obsessions, life is distorted, the mind is degraded.

Being the last to have joined the castrated, social democrat rich of Europe, they are the most gullible, the most vulgar and they suffer the most from this newly acquired absurdity. It's accepted only because their sole comparison is with their previous poverty.

This is a long introduction which has almost killed my style but which should tell the reader that he is very lucky if his only problem is to know just where his next acid is coming from.

The example of Italy, the most repressed of the "not poverty stricken countries", the rotten apple with the golden skin, where to be young is a sin and to be old is deadly, should show them how desperately they're needed. Entrenched in Portobello Rd, barricaded in Kings Rd, surrounded by photographers' flashes and miserable, mercenary flattery you forget your undeveloped brother: the teenagers wasting their spunk on their handkerchief, the young cunts rusting, the forlorn hands never finishing the job, the misery of the segregation of the sexes, the tyranny of garters, the injustice of coitus interruptus, the darkness of organs never shown, the mental fatigue of the unachieved. Oh! you wouldn't have time for your daisies, there where the bread is so meagre, where every male eye spells danger and every female eye spells unwillingness.

It's very easy to sleep with comfortable dollies and proclaim the psychedelic era. Hyde Park may be conquered but the parks in Milan are still in the hands of the enemy.

You should have been there when the police raided and destroyed the first beatnik camp (two thousand strong) in Via Ripamonti in Milan, early this summer. There aren't any hippies there yet, it's too early for joy, it's still time for anger. You ask for democracy of love, they ask for freedom of sex.

You should advocate here-and-now flower guerrillas in Europe, and England should be like Cuba. Bring the flowers to sunny Italy, darkened by secular oppression. Don't just send the slogans (make love, not war) don't just send the generals (the pop groups). Here they are tired of listening to the words of the Beatles, those Lenins of the mind promising an impossible paradise. Italian

teenagers need help - quickly. Don't send medicines (the pill), or small arms (records), send men (girls).

The Pope, (Allen Ginsberg) has already been here (to Spoleto), and was charged with obscenity by Italian law. He will stand trial in November. In Spoleto, a small, beautiful town in central Italy, the weather will be mild, the judges will be bastards - let's go down.

We have only one thing to gain: our consciousness, nothing to lose but our minds.

Let the old asses worry, let them drink petrol and smoke pound notes.
See: the old man talking fondly to his telly be - longs to another geological era, to the era of big wars and small pleasures. He must disappear, like the dinosaurs. We won't need passports to piss from trees, we won't need old currency to lay new women, we won't need teachers to show us the way. We'll be given chocolate sixpences for every smile, coppers will be employed to keep the rain out of our sleeping bags, bankers will clean our stained sheets - when the time will come.
But now is the time to preach and convince, the time to fuck hard and sleep rough. Now is the time to come to Italy, en masse.

For every black priest Rome breeds we want three hippies, one masculine, one feminine, one neuter, this is our programme. As long as Rome is still in enemy hands, London is in danger. From the top of Primrose Hill, on clear nights, you can see, if you stretch your eyes, platoons of Italian mothers armed with vacuum cleaners, the Virgin Mary their guide. Their breath is of poisonous gas, their eyes smile like napalm, their cunts are stuffed with hand grenades, their nails are made of phosphorous. How can you sleep with so many nuns around?

Our only salvation, our only hope is to unite, to form a new International: to help our brothers in need of a fuck, of a laugh, of anything and everything.

I've told you this about Italy so you'll go there to help them. You don't need addresses. I won't give you any.

Grow and spread the flower, grow and multiply, the numbers of heavens are infinite for each man. The crows will die.

In Bed With The Americans   by Polly Peachum

The American is a very clean sort of person. (There are some who say he has to be, because cleanliness is about the only thing he has going for him.) At the laundromat, his oversized boxer shorts and interlock undershirts are never just bleached - they're double bleached. He sports what must be the driest armpits in all of Christendom. And no American bathroom cabinet is complete without its family size bottle of mouthwash. (Recently, a new mouthwash 'very concentrated golden breath drops, entered the market. There is no doubt that part of its appeal was the subliminal suggestion that unheard of sexual successes wait the Man with the Golden Breath.) The female of the species, against all sorts of reasonable medical advice, douches once, or even twice a day with a Tennessee-made powder put out in individual pre-measured packettes that are guaranteed to make her feel more than just clean. The packettes like the concentrated breath drops are conveniently miniaturised for eary portability, You are intended to tend to your breath and what not, the way you might reapply your lipstick-namely, often. At home, hung defiantly behind every All-American girl's bathroom door are yards and yards of terrifying equipment, to bear testimony, I suppose, to a routine of relentless cleansing, not to mention the owner's sexual emancipation and, no doubt, availability. It is no surprise, then, to learn that mere seconds after the final blinding moment of ecstasy, Mister and Miss Clean race each other to the bathroom with a ferocity and competitiveness unmatched anywhere in or out of the animal kingdom. No American male or female ever wants to be unclean a second longer than necessary - no matter what the circumstances. When opportunities for contamination are likely to be frequent, a two-bathroom dwelling is chosen. It is the only reasonable explanation for the new system which provides one bedroom apartments with His and Her bathrooms. (A Texas store does His n' Her bath-tubs).

This probably also explains why many American resort hotels which specialise in honeymooners see fit to present as their chief attraction

circular Roman baths - tiled sunken and six feet in diameter. One place in Pennsylvania goes so far as to pass over, in its advertisements, its colour TV, heated pool, late-late-late sleepyhead breakfasts, roaring log fires and high fidelity mood music, in favour of a full paged picture of a heartshaped bathtub. One can only presume that fastidious honeymooners prefer to start their married life with the cleanest sort of copulation - in a bathtub, heartshaped to provide a touch of romance for those who may find it still a little too conjugal for embraces.

Without a doubt, behind this preoccupation with cleanliness is a great national eagerness not to offend. It has not yet occurred to Americans that being obsessively preoccupied with offending is even more offensive. (When an American woman gently inquires of her partner during intercourse Have you slimed yet? she betrays a passion for cleanliness at least 100 points more offensive than the mildly perspiry armpits she worries about so incessantly. If her partner is not American that is. If he is, he might very well reply, equally tenderly, NO, honey, have you?).

It has been suggested that cleanliness in these cases is nothing more than impersonality. The ideal American coupling, one feels, is that of two neutral plastic-fresh bodies that try to leave each other as untouched as possible both physically and emotionally. (In the Underground Uplift Button Shop, a button says 'Love is alive and well in Mexico City'. 'It just doesn't want to get involved'. 'Follow me, if you want uncomplicated Love' says another. Americans as lovers are very much the same as Americans as tourists. Getting there is half the fun, did after all start off as an American tourist slogan. The American tourist likes to steep himself in the whole business of travel. He buys countless guidebooks, even learns the language, gets all excited, but, once he gets there somehow never does get to eat much of the food or talk to the natives. Afterwards, though, he does talk about it a lot. At least, he makes a point of boasting he's been there, though he'll also express his dis-

appointment on many occasions and discourage others from following his steps.

So the lover. He does not like to take no for an answer. Money is never any object. (The Americans have a contemptuous term for the girl who puts out without being bought in some way first. As one girl here said, 'I'd rather be a whore than a freebie'.) And of course, for the country of sex there are many guidebooks. The lovers, like the tourists, like their guidebooks systematic. Listen to the blurb on the back of Robert Street's best selling paperback of Modern Sex Techniques. It starts, 'With admirable frankness, the authors present detailed step by step instructions for achieving mutual sexual satisfaction. These include a directive to be carried out on the bridal night, which has the groom comparing the book's diagrams of the female reproductive system with its real life counterpart.

Not that the American passion for efficiency is always such a bad thing. There is a type of American made to order for the age of computers who because he likes to know all the answers, asks all the questions. We have seen their questionnaires on other topics. The erotic questionnaire is just as detailed. 'Do you have a favourite position?' 'Is there any position of caress you particularly like/dislike?'

But the goal of the questioner is not a bout of prolonged pleasure with less of the usual awkward misunderstandings. It is orgasm for both parties. ('Orgasms, for sale rent or trade' is a popular button,) the Big 'O' - the only measure of sexual success American men (and women) will accept, and a favour few American women are willing to make available to any but a chosen few. (They don't mind cutting off their noses to spite their faces if it means bringing down a male ego a couple of notches. That's the battle of the sexes for you.') What happens, then, is that after several encounters with this sort of woman,

(the first is invariably, if only symbolically, with his mother) many American men will give up. They either become homosexual or merely passive. Like the man who had me on the brink of finally yielding to his impressive blandishments when he ruined everything by sinking gracefully back on the bed, flinging out his arms and exhorting with more than a trace of coquetishness: 'Do something spectacular!)

Being young and inexperienced I imagined he wanted me to don a spangled Uncle Sam costume and do a tap dance on his bared and waiting jelly belly, but Americans aren't kinky like the English, and all he meant was 'Do anything, the more interesting, the better, but just get the responsibility off MY tired shoulders! In a country where women like to win, no man wants to be in a position of always being the loser.

It is no accident that the American man's term for 'scoring' with the opposite sex is 'getting laid', as in, 'I got laid last night.' ('What are you going to do to me?' I once heard a man ask a woman in a Times Square bar.) Passive, perhaps, but at least no one's going to tell him he's no good in bed. This naturally accounts for the strong oral motif in American wall writings. Buttons that say "Dracula sucks,and "LXIX"" far outsell 'Frodo lives', 'END THE WAR IN VIETNAM', and 'I FEEL SEXY, HOW ABOUT YOU?'

Andy Warhol's film, BLOWJOB never fails to draw large crowds, even though it consists of nothing more than thirty-three minutes of the head and shoulders of a young man whose facial expression rarely varies. (Why should it? He doesn't want to get involved.) No American man does. Though all are in analysis because they are looking for a meaningful relationship. And with the acute man shortage in America, in the cities anyway, no man has to. I think it was Tom Wolfe who commented that American men are now developing all the

traits of a spoiled and much sought after woman.

Why not when one of the country's most successful magazines Cosmopolitan is written around this premise?

(No wonder they can afford to sit back and say 'Do something spectacular', or as in another case, 'Say something dirty').

The success of Cosmopolitan was matched by Sex and the Single Man only because women bought it to see what they could learn. Meanwhile American men are invariably puffy and unimaginatively dressed with only one redeeming feature, good skin, but even that is a disadvantage. For one good reason, it simply heightens the resemblance all of them bear to their mothers.

MICHAEL CRAWFORD   JOHN LENNON

HOW I WON THE WAR x

Co-starring
ROY **KINNEAR** · LEE **MONTAGUE** · JACK **MacGOWRAN**

MICHAEL **HORDERN** · JACK **HEDLEY** · Also starring KARL MICHAEL **VOGLER**

SCREENPLAY BY **CHARLES WOOD** · BASED ON THE NOVEL BY **PATRICK RYAN** · PRODUCED AND DIRECTED BY **RICHARD LESTER** · ASSOCIATE PRODUCER **DENIS O'DELL**

EASTMAN COLOUR   A Petersham Films Ltd, Production

If you think Richard Lester's 'HOW I WON THE WAR' is just another war film— forget it.

NOW SHOWING LONDON PAVILION

Advertisement

Switch on to **Penthouse** this month and devour Michael Thomas's
5,000-word celebration of hippiedom, the fullest, liveliest, most understanding
article on the world of the Flower People yet published in the British press. And,
for Marshall McLuhan's non-readers, skip the words and relish the pictures—five solid
pages of hippie reportage in full colour.

Get hip, get Penthouse, the record-breaking magazine for men:
record-breaking sale (ABC 160,437), record-breaking number of colour
pages, record-breaking frankness in its famous Forum and other features.
Also: gorgeous nudes, sexy science fiction, outspoken comment,
Kingsley Amis interview, violence in ancient Rome, and a final instalment
of Al Capone serial.
October   Five shillings

Other Scenes

Pirate radio – and its inevitable successor pirate television – could have brought down this government if the stations had stuck together on a point of principle rather than gutlessly giving up the ghost. Its advertisers, even more disgustingly, are going to great lengths to disassociate themselves even when they get free ads. Boycott all advertisers who write letters to newspapers with disclaimers. The irony is that there's so much money to be made from commercial radio that the next government – a Tory one, inevitably – will undoubtedly sponsor it. Transferred to the United States pirate radio and television will be a major weapon against the U. S. establishment as soon as stations start broadcasting from the ghettoes of Watts, Harlem and Detroit.

The bumbling, let-the-customer-wait British telephone service introduced a curious new system a few months ago – a policy of charging 3Os for uncompleted transatlantic calls that were made collect" (i.e. transferring the charge). If, for example, you make a call to your publisher in New York and his secretary understandably won't accept the call because he's not there you'll be charged 3Os for the call anyway. The bumbling, let-the-customer-wait british telephone service justifies this on the grounds that they've had to do the "work" of trying to get the call but, of course, they would have done the work anyway and nobody minds paying for a call if it IS completed. The new system marks a subtle change in telephone company attitudes: once you paid for talking to a person, now you have to pay to find out that he's not there. Will the British telephone subscriber complain? Not likely. That's why charges like this can be safely imposed.

Time & Tide, which likes to think of itself as Britain's only news magazine, has undergone a facelifting recently and comes out basically Rightwing and slick – but with some interesting features. It doesn't, for example, promote a straight reactionary line and some of its more simple-minded readers had this not only confused but disquieting. There's nothing that bothers simple, prejudiced minds more than to find someone who doesn't share their opinions but not all of them ...

"How do you like it so far?"....Hatemonger named Andrew Fergus, writing in Scotland's Sunday Mail (he's described as 'Scotland's most outspoken writer', if you care) says he's had a bellyful of the Beatles. "Even the death of their friend Brian Epstein hasn't taught them humility", he whines. Multi-millionaire musical geniuses don't really need to learn humility, one might suggest. Even from a pompous Glasgow hack who heads his column: "My Advice to the Beatles" ... The publishers of the glossy mag "Antique Finder" are turning an almost-neglected sport into an artistic joy. Their "Portobello Finder" (6s from 39b Harrington Rd, SW7) is more imaginatively produced than any such magazine has a right to be .... Tom Wolfe's next book is on SF's Haight-Ashbury scene....Israel's best zoo, the Biblical Zoo in Jerusalem, is building a reptile house in response to requests from all the new Arab Tourists. "This is probably due to the prominent place occupied by snakes in Arab folklore", a zoo biologist is quoted as saying in September's "Jewish Observer & Middle East Review"....Anthony Lejeune writing in Daily Telegraph magazine: "Without doubt this is the worst, the most dictatorial, the most untrustworthy, the most contemptible administration beneath which our unhappy country has languished for at least a century"...Insider's Newsletter says that one week before the Israeli war broke out last June the head of Israel's airforce got a call from a security officer to say: "There's a journalist here trying to file a story to London that we could destroy the Egyptian air force in 7O minutes. What should I do?" The journalist was Winston Churchill II and he was persuaded to drop his story.

particular must be acknowledged as a poet of greatness - far more so than say, Walt Whitman, whose influence can be detected in Dylan's early work. (It is, for example, prominent in the long, piled-up lines of 'A Hard Rain's A-Gonna Fall'.)

"Art," as Collingwood somewhat pompously suggests, "is the community's medicine against the worst disease of mind, the corruption of consciousness." Eliot, unquestionably, has exercised his responsibility in this direction and is very far from fighting for the captaincy of the Titanic. Dylan's claim to validity as an artist must ultimately stand or fall by his acceptance or rejection of this same responsibility. So too must the measure of his _success_ as an artist be the quality of perception which he brings to bear in the struggle against this corruption of consciousnes

It may be said that Dylan's claim _is_ valid and his success appreciable.

WHAT IS it? it?

—THAT CAN SLOW DOWN YOUR THINKING
—CAN TAKE THE EDGE OFF YOUR APPETITE
—CAN CAUSE COLDS TO HANG FOR WEEKS
—CAN MAKE WORK (LITERALLY!) A "HEADACHE"
—CAN SPOIL ENJOYMENT OF SMOKING
—AND IT'S USUALLY BLAMED ON THE WEATHER!

You'll find the answer
IN YOUR HEAD
IT SURVIVES IF _you_ SUBSCRIBE!

SUBSCRIBE OR DIE!

RATE FOR ONE YEAR ....

NAME ....

ADDRESS ....

....

Cut me out and send to: INTERNATIONAL
TIMES, 102 SOUTHAMPTON ROW, W.C.1

YEARLY SUBSCRIPTION RATE

U.K. & Northern Ireland	£3	Italy	4,175 Lire
Belgium	350 Francs	Morocco	35 Dirham
Canada	$7	Netherlands	24 Guilders
Denmark	46 Kroner	Sweden	35 Kr.
France	35 New Francs	Spain	400 Pesetas
Germany	27 Deutschmarks	Switzerland	30 Francs
Greece	200 Dr.	U.S.A.	$7

owever premature Time magazine's comments might have been about swinging London there's no doubt that England is on the verge of its most exciting cultural revolution for many years. Everything is starting to come together: an exciting winter is coming up. Many more of America's social and cultural guerillas have had their effect– Grogan with plans for a Digger group; Andy Warhol; Frank Zappa; numerous film makers, writers and rock go groups. More light shows and freak out centers are planned; more gathering places for the English tribe.

From past experience in Greenwich Village, Haight Ashbury and L. A.'s Fairfax–Melrose districts, it would seem that the single most important requirement in London at the moment is for a COMMUNITY. Weekend meetings at UFO & Middle Earth (defunct?) and similar are all very well & the Saturday gatherings on Portobello and Kings Roads are very colorful – but still only transitory. What's needed is a place where like–minded people can live together and congregate in a specific area; an area where rents are low and big houses or buildings are available for ashrams or smaller collectives. Chelsea would be ideal but it's too expensive; Battersea might be better but isn't terribly accessible.

There's talk of converting some of the disused warehouses in the Covent Garden area into studios etc. but this isn't entirely practical for several reasons not the least of which is that some kind of zoning laws are obviously going to be applied to the area when the market moves out (in 1970) and money is going to talk. Also it's a gloomy area and isn't condusive to milling about. At the present time, Notting Hill Gate and the Portobello Road area looks like a better bet if it can be turned into an all–week scene.

How can such a community be strengthened and struct– ured? Firstly by Digger action to ensure that it isn't turned into a high–priced, boutique–filled tourist area too fast. Lots of free things, all–night coffee houses and delicatessens. New undergound newspapers – the more the better – and publications devoted to the experimental and avant garde. An underground movie theatre operating as a cooperative to show the work of all members as well as the best of the American and European underground.

There are problems in the way of underground publishing here that don't exist in America. Printing in the States is faster, cheaper and with less interference from the printers who, in England, take it upon themselves to act as censors. Miles says that America's photo offset revolution is being delayed here because all the offset equipment is owned by big firms who pay royalties to U.S. companies to use the process. Okay then, other breakthroughs must be made: some kind of a mimeographed publication can be effectively published and distributed – like Haight– Ashbury's famous Communications Company that rushes mimeo–ed "newspapers" onto the streets with several editions daily.

Finally, a major issue that the new community has to face is what is to be the nature of its relationship with the squarer and not–necessarily–sympathetic community around it? Ideally, the drop out society shouldn't have to think about such bring–down matters: a group of friendly anarchists, full of love, peace, flowers and social revolution ought to be able to do its own thing without outside interference.

But realistically, wherever such a community starts its members will always make some of the neighbours uptight: some don't like to see inter–racial couples, long–haired 'freaks' & minimally– dressed 'teeny– boppers'; they can't stand either the all–night parties or the gentle tinkling outside; some abhor incense & are frightened of...pot. All these are personified in and represented by the police who take it upon themselves to harass, frame and divide such happy groups.

How can they be handled? By responsible political action & sympathetic lawyers. If you are in on the beginning of a 'community' – however freaky– always make sure that there is someone willing to represent you in the politics game. Some love that stupid scene so let them play it. The only thing that cuts any ice with authority is, unfortunately, power – and power is any group that appears to have a spokesman. It may not be nescessary to actually deliver votes just so long as they seem to be potentially available.

There are many ingredients necessary for a revolution. The extremists, by making outrageous demands, condition the Establishment to settle for more than they would normally agree to. The politicians – OUR Politicians – do the settling. And the rest of us (hope'fully) live in peace.

A Review of 'The Science of Being and Art of Living'   by His Holiness Maharishi Mahesh Yogi

hile at first sight this might seem just a simplified variety of the westernised Hinduism that has sold fairly well over the last 100 years, His Holiness quickly distinguishes himself from such previous solvers of the problems of Man and the Universe as Gurdjieff and Ouspensky. For, while he asks for no sweat, blood or tears (his way being not straight and narrow but broad and easy), yet he promises the most amazing results. He 'deals with the fundamentals of all problems of life' and knows 'one solution to eradicate all suffering' (p. 19). While this claim itself would be enough to condemn the book for some, others may like to hear more.

His Holiness unoriginally, considers Einstein's Relativity Theory a good starting point for such an excursion and he gives it a couple of hundred words at the beginning. 'The physical sciences', he has noticed, 'inform us the whole of creation is built up of layers of energy, one inside the other'. I myself had not heard of this before, and it is a measure of His Holiness's breadth of culture that he is able to inform us in this fashion. The revolution started by Einstein has put to the scientists the view that 'there might exist some fundamental form of energy, which is absolutely stable and more subtle than any other form of energy. The relative would then arise as perturbations of this absolute energy, and all forms of physical energy would be manifestations of this absolute state of unmanifested energy' (p. 26). And indeed His Holiness is able to assure us that the scientists have not gone wrong and that there is such a fundamental form, though he first heard about it, not from the scientists, but from His Divinity Swami Brahmananda Saraswati, Jagadguru Bhagwan Shankaracharya, 'the most illustrious of the Jagadguru Shankaracharyas of India. Manifestly, it would be

irrational to reject such a congruence of the scientists of the West with His Divinity of the East.

His Holiness reiterates that it will only be possible to discover the one solution by transcendental meditation under the guidance of a teacher from the Spiritual Regeneration Movement, for which you will be charged 'one week's net income' (husband and wife treated as one, and a meditate-now-and-pay-later scheme available). It is not possible fully to understand even the published book by the light of your own unaided reason (p. 58). Recognizing this, however, there are still passages which are puzzling. For example, it is unclear how the 'fundamental form of energy' referred to above can be both 'absolutely stable' and also exhibit 'perturbations', or how anything can be a manifestation of something which is itself unmanifested.

Some of his claims, moreover, might not pass unchallenged. for example: in his discussion of architecture and money, on pp. 75-6, he says, with special reference to the money got from the sale of alcohol or tobacco, that 'any house built with it, has an over-all depressing effect'. Yet I myself know two millionaires who live in

such houses, and who do not appear depressed.

There are many other passages that are open to serious question, however, set against these the book contains a lot of simple uplift after the fashion of St. Matthew's Christian Gospel (e.g., pp. 95-101). Here we are enjoined to develop all 'a loving, kind and sympathetic heart', which seems quite excellent if not wholly without adumbration. And indeed if there be any who are anxious to expose themselves to conventional Christian uplift, while doing so in a slightly exotic atmosphere, then the Spiritual Regeneration Movement may suit them very well. On the other hand, some species of Christianity specifically reject the view that life should not be a struggle (p. 258), and that it is not a simple matter to jump to glory. But all such idle cavilling is swept away by the breathtakingly beautiful suggestion, on p. 275, that God is like butter. The conception is subtle and yet, like all supremely logical achievements, bewitching in its simplicity. The impersonal God, it seems, permeates the entire field of creation as butter permeates milk and, just as 'if the level of the butter is to be reached in milk, it is necessary to enter into the subtle strata of milk', so also the only way to realise God is 'to enter into the subtle strata of anything'. Possibly His Holiness would not claim this as the easiest passage in his book; but I do not doubt that anybody who can once understand its truth will quickly discover the one solution of all suffering.

Meanwhile, for those who cannot afford a week's wages (net) for the study of philosophy, I should recommend the Workers' Educational Association, which is now enrolling people for the next session at 25/-.

CRYSTAL WINGS AND POWDERED DREAMFLAKES DUST MY PATH WITH SWEET
DELUSIONS
HAMA
BLOODY TWO DAY DEADLINE NOTICE...
THEY MUST THINK I'M A MACHINE...
ONE MORE GIG LIKE THIS...
AND I'LL CRACK-UP!
BLASTED HEADACHE IS COMING BACK, EYESTRAIN....
SPA-FON!
....MOST PROBABLY LACK OF SLEEP, MY HEAD FEELS FUNNY, WEIGHTLESS....
COME ON MATE! WE'VE GOT TO GET OUT OF HERE! THEY'RE COMING!
WHAT.... GOOD LORD! GET AWAY FROM ME!

the body's heat regulator, the hypothalamus, the thing in the brain that oversees blood temperature, and pushes blood closer to the surface so the body can be cooled. When it fails the blood becomes overheated. Temperature rises rapidly. Convulsions, vomiting and coma follow. Death next. At 106° the globulin in your nerve cells begins to coagulate. In other words you cook. It's called sunstroke.

Sunlight is no place for beginners. Or anyone else for that matter. It can't possibly do you any good. If you have been told something about Vitamin D, forget it, you get all you need by drinking milk occasionally or by sitting in a sunlit room by the window. Reflected light is sufficient. And too much Vitamin D results in kidney failure.

Some argue that a bronzed appearance will help get rid of their depression, hide pimples and make them desirable people. Maybe, but their skin will certainly have: Thickened, Coarsened, Lost elasticity, Discoloured in the process. Women of 40 who have spent much of their time in the sun will have the skin of a 40 year old.

Ever thought about the nature of sunburn itself? Its pathology is the same as a first degree burn. The oedema (swelling) may be so great that blisters form. Keep it up and the whole skin lifts. The skin goes red and swells. Fluid in the body leak away and slowly you die. If you don't go as far as that and it doesn't scar. In any case the mobility of your joints will be diminished.

As you come back from a Mediterranean summer holiday you notice the raised roughened areas on the back of your hands or on your face. by skin contractions. It's skin cancer. Not the worst kind though. If treated before it turns into an ulcer it probably won't spread. Once it metastasises and gets into the blood stream growths spring up. one of the black moles you've always worried about has changed shape and colour. The body is eaten away. Nor the worse kind though. What you have is a form of (fairly rare) cancer called malignant melanoma. It delights the medical profession with its implacable malignancy and ability to spread around the body.

through a woman with its insidious beginning, making her hair grey before its time, an extra growth of hair on her face, arms and legs, a rare condition.

a big too long, your retina has a blind area in the sun. Don't wear sunglasses. It will give your retina a severe blind spot. the brain haemorrhages. the blood vessels burst. As the temperature rises. heat stroke. in extreme it becomes cramps, vomiting. Without it there will be. Salt also is needed. Will not help. Drinking water. (from perspiration.) loses too much fluid the body. heat exhaustion. commonly produces. strenuous work in hot weather. has been calculated as being 350 fahrenheit. The ideal temperature for mental work, not dissimilar to a maximum, and giving rise to large, grey, and wary patches of skin growing tufts of hair.

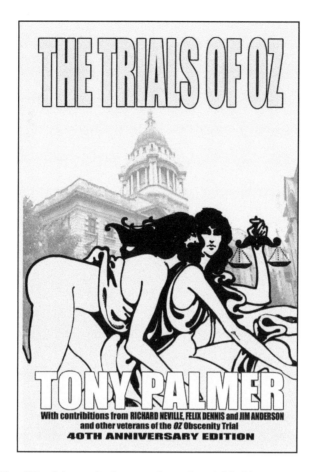

The *OZ* trial was the longest obscenity trial in history. It was also one of the worst reported. With minor exceptions, the Press chose to rewrite what had occurred, presumably to fit in with what seemed to them the acceptable prejudices of the times. Perhaps this was inevitable.

The proceedings dragged on for nearly six weeks in the hot summer of 1971 when there were, no doubt, a great many other events more worthy of attention. Against the background of murder in Ulster, for example, the *OZ* affair probably fades into its proper insignificance. Even so, after the trial, when some newspapers realised that maybe something important had happened, it became more and more apparent that what was essential was for anyone who wished to be able to read what had actually been said. Trial and judgment by a badly informed press became the order of the day. This 40th Anniversary edition includes new material by all three of the original defendants, the prosecuting barrister, one of the *OZ* schoolkids, and even the daughters of the judge. There are also many illustrations including unseen material from Felix Dennis' own collection...

ALSO AVAILABLE FROM GONZO MULTIMEDIA

Books

There is still such a thing as alternative Publishing

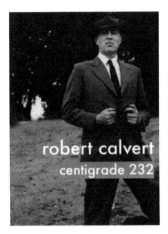

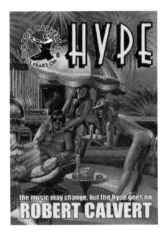

Robert Newton Calvert: Born 9 March 1945, Died 14 August 1988 after suffering a heart attack. Contributed poetry, lyrics and vocals to legendary space rock band Hawkwind intermittently on five of their most critically acclaimed albums, including Space Ritual (1973), Quark, Strangeness & Charm (1977) and Hawklords (1978). He also recorded a number of solo albums in the mid 1970s. CENTIGRADE 232 was Robert Calvert's first collection of poems.

Hype   'And now, for all you speeding street smarties out there, the one you've all been waiting for, the one that'll pierce your laid back ears, decoke your sinuses, cut clean thru the schlock rock, MOR/crossover, techno flash mind mush. It's the new Number One with a bullet … with a bullet … It's Tom, Supernova, Mahler with a pan galactic biggie …' And the Hype goes on. And on. Hype, an amphetamine hit of a story by Hawkwind collaborator Robert Calvert. Who's been there and made it back again. The debriefing session starts here.

Rick Wakeman is the world's most unusual rock star, a genius who has pushed back the barriers of electronic rock. He has had some of the world's top orchestras perform his music, has owned eight Rolls Royces at one time, and has broken all the rules of composing and horrified his tutors at the Royal College of Music. Yet he has delighted his millions of fans. This frank book, authorised by Wakeman himself, tells the moving tale of his larger than life career.

"So many books, so little time."
Frank Zappa

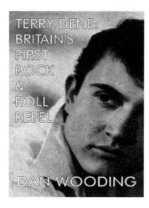

There are nine Henrys, pur
ported to be the world's
first cloned cartoon charac
ter. They live in a strange
lo fi domestic surrealist
world peopled by talking
rock buns and elephants on
wobbly stilts.

They mooch around in their
minimalist universe suffer
ing from an existential
crisis with some genetically
modified humour thrown in.

Marty Wilde on Terry Dene: "Whatever
happened to Terry becomes a great deal
more comprehensible as you read of the
callous way in which he was treated by
people who should have known better
many of whom, frankly, will never know
better   of the sad little shadows of
the past who eased themselves into
Terry's life, took everything they
could get and, when it seemed that all
was lost, quietly left him — Dan Wood
ing's book tells it all."

Rick Wakeman: "There have
always been certain 'careers'
that have fascinated the
public, newspapers, and the
media in general. Such
include musicians, actors,
sportsmen, police, and not
surprisingly, the people who
give the police their employ
ment: The criminal. For the
man in the street, all these
careers have one thing in
common: they are seemingly
beyond both his reach and,
in many cases, understanding
and as such, his only associ
ation can be through the
media of newspapers or tele
vision. The police, however,
will always require the ser
vices of the grass, the
squealer, the snitch, (call
him what you will), in order
to assist in their investiga
tions and arrests; and amaz
ingly, this is the area that
seldom gets written about."

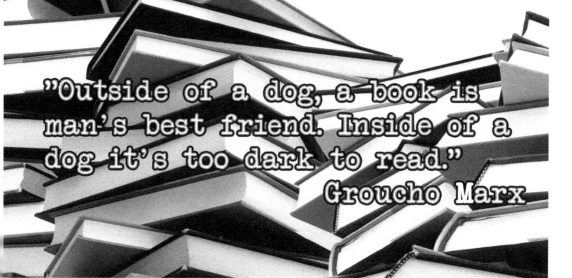

"Outside of a dog, a book is
man's best friend. Inside of a
dog it's too dark to read."
Groucho Marx

Bill Harkleroad joined Captain Beef heart's Magic Band at a time when they were changing from a straight ahead blues band into something completely different. Through the vision of Don Van Vliet (Captain Beefheart) they created a new form of music which many at the time considered atonal and difficult, but which over the years has continued to exert a powerful influence. Beefheart re christened Harkleroad as Zoot Horn Rollo, and they embarked on recording one of the classic rock albums of all time Trout Mask Replica - a work of unequalled daring and inventiveness.

Politics, paganism and .... Vlad the Impaler. Selected stories from CJ Stone from 2003 to the present. Meet Ivor Coles, a British Tommy killed in action in September 1915, lost, and then found again. Visit Mothers Club in Erdington, the best psyche delic music club in the UK in the '60s. Celebrate Robin Hood's Day and find out what a huckle duckle is. Travel to Stonehenge at the Summer Solstice and carouse with the hippies. Find out what a Ranter is, and why CJ Stone thinks that he's one. Take LSD with Dr Lilly, the psychedelic scientist. Meet a headless soldier or the ghost of Elvis Presley in Gabalfa, Cardiff. Journey to Whitstable, to New York, to Malta and to Transylvania, and to many other places, real and imagined, polit ical and spiritual, transcendent and mundane. As The Independent says, Chris is "The best guide to the underground since Charon ferried dead souls across the Styx."

This is is the first in the highly acclaimed vampire novels of the late Mick Farren. Victor Renquist, a surprisingly urbane and likable leader of a colony of vampires which has existed for centuries in New York is faced with both admin istrative and emotional prob lems. And when you are a vampire, administration is not a thing which one takes lightly.

"The person, be it gentleman or lady, who has not pleasure in a good novel, must be intolerably stupid."

Jane Austen

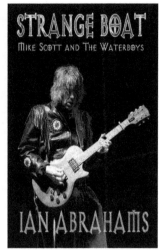

Los Angeles City of Angels, city of dreams. But
sometimes the dreams become nightmares. Having fled
New York, Victor Renquist and his small group of
Nosferatu are striving to re establish their colony.
They have become a deeper, darker part of the
city's nightlife. And Hollywood's glitterati are hot
on the scent of a new thrill, one that outshines all
others   immortality. But someone, somewhere, is med
dling with even darker powers, powers that even the
Nosferatu fear. Someone is attempting to summon the
entity of ancient evil known as Cthulhu. And Ren
quist must overcome dissent in his own colony, solve
the riddle of the Darklost (a being brought part
way along the Nosferatu path and then abandoned)
and combat powerful enemies to save the world   of
humans!

Canadian born Corky Laing is probably best
known as the drummer with Mountain. Corky
joined the band shortly after Mountain played
at the famous Woodstock Festival, although he
did receive a gold disc for sales of the
soundtrack album after over dubbing drums on
Ten Years After's performance. Whilst with
Mountain Corky Laing recorded three studio
albums with them before the band split. Follow
ing the split Corky, along with Mountain gui
tarist Leslie West, formed a rock three piece
with former Cream bassist Jack Bruce. West,
Bruce and Laing recorded two studio albums and
a live album before West and Laing re formed
Mountain, along with Felix Pappalardi. Since
1974 Corky and Leslie have led Mountain
through various line ups and recordings, and
continue to record and perform today at numer
ous concerts across the world. In addition to his
work with Mountain, Corky Laing has recorded
one solo album and formed the band Cork with
former Spin Doctors guitarist Eric Shenkman,
and recorded a further two studio albums with
the band, which has also featured former Jimi
Hendrix bassist Noel Redding. The stories are
told in an incredibly frank, engaging and
amusing manner, and will appeal also to those
people who may not necessarily be fans of

To me there's no difference between Mike Scott and
The Waterboys; they both mean the same thing. They
mean myself and whoever are my current travel
ling musical companions" Mike Scott Strange Boat
charts the twisting and meandering journey of
Mike Scott, describing the literary and spiritual
references that inform his songwriting and explor
ing the multitude of locations and cultures in
which The Waterboys have assembled and reflected
in their recordings. From his early forays into the
music scene in Scotland at the end of the 1970s, to
his creation of a 'Big Music' that peaked with the
hit single 'The Whole of the Moon' and onto the
Irish adventure which spawned the classic Fisher
man's Blues, his constantly restless creativity has
led him through a myriad of changes. With his
revolving cast of troubadours at his side, he's
created some of the most era defining records of
the 1980s, reeled and jigged across the Celtic
heartlands, reinvented himself as an electric
rocker in New York, and sought out personal
renewal in the spiritual calm of Findhorn's Scot
tish highland retreat. Mike Scott's life has been a
tale of continual musical exploration entwined
with an ever evolving spirituality. "An intriguing
portrait of a modern musician" (Record Collector).

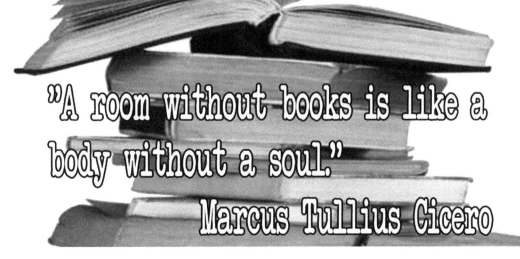

"A room without books is like a body without a soul."
Marcus Tullius Cicero

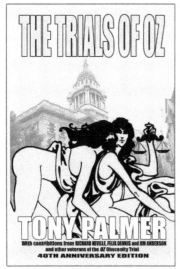

The OZ trial was the longest obscenity trial in history. It was also one of the worst reported. With minor exceptions, the Press chose to rewrite what had occurred, presumably to fit in with what seemed to them the acceptable prejudices of the times. Perhaps this was inevitable. The proceedings dragged on for nearly six weeks in the hot summer of 1971 when there were, no doubt, a great many other events more worthy of attention. Against the background of murder in Ulster, for example, the OZ affair probably fades into its proper insignificance. Even so, after the trial, when some newspapers realised that maybe something important had happened, it became more and more apparent that what was essential was for anyone who wished to be able to read what had actually been said. Trial and judgment by a badly informed press became the order of the day. This 40th Anniversary edition includes new material by all three of the original defendants, the prosecuting barrister, one of the OZ schoolkids, and even the daughters of the judge. There are also many illustrations including unseen material from Felix Dennis' own collection...

Merrell Fankhauser has led one of the most diverse and interesting careers in music. He was born in Louisville, Kentucky, and moved to California when he was 13 years old. Merrell went on to become one of the innovators of surf music and psychedelic folk rock. His travels from Hollywood to his 15 year jungle experience on the island of Maui have been documented in numerous music books and magazines in the United States and Europe. Merrell has gained legendary international status throughout the field of rock music; his credits include over 250 songs published and released. He is a multi talented singer/songwriter and unique guitar player whose sound has delighted listeners for over 35 years. This extraordinary book tells a unique story of one of the founding fathers of surf rock, who went on to play in a succession of progressive and psychedelic bands and to meet some of the greatest names in the business, including Captain Beefheart, Randy California, The Beach Boys, Jan and Dean... and there is even a run in with the notorious Manson family.

On September 19, 1985, Frank Zappa testified before the United States Senate Commerce, Technology, and Transportation committee, attacking the Parents Music Resource Center or PMRC, a music organization co founded by Tipper Gore, wife of then senator Al Gore. The PMRC consisted of many wives of politicians, including the wives of five members of the committee, and was founded to address the issue of song lyrics with sexual or satanic content. Zappa saw their activities as on a path towards censorship,and called their proposal for voluntary labelling of records with explicit content "extortion" of the music industry. This is what happened.

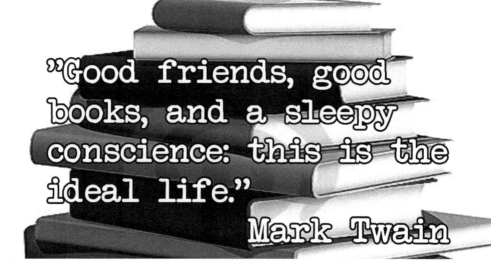

"Good friends, good books, and a sleepy conscience: this is the ideal life." Mark Twain

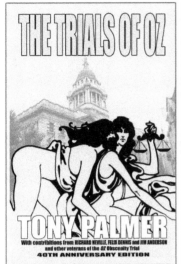

The OZ trial was the longest obscenity trial in history. It was also one of the worst reported. With minor exceptions, the Press chose to rewrite what had occurred, presumably to fit in with what seemed to them the acceptable prejudices of the times. Perhaps this was inevitable. The proceedings dragged on for nearly six weeks in the hot summer of 1971 when there were, no doubt, a great many other events more worthy of attention. Against the background of murder in Ulster, for example, the OZ affair probably fades into its proper insignificance. Even so, after the trial, when some newspapers realised that maybe something important had happened, it became more and more apparent that what was essential was for anyone who wished to be able to read what had actually been said. Trial and judgment by a badly informed press became the order of the day. This 40th Anniversary edition includes new material by all three of the original defendants, the prosecuting barrister, one of the OZ schoolkids, and even the daughters of the judge. There are also many illustrations including unseen material from Felix Dennis' own collection...

Merrell Fankhauser has led one of the most diverse and interesting careers in music. He was born in Louisville, Kentucky, and moved to California when he was 13 years old. Merrell went on to become one of the innovators of surf music and psychedelic folk rock. His travels from Hollywood to his 15 year jungle experience on the island of Maui have been documented in numerous music books and magazines in the United States and Europe. Merrell has gained legendary international status throughout the field of rock music; his credits include over 250 songs published and released. He is a multi talented singer/songwriter and unique guitar player whose sound has delighted listeners for over 35 years. This extraordinary book tells a unique story of one of the founding fathers of surf rock, who went on to play in a succession of progressive and psychedelic bands and to meet some of the greatest names in the business, including Captain Beefheart, Randy California, The Beach Boys, Jan and Dean... and there is even a run in with the notorious Manson family.

On September 19, 1985, Frank Zappa testified before the United States Senate Commerce, Technology, and Transportation committee, attacking the Parents Music Resource Center or PMRC, a music organization co founded by Tipper Gore, wife of then senator Al Gore. The PMRC consisted of many wives of politicians, including the wives of five members of the committee, and was founded to address the issue of song lyrics with sexual or satanic content. Zappa saw their activities as on a path towards censorship and called their proposal for voluntary labelling of records with explicit content "extortion" of the music industry. This is what happened.

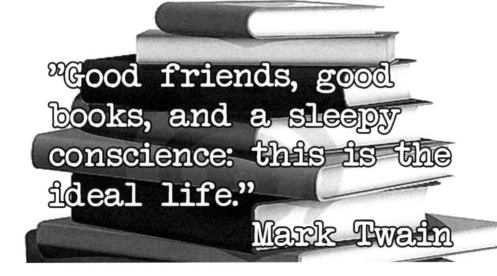

"Good friends, good books, and a sleepy conscience: this is the ideal life." Mark Twain

Lightning Source UK Ltd.
Milton Keynes UK
UKHW05f1357060818
326816UK00003B/38/P

CW00537060

The British Boxing
Board of Control

BOXING
YEARBOOK
2002

'The Boxing Bible'

Edited and Compiled by
Barry J. Hugman

Exxus Publication

The British Boxing Yearbook
is produced in association with
The British Boxing Board of Control

First Published in Great Britain in 2001 by
Exxus Limited
18 St Philip Square
London
SW8 3RS

© 2001 Exxus Ltd

www.exxus.co.uk

All rights reserved. No part of this publication may be reproduced, stored in a
retrieval system, or transmitted, in any form or by any means without the prior
written permission of the publisher, nor be otherwise circulated in any form of
binding or cover other than that in which it is published and without a similar
condition, including this condition, being imposed on the subsequent purchaser.

The CIP catalogue record for this book
Is available from the British Library

Front Cover: Joe Calzaghe (Les Clark)
Back Cover: Colin Dunne v Billy Schwer (Les Clark)

ISBN: 0-946531-28-5

Typeset and Designed by
Typecast (Artwork and Design)
8 Mudford Road
Yeovil, Somerset BA21 4AA

Distributed by Book Representation and Distribution Ltd
Hadleigh Hall, London Road, Hadleigh, SS7 2DE
Tel: 01702 552912
Fax 01702 556065
E-mail: mail@bookreps.com
www.bookreps.com

Printed and Bound in Great Britain by
Butler & Tanner Ltd, Frome and London

Contents

ST. ANDREWS SPORTING CLUB

EXCLUSIVE GENTLEMEN'S CLUB
AND
THE HOME OF SCOTTISH BOXING

2001/2002 Fixture List

Monday 17th September 2001

Monday 22nd October 2001

Monday 19th November 2001

Saturday 8th December 2001
(Ladies Night Dinner/Dance)

Monday 21st January 2002
(Burns Night)

Monday 18th February 2002

Monday 18th March 2002

Monday 22nd April 2002

Saturday 11th May 2002
(Summer Ball)

Monday 3rd June 2002

TEAM 2001

FLYWEIGHT
Jason Booth
British & Commonwealth Champion

Dale Robinson
Central Area Champion

BANTAMWEIGHT
Jose Sanjuanelo
I.B.O. World Champion

Nicky Booth
British & Commonwealth Champion

Ady Lewis
Former British &
Commonwealth Champion

Walker Logue

Jamil Hussain

FEATHERWEIGHT
Barry Hawthorne

SUPER-FEATHER-WEIGHT
Affif Djelti
I.B.O. World Champion

Charles Shepherd
Former I.B.O. Champion

Alex Moon
Commonwealth Champion

Craig Docherty
Undefeated

Andrew Ferrans

LIGHTWEIGHT
Bobby Vanzie
British Champion

James Armah
Commonwealth Champion

LIGHT-WELTERWEIGHT
Gary Ryder
Undefeated

WELTERWEIGHT
Jawaid Khaliq
I.B.O. World Champion

Derek Roche
Former British Champion

James Hare
Undefeated

Paul Burns

James Docherty
Undefeated

Darren Spencer

Lee Sharp

Emmanuel Marcos

LIGHT-MIDDLEWEIGHT
Joe Townsley
Former I.B.O. Inter-Continental Champion

Scott Millar

David Keir

MIDDLEWEIGHT
Biagio Falcone

SUPER-MIDDLEWEIGHT
Dean Cockburn

LIGHT-HEAVYWEIGHT
Joe Gillon
Undefeated

CRUISERWEIGHT
Tony Moran

HEAVYWEIGHT
Mark Hobson

Administrative Offices: Holiday Inn, Bothwell St, Glasgow G2 7EN, Scotland
Tel: +44 (0)141 248 5461 and +44 (0)141 275 4265
Fax: +44 (0)141 248 5922 E.mail: gilmourjnr@aol.com
DIRECTOR: TOMMY GILMOUR Jnr

Acknowledgements

Now in its 18th year, with the *British Boxing Yearbook* going from strength to strength, it is once again my pleasure to thank all of those who have helped to establish the *Yearbook* as an essential annual for the sport, and one that in its own way is just as important to the boxing public as receiving *Boxing News* every week.

As in previous years, I am indebted to the BBBoC's General Secretary, Simon Block, for his continued support and help in placing information at my disposal, and being of assistance when required. His assistant, Robert Smith, who is also the Southern Area Secretary and a former pro fighter of note, was again extremely helpful, as was Jackie Pease-Cox, Lyndsay Foster and Christine Venturelli, who took on all kinds of tasks such as supplying new fighters' complete details, plus changes of manager, and updating license holders' names and addresses, etc. I would also like to extend my thanks to the Board's Geoff Born, an old favourite of the famous Lynn ABC, who has also helped with certain aspects of the *Yearbook* in the past.

Once again, I would like to thank Bernard Hart, the Managing Director of Lonsdale Sports Equipment Ltd, for his efforts on behalf of the *Yearbook*, especially in organising the annual British Boxing Board of Control Awards Luncheon where the book will be launched. He was ably supported in this exercise by Kymberly Taylor and Peter Chapman. At the same time, I would like to thank Jonathan Ticehurst, the Managing Director of the Sports Division of Windsor Insurance Brokers Ltd, for his continued support and sponsorship of the *Yearbook*.

Ron Olver has been with the *Yearbook* from day one and, as ever, remains a tower of strength with his help and support, despite health problems and finding it difficult to get around. Once again, Ron has produced the Directory of Ex-Boxers' Associations and Obituaries, an exercise tinged with sadness as many of the fighters and personalities of the ring who departed during the past 12 months would have been long-time friends. A former Assistant Editor of both *Boxing News* and *Boxing World*, he is also well known as the British correspondent of the *Ring*; the author of *The Professionals*; for producing the boxing section within *Encyclopedia Britannica*; his work on *Boxing*, Foyles' library service; and as the former co-editor of the *Boxing News Annual*. His honorary work which includes being the Chairman of the BBBoC Charity Grants' Committee; the Vice-President of many ex-boxers' associations; the Public Relations Officer of the London Ex-Boxers' Association; membership of the Commonwealth Boxing Council as New Zealand's representative; and the International Hall of Fame – has, in recent years, seen him honoured by the Boxing Writers' Club, the BBBoC, and the Commonwealth Boxing Council. He has recently been further honoured by the Boxing Writers' Club, who have made him an Honorary Life Member. It was due to Ron's promptings that the ex-boxers' associations came into being as we now know them, and he will always be remembered by the *Boxing News'* readership as the man responsible for the 'Old Timers' page, now in its 34th year.

Members of the *Yearbook* 'team' who wrote articles for this year's edition and who have recently published, or are in the process of publishing their own books are: John Jarrett (*Dynamite Gloves*); Bob Lonkhurst (*Gentleman Jack: The Life and Career of Jack Petersen* and *Golden Boy* – the biography of Terry Spinks); and Ralph Oates (*The Heavyweight Boxing Quizbook*).

As in last year's *Yearbook*, Melanie Lloyd, an extremely promising boxing writer, has produced another splendid article, this time chronicling the life and times of the legendary Max Schmeling. She is joined by another lady boxing writer, Tracey Pollard, while we welcome back Chris Kempson, who details highlights among the amateurs.

Other important men that the *Yearbook* relies heavily upon every year are Bob Yalen, who covers boxing with ABC across the world and looks after the World Title Bouts' section; Harold Alderman, an unsung hero who has spent over 40 years researching the early days of boxing through to modern times; and Eric Armit, who is a leading authority of boxers' records throughout the world, and who is responsible for the 'World Scene' column within *Boxing News*.

Regarding photographs, as in previous years the great majority were produced by Les Clark (he also writes the Boxing Quiz with a Few Below the Belt within these pages), who has possibly the largest library of both action and poses from British rings. If anyone requires a copy of a photo that has appeared in the *Yearbook* credited to Les, or requires a list, he can be reached at 352 Trelawney Avenue, Langley, Bucks SL3 7TS. Other photos were supplied by my good friends, Derek Rowe and Harry Goodwin.

Also, additional help came from Neil Blackburn (who yet again provided information to make the Obituaries section as complete as possible); Mrs Enza Jacoponi, the Secretary of the European Boxing Union (EBU Championship data covering the past 12 months); Simon Block (Commonwealth and British Championship data); Patrick Myler (Irish amateur boxing information); Ray Allen (Welsh amateur boxing information); Mick Taylor, Sid Turp, Keith Ayres, Tommy Johnson, Mick Ryan, Ray Black, Dave Carris, Bob Wright, Peter Foley and Dave Cockell (ABA Championship information); Mary Coppleston and Dudley Saville (British Junior Championship information); and Dai Corp, John Jarrett, Brian McAllister, Ken Morton, Les Potts, and Robert Smith (Area title data). Although the research on world title bouts since gloves continues to wind down, I would again like to praise the efforts of men such as Tracy Callis, Luckett Davis, John Hogg, and Robert Soderman who are always available to help track down old fighters' records.

Finally, my thanks go to Jean Bastin, who continued the good work in typesetting and design, and my wife, Jennifer, who looks after the proof reading.

TARA BOXING PROMOTIONS & MANAGEMENT

Doughty's Gym, Princess Road, Shaw, Oldham OL2 7AZ
Tel/Fax: 01706-845753 (Office)   Tel: 01706-846762 (Gym)

Jack Doughty with left to right: Ady Lewis, Bobby Vanzie and Charles Shepherd

Trainer/Manager: JACK DOUGHTY
Trainers: Godfrey Brown, Eamonn Vickers, Ray Ashton, Glen Crawford, Chris Fuller
Matchmaker: John Gaynor M.C: Michael Pass

BOXERS

Shinny Bayaar - Flyweight
•Ady Lewis - Former British & Commonwealth Fly & Bantamweight Champion
Choi Tseveenpurev - Super-Bantamweight
•Charles Shepherd - Former British, Commonwealth & IBO World
Super-Featherweight Champion
Amjed Mahmood - Super-Featherweight
Mark Hargreaves - Super-Featherweight
•Bobby Vanzie British Lightweight Champion
Shaun Horsfall - Welterweight
Lee Murtagh - Light-Middleweight
Wayne Shepherd - Light-Middleweight
Mike Whittaker - Middleweight
Gary Dixon - Middleweight
•Co-managed

Introduction

by Barry J. Hugman

It only seems a short while ago that I wrote a few words for the last *British Boxing Yearbook*, but here we go again, this time round welcoming the readership, both new and old, to the 18th edition. The format hasn't changed dramatically, as myself and the team continue to monitor and update the current goings on, while also continuing to research the past and pass on our findings in much detail.

Starting with the modern era, once again we have decided to stay with the way we list Current British Based-Boxers: Complete Records. The decision to have one alphabet instead of separating champions, being taken on the grounds that because there are so many champions these days – British, Commonwealth, European, IBF, WBA, WBC, WBO, and more recently WBU, IBO, WBF, etc, etc, and a whole host of Inter-Continental and International titles – it would cause confusion rather than what was really intended. If you wish to quickly locate whether or not a boxer fought during the past season (1 July 2000 to 30 June 2001) then the Boxers' Record Index at the back of the *Yearbook* is the place to look.

Regarding records, if a fighter is counted out standing up we have continued to show it as a stoppage rather than that of a kayo, as in fights where the referee dispenses with the count. Thus fights are recorded as count outs (the count being tolled with the fighter still on the canvas), retirements (where a fighter is retired on his stool) and referee stopped contest. Of course, other types of decisions would take in draws, no contests, and no decisions. In these days of health and safety fears, more and more boxers are being counted out standing up, especially when a referee feels that the man on the receiving end is unable to defend himself adequately. One of the reasons that we have yet to discriminate between cut-eye stoppages and other types of endings, is because a fighter who is stopped because of cuts is often on his way to a defeat in the first place. Thus, if you want to get a true reflection on the fight it is probably better to consult the trade paper, *Boxing News*, rather than rely on a referee's decision to tell you all you want to know, the recorded result merely being a guide.

Continuing the trend set in the first edition, there are always new articles to match the old favourites. Regular features such as Home and Away With British Boxers During 2000-2001 (John Jarrett), A-Z of Current World Champions (Eric Armit), Highlights From the 2000-2001 Amateur Season (Chris Kempson), Directory of Ex-Boxers' Associations and Obituaries (Ron Olver) and two regular quizzes (Ralph Oates and Les Clark) being supported this year with interesting articles such as Tommy 'Smiler' Proffitt: Still Going Strong (Tracey Pollard), Terry Spinks: The Forgotten Olympian (Bob Lonkhurst), Graham Moughton: Mister Boxing (Ralph Oates) and A Tribute to Max Schmeling (Melanie Lloyd).

Elsewhere, hopefully, you will find all you want to know about British (Area), Commonwealth, European and world title bouts that took place in 2000-2001, along with the amateur championships that were held in England, Scotland, Wales and Ireland.

Historically, what was started two years ago under the heading of Early Gloved Boxing has now been extended to 138lbs. Due to Harold Alderman painstakingly piecing together results for the pre-Lonsdale Belt and named weight-division period, boxing in those far-flung days should become clearer. There are still many who believe as gospel much of what was reported down the ages by 'respected' men such as Nat Fleischer, the owner of *The Ring* Magazine and the *Ring Record Book*, and then copied by numerous historians who failed to grasp what the sport was really like before the First World War.

Basically, boxing prior to the period in question was a shambles, following bare fists with an assortment of driving gloves, knuckle gloves, and two-ounce gloves, etc, until it arrived at what we recognise today. There were no Commissions, newspapermen becoming all powerful by naming their own champions at all kinds of weights, and in much of America the sport was illegal, no-decision contests rescuing it from being abolished. If you thought today was dire, then boxing prior to that period was almost impossible in all divisions bar the heavyweights. Because travel was difficult and news travelled slowly, fighters were able to move from town to town proclaiming themselves to be the best and 'ringers' constantly prevailed. With today's research being aided by access to early newspapers, and the use of computers, it is becoming clear that men like Fleischer 'took' the best fighters of the day and then 'fitted' them into the named weight divisions we now know so well. If that is still as clear as mud, then turn to the pages in question.

Finally, I would like to thank you all for your continued support of the *British Boxing Yearbook* and, at the same time, place on record my gratitude to Lonsdale's Bernard Hart and Windsor's Jonathan Ticehurst for their support of the *Yearbook* during these difficult times for the BBBoC.

Abbreviations and Definitions used in the record sections of the Yearbook:
PTS (Points), CO (Count Out), RSC (Referee Stopped Contest), RTD (Retired), DIS (Disqualification), NC (No Contest), ND (No Decision).

British Boxing Board of Control Ltd: Structure

(Members of the World Boxing Council, World Boxing Association, International Boxing Federation, World Boxing Organisation, Commonwealth Boxing Council and European Boxing Union)

PRESIDENT	Leonard E. Read, QPM
CHAIRMAN	Lord Brooks of Tremorfa, DL
VICE CHAIRMAN	His Honour Alan Simpson, MA, Oxon
GENERAL SECRETARY	Simon Block
ADMINISTRATIVE STEWARDS	Dr Oswald Ross
	Dennis Lockton
	Lincoln Crawford, OBE
	Charles Giles
	John Handelaar
	Judith Rollestone
	Nicky Piper
	Dr Adrian Whiteson, OBE
	Billy Walker
	Rt. Hon. Lord Pendry
	David Roden
HONORARY STEWARDS*	Dr James Shea
	Mary Peters, DBE
	Frank Butler, OBE
	Bill Sheeran
	Sir Henry Cooper, OBE, KSG
	Robert Graham, BEM
STEWARDS OF APPEAL*	Robin Simpson, QC
	Peter Richards
	John Mathew, QC
	Nicholas Valios, QC
	William Tudor John
	Geoffrey Finn
	His Honour Brian Capstick, QC
	Colin Ross-Munroe, QC
	Prof. Andrew Lees
HEAD OFFICE	Jack Petersen House
	52a Borough High Street
	London SE1 1XN
	Tel. 0207 403 5879
	Fax. 0207 378 6670
	E-mail: sblock@bbbofc.com
	Website: www.bbbofc.com

* Not directors of the company

AREA COUNCILS - AREA SECRETARIES

AREA NO 1 (SCOTLAND)
Brian McAllister
11 Woodside Crescent, Glasgow G3 7UL
Telephone 0141 3320392

AREA NO 2 (NORTHERN IRELAND)
John Campbell
8 Mount Eden Park, Belfast, Northern Ireland BT9 6RA
Telephone 01232 683310

AREA NO 3 (WALES)
Dai Corp
13 Hill Crest, Brynna, Llanharan, Pontyclun,
Mid Glamorgan CF7 9SN
Telephone 01443 226465

AREA NO 4 (NORTHERN)
(Northumberland, Cumbria, Durham, Cleveland, Tyne and Wear, North Yorkshire [north of a line drawn from Whitby to Northallerton to Richmond, including these towns].)
John Jarrett
5 Beechwood Avenue, Gosforth, Newcastle upon Tyne NE3 5DH
Telephone 0191 285 6556

AREA NO 5 (CENTRAL)
(North Yorkshire [with the exception of the part included in the Northern Area - see above], Lancashire, West and South Yorkshire, Greater Manchester, Merseyside and Cheshire, Isle of Man, North Humberside.)
James Walker
1 Whinby Croft, Dodworth, Barnsley, South Yorkshire S75 3TN
Telephone 01226 242700

AREA NO 6 (SOUTHERN)
(Bedfordshire, Berkshire, Buckinghamshire, Cambridgeshire, Channel Islands, Isle of Wight, Essex, Hampshire, Kent, Hertfordshire, Greater London, Norfolk, Suffolk, Oxfordshire, East and West Sussex.)
Robert W. Smith
British Boxing Board of Control
Jack Petersen House, 52a Borough High Street, London SE1 1XN
Telephone 0207 4035879

AREA NO 7 (WESTERN)
(Cornwall, Devon, Somerset, Dorset, Wiltshire, Avon, Gloucestershire.)
Dai Corp
13 Hill Crest, Brynna, Llanharan, Pontyclun,
Mid Glamorgan CF7 9SN
Telephone 01443 226465

AREA NO 8 (MIDLANDS)
(Derbyshire, Nottinghamshire, Lincolnshire, Salop, Staffordshire, Herefordshire and Worcestershire, Warwickshire, West Midlands, Leicestershire, South Humberside, Northamptonshire.)
Alec Kirby
105 Upper Meadow Road, Quinton, Birmingham B32
Telephone 0121 421 1194

Foreword

by Simon Block *(General Secretary, British Boxing Board of Control)*

Another year gone by and another *Yearbook* to enjoy. A great job once again from Barry and the team.

As always in the roller coaster world of boxing, it was a year with highs and lows. Three of our shining lights were toppled from their positions. With one, Paul Ingle, there were near tragic consequences, but the Board's current ringside requirements, under the supervision of the Central Area Chief Medical Officer, Dr Graham Stead, which had been diligently effected by promoter Frank Warren's staff, enabled Paul to be scanned and undergoing surgery in around 45 minutes from the end of the contest. Consequently, his expectation of recovery is good and I was so pleased to see Paul back at ringside assisting Steve Pollard in Sheffield last July.

The defeats of Lennox Lewis and Naseem Hamed, two of Britain's most successful boxers ever, removed them from their positions of eminence in their respective weight divisions. Both, I believe, are capable of making it back to the top.

The Board's concern about boxers rapidly losing weight prior to contests has not been solved by the introduction a few years ago of holding weigh-ins 24 hours prior to the tournament. Early in 2001, following a formal inquiry, the Board introduced check weights which would be mandatory for all championship contests and random in gymnasiums. The effect of championship weight checks, despite initial criticism from some quarters, have proved extremely beneficial and some boxers have publicly acknowledged that they have made the weight easier than before. Random weight checking in gymnasiums has not yet been established long enough for any effectiveness to become apparent, but by next season it may be possible to draw conclusions from the results.

Hospitalisation of the former IBO world champion, Billy Schwer, and British light-middleweight challenger, James Lowther, reminds us all that we can never become complacent and that the dangers of the sport will always be with us. Thankfully, neither required surgery and both appear to have made excellent recovery.

Despite the foregoing our sport still prospers. Johnny Nelson and Joe Calzaghe became our leading world champions and there is plenty of talent behind them like Clinton Woods, Howard Eastman, Colin Dunne, Michael Brodie, Richard Hatton, Eamonn Magee, Michael Ayers, Michael Gomez, Scott Harrison and Alex Arthur. The prospect of domestic pairings at heavyweight between the champion, Danny Williams, Herbie Hide and amateur star Audley Harrison looks appealing. Our light-middleweight division headed by Wayne Alexander and including Commonwealth champion, Richard Williams, IBF champion Takaloo, WBF champion Steve Roberts and, despite the Takaloo defeat, Anthony Farnell, has the potential for some further excellent domestic clashes. Similarly, in the flyweight division we have two world champions in Peter

Culshaw and Damaen Kelly, with British and Commonwealth champion, Jason Booth, making up the triumvirate. Are we likely to see any matches from these potential pairings? Or is it the case that politics and TV obligations will prevent fans from finding out just who is the best in Britain. The proliferation of 'World' and 'Inter-Continental' type titles have opened up opportunities for a lot of boxers and promoters, but it has also permitted young stars to circumvent good domestic competition to the detriment of the sport as a whole. To people outside boxing it must appear ridiculous that we have 'World' champions who have not yet proved themselves the best in their own 'Area' let alone the country.

In September of last year, the Board learned that it had lost its Appeal against the judgement of the Court in the Michael Watson case, but leave for further Appeal to the House of Lords was granted. The Board's Administrators, Hacker Young, and Michael Watson's solicitors got together and, at the time of writing, both parties have applied to the House of Lords for a stay of proceedings to see whether a settlement is possible.

Here at the Board, our long-standing Chief Medical Officer, Vice President and Chairman of the Board's Charity, Dr Adrian Whiteson OBE, who for a quarter of a century or more has been the leading boxing Medical Official, has stepped down from these roles in view of his increasing commitments to his practice and other charity work, and the Northern Ireland Area Chief Medical Officer, Dr George O'Neill, becomes the new Acting Chief Medical Officer. Adrian will remain a Steward and will continue to be on hand for us. Lord Brooks of Tremorfa, the Chairman of the Board and also Chairman of the Board's Charity, continues to keep me on a relatively steady course both in my capacity as General Secretary and now as the new Secretary of the Charity.

Finally, with all the good boxing people who passed away during the last 12 months I was particularly saddened by the death of Howard Winstone MBE. It was Howard's success in the 1960s that inspired me to take up boxing in the first place and, although I never got further than being a novice amateur having only a handful of contests, it was his example that kept me in the sport, leading to the position I currently hold. I was extremely pleased to obtain for his widow, Bronwen, thanks to the kindness of the WBC President, Jose Sulaiman, a special World Championship Belt incorporating his picture alongside those of Muhammad Ali and Joe Louis.

That's the report from the Board, now enjoy the book.

MATCHROOM SPORT and PRINCE PROMOTIONS
combine to present

'RINGSIDE BOXING'

EUROPE'S LEADING BOXING PROMOTERS

Promoting competitive, exciting boxing contests

Check out our website for the latest news and results;
boxer profiles and records

www.matchroomsport.com.uk

Prince Promotions, 172 Psalter Lane, Sheffield S11 8UR
Telephone: 0114 220 3015. Fax: 0114 220 3010

Matchroom Sport, 10 Western Road, Romford, Essex RM1 3JT
Telephone: 01708 782200. Fax: 01708 723425

British Boxing Board of Control Awards

The Awards, inaugurated in 1984 in the form of statuettes of boxers, and designed by Morton T. Colver, are supplied by Len Fowler Trophies of Holborn. Len was an early post-war light-heavyweight favourite. As in 2000, the Awards Ceremony, which has reverted back to a luncheon format, is due to be held this coming Autumn in London and will again be hosted by the Lonsdale International Sporting Club's Bernard Hart, the Managing Director of Lonsdale Sports Equipment Ltd, and sponsor of the Awards.

British Boxer of the Year: The outstanding British Boxer at any weight. 1984: Barrry McGuigan. 1985: Barry McGuigan. 1986: Dennis Andries. 1987: Lloyd Honeyghan. 1988: Lloyd Honeyghan. 1989: Dennis Andries. 1990: Dennis Andries. 1991: Dave McAuley. 1992: Colin McMillan. 1993: Lennox Lewis. 1994: Steve Robinson. 1995: Nigel Benn. 1996: Prince Naseem Hamed. 1997: Robin Reid. 1998: Carl Thompson. 1999: Billy Schwer. 2000: Glenn Catley.

British Contest of the Year: Although a fight that took place in Europe won the 1984 Award, since that date, the Award, presented to both participants, has applied to the best all-action contest featuring a British boxer in a British ring. 1984: Jimmy Cable v Said Skouma. 1985: Barry McGuigan v Eusebio Pedroza. 1986: Mark Kaylor v Errol Christie. 1987: Dave McAuley v Fidel Bassa. 1988: Tom Collins v Mark Kaylor. 1989: Michael Watson v Nigel Benn. 1990: Orlando Canizales v Billy Hardy. 1991: Chris Eubank v Nigel Benn. 1992: Dennis Andries v Jeff Harding. 1993: Andy Till v Wally Swift Jnr. 1994: Steve Robinson v Paul Hodkinson. 1995: Steve Collins v Chris Eubank. 1996: P. J. Gallagher v Charles Shepherd. 1997: Spencer Oliver v Patrick Mullings. 1998: Carl Thompson v Chris Eubank. 1999: Shea Neary v Naas Scheepers. 2000: Simon Ramoni v Patrick Mullings.

Overseas Boxer of the Year: For the best performance by an overseas boxer in a British ring. 1984: Buster Drayton. 1985: Don Curry. 1986: Azumah Nelson. 1987: Maurice Blocker. 1988: Fidel Bassa. 1989: Brian Mitchell. 1990: Mike McCallum. 1991: Donovan Boucher. 1992: Jeff Harding. 1993: Crisanto Espana. 1994: Juan Molina. 1995: Mike McCallum. 1996: Jacob Matlala. 1997: Ronald Wright. 1998: Tim Austin. 1999: Vitali Klitschko. 2000: Keith Holmes.

Special Award: Covers a wide spectrum, and is an appreciation for service's to boxing. 1984: Doctor Adrian Whiteson. 1985: Harry Gibbs. 1986: Ray Clarke. 1987: Hon. Colin Moynihan. 1988: Tom Powell. 1989: Winston Burnett. 1990: Frank Bruno. 1991: Muhammad Ali. 1992: Doctor Oswald Ross. 1983: Phil Martin. 1994: Ron Olver. 1995: Gary Davidson. 1996: Reg Gutteridge and Harry Carpenter. 1997: Miguel Matthews and Pete Buckley. 1998: Mickey Duff and Tommy Miller. 1999: Jim Evans and Jack Lindsey. 2000: Henry Cooper.

Sportsmanship Award: This Award recognises boxers who set a fine example, both in-and-out of the ring. 1986: Frank Bruno. 1987: Terry Marsh. 1988: Pat Cowdell. 1989: Horace Notice. 1990: Rocky Kelly. 1991: Wally Swift Jnr. 1992: Duke McKenzie. 1993: Nicky Piper. 1994: Francis Ampofo. 1995: Paul Wesley. 1996: Frank Bruno. 1997: Lennox Lewis. 1998: Johnny Williams. 1999: Brian Coleman. 2000: Michael Ayers and Wayne Rigby.

Glenn Catley (left) receives the 2000 BBBoC 'British Boxer of the Year' Award from the BBBoC General Secretary, Simon Block

Les Clark

PANIX PROMOTIONS LTD
PANIX ACADEMY
18 THEYDON ROAD
LONDON E5 9NA
Tel: 0208 806 8700
Fax: 0208 806 2797

website address: www.panixpromotions.com

Boxing and the Need For Insurance

by Jonathan Ticehurst (Managing Director, Sports Division of Windsor Insurance Brokers Ltd)

To all of us in the insurance industry, our clients are of paramount importance. But, in our case, not only are they important, they are also in the public eye – because our speciality is professional sports and, in particular, boxing.

Boxing is, of course, a national sport, enjoyed at amateur level through schools and clubs by thousands of people and watched at top professional level by millions worldwide through the eyes of television.

How many of us see claims, or potential claims, occurring on television, or read about them in the papers before we get to the office? Millions have seen both promising, mature and lucrative careers ended in a matter of seconds as we have watched late night title fights and supporting bouts from our sitting room chairs.

Many people might wonder how such a direct contact sport can possibly qualify for Accident and Injury insurance cover. The answer lies in the definition of 'injury' and the definition of 'disablement'. For many years, the British Boxing Board of Control has provided and paid for a Personal Accident Policy for every one of its licensed boxers. This includes overseas boxers who have acquired a temporary licence for the purposes of fighting in this country in specific bouts. Traditionally, that policy provided cover for death, blindness, deafness and loss of limbs or parts of limbs whilst the licensed boxer was in the ring or climbing into or out of the ring.

Windsor have been managing the insurance affairs of the world of professional football and cricket for 20 years or more. During this time, various policies have paid out millions of pounds against claims by the national associations, the leagues, the clubs and counties, in respect of players who have gone out of the game early through injury. Some names you will only remember, others you may well have seen or, in early days, even played with, like Ian Storey-Moore, Steve Coppell, Gary Bailey, Alan Brazil, John O'Neill, Norman Whiteside, Gary Stevens, Siggi Jonsson, Mick McCarthy, Paul Elliott, John Fashanu, 'Syd' Lawrence, Paul Downton, Nigel Felton, Rodney Ontong and many others.

It was, perhaps, no surprise, therefore, that the Board should turn to Windsor in the course of its review of the insurance cover which has been available historically for boxers. The London insurance market is nothing if not imaginative and when brokers who are experts in their field put their heads together with underwriters who have made it their business to specialise in a particular class of insurance worldwide, then almost anything is possible at an affordable premium. The result was that the Board has now been able to include within their policy the all-important additional cover of Permanent & Total Disablement.

Experience has taught us that where an association, a federation, or affinity body takes out insurance for the benefit of its membership, then any individual member who needs additional or more wide-ranging cover for his own particular needs, should be able to buy his or her own cover as an extension to the group cover. That is what happens in football, cricket and many other sports. The Board's policy provides basic benefits for its licensed members and, although the benefits could not be, and, as is generally known, was never intended to be, regarded as a 'retirement fund', the policy is a very important starting point.

The Professional Boxers' Association recognised the hard work and imagination that the Board put into their new policy and were quick to endorse its value to all their members. Perhaps, more importantly, the PBA then worked closely with Windsor in designing tailor-made additional insurance cover which could be purchased, through their association, by members individually.

It is an ideal arrangement. The British Boxing Board of Control, through their own funds, are providing a general benefit for all their licensed boxers which can act as a platform for individual members to buy top-up cover, at their own expense, to suit their own particular requirements and financial obligations. The insurance wraps itself around the actual business of boxing and those in it and responds directly to the risks associated with it. It may be marginally more expensive than 'off the shelf' Accident & Injury policies, but then "off the shelf" policies will not respond to the peculiarities and the particular risks associated with a sport having such pugnacious characteristics.

Between them, the Board and the PBA have taken a giant leap forward for the benefit of all professional boxers. We, at Windsor, are happy that another high profile professional sport has the protection from the insurance market that it needs and deserves.

EVANS-WATERMAN PROMOTIONS

Licensed to the British Boxing Board of Control

Members of the Professional Boxing Promoters' Association

88 WINDSOR ROAD
MAIDENHEAD
BERKS SL6 2DJ
Tel: 01628 623640   Fax: 01628 684633

<table>
<tr><td colspan="4">HEAVYWEIGHTS</td></tr>
<tr><td>Jacklord Jacobs</td><td>– Surbiton</td><td>–</td><td>8-10 Rounds</td></tr>
<tr><td>Tim Puller</td><td>– USA</td><td>–</td><td>8-10 Rounds</td></tr>
<tr><td>Roman Greenberg</td><td>– Israel</td><td>–</td><td>Debut</td></tr>
<tr><td>Peter Horacek</td><td>– Maidenhead</td><td>–</td><td>6-8 Rounds</td></tr>
</table>

CRUISERWEIGHT
Graham Nolan — Maidenhead — Debut

LIGHT-HEAVYWEIGHT
Gareth Hogg — Torquay — 6-8 Rounds

MIDDLEWEIGHTS
Alan Gilbert — Crawley — 8-10 Rounds
Matthew Barr — Walton — 6-8 Rounds

LIGHT-MIDDLEWEIGHTS
Adrian Chase — St Albans — 6-8-10 Rounds
Chrissy Howarth — Bracknell — 4-6 Rounds

WELTERWEIGHTS
Geoff McCreesh — Bracknell — 8-10 Rounds
Dewey Welliver — USA — 8-10 Rounds

LIGHT-WELTERWEIGHTS
Sammy Smith — Bracknell — 6-8 Rounds
Iain Eldridge — Watford — 6-8 Rounds
Wee Barry — Stanmore — 4 Rounds

LIGHTWEIGHT
Chris McDonagh — Maidenhead — Debut

FEATHERWEIGHTS
Jezz D'Agostino — Peterborough — 4-6 Rounds
Mickey Bowden — Forest Hill — 4-6 Rounds
Nickoli Melordovich — Israel — 8-10 Rounds

SUPER-BANTAMWEIGHT
Sergio Devakov — Israel — 8-10-12 Rounds

BANTAMWEIGHT
Jamie Yelland — Finchley — 6-8 Rounds

FLYWEIGHT
Darren Taylor — Bracknell — 6-8 Rounds

JIM EVANS STABLE OF TRAINERS:-
Johnny Bloomfield
Freddie Barr
Derek Andrews
Paul Rees
Barney Keen

WEST LONDON'S FASTEST RISING STABLE

Tommy 'Smiler' Proffitt: Still Going Strong

by Tracey Pollard

In 1933, Tom Proffitt, a boxer, bought his six-year-old son a little pair of boxing gloves for Christmas, probably hoping to nudge him in the right direction. Well, it certainly did the trick. Young Tommy's boxing prowess would lead to him being rated fourth in the world, and being instrumental in the creation of the Manchester Ex-Boxers' Association, attending the first-ever meeting, and remaining actively involved to this day.

Back then, Tommy's sparring took place in the garden of his home in Market Street, Droylsden (near Manchester). He sparred with his young friends and his first fight was against one of those friends, Vic 'Cyclone' Cheatham, who he would defeat a second time as an 11-year old. It was also at this time that he became known as 'Smiler Proffitt' and if you should meet Tommy today you would see that the name still fits.

Tommy's first club was Droylsden Lads' Club on Herbert Street with trainer, Jack Pearson. Tommy had seen two lads with medals for boxing and he was utterly confident that he could beat them. When he arrived at the club, Jack recognised that this was the son of Tom Proffitt who he had fought at the Alhambra Palace in Openshaw. Tommy thought a lot of Jack and when he died, 14-year-old Tommy stopped boxing and didn't return to the sport for nearly three years. Then he joined the Wheeler Street Youth Centre where he would win his first medal as the Manchester Youth Centre Champion. By the time he was 17 he had added further medals to his collection for winning the North-West Command Air Training Corp Boxing Association Championship in 1943 and 1944.

Within weeks of being called up after a bad illness, Tommy fought Ronnie Bissell, the ABA, RAF and Imperial Services champion, in the final of the RAF Championships. He lost on points, but later, as a professional, he would defeat him three times, stopping him twice. Tommy then spent a frustrating nine months with no boxing as part of an Aircraft Maintenance Unit, but when he was sent to Cosford on a flight mechanics' course he got his chance. The RAF team arrived to train for the Britannia Shield and Tommy managed to get excused from a lecture to go to the gym. He told the Sergeant in charge that he could beat the bantamweight who was in the ring and he did just that. He went on to beat a Golden Gloves State champion to win the Shield and narrowly missed winning a second shield by one eighth of a point.

Tommy also received medals as the RAF individual featherweight champion in 1946, the RAF ABA champion in Dublin 1947, and for boxing for Wales against the Army in the Army Boxing Association Championships in Aldershot in 1947.

Tommy seen putting the Canadian champion, Fernando Gagnon, on the seat of his pants during a second-round victory at Newcastle on 5 May 1950

Back on Civvy Street, Tommy joined the LNER club in Higher Openshaw, where he would beat the Imperial Services champion to win the Northern Counties ABA title. This was swiftly followed by victory in the semi-finals and the finals to become the ABA champion and Olympic representative.

Tommy was joined in the 1948 Olympic team by Peter Keenan (who he would later face in the final eliminator for the British pro title), Jack Gardner and silver medallist, Johnny Wright, who lost the gold to none other than, Laszlo Papp. Sadly, Johnny passed away recently. Tommy was himself beaten in a preliminary round.

Harold 'Boy' Bolton was Tommy's trainer for the ABAs and he later took him to Len Steele's gym on Taunton Road in Ashton-under-Lyne to turn professional. Tommy would spend the next 18 months at Len's place, alongside fighters like Ken Daniels, Tony Lord, Johnny Sullivan, Harry Warner, Jackie Standing and Paul Dunne. During this time he would have about 17 fights with just three losses and reach number seven in the British ratings.

It was at Len's that Tommy met trainer, Jack Bates, who was training Johnny Cusick at the time. Jack had also trained champions such as Jackie Brown, Johnny King and Jock McAvoy. He bought Tommy's contract from Len and trained him in a shop next to 'Harry the Barbers' on Rochdale Road, which they turned into a gym.

In March 1950, Tommy, rated one of the hardest punching men in the world at his weight, received a *Boxing News* Certificate of Merit for his defeat of the Canadian, Charlie Savard, in fine style inside five rounds. His second-round stoppage of Fernando Gagnon was a turning point for Tommy. Gagnon had just gone 15 rounds with world champion, Vic Toweel, and victory catapulted Tommy to fourth place in the world ratings. After defeating Michel Dicky, the Belgian champion, by KO in the seventh, Tommy faced Bobby Boland in an eliminator for the British bantamweight title. Tommy had won his last 11 fights since losing to Boland in August 1949, but had beaten him two months earlier. This time he won and was now number one in the British ratings. This was followed by victory over the Italian champion, Tino Cardinale. He now faced Peter Keenan in the final eliminator for the British title. Sadly, he was knocked out in the second round and Keenan went on to win the title.

Tommy's career continued with a further 11 wins and four losses, including a victory over Mickey McKay, the South African champion, who had often sparred with the lads at Len Steele's gym. There now followed two contests with the legendary Nigerian, Hogan 'Kid' Bassey. The first ended in a points win for Bassey, but not before he had been rocked by a lovely right from Tommy, and in the return Tommy retired at the end of the seventh. Bassey would of course become the world champion. Tommy was still rated number two in the country when he suffered his next two defeats, the first to Empire champion, Jake Tuli, and the second to John Kelly, who very quickly went on to become British and European champion. No shame there then but Tommy decided it was time to hang up the gloves. He had won 34 of his 47 contests, with one draw.

He ran the LNER club in Gorton and later assisted at the Collyhurst and Moston Lads' Club with Brian Hughes. He also attended the first-ever meeting of an Ex-Boxers' Association in Great Britain which took place at the Palais de Danse in Ashton-under-Lyne, at a benefit for Jock McAvoy. Also present were Jackie Brown, Harold Smithson, Len Steele and Tony Lord, among others. Over the next 25 years, Tommy would serve as Chairman, Vice-Chairman and President of the Manchester Ex-Boxers' Association, the position he has held for the last three years.

Tommy now lives quietly in Droylsden with his wife, Hilda. They have been married for 50 years and have two daughters, Janice and Christine, and four grandchildren, including one grandson who strangely seems to prefer football!

Tracey is a local freelance journalist who covers boxing through a weekly column in the Manchester-based Reporter & Chronicle Newspaper Group. Her interest in boxing and putting words to paper is helped by the fact that Manchester is a boxing hot-bed right now, with men like Richard Hatton and Michael Brodie having gravitated to world class, while there are many more young aspiring fighters being trained locally. In short, the north west is buzzing. Tracey first met Tommy Proffitt when she was writing an article on his original trainer, Len Steele, which formed part of a series on local trainers and included Ken Daniels, Billy Graham, Bob Shannon, Brian Hughes and Jack Doughty. Charlie Grice, a good quality pro and amateur welterweight of the 1960s, kicked off a further series on local amateur trainers, and in a recent feature she looked back in time to write about Sam Hurst, the 'Stalybridge Infant', a leading bare-knuckle fighter who claimed the championship on beating Tom Paddock in 1860.

Tommy as he is today   Harry Goodwin

Terry Spinks: The Forgotten Olympian

by Bob Lonkhurst

Everybody knows that life is full of injustices and there is one rule for the rich and another for the poor. Most of us can relate countless tales along those lines, not just in sport but everyday life. After initial anger and disappointment, however, they generally fade into obscurity and life moves on. Yet there is one injustice which I and many other people cannot accept. It relates to the failure of successive governments, and whoever else is responsible, to bestow an MBE or similar honour upon former Olympic gold medallist, Terry Spinks.

In 1956, at the age of just 18, Spinks went to Melbourne and within the space of only seven days beat five of the world's best amateur boxers to win the Olympic flyweight gold medal. It was only his first season as a senior and three months earlier the selection committee had considered him too young and inexperienced to compete in such a prestigious competition.

Other British gold medal winners at boxing, Dick McTaggart, also in 1956, and Chris Finnegan (1968), quite rightly duly received honours. So too did Audley Harrison and every other gold medal winner from the 2000 Olympics at Sydney. Yet despite repeated nominations and an energetic campaign on his behalf, Spinks continues to be overlooked. It is an outrage which should be rectified without further delay.

Throughout the East End there is more than just disappointment – there is sheer anger at the injustice. That anger is not just confined to boxing fans but to people from all walks of life, old and young. Many remember Terry's incredible achievement back in 1956, while others have read or been told about it. People want to know why he is not considered worthy of being honoured because almost 45 years since returning to Canning Town a hero, he is still idolised. He is in constant demand for autographs, photographs and personal appearances because his achievement is part of East-End folk lore.

Born in 1938, Terry was evacuated to Kent at the start of the war. On returning to the stricken East End in 1945, it wasn't long before he got involved in scraps with other youngsters. He started boxing at the age of nine when a teacher at his school asked if any boys wanted to join a local club. Thinking it would get him out of some lessons he immediately put up his hand.

Apart from boxing at school, Spinks joined the Tate & Lyle Club where he trained under former professional boxer, Billy 'Kid' Brookes, for about a year. He then moved to West Ham, one of the finest amateur boxing clubs in the country, which had produced many schoolboy, National Association of Boys Clubs and ABA champions.

Despite being so small that he had difficulty climbing through the ropes, Terry progressed well. Coached by ex-professional Jackie Gubbins three times a week, he had incredible speed and a wonderful left jab. He was given great encouragement by older boys at the club and became very friendly with Dennis and Ron Hinson, Terry Brown, Terry Gill, Jackie Bowers and the Enifer brothers, Roy and Danny, all of whom were quality boxers.

Spinks won a succession of West Ham schoolboy championships, and the only boy to beat him in a final was Jackie Bowers, now a successful trainer at the Peacock gym. In 1953 he became Essex schoolboy champion and progressed to the English national finals at Wembley, where he won a Junior B, five stone 11 lbs championship.

With his father being a bookmaker it was perhaps not surprising that Terry had a love of horses. He desperately wanted to become a jockey, and in July 1953 was taken on as a stable lad at the Newmarket stable of Marcus Marsh. Shortly after he arrived, entries were invited for a forth-coming stable lads boxing competition, so he promptly put his name down.

The top jockey at the stable was Charlie Smirke, who in his younger days had been a good boxer. He asked Terry to keep quiet about being a schoolboy champion and being the new boy he conformed. After he won the championship Spinks realised the need for secrecy, because Charlie pulled him aside and gave him 'a nice few quid'. He knew Terry's quality and laid out plenty of bets on him and received a good return.

A champion boxer was good prestige for the stable and, during the two and a half years he was at Newmarket, Spinks entered every lads competition he could. He won all but one and the only man to beat him was his good friend Tony Rawlinson, a four times Liverpool schoolboy champion. Today a host of trophies grace Terry's cabinet as a reminder of the good times he had in stable lads competitions.

There was one competition at Newmarket during 1955 when Terry didn't have an opponent. Instead he boxed a three-rounds exhibition with British and European flyweight champion, Dai Dower, who was there as guest of honour. Dai was extremely impressed with Terry's ability and followed his career with great interest.

Terry's time as a stable lad came to an end during the autumn of 1955, due to weight problems. Left with no alternative he returned home to Canning Town and took a series of jobs, none of which motivated him greatly. After horses his only love was boxing so he rejoined the West Ham club, re-affiliated with the ABA, and embarked on his first season as a senior.

He entered the 1956 ABA championships and his first success was winning the North-East London Divs flyweight title at York Hall by outpointing John Holt of Repton. A few weeks later he won the London Championship at the Royal Albert Hall, which put him into the ABA semi finals at Wembley.

The critics didn't fancy his chances because his opponent was Army and Imperial Services champion, Alex Ambrose. He had lost just two of his last 15 contests that season, both due to cuts, and was already being chased by a number of professional managers. Spinks, however, was unconcerned about his opponent's reputation and boxed brilliantly to win on points. Writing in a late edition of the *London Evening Standard*, Reg Gutteridge predicted: "Spinks could well be the shock of the championships".

In the final, Terry faced 26-years-old Peter Walsh (Royal Northern), who had been trying to win an ABA title for six years. Men such as John Smillie, Chick Brogan, Dick Currie, Frankie Jones and Jimmy Quinn, had barred his way and went on to become successful professionals. Walsh took boxing so seriously that he had to beat his twin brother John to win an Army Egyptian final seven years earlier.

Dominating the fight from the start, Spinks took Walsh out of his stride. He used his left hand to good effect and boxed brilliantly throughout the three rounds to take a comfortable points decision. The 18-years-old East End lad had confounded the critics by beating two of the outstanding flyweights in Britain to become ABA champion at his first attempt.

Most national newspapers reported his victory and there were comments that he had boxed like Sammy McCarthy when he became British featherweight champion a few years earlier. Few people knew, however, that Sammy was Terry's idol and they had become good friends.

Terry's success brought immediate reward because when Derek Lloyd went down with tonsillitis, he was drafted into the ABA team for a two-match trip to Poland. His first contest was just nine days after winning the ABA title and he was considered extremely unlucky to suffer his first defeat in nine contests at senior level.

His opponent was Henryk Kukier, a vastly experienced boxer who had won the European flyweight championship at Warsaw in 1953. Although it was his first international, Spinks gave a delightful display in a cat and mouse contest, only to lose by a majority decision. In a steamy Turkish-bath atmosphere beneath the glass topped roof of the Gwardia Stadium at Warsaw, he was the hero in the team's 8-2 defeat by the Poles.

The decision in favour of the Polish boxer was extremely unpopular with the home supporters, who mobbed Terry as he left the ring. Their reaction was a clear indication of how well he had performed. In fact, he received more punishment from slaps on the back as he made his way back to the dressing room than he did during three rounds in the ring. After the fight, the Polish national coach, Felix Stamm, said he believed Terry was the best British amateur since Dai Dower, and had the ability to do well at the forthcoming Olympics if selected.

The second match of the Polish tour was two days later at Gdansk. Although the ABA were beaten 5-4, Spinks

Terry (right) outpointed Finland's Ossi Palvalin in Helsinki ahead of being selected for Britain's 1956 Olympic team

again performed admirably. Using his fantastic speed and boxing skill, he outpointed Janusz Litke who took a real hiding. He was floored in the second round and also sustained cuts around both eyes. Terry was again mobbed by the large Polish crowd as he left the ring.

The ABA selectors had no hesitation picking Spinks for a trip to Russia and Finland where three international matches were scheduled in nine days. In his first contest of the tour, Terry faced a mammoth task when he faced the 22-years-old USSR champion, Vladimir Stolnikov. Despite battling bravely he took a bit of a hiding and lost a unanimous decision.

Three days later he faced Viktor Bystrov and, despite losing several pounds in weight due to the humid conditions, he had lost none of his strength. Spinks did most of the attacking and often rocked the Soviet with heavy, accurate punches. The Russian countered well and although Terry had a good last round he lost a unanimous decision. It was not well received by the crowd of 20,000 and Spinks, nicknamed 'Baby-Doll' by the Muscovites, was cheered all the way to the dressing room.

Although he had lost two demanding contests within three days Terry suffered no ill effects. Five days later he boxed brilliantly at Helsinki to outpoint Ossi Palvalin in the ABA's 6-4 victory over Finland.

Victories for London in Berlin and Hanover were followed by success for West Ham against a Swiss and German select team at Basle. After Terry's fight in Berlin, Sydney Hulls, writing in the *Daily Express*, insisted that Spinks must be picked for the Olympic Games in Melbourne. "Rarely have I seen any boxer, amateur or professional, take command of a bout so completely as Spinks did".

The selectors, however, took the view that Terry was too young and inexperienced to compete in a tournament of such importance. They clearly failed to recognise or consider the maturity of his performances at international level during the preceding four months.

The situation infuriated a number of prominent London boxing journalists. In particular, Reg Gutteridge of the *Evening News* had tremendous admiration for Spinks and, with the help of Walter Bartleman of the *Star* and Sydney Hulls of *The Daily Express*, he started a campaign in support of his nomination. Almost daily something was written in one of the papers urging the selectors to re-consider.

The power of the media was effective and at the end of September 1956, Terry was drafted into the British team of six. He had never given up hope of being selected and remained in constant training. To keep in shape he took three fights within the space of two weeks, as well as embarking on a rigorous training programme devised by West Ham coach, Billy Walker. It had to be that way because, despite the importance of the Olympic Games, the ABA made no arrangements for specialist training or sparring. Everything was left to the individual boxers and their trainers.

After convincingly beating boxers from Pakistan and Argentina in his opening two contests, Terry was really put to the test in the quarter-final. Drawn against his old foe, Vladimir Stolnikov, his team mates detected signs of anxiety about him. The night before the contest he had a nightmare and fell out of bed. Nobody doubted his ability but some kidology was clearly needed. More experienced members of the team convinced him that the Russian was having weight problems and wouldn't be able to cope with a fast pace.

The ploy paid off because by using his superior speed the Londoner piled up the points using hit and run tactics. His left jab was brilliant and he kept away from Stolnikov's stiff counter punches. As the Russian tired in the final round, Terry piled on the pressure to take a well-earned decision. "This was one fight I desperately wanted to win", said a relieved Spinks. "I am delighted with the result".

An equally fleet-footed performance against Rene Libeer of France the following night took Terry into the Olympic final. His opponent was Mircia Dobrescu, a tough 26-years-old Romanian who had beaten Johnny Caldwell in the semi final. Everything pointed to victory for Dobrescu, thought to be the fresher by virtue of a bye in the first round of the competition. He was vastly more experienced than Spinks, having reached the semi finals of the 1952 Olympics at Helsinki, winning gold at the 1954 World University Games and being narrowly beaten in the finals of the 1955 European Championships in Berlin.

Described as a 'Pocket Marciano', the Romanian was a muscular, barrel-chested little man, and although he stood only five foot tall, was built like a tank. In comparison, Spinks looked pale and lean, his choirboy looks giving the impression of a boy facing a man. Appearances and reputations, however, held no fear for Terry. Having grown up on the streets of the East End, he had his own brand of toughness. Places don't come much tougher than Canning Town, where he was getting into scraps soon after starting school.

Spinks didn't know the meaning of fear and when he faced Dobrescu at the opening bell he was calm and very focused. Although the Romanian attacked strongly to the body and attempted to swamp him with wide rushes, Terry moved well and counter-punched. As the round wore on he stood his ground and hit back with solid punches rocking Dobrescu back on to his heels. At the bell there was an air of satisfaction about Spinks as he went to his corner.

The second round was quieter and although Terry was under constant pressure he did not panic. Boxing with a maturity beyond his years he continued to move and jab to pick up the points.

The Londoner was really pumped up as he stood in his corner awaiting the bell for the final round. Dobrescu, who never stopped attacking throughout the fight, went after Spinks throwing punches from all angles. Many missed and the good boxing came from the youngster. Moving skilfully around the ring, he side-stepped the bobbing, weaving Romanian who often punched thin air. Good left jabs to head and body made Dobrescu shake his head in despair. The accuracy of Spinks' punches caught the judges eyes and he was awarded a majority decision.

It was an incredible performance against all the odds.

Being the first final of the evening, it meant that Spinks became the first Briton to win an Olympic gold medal for 32 years. He was also the first British boxer ever to win gold in the flyweight division. The fans had taken him to their hearts and thunderous cheers rang out around the Melbourne Sports Arena as he stood on the podium holding his medal aloft.

Terry's victory was a great incentive for the British team, and Dick McTaggart won gold in the lightweight division, Tommy Nicholls took silver, while Nicky Gargano and John McCormack won bronze. McTaggart won the Val Barker trophy for being the most stylish boxer of the Games, and Spinks was voted runner-up.

The following week Spinks arrived home in Canning Town to the most incredible welcome. The entire area was ablaze with Union Jacks of all sizes. Bunting and flags hung from windows and lamp-posts and, as he stepped from his car, he was hoisted on to the shoulders of neighbours and carried up and down Morgan Street where he lived with his parents. The little street off the busy Barking Road became alive with reporters, photographers and newsreel teams. The Duke of Edinburgh sent his chauffeur to Terry's house with a case of champagne and a message of congratulations.

Some local children were given the day off school to celebrate Terry's success. When a group gathered in the street outside his house, he took the gold medal out to show them. Later, the same day, he took it to his old school at Ashburton Road to show the staff and pupils.

Becoming an Olympic champion made the 18-years-old Canning Town boy an instant hero. He was invited to a succession of luncheons and dinners, appeared as a guest on a host of television programmes, including *Sports Desk*, *Top of the Pops* and *Six-Five Special*. On each occasion a chauffeur-driven car collected him from Morgan Street and took him home afterwards.

He appeared on stage at the Victoria Palace Theatre with the Crazy Gang, and visited London Zoo for a photo shoot after a baby giraffe born there was named after him. A cycling club elected him as their President, Holiday Camp boss Billy Butlin offered him a job as a Physical Training Instructor, and top greyhound trainers invited him to be photographed exercising dogs due to run at West Ham Stadium.

Terry mixed with the rich and famous and was in great demand for personal appearances. Together, with football international, Stanley Matthews, he was guest of honour at a Variety Club of Britain Luncheon at the Savoy Hotel. They were also guests of the National Sporting Club at a dinner at The Cafe Royal and when Spinks was introduced by Donald Campbell the ovation lasted for over two minutes.

In January 1957, Terry was invited to have his effigy in wax exhibited at Madame Tussauds. Once completed it stood alongside other sporting greats, including Gordon Richards, Freddie Mills and Sammy McCarthy. The following month, West Ham Council unanimously agreed to honour Spinks for his Olympic success. At a special ceremony at Stratford Town Hall he was presented with an illuminated address and given the Freedom of the Borough. Seven days later he was a guest at a prestigious luncheon at the Mansion House to honour a visit to the City of London by the Duke of Edinburgh.

Turning professional was the natural progression for Spinks and, following his return from Melbourne, he received offers from most top managers and promoters in London. Somewhat surprisingly, he favoured his close friend, Sammy McCarthy, to guide him. In early March 1957 Sammy was featured in a BBC television programme, *This is Your Life*, and officially announced his retirement from the ring. Spinks was a guest and asked Sammy to be his manager. The former featherweight champion agreed and promptly enlisted the help of his former business adviser, Jarvis Astaire.

Terry had his first professional fight on Jack Solomons' bill at Harringay on 9 April. He was paid £250 and beat Jim Loughrey of Belfast, who was stopped when he sustained a badly-cut eye in the fourth round. It was a workmanlike performance by the former Olympic champion against a rough fighter who, in his previous contest, was narrowly outpointed over 12 rounds for the Northern Ireland flyweight title.

Spinks progressed well in the paid ranks and won his first 19 contests in the space of 16 months. The only real cause for concern was the fact that he was susceptible to cuts, something he had never been prone to as an amateur. His first defeat as a professional came on 28 August 1958 when he was stopped on a cut eye by Billy Rafferty at Paisley Ice Rink. Already well behind on points by the fifth round, Terry tried to mix it and an injury sustained in his previous contest against Terry Toole re-opened, prompting the referee to intervene.

After a break of five weeks, Spinks faced Eddie O'Connor at Shoreditch on 7 October. He was also lined up to meet Dai Dower in a mouth-watering ten rounder on the last night at Harringay show on 28 October. Although he outpointed O'Connor, he was cut on the left eyelid in the final minute of the fight and, despite treatment for the injury at Moorfields Eye Hospital, had to withdraw from the contest with Dower.

Since turning professional Terry had been trained by Snowy Buckingham but Sammy McCarthy and Jarvis Astaire felt that if he was to progress to championship level some changes were needed. Buckingham was replaced by Jimmy Davis, a former middleweight from Bethnal Green. A veteran of almost 100 contests, Jimmy was known for his ringcraft and defensive skills. He introduced new training methods devised to avoid situations liable to cause eye injuries.

Initially, everything went well and Spinks won his next eight contests in seven months. Among his victims was the Canadian champion, Pat Supple, who had replaced him at Harringay and beaten Dai Dower. Terry also soundly beat the vastly experienced Belgian, Pierre Cossemyns, who had given him many anxious moments in an eight rounder the previous year. He, in fact, had so much respect for Cossemyns that when he bought himself a large black poodle dog, he named it Pierre.

By the middle of 1959, Spinks was a natural contender for the British featherweight championship held by Bobby Neill, and it was believed to be only a matter of time before the fight was made. The Board of Control, however, had other ideas, and Sammy McCarthy and Jimmy Davis were called before the Southern Area Council to explain why their boxer had been overweight for four of his last seven contests. Although he didn't mention it, Sammy knew that Terry was totally undisciplined when it came to diet. He had a liking for all the wrong food and even when in training thought nothing of devouring bars of chocolate, cream cakes and bottles of ginger beer.

The Council decided to monitor the situation and warned that if Terry continued to exceed contracted weights, a more serious view would be taken. In the meantime, he would not be recognised as the official contender for the British featherweight title.

Spinks against Bobby Neil, however, was a fight the public desperately wanted. Jack Solomons therefore matched them over ten rounds in a non-title fight at Wembley on 2 June, advertising it as 'The most controversial contest since Eric Boon v Arthur Danahar'.

Spinks set an incredible pace and by the end of round four was well ahead. Bobby improved during the fifth and sixth when he slowed Terry with good jabs and uppercuts. The seventh was an incredible round in which the champion was sent reeling on a number of occasions as Spinks sought to end it.

Although he remained in control during the eighth, Terry was badly cut above his right eye and appeared to be tiring. Bobby's punches carried greater power but he too was in a bad way, cut and exhausted. In one desperate effort in round nine, however, he slammed in heavy punches to Terry's head and stomach, driving him into a corner. A right to the jaw and left hook to the stomach sent him crashing to the floor to be counted out.

It was one of the most dramatic endings to the fiercest featherweight contest seen in a British ring for many years. There were just two seconds of the ninth round remaining and many boxing writers saw the ending as a climax that could be compared to Boon and Danahar 20 years earlier. Writing in the *Daily Mirror*, Peter Wilson gave Spinks seven rounds with the fifth even. Summing it up he wrote: "In all the thousands of fights I have seen, I have never witnessed a finish to compare with this".

Despite Terry's defeat, Sammy McCarthy felt his performance warranted a shot at the title. Although agreement was made with Neill's camp, the Board of Control ordered Spinks to meet John O'Brien of Scotland in an eliminator. The fight was made for Wembley on 15 September, but Spinks surprisingly agreed to have a warm up against Derry Treanor at Streatham two weeks earlier. It was poor judgement because he failed to re-capture the form shown against Neill and was well outpointed. Worse was to follow because O'Brien also beat him on points, causing a serious set-back to his plans.

After a three month break, Terry eased back with victories over George Dormer and Junior Cassidy, then in January 1960 outpointed Johnny Kidd over 12 rounds in a title eliminator. Despite his victory, the Board of Control had concerns about Terry's physical condition. He had again been overweight at the official weigh-in and by the end of the contest was almost at the point of exhaustion.

McCarthy was again called before the Southern Area Council, but insisted that Terry had misjudged his weight in the days leading up to the fight and could make the featherweight limit with ease. The Council, however, ruled that he must have two contests not exceeding ten rounds before consideration could be given to him meeting Bobby Neill for the title.

Spinks proved his fitness in a ten rounds draw with Roy Jacobs, followed by a points victory over Dave Croll. His long awaited title shot against Bobby Neill finally went ahead at the Royal Albert Hall on 27 September, but again ended amid controversy.

As with their first fight, Spinks boxed brilliantly and built up a big lead. Neill, however, was still strong and biding his time, believing Terry would run out of gas.

The fight was at a fascinating stage towards the end of round seven when, suddenly, Neill emerged from a clinch with blood streaming from a cut above his left eye. Referee Ike Powell stopped the action, inspected the injury and called the fight off just as the bell ended the round. Arguments raged over the fact that the corner were not given the opportunity to treat the injury. At a subsequent meeting, the Board of Control ordered a rematch, which took place at Wembley on 22 November 1960 on a winner-take-all basis.

The fight followed the familiar pattern of previous encounters, with Spinks setting a fast pace as Bobby patiently waited, while looking to unload his heavier punches. It was another absorbing contest and by round nine both men were showing signs of battle. Spinks, however, showed no signs of weakening and, as they entered the final three rounds, he looked the fresher and stronger of the two.

By round 13, Bobby had nothing to offer and Spinks was told to go all out for victory. He hammered the former champion unmercifully before knocking him out in round 14. It was a great victory for Terry but, sadly, Bobby later collapsed and was taken to hospital, where a blood clot was removed from his brain. His career was over, but fortunately he made a remarkable recovery and remained in boxing for many years.

Spinks reign as champion came to an end in May the following year, when the great Howard Winstone forced him to retire after ten rounds at Wembley. Ever respectful of his conquerer, Terry remarked years later: "He had the fastest and most accurate left jab ever. I don't think I could have licked him on my best night".

Although he carried on fighting for another 18 months, Terry's best days were behind him, and he announced his retirement from the ring in December 1962. He admitted that he was taking punches he would have avoided a couple of years earlier, so it was time to call it a day.

From that point in time, Terry's life became a roller-coaster ride. Like many other boxers he soon fell foul of the Inland Revenue because he hadn't paid sufficient tax on his ring earnings. The outcome was that, in 1964, he was declared bankrupt, which was hurtful and embarrassing. Yet he was never a quitter and picked himself up by working hard cleaning statues and mini-cabbing. More importantly, he retained his character, self respect and popularity.

Terry stayed close to the fight game and in 1972 was invited to train the South Korean team for the Munich Olympics. Two of his boxers reached the quarter-finals and all won their first-series contests. The trip to Munich was not without its dangers because he was only a few yards from the horrific assassinations of Israeli athletes.

On returning to England, Terry spent a year at the West Ham club coaching youngsters before taking out a professional trainers licence. Working mostly at The Thomas A' Becket gym, he guided Johnny Cheshire, Albert Hillman, Johnny Claydon and Dave Smith to British title fights, and helped Claydon, Hillman, Smith and Alex Tompkins win Southern Area championships.

Terry left the fight game in 1981 to pursue a career as a licensee. He ran successful pubs at Upchurch and Worthing until 1992 when his health began to deteriorate. In August the following year he was admitted to Newham General Hospital, where he was diagnosed as having a form of brain damage. After three months he was transferred to a specialist clinic, until March 1995 when he went to live with his cousin Rosemary Ellmore at Chadwell Heath.

Due largely to Rosemary's love, patience and caring, Terry has made a steady recovery and now leads an active life. He is a Vice-President of the London Ex-Boxers' Association, attends amateur and professional boxing shows and remains closely connected with his old club, West Ham. He also works hard for charity, something which has been high on his agenda throughout his life.

Winning the Olympic gold medal was an incredible achievement by Spinks, because he did it in an era when boxers from Eastern European countries never turned professional. The top men invariably had the experience of more than 200 contests and represented their countries on many occasions. In reality, an 18-years-old British amateur was not in the same league, but Terry Spinks proved to be an exception. Yet his Olympic success was not a 'one-off' – it was part of his massive contribution to a difficult and sometimes controversial sport.

Spinks remains the only British boxer ever to have won a schoolboy championship, ABA title, Olympic gold medal and a British professional title. The chances of anyone repeating his success are extremely remote. Amazingly, his achievements have been overlooked, or ignored, by those responsible for awarding honours. It is a situation which has for years angered followers of boxing and many outside the sport as well.

In an interview with the *Sunday Telegraph* in June 2000, Sir Henry Cooper said: "Why Terry is still waiting for his gong after all these years is beyond me".

Chris Finnegan added his weight to public opinion when he told Colin Hart of *The Sun*: "It is diabolical that Terry has been left out, and I would do anything to help right this wrong. I can't understand why the authorities have insulted a great champion like this".

In and out of the ring, Terry has always been a model professional – no bad mouthing of opponents or disputing decisions of referees. He is an honourable man, and even 40 years after retirement from boxing his popularity remains as high as ever. Sadly, his only enemies appear to be the individuals who award New Year and Birthday Honours.

Two great rivals, Terry (left) and Bobby Neill meet up many years after their three exciting encounters, the last of which ended Bobby's career

"GENTLEMAN OF THE RING" The Life and Career of Jack Petersen, by Bob Lonkhurst

A meticulously researched biograpy of one of Britain's most popular heavyweight champions who became arguably the most respected and influential man in the history of Welsh sport.

Written with insight and affection, the book chronicles his entire ring career and contains vivid descriptions of all his big fights, in particular his epic encounters with German strongman, Walter Neusel.

Published in May 2001 – the hardback with dust wrapper and profusely illustrated – is obtainable only from the author, 6 Drayton Avenue, Potters Bar, Herts, EN6 2LF. Price £16.95 plus £3 post and packing.

(EAST-END IDOL: The Amazing Story of Terry Spinks, by Bob Lonkhurst, will be published in the spring of 2002)

Graham Moughton: Mister Boxing

by Ralph Oates

As we move through the stages of life we gain a most valuable asset called experience. It is made up of lessons learnt and mistakes made. In many ways the said experience is as valuable as gold dust, since it helps us to endure and indeed cope with similar situations should they ever arise again, which often they inevitably do. In the fight game, experience can be both hard and painful to acquire, but nevertheless the bumpy road to boxing knowledge must be travelled upon in the hope that each telling moment in the business will build the education bank to a high level, which will duly lead to success in the square ring. No one said it would be easy is an expression we often hear today, with reference to certain problems which are encountered in various other walks of life. This is surely more so for boxing.

Graham Moughton is a man who has travelled many roads these past years, enriching his fistic knowledge on all

fronts. Before moving on to the professional side of the sport as a promoter, manager and trainer, he was a former first-class amateur boxer, who experienced the thrill of battle in the ring, the glory of victory and the bitter pain of defeat.

In a promoter capacity he has experienced the difficulties of putting a fight card together, coupled in retrospect with the delight of a successful evening. An example of this took place on 23 February at the Broadway Theatre in Barking, Essex. Graham presented a dinner show which was part of Jason Leonard's testimonial year. Jason, of course, is the most capped England rugby player of all time. Not only did Moughton put on a quality card he also had the former world, European, British and Commonwealth light-heavyweight champion, John Conteh, as a guest speaker. The man from Liverpool was excellent in this capacity. Also present on the night was the former

Graham (right), who represented Bermuda at welter in the 1974 World Cup, seen in action that year against the Canadian, Jope Martinez

hard-punching world flyweight king, Charlie Magri, plus former world welterweight title holders, John H. Stracey and Lloyd Honeyghan. Former British featherweight champion and 1956 Olympic Games flyweight gold medal winner, Terry Spinks, and former world featherweight title holder, Colin McMillan, enriched the night's impressive line up. The fans were most certainly given a treat and went home happy.

In the role of trainer, Graham has experienced the joy of his charge improving with each bout. At the moment, Colin Lynes is being put through his paces and the fighter, who has championship potential written all over him, is moving in an upwards direction under Graham's tuition.

As a manager, Moughton has endured the nerve-racking ordeal of accepting and agreeing the right kind of fight for his boxer. Being a manager is not an easy task. It is like walking a tight rope knowing that one wrong decision can set your man's career back, if not ruin it forever. Clearly, Graham can be called with every justification 'Mister Boxing' – the man has learnt his trade the hard way. On behalf of the *Yearbook*, I carried out this interview.

(Ralph Oates) When were you born?

(Graham Moughton) on 2 December 1948.

(RO) How old were you when you first started to box?

(GM) I was nine years of age.

(RO) So you started to box when at school?

(GM) Yes I did, and I enjoyed it. I won three schoolboy titles and it was an excellent grounding for what lay ahead.

(RO) What made you take up boxing?

(GM) Both my father and grandfather had boxed. My grandfather in fact had over 500 professional bouts during his career and was once matched with Johnny Coulon for the world bantamweight championship. Coulon had won the vacant title on 6 March 1910, knocking out Jim Kendrick in round 19 and was later elected to the Hall of Fame in 1973, so he was some fighter. Sadly, however, my grandfather injured his arm and the fight had to be called off. The bout wasn't rescheduled so my grandfather, Bert Moughton, from Dublin, via Norfolk, missed his chance.

(RO) How many amateur bouts did you have?

(GM) Over a period of 23 years I took part in over 273 bouts, meeting along the way many good fighters. Men like 'Sugar' Ray Leonard, Ayub Kalule, John H. Stracey and Terry Marsh all went on to become world champions in the professional ranks.

(RO) In which stance did you box?

(GM) Orthodox.

(RO) Many fighters do not like boxing southpaws and how did you feel about crossing gloves with them?

(GM) I had no problem with them. If you prepare for the style correctly you should be able to cope. It's like any other boxer you meet. You must put in the work if you want to win and, in truth, if you are going to be a champion of any kind you must be able to handle southpaws. A class man will meet and defeat both southpaw and orthodox. You just cannot pick and choose.

(RO) Which clubs did you box for?

(GM) Repton, Monteagle and West Ham.

(RO) When you boxed 'Sugar' Ray Leonard, did you have a feeling that he would go on and become a little special?

(GM) Yes I did. He had some very good moves which many fans may have appreciated, but believe me you both notice and appreciate them even more when you were in the ring doing battle with him. Leonard had that little bit of magic and, of course, talent that separated him from the rest. However, I was quite happy with my performance against 'Sugar Ray' on the night.

(RO) You boxed in the 1972 Olympic Games and thus had an excellent amateur pedigree. Why did you not turn professional?

(GM) I would have turned professional with Terry Lawless, but various problems over a period of four to five years really held me back. For example, I had an operation on my left knuckle and if that wasn't enough I also had some kind of acid substance in my eye. They say that time waits for no man, this is also true of boxers. By the time my problems cleared up I was about 25 years of age, so I decided to stay in the amateurs and enjoy the sport. I must, however, admit I still get many moments when I wonder just how far I would have gone in the paid ranks. Terry, of course, produced a number of world, European and British champions at various weights and it's possible that I could have been one of them.

(RO) Who was your most difficult opponent?

(GM) On the night it could have been Ireland's Jim McCourt or the American, Davey Armstrong.

(RO) What made you become a promoter?

(GM) All in all I have been in this business for 43 years, one way or another, and it really was something I wanted to do.

(RO) What made you decide to become a trainer?

(GM) Once again it was something I wanted to do. It also gives you a good feeling to help youngsters on the way up.

(RO) What made you become a manager?

(GM) This seemed to be the next natural step.

(RO) Are any members of your family involved in boxing at this present time?

(GM) My son Tom had a couple of bouts for Repton and was unbeaten, but he is not fighting at the moment.

(RO) How long have you been married?

(GM) Wendy and I were married on 7 December 1974.

(RO) Is Wendy a boxing fan?

(GM) Being married to me she would have to be. In fact, Wendy has a promoters' licence which she has yet to use.

(RO) You have two sons I understand?

(GM) Yes, Tom and Lee.

(RO) What quality do you look for in a boxer before you decide to manage him?

(GM) Ability and dedication are the two main assets I look for. However, a fighter's personality can also be a big factor in my view.

(RO) How do you feel about female involvement in the sport?

(GM) Just as long as it's controlled medically, I've no problem with women boxing. I understand on one occasion in the USA that a lady boxer was found to be pregnant when having her medical for a promotion. Just imagine the

terrible circumstances had the pregnancy not been detected. The outcome would have been tragic for both the lady in question and the sport in general.

(RO) Earlier this year, Lalia Ali outpointed Jacqui Frazier-Lyde over eight rounds. Do you think this contest advanced the cause of women's boxing?

(GM) I suppose it did in someways, since the bout was given a great deal of media coverage due mostly to the fact that they were daughters of well-known fathers – Muhammad Ali and Joe Frazier. In truth, they both gave it their best shot and I dare say a return will be made in the future, which in turn will attract even more press coverage.

(RO) Who is your favourite old-time fighter?

(GM) There are so many in different era's but if pushed I would have to go for 'Sugar' Ray Robinson. He had it all. The boxing skill, punch and courage when the chips were down. You can still appreciate the class of the man on old fight films which are shown from time to time. Class does not deteriorate with the passing of time.

(RO) Who is your favourite modern-day fighter?

(GM) Of the boxers still active it has to be Felix Trinidad. This man has the power and the boxing ability, and is dangerous when hurt. He also generates excitement when in action. More of his fights should be shown on television. If I may go back a few years to the 1970s, Wilfredo Gomez, the former WBC world super-bantamweight champion, was another fighter whom I admired. Gomez, for my money, had that special talent in being a good boxer and puncher.

(RO) Who in your opinion was the best heavyweight champion in the history of the sport?

(GM) There are of course a number of names which come to mind, Joe Louis, Rocky Marciano and Jack Dempsey, etc. They all had a special quality which made them stand out above the rest in their time period. However, I would go for Muhammad Ali without question.

(RO) Which is your favourite world heavyweight title fight?

(GM) There have been a number over the years, but I think that if pressed I would go for the Muhammad Ali – Joe Frazier bout which took place on 1 October 1975 in Manila (The Thriller in Manila). Both fighters gave 100 percent and more. Frazier, of course, retired in round 14, but this was no disgrace. It is interesting to note that Joe and Ali were never the same after this encounter.

(RO) How do you feel about the boxers who continue to fight on, even when middle aged?

(GM) I feel really sorry, since many of them should be in a position to call it a day and hence retire from the active side of the sport. They could use their experience in some other capacity, such as training, etc.

(RO) What changes if any would you like to see made in the sport?

(GM) I would like to see no more than two governing bodies. At the moment there are a vast number of organisations which makes boxing a farce. Winning a world title should be an achievement, something which is difficult to obtain, which in turn makes it all the more valuable when won. Let's be honest, we sometimes have

boxers contesting a version of the world title who have not earned the right to do so in the first place. This does not put the sport in a very good light, and how many fans today can name all the world champions? Few, if any.

(RO) How do you feel about there being so many weight divisions in the sport today?

(GM) I have no problems with the extra weight divisions and, in truth, many of them are necessary.

(RO) What annoys you most in boxing?

(GM) The way the smaller promoters are left to battle on without the assistance of television. Many of the small hall promotions present some excellent fights which send the fans home happy. If TV money was provided, many promoters would be able to more than compete with the big boys in the game. Television would also profit since they would be gaining both value and entertainment, which in turn would be good also for them. Let's not forget that a number of good fighters have come from small halls over the years and viewers may well be treated to seeing a future champion on the way up. Also, a number of journeymen can put on some fine performances.

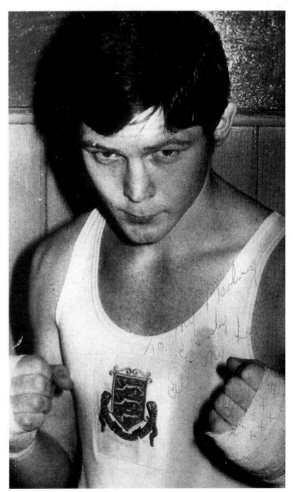

Graham in boxing pose

(RO) How do you feel boxers today compare with past boxers with both their skill and technique?

(GM) From the early '60s I would put most of the top fighters at any weight on a par with many of today's boxers. In some cases they may have been even better, since they had much more competition and were thus able to learn their trade.

(RO) You are a promoter, trainer and manager – which role do you enjoy the most?

(GM) Promoting would be first, followed by training, then managing.

(RO) Do you have a favourite weight division?

(GM) Yes I do – light-welterweight. There is quite a lot of talent at the poundage in Britain and, indeed, the world as well. There can be some very exciting matches made in the future at domestic level and also at world level.

(RO) Do you have a hobby?

(GM) Fishing. I find it very restful.

(RO) What is the best advice you have been given in boxing?

(GM) Teddy Lewis, my first trainer at Monteagle ABC as a junior, taught me to always believe in myself, while Jackie Bowes, at Repton ABC, believed that you should look after your hands and ensure that they are bandaged correctly.

(RO) Have you ever had any awkward moments in the sport?

(GM) No. I can honestly say that I have enjoyed every single moment in boxing without a doubt.

(RO) Apart from boxing what is your favourite sport?

(GM) Boxing is the only sport I enjoy.

(RO) What would you say was your proudest moment in boxing to date?

(GM) I would have to say being captain of the British Olympic boxing team.

(RO) Do you still keep fit by jogging, etc?

(GM) No, I don't excercise at all now. However, to my credit, I don't smoke or drink and I work the pads most days, which can keep you very fit, believe me.

(RO) What answer would you give those who would like to ban boxing?

(GM) Understand the sport first, before being quick to condemn. Visit a few of the gyms, talk to a few fighters, watch them train, and observe the many good things which come from the game. Don't just look at the negatives, look also at the positive side of the sport. Boxing has given many kids an opportunity in life.

(RO) Over the years there have been many films made about boxing – some good, some bad. Do you have a favourite?

(GM) Yes I think I would go for *The Champ*, which had Jon Voight in the leading role.

(RO) I understand that both Wendy and yourself are soon to be grandparents?

(GM) Yes, that's right by courtesy of our son, Lee. We are all waiting keenly for the happy event.

(RO) What advice would you give to anyone embarking upon a career in boxing?

(GM) To both amateurs or professionals I would say dedicate yourself completely to the sport. You must live in the gym, listen to your trainers, and remember there are no short cuts. Be confident and aim for the top.

(RO) If you had your time over again, what would you do differently?

(GM) I would have gone professional, even at a later age.

(RO) What is your ultimate aim in boxing?

(GM) To find a sponsor and thus be able to promote even better shows in the future.

There is no doubt that over the years Graham Moughton has made a great contribution to British Boxing and is continuing to do so, and for this the man should be given every ounce of praise and encouragement. Graham is boxing through and through and loves the sport, which he serves with both honour and dignity. It is to be hoped that he will one day be given a chance to present one of his promotions on TV, something he really deserves. Having spoken to Graham on various occasions, I know that he has many good ideas with regards to certain contests which he would like to make. If TV money was made available, he would thus be able to put his plans into action. In fact, if many small hall promoters could be given a slot on TV the sport could well benefit in the long run, since over the years some fine fighters have turned in some exciting performances on the night. They say good things come to he who waits. I really hope that's true, and I further hope that good things come Graham Moughton's way soon as he deserves every success. He has paid his dues and knows the sport from back to front. On behalf of the *Yearbook*, I wish Graham and family the very best for the future.

THE HEAVYWEIGHT BOXING QUIZBOOK

Written and compiled by Ralph Oates

Over 2000 questions about the heavyweight division from boxing's leading quizbook compiler

*"Being a former heavyweight boxer I can appreciate and enjoy the questions presented in **The Heavyweight Boxing Quizbook** by Ralph Oates. It's ideal for the fans of the sport."*
BILLY WALKER

Following a delay, The Parrs Wood Press are pleased to announce that the above book will be available from all leading bookshops in November or by Mail Order
£7.99 POST FREE (UK only) from:

The Parrs Wood Press
FREEPOST
Manchester M15 9PW

(Make cheques payable to The Parrs Wood Press)

A Tribute to Max Schmeling

by Melanie Lloyd

Many moons ago I became interested in boxing. My early fascination blossomed as I learned about fighters of the past. There is one in particular whose life story and boxing career continues to captivate me. At the age of 96 he is the oldest surviving world heavyweight champion. His name is Max Schmeling. A few years ago I decided that I would either take an evening degree in English Literature or write a book about boxing. I applied to Kingston University and wrote to Max the same day. Two weeks later I received two letters, a glossy package from the university and a short note with an autographed photograph from Max Schmeling. There was no contest. I am now at the closing stage of my book and this is my personal tribute to Max Schmeling.

Maximilian Adolph Otto Siegfried Schmeling was born on 28 September 1905 in Klein-Luckow, near Berlin. Because of his nationality and the timing of his birth, he would become one of the most misunderstood sportsmen of all time. Not only did he face some of the finest heavyweights about, including Joe Louis, twice, but the scornful reaction of a world taken in by the awful Nazi propaganda machine.

Max stood over six foot tall and as a heavyweight, came in at around 195 pounds. His dark hair, dusky looks and haunting deep-set eyes, together with his rather shy smile projected a distinctive kind of charm. He bore a striking resemblance to Jack Dempsey and these two would become good friends, occasionally known to play practical jokes on an unsuspecting public. Their favourite prank was to appear together, dressed identically.

It was perhaps no great coincidence then that Max's love affair with boxing began when as a young boy, he saw Dempsey's fight with Georges Carpentier at the cinema. He was so enchanted that he returned every night that week, eventually persuading his father to accompany him. Seeing perhaps for the first time his son's heartfelt enthusiasm for boxing, Max's father agreed that he take lessons. The star-struck son wasted no time in procuring a pair of second-hand gloves which he hung over his bed. But little was Max or his father to know that he would eventually become world heavyweight champion during a professional career comprising 70 fights, 56 wins, 38 by stoppage.

As an amateur, Max reached the finals of the West German light-heavyweight division in 1924. Arthur Bülow, editor of the *Boxsport* magazine, was present at ringside and was so impressed by the 19-year old that he became his advisor. Max soon signed with manager, Hugo Abels. His first professional fight was in August 1924 at light-heavyweight and he stopped heavily favoured Jean Czapp in Dusseldorf in the sixth round. By the end of the year Max had participated in ten fights, his only loss being to heavy

hitting Max Dieckmann, a score that he would go on to settle. In 1925 he had ten more fights, his big right hand rapidly becoming his trademark.

Max and Hugo Abels decided to go into the ice-cream business. However, their partnership was destined to be a short one. Shortly after they began trading Max became acquainted with Kate Sandwina of the Busch Circus, who was billed as 'The World's Strongest Woman'. He started teaching Kate's son to box and went off with the circus for a month. When he returned to Cologne Abels had sold the business behind his back, so Max left him and Arthur Bülow became his manager.

A young Max Schmeling in suitable pose

He spent Summer 1926 in Berlin where he met his new trainer, Max Machon, a relationship that was to stand the test of time. In July 1926 Max scored a first-round knockout over August Vengehr. Two months later he stopped Max Dieckmann in 30 seconds for the German light-heavyweight title. That week, *Boxsport* opened with glowing accolades of the victory. And a star was born.

Max had ten fights during the next ten months, winning them all, eight by knockout. In June 1927 he became the first German to win the European light-heavyweight title, stopping the Belgian, Fernand Delarge, in the 14th round. After the Delarge victory Max sailed to London to see Mickey Walker fight Tommy Milligan. As he passed through the turnstile an usher tipped his hat and said, "Pass through Mr Dempsey". This was the first time Max had genuinely been mistaken for Dempsey and he loved it.

His career continued to flourish and in January 1928 he won by a first-round knockout over Michele Bonaglia of Italy. As the count finished, the ecstatic crowd at the Berlin Sports Palace leapt to its feet and sang the German National Anthem. Max glowed with pride.

But along with his new found fame and popularity came many invitations from Germany's 'in crowd'. Max was initially quite shy of his new, exotic friends as they drew him further into their glamorous midst. He knew so little of their world. But gradually he formed close friendships with a colourful bunch of artists, sculptors, writers, racing drivers and actors. They were a happy-go-lucky crowd and Max began to succumb to tempting, late night alternatives to early nights and rigorous training. He paid the price in February 1928 when he was knocked out in one round by the British fighter and previous points victim, Gypsy Daniels. Max decided to move up to the heavyweight division and in April 1928, he fought Franz Diener in Berlin for the German heavyweight title. This time he stepped through the ropes in immaculate physical and mental condition to score a clear 15-round points win. But victory came at great cost. Max's left thumb had been fractured during the first round and the bone had splintered. The doctors forbade him to defend his titles, but the German media turned on their champion viciously, claiming he was unwilling to fight, calling him arrogant. In May 1928 the boxing authorities stripped him of his titles for failure to defend. The following day Max headed for New York.

First impressions of America would remain with Max always. As the massive liner *New York* reached the harbour, swarms of reporters enveloped the decks like angry insects, eager to discover any celebrities on board. Passing ships blasted their sirens in welcome. Crowds waved and shouted greetings from the shore. Max and Arthur Bülow took a room at the Hotel Ransby which Max was delighted to discover had previously been occupied by both Jack Dempsey and Gene Tunney. Bülow was convinced that his fighter would be in great demand in

America and decided they should play the waiting game. But New York was flooded with European fighters, none of which had impressed against the tough Americans. The phone remained ominously silent. Meanwhile, back in Germany the media sustained their attack, demanding Max have a rematch with Franz Diener. Max's hand was still causing him a lot of pain and Bülow remained adamant that they should sit and wait. Finances began to dwindle and the pair were forced to vacate their room at the Ransby, moving into a cheap waterside bungalow.

At his darkest hour Max met a wonderful lady called Madame Bey who ran a famous training camp in New Jersey. She immediately realized that his hand urgently needed treatment and arranged for him to have an operation. It was through Madame Bey that Max met Joe Jacobs, a short, vivacious American-Jewish gentleman with a penchant for huge cigars. Max was getting frustrated with Bülow's inactivity and when Jacobs expressed an interested in becoming his manager Max readily agreed. Jacobs, convinced that his new find was something truly special, worked for no fee until Bülow's contract ended. Despite coming from different worlds, their fighter-manager relationship would become one of the strongest in history. Their friendship lasted until the day Joe died.

When Max knocked out Joe Monte at Madison Square Garden in November 1928, fight promoter, Tex Rickard, was sitting at ringside and leapt from his seat as Monte went down, yelling: "What a right hand"! The next day Rickard's phrase was splashed across every newspaper in America. Joe Jacobs wasted no time in capitalising with a relentless publicity campaign, naming his new fighter, 'The Black Ulan', Max's raven hair and brooding looks carrying it off to perfection. Jacobs arranged endless visits to schools and hospitals and exploited Max's startling resemblance to Jack Dempsey relentlessly.

In January 1929, Max fought Joe Sykra. At one point during the fight Sykra went down and it didn't look as if he was going to make the count. Max instinctively rushed over to help him to his feet. Max eventually won the fight on points but his earlier compassion won him the heart of the Madison Square Garden crowd. Eighteen days later he knocked out Italian-American Pietro Corri in 59 seconds. Next came his biggest fight yet. He stopped Johnny Risko in nine at Madison Square Garden. Risko was a big light who had never been down and had just beaten Max Baer. A few days later, Tex Rickard, the man who had launched Max's American career with a single phrase died. The whole fight fraternity was devastated.

After beating Risko, Max returned to Germany, where he was welcomed home with open arms. Cheering crowds and reception committees greeted him everywhere he went. The German Boxing Commission could not reinstate his titles fast enough. But he had not forgotten his homeland's earlier rejection, accepting her renewed warmth cautiously. While he enjoyed a short break from the ring Max was persuaded, much against his better judgement, to appear in the film, *Love in the Ring*, which was originally planned to be a silent movie. Unfortunately, plans changed and to his utter horror, he even had to sing a song!

On a much darker note, Adolf Hitler's influence had begun to impact upon Germany. But the rest of the world still believed he was nothing more than a mad man, no real threat to anybody. Only the minorities who remained trapped in Germany were becoming completely aware of the catastrophic truth.

Meanwhile, in America the world heavyweight champion, Gene Tunney, had decided to step down from his throne. Boxing needed a new heavyweight champion and the search began in earnest. Max, for his part in the elimination process, was to fight Paolino Uzcudun of Spain. Once again he set sail for America. In June 1929 he beat Uzcudun on points before a Yankee Stadium crowd of forty thousand. By the end of 1929, *Ring Magazine* ranked him next in line to Jack Sharkey, the leading heavyweight contender and one tough customer. Max's camp were led to believe that the Uzcudun victory automatically entitled him to a fight with Sharkey for the world title, but the New York Boxing Commission had other ideas. Max was informed that first, he must first fight Phil Scott of England. He refused and the commission tried to force the issue by suspending his licence. Max decided to return to Germany, telling them, "If I stay and give in, I'll become your puppet". Jacobs immediately flew into action with an extremely loud and proud publicity campaign called 'Bring Max over', leaving little clouds of cigar smoke behind him like calling cards everywhere he went. The commission rapidly relented, declaring that Max should fight Sharkey straight away. Jacobs travelled to Germany to deliver the news to Max personally. Together, they had won this

Max became the first heavyweight champion to win the title on a foul. Our picture shows Jack Sharkey just about to land the low blow that handed the title to the German on 12 June 1930

battle. Now Max must win his fight with Sharkey to become world heavyweight champion. It was scheduled for 12 June 1930 at the Yankee Stadium, New York.

Sharkey was known for flying into a rage during a fight, making things personal. As the date approached both fighters had a lot of fun with the publicity machine, each striving to come up with the worst insults and greatest boasts. And then the night that Max had been working for finally arrived. Thousands of fans queued up all night outside the stadium desperate for tickets. Many were turned away. Private aeroplanes were chartered to carry the rich and famous to ringside seats. When the fighters entered the stadium the crowd of almost eighty thousand erupted into a thunderous greeting, many of them waving lit matches and lighters, radiating a golden cloud. The fight commenced. Sharkey won the first three rounds and in the fourth Max came out on the attack. Then Sharkey's famous temper got the better of him and he landed a desperate low blow. Max crumpled to the canvas in agony. Screams of "Foul!" from the German corner pierced the air as their man lay shattered. The count reached six and the bell went. As Joe Jacobs stood in the centre of the ring, arguing furiously with Sharkey's manager the massive crowd suddenly became silent. Then referee Jim Crowley announced that Sharkey had been disqualified. Max Schmeling had become the first fighter to win the world heavyweight championship on a foul. Max was held up by his corner for Crowley to raise his hand. He was devastated for he believed that he could have won the fight squarely. The nature of his victory, coupled with his nationality (the first non-American world heavyweight champion since Tommy Burns 20 years earlier), made his victory unpopular with everybody. He returned to Germany, finding only cold comfort. The media had turned on him again, ridiculing their new champion for the nature of his victory. At a time when he should have been as high as a kite, Max became very depressed and locked himself away in a flat in Berlin, agreeing only to see his closest friends.

One night, a good friend persuaded the dejected world champion out of his reclusive shell. They took a trip to the cinema to see the new big film in Germany, *The Girl from Rummelplatz*. The leading lady, Anny Ondra, happened to be Max's next-door neighbour and by the time the film was over, our hero had fallen head over heels in love with the girl next door. Max was much too shy to approach Anny himself, so he persuaded his friend, the boxing promoter, Paul Damski, to call on her for him. Damski explained, "Herr Schmeling may be the world champion, but he's too scared to approach you himself". Anny laughingly agreed to meet Max the next day, his birthday, for afternoon tea. Every day after that Max left a bouquet of flowers on the bonnet of her Blue Cadillac before embarking on his morning run. For the record, Paul Damski would later be forced to flee Germany because he was Jewish.

Meanwhile, the German media continued to berate Max's world title. The first time he attended a boxing evening with Anny he suffered the acute humiliation of being booed by the crowd, right before the eyes of his new love.

In 1931 the New York Boxing Commission ordered that Max fight the 'Georgia Peach', William 'Young' Stribling, a man who began his boxing career at bantamweight and fought his way to heavyweight through every division. Stribling had notched up over 270 fights, knocking out 126 of his opponents, the highest KO record next to that of Archie Moore. The fight was scheduled for 3 July 1931. Max set up training camp in Cleveland and every evening, at exactly the same time, a light aircraft would appear. The plane would circle the camp a few times and perform an array of daring airborne antics before disappearing into the distance. The pilot was one 'Young' Stribling. It was a tremendously tough fight, both fighters determined to win. In the last minute Max scored a sensational knockout. When the count was over Max gently lifted Stribling from the canvas to carry him to his corner. Tragically, Stribling died a few months later in a motorcycle accident. His wife was giving birth and he was on his way to her when he crashed the bike. He was 28 years old.

A re-match with Jack Sharkey was scheduled for 21 June 1932. A new stadium was built for the fight in New York and all seventy thousand seats were sold. The fight went the distance and almost everybody present believed that Max had won it. But, to the disbelief of the crowd and media present, Max lost his world title almost as controversially as he had won it. Sharkey was announced the new world heavyweight champion. Joe Jacobs jumped into the ring and indignantly shrieked, "We wuz robbed". Max sportingly congratulated Sharkey, even managing a smile. Years later, Gunboat Smith, Sharkey's best friend, who refereed the fight, would admit, "I knew the best man lost".

Following that, in September 1932, Max fought the top contender, Mickey Walker. Max was taller, heavier and younger than the American and knocked him down in the first minute of the first round and several times after that. His repeated appeals to the referee to stop the fight were ignored until Walker was unable to come out for the ninth. Max returned to his homeland to propose to Anny, who happily accepted.

But Germany was a rapidly changing place where another fight was breaking out and the big money was on the Brown Shirts. There was no referee to monitor the intimidation, the bloody street battles and the lynchings. On 30 January 1933, Reich President von Hindenburg named Adolph Hitler to the office of Reich Chancellor. One evening, a few months later, Max was dining out with friends. An SA Officer entered the restaurant and declared that Adolph Hitler had ordered Max Schmeling's presence for dinner. Max explained that he had already eaten but would gladly meet with the Führer and left with the officer. They arrived at the Chancellery and Hitler, surrounded by many of his Cabinet ministers, deftly steered the conversation to America. "If anyone over there asks how it's going in Germany, you can reassure the doomsayers that everything is moving along quite peacefully".

There was just one fight in 1933, Max returning to America to take on 'The Clown Prince', Max Baer, in June. But the joker was in a seriously dangerous mood that night. Max had no chance, referee Arthur Donovan stopping the fight in the tenth round. A month later Max and Anny got married. At their wedding ceremony, it suddenly became painfully clear how many of their friends were no longer around. Hitler made his presence strongly felt by presenting the happy couple with a Japanese Maple as a wedding gift. In the meantime, Anny's film production company, *Ondra-Lamac Productions*, was being forced into liquidation because she had Jewish and Czech partners.

In February 1934 Max suffered a humiliating defeat at the hands of Steve 'Hurricane' Hamas in Philadelphia. Hamas was considered to be mediocre opposition and on the back of the Baer defeat things were looking bleak for our man. Four months later he was awarded a draw against Paolino Uzcudun in Barcelona. Many of Paolino's staunch supporters believed that Max had done enough to win and Spanish newspaper *La Vanguardia* declared, "There can be no more decisions like this one, which hurts the prestige of Paolino, Spain, and the sport of boxing".

Back in America, Jack Sharkey had lost his title to Primo Carnera. Max Baer had taken it off Carnera and a strong young contender named Walter Neusel was baying at the door. Neusel was managed by Paul Damski (Max and Anny's matchmaker) and had fought a series of hard victories in America. The scene was set for 'The Black Ulan' and 'The German Tiger' to do battle. The fight took place in Hamburg in August 1934 before a crowd of ninety thousand. Damski could not be in Germany with Neusel for fear of being arrested by the Gestapo. It was a ferocious fight and Max stopped Neusel in the ninth round.

Back in the USA, Max Baer lost his title in a surprise defeat to James Braddock. However, the latest big name on the tip of everybody's tongue was a young black man called Joe Louis.

The opportunity to settle a score came in March 1935 when Max fought a re-match with Steve Hamas in Hamburg. A few days before the fight, Joe Jacobs arrived in Germany. When he reached the hotel the desk clerk refused him admission, explaining that the Jews could not be accommodated. Max was called to the scene and, at first, he innocently thought his booking had been overlooked. Slowly, the real reason for the clerk's attitude dawned on him and fury set in. "You mean you can't give him a room because he's a Jew? You don't know who Herr Jacobs is! When this shows up in the New York papers, then you've seen your last American guest. And you can be sure that my guests will never stay here again". The terrified clerk decided that Jacobs should have his room after all. A few days later Max stopped Hamas in the ninth. As the decision was announced, twenty-five thousand fans stood and sang the German National Anthem, raising their arms in the Nazi salute. Then Joe Jacobs did something that insulted the Third Reich, deeply and for all time. He jumped into the ring and, bemused by the sea of raised arms, raised his own arm with the ever-present cigar between the fingers! Photographs of this image were published all over the world. Max was immediately summoned to the office of the Reich Minister of Sports, Hans Tschammer, who angrily demanded that Jacobs be immediately dismissed. Max remained calm while Tschammer repeatedly interrogated his loyalty to the Third Reich. A few days later he received an official letter from the Reich Ministry demanding that he sever all contact with Jacobs. Max never replied. He sought and was granted a meeting with Adolph Hitler to request official permission to continue his association with Jacobs. He explained "I really need Joe Jacobs. I owe all my success in America to him". Hitler was furious that Max had dared to mention a Jew in a favourable light. From that moment Max started making dangerous enemies at the Reich office. In April 1935, it was reported in the *New York Times*, "The refusal of Max Schmeling and Walter Neusel, after years of warning, to discharge their Jewish managers 'In the interests of Germanhood' has angered the Nazi newspaper, the *Fraenkische Tageszeitung*. The paper particularly scores Joe Jacobs, Schmeling's American manager, for recently giving the Nazi salute with a 'smoking cigar' between the fingers of the saluting hand".

Then Max managed to secure a fight with the main man, Joe Louis, which angered Hitler even more. The dictator didn't believe that Max had a chance against Louis and felt it unthinkable that a prominent German citizen should loose to a negro. Max returned to America to prepare for the fight that few believed he could win. One young reporter named Bill Farnsworth spoke in his favour, maintaining that Louis was over trained. Another person who amused everybody with the prediction that Max would win by knockout was Marlene Dietrich. The odds crept up in Louis' favour but Max wasn't listening. He studied Louis's fight films over and over again. His diligence was rewarded with the discovery of a vital flaw in Louis' style. When the bomber threw his short, powerful left hook, he would drop his left for a fraction of a second, leaving him open to a right cross over the top, Max's best punch! Max appeared amused as he declared at a pre-fight press conference, "I saw something". When he was quizzed by reporters about what it was he had seen, he smilingly refused to elaborate.

On 19 June 1936 at the Yankee Stadium before a crowd of forty-five thousand, Max Schmeling did the unbelievable. He stopped Joe Louis in round 12. There have been many great upsets over the years but this was one of the biggest ever. Max's plan worked, his right hand finding it's target over and over again. Louis, younger by 11 years, gave the

German plenty of trouble along the way. Max got the shock of his life when he felt Louis' power for the first time. The younger man was out on his feet several times, but 'The Brown Bomber' defiantly refused to cave in. Max floored him for the second and last time in the 12th. When Louis fell to the canvas his face was a picture of bewilderment that seemed to say, "Hold on, this wasn't in the script"! As Arthur Donovan counted the fallen Louis out Max raced over to help carry him to his stool. And so, Max Schmeling became the first man to beat Joe Louis. The *Daily Telegraph* reported that the blow by blow report on the fight was so exciting, 'that 12 people died while listening to it'.

Against all the odds, Schmeling sensationally handed Joe Louis, considered invincible by many, a 12-round shellacking on 19 June 1936

Schmeling and his handlers celebrate the victory over Joe Louis

Max returned home to find himself back in favour with the German public. Hitler declared to the world that he always knew Max Schmeling would beat the negro, Joe Louis. With those words the Führer making Max as much a victim of the Nazi party as anybody. All over the world his name became tarnished, he was called a Nazi and a fascist. Max, however, was always prepared to speak his mind. He gave post-fight interviews praising Louis, calling him a great boxer and declaring the fight the hardest of his career.

As a result of the Louis victory Max was lined up to fight world champion, Jim Braddock. The contract was signed and the date set for June 1937. During his training Max received a visit from Gene Tunney, who warned, "Be ready for anything, Max. You don't know what's possible in this country". The former world champion turned out to be right. Joe Louis' managers offered Braddock a staggering deal to renege on his contract with Max and fight Joe Louis instead. The money making machine had its way and Max was blatantly side-stepped. In protest he turned up alone to weigh in for the fight that would never happen, but nobody cared. A day later, Max was scheduled to make a coast-to-coast radio broadcast but it was blocked by the boxing commission who felt his opinions of them might be too brutally close to the truth. They offered him a substitute speech which he adamantly refused. Braddock for his part got fined $1,000, small change when you consider the contract he had signed to fight Louis was worth almost $300,000, plus ten percent of all profits from Joe Louis' future fights. Max lost $25,000 in travelling and training expenses. To add insult to injury, Louis' managers capitalised on the fact that Max was from Nazi Germany, stating that public opinion would not tolerate the fight. Louis knockout Braddock out in the eighth round to become the next heavyweight champion of the world.

Max knew that his fighting days could not last for ever and he and Anny found distraction from a world that raged around them by planning their future, investing in a farm. Their new neighbours were the Thoraks, a sculptor named Josef and his Jewish wife. Under the Nuremberg Laws of 1935 that prohibited a German citizen from cohabiting with a Jew, Frau Thorak had been ordered to leave her home. One night the Gestapo surrounded the house. The next day Max paid a visit to the Reich Minister of Propaganda, Joseph Goebbels, urging him to show leniency to Frau Thorak. Goebbels was initially reluctant to listen but Max persisted with his appeal and it paid off. Frau Thorak was allowed to remain free and live in her hometown in return for her assurance that she would in future obey the law and have no further contact with her husband. Josef Thorak later separated from his wife permanently and became an official sculptor for the Third Reich.

Max had one more fight in mind, a re-match with Joe Louis, and he would happily retire from boxing for ever. He got his wish on 22 June 1938. The reception Max received as he sailed into New York harbour aboard *The Bremen* broke his heart. Crowds of demonstrators waved signs and shouted anti-Nazi slogans. Throughout his stay he was taunted, insulted, and received mountains of hate-mail. He could not believe that America, the country he had come to consider his second home, could treat him in this way. The media used every opportunity to portray him as a Nazi, an image that he neither wanted nor believed in. Louis, on the other hand, was portrayed a symbol of the American way. A syndicated statement was released on Louis' behalf the day before the fight which read, "Tonight I not only fight the battle of my life to revenge the lone blot on my record, but I fight for America against the challenge of a foreign invader, Max Schmeling. This isn't just one man against another or Joe Louis boxing Max Schmeling; it is the good old USA versus Germany". Ironic really when you consider that in 'the good old USA' Louis was a second class citizen. The night before the fight a telegram arrived from Hitler to Max, addressing him as 'The New Heavyweight Champion of the World.' The American public became even more enraged, aligning themselves firmly behind Louis.

When fight night arrived Joe Jacobs was forbidden to see his charge. Max sat and waited in his dressing room to be called to the ring, completely alone. On his way through the arena many of the crowd of seventy-five thousand hurled abuse and pelted him with missiles. Louis paced the ring like a caged panther, shrugging off his robe angrily as if he truly had a personal score to settle here tonight. The fight lasted just 124 seconds, during which time Max's vertebrae was broken in two places. As the carnage was taking place, Max Machon jumped into the ring, screaming: "I'm not letting my man get beaten to death. Don't you have eyes? He's had enough". When it was over Max dragged himself across to Louis' corner smiling bravely as he shook the champion's hand. Then he collapsed. He was taken directly to hospital where he stayed for three months. He received few visitors. Joe

Roles reversed. Max Schmeling crashes to the floor during his savage beating at the hands of Joe Louis on 22 June 1938

Louis tried but he was turned away. Anny was desperate to be at her husband's side but, afraid of the reception that she might receive from the American people, Max forbade her to come to him, insisting she remain in Germany. He returned to her three months later, on a stretcher.

In July 1939, Max stepped back into the ring to knock out Adolph Heuser in one round and become European heavyweight champion. Two months later war broke out in Europe. Max was conscripted into a paratrooper regiment, which was a big shock to him because entertainers, sports personalities and men over 35 were not being called. His 'old friends' at the Reich Ministry of Sport had engineered his calling. A few days later he was told that Joe Jacobs had died of heart attack. He was 41 years old.

Germany invaded Greece in April 1941. A few weeks later the German army launched a massive airborne assault on the island of Crete. Max's unit took part in a night-time parachute drop and he landed awkwardly. In agony and under heavy gun fire, he managed to crawl forward passing out many times on the way, miraculously finding his unit the next day. When he had recovered sufficiently to walk with two canes he was commanded to escort an injured British prisoner to a different base. He was ordered not to speak to the Englishman during the journey but, as soon as the pair were out of sight of the command post, they wordlessly linked arms for support. The English soldier recognised Max and explained that he came from Brighton and he was a friend of the Welsh heavyweight, Tommy Farr.

A few months later Max attracted the further wrath of the Reich. He gave an interview to journalist, Bill Flannery, telling the Americans that he had no problem with the way the British soldiers had conducted themselves during the war. Goebbels was furious and ordered a military court summons to be issued. Max was arrested and interrogated for hours. The case against him was never progressed but Goebbels issued the order that the German press must never again print the name Max Schmeling'. The Reich Ministry of Sports banned him from a rematch with Walter Neusel and Max decided to relinquish his European title, announcing that his boxing career was over.

Three and a half years after he had been drafted into the paratroopers, Max was discharged. He returned to his farm to be with Anny. Their estate was situated far from most of the bombing and the couple took in many of their friends' children in an effort to keep them safe. For a while, their home was full of the sounds of laughter and children playing. Max continued to help Jewish people in trouble whenever possible by using what remaining influence he held with the Gestapo, often at risk to his own life. He had long since fallen out of favour with the higher Nazi powers but he appealed to old friends from the past, relying on a sense of humanity that surprisingly still remained, in some cases. He also made a series of visits to Prisoner Of War Camps. Across the Atlantic, Joe Louis was doing the same for German prisoners.

In 1945 the Nazi regime collapsed totally as Russian troops marched through Germany. Max and Anny were forced to flee virtually in the clothes they stood up in, knowing their home was gone for ever. Eventually, they made their way to Hamburg where Max set up a publishing company with two old friends, John Jahr and Axel Springer. While they awaited a licence, Max gave an interview to the *Daily Express* stating that he fully expected to receive a publishing licence from the Military Government. He was arrested immediately for 'making a false statement regarding a member of the Military Government'. He spent the next few weeks in jail until the case was heard and he was freed. Soon afterwards he was arrested again, this time because he had acquired a property without applying for a building permit. He was heavily fined and sentenced to three months in prison, every day of which he served. Stripped of their property and most of their money, life for Max and Anny became quite desperate. Max took on some refereeing work to keep the wolf from the door, but he soon realised that the only way he was going to make any serious money was as a fighter. He travelled to Berlin and persuaded Max Machon, who was initially strongly against the idea, to train him. Max trained like he had never trained before.

On 28 September 1947, his 42nd birthday, Max Schmeling stepped through the ropes for the first time in eight years to stop Werner Vollmer in seven rounds. He had four more fights, including a points defeat at the hands of his old foe Neusel, the last of which took place in Berlin against Richard Vogt on 31 October 1948. He lost a points decision and announced his retirement from boxing while he waited for the verdict, this time for ever. The money from these last fights was enough to buy a piece of land in Hollenstedt where he still lives today. In a beautifully timed business move, he also got in on the ground floor of the European launch of Coca-Cola. A far more lucrative venture than the ice cream partnership with Hugo Abels all those years ago, especially as he went on to become president of the company.

In 1954 Max returned to America. His first stop was a Jewish cemetery in New York to pay his quiet respects at the graveside of his old mentor and friend, Joe Jacobs. Then he travelled to Chicago to visit another old friend, Joe Louis. The moment these two wonderful warriors came face to face they warmly embraced.

Melanie Lloyd is a freelance boxing writer who is currently completing her first book, which should be on the shelves by the end of 2002. The book is entirely based on personal interviews with professional boxers from the past and present, including Jimmy Tibbs, James Cook, Crawford Ashley, Billy Walker, Alan Minter, and the late, great Howard Winstone. Also, for some years, Melanie has been closely involved with Foley ABC in the capacity of Press Secretary and Secretary.

STEVE JAMES
International Agent
Licensed by The British Boxing Board of Control

Telephone (01933) 222241
Fax (01933) 442775
Mobile 0771 875 6677

Home and Away With British Boxers During 2000-2001

by John Jarrett

JULY

The King came home in style after six years in exile and twelve thousand of his subjects welcomed him to the London Arena where he was to joust with the 'White Buffalo' from South Africa, Frans Botha. World heavyweight champion Lennox Lewis was back in town to defend his title and you had to think of the last time, September 1994, when Lewis was in London and Oliver McCall came from America to challenge for his WBC title. McCall knocked Lewis down in the second round and when he got up the referee said Oliver McCall was the winner and new champion.

Lennox remembered the old cliche, if you can't beat 'em, join 'em! The great American trainer, Emanuel Steward, had prepared McCall for the Lewis fight, so Lennox brought Steward on board and hasn't looked back since. He regained the title and beat Evander Holyfield in a unification match that was voted a draw. Lennox won the rematch to become WBC, WBA, and IBF champion, but the WBA got their bauble back when Lewis refused to meet their mandatory challenger, John Ruiz.

So when Lennox stepped into the ring at the London Arena to fight Botha, he was still recognised as the heavyweight champion of the world, regardless of which belts he used to hold his pants up. For the record, he held WBC, IBF, and IBO belts. After five minutes and 39 seconds, Lewis still held those belts. The South African, who had troubled Mike Tyson for the best part of five rounds, was belted through the ropes in the second round and the referee called it off before the champion could do any more damage.

It was a different story when Michael Ayers defended his IBO lightweight title against the former British champion, Wayne Rigby, in Manchester. The fighters themselves stopped this one after the American third man, Arthur Mercante, had been willing to let them carry on. It had been a tremendous fight every second of the way with first one then the other on the verge of defeat and, although they were still on their feet in round ten, both had been smashed to the canvas along the way. Ayers had lasted the better of the two and Rigby, punched to a standstill in the dying seconds of the tenth round, had nothing left. They both knew it was over, and it was.

You never can tell in this business. Michael Brodie, undefeated European super-bantamweight champion with a crack at the WBC title lined up next, put his crown on the line for the French southpaw, Mustapha Hame, in his hometown, Manchester. Michael was the puncher in this one, 19 early wins in 28, while the visitor had a spotty 18-14-3 pro log with only five stoppages. So what happened. First round, left over the top, and Brodie was on the deck! Michael got up, dusted himself off, and dusted off the Frenchman with a superb left hook in round four. But, like I say, you never can tell in this business.

Another little guy with a big punch is the British super-featherweight champion, Michael Gomez, and it was all too much for challenger Carl Greaves, who was blasted out with a left hook in round two at Widnes. Putting a third notch on his Lonsdale Belt, Gomez took his record to 21-3 (13) and was looking for a crack at a world title. Patience, son.

Bristol's Adrian Stone had honed his skills in American gyms and rings and it showed when he destroyed the former undefeated British welterweight champion, Geoff McCreesh, in the sixth round of a thriller on the London Arena card. McCreesh, as usual, fought with his heart, but had been decked three times and was bleeding from a cut left eye when it was stopped. In retaining his IBO light-middleweight title, Stone moved to 28-3-2... Noel Wilders turned back the challenge of veteran Paul Lloyd to keep his IBO bantamweight title with a unanimous decision, but finished with a nasty cut over his left eye...Defending his IBO Inter-Continental featherweight title, Scott Harrison whipped the former IBF champion, Tom Johnson, over 12 rounds. The American doesn't go 'Boom-Boom' any more, but it took a puncher like Naseem Hamed to stop him in 59 fights and it was a fine victory for Harrison in only his 13th contest.

Out of the ring for 17 months and with a big fight with Billy Schwer lined up, the WBU lightweight champion, Colin Dunne, got back in the groove with a couple of warm-up jobs, knocking out Leonti Voronchuk in four rounds at the York Hall and forcing Rakhim Mingaleev to retire on his stool after five rounds at the Elephant and Castle. There was a similar ending to the top of the bill fight that night when the Russian, Ahmet Dottouev, refused to answer the bell for the fifth, leaving the British and WBA International middleweight champion, Howard Eastman, still unbeaten in 29 pro fights.

AUGUST

After the King comes the Prince. Britain's other world champion, Naseem Hamed, gambled his WBO featherweight crown against the American, Augie Sanchez, in a bingo hall somewhere in Connecticut and came out a winner, but the gamble almost didn't pay off for the showman from Sheffield. The kid from Las Vegas nearly hit the jackpot in the second round when he nailed Naz with a solid right hand, then a good left hook, and a big right to the head sent the champion tumbling to the canvas.

For some reason the referee didn't call it a knockdown, but it was still a big round for the unheralded challenger and the crowd, behind the Brit when he entered the ring, were now chanting for the young American. Hamed, his nose bleeding, was wild as he tried to take the kid out with big shots and Sanchez was holding his own through the third. The power, however, was with the champion, and this was the deciding factor. In round four, Naz hurt the

American, before sending him crashing to the canvas for a dramatic finish.

In racking up his 35th straight triumph, 31 inside schedule, Hamed's performance was flawed and gave cause for concern if and when he gets in with either (or both) of the Mexican stars, Marco Antonio Barrera and Erik Morales. Going off the Sanchez fight, Naz wouldn't be a safe bet against either, but then my Daddy told me never to bet on fights anyway.

On the Naz bill, Jane Couch, the feisty 'Fleetwood Assassin', caught a tartar in the American, Liz Mueller, who took a unanimous decision after an excellent six-twos. Jane tried to outwork her rival but lacked the power of the American, who made a big impression in only her fifth contest. Couch dropped to 13-3 but her WBF title was not on the line.

Joe Calzaghe finally got his act together with a fifth-round stoppage of the American challenger, Omar Sheika, at Wembley Grand Hall to retain his WBO super-middleweight title for the sixth time. Although Sheika's interest in the proceedings was terminated because of bad cuts over both eyes caused by accidental head clashes, Calzaghe deserved his victory, and the American referee confirmed he had stopped it to save Sheika taking too much punishment. After a series of injuries and postponements, Calzaghe was back on track and looking for bigger things, still undefeated after 29 contests, 24 inside schedule.

Also on the bill was the mandatory challenger for Calzaghe's title, the German, Mario Veit, who sent Nottingham's Errol McDonald into retirement inside three rounds. Veit is the WBO Inter-Continental champion, has height and reach over Calzaghe, and is still unbeaten…The Warley veteran, Howard Clarke, gave it his best shot when up against Takaloo for the vacant IBF Inter-Continental light-middleweight title, but the Margate Iranian was too sharp and came out with the unanimous decision and the title after 12 good rounds…Hartlepool lightweight, Alan Temple, was hoping his third British title eliminator would be third time lucky, but he was doomed to disappointment as the Harlow tree surgeon, Steve Murray, chopped him down inside two rounds.

Just seven weeks after his war with Wayne Rigby, the IBO lightweight champion, Michael Ayers, put his title on the line again, at Brentwood. They had their answer after a mere 99 seconds and his French opponent, Mehdi Labdouni, was the first to applaud the champion, while sitting on the canvas courtesy of a smashing right hand from the 35-year-old Londoner…To make up for that quickie, Steve Roberts and Scott Dixon staged a war for the vacant WBF light-middleweight title, with the West Ham southpaw hammering his way to victory in round nine. Dixon, the Scott from Hamilton, was decked four times and had nothing left when the final left uppercut went in, but he had fought his heart out. No man could have done more…Columbia's Newton Villareal produced the big punch to end the IBO light-welterweight title ambitions of Chris Barnett in round three on the Brentwood bill, after the Wolverhampton man had flattered to deceive in the

opening round…Last time in the ring, Adrian Dodson bit off more than he could chew when he was disqualified for getting his teeth into Alain Bonnamie in a Commonwealth middleweight title bout. His suspension lifted, the Islington man returned against the former British title challenger (light-middleweight), Paul Wesley, who came in for Oscar Checa. The bout was cut to four rounds and Dodson won them all over the cagey veteran.

At the Baths Hall in Scunthorpe, the local favourite, Jim Betts, took his unbeaten tally to 12-0 when he hammered the former Central Area flyweight champion, Dave Coldwell, into a second-round stoppage to win the British Masters title. The contest was also an eliminator for the British flyweight championship. Betts is a man to watch…

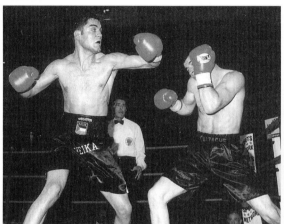

Joe Calzaghe (right) seen in action against America's Omar Sheika   Les Clark

SEPTEMBER

Michael Brodie had big plans for the weekend – to beat the American, Willie Jorrin, for the vacant WBC super-bantamweight championship and marry long-time partner, Donna, before taking a few days away with her and the two kids.

But that Saturday night at Bowlers in Manchester it all went horribly wrong. With his fans roaring him on, local hero Brodie outboxed and outpunched the American, but at the end of 12 rounds, two myopic officials gave the fight and the championship belt to Willie Jorrin. In 29 professional fights, Michael Brodie had been punch-perfect, winning all 29, 20 inside schedule, while collecting British, Commonwealth, and European titles, and that night in Manchester he won the WBC world title, although Jorrin went home to California with the belt. He, and not Michael Brodie, was the champion of the world!

Bristol super-middleweight Glenn Catley is not good for manager Chris Sanigar's nerves. In December 1999, Chris took his tiger to Montreal for a WBC final eliminator against Eric Lucas and Glenn needed a big punch to win it in the final round. It was the same story when he went to Frankfurt to meet the champion, Markus Beyer, manager Chris being down to his last fingernail when Catley landed the bomb in the final round to win the title. Now the "Bristol Boys" were in South Africa to give the veteran, Dingaan Thobela, a shot at the crown and Chris was happier going into this one. The 'Rose of Soweto', still thorny, was growing old, 34-years-old, his golden years as a lightweight a distant memory.

Well, this night at the Carnival City Arena in Brakpan, the 'Rose' was blooming again, taking everything Catley threw at him, which was plenty, and fighting back, and as they came up for the final round, Sanigar was feasting on fingernails again. Once again it was a sensational finish, but this time it was Catley who was smashed to the floor. He managed to struggle to his feet but it was too late and Dingaan Thobela was the new champion! There was, however, a controversial cloud hanging over his head. Catley claimed that in a photograph of Thobela celebrating in the ring, there was a square edge to the bandages on the South African's left fist! Thobela had never been known as a puncher, yet Glenn said: "It was like being hit by a plank of wood". Catley and Sanigar took their case to the WBC Convention a few weeks later and an investigation was ordered. The result was that although it was ruled Thobela's bangages were illegal, the South African was allowed to keep the title, although the supervisor and the American referee were both suspended for a year. Glenn was made mandatory challenger to the winner of Thobela's first defence against the Canadian, Dave Hilton, but was not too happy. "Thobela should have been disqualified," he said on his return to Bristol.

The young Manchester hero, Anthony Farnell, was given a stiff argument by a Mexican, Juan Carlos Sanchez, when defending his WBO Inter-Continental light-middle-weight title for the third time at the Wythenshawe Forum, and had to be content with a decision as he took his pro log to 23-0, 16 early.

At York Hall, the British middleweight champion, Howard Eastman, took a decision over an Australian, Sam Soliman, to add the Commonwealth title to his collection and take his unbeaten run to 30-0, 27 inside, but didn't look worthy of his WBA number-one rating...A week later, at York Hall, Manchester's young lion, Richard Hatton, was also collecting titles, adding the WBA Inter-Continental light-welterweight belt to the WBO one he already held, when hammering the Italian, Giuseppe Lauri, to a fifth-round defeat. Still undefeated after 21 fights, 17 early, Richard looked ready for his shot at the vacant British title against Jonathan Thaxton. In a four rounder on the bill, Richard's younger brother, Matthew, made a winning pro debut with a decision over Cardiff's Dave White.

Carl Thompson, at 36, still had enough stuff left to see off the challenge of Russia's Alexei Iliin at the Barnsley Metrodome to retain his European cruiserweight title with a crushing second-round stoppage. He came out of the ring looking for a world title shot...Damaen Kelly had given up his European flyweight title to fight the South African, Zolile Mbityi, for his IBO championship at Peterborough, and although the Belfast man came out a points winner his performance left a lot to be desired...Another second-division title on the line saw WBF middleweight champion,

Delroy Leslie, lose his belt to the 38-year-old Peckham veteran, Lester Jacobs, in Hammersmith after a cut on his left eye brought the referee's intervention in round eight...The Bradford southpaw, Bobby Vanzie, retained his Commonwealth lightweight title at Bowlers, Manchester, when he dropped Trinidad's Joseph Charles, another southpaw, three times for a sixth-round stoppage.

The Carlisle super-featherweight, Charles Shepherd, tried his terrier-like tactics on Ghana's James Armah in Glasgow, with the vacant Commonwealth title on the line. However, the African refused to buckle and by the eighth round Shepherd had a swelling under his right eye which hampered his vision, and when blood ran from two cuts in the ninth, the Cumbrian clouter was pulled out at the end of the round...Eye injuries also brought an end to the championship reign of little Ady Lewis, leaving Belfast's Tommy Waite as the new British and Commonwealth bantamweight champion when the referee intervened in round four of their clash in Manchester. Lewis had looked on top before a nasty cut appeared on his right eyelid and prompted the stoppage.

To the relief of ring announcers, Tokunbo Owomoyela adopted the ring name of Toks Owoh when he started fighting for money in 1995. Having lost only one of his 16 pro fights, he was hoping to hear his name announced as the new IBF Inter-Continental super-middleweight champion at the end of his fight with the Florida-based Jamaican, Glencoffe Johnson, at York Hall. Unfortunately, the veteran had too much of everything and Owoh was rescued by the referee in the sixth round after taking a terrific left hook.

The former two-time WBO champion, Paul Weir, bounced back at 33 to win an excellent eight-threes flyweight bout over Delroy Spencer at Chigwell...At the other end of the scale, the Commonwealth heavyweight champion, Danny Williams, hammered hapless Quinn Navarre to a one-sided defeat in six rounds at York Hall.

Richard Hatton (left) had little trouble in deposing with the Italian, Giuseppe Lauri, last September   Les Clark

OCTOBER

The WBU lightweight championship contest between Colin Dunne, the champion, and Billy Schwer at the Wembley Conference Centre figured to be a barn-burner, and it was! The fight exceeded all expectations, all but those of Billys and his team who hoped to come out winners after 12 tremendous rounds. Although Schwer lost by a split decision, there were people there who thought he had done enough to win, including one of the officials, but it was not to be. Dunne fought out of his skin, this being his night, and Billy Schwer was not going to rain on his parade.

Schwer looked a division bigger than Dunne, even though he scaled the same weight as the champion. "It was murder", said Billy, referring to his battle with the scales. "I just couldn't dig deep when I needed to". He still gave Dunne a helluva fight, but Colin was able to top everything Billy tried, giving a career-best performance while taking his pro log to 32-1. There was another remarkable fight in the Wembley ring a week later when the Commonwealth heavyweight champion, Danny Williams, was due to fight Mike Holden. When Holden came down with a virus, the Southern Area champion, Mark Potter, stepped in and the vacant British title was tossed into the pot along with Danny's two belts. (He also held the WBO Inter-Continental title). Potter grabbed his chance and promptly dumped Danny on the deck in the very first round, although referee John Coyle called it a slip.

Potter was down in the second round, being dropped by a body shot that Coyle called low. In the third, Danny's right shoulder popped out and Potter was not slow to take advantage, winning the round big. Round four and Potter was down again from a low blow, with Williams losing two points. The shoulder had gone back in, but in the sixth it came out again leaving Williams one handed. But it was a good hand, the left uppercut, with which he hit Potter to send him to the floor. Mark got up as ringsiders looked on in amazement and Danny smashed a left hook on his chin to drop him again. He beat the count but when he went over a third time it was stopped and Danny Williams, his right shoulder dislocated, was a one-armed-winner!

In another war on the Wembley card, unbeaten Richard Hatton was staring at his first pro defeat in 22 fights after sustaining a bloody left eye in the opening minute of his bout with Jonathan Thaxton for the vacant British light-welterweight championship. Yet this fine young fighter got on with his job, leaving his injury in the competent hands of Mick Williamson and his fate in the hands of a lenient referee, Paul Thomas. Both came through for the 'Manchester Hitman' and at the final bell he had the decision and the title. It takes two to tango and Thaxton fought his heart out, but at the finish there could be only one winner. But with his vulnerable eyebrows, Hatton is a flawed diamond.

Like the WBO, the WBU seems to have found a welcome home in Britain and we gained another champion in Jason Rowland, wearing the light-welterweight crown as a result of a points victory over Russia's Viktor Baranov at Wembley. Jason sustained a nasty split lip in the opening minute but, fortunately, it didn't get any worse and he got better.

Nicky Booth completed a fine family double when he took the British and Commonwealth bantamweight titles off the 30-day champ, Tommy Waite, in Liverpool, his elder brother, Jason, having already won the British and Commonwealth flyweight titles. The Nottingham brothers thus became the first to hold British championships simultaneously since John and George Feeney 15 years previously, and was a long overdue success for their manager, Mike Shinfield. It never rains but it pours, Mike! Also on the Liverpool bill, Bobby Vanzie retained his Commonwealth lightweight title with an eighth-round stoppage of Ghana's Laatekwei Hammond, but he failed to impress and was decked twice himself before finding a big right hand to bring about the ending. Harry Dhami put a second notch on the Lonsdale Belt when defending the welterweight title with a points win over Malcolm Melvin...The comeback of Paul 'Silky' Jones picked up speed as he stopped France's Olivier Beard in 47 seconds to win the vacant WBC International super-middleweight belt.

The amazing French veteran, 41-year-old Affif Djelti, turned back another British hopeful when Dean Pithie went down for the count in the sixth round before his local fans at the Coventry Skydome. Djelti thus retained the IBO super-featherweight title he had taken off Charles Shepherd and defended against Ian McLeod on previous visits... Johnny Nelson smashed the Australian challenger, Adam Watt, to the canvas in round five to keep his WBO cruiser-weight title, but is still only a big fish in a little pond... Mixed fortunes in foreign rings as Michael Gomez took a decision off Awel Abdulai in Harrisburg, Pennsylvania, while Ali Forbes was out of luck in Cologne when losing on points to Thomas Ulrich, and Glenn McClarnon was also on the wrong end of the decision when boxing Alan Vester for his IBF Inter-Continental light-welterweight title at Aarhus, Denmark.

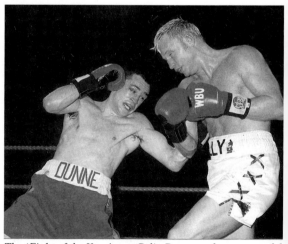

The 'Fight of the Year' saw Colin Dunne make a successful defence of his WBO lightweight title against popular Billy Schwer

Les Clark

NOVEMBER

It was due to be another lavish spectacle in garish, glitzy Las Vegas, it was to be David versus Goliath, but the capacity crowd at the Mandalay Bay Events Center wished they had stayed in the casino. At least there was a chance of hitting the jackpot in the casino, which is more than David Tua had when he challenged Lennox Lewis for the WBC, IBF, and IBO world heavyweight championships. This David had no stone in his slingshot and without that the giant was odds on to win. He did. Easily.

An explosive left hook had earned Tua the number one spot in the IBF ratings, but when the opening bell brought them from their corners all Lewis had in front of him was a fat little man with a funny haircut. With a spear and a shield, the Samoan warrior had a chance, but the rules of the Nevada State Athletic Association allowed only gloves and a gumshield. With a seven inch height and 15 inch reach advantage, Lewis played with his opponent like a cat with a mouse for 12 rounds. Usually the cat gets bored and goes for the kill, but Lennox was content to take Tua along to the final bell to win a lopsided decision, a fat purse, but little else.

Fireworks were expected when Shea Neary went in against Eamonn Magee for his Commonwealth light-welterweight title at Belfast, but it was the crowd in the Waterfront Hall that erupted when Roy Francis raised Magee's hand at the end of 12 less than exciting rounds. The tough Liverpool man was not the two-fisted terrier of his days as WBU champion, but he still looked to have done enough to take the decision and the title. But it was not to be.

In another Commonwealth title bout on the card, at featherweight, Ghana's Eric Odumasi had Azumah Nelson sitting by his corner offering encouragement as he went after Scott Harrison's crown. Eric should have changed places with Azumah. He didn't, and came out a sorry loser. Trailing on points going into the final round, the Ghanaian was dropped by a left hook and when he got up the referee called it off, Harrison improving to 12-1-1.

Charles Shepherd was out of luck again in trying to get hold of another title, losing a decision to unbeaten Tontcho Tontchev, the Bulgarian retaining his WBA Inter-Continental super-featherweight championship. The Carlisle man has held British, Commonwealth, IBO, and IBO Inter-Continental belts, but he was well beaten in this one...There was no joy for another Bulgarian on the Belfast card as Peter Culshaw easily retained his WBU flyweight title with a first-round knockout of Dimitar Alipiev, taking his pro log to 19-1-1...The former British welterweight champion, Derek Roche, tried to move up and take Adrian Dodson's IBO light-middleweight crown from the Bristolian's shaven head, but was outpunched, dropped and stopped in round two. Dodson was impressive!

A couple of weeks away from his 35th birthday, Drew Docherty suffered a sixth-round stoppage defeat when trying to take the British super-bantamweight title from Michael Alldis at York Hall. A former undefeated champion at the weight, as well as being a British bantamweight champion, the feisty little Scot had challenged at Common-wealth, European, and WBO level in a fine 11-year pro career that was suddenly history.

The luckiest fight fans in the UK must be the patrons of York Hall in Bethnal Green, with promotions just about every week! They turned out to cheer the Hackney flyweight, Ian Napa, as he went after Jason Booth's British and Commonwealth titles, but the challenger found the champion a little too slick over 12 rounds and the Nottingham man was a good winner as he took his record to 19-1, his only defeat being to European champion, David Guerault.

At 31, Steve Robinson still has some tread on his tyres and was just pipped on the post as South Africa's Cassius Baloyi took the checkered flag after 12 laps at the Ebbw Vale Leisure Centre. The veteran decked the WBU champion in the second round, but Cassius fought back in a thriller to just get up on the line.

Harry Dhami retained his British welterweight title with a clear points victory over Spencer McCracken at the Aston Villa Leisure Centre. Six feet tall, and with a ramrod jab, the champion had too much of everything as he won his second title defence. On the same bill, Nottingham's Jawaid Khaliq took the vacant Commonwealth welterweight belt with a skilled performance against New Zealand's Sean Sullivan to set up a double title battle with Dhami...Anthony Farnell put another notch on his belt at the Wythenshawe Forum when he stopped Scott Dixon in round seven to retain his WBO Inter-Continental light-middleweight title and record his 24th straight win...The British light-heavyweight champion, Neil Simpson, was in devastating form at Dagenham as he blasted Mark Delaney out of the picture in just 60 seconds of round one to keep his title, while David Starie kept his Commonwealth super-middleweight title with a fine display, outboxing and outpunching Australia's Guy Waters to defeat in the sixth.

DECEMBER

This would be the worst Christmas of all for Paul Ingle who lay in a hospital bed nine days after being knocked out in what would be his last fight, nine days after a brain operation that hopefully would save his life. It would also be the worst Christmas of all for Mbulelo Botile, the South African fighter whose hammering punches sent Paul Ingle to that hospital bed, along with all the relatives and friends of these two brave little warriors. Their prayers were that Paul Ingle receive the greatest gift of all at this traditional time of giving, the gift of life itself.

Hindsight makes experts of all of us. Ingle had trouble making the weight...He didn't seem himself during the fight...He should have not have been allowed to come up for the 12th and final round after being floored heavily at the end of round 11.

"If I knew what was going to happen I would never have sent him back out", said his manager, Frank Maloney, afterwards. Ironically, being knocked out in that fateful round probably saved Ingle's life, for as trainer Steve Pollard stated: "If he hadn't been knocked out, he might have gone home after a brief examination...Had he left that arena with the bleeding already started, he would have been dead the next day".

Paul had battled through three wars prior to this one with the former IBF bantamweight champion from the

African continent, long distance wars with Naseem Hamed (11 rounds), with Manuel Medina (12 rounds), and with Junior Jones (11 rounds). Maybe they suddenly caught up with the gutsy little scrapper from Scarborough.

While Paul Ingle was beginning his fight for life, Joe Calzaghe was winning the fight of his life in that same Sheffield ring, retaining his WBO super-middleweight championship with a fine display against the former WBC titleholder, Richie Woodhall, who gave his all before Roy Francis pulled him out 28 seconds into the tenth round. It was Roy's final action in a British ring, having turned 65, and in the immediate aftermath of the fight it looked like the last fight for Woodhall as he contemplated retirement.

It was an excellent performance by the Newbridge southpaw following his stoppage of Omar Sheika and it looked as though he was finally back on top of his game after several disappointing fights and injury problems. In taking his pro log to 30-0, Calzaghe didn't put a glove wrong and the drums started beating for a match with the American super star, Roy Jones.

There were five title bouts on this Sheffield show and none more brutal than the battle of attrition between Bruce Scott and John 'Buster' Keeton for the vacant British cruiserweight crown. In front of his hometown supporters, Keeton fought out of his skin and was looking to be on his way to the title when Scott blasted him to the canvas in the sixth round with a right uppercut...Newark's Esham Pickering was no match for the WBO bantamweight champion, Mauricio Martinez, and was on his way to the

showers in just 72 seconds of round one...Belfast's Neil Sinclair was also out of his league when trying for the WBO welterweight title even though he floored Daniel Santos in the opening round after being down himself. In round two, however, the Puerto Rican champion did the business with a short left and Neil was out for the count.

The dream came true for Michael Gomez at Widnes when he beat off the gritty challenge of Scotland's Ian McLeod to retain his British super-featherweight championship and thus win the coveted Lonsdale Belt outright. Both suffered eye injuries in a gruelling fight that saw Gomez move to 23-3 and start looking for a world title shot.

At Southwark, the British super-middleweight champion, David Starie, had no trouble retaining his title against the challenge of Alex Mason, the Wolverhampton man being counted out in round three...Fight of the night saw the Chatham southpaw, John Armour, take the vacant WBU bantamweight title after 12 terrific rounds with the veteran, Francis Ampofo. It was a typical Armour performance as he finished with four facial cuts requiring 13 stitches and the fans were as exhausted as the two warriors at the final bell.

Twenty-four hour substitute Mike Gormley made it to the National Sports Centre at Crystal Palace in time for his bout with Robin Reid for the vacant WBF super-middleweight title, then had to wait another quarter of an hour before the former WBC champion climbed into the ring. Reid didn't keep Mike waiting much longer, however, and it was all over in 100 seconds!

John Armour (right) and Francis Ampofo seen at close quarters during their WBU bantamweight title fight　　Les Clark

York Hall was the scene of a fight for the vacant IBO welterweight title with America's Willy Wise knowing too much for Darren Bruce to take a unanimous decision. On the same card, West Ham's Steve Roberts took his pro log to 22-0 as he retained his WBF light-middleweight title with a seventh-round stoppage of the Frenchman, Mohammed Hissani. In Tallhassee, Florida, big Henry Akinwande won something called the WBC FeCarBox heavyweight title when he flattened Kenny Craven at a local nightclub. Big deal!

JANUARY

It certainly was a Happy New Year for Coventry's British light-heavyweight champion, Neil Simpson, as he blasted out Zimbabwe's Hastings Rasani in four rounds at the local Skydome just two days into the new millennium. It was what our American cousins used to call a 'Pier Six Brawl', with Simpson decked four times in the opening two rounds before getting his act together and belting Rasani into dreamland just before the bell ended round four. The referee carried on counting, Rasani didn't get up, and Neil Simpson was the new Commonwealth champion.

Romanian-born Canadian, Tony Badea, was the Commonwealth light-middleweight champion when he came to the ring at the Crawley Leisure Centre to fight Richard Williams. Tony, who likes to be known as 'Bad Boy' Badea, received a good spanking and went home minus his title as Williams emerged as the new face of 2001. The boy from Stockwell had won ten of his 11 fights, nine inside schedule, and he won this one in a breeze. The tough Canuck was blasted to the canvas twice in round

three before it was called off and everyone went home talking about Richard Williams!

Anthony Farnell was given a stubborn argument by the Argentine welterweight champion, Sergio Acuna, at the Wythenshawe Forum but came through after 12 tough rounds to take the unanimous decision and retain his WBO Inter-Continental light-middleweight title for the fifth time. The 22-year-old Manchester boy went off like a train in the first half of the fight, which was just as well as Sergio finished like a train to earn his share of the applause. It was close, but Farnell won it to stay on track for bigger things.

After rocking the Brazilian challenger, George Arias, in the first round, the WBO cruiserweight champion, Johnny Nelson, settled for a safe journey home and was a runaway points winner at the York Hall, retaining his title for the seventh time. At 34, with 51 fights in the book, Nelson is like a star of the West End who prefers working in repertory.

On the Crawley show, the British super-bantamweight champion, Michael Alldis, boxed a six rounder with France's Salem Bouita, who faded after a good start and was beaten in the final round. A clash of heads saw Salem turn away, while Alldis grabbed his chance and dropped his man with a left hook, the referee calling it off when Bouita got up...Gary Lockett made it 9-0, dumping the French southpaw, Abdel Mehidi, three times for a second-round stoppage...Southern Area light-middleweight champion Delroy Mellis repeated a previous victory over his challenger, Alan Gilbert, retaining his title with another third-round stoppage and looking good doing it.

The Belfast southpaw, Brian Magee, reached the top

Australia's Nedal Hussein (left) looked good when taking out Delroy Pryce last January   Les Clark

level an an amateur and at the Bushfield Sports Centre in Peterborough he set his feet firmly on the ladder to professional success when he took a unanimous decision over Leicester's Neil Linford. Up for grabs was the vacant IBO Inter-Continental super-middleweight belt and Magee was able to overcome a hand injury and box his way to victory, taking his pro log to 12-0...A Commonwealth light-heavyweight title eliminator saw the Brockley-based Nigerian, Peter Oboh, punch too hard and too often for Chris Davies, and it was stopped in round eight as the Welshman dropped to his knees.

Marking time for a return bout with the British and Commonwealth champion, Neil Simpson, Lewisham's Mark Baker kept his name in the frame with an eight-round decision over Sheffield's Andy Manning at York Hall...On the York Hall bill a week later, the Hussein brothers from Australia chalked up a double, with Nedal, the Commonwealth super-bantamweight champion, belting out Welshman Delroy Pryce with a body shot in the third round of a non-title bout, while bantamweight Hussein forced the Belfast southpaw, Stevie Quinn, to retire after just two rounds with a badly-cut left eye...Twice a Welsh ABA champion, Nathan King bit off more than he could chew in his professional debut when he went in with Tony Oakey at light-heavyweight. The Portsmouth man was himself a former double ABA champion, at heavy and cruiser, was unbeaten in nine starts as a money fighter, and had too much for the Mountain Ash youngster, when coming out with the decision over six rounds.

FEBRUARY

I wouldn't be surprised if Jack Doughty put out a contract on James Armah, after Ghana's 'Bukom Fire' completed a Commonwealth double over Doughty's fighters when sneaking a tight decision over Bobby Vanzie in Manchester to take the lightweight title. This was five months after Armah stopped Charles Shepherd in nine rounds on facial injuries in Glasgow for the super-featherweight championship.

In a contest that left a lot to be desired, Armah outlasted Vanzie, who was docked a point for holding in the fifth round which probably cost him his title, referee Mickey Vann giving it to the African 115-114. At the end of the night, Bobby still had his British title and Armah still had his unbeaten record, 11-0.

Another title upset this month saw Michael Gomez blow his WBO Inter-Continental super-featherweight championship to the Hungarian southpaw, Laszio Bognar, at Widnes, the fight being stopped in round nine with Gomez almost out on his feet. Gomez blew more than just a second-division title. Unbeaten in four years, the 23-year-old Manchester boy was being groomed for bigger things – 23-3 as a pro and already winner outright of the Lonsdale Belt. So what happened? Reports of the fight indicated that Gomez looked unfit and it was claimed he had been suffering from flu. Michael did floor his opponent in round five but the effort seemed to take more out of him than it did Bognar. Whatever, if Gomez was weight-drained, unfit, unwell, he and his connections gambled, and lost!

It was a wonderful night for the Booth brothers at Nottingham as they made British boxing history in being the first brothers to contest major championships on the same bill. Jason, the British and Commonwealth flyweight champion, defended the latter bauble against Zambian-born Nokuthula Tshabangu, who folded inside two rounds after taking a right uppercut and two left hooks. His younger brother, Nicky, had a tougher task against the former champion, Ady Lewis, before stopping the Bury man in round seven of a mini-war to retain his British and Commonwealth bantamweight titles.

The Belfast boxing master, Damaen Kelly, turned in a punch-perfect performance at York Hall in retaining his IBO flyweight championship against the Mexican southpaw, Paulino Villalobos, with a lop-sided unanimous decision. Having suffered horrendous cuts in previous contests, Kelly played it safe and was never in any danger as he took his record to 14-1.

A week later, the York Hall crowd saw Takaloo hang on to his IBF Inter-Continental light-middleweight championship in a close one with James Lowther, many considering the Leeds' man a winner. He was the better boxer of the two, with the Kent-Iranian having the power. Takaloo emerged with his title intact but with a broken bone in his right wrist.

Boxing is a young man's game but you wouldn't know it if you saw 36-year-old Carl Thompson bombing out a 40-year-old grandfather, Uriah Grant, inside five rounds to take the IBO cruiserweight title in the Manchester ring. The Jamaican from Miami made it exciting while he was on his feet, but Thompson had him on the canvas three times before it was stopped in the fifth. Thompson, who lost his WBO title to Johnny Nelson on a controversial stoppage two years previously, dreams of fighting Nelson again.

Back in the ring after being robbed in his fight for the vacant WBC super-bantamweight title against Willie Jorrin, Michael Brodie kept his name in the frame with a ruthless display to stop Mexico's Sergio Aguila in four rounds, a superb body shot taking his pro log to 30-1.

The British and Commonwealth middleweight champion, Howard Eastman, gave a chunk of weight and a beating to Mark Baker, who stepped in at the last minute to save the Sky TV show at Hull City Hall. The champion was too sharp and hit too hard for Baker who retired at the end of round five...Another late substitute was the British light-middleweight champion, Wayne Alexander, who agreed to challenge Harry Simon for the Namibian's WBO championship at Widnes. Due to meet WBO welterweight champ, Daniel Santos, of Puerto Rico, then New Orleans' Robbie Allen, Simon finally faced Alexander, who gave it a good try but suffered broken knuckles on both hands and was rescued after being dropped in the fifth.

One of a talented group of former amateur stars putting Hartlepool back on the boxing map, Ian Cooper hammered Mike White into a thrilling ninth-round stoppage to win the Northern Area super-middleweight title in only his fifth pro contest...The Reading heavyweight, Michael Sprott, had a big job on his hands, literally, when he faced up to a German giant, Timo Hoffmann, at York Hall. Conceding almost three stone to his 6'8" opponent, Sprott dug deep and finished well to take a narrow decision and ruin Hoffmann's British debut.

MARCH

Fight of the month! Hell, this could be the 'Fight of the Year' again, just as it was in 2000. The ageless wonder, Michael Ayers, retained his IBO lightweight title in another thriller with former British champion, Wayne Rigby, at the Wembley Conference Centre, taking a close but unanimous decision after 12 blistering rounds. Stopped in the tenth first time around, the Manchester man was better prepared this time but it still wasn't enough to beat Ayers, at 36 and defending his title for the sixth time, to take his record to 31-3.

Another veteran still filled with the lust for battle was Ali Forbes, still plugging away at the age of 40. Matched against the former WBC light-heavyweight champion, Montell Griffin, on the Sheffield card, the Sydenham man was moved into the main event against Clinton Woods when Michael Nunn pulled out of the WBC final eliminator for the third, and final, time. His replacement, Greg Wright, was another no-show so Forbes, a former British super-middleweight champion, stepped up to fight Woods for the vacant WBC International light-heavy crown.

Former unbeaten British, Commonwealth, and European champion, Woods lives for the day he gets to fight super-star Roy Jones, but if and when that happens he will have to do better than he did against the veteran Forbes who retired on his stool after ten rounds. Winning for the 29th time in 30 starts, the Sheffield star was well on top and floored Ali in the tenth, but Roy Jones is something else…

The Commonwealth featherweight champion, Scott Harrison, collected the vacant British title with an easy victory over the former British super-bantamweight titleholder, Richie Wenton, who had nothing left when it was stopped in round four on the Sheffield card. Taking his record to 13-1-1, the Glasgow man had too much of everything for the 33-year-old Liverpudlian who had survived a first round knockdown…British and Commonwealth super-middleweight champion, David Starie, strolled to a three-round victory when Andrew Flute, boxing for the first time in over two years, retired with a shoulder injury in this non-title bout…The Lincoln southpaw, Lee Swaby, provided stubborn resistance to the former British, Commonwealth, and European light-heavy champion, Crawford Ashley, who had to settle for a points win in this his second comeback bout after two years out.

Richard Hatton did it again! The 22-year-old 'Manchester Hitman' blasted out the lanky Canadian, Tony Pep, in four rounds to win the vacant WBU light-welterweight title at the Wembley Conference Centre. Pep, a pumped-up lightweight, came in at short notice and never

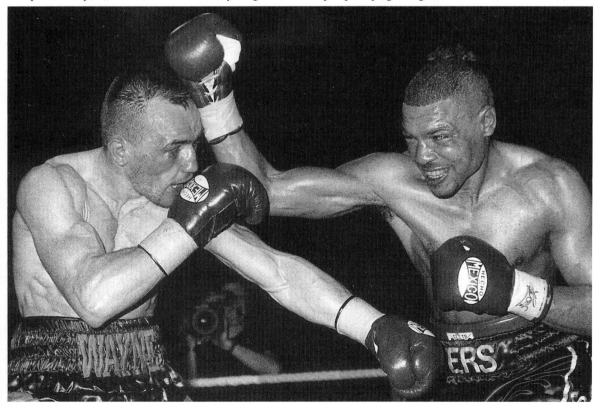

Wayne Rigby (left) v Michael Ayers second time round, again for the IBO lightweight title, proved almost as good as the first
Les Clark

looked like winning, not even when Hatton sustained his obligatory cut eye. Richard knocked Tony down three times and the latter only got up twice.

At Glasgow's Bellahuston Leisure Centre, Carlisle's Charles Shepherd was tamed over 12 rounds by Alex Moon, the Liverpool man picking up the vacant Commonwealth super-featherweight title in a gruelling war of attrition…In the main event, Keith Knox found his all-out aggression just not good enough against the skills of the IBO light-flyweight champion, Jose Garcia, and the Columbian came out with a split decision and his title intact. The Bonnyrigg butcher gave his all before losing possibly his last title shot.

The British cruiserweight champion, Bruce Scott, avenged an amateur defeat, retained his title, and added the vacant Commonwealth crown to his collection at York Hall when he forced his London rival, Garry Delaney, to retire after three rounds with his left eye hammered shut. He also won a Lonsdale Belt outright, with Delaney making little impression in the time it lasted. There were mixed fortunes for our boys overseas as Michael Sprott failed to repeat his February decision over Timo Hoffmann in Magdeburg. Again it was close, so it was no surprise when the points favoured Hoffmann…It was better luck for the fighting Irish in Worcester, Massachusetts, as Jim Rock knocked out Holly Elliott in six rounds and Cathal O'Grady stopped Jose Torres inside three rounds.

In Manchester, the WBO Inter-Continental light-middleweight champion, Anthony Farnell, had an early night as he outclassed America's Shakir Ashanti to retain his title, it being stopped in round two. On the undercard, the former two-time English ABA lightweight champion, Andy McLean, got his feet wet when he took a clear decision over Steve Hanley in his debut.

West Ham's Steve Roberts is the only one they're all going to watch, going off his sensational first-round demolition of the Argentine hard man, Sergio Acuna, at Wembley. Retaining his IBO super-middleweight belt and taking his unbeaten run to 23-0, Steve blasted Acuna to the canvas three times to bring the referee's intervention. It was the first stoppage for Acuna, who had taken Anthony Farnell the distance just two months previously…Adrian Dodson got his career back on track with a devastating third-round knockout of Paul Jones to win the IBO super-middleweight title.

APRIL

I suppose the worst thing a fighter can do is believe his own publicity. Naseem Hamed talked the talk, and for nine years as a professional fighter he walked the walk. He was undefeated European bantamweight champion, undefeated WBC International super-bantamweight champion, WBO featherweight champion for over five years, and also one-time holder of the IBF and WBC featherweight titles. He was undefeated in 35 professional fights and in only four of them was it necessary to go to the scorecards. Many thought he was invincible, and you couldn't blame him for thinking that.

Billy Schwer (left) finally gained a world title for his hard labours when beating Newton Villareal for the IBO light-welter title

Les Clark

Las Vegas is a gambling town, a town of winners and losers, break the bank or it breaks you. Vegas had become the fight capital of the world and that was where Naz had to go to claim his place in the pantheon of pugilism. Beat the fearsome Mexican warrior, Marco Antonio Barrera, and he would finally be accepted by a nation weaned on Dempsey, Louis, Armstrong, Robinson, Canzoneri, Pep and Saddler. He could do it, he had the punch, it came at you from crazy angles and you didn't want to be there when it arrived!

Marco Antonio Barrera knew all about the punch, he wasn't a bad puncher himself. But he could also box and that was what he did that night out there on the Strip. He boxed Hamed's socks off over 12 fascinating rounds to hand the 27-year-old Naz his first defeat since he was a skinny 15-year-old kid back home in Sheffield. The Prince had just come from Mecca, but Marco had come from Mexico and that made the difference.

With the British fight trade still reeling from the Naz defeat, the knockout punch came a fortnight later when our other mega-star, Lennox Lewis, landed on the flat of his broad back in a South African ring, courtesy of a big right hand thrown by the unfancied American, Hasim Rahman. When Lewis got up, he was the ex-heavyweight champion of the world! But whereas it was accepted that Hamed had been beaten by a better man, it was almost universally agreed that Lewis had been beaten by himself. He had taken Rahman lightly, he hadn't arrived in South Africa in time to become properly acclimatised, his preparation was poor and his performance was sloppy. And when that big right hand landed on his chin in round five his resistance was lower than a snake's belly. Brakpan, like Las Vegas, was a place of broken dreams, and a place where dreams come true. When Lewis got off the canvas, he didn't know where he was. Rahman knew where he was, he was in heaven!

It was left to Joe Calzaghe to restore the faith as he ruthlessly destroyed the lanky German challenger, Mario Veit, in just 112 seconds to retain his WBO super-middleweight title and send his Cardiff fans home happy. It was Joe's finest victory in his unbeaten 31-fight pro career and at long last the Welsh southpaw looked ready to take on the world, maybe even get the fight he dreamed of, with Roy Jones. Veit was Joe's mandatory challenger, also unbeaten in 30 fights, but he was never in the hunt, smashed to the canvas twice before the referee called it off at 1.52 of round one…On the undercard, undefeated Gavin Rees from Newbridge took his pro log to 11-0 and picked up the WBO Inter-Continental featherweight title with an easy victory over Bulgaria's Vladimir Borov, who was rescued by the third man in round four.

The fight Howard Eastman had been looking for finally came along and he rose to the occasion with his finest performance, hammering the resistance out of Robert McCracken in ten thrilling rounds at Wembley, thus adding the vacant European middleweight title to his British and Commonwealth belts and consolidating his WBA number one ranking. The Brummie gave everything he had, but was dropped by a right uppercut in the tenth and when he got up it was stopped. McCracken announced his retirement as Eastman moved his pro record to 32-0.

Wembley Conference Centre was also the scene of a gruelling fight for the IBO light-welterweight title between the champion, Newton Villareal, and Luton's Billy Schwer, with the former British, Commonwealth and European lightweight champion finally gaining a world title, of sorts, with a unanimous decision over the awkward Columbian…On the same bill, West Ham's Steve Roberts retained his WBF light-middleweight title with a stunning two-rounds stoppage of the former WBC champion, Keith Mullings, to keep his unbeaten tag at 24-0…It was not such a happy evening for Adrian Dodson, with the London southpaw being knocked out in the fifth round and blowing his IBO super-middleweight title to the Argentinian hard man, Ramon Britez.

At Liverpool, local taxi driver Alex Moon took the chequered flag as he led the Australian champion, Karim Nashar, throughout the 12 laps to retain his Commonwealth super-featherweight title, while Huddersfield's Mark Hobson found Sebastiaan Rothmann a tough assignment, the South African retaining his WBU cruiserweight title when forcing the Yorkshireman to retire after nine hard rounds.

MAY

The black trunks worn by the American heavyweight, Mike Middleton, when he climbed into the Wembley ring to face Audley Harrison bore the legend, 'Ristorante Francesco – Tampa Bay'. I hope the food served there is better than the fistic fare served up by Middleton for Britain's Olympic gold medallist to feed on in his much-ballyhooed professional debut. Harrison chewed up this hunk of beefsteak in just two minutes and 45 seconds and left the table still hungry.

Mike Middleton was 33-years-old, 16 stones and reportedly six feet tall, which would have been a big heavyweight 40 or 50 years ago, but not by today's standards, however. Audley Harrison towers a magnificent six-five in his size 16 ring boots and bounces the scales at a solid 18st 8lbs. That's a big heavyweight today! So, if they were getting a stiff for him to roll over the least they could have done was get a big stiff. That way it wouldn't have looked so bad, especially to the celebrity crowd who turned up at Wembley and to the millions watching free on BBC television. To make any sort of a dent in Harrison, the Gulf War veteran would have needed heavy artillery.

If the main event was a disappointment, the chief supporting contest was not much better, as Robin Reid had a walk in the park, dismantling Russia's Roman Babaev inside three effortless rounds to retain his WBF super-middleweight belt, which is good for holding your pants up and not much more. After Reid dropped his man twice in the third round it was stopped.

Bobby Vanzie showed why and how he is a champion when he climbed off the deck to finish his challenger, Steve Murray, in the seventh round to keep his British title. That Saturday night at the Lee Valley Leisure Centre in Edmonton, the Harlow lightweight smashed Vanzie to the canvas twice in the opening round and Bobby was glad to hear the bell. The Bradford southpaw fought his way back into the fight and it was rough and untidy at times with

Bobby being docked a point in the sixth for holding. In the seventh, the champion made the points academic when he sent Steve crashing to the canvas. The challenger gamely got to his feet but was a sitting duck and as Vanzie moved in the referee called it off. After 16 straight wins, it was a fight too far for Murray.

I remember seeing Alvin 'Slick' Miller box a six rounder in Hartlepool back in 1995. The Doncaster man didn't win that night, in fact he didn't win a fight until June of 1998, following 13 losses and two draws. Alvin started the year 2001 with only three wins in 26 pro fights, but whatever he drank to see in the New Year worked a treat. Miller knocked out Scott Baker, stopped Hughie Robertson, was stopped himself by Colin McKenna, then on the Edmonton show a week before his 33rd birthday, the veteran hammered the former amateur star, Danny Percival, to a stunning first-round knockout defeat. Alvin has been stopped 12 times in 22 losing fights, but his six wins have all been via the short route. The guy ain't no Billy Conn, but if he hits you right you're having an early shower!

Four months after decking Neil Simpson four times in the first two rounds, only to be stopped himself when contesting the vacant Commonwealth light-heavyweight title, Zimbabwe's Hastings Rasani was given another chance when the title again became vacant, against Portsmouth's unbeaten Tony Oakey at Barnsley. This time, the lanky African lasted into the tenth round before a fired-up Oakey dropped him with a left hook. Rasani got up but he was all through, and it was stopped as Tony became champion of the Commonwealth after just 12 winning fights.

Another fighter from the African continent in Harrison Methula found the Commonwealth light-welterweight champion, Eamonn Magee, too much of a handful and was stopped in round seven of their fight at Plymouth. Also on the card was the local hero, Scott Dann, who sent his fans home happy as he dismantled South Africa's Elvis Adonisi in the seventh to win the vacant IBO Inter-Continental middleweight title. A box-office favourite, Scott won for the 12th time and showed promise…The British Masters super-bantamweight title was on the line when Sunderland's John Barnes gave Frankie DeMilo, the champion, a run for his money before losing on points.

In a return match, in the same ring in Legranes, again for the vacant European featherweight title, Steve Robinson met the Spaniard, Manuel Calvo, but this time the decision went to the local by a majority vote after 12 rounds of an absorbing encounter. Calvo, who was able to nulify Robinson's body-punching capability, just about deserved the win.

One of the better female fighters in the country is Michelle Sutcliffe of Leeds and her fans packed the local Town Hall to cheer her to victory over the outgunned Bulgarian, Marietta Ivanova, who was floored and stopped in round five as Michelle retained her WBF flyweight title and picked up the vacant IFBA belt. It was a good performance from the lass from Leeds. Say what you like, some of these gals can fight!

JUNE

Mixed fortunes this month for the battling Booth brothers of Nottingham. With the hometown fans cheering him on, British and Commonwealth bantamweight champion Nicky took care of business in a non-title bout with his local rival, Kevin Gerowski, who was hammered for three rounds before Nicky's body shots floored him in round four and it was stopped. A couple of weeks later, Jason was in action, albeit on a different level. As the British and Commonwealth flyweight champion, he was trying for the second time to add the European title to his collection when going in against Alexander Mahmutov in Madrid. He almost pulled it off.

Having failed in a previous attempt, when beaten by France's David Guerault two years previously, his only defeat in 21 fights, Jason was up for this one and he outboxed the Russian veteran most of the way. But he didn't stick to his boxing and Mahmutov's more aggressive style caught the eyes of the judges and saved his title with a unanimous decision. Pressing for a rematch before leaving for home, Booth was upbeat and already thinking of third time lucky. When you are 23, you can think like that.

The ladies were up in arms at the Wembley Conference Centre, with Jane Couch having her hands full against Viktoria Oleynikov of the Ukraine before earning a four-rounds decision, while Cathy Brown had an easy ride in stopping mismatched Romona Gughie from Romania in three one-sided rounds. And in Derby there was no 'coming out' for the debutante, Juliet Winter, not after four rounds with Sara Hall anyway.

At York Hall, Hackney's Ian Napa found himself in trouble when he tried to take the WBU flyweight belt from around the slim waist of the Liverpool stylist, Peter Culshaw. Making his sixth defence, Culshaw turned in a brilliant performance to chop down the little fellow from Zimbabwe in round eight to keep his title and take his pro log to 20-1-1. Napa had given the Commonwealth champion, Jason Booth, a stiff argument over 12 rounds in the same ring seven months previously, but he could do nothing with Culshaw this night.

It was a good night also for big Danny Williams, his right arm back in its socket, as he destroyed the unbeaten New Zealander, Kali Meehan, in a division record 32

The old man of boxing, Lester Jacobs (left), made a successful first defence of the WBF middles title when knocking out the stubborn Jason Collins   Les Clark

seconds of the first round to retain his Commonwealth heavyweight title. The visitor was sent crashing twice from right hands before it was called off.

Other first-round winners this month were Henry Akinwande, still plugging away on the American club circuit, taking out Maurice Harris with a right-hand smash in Cincinnati…Belfast's Darren Corbett starting the comeback in an ice skating rink in Yonkers, New York, where a big left hook disposed of Tyler Hughes in just 19 seconds!…At the Wembley Conference Centre, two fat guys met in a scheduled four rounder and it was all over at 2.38 of round one, the massive American, Butterbean, flattening Shane Woollas with a roundhouse right and the Doncaster man being out before he hit the deck. The ring floor stood up well under the heaviest matchup ever staged in Britain, with Butterbean at 25st 13lbs and Woollas a mere 19st 1lb, making it a combined 45 stones! Makes Tony Galento look like 'Slimmer of the Week' at his local Weightwatchers' meeting.

Lester Jacobs is something else. The Peckham boxer is 39 years old, unbeaten in 27 pro fights, WBF middleweight champion, promotes his own fights, yet is still Lester "Who?" to most boxing fans! At the Paragon Hotel, Earls Court, Jacobs did it again when he took care of his Walsall challenger, Jason Collins, inside nine rounds. Promoter Jacobs doesn't forget those other old timers still out there. In his chief supporting contest he had the former British super-middleweight champion, Ali Forbes, at 40, taking a close one from Mark Williams over four rounds.

In Nottingham, the Commonwealth welterweight champion, Jawaid Khaliq, took the IBO title from an American veteran, Willy Wise, while surviving a badly cut left eye to come out with a points decision. Khaliq, in becoming the IBO 'Champion of the World' will have to forfeit his Commonwealth title, no matter what you think of his new bauble. It's geting to where one guy asks his pal, "who is the world champ?" and his pal says, "who isn't!".

On the Wembley bill, Sven Hamer fought out of his skin against Elvis Michailenko for something called the WBF Pan-European light-heavyweight championship, which of course just happened to be vacant. Or maybe they just pulled that one out of the air! Anyway, title or not, it was a good fight and Michailenko, from Latvia via London, looked like he might do something one day…In Dagenham, the WBU lightweight champion, Colin Dunne, kept his hand in when he easily took care of Barrie Kelley, lefts to the body sinking the Welsh lad in the second and finally in round three. One of our better fighters, Dunne took his pro log to 33-1, with 22 finishing early.

John Jarrett's new book DYNAMITE GLOVES recently exploded in a book shop near you. With 273 pages of punch-packed prose it gives a fascinating new look at some old favourites, guys like 'Terrible' Terry McGovern, 'Mighty Atom' Jimmy Wilde, 'Manassa Mauler' Jack Dempsey, 'Michigan Assassin' Stanley Ketchel, 'Rochdale Thunderbolt' Jock McAvoy, 'Brown Bomber' Joe Louis, through to the murderous punching Rocky Graziano and granite-jawed Rocky Marciano. It's

Facts and Figures, 2000-2001

There were 643 (609 in 1999-2000) British-based boxers who were active between 1 July 2000 and 30 June 2001, spread over 191 (187 in 1999-2000) promotions held in Britain, not including the Republic of Ireland, during the same period. The above figure comprised 494 boxers already holding licenses or having been licensed previously, and 149 (115 in 1999-2000) new professionals. There are now seven licenced women boxers – Cathy Brown, Jane Couch, Audrey Guthrie, Sara Hall, Michelle Sutcliffe, Jan Wild and Juliette Winter. Also included are two foreign-born boxers, Ossie Duran (Ghana) and Peter Oboh (Nigeria), who began their careers elsewhere but are now domiciled in Britain.

Unbeaten during season (minimum qualification: 6 contests): 8: Gavin Down, Leo O'Reilly, David Walker. 7: Matthew Hatton, Michael Hunter, John McDermott, Lee Meager (1 draw), Darren Melville, Elvis Michailenko (1 draw), James Rooney. 6: Ricky Eccleston, Dale Robinson.

Longest unbeaten sequences (minimum qualification: 10 contests): 32: Howard Eastman. 31: Joe Calzaghe. 28: Lester Jacobs. 26: Anthony Farnell. 25: Steve Roberts. 23: Richard Hatton. 20: Noel Wilders. 18: Gavin Down, James Hare (1 draw). 16: Oscar Hall (1 draw). 14: Nicky Cook, Tony Mulholland (1 draw), Johnny Nelson. 13: Michael Bowen, Harry Dhami, Craig Docherty (1 draw), Graham Earl, Colin Lynes, Thomas McDonagh, Jim Rock. 12: Scott Dann, Colin Dunne, Matthew Ellis (1 draw), Michael Jones, Willie Limond, Gary Lockett, Brian Magee, Jamie Moore, Tony Oakey. 11: Tony Behan, Steven Bendall, Paul Halpin (1 draw), Scott Harrison (1 draw), Franny Hogg, Michael Jennings, Bradley Pryce, Gavin Rees, Mehrdud Takaloo. 10: Nicky Booth, Jesse James Daniel, James Docherty, Barry Hughes, Jawaid Khaliq, Kevin Lear, Eamonn Magee, Liam Maltby, Gerard Murphy, James Rooney, David Walker, Richard Williams, Clinton Woods.

Most wins during season (minimum qualification: 6 contests): 8: Gavin Down, Leo O'Reilly, David Walker. 7: Matthew Hatton, Michael Hunter, John McDermott, Darren Melville. 6: Francis Barrett, Kevin Bennett, Ricky Eccleston, Lee Meager, Elvis Michailenko, Chris Nembhard, Dale Robinson.

Most contests during season (minimum qualification: 10 contests): 20: Keith Jones. 17: Pete Buckley. 16: Paul Bonson, Ernie Smith. 15: Brian Coleman. 14: Harry Butler. 13: Steve Hanley, Anthony Hanna, Arv Mittoo, Lee Williamson. 12: Paul Denton, David Kirk, Ram Singh. 11: Darren Ashton, Dave Hinds, Mark Ramsey, Nigel Senior. 10: Ojay Abrahams, John Barnes, Jason Collins, Dave Travers.

Most contests during career (minimum qualification: 50 contests): 168: Pete Buckley. 131: Brian Coleman. 110: Miguel Matthews. 104: Nigel Rafferty. 102: Tony Booth. 75: Martin Jolley. 70: Anthony Hanna, Karl Taylor. 67: Nigel Senior. 65: Keith Jones. 64: Paul Wesley. 62: Mark Dawson. 61: Mark Ramsey. 59: Arv Mittoo. 58: Michael Alexander. 56: Michael Pinnock, Leigh Wicks. 55: Paul Bonson, Gary Williams. 53: Ojay Abrahams. 52: Chris Jickells, Johnny Nelson, Wayne Shepherd. 50: Darren Ashton, Jason Barker, Gary Flear, Ram Singh.

Stop Press: Results for July/August 2001

Royal National Hotel, Bloomsbury, London - 4 July (Promoter: David Casey)
Chill John w pts 4 Steve Hanley. Harry Butler w rsc 4 Darren Covill. Calvin Stonestreet w pts 4 Earl Ling.

The Velodrome, Manchester - 7 July (Promoter: Sports Network)
Richard Hatton w co 4 Jason Rowland (WBU L. Welterweight Title). Mehrdud Takaloo w rsc 1 Anthony Farnell (WBU L. Middleweight Title). Michael Gomez w rsc 3 Laszlo Bognar (WBO Inter-Continental S. Featherweight Title). Scott Dixon w rsc 5 Jamie Moore (WBO International L. Middleweight Title). Wayne Pinder w rtd 5 Ian Toby. Thomas McDonagh w pts 6 Paul Denton. Michael Jennings w pts 6 David Kirk. Wayne Elcock w pts 4 Darren Rhodes. Anthony Hughes w rsc 1 Daniel Ring. Darren Cleary w pts 4 Marty Kayes. David Barnes w rsc 2 Trevor Smith. Colin Toohey w pts 4 Jason Nesbitt.

Amsterdam, Holland - 7 July
Derek Roche w rsc 4 Zoltan Szili. Gary Hibbert w rsc 1 Gaeten Trovato.

Montreal, Canada - 10 July
Eric Lucas w rsc 7 Glenn Catley (WBC S. Middleweight Title). Gareth Hogg w rsc 1 Kevin Rainey.

Houston, Texas, USA - 12 July
Matthew Ellis w pts 6 Ronnie Smith.

The Conference Centre, Wembley - 14 July (Promoter: Ringside)
Pablo Sarmiento w rsc 11 Billy Schwer (IBO L. Welterweight Title). Jose Sanjuanelo w rsc 9 Nicky Booth (IBO Bantamweight Title). Patrick Mullings w pts 12 Michael Alldis (British S. Bantamweight Title). Isaac Sebaduka w rsc 5 Charles Shepherd. Matthew Barney w pts 8 Robert Milewics. Mark Ramsey w pts 6 Darren Bruce. Gary Lockett w rsc 1 Howard Clarke. Wayne Rigby w co 3 Keith Jones. Brett James w pts 6 Lee Williamson. Lee Byrne w pts 4 Arv Mittoo.

Olympia, Liverpool - 14 July (Promoter: Harding)
Robin Reid w rsc 4 Soon Botes (WBF S. Middleweight Title). Garry Delaney w rsc 10 Chris P. Bacon (British Masters Cruiserweight Title). Herbie Hide w rsc 3 Alexei Osokin. Dean Pithie w pts 4 Jason White. David Walker w pts 4 David White. Dazzo Williams w rsc 3 Dimitri Gorodetsky. Eric Teymour w rsc 2 Dean Ashton.

Ponds Forge International Sports Centre, Sheffield - 21 July (Promoter: Sports Network)
Johnny Nelson w pts 12 Marcelo Dominguez (WBO Cruiserweight Title). Roman Karmazin w pts 6 Viktor Fesetchko. Noel Wilders w pts 6 Chris Emanuele. Junior Witter w co 5 Alan Temple. Ryan Rhodes w pts 6 Youri Tsarenko. Bradley Pryce w rsc 5 Stuart Patterson. Gavin Rees w rsc 2 Nigel Senior. Dimitri Kirilov w pts 6 Nathan Sting. Alex Arthur w pts 4 Rakhim Mingaleev. Matthew Hatton w rsc 2 Ram Singh. Damon Hague w pts 4 Leigh Wicks. Ruben Groenewald w rsc 4 Terry Morrill. John Keeton w pts 4 Radcliffe Green. Gavin Down w rsc 1 Tommy Peacock. Scott Miller w pts 4 Pete Buckley.

Las Vegas, USA
Shane Mosley w rsc 3 Adrian Stone (WBC Welterweight Title).

Brakpan, South Africa - 25 July
David Starie w rsc 3 Bruno Godoy.

Paradise Rooms, Blackpool - 26 July (Promoter: Louis Veitch)
Lee Blundell w rsc 4 Harry Butler. Mark Winters w rsc 4 Joel Viney. Alan Campbell w pts 6 Brian Gifford. Lee Woodruff w rsc 1 Paul Martin. Gary Dixon w pts 6 Michael Thompson. Andy Abrol w pts 6 Ernie Smith. Eamonn Glennon w pts 6 Adam Cale.

Don Valley Stadium, Sheffield - 27 July (Promoters: Dennis Hobson/Panix)
Clinton Woods w pts 6 Paul Bonson. Mark Krence w pts 4 Shane Woollas. Mark Brookes w pts 4 Michael Pinnock. Dean Walker w rsc 4 Chris Duggan. Chris Hall w pts 4 Duncan Armstrong.

Conference Centre, Wembley - 28 July (Promoter: Sports Network)
Danny Williams w co 4 Julius Francis (British & Commonwealth Heavyweight Titles). Bruce Scott w pts 12 Rene Janvier (WBU International Cruiserweight Title). Alexander Vasiliev w rsc 7 Mark Potter (WBU International Heavyweight Title). Wayne Alexander w pts 8 Viktor Fesetchko. Gary Logan w rsc 4 Ojay Abrahams. Jonathan Thaxton w pts 4 David Kirk. Kevin Lear w pts 4 Pete Buckley. Matt Legg w pts 4 Mal Rice. Martin Power w rsc 3 Andrew Greenaway. Ross Minter w pts 4 Lee Williamson.

York Hall, Bethnal Green, London - 31 July (Promoter: Panix)
Damaen Kelly w rsc 4 Sipho Mantyi. Brian Magee w rsc 6 Chris Nembhard. Costas Katsantonis w rsc 4 Woody Greenaway. Allan Foster w pts 6 Mark Snipe. Ted Bami w pts 6 Lance Crosby. Lee Meager w pts 6 Steve Hanley. Jamie Yelland w rsc 5 Paddy Folan. Lee Swaby w pts 4 Stephane Allouane. Mark Alexander w pts 4 Damien Dunnion. Eric Teymour w rsc 1 Leigh Wicks. Neil Hosking w rsc 2 Slick Miller.

Montego Bay, Jamaica - 31 July
Jane Couch w pts 4 Shakurah Witherspoon.

Little Rock, Arkansas, USA - 11 August
Kevin McBride w pts 10 Willie Phillips.

Town Hall, Dewsbury - 18 August (Promoter: Alma Ingle)
Steve Conway w pts 8 Keith Jones. Oscar Hall w pts 6 David White. Jesse James Daniel w pts 6 Jason White. Simeon Cover w pts 6 Rob Stevenson. Mark Bowen w rsc 1 Mally McIver.

Hammanskraal, South Africa - 22 August
Steven Bendall w rsc 1 Bert Bado.

The Bank Quay, Warrington - 26 August (Promoter: Showsport International)
Peter Merrall w pts 6 Adam Cale. Lee Holmes w pts 6 Neil Read. Neil Bonner w rsc 1 Colin McCash.

Diary of British Boxing Tournaments, 2000-2001

Tournaments are listed by date, town, venue, and promoter, and cover the period 1 July 2000 - 30 June 2001

Code: SC = Sporting Club

Date	Town	Venue	Promoters
01.07.00	Southwark	Elephant & Castle Leisure Centre	World Sports Organisation/Pyle
01.07.00	Manchester	Bowler's Arena	Ringside Sporting Promotions
04.07.00	Tooting	The Leisure Centre	Mason
07.07.00	Chigwell	Prince Regent Hotel	Burns
08.07.00	Widnes	Kingsway Leisure Centre	Sports Network
08.07.00	Rotherham	Herringthorpe Leisure Centre	Rhodes
13.07.00	Bethnal Green	York Hall	Panix Promotions
15.07.00	Millwall	London Arena	Panix Promotions
15.07.00	Norwich	Sports Village	Ingle
22.07.00	Watford	Brickett Wood Leisure Centre	Evans-Waterman Promotions
23.07.00	Hartlepool	Seaton Carew Mayfair Suite	Garside
25.07.00	Southwark	Elephant & Castle Leisure Centre	Panix Promotions
12.08.00	Wembley	Grand Hall	Sports Network
13.08.00	Nottingham	Victoria Baths	Ingle
19.08.00	Brentwood	International Leisure Centre	Ringside Sporting Promotions
30.08.00	Scunthorpe	The Baths	Ingle
04.09.00	Manchester	Wythenshawe Forum	Sports Network
08.09.00	Hammersmith	Novotel Hotel	Harding
08.09.00	Bristol	Whitchurch Leisure Centre	Golden Fists Promotions
09.09.00	Manchester	Bowler's Arena	Ringside Sporting Promotions
09.09.00	Newark	Grove Leisure Centre	Ashton
10.09.00	Walsall	Town Hall	Bradley
16.09.00	Bethnal Green	York Hall	Panix Promotions
18.09.00	Glasgow	Posthouse Hotel	St Andrew's SC
21.09.00	Bloomsbury	Royal National Hotel	Jacobs
22.09.00	Wrexham	Plas Madoc Centre	Showsport International
23.09.00	Bethnal Green	York Hall	Sports Network
24.09.00	Shaw	Tara Leisure Centre	Tara Promotions
25.09.00	Barnsley	The Metrodome	Ringside Sporting Promotions
28.09.00	Kensington	Royal Gardens Hotel	Pyle
29.09.00	Bethnal Green	York Hall	Peacock Promotions
30.09.00	Peterborough	Bushfield Leisure Centre	Panix Promotions/Sanders
30.09.00	Chigwell	Prince Regent Rooms	Burns
01.10.00	Hartlepool	Seaton Carew Mayfair Suite	Garside
02.10.00	Glasgow	Thistle Hotel	Morrison
05.10.00	Sunderland	Swallow Hotel	Conroy
06.10.00	Maidstone	Leisure Centre	Golden Fists Promotions
07.10.00	Doncaster	The Dome	Golden Fists Promotions
09.10.00	Liverpool	Everton Park Leisure Centre	Ringside Sporting Promotions
09.10.00	Birmingham	Burlington Hotel	Cowdell
10.10.00	Brierley Hill	Copthorne Hotel	Midland SC
14.10.00	Wembley	Conference Centre	Panix Promotions
20.10.00	Belfast	Ulster Hall	Murray
20.10.00	Manchester	Palace Hotel	Viking International Promotions
21.10.00	Wembley	Conference Centre	Sports Network
21.10.00	Sheffield	Don Valley Stadium	Hobson
22.10.00	Streatham	Caesar's Nightclub	Honeyghan
23.10.00	Glasgow	Posthouse Hotel	St Andrew's SC
26.10.00	Stoke	Moat House Hotel	Brogan
26.10.00	Clydach	Manor Park Country House	SC of Wales
28.10.00	Coventry	The Sky Dome	Ringside Sporting Promotions

31.10.00	Hammersmith	Novotel Hotel	Harding
02.11.00	Kensington	Royal Gardens Hotel	Pyle
03.11.00	Ebbw Vale	The Leisure Centre	Golden Fists Promotions
04.11.00	Bethnal Green	York Hall	Matchroom
04.11.00	Derby	Pennine Hotel	Ingle
06.11.00	Wolvehampton	Civic Hall	Bradley
10.11.00	Glasgow	Thistle Hotel	Morrison
10.11.00	Mayfair	Marriott Hotel	Peacock Promotions
11.11.00	Belfast	Waterfront Hall	Panix Promotions/Munro & Hyland
12.11.00	Manchester	Palace Hotel	Viking International Promotions
13.11.00	Bethnal Green	York Hall	Sports Network
16.11.00	Hull	Quality Royal Hotel	Ulyatt
18.11.00	Dagenham	Goresbrook Leisure Centre	Panix Promotions
19.11.00	Chesterfield	Queens Park Sports Centre	Ingle/Ashton
20.11.00	Glasgow	Posthouse Hotel	St Andrew's SC
23.11.00	Bayswater	Hilton Hotel	Evans-Waterman Promotions
24.11.00	Hull	The University	Hull & District SC
24.11.00	Darlington	Dolphin Leisure Centre	Walker
25.11.00	Manchester	Wythenshawe Leisure Centre	Sports Network
27.11.00	Birmingham	Aston Villa Leisure Centre	Ringside Sporting Promotions
28.11.00	Brierley Hill	Copthorne Hotel	Midland SC
30.11.00	Blackpool	De Vere Hotel	Veitch
30.11.00	Peterborough	Moat House Hotel	Sanders
30.11.00	Bloomsbury	Royal National Hotel	Jacobs
01.12.00	Peterborough	Bushfield Leisure Centre	Golden Fists Promotions
02.12.00	Bethnal Green	York Hall	Ringside Sporting Promotions
02.12.00	Chigwell	Prince Regent Hotel	Burns
03.12.00	Shaw	Tara Leisure Centre	Tara Promotions
04.12.00	Bradford	Hilton Hotel	Yorkshire Executive SC
05.12.00	Nottingham	Albany Hotel	Gill
07.12.00	Sunderland	Swallow Hotel	Conroy
07.12.00	Stoke	Moat House Hotel	Brogan
08.12.00	Crystal Palace	National Sports Centre	Harding
09.12.00	Southwark	Elephant & Castle Leisure Centre	Panix Promotions
11.12.00	Widnes	Kingsway Leisure Centre	Sports Network
11.12.00	Birmingham	Burlington Hotel	Cowdell
11.12.00	Cleethorpes	Winter Gardens	Dalton
11.12.00	Sheffield	Holiday Inn Hotel	Hobson
12.12.00	Clydach	Manor Park Country House	SC of Wales
16.12.00	Sheffield	The Arena	Sports Network
17.12.00	Glasgow	Thistle Hotel	Morrison
02.01.01	Coventry	The Sky Dome	Harding
15.01.01	Manchester	Wythenshawe Forum	Sports Network
20.01.01	Bethnal Green	York Hall	Panix Promotions
22.01.01	Glasgow	Posthouse Hotel	St Andrew's SC
23.01.01	Crawley	The Leisure Centre	Matchroom
27.01.01	Bethnal Green	York Hall	Sports Network
28.01.01	Wolverhampton	The Light Bar	Bradley
29.01.01	Peterborough	Bushfield Leisure Centre	Panix Promotions
31.01.01	Piccadilly	Café Royal	National SC
02.02.01	Portsmouth	Mountbatton Centre	Sanigar
03.02.01	Brighton	Hove Town Hall	Davies
03.02.01	Manchester	Bowler's Arena	Ringside Sporting Promotions
04.02.01	Queensferry	Deeside Leisure Centre	Showsport International
05.02.01	Hull	City Hall	Panix Promotions
05.02.01	Bradford	Hilton Hotel	Yorkshire Executive SC
10.02.01	Widnes	Kingsway Leisure Centre	Sports Network

11.02.01	Hartlepool	Seaton Carew Mayfair Suite	Garside
13.02.01	Brierley Hill	Copthorne Hotel	Midland SC
15.02.01	Glasgow	Thistle Hotel	Morrison
17.02.01	Bethnal Green	York Hall	Panix Promotions
18.02.01	Southwark	Elephant & Castle Leisure Centre	TKO Promotions
19.02.01	Glasgow	Posthouse Hotel	St Andrew's SC
22.02.01	Sunderland	Swallow Hotel	Conroy
23.02.01	Irvine	Volunteer Rooms	St Andrew's SC
23.02.01	Barking	Broadway Theatre	Moughton
24.02.01	Bethnal Green	York Hall	Sports Network
25.02.01	Derby	Pennine Hotel	Ingle
25.02.01	Streatham	Caesar's Nightclub	Honeyghan
26.02.01	Nottingham	Harvey Hadden Leisure Centre	Ringside Sporting Promotions
28.02.01	Kensington	Royal Gardens Hotel	World Sports Organisation/Pyle
03.03.01	Wembley	Conference Centre	Ringside Sporting Promotions
06.03.01	Yarm	Tall Trees Hotel	Spensley
08.03.01	Stoke	Moat House Hotel	Brogan
08.03.01	Blackpool	The Tower	Veitch
09.03.01	Millwall	Britannia Hotel	Peacock Promotions
10.03.01	Bethnal Green	York Hall	Sports Network
12.03.01	Birmingham	Burlington Hotel	Cowdell
13.03.01	Plymouth	The Pavilions	Panix Promotions/Sanigar
16.03.01	Portsmouth	Mountbatton Centre	Sanigar
17.03.01	Manchester	Wythenshawe Forum	Sports Network
18.03.01	Shaw	Tara Leisure Centre	Tara Promotions
19.03.01	Glasgow	Posthouse Hotel	St Andrew's SC
20.03.01	Leeds	Elland Road (Marquee)	Yorkshire Executive SC
20.03.01	Glasgow	Bellahouston Leisure Centre	St Andrew's SC/Ringside Sporting Promotions
24.03.01	Sheffield	Ponds Forge Leisure Centre	Panix Promotions
24.03.01	Newark	Grove Leisure Centre	Ingle/Ashton
24.03.01	Chigwell	Prince Regent Hotel	Burns
26.03.01	Wembley	Conference Centre	Sports Network
26.03.01	Peterborough	Moat House Hotel	Sanders
27.03.01	Brierley Hill	Copthorne Hotel	Midland SC
28.03.01	Piccadilly	Café Royal	Golden Fists Promotions
29.03.01	Hammersmith	Novotel Hotel	Jacobs
01.04.01	Wolverhampton	The Light Bar	Bradley
01.04.01	Alfreton	The Leisure Centre	Ashton/Ingle
01.04.01	Southwark	Elephant & Castle Leisure Centre	TKO Promotions
03.04.01	Bethnal Green	York Hall	Sports Network
07.04.01	Wembley	Conference Centre	Ringside Sporting Promotions
08.04.01	Wrexham	Brymbo Sports & Social Club	Showsport International
09.04.01	Bradford	Hilton Hotel	Yorkshire Executive SC
10.04.01	Wembley	Conference Centre	Panix Promotions
20.04.01	Millwall	Britannia Hotel	Peacock Promotions
22.04.01	Streatham	Caesar's Nightclub	Honeyghan
24.04.01	Liverpool	Olympia	Ringside Sporting Promotions/ Golden Fists Promotions
26.04.01	Kensington	Royal Gardens Hotel	World Sports Organisation/Pyle
26.04.01	Gateshead	The Leisure Centre	Golden Fists Promotions
27.04.01	Glasgow	Thistle Hotel	Morrison
28.04.01	Cardiff	International Arena	Sports Network
30.04.01	Glasgow	Posthouse Hotel	St Andrew's SC
05.05.01	Edmonton	Lee Valley Leisure Centre	Sports Network
05.05.01	Brighton	Hove Town Hall	Davies
06.05.01	Hartlepool	Seaton Carew Mayfair Suite	Garside
08.05.01	Barnsley	The Metrodome	Ringside Sporting Promotions

10.05.01	Sunderland	Swallow Hotel	Conroy
12.05.01	Plymouth	The Pavilions	Panix Promotions
17.05.01	Leeds	Irish Centre	Walker
19.05.01	Wembley	The Arena	Harding
20.05.01	Wolverhampton	The Light Bar	Bradley
21.05.01	Birmingham	Burlington Hotel	Cowdell
24.05.01	Kensington	Royal Gardens Hotel	World Sports Organisation/Pyle
24.05.01	Glasgow	Moat House Hotel	GSC Promotions
26.05.01	Bethnal Green	York Hall	Ringside Sporting Promotions
27.05.01	Manchester	Palace Hotel	Viking International Promotions
02.06.01	Wakefield	Light Waves Leisure Centre	Panix Promotions
03.06.01	Southwark	Elephant & Castle Leisure Centre	TKO Promotions
03.06.01	Hanley	The Void	Brogan
04.06.01	Glasgow	Posthouse Hotel	St Andrew's SC
04.06.01	Hartlepool	Borough Hall	Ringside Sporting Promotions
08.06.01	Hull	The University	Hull & District SC
09.06.01	Bethnal Green	York Hall	Sports Network
10.06.01	Ellesmere Port	Civic Hall	Showsport International
11.06.01	Nottingham	Harvey Hadden Leisure Centre	Ringside Sporting Promotions
15.06.01	Millwall	Britannia Hotel	Peacock Promotions
16.06.01	Dagenham	Goresbrook Leisure Centre	Burns
16.06.01	Wembley	Conference Centre	World Sports Organisation/Pyle
16.06.01	Derby	Pennine Hotel	Ingle
18.06.01	Bradford	Hilton Hotel	Yorkshire Executive SC
21.06.01	Earls Court	Paragon Hotel	Jacobs
21.06.01	Sheffield	Grosvenor Hotel	Rhodes
23.06.01	Peterborough	Bushfield Leisure Centre	Panix Promotions/Sanders

Clinton Woods (right) forced Ali Forbes to retire on his stool at the end of the tenth round of their battle to decide the vacant WBC International light-heavyweight title at Sheffield's Ponds Forge Leisure Centre on 24 March   Les Clark

Active British-Based Boxers: Career Records

Shows the complete record for all British-based boxers who have been active between 1 July 2000 and 30 June 2001. Names in brackets are real names, where they differ from ring names, and the first place name given is the boxer's domicile. Boxers are either shown as being self-managed or with a named manager, the information being supplied by the BBBoC shortly before going to press. Also included are foreign-born fighters who made their pro debuts in Britain, along with others like Peter Oboh (Nigeria) and Ossie Duran (Ghana) who, although starting their careers elsewhere, now hold BBBoC licenses.

Ojay Abrahams

Watford. *Born* Lambeth, 17 December, 1964
British Masters L. Middleweight
Champion. Ht. 5'8½"
Manager Self

21.09.91	Gordon Webster W RSC 3 Tottenham
26.10.91	Mick Reid W RSC 5 Brentwood
26.11.91	John Corcoran W PTS 6 Bethnal Green
21.01.92	Dave Andrews DREW 6 Norwich
31.03.92	Marty Duke W RSC 2 Norwich
19.05.92	Michael Smyth L PTS 6 Cardiff
16.06.92	Ricky Mabbett W PTS 6 Dagenham
13.10.92	Vince Rose L RSC 3 Mayfair
30.01.93	Vince Rose DREW 6 Brentwood
19.05.93	Ricky Mabbett L RSC 4 Leicester
18.09.93	Ricky Mabbett L PTS 6 Leicester
09.12.93	Nick Appiah W PTS 6 Watford
24.01.94	Errol McDonald W RSC 2 Glasgow
09.02.94	Vince Rose W PTS 6 Brentwood
23.05.94	Spencer McCracken L PTS 6 Walsall
11.06.94	Darren Dyer W RSC 1 Bethnal Green
29.09.94	Gary Logan L PTS 10 Bethnal Green *(Southern Area Welterweight Title Challenge)*
13.12.94	Geoff McCreesh L PTS 6 Potters Bar
11.02.95	Gary Murray L PTS 8 Hamanskraal, South Africa
17.07.95	Andreas Panayi L PTS 8 Mayfair
02.10.95	Larbi Mohammed L RTD 5 Mayfair
08.12.95	Jason Beard W CO 2 Bethnal Green
09.04.96	Kevin Thompson W RSC 3 Stevenage
07.05.96	Harry Dhami L RSC 5 Mayfair *(Vacant Southern Area Welterweight Title)*
12.11.96	Spencer McCracken L PTS 8 Dudley
22.04.97	Paul King W RSC 4 Bethnal Green
29.05.97	Paul Ryan L RSC 3 Mayfair
30.06.97	Ahmet Dottuev L RSC 4 Bethnal Green
08.11.97	Anthony McFadden L PTS 8 Southwark
24.03.98	Leigh Wicks W PTS 6 Bethnal Green
28.04.98	Jim Webb W RSC 2 Belfast
10.09.98	Delroy Leslie L PTS 10 Acton *(Vacant Southern Area L. Middleweight Title)*
19.12.98	Michael Jones L PTS 6 Liverpool
23.01.99	Wayne Alexander L DIS 1 Cheshunt *(Vacant Southern Area L. Middleweight Title)*
01.05.99	Wayne Alexander L RSC 3 Crystal Palace
26.06.99	Geoff McCreesh L PTS 8 Millwall
05.10.99	Hussain Osman L PTS 4 Bloomsbury
23.10.99	Paul Samuels L PTS 8 Telford
18.01.00	Howard Eastman L RSC 2 Mansfield
23.03.00	Pedro Thompson DREW 6 Bloomsbury
08.04.00	Anthony Farnell L PTS 8 Bethnal Green
16.05.00	Ryan Rhodes L PTS 6 Warrington
23.05.00	Alexandru Andrei L PTS 6 Paris, France
04.07.00	Lester Jacobs L PTS 4 Tooting
21.09.00	Harry Butler W PTS 6 Bloomsbury
07.10.00	Kofi Jantuah L RTD 3 Doncaster
25.11.00	Donovan Smillie W RSC 2 Manchester
16.12.00	Marlon Hayes L RTD 6 Sheffield
15.01.01	Gordon Behan DREW 6 Manchester
24.02.01	Ruben Groenewald L PTS 6 Bethnal Green
22.04.01	Harry Butler W PTS 6 Streatham
17.05.01	Lee Murtagh W RSC 2 Leeds *(Vacant British Masters L. Middleweight Title)*
21.06.01	Charden Ansoula L PTS 4 Earls Court

Career: 53 contests, won 18, drew 4, lost 31.

Ojay Abrahams Les Clark

Andy Abrol

Blackpool. *Born* Middlesbrough, 19 October, 1973
Welterweight. Ht. 5'10"
Manager L. Veitch

08.03.01	Chris Steele W RSC 6 Blackpool
18.03.01	Paddy Martin W RSC 3 Shaw

Career: 2 contests, won 2.

Babatunde Ajayi

Peckham. *Born* London, 10 July, 1974
Welterweight. Ht. 5'7¾"
Manager K. Asante

18.02.01	Brian Gifford W RSC 1 Southwark
01.04.01	Arv Mittoo W PTS 6 Southwark
03.06.01	Ernie Smith W PTS 4 Southwark

Career: 3 contests, won 3.

Henry Akinwande

Dulwich. *Born* London, 12 October, 1965
WBC FeCarBox Heavyweight Champion.
Former Undefeated WBO, European &
Commonwealth Heavyweight Champion.
Ht. 6'7"
Manager Self

04.10.89	Carlton Headley W CO 1 Kensington
08.11.89	Dennis Bailey W RSC 2 Wembley
06.12.89	Paul Neilson W RSC 1 Wembley
10.01.90	John Fairbairn W RSC 1 Kensington
14.03.90	Warren Thompson W PTS 6 Kensington
09.05.90	Mike Robinson W CO 1 Wembley
10.10.90	Tracy Thomas W PTS 6 Kensington
12.12.90	Francois Yrius W RSC 1 Kensington
06.03.91	J. B. Williamson W RSC 2 Wembley
06.06.91	Ramon Voorn W PTS 8 Barking
28.06.91	Marshall Tillman W RSC 1 Wembley
09.10.91	Gypsy John Fury W CO 3 Manchester *(Elim. British Heavyweight Title)*
06.12.91	Tim Bullock W CO 3 Dusseldorf, Germany
28.02.92	Young Joe Louis W RSC 3 Issy les Moulineaux, France
26.03.92	Tucker Richards W RSC 2 Telford
10.04.92	Lumbala Tshimba W PTS 8 Carquefou, France
05.06.92	Kimmuel Odum W DIS 6 Marseille, France
18.07.92	Steve Garber W RTD 2 Manchester
19.12.92	Axel Schulz DREW 12 Berlin, Germany *(Vacant European Heavyweight Title)*
18.03.93	Jimmy Thunder W PTS 12 Lewisham *(Vacant Commonwealth Heavyweight Title)*
01.05.93	Axel Schulz W PTS 12 Berlin, Germany *(Vacant European Heavyweight Title)*
06.11.93	Frankie Swindell W PTS 10 Sun City, South Africa
01.12.93	Biagio Chianese W RSC 4 Kensington *(European Heavyweight Title Defence)*
05.04.94	Johnny Nelson W PTS 10 Bethnal Green
23.07.94	Mario Schiesser W CO 7 Berlin, Germany *(European Heavyweight Title Defence)*
08.04.95	Calvin Jones W CO 2 Las Vegas, USA
22.07.95	Stanley Wright W RSC 2 Millwall
16.12.95	Tony Tucker W PTS 10 Philadelphia, USA
27.01.96	Brian Sergeant W RSC 1 Phoenix, USA

23.03.96 Gerard Jones W DIS 7 Miami, USA
29.06.96 Jeremy Williams W CO 3 Indio, USA
(*Vacant WBO Heavyweight Title*)
09.11.96 Alexander Zolkin W RSC 10 Las
Vegas, USA
(*WBO Heavyweight Title Defence*)
11.01.97 Scott Welch W PTS 12 Nashville, USA
(*WBO Heavyweight Title Defence*)
12.07.97 Lennox Lewis L DIS 5 Lake Tahoe, USA
(*WBC Heavyweight Title Challenge*)
13.12.97 Orlin Norris W PTS 12 Pompano
Beach, USA
(*Final Elim. WBA Heavyweight Title*)
06.03.99 Reynaldo Minus W RSC 2 St Paul, USA
15.05.99 Najeed Shaheed W RSC 9 Miami, USA
22.02.00 Chris Serengo W RSC 1 Capetown,
South Africa
25.05.00 Russull Chasteen W CO 5 Tunica, USA
08.12.00 Ken Craven W CO 1 Tallahassee, USA
(*Vacant WBC FeCarBox Heavyweight
Title*)
17.03.01 Peter McNeeley W CO 2 Tallahassee,
Florida, USA
16.06.01 Maurice Harris W CO 1 Cincinnati, USA
Career: 42 contests, won 40, drew 1, lost 1.

Mark Alexander

Finsbury Park. *Born* Hackney, 18
November, 1975
Featherweight. Ht. 5'9½"
Manager A. Gee

10.04.01 Steve Hanley W PTS 4 Wembley
Career: 1 contest, won 1.

Michael Alexander

Doncaster. *Born* Doncaster, 31 August, 1971
Middleweight. Ht. 5'9"
Manager J. Rushton

25.01.93 Tim Hill W PTS 6 Bradford
09.03.93 J. T. Kelly L PTS 6 Hartlepool
29.04.93 Pete Roberts W RSC 2 Hull
06.05.93 Ian Noble W PTS 6 Hartlepool
28.06.93 Mick Hoban W PTS 6 Morecambe
04.10.93 Micky Hall L CO 1 Bradford
28.11.93 Everald Williams L PTS 6 Southwark
28.02.94 Paul Hughes W PTS 6 Manchester
28.03.94 Laurence Roche W PTS 6 Cleethorpes
20.05.94 Andrew Morgan W PTS 6 Neath
13.06.94 Laurence Roche L PTS 6 Bradford
26.09.94 Derek Roche L RSC 6 Bradford
21.11.94 Alan Peacock L RSC 1 Glasgow
06.03.95 Brian Dunn L CO 5 Bradford
26.02.96 Charlie Paine W PTS 6 Manchester
05.03.96 John Jones L PTS 6 Barrow
29.03.96 Cam Raeside L PTS 6 Doncaster
22.04.96 Peter Reid L PTS 6 Cleethorpes
03.05.96 Andy Davidson W RTD 2 Sheffield
10.05.96 Tony Mock W PTS 6 Liverpool
03.06.96 Tommy Quinn L PTS 6 Glasgow
24.06.96 Lee Murtagh L PTS 6 Bradford
29.07.96 Brian Dunn W PTS 6 Skegness
06.09.96 Paul Burns L RSC 4 Liverpool
28.10.96 Stuart Dunn W PTS 6 Leicester
10.11.96 Joe Townsley L PTS 8 Glasgow
26.11.96 George Richards W PTS 8
Wolverhampton
03.12.96 James Donoghue L PTS 6 Yarm
21.01.97 Anthony van Niekerk L PTS 8
Hammanskraal, South Africa
17.02.97 Derek Roche L DIS 4 Bradford
03.03.97 George Richards L PTS 8 Birmingham
14.03.97 Joe Townsley L PTS 6 Irvine
15.04.97 Darren Sweeney L RSC 6 Edgbaston
(*Vacant All-Ireland Middleweight Title*)

22.05.97 Howard Clarke L RSC 3 Solihull
19.07.97 Paul Ryan L CO 1 Wembley
02.09.97 Richard Williams W PTS 4 Southwark
13.09.97 Mehrdud Takaloo L PTS 4 Millwall
04.10.97 Junior Witter L PTS 4 Hannover,
Germany
21.11.97 Brian Dunn W RSC 4 Hull
29.11.97 Anas Oweida L PTS 4 Norwich
08.12.97 Carlton Williams L PTS 8 Leicester
15.12.97 Shamus Casey W PTS 6 Cleethorpes
12.01.98 Joni Nyman W PTS 6 Helsinki, Finland
21.01.98 Barry Thorogood L PTS 8 Stoke
28.02.98 Fighting Nordin L RSC 1 Dortmund,
Germany
05.04.98 Jeff Finlayson W PTS 6 Shaw
25.04.98 Jason Papillion L RSC 4 Cardiff
30.05.98 Scott Dann L PTS 4 Bristol
21.07.98 Ahmet Onar L RSC 1 Widnes
07.10.98 Gordon Behan L PTS 8 Stoke
17.10.98 Zoltan Sarossy L RSC 3 Manchester

23.03.99 George Richards L PTS 8
Wolverhampton
17.04.99 Jim Rock L RSC 1 Dublin
(*Vacant All-Ireland S. Middleweight
Title*)
07.10.00 Harry Butler W PTS 6 Doncaster
21.10.00 Ryan Rhodes L PTS 6 Wembley
03.12.00 Lee Murtagh L PTS 6 Shaw
17.12.00 Lawrence Murphy L PTS 6 Glasgow
02.01.01 Viktor Oganov L RSC 4 Coventry
Career: 58 contests, won 19, lost 39.

Wayne Alexander

Croydon. *Born* Tooting, 17 July, 1973
British L. Middleweight Champion. Former
Undefeated Southern Area L. Middleweight
Champion. Ht. 5'8¾"
Manager F. Warren

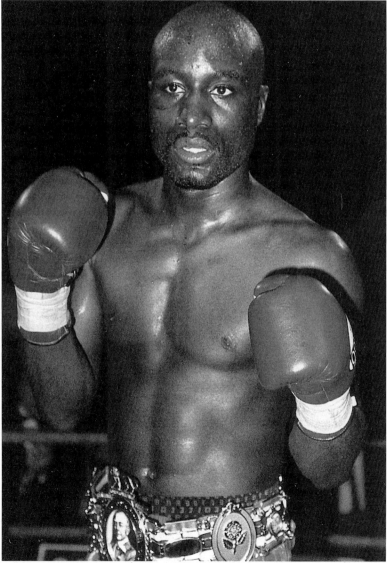

Wayne Alexander   Les Clark

10.11.95	Andrew Jervis W RTD 3 Derby
13.02.96	Paul Murray W PTS 4 Bethnal Green
11.05.96	Jim Webb W RSC 2 Bethnal Green
13.07.96	John Janes W RSC 3 Bethnal Green
05.06.97	Prince Kasi Kaihau W CO 4 Bristol
29.11.97	John Janes W RSC 1 Norwich
21.03.98	Darren Covill W RSC 2 Bethnal Green
09.05.98	Pedro Carragher W CO 2 Sheffield
14.07.98	Lindon Scarlett W RSC 5 Reading
05.12.98	Jimmy Vincent W RSC 3 Bristol
23.01.99	Ojay Abrahams W DIS 1 Cheshunt
	(Vacant Southern Area
	L. Middleweight Title)
01.05.99	Ojay Abrahams W RSC 3 Crystal
	Palace
07.08.99	George Richards W RSC 2 Dagenham
19.02.00	Paul Samuels W RSC 3 Dagenham
	(Vacant British L. Middleweight Title)
12.08.00	Paul Denton W RSC 1 Wembley
10.02.01	Harry Simon L RSC 5 Widnes
	(WBO L. Middleweight Title
	Challenge)

Career: 16 contests, won 15, lost 1.

Michael Alldis   Les Clark

Michael Alldis

Crawley. *Born* London, 25 May, 1968
British S. Bantamweight Champion.
Former Undefeated British Masters S.
Bantamweight Champion. Ht. 5'6"
Manager B. Hearn

15.09.92	Ceri Farrell W RSC 3 Crystal Palace
10.11.92	Kid McAuley W PTS 6 Dagenham
12.12.92	Kid McAuley W CO 1 Muswell Hill
16.02.93	Ceri Farrell W CO 1 Tooting
29.06.93	Ady Benton L DIS 3 Mayfair
28.09.93	Alan Ley W PTS 6 Bethnal Green
06.11.93	Pete Buckley W PTS 8 Bethnal Green
09.04.94	Fernando Lugo W CO 1 Bethnal Green
11.06.94	Conn McMullen W PTS 8 Bethnal Green
20.12.94	Pete Buckley W PTS 6 Bethnal Green
17.02.95	Miguel Matthews W PTS 8 Crawley
25.03.95	Chip O'Neill W RSC 2 Chester
13.06.95	Laureano Ramirez L PTS 12 Basildon
	(Vacant WBO Inter-Continental
	S. Bantamweight Title)

25.11.95	Conn McMullen W CO 4 Dagenham
13.01.96	Garry Burrell W RSC 7 Halifax
14.02.96	Billy Hardy L PTS 12 Sunderland
	(Commonwealth Featherweight Title
	Challenge)
04.04.97	Ervine Blake W RSC 3 Brighton
28.04.97	Paul Ingle L RTD 11 Hull
	(British Featherweight Title Challenge)
06.01.98	Luigi Mancini L RSC 4 Brighton
03.10.98	Jason Thomas W PTS 6 Crawley
15.12.98	Simon Ramoni L RSC 2 Durban, South
	Africa
	(IBO S. Bantamweight Title Challenge)
27.04.99	Garry Burrell W RSC 1 Bethnal Green
29.06.99	David Jeffrey W CO 1 Bethnal Green
	(British Masters S. Bantamweight
	Final)
06.11.99	Patrick Mullings W PTS 12 Bethnal
	Green
	(Vacant British S. Bantamweight Title)
24.01.00	Shaun Anderson W PTS 12 Glasgow
	(British S. Bantamweight Title
	Defence)
16.06.00	Bagdad Touama W RSC 4 Bloomsbury
04.11.00	Drew Docherty W RSC 6 Bethnal
	Green
	(British S. Bantamweight Title
	Defence)
23.01.01	Salem Bouita W RSC 6 Crawley

Career: 28 contests, won 22, lost 6.

Carl Allen

Wolverhampton. *Born* Wolverhampton, 20
November, 1969
S. Featherweight. Midlands Area S.
Bantamweight Champion. Ht. 5'7¼"
Manager Self

26.11.95	Gary Jenkinson W PTS 6 Birmingham
29.11.95	Jason Squire L PTS 6 Solihull
17.01.96	Andrew Robinson L PTS 6 Solihull
13.02.96	Ervine Blake W RSC 5
	Wolverhampton
21.02.96	Ady Benton L PTS 6 Batley
29.02.96	Chris Jickells W PTS 6 Scunthorpe
27.03.96	Jason Squire DREW 6 Whitwick
26.04.96	Paul Griffin L RSC 3 Cardiff
30.05.96	Roger Brotherhood W RSC 5 Lincoln
26.09.96	Matthew Harris W PTS 10 Walsall
	(Midlands Area S. Bantamweight Title
	Challenge)
07.10.96	Emmanuel Clottey L RTD 3 Lewisham
21.11.96	Miguel Matthews W PTS 8 Solihull
30.11.96	Floyd Havard L RTD 3 Tylorstown
29.01.97	Pete Buckley W PTS 8 Stoke
11.02.97	David Morris DREW 8
	Wolverhampton
28.02.97	Ian McLeod L RTD 3 Kilmarnock
21.05.97	David Burke L PTS 4 Liverpool
30.06.97	Duke McKenzie L PTS 8 Bethnal
	Green
12.09.97	Brian Carr L PTS 8 Glasgow
04.10.97	Sergei Devakov L PTS 6 Muswell Hill
03.12.97	Chris Lyons W PTS 8 Stoke
21.05.98	Roy Rutherford L PTS 6 Solihull
09.06.98	Scott Harrison L RSC 6 Hull
30.11.98	Gary Hibbert L PTS 4 Manchester
09.12.98	Chris Jickells W RSC 3 Stoke
04.02.99	Mat Zegan L PTS 4 Lewisham
17.03.99	Craig Spacie W PTS 8 Stoke
08.05.99	Phillip Ndou L RSC 2 Bethnal Green
14.06.99	Pete Buckley W PTS 6 Birmingham
22.06.99	David Lowry L PTS 4 Ipswich
11.10.99	Lee Williamson L PTS 6 Birmingham

19.10.99	Tontcho Tontchev L CO 2 Bethnal Green	
20.12.99	Nicky Cook L CO 3 Bethnal Green	
08.02.00	Lee Williamson W PTS 8 Wolverhampton	
29.02.00	Bradley Pryce L PTS 4 Widnes	
28.03.00	Lee Williamson W PTS 8 Wolverhampton	
16.05.00	Bradley Pryce L RSC 3 Warrington	
24.06.00	Michael Gomez L CO 2 Glasgow	
10.10.00	Steve Hanley W PTS 8 Brierley Hill	
05.02.01	Lee Meager DREW 6 Hull	
12.03.01	Pete Buckley W PTS 6 Birmingham	
27.03.01	Pete Buckley W PTS 8 Brierley Hill	

Career: 42 contests, won 16, drew 3, lost 23.

Adnan Amar

Nottingham. *Born* Nottingham, 17 February, 1983
Lightweight. Ht. 5'9"
Manager M. Shinfield

11.06.01	Steve Hanley W PTS 4 Nottingham	

Career: 1 contest, won 1.

Francis Ampofo   Les Clark

Francis Ampofo

Bethnal Green. *Born* Ghana, 5 June, 1967
Former IBO Inter-Continental Bantamweight Champion. Former Undefeated British Flyweight Champion. Former Commonwealth Flyweight Champion. Ht. 5'1½"
Manager D. Powell

30.01.90	Neil Parry W PTS 6 Bethnal Green
06.03.90	Robbie Regan L PTS 6 Bethnal Green
29.05.90	Eric George W RSC 3 Bethnal Green
12.09.90	Eric George W CO 2 Bethnal Green
26.03.91	Ricky Beard W PTS 8 Bethnal Green
22.06.91	Neil Johnston W RSC 2 Earls Court
03.09.91	Robbie Regan W RSC 11 Cardiff *(British Flyweight Title Challenge)*
17.12.91	Robbie Regan L PTS 12 Cardiff *(British Flyweight Title Defence)*
25.02.92	Ricky Beard W PTS 8 Crystal Palace
16.06.92	Shaun Norman RSC 4 Dagenham
22.12.92	James Drummond W PTS 12 Mayfair *(Vacant British Flyweight Title)*
17.02.93	Alberto Cantu W RSC 5 Bethnal Green
29.06.93	Albert Musankabala W RSC 3 Mayfair *(Vacant Commonwealth Flyweight Title)*
11.06.94	Jacob Matlala L RTD 9 Bethnal Green *(WBO Flyweight Title Challenge)*
20.09.94	James Drummond W RSC 3 Musselburgh *(British Flyweight Title Defence)*
20.12.94	Daren Fifield W RSC 2 Bethnal Green *(British Flyweight Title Defence. Commonwealth Flyweight Title Challenge)*
06.03.95	Danny Ward L CO 12 Mayfair *(Commonwealth Flyweight Title Defence)*
27.11.96	Rowan Williams W PTS 6 Bethnal Green
08.04.97	Vince Feeney L PTS 10 Bethnal Green *(Vacant Southern Area Bantamweight Title)*
19.09.97	Gary Hickman W RSC 2 Southend
25.10.97	Paul Lloyd L PTS 12 Queensferry *(Commonwealth Bantamweight Title Challenge. Vacant British Bantamweight Title)*
08.09.98	Graham McGrath W RTD 3 Bethnal Green
25.01.99	Shaun Anderson W RSC 9 Glasgow *(Vacant IBO Inter-Continental Bantamweight Title)*
30.10.99	Noel Wilders L PTS 12 Peterlee *(Vacant British Bantamweight Title)*
01.04.00	Ady Lewis L PTS 12 Bethnal Green *(Vacant British & Commonwealth Bantamweight Titles)*
09.12.00	John Armour L PTS 12 Southwark *(Vacant WBU Bantamweight Title)*

Career: 26 contests, won 17, lost 9.

Shaun Anderson

Maybole. *Born* Girvan, 20 September, 1969
S. Bantamweight. Scottish Bantamweight Champion. Ht. 5'5"
Manager T. Gilmour

29.05.92	Tucker Thomas W RSC 1 Glasgow
11.09.92	Mark Hargreaves W PTS 6 Glasgow
10.12.92	Graham McGrath W PTS 6 Glasgow
29.01.93	Graham McGrath W PTS 6 Glasgow
26.03.93	Dave Campbell W RSC 5 Glasgow
30.04.93	Paul Kelly W RSC 5 Glasgow
14.05.93	Kid McAuley W PTS 8 Kilmarnock
29.05.93	Ronnie Stephenson W PTS 6 Paisley
09.09.93	Graham McGrath W PTS 8 Glasgow
19.12.93	Pete Buckley W PTS 6 Glasgow
13.04.94	Paul Wynn DREW 6 Glasgow
13.05.94	Paul Wynn L PTS 8 Kilmarnock
08.09.94	Graham McGrath W PTS 8 Glasgow
23.09.94	Johnny Armour L RSC 11 Bethnal Green *(Commonwealth Bantamweight Title Challenge)*
18.11.94	James Murray L PTS 10 Glasgow *(Vacant Scottish Bantamweight Title)*
21.01.95	Brian Carr L PTS 6 Glasgow
04.03.95	Shaun Norman W PTS 6 Livingston
21.04.95	Donnie Hood W PTS 8 Glasgow
12.05.95	Warren Bowers L RSC 7 Bethnal Green
25.11.95	Spencer Oliver L RSC 3 Dagenham
16.03.96	Colin Innes W PTS 4 Glasgow
24.04.96	Ady Benton L PTS 6 Solihull
06.11.96	Donnie Hood W PTS 6 Glasgow

27.01.97	Lyndon Kershaw L PTS 8 Glasgow	
28.02.97	Benny Jones W PTS 6 Kilmarnock	
17.03.97	Neil Parry W RTD 4 Glasgow	
20.04.97	Noel Wilders L PTS 6 Leeds	
28.04.97	Graham McGrath W PTS 6 Glasgow	
14.10.97	Neil Armstrong W RSC 10 Kilmarnock	

14.10.97 Neil Armstrong W RSC 10 Kilmarnock
(Vacant Scottish Bantamweight Title)
24.11.97 Anthony Hanna W PTS 8 Glasgow
27.02.98 Matthew Harris W PTS 6 Irvine
01.06.98 Louis Veitch W PTS 6 Glasgow
08.11.98 Marty Chestnut W PTS 8 Glasgow
11.12.98 Brendan Bryce L PTS 6 Prestwick
25.01.99 Francis Ampofo L RSC 9 Glasgow
(Vacant IBO Inter-Continental Bamtamweight Title)
26.02.99 Brendan Bryce W RSC 2 Irvine
03.04.99 Kevin Gerowski W PTS 4 Carlisle
18.10.99 Kevin Gerowski W PTS 6 Glasgow
24.01.00 Michael Alldis L PTS 12 Glasgow
(British S. Bantamweight Title Challenge)
19.02.00 Paul Quarmby W PTS 6 Prestwick
03.03.00 Nicky Booth L PTS 6 Irvine
06.06.00 Chris Emanuele W PTS 6 Motherwell
23.10.00 John Barnes L PTS 6 Glasgow
19.03.01 John Barnes L PTS 6 Glasgow
Career: 44 contests, won 28, drew 1, lost 15.

Simon Andrews

Plymouth. *Born* Birmingham, 24 April, 1970
L. Heavyweight. Ht. 5'9½"
Manager Self

19.09.95 J. P. Matthews L RSC 3 Plymouth
13.11.95 Carl Winstone L PTS 6 Barnstaple
03.12.95 Jason Hart L PTS 6 Southwark
12.02.96 Neville Smith L RSC 3 Heathrow
04.04.96 Jetty Williams W PTS 6 Plymouth
10.05.96 Graham Townsend L RSC 5 Wembley
18.10.96 Gareth Thomas W RSC 5 Barnstaple
07.11.96 Gary Reyniers DREW 6 Battersea
10.12.96 Gareth Thomas W RSC 4 Plymouth
15.02.97 Neville Smith L PTS 4 Tooting
19.04.97 Peter Vosper L PTS 10 Plymouth
(Vacant Western Area L. Heavyweight Title)
12.07.97 Markus Beyer L RSC 5 Earls Court
02.12.97 Gary Reyniers L PTS 6 Windsor
24.02.98 Alex Mason L PTS 6 Edgbaston
24.03.98 Gordon Behan L RSC 6 Wolverhampton
24.09.98 Alex Mason L PTS 8 Edgbaston
17.03.99 Matthew Barney L RTD 4 Kensington
03.10.99 Damon Hague L PTS 6 Chesterfield
20.11.99 Damon Hague L RSC 4 Grantham
27.02.00 Matt Mowatt L PTS 6 Plymouth
29.03.00 Gareth Hogg L RSC 5 Piccadilly
02.06.00 Steven Bendall L RSC 5 Ashford
25.02.01 Joe Brame L RSC 5 Streatham
12.05.01 Freddie Yemofio W PTS 4 Plymouth
Career: 24 contests, won 4, drew 1, lost 19.

John Armour

Chatham. *Born* Chatham, 26 October, 1968
WBU Bantamweight Champion. Former Undefeated European & Commonwealth Bantamweight Champion. Ht. 5'4¾"
Manager Self

24.09.90 Lupe Castro W PTS 6 Lewisham
31.10.90 Juan Camero W RSC 4 Crystal Palace
21.01.91 Elijro Mejia W RSC 1 Crystal Palace

30.09.91 Pat Maher W CO 1 Kensington
29.10.91 Pete Buckley W PTS 6 Kensington
14.12.91 Gary Hickman W RSC 6 Bexleyheath
25.03.92 Miguel Matthews W PTS 6 Dagenham
30.04.92 Ndabe Dube W RSC 12 Kensington
(Vacant Commonwealth Bantamweight Title)
17.10.92 Mauricio Bernal W PTS 8 Wembley
03.12.92 Albert Musankabala W RSC 5 Lewisham
(Commonwealth Bantamweight Title Defence)
28.01.93 Ricky Romero W CO 1 Southwark
10.02.93 Morgan Mpande W PTS 12 Lewisham
(Commonwealth Bantamweight Title Defence)
09.06.93 Boualem Belkif W PTS 10 Lewisham
01.12.93 Karl Morling W CO 3 Kensington

14.01.94 Rufus Adebayo W RSC 7 Bethnal Green
(Commonwealth Bantamweight Title Defence)
23.09.94 Shaun Anderson W RSC 11 Bethnal Green
(Commonwealth Bantamweight Title Defence)
14.02.95 Tsitsi Sokutu W RSC 7 Bethnal Green
(Commonwealth Bantamweight Title Defence)
19.04.95 Antonio Picardi W RSC 8 Bethnal Green
(Vacant European Bantamweight Title)
19.05.95 Matthew Harris W RSC 3 Southwark
29.11.95 Redha Abbas W CO 5 Bethnal Green
(European Bantamweight Title Defence)

John Armour   Les Clark

57

17.12.96 Lyndon Kershaw W RSC 8 Bethnal Green
29.01.97 Petrica Paraschiv W PTS 12 Bethnal Green
(Vacant Interim WBC International Bantamweight Title)
20.05.97 Anatoly Kvitko W RSC 8 Gillingham
28.11.97 Ervine Blake W PTS 10 Bethnal Green
12.12.98 Carlos Navarro L RSC 4 Southwark
(WBU S. Bantamweight Title Challenge)
19.06.99 Mohamed Ouzid W RSC 5 Dublin
25.07.00 Alexander Tiranov W PTS 8 Southwark
09.12.00 Francis Ampofo W PTS 12 Southwark
(Vacant WBU Bantamweight Title)
Career: 28 contests, won 27, lost 1.

Duncan Armstrong

South Shields. *Born* South Shields, 29 November, 1977
Lightweight. Ht. 5'10"
Manager T. Callighan

26.11.99 Chris Hall L PTS 6 Wakefield
02.03.00 Joel Viney L PTS 6 Blackpool
28.03.00 Dave Travers W PTS 6 Wolverhampton
06.06.00 Andrew Ferrans L PTS 6 Motherwell
23.07.00 James Rooney L RSC 3 Hartlepool
20.11.00 Andrew Ferrans L PTS 6 Glasgow
05.12.00 Dave Cotterill L PTS 6 Nottingham
26.02.01 Inderpaul Sandhu L PTS 4 Nottingham
19.03.01 Pete Buckley W PTS 6 Glasgow
09.04.01 Leo Turner L PTS 6 Bradford
Career: 10 contest, won 2, lost 8.

(Shaun) Lee Armstrong

Huddersfield. *Born* Hartlepool, 18 October, 1972
Lightweight. Central Area S. Featherweight Champion. Ht. 5'8"
Manager Self

26.04.96 Daryl McKenzie W RSC 4 Glasgow
10.05.96 Charlie Rumbol W PTS 6 Wembley
23.05.96 Ian Richardson W PTS 6 Queensferry
04.10.96 Michael Gibbons W RSC 3 Wakefield
18.11.96 Garry Burrell W PTS 6 Glasgow
20.02.97 Carl Greaves W RSC 4 Mansfield
10.04.97 Chris Lyons W PTS 6 Sheffield
28.04.97 Hugh Collins W RTD 5 Glasgow
26.06.97 Garry Burrell W PTS 6 Sheffield
06.10.97 Roger Sampson L PTS 6 Bradford
13.11.97 Graeme Williams W PTS 6 Bradford
30.11.97 Gary Jenkinson W PTS 6 Shaw
06.02.98 Nigel Leake W PTS 6 Wakefield
05.04.98 John T. Kelly W PTS 4 Shaw
21.05.98 Pete Buckley W PTS 6 Bradford
14.06.98 Pete Buckley W PTS 6 Shaw
23.10.98 Nigel Leake W RSC 3 Wakefield
(Vacant Central Area S. Featherweight Title)
11.12.98 Ian McLeod L RSC 8 Prestwick
(IBO Inter-Continental S. Featherweight Title Challenge)
21.02.99 Bobby Lyndon W RSC 5 Bradford
03.04.99 John T. Kelly L PTS 6 Carlisle
25.04.99 Chris Lyons W PTS 8 Leeds
02.10.99 Jamie McKeever DREW 6 Cardiff
14.11.99 Keith Jones W PTS 6 Bradford
11.12.99 Jason Dee L RSC 4 Merthyr
21.02.00 Gary Flear W PTS 8 Glasgow

27.03.00 Sebastian Hart L CO 4 Barnsley
24.09.00 Dave Travers W PTS 6 Shaw
23.10.00 Craig Docherty DREW 8 Glasgow
Career: 28 contests, won 20, drew 2, lost 6.

Alex Arthur

Edinburgh. *Born* Edinburgh, 26 June, 1978
S. Featherweight. Ht. 5'9"
Manager F. Warren/F. Maloney

25.11.00 Richmond Asante W RSC 1 Manchester
10.02.01 Eddie Nevins W RSC 1 Widnes
26.03.01 Woody Greenaway W RTD 2 Wembley
28.04.01 Dafydd Carlin W PTS 4 Cardiff
Career: 4 contests, won 4.

Richmond Asante

East Ham. *Born* Ghana, 7 July, 1976
Featherweight. Ht. 5'5¹/₂"
Manager D. Powell

25.11.00 Alex Arthur L RSC 1 Manchester
18.02.01 Gareth Wiltshaw W PTS 4 Southwark
01.04.01 Stevie Quinn L PTS 4 Southwark
03.06.01 Steve Gethin W PTS 4 Southwark
Career: 4 contests, won 2, lost 2.

(Gary) Crawford Ashley (Crawford)

Leeds. *Born* Leeds, 20 May, 1964
Cruiserweight. Former British, Commonwealth & European L. Heavyweight Champion. Former Undefeated Central Area L. Heavyweight Champion. Ht. 6'3"
Manager Self

26.03.87 Steve Ward W RSC 2 Merton
29.04.87 Lee Woolis W RSC 3 Stoke
14.09.87 Glazz Campbell L PTS 8 Bloomsbury
07.10.87 Joe Frater W RSC 4 Burnley
28.10.87 Ray Thomas W RSC 1 Stoke
03.12.87 Jonjo Greene W RSC 7 Leeds
04.05.88 Johnny Nelson L PTS 8 Solihull
15.11.88 Richard Bustin W CO 3 Norwich
22.11.88 Cordwell Hylton W CO 3 Basildon
24.01.89 John Foreman W RSC 4 Kings Heath
08.02.89 Lavell Stanley W CO 1 Kensington
28.03.89 Blaine Logsdon L RSC 2 Glasgow
10.05.89 Serg Fame W RTD 7 Solihull
31.10.89 Carl Thompson W RSC 6 Manchester
(Vacant Central Area L. Heavyweight Title)
24.01.90 Brian Schumacher W RSC 3 Preston
(Central Area L. Heavyweight Title Defence)
25.04.90 Dwain Muniz W RSC 1 Brighton
26.11.90 John Williams W RSC 1 Mayfair
12.02.91 Melvin Ricks W CO 1 Belfast
01.03.91 Graciano Rocchigiani L PTS 12 Dusseldorf, Germany
(Vacant European L. Heavyweight Title)
25.07.91 Roy Skeldon W RSC 7 Dudley
(Vacant British L. Heavyweight Title)
30.01.92 Jim Peters W RSC 1 Southampton
(British L. Heavyweight Title Defence)
25.04.92 Glazz Campbell W RSC 8 Belfast
(British L. Heavyweight Title Defence)
23.09.92 Yawe Davis DREW 12 Campione d'Italia, Italy
(Vacant European L. Heavyweight Title)

23.04.93 Michael Nunn L RSC 6 Memphis, USA
(WBA S. Middleweight Title Challenge)
29.01.94 Dennis Andries L RTD 4 Cardiff
19.11.94 Nicky Piper W PTS 12 Cardiff
(Vacant British L. Heavyweight Title)
25.02.95 Hunter Clay W RTD 3 Millwall
01.04.95 Virgil Hill L PTS 12 Stateline, USA
(WBA L. Heavyweight Title Challenge)
01.07.95 Lenzie Morgan W PTS 8 Kensington
24.11.95 Jesus Castaneda W RSC 3 Manchester
10.02.96 Frank Minton W RSC 1 Cottbus, Germany
02.03.96 Ray Kane W CO 2 Newcastle
11.12.96 Tony Booth W RSC 1 Southwark
11.01.97 Peter Kamarenko W RSC 1 Bethnal Green
01.03.97 Roberto Dominguez W CO 3 Liverpool
(Vacant European L. Heavyweight Title)
31.05.97 Pascal Warusfel W PTS 12 Paris, France
(European L. Heavyweight Title Defence)
04.10.97 Ole Klemetsen L RSC 2 Muswell Hill
(European L. Heavyweight Title Defence)
14.03.98 Monty Wright W RSC 2 Bethnal Green
(British L. Heavyweight Title Defence)
09.06.98 Tony Booth W RSC 6 Hull
(British L. Heavyweight Title Defence. Vacant Commonwealth L. Heavyweight Title)
26.09.98 Jo Siluvangi W PTS 12 York
(Vacant European L. Heavyweight Title)
13.03.99 Clinton Woods L RSC 8 Manchester
(British, Commonwealth & European L. Heavyweight Title Defences)
05.02.01 Shane Woollas W RSC 4 Hull
24.03.01 Lee Swaby W PTS 8 Sheffield
Career: 43 contests, won 33, drew 1, lost 9.

Matthew Ashmole　　　　Les Clark

Matthew Ashmole

Swansea. *Born* Swansea, 5 May, 1980
Middleweight. Ht. 5'11"
Manager Self

12.08.00 P.J.Maxwell L RSC 3 Wembley
28.09.00 Karim Hussine L PTS 4 Kensington
26.10.00 Harry Butler L PTS 6 Clydach
16.11.00 Brendan Rollinson L PTS 6 Hull
Career: 4 contests, lost 4.

Darren Ashton

Stoke. *Born* Stoke, 26 February, 1969
Cruiserweight. Midlands Area
L. Heavyweight Champion. Former
Undefeated Midlands Area
S. Middleweight Champion. Ht. 6'1"
Manager Self

13.10.93 Tony Colclough W RSC 1 Stoke
08.12.93 Nigel Rafferty W PTS 6 Stoke
23.03.94 L. A. Williams W PTS 6 Stoke
23.05.94 Nigel Rafferty W PTS 6 Walsall
30.11.94 Carlos Christie L PTS 6 Solihull
04.03.95 John Wilson NC 3 Livingston
06.05.95 Dale Nixon W RSC 4 Shepton Mallet
13.05.95 Stefan Wright W PTS 6 Glasgow
11.10.95 Neil Simpson L RSC 3 Solihull
17.11.95 Mark Baker L RSC 1 Bethnal Green
12.01.96 Frederic Alvarez L PTS 6 Copenhagen, Denmark
27.05.96 Harri Hakulinen L PTS 4 Helsinki, Finland
09.07.96 Chris Johnson L RSC 1 Bethnal Green
08.02.97 Paul Bowen L PTS 4 Millwall
04.04.97 Mark Snipe W RSC 2 Brighton
26.06.97 Clinton Woods L PTS 6 Sheffield
02.09.97 Adrian Strachan W PTS 4 Southwark
15.09.97 Darren Dorrington W DIS 2 Bristol
21.11.97 Stuart Fleet W RSC 4 Hull
  *(Vacant Midlands Area
  S. Middleweight Title)*
07.02.98 Sven Hamer L RSC 2 Cheshunt
27.03.98 Toks Owoh L RSC 2 Telford
16.05.98 Ali Forbes L PTS 6 Chigwell
23.05.98 Howard Eastman L RSC 4 Bethnal Green
23.09.98 Bobby Banghar L RSC 2 Bloomsbury
13.11.98 Graham Townsend L DIS 6 Brighton
30.11.98 Mervyn Penniston-John L PTS 4
19.12.98 Ole Klemetsen L RSC 2 Liverpool
11.02.99 Alex Mason W PTS 10 Dudley
  (Vacant Midlands Area L. Heavyweight Title)
13.03.99 Glenn Williams L PTS 4 Manchester
17.05.99 Tony Booth L PTS 6 Cleethorpes
04.06.99 Lee Osie Manuel L RSC 5 Vigo, Spain
  (Transcontinental L. Heavyweight Title Challenge)
31.07.99 Darren Corbett L RSC 2 Carlisle
09.10.99 Glenn Williams L PTS 6 Manchester
28.10.99 Warren Stowe W PTS 6 Burnley
04.12.99 Mike Gormley L PTS 4 Manchester
21.02.00 Tony Oakey L PTS 4 Southwark
04.03.00 Neil Linford L PTS 6 Peterborough
20.03.00 Brian Magee L RTD 5 Mansfield
29.05.00 Roy Finlay L PTS 6 Manchester
21.10.00 Tony Oakey L PTS 4 Wembley
31.10.00 Konstantin Schvets L RSC 1 Hammersmith
30.11.00 Neil Linford L PTS 4 Peterborough

08.12.00 Delroy Leslie L RTD 3 Crystal Palace
27.01.01 Peter Haymer L PTS 4 Bethnal Green
17.02.01 Faisal Mohammed L RSC 1 Bethnal Green
28.03.01 Michael Pinnock DREW 6 Piccadilly
20.04.01 Tony Griffiths W PTS 4 Millwall
28.04.01 Enzo Maccaranelli L CO 1 Cardiff
27.05.01 Lee Whitehead W RSC 2 Manchester
15.06.01 Garry Delaney L RTD 4 Millwall
  (Vacant British Masters Cruiserweight Title)
Career: 50 contests, won 14, drew 1, lost 34, no contest 1.

Dean Ashton

Stoke. *Born* Stoke, 26 November, 1967
L. Heavyweight. Ht. 5'9"
Manager Self

13.10.93 Phil Ball W PTS 6 Stoke
08.12.93 Mark Hale W RSC 1 Stoke
23.03.94 Shaun McCrory DREW 6 Stoke
23.05.94 Mark Smallwood L RTD 3 Walsall
28.03.98 Andy Wright L RSC 2 Crystal Palace
16.05.98 Earl Ling DREW 6 Chigwell
02.07.98 Earl Ling W RSC 2 Ipswich
17.09.98 Peter Mitchell L PTS 6 Brighton
25.10.98 Mike Whittaker L PTS 6 Shaw
13.11.98 Jimmy Millen W RSC 3 Brighton
30.11.98 Mike Gormley L PTS 4 Manchester
14.12.98 Damon Hague L PTS 6 Cleethorpes
19.01.99 Adrian Houldey W PTS 8 Ipswich
22.02.99 John Docherty L PTS 6 Glasgow
13.03.99 Brian Magee L RSC 2 Manchester
22.04.99 Alex Mason L PTS 10 Dudley
  (Vacant Midlands Area S. Middleweight Title)
26.06.99 Frode Steinsvik L RSC 2 Millwall
19.09.99 Lee Blundell L RSC 4 Shaw
28.10.99 Mike Whittaker L PTS 6 Burnley
14.11.99 Danny Thornton L PTS 4 Bradford
01.12.99 Ian Cooper L PTS 4 Yarm
14.12.99 Peter Federenko L PTS 4 Coventry
22.01.00 Gordon Behan L RSC 2 Birmingham
20.03.00 Ivan Botton L RSC 2 Mansfield
11.05.00 Ian Toby L PTS 6 Sunderland
22.05.00 Edwin Cleary DREW 4 Coventry
29.05.00 Darren Rhodes L RSC 3 Manchester
25.07.00 Butch Lesley L PTS 6 Southwark
08.09.00 Richard Williams L RSC 1 Hammersmith
12.11.00 Alan Page L RSC 2 Manchester
23.02.01 Tony Griffiths L PTS 8 Barking
28.03.01 Wayne Asker L PTS 6 Piccadilly
20.04.01 Elvis Michailenko L RSC 4 Millwall
27.05.01 Wayne Pinder L PTS 6 Manchester
16.06.01 Damon Hague W DIS 1 Derby
Career: 35 contests, won 6, drew 3, lost 26.

Wayne Asker

Bury St Edmunds. *Born* Bury St Edmunds, 20 November, 1975
S. Middleweight. Ht. 5'9"
Manager Self

02.07.98 Dennis Griffin W PTS 4 Ipswich
03.10.98 Delroy Mellis W PTS 6 Crawley
19.01.99 David Baptiste W PTS 6 Ipswich
09.05.99 Hussan Osman L PTS 4 Bracknell
22.06.99 David Baptiste L PTS 4 Ipswich
28.03.01 Dean Ashton W PTS 6 Piccadilly
Career: 6 contests, won 4, lost 2.

Michael Ayers

Tooting. *Born* London, 26 January, 1965
IBO Lightweight Champion. Former
Undefeated British, WBC International &
Southern Area Lightweight Champion.
Ht. 5'8"
Manager B. Hearn

16.05.89 Young Joe Rafiu W RSC 5 Wandsworth
27.06.89 Greg Egbuniwe W CO 1 Kensington
15.11.89 Mille Markovic W RSC 2 Lewisham
05.12.89 Darren Mount W RSC 2 Catford
26.04.90 Nick Hall W CO 3 Wandsworth
04.06.91 Stuart Rimmer W CO 1 Bethnal Green
22.06.91 Wayne Weekes W RSC 6 Earls Court
  (Vacant Southern Area Lightweight Title)
21.09.91 Peter Till W RSC 5 Tottenham
  (Elim. British Lightweight Title)
28.01.92 Jorge Pompey W PTS 8 Hamburg, Germany
19.02.92 Rudy Valentino W RSC 7 Muswell Hill
  (Southern Area Lightweight Title Defence. Elim. British Lightweight Title)
27.06.92 Sugar Gibiliru W RSC 6 Quinta do Lago, Portugal
13.10.92 Scott Brouwer W RSC 4 Mayfair
  (Vacant WBC International Lightweight Title)
20.02.93 Danny Myburgh W RSC 5 Earls Court
  (WBC International Lightweight Title Defence)
16.04.93 Giovanni Parisi L PTS 12 Rome, Italy
  (WBO Lightweight Title Challenge)
24.05.94 Karl Taylor DREW 8 Sunderland
30.09.94 John O. Johnson W RSC 3 Bethnal Green
07.11.94 Bamana Dibateza W PTS 6 Bethnal Green
17.02.95 Paul Burke W RSC 6 Crawley
  (Vacant British Lightweight Title)
31.03.95 Karl Taylor W RSC 8 Crystal Palace
  (British Lightweight Title Defence)
23.05.95 Charles Shepherd W RSC 3 Potters Bar
  (British Lightweight Title Defence)
30.09.95 Dave Anderson W RTD 7 Basildon
  (British Lightweight Title Defence)
27.09.96 Tony Swift W RSC 5 Stevenage
20.11.96 Colin Dunne W RSC 9 Wembley
  (British Lightweight Title Defence)
21.03.98 Alan Temple W RSC 2 Bethnal Green
30.05.98 Anthony Maynard L PTS 8 Bristol
06.11.98 Steve Tuckett W RSC 5 Mayfair
03.12.98 Roger Sampson L PTS 6 Mayfair
12.01.99 Jean Gomis W RTD 5 Bethnal Green
12.03.99 Luis Flores W RSC 4 Bethnal Green
  (Vacant IBO Lightweight Title)
25.05.99 Mkhuseli Kondile W CO 3 Mayfair
  (IBO Lightweight Title Defence)
02.10.99 Pablo Sarmiento W RSC 6 Cardiff
  (IBO Lightweight Title Defence)
20.12.99 Tony Miller W RSC 10 Bethnal Green
  (IBO Lightweight Title Defence)
01.07.00 Wayne Rigby W RSC 10 Manchester
  (IBO Lightweight Title Defence)
19.08.00 Mehdi Labdouni W CO 1 Brentwood
  (IBO Lightweight Title Defence)
03.03.01 Wayne Rigby W PTS 12 Wembley
  (IBO Lightweight Title Defence)
Career: 35 contests, won 31, drew 1, lost 3.

Chris P. Bacon

Manchester. *Born* Australia, 8 October, 1969
Cruiserweight. Former Undefeated WBF European S. Cruiserweight Champion. Ht. 6'0"
Manager Self

21.12.97	Tim Brown W PTS 6 Salford	
23.02.98	Tim Brown W PTS 6 Salford	
08.05.98	Lee Swaby W RSC 3 Manchester	
30.05.98	Phill Day W RSC 4 Bristol	
17.07.98	Lee Swaby W PTS 6 Mere	
18.09.98	Kevin Mitchell W RSC 1 Manchester	
16.10.98	Luke Simpkin W PTS 6 Salford	
16.11.98	Paul Bonson W PTS 8 Glasgow	
25.02.99	Israel Ajose W PTS 10 Kentish Town	

(Vacant WBF European S. Cruiserweight Title)

19.06.99	Kelly Oliver L PTS 8 Dublin
09.10.99	Chris Woollas W PTS 4 Manchester
03.02.01	Collice Mutizwa W RSC 1 Manchester

Career: 12 contests, won 11, lost 1.

Martyn Bailey

Wrexham. *Born* Wrexham, 16 January, 1976
L. Middleweight. Ht. 5'8"
Manager Self

07.10.99	John Marsden W PTS 6 Sunderland
27.11.99	Lee Molloy L RSC 2 Liverpool
18.02.00	Donovan Davey W PTS 6 Pentre Halkyn
06.03.00	Richard Inquieti L RSC 5 Bradford
05.05.00	Richard Inquieti W PTS 6 Pentre Halkyn
22.09.00	David Smales W RSC 3 Wrexham
28.11.00	Paul Martin W PTS 6 Brierley Hill
04.02.01	Pedro Thompson W PTS 6 Queensferry
08.04.01	Peter Dunn W PTS 6 Wrexham
10.06.01	Robert Burton DREW 6 Ellesmere Port

Career: 10 contests, won 7, drew 1, lost 2.

Mark Baker

Sidcup. *Born* Farnborough, 14 July, 1969
Former Undefeated WBF L. Heavyweight Champion. Former Undefeated Southern Area Middleweight Champion. Ht. 5'9½"
Manager Self

07.09.92	Jason McNeill W RSC 2 Bethnal Green
15.10.92	Graham Jenner W RTD 4 Lewisham
03.12.92	Adrian Wright W RSC 1 Lewisham
10.02.93	Paul Hanlon W RSC 2 Lewisham
26.04.93	Karl Mumford W CO 1 Lewisham
15.06.93	Alan Baptiste W PTS 6 Hemel Hempstead
14.01.94	Karl Barwise L PTS 6 Bethnal Green
11.03.94	Graham Jenner W RSC 2 Bethnal Green
26.04.94	Jerry Mortimer W PTS 6 Bethnal Green
23.09.94	Alan Baptiste W RSC 1 Bethnal Green
17.10.94	Steve Thomas W RSC 5 Mayfair
27.10.94	Chris Richards W PTS 6 Milwall

13.12.94	Stinger Mason W RSC 4 Ilford	
20.01.95	Mark Dawson W RSC 3 Bethnal Green	
17.11.95	Darren Ashton W RSC 1 Bethnal Green	
13.01.96	Mark Dawson W RSC 3 Halifax	
05.03.96	Sven Hamer W PTS 10 Bethnal Green	

(Vacant Southern Area Middleweight Title)

14.10.96	John Duckworth W RSC 6 Mayfair	
27.03.97	Heath Todd W RSC 5 Dubai	
30.06.97	Mark Delaney W PTS 10 Bethnal Green	

(Elim. British S. Middleweight Title)

08.10.97	Robert Peel W RSC 5 Poplar
06.12.97	Clinton Woods L PTS 12 Wembley

(Vacant Commonwealth S. Middleweight Title)

07.03.98	Dean Francis L RSC 12 Reading

(British & WBO Inter-Continental S. Middleweight Title Challenges)

04.02.99	Danny Juma W PTS 6 Lewisham
29.04.99	Errol McDonald W PTS 10 Bethnal Green
22.06.99	David Starie L PTS 12 Ipswich

(British & Commonwealth S. Middleweight Title Challenges)

09.03.00	Ali Forbes W PTS 12 Bethnal Green

(Vacant WBF L. Heavyweight Title)

22.05.00	Neil Simpson L PTS 12 Coventry

(Vacant British & Commonwealth L. Heavyweight Titles)

09.12.00	Paul Bonson W PTS 6 Southwark
20.01.01	Andy Manning W PTS 8 Bethnal Green
05.02.01	Howard Eastman L RTD 5 Hull
10.04.01	Tony Booth W PTS 4 Wembley

Career: 32 contests, won 26, lost 6.

Scott Baker   Les Clark

Scott Baker

Walthamstow. *Born* Londonderry, 29 August, 1977
Cruiserweight. Ht. 6'2"
Manager R. Davies

22.06.99	Adam Cale W PTS 4 Ipswich	
13.09.99	Georgie Stevens L PTS 4 Bethnal Green	
01.10.99	Jason Brewster W RTD 5 Cleethorpes	
16.06.00	Adam Cale W PTS 4 Bloomsbury	
08.09.00	Mark Dawson L RSC 3 Hammersmith	
03.02.01	Slick Miller L RSC 4 Brighton	

Career: 6 contests, won 3, lost 3.

Ted Bami (Minsende)

Brixton. *Born* Zaire, 2 March, 1978
L. Welterweight. Ht. 5'7"
Manager Self

26.09.98	Des Sowden W RSC 1 Southwark
11.02.99	Gary Reid W RSC 2 Dudley
10.03.00	David Kehoe W PTS 4 Bethnal Green
08.09.00	Jacek Bielski L RSC 6 Hammersmith
29.03.01	Keith Jones W PTS 4 Hammersmith
05.05.01	Francis Barrett W PTS 6 Edmonton

Career: 6 contests, won 5, lost 1.

Ted Bami   Les Clark

(Ratesh) Bobby Banghar

Bedford. *Born* Bedford, 30 June, 1977
L. Middleweight. Ht. 5'10¾"
Manager T. Toole

02.12.97	Mark Dawson W PTS 4 Swansea
27.01.98	Neville Smith DREW 4 Piccadilly
06.02.98	Carl Nicholson W RSC 3 Wakefield
26.03.98	Robert Peel W PTS 4 Piccadilly
30.04.98	Michael Pinnock W PTS 6 Purfleet
14.06.98	Paul Carr W PTS 6 Golders Green
23.09.98	Darren Ashton W RSC 2 Bloomsbury
21.11.98	Errol McDonald L CO 6 Southwark
26.02.99	Graham Townsend W PTS 6 Bethnal Green
20.05.99	Matthew Barney L RSC 5 Kensington

(Vacant British Masters S. Middleweight Title)

30.09.00	Leigh Wicks W PTS 4 Peterborough
24.03.01	Ernie Smith W PTS 4 Chigwell
16.06.01	Ernie Smith W PTS 4 Dagenham

Career: 13 contests, won 9, drew 1, lost 3.

David Baptiste

Balham. *Born* Luton, 5 March, 1966
L. Middleweight. Ht. 5'7"
Manager Self

20.09.96	Robbie Dunn W CO 2 Tooting	
08.11.97	Darren Covill L PTS 4 Southwark	
04.03.98	Scott Garrett L PTS 6 Bloomsbury	
02.07.98	Mark Weller L PTS 4 Ipswich	
08.08.98	Darren Christie L PTS 4 Scarborough	
12.10.98	Ray Newby L RSC 6 Nottingham	
30.11.98	Neil Linford L PTS 4 Peterborough	
12.12.98	Shane Thomas W RSC 2 Chester	
19.12.98	Paolo Roberto L RSC 6 Liverpool	
19.01.99	Wayne Asker L PTS 6 Ipswich	
26.02.99	Joel Ani W RSC 5 Longford	
13.03.99	Brian Knudsen L RSC 4 Manchester	
29.04.99	Sergei Dzindziruk L RTD 2 Bethnal Green	
22.06.99	Wayne Asker W PTS 4 Ipswich	
21.07.99	Lester Jacobs L RSC 2 Bloomsbury	
15.09.99	James Lowther W RSC 3 Harrogate	
26.11.99	Adrian Chase L RSC 2 Bayswater *(Vacant British Masters Welterweight Title)*	
29.02.00	Jamie Moore L RSC 3 Manchester	
07.04.00	Jason Williams L PTS 6 Bristol	
06.05.00	Zoltan Sarossy L PTS 8 Neuss, Germany	
29.05.00	Thomas McDonagh L PTS 6 Manchester	
16.09.00	Kevin McCarthy W RSC 6 Bethnal Green	
04.11.00	Gary Lockett L PTS 4 Bethnal Green	
11.11.00	Jim Rock L PTS 4 Belfast	
30.11.00	Lester Jacobs L RSC 3 Bloomsbury	
02.02.01	Paul Dyer L PTS 10 Portsmouth *(Vacant Southern Area Welterweight Title)*	
23.02.01	Chris Nembhard L PTS 8 Barking	
17.03.01	Thomas McDonagh L PTS 4 Manchester	
26.03.01	Clive Johnson L PTS 6 Peterborough	

Career: 29 contests, won 6, lost 23.

Jason Barker

Sheffield. *Born* Chesterfield, 1 June, 1973
L. Heavyweight. Scottish S. Middleweight
Champion. Ht. 6'0"
Manager Self

30.01.92	Nicky Lucas W PTS 6 Southampton	
12.02.92	Roger Hunte L RTD 4 Wembley	
29.04.92	Dave Lovell L PTS 6 Stoke	
03.06.92	John O. Johnson L PTS 6 Newcastle under Lyne	
07.07.92	Patrick Loughran L PTS 6 Bristol	
21.10.92	Brian Coleman L PTS 6 Stoke	
02.11.92	Shea Neary L RSC 3 Liverpool	
09.12.92	John O. Johnson L PTS 8 Stoke	
28.01.93	Jason Beard L RSC 3 Southwark	
22.04.93	Marco Fattore L PTS 6 Mayfair	
12.05.93	Shaba Edwards W PTS 6 Stoke	
14.06.93	Delroy Leslie L RTD 3 Bayswater	
21.09.95	Jamie Gallagher L RSC 2 Sheffield	
20.10.95	Wesley Jones W RSC 2 Mansfield	
22.11.95	Darren Covill W PTS 4 Sheffield	
08.12.95	James Donoghue L PTS 6 Leeds	
05.02.96	Darren Covill L RSC 1 Bexleyheath	
03.05.96	Shamus Casey W RSC 1 Sheffield	
09.05.96	Hughie Davey L PTS 6 Sunderland	
08.10.96	Alvar Coppard W RSC 3 Battersea	
26.11.96	Ray Newby W PTS 6 Sheffield	
03.12.96	Phil Epton W RSC 1 Yarm	

24.02.97	Humphrey Harrison W CO 6 Manchester	
03.03.97	Ricky Mabbett W PTS 6 Leicester	
17.03.97	Billy Collins L PTS 6 Glasgow	
20.05.97	Panayiotis Panayiotiou L PTS 6 Edmonton	
30.11.97	Derek Wormald L PTS 6 Shaw	
01.02.98	Willie Quinn L RSC 4 Glasgow *(Vacant Scottish S. Middleweight Title)*	
17.03.98	Jimmy Steel W PTS 6 Sheffield	
30.04.98	Craig Winter L PTS 6 Pentre Halkyn	
12.05.98	James Lowther L PTS 4 Leeds	
20.09.98	Jon Penn L PTS 6 Sheffield	
03.10.98	Peter Mitchell W RSC 2 Crawley	
30.11.98	Carlton Williams W PTS 8 Leicester	
04.02.99	Howard Eastman L RSC 6 Lewisham	
02.05.99	Derek Wormald L PTS 8 Shaw	
17.05.99	Neil Linford W RSC 3 Peterborough	
07.06.99	John Docherty L PTS 10 Glasgow *(Vacant Scottish Middleweight Title)*	
19.06.99	Ali Ennebati L CO 1 Sedan, France	
20.08.99	Cornelius Carr L RSC 3 Bloomsbury	
09.10.99	Ahmet Oner L CO 3 Oberhausen, Germany	
25.02.00	Ganny Dovidovas DREW 4 Newmarket	
18.03.00	Willie Quinn L RTD 2 Glasgow	
20.05.00	Clint Johnson W RSC 1 Rotherham	
12.06.00	Brian Magee L PTS 8 Belfast	
08.07.00	Paul Jones L RSC 5 Rotherham	
08.09.00	Steven Bendall L PTS 6 Bristol	
02.10.00	Biagio Falcone W PTS 10 Glasgow *(Vacant Scottish S.Middleweight Title)*	
21.10.00	Jamie Warters L PTS 4 Sheffield	
02.12.00	Butch Lesley L RSC 1 Chigwell	

Career: 50 contests, won 17, drew 1, lost 32.

John Barnes

Sunderland. *Born* Sunderland, 7 July, 1975
S. Bantamweight. Ht. 5'6¹/₂"
Manager T. Conroy

02.10.97	Nicky Wilders W PTS 6 Sunderland	
04.12.97	Sean Grant W PTS 6 Sunderland	
26.01.98	Alston Buchanan L PTS 6 Glasgow	
07.05.98	Kevin Gerowski W PTS 6 Sunderland	
06.05.99	Simon Chambers W PTS 6 Sunderland	
12.07.99	Mark Payne L PTS 4 Coventry	
20.09.99	Craig Docherty L PTS 6 Glasgow	
30.10.99	Paul Quarmby W PTS 4 Peterlee	
27.11.99	Nicky Cook L PTS 6 Liverpool	
07.02.00	Jezz D'Agostino W PTS 4 Peterborough	
24.02.00	Sebastian Hart L PTS 6 Sunderland	
04.03.00	Jezz D'Agostino W PTS 4 Peterborough	
20.03.00	Andrew Ferrans DREW 6 Glasgow	
01.04.00	Marc Callaghan L PTS 4 Bethnal Green	
11.05.00	Nigel Senior W PTS 6 Sunderland	
01.07.00	Jason Booth L PTS 6 Manchester	
25.09.00	Dale Robinson L PTS 4 Barnsley	
05.10.00	Steve Brook W PTS 6 Sunderland	
23.10.00	Shaun Anderson W PTS 6 Glasgow	
31.10.00	Jamie Yelland L PTS 6 Hammersmith	
20.11.00	Barry Hawthorne L PTS 6 Glasgow	
19.03.01	Shaun Anderson W PTS 6 Glasgow	
07.04.01	Jamie Yelland L PTS 4 Wembley	
30.04.01	Chris Emanuele W PTS 4 Glasgow	
12.05.01	Frankie DeMilo L PTS 10 Plymouth *(British Masters S. Bantamweight Title Challenge)*	

Career: 25 contests, won 12, drew 1, lost 12.

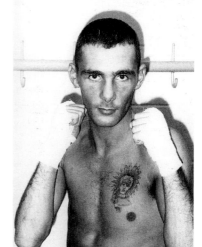

John Barnes   Les Clark

Chris Barnett

Manchester. *Born* Coventry, 15 July, 1973
Former Undefeated IBO International L.
Welterweight Champion. Ht. 5.5½"
Manager Self

18.02.95	Wayne Jones W RSC 5 Shepton Mallet	
24.11.95	Brian Coleman W RSC 4 Manchester	
09.04.96	Charlie Paine W RSC 2 Salford	
25.10.96	John Smith W PTS 6 Mere	
22.12.96	Wayne Shepherd W PTS 6 Salford	
18.01.97	Kid McAuley W RTD 3 Manchester	
24.02.97	Jay Mahoney L PTS 6 Manchester	
20.03.97	Mike Watson W RSC 2 Salford	
08.05.98	David Kirk W PTS 6 Manchester	
17.07.98	Ivan Walker W RSC 1 Mere	
17.10.98	Trevor Smith W RSC 4 Manchester	
10.07.99	Karim Bouali DREW 6 Southwark	
09.10.99	Mick Mulcahy W RSC 2 Manchester	
27.11.99	Glenn McClarnon W PTS 12 Liverpool *(Vacant IBO International L. Welterweight Title)*	
29.02.00	Victor Barinov L PTS 8 Manchester	
19.08.00	Newton Villareal L RSC 3 Brentwood *(IBO L.Welterweight Title Challenge)*	

Career: 16 contests, won 12, drew 1, lost 3.

Matthew Barney

Southampton. *Born* Fareham, 25 June, 1974
Southern Area & British Masters S.
Middleweight Champion. Ht. 5'10³/₄"
Manager G. Evans

04.06.98	Adam Cale W PTS 6 Barking	
23.07.98	Adam Cale W PTS 6 Barking	
02.10.98	Dennis Doyley W PTS 4 Cheshunt	
22.10.98	Kevin Burton W PTS 6 Barking	
07.12.98	Freddie Yemofio W PTS 4 Acton	
17.03.99	Simon Andrews W RTD 4 Kensington	
09.05.99	Gareth Hogg W PTS 4 Bracknell	
20.05.99	Bobby Banghar W RSC 5 Kensington *(British Masters S. Middleweight Final)*	

05.06.99 Paul Bowen DREW 10 Cardiff
(Southern Area S. Middleweight Title Challenge)
20.08.99 Adam Cale W PTS 4 Bloomsbury
05.10.99 Delroy Leslie L PTS 10 Bloomsbury
(Vacant Southern Area Middleweight Title)
15.04.00 Mark Dawson W PTS 6 Bethnal Green
06.05.00 Jason Hart W PTS 10 Southwark
(Vacant Southern Area S. Middleweight Title)
30.09.00 Neil Linford L PTS 10 Peterborough
(Elim. British S. Middleweight Title)
02.02.01 Darren Covill W PTS 6 Portsmouth
16.03.01 Matt Mowatt W RSC 1 Portsmouth
(British Masters S. Middleweight Title Defence)
Career: 16 contests, won 13, drew 1, lost 2.

Matthew Barr

Walton. *Born* Kingston, 22 May, 1977
L. Middleweight. Ht. 5'11"
Manager Self

02.12.97 Keith Palmer L RSC 3 Windsor
23.02.98 Martin Cavey W RSC 1 Windsor
14.05.98 Gerard Lawrence L RSC 1 Acton
29.10.98 Sonny Thind W RSC 2 Bayswater
20.05.99 Paul Knights L RSC 1 Barking
31.10.99 Allan Gray W PTS 4 Raynes Park
25.02.00 John Humphrey W RSC 1 Newmarket
06.05.00 Ernie Smith W PTS 4 Southwark
22.10.00 Ernie Smith W PTS 4 Streatham
23.11.00 Harry Butler W PTS 4 Bayswater
Career: 10 contests, won 7, lost 3.

Francis Barrett   Les Clark

Francis Barrett

Wembley. *Born* Galway, 7 February, 1977
L. Welterweight. Ht. 5'7"
Manager F. Warren

12.08.00 Mohamed Helel W PTS 4 Wembley
23.09.00 Trevor Smith W RSC 1 Bethnal Green
21.10.00 Keith Jones W PTS 4 Wembley

24.02.01 David White W PTS 4 Bethnal Green
10.03.01 Karl Taylor W RSC 3 Bethnal Green
26.03.01 Tony Montana W PTS 4 Wembley
05.05.01 Ted Bami L PTS 6 Edmonton
Career: 7 contests, won 6, lost 1.

Kevin Barrett

Hackney. *Born* Hackney, 15 October, 1973
Cruiserweight. Ht. 5'9"
Manager B. Lawrence

27.01.01 Mark McManus W RSC 1 Bethnal Green
10.04.01 Brian Gascoigne W RSC 1 Wembley
Career: 2 contests, won 2.

(Martin) Wee Barry (Moore)

Staines. *Born* Limavaay, Ireland, 5 April, 1971
Lightweight. Ht. 5'6½"
Manager Self

24.07.92 Jose Hernandez L RSC 1 New York City, USA
30.10.95 Martin Evans L PTS 6 Heathrow
12.02.96 Martin Evans W RSC 4 Heathrow
07.11.96 Dean Murdoch L PTS 6 Battersea
02.12.97 Brian Gentry L PTS 6 Windsor
20.02.98 Scott Buckzeiger L RSC 4 USA
24.04.98 Thomas Barker W RTD 2 Plymouth, USA
07.12.98 Jezz D'Agostino L PTS 6 Acton
09.05.99 Des Sowden L DIS 2 Bracknell
22.05.99 David Lowry L RTD 1 Belfast
26.06.99 Eddie McAloney W PTS 4 Boston, USA
11.12.99 Shamir Reyes L CO 1 Tunica, USA
04.05.00 Scotty Buck L PTS 6 Detroit, USA
05.08.00 Daniel Mitchell L PTS 4 Uncasville, USA
16.06.01 Ron Greer L RSC 3 New York City, USA
Career: 15 contests, won 3, lost 12.

Gary Beardsley

Belper. *Born* Belper, 18 July, 1968
British Masters Middleweight Champion.
Ht. 5'10"
Manager J. Ashton

09.02.95 Shaun Stokes W RSC 3 Doncaster
01.03.95 Eddie Haley W RSC 1 Glasgow
06.03.95 Stefan Scriggins L PTS 6 Leicester
15.03.95 Jamie Gallagher W PTS 6 Stoke
20.10.95 Dewi Roberts W PTS 6 Mansfield
22.11.95 Richard Swallow DREW 6 Sheffield
06.12.95 John Smith W PTS 8 Stoke
06.02.96 Georgie Smith L RSC 1 Basildon
22.03.96 Mark Legg W PTS 6 Mansfield
09.12.96 Derek Roche L RSC 2 Bradford
16.01.97 Steve Levene L PTS 6 Solihull
29.01.97 Howard Clarke L PTS 6 Stoke
20.11.99 William Webster W PTS 6 Grantham
18.01.00 Mike Duffield W RTD 2 Mansfield
09.04.00 Matt Mowatt W PTS 6 Alfreton
01.07.00 Wayne Pinder L PTS 4 Manchester
19.11.00 Matt Mowatt W PTS 10 Chesterfield
(Vacant British Masters Middleweight Title)
08.12.00 Cornelius Carr L PTS 4 Crystal Palace
25.02.01 William Webster W PTS 6 Derby
Career: 19 contests, won 11, drew 1, lost 7.

Jimmy Beech

Walsall. *Born* Walsall, 19 January, 1979
S. Featherweight. Ht. 5'7"
Manager Self

23.06.99 Ike Halls W RTD 2 West Bromwich
03.09.99 Tom Wood W PTS 6 West Bromwich
07.04.00 Willie Limond L RSC 2 Glasgow
28.01.01 Lenny Hodgkins W PTS 6 Wolverhampton
Career: 4 contests, won 3, lost 1.

Gordon Behan

Leamington. *Born* Dublin, 13 February, 1976
Midlands Area Middleweight Champion.
Ht. 5'10¾"
Manager Self

24.04.96 Michael Pinnock W PTS 6 Solihull
03.06.96 Peter Mitchell DREW 6 Birmingham
07.03.97 James Lowther L PTS 6 Northampton
15.01.98 Carlton Williams W RSC 7 Solihull
24.02.98 Phil Ball W PTS 6 Edgbaston
24.03.98 Simon Andrews W RSC 6 Wolverhampton
07.10.98 Michael Alexander W PTS 8 Stoke
26.11.98 Mike Duffield W RSC 3 Edgbaston
(Vacant Midlands Area Middleweight Title)
25.03.99 Matt Galor W RSC 9 Edgbaston
(Midlands Area Middleweight Title Defence)
27.05.99 Robert Wright W PTS 10 Edgbaston
(Midlands Area Middleweight Title Defence)
22.01.00 Dean Ashton W RSC 2 Birmingham
17.04.00 Michael Pinnock W PTS 6 Birmingham
22.05.00 Yuri Filipko W RSC 2 Coventry
15.01.01 Ojay Abrahams DREW 6 Manchester
Career: 14 contests, won 11, drew 2, lost 1.

Steven Bendall

Coventry. *Born* Coventry, 1 December, 1973
Middleweight. Ht. 6'0"
Manager Self

15.05.97 Dennis Doyley W RSC 2 Reading
13.09.97 Gary Reyniers W PTS 4 Millwall
27.02.99 Israel Khumalo W PTS 4 Oldham
02.07.99 Darren Covill W RTD 3 Bristol
24.09.99 Sean Pritchard W PTS 6 Merthyr
03.12.99 Ian Toby W PTS 6 Peterborough
07.04.00 Des Sowden W RSC 3 Bristol
02.06.00 Simon Andrews W RSC 5 Ashford
08.09.00 Jason Barker W PTS 6 Bristol
03.11.00 Eddie Haley W RSC 1 Ebbw Vale
01.12.00 Peter Mitchell W PTS 8 Peterborough
Career: 11 contests, won 11.

Kevin Bennett

Hartlepool. *Born* Birmingham, 15 August, 1975
L. Welterweight. Ht. 5'7"
Manager M. Marsden

01.12.99 Karim Bouali W PTS 4 Yarm
28.03.00 Les Frost W RSC 2 Hartlepool
25.06.00 Steve Hanley W PTS 6 Wakefield
23.07.00 Gary Reid W RSC 4 Hartlepool
28.10.00 Gary Harrison W RTD 2 Coventry

27.11.00	Keith Jones W PTS 4 Birmingham
23.01.01	Tommy Peacock W RSC 5 Crawley
03.03.01	Iain Eldridge W PTS 6 Wembley
08.05.01	Keith Jones W PTS 6 Barnsley
04.06.01	Gary Ryder L RSC 6 Hartlepool

Career: 10 contests, won 9, lost 1.

Kevin Bennett   Les Clark

Billy Bessey

Hartlepool. *Born* Portsmouth, 8 January, 1974
Heavyweight. Ht. 6'1"
Manager D. Garside

01.10.00	Paul Fiske W PTS 6 Hartlepool
26.02.01	Mark Hobson L PTS 4 Nottingham
06.05.01	Luke Simpkin W PTS 6 Hartlepool
04.06.01	Gary Williams W PTS 4 Hartlepool

Career: 4 contests, won 3, lost 1.

Jim Betts

Scunthorpe. *Born* Tickhill, 6 October, 1977
British Masters Flyweight Champion. Ht. 5'6½"
Manager M. Marsden

26.03.98	Des Gargano W PTS 6 Scunthorpe
13.05.98	David Jeffrey W RSC 3 Scunthorpe
05.06.98	Chris Price W PTS 6 Hull
11.09.98	Marty Chestnut W PTS 6 Newark
16.10.98	Marty Chestnut W PTS 6 Salford
28.11.98	Ola Dali W PTS 4 Sheffield
17.05.99	Dave Travers W RTD 4 Cleethorpes
17.07.99	Ross Cassidy W RSC 1 Doncaster
27.09.99	Graham McGrath W PTS 6 Cleethorpes
19.02.00	Chris Price W PTS 6 Newark
19.06.00	Chris Price W PTS 4 Burton
30.08.00	David Coldwell W RSC 2 Scunthorpe *(Vacant British Masters Flyweight Title. Elim. British Flyweight Title)*
26.02.01	Chris Emanuele L PTS 6 Nottingham
08.05.01	Sean Grant W RSC 3 Barnsley
11.06.01	Daniel Ring W PTS 6 Nottingham

Career: 15 contests, won 14, lost 1.

Lee Bird

Doncaster. *Born* Doncaster, 17 June, 1971
L. Middleweight. Ht. 5'6"
Manager Self

13.02.96	Paul Bowen L RSC 2 Bethnal Green
27.09.96	Mark Owens W PTS 6 Hull
24.10.96	Michael Monaghan L RSC 6 Lincoln
19.06.97	Shaun O'Neill L PTS 6 Scunthorpe
12.07.97	Matthew Tait L PTS 6 Earls Court
18.09.97	Kevin Lang L RSC 2 Alfreton
15.05.98	Matt Scriven L RSC 5 Nottingham
15.06.98	David Smales L RSC 1 Bradford
17.09.98	Lawrence Murphy L RSC 3 Glasgow
24.10.98	Gary Lockett L RSC 2 Liverpool
27.11.98	Brian Swain W PTS 6 Hull
07.12.98	Paul Swindles W PTS 6 Nottingham
22.01.99	Wayne Shepherd L PTS 6 Carlisle
16.02.99	Allan Gray L PTS 6 Brentford
28.02.99	Wayne Pinder L RSC 5 Shaw
22.04.99	Shane Junior W RSC 2 Dudley
02.05.99	Mick Mulcahy L RSC 2 Shaw
23.06.99	Peter Nightingale L PTS 6 West Bromwich
20.09.99	Oleg Kudinov L CO 3 Peterborough
06.11.99	Richard Williams L RSC 4 Bethnal Green
12.12.99	Harry Dhami L PTS 6 Chigwell
15.01.00	Jawaid Khaliq L RSC 4 Doncaster
13.08.00	Gavin Down L PTS 6 Nottingham
30.09.00	John Tiftik L PTS 6 Chigwell
24.11.00	Rob Stevenson L PTS 6 Hull
11.12.00	Brian Coleman L CO 4 Cleethorpes
24.03.01	Francie Doherty L RSC 3 Sheffield

Career: 27 contests, won 4, lost 23.

Lee Blundell

Wigan. *Born* Wigan, 11 August, 1971
Middleweight. Central Area L. Middleweight Champion. Ht. 6'2"
Manager L. Veitch

25.04.94	Robert Harper W RSC 2 Bury
20.05.94	Freddie Yemofio W RSC 6 Acton
08.09.94	Gordon Blair DREW 6 Glasgow
07.12.94	Kesem Clayton W RTD 2 Stoke
18.02.95	Glenn Catley L RSC 6 Shepton Mallet
11.12.95	Martin Jolley W PTS 6 Morecambe
16.03.97	Martin Jolley W PTS 6 Shaw
08.05.97	Paul Jones L RSC 4 Mansfield
19.09.99	Dean Ashton W RSC 4 Shaw
28.10.99	Jason Collins DREW 6 Burnley
06.12.99	Danny Thornton W PTS 6 Bradford
05.03.00	Ian Toby W RTD 3 Shaw
21.05.00	Phil Epton W RSC 2 Shaw
30.11.00	Danny Thornton W RSC 8 Blackpool *(Vacant Central Area L. Middleweight Title)*
08.03.01	Paul Wesley W RSC 3 Blackpool
03.04.01	Spencer Fearon W PTS 6 Bethnal Green

Career: 16 contests, won 12, drew 2, lost 2.

Neil Bonner

Abergele. *Born* Enfield, 13 October, 1975
L. Middleweight. Ht. 5'9"
Manager J. Davies

22.09.00	Drea Dread W RSC 4 Wrexham
03.11.00	James Lee L PTS 4 Ebbw Vale
04.02.01	Richard Inquieti W PTS 6 Queensferry

Career: 3 contests, won 2, lost 1.

Neil Bonner   Les Clark

Paul Bonson

Featherstone. *Born* Castleford, 18 October, 1971
Cruiserweight. Former Central Area L. Heavyweight Champion. Ht. 5'10"
Manager M. Marsden

04.10.96	Michael Pinnock W PTS 6 Wakefield
14.11.96	Michael Pinnock DREW 6 Sheffield
22.12.96	Pele Lawrence DREW 6 Salford
20.04.97	Shamus Casey W PTS 6 Leeds
26.06.97	Andy Manning L PTS 6 Sheffield
19.09.97	Mike Gormley W PTS 6 Salford
03.10.97	Rudi Marcussen L PTS 4 Copenhagen, Denmark
03.12.97	Alex Mason DREW 6 Stoke
14.12.97	Willie Quinn L RSC 4 Glasgow
15.01.98	Alex Mason L PTS 6 Solihull
13.02.98	Peter Mason L PTS 4 Seaham
23.02.98	Martin McDonough W PTS 6 Windsor
07.03.98	Michael Bowen L PTS 6 Reading
14.03.98	Alain Simon L PTS 6 Pont St Maxence, France
08.04.98	Tim Brown DREW 4 Liverpool
21.05.98	Mark Hobson L PTS 6 Bradford
21.06.98	Kenny Rainford L PTS 6 Liverpool
01.09.98	Roberto Dominguez L PTS 8 Vigo, Spain
23.10.98	Rob Galloway W PTS 6 Wakefield
16.11.98	Chris P. Bacon L PTS 8 Glasgow
11.12.98	Robert Zlotkowski L PTS 4 Prestwick
20.12.98	Glenn Williams L PTS 6 Salford
24.04.99	Kenny Gayle DREW 4 Peterborough
29.05.99	Dave Johnson L PTS 6 South Shields
19.06.99	Sebastiaan Rothmann L PTS 8 Dublin
12.07.99	Jim Twite L PTS 6 Coventry
07.08.99	Juan Nelongo L PTS 8 Arona, Tenerife
11.09.99	Mark Hobson L PTS 4 Sheffield
02.10.99	Enzo Maccarinelli L PTS 4 Cardiff
16.10.99	Robert Zlotkowski L PTS 6 Bethnal Green
27.10.99	Peter McCormack W PTS 6 Birmingham
04.12.99	Glenn Williams W PTS 4 Manchester

11.12.99 Chris Davies L PTS 4 Merthyr
05.02.00 Paul Maskell L PTS 4 Bethnal Green
11.03.00 Tony Booth L PTS 4 Kensington
26.03.00 Wayne Buck L PTS 8 Nottingham
29.04.00 Cathal O'Grady L PTS 4 Wembley
13.05.00 Mark Hobson L PTS 4 Barnsley
25.06.00 Andy Manning W PTS 10 Wakefield
(Vacant Central L. Heavyweight Title)
08.09.00 Robert Milewicz L PTS 4 Hammersmith
21.10.00 Jon Penn L PTS 6 Sheffield
12.11.00 Glenn Williams L PTS 10 Manchester
(Central Area L.Heavyweight Title Defence)
24.11.00 Alex Mason L PTS 6 Darlington
09.12.00 Mark Baker L PTS 6 Southwark
23.01.01 Calvin Stonestreet W PTS 4 Crawley
03.02.01 Tony Dodson L PTS 4 Manchester
18.02.01 Butch Lesley L PTS 6 Southwark
13.03.01 Konstantin Schvets L PTS 6 Plymouth
07.04.01 Rob Hayes-Scott L PTS 4 Wembley
26.04.01 Mike White L PTS 6 Gateshead
17.05.01 Clint Johnson W PTS 6 Leeds
24.05.01 Sven Hamer L PTS 4 Kensington
04.06.01 Joe Gillon DREW 6 Glasgow
11.06.01 Darren Chubbs L PTS 4 Nottingham
21.06.01 Michael Pinnock W PTS 6 Sheffield
Career: 55 contests, won 11, drew 6, lost 38.

Jason Booth

Nottingham. *Born* Nottingham, 7 November, 1977
British & Commonwealth Flyweight Champion. Ht. 5'4"
Manager Self

13.06.96 Darren Noble W RSC 3 Sheffield
24.10.96 Marty Chestnut W PTS 6 Lincoln
27.11.96 Jason Thomas W PTS 4 Swansea
18.01.97 David Coldwell W PTS 4 Swadlincote
07.03.97 Pete Buckley W PTS 6 Northampton
20.03.97 Danny Lawson W RSC 3 Newark
10.05.97 Anthony Hanna W PTS 6 Nottingham
19.05.97 Chris Lyons W PTS 6 Cleethorpes
31.10.97 Mark Reynolds W PTS 6 Ilkeston
31.01.98 Anthony Hanna W PTS 6 Edmonton

20.03.98 Louis Veitch W CO 2 Ilkeston
(Elim. British Flyweight Title)
09.06.98 Dimitar Alipiev W RSC 2 Hull
17.10.98 Graham McGrath W RSC 4 Manchester
07.12.98 Louis Veitch W RSC 5 Cleethorpes
08.05.99 David Guerault L PTS 12 Grande Synthe, France
(European Flyweight Title Challenge)
12.07.99 Mark Reynolds W RSC 3 Coventry
16.10.99 Keith Knox W RSC 10 Belfast
(British & Commonwealth Flyweight Title Challenges)
22.01.00 Abie Mnisi W PTS 12 Birmingham
(Commonwealth Flyweight Title Defence)
01.07.00 John Barnes W PTS 6 Manchester
13.11.00 Ian Napa W PTS 12 Bethnal Green
(British & Commonwealth Flyweight Title Defences)
26.02.01 Nokuthula Tshabangu W CO 2 Nottingham
(Commonwealth Flyweight Title Defence)
30.06.01 Alexander Mahmutov L PTS 12 Madrid, Spain
(European Flyweight Title Challenge)
Career: 22 contests, won 20, lost 2.

Nicky Booth

Nottingham. *Born* Nottingham, 21 January, 1980
British & Commonwealth Bantamweight Champion. Ht. 5'5"
Manager M. Shinfield

26.02.98 Shane Mallon W RSC 4 Hull
15.05.98 Marty Chestnut W PTS 6 Nottingham
14.07.98 Ian Napa L PTS 6 Reading
11.09.98 Anthony Hanna DREW 6 Cleethorpes
25.11.98 Anthony Hanna L PTS 6 Clydach
30.04.99 Delroy Spencer W PTS 6 Scunthorpe
06.06.99 Delroy Spencer W PTS 4 Nottingham
20.09.99 Russell Laing W PTS 8 Glasgow
03.12.99 David Jeffrey W PTS 4 Peterborough
03.03.00 Shaun Anderson W PTS 6 Irvine

22.05.00 Gareth Payne W PTS 4 Coventry
24.09.00 Gary Ford W PTS 6 Shaw
09.10.00 Tommy Waite W PTS 12 Liverpool
(British & Commonwealth Bantamweight Title Challenges)
26.02.01 Ady Lewis W RSC 7 Nottingham
(British & Commonwealth Bantamweight Title Defences)
11.06.01 Kevin Gerowski W RSC 4 Nottingham
Career: 15 contests, won 12, drew 1, lost 2.

Tony Booth

Hull. *Born* Hull, 30 January, 1970
Former Undefeated British Masters L. Heavyweight Champion. Former Undefeated British Central Area Cruiserweight Champion. Ht. 5'11¼"
Manager M. Dalton

08.03.90 Paul Lynch L PTS 6 Watford
11.04.90 Mick Duncan W PTS 6 Dewsbury
26.04.90 Colin Manners W PTS 6 Halifax
16.05.90 Tommy Warde W PTS 6 Hull
05.06.90 Gary Dyson W PTS 6 Liverpool
05.09.90 Shaun McCrory L PTS 6 Stoke
08.10.90 Bullit Andrews W RSC 3 Cleethorpes
23.01.91 Darron Griffiths DREW 6 Stoke
06.02.91 Shaun McCrory L PTS 6 Liverpool
06.03.91 Billy Brough L PTS 6 Glasgow
18.03.91 Billy Brough W PTS 6 Glasgow
28.03.91 Neville Brown L PTS 6 Alfreton
17.05.91 Glenn Campbell L RSC 2 Bury
(Central Area S. Middleweight Title Challenge)
25.07.91 Paul Murray W PTS 6 Dudley
01.08.91 Nick Manners DREW 8 Dewsbury
11.09.91 Jim Peters L PTS 8 Hammersmith
28.10.91 Eddie Smulders L RSC 6 Arnhem, Holland
09.12.91 Steve Lewsam L PTS 8 Cleethorpes
30.01.92 Serg Fame W PTS 6 Southampton
12.02.92 Tenko Ernie W RSC 4 Wembley
05.03.92 John Beckles W RSC 6 Battersea
26.03.92 Dave Owens W PTS 6 Hull
08.04.92 Michael Gale L PTS 8 Leeds
13.05.92 Phil Soundy W PTS 6 Kensington
02.06.92 Eddie Smulders L RSC 1 Rotterdam, Holland
18.07.92 Maurice Core L PTS 6 Manchester
07.09.92 James Cook L PTS 8 Bethnal Green
30.10.92 Roy Richie DREW 6 Istrees, France
18.11.92 Tony Wilson DREW 8 Solihull
25.12.92 Francis Wanyama L PTS 6 Izegem, Belgium
09.02.93 Tony Wilson W PTS 8 Wolverhampton
01.05.93 Ralf Rocchigiani DREW 8 Berlin, Germany
03.06.93 Victor Cordoba L PTS 8 Marseille, France
23.06.93 Tony Behan W PTS 6 Gorleston
01.07.93 Michael Gale L PTS 8 York
17.09.93 Ole Klemetsen L PTS 8 Copenhagen, Denmark
07.10.93 Denzil Browne DREW 8 York
02.11.93 James Cook L PTS 8 Southwark
12.11.93 Carlos Christie W PTS 6 Hull
28.01.94 Francis Wanyama L RSC 2 Waregem, Belgium
(Vacant Commonwealth Cruiserweight Title)
26.03.94 Torsten May L PTS 6 Dortmund, Germany
21.07.94 Mark Prince L RSC 3 Battersea
24.09.94 Johnny Held L PTS 8 Rotterdam, Holland

Nicky (left) and Jason Booth   Les Clark

07.10.94 Dirk Wallyn L PTS 6 Waregem, Belgium
27.10.94 Dean Francis L CO 1 Bayswater
23.01.95 Jan Lefeber L PTS 8 Rotterdam, Holland
07.03.95 John Foreman L PTS 6 Edgbaston
27.04.95 Art Stacey W PTS 10 Hull
(Vacant Central Area Cruiserweight Title)
04.06.95 Montell Griffin L RSC 2 Bethnal Green
06.07.95 Nigel Rafferty W RSC 7 Hull
22.07.95 Mark Prince L RSC 2 Millwall
06.09.95 Leif Keiski L PTS 8 Helsinki, Finland
25.09.95 Neil Simpson W PTS 8 Cleethorpes
06.10.95 Don Diego Poeder L RSC 2 Waregem, Belgium
11.11.95 Bruce Scott L RSC 3 Halifax
16.12.95 John Marceta L RSC 2 Cardiff
20.01.96 Johnny Nelson L RSC 2 Mansfield
15.03.96 Slick Miller W PTS 6 Hull
27.03.96 Neil Simpson L PTS 6 Whitwick
17.05.96 Mark Richardson W RSC 2 Hull
13.07.96 Bruce Scott L PTS 8 Bethnal Green
03.09.96 Paul Douglas L PTS 6 Belfast
14.09.96 Kelly Oliver L RSC 2 Sheffield
06.11.96 Martin Jolley W PTS 4 Hull
22.11.96 Slick Miller W RSC 5 Hull
11.12.96 Crawford Ashley L RSC 1 Southwark
18.01.97 Kelly Oliver L RSC 4 Swadlincote
27.02.97 Kevin Morton L PTS 6 Hull
25.03.97 Nigel Rafferty DREW 8 Wolverhampton
04.04.97 John Wilson L PTS 6 Glasgow
16.04.97 Robert Norton L RSC 4 Bethnal Green
15.05.97 Phill Day W PTS 4 Reading
11.09.97 Steve Bristow L PTS 4 Widnes
22.09.97 Martin Langtry W PTS 4 Cleethorpes
04.10.97 Bruce Scott W PTS 8 Muswell Hill
28.11.97 Martin Jolley L PTS 6 Hull
15.12.97 Nigel Rafferty W PTS 6 Cleethorpes
06.03.98 Peter Mason W RSC 3 Hull
09.06.98 Crawford Ashley L RSC 6 Hull
(British L. Heavyweight Title Challenge. Vacant Commonwealth L. Heavyweight Title)
18.07.98 Omar Sheika W PTS 8 Sheffield
26.09.98 Toks Owoh L PTS 6 Norwich
29.10.98 Nigel Rafferty W PTS 8 Bayswater
14.12.98 Sven Hamer L PTS 6 Cleethorpes
05.01.99 Ali Saidi W RSC 4 Epernay, France
17.05.99 Darren Ashton W PTS 6 Cleethorpes
12.07.99 Neil Simpson L PTS 10 Coventry
(Elim. British L. Heavyweight Title)
27.09.99 Adam Cale W PTS 6 Cleethorpes
16.10.99 Cathal O'Grady L CO 4 Belfast
18.01.00 Michael Sprott L PTS 6 Mansfield
12.02.00 Thomas Hansvoll L PTS 6 Sheffield
29.02.00 John Keeton L RSC 2 Widnes
09.04.00 Greg Scott-Briggs W PTS 10 Alfreton
(Vacant British Masters L. Heavyweight Title)
15.05.00 Michael Pinnock W PTS 6 Cleethorpes
19.06.00 Toks Owoh L RSC 3 Burton
08.09.00 Dominic Negus W PTS 6 Bristol
30.09.00 Robert Norton L RSC 3 Peterborough
31.10.00 Firat Aslan L RSC 2 Hammersmith
11.12.00 Mark Krence L PTS 6 Sheffield
05.02.01 Denzil Browne L RSC 5 Hull
(Vacant Central Area Cruiserweight Title)
01.04.01 Kenny Gayle DREW 4 Southwark
10.04.01 Mark Baker L PTS 4 Wembley
16.06.01 Butch Lesley L RSC 3 Dagenham
Career: 102 contests, won 36, drew 8, lost 58.

Elias Boswell
Blackpool. *Born* Carlisle, 27 July, 1977
L. Welterweight. Ht. 5'9"
Manager L. Veitch

02.03.00 Chris Steele L RSC 4 Blackpool
09.06.00 Dave Hinds L RSC 5 Blackpool
08.03.01 Mark Halstead L RSC 5 Blackpool
Career: 3 contests, lost 3.

Alan Bosworth
Northampton. *Born* Northampton, 31 December, 1967
L. Welterweight. Ht. 5'7"
Manager N. Christian

17.10.95 Simon Hamblett W RSC 2 Wolverhampton
29.10.95 Shaun Gledhill W PTS 6 Shaw
16.11.95 Brian Coleman W PTS 6 Evesham
23.11.95 David Thompson W RSC 4 Tynemouth
13.01.96 Jason Blanche W PTS 6 Halifax
31.01.96 Arv Mittoo W PTS 6 Stoke
16.02.96 John Docherty W PTS 6 Irvine
24.03.96 Scott Walker DREW 6 Shaw
16.05.96 Yifru Retta W PTS 6 Dunstable
07.03.97 Wayne Rigby L RSC 5 Northampton
09.09.97 Colin Dunne L RSC 8 Bethnal Green
31.10.98 Alan Temple L PTS 6 Basingstoke
26.02.99 Des Sowden W PTS 6 Longford
13.03.99 Paul Burke L PTS 6 Manchester
24.04.99 Jan Bergman L RSC 6 Munich, Germany
02.07.99 Keith Jones W PTS 6 Bristol
24.09.99 Woody Greenaway L PTS 6 Merthyr
03.12.99 Darren Underwood W CO 5 Peterborough
20.01.00 Brian Coleman W PTS 6 Piccadilly
24.03.00 Allan Vester L PTS 12 Aarhus, Denmark
(IBF Inter-Continental L. Welterweight Title Challenge)
28.04.00 George Scott L PTS 8 Copenhagen, Denmark
02.06.00 Mohamed Helel W PTS 6 Ashford
25.07.00 Shea Neary L PTS 6 Southwark
01.12.00 David Kirk DREW 8 Peterborough
13.03.01 Eamonn Magee L RSC 5 Plymouth
23.06.01 Keith Jones W PTS 6 Peterborough
Career: 26 contests, won 14, drew 2, lost 10.

Ivan Botton
Newark. *Born* Nottingham, 8 October, 1979
Cruiserweight. Ht. 6'1¼"
Manager D. Smith

20.03.00 Dean Ashton W RSC 2 Mansfield
11.05.00 Matthew Pepper W RSC 4 Newark
29.01.01 Michael Pinnock L PTS 4 Peterborough
02.06.01 Adam Cale W PTS 4 Wakefield
Career: 4 contests, won 3, lost 1.

Karim Bouali
Canning Town. *Born* France, 19 June, 1973
WBU International L. Welterweight Champion. Ht. 5'6"
Manager A. Bowers

10.11.98 Imed Benkalifa L PTS 4 Grand Synthe, France
20.05.99 Hussain Osman L PTS 4 Barking
26.06.99 Kevin McIntyre W RTD 1 Glasgow

10.07.99 Chris Barnett DREW 6 Southwark
27.09.99 Brian Gifford W RSC 3 Cleethorpes
01.12.99 Kevin Bennett L PTS 4 Yarm
25.02.00 Dennis Griffin W RSC 2 Newmarket
02.03.00 Tommy Peacock W PTS 4 Birkenhead
09.03.00 Ross McCord W RSC 1 Bethnal Green
08.09.00 Jason Williams W RSC 5 Bristol
21.09.00 Gary Reid W PTS 4 Bloomsbury
10.11.00 Paul Burns W RSC 3 Mayfair
09.03.01 Franck Benoni W RSC 8 Millwall
(Vacant WBU International L. Welterweight Title)
Career: 13 contests, won 9, drew 1, lost 3.

Micky Bowden
Forest Hill. *Born* Lewisham, 30 June, 1975
Featherweight. Ht. 5'8"
Manager Self

25.02.99 Kevin Gerowski W PTS 4 Kentish Town
09.05.99 Graham McGrath W RSC 4 Bracknell
07.08.99 Brendan Bryce W PTS 4 Dagenham
26.05.01 Anthony Hanna W PTS 4 Bethnal Green
Career: 4 contests, won 4.

Mark Bowen
Bilston. *Born* Wolverhampton, 11 September, 1974
Lightweight. Ht. 5'7"
Manager P. Bowen

08.03.01 Woody Greenaway DREW 6 Stoke
Career: 1 contest, drew 1.

Michael Bowen
West Ham. *Born* Forest Gate, 14 November, 1974
S. Middleweight. Ht. 6'0½"
Manager Self

02.06.95 Robert Harper W PTS 6 Bethnal Green
09.12.95 Peter Varnavas W CO 3 Bethnal Green
13.02.96 Henry Price W RSC 1 Millwall
13.04.96 Danny Ryan W RSC 2 Wythenshawe
11.05.96 Mark Dawson W PTS 4 Bethnal Green
25.02.97 Mark Dawson W RSC 4 Sheffield
29.11.97 Peter Mason W RSC 2 Norwich
24.01.98 Martin Jolley W RSC 5 Cardiff
07.03.98 Paul Bonson W PTS 6 Reading
14.11.98 Robert Peel W RTD 4 Cheshunt
03.04.99 Glenn Williams W RSC 8 Kensington
25.07.00 Jason Hart W RSC 1 Southwark
26.03.01 Jon Penn W RSC 5 Wembley
Career: 13 contests, won 13.

Paul Bowen
West Ham. *Born* Barking, 14 May, 1973
Former Undefeated Southern Area S. Middleweight Champion. Ht. 6'0"
Manager Self

13.02.96 Lee Bird W RSC 2 Bethnal Green
13.04.96 Pat Durkin W RSC 3 Wythenshawe
13.07.96 Mark Dawson W RSC 3 Bethnal Green
08.02.97 Darren Ashton W PTS 4 Millwall
29.11.97 Ian Toby W RSC 4 Norwich
17.01.98 Mark Dawson W PTS 4 Bristol
16.05.98 Eddie Knight W RSC 3 Bethnal Green
10.10.98 Enzo Giordano W RSC 10 Bethnal Green
(Vacant Southern Area S. Middleweight Title)

27.02.99	Phil Epton W RSC 2 Oldham	
05.06.99	Matthew Barney DREW 10 Cardiff	

(Southern Area S. Middleweight Title Defence)

25.07.00	Andy Manning W PTS 4 Southwark
18.11.00	Paul Wesley W PTS 4 Dagenham
03.04.01	Ruben Groenewald L PTS 6 Bethnal Green

Career: 13 contests, won 11, drew 1, lost 1.

Matthew Bowers

Southampton. *Born* Fareham, 3 September, 1973
Middleweight. Ht. 5'7½"
Manager J. Bishop

23.09.00	Spencer Fearon L RSC 2 Bethnal Green
22.10.00	Sol Gilbert W RSC 1 Streatham

Career: 2 contests, won 1, lost 1.

Shaun Bowes

Esh Winning. *Born* Durham, 4 October, 1973
Cruiserweight. Ht. 5'10"
Manager G. McCrory

26.04.01	Tony Moran W PTS 6 Gateshead

Career: 1 contest, won 1.

Christian Brady

Birmingham. *Born* Birmingham, 23 July, 1970
Midlands Area Welterweight Champion. Ht. 5'8"
Manager Self

02.12.96	Shaun Gledhill W RTD 3 Birmingham
03.03.97	Vic Broomhead W PTS 6 Birmingham
09.06.97	Tony Smith W RSC 4 Birmingham
06.10.97	David Kirk W PTS 6 Birmingham
08.12.97	Craig Kelley W PTS 8 Birmingham
02.03.98	Craig Kelley W RTD 5 Birmingham
08.06.98	Dean Bramhald W PTS 6 Birmingham
12.10.98	Brian Coleman W PTS 6 Birmingham
26.10.98	Darren McInulty W PTS 6 Manchester
26.11.98	Dewi Roberts W RSC 7 Edgbaston
13.03.00	Harry Butler W PTS 6 Birmingham
15.05.00	Delroy Mellis L RSC 6 Birmingham
21.05.01	Matt Scriven W RSC 5 Birmingham

(Vacant Midlands Area Welterweight Title)

Career: 13 contests, won 12, lost 1.

Joe Brame

London. *Born* Portsmouth, 2 October, 1975
L. Heavyweight. Ht. 5'8¼"
Manager J. Bishop

25.02.01	Simon Andrews W RSC 5 Streatham

Career: 1 contest, won 1.

Jason Brewster

Coseley. *Born* Wolverhampton, 6 February, 1971
Heavyweight. Ht. 6'1"
Manager C. Flute

23.06.99	Mark Williams DREW 6 West Bromwich
03.09.99	Adam Cale W PTS 6 West Bromwich
01.10.99	Scott Baker L RTD 5 Cleethorpes

18.02.00	Nigel Rafferty L PTS 6 West Bromwich
11.05.00	Tony Dowling L RSC 2 Newark
09.06.00	Paul Richardson L PTS 6 Blackpool
10.09.00	Adam Cale W PTS 4 Walsall
06.11.00	Nigel Rafferty W PTS 8 Wolverhampton
13.11.00	Mark McManus L RTD 2 Bethnal Green
01.04.01	Paul Richardson L RSC 4 Wolverhampton
20.05.01	Kevin Burton W PTS 6 Wolverhampton

Career: 11 contests, won 4, drew 1, lost 6.

Jason Brewster   Les Clark

Michael Brodie

Manchester. *Born* Manchester, 10 May, 1974
Former Undefeated British, European & Commonwealth S. Bantamweight Champion. Ht. 5'6"
Manager J. Trickett

03.10.94	Graham McGrath W RSC 5 Manchester
20.10.94	Chip O'Neill W CO 3 Middleton
28.11.94	Muhammad Shaffique W CO 2 Manchester
13.12.94	Pete Buckley W PTS 6 Potters Bar
16.02.95	G. G. Goddard W PTS 6 Bury
03.04.95	Garry Burrell W RSC 4 Manchester
05.05.95	G. G. Goddard W PTS 6 Swansea
17.05.95	Ian Reid W RSC 3 Ipswich
10.06.95	Chris Clarkson W PTS 6 Manchester
14.11.95	Niel Leggett W CO 1 Bury
25.11.95	Karl Morling W RSC 1 Dagenham
18.12.95	Marty Chestnut W RTD 3 Mayfair
26.02.96	Bamana Dibateza W PTS 6 Manchester
13.04.96	John Sillo W CO 1 Liverpool
07.05.96	Elvis Parsley W RSC 1 Mayfair
06.07.96	Colin Innes W RSC 2 Manchester

19.09.96	Ervine Blake W RSC 4 Manchester
09.11.96	Miguel Matthews W PTS 6 Manchester
22.03.97	Neil Swain W RSC 10 Wythenshawe

(Vacant British S. Bantamweight Title)

30.08.97	Pete Buckley W PTS 8 Cheshunt
01.11.97	Wilson Docherty W CO 4 Glasgow

(British S. Bantamweight Title Defence. Vacant Commonwealth S. Bantamweight Title)

31.01.98	Brian Carr W RSC 10 Edmonton

(British & Commonwealth S. Bantamweight Title Defences)

23.05.98	Simon Ramoni W PTS 12 Bethnal Green

(Commonwealth S. Bantamweight Title Defence)

17.10.98	Sergei Devakov W PTS 12 Manchester

(European S. Bantamweight Title Challenge)

13.03.99	Salim Medjkoune W RSC 9 Manchester

(European S. Bantamweight Title Defence)

31.07.99	Serge Poilblan W RSC 12 Carlisle

(European S. Bantamweight Title Defence)

01.10.99	Drew Docherty W RSC 6 Bethnal Green

(European S. Bantamweight Title Defence)

26.02.00	Salim Medjkoune W RSC 9 Carlisle

(European S. Bantamweight Title Defence)

01.07.00	Mustapha Hame W CO 4 Manchester

(European S.Bantamweight Title Defence)

09.09.00	Willie Jorrin L PTS 12 Manchester

(Vacant WBC S.Bantamweight Title)

03.02.01	Sergio Aguila W RSC 4 Manchester

Career: 31 contests, won 30, lost 1.

Steve Brook

Pontefract. *Born* Pontefract, 6 August, 1975
Featherweight. Ht. 5'8"
Manager C. Aston

15.09.99	Peter Allen W PTS 6 Harrogate
26.11.99	Tom Wood W PTS 6 Wakefield
09.12.99	Tom Wood W PTS 6 Sunderland
24.01.00	Barry Hawthorne DREW 4 Glasgow
05.02.00	Marc Callaghan L RSC 2 Bethnal Green
26.03.00	Nigel Senior W PTS 6 Nottingham
17.04.00	Nigel Senior W PTS 6 Bradford
18.09.00	Andrew Ferrans L PTS 6 Glasgow
05.10.00	John Barnes L PTS 6 Sunderland
20.10.00	Kevin England W PTS 6 Manchester

Career: 10 contests, won 6, drew 1, lost 3.

Casey Brooke

Great Wyrley. *Born* Birmingham, 8 July, 1971
Welterweight. Ht. 5'11"
Manager Self

06.06.00	Arv Mittoo L PTS 6 Brierley Hill
07.07.00	John Tiftik L RSC 2 Chigwell
10.10.00	Rene Grayel L PTS 6 Brierley Hill
28.11.00	Rene Grayel L PTS 6 Brierley Hill
03.02.01	Gary Harrison L PTS 6 Brighton
12.03.01	Tony Smith L PTS 6 Birmingham

Career: 6 contests, lost 6.

Mark Brookes

Swinton. *Born* Doncaster, 1 December, 1979
S. Middleweight. Ht. 6'0"
Manager D. Hobson

21.10.00 Rob Galloway W RSC 5 Sheffield
11.12.00 Jimmy Steel W PTS 6 Sheffield
24.03.01 Matthew Pepper W RSC 1 Sheffield
18.06.01 Clint Johnson W PTS 6 Bradford
Career: 4 contests, won 4.

Cathy Brown

Peckham. *Born* Leeds, 28 July, 1970
WBF European Flyweight Champion. Ht. 5'2"
Manager Self

31.10.99 Veerle Braspenningsx W PTS 5 Raynes Park
05.02.00 Veerle Braspenningsx W RSC 6 Sint-Truiden, Belgium
01.07.00 Jan Wild W PTS 6 Southwark
 (Vacant WBF European Flyweight Title)
31.10.00 Viktoria Vargal W RSC 3 Hammersmith
28.02.01 Marietta Ivanova W PTS 4 Kensington
26.04.01 Oksana Vasilieva L PTS 4 Kensington
16.06.01 Romona Gughie W RSC 3 Wembley
Career: 7 contests, won 6, lost 1.

Damien Brown

March. *Born* Peterborough, 3 November, 1978
L. Middleweight. Ht. 5'10"
Manager C. Sanigar

05.03.00 Julian Kacanolli W PTS 6 Peterborough
01.12.00 Ross Murray L CO 1 Peterborough
Career: 2 contests, won 1, lost 1.

Damien Brown   Les Clark

Denzil Browne

Leeds. *Born* Leeds, 21 January, 1969
Central Area Cruiserweight Champion. Ht. 6'2½"
Manager D. Smith

18.10.90 Mark Bowen W PTS 6 Dewsbury
29.11.90 R. F. McKenzie L PTS 6 Sunderland
13.12.90 Gary Railton W RSC 2 Dewsbury
21.02.91 Mark Bowen W PTS 6 Walsall
21.03.91 R. F. McKenzie W PTS 6 Dewsbury
09.05.91 Darren McKenna W PTS 6 Leeds
27.06.91 Steve Yorath W PTS 6 Leeds
01.08.91 Tony Colclough W RSC 1 Dewsbury
09.10.91 R. F. McKenzie L PTS 6 Manchester
30.10.91 Gus Mendes W RSC 6 Leeds
23.01.92 Darren McKenna W PTS 6 York
19.03.92 Ian Bulloch W PTS 8 York
23.09.92 Steve Yorath W PTS 8 Leeds
29.10.92 Sean O'Phoenix W RSC 4 Leeds
25.02.93 Cordwell Hylton W PTS 8 Bradford
22.04.93 Dave Muhammed W PTS 8 Mayfair
01.07.93 Steve Osborne W RSC 1 York
07.10.93 Tony Booth DREW 8 York
01.12.93 Lennie Howard W RSC 6 Kensington
26.10.94 Steve Lewsam W CO 2 Leeds
21.01.95 Dennis Andries L RSC 11 Glasgow
 (Vacant British Cruiserweight Title)
08.07.95 Bobbi Joe Edwards L PTS 8 York
11.11.95 John Keeton L RSC 4 Halifax
13.01.96 Albert Call W PTS 6 Halifax
04.06.96 Bobbi Joe Edwards W PTS 10 York
 (Vacant Central Area Cruiserweight Title)
25.03.97 Chris Okoh L PTS 12 Lewisham
 (Commonwealth Cruiserweight Title Challenge)
05.02.01 Tony Booth W RSC 5 Hull
 (Vacant Central Area Cruiserweight Title)
02.06.01 Lee Swaby DREW 8 Wakefield
Career: 28 contests, won 20, drew 2, lost 6.

(Taiwo) Ty Browne

Portsmouth. *Born* London, 28 June, 1977
Middleweight. Ht. 5'8¾"
Manager R. Davies

03.02.01 Chris Duggan W RSC 1 Brighton
05.05.01 Leigh Wicks W PTS 6 Brighton
Career: 2 contests, won 2.

Darren Bruce

Grays. *Born* Orsett, 1 December, 1972
Former Undefeated IBO Inter-Continental Welterweight Champion. Ht. 5'11"
Manager B. Hearn

28.11.97 Noel Henry W RSC 1 Bethnal Green
27.01.98 Darren McInulty W PTS 4 Bethnal Green
11.03.98 Kevin Lang W RSC 6 Bethnal Green
02.05.98 Harry Butler W RSC 6 Kensington
05.06.98 Leigh Wicks W PTS 6 Southend
08.09.98 Darren McInulty W CO 1 Bethnal Green
31.10.98 Shaun O'Neill W RSC 1 Southend
06.11.98 Delroy Mellis W RTD 3 Mayfair
11.12.98 John Green W RSC 1 Cheshunt
26.02.99 George Richards W PTS 6 Coventry
27.04.99 Dennis Berry W RSC 3 Bethnal Green
29.06.99 Frederic Noto L PTS 10 Bethnal Green

16.10.99 Charlie Kane W RTD 5 Bethnal Green
 (Vacant IBO Inter-Continental Welterweight Title)
05.02.00 Michael Smyth W CO 5 Bethnal Green
 (IBO Inter-Continental Welterweight Title Defence)
11.03.00 Mark Ramsey DREW 6 Kensington
02.12.00 Willy Wise L PTS 12 Bethnal Green
 (Vacant IBO Welterweight Title)
Career: 16 contests, won 13, drew 1, lost 2.

Steve Brumant

Birmingham. *Born* Birmingham, 18 May, 1971
L. Middleweight. Ht. 5'7"
Manager Self

18.09.97 Gerard Lawrence W CO 1 Alfreton
24.01.98 Anthony Farnell L PTS 4 Cardiff
28.04.98 Nicky Bardle W RSC 3 Brentford
24.03.99 Paul Dyer L PTS 4 Bayswater
20.05.99 David Kirk L PTS 4 Kensington
30.09.99 Delroy Mellis W PTS 6 Kensington
26.11.99 Scott Garrett W RSC 4 Bayswater
19.12.99 Wahid Fats L PTS 6 Salford
19.04.00 Karim Hussine L PTS 4 Kensington
24.06.00 Gerard Murphy L PTS 4 Glasgow
10.10.00 Jason Samuels L PTS 6 Brierley Hill
Career: 11 contests, won 4, lost 7.

Andrew Buchanan

West Denton. *Born* Newcastle, 24 March, 1980
Middleweight. Ht. 6'0"
Manager G. McCrory

01.12.00 Paul Johnson W PTS 4 Peterborough
28.03.01 Wayne Shepherd W RSC 2 Piccadilly
26.04.01 Steve Timms W RSC 4 Gateshead
Career: 3 contests, won 3.

Andrew Buchanan   Les Clark

Paul Buchanan

West Denton. *Born* Newcastle, 23 October, 1981
L. Heavyweight. Ht. 5'10"
Manager G. McCrory

31.01.01 Gary Jones W RTD 1 Piccadilly
26.04.01 Lee Woodruff W PTS 6 Gateshead
Career: 2 contests, won 2.

Pete Buckley

Birmingham. *Born* Birmingham, 9 March, 1969
L. Welterweight. Former Undefeated Midlands Area S. Featherweight Champion. Former Midlands Area S. Bantamweight Champion. Ht. 5'8"
Manager Self

04.10.89 Alan Baldwin DREW 6 Stafford
10.10.89 Ronnie Stephenson L PTS 6 Wolverhampton
30.10.89 Robert Braddock W PTS 6 Birmingham
14.11.89 Neil Leitch W PTS 6 Evesham
22.11.89 Peter Judson W PTS 6 Stafford
11.12.89 Stevie Woods W PTS 6 Bradford
21.12.89 Wayne Taylor W PTS 6 Kings Heath
10.01.90 John O'Meara W PTS 6 Kensington
19.02.90 Ian McGirr L PTS 6 Birmingham
27.02.90 Miguel Matthews DREW 6 Evesham
14.03.90 Ronnie Stephenson DREW 6 Stoke
04.04.90 Ronnie Stephenson L PTS 8 Stafford
23.04.90 Ronnie Stephenson W PTS 6 Birmingham
30.04.90 Chris Clarkson L PTS 8 Mayfair
17.05.90 Johnny Bredahl L PTS 6 Aars, Denmark
04.06.90 Ronnie Stephenson W PTS 8 Birmingham
28.06.90 Robert Braddock W RSC 5 Birmingham
01.10.90 Miguel Matthews W PTS 8 Cleethorpes
09.10.90 Miguel Matthews L PTS 8 Wolverhampton
17.10.90 Tony Smith W PTS 6 Stoke
29.10.90 Miguel Matthews W PTS 8 Birmingham
21.11.90 Drew Docherty L PTS 8 Solihull
10.12.90 Neil Leitch W PTS 8 Birmingham
10.01.91 Duke McKenzie L RSC 5 Wandsworth
18.02.91 Jamie McBride L PTS 8 Glasgow
04.03.91 Brian Robb W RSC 7 Birmingham
26.03.91 Neil Leitch DREW 8 Wolverhampton
01.05.91 Mark Geraghty W PTS 8 Solihull
05.06.91 Brian Robb W PTS 10 Wolverhampton
*(Vacant Midlands Area
S. Featherweight Title)*
09.09.91 Mike Deveney L PTS 8 Glasgow
24.09.91 Mark Bates W RTD 5 Basildon
29.10.91 John Armour L PTS 6 Kensington
14.11.91 Mike Deveney L PTS 6 Edinburgh
28.11.91 Craig Dermody L PTS 6 Liverpool
19.12.91 Craig Dermody L PTS 6 Oldham
18.01.92 Alan McKay DREW 8 Kensington
20.02.92 Brian Robb W RSC 10 Oakengates
*(Midlands Area S. Featherweight Title
Defence)*
27.04.92 Drew Docherty L PTS 8 Glasgow
15.05.92 Ruben Condori L PTS 10 Augsburg, Germany
29.05.92 Donnie Hood L PTS 8 Glasgow

07.09.92 Duke McKenzie L RTD 3 Bethnal Green
12.11.92 Prince Naseem Hamed L PTS 6 Liverpool
19.02.93 Harald Geier L PTS 12 Vienna, Austria
(Vacant WBA Penta-Continental S. Bantamweight Title)
26.04.93 Bradley Stone L PTS 8 Lewisham
18.06.93 Eamonn McAuley L PTS 6 Belfast
01.07.93 Tony Silkstone L PTS 8 York
06.10.93 Jonjo Irwin L PTS 8 Solihull
25.10.93 Drew Docherty L PTS 8 Glasgow
06.11.93 Michael Alldis L PTS 8 Bethnal Green
30.11.93 Barry Jones L PTS 4 Cardiff
19.12.93 Shaun Anderson L PTS 6 Glasgow
22.01.94 Barry Jones L PTS 8 Cardiff
29.01.94 Prince Naseem Hamed L RSC 4 Cardiff
10.03.94 Tony Falcone L PTS 4 Bristol
29.03.94 Conn McMullen W PTS 6 Bethnal Green
05.04.94 Mark Bowers L PTS 6 Bethnal Green
13.04.94 James Murray L PTS 6 Glasgow
06.05.94 Paul Lloyd L PTS 6 Liverpool
03.08.94 Greg Upton L PTS 6 Bristol
26.09.94 John Sillo L PTS 6 Liverpool
05.10.94 Matthew Harris L PTS 6 Wolverhampton
07.11.94 Marlon Ward L PTS 4 Piccadilly
23.11.94 Justin Murphy L PTS 4 Piccadilly
29.11.94 Neil Swain L PTS 4 Cardiff
13.12.94 Michael Brodie L PTS 6 Potters Bar
20.12.94 Michael Alldis L PTS 6 Bethnal Green
10.02.95 Matthew Harris W RSC 6 Birmingham
*(Midlands Area S. Bantamweight Title
Challenge)*
23.02.95 Paul Ingle L PTS 8 Southwark
20.04.95 John Sillo L PTS 6 Liverpool
27.04.95 Paul Ingle L PTS 8 Bethnal Green
09.05.95 Ady Lewis L PTS 4 Basildon
23.05.95 Spencer Oliver L PTS 4 Potters Bar
01.07.95 Dean Pithie L PTS 4 Kensington
21.09.95 Patrick Mullings L PTS 6 Battersea
29.09.95 Marlon Ward L PTS 4 Bethnal Green
25.10.95 Matthew Harris L PTS 10 Telford
*(Midlands Area S. Bantamweight Title
Defence)*
08.11.95 Vince Feeney L PTS 8 Bethnal Green
28.11.95 Barry Jones L PTS 6 Cardiff
15.12.95 Patrick Mullings L PTS 4 Bethnal Green
05.02.96 Patrick Mullings L PTS 8 Bexleyheath
09.03.96 Paul Griffin L PTS 4 Millstreet
21.03.96 Colin McMillan L RSC 3 Southwark
14.05.96 Venkatesan Deveraju L PTS 4 Dagenham
29.06.96 Matt Brown W RSC 1 Erith
03.09.96 Vince Feeney L PTS 4 Bethnal Green
28.09.96 Fabrice Benichou L PTS 8 Barking
09.10.96 Gary Marston DREW 8 Stoke
06.11.96 Neil Swain L PTS 4 Tylorstown
29.11.96 Alston Buchanan L PTS 8 Glasgow
22.12.96 Brian Carr L PTS 6 Glasgow
11.01.97 Scott Harrison L PTS 4 Bethnal Green
29.01.97 Carl Allen L PTS 8 Stoke
12.02.97 Ronnie McPhee L PTS 6 Glasgow
25.02.97 Dean Pithie L PTS 4 Sheffield
07.03.97 Jason Booth L PTS 6 Northampton
20.03.97 Thomas Bradley W PTS 6 Newark
08.04.97 Sergei Devakov L PTS 6 Bethnal Green
25.04.97 Matthew Harris L PTS 6 Cleethorpes
08.05.97 Gregorio Medina L RTD 2 Mansfield
13.06.97 Mike Deveney L PTS 6 Paisley

19.07.97 Richard Evatt L PTS 4 Wembley
30.08.97 Michael Brodie L PTS 8 Cheshunt
06.10.97 Brendan Bryce W PTS 6 Piccadilly
20.10.97 Kelton McKenzie L PTS 6 Leicester
20.11.97 Ervine Blake L PTS 8 Solihull
06.12.97 Danny Adams L PTS 4 Wembley
13.12.97 Gary Thornhill L PTS 6 Sheffield
31.01.98 Scott Harrison L PTS 4 Edmonton
05.03.98 Steve Conway L PTS 6 Leeds
18.03.98 Ervine Blake L PTS 8 Stoke
26.03.98 Graham McGrath W RTD 4 Solihull
11.04.98 Salim Medjkoune L PTS 6 Southwark
18.04.98 Tony Mulholland L PTS 4 Manchester
27.04.98 Alston Buchanan L PTS 8 Glasgow
11.05.98 Jason Squire W RTD 2 Leicester
21.05.98 Lee Armstrong L PTS 6 Bradford
06.06.98 Tony Mulholland L PTS 6 Liverpool
14.06.98 Lee Armstrong L PTS 6 Shaw
21.07.98 David Burke L PTS 6 Widnes
05.09.98 Michael Gomez L PTS 6 Telford
17.09.98 Brian Carr L PTS 6 Glasgow
03.10.98 Justin Murphy L PTS 6 Crawley
05.12.98 Lehlohonolo Ledwaba L PTS 8 Bristol
19.12.98 Acelino Freitas L RTD 3 Liverpool
09.02.99 Chris Jickells L PTS 6 Wolverhampton
16.02.99 Franny Hogg L PTS 6 Leeds
26.02.99 Richard Evatt L RSC 5 Coventry
17.04.99 Martin O'Malley L RSC 3 Dublin
29.05.99 Richie Wenton L PTS 6 Halifax
14.06.99 Carl Allen L PTS 6 Birmingham
26.06.99 Paul Halpin L PTS 4 Millwall
15.07.99 Salim Medjkoune L PTS 6 Peterborough
07.08.99 Steve Murray L PTS 6 Dagenham
12.09.99 Kevin Gerowski L PTS 6 Nottingham
20.09.99 Mat Zegan L PTS 6 Peterborough
02.10.99 Jason Cook L PTS 4 Cardiff
09.10.99 Brian Carr L PTS 6 Manchester
19.10.99 Gary Steadman L PTS 4 Bethnal Green
27.10.99 Miguel Matthews W PTS 8 Birmingham
20.11.99 Carl Greaves L PTS 10 Grantham
*(British Masters S. Featherweight Title
Challenge)*
11.12.99 Gary Thornhill L PTS 6 Liverpool
29.01.00 Bradley Pryce L PTS 4 Manchester
19.02.00 Gavin Rees L PTS 4 Dagenham
29.02.00 Tony Mulholland L PTS 4 Widnes
20.03.00 Carl Greaves L PTS 4 Mansfield
27.03.00 James Rooney L PTS 4 Barnsley
08.04.00 Delroy Pryce L PTS 4 Bethnal Green
17.04.00 Franny Hogg L PTS 8 Glasgow
11.05.00 Craig Spacie L PTS 4 Newark
25.05.00 Jimmy Phelan DREW 6 Hull
19.06.00 Delroy Pryce L PTS 4 Burton
01.07.00 Richard Evatt L PTS 4 Manchester
16.09.00 Lee Meager L PTS 4 Bethnal Green
23.09.00 Gavin Rees L PTS 4 Bethnal Green
02.10.00 Brian Carr L PTS 4 Glasgow
14.10.00 Gareth Jordan L PTS 4 Wembley
13.11.00 Kevin Lear L PTS 6 Bethnal Green
24.11.00 Lee Williamson L PTS 6 Hull
09.12.00 Leo O'Reilly L PTS 4 Southwark
15.01.01 Eddie Nevins L PTS 4 Manchester
23.01.01 David Burke L PTS 4 Crawley
31.01.01 Tony Montana L PTS 6 Piccadilly
19.02.01 Kevin England W PTS 6 Glasgow
12.03.01 Carl Allen L PTS 6 Birmingham
19.03.01 Duncan Armstrong L PTS 6 Glasgow
27.03.01 Carl Allen L PTS 8 Brierley Hill
05.05.01 Danny Hunt L PTS 4 Edmonton
09.06.01 Gary Thornhill L PTS 4 Bethnal Green
Career: 168 contests, won 27, drew 7, lost 134.

David Burke

Liverpool. *Born* Liverpool, 3 February, 1975
Lightweight. Ht. 5'9"
Manager J. Hyland

01.03.97	Ervine Blake W PTS 4 Liverpool
21.05.97	Carl Allen W PTS 4 Liverpool
26.09.97	Rudy Valentino W PTS 4 Liverpool
12.03.98	Bamana Dibateza W PTS 6 Liverpool
08.04.98	John O. Johnson W RSC 1 Liverpool
23.05.98	Mike Deveney W PTS 6 Bethnal Green
21.07.98	Pete Buckley W PTS 6 Widnes
24.10.98	Gary Flear W PTS 6 Liverpool
12.12.98	Justin Murphy W RSC 4 Southwark
05.03.99	Alan Temple W PTS 8 Liverpool
15.05.99	Marian Leonardu L RSC 3 Blackpool
19.06.99	Chris Williams W RTD 1 Dublin
13.12.99	Chris Jickells W PTS 6 Glasgow
09.03.00	Woody Greenaway W RSC 2 Liverpool
23.01.01	Pete Buckley W PTS 4 Crawley
03.02.01	Keith Jones W PTS 4 Manchester
03.03.01	Marco Fattore W RSC 1 Wembley
24.04.01	Jason Dee W RSC 1 Liverpool
26.05.01	Matthew Zulu W PTS 6 Bethnal Green

Career: 19 contests, won 18, lost 1.

Paul Burns

Liverpool. *Born* Liverpool, 15 July, 1971
Welterweight. Ht. 5'9½"
Manager T. Gilmour

16.06.95	Mick Mulcahy W RSC 3 Liverpool
08.09.95	Peter Varnavas W RSC 3 Liverpool
24.11.95	Donovan Davey W PTS 6 Chester
03.02.96	Rick North W PTS 4 Liverpool
06.09.96	Michael Alexander W RSC 4 Liverpool
03.12.96	Charlie Paine W PTS 6 Liverpool
26.09.97	Andreas Panayi W PTS 6 Liverpool
28.11.97	Ray Newby W PTS 6 Bethnal Green
12.03.98	Mustapha Belizid L PTS 8 Liverpool
08.04.98	Prince Kasi Kaihau L RSC 2 Liverpool
05.03.99	Harry Butler W RSC 5 Liverpool
15.05.99	Harry Dhami L PTS 8 Blackpool
09.03.00	Brian Coleman W PTS 6 Liverpool
10.11.00	Karim Bouali L RSC 3 Mayfair
24.04.01	Paul Denton W PTS 4 Liverpool

Career: 15 contests, won 11, lost 4.

Kevin Burton

Doncaster. *Born* Doncaster, 20 February, 1965
Cruiserweight. Ht. 5'10½"
Manager J. Rushton

10.05.93	Pat McNamara W RSC 2 Cleethorpes
07.06.93	Tony Colclough W PTS 6 Walsall
20.09.93	Bullit Andrews W PTS 6 Cleethorpes
30.09.93	Tony Colclough W DIS 5 Walsall
13.12.93	Tony Colclough W RSC 3 Doncaster
07.03.94	Bullit Andrews W RSC 1 Doncaster
07.04.94	Johnny Hooks L PTS 6 Walsall
10.05.94	Declan Faherty L RSC 4 Doncaster
12.10.94	Tony Colclough W PTS 6 Stoke
25.10.94	Chris Nurse W RSC 1 Edgbaston
12.12.94	Jem Jackson W RSC 4 Doncaster
09.02.95	Dave Battey L PTS 6 Doncaster
05.05.95	Dave Battey L PTS 6 Doncaster
16.05.95	Clinton Woods L PTS 6 Cleethorpes
14.06.95	Clinton Woods L RSC 6 Batley
28.07.95	Paul Murray W PTS 6 Epworth
25.09.95	Robert Harper W DIS 4 Cleethorpes

11.10.95	John Kaighin L CO 1 Stoke
26.01.96	Paul Murray W PTS 6 Doncaster
26.02.96	Lee Whitehead L PTS 6 Manchester
24.04.96	David Jules L PTS 6 Stoke
11.05.96	Frederik Alvarez L RSC 1 Bethnal Green
09.10.96	Zak Goldman W PTS 6 Stoke
09.12.96	P.R. Mason L PTS 6 Bradford
24.03.97	Harri Hakulinen L RSC 3 Helsinki, Finland
16.05.97	Alex Carey W PTS 6 Hull
10.07.97	Edwin Cleary L RSC 1 Doncaster
18.08.97	Edwin Cleary L PTS 6 Nottingham
22.11.97	Lee Whitehead DREW 4 Manchester
29.11.97	Warren Barnes DREW 4 Norwich
05.03.98	Nick Manners L RSC 1 Leeds *(Central Area L. Heavyweight Title Challenge)*
07.10.98	Adam Cale L PTS 6 Stoke
22.10.98	Matthew Barney L PTS 6 Barking
26.11.98	Stevie Pettit L PTS 8 Edgbaston
14.12.98	Barry Thorogood L PTS 8 Birmingham
09.02.99	Adam Cale L PTS 8 Wolverhampton
22.04.99	Nigel Rafferty L PTS 6 Dudley
17.07.99	Ahmet Oner L CO 2 Dusseldorf, Germany
18.02.01	Rob Hayes-Scott L RSC 1 Southwark
20.05.01	Jason Brewster L PTS 6 Wolverhampton
16.06.01	Steven Spartacus L RSC 1 Dagenham

Career: 41 contests, won 14, drew 2, lost 25.

Pinky Burton

Sheffield. *Born* Perth, 13 December, 1979
L. Heavyweight. Ht. 5'11½"
Manager F. Warren

28.04.01	Nathan King L PTS 4 Cardiff

Career: 1 contest, lost 1.

Robert Burton

Barnsley. *Born* Barnsley, 1 April, 1971
L. Middleweight. Ht. 5'9"
Manager T. Schofield

05.02.01	Gavin Pearson W RSC 3 Bradford
23.02.01	Scott Millar W CO 5 Irvine
20.03.01	Peter Dunn W PTS 6 Leeds
08.05.01	Arv Mittoo W PTS 4 Barnsley
10.06.01	Martyn Bailey DREW 6 Ellesmere Port

Career: 5 contests, won 4, drew 1.

Harry Butler

Worcester. *Born* Wisbech, 12 August, 1977
Middleweight. Ht. 5'8"
Manager Self

19.07.97	Mehrdud Takaloo L RSC 1 Wembley
30.08.97	Patrick Pasi L PTS 4 Cheshunt
26.09.97	Darren Williams L PTS 6 Port Talbot
21.10.97	John Green L PTS 6 Yarm
15.11.97	Michael Jones L PTS 4 Bristol
02.12.97	Ross McCord W RSC 3 Swansea
13.12.97	Hercules Kyvelos L PTS 4 Sheffield
06.01.98	Alan Gilbert L PTS 4 Brighton
13.02.98	Gareth Hogg L RSC 3 Weston super Mare
14.03.98	Sonny Thind L PTS 4 Bethnal Green
03.04.98	Jon Foster L PTS 6 Ebbw Vale
18.04.98	Anthony Farnell L PTS 6 Manchester
02.05.98	Darren Bruce L RSC 6 Kensington
04.06.98	Adrian Houldey L PTS 6 Dudley
14.06.98	Gerard Lawrence L PTS 6 Golders Green

08.08.98	Sonny Pollard W RSC 4 Scarborough
05.09.98	Jawaid Khaliq L PTS 4 Telford
26.09.98	James Lowther L RSC 6 York
21.11.98	Brian Knudsen L RSC 4 Southwark
18.02.99	Clive Johnson L PTS 6 Barking
05.03.99	Paul Burns L RSC 5 Liverpool
23.04.99	Jason Williams L RSC 7 Clydach
26.06.99	Lawrence Murphy L RSC 1 Glasgow
19.09.99	Mick Mulcahy L PTS 6 Shaw
14.10.99	Lester Jacobs L PTS 6 Bloomsbury
06.11.99	Junior Witter L PTS 6 Widnes
06.12.99	Malcolm Melvin L PTS 8 Birmingham
20.12.99	Richard Williams L RSC 1 Bethnal Green
26.02.00	Jason Cook L PTS 6 Swansea
13.03.00	Christian Brady L PTS 6 Birmingham
20.03.00	Jamie Moore L RSC 2 Mansfield
15.05.00	Ernie Smith W PTS 6 Birmingham
26.05.00	Barry Connell L PTS 4 Glasgow
21.09.00	Ojay Abrahams L PTS 6 Bloomsbury
07.10.00	Michael Alexander L PTS 6 Doncaster
26.10.00	Matthew Ashmole W PTS 6 Clydach
23.11.00	Matthew Barr L PTS 4 Bayswater
30.11.00	Shpetim Hoti W PTS 4 Bloomsbury
11.12.00	Jimmy Vincent L PTS 6 Birmingham
28.01.01	Peter Jackson L PTS 6 Wolverhampton
10.02.01	Thomas McDonagh L PTS 6 Widnes
24.02.01	Spencer Fearon L PTS 4 Bethnal Green
09.03.01	John Humphrey L RSC 1 Millwall
22.04.01	Ojay Abrahams L PTS 6 Streatham
05.05.01	Liam Lathbury L PTS 6 Brighton
19.05.01	Delroy Leslie L PTS 6 Wembley
21.06.01	Shpetim Hoti W PTS 4 Earls Court

Career: 47 contests, won 6, lost 41.

Paul Buttery

Preston. *Born* Preston, 12 May, 1977
Heavyweight. Ht. 6'2½"
Manager B. Devine

03.02.01	Luke Simpkin L RSC 1 Manchester
24.04.01	Dave Faulkner W CO 1 Liverpool

Career: 2 contests, won 1, lost 1.

Terry Butwell

Bethnal Green. *Born* Mile End, 26 June, 1978
L. Welterweight. Ht. 5'7½"
Manager Self

14.06.98	Mark Halstead W PTS 6 Golders Green
23.07.98	Woody Greenaway L PTS 6 Barking
09.12.00	Lee Williamson W PTS 4 Southwark

Career: 3 contests, won 2, lost 1.

Lee Byrne

Manchester. *Born* Manchester, 23 July, 1981
L. Welterweight. Ht. 5'7"
Manager J. Trickett

09.09.00	Ram Singh W RSC 2 Manchester

Career: 1 contest, won 1.

Tony Byrne

Preston. *Born* Preston, 17 November, 1978
L. Middleweight. Ht. 5'7"
Manager M. Goodall

10.06.01	Paul Lomax W PTS 6 Ellesmere Port

Career: 1 contest, won 1.

Adam Cale

Worcester. *Born* Worcester, 11 April, 1972
Cruiserweight. Ht. 6'2"
Manager Self

04.06.98	Matthew Barney L PTS 6 Barking
23.07.98	Matthew Barney L PTS 6 Barking
07.10.98	Kevin Burton W PTS 6 Stoke
31.10.98	Faisal Mohammed L RSC 2 Basingstoke
09.02.99	Kevin Burton W PTS 8 Wolverhampton
26.02.99	Neil Simpson L RSC 3 Coventry
27.05.99	Carl Smallwood L PTS 6 Edgbaston
06.06.99	Wayne Buck L PTS 6 Nottingham
22.06.99	Scott Baker L PTS 4 Ipswich
20.08.99	Matthew Barney L PTS 4 Bloomsbury
03.09.99	Jason Brewster L PTS 6 West Bromwich
20.09.99	Kenny Gayle L PTS 4 Peterborough
27.09.99	Tony Booth L PTS 6 Cleethorpes
11.10.99	Stevie Pettit L PTS 6 Birmingham
20.10.99	Stevie Pettit L PTS 6 Stoke
08.12.99	Nigel Rafferty L PTS 6 Stoke
12.02.00	Tony Dowling L PTS 4 Sheffield
26.02.00	Chris Davies L RSC 4 Swansea
18.05.00	Elvis Michailenko L PTS 4 Bethnal Green
16.06.00	Scott Baker L PTS 4 Bloomsbury
10.09.00	Jason Brewster L PTS 4 Walsall
21.10.00	Scott Lansdowne L RSC 5 Sheffield
25.11.00	Peter Haymer L RSC 1 Manchester
22.04.01	Radcliffe Green L CO 5 Streatham
02.06.01	Ivan Botton L PTS 4 Wakefield

Career: 25 contests, won 2, lost 23.

Marc Callaghan

Barking. *Born* Barking, 13 November, 1977
Featherweight. Ht. 5'6"
Manager B. Hearn

08.09.98	Kevin Sheil W PTS 4 Bethnal Green
31.10.98	Nicky Wilders W RSC 1 Southend
12.01.99	Nicky Wilders W RTD 2 Bethnal Green
12.03.99	Peter Allen W PTS 4 Bethnal Green
25.05.99	Simon Chambers L RSC 1 Mayfair
16.10.99	Nigel Leake W PTS 4 Bethnal Green
20.12.99	Marc Smith W PTS 4 Bethnal Green
05.02.00	Steve Brook W RSC 2 Bethnal Green
01.04.00	John Barnes W PTS 4 Bethnal Green
19.08.00	Anthony Hanna W PTS 4 Brentwood
09.10.00	Jamie McKeever L PTS 6 Liverpool
04.11.00	Nigel Senior W RSC 4 Bethnal Green
03.03.01	Anthony Hanna W PTS 6 Wembley
26.05.01	Roy Rutherford L RSC 3 Bethnal Green

Career: 14 contests, won 11, lost 3.

Joe Calzaghe

Newbridge. *Born* Hammersmith, 23 March, 1972
WBO S. Middleweight Champion. Former Undefeated British S. Middleweight Champion. Ht. 5'11"
Manager F. Warren

01.10.93	Paul Hanlon W RSC 1 Cardiff
10.11.93	Stinger Mason W RSC 1 Watford
16.12.93	Spencer Alton W RSC 2 Newport
22.01.94	Martin Rosamond W RSC 1 Cardiff
01.03.94	Darren Littlewood W RSC 1 Dudley
04.06.94	Karl Barwise W RSC 1 Cardiff
01.10.94	Mark Dawson W RSC 1 Cardiff
30.11.94	Trevor Ambrose W RSC 2 Wolverhampton
14.02.95	Frank Minton W CO 1 Bethnal Green
22.02.95	Bobbi Joe Edwards W PTS 8 Telford
19.05.95	Robert Curry W RSC 1 Southwark
08.07.95	Tyrone Jackson W RSC 4 York
30.09.95	Nick Manners W RSC 4 Basildon
28.10.95	Stephen Wilson W RSC 8 Kensington *(Vacant British S. Middleweight Title)*
13.02.96	Guy Stanford W RSC 1 Cardiff
13.03.96	Anthony Brooks W RSC 2 Wembley
20.04.96	Mark Delaney W RSC 5 Brentwood *(British S. Middleweight Title Defence)*
04.05.96	Warren Stowe W RTD 2 Dagenham
15.05.96	Pat Lawlor W RSC 2 Cardiff
21.01.97	Carlos Christie W CO 2 Bristol
22.03.97	Tyler Hughes W CO 1 Wythenshawe
05.06.97	Luciano Torres W RSC 3 Bristol
11.10.97	Chris Eubank W PTS 12 Sheffield *(Vacant WBO S. Middleweight Title)*
24.01.98	Branco Sobot W RSC 3 Cardiff *(WBO S. Middleweight Title Defence)*
25.04.98	Juan Carlos Gimenez W RTD 9 Cardiff *(WBO S. Middleweight Title Defence)*
13.02.99	Robin Reid W PTS 12 Newcastle *(WBO S. Middleweight Title Defence)*

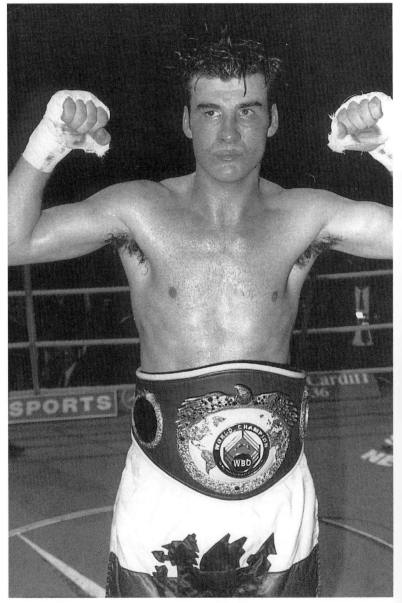

Joe Calzaghe　　　　　　　　　　　　　　　Les Clark

05.06.99 Rick Thornberry W PTS 12 Cardiff
(WBO S. Middleweight Title Defence)
29.01.00 David Starie W PTS 12 Manchester
(WBO S, Middleweight Title Defence)
12.08.00 Omar Sheika W RSC 5 Wembley
(WBO S.Middleweight Title Defence)
16.12.00 Richie Woodhall W RSC 10 Sheffield
(WBO S. Middleweight Title Defence)
28.04.01 Mario Veit W RSC 1 Cardiff
(WBO S. Middleweight Title Defence)
Career: 31 contests, won 31.

Alan Campbell

Kirkham. *Born* Greenock, 5 April, 1974
L. Middleweight. Ht. 5'11"
Manager L. Veitch

08.03.01 Richard Inquieti W PTS 6 Blackpool
Career: 1 contest, won 1.

Tom Cannon

Coatbridge. *Born* Bellshill, 18 March, 1980
L. Heavyweight. Ht. 5'11¹/₂"
Manager R. Bannon

15.06.01 Valery Odin L PTS 4 Millwall
Career: 1 contest, lost 1.

Dafydd Carlin

Belfast. *Born* Brecon, 2 August, 1978
S. Featherweight. Ht. 5'6"
Manager A. Wilton

01.04.01 Paddy Folan W PTS 4 Southwark
28.04.01 Alex Arthur L PTS 4 Cardiff
03.06.01 Dave Hinds W PTS 4 Southwark
Career: 3 contests, won 2, lost 1.

Brian Carr

Moodiesburn. *Born* Glasgow, 20 June,
1969
S. Bantamweight. Scottish Featherweight
Champion. Ht. 5'6"
Manager A. Morrison

18.12.94 Fred Reeve W CO 2 Glasgow
21.01.95 Shaun Anderson W PTS 6 Glasgow
04.03.95 G. G. Goddard W PTS 8 Livingston
13.05.95 Paul Wynn W RTD 2 Glasgow
08.06.95 Abdul Manna W PTS 6 Glasgow
13.10.95 Muhammad Shaffique W PTS 6
Glasgow
17.12.95 Abdul Mannon W PTS 8 Glasgow
16.03.96 Chip O'Neill W PTS 4 Glasgow
26.04.96 Mike Deveney W PTS 10 Glasgow
(Vacant Scottish Featherweight Title)
20.09.96 Fred Reeve W RSC 3 Glasgow
06.11.96 Mike Deveney W PTS 10 Glasgow
(Scottish Featherweight Title Defence)
22.12.96 Pete Buckley W PTS 6 Glasgow
04.04.97 Lyndon Kershaw W PTS 10 Glasgow
(Elim. British S. Bantamweight Title)
05.07.97 Kevin Sheil W PTS 5 Glasgow
12.09.97 Carl Allen W PTS 8 Glasgow
01.11.97 Steve Conway W PTS 6 Glasgow
31.01.98 Michael Brodie L RSC 10 Edmonton
(British & Commonwealth
S. Bantamweight Title Challenges)
17.09.98 Pete Buckley W PTS 6 Glasgow
06.02.99 Patrick Mullings L PTS 12 Halifax
(Vacant British S. Bantamweight Title)
27.02.99 Fondil Madani W CO 3 Bethnal Green

09.04.99 Keith Jones W PTS 8 Glasgow
26.06.99 Cassius Baloyi L RTD 9 Glasgow
(WBU Featherweight Title Challenge)
09.10.99 Pete Buckley W PTS 6 Manchester
12.11.99 Harry Woods W PTS 6 Glasgow
11.12.99 Lee Williamson DREW 6 Liverpool
18.03.00 Nedal Hussein L PTS 12 Glasgow
(Vacant Commonwealth
S. Bantamweight Title)
26.05.00 Ian Turner W PTS 6 Glasgow
24.06.00 Dave Hinds W PTS 4 Glasgow
02.10.00 Pete Buckley W PTS 4 Glasgow
Career: 29 contests, won 24, drew 1, lost 4.

(John) Cornelius Carr

Middlesbrough. *Born* Middlesbrough, 9
April, 1969
Former Undefeated WBF Middleweight
Champion. Former Undefeated British S.
Middleweight Champion. Ht. 5'9½"
Manager Self

22.09.87 Paul Burton W RSC 5 Bethnal Green
28.11.87 Dave Heaver W RSC 2 Windsor
12.01.88 Shamus Casey W RSC 6 Cardiff
27.01.88 Kesem Clayton W PTS 6 Bethnal
Green
29.03.88 Darren Parker W RSC 1 Bethnal Green
12.04.88 Franki Moro W PTS 6 Cardiff
10.05.88 Andy Catesby W RSC 5 Tottenham
15.11.88 Skip Jackson W CO 1 Norwich
20.12.88 Kevin Hayde W PTS 6 Swansea
22.03.89 George Bocco L RSC 3 Reading
24.10.89 Carlo Colarusso W RTD 4 Watford
20.02.90 Peter Gorny W RSC 4 Millwall
21.04.90 Franki Moro W PTS 8 Sunderland
26.09.90 John Maltreaux W CO 1 Metairie, USA
27.10.90 Jerry Nestor W CO 1 Greenville, USA
16.02.91 Frank Eubanks W RSC 5 Thornaby
02.03.91 Carlo Colarusso W PTS 8 Darlington
18.05.91 Paul Burton W RSC 3 Verbania, Italy
06.09.91 Marvin O'Brien W RSC 7 Salemi, Italy
29.10.92 Alan Richards W PTS 8 Bayswater
24.04.93 Graham Burton W PTS 6 Birmingham
19.05.93 Stan King W PTS 8 Sunderland
22.09.93 Horace Fleary W PTS 8 Wembley
11.03.94 James Cook W PTS 12 Bethnal Green
(British S. Middleweight Title
Challenge)
04.02.95 Colin Manners W PTS 8 Cardiff
13.05.95 Chris Richards W RTD 3 Glasgow
07.07.95 Barry Thorogood W RSC 6 Cardiff
25.11.95 Steve Collins L PTS 12 Dublin
(WBO S. Middleweight Title
Challenge)
02.03.96 Danny Juma W PTS 8 Newcastle
14.03.97 Dean Francis L RSC 7 Reading
(WBO Inter-Continental S.
Middleweight Title Challenge)
10.09.98 Darren Covill W RTD 2 Acton
27.10.98 Danny Juma W PTS 6 Brentford
25.11.98 Jimmy Vincent W PTS 6 Streatham
20.02.99 Steve Foster W PTS 12 Thornaby
(Vacant WBF Middleweight Title)
20.08.99 Jason Barker W RSC 3 Bloomsbury
31.10.99 Dingaan Thobela W PTS 12 Raynes
Park
(WBF Middleweight Title Defence)
08.12.00 Gary Beardsley W PTS 4 Crystal
Palace
28.02.01 Sam Soliman L PTS 6 Kensington
Career: 38 contests, won 34, lost 4.

Henry Castle

Salisbury. *Born* Southampton, 7 February,
1979
Featherweight. Ht. 5'6³/₄"
Manager K. Sanders

29.01.01 Jason Nesbitt W CO 6 Peterborough
26.03.01 Eddie Nevins W RSC 2 Peterborough
Career: 2 contests, won 2.

Henry Castle   Les Clark

Glenn Catley

Bristol. *Born* Sodbury, 15 March, 1972
Former WBC S. Middleweight Champion.
Former Undefeated IBF & WBO Inter-
Continental S. Middleweight Champion.
Former Undefeated British Middleweight
Champion. Former WBC International
Middleweight Champion. Ht. 5'8"
Manager C. Sanigar/F. Warren

27.05.93 Rick North W PTS 4 Bristol
26.06.93 Chris Vassiliou W CO 2 Keynsham
31.08.93 Marty Duke W RSC 2 Croydon
13.09.93 Barry Thorogood W PTS 4 Bristol
03.11.93 Marty Duke W RSC 1 Bristol
13.12.93 Shamus Casey W PTS 4 Bristol
10.03.94 Mark Cichocki W PTS 6 Bristol
23.03.94 Carlo Colarusso L RSC 5 Cardiff
25.05.94 Chris Davies W RSC 1 Bristol
02.07.94 Martin Jolley W RSC 1 Keynsham
22.11.94 Kirkland Laing W RSC 5 Bristol
18.02.95 Lee Blundell W RSC 6 Shepton Mallet
06.05.95 Mark Dawson W RSC 5 Shepton
Mallet
28.07.95 Kevin Adamson W CO 1 Bristol
02.09.95 Quinn Paynter W RSC 1 Wembley
30.09.95 John Duckworth W RSC 3 Cardiff
28.10.95 Carlos Christie W PTS 8 Bristol
10.11.95 Carlos Christie W CO 3 Bristol
16.12.95 Peter Vosper W RSC 2 Cardiff
26.04.96 Lee Crocker W RSC 2 Cardiff
19.10.96 Paul Wesley W RSC 7 Bristol
21.01.97 George Bocco W RTD 4 Bristol
(Vacant WBC International
Middleweight Title)

05.06.97 Andras Galfi L RSC 7 Bristol
*(WBC International Middleweight Title
Defence)*
17.01.98 Neville Brown W RTD 8 Bristol
(British Middleweight Title Challenge)
05.09.98 Richie Woodhall L PTS 12 Telford
(WBC S. Middleweight Title Challenge)
24.10.98 Andras Galfi W PTS 12 Bristol
*(Vacant WBO Inter-Continental
S. Middleweight Title)*
05.12.98 Andrew Flute W RSC 5 Bristol
*(Vacant IBF Inter-Continental
S. Middleweight Title)*
10.12.99 Eric Lucas W RSC 12 Montreal,
Canada
*(Final Elim. WBC S. Middleweight
Title)*
06.05.00 Markus Beyer W RSC 12 Frankfurt,
Germany
(WBC S. Middleweight Title Challenge)
01.09.00 Dingaan Thobela L CO 12 Brakpan,
South Africa
(WBC S.Middleweight Title Defence)
Career: 30 contests, won 26, lost 4.

Adrian Chase

St Albans. *Born* St Albans, 18 October, 1968
Former Undefeated British Masters
Welterweight Champion. Ht. 5'9"
Manager Self

06.05.93 Jason Campbell W CO 2 Bayswater
24.06.93 Delwyn Panayiotiou W CO 1 Watford
23.02.94 Dennis Griffin W PTS 6 Watford
16.05.94 Tony Gibbs W PTS 6 Heathrow
21.07.94 Steve Burton W PTS 6 Battersea
19.11.94 Wayne Jones W PTS 6 Heathrow
21.04.95 Juha Temonen L PTS 4 Pori, Finland
28.10.95 Tom Welsh L RSC 2 Bristol
03.12.95 Delroy Leslie L RSC 4 Southwark
12.02.96 Marc Smith W CO 1 Heathrow
21.03.96 Peter Richardson L RSC 2 Southwark
07.11.96 Gary Hiscox W PTS 4 Battersea
15.02.97 Ray Newby L PTS 6 Tooting
27.01.98 Paul Knights W RSC 1 Bethnal Green
23.02.98 Jason Williams L PTS 6 Windsor
28.04.98 Paul Miles L PTS 6 Brentford
28.08.98 Corey Johnson L CO 4 Southfield,
USA
18.11.99 David Kirk L PTS 10 Mayfair
*(Vacant WBF EuropeanWelterweight
Title)*
26.11.99 David Baptiste W RSC 2 Bayswater
*(Vacant British Masters Welterweight
Title*
27.05.00 Kevin McCarthy L RSC 4 Southwark
*(Vacant Southern Area Welterweight
Title)*
12.08.00 Neil Sinclair L RSC 2 Wembley
Career: 21 contests, won 10, lost 11.

Stephen Chinnock

Rugeley. *Born* Lichfield, 4 December, 1975
Featherweight. Ht. 5'10"
Manager Self

10.09.00 Neil Read W RSC 5 Walsall
06.11.00 Jason Nesbitt W PTS 6
Wolverhampton
27.11.00 Jason White W PTS 4 Birmingham
20.05.01 Gareth Wiltshaw W PTS 6
Wolverhampton
Career: 4 contests, won 4.

Stephen Chinnock   Les Clark

Darren Chubbs

Southport. *Born* Southport, 4 October, 1968
Heavyweight. Ht. 6'3"
Manager B. Devine

09.10.00 Geoff Hunter W RSC 3 Liverpool
08.12.00 Eamonn Glennon W PTS 4 Crystal
Palace
24.04.01 Luke Simpkin W PTS 4 Liverpool
11.06.01 Paul Bonson W PTS 4 Nottingham
Career: 4 contests, won 4.

Darren Chubbs   Les Clark

Howard Clarke

Warley. *Born* London, 23 September, 1967
L. Middleweight. Ht. 5'10"
Manager Self

15.10.91 Chris Mylan W PTS 4 Dudley
09.12.91 Claude Rossi W RSC 3 Brierley Hill
04.02.92 Julian Eavis W PTS 4 Alfreton
03.03.92 Dave Andrews W RSC 3 Cradley
Heath
21.05.92 Richard O'Brien W CO 1 Cradley
Heath
29.09.92 Paul King W PTS 6 Stoke
27.10.92 Gordon Blair L RSC 4 Cradley Heath
16.03.93 Paul King W PTS 6 Edgbaston
07.06.93 Dean Bramhald W RTD 2 Walsall
29.06.93 Paul King W PTS 6 Edgbaston
06.10.93 Julian Eavis L PTS 8 Solihull
30.11.93 Julian Eavis W PTS 8 Wolverhampton
08.02.94 Nigel Bradley W RTD 6
Wolverhampton
18.04.94 Andy Peach W PTS 6 Walsall
28.06.94 Dennis Berry L RSC 3 Edgbaston
12.10.94 Julian Eavis W PTS 8 Stoke
25.10.94 Andy Peach W RSC 3 Edgbaston
02.11.94 Julian Eavis W PTS 8 Birmingham
29.11.94 Julian Eavis W PTS 6 Cannock
07.12.94 Peter Reid W PTS 8 Stoke
25.01.95 Dennis Berry L PTS 8 Stoke
08.03.95 Andrew Jervis W PTS 6 Solihull
11.05.95 David Bain W RSC 1 Dudley
20.09.95 Michael Smyth DREW 6 Ystrad
02.10.95 Nigel Wenton L PTS 6 Mayfair
02.12.96 Martin Smith W PTS 8 Birmingham
29.01.97 Gary Beardsley W PTS 6 Stoke
11.02.97 Prince Kasi Kaihau L RSC 4
Wolverhampton
19.03.97 Mark Cichocki W PTS 6 Stoke
15.04.97 Prince Kasi Kaihau W PTS 6
Edgbaston
30.04.97 Allan Gray W PTS 8 Acton
22.05.97 Michael Alexander W RSC 3 Solihull
21.06.97 Paul Samuels L PTS 8 Cardiff
09.09.97 Harry Dhami L PTS 8 Bethnal Green
05.11.97 Andras Galfi W PTS 8 Tenerife
27.01.98 Mack Razor L PTS 8 Hammanskraal,
South Africa
23.03.98 Lindon Scarlett DREW 6 Crystal
Palace
18.07.98 Jason Papillion W PTS 8 Sheffield
13.03.99 Fernando Vargas L RSC 4 New York
City, USA
(IBF L. Middleweight Title Challenge)
05.11.99 Michael Rask L PTS 12 Aalberg,
Denmark
*(WBA Inter-Continental
L. Middleweight Title Challenge)*
29.05.00 Anthony Farnell L PTS 12 Manchester
*(WBO Inter-Continental
L. Middleweight Title Challenge)*
12.08.00 Mehrdud Takaloo L PTS 12 Wembley
*(Vacant IBF Inter-Continental
L.Middleweight Title)*
04.11.00 Richard Williams L CO 4 Bethnal
Green
16.12.00 Ryan Rhodes L PTS 6 Sheffield
03.02.01 Michael Jones L PTS 4 Manchester
26.02.01 Jawaid Khaliq L PTS 6 Nottingham
07.04.01 Gary Lockett L RSC 2 Wembley
06.05.01 Ian Cooper L PTS 6 Hartlepool
04.06.01 James Docherty L PTS 6 Hartlepool
Career: 49 contests, won 26, drew 2, lost 21.

Craig Clayton

Great Wyrley. *Born* Wolverhampton, 21 March, 1974
S. Middleweight. Ht. 5'11"
Manager Self

24.09.98	Kevin Lang W PTS 6 Edgbaston
24.11.98	Kid Halls L PTS 6 Wolverhampton
22.04.99	Pedro Thompson L PTS 6 Dudley
12.10.99	Rene Grayel W PTS 6 Wolverhampton
30.11.99	Tony Smith W PTS 6 Wolverhampton
08.12.99	Tony Smith W PTS 6 Stoke
24.02.00	Rene Grayel W PTS 6 Edgbaston
10.10.00	Reece McAllister L RSC 4 Brierley Hill

Career: 8 contests, won 5, lost 3.

Darren Cleary

Salford. *Born* Salford, 28 February, 1980
Flyweight. Ht. 5'5"
Manager S. Foster/S. Wood

27.05.01 Marty Kayes W PTS 4 Manchester
Career: 1 contest, won 1.

David Coldwell

Sheffield. *Born* Calcutta, India, 6 July, 1975
Former Undefeated Central Area Flyweight Champion. Ht. 5'3"
Manager D. Ingle

23.09.96 Marty Chestnut W PTS 6 Cleethorpes
24.10.96 Benny Jones L PTS 6 Lincoln
16.12.96 Darren Noble L PTS 6 Cleethorpes
18.01.97 Jason Booth L PTS 4 Swadlincote
20.02.97 Ross Cassidy L PTS 6 Mansfield
14.03.97 Willie Smith W RSC 5 Hull
25.03.97 Graham McGrath L PTS 6 Wolverhampton
03.05.97 Mickey Cantwell L PTS 8 Manchester
10.07.97 Andy Roberts L RSC 3 Doncaster
(Vacant Central Area Flyweight Title)
04.12.97 Andy Roberts W PTS 6 Doncaster
23.02.98 Anthony Hanna L PTS 6 Salford
02.03.98 Graham McGrath L PTS 6 Birmingham
14.10.98 Louis Veitch W PTS 10 Blackpool
(Central Area Flyweight Title Challenge)
12.12.98 Jose Antonio Lopez L PTS 12 Zaragoza, Spain
(Vacant WBA Inter-Continental Flyweight Title)
01.05.99 Mickey Cantwell L PTS 6 Crystal Palace
17.07.99 Terry Gaskin W CO 5 Doncaster
(Central Area Flyweight Title Defence)
28.11.99 Tommy Craig W PTS 4 Chesterfield
24.06.00 Hussein Hussein L RSC 1 Glasgow
30.08.00 Jim Betts L RSC 2 Scunthorpe
(Vacant British Masters Flyweight Title. Elim. British Flyweight Title)

Career: 19 contests, won 6, lost 13.

Brian Coleman

Birmingham. *Born* Birmingham, 27 July, 1969
Welterweight. Ht. 5'11"
Manager Self

21.11.91 Jamie Morris DREW 6 Stafford
11.12.91 Craig Hartwell DREW 6 Leicester

22.01.92 John O. Johnson L PTS 6 Stoke
20.02.92 Davy Robb L PTS 6 Oakengates
31.03.92 Blue Butterworth L PTS 6 Stockport
17.05.92 Korso Aleain L RSC 5 Harringay
17.09.92 Nicky Bardle L RSC 4 Watford
21.10.92 Jason Barker W PTS 6 Stoke
10.12.92 A. M. Milton DREW 4 Bethnal Green
31.03.93 A. M. Milton L PTS 4 Bethnal Green
26.04.93 Jason Beard L PTS 6 Lewisham
06.05.93 Mark Allen W PTS 6 Walsall
18.05.93 Sean Metherell DREW 6 Kettering
27.05.93 Blue Butterworth L PTS 6 Burnley
23.06.93 Jonathan Thaxton L PTS 8 Gorleston
11.08.93 Steve Howden L RSC 4 Mansfield
13.09.93 Mick Hoban L PTS 6 Middleton
01.12.93 A. M. Milton L PTS 4 Bethnal Green
08.12.93 Chris Pollock W PTS 6 Stoke
16.12.93 Mark Newton L PTS 6 Newport
11.01.94 Paul Knights L RSC 4 Bethnal Green
08.02.94 Andy Peach W PTS 6 Wolverhampton
18.02.94 Cam Raeside L PTS 6 Leicester
08.03.94 Chris Pollock L PTS 6 Edgbaston
29.03.94 P. J. Gallagher L PTS 6 Bethnal Green
14.04.94 Cham Joof L PTS 6 Battersea
02.06.94 Scott Walker L CO 1 Middleton
12.09.94 Shabba Edwards L PTS 6 Mayfair
19.09.94 Mark Breslin L CO 1 Glasgow
09.11.94 Kenny Scott L PTS 6 Stafford
23.11.94 Billy McDougall W PTS 4 Piccadilly
29.11.94 Warren Stephens W PTS 6 Wolverhampton
09.12.94 Danny Stevens L RTD 2 Bethnal Green
24.01.95 Wayne Jones L PTS 6 Piccadilly
07.02.95 Alan Temple L PTS 6 Ipswich
23.02.95 Darren Covill L PTS 4 Southwark
16.03.95 Paul Knights L RSC 2 Basildon
02.07.95 Tommy Lawler L PTS 4 Dublin
08.09.95 George Naylor L PTS 6 Liverpool
27.09.95 Allan Gray L PTS 6 Bethnal Green
20.10.95 Mikael Nilsson L PTS 4 Ipswich
02.11.95 Marco Fattore W PTS 6 Mayfair
16.11.95 Alan Bosworth L PTS 6 Evesham
24.11.95 Chris Barnett L PTS 6 Manchester
02.12.95 Neil Sinclair L RTD 1 Belfast
20.01.96 James Hare L PTS 6 Mansfield
29.01.96 Dave Fallon L PTS 6 Piccadilly
13.02.96 Martin Holgate L PTS 4 Bethnal Green
21.02.96 Marco Fattore W PTS 6 Piccadilly
13.03.96 Paul Samuels L PTS 6 Wembley
03.04.96 Ian Honeywood L PTS 6 Bethnal Green
20.04.96 Ray Robinson L PTS 6 Brentwood
24.05.96 Scott Dixon L PTS 8 Glasgow
08.06.96 Mark Winters L PTS 4 Newcastle
06.07.96 Nick Boyd L PTS 4 Manchester
16.08.96 Charlie Paine W PTS 6 Liverpool
27.08.96 Dave Brazil L RTD 6 Windsor
19.09.96 Ricky Sackfield W RSC 3 Manchester
27.09.96 Nicky Bardle L PTS 4 Stevenage
08.10.96 Marcus McCrae W PTS 6 Battersea
09.11.96 Mark Haslam L PTS 6 Manchester
27.11.96 Bernard Paul L PTS 6 Bethnal Green
09.12.96 Wayne Windle L PTS 6 Chesterfield
18.01.97 Paul Burke L PTS 6 Manchester
19.02.97 Anthony Campbell L PTS 6 Acton
25.03.97 Craig Stanley DREW 4 Lewisham
03.04.97 Kevin McCarthy L PTS 6 Wembley
22.04.97 Georgie Smith L PTS 6 Bethnal Green
19.05.97 John O.Johnson DREW 6 Cleethorpes
02.06.97 Steve McLevy W RSC 5 Glasgow
02.08.97 Junior Witter L PTS 4 Barnsley
13.09.97 Jason Rowland L PTS 8 Millwall
04.10.97 Everald Williams L PTS 4 Muswell Hill

24.10.97 Anthony Maynard L CO 1 Birmingham
27.01.98 Kevin McCarthy L PTS 6 Streatham
23.02.98 Kevin McKillan L PTS 6 Salford
05.03.98 Junior Witter L PTS 6 Leeds
24.03.98 Jon Harrison DREW 6 Wolverhampton
03.04.98 Peter Nightingale L PTS 6 West Bromwich
23.04.98 Marc Smith W PTS 6 Edgbaston
06.05.98 Stuart Rimmer L PTS 6 Blackpool
18.05.98 Steve Conway L PTS 6 Cleethorpes
26.05.98 Rimvidas Billius L PTS 4 Mayfair
06.06.98 Jamie McKeever L PTS 6 Liverpool
18.06.98 Shaun Stokes L PTS 6 Sheffield
12.09.98 Graham Earl L PTS 4 Bethnal Green
03.10.98 Peter Nightingale L PTS 6 West Bromwich
12.10.98 Christian Brady L PTS 6 Birmingham
22.10.98 Colin Lynes L RSC 2 Barking
25.11.98 Arv Mittoo W PTS 6 Clydach
07.12.98 Gavin Down L PTS 6 Manchester
21.01.99 Dennis Griffin W PTS 6 Piccadilly
06.02.99 Tontcho Tontchev L PTS 6 Halifax
26.02.99 Peter Nightingale L PTS 6 West Bromwich
08.03.99 Sammy Smith W PTS 8 Birmingham
25.03.99 Ernie Smith W PTS 6 Edgbaston
03.04.99 Richard Hatton L CO 2 Kensington
27.05.99 Ernie Smith L PTS 6 Edgbaston
04.06.99 Steve Conway L PTS 6 Hull
26.06.99 Steve Murray L PTS 6 Millwall
07.08.99 Jonathan Thaxton L PTS 6 Dagenham
13.09.99 Bobby Vanzie L PTS 6 Bethnal Green
27.09.99 Steve Conway L PTS 6 Leeds
24.10.99 Peter Nightingale L PTS 10 Wolverhampton
(Midlands Area Welterweight Title Challenge)
06.11.99 Jacek Bielski L PTS 4 Bethnal Green
22.11.99 Sonny Thind W RSC 5 Piccadilly
30.11.99 Ernie Smith W PTS 8 Wolverhampton
11.12.99 Oscar Hall L PTS 6 Liverpool
20.01.00 Alan Bosworth L PTS 6 Piccadilly
12.02.00 Shaun Stokes W PTS 4 Sheffield
24.02.00 Ernie Smith W PTS 6 Edgbaston
09.03.00 Paul Burns L PTS 6 Liverpool
25.03.00 Michael Jennings L PTS 6 Liverpool
16.05.00 Michael Jennings L PTS 6 Warrington
25.05.00 Lee Molyneux L PTS 6 Peterborough
19.06.00 Gavin Down L PTS 4 Burton
19.08.00 Glenn McClarnon L PTS 6 Brentwood
25.09.00 Derek Roche L PTS 6 Barnsley
14.10.00 Colin Lynes L PTS 6 Wembley
31.10.00 Ivan Kirpa L RSC 3 Hammersmith
02.12.00 John Tiftik L PTS 4 Chigwell
11.12.00 Lee Bird W CO 4 Cleethorpes
23.01.01 Paul Knights L PTS 6 Crawley
03.02.01 Darren Spencer L PTS 6 Manchester
10.02.01 Carl Wall L RSC 4 Widnes
17.03.01 Bradley Pryce L PTS 4 Manchester
26.03.01 Ross Minter L PTS 4 Wembley
28.04.01 Ismail Khalil L PTS 4 Cardiff
08.05.01 Gavin Wake L PTS 4 Barnsley
21.05.01 Ernie Smith L PTS 6 Birmingham
09.06.01 Matthew Hatton L RTD 2 Bethnal Green

Career: 131 contests, won 22, drew 7, lost 102.

Jason Collins

Walsall. *Born* Walsall, 5 December, 1972
Middleweight. Ht. 5'9"
Manager Self

18.02.99 Biagio Falcone L PTS 6 Glasgow
17.03.99 Stuart Harper W RSC 2 Stoke
06.06.99 Jon Foster DREW 6 Nottingham
15.08.99 Matt Galer W PTS 6 Derby
28.10.99 Lee Blundell DREW 6 Burnley
20.11.99 Dennis Berry L PTS 6 Grantham
15.01.00 Martin Jolley W RTD 1 Doncaster
18.02.00 Oscar Hall DREW 6 West Bromwich
27.02.00 Jawaid Khaliq L PTS 6 Leeds
05.03.00 Wayne Shepherd W PTS 6 Shaw
21.03.00 Sharden Ansoula W PTS 6 Telde, Gran
Canaria
21.05.00 Neville Brown L RSC 2 Derby
08.07.00 Darren Rhodes DREW 4 Widnes
04.09.00 Darren Rhodes W PTS 4 Manchester
01.10.00 Juergen Braehmer L CO 1 Hamburg,
Germany
13.11.00 Mehrdud Takaloo L RSC 2 Bethnal
Green
16.12.00 Louis Swales DREW 4 Sheffield
27.01.01 Spencer Fearon W PTS 4 Bethnal
Green
26.03.01 P.J. Maxwell W PTS 4 Wembley
20.04.01 Jim Rock L PTS 6 Dublin
08.06.01 Leigh Wicks W PTS 4 Hull
21.06.01 Lester Jacobs L CO 9 Earls Court
(WBF Middleweight Title Challenge)
Career: 22 contests, won 9, drew 5, lost 8.

Danny Connelly

Glasgow. *Born* Glasgow, 14 May, 1971
Lightweight. Ht. 5'4¹/₂"
Manager Self

10.12.90 Tommy Smith W PTS 6 Glasgow
31.05.91 Miguel Matthews W PTS 8 Glasgow
29.05.92 Lee Fox W PTS 6 Glasgow
10.11.00 Willie Limond L PTS 6 Glasgow
28.11.00 Steve Saville L PTS 8 Brierley Hill
11.12.00 Matthew Hatton L PTS 4 Widnes
15.02.01 Dave Stewart L PTS 6 Glasgow
Career: 7 contests, won 3, lost 4.

Danny Connelly   Les Clark

Tony Conroy

Coventry. *Born* Coventry, 18 December,
1977
L. Welterweight. Ht. 5'9"
Manager J. Harding/J. Griffin

22.10.99 Mark Halstead W PTS 4 Coventry
24.02.00 Dave Gibson W PTS 4 Edgbaston
22.05.00 Dave Hinds W PTS 4 Coventry
28.10.00 Chris Hall W RSC 1 Coventry
02.01.01 Woody Greenaway W PTS 4 Coventry
Career: 5 contests, won 5.

Tony Conroy   Les Clark

Steve Conway

Dewsbury. *Born* Hartlepool, 6 October, 1977
Lightweight. Ht. 5'8"
Manager J. Ingle

21.02.96 Robert Grubb W PTS 6 Batley
24.04.96 Ervine Blake W PTS 6 Solihull
20.05.96 Chris Lyons W PTS 6 Cleethorpes
30.05.96 Ram Singh W PTS 6 Lincoln
03.02.97 Jason Squire W PTS 6 Leicester
11.04.97 Marc Smith W PTS 4 Barnsley
22.09.97 Arv Mittoo W PTS 6 Cleethorpes
09.10.97 Arv Mittoo W PTS 6 Leeds
01.11.97 Brian Carr L PTS 6 Glasgow
14.11.97 Brendan Bryce W PTS 6 Mere
04.12.97 Kid McAuley W RSC 5 Doncaster
15.12.97 Nicky Wilders W PTS 6 Cleethorpes
05.03.98 Pete Buckley W PTS 6 Leeds
25.04.98 Dean Phillips W PTS 6 Cardiff
09.05.98 Gary Flear W PTS 4 Sheffield
18.05.98 Brian Coleman W PTS 6 Cleethorpes
05.09.98 Benny Jones W PTS 4 Telford
19.12.98 Gary Thornhill L RSC 9 Liverpool
*(WBO Inter-Continental
S. Featherweight Title Challenge)*
04.06.99 Brian Coleman W PTS 6 Hull
27.09.99 Brian Coleman W PTS 6 Leeds
27.02.00 Chris Price W RTD 3 Leeds
21.03.00 Pedro Miranda L RSC 3 Telde, Gran
Canaria
15.07.00 Arv Mittoo W PTS 6 Norwich
20.10.00 Junior Witter L RTD 4 Belfast

25.02.01 Ram Singh W RSC 2 Derby
02.06.01 Jimmy Phelan W PTS 4 Wakefield
Career: 26 contests, won 22, lost 4.

(Adrian) Adey Cook

Hull. *Born* Hull, 24 May, 1968
Heavyweight. Ht. 5'10¹/₂"
Manager Self

21.04.98 Paul Fiske W RSC 3 Edmonton
09.06.98 Marat Tekouev L RSC 1 Hull
18.12.99 Danny Watts L RSC 1 Southwark
30.11.00 Wes Thompson W RSC 4 Bloomsbury
05.02.01 Paul Fiske W PTS 4 Hull
Career: 5 contests, won 3, lost 2.

Jason Cook

Maesteg. *Born* Maesteg, 27 February, 1975
Lightweight. Welsh L. Welterweight
Champion. Ht. 5'9"
Manager B. Hearn

11.10.96 Brian Robb W RSC 2 Mayfair
27.11.96 Andrew Reed W RSC 3 Bethnal Green
27.05.97 Marc Smith W PTS 4 Mayfair
31.10.97 Marc Smith W PTS 4 Mayfair
24.01.98 David Kirk W RSC 3 Cardiff
26.05.98 Trevor Smith L RSC 1 Mayfair
23.02.99 Darren Woodley W RSC 4 Cardiff
28.05.99 Dave Hinds W RSC 1 Liverpool
02.10.99 Pete Buckley W PTS 4 Cardiff
11.12.99 Woody Greenaway W RSC 1 Merthyr
(Vacant Welsh L. Welterweight Title)
26.02.00 Harry Butler W PTS 6 Swansea
17.04.00 Andrei Sinepupov W RTD 3
Birmingham
12.05.00 Keith Jones W PTS 10 Swansea
(Welsh L. Welterweight Title Defence)
09.10.00 Assen Vasilev W PTS 6 Liverpool
17.02.01 Dariusz Snarski W PTS 8 Kolbrzeg,
Poland
Career: 15 contests, won 14, lost 1.

Nicky Cook

Dagenham. *Born* Stepney, 13 September,
1979
Featherweight. Ht. 5'6¹/₂"
Manager J. Harding

11.12.98 Sean Grant W CO 1 Cheshunt
26.02.99 Graham McGrath W CO 2 Coventry
27.04.99 Vasil Paskelev W CO 1 Bethnal Green
25.05.99 Wilson Acuna W PTS 4 Mayfair
12.07.99 Igor Sakhatarov W PTS 4 Coventry
20.08.99 Vlado Varhegyi W PTS 4 Bloomsbury
27.11.99 John Barnes W PTS 6 Liverpool
20.12.99 Carl Allen W CO 3 Bethnal Green
10.03.00 Chris Jickells W RSC 1 Bethnal Green
27.05.00 Anthony Hanna W PTS 6 Mayfair
16.06.00 Salem Bouaita W PTS 6 Bloomsbury
04.11.00 Vladimir Borov W RSC 1 Bethnal
Green
08.12.00 Rakhim Mingaleev W PTS 8 Crystal
Palace
19.05.01 Foudil Madani W RSC 1 Wembley
Career: 14 contests, won 14.

Ian Cooper

Hartlepool. *Born* Hartlepool, 3 May, 1974
Northern Area S. Middleweight Champion.
Ht. 5'11"
Manager D. Garside

01.12.99 Dean Ashton W PTS 4 Yarm
09.06.00 Richie Jenkins W PTS 6 Blackpool
23.07.00 Martin Jolley W PTS 6 Hartlepool
01.10.00 Ian Toby W RSC 4 Hartlepool
11.02.01 Mike White W RSC 9 Hartlepool
(Vacant Northern Area S.Middleweight Title)
06.05.01 Howard Clarke W PTS 6 Hartlepool
Career: 6 contests, won 6.

Darren Corbett

Belfast. *Born* Belfast, 8 July, 1972
IBO Inter-Continental L. Heavyweight Champion. Former Commonwealth, IBO Inter-Continental & All-Ireland Cruiserweight Champion. Ht. 5'11"
Manager Self

10.12.94 David Jules W RSC 1 Manchester
13.12.94 Carl Gaffney W RSC 1 Potters Bar
21.02.95 Steve Garber W PTS 6 Sunderland
18.03.95 Gary Williams DREW 6 Millstreet
14.04.95 Dennis Bailey W RSC 2 Belfast
27.05.95 R. F. McKenzie L PTS 6 Belfast
26.08.95 Nigel Rafferty W PTS 6 Belfast
07.10.95 Nigel Rafferty W PTS 6 Belfast
02.12.95 Bobbi Joe Edwards W PTS 6 Belfast
07.05.96 Cliff Elden W RSC 1 Mayfair
28.05.96 Darren Fearn W RSC 1 Belfast
03.09.96 Chris Woollas W RSC 7 Belfast
05.11.96 Ray Kane W RSC 5 Belfast
(Vacant All-Ireland Cruiserweight Title)
17.12.96 Chris Woollas W RSC 1 Doncaster
28.01.97 Nigel Rafferty W PTS 10 Belfast
(All-Ireland Cruiserweight Title Defence)
29.04.97 Noel Magee W CO 2 Belfast
(All-Ireland Cruiserweight Title Defence)
02.06.97 Chris Okoh W RSC 3 Belfast
(Commonwealth Cruiserweight Title Challenge)
17.10.97 Hector Sanjuro W PTS 6 Ledyard, USA
20.12.97 Robert Norton W PTS 12 Belfast
(Commonwealth Cruiserweight Title Defence)
21.02.98 Dirk Wallyn W PTS 10 Belfast
28.04.98 Konstantin Ochrej W RSC 4 Belfast
(Vacant IBO Inter-Continental Cruiserweight Title)
26.05.98 Roberto Dominguez W CO 1 Mayfair
(IBO Inter-Continental Cruiserweight Title Defence)
28.11.98 Bruce Scott L RSC 10 Belfast
(Commonwealth Cruiserweight Title Defence. Vacant British Cruiserweight Title)
10.04.99 Stephane Allouane L RSC 9 Manchester
(Vacant IBO Inter-Continental Cruiserweight Title)
31.07.99 Darren Ashton W RSC 2 Carlisle
14.12.99 Neil Simpson W PTS 12 Coventry
(Vacant IBO Inter-Continental L. Heavyweight Title)
25.03.00 Lennox Lewis W RSC 2 Liverpool
(IBO Inter-Continental L. Heavyweight Title Defence)
16.06.01 Tyler Hughes W RSC 1 New York City, USA
Career: 28 contests, won 24, drew 1, lost 3.

Danny Costello

Norwood. *Born* Lambeth, 21 August, 1975
Flyweight. Ht. 5'6½"
Manager Self

26.10.96 Henry Jones W RSC 3 Liverpool
24.10.98 Ross Cassidy W PTS 4 Liverpool
10.03.00 Lennie Hodgkins W PTS 4 Chigwell
14.10.00 Anthony Hanna DREW 4 Wembley
02.12.00 Sean Green W PTS 4 Chigwell
16.06.01 Sean Green L RSC 3 Dagenham
Career: 6 contests, won 4, drew 1, lost 1.

Dave Cotterill

Hemsworth. *Born* Pontefract, 25 April, 1977
Lightweight. Ht. 5'8"
Manager S. Butler

26.10.00 Leo Turner L PTS 6 Stoke
04.11.00 Scott Spencer L PTS 4 Bethnal Green
30.11.00 Joel Viney W RSC 1 Blackpool
05.12.00 Duncan Armstrong W PTS 6 Nottingham
23.02.01 Andrew Ferrans W RSC 2 Irvine
30.04.01 Andrew Ferrans L RSC 1 Glasgow
18.06.01 Nigel Senior W PTS 6 Bradford
Career: 7 contests, won 4, lost 3.

Dave Cotterill   Les Clark

Jane Couch

Fleetwood. *Born* Fleetwood, 12 August, 1968
WBF Lightweight Champion. Former Undefeated WIBF & WBF Welterweight Champion. Ht. 5'7"
Manager Tex Woodward

30.10.94 Kalpna Shah W RSC 2 Wigan
29.01.95 Fosteres Joseph W PTS 6 Fleetwood
18.04.95 Jane Johnson W RSC 4 Fleetwood
01.07.95 Julia Shirley W PTS 6 Fleetwood
24.05.96 Sandra Geiger W PTS 10 Copenhagen, Denmark
(WIBF Welterweight Title Challenge)

01.03.97 Andrea Deshong W RSC 7 New Orleans, USA
(WIBF Welterweight Title Defence)
24.08.97 Leah Mellinger W PTS 10 Connecticut, USA
(WIBF Welterweight Title Defence)
24.10.97 Dora Webber L PTS 6 Mississippi, USA
10.01.98 Dora Webber L PTS 10 Atlantic City, USA
25.11.98 Simone Lukic W RSC 2 Streatham
20.02.99 Marisch Sjauw W PTS 10 Thornaby
(WIBF Welterweight Title Defence. Vacant WBF Welterweight Title)
01.04.99 Heike Noller W PTS 8 Birmingham
31.10.99 Sharon Anyos W PTS 10 Raynes Park
(Vacant WBF Lightweight Title)
09.03.00 Michelle Straus W RSC 3 Bethnal Green
01.07.00 Galina Gumliska W RSC 6 Southwark
(WBF Lightweight Title Defence)
19.08.00 Liz Mueller L PTS 6 Mashantucket, Connecticut, USA
16.06.01 Viktoria Oleynikov W PTS 4 Wembley
Career: 17 contests, won 14, lost 3.

Mickey Coveney

West Ham. *Born* London, 26 November, 1981
Featherweight. Ht. 5'4"
Manager F. Maloney

12.06.00 Stevie Quinn W PTS 4 Belfast
30.11.00 Gareth Wiltshaw W PTS 4 Peterborough
24.02.01 Dazzo Williams L CO 1 Bethnal Green
03.06.01 Gareth Wiltshaw W PTS 4 Southwark
Career: 4 contests, won 3, lost 1.

Simeon Cover

Worksop. *Born* Clapton, 12 March, 1978
S. Middleweight. Ht. 5'11"
Manager D. Ingle

28.03.01 Danny Smith L PTS 6 Piccadilly
Career: 1 contest, lost 1.

Darren Covill

Welling. *Born* Welling, 11 April, 1970
S. Middleweight. Ht. 5'8"
Manager Self

23.02.95 Brian Coleman W PTS 4 Southwark
19.05.95 Allan Gray L PTS 6 Southwark
04.06.95 Dick Hanns-Kat W RSC 3 Bethnal Green
14.09.95 Gavin Barker W CO 1 Battersea
21.09.95 Shaun Stokes L PTS 6 Sheffield
22.11.95 Jason Barker L PTS 4 Sheffield
05.02.96 Jason Barker W RSC 1 Bexleyheath
21.03.96 Paul Miles L PTS 4 Southwark
11.07.97 Leigh Wicks W RSC 2 Brighton
26.09.97 Jason Williams L PTS 6 Port Talbot
08.10.97 Steve Roberts L PTS 6 Poplar
08.11.97 David Baptiste W PTS 4 Southwark
06.12.97 Ali Khattab L PTS 4 Wembley
31.01.98 Paolo Roberto L PTS 6 Edmonton
13.02.98 John Docherty W RSC 1 Barrhead
21.03.98 Wayne Alexander L RSC 2 Bethnal Green
04.06.98 Darren McInulty DREW 6 Barking

10.09.98	Cornelius Carr L RTD 2 Acton
25.11.98	Leigh Wicks L PTS 4 Streatham
16.01.99	Anthony McFadden L RSC 2 Bethnal Green
18.02.99	Adrian Stone L RSC 2 Barking
24.03.99	Lester Jacobs L RSC 2 Bayswater
02.07.99	Steven Bendall L RTD 3 Bristol
27.02.00	Gareth Hogg L RSC 3 Plymouth
02.02.01	Matthew Barney L PTS 6 Portsmouth
24.03.01	Allan Foster L RTD 3 Sheffield
12.05.01	Hughie Doherty L PTS 4 Plymouth

Career: 27 contests, won 7, drew 1, lost 19.

Chris Crook

Haslingden. *Born* Rossendale, 30 July, 1972
S. Middleweight. Ht. 5'10"
Manager Self

29.05.99	Mike White L PTS 6 South Shields
24.02.00	Andy Vickers W PTS 6 Sunderland
25.03.00	Joey Ainscough L PTS 4 Liverpool
01.04.00	Steve Roberts L RSC 3 Bethnal Green
08.07.00	Paul Owen L RSC 1 Rotherham
05.10.00	Mike White L RSC 4 Sunderland

Career: 6 contests, won 1, lost 5.

Lance Crosby

Hull. *Born* Hull, 15 June, 1974
L. Welterweight. Ht. 5'8½"
Manager D. Smith

20.03.00	Delroy Mellis W PTS 4 Mansfield
25.05.00	Trevor Smith W PTS 6 Hull
16.11.00	Arv Mittoo W RSC 3 Hull
05.02.01	David White DREW 4 Hull
02.06.01	Woody Greenaway W PTS 6 Wakefield

Career: 5 contests, won 4, drew 1.

Peter Culshaw

Liverpool. *Born* Liverpool, 15 May, 1973
WBU Flyweight Champion. Former Undefeated WBU International S. Flyweight Champion. Former Commonwealth Flyweight Champion. Former Undefeated Central Area Flyweight Champion. Ht. 5'6"
Manager Self

02.07.93	Graham McGrath W PTS 6 Liverpool
28.09.93	Vince Feeney W PTS 6 Liverpool
11.12.93	Nick Tooley W RSC 1 Liverpool
25.02.94	Des Gargano W PTS 6 Chester
06.05.94	Neil Swain W PTS 6 Liverpool
26.09.94	Daryl McKenzie W PTS 6 Liverpool
20.04.95	Rowan Williams W CO 6 Liverpool
29.09.95	Maxim Pougatchev DREW 8 Liverpool
05.03.96	Louis Veitch W RSC 3 Barrow *(Central Area Flyweight Title Challenge)*
13.04.96	Lyndon Kershaw W RSC 3 Liverpool
25.06.96	Danny Ward W RSC 3 Stevenage *(Commonwealth Flyweight Title Challenge)*
27.09.96	James Wanene W RSC 7 Stevenage *(Commonwealth Flyweight Title Defence)*
02.08.97	Jason Thomas W PTS 8 Barnsley
11.09.97	Ady Lewis L RSC 8 Widnes *(Commonwealth Flyweight Title Defence. British Flyweight Title Challenge)*
12.03.98	Foudil Madani W RSC 4 Liverpool *(Vacant WBU International S. Flyweight Title)*
24.10.98	Mzukisi Marali W RSC 7 Liverpool *(Vacant WBU Flyweight Title)*
05.03.99	Zolile Mbityi W PTS 12 Liverpool *(WBU Flyweight Title Defence)*
15.05.99	Adrian Ochoa W RSC 9 Blackpool *(WBU Flyweight Title Defence)*
09.03.00	Oscar Andrade W PTS 12 Liverpool *(WBU Flyweight Title Defence)*
24.05.00	Jake Matlala W PTS 12 Carnival City, South Africa *(WBU Flyweight Title Defence)*
11.11.00	Dimitar Alipiev W CO 1 Belfast *(WBU Flyweight Title Defence)*
09.06.01	Ian Napa W RSC 8 Bethnal Green *(WBU Flyweight Title Defence)*

Career: 22 contests, won 20, drew 1, lost 1.

Jane Couch (left) versus Viktoria Oleynikov

Les Clark

D

(Gerardo) Jezz D'Agostino

Peterborough. *Born* Peterborough, 4
September, 1972
Featherweight. Ht. 5'5"
Manager Self

03.04.97	David Jeffrey L PTS 6 Wembley
28.11.97	Brendan Bryce W RSC 5 Bethnal Green
28.03.98	Brendan Bryce W PTS 6 Crystal Palace
07.12.98	Wee Barry W PTS 6 Acton
25.02.99	Wayne Jones W PTS 6 Kentish Town
07.08.99	David Jeffrey W PTS 4 Dagenham
07.02.00	John Barnes L PTS 4 Peterborough
04.03.00	John Barnes L PTS 4 Peterborough
22.07.00	Alex Stewart L PTS 4 Watford

Career: 9 contests, won 5, lost 4.

(Daniel) Jesse James Daniel (James)

Leeds. *Born* Leeds, 21 July, 1975
Lightweight. Ht. 5'9"
Manager J. Ingle

17.05.99	Dave Hinds W PTS 6 Cleethorpes
15.08.99	Graham McGrath W PTS 6 Derby
27.09.99	Marc Smith W PTS 6 Cleethorpes
13.12.99	Sean Grant W RSC 5 Cleethorpes
27.02.00	Les Frost W PTS 6 Leeds
15.05.00	Chris Jickells W PTS 6 Cleethorpes
29.05.00	Gary Flear W PTS 4 Manchester
04.09.00	Steve Hanley W PTS 4 Manchester
07.10.00	Arv Mittoo W PTS 4 Doncaster
19.11.00	Chris Price W PTS 4 Chesterfield

Career: 10 contests, won 10.

Jesse James Daniel   Les Clark

Scott Dann

Plymouth. *Born* Plymouth, 23 July, 1974
IBO Inter-Continental Middleweight
Champion. Ht. 5'10½"
Manager C. Sanigar/F. Warren

15.11.97	Jon Rees W RSC 1 Bristol
25.04.98	Israel Khumalo W RSC 3 Cardiff
30.05.98	Michael Alexander W PTS 4 Bristol
14.07.98	Richard Glaysher W RSC 1 Reading
24.10.98	James Donoghue W PTS 6 Bristol
27.02.00	James Donoghue W RSC 1 Plymouth
07.04.00	Martin Jolley W RSC 2 Bristol
08.09.00	Sean Pritchard W RSC 5 Bristol
06.10.00	Peter Mitchell W RSC 3 Maidstone
03.11.00	Anthony Ivory W PTS 8 Ebbw Vale
13.03.01	Jason Hart W RSC 2 Plymouth
12.05.01	Elvis Adonesi W CO 7 Plymouth
	(Vacant IBO Inter-Continental Middleweight Title)

Career: 12 contests, won 12.

Shaune Danskin

Peterborough. *Born* Spalding, 28
December, 1975
L. Welterweight. Ht. 5'5"
Manager M. Goodall

08.12.95	Gary Jenkinson L PTS 6 Leeds
19.02.96	Paul Hamilton L CO 2 Glasgow
04.10.96	Nicky Wilders L PTS 6 Wakefield
24.05.01	Martin Watson L RSC 3 Glasgow

Career: 4 contests, lost 4.

Chris Davies

Blaenclydach. *Born* Pontypridd, 24 August,
1974
L. Heavyweight. Ht. 5'9"
Manager D. Gardiner

27.04.94	Craig Joseph L PTS 6 Solihull
25.05.94	Glenn Catley L RSC 1 Bristol
29.05.96	Mark Hickey W RSC 1 Ebbw Vale
19.07.96	Michael Pinnock W PTS 6 Ystrad
31.08.96	James Branch L PTS 4 Dublin
02.10.96	Neil Simpson L PTS 4 Cardiff
02.10.99	Carl Nicholson W CO 1 Cardiff
22.10.99	Jim Twite W CO 1 Coventry
30.10.99	Ganny Dovidavas W PTS 4 Southwark
11.12.99	Paul Bonson W PTS 4 Merthyr
26.02.00	Adam Cale W RSC 4 Swansea
18.03.00	Neville Brown W RSC 2 Glasgow
11.04.00	Lee Manuel Ossie L PTS 10 Vigo, Spain
12.06.00	Cathal O'Grady W RSC 1 Belfast
29.01.01	Peter Oboh L RSC 8 Peterborough
	(Elim. Commonwealth L. Heavyweight Title)

Career: 15 contests, won 9, lost 6.

Mark Dawson (Lee)

Burton. *Born* Burton, 26 February, 1971
Cruiserweight. Ht. 5'8"
Manager W. Swift

03.06.92	Rick North W PTS 6 Newcastle under Lyme
09.09.92	Jimmy Vincent W PTS 6 Stoke
29.09.92	Steve Goodwin L RSC 1 Stoke
28.10.92	Steve McNess W RSC 2 Kensington
07.12.92	Steve Goodwin W PTS 6 Mayfair
27.01.93	Rick North W PTS 8 Stoke
15.02.93	John Bosco L PTS 6 Mayfair

27.02.93	Robin Reid L RSC 1 Dagenham
30.03.93	Matthew Turner L PTS 6 Cardiff
12.05.93	Steve Goodwin L PTS 10 Stoke
	(Vacant Midlands Area L. Middleweight Title)
27.05.93	Derek Wormald L RTD 5 Burnley
10.11.93	John Bosco L RTD 4 Watford
15.03.94	Stinger Mason W RSC 6 Stoke
22.03.94	Geoff McCreesh L PTS 6 Bethnal Green
05.09.94	Tony Griffiths W PTS 6 Brentwood
17.09.94	Mark Delaney L PTS 6 Crawley
01.10.94	Joe Calzaghe L RSC 1 Cardiff
29.11.94	Andrew Flute L PTS 8 Cannock
07.12.94	John Duckworth W PTS 6 Stoke
20.01.95	Mark Baker L RSC 3 Bethnal Green
08.03.95	Lester Jacobs L PTS 6 Bloomsbury
30.03.95	David Starie L RSC 1 Bethnal Green
06.05.95	Glenn Catley L RSC 5 Shepton Mallet
10.06.95	Ryan Cummings W RSC 3 Manchester
01.07.95	Shaun Cummins L PTS 8 Kensington
22.07.95	Lester Jacobs L PTS 4 Millwall
06.09.95	Robert Harper W PTS 6 Stoke
15.09.95	Jason Matthews L RSC 3 Mansfield
25.10.95	Jetty Williams W PTS 6 Telford
10.11.95	Ryan Rhodes L PTS 6 Derby
25.11.95	Danny Ryan L PTS 4 Dublin
02.12.95	Frederik Alvarez L RTD 1 Belfast
13.01.96	Mark Baker L RSC 3 Halifax
04.03.96	Harri Hakulinen L PTS 4 Helsinki, Finland
13.04.96	Paul Wright L PTS 6 Liverpool
11.05.96	Michael Bowen L PTS 4 Bethnal Green
31.05.96	Peter H. Madsen L PTS 4 Copenhagen, Denmark
08.06.96	Robin Reid L RSC 5 Newcastle
13.07.96	Paul Bowen L RSC 3 Bethnal Green
18.01.97	Lee Whitehead L PTS 6 Manchester
03.02.97	Peter Mason L PTS 4 Sunderland
25.02.97	Michael Bowen L RSC 4 Sheffield
21.11.97	Terry Morrill L PTS 6 Hull
02.12.97	Bobby Banghar L PTS 4 Swansea
21.12.97	Lee Whitehead W RSC 4 Salford
17.01.98	Paul Bowen L PTS 4 Bristol
27.11.98	Michael Monaghan L PTS 6 Nottingham
23.01.99	Jason Matthews L RSC 1 Cheshunt
26.02.99	Tony Griffiths L PTS 4 Bethnal Green
06.03.99	Tony Oakey L PTS 4 Southwark
02.05.99	Donovan Smillie L PTS 6 Shaw
15.05.99	Roy Finlay L PTS 4 Blackpool
27.11.99	Joey Ainscough L PTS 4 Liverpool
04.12.99	Donovan Smillie L PTS 4 Manchester
22.01.00	Tony Dodson L PTS 4 Birmingham
07.02.00	Neil Linford L PTS 4 Peterborough
21.02.00	Tomasz Adamek L RSC 3 Southwark
01.04.00	Dean Doyle L PTS 4 Bethnal Green
15.04.00	Matthew Barney L PTS 6 Bethnal Green
09.06.00	Eamonn Glennon W PTS 6 Blackpool
08.09.00	Scott Baker W RSC 3 Hammersmith
25.09.00	Mark Hobson L CO 1 Barnsley

Career: 62 contests, won 14, lost 48.

Rocky Dean

Thetford. *Born* Bury St Edmonds, 17 June,
1978
Bantamweight. Ht. 5'5"
Manager A. Bowers

14.10.99	Lennie Hodgkins W PTS 6 Bloomsbury
30.10.99	Lennie Hodgkins W PTS 6 Southwark

18.05.00 Danny Lawson W RSC 1 Bethnal Green
29.09.00 Anthony Hanna W PTS 4 Bethnal Green
10.11.00 Chris Jickells L RSC 1 Mayfair
Career: 5 contests, won 4, lost 1.

Jason Dee (Davies)

Pontardawe. *Born* Londonderry, 18 August, 1972
Lightweight. Ht. 5'7"
Manager B. Hearn

11.10.96 Danny Thomas W RSC 3 Mayfair
28.04.97 David Jay W RSC 3 Enfield
08.10.97 Andrew Reed W RSC 1 Poplar
18.11.97 Dewi Roberts W PTS 4 Mansfield
27.01.98 Mark McGowan L RSC 1 Piccadilly
06.11.98 Gary Jenkinson W RSC 2 Mayfair
23.02.99 Woody Greenaway W CO 6 Cardiff
31.07.99 Stefy Bull W RSC 4 Carlisle
02.10.99 Keith Jones W RSC 5 Cardiff
11.12.99 Lee Armstrong W RSC 4 Merthyr
24.04.01 David Burke L RSC 1 Liverpool
Career: 11 contests, won 9, lost 2.

Garry Delaney

West Ham. *Born* Newham, 12 August, 1970
British Masters Cruiserweight Champion. Former Commonwealth, WBO Inter-Continental & Southern Area L. Heavyweight Champion. Ht. 6'3"
Manager A. Bowers

02.10.91 Gus Mendes W RSC 1 Barking
23.10.91 Joe Frater W RSC 1 Bethnal Green
13.11.91 John Kaighin W PTS 6 Bethnal Green
11.12.91 Randy B. Powell W RSC 1 Basildon
11.02.92 Simon Harris DREW 8 Barking
12.05.92 John Williams W PTS 6 Crystal Palace
16.06.92 Nigel Rafferty W CO 5 Dagenham
15.09.92 Gil Lewis W CO 2 Crystal Palace
06.10.92 Simon McDougall W PTS 8 Antwerp, Belgium
10.11.92 John Oxenham W CO 5 Dagenham
12.12.92 Simon McDougall W PTS 8 Muswell Hill
30.01.93 Simon Collins W PTS 8 Brentwood
28.09.93 Glazz Campbell W CO 6 Bethnal Green
(Southern Area L. Heavyweight Title Challenge)
06.11.93 John Kaighin W CO 1 Bethnal Green
21.12.93 Ray Albert W RSC 3 Mayfair
(Vacant WBO Inter-Continental L. Heavyweight Title)
11.01.94 Jim Murray W RSC 7 Bethnal Green
(WBO Inter-Continental L. Heavyweight Title Defence)
09.04.94 Simon Harris W CO 6 Bethnal Green
(WBO Inter-Continental & Southern Area L. Heavyweight Title Defences)
09.07.94 Sergio Merani W PTS 12 Earls Court
(WBO Inter-Continental L. Heavyweight Title)
30.09.94 Arigoma Chiponda W CO 2 Bethnal Green
(Vacant Commonwealth L. Heavyweight Title)
18.03.95 Ernest Mateen W RTD 7 Millstreet
(Vacant WBO Inter-Continental L. Heavyweight Title)

09.05.95 Noel Magee L RTD 7 Basildon
(Commonwealth L. Heavyweight Title Defence)
06.02.96 Francis Wanyama W PTS 6 Basildon
09.04.96 Joey Paladino W RSC 1 Stevenage
07.02.97 John Kiser W PTS 6 Las Vegas, USA
04.03.97 Peter Oboh W DIS 8 Southwark
27.09.97 Julius Francis L RSC 6 Belfast
(Vacant British Heavyweight Title. Commonwealth Heavyweight Title Challenge)
05.06.98 Darron Griffiths W PTS 6 Southend
23.01.99 John Keeton L PTS 12 Cheshunt
(Vacant WBO Inter-Continental Cruiserweight Title)
01.05.99 Tim Brown W PTS 8 Crystal Palace
04.09.99 Lee Swaby W PTS 8 Bethnal Green
29.04.00 Jesper Kristiansen L RTD 10 Varde, Denmark
(Vacant WBO Inter-Continental Cruiserweight Title)
06.10.00 Dominic Negus W PTS 10 Maidstone
(Southern Area Cruiserweight Title Challenge)
10.03.01 Bruce Scott L RTD 3 Bethnal Green
(British Cruiserweight Title Challenge. Vacant Commonwealth Cruiserweight Title)
15.06.01 Darren Ashton W RTD 4 Millwall
(Vacant British Masters Cruiserweight Title)
Career: 34 contests, won 28, drew 1, lost 5.

Mark Delaney

West Ham. *Born* London, 1 December, 1971
L. Heavyweight. Former Undefeated WBO Inter-Continental S. Middleweight Champion. Ht. 5'11"
Manager Self

05.10.93 Lee Sara W RTD 5 Mayfair
11.01.94 Jason McNeill W RSC 2 Bethnal Green
22.01.94 Graham Jenner W RTD 3 Belfast
09.02.94 Tony Colclough W RSC 4 Brentwood
19.03.94 Paul Murray W CO 3 Millwall
09.04.94 Tim Robinson W RSC 2 Bethnal Green
11.06.94 Ernie Loveridge W RSC 5 Bethnal Green
09.07.94 Eddie Knight W CO 4 Earls Court
17.09.94 Mark Dawson W PTS 6 Crawley
30.09.94 Jerry Mortimer W RSC 3 Bethnal Green
07.11.94 Martin Jolley W RSC 3 Bethnal Green
23.11.94 Marvin O'Brien W RTD 1 Irvine
20.12.94 Martin Jolley W RSC 4 Bethnal Green
17.02.95 Peter Vosper W RSC 1 Crawley
16.03.95 Carlos Christie W CO 1 Basildon
31.03.95 Trevor Ambrose W RSC 1 Crystal Palace
09.05.95 Eddie Knight W RSC 2 Basildon
30.09.95 Andrew Flute W PTS 12 Basildon
(Vacant WBO Inter-Continental S. Middleweight Title)
28.10.95 Hunter Clay W RTD 2 Kensington
14.11.95 Armando Rodriguez W PTS 12 Bury
(WBO Inter-Continental S. Middleweight Title Defence)
23.01.96 Darron Griffiths W PTS 12 Bethnal Green
(WBO Inter-Continental S. Middleweight Title Defence)

20.04.96 Joe Calzaghe L RSC 5 Brentwood
(British S. Middleweight Title Challenge)
27.11.96 John Duckworth W RSC 5 Bethnal Green
08.03.97 Butch Lesley W PTS 6 Brentwood
30.06.97 Mark Baker L PTS 10 Bethnal Green
(Elim. British S. Middleweight Title)
08.09.98 Robert Peel W PTS 6 Bethnal Green
10.07.99 Tony Griffiths W PTS 6 Southwark
18.12.99 Ali Forbes W PTS 8 Southwark
18.11.00 Neil Simpson L RSC 1 Dagenham
(British L.Heavyweight Title Challenge)
Career: 29 contests, won 26, lost 3.

(Mtabingwa) Frankie DeMilo

Bristol. *Born* Rwanda, 6 April, 1974
British Masters & Western Area S. Bantamweight Champion. Ht. 5'7½"
Manager C. Sanigar

26.02.99 Danny Lawson W PTS 6 Longford
17.03.99 Daniel Ring W RSC 2 Kensington
02.07.99 Graham McGrath W PTS 4 Bristol
24.09.99 Jason Thomas L RSC 2 Merthyr
22.11.99 Anthony Hanna W PTS 6 Piccadilly
03.12.99 Ian Turner W PTS 6 Peterborough
20.01.00 David Jeffrey W RSC 8 Piccadilly
(Vacant Western Area S. Bantamweight Title)
29.03.00 Jason Thomas W RSC 8 Piccadilly
(Vacant British Masters S. Bantamweight Title)
02.06.00 Kevin Gerowski W RSC 7 Ashford
(British Masters S. Bantamweight Title Defence)
08.09.00 Harry Woods W RTD 6 Bristol
(British Masters S.Bantamweight Title Defence)
03.11.00 Ian Turner W PTS 10 Ebbw Vale
(British Masters S.Bantamweight Title Defence)
12.05.01 John Barnes W PTS 10 Plymouth
(British Masters S. Bantamweight Title Defence)
Career: 12 contests, won 11, lost 1.

Paul Denton (Ramsey)

Birmingham. *Born* Birmingham, 12 April, 1970
Welterweight. Ht. 5'10"
Manager Self

18.03.93 Mark O'Callaghan W RSC 4 Lewisham
29.04.93 Dave Maj DREW 6 Mayfair
11.08.93 Billy McDougall W PTS 6 Mansfield
01.10.93 Ferid Bennecer W CO 3 Waregem, Belgium
01.12.93 Brian Hickey W CO 1 Kensington
28.01.94 Youssef Bakhouche L PTS 6 Waregem, Belgium
07.05.94 Viktor Fesechko L PTS 6 Dnepropetrousk, Ukraine
23.09.94 Roy Rowland W RSC 5 Bethnal Green
03.01.95 Patrick Charpentier L RSC 4 Epernay, France
25.02.95 Paul Ryan L RSC 4 Millwall
25.11.95 Michael Carruth L PTS 8 Dublin
03.02.96 George Naylor W RSC 3 Liverpool
26.04.96 Ross Hale W RSC 4 Cardiff
15.11.96 Frank Olsen L RSC 4 Nestved, Denmark

14.03.97	Mark Winters L PTS 8 Reading
13.06.97	Alan McDowall DREW 6 Paisley
21.03.98	Naas Scheepers L PTS 8 Hammanskraal, South Africa
19.09.98	Neil Sinclair L RSC 1 Dublin
19.12.98	Richard Hatton L RSC 6 Liverpool
16.02.99	Steve Tuckett L PTS 6 Leeds
27.02.99	Michael Carruth L RSC 5 Bethnal Green
27.05.00	Jacek Bielski L PTS 6 Mayfair
19.06.00	Oscar Hall L PTS 4 Burton
08.07.00	Michael Jennings L PTS 6 Widnes
12.08.00	Wayne Alexander L RSC 1 Wembley
02.10.00	Kevin McIntyre L PTS 6 Glasgow
18.11.00	Pavel Melnikov L PTS 4 Dagenham
01.12.00	Paul Dyer L PTS 4 Peterborough
11.12.00	Michael Jennings L PTS 4 Widnes
17.02.01	David Walker L PTS 4 Bethnal Green
26.02.01	James Hare L PTS 4 Nottingham
07.04.01	Brett James L PTS 4 Wembley
24.04.01	Paul Burns L PTS 4 Liverpool
08.05.01	Derek Roche L PTS 6 Barnsley
27.05.01	Jamie Moore L RSC 3 Manchester

Career: 35 contests, won 7, drew 2, lost 26.

Reagan Denton

Sheffield. *Born* Sheffield, 26 June, 1978
L. Middleweight. Ht. 5'11"
Manager Self

15.05.99	Pedro Thompson W PTS 4 Sheffield
15.11.99	Colin Vidler W PTS 4 Bethnal Green
25.09.00	William Webster W PTS 4 Barnsley

Career: 3 contests, won 3.

Reagan Denton   Les Clark

(Hardip) Harry Dhami

Gravesend. *Born* Gravesend, 17 April, 1972
British Welterweight Champion. Former
Undefeated Southern Area Welterweight
Champion. Ht. 5'10"
Manager T. Toole

29.10.92	Johnny Pinnock W PTS 6 Hayes
20.05.94	Nick Appiah W RSC 4 Acton

27.05.94	Chris Vassiliou W RSC 5 Ashford
11.10.94	Steve McNess DREW 6 Bethnal Green
09.11.94	Clay O'Shea L PTS 6 Millwall
30.11.94	Robert Wright L PTS 8 Wolverhampton
17.11.95	John Bosco L PTS 6 Bethnal Green
08.12.95	Nicky Thurbin L PTS 8 Bethnal Green
25.04.96	Chris Pollock W PTS 6 Mayfair
07.05.96	Ojay Abrahams W RSC 5 Mayfair *(Vacant Southern Area Welterweight Title)*
20.11.96	Andy Peach W RTD 3 Wembley
14.03.97	Paul Dyer W PTS 10 Reading *(Southern Area Welterweight Title Defence)*
20.05.97	Paul Miles W RTD 2 Gillingham *(Southern Area Welterweight Title Defence)*

09.09.97	Howard Clarke W PTS 8 Bethnal Green
26.09.98	Allan Gray W PTS 10 Southwark *(Southern Area Welterweight Title Defence)*
12.12.98	Kevin McCarthy W PTS 10 Southwark *(Southern Area Welterweight Title Defence)*
15.05.99	Paul Burns W PTS 8 Blackpool
12.12.99	Lee Bird W PTS 6 Chigwell
27.03.00	Derek Roche W PTS 12 Barnsley *(British Welterweight Title Challenge)*
14.10.00	Malcolm Melvin W PTS 12 Wembley *(British Welterweight Title Defence)*
27.11.00	Spencer McCracken W PTS 12 Birmingham *(British Welterweight Title Defence)*

Career: 21 contests, won 16, drew 1, lost 4.

Harry Dhami   Les Clark

Haroon Din
Sheffield. *Born* Middlesbrough, 21 May, 1978
S. Featherweight. Ht. 5'8"
Manager D. Ingle

21.09.98	Les Frost L PTS 6 Cleethorpes	
14.12.98	Les Frost L RSC 1 Cleethorpes	
02.05.99	Amjid Mahmood W PTS 6 Shaw	
20.05.00	Dave Travers W PTS 6 Leicester	
24.06.00	Willie Limond L PTS 4 Glasgow	
30.08.00	Leon Dobbs W CO 1 Scunthorpe	
19.11.00	Carl Greaves L RSC 4 Chesterfield	

Career: 7 contests, won 3, lost 4.

Gary Dixon
Carlisle. *Born* Carlisle, 2 November, 1974
Middleweight. Ht. 5'10¹/₂"
Manager J. Doughty

18.03.01	Jamie Logan W PTS 6 Shaw	
10.05.01	Paul Owen L RSC 3 Sunderland	

Career: 2 contests, won 1, lost 1.

Scott Dixon
Hamilton. *Born* Hamilton, 28 September, 1976
L. Middleweight. Former Undefeated Commonwealth Welterweight Champion. Former Undefeated WBB & Scottish Welterweight Champion. Ht. 5'9"
Manager A. Bowers

13.10.95	Andrew Smith W PTS 4 Glasgow	
17.12.95	Martin Evans W RSC 4 Glasgow	
12.02.96	Colin Innes W PTS 6 Glasgow	
16.03.96	Ian Richardson W PTS 4 Glasgow	
26.04.96	Andy Green W RSC 5 Glasgow	
24.05.96	Brian Coleman W PTS 6 Glasgow	
20.09.96	Alan Temple W PTS 4 Glasgow	
06.11.96	Rocky Ferrari DREW 6 Glasgow	
22.12.96	Marc Smith W PTS 6 Glasgow	
04.04.97	Jimmy Phelan W PTS 6 Glasgow	
16.05.97	Dean Bramhald W PTS 6 Glasgow	
13.06.97	Chris Price W PTS 6 Paisley	
05.07.97	Mark McGowan W PTS 4 Glasgow	
12.09.97	Gerard Murphy W PTS 8 Brighton	
01.11.97	Nigel Bradley W PTS 4 Glasgow	
12.11.97	John Green DREW 8 Glasgow	
14.12.97	Tony Walton W PTS 6 Glasgow	
27.02.98	Chris Saunders W PTS 10 Glasgow	
	(Elim. British Welterweight Title)	
19.09.98	Michael Carruth L PTS 12 Dublin	
	(Vacant WAA Welterweight Title)	
13.11.98	Lee Molyneux W PTS 4 Brighton	
26.02.99	Edwin Murillo W CO 6 Bethnal Green	
	(WBB Welterweight Title Challenge)	
07.06.99	Mark Ramsey W PTS 8 Glasgow	
22.10.99	Derek Roche L PTS 12 Coventry	
	(British Welterweight Title Challenge)	
05.02.00	Sean Sullivan W PTS 12 Bethnal Green	
	(Vacant Commonwealth Welterweight Title)	
06.06.00	Charlie Kane W RSC 6 Motherwell	
	(Commonwealth Welterweight Title Defence. Vacant Scottish Welterweight Title)	
24.06.00	Leith Wicks W PTS 4 Glasgow	
19.08.00	Steve Roberts L RSC 9 Brentwood	
	(Vacant WBF L. Middleweight Title)	
25.11.00	Anthony Farnell L RSC 7 Manchester	
	(WBO Inter-Continental L. Middleweight Title Challenge)	
20.03.01	Wayne Shepherd W PTS 6 Glasgow	
27.04.01	Anders Styve L PTS 4 Aalborg, Denmark	
18.05.01	Ruben Varon W RSC 5 Guadalajara, Spain	

Career: 31 contests, won 24, drew 2, lost 5.

Leon Dobbs
Scunthorpe. *Born* Beverley, 28 March, 1977
S. Featherweight. Ht. 5'8³/₄"
Manager Self

05.06.98	Bobby Lyndon L PTS 6 Hull	
07.12.98	Amjid Mahmood L RSC 2 Manchester	
18.02.99	Barry Hughes L RSC 1 Glasgow	
30.08.00	Haroon Din L CO 1 Scunthorpe	
26.10.00	Kevin Gerowski L CO 1 Stoke	

Career: 5 contests, lost 5.

Craig Docherty
Glasgow. *Born* Glasgow, 27 September, 1979
S. Featherweight. Ht. 5'7"
Manager T. Gilmour

16.11.98	Kevin Gerowski W PTS 6 Glasgow	
22.02.99	Des Gargano W PTS 6 Glasgow	
19.04.99	Paul Quarmby W RSC 4 Glasgow	
07.06.99	Simon Chambers W PTS 6 Glasgow	
20.09.99	John Barnes W PTS 6 Glasgow	
15.11.99	Peter Allen W RSC 1 Glasgow	
24.01.00	Lee Williamson W PTS 6 Glasgow	
19.02.00	Steve Hanley W PTS 6 Prestwick	
05.06.00	Sebastian Hart W RSC 1 Glasgow	
23.10.00	Lee Armstrong DREW 8 Glasgow	
22.01.01	Nigel Senior W RSC 4 Glasgow	
20.03.01	Jamie McKeever W RSC 3 Glasgow	
11.06.01	Rakhim Mingaleev W PTS 8 Nottingham	

Career: 13 contests, won 12, drew 1.

(Andrew) Drew Docherty
Condorrat. *Born* Glasgow, 29 November, 1965
Former Undefeated British S. Bantamweight Champion. Former British Bantamweight Champion. Ht. 5'6"
Manager T. Gilmour

14.09.89	Gordon Shaw W PTS 6 Motherwell	
23.11.89	Chris Clarkson W PTS 6 Motherwell	
09.05.90	Rocky Lawlor DREW 8 Solihull	
03.10.90	Steve Robinson W PTS 8 Solihull	
21.11.90	Pete Buckley W PTS 8 Solihull	
14.11.91	Stevie Woods W RSC 1 Edinburgh	
27.01.92	Neil Parry W RSC 4 Glasgow	
27.04.92	Pete Buckley W PTS 8 Glasgow	
01.06.92	Joe Kelly W RSC 5 Glasgow	
	(British Bantamweight Title Challenge)	
25.01.93	Donnie Hood W PTS 12 Glasgow	
	(British Bantamweight Title Defence)	
26.04.93	Russell Davison W PTS 8 Glasgow	
25.10.93	Pete Buckley W PTS 8 Glasgow	
02.02.94	Vincenzo Belcastro L PTS 12 Glasgow	
	(European Bantamweight Title Challenge)	
09.07.94	Conn McMullen W PTS 8 Earls Court	
20.09.94	Miguel Matthews W PTS 8 Musselburgh	
23.11.94	Ady Benton W PTS 12 Irvine	
	(British Bantamweight Title Defence)	
17.02.95	Alfred Kotey L RSC 4 Cumbernauld	
	(WBO Bantamweight Title Challenge)	
13.10.95	James Murray W CO 12 Glasgow	
	(British Bantamweight Title Defence)	
20.01.96	Daniel Jimenez L PTS 12 Mansfield	
	(WBO Bantamweight Title Challenge)	
14.03.97	Johnny Bredahl L RSC 3 Odense, Denmark	
	(European Bantamweight Title Challenge)	
26.09.98	Paul Lloyd L PTS 12 York	
	(British & Commonwealth Bantamweight Title Challenges)	
24.04.99	Patrick Mullings W PTS 12 Peterborough	
	(British S. Bantamweight Title Challenge)	
01.10.99	Michael Brodie L RSC 6 Bethnal Green	
	(European S. Bantamweight Title Challenge)	
04.11.00	Michael Alldis L RSC 6 Bethnal Green	
	(British S. Bantamweight Title Challenge)	

Career: 24 contests, won 16, drew 1, lost 7.

James Docherty
Edinburgh. *Born* Edinburgh, 4 April, 1977
L. Middleweight. Ht. 6'0¹/₂"
Manager Self

27.04.98	Shaun O'Neill W PTS 6 Glasgow	
19.10.98	Ram Singh W PTS 6 Glasgow	
22.02.99	Brian Dunn W PTS 6 Glasgow	
19.04.99	Shaun O'Neill W RSC 3 Glasgow	
15.11.99	Wayne Shepherd W PTS 8 Glasgow	
20.03.00	Matt Scriven W PTS 8 Glasgow	
17.04.00	Dean Nicholas W RSC 6 Glasgow	
06.06.00	Jon Foster W PTS 6 Motherwell	
20.03.01	Matt Scriven W RSC 1 Glasgow	
04.06.01	Howard Clarke W PTS 6 Hartlepool	

Career: 10 contests, won 10.

Adrian Dodson
Islington. *Born* Georgetown, Guyana, 20 September, 1970
S. Middleweight. Former IBO S. Middleweight Champion. Former Undefeated WBO Inter-Continental L. Middleweight Champion. Ht. 5'10"
Manager Self

31.03.93	Chris Mulcahy W RSC 1 Bethnal Green	
14.04.93	Rick North W RTD 1 Kensington	
06.05.93	Greg Wallace W RSC 3 Las Vegas, USA	
23.06.93	Russell Washer W PTS 6 Edmonton	
22.09.93	Robert Peel W CO 1 Bethnal Green	
23.10.93	Julian Eavis W RSC 4 Cardiff	
26.02.94	Shamus Casey W CO 1 Earls Court	
12.03.94	Danny Juma W PTS 6 Cardiff	
09.04.94	Stuart Dunn W RSC 1 Mansfield	
04.06.94	Andrew Jervis W RSC 2 Cardiff	
10.09.94	Colin Pitters W PTS 6 Birmingham	
25.02.95	Lloyd Honeyghan W RSC 3 Millwall	
07.10.95	Hughes Daigneault W RSC 4 Belfast	
	(Vacant WBO Inter-Continental L. Middleweight Title)	
02.12.95	Craig Snyder W RSC 8 Belfast	
	(WBO Inter-Continental L. Middleweight Title Defence)	

04.05.96 John Bosco W RSC 7 Dagenham
*(WBO Inter-Continental
L. Middleweight Title Defence)*
27.11.96 Anthony Joseph W CO 1 Bethnal
Green
*(WBO Inter-Continental
L. Middleweight Title Defence)*
29.01.97 Rachid Serdjane W DIS 5 Bethnal
Green
29.04.97 Viktor Fessetchko W RSC 3 Belfast
19.12.97 Ronald Wright L RTD 6 Millwall
*(WBO L. Middleweight Title
Challenge)*
24.03.98 Nestor Tobias W RSC 4 Bethnal Green
28.08.98 Israel Ponce W RSC 2 Atlantic City,
USA
08.09.98 Mpush Makambi L CO 11 Bethnal
Green
(Vacant IBO Middleweight Title)
11.12.98 Mpush Makambi L RSC 8 Prestwick
(IBO Middleweight Title Challenge)
27.04.99 Orlando Wiet W PTS 10 Bethnal Green
29.06.99 Derek Wormald W PTS 6 Bethnal
Green
20.08.99 Lorant Szabo W PTS 8 Bloomsbury
05.10.99 Alain Bonnamie L DIS 12 Bloomsbury
*(Vacant Commonwealth Middleweight
Title)*

19.08.00 Paul Wesley W PTS 4 Brentwood
03.03.01 Paul Jones W CO 3 Wembley
(Vacant IBO S.Middleweight Title)
07.04.01 Ramon Britez L CO 5 Wembley
(IBO S. Middleweight Title Defence)
Career: 30 contests, won 25, lost 5.

Tony Dodson
Liverpool. *Born* Liverpool, 2 July, 1980
S. Middleweight. Ht. 6'0½"
Manager B. Devine

31.07.99 Michael McDermott W RTD 1 Carlisle
02.10.99 Sean Pritchard W RSC 3 Cardiff
22.01.00 Mark Dawson W PTS 4 Birmingham
11.03.00 Paul Bonson W PTS 4 Kensington
19.08.00 Jimmy Steel W RSC 3 Brentwood
09.09.00 Danny Southam W RSC 2 Manchester
09.10.00 Elvis Michailenko DREW 6 Liverpool
03.02.01 Paul Bonson W PTS 4 Manchester
Career: 8 contests, won 7, drew 1.

Francie Doherty
Wellingborough. *Born* Cardiff, 12 October,
1977
Middleweight. Ht. 5'6"
Manager K. Sanders

29.01.01 Freddie Yemofio W RSC 4
Peterborough
24.03.01 Lee Bird W RSC 3 Sheffield
23.06.01 Conroy McIntosh W PTS 4
Peterborough
Career: 3 contests, won 3.

Hughie Doherty
Wellingborough. *Born* Greenwich, 25 July,
1982
S. Middleweight. Ht. 5'10"
Manager K. Sanders

29.01.01 Tommy Matthews W PTS 4
Peterborough
12.05.01 Darren Covill W PTS 4 Plymouth
Career: 2 contests, won 2.

James Donoghue
Middlesbrough. *Born* Middlesbrough, 12
January, 1973
Middleweight. Ht. 5'9"
Manager G. Robinson

15.09.95 George Wilson W PTS 6 Darlington
08.12.95 Jason Barker W PTS 6 Leeds
19.03.96 Ernie Loveridge W PTS 6 Leeds
28.10.96 Billy Collins W PTS 6 Glasgow
03.12.96 Michael Alexander W PTS 6 Yarm
04.03.97 Andrew Jervis W RSC 4 Yarm
21.10.97 Andreas Panayi L PTS 8 Yarm
24.10.98 Scott Dann L PTS 6 Bristol
01.12.98 Charlie Paine W PTS 6 Yarm
11.12.98 Frederic Serrat L RTD 6 Nice, France
27.02.00 Scott Dann L RSC 1 Plymouth
12.11.00 Wayne Pinder L PTS 6 Manchester
Career: 12 contests, won 7, lost 5.

Francie Doherty Les Clark

Tony Dowling Les Clark

Tony Dowling
Lincoln. *Born* Lincoln, 5 January, 1976
Cruiserweight. Ht. 6'2"
Manager J. Ashton

22.03.96 Slick Miller W RSC 4 Mansfield

30.05.96 Nigel Rafferty W PTS 6 Lincoln
29.07.96 Albert Call L RSC 4 Skegness
12.02.00 Adam Cale W PTS 4 Sheffield
20.03.00 Danny Southam W PTS 4 Mansfield
11.05.00 Jason Brewster W RSC 2 Newark
08.07.00 Slick Miller W PTS 4 Widnes
09.09.00 Lee Swaby L RSC 9 Newark
(Vacant British Masters Cruiserweight
Title)
20.04.01 Cathal O'Grady L RSC 1 Dublin
Career: 9 contests, won 6, lost 3.

Gavin Down

Chesterfield. *Born* Chesterfield, 2 February, 1977
Midlands Area & British Masters L. Welterweight Champion. Ht. 5'9"
Manager J. Ingle

21.09.98 Peter Lennon W RSC 1 Cleethorpes
27.11.98 Trevor Tacy L PTS 6 Nottingham
07.12.98 Brian Coleman W PTS 6 Manchester
26.02.99 Brian Gifford W PTS 6 West Bromwich
27.03.99 Lee Molyneux W PTS 4 Derby
15.05.99 Les Frost W RSC 1 Sheffield
27.06.99 Lee Molyneux W PTS 6 Alfreton
03.10.99 Ernie Smith W RSC 1 Chesterfield
28.11.99 Dave Gibson W PTS 6 Chesterfield
09.04.00 Sammy Smith W PTS 6 Alfreton
21.05.00 Arv Mittoo W PTS 6 Derby
19.06.00 Brian Coleman W PTS 4 Burton
13.08.00 Lee Bird W PTS 6 Nottingham
30.08.00 Ram Singh W PTS 6 Scunthorpe
04.11.00 Sebastian Hart W RSC 4 Derby
19.11.00 David Kirk W PTS 10 Chesterfield
(Vacant British Masters
L. Welterweight Title)
11.12.00 Dave Gibson W RSC 5 Cleethorpes
25.02.01 Jay Mahoney W RSC 1 Derby
01.04.01 Steve Saville W RSC 3 Alfreton
(Vacant Midlands Area
L. Welterweight Title)
16.06.01 Arv Mittoo W PTS 6 Derby
Career: 20 contests, won 19, lost 1.

Gavin Down   Les Clark

(Andre) Drea Dread (Francis)

Nottingham. *Born* Nottingham, 4 November, 1969
Welterweight. Ht. 5'11"
Manager J. Gill

22.09.00 Neil Bonner L RSC 4 Wrexham
Career: 1 contest, lost 1.

Mike Duffield

Cleethorpes. *Born* Cleethorpes, 9 April, 1969
S. Middleweight. Ht. 6'2½"
Manager Self

22.09.97 Ian Toby L PTS 6 Cleethorpes
21.10.97 Ian Toby W PTS 6 Yarm
14.11.97 Mike Gormley L RSC 2 Mere
15.12.97 Jon Penn L RSC 2 Cleethorpes
16.03.98 Matt Galer L PTS 6 Nottingham
28.04.98 Gary Reyniers DREW 6 Brentford
18.05.98 Carlton Williams W PTS 6 Cleethorpes
17.07.98 Mike White W PTS 6 Mere
21.09.98 Phil Ball W RSC 2 Cleethorpes
26.11.98 Gordon Behan L RSC 3 Edgbaston
(Vacant Midlands Area Middleweight
Title)
18.02.99 Lawrence Murphy L RSC 2 Glasgow
29.05.99 Eddie Haley L RSC 6 South Shields
28.11.99 Martin Jolley W PTS 6 Chesterfield
18.01.00 Gary Beardsley L RTD 2 Mansfield
15.05.00 William Webster L PTS 6 Birmingham
15.07.00 Earl Ling L PTS 6 Norwich
30.08.00 Matthew Pepper W RSC 4 Scunthorpe
04.11.00 Damon Hague L RSC 3 Derby
(Vacant WBF European
S. Middleweight Title)
Career: 18 contests, won 6, drew 1, lost 11.

Chris Duggan

Coatbridge. *Born* Glasgow, 26 May, 1981
L. Middleweight. Ht. 5'10½"
Manager P. Cowdell

03.02.01 Ty Browne L RSC 1 Brighton
Career: 1 contest, lost 1.

Peter Dunn

Pontefract. *Born* Doncaster, 15 February, 1975
Welterweight. Ht. 5'8"
Manager Self

08.12.97 Leigh Daniels W PTS 6 Bradford
15.05.98 Peter Lennon W PTS 6 Nottingham
18.09.98 Jan Cree L RSC 5 Belfast
23.10.98 Bobby Lyndon W PTS 6 Wakefield
03.12.98 Craig Smith L RSC 3 Sunderland
17.03.99 Des Sowden W PTS 6 Kensington
15.05.99 Ray Wood DREW 4 Blackpool
29.05.99 Dean Nicholas L PTS 6 South Shields
01.10.99 Jon Honney L PTS 4 Bethnal Green
18.10.99 Jan Cree W PTS 6 Glasgow
26.11.99 Gavin Pearson DREW 6 Wakefield
18.02.00 John T. Kelly L PTS 6 Pentre Halkyn
11.03.00 Iain Eldridge L RSC 2 Kensington
18.09.00 Joe Miller L PTS 6 Glasgow
26.10.00 Ram Singh W PTS 6 Stoke
27.11.00 Young Muttley L RSC 3 Birmingham
22.02.01 Darren Spencer W PTS 6 Sunderland
03.03.01 Glenn McClarnon L PTS 4 Wembley

20.03.01 Robert Burton L PTS 6 Leeds
08.04.01 Martyn Bailey L PTS 6 Wrexham
17.05.01 Gavin Pearson L PTS 6 Leeds
Career: 21 contests, won 7, drew 2, lost 12.

Peter Dunn   Les Clark

Colin Dunne

Holloway. *Born* Liverpool, 19 September, 1970
WBU Lightweight Champion. Former Undefeated Southern Area Lightweight Champion. Ht. 5'6"
Manager T. Toole

07.12.93 Mark O'Callaghan W RSC 1 Bethnal Green
14.01.94 Wayne Jones W RSC 3 Bethnal Green
04.03.94 Malcolm Thomas W CO 1 Bethnal Green
26.04.94 Steve Burton W CO 2 Bethnal Green
17.05.94 Phil Found W PTS 6 Kettering
23.09.94 Steve Howden W CO 1 Bethnal Green
11.10.94 Jimmy Phelan W PTS 6 Bethnal Green
09.11.94 Mark O'Callaghan W RSC 2 Millwall
09.12.94 David Thompson W RSC 3 Bethnal Green
20.01.95 Chris Aston W RSC 4 Bethnal Green
03.03.95 Marco Fattore W RSC 3 Bethnal Green
19.04.95 Rudy Valentino W PTS 6 Bethnal Green
12.05.95 Chris Aston W RSC 4 Bethnal Green
27.09.95 Steve Howden W RSC 4 Bethnal Green
28.10.95 Chris Clarkson W RSC 4 Kensington
08.12.95 Jonathan Thaxton W RSC 5 Bethnal Green
(Vacant Southern Area Lightweight
Title)
05.03.96 Rudy Valentino W RSC 4 Bethnal Green
03.04.96 Kino Rodriguez W RSC 2 Bethnal Green
10.05.96 Lajos Nagy W RSC 5 Wembley

03.07.96 Marian Stoica W PTS 8 Wembley
24.10.96 Bamana Dibateza W PTS 8 Wembley
20.11.96 Michael Ayers L RSC 9 Wembley
(British Lightweight Title Challenge)
24.04.97 Lewis Reynolds W CO 4 Mayfair
(Southern Area Lightweight Title Defence)
30.06.97 Demir Nanev W RSC 8 Bethnal Green
09.09.97 Alan Bosworth W RSC 8 Bethnal Green
28.11.97 Zoltan Kalocsai W PTS 12 Bethnal Green
(Vacant WBU Lightweight Title)
23.05.98 Emmanuel Clottey W PTS 12 Bethnal Green

(WBU Lightweight Title Defence)
21.07.98 Affif Djelti W PTS 12 Widnes
(WBU Lightweight Title Defence)
12.12.98 Sedat Puskullu W RSC 3 Southwark
27.02.99 Phillip Holiday W PTS 12 Bethnal Green
(WBU Lightweight Title Defence)
13.07.00 Leonti Voronchuk W CO 4 Bethnal Green
25.07.00 Rakhim Mingaleev W RTD 5 Southwark
14.10.00 Billy Schwer W PTS 12 Wembley
(WBU Lightweight Title Defence)
16.06.01 Barrie Kelley W CO 3 Dagenham
Career: 34 contests, won 33, lost 1.

Colin Dunne   Les Clark

(Osumanu) Ossie Duran (Yahaya)

London. *Born* Accra, Ghana, 23 April, 1977
WBF European Welterweight Champion. Former Undefeated Ghanaian Lightweight Champion. Ht. 5'10"
Manager Self

28.08.96 Dick Dotse W RSC 4 Togo
20.09.96 Victor Abbey W RSC 2 Ivory Coast
30.11.96 David Allotey W PTS 8 Accra, Ghana
28.12.96 Neuziwere Apolo W RSC 1 Accra, Ghana
05.03.97 Ike Obi L PTS 10 Nigeria
26.04.97 Abas de Souza W RSC 6 Benin
28.06.97 Tony Danso DREW 12 Accra, Ghana
(Ghanaian Lightweight Title Challenge)
06.09.97 Iron Cutter W RSC 2 Accra, Ghana
04.10.97 Tony Danso W PTS 12 Accra, Ghana
(Ghanaian Lightweight Title Challenge)
06.06.98 David Tetteh L PTS 12 Accra, Ghana
(Commonwealth Lightweight Title Challenge)
09.03.00 Ganny Dovidovas L PTS 4 Bethnal Green
19.04.00 Vincent Nobela W PTS 6 Kensington
28.09.00 Mark Ramsey W RSC 2 Kensington
31.10.00 Yuri Tsarenko W PTS 4 Hammersmith
28.02.01 David Kirk W PTS 8 Kensington
(Vacant WBF European Welterweight Title)
26.04.01 Geoff McCreesh W PTS 6 Kensington
Career: 16 contests, won 12, drew 1, lost 3.

Paul Dyer

Portsmouth. *Born* Portsmouth, 11 July, 1970
Southern Area Welterweight Champion. Ht. 5'11½"
Manager C. Sanigar/G. Evans

24.09.91 Mick Reid W PTS 6 Basildon
19.11.91 Dave Andrews W PTS 6 Norwich
23.02.93 Kevin Mabbutt L PTS 6 Kettering
17.06.94 Dewi Roberts W PTS 6 Plymouth
27.10.94 George Wilson W PTS 4 Bayswater
25.01.95 John Janes W PTS 6 Cardiff
08.03.95 Anthony Huw Williams W PTS 6 Cardiff
06.05.95 Wahid Fats W PTS 4 Shepton Mallet
15.09.95 Mark Ramsey W PTS 6 Mansfield
16.12.95 Dennis Gardner W RSC 1 Cardiff
26.01.96 Danny Quacoe W PTS 6 Brighton
30.11.96 Mark Winters L PTS 6 Tylorstown
09.12.96 Paul Miles W PTS 6 Bristol
08.02.97 Michael Carruth L PTS 4 Millwall
14.03.97 Harry Dhami L PTS 10 Reading
(Southern Area Welterweight Title Challenge)
24.03.99 Steve Brumant W PTS 4 Bayswater
16.10.99 Neil Sinclair L RSC 8 Belfast
16.05.00 Neil Sinclair L RSC 6 Warrington
01.12.00 Paul Denton W PTS 4 Peterborough
02.02.01 David Baptiste W PTS 10 Portsmouth
(Vacant Southern Area Welterweight Title)
16.03.01 Peter Nightingale W PTS 6 Portsmouth
Career: 21 contests, won 15, lost 6.

Graham Earl

Luton. *Born* Luton, 26 August, 1978
Southern Area Lightweight Champion. Ht.
5'5¾"
Manager F. Maloney

02.09.97	Mark O'Callaghan W RSC 2 Southwark
06.12.97	Mark McGowan W PTS 4 Wembley
11.04.98	Danny Lutaaya W RSC 2 Southwark
23.05.98	David Kirk W PTS 4 Bethnal Green
12.09.98	Brian Coleman W PTS 4 Bethnal Green
10.12.98	Marc Smith W RSC 1 Barking
16.01.99	Lee Williamson W RSC 4 Bethnal Green
08.05.99	Benny Jones W PTS 6 Bethnal Green
15.07.99	Simon Chambers W CO 6 Peterborough
04.03.00	Ivo Golakov W RSC 1 Peterborough
29.04.00	Marco Fattore W PTS 6 Wembley
21.10.00	Lee Williamson W RSC 3 Wembley
10.03.01	Brian Gentry W RSC 8 Bethnal Green *(Vacant Southern Area Lightweight Title)*

Career: 13 contests, won 13.

Howard Eastman

Battersea. *Born* New Amsterdam, Guyana,
8 December, 1970
British, Commonwealth & European
Middleweight Champion. Former
Undefeated IBO Inter-Continental & WBA
Inter-Continental Middleweight Champion.
Former Undefeated Southern Area
Middleweight Champion. Ht. 5'11"
Manager Self

06.03.94	John Rice W RSC 1 Southwark
14.03.94	Andy Peach W PTS 6 Mayfair
22.03.94	Steve Phillips W RSC 5 Bethnal Green
17.10.94	Barry Thorogood W RSC 6 Mayfair
06.03.95	Marty Duke W RSC 1 Mayfair
20.04.95	Stuart Dunn W RSC 2 Mayfair
23.06.95	Peter Vosper W RSC 1 Bethnal Green
16.10.95	Carlo Colarusso W RSC 1 Mayfair
29.11.95	Brendan Ryan W RSC 2 Bethnal Green
31.01.96	Paul Wesley W RSC 1 Birmingham
13.03.96	Steve Goodwin W RSC 5 Wembley
29.04.96	John Duckworth W RSC 5 Mayfair
11.12.96	Sven Hamer W RSC 10 Southwark *(Vacant Southern Area Middleweight Title)*
18.02.97	John Duckworth W CO 7 Cheshunt
25.03.97	Rachid Serdjane W RSC 7 Lewisham
14.02.98	Vitali Kopitko W PTS 8 Southwark
28.03.98	Terry Morrill W RTD 4 Hull
23.05.98	Darren Ashton W RSC 4 Bethnal Green
30.11.98	Steve Foster W RSC 7 Manchester *(Vacant British Middleweight Title)*
04.02.99	Jason Barker W RSC 6 Lewisham
06.03.99	Jon Penn W RSC 3 Southwark *(Vacant IBO Inter-Continental S. Middleweight Title)*
22.05.99	Roman Babaev W RSC 6 Belfast *(WBA Inter-Continental Middleweight Title Challenge)*
10.07.99	Teimouraz Kikelidze W RSC 6 Southwark *(WBA Inter-Continental Middleweight Title Defence)*
13.09.99	Derek Wormald W RSC 3 Bethnal Green *(British Middleweight Title Defence)*
13.11.99	Mike Algoet W RSC 8 Hull *(WBA Inter-Continental Middleweight Title Defence)*
18.01.00	Ojay Abrahams W RSC 2 Mansfield
04.03.00	Viktor Fessetchko W RTD 4 Peterborough
29.04.00	Anthony Ivory W RTD 6 Wembley
25.07.00	Ahmet Dottouev W RTD 5 Southwark *(WBA International Middleweight Title Defence)*
16.09.00	Sam Soliman W PTS 12 Bethnal Green *(Commonwealth Middleweight Title Challenge)*
05.02.01	Mark Baker W RTD 5 Hull
10.04.01	Robert McCracken W RSC 10 Wembley *(British & Commonwealth Middleweight Title Defences. Vacant European Middleweight Title)*

Career: 32 contests, won 32.

Ricky Eccleston

Liverpool. *Born* Liverpool, 22 September,
1981
Lightweight. Ht. 5'8½"
Manager B. Devine

01.07.00	Dave Hinds W PTS 4 Manchester
09.09.00	Billy Smith W PTS 4 Manchester
09.10.00	Nigel Senior W PTS 4 Liverpool
27.11.00	Dave Hinds W PTS 4 Birmingham
03.02.01	Steve Hanley W PTS 4 Manchester
24.04.01	Gary Flear W PTS 4 Liverpool

Career: 6 contests, won 6.

Ricky Eccleston   Les Clark

Chris Edwards

Stoke. *Born* Stoke, 6 May, 1976
Flyweight. Ht. 5'3"
Manager Self

03.04.98	Chris Thomas W RSC 2 Ebbw Vale
21.09.98	Russell Laing L PTS 6 Glasgow
26.02.99	Delroy Spencer L PTS 6 West Bromwich
17.04.99	Stevie Quinn L RSC 4 Dublin
19.10.99	Lee Georgiou L RSC 2 Bethnal Green
03.12.99	Daniel Ring L PTS 4 Peterborough
15.05.00	Paddy Folan L PTS 6 Bradford
07.10.00	Andy Roberts W PTS 4 Doncaster
27.11.00	Levi Pattison W PTS 4 Birmingham
16.03.01	Jamie Evans L PTS 6 Portsmouth
03.06.01	Darren Taylor DREW 6 Hanley

Career: 11 contests, won 3, drew 1, lost 7.

Jason Edwards

Wrexham. *Born* Wrexham, 1 January, 1978
Featherweight. Ht. 5'4½"
Manager Self

15.11.99	Barry Hawthorne L PTS 6 Glasgow

Howard Eastman (right) pictured defeating Robert McCracken   Les Clark

05.05.00 Henry Jones W PTS 6 Pentre Halkyn
22.09.00 Nigel Senior L PTS 6 Wrexham
08.04.01 Gareth Wiltshaw W PTS 6 Wrexham
10.06.01 Tasawar Khan W PTS 6 Ellesmere Port
Career: 5 contests, won 3, lost 2.

Andy Egan
Coventry. *Born* Coventry, 16 September, 1977
Welterweight. Ht. 5'8¾"
Manager J. Griffin/J. Harding

02.01.01 Gareth Jones L PTS 4 Coventry
Career: 1 contest, lost 1.

Iain Eldridge
Watford. *Born* Watford, 26 February, 1975
L. Welterweight. Ht. 5'8"
Manager Self

18.11.99 Des Sowden W RSC 4 Mayfair
21.02.00 Lee Sharp L PTS 6 Glasgow
11.03.00 Peter Dunn W RSC 2 Kensington
22.07.00 Ross McCord W RSC 2 Watford
19.08.00 Karl Taylor W PTS 4 Brentwood
03.03.01 Kevin Bennett L PTS 6 Wembley
Career: 6 contests, won 4, lost 2.

Matthew Ellis
Blackpool. *Born* Oldham, 12 April, 1974
Heavyweight. Ht. 5'11¾"
Manager J. Hyland

03.02.96 Laurent Rouze W CO 1 Liverpool
01.04.96 Ladislav Husarik W RTD 4 Den Bosch, Holland
06.09.96 Darren Fearn W RSC 6 Liverpool
26.10.96 Daniel Beun W RSC 1 Liverpool
01.03.97 Yuri Yelistratov L RSC 5 Liverpool
20.07.97 Ricardo Phillips W PTS 4 Indio, USA
26.09.97 Albert Call DREW 6 Liverpool
12.03.98 Yuri Yelistratov W RSC 1 Liverpool
21.07.98 Chris Woollas W RSC 5 Widnes
24.10.98 Peter Hrivnak W RSC 1 Liverpool
12.12.98 Harry Senior W PTS 8 Southwark
27.02.99 Michael Murray W PTS 8 Bethnal Green
15.05.99 Biko Botowamungu W PTS 8 Blackpool
27.05.00 Alex Vasiliev W CO 4 Southwark
16.09.00 Dimitri Bakhtov W PTS 4 Bethnal Green
18.11.00 Chris Woollas W PTS 4 Dagenham
17.02.01 Alexei Osokin W PTS 8 Bethnal Green
Career: 17 contests, won 15, drew 1, lost 1.

Keith Ellwood
Edinburgh. *Born* Edinburgh, 14 December, 1979
L. Middleweight. Ht. 6'1"
Manager A. Morrison

02.10.00 Pedro Thompson W RSC 3 Glasgow
15.02.01 Chris Nembhard L RSC 2 Glasgow
Career: 2 contests, won 1, lost 1.

Stuart Elwell
Darlaston. *Born* Walsall, 14 December, 1977
Welterweight. Ht. 5'9"
Manager Self

06.11.00 Ernie Smith W PTS 6 Wolverhampton

28.01.01 Arv Mittoo W PTS 6 Wolverhampton
01.04.01 Richard Inquieti W PTS 6 Wolverhampton
Career: 3 contests, won 3.

Stuart Elwell   Les Clark

(Christoforo) Chris Emanuele
Nuneaton. *Born* Nuneaton, 26 November, 1973
Bantamweight. Ht. 5'5¼"
Manager Self

08.12.97 Marty Chestnut W PTS 6 Leicester
17.01.98 Stephen Oates L RSC 4 Bristol
18.05.98 Anthony Hanna L RSC 3 Cleethorpes
11.09.98 Dave Travers L RSC 2 Newark
27.11.98 Terry Gaskin W PTS 6 Nottingham
21.02.99 Paddy Folan DREW 6 Bradford
17.05.99 Daniel Ring DREW 6 Cleethorpes
17.07.99 Andy Roberts W PTS 4 Doncaster
26.11.99 Paddy Folan W RSC 5 Wakefield
11.03.00 Jamie Yelland L PTS 4 Kensington
17.04.00 Tommy Waite L PTS 6 Bradford
20.05.00 Sean Grant W RSC 5 Rotherham
06.06.00 Shaun Anderson L PTS 6 Motherwell
08.07.00 Tiger Singh W RSC 1 Rotherham
13.07.00 Lee Georgiou W CO 1 Bethnal Green
01.10.00 Michael Hunter L PTS 6 Hartlepool
28.10.00 Gareth Payne L CO 1 Coventry
26.02.01 Jim Betts W PTS 6 Nottingham
17.03.01 Stephen Oates L PTS 8 Manchester
30.04.01 John Barnes L PTS 4 Glasgow
15.06.01 John Mackay W RSC 4 Millwall
Career: 21 contests, won 9, drew 2, lost 10.

Kevin England
Sheffield. *Born* Sheffield, 12 October, 1973
S. Featherweight. Ht. 5'5½"
Manager Self

08.07.00 Gareth Wiltshaw DREW 6 Rotherham
20.10.00 Steve Brook L PTS 6 Manchester
19.02.01 Pete Buckley L PTS 6 Glasgow
Career: 3 contests, drew 1, lost 2.

Gary Evans
Portsmouth. *Born* Portsmouth, 7 July, 1982
Bantamweight. Ht. 5'5"
Manager C. Sanigar/G. Evans

02.02.01 Daniel Ring L RSC 4 Portsmouth
Career: 1 contest, lost 1.

Gwyn Evans
Portsmouth. *Born* Portsmouth, 10 December, 1978
Flyweight. Ht. 5'5"
Manager C. Sanigar/G. Evans

30.10.98 Delroy Spencer W PTS 4 Peterborough
02.02.01 Tommy Thomas W RSC 4 Portsmouth
16.03.01 Ankar Miah W PTS 6 Portsmouth
05.05.01 Andrew Greenaway DREW 6 Brighton
Career: 4 contests, won 3, drew 1.

Jamie Evans
Portsmouth. *Born* Portsmouth, 10 December, 1978
Flyweight. Ht. 5'2¼"
Manager C. Sanigar/G. Evans

21.11.98 Delroy Spencer L PTS 4 Southwark
22.06.99 Mark Reynolds W PTS 4 Ipswich
26.02.00 Lennie Hodgkins W PTS 4 Swansea
20.03.00 Keith Knox L PTS 6 Glasgow
15.07.00 Ian Napa L PTS 4 Millwall
02.02.01 Danny Lawson W RSC 1 Portsmouth
16.03.01 Chris Edwards W PTS 6 Portsmouth
Career: 7 contests, won 4, lost 3.

Richard Evatt
Coventry. *Born* Coventry, 26 August, 1973
S. Featherweight. Former IBO Inter-Continental Featherweight Champion. Ht. 5'6"
Manager B. Hearn

18.12.95 Kevin Sheil W RSC 1 Mayfair
06.02.96 Joe Donohoe W RSC 2 Basildon
09.04.96 Fred Reeve W RSC 1 Stevenage
20.04.96 Wayne Jones W RSC 2 Brentwood
04.05.96 Miguel Matthews W PTS 6 Dagenham
27.11.96 Brian Robb W RSC 2 Bethnal Green
17.12.96 Andrew Robinson W RSC 2 Doncaster
08.03.97 Brian Robb W CO 3 Brentwood
19.07.97 Pete Buckley W PTS 4 Wembley
19.09.97 Demir Nanev W RSC 1 Southend
18.11.97 Rudy Valentino W RSC 3 Mansfield
27.01.98 Hendrik Makolane W RSC 1 Bethnal Green
23.02.98 Mzukisi Oliphant W RSC 7 Glasgow
(Vacant IBO Inter-Continental Featherweight Title)
11.12.98 John T. Kelly W RSC 2 Cheshunt
12.01.99 Keith Jones W CO 3 Bethnal Green
13.02.99 Smith Odoom L PTS 12 Jastrzebie, Poland
(IBO Inter-Continental Featherweight Title Defence)
26.02.99 Pete Buckley W RSC 5 Coventry
10.04.99 Junior Jones L RSC 11 Manchester
(Vacant IBO Featherweight Title)
22.10.99 Mick O'Malley L RTD 1 Coventry
(Vacant Commonwealth S. Featherweight Title)
17.04.00 Isaac Sebaduka L RSC 2 Birmingham
01.07.00 Pete Buckley W PTS 4 Manchester
19.08.00 Keith Jones W PTS 6 Brentwood
28.10.00 Roy Rutherford W PTS 10 Coventry
07.04.01 Rakhim Mingaleev W PTS 4 Wembley
Career: 24 contests, won 20, lost 4.

85

Andrew Facey

Sheffield. *Born* Wolverhampton, 20 May, 1972
S. Middleweight. Ht. 6'0"
Manager D. Ingle

06.12.99 Peter McCormack W CO 2 Birmingham
09.06.00 Matthew Pepper W RSC 1 Hull
04.11.00 Earl Ling W PTS 6 Derby
11.12.00 Gary Jones W PTS 6 Cleethorpes
10.02.01 Louis Swales W RSC 3 Widnes
17.03.01 Darren Rhodes L PTS 4 Manchester
24.03.01 Matthew Tait W PTS 4 Chigwell
16.06.01 Earl Ling DREW 6 Derby
Career: 8 contests, won 6, drew 1, lost 1.

Biagio Falcone

Falkirk. *Born* Edinburgh, 1 February, 1973
Middleweight. Ht. 5'9"
Manager T. Gilmour

24.04.98 Mark Owens W PTS 6 Glasgow
17.09.98 Mark Owens W PTS 6 Glasgow
18.02.99 Jason Collins W PTS 6 Glasgow
09.04.99 Ian Toby W RSC 3 Glasgow
26.06.99 Ian Toby W PTS 4 Glasgow
04.10.99 Pedro Carragher W PTS 6 Glasgow
12.11.99 William Webster W PTS 6 Glasgow
13.12.99 William Webster W RSC 1 Glasgow
24.02.00 Mike Watson W RSC 2 Glasgow
18.03.00 Ernie Smith W PTS 4 Glasgow
08.04.00 Mehrdud Takaloo L RTD 4 Bethnal Green
26.05.00 Ernie Smith W PTS 4 Glasgow
02.10.00 Jason Barker L PTS 10 Glasgow
(Vacant Scottish S.Middleweight Title)
30.04.01 Ian Toby W RSC 2 Glasgow
Career: 14 contests, won 12, lost 2.

Biagio Falcone   Les Clark

Anthony Farnell   Les Clark

Anthony Farnell

Manchester. *Born* Manchester, 1 July, 1978
WBO Inter-Continental L. Middleweight Champion. Ht. 5'10"
Manager F. Warren

03.05.97 Lee Molyneux W PTS 4 Manchester
02.08.97 Martin Renaghan W RSC 3 Barnsley
20.09.97 Dominique van der Steene W CO 1 Aachen, Germany
13.12.97 Paul Scott W RSC 3 Sheffield
24.01.98 Steve Brumant W PTS 4 Cardiff
21.03.98 Hughie Davey W PTS 6 Bethnal Green
18.04.98 Harry Butler W PTS 6 Manchester
09.05.98 David Thompson W CO 1 Sheffield
18.07.98 Lee Molyneux W CO 3 Sheffield
05.09.98 Darren Williams W RTD 4 Telford
31.10.98 Mark Richardson W PTS 6 Atlantic City, USA
28.11.98 George Richards W RSC 7 Sheffield
19.12.98 Koba Kulu W RTD 5 Liverpool
27.02.99 Koba Kulu W RSC 1 Oldham
01.05.99 Alan Gilbert W RSC 8 Crystal Palace
29.05.99 John Long W RSC 6 Halifax
(Vacant WBO Inter-Continental L. Middleweight Title)
07.08.99 Israel Ponce W RSC 3 Atlantic City, USA
09.10.99 Javier Santibanez W CO 1 Manchester
(WBO Inter-Continental L. Middleweight Title Defence)
27.11.99 Marino Monteyne W CO 6 Lubeck, Germany
29.01.00 Ian Toby W RSC 3 Manchester
08.04.00 Ojay Abrahams W PTS 8 Bethnal Green
29.05.00 Howard Clarke W PTS 12 Manchester
(WBO Inter-Continental L. Middleweight Title Defence)
04.09.00 Juan Carlos Sanchez W PTS 12 Manchester
(WBO Inter-Continental L. Middleweight Title Defence)
25.11.00 Scott Dixon W RSC 7 Manchester
(WBO Inter-Continental L. Middleweight Title Defence)
15.01.01 Sergio Acuna W PTS 12 Manchester

(WBO Inter-Continental L. Middleweight Title Defence)
17.03.01 Shakir Ashanti W RSC 2 Manchester
(WBO Inter-Continental L. Middleweight Title Defence)
Career: 26 contests, won 26.

Marco Fattore

Watford. *Born* Italy, 17 October, 1968
Lightweight. Ht. 5'8"
Manager Self

03.09.92 Jason White W RSC 1 Dunstable
19.10.92 Carlos Domonkos W RTD 4 Mayfair
07.12.92 Steve Patton W RSC 6 Mayfair
15.02.93 Jason Hutson W PTS 6 Mayfair
29.03.93 T. J. Smith DREW 6 Mayfair
22.04.93 Jason Barker W PTS 6 Mayfair
04.10.93 Andrew Bloomer W PTS 6 Mayfair
10.11.93 Lee Fox W PTS 6 Watford
09.12.93 Jason Hutson DREW 6 Watford
10.03.94 Simon Frailing DREW 6 Watford
28.04.94 Andrew Reed DREW 6 Mayfair
12.09.94 Keith Jones W PTS 6 Mayfair
30.11.94 Kid McAuley L PTS 6 Solihull
03.03.95 Colin Dunne L RSC 3 Bethnal Green
25.05.95 P. J. Gallagher L RSC 5 Reading
02.11.95 Brian Coleman L PTS 6 Mayfair
22.11.95 Marc Smith L PTS 6 Mayfair
29.01.96 Ram Singh DREW 6 Piccadilly
21.02.96 Brian Coleman L PTS 6 Piccadilly
02.04.96 Matt Brown L PTS 4 Southwark
07.10.96 Richie Edwards L PTS 6 Lewisham
11.12.96 Craig Stanley L PTS 4 Southwark
28.01.97 Vince Burns W PTS 6 Piccadilly
24.03.97 Jose Tuominen L RSC 3 Helsinki, Finland
23.10.97 Arv Mittoo L PTS 6 Mayfair
11.11.97 Daniel James L RSC 3 Bethnal Green
18.12.99 Jon Honney L PTS 4 Southwark
18.01.00 Craig Spacie L RTD 1 Mansfield
29.02.00 Wahid Fats L PTS 4 Manchester
13.03.00 Kevin Lear L PTS 4 Bethnal Green
23.03.00 Dave Hinds W PTS 6 Bloomsbury
29.04.00 Graham Earl L PTS 6 Wembley
11.05.00 Carl Greaves L PTS 8 Newark
12.06.00 P. J. Gallagher L PTS 6 Belfast
01.07.00 Gary Hibbert L PTS 4 Manchester
22.07.00 Dave Tatton L RSC 2 Watford
30.09.00 Liam Maltby L PTS 6 Peterborough
14.10.00 Leo O'Reilly L PTS 4 Wembley
21.10.00 Jan Jensen L PTS 4 Wembley
11.11.00 Tomas Jansson L RSC 4 Belfast
18.02.01 Jason Hall L PTS 6 Southwark
03.03.01 David Burke L RSC 1 Wembley
Career: 42 contests, won 10, drew 5, lost 27.

Dave Faulkner

Barnsley. *Born* Hemsworth, 22 September, 1972
Heavyweight. Ht. 6'3"
Manager T. Schofield

27.03.00 Paul Fiske L PTS 4 Barnsley
15.05.00 Nigel Rafferty L PTS 6 Bradford
08.07.00 Huggy Osman DREW 6 Rotherham
25.09.00 Eamonn Glennon L PTS 4 Barnsley
30.11.00 Paul Richardson L PTS 6 Blackpool
07.12.00 Paul Fiske L RTD 4 Sunderland
22.02.01 Paul Fiske L PTS 6 Sunderland
08.03.01 Paul Richardson L RSC 2 Blackpool
24.04.01 Paul Buttery L CO 1 Liverpool
Career: 9 contests, drew 1, lost 8.

Spencer Fearon

Forest Hill. *Born* London, 20 December, 1973
Middleweight. Ht. 6'0"
Manager Self

28.06.97	Mark Sawyers W PTS 4 Norwich
13.09.97	Danny Quacoe W PTS 4 Millwall
21.03.98	Perry Ayres W PTS 4 Bethnal Green
16.05.98	Danny Quacoe W PTS 4 Bethnal Green
26.09.98	Rob Stevenson W CO 2 Norwich
14.11.98	Prince Kasi Kaihau W CO 5 Cheshunt
23.01.99	George Richards L PTS 6 Cheshunt
08.04.00	Leigh Wicks W PTS 4 Bethnal Green
12.08.00	Freddie Yemofio W RSC 4 Wembley
23.09.00	Matthew Bowers W RSC 2 Bethnal Green
27.01.01	Jason Collins L PTS 4 Bethnal Green
24.02.01	Harry Butler W PTS 4 Bethnal Green
03.04.01	Lee Blundell L PTS 6 Bethnal Green
03.06.01	Gary Logan L RSC 2 Southwark
	(Vacant Southern Area Middleweight Title)

Career: 14 contests, won 10, lost 4.

Andrew Ferrans

New Cumnock. *Born* Irvine, 4 February, 1981
S. Featherweight. Ht. 5'9"
Manager T. Gilmour

19.02.00	Chris Lyons W PTS 6 Prestwick
03.03.00	Gary Groves W RSC 1 Irvine
20.03.00	John Barnes DREW 6 Glasgow
06.06.00	Duncan Armstrong W PTS 6 Motherwell
18.09.00	Steve Brook W PTS 6 Glasgow
20.11.00	Duncan Armstrong W PTS 6 Glasgow
23.02.01	Dave Cotterill L RSC 2 Irvine
30.04.01	Dave Cotterill W RSC 1 Glasgow
04.06.01	Jason Nesbitt W RSC 2 Glasgow

Career: 9 contests, won 7, drew 1, lost 1.

(Benjamin) Paul Fiske (Thomas)

Newcastle. *Born* Norwich, 10 March, 1969
Heavyweight. Ht. 6'4"
Manager T. Conroy

21.04.98	Adey Cook L RSC 3 Edmonton
29.10.98	Gordon Minors L RSC 3 Newcastle
03.12.98	Tommy Bannister L CO 1 Mayfair
10.06.99	Phil Reid W RSC 2 Hartlepool
07.10.99	Gary Williams L PTS 6 Sunderland
09.12.99	Gary Williams L PTS 6 Sunderland
24.02.00	Brodie Pearmaine W PTS 6 Sunderland
06.03.00	Huggy Osman L PTS 6 Bradford
27.03.00	Dave Faulkner W PTS 4 Barnsley
11.05.00	Geoff Hunter W PTS 6 Sunderland
09.06.00	Craig Bowen-Price L RSC 1 Blackpool
01.10.00	Billy Bessey L PTS 6 Hartlepool
07.12.00	Dave Faulkner W RTD 4 Sunderland
22.01.01	Paul Richardson L PTS 6 Glasgow
05.02.01	Adey Cook L PTS 4 Hull
22.02.01	Dave Faulkner W PTS 6 Sunderland
26.05.01	Dominic Negus L CO 1 Bethnal Green

Career: 17 contests, won 6, lost 11.

Gary Flear

Birmingham. *Born* Birmingham, 28 May, 1965
L. Welterweight. Former Undefeated British Masters Lightweight Champion. Ht. 5'8"
Manager Self

20.09.84	Wayne Trigg W PTS 4 Dudley
10.10.84	Neville Fivey W PTS 6 Stoke
29.10.84	Muhammad Lovelock L PTS 6 Birmingham
07.11.84	Ray Newby W PTS 6 Evesham
19.11.84	Henry Arnold W RSC 5 Leicester
27.11.84	Andy Williams DREW 6 Wolverhampton
10.12.84	Nicky Day W PTS 6 Birmingham
04.02.85	Tyrell Wilson W CO 2 Birmingham
12.02.85	Peter Bowen W PTS 6 Wolverhampton
20.02.85	George Jones W PTS 6 Stafford
04.03.85	Teddy Anderson W RSC 5 Birmingham
20.03.85	Tommy Frankham W PTS 6 Solihull
22.04.85	George Jones W PTS 8 Birmingham
08.05.85	Michael Marsden W RTD 5 Solihull
20.05.85	Edward Lloyd W PTS 8 Nottingham
23.09.85	Peter Bradley L PTS 6 Mayfair
02.10.85	Paul Cook W PTS 8 Solihull
15.10.85	Dave Henderson W PTS 8 Wolverhampton
06.11.85	George Jones W PTS 8 Evesham
20.11.85	George Kerr W PTS 8 Solihull
09.12.85	Gerry Beard W PTS 8 Birmingham
22.01.86	Andy Mayers W PTS 8 Solihull
11.02.86	Lenny Gloster W PTS 8 Wolverhampton
27.02.86	Errol McDonald L RSC 5 Bethnal Green
21.04.86	Dean Barclay L RSC 1 Birmingham
28.05.86	Billy Edwards W PTS 8 Lewisham
03.10.91	Chris Saunders W PTS 6 Burton
06.10.97	Chris Lyons W PTS 6 Piccadilly
27.10.97	Isaac Sebaduka W PTS 6 Nottingham
20.11.97	Elvis Parsley L PTS 6 Solihull
27.03.98	Anthony Maynard L RSC 9 Telford
	(Vacant Midlands Area Lightweight Title)
09.05.98	Steve Conway L PTS 4 Sheffield
01.06.98	Bobby Vanzie L PTS 6 Manchester
24.10.98	David Burke L PTS 6 Liverpool
12.01.99	David Kehoe W PTS 4 Bethnal Green
06.03.99	Stephen Smith L RTD 7 Southwark
	(Vacant IBO Inter-Continental Lightweight Title)
12.10.99	Steve Saville L RSC 6 Wolverhampton
11.12.99	Tony Mulholland L PTS 4 Liverpool
21.02.00	Lee Armstrong L PTS 8 Glasgow
18.03.00	Barry Hughes L RSC 4 Glasgow
29.05.00	Jesse James Daniel L PTS 4 Manchester
12.06.00	David Lowry L PTS 4 Belfast
01.07.00	Jamie McKeever L PTS 4 Manchester
15.07.00	Bradley Pryce L RSC 1 Millwall
08.09.00	Brian Gentry W RSC 6 Hammersmith
	(Vacant British Masters Lightweight Title)
11.11.00	David Lowry W PTS 4 Belfast
18.11.00	David Walker L PTS 4 Dagenham
02.12.00	James Rooney L PTS 4 Bethnal Green
01.04.01	Jason Hall L PTS 8 Southwark
24.04.01	Ricky Eccleston L PTS 4 Liverpool

Career: 50 contests, won 28, drew 1, lost 21.

Mark Florian

Bury St Edmunds. *Born* Bury St Edmunds, 12 January, 1975
Welterweight. Ht. 5'7"
Manager G. Holmes

30.09.00	Arv Mittoo W PTS 4 Peterborough

Career: 1 contest, won 1.

Mark Florian Les Clark

Andrew Flute

Coseley. Born Wolverhampton, 5 March, 1970
S. Middleweight. Ht. 6'1"
Manager N. Christian

24.05.89	Stinger Mason W PTS 6 Hanley
24.10.89	Paul Murray W RSC 3 Wolverhampton
22.03.90	Dave Maxwell W RSC 5 Wolverhampton
24.05.90	Spencer Alton L RSC 1 Dudley
18.09.90	Tony Hodge W CO 2 Wolverhampton
24.10.90	Nigel Rafferty W CO 6 Dudley
27.11.90	Paul Burton L PTS 6 Stoke
13.03.91	Robert Peel W PTS 6 Stoke
10.04.91	Russell Washer W PTS 6 Wolverhampton
14.05.91	Alan Richards W PTS 8 Dudley
16.10.91	Karl Barwise L RSC 8 Stoke
05.12.91	Richard Okumu DREW 8 Cannock
17.03.92	Graham Burton W PTS 8 Wolverhampton
28.04.92	Paul Smith W RSC 5 Wolverhampton
20.01.93	Glen Payton W RSC 4 Wolverhampton
16.03.93	Mark Hale W RSC 2 Wolverhampton
24.04.93	Steve Thomas W RSC 1 Birmingham
21.10.93	Terry Magee W RSC 6 Bayswater
26.01.94	Neville Brown L RTD 7 Wolverhampton
	(British Middleweight Title Challenge)
16.03.94	Graham Burton W PTS 6 Birmingham
29.10.94	Carlos Christie L PTS 8 Cannock
29.11.94	Mark Dawson W PTS 8 Cannock
17.01.95	Chris Richards W PTS 6 Worcester
11.05.95	Paul Murray W PTS 6 Dudley
30.09.95	Mark Delaney L PTS 12 Basildon
	(Vacant WBO Inter-Continental S. Middleweight Title)
16.03.96	Robin Reid L RSC 7 Glasgow
25.05.96	Norbert Nieroba L RTD 4 Leipzig, Germany
28.09.96	Leif Keiski L PTS 8 Barking
24.10.96	Carlos Christie L PTS 10 Mayfair
	(Midlands Area S. Middleweight Title Challenge)
15.02.97	Markus Beyer L PTS 6 Vienna, Austria

01.06.97	Sven Ottke L PTS 6 Riesa, Germany	
03.04.98	Octavian Stoica W PTS 6 West Bromwich	
04.06.98	Martin Jolley W PTS 6 Dudley	
03.10.98	Darren Littlewood W PTS 6 West Bromwich	
05.12.98	Glenn Catley L RSC 5 Bristol	
	(Vacant IBF Inter-Continental S. Middleweight Title)	
26.02.99	Errol McDonald W RSC 4 West Bromwich	
24.03.01	David Starie L RTD 3 Sheffield	

Career: 37 contests, won 22, drew 1, lost 14.

(Patrick) Paddy Folan (Powders)

Huddersfield. *Born* Birmingham, 25 June, 1972
Featherweight. Ht. 5'7"
Manager Self

25.10.98	Waj Khan W PTS 6 Shaw
26.11.98	Daniel Ring DREW 6 Bradford
07.12.98	Kevin Gerowski L PTS 6 Bradford
21.02.99	Chris Emanuele DREW 6 Bradford
19.04.99	Gary Groves L CO 1 Bradford
19.09.99	Gary Ford L PTS 6 Shaw
14.11.99	Shane Mallon W PTS 6 Bradford
26.11.99	Chris Emanuele L RSC 5 Wakefield
05.03.00	Gary Ford L PTS 6 Shaw
15.05.00	Chris Edwards W PTS 6 Bradford
25.06.00	Levi Pattison L PTS 6 Wakefield
30.11.00	Neil Read W PTS 6 Blackpool
07.12.00	John-Paul Ryan L PTS 6 Stoke
11.02.01	Michael Hunter L RSC 6 Hartlepool
20.03.01	Sean Grant DREW 6 Leeds
01.04.01	Dafydd Carlin L PTS 4 Southwark
09.04.01	Sean Grant L PTS 6 Bradford
10.06.01	Lee Holmes L PTS 6 Ellesmere Port

Career: 18 contests, won 4, drew 3, lost 11.

Ali Forbes

Sydenham. *Born* London, 7 March, 1961
L. Heavyweight. Former British S. Middleweight Champion. Former Undefeated Southern Area S. Middleweight Champion. Ht. 5'9"
Manager Self

16.02.89	David Haycock W RSC 4 Battersea
22.06.90	Andy Marlow W RTD 4 Gillingham
26.09.90	Peter Vosper W PTS 6 Mayfair
06.02.91	Adrian Wright W PTS 6 Battersea
03.04.91	Karl Barwise W RTD 4 Bethnal Green
16.05.91	Quinn Paynter DREW 6 Battersea
01.06.91	Paul McCarthy W CO 2 Bethnal Green
11.03.92	Ian Strudwick L PTS 10 Solihull
	(Southern Area S. Middleweight Title Challenge)
29.10.92	Nick Manners W RSC 3 Leeds
28.11.93	Carlos Christie W CO 4 Southwark
06.03.94	Richard Bustin W PTS 10 Southwark
	(Vacant Southern Area S. Middleweight Title)
29.09.94	Darron Griffiths W PTS 12 Bethnal Green
	(Final Elim. British S. Middleweight Title)
23.01.95	Fidel Castro W PTS 12 Bethnal Green
	(Vacant British S. Middleweight Title)
27.04.95	Sammy Storey L PTS 12 Bethnal Green
	(British S. Middleweight Title Defence)

16.05.98	Darren Ashton W PTS 6 Chigwell
21.11.98	David Starie L CO 11 Southwark
	(Commonwealth S. Middleweight Title Challenge. Vacant British S. Middleweight Title)
18.12.99	Mark Delaney L PTS 8 Southwark
09.03.00	Mark Baker L PTS 12 Bethnal Green
	(Vacant WBF L. Heavyweight Title)
14.10.00	Thomas Ulrich L PTS 8 Cologne, Germany
24.03.01	Clinton Woods L RTD 10 Sheffield
	(Vacant WBC International L. Heavyweight Title)
21.06.01	Mark Williams W PTS 4 Earls Court

Career: 21 contests, won 13, drew 1, lost 7.

Gary Ford

Oldham. *Born* Oldham, 27 July, 1973
Bantamweight. Ht. 5'1"
Manager J. Doughty

19.09.99	Paddy Folan W PTS 6 Shaw
05.03.00	Paddy Folan W PTS 6 Shaw
21.05.00	Andy Roberts DREW 6 Shaw
24.09.00	Nicky Booth L PTS 6 Shaw
18.03.01	Andrew Greenaway W RSC 1 Shaw
17.05.01	Levi Pattison L RSC 5 Leeds

Career: 6 contests, won 3, drew 1, lost 2.

Allan Foster

Northampton. *Born* Kilmarnock, 8 November, 1973
S. Middleweight. Ht. 5'11"
Manager C. Sanigar

03.12.99	Steve Timms W RSC 4 Peterborough
05.03.00	Richie Jenkins W PTS 6 Peterborough
02.06.00	Leigh Wicks W PTS 4 Ashford
06.10.00	Paul Johnson W PTS 4 Maidstone
01.12.00	Michael Pinnock W PTS 4 Peterborough
17.02.01	Tommy Matthews W PTS 4 Bethnal Green
24.03.01	Darren Covill W RTD 3 Sheffield

Career: 7 contests, won 7.

Jon Foster

Nottingham. *Born* Nottingham, 18 October, 1979
L. Middleweight. Ht. 6'1"
Manager Self

31.10.97	David Thompson W RSC 4 Ilkeston
26.11.97	Billy McDougall W RSC 2 Stoke
20.03.98	Phil Molyneux W PTS 6 Ilkeston
03.04.98	Harry Butler W PTS 6 Ebbw Vale
23.04.98	Hughie Davey L PTS 8 Newcastle
11.09.98	Brian Dunn W RTD 3 Cleethorpes
07.12.98	Darren Christie W RSC 6 Cleethorpes
06.06.99	Jason Collins DREW 6 Nottingham
20.09.99	Joe Townsley L PTS 6 Glasgow
11.12.99	Jacek Bielski L PTS 6 Merthyr
12.02.00	Zoltan Sarossy L RSC 1 Sheffield
06.06.00	James Docherty L PTS 6 Motherwell
24.09.00	Lee Murtagh L PTS 6 Shaw

Career: 13 contests, won 6, drew 1, lost 6.

Julius Francis

Woolwich. *Born* Peckham, 8 December, 1964
Former Undefeated Commonwealth

Heavyweight Champion. Former British Heavyweight Champion. Former Undefeated Southern Area Heavyweight Champion. Ht. 6'2"
Manager Self

23.05.93	Graham Arnold W RSC 5 Brockley
23.06.93	Joey Paladino W CO 4 Edmonton
24.07.93	Andre Tisdale W PTS 4 Atlantic City, USA
28.08.93	Don Sargent W RSC 2 Bismark, USA
01.12.93	John Keeton W PTS 4 Bethnal Green
27.04.94	Manny Burgo W PTS 4 Bethnal Green
25.05.94	John Ruiz L CO 4 Bristol
12.11.94	Conroy Nelson W RSC 4 Dublin
23.11.94	Gary Charlton W RSC 1 Piccadilly
23.02.05	Damien Caesar W RSC 8 Southwark
	(Vacant Southern Area Heavyweight Title)
27.04.95	Keith Fletcher W PTS 10 Bethnal Green
	(Southern Area Heavyweight Title Defence)
25.05.95	Steve Garber W PTS 8 Reading
01.07.95	Scott Welch L RSC 10 Kensington
	(Southern Area Heavyweight Title Defence. Final Elim. British Heavyweight Title)
24.10.95	Neil Kirkwood W RSC 7 Southwark
30.11.95	Nikolai Kulpin L PTS 10 Saratov, Russia
05.02.96	Michael Murray L PTS 10 Bexleyheath
	(Elim. British Heavyweight Title)
09.04.96	Damien Caesar W CO 1 Stevenage
	(Vacant Southern Area Heavyweight Title)
07.05.96	Darren Fearn W PTS 8 Mayfair
09.07.96	Mike Holden W PTS 10 Bethnal Green
28.09.96	James Oyebola W RSC 5 Barking
	(Southern Area Heavyweight Title Defence)
15.02.97	Zeljko Mavrovic L RSC 8 Vienna, Austria
	(European Heavyweight Title Challenge)
30.06.97	Joseph Chingangu W PTS 12 Bethnal Green
	(Vacant Commonwealth Heavyweight Title)
27.09.97	Garry Delaney W RSC 6 Belfast
	(Commonwealth Heavyweight Title Defence. Vacant British Heavyweight Title)
28.02.98	Axel Schulz L PTS 12 Dortmund, Germany
18.04.98	Vitali Klitschko L RSC 2 Aachen, Germany
30.01.99	Pele Reid W RSC 3 Bethnal Green
	(British & Commonwealth Heavyweight Title Defences)
03.04.99	Danny Williams W PTS 12 Kensington
	(British & Commonwealth Heavyweight Title Defences)
26.06.99	Scott Welch W PTS 12 Millwall
	(British & Commonwealth Heavyweight Title Defences)
29.01.00	Mike Tyson L RSC 2 Manchester
13.03.00	Mike Holden L PTS 12 Bethnal Green
	(British Heavyweight Title Defence)
03.04.01	Mike Holden W PTS 12 Bethnal Green
	(Final Elim. British Heavyweight Title)

Career: 31 contests, won 22, lost 9.

Patrick Gallagher

Islington. *Born* Manchester, 23 July, 1971
Lightweight. Ht. 5'7½"
Manager Self

22.12.92	Karl Taylor W RSC 3 Mayfair
20.02.93	Joe Fannin W RTD 1 Earls Court
21.12.93	Karl Taylor W PTS 6 Mayfair
11.01.94	Mark Antony W RSC 3 Bethnal Green
15.03.94	Karl Taylor W PTS 6 Mayfair
07.11.94	Rudy Valentino W PTS 6 Bethnal Green
27.05.95	Paul Burke L PTS 8 Belfast
27.01.98	Elvis Parsley W CO 3 Bethnal Green
11.03.98	David Kirk W PTS 6 Bethnal Green
28.04.98	Ian McLeod L RSC 7 Belfast
	(Vacant IBO Inter-Continental S. Featherweight Title)
27.04.99	Demir Nanev W RSC 3 Bethnal Green
28.04.01	Gareth Jordan W PTS 4 Cardiff

Career: 12 contests, won 10, lost 2.

(Patrick) P. J. Gallagher

Wood Green. *Born* Manchester, 14 February, 1973
Lightweight. Former Undefeated British & WBC International S. Featherweight Champion. Former Undefeated Southern Area S. Featherweight Champion. Ht. 5'7"
Manager F. Maloney

15.09.93	John T. Kelly W RSC 2 Bethnal Green
13.10.93	Mike Morrison W PTS 4 Bethnal Green
01.12.93	Mark Antony W PTS 4 Bethnal Green
09.02.94	Simon Hamblett W RSC 1 Bethnal Green
29.03.94	Brian Coleman W PTS 6 Bethnal Green
15.06.94	Mark O'Callaghan W RSC 4 Southwark
29.09.94	Anthony Campbell W PTS 6 Bethnal Green
12.11.94	Karl Taylor W PTS 6 Dublin
23.01.95	David Thompson W RSC 1 Bethnal Green
30.03.95	Phil Found W PTS 6 Bethnal Green
25.05.95	Marco Fattore W RSC 5 Reading
02.07.95	Chris Clarkson W RSC 3 Dublin
29.09.95	Marc Smith W RSC 3 Bethnal Green
08.11.95	Justin Murphy W RSC 6 Bethnal Green
	(Vacant Southern Area S. Featherweight Title & Elim. British S. Featherweight Title)
19.01.96	Rakhim Mingaleev W PTS 12 Bracknell
	(Vacant WBC International S. Featherweight Title)
22.04.96	Dave McHale W RSC 10 Crystal Palace
	(Vacant British S. Featherweight Title)
29.06.96	Charles Shepherd W PTS 12 Erith
	(British S. Featherweight Title Defence)
18.02.97	Bamana Dibateza L PTS 8 Cheshunt
12.06.00	Marco Fattore W PTS 6 Belfast
25.07.00	David Kehoe W PTS 6 Southwark

Career: 20 contests, won 19, lost 1.

Rob Galloway

Barnsley. *Born* Barnsley, 30 May, 1974
Cruiserweight. Ht. 5'11"
Manager Self

17.02.98	Clint Johnson L PTS 6 Leeds
15.05.98	Johnny Hooks L PTS 6 Nottingham
20.09.98	Clint Johnson L PTS 6 Sheffield
23.10.98	Paul Bonson L PTS 6 Wakefield
03.12.98	Tony Rowbotham L PTS 6 Hull
20.12.98	Mike White L PTS 6 Salford
01.02.99	Shamus Casey L PTS 6 Bradford
26.02.99	Joe Gillon L PTS 6 Irvine
05.03.99	Brian Kilbride L PTS 4 Liverpool
19.04.99	Joe Gillon L PTS 6 Glasgow
29.05.99	Darren Kirby L PTS 6 South Shields
14.06.99	Lee Simpkin DREW 6 Bradford
12.09.99	Lee Simpkin L RSC 4 Nottingham
30.10.99	Andy Vickers L PTS 6 Peterlee
26.11.99	Kent Davis W PTS 6 Hull
06.12.99	Eamonn Glennon L PTS 6 Bradford
20.12.99	Paul Maskell L RSC 1 Bethnal Green
02.03.00	Eamonn Glennon L PTS 6 Blackpool
14.04.00	Kent Davis L PTS 6 Manchester
09.06.00	Kent Davis L CO 3 Hull
21.10.00	Mark Brookes L RSC 5 Sheffield

Career: 21 contests, won 1, drew 1, lost 19.

Al Garrett (Garrity)

Glasgow. *Born* Glasgow, 21 December, 1966
S. Featherweight. Ht. 5'5½"
Manager T. Gilmour

23.09.91	Robert Braddock DREW 6 Glasgow
09.12.91	Chris Jickells L RSC 2 Bradford
18.11.92	Colin Innes DREW 6 Solihull
02.03.94	Daryl McKenzie L PTS 6 Glasgow
25.04.94	Daryl McKenzie W PTS 6 Glasgow
16.05.94	Dave Clavering L RTD 4 Morecambe
20.11.00	Gareth Wiltshaw W PTS 6 Glasgow

Career: 7 contests, won 2, drew 2, lost 3.

Brian Gascoigne

Kirkby in Ashfield. *Born* Kirkby in Ashfield, 4 June, 1970
Cruiserweight. Ht. 6'5"
Manager M. Shinfield

23.11.98	Lennox Williams W RSC 3 Piccadilly
30.04.99	Shane Woollas DREW 6 Scunthorpe
03.10.99	Lee Swaby DREW 6 Chesterfield
06.12.99	Mark Hobson L RSC 3 Bradford
09.04.00	Nigel Rafferty W PTS 6 Alfreton
25.06.00	Danny Southam L RSC 4 Wakefield
04.12.00	Huggy Osman L PTS 6 Bradford
10.04.01	Kevin Barrett L RSC 1 Wembley

Career: 8 contests, won 2, drew 2, lost 4.

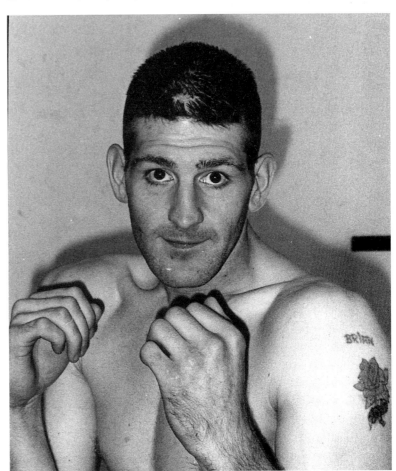

Brian Gascoigne   Les Clark

(Terrace) Terry Gaskin

Doncaster. *Born* Doncaster, 20 October, 1974
Former Central Area Flyweight Champion.
Ht. 5'4"
Manager Self

28.03.94	Keith Knox L PTS 6 Musselburgh
09.05.94	Tiger Singh L RSC 2 Bradford
26.09.94	Ian Baillie W RSC 3 Bradford
29.10.94	Neil Parry L PTS 6 Cannock
28.11.94	Tiger Singh L PTS 6 Manchester
08.12.94	Ian Baillie W RTD 3 Hull
11.03.95	Neil Parry DREW 6 Barnsley
22.03.95	Neil Parry L PTS 8 Stoke
19.05.95	Shaun Hall L RSC 3 Leeds
21.09.95	Darren Noble DREW 6 Sheffield
20.10.95	Steve Williams L PTS 6 Mansfield
12.05.97	Paul Squire DREW 6 Leicester
20.10.97	Tiny Pope W CO 3 Leicester
04.12.97	Chris Thomas W PTS 6 Doncaster
13.12.97	Zoltan Lunka L CO 2 Hamburg, Germany
27.11.98	Chris Emanuele L PTS 6 Nottingham
18.03.99	Andy Roberts W RSC 8 Doncaster
17.07.99	David Coldwell L CO 5 Doncaster
	(Central Area Flyweight Title Challenge)
15.01.00	Andy Roberts W RSC 8 Doncaster
	(Vacant Central Area Flyweight Title)
08.05.01	Dale Robinson L RTD 3 Barnsley
	(Central Area Flyweight Title Defence)

Career: 20 contests, won 6, drew 3, lost 11.

Kenny Gayle   Les Clark

Kenny Gayle

Harrow. *Born* Park Royal, 6 March, 1969
Cruiserweight. Ht. 5'9¼"
Manager Self

24.03.99	Mark Williams DREW 6 Bayswater
24.04.99	Paul Bonson DREW 4 Peterborough

17.05.99	Israel Khumalo W RSC 2 Peterborough
20.09.99	Adam Cale W PTS 4 Peterborough
01.10.99	Geoff Hunter W PTS 6 Cleethorpes
31.10.99	Chris Okoh W PTS 6 Raynes Park
10.12.99	Konstantin Okhrey L RSC 5 Nicosia, Cyprus
04.07.00	Mark Williams W PTS 4 Tooting
13.02.01	Simon Bakinde L CO 2 Pont Audemir, France
01.04.01	Tony Booth DREW 4 Southwark

Career: 10 contests, won 5, drew 3, lost 2.

Brian Gentry

Morden. *Born* Balham, 2 January, 1975
Lightweight. Ht. 5'6"
Manager B. Baker

29.11.95	Des Gargano W PTS 4 Southwark
20.09.96	Stevie Bolt W RSC 3 Tooting
07.11.96	Wayne Jones L PTS 6 Battersea
15.02.97	David Jeffrey W PTS 6 Tooting
02.12.97	Wee Barry W PTS 6 Windsor
03.10.98	Benny Jones W PTS 6 Crawley
25.11.98	Des Sowden W RSC 6 Streatham
24.03.99	Wayne Jones W PTS 6 Bayswater
21.07.99	Arv Mittoo W RSC 4 Bloomsbury
31.10.99	Dennis Griffin W PTS 4 Raynes Park
06.05.00	Dean Murdoch W RSC 3 Southwark
08.09.00	Gary Flear L RSC 6 Hammersmith
	(Vacant British Masters Lightweight Title)
10.03.01	Graham Earl L RSC 8 Bethnal Green
	(Vacant Southern Area Lightweight Title)
22.04.01	Keith Jones W PTS 8 Streatham

Career: 14 contests, won 11, lost 3.

Lee Georgiou

Romford. *Born* Rush Green, 25 April, 1977
Flyweight. Ht. 5'2½"
Manager F. Maloney

19.10.99	Chris Edwards W RSC 2 Bethnal Green
29.11.99	Delroy Spencer W PTS 4 Wembley
15.04.00	Delroy Spencer W PTS 4 Bethnal Green
13.07.00	Chris Emanuele L CO 1 Bethnal Green

Career: 4 contests, won 3, lost 1.

Kevin Gerowski

Nottingham. *Born* Leicester, 6 February, 1971
Bantamweight. Ht. 5'4½"
Manager J. Gill

07.05.98	John Barnes L PTS 6 Sunderland
12.10.98	Brendan Bryce W PTS 6 Nottingham
16.11.98	Craig Docherty L PTS 6 Glasgow
28.11.98	Barry Waite L PTS 4 Belfast
07.12.98	Paddy Folan W PTS 6 Bradford
22.01.99	Ady Benton W PTS 4 Carlisle
25.02.99	Micky Bowden L PTS 4 Kentish Town
22.03.99	Alston Buchanan L PTS 6 Glasgow
03.04.99	Shaun Anderson L PTS 4 Carlisle
17.04.99	Willie Valentine L PTS 6 Dublin
06.06.99	Waj Khan W PTS 6 Nottingham
12.09.99	Pete Buckley W PTS 6 Nottingham
01.10.99	Salim Medjkoune L PTS 6 Bethnal Green
18.10.99	Shaun Anderson L PTS 6 Glasgow

27.11.99	Tommy Waite W PTS 6 Liverpool
13.12.99	Sean Green W PTS 6 Cleethorpes
19.02.00	Esham Pickering L PTS 10 Newark
	(Vacant British Masters Bantamweight Title. Elim. British Bantamweight Title)
02.06.00	Frankie DeMilo L RSC 7 Ashford
	(British Masters S. Bantamweight Title Challenge)
26.10.00	Leon Dobbs W CO 1 Stoke
05.12.00	Jason Thomas W PTS 8 Nottingham
11.06.01	Nicky Booth L RSC 4 Nottingham

Career: 21 contests, won 9, lost 12.

Steve Gethin

Walsall. *Born* Walsall, 30 July, 1978
Featherweight. Ht. 5'9"
Manager Self

03.09.99	Ike Halls W RSC 3 West Bromwich
24.10.99	Ricky Bishop W RSC 4 Wolverhampton
22.01.00	Sebastian Hart L PTS 4 Birmingham
10.09.00	Nigel Senior DREW 6 Walsall
03.06.01	Richmond Asante L PTS 4 Southwark

Career: 5 contests, won 2, drew 1, lost 2.

Dave Gibson

St Helens. *Born* Whiston, 27 February, 1971
Welterweight. Ht. 5'11"
Manager Self

28.11.97	Jon Dodsworth L PTS 6 Hull
08.12.97	Trevor Smith L PTS 6 Leicester
06.03.98	Perry Ayres L PTS 6 Hull
21.09.98	Tony Smith W RSC 6 Cleethorpes
17.04.99	Bernard McComiskey L PTS 4 Dublin
17.05.99	Brian Gifford L PTS 6 Cleethorpes
14.06.99	Ernie Smith L PTS 6 Birmingham
27.09.99	Oscar Hall L PTS 6 Leeds
20.10.99	David Kirk L PTS 6 Stoke
28.11.99	Gavin Down L PTS 6 Chesterfield
24.02.00	Tony Conroy L PTS 4 Edgbaston
05.03.00	Shaun Horsfall L PTS 6 Shaw
13.03.00	Steve Saville L RSC 6 Birmingham
09.06.00	Oscar Hall L PTS 6 Hull
15.07.00	Ram Singh W PTS 6 Norwich
30.08.00	Richard Holden L PTS 6 Scunthorpe
09.09.00	Trevor Smith L PTS 6 Newark
09.10.00	Ernie Smith L PTS 6 Birmingham
12.11.00	Ray Wood L PTS 6 Manchester
24.11.00	Tony Montana L PTS 6 Hull
11.12.00	Gavin Down L RSC 5 Cleethorpes

Career: 21 contests, won 2, lost 19.

Brian Gifford

Hull. *Born* Hull, 27 January, 1972
Welterweight. Ht. 5'6"
Manager M. Toomey

26.02.99	Gavin Down L PTS 6 West Bromwich
05.03.99	Ray Wood L CO 2 Liverpool
22.04.99	Lee Williamson L PTS 6 Dudley
17.05.99	Dave Gibson W PTS 6 Cleethorpes
29.05.99	Oscar Hall L RSC 1 Halifax
27.09.99	Karim Bouali L RSC 3 Cleethorpes
18.02.01	Babatunde Ajayi L RSC 1 Southwark
10.05.01	Gary Greenwood L PTS 6 Sunderland
08.06.01	Ram Singh L PTS 6 Hull
23.06.01	Ram Singh DREW 4 Peterborough

Career: 10 contests, won 1, drew 1, lost 8.

Alan Gilbert

Crawley. *Born* Bromley, 17 November, 1970
L. Middleweight. Ht. 5'11"
Manager Self

02.12.97	Martin Cavey W RSC 1 Windsor
06.01.98	Harry Butler W PTS 4 Brighton
23.02.98	Jon Harrison W PTS 6 Windsor
21.04.98	Paul Henry L PTS 4 Edmonton
08.08.98	Lee Murtagh L PTS 4 Scarborough
03.10.98	C. J. Jackson W RSC 3 Crawley
25.02.99	Justin Simmons W RSC 5 Kentish Town
01.05.99	Anthony Farnell L RSC 8 Crystal Palace
07.08.99	Wayne Shepherd DREW 8 Dagenham
	(Vacant British Masters
	L. Middleweight Title)
11.03.00	Michael Jones L RTD 3 Kensington
12.06.00	Jim Rock L PTS 6 Belfast
22.07.00	Delroy Mellis L RSC 3 Watford
	(Vacant Southern Area L.Middleweight
	Title)
23.01.01	Delroy Mellis L RSC 3 Crawley
	(Southern Area L. Middleweight Title
	Challenge)

Career: 13 contests, won 5, drew 1, lost 7.

Sol Gilbert

Brighton. *Born* London, 27 July, 1975
Middleweight. Ht. 5'11"
Manager R. Davies

22.10.00	Matthew Bowers L RSC 1 Streatham

Career: 1 contest, lost 1.

Joe Gillon

Motherwell. *Born* Motherwell, 24 April, 1977
L. Heavyweight. Ht. 6'3"
Manager T. Gilmour

26.02.99	Rob Galloway W PTS 6 Irvine
19.04.99	Rob Galloway W PTS 6 Glasgow
23.10.00	Clint Johnson W CO 4 Glasgow
20.03.01	Michael Pinnock W PTS 6 Glasgow
04.06.01	Paul Bonson DREW 6 Glasgow

Career: 5 contests, won 4, drew 1.

Eamonn Glennon

Blackpool. *Born* Blackpool, 12 February, 1970
Heavyweight. Ht. 5'10"
Manager L. Veitch

06.12.99	Rob Galloway W PTS 6 Bradford
02.03.00	Rob Galloway W PTS 6 Blackpool
09.06.00	Mark Dawson L PTS 6 Blackpool
25.09.00	Dave Faulkner W PTS 4 Barnsley
08.12.00	Darren Chubbs L PTS 4 Crystal Palace
27.01.01	John McDermott L RSC 1 Bethnal Green
10.03.01	Danny Percival L PTS 4 Bethnal Green
22.04.01	Colin Kenna L PTS 4 Streatham
30.04.01	Lee Swaby L PTS 6 Glasgow

Career: 9 contests, won 3, lost 6.

Michael Gomez (Armstrong)

Manchester. *Born* Dublin, 21 June, 1977
British S. Featherweight Champion. Former
WBO Inter-Continental S. Featherweight
Champion. Former Undefeated Central
Area & IBF Inter-Continental
Featherweight Champion.
Ht. 5'5"
Manager F. Warren

10.06.95	Danny Ruegg W PTS 6 Manchester
15.09.95	Greg Upton L PTS 4 Mansfield
24.11.95	Danny Ruegg L PTS 4 Manchester
19.09.96	Martin Evans W RSC 1 Manchester
09.11.96	David Morris W PTS 4 Manchester
22.03.97	John Farrell W RSC 2 Wythenshawe
03.05.97	Chris Williams L PTS 4 Manchester
11.09.97	Wayne Jones W RSC 2 Widnes
18.04.98	Benny Jones W PTS 4 Manchester
16.05.98	Craig Spacie W RSC 3 Bethnal Green
05.09.98	Pete Buckley W PTS 6 Telford
14.11.98	David Jeffrey W RSC 1 Cheshunt
19.12.98	Kevin Sheil W RSC 4 Liverpool
13.02.99	Dave Hinds W PTS 6 Newcastle
27.02.99	Chris Jickells W RSC 5 Oldham
	(Vacant Central Area Featherweight
	Title)

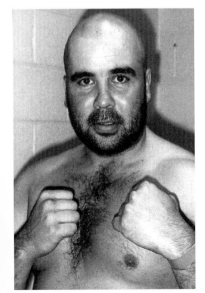

Eamonn Glennon　　　Les Clark　　　*Michael Gomez*　　　Harry Goodwin

29.05.99 Nigel Leake W RSC 2 Halifax
(*Vacant IBF Inter-Continental Featherweight Title*)
07.08.99 William Alverzo W PTS 6 Atlantic City, USA
04.09.99 Gary Thornhill W RSC 2 Bethnal Green
(*Vacant British S. Featherweight Title*)
06.11.99 Jose Juan Manjarrez W PTS 12 Widnes
(*WBO Inter-Continental S. Featherweight Title Defence*)
11.12.99 Oscar Galindo W RSC 11 Liverpool
(*WBO Inter-Continental S. Featherweight Title Defence*)
29.01.00 Chris Jickells W RSC 4 Manchester
29.02.00 Dean Pithie W PTS 12 Widnes
(*British S. Featherweight Title Defence*)
24.06.00 Carl Allen W CO 2 Glasgow
08.07.00 Carl Greaves W CO 2 Widnes
(*British S. Featherweight Title Defence*)
19.10.00 Awel Abdulai W PTS 8 Harrisburg, USA
11.12.00 Ian McLeod W PTS 12 Widnes
(*British S.Featherweight Title Defence*)
10.02.01 Laszlo Bognar L RSC 9 Widnes
(*WBO Inter-Continental S. Featherweight Title Defence*)
Career: 27 contests, won 23, lost 4.

Mike Gormley

Salford. *Born* Salford, 2 November, 1965
Former Undefeated Central Area S. Middleweight Champion. Ht. 6'0"
Manager S. Foster/S. Wood

25.04.97 Robert Peel W PTS 6 Mere
02.09.97 Michael Pinnock W PTS 6 Manchester
19.09.97 Paul Bonson L PTS 6 Salford
14.11.97 Mike Duffield W RSC 2 Mere
27.11.97 Darren Murphy W RSC 2 Bloomsbury
21.12.97 Jimmy Steel W PTS 6 Salford
08.05.98 Peter Federenko L CO 1 Manchester
17.07.98 John O'Byrne W PTS 6 Mere
18.09.98 Glenn Williams W RSC 2 Manchester
(*Vacant Central Area S. Middleweight Title*)
30.11.98 Dean Ashton W PTS 4 Manchester
02.07.99 Michael Pinnock W RSC 6 Manchester
04.12.99 Darren Ashton W PTS 4 Manchester
29.02.00 Jimmy Steel W RSC 3 Manchester
08.12.00 Robin Reid L RSC 1 Crystal Palace
(*Vacant WBF S.Middleweight Title*)
Career: 14 contests, won 11, lost 3.

Jimmy Gould

Coseley. *Born* Wolverhampton, 8 July, 1977
L. Welterweight. Ht. 5'10"
Manager Self

23.06.99 Benny Jones W PTS 6 West Bromwich
03.09.99 Dave Travers W PTS 6 West Bromwich
06.11.00 Jon Honney W PTS 6 Wolverhampton
28.01.01 David White W PTS 6 Wolverhampton
20.05.01 Keith Jones W PTS 6 Wolverhampton
Career: 5 contests, won 5.

Jimmy Gould   Les Clark

Darrell Grafton

Chesterfield. *Born* Chesterfield, 14 July, 1974
L. Middleweight. Ht. 5'10"
Manager M. Shinfield

11.06.01 Chris Steele W RSC 1 Nottingham
Career: 1 contest, won 1.

Sean Grant

Newton Aycliffe. *Born* Bishop Auckland, 18 January, 1971
S. Bantamweight. Ht. 5'6"
Manager Self

04.12.97 John Barnes L PTS 6 Sunderland
03.02.98 Graham McGrath W PTS 6 Yarm
30.04.98 Peter Allen W PTS 6 Pentre Halkyn
18.07.98 Noel Wilders L RSC 4 Sheffield
19.09.98 Willie Valentine L PTS 4 Dublin
11.12.98 Nicky Cook L CO 1 Cheshunt
29.05.99 Gary Groves W PTS 6 South Shields
29.06.99 Barry Waite L RSC 3 Bethnal Green
16.10.99 David Lowry L RSC 1 Belfast
13.12.99 Jesse James Daniel L RSC 5 Cleethorpes
22.01.00 Gareth Payne L RSC 1 Birmingham
20.05.00 Chris Emanuele L RSC 5 Rotherham
23.07.00 Michael Hunter L PTS 6 Hartlepool
20.10.00 Stevie Quinn L RSC 2 Belfast
20.03.01 Paddy Folan DREW 6 Leeds
09.04.01 Paddy Folan W PTS 6 Bradford
08.05.01 Jim Betts L RSC 3 Barnsley
09.06.01 Martin Power L PTS 4 Bethnal Green
Career: 18 contests, won 4, drew 1, lost 13.

Allan Gray

Putney. *Born* Roehampton, 4 August, 1971
L. Middleweight. Ht. 5'9"
Manager D. Mancini

19.05.95 Darren Covill W PTS 6 Southwark
23.06.95 Wayne Jones W PTS 6 Bethnal Green
27.09.95 Brian Coleman W PTS 6 Bethnal Green

28.10.95 John O. Johnson W PTS 6 Kensington
29.11.95 Justin Simmons L PTS 6 Bethnal Green
08.12.95 Mike Watson W PTS 8 Bethnal Green
15.03.96 Mike Watson DREW 6 Dunstable
29.04.96 Mike Watson W PTS 6 Mayfair
03.07.96 Jon Harrison W PTS 6 Wembley
24.10.96 Costas Katsantonis W PTS 6 Mayfair
29.01.97 Gary Hiscox W PTS 6 Bethnal Green
19.02.97 Costas Katsantonis W PTS 6 Acton
30.04.97 Howard Clarke L PTS 8 Acton
27.01.98 Peter Nightingale W PTS 6 Streatham
26.09.98 Harry Dhami L PTS 10 Southwark
(*Southern Area Welterweight Title Challenge*)
16.02.99 Lee Bird W PTS 6 Brentford
31.10.99 Matthew Barr L PTS 4 Raynes Park
15.04.00 Jim Rock L PTS 10 Bethnal Green
(*Vacant All-Ireland L. Middleweight Title*)
22.10.00 Delroy Mellis L RSC 6 Streatham
(*Southern Area L.Middleweight Title Challenge*)
Career: 19 contests, won 12, drew 1, lost 6.

Rene Grayel

Doncaster. *Born* France, 12 August, 1971
Welterweight. Ht. 5'9"
Manager J. Rushton

18.03.99 Tony Smith DREW 6 Doncaster
12.10.99 Craig Clayton L PTS 6 Wolverhampton
24.02.00 Craig Clayton L PTS 6 Edgbaston
10.10.00 Casey Brooke W PTS 6 Brierley Hill
28.11.00 Casey Brooke W PTS 6 Brierley Hill
Career: 5 contests, won 2, drew 1, lost 2.

Carl Greaves

Newark. *Born* Nottingham, 12 June, 1976
Midlands Area & British Masters S. Featherweight Champion. Ht. 5'7"
Manager Self

22.03.96 Paul Hamilton W PTS 6 Mansfield
30.05.96 Kevin Sheil W PTS 6 Lincoln
02.10.96 Robert Grubb W PTS 8 Stoke
01.11.96 Benny Jones W PTS 6 Mansfield
26.11.96 Danny Ruegg W RTD 4 Sheffield
04.12.96 Des Gargano W PTS 6 Stoke
20.02.97 Lee Armstrong L RSC 4 Mansfield
10.04.97 Kevin Sheil W PTS 6 Sheffield
08.05.97 Benny Jones L RSC 4 Mansfield
10.07.97 Stefy Bull L PTS 6 Doncaster
18.08.97 Graham McGrath W PTS 6 Nottingham
06.10.97 Ervine Blake L PTS 10 Birmingham
(*Vacant Midlands Area S. Featherweight Title*)
30.10.97 Graham McGrath W PTS 6 Newark
18.11.97 Garry Burrell W CO 4 Mansfield
07.05.98 John T. Kelly W PTS 6 Sunderland
14.10.98 Andrew Robinson W PTS 6 Stoke
02.12.98 Graham McGrath W PTS 6 Stoke
18.03.99 Ernie Smith W PTS 6 Doncaster
27.06.99 Chris Jickells W PTS 10 Alfreton
(*British Masters S. Featherweight Final*)
20.11.99 Pete Buckley W PTS 10 Grantham
(*British Masters S. Featherweight Title Defence*)
18.01.00 Keith Jones W PTS 6 Mansfield
19.02.00 Marc Smith W PTS 6 Newark
20.03.00 Pete Buckley W PTS 4 Mansfield

11.05.00 Marco Fattore W PTS 8 Newark
08.07.00 Michael Gomez L CO 2 Widnes
  (British S. Featherweight Title
  Challenge)
09.09.00 Dave Hinds W PTS 6 Newark
19.11.00 Haroon Din W RSC 4 Chesterfield
24.03.01 Nigel Senior W CO 6 Newark
  (Vacant Midlands Area
  S. Featherweight Title)
16.06.01 Dave Hinds W PTS 6 Derby
Career: 29 contests, won 24, lost 5.

(Roger) Radcliffe Green

Balham. *Born* Jamaica, 24 November, 1973
Cruiserweight. Ht. 5'9½"
Manager I. Akay

26.03.01 Peter Haymer L PTS 4 Wembley
22.04.01 Adam Cale W CO 5 Streatham
03.06.01 Rob Hayes-Scott W RSC 4 Southwark
Career: 3 contests, won 2, lost 1.

Sean Green

Rotherham. *Born* Doncaster, 2 November, 1977
Bantamweight. Ht. 5'6"
Manager J. Rushton

17.12.96 Willie Smith W PTS 6 Doncaster
17.02.97 Jason Whitaker W PTS 6 Bradford
24.02.97 Neil Armstrong L PTS 6 Glasgow
08.05.97 Ross Cassidy DREW 6 Mansfield
27.09.97 Tommy Waite W RSC 3 Belfast
24.10.97 Graham McGrath DREW 6 Birmingham
04.12.97 Jason Thomas DREW 4 Doncaster
21.01.98 Graham McGrath W PTS 6 Stoke
19.03.98 Steve Williams L PTS 6 Doncaster
06.05.98 Louis Veitch W PTS 6 Blackpool
10.10.98 Ian Napa L PTS 6 Bethnal Green
09.12.98 Graham McGrath W PTS 6 Stoke
21.05.99 Chris Jickells W PTS 6 Glasgow
01.06.99 Samir Laala L RSC 3 Levallois, France
27.10.99 Graham McGrath W PTS 6 Birmingham
30.11.99 Phil Lashley W PTS 6 Wolverhampton
13.12.99 Kevin Gerowski L PTS 6 Cleethorpes
15.01.00 Levi Pattison W PTS 4 Doncaster
07.10.00 Hussein Hussein L RSC 1 Doncaster
02.12.00 Danny Costello L PTS 4 Chigwell
16.06.01 Danny Costello W RSC 3 Dagenham
Career: 21 contests, won 11, drew 3, lost 7.

Andy Greenaway

Gelligaer. *Born* Caerphilly, 13 January, 1974
Bantamweight. Ht. 5'1"
Manager D. Gardiner

12.12.00 Danny Lawson W PTS 6 Clydach
18.03.01 Gary Ford L RSC 1 Shaw
05.05.01 Gwyn Evans DREW 6 Brighton
27.05.01 Anthony Hughes L PTS 4 Manchester
Career: 4 contests, won 1, drew 1, lost 2.

(Paul) Woody Greenaway

Gelligaer. *Born* Gelligaer, 5 February, 1972
Lightweight. Ht. 5'7"
Manager Self

23.07.98 Terry Butwell W PTS 6 Barking
17.09.98 Pat Larner L RSC 3 Brighton
13.11.98 Daniel James L PTS 4 Brighton

24.11.98 Ernie Smith W PTS 6 Wolverhampton
07.12.98 Barry Hughes L PTS 6 Acton
14.12.98 Steve Saville W PTS 6 Birmingham
23.02.99 Jason Dee L CO 6 Cardiff
03.04.99 Steve Murray L CO 2 Kensington
26.06.99 Nwajcvenki Sambo L PTS 6 Glasgow
15.07.99 Koba Gogoladze L RSC 2 Peterborough
24.09.99 Alan Bosworth W PTS 6 Merthyr
22.10.99 Roy Rutherford L PTS 4 Coventry
06.11.99 Jason Hall L RSC 5 Bethnal Green
11.12.99 Jason Cook L RSC 1 Mayfair
  (Vacant Welsh L. Welterweight Title)
26.02.00 Ross McCord W PTS 4 Swansea
09.03.00 David Burke L RSC 2 Liverpool
19.04.00 Nono Junior L PTS 4 Kensington
12.05.00 Dave Tatton L PTS 4 Swansea
30.05.00 Manzo Smith L PTS 4 Kensington
09.09.00 Gary Hibbert L PTS 4 Clydach
26.10.00 Barrie Kelley L PTS 6 Clydach
06.11.00 Steve Saville L CO 5 Wolverhampton
12.12.00 Ross McCord W PTS 6 Clydach
02.01.01 Tony Conroy L PTS 4 Coventry
05.02.01 Leo O'Reilly L CO 1 Hull
08.03.01 Mark Bowen DREW 6 Stoke
16.03.01 Jon Honney L PTS 6 Portsmouth
26.03.01 Alex Arthur L RTD 2 Wembley
27.04.01 Dave Stewart L PTS 6 Glasgow
05.05.01 Chill John L PTS 6 Brighton
19.05.01 Mark Hawthorne L PTS 4 Wembley
02.06.01 Lance Crosby L PTS 6 Wakefield
11.06.01 Anthony Maynard L PTS 4 Nottingham
21.06.01 Ajose Olusegun L RSC 1 Earls Court
Career: 34 contest, won 7, drew 1, lost 26.

Gary Greenwood

Hinckley. *Born* Leicester, 9 December, 1974
L. Welterweight. Ht. 5'8"
Manager J. Weaver

09.03.00 Ray Wood W PTS 4 Liverpool
03.12.00 Tony Montana DREW 6 Shaw
13.02.01 Dave Travers W PTS 6 Brierley Hill
10.05.01 Brian Gifford W PTS 6 Sunderland
23.06.01 Jay Mahoney L PTS 4 Peterborough
Career: 5 contests, won 3, drew 1, lost 1.

Darron Griffiths

Porth. *Born* Pontypridd, 11 February, 1972
Welsh Cruiserweight Champion. Former
Undefeated Welsh S. Middleweight
Champion. Ht. 6'0"
Manager J. Harding/J. Griffin

26.11.90 Colin Ford DREW 6 Mayfair
04.12.90 Kevin Adamson W RSC 4 Southend
23.01.91 Tony Booth DREW 6 Stoke
06.03.91 Barry Messam W PTS 6 Croydon
10.04.91 John Kaighin W PTS 6 Newport
25.04.91 Michael Graham W RSC 2 Mayfair
02.05.91 Carlton Myers W RTD 5 Kensington
21.10.91 John Ogiste W PTS 6 Mayfair
11.12.91 Adrian Wright W PTS 6 Stoke
22.01.92 Richard Okumu W PTS 8 Solihull
17.02.92 John Ogiste W RSC 5 Mayfair
29.04.92 Colin Manners DREW 8 Solihull
30.09.92 Colin Manners W PTS 10 Solihull
  (Elim. British Middleweight Title)
28.10.92 Antonio Fernandez W PTS 10 Cardiff
  (Elim. British Middleweight Title)
24.03.93 John Kaighin W RSC 6 Cardiff
  (Vacant Welsh S. Middleweight Title)

22.01.94 Carlos Christie W PTS 8 Cardiff
09.02.94 Paul Hitch W PTS 6 Bethnal Green
23.03.94 Karl Barwise W PTS 8 Cardiff
27.04.94 Ray Webb W RSC 6 Bethnal Green
  (Elim. British S. Middleweight Title)
15.06.94 Nigel Rafferty W RSC 4 Southwark
29.09.94 Ali Forbes L PTS 12 Bethnal Green
  (Final Elim. British S. Middleweight
  Title)
22.11.94 Dean Francis L RTD 1 Bristol
05.05.95 Wayne Ellis W PTS 10 Swansea
  (Welsh S. Middleweight Title Defence)
29.09.95 Andy Till W RSC 3 Bethnal Green
23.01.96 Mark Delaney L PTS 12 Bethnal Green
  (WBO Inter-Continental S.
  Middleweight Title Challenge)
02.04.96 Chris Johnson L RTD 3 Southwark
26.02.97 Yuri Filipko W PTS 8 Cardiff
14.11.97 Ivan Camacho L PTS 6 Copenhagen, Denmark
28.02.98 Norbert Nieroba L PTS 8 Dortmund, Germany
05.06.98 Garry Delaney L PTS 6 Southend
23.02.99 Tim Redman W CO 7 Cardiff
  (Vacant Welsh Cruiserweight Title)
15.05.99 Cathal O'Grady W RSC 5 Blackpool
01.02.00 Bernard Bagci DREW 8 Paris, France
06.05.00 Rudiger May L PTS 8 Frankfurt, Germany
18.11.00 Robert Norton L PTS 10 Dagenham
  (Elim. British Cruiserweight Title)
Career: 35 contests, won 22, drew 4, lost 9.

Tony Griffiths

Millwall. *Born* Tower Hamlets, 16 April, 1969
S. Middleweight. Ht. 5'9½"
Manager A. Bowers

28.06.94 Tim Robinson W RSC 6 Mayfair
05.09.94 Mark Dawson L PTS 6 Brentwood
13.06.95 Andy Farr L RSC 4 Basildon
13.11.98 Jimmy Steel W PTS 4 Brighton
26.02.99 Mark Dawson W PTS 4 Bethnal Green
10.07.99 Mark Delaney L PTS 6 Southwark
10.11.00 Michael Pinnock W PTS 4 Mayfair
23.02.01 Dean Ashton W PTS 8 Barking
20.04.01 Darren Ashton L PTS 4 Millwall
Career: 9 contests, won 5, lost 4.

Gary Groves

Walsall. *Born* Walsall, 17 November, 1969
S. Bantamweight. Ht. 5'6"
Manager M. Shinfield

21.02.99 Mark Hudson L RSC 3 Bradford
19.04.99 Paddy Folan W CO 1 Bradford
27.04.99 Gary Steadman L RSC 2 Bethnal Green
29.05.99 Sean Grant L PTS 6 South Shields
08.02.00 Neil Read L PTS 6 Wolverhampton
03.03.00 Andrew Ferrans L RSC 1 Irvine
24.11.00 Michael Hunter L RSC 2 Darlington
Career: 7 contests, won 1, lost 6.

Audrey Guthrie

Newcastle. *Born* Newcastle, 19 April, 1964
Bantamweight. Ht. 5'0"
Manager G. Robinson

01.12.99 Jan Wild L PTS 4 Yarm
01.04.01 Sara Hall L RSC 2 Alfreton
Career: 2 contests, lost 2.

Damon Hague (Wheatley)

Derby. *Born* Derby, 29 October, 1970
WBF European S. Middleweight
Champion. Ht. 6'0"
Manager D. Ingle

27.11.98	Jimmy Steel DREW 6 Nottingham	
14.12.98	Dean Ashton W PTS 6 Cleethorpes	
26.02.99	Adrian Houldey W RSC 5 West Bromwich	
27.03.99	Mark Owens W RSC 2 Derby	
15.05.99	Michael Pinnock W PTS 4 Sheffield	
27.06.99	Mark Owens W RSC 5 Alfreton	
15.08.99	Ian Toby W PTS 6 Derby	
03.10.99	Simon Andrews W PTS 6 Chesterfield	
20.11.99	Simon Andrews W RSC 4 Grantham	
15.01.00	Matthew Pepper W CO 1 Doncaster	
09.04.00	Matthew Pepper W RSC 3 Alfreton	
21.05.00	Martin Jolley W PTS 6 Derby	
19.06.00	William Webster W PTS 4 Burton	
13.08.00	Martin Jolley W RTD 1 Nottingham	
04.11.00	Mike Duffield W RSC 3 Derby	

*(Vacant WBF European
S. Middleweight Title)*

25.02.01	Rob Stevenson W PTS 8 Derby	
16.06.01	Dean Ashton L DIS 1 Derby	

Career: 17 contests, won 15, drew 1, lost 1.

Eddie Haley

North Shields. *Born* South Shields, 25
August, 1965
Northern Area Middleweight Champion.
Ht. 5'9"
Manager T. Callighan

06.06.94	Brian Dunn W PTS 6 Glasgow	
25.10.94	Sven Hamer L RSC 4 Southwark	
30.11.94	Roy Chipperfield W RSC 3 Solihull	
23.01.95	Billy Collins L RSC 4 Glasgow	
01.03.95	Gary Beardsley L RSC 1 Glasgow	
27.04.95	Gary Silvester W RSC 2 Hull	
19.05.95	James Lowther L RSC 5 Leeds	
21.05.98	Jon Penn L RSC 2 Bradford	
29.10.98	Ian Toby W PTS 10 Newcastle	

*(Vacant Northern Area Middleweight
Title)*

13.02.99	Ian Toby W RSC 6 Newcastle	

*(Northern Area Middleweight Title
Defence)*

29.05.99	Mike Duffield W RSC 6 South Shields	
23.10.99	Toks Owoh L RSC 3 Telford	
15.01.00	Ryan Rhodes L RSC 5 Doncaster	
17.04.00	Dave Johnson W RSC 6 Glasgow	

*(Northern Area Middleweight Title
Defence)*

03.11.00	Steven Bendall L RSC 1 Ebbw Vale	

Career: 15 contests, won 7, lost 8.

Chris Hall

Sheffield. *Born* Sheffield, 25 September,
1980
L. Welterweight. Ht. 5'7"
Manager G. Rhodes

11.09.99	Ricky Bishop W PTS 4 Sheffield	
26.11.99	Duncan Armstrong W PTS 6 Wakefield	

18.03.00	Kevin McIntyre L RSC 3 Glasgow	
20.05.00	Craig Goodman W PTS 6 Rotherham	
28.10.00	Tony Conroy L RSC 1 Coventry	

Career: 5 contests, won 3, lost 2.

Jason Hall

Hanwell. *Born* Perivale, 19 November,
1975
Lightweight. Ht. 5'8½"
Manager F. Maloney

19.04.97	Johannes Musa W RSC 3 Las Vegas, USA	
06.06.97	Raul Basulto L RSC 10 Las Vegas, USA	
30.07.97	Mark Chang w pts 4 Las Vegas, USA	
27.06.98	Andrew Poulos W PTS 4 Vancouver, Canada	
29.06.99	Brendan Ahearne W PTS 6 Bethnal Green	
20.08.99	Keith Jones W PTS 6 Bloomsbury	
05.10.99	John Paul Temple W PTS 6 Bloomsbury	
06.11.99	Woody Greenaway W RSC 5 Bethnal Green	
10.03.00	Arv Mittoo L RSC 3 Bethnal Green	
18.02.01	Marco Fattore W PTS 6 Southwark	
01.04.01	Gary Flear W PTS 8 Southwark	
28.04.01	Bradley Pryce L PTS 12 Cardiff	

*(Vacant WBO Inter-Continental
Lightweight Title)*

Career: 12 contests, won 9, lost 3.

Nick Hall

Darlington. *Born* Darlington, 9 November,
1968
L. Middleweight. Ht. 5'9"
Manager Self

14.09.89	Paul Charters W PTS 6 Motherwell	
24.10.89	Paul Day L CO 4 Watford	
21.03.90	Mark Antony W PTS 6 Solihull	
03.04.90	Steve Griffith W RSC 2 Canvey Island	
26.04.90	Michael Ayers L CO 3 Wandsworth	
03.10.90	Mike Morrison W PTS 8 Solihull	
18.10.90	Peter Till L PTS 6 Birmingham	
03.11.93	Young Gully W RSC 2 Bristol	
25.01.94	Nick Appiah W PTS 4 Piccadilly	
25.10.94	Gary Logan DREW 8 Southwark	
08.12.97	David Kirk W PTS 6 Nottingham	
24.03.98	Darren McInulty W PTS 6 Wolverhampton	
01.04.01	Peter Nightingale DREW 6 Wolverhampton	

Career: 13 contests, won 8, drew 2, lost 3

(Michael) Oscar Hall

Darlington. *Born* Darlington, 8 November,
1974
Welterweight. Ht. 5'9"
Manager D. Ingle

09.05.98	Trevor Smith W PTS 4 Sheffield	
27.02.99	Lee Molyneux W PTS 4 Oldham	
15.05.99	Chris Price W PTS 4 Sheffield	
29.05.99	Brian Gifford W RSC 1 Halifax	
04.06.99	Arv Mittoo W PTS 6 Hull	
27.09.99	Dave Gibson W PTS 6 Leeds	
11.12.99	Brian Coleman W PTS 6 Liverpool	
18.02.00	Jason Collins DREW 6 West Bromwich	
02.03.00	Ernie Smith W PTS 6 Birkenhead	

09.06.00	Dave Gibson W PTS 6 Hull	
19.06.00	Paul Denton W PTS 4 Burton	
13.08.00	Lee Molyneux W PTS 6 Nottingham	
04.11.00	Ram Singh W PTS 6 Derby	
24.11.00	Dean Nicholas W PTS 6 Darlington	
11.12.00	Ram Singh W PTS 6 Derby	
16.06.01	David Kirk W PTS 6 Derby	

Career: 16 contests, won 15, drew 1.

Sara Hall

Chesterfield. *Born* Chesterfield, 4
December, 1970
Bantamweight. Ht. 5'1"
Manager J. Ashton

30.06.98	Jolene Blackshear L RSC 5 Atlantic City, USA	
01.04.01	Audrey Guthrie W RSC 2 Alfreton	
16.06.01	Juliette Winter W RTD 4 Derby	

Career: 3 contests, won 2, lost 1.

(Michael) Kid Halls

Walsall. *Born* Bloxwich, 2 October, 1975
L. Middleweight. Ht. 5'9"
Manager D. Poston

24.11.98	Craig Clayton W PTS 6 Wolverhampton	
11.02.99	Andy Kemp W RSC 1 Dudley	
26.02.99	Brian Swain W RSC 5 West Bromwich	
29.04.99	Oleg Kudinov L RSC 2 Bethnal Green	
19.06.99	Gary Lockett L CO 1 Dublin	
15.01.01	Thomas McDonagh L RSC 4 Manchester	

Career: 6 contests, won 3, lost 3.

Paul Halpin

Brighton. *Born* Brighton, 4 August, 1974
S. Featherweight. Former Undefeated
Southern Area Featherweight Champion.
Ht. 5'5"
Manager F. Warren

04.04.97	Graham McGrath W PTS 6 Brighton	
20.05.97	David Jeffrey W PTS 6 Gillingham	
11.07.97	Wayne Jones W RSC 5 Brighton	
08.10.97	Greg Upton DREW 4 Poplar	
27.02.98	Taffy Evans W RSC 3 Brighton	
16.05.98	Chris Lyons W PTS 6 Chigwell	
26.02.99	Justin Murphy W RSC 2 Bethnal Green	

*(Vacant Southern Area Featherweight
Title)*

26.06.99	Pete Buckley W PTS 4 Millwall	
15.11.99	Chris Jickells W PTS 6 Bethnal Green	
19.06.00	Chris Jickells W RSC 4 Burton	
12.08.00	Eddie Nevins W PTS 6 Wembley	

Career: 11 contests, won 10, drew 1.

Mark Halstead

Halifax. *Born* Halifax, 14 July, 1974
L. Welterweight. Ht. 5'7"
Manager Self

30.03.98	Leigh Daniels DREW 6 Bradford	
14.06.98	Terry Butwell L PTS 6 Golders Green	
12.10.98	Mark Harrison DREW 6 Bradford	
25.11.98	Malcolm Thomas L PTS 6 Clydach	
07.12.98	Gavin McGill L PTS 6 Nottingham	
01.02.99	Les Frost DREW 6 Bradford	
21.05.99	Ram Singh DREW 6 Glasgow	
04.06.99	Chris Price DREW 6 Hull	
01.10.99	Dale Lowe L PTS 6 Cleethorpes	

22.10.99 Tony Conroy L PTS 4 Coventry
26.11.99 Kevin Abdy W PTS 6 Wakefield
11.12.99 Dariusz Snarski L PTS 6 Merthyr
08.03.01 Elias Boswell W RSC 5 Blackpool
Career: 13 contests, won 2, drew 5, lost 6.

Prince Naseem Hamed
Sheffield. *Born* Sheffield, 12 February, 1974
Former Undefeated WBO, IBF & WBC Featherweight Champion. Former Undefeated WBC International S. Bantamweight Champion. Former Undefeated European Bantamweight Champion. Ht. 5'3"
Manager Self

14.04.92 Ricky Beard W CO 2 Mansfield
25.04.92 Shaun Norman W RSC 2 Manchester
23.05.92 Andrew Bloomer W RSC 2 Birmingham
14.07.92 Miguel Matthews W RSC 3 Mayfair
07.10.92 Des Gargano W RSC 4 Sunderland
12.11.92 Pete Buckley W PTS 6 Liverpool
24.02.93 Alan Ley W CO 2 Wembley
26.05.93 Kevin Jenkins W RSC 3 Mansfield
24.09.93 Chris Clarkson W CO 2 Dublin
29.01.94 Pete Buckley W RSC 4 Cardiff
09.04.94 John Miceli W CO 1 Mansfield
11.05.94 Vincenzo Belcastro W PTS 12 Sheffield
(European Bantamweight Title Challenge)
17.08.94 Antonio Picardi W RSC 3 Sheffield
(European Bantamweight Title Defence)
12.10.94 Freddy Cruz W RSC 6 Sheffield
(Vacant WBC International S. Bantamweight Title)
19.11.94 Laureano Ramirez W RTD 3 Cardiff
(WBC International S. Bantamweight Title Defence)
21.01.95 Armando Castro W RSC 4 Glasgow
(WBC International S. Bantamweight Title Defence)
04.03.95 Sergio Liendo W RSC 2 Livingston
(WBC International S. Bantamweight Title Defence)
06.05.95 Enrique Angeles W CO 2 Shepton Mallet
(WBC International S. Bantamweight Title Defence)
01.07.95 Juan Polo Perez W CO 2 Kensington
(WBC International S. Bantamweight Title Defence)
30.09.95 Steve Robinson W RSC 8 Cardiff
(WBO Featherweight Title Challenge)
16.03.96 Said Lawal W RSC 1 Glasgow
(WBO Featherweight Title Defence)
08.06.96 Daniel Alicea W RSC 2 Newcastle
(WBO Featherweight Title Defence)
31.08.96 Manuel Medina W RSC 11 Dublin
(WBO Featherweight Title Defence)
09.11.96 Remigio Molina W RSC 2 Manchester
(WBO Featherweight Title Defence)
08.02.97 Tom Johnson W RSC 8 Millwall
(WBO Featherweight Title Defence. IBF Featherweight Title Challenge)
03.05.97 Billy Hardy W RSC 1 Manchester
(WBO & IBF Featherweight Title Defences)
19.07.97 Juan Cabrera W RSC 2 Wembley
(WBO Featherweight Title Defence)

11.10.97 Jose Badillo W RSC 7 Sheffield
(WBO Featherweight Title Defence)
19.12.97 Kevin Kelley W CO 4 New York City, USA
(WBO Featherweight Title Defence)
18.04.98 Wilfredo Vasquez W RSC 7 Manchester
(WBO Featherweight Title Defence)
31.10.98 Wayne McCullough W PTS 12 Atlantic City, USA
(WBO Featherweight Title Defence)
10.04.99 Paul Ingle W RSC 11 Manchester
(WBO Featherweight Title Defence)
22.10.99 Cesar Soto W PTS 12 Detroit, USA
(WBO Featherweight Title Defence. WBC Featherweight Title Challenge)
11.03.00 Vuyani Bungu W CO 4 Kensington
(WBO Featherweight Title Defence)
19.08.00 Augie Sanchez W RSC 4 Mashantucket, Connecticut, USA
(WBO Featherweight Title Defence)
07.04.01 Marco Antonio Barrera L PTS 12 Las Vegas, USA
(Vacant IBO Featherweight Title)
Career: 36 contests, won 35, lost 1.

Sven Hamer
Margate. *Born* Margate, 6 June, 1973
Former Undefeated WBF European L. Heavyweight Champion. Ht. 5'11"
Manager Self

25.10.94 Eddie Haley W RSC 4 Southwark
07.11.94 Shamus Casey W PTS 4 Piccadilly
23.11.94 Andy Ewen W RSC 1 Piccadilly
20.12.94 Tony Velinor W RSC 4 Bethnal Green
24.01.95 Delroy Matthews L PTS 6 Piccadilly
28.07.95 Russell Washer W PTS 6 Bristol
09.12.95 Jason Matthews L RSC 6 Bethnal Green
05.03.96 Mark Baker L PTS 10 Bethnal Green
(Vacant Southern Area Middleweight Title)
11.12.96 Howard Eastman L RSC 10 Southwark
(Vacant Southern Area Middleweight Title)
14.03.97 Brian Galloway W CO 1 Reading
15.05.97 Stinger Mason W CO 5 Reading
05.07.97 John Wilson W RSC 4 Glasgow
27.10.97 Willie Quinn W RSC 1 Musselburgh
(Elim. British S. Middleweight Title)
29.11.97 Toks Owoh L PTS 8 Norwich
07.02.98 Darren Ashton W RSC 6 Cheshunt
09.05.98 Mark Smallwood L PTS 8 Sheffield
23.09.98 Robert Peel W RSC 1 Bloomsbury
25.11.98 Greg Scott-Briggs W CO 2 Streatham
14.12.98 Tony Booth L PTS 6 Cleethorpes
20.05.99 Greg Scott-Briggs L RSC 5 Kensington
30.09.99 Terry Morrill W PTS 6 Kensington
31.10.99 Vitali Kopitko W PTS 10 Raynes Park
(Vacant WBF European L. Heavyweight Title)
24.05.01 Paul Bonson W PTS 4 Kensington
16.06.01 Elvis Michailenko L RSC 6 Wembley
(Vacant WBF European L. Heavyweight Title)
Career: 24 contests, won 15, lost 9.

Gary Hamilton
Belfast. *Born* Belfast, 27 May, 1980
L. Welterweight. Ht. 5'8½"
Manager P. McCausland

20.10.00 Gyula Szabo W PTS 4 Belfast
10.12.00 Patrick Dominguez L RSC 3 Elgin, Illinois, USA
Career: 2 contests, won 1, lost 1.

Steve Hanley
Redditch. *Born* Bromsgrove, 30 April, 1970
Lightweight. Ht. 5'8"
Manager Self

15.11.99 Kevin Lear L RSC 1 Bethnal Green
13.12.99 Willie Limond L PTS 6 Glasgow
08.02.00 Barrie Kelley L PTS 6 Wolverhampton
19.02.00 Craig Docherty L PTS 6 Prestwick
05.03.00 Mark Hargreaves W RTD 4 Shaw
25.03.00 Tony Mulholland L PTS 6 Liverpool
13.04.00 Danny Hunt L PTS 4 Holborn
25.05.00 Liam Maltby L PTS 4 Peterborough
06.06.00 Barrie Kelley W RSC 5 Brierley Hill
25.06.00 Kevin Bennett L PTS 6 Wakefield
15.07.00 Jan Jansen L RSC 1 Millwall
04.09.00 Jesse James Daniel L PTS 4 Manchester
25.09.00 Franny Hogg L PTS 6 Barnsley
10.10.00 Carl Allen L PTS 8 Brierley Hill
13.11.00 Gavin Rees L RSC 1 Bethnal Green
03.02.01 Ricky Eccleston L PTS 4 Manchester
10.02.01 Scott Miller L RSC 3 Widnes
17.03.01 Andy McLean L PTS 4 Manchester
24.03.01 Mally McIver L PTS 4 Sheffield
03.04.01 Kevin Lear L PTS 6 Bethnal Green
10.04.01 Mark Alexander L PTS 4 Wembley
04.06.01 James Rooney L PTS 4 Hartlepool
11.06.01 Adnan Amar L PTS 4 Nottingham
Career: 23 contests, won 2, lost 21.

Anthony Hanna
Birmingham. *Born* Birmingham, 22 September, 1974
S. Bantamweight. Midlands Area Flyweight Champion. Ht. 5'6"
Manager Self

19.11.92 Nick Tooley L PTS 6 Evesham
10.12.92 Daren Fifield L RSC 6 Bethnal Green
11.05.93 Tiger Singh W PTS 6 Norwich
24.05.93 Lyndon Kershaw L PTS 6 Bradford
16.09.93 Chris Lyons W PTS 6 Southwark
06.10.93 Tiger Singh W PTS 6 Solihull
03.11.93 Mickey Cantwell L PTS 8 Bristol
25.01.94 Marty Chestnut W PTS 4 Piccadilly
10.02.94 Allan Mooney W RTD 1 Glasgow
13.04.94 Allan Mooney L PTS 6 Glasgow
22.04.94 Jesper Jensen L PTS 5 Aalborg, Denmark
03.08.94 Paul Ingle L PTS 6 Bristol
01.10.94 Mark Hughes L PTS 4 Cardiff
30.11.94 Shaun Norman W PTS 10 Solihull
(Vacant Midlands Area Flyweight Title)
24.02.95 Darren Greaves W RSC 5 Weston super Mare
06.03.95 Mark Hughes L PTS 6 Mayfair
27.04.95 Mickey Cantwell L PTS 6 Bethnal Green
05.05.95 Mark Cokely W RSC 4 Swansea
04.06.95 Mark Reynolds L PTS 10 Bethnal Green
(Elim. British Flyweight Title)
02.07.95 Mickey Cantwell L PTS 6 Dublin
02.11.95 Shaun Norman DREW 10 Mayfair
(Midlands Area Flyweight Title Defence)

31.01.96	Marty Chestnut DREW 6 Stoke
20.03.96	Harry Woods L PTS 6 Cardiff
22.04.96	Neil Parry W PTS 6 Manchester
14.05.96	Dharmendra Singh Yadav L PTS 4 Dagenham
08.10.96	Marty Chestnut W PTS 6 Battersea
11.12.96	Mark Reynolds DREW 8 Southwark
28.01.97	Colin Moffett L PTS 4 Belfast
28.02.97	Paul Weir L PTS 8 Kilmarnock
14.03.97	Jesper Jensen L PTS 6 Odense, Denmark
30.04.97	Clinton Beeby DREW 6 Acton
10.05.97	Jason Booth L PTS 6 Nottingham
02.06.97	Keith Knox L PTS 6 Glasgow
14.10.97	Louis Veitch L PTS 6 Kilmarnock
27.10.97	Russell Laing W PTS 4 Musselburgh
13.11.97	Noel Wilders L PTS 6 Bradford
24.11.97	Shaun Anderson L PTS 8 Glasgow
20.12.97	Damaen Kelly L PTS 4 Belfast
31.01.98	Jason Booth L PTS 6 Edmonton
23.02.98	David Coldwell W PTS 6 Salford
19.03.98	Andy Roberts L PTS 6 Doncaster
18.05.98	Chris Emanuele W RSC 3 Cleethorpes
11.09.98	Nicky Booth DREW 6 Cleethorpes
18.09.98	Colin Moffett DREW 4 Belfast
29.10.98	Nick Tooley W RTD 6 Bayswater
25.11.98	Nicky Booth W PTS 6 Clydach
21.01.99	Ola Dali W PTS 6 Piccadilly
13.03.99	Damaen Kelly L PTS 12 Manchester *(Vacant British Flyweight Title. Commonwealth Flyweight Title Challenge)*
24.04.99	Noel Wilders L PTS 6 Peterborough
07.06.99	Alston Buchanan W RSC 3 Glasgow
29.06.99	Tommy Waite L PTS 4 Bethnal Green
16.10.99	Stevie Quinn W PTS 4 Belfast
22.11.99	Frankie DeMilo L PTS 6 Piccadilly
04.12.99	Ady Lewis L PTS 6 Manchester
19.02.00	Ian Napa L PTS 6 Dagenham
13.03.00	Mzukisi Sikali L PTS 6 Bethnal Green
27.05.00	Nicky Cook L PTS 6 Mayfair
25.07.00	David Lowry L PTS 4 Southwark
19.08.00	Marc Callaghan L PTS 4 Brentwood
29.09.00	Rocky Dean L PTS 4 Bethnal Green
07.10.00	Oleg Kiryukhin L PTS 6 Doncaster
14.10.00	Danny Costello DREW 4 Wembley
31.10.00	Dmitri Kirilol L PTS 6 Hammersmith
10.02.01	Tony Mulholland L PTS 4 Widnes
19.02.01	Alex Moon L PTS 6 Glasgow
03.03.01	Marc Callaghan L PTS 6 Wembley
24.04.01	Silence Mabuza L PTS 6 Liverpool
06.05.01	Michael Hunter L PTS 4 Hartlepool
26.05.01	Micky Bowden L PTS 4 Bethnal Green
04.06.01	Michael Hunter L PTS 4 Hartlepool

Career: 70 contests, won 18, drew 7, lost 45.

James Hare

Robertown. *Born* Dewsbury, 16 July, 1976
Welterweight. Ht. 5'6"
Manager T. Gilmour/C. Aston

20.01.96	Brian Coleman W PTS 6 Mansfield
25.06.96	Mike Watson W PTS 4 Mansfield
13.07.96	Dennis Griffin W RSC 4 Bethnal Green
14.09.96	Paul Salmon W RSC 4 Sheffield
14.12.96	Jon Harrison W PTS 4 Sheffield
25.02.97	Kid McAuley W PTS 4 Sheffield
12.04.97	Andy Peach W RSC 1 Sheffield
13.12.97	Costas Katsantonis W RSC 3 Sheffield
09.05.98	Peter Nightingale W PTS 4 Sheffield
18.07.98	Karl Taylor W PTS 4 Sheffield
28.11.98	Peter Nightingale W PTS 6 Sheffield
15.05.99	Lee Williamson W RSC 2 Sheffield

23.10.99	Mark Winters DREW 6 Telford
23.10.00	Dean Nicholas W RSC 1 Glasgow
23.01.01	Mark Ramsey W PTS 6 Crawley
26.02.01	Paul Denton W PTS 4 Nottingham
08.05.01	Jessy Moreaux W RSC 3 Barnsley
26.05.01	John Humphrey W RSC 7 Bethnal Green
	(Elim. British Welterweight Title)

Career: 18 contests, won 17, drew 1.

James Hare   Harry Goodwin

Audley Harrison

Edmonton. *Born* Park Royal, 26 October, 1971
Heavyweight. Ht. 6'4¾"
Manager C. McMillan

19.05.01	Michael Middleton W RSC 1 Wembley

Career: 1 contest, won 1.

Audley Harrison   Les Clark

Gary Harrison

Swadlincote. *Born* Burton, 26 May, 1969
Welterweight. Ht. 5'8"
Manager R. Davies

20.05.99	Chris Lyons W PTS 6 Barking
29.04.00	Mike Yikealo L PTS 4 Wembley
13.07.00	Costas Katsantonis L PTS 4 Bethnal Green
28.10.00	Kevin Bennett L RTD 2 Coventry
03.02.01	Casey Brooke W PTS 6 Brighton
05.05.01	Jason McElligott W PTS 6 Brighton

Career: 6 contests, won 3, lost 3.

Jon Harrison

Plymouth. *Born* Scunthorpe, 18 March, 1977
L. Middleweight. Ht. 5'11½"
Manager N. Christian

13.01.96	Mark Haslam L PTS 6 Manchester
13.02.96	Paul Samuels L CO 1 Cardiff
16.05.96	Dave Fallon W RSC 4 Dunstable
03.07.96	Allan Gray L PTS 6 Wembley
01.10.96	Cam Raeside L PTS 6 Birmingham
07.11.96	Nicky Bardle L PTS 6 Battersea
14.12.96	James Hare L PTS 4 Sheffield
19.04.97	Jason Williams W PTS 6 Plymouth
11.07.97	Pat Larner L PTS 6 Brighton
07.10.97	Paul Salmon L PTS 6 Plymouth
23.02.98	Alan Gilbert L PTS 6 Windsor
24.03.98	Brian Coleman DREW 6 Wolverhampton
14.07.98	Jason Williams L RTD 2 Reading
12.05.01	Ernie Smith W PTS 4 Plymouth

Career: 14 contests, won 3, drew 1, lost 10.

Scott Harrison

Cambuslang. *Born* Bellshill, 19 August, 1977
British, Commonwealth & IBO Inter-Continental Featherweight Champion. Ht. 5'7"
Manager F. Maloney

07.10.96	Eddie Sica W RSC 2 Lewisham
11.01.97	Pete Buckley W PTS 4 Bethnal Green
25.03.97	David Morris W PTS 4 Lewisham
04.10.97	Miguel Matthews L RSC 4 Muswell Hill
16.12.97	Stephane Fernandez DREW 6 Grand Synthe, France
31.01.98	Pete Buckley W PTS 4 Edmonton
09.06.98	Carl Allen W RSC 6 Hull
17.10.98	Rakhim Mingaleev W PTS 8 Manchester
06.03.99	John Matthews W RSC 4 Southwark
10.07.99	Smith Odoom W PTS 12 Southwark *(IBO Inter-Continental Featherweight Title Challenge)*
24.01.00	Patrick Mullings W PTS 12 Glasgow *(Commonwealth Featherweight Title Challenge)*
29.04.00	Tracy Harris Patterson W PTS 10 New York City, USA
15.07.00	Tom Johnson W PTS 12 Millwall *(IBO Inter-Continental Featherweight Title Defence)*
11.11.00	Eric Odumasi W RSC 12 Belfast *(Commonwealth Featherweight Title Defence)*
24.03.01	Richie Wenton W RSC 4 Sheffield *(Vacant British Featherweight Title. Commonwealth Featherweight Title Defence)*

Career: 15 contests, won 13, drew 1, lost 1.

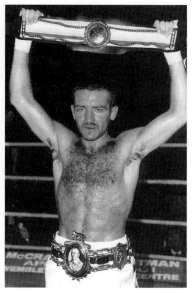

Scott Harrison   Les Clark

Jason Hart

Bromley. *Born* Beckenham, 23 January, 1970
S. Middleweight. Ht. 5'9½"
Manager Self

02.06.94	Paul Matthews L RSC 3 Tooting
28.07.94	Julian Eavis W PTS 6 Tooting
30.09.94	Freddie Yemofio W PTS 6 Bethnal Green
31.03.95	Andy Ewen W PTS 6 Crystal Palace
20.09.95	Steve Roberts L RSC 5 Potters Bar
03.12.95	Simon Andrews W PTS 6 Southwark
30.01.96	Ernie Loveridge W PTS 6 Barking
05.03.96	Martin Jolley W PTS 6 Bethnal Green
03.04.96	Michael Pinnock W PTS 6 Bethnal Green
24.10.96	Graham Townsend L RSC 5 Mayfair *(Vacant Southern Area S. Middleweight Title)*
13.04.97	Sven Ottke L RSC 2 Cologne, Germany
20.05.97	Johnny Hooks W PTS 6 Gillingham
28.03.98	Rob Stevenson W PTS 6 Crystal Palace
30.05.98	Darren Dorrington L RTD 2 Bristol
26.09.98	Jimmy Hawk DREW 6 Southwark
25.11.98	Lester Jacobs L RSC 6 Streatham *(Vacant WBF European Middleweight Title)*
05.11.99	Evans Ashira L RTD 3 Aalberg, Denmark
06.05.00	Matthew Barney L PTS 10 Southwark *(Vacant Southern Area S. Middleweight Title)*
25.07.00	Michael Bowen L RSC 1 Southwark
13.03.01	Scott Dann L RSC 2 Plymouth

Career: 20 contests, won 9, drew 1, lost 10.

Sebastian Hart

Wisbech. *Born* Burnley, 10 May, 1980
S. Featherweight. Ht. 5'4"
Manager B. Lee

26.11.99	Gary Wilson W PTS 6 Wakefield

08.12.99	Phil Lashley W RSC 3 Stoke
22.01.00	Steve Gethin W PTS 4 Birmingham
24.02.00	John Barnes W PTS 6 Sunderland
05.03.00	Chris Lyons W PTS 6 Peterborough
27.03.00	Lee Armstrong W CO 4 Barnsley
13.05.00	James Rooney L PTS 6 Barnsley
05.06.00	Craig Docherty L RSC 1 Glasgow
04.11.00	Gavin Down L RSC 4 Derby

Career: 9 contests, won 6, lost 3.

Mark Haslam

Manchester. *Born* Bury, 20 October, 1969
Welterweight. Ht. 5'8"
Manager S. Foster

12.06.95	Steve Burton W PTS 6 Manchester
15.09.95	Thomas Bradley W CO 4 Mansfield
24.11.95	Anthony Campbell L PTS 4 Manchester
13.01.96	Jon Harrison W PTS 6 Manchester
09.04.96	Pete Roberts W CO 2 Salford
25.10.96	Andrew Robinson W RTD 4 Mere
09.11.96	Brian Coleman W PTS 6 Manchester
22.03.97	Mark Richards DREW 4 Wythenshawe
17.11.97	Tommy Peacock L DIS 5 Manchester
16.10.98	Arv Mittoo W PTS 6 Salford
20.12.98	Mark Harrison W RSC 3 Salford
13.03.99	Gary Hibbert L PTS 10 Salford *(Vacant Central Area Lightweight Title)*
20.05.99	Colin Lynes L PTS 4 Barking
04.12.99	Wayne Rigby L CO 3 Manchester
11.06.00	Dave Tatton W PTS 4 Salford
10.02.01	Michael Jennings L RSC 2 Widnes

Career: 16 contests, won 9, drew 1, lost 6.

Matthew Hatton

Manchester. *Born* Stockport, 15 May, 1981
L. Welterweight. Ht. 5'8½"
Manager F. Warren

23.09.00	David White W PTS 4 Bethnal Green
25.11.00	David White W PTS 4 Manchester
11.12.00	Danny Connelly W PTS 4 Widnes
15.01.01	Keith Jones W PTS 4 Manchester
10.02.01	Karl Taylor W PTS 4 Widnes
17.03.01	Assen Vassilev W RSC 5 Manchester
09.06.01	Brian Coleman W RTD 2 Bethnal Green

Career: 7 contests, won 7.

Matthew Hatton   Les Clark

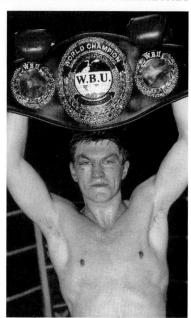

Richard Hatton   Les Clark

Richard Hatton

Manchester. *Born* Stockport, 6 October, 1978
WBU L. Welterweight Champion. Former Undefeated British, WBO Inter-Continental & Central Area L. Welterweight Champion. Ht. 5'7½"
Manager Self

11.09.97	Kid McAuley W RTD 1 Widnes
19.12.97	Robert Alvarez W PTS 4 New York City, USA
17.01.98	David Thompson W RSC 1 Bristol
27.03.98	Paul Salmon W RSC 1 Telford
18.04.98	Karl Taylor W RSC 1 Manchester
30.05.98	Mark Ramsey W PTS 6 Bristol
18.07.98	Anthony Campbell W PTS 6 Sheffield
19.09.98	Pascal Montulet W CO 2 Oberhausen, Germany
31.10.98	Kevin Carter W RSC 1 Atlantic City, USA
19.12.98	Paul Denton W RSC 6 Liverpool
27.02.99	Tommy Peacock W RSC 2 Oldham *(Vacant Central Area L. Welterweight Title)*
03.04.99	Brian Coleman W CO 2 Kensington
29.05.99	Dillon Carew W RSC 5 Halifax *(Vacant WBO Inter-Continental L. Welterweight Title)*
17.07.99	Mark Ramsey W PTS 6 Doncaster
09.10.99	Bernard Paul W RTD 4 Manchester *(WBO Inter-Continental L. Welterweight Title Defence)*
11.12.99	Mark Winters W RSC 4 Liverpool *(WBO Inter-Continental L. Welterweight Title Defence)*
29.01.00	Leoncio Garces W RSC 3 Manchester
25.03.00	Pedro Teran W RSC 4 Liverpool *(WBO Inter-Continental L. Welterweight Title Defence)*
16.05.00	Ambioris Figuero W RSC 4 Warrington *(WBO Inter-Continental L. Welterweight Title Defence)*

10.06.00 Gilbert Quiros W CO 2 Detroit, USA
*(WBO Inter-Continental
L. Welterweight Title Defence)*
23.09.00 Giuseppe Lauri W RSC 5 Bethnal Green
*(WBO Inter-Continental
L. Welterweight Title Defence. WBA
Inter-Continental L. Welterweight Title
Challenge)*
21.10.00 Jonathan Thaxton W PTS 12 Wembley
(Vacant British L.Welterweight Title)
26.03.01 Tony Pep W CO 4 Wembley
(Vacant WBU L. Welterweight Title)
Career: 23 contests, won 23.

Barry Hawthorne

Port Glasgow. *Born* Greenock, 21 July, 1978
Featherweight. Ht. 5'9"
Manager T. Gilmour

18.10.99 Paul Quarmby W PTS 6 Glasgow
15.11.99 Jason Edwards W PTS 6 Glasgow
24.01.00 Steve Brook DREW 4 Glasgow
19.02.00 Stevie Quinn L RSC 5 Prestwick
06.06.00 Nigel Senior W PTS 6 Motherwell
18.09.00 Nigel Leake W RSC 4 Glasgow
20.11.00 John Barnes W PTS 6 Glasgow
04.06.01 Joel Viney W PTS 8 Glasgow
Career: 8 contests, won 6, drew 1, lost 1.

Mark Hawthorne

Lowestoft. *Born* Great Yarmouth, 20
March, 1973
Lightweight. Ht. 5'7¾"
Manager J. Harding

10.03.00 Dean Murdoch W RSC 1 Bethnal
Green
17.04.00 David Kehoe W PTS 4 Birmingham
19.05.01 Woody Greenaway W PTS 4
Wembley
Career: 3 contests, won 3.

Darren Hayde

Cardiff. *Born* Cardiff, 29 July, 1979
Bantamweight. Ht. 5'8"
Manager K. Hayde

13.07.00 Delroy Spencer L PTS 4 Bethnal
Green
Career: 1 contest, lost 1.

Rob Hayes-Scott

Kennington. *Born* Lambeth, 4 January, 1976
Cruiserweight. Ht. 6'0"
Manager T. Follett

18.02.01 Kevin Burton W RSC 1 Southwark
07.04.01 Paul Bonson W PTS 4 Wembley
03.06.01 Radcliffe Green L RSC 4 Southwark
Career: 3 contests, won 2, lost 1.

Peter Haymer

Enfield. *Born* London, 10 July, 1978
L. Heavyweight. Ht. 6'1¼"
Manager F. Maloney

25.11.00 Adam Cale W RSC 1 Manchester
27.01.01 Darren Ashton W PTS 4 Bethnal Green
10.03.01 Daniel Ivanov W CO 2 Bethnal Green
26.03.01 Radcliffe Green W PTS 4 Wembley
05.05.01 Terry Morrill W PTS 4 Edmonton
Career: 5 contests, won 5.

Peter Haymer   Les Clark

Mohamed Helel

Hartlepool. *Born* Tunisia, 16 May, 1974
L. Welterweight. Ht. 5'5½"
Manager G. Robinson

21.05.99 Kevin McIntyre L PTS 6 Glasgow
10.06.99 Gareth Dooley W RSC 1 Hartlepool
06.11.99 Tommy Peacock L PTS 4 Widnes
22.11.99 Arv Mittoo W PTS 6 Piccadilly
01.12.99 Jason Vlasman L PTS 4 Yarm
29.03.00 Stephen Carr L PTS 6 Piccadilly
02.06.00 Alan Bosworth L PTS 6 Ashford
12.08.00 Francis Barrett L PTS 4 Wembley
12.11.00 Eddie Nevins L PTS 4 Manchester
19.02.01 Gary Ryder L RSC 1 Glasgow
Career: 10 contests, won 2, lost 8.

Gary Hibbert   Harry Goodwin

Gary Hibbert

Oldham. *Born* Oldham, 5 February, 1975
Central Area Lightweight Champion.
Ht. 5'8½"
Manager B. Hearn

02.06.96 John T. Kelly W PTS 6 Shaw

13.10.96 Sean Morrison W RSC 2 Shaw
16.03.97 David Kirk W PTS 6 Shaw
08.06.97 Bamana Dibateza W PTS 4 Shaw
18.09.98 Jimmy Phelan W PTS 6 Manchester
17.10.98 Dennis Griffin W RSC 4 Manchester
30.11.98 Carl Allen W PTS 4 Manchester
13.03.99 Mark Haslam W PTS 10 Manchester
(Vacant Central Area Lightweight Title)
01.07.00 Marco Fattore W PTS 4 Manchester
09.09.00 Woody Greenaway W RSC 2
Manchester
03.02.01 Franck Benoni L PTS 6 Manchester
04.06.01 Alan Temple L PTS 6 Hartlepool
Career: 12 contests, won 10, lost 2.

Dave Hinds

Birmingham. *Born* Leicester, 5 January, 1971
L. Welterweight. Ht. 5'5"
Manager Self

19.09.95 Martin Evans W RSC 5 Plymouth
08.11.95 Wayne Pardoe L CO 4 Walsall
04.04.96 Paul Salmon L RTD 5 Plymouth
06.10.97 Eddie Sica L RSC 1 Piccadilly
25.11.97 Graham McGrath W PTS 6
Wolverhampton
06.12.97 Adam Spelling W RSC 1 Wembley
27.01.98 Malcolm Thomas L PTS 6 Piccadilly
06.03.98 Jon Dodsworth W RSC 1 Hull
12.03.98 Jamie McKeever L PTS 4 Liverpool
20.03.98 John O'Johnson L PTS 6 Ilkeston
23.04.98 Roy Rutherford L RSC 5 Edgbaston
26.05.98 David Kehoe L RSC 5 Mayfair
07.10.98 Steve Saville L PTS 6 Stoke
26.10.98 Eddie Nevins L PTS 6 Manchester
26.11.98 Steve Saville L PTS 6 Edgbaston
07.12.98 Danny Bell L PTS 6 Nottingham
13.02.99 Michael Gomez L PTS 6 Newcastle
23.04.99 Mark Ramsey L PTS 6 Clydach
17.05.99 Jesse James Daniel L PTS 6 Cleethorpes
28.05.99 Jason Cook L RSC 1 Liverpool
17.07.99 Bradley Pryce L PTS 4 Doncaster
03.09.99 Young Muttley L RSC 4 West Bromwich
13.11.99 Humberto Soto L PTS 6 Hull
11.12.99 Gavin Rees L PTS 2 Liverpool
07.02.00 Liam Maltby L PTS 4 Peterborough
13.03.00 Danny Hunt L PTS 4 Bethnal Green
23.03.00 Marco Fattore L PTS 6 Bloomsbury
13.05.00 Alan Kershaw L PTS 4 Barnsley
22.05.00 Tony Conroy L PTS 4 Coventry
09.06.00 Elias Boswell W RSC 5 Blackpool
24.06.00 Brian Carr L PTS 4 Glasgow
01.07.00 Ricky Eccleston L PTS 4 Manchester
25.07.00 Kevin Lear L PTS 6 Southwark
09.09.00 Carl Greaves L PTS 6 Newark
16.09.00 Leo O'Reilly L RSC 2 Bethnal Green
27.11.00 Ricky Eccleston L PTS 4 Birmingham
04.12.00 Gavin Pearson L PTS 6 Bradford
11.12.00 Miguel Matthews W PTS 6 Birmingham
11.02.01 James Rooney L PTS 6 Hartlepool
26.03.01 Kevin Lear L CO 1 Wembley
03.06.01 Dafydd Carlin L PTS 4 Southwark
16.06.01 Carl Greaves L PTS 6 Derby
Career: 42 contests, won 6, lost 36.

Mark Hobson

Huddersfield. *Born* Workington, 7 May, 1976
Cruiserweight. Ht. 6'5"
Manager C. Aston/T. Gilmour

09.06.97 Michael Pinnock W PTS 6 Bradford
06.10.97 P. R. Mason W PTS 6 Bradford
13.11.97 P. R. Mason W PTS 6 Bradford
27.02.98 Colin Brown DREW 6 Irvine

21.05.98	Paul Bonson W PTS 6 Bradford
15.06.98	Martin Jolley W RSC 3 Bradford
25.10.98	Mark Snipe W RSC 3 Shaw
26.11.98	Danny Southam W RSC 5 Bradford
19.04.99	Mark Levy L PTS 8 Bradford
11.09.99	Paul Bonson W PTS 4 Sheffield
06.12.99	Brian Gascoigne W RSC 3 Bradford
11.03.00	Nikolai Ermenkov W RSC 3 Kensington
27.03.00	Luke Simpkin W PTS 4 Barnsley
13.05.00	Paul Bonson W PTS 4 Barnsley
25.09.00	Mark Dawson W CO 1 Barnsley
26.02.01	Billy Bessey W PTS 4 Nottingham
24.04.01	Sebastiaan Rothmann L RTD 9 Liverpool
	(WBU Cruiserweight Title Challenge)

Career: 17 contests, won 14, drew 1, lost 2.

Scott Hocking

Plymouth. *Born* Plymouth, 7 December, 1980
Lightweight. Ht. 5'6"
Manager N. Christian

25.02.01	Chill John L RSC 4 Streatham

Career: 1 contest, lost 1.

Scott Hocking   Les Clark

Lennie Hodgkins

Worcester. *Born* Bewdley, 10 March, 1977
S. Featherweight. Ht. 5'5"
Manager D. Gardiner

12.07.99	Gareth Payne L PTS 4 Coventry
14.10.99	Rocky Dean L PTS 6 Bloomsbury
30.10.99	Rocky Dean L PTS 6 Southwark
12.11.99	Willie Limond L RTD 1 Glasgow
26.02.00	Jamie Evans L PTS 4 Swansea
10.03.00	Danny Costello L PTS 4 Chigwell
25.03.00	Barry Waite L PTS 4 Liverpool
21.05.00	Eddie Nevins L RSC 1 Shaw
24.09.00	Steve Sharples L PTS 6 Shaw
28.01.01	Jimmy Beech L PTS 6 Wolverhampton
13.03.01	Lee Meager L RSC 3 Plymouth

Career: 11 contests, lost 11.

Franny Hogg

Leeds. *Born* Belfast, 8 March, 1973
Lightweight. Ht. 5'8"
Manager T. O'Neill/T. Gilmour

06.12.96	Les Frost W PTS 6 Leeds
16.12.96	Gary Jenkinson W RSC 2 Cleethorpes
24.03.97	Tomas Jansson L PTS 4 Helsinki, Finland
13.06.97	Vic Broomhead W RSC 2 Leeds
11.11.97	Ram Singh W PTS 6 Leeds
17.02.98	John T. Kelly W PTS 4 Leeds
12.05.98	Benny Jones W PTS 6 Leeds
21.11.98	John T. Kelly W PTS 6 Leeds
16.02.99	Pete Buckley W PTS 6 Leeds
25.04.99	Peter Leachman W PTS 6 Leeds
04.12.99	Keith Jones W PTS 4 Manchester
17.04.00	Pete Buckley W PTS 8 Glasgow
13.05.00	Barrie Kelley W PTS 6 Barnsley
25.09.00	Steve Hanley W PTS 6 Barnsley

Career: 14 contests, won 13, lost 1.

Gareth Hogg

Torquay. *Born* Newton Abbott, 21 October, 1977
L. Heavyweight. Ht. 6'2"
Manager C. Sanigar

13.02.98	Harry Butler W RSC 3 Weston super Mare
09.05.99	Matthew Barney L PTS 4 Bracknell
07.08.99	Clive Johnson W PTS 4 Dagenham
27.02.00	Darren Covill W RSC 3 Plymouth
29.03.00	Simon Andrews W RSC 5 Piccadilly
12.05.01	Oddy Papantoniou W RSC 2 Plymouth

Career: 6 contests, won 5, lost 1.

Mike Holden

Manchester. *Born* Ashton under Lyme, 13 March, 1968
Former Undefeated British Heavyweight Champion. Ht. 6'4"
Manager Self

04.10.94	Gary Williams W RSC 4 Mayfair
20.12.94	Pat Passley L RTD 3 Bethnal Green
07.10.95	R. F. McKenzie W RSC 2 Belfast
14.11.95	Michael Murray L PTS 6 Bury
09.07.96	Julius Francis L PTS 10 Bethnal Green
28.09.96	Mikael Lindblad W PTS 6 Barking
26.06.97	Israel Ajose W RSC 1 Salford
02.09.97	Mika Kihlstrom W RSC 1 Southwark
12.12.98	Nigel Rafferty W RTD 2 Chester
08.05.99	Harry Senior L PTS 8 Bethnal Green
15.07.99	Derek McCafferty W RSC 1 Peterborough
13.03.00	Julius Francis W PTS 12 Bethnal Green
	(British Heavyweight Title Challenge)
03.04.01	Julius Francis L PTS 10 Bethnal Green
	(Final Elim. British Heavyweight Title)

Career: 13 contests, won 8, lost 5.

Richard Holden

Mexborough. *Born* Mexborough, 14 November, 1975
Welterweight. Ht. 5'10"
Manager J. Ingle

13.12.99	Craig Goodman W PTS 6 Cleethorpes
19.02.00	Craig Goodman W PTS 6 Newark
15.05.00	David Smales DREW 6 Cleethorpes

30.08.00	Dave Gibson W PTS 6 Scunthorpe
19.11.00	Ram Singh W PTS 6 Chesterfield
24.03.01	Arv Mittoo W PTS 6 Newark

Career: 6 contests, won 5, drew 1.

Lee Holmes

Ellesmere Port. *Born* Chester, 18 April, 1975
Bantamweight. Ht. 5'6"
Manager M. Goodall

10.06.01	Paddy Folan W PTS 6 Ellesmere Port

Career: 1 contest, won 1.

Jon Honney

Basingstoke. *Born* Basingstoke, 6 August, 1975
L. Welterweight. Ht. 5'7"
Manager Self

01.10.99	Peter Dunn W PTS 4 Bethnal Green
18.12.99	Marco Fattore W PTS 4 Southwark
21.02.00	Costas Katsantonis L RSC 1 Southwark
13.07.00	Mickey Yikealo L PTS 4 Bethnal Green
29.09.00	Manzo Smith L PTS 4 Bethnal Green
06.11.00	Jimmy Gould L PTS 6 Wolverhampton
16.03.01	Woody Greenaway W PTS 6 Portsmouth

Career: 7 contests, won 3, lost 4.

Shaun Horsfall

Colne. *Born* Burnley, 15 November, 1975
L. Middleweight. Ht. 5'7"
Manager J. Doughty

19.09.99	Danny Bance W PTS 6 Shaw
28.10.99	Lee Molyneux W PTS 6 Burnley
05.03.00	Dave Gibson W PTS 6 Shaw
21.05.00	Tony Smith W RSC 4 Shaw
24.09.00	Ernie Smith W PTS 6 Shaw
03.12.00	Ernie Smith W PTS 6 Shaw

Career: 6 contests, won 6.

Shpetim Hoti

New Cross. *Born* Montenegro, 29 November, 1974
L. Heavyweight. Ht. 5'11 1/2"
Manager A. Gee

21.09.00	Elvis Michailenko L PTS 4 Bloomsbury
30.11.00	Harry Butler L PTS 4 Bloomsbury
21.06.01	Harry Butler L PTS 4 Earls Court

Career: 3 contests, lost 3.

Anthony Hughes

Manchester. *Born* Salford, 8 May, 1981
S. Bantamweight. Ht. 5'6"
Manager S. Foster/S. Wood

27.05.01	Andrew Greenaway W PTS 4 Manchester

Career: 1 contest, won 1.

Barry Hughes

Glasgow. *Born* Glasgow, 18 November, 1978
Lightweight. Ht. 5'8"
Manager Self

07.12.98	Woody Greenaway L PTS 6 Acton

18.02.99 Leon Dobbs W RSC 1 Glasgow
09.04.99 Gareth Dooley W PTS 6 Glasgow
26.06.99 Des Sowden W CO 1 Glasgow
04.10.99 Tony Smith W RSC 5 Glasgow
12.11.99 Brendan Ahearne W RSC 5 Glasgow
13.12.99 Jason Vlasman W RSC 2 Glasgow
24.02.00 Nono Junior W RSC 1 Glasgow
18.03.00 Gary Flear W RSC 4 Glasgow
07.04.00 Billy Smith W PTS 6 Glasgow
12.08.00 Dave Travers W PTS 4 Wembley
Career: 11 contests, won 10, lost 1.

John Humphrey

Newmarket. *Born* Kings Lynn, 24 July, 1980
British Masters Welterweight Champion.
Ht. 6'2"
Manager A. Bowers

20.05.99 Arv Mittoo W PTS 6 Barking
13.09.99 Les Frost W CO 1 Bethnal Green
05.10.99 David Kehoe W PTS 4 Bloomsbury
06.11.99 Emmanuel Marcos W PTS 4 Bethnal Green
25.02.00 Matthew Barr L RSC 1 Newmarket
18.05.00 Lee Molyneux W PTS 6 Bethnal Green
29.09.00 Chris Henry W RSC 4 Bethnal Green
15.02.01 Kevin McIntyre W RSC 4 Glasgow
09.03.01 Harry Butler W RSC 1 Millwall
20.04.01 Mark Ramsey W PTS 10 Millwall
(Vacant British Masters Welterweight Title)
26.05.01 James Hare L RSC 7 Bethnal Green
(Elim. British Welterweight Title)
Career: 11 contests, won 9, lost 2.

John Humphrey   Les Clark

Danny Hunt

Southend. *Born* Rochford, 1 May, 1981
Lightweight. Ht. 5'7"
Manager F. Maloney

29.11.99 Chris Lyons W PTS 4 Wembley
13.03.00 Dave Hinds W PTS 4 Bethnal Green
13.04.00 Steve Hanley W PTS 4 Holborn

13.07.00 Dave Travers W PTS 4 Bethnal Green
27.01.01 Lee Williamson L RSC 2 Bethnal Green
03.04.01 Lee Williamson W PTS 4 Bethnal Green
05.05.01 Pete Buckley W PTS 4 Edmonton
Career: 7 contests, won 6, lost 1.

Danny Hunt   Les Clark

Geoff Hunter

Salford. *Born* Runcorn, 28 October, 1969
Heavyweight. Ht. 6'0¾"
Manager Self

13.01.96 Slick Miller DREW 6 Halifax
04.10.96 Tim Redman L CO 5 Pentre Halkyn
20.11.96 Michael Sprott L RSC 1 Wembley
15.05.97 Gavin McGhin L PTS 6 Sunderland
04.10.97 Rune Lillebuen L RSC 3 Muswell Hill
21.04.98 Mark Potter L RSC 1 Edmonton
01.10.99 Kenny Gayle L PTS 6 Cleethorpes
18.10.99 Huggy Osman L PTS 6 Bradford
09.12.99 Scott Lansdowne L PTS 6 Sheffield
25.03.00 Tommy Bannister L PTS 4 Liverpool
11.05.00 Paul Fiske L PTS 6 Sunderland
15.07.00 Johan Thorbjoernsson L PTS 4 Millwall
09.10.00 Darren Chubbs L RSC 3 Liverpool
13.11.00 John McDermott L RSC 1 Bethnal Green
Career: 14 contests, drew 1, lost 13.

Michael Hunter

Hartlepool. *Born* Hartlepool, 5 May, 1978
S. Bantamweight. Ht. 5'7½"
Manager D. Garside

23.07.00 Sean Grant W PTS 6 Hartlepool
01.10.00 Chris Emanuele W PTS 6 Hartlepool
24.11.00 Gary Groves W RSC 2 Darlington
09.12.00 Chris Jickells W PTS 4 Southwark
11.02.01 Paddy Folan W RSC 6 Hartlepool
06.05.01 Anthony Hanna W PTS 4 Hartlepool
04.06.01 Anthony Hanna W PTS 4 Hartlepool
Career: 7 contests, won 7.

Michael Hunter   Les Clark

Karim Hussine

Balham. *Born* Tunisia, 22 March, 1970
L. Middleweight. Ht. 5'9"
Manager H. Holland

19.04.00 Steve Brumant W PTS 4 Kensington
01.07.00 Leigh Wicks W PTS 6 Southwark
28.09.00 Matthew Ashmole W PTS 4 Kensington
27.04.01 R.J.Karstens L PTS 6 Lake Tahoe, USA
Career: 4 contests, won 3, lost 1.

Karim Hussine   Les Clark

I J

Paul Ingle

Scarborough. *Born* Scarborough, 22 June, 1972
Former IBF Featherweight Champion. Former Undefeated British, Commonwealth, European & IBF Inter-Continental Featherweight Champion. Ht. 5'5"
Manager Self

23.03.94	Darren Noble W RSC 3 Cardiff
27.04.94	Graham McGrath W PTS 4 Bethnal Green
25.05.94	Neil Swain W CO 4 Bristol
03.08.94	Anthony Hanna W PTS 6 Bristol
24.11.94	Graham McGrath W PTS 6 Hull
23.02.95	Pete Buckley W PTS 8 Southwark
27.04.95	Pete Buckley W PTS 8 Bethnal Green
16.06.95	Des Gargano W RSC 2 Southwark
29.09.95	Miguel Matthews W RSC 4 Bethnal Green
15.12.95	Damir Nanev W RSC 5 Bethnal Green
05.02.96	Greg Upton W RSC 10 Bexleyheath
29.06.96	Ervine Blake W RSC 2 Erith
03.09.96	Brian Robb W RSC 2 Bethnal Green
06.11.96	Chris Jickells W RSC 4 Hull
11.01.97	Colin McMillan W RSC 8 Bethnal Green
	(British Featherweight Title Challenge)
28.04.97	Michael Alldis W RTD 11 Hull
	(British Featherweight Title Defence)
11.10.97	Jonjo Irwin W RTD 8 Sheffield
	(British Featherweight Title Defence. Commonwealth Featherweight Title Challenge)
28.03.98	Trust Ndlovu W PTS 12 Hull
	(Commonwealth Featherweight Title Defence)
09.06.98	Moussa Sangare W RTD 10 Hull
	(Vacant IBF Inter-Continental Featherweight Title)
08.08.98	Rakhim Mingaleev W CO 4 Scarborough
	(IBF Inter-Continental Featherweight Title Defence)
26.09.98	Billy Hardy W RSC 8 York
	(Commonwealth & IBO Inter-Continental Featherweight Title Defences. European Featherweight Title Challenge)
10.04.99	Prince Naseem Hamed L RSC 11 Manchester
	(WBO Featherweight Title Challenge)
13.11.99	Manuel Medina W PTS 12 Hull
	(IBF Featherweight Title Challenge)
29.04.00	Junior Jones W RSC 11 New York City, USA
	(IBF Featherweight Title Defence)
16.12.00	Mbulelo Botile L RSC 12 Sheffield
	(IBF Featherweight Title Defence)

Career: 25 contests, won 23, lost 2.

Richard Inquieti

Nottingham. *Born* Langley Mill, 19 October, 1968
L. Middleweight. Ht. 6'3¼"
Manager Self

30.09.96	Peter Varnavas L CO 2 Manchester
20.02.97	Paul Johnson W PTS 6 Mansfield
12.03.97	Tony Smith W RSC 2 Stoke
19.03.97	Andy Peach L RSC 1 Stoke
18.08.97	Jawaid Khaliq L RSC 5 Nottingham
18.09.97	Danny Bell L RSC 1 Alfreton
11.11.97	Trevor Smith L RSC 3 Edgbaston
08.12.97	Danny Bell L RSC 1 Nottingham
07.10.98	Sean O'Sullivan W PTS 6 Stoke
29.10.98	Dean Nicholas L RSC 1 Newcastle
02.12.98	Martyn Thomas L RSC 3 Stoke
25.03.99	Shane Junior L CO 2 Edgbaston
06.03.00	Martyn Bailey W RSC 5 Bradford
28.03.00	David Smales W PTS 6 Hartlepool
05.05.00	Martyn Bailey L PTS 6 Pentre Halkyn
20.11.00	Darren Spencer L RSC 1 Glasgow
04.02.01	Neil Bonner L PTS 6 Queensferry
23.02.01	Dean Nicholas L PTS 6 Irvine
08.03.01	Alan Campbell L PTS 6 Blackpool
01.04.01	Stuart Elwell L PTS 6 Wolverhampton
09.04.01	Gavin Wake L PTS 6 Bradford
20.04.01	Darren Williams L PTS 6 Dublin
03.06.01	Nicky Leech L PTS 6 Hanley

Career: 23 contests, won 5, lost 18.

Peter Jackson

Halesowen. *Born* Wordsley, 27 January, 1976
S. Middleweight. Ht. 5'11"
Manager D. Bradley

28.01.01	Harry Butler W PTS 6 Wolverhampton
01.04.01	Jamie Logan W PTS 6 Wolverhampton
20.05.01	Jamie Logan W PTS 6 Wolverhampton

Career: 3 contests, won 3.

Jacklord Jacobs

Kingston. *Born* Nigeria, 1 January, 1970
British Masters Heavyweight Champion. Ht. 6'1"
Manager J. Evans

03.03.94	Cordwell Hylton W RSC 3 Ebbw Vale
30.07.94	Cordwell Hylton W RSC 4 Bethnal Green
01.11.94	Bobby Anderson DREW 4 Las Vegas, USA
14.11.95	John Pierre W PTS 6 Yarm
05.02.96	Tim Redman DREW 6 Bexleyheath
22.04.96	Chris Woollas DREW 4 Crystal Palace
27.08.96	Andrew Benson L CO 2 Windsor
22.01.00	Pele Reid W RSC 2 Birmingham
23.11.00	Gordon Minors W RSC 4 Bayswater
	(Vacant British Masters Heavyweight Title)

Career: 9 contests, won 5, drew 3, lost 1.

Lester Jacobs

Peckham. *Born* London, 29 January, 1962
WBF Middleweight Champion. Former Undefeated WBF European Middleweight Champion. Ht. 5'7"
Manager Self

01.03.89	Peter Vosper W PTS 6 Bethnal Green
29.03.89	Reuben Thurley W RSC 4 Bethnal Green
30.01.90	David Brown W PTS 6 Battersea
12.09.90	Peter Gorny W RSC 2 Battersea
18.10.90	Alan Pennington W RSC 2 Wandsworth
20.03.91	Karl Barwise W PTS 6 Battersea
16.05.91	Paul McCarthy W PTS 6 Battersea

11.09.91	John Kaighin W RSC 2 Hammersmith
05.03.92	John Kaighin W RSC 1 Battersea
17.05.92	Marvin O'Brien W PTS 6 Harringay
16.11.94	Stinger Mason W PTS 6 Bloomsbury
23.02.95	Paul Murray W RSC 2 Southwark
08.03.95	Mark Dawson W PTS 6 Bloomsbury
22.07.95	Mark Dawson W PTS 4 Millwall
02.09.95	Butch Lesley W PTS 4 Wembley
27.11.97	Leigh Wicks W PTS 6 Bloomsbury
04.03.98	Mike Whittaker W RSC 3 Bloomsbury
23.09.98	Paul Wesley W CO 4 Bloomsbury
25.11.98	Jason Hart W RSC 6 Streatham
	(Vacant WBF European Middleweight Title)
24.03.99	Darren Covill W RSC 2 Bayswater
21.07.99	David Baptiste W RSC 2 Bloomsbury
14.10.99	Harry Butler W PTS 6 Bloomsbury
23.03.00	Paul Wesley W PTS 6 Bloomsbury
04.07.00	Ojay Abrahams W PTS 4 Tooting
08.09.00	Delroy Leslie W RSC 8 Hammersmith
	(WBF Middleweight Title Challenge)
30.11.00	David Baptiste W RSC 3 Bloomsbury
29.03.01	Leigh Wicks W PTS 6 Hammersmith
21.06.01	Jason Collins W CO 9 Earls Court
	(WBF Middleweight Title Defence)

Career: 28 contests, won 28.

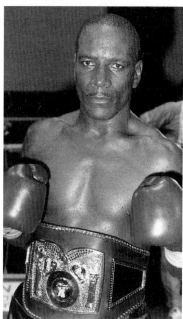

Lester Jacobs   Les Clark

Brett James (Eleftheriou)

St Pancras. *Born* London, 3 November, 1975
Welterweight. Ht. 5'8"
Manager D. Powell

20.01.00	Colin Vidler W PTS 6 Piccadilly
21.02.00	Julian Kacanolli W PTS 4 Southwark
04.07.00	Colin Vidler W PTS 4 Tooting
04.11.00	Matt Scriven W RTD 1 Bethnal Green
20.01.01	Jay Mahoney W PTS 4 Bethnal Green
07.04.01	Paul Denton W PTS 4 Wembley
16.06.01	Karl Taylor DREW 4 Wembley

Career: 7 contests, won 6, drew 1.

Daniel James

Newmarket. *Born* Lincoln, 15 December, 1975
Southern Area L. Welterweight Champion.
Ht. 5'9"
Manager A. Bowers

24.10.96	Shaba Edwards W PTS 6 Wembley
20.11.96	Costas Katsantonis W PTS 6 Wembley
11.02.97	Vince Burns W CO 2 Bethnal Green
03.04.97	Mark Allen W RSC 4 Wembley
09.09.97	Peter Nightingale W PTS 6 Bethnal Green
11.11.97	Marco Fattore W RSC 3 Bethnal Green
13.11.98	Woody Greenaway W PTS 4 Brighton
26.02.99	Tony Swift W PTS 6 Bethnal Green
20.05.99	Delroy Mellis W PTS 4 Barking
16.10.99	Steve Tuckett W RSC 1 Bethnal Green
25.02.00	John Paul Temple W PTS 10 Newmarket *(Vacant Southern Area L. Welterweight Title)*
06.10.00	Stephen Carr L RTD 5 Maidstone

Career: 12 contests, won 11, lost 1.

Michael Jennings

Chorley. *Born* Preston, 9 September, 1977
Welterweight. Ht. 5'9¹/₂"
Manager F. Warren

15.05.99	Tony Smith W RSC 1 Blackpool
11.12.99	Lee Molyneux W PTS 4 Liverpool
29.02.00	Lee Molyneux W PTS 6 Widnes
25.03.00	Brian Coleman W PTS 6 Liverpool
16.05.00	Brian Coleman W PTS 6 Warrington
29.05.00	William Webster W PTS 6 Manchester
08.07.00	Paul Denton W PTS 6 Widnes
04.09.00	Mark Ramsey W PTS 6 Manchester
25.11.00	Ernie Smith W PTS 4 Manchester
11.12.00	Paul Denton W PTS 6 Widnes
10.02.01	Mark Haslam W RSC 2 Widnes

Career: 11 contests, won 11.

Michael Jennings   Harry Goodwin

Daniel James   Les Clark

Chris Jickells

Brigg. *Born* Scunthorpe, 26 March, 1971
Former Undefeated Central Area
Featherweight Champion.
Ht. 5'5"
Manager Self

18.11.91	Tony Smith W RSC 4 Manchester
09.12.91	Al Garrett W RSC 2 Bradford
15.01.92	Ronnie Stephenson L PTS 6 Stoke
30.03.92	Colin Innes W RSC 3 Bradford
29.04.92	Kevin Middleton W RSC 6 Solihull
01.06.92	Dave McHale L RSC 4 Glasgow
12.10.92	Ian McGirr W RSC 3 Bradford
10.02.93	Kevin Middleton L CO 1 Lewisham
07.06.93	Wilson Docherty L RSC 5 Glasgow
02.11.93	Mark Bowers L RSC 3 Southwark
21.03.94	Mike Deveney L RSC 5 Glasgow
26.09.94	Dave Clavering L PTS 6 Morecambe
11.10.94	Yifru Retta L PTS 6 Bethnal Green
11.11.94	Dennis Holback Pedersen L PTS 6 Randers, Denmark
23.11.94	Ian McLeod L PTS 6 Irvine
04.02.95	Neil Swain L PTS 6 Cardiff
04.03.95	Paul Griffin L RSC 5 Livingston
30.06.95	Graham McGrath W PTS 4 Doncaster
28.07.95	Graham McGrath W PTS 6 Epworth
11.10.95	Gary Marston L PTS 8 Stoke
25.10.95	Barry Jones L PTS 6 Cardiff
29.11.95	Miguel Matthews L PTS 6 Solihull

22.01.96	Ian McLeod L PTS 8 Glasgow
29.02.96	Carl Allen L PTS 6 Scunthorpe
01.04.96	Kid McAuley W PTS 6 Bradford
03.05.96	Trevor Sumner W RSC 5 Sheffield
	(Vacant Central Area Featherweight Title)
25.05.96	Stephen Smith L RSC 3 Leipzig, Germany
25.06.96	Gary Thornhill L PTS 6 Stevenage
06.11.96	Paul Ingle L RSC 4 Hull
13.10.98	Dave Travers W PTS 6 Wolverhampton
14.11.98	Stephen Oates L PTS 6 Cheshunt
09.12.98	Carl Allen L RSC 3 Stoke
09.02.99	Pete Buckley W PTS 6 Wolverhampton
27.02.99	Michael Gomez L RSC 5 Oldham
	(Vacant Central Area Featherweight Title)
21.05.99	Sean Green L PTS 6 Glasgow
27.06.99	Carl Greaves L PTS 10 Alfreton
	(British Masters S. Featherweight Final)
07.08.99	Gary Thornhill L RSC 4 Dagenham
19.09.99	Mark Hargreaves L RSC 3 Shaw
20.10.99	Chris Lyons W PTS 6 Stoke
15.11.99	Paul Halpin L PTS 6 Bethnal Green
01.12.99	Nigel Senior W RSC 2 Stoke
13.12.99	David Burke L PTS 6 Glasgow
29.01.00	Michael Gomez L RSC 4 Manchester
10.03.00	Nicky Cook L RSC 1 Bethnal Green
15.05.00	Jesse James Daniel L PTS 6 Cleethorpes
19.06.00	Paul Halpin L RSC 4 Burton
14.10.00	Lee Meager L PTS 4 Wembley
21.10.00	Delroy Pryce L PTS 4 Wembley
10.11.00	Rocky Dean W RSC 1 Mayfair
09.12.00	Michael Hunter L PTS 4 Southwark
16.12.00	Stephen Oates L PTS 4 Sheffield
15.01.01	Gavin Rees L RSC 2 Manchester

Career: 52 contests, won 14, lost 38.

(Garnet) Chill John

Brighton. *Born* St Vincent, 11 August, 1977
Welterweight. Ht. 5'7"
Manager R. Davies

22.10.00	Paul Philpott W PTS 6 Streatham
03.02.01	Dave Travers W PTS 4 Brighton
25.02.01	Scott Hocking W RSC 4 Streatham
05.05.01	Woody Greenaway W PTS 6 Brighton

Career: 4 contests, won 4.

Clint Johnson

Leeds. *Born* Leeds, 13 April, 1974
Cruiserweight. Ht. 6'2"
Manager T. O'Neill

11.11.97	Jon Penn W RSC 2 Leeds
04.12.97	John O'Byrne L PTS 6 Sunderland
17.02.98	Rob Galloway W PTS 6 Leeds
20.09.98	Rob Galloway W PTS 6 Sheffield
29.10.98	Mike White L PTS 6 Newcastle
06.11.98	Gerard Zdiarski W PTS 4 Mayfair
07.12.98	Carl Nicholson W PTS 6 Bradford
16.02.99	Danny Southam L RSC 5 Leeds
15.09.99	Steve Loftus W PTS 6 Harrogate
28.03.00	Martin Jolley W PTS 6 Hartlepool
17.04.00	Alex Mason L PTS 6 Birmingham
20.05.00	Jason Barker L RSC 1 Rotherham
23.10.00	Joe Gillon L CO 4 Glasgow
17.05.01	Paul Bonson L PTS 6 Leeds
18.06.01	Mark Brookes L PTS 6 Bradford

Career: 15 contests, won 7, lost 8.

Clive Johnson

Basingstoke. *Born* Botswana, 18 October, 1977
L. Middleweight. Ht. 5'10"
Manager C. Sanigar

18.02.99	Harry Butler W PTS 6 Barking
20.05.99	Joe Skeldon W PTS 6 Barking
07.08.99	Gareth Hogg L PTS 4 Dagenham
09.10.99	Jamie Moore L RSC 3 Manchester
07.04.00	Kevin Lang W RSC 1 Bristol
08.09.00	Chris Henry L PTS 4 Bristol
06.10.00	Colin Vidler L PTS 6 Maidstone
26.03.01	David Baptiste W PTS 6 Peterborough

Career: 8 contests, won 4, lost 4.

Paul Johnson

Cardiff. *Born* Cardiff, 28 May, 1975
Middleweight. Ht. 6'0"
Manager C. Sanigar

07.04.00	Pedro Carragher W PTS 4 Bristol
12.05.00	Richie Jenkins L PTS 4 Swansea
06.10.00	Allan Foster L PTS 4 Maidstone

Clint Johnson Les Clark

103

01.12.00 Andrew Buchanan L PTS 4
Peterborough

Career: 4 contests, won 1, lost 3.

Paul Johnson   Les Clark

Martin Jolley

Chesterfield. *Born* Chesterfield, 22
November, 1967
S. Middleweight. Ht. 5'11½"
Manager Self

10.03.92 Gypsy Johnny Price W RSC 3 Bury
06.04.92 Sean Byrne L RSC 6 Northampton
11.05.92 Mark Hale W PTS 6 Coventry
08.09.92 Brian McGloin W PTS 6 Doncaster
05.10.92 Mark Hale W RSC 4 Bardon
14.10.92 Carl Smallwood W PTS 6 Stoke
02.11.92 Bobby Mack L PTS 6 Wolverhampton
24.11.92 Phil Ball DREW 6 Doncaster
02.02.93 Mark McBiane W RSC 5 Derby
23.02.93 Phil Ball W RSC 5 Doncaster
12.05.93 Marvin O'Brien W PTS 6 Sheffield
08.06.93 Paul Hanlon W PTS 6 Derby
22.09.93 Nigel Rafferty L PTS 6 Chesterfield
29.10.93 Mads Larsen L CO 2 Korsoer,
Denmark
02.12.93 Darren Littlewood L PTS 6 Evesham
17.03.94 Paul Hitch W RSC 2 Lincoln
25.04.94 Derek Wormald L RSC 4 Bury
24.05.94 Dave Johnson L PTS 6 Sunderland
17.06.94 Dean Francis L PTS 6 Plymouth
02.07.94 Glenn Catley L RSC 1 Keynsham
23.09.94 Gilbert Jackson L CO 3 Bethnal Green
24.10.94 Craig Joseph L PTS 6 Bradford
07.11.94 Mark Delaney L RSC 3 Bethnal Green
12.12.94 Darren Littlewood L PTS 6
Cleethorpes
20.12.94 Mark Delaney L RSC 4 Bethnal Green
17.02.95 Willie Quinn L CO 5 Cumbernauld
11.05.95 Darren Sweeney L PTS 6 Dudley
19.05.95 Steve McNess L PTS 6 Southwark
10.06.95 Robin Reid L CO 1 Manchester

27.09.95 Steve McNess W RTD 4 Bethnal Green
29.10.95 Warren Stowe L PTS 6 Shaw
13.11.95 Peter Vosper W PTS 6 Barnstaple
23.11.95 Dave Johnson L PTS 6 Tynemouth
11.12.95 Lee Blundell L PTS 6 Morecambe
26.01.96 Ryan Rhodes L CO 3 Brighton
05.03.96 Jason Hart L PTS 6 Bethnal Green
16.03.96 Willie Quinn L RSC 4 Glasgow
11.05.96 Ryan Rhodes L RSC 2 Bethnal Green
25.06.96 Jason Matthews L RSC 3 Mansfield
20.09.96 Neville Smith L RSC 3 Tooting
06.11.96 Tony Booth L PTS 4 Hull
06.12.96 James Lowther L PTS 6 Leeds
22.12.96 Lee Whitehead DREW 6 Salford
31.01.97 Craig Winter L RSC 3 Pentre Halkyn
07.03.97 Raziq Ali L PTS 6 Northampton
16.03.97 Lee Blundell L PTS 6 Shaw
20.04.97 David Radford L PTS 8 Leeds
03.05.97 Paschal Collins L PTS 6 Manchester
10.05.97 Johnny Hooks DREW 6 Nottingham
20.05.97 Eddie Knight L PTS 6 Gillingham
26.06.97 Lee Whitehead L PTS 6 Salford
12.07.97 Monty Wright L RSC 1 Earls Court
18.09.97 Michael Pinnock DREW 6 Alfreton
08.10.97 George Richards L PTS 8 Stoke
11.11.97 Butch Lesley L PTS 6 Bethnal Green
28.11.97 Tony Booth L PTS 6 Hull
10.01.98 Butch Lesley L PTS 4 Bethnal Green
24.01.98 Michael Bowen L RSC 5 Cardiff
11.03.98 Jason Ratcliff L PTS 6 Bethnal Green
18.04.98 Ahmed Oener L RSC 4 Duisberg,
Germany
04.06.98 Andrew Flute L PTS 6 Dudley
15.06.98 Mark Hobson L RSC 3 Bradford
28.11.99 Mike Duffield L PTS 6 Chesterfield
08.12.99 Prince Kasi Kaihau W PTS 8 Stoke
15.01.00 Jason Collins L RTD 1 Doncaster
24.02.00 Alex Mason L PTS 10 Edgbaston
*(Midlands Area S. Middleweight Title
Challenge)*
13.03.00 Tony Oakey L PTS 6 Bethnal Green
28.03.00 Clint Johnson L PTS 6 Hartlepool
07.04.00 Scott Dann L RSC 2 Bristol
21.05.00 Damon Hague L PTS 6 Derby
02.06.00 Eddie Knight L RSC 5 Ashford
23.07.00 Ian Cooper L PTS 6 Hartlepool
13.08.00 Damon Hague L RTD 1 Nottingham
30.09.00 Steven Spartacas L PTS 6 Chigwell
09.10.00 Lee Molloy L PTS 4 Liverpool

Career: 75 contests, won 13, drew 4, lost 58.

Gareth Jones

Merthyr. *Born* Aberdare, 4 May, 1981
Welterweight. Ht. 5'10"
Manager D. Gardiner

12.12.00 Darren Williams DREW 6 Clydach
02.01.01 Andy Egan W PTS 4 Coventry

Career: 2 contests, won 1, drew 1.

Gary Jones

Birmingham. *Born* Birmingham, 26
October, 1976
Middleweight. Ht. 6'1"
Manager Self

15.07.00 Danny Smith L RSC 1 Norwich
16.09.00 Liam Lathbury L RSC 5 Bethnal Green
11.12.00 Andrew Facey L PTS 6 Cleethorpes
31.01.01 Paul Buchanan L RTD 1 Piccadilly

Career: 4 contests, lost 4.

Gary Jones   Les Clark

Keith Jones

Cefn Hengoed. *Born* Bradwell, 4
December, 1968
L. Welterweight. Former Undefeated
British Masters Lightweight Champion.
Ht. 5'5¾"
Manager Self

17.05.94 Abdul Mannon L PTS 6 Kettering
13.06.94 G. G. Goddard L PTS 6 Liverpool
21.07.94 G. G. Goddard L RSC 1 Battersea
12.09.94 Marco Fattore L PTS 6 Mayfair
29.09.94 Marlon Ward L PTS 4 Bethnal Green
21.10.94 James Murray L CO 3 Glasgow
27.11.94 Daniel Lutaaya L CO 1 Southwark
03.09.96 Benny May W RSC 2 Bethnal Green
18.09.96 Kevin Sheil W PTS 4 Tylorstown
04.10.96 Andy Ross DREW 6 Pentre Halkyn
18.10.96 Wayne Jones DREW 6 Barnstaple
06.11.96 Robert Grubb W PTS 4 Tylorstown
22.11.96 Tony Mulholland L PTS 4 Liverpool
03.12.96 Alex Moon L RTD 5 Liverpool
21.01.97 Greg Upton DREW 6 Bristol
26.02.97 Greg Upton L PTS 4 Cardiff
07.03.97 Dean Murdoch L PTS 6 Weston super
Mare
20.03.97 Kevin Sheil DREW 8 Solihull
04.04.97 Tony Mulholland L PTS 4 Liverpool
22.05.97 Darrell Easton L PTS 4 Southwark
02.10.98 Dean Pithie L PTS 8 Cheshunt
10.10.98 Steve Murray L RSC 4 Bethnal Green
21.11.98 Mat Zegan L PTS 4 Southwark
30.11.98 Eddie Nevins L PTS 4 Manchester
14.12.98 Roy Rutherford L PTS 6 Birmingham
12.01.99 Richard Evatt L CO 3 Bethnal Green
23.02.99 Simon Chambers DREW 4 Cardiff
12.03.99 Maurycy Gojko L PTS 4 Bethnal Green
09.04.99 Brian Carr L PTS 8 Glasgow
23.04.99 Dewi Roberts W PTS 6 Clydach
01.05.99 Steve Murray L RSC 6 Crystal Palace
04.06.99 Luis Navarro L RSC 5 Malaga, Spain
02.07.99 Alan Bosworth L PTS 6 Bristol
15.07.99 Tomas Jansson L PTS 4 Peterborough

20.08.99 Jason Hall L PTS 6 Bloomsbury
02.10.99 Jason Dee L RSC 5 Cardiff
06.11.99 Isaac Sebaduka W PTS 4 Bethnal Green
14.11.99 Lee Armstrong L PTS 6 Bradford
04.12.99 Franny Hogg L PTS 4 Manchester
14.12.99 Roy Rutherford L PTS 4 Coventry
18.01.00 Carl Greaves L PTS 6 Mansfield
29.01.00 Steve Murray L PTS 4 Manchester
27.02.00 Mark McGowan W RSC 7 Plymouth
(British Masters Lightweight Title Challenge)
25.03.00 Alex Moon L PTS 6 Liverpool
12.05.00 Jason Cook L PTS 10 Swansea
(Welsh L. Welterweight Title Challenge)
01.07.00 Matty Leonard W RSC 4 Southwark
25.07.00 Koba Gogoladze L PTS 4 Southwark
19.08.00 Richard Evatt L PTS 6 Brentwood
16.09.00 David Walker L PTS 6 Bethnal Green
21.10.00 Francis Barrett L PTS 4 Wembley
16.11.00 Jimmy Phelan DREW 6 Hull
27.11.00 Kevin Bennett L PTS 4 Birmingham
11.12.00 Steve Saville L PTS 8 Birmingham
02.01.01 Mark Payne L PTS 6 Coventry
15.01.01 Matthew Hatton L PTS 4 Manchester
03.02.01 David Burke L PTS 4 Manchester
10.02.01 Nigel Wright L PTS 4 Widnes
23.02.01 Darren Melville L PTS 4 Barking
29.03.01 Ted Bami L PTS 4 Hammersmith
10.04.01 Dean Pithie L PTS 4 Wembley
22.04.01 Brian Gentry L PTS 8 Streatham
08.05.01 Kevin Bennett L PTS 6 Barnsley
20.05.01 Jimmy Gould L PTS 6 Wolverhampton
02.06.01 Mally McIver L PTS 6 Wakefield
23.06.01 Alan Bosworth L PTS 6 Peterborough
Career: 65 contests, won 7, drew 6, lost 52.

Michael Jones

Liverpool. *Born* Liverpool, 14 November, 1974
L. Middleweight. Ht. 6'0¼"
Manager J. Trickett

15.11.97 Harry Butler W PTS 4 Bristol
17.01.98 Martin Cavey W CO 1 Bristol
07.03.98 Darren McInulty W PTS 4 Reading
25.04.98 Koba Kulu W RSC 3 Cardiff
06.06.98 G. L. Booth W RSC 2 Liverpool
10.10.98 Mehrdud Takaloo W PTS 6 Bethnal Green
19.12.98 Ojay Abrahams W PTS 6 Liverpool
26.06.99 Paul King W PTS 6 Glasgow
11.03.00 Alan Gilbert W RTD 3 Kensington
02.06.00 Mohammed Boualleg W PTS 8 Ashford
03.02.01 Howard Clarke W PTS 4 Manchester
24.04.01 Judicael Bedel W PTS 6 Liverpool
Career: 12 contests, won 12.

Paul Jones

Sheffield. *Born* Sheffield, 19 November, 1966
Former Undefeated WBC International S. Middleweight Champion. Former Commonwealth Middleweight Champion. Former Undefeated WBO, WBO Inter-Continental & Central Area L. Middleweight Champion. Ht. 6'0"
Manager Self

08.12.86 Paul Gillings W PTS 6 Liverpool

28.10.87 Pat Durkin W PTS 4 Sheffield
10.11.87 David Binns L PTS 6 Batley
11.01.88 Humphrey Harrison L PTS 8 Manchester
27.09.88 George Sponagle DREW 8 Halifax, Canada
07.12.88 Jimmy Thornton W PTS 6 Stoke
23.01.89 Donovan Boucher L DIS 6 Toronto, Canada
13.03.89 Dale Moreland W PTS 6 Toronto, Canada
30.03.89 Benoit Boudreau W PTS 10 Moncton, Canada
19.04.89 Tony Collier W CO 3 Toronto, Canada
06.06.89 George Sponagle L PTS 8 Halifax, Canada
06.09.89 Kid Ford W PTS 6 Mississouga, Canada
13.11.89 Ian Midwood-Tate W RSC 4 Manchester
08.12.89 Antoine Tarver L PTS 4 Doncaster
06.03.90 Antonio Fernandez W PTS 8 Stoke
22.03.90 Darren Pilling W RTD 7 Gateshead
26.04.90 Newton Barnett W PTS 8 Mayfair
20.05.90 Jim Beckett W CO 1 Sheffield
22.05.90 Wayne Ellis L PTS 6 St Albans
14.11.90 Jason Rowe W PTS 10 Sheffield
(Central Area L. Middleweight Title Challenge)
12.03.91 Tony Velinor W PTS 8 Mansfield
16.08.91 Hugo Marinangelli L CO 2 Marbella, Spain
01.10.91 Simon Eubank W CO 6 Sheffield
14.04.92 Paul Lynch W RSC 3 Mansfield
19.05.92 Trevor Ambrose W PTS 6 Cardiff
02.06.92 Patrick Vungbo W PTS 10 Rotterdam, Holland
19.09.92 Ernie Loveridge W PTS 6 Glasgow
24.11.92 Paul Wesley L RSC 2 Doncaster
17.01.95 Julian Eavis W RSC 4 Worcester
06.03.95 Peter Waudby W PTS 6 Mayfair
14.04.95 Damien Denny W CO 1 Belfast
(Vacant WBO Inter-Continental L. Middleweight Title)
26.08.95 Danny Juma W PTS 12 Belfast
(WBO Inter-Continental L. Middleweight Title Defence)
02.10.95 Eric Spalding W RSC 2 Mayfair
(WBO Inter-Continental L. Middleweight Title Defence)
22.11.95 Verno Phillips W PTS 12 Sheffield
(WBO L. Middleweight Title Challenge)
14.12.96 Ryan Rhodes L RSC 8 Sheffield
(Vacant British L. Middleweight Title)
08.05.97 Lee Blundell W RSC 4 Mansfield
31.10.97 Johnson Tshuma L PTS 12 Mayfair
(Vacant Commonwealth Middleweight Title)
24.03.98 Johnson Tshuma W PTS 12 Bethnal Green
(Commonwealth Middleweight Title Challenge)
27.02.99 Jason Matthews L DIS 7 Oldham
(Commonwealth Middleweight Title Defence)
20.05.00 Ganny Dovidovas W PTS 6 Rotherham
08.07.00 Jason Barker W RSC 5 Rotherham
09.10.00 Olivier Beard W RSC 1 Liverpool
(Vacant WBC International S.Middleweight Title)
03.03.01 Adrian Dodson L CO 3 Wembley
(Vacant IBO S.Middleweight Title)
Career: 43 contests, won 30, drew 1, lost 12.

Cham Joof

Brixton. *Born* London, 19 November, 1968
L. Middleweight. Former Undefeated Southern Area Lightweight Champion. Ht. 5'8"
Manager Self

22.02.93 Chris Saunders W PTS 4 Eltham
04.04.93 Anthony Wanza W RSC 2 Brockley
14.04.93 Mike Morrison W PTS 4 Kensington
23.05.93 Charles Shepherd L PTS 4 Brockley
25.06.93 Scott Smith W RTD 2 Battersea
14.08.93 Mark Allen W RSC 3 Hammersmith
20.01.94 Phil Found W RSC 1 Battersea
14.04.94 Brian Coleman W CO 3 Battersea
22.05.94 Felix Kelly W RSC 5 Crystal Palace
(Southern Area Lightweight Title Challenge)
25.02.95 Tony Foster W PTS 8 Millwall
06.05.95 Karl Taylor L PTS 8 Shepton Mallet
01.07.95 Tanveer Ahmed L PTS 6 Kensington
13.01.96 Paul Burke L RSC 2 Manchester
01.07.00 Delroy Mellis DREW 6 Southwark
Career: 14 contests, won 9, drew 1, lost 4.

Gareth Jordan

Monmouth. *Born* Usk, 19 December, 1971
Lightweight. Ht. 5'6¾"
Manager Self

02.11.92 Con Cronin W RSC 2 Wolverhampton
04.12.92 Jason White W RSC 2 Telford
16.03.93 Lee Fox W RSC 3 Wolverhampton
26.05.93 Mark O'Callaghan W RSC 3 Mansfield
27.10.93 Dave Madden W RSC 5 West Bromwich
16.12.93 Phil Found W PTS 6 Newport
04.06.94 T. J. Smith W RSC 1 Cardiff
01.10.94 Wayne Jones W RSC 2 Cardiff
30.11.94 Kevin McKenzie W PTS 6 Wolverhampton
04.02.95 Mark O'Callaghan W RSC 2 Cardiff
21.04.95 Peter Till W PTS 6 Dudley
07.07.95 Kelton McKenzie W PTS 4 Cardiff
25.10.95 Mervyn Bennett L PTS 10 Cardiff
(Welsh Lightweight Title Challenge)
13.02.96 Bamana Dibateza W PTS 8 Cardiff
16.05.96 Billy Schwer L RSC 3 Dunstable
03.04.97 Anthony Campbell W PTS 6 Wembley
07.07.00 Billy Smith W PTS 6 Chigwell
14.10.00 Pete Buckley W PTS 4 Wembley
28.04.01 Patrick Gallagher L PTS 4 Cardiff
Career: 19 contests, won 16, lost 3.

(Fation) Nono Junior (Kacanolli)

Hayes. *Born* Kosovo, 20 October, 1977
Lightweight. Ht. 5'7"
Manager D. Currivan

18.11.99 Darren Woodley W RSC 1 Mayfair
19.12.99 Gary Reid W PTS 6 Salford
24.02.00 Barry Hughes L RSC 1 Glasgow
19.04.00 Woody Greenaway W PTS 4 Kensington
30.05.00 Phil Lashley W CO 2 Kensington
24.06.00 Steve Murray L RSC 4 Glasgow
10.03.01 Ivan Kirpa L RSC 1 Bethnal Green
Career: 7 contests, won 4, lost 3.

Prince Kasi Kaihau

Doncaster. *Born* Doncaster, 3 October, 1967
L. Middleweight. Ht. 5'11"
Manager J. Rushton

12.10.93	Prince Louis W PTS 6 Wolverhampton
24.11.93	Steve Levene W PTS 6 Solihull
13.12.93	Rob Stevenson W RSC 5 Doncaster
07.03.94	Steve Levene W RSC 3 Doncaster
10.05.94	Billy McDougall W RTD 4 Doncaster
12.09.94	Rick North W PTS 6 Doncaster
12.10.94	Andy Peach W PTS 6 Stoke
30.11.94	Billy McDougall W PTS 6 Solihull
12.12.94	Andy Peach W PTS 6 Doncaster
28.03.95	David Bain L PTS 6 Wolverhampton
05.05.95	Andy Peach W PTS 6 Doncaster
02.11.95	Robbie Bell L PTS 6 Houghton le Spring
26.01.96	Ozzy Orrock W RSC 5 Doncaster
29.03.96	Chris Pollock L RSC 2 Doncaster
10.05.96	Jon Stocks L PTS 6 Liverpool
28.05.96	Neil Sinclair L RSC 2 Belfast
26.09.96	Joe Townsley L PTS 8 Glasgow
07.10.96	Carl Winstone W RSC 5 Birmingham
24.10.96	George Richards L PTS 6 Birmingham
09.12.96	Stuart Dunn W RSC 2 Leicester
16.01.97	George Richards L PTS 8 Solihull
11.02.97	Howard Clarke W RSC 4 Wolverhampton
27.02.97	Terry Morrill L PTS 6 Hull
15.04.97	Howard Clarke L PTS 6 Edgbaston
25.04.97	Brian Dunn W RSC 1 Cleethorpes
05.06.97	Wayne Alexander L CO 4 Bristol
08.10.97	Alex Mason DREW 6 Stoke
20.10.97	Carlton Williams DREW 6 Leicester
21.11.97	Peter Waudby DREW 6 Hull
06.12.97	Ahmet Oner L PTS 4 Offenbach, Germany
13.12.97	Harry Simon L RSC 4 Sheffield
24.01.98	Paul Samuels L CO 3 Cardiff
27.03.98	Spencer McCracken L PTS 8 Telford
08.04.98	Paul Burns W RSC 2 Liverpool
30.05.98	Jason Williams L CO 2 Bristol
18.09.98	Jim Webb L RSC 4 Belfast
14.11.98	Spencer Fearon L CO 5 Cheshunt
21.05.99	Gerard Murphy L PTS 6 Glasgow
04.10.99	Brian Dunn W RSC 2 Glasgow
23.10.99	Mehrdud Takaloo L RSC 3 Telford
08.12.99	Martin Jolley L PTS 8 Stoke
12.11.00	Jamie Moore L RSC 2 Manchester
17.12.00	Gerard Murphy L PTS 6 Glasgow

Career: 43 contests, won 17, drew 3, lost 23.

Costas Katsantonis

St Pancras. *Born* London, 16 October, 1970
L. Welterweight. Ht. 5'8"
Manager Self

09.07.96	Gilbert Eastman L RSC 1 Bethnal Green
28.09.96	Jason Campbell W PTS 6 Barking
24.10.96	Allan Gray L PTS 6 Mayfair
20.11.96	Daniel James L PTS 6 Wembley
19.02.97	Allan Gray L PTS 6 Acton
30.04.97	Kevin McCarthy W RSC 6 Acton
13.12.97	James Hare L RSC 3 Sheffield
21.02.98	Martin Renaghan L PTS 4 Belfast

21.02.00	Jon Honney W RSC 1 Southwark
13.07.00	Gary Harrison W PTS 4 Bethnal Green
18.11.00	Peter Richardson L PTS 4 Dagenham
17.02.01	Trevor Smith W RSC 3 Bethnal Green
10.04.01	Karl Taylor W PTS 4 Wembley

Career: 13 contests, won 6, lost 7.

Costas Katsantonis   Les Clark

Marty Kayes

Downpatrick. *Born* Ashton under Lyne, 16
December, 1975
Flyweight. Ht. 5'5½"
Manager N. Nobbs

27.05.01	Darren Cleary L PTS 4 Manchester

Career: 1 contest, lost 1.

John Keeton

Sheffield. *Born* Sheffield, 19 May, 1972
Former Undefeated WBO Inter-Continental
Cruiserweight Champion. Ht. 6'0"
Manager D. Ingle

11.08.93	Tony Colclough W RSC 1 Mansfield
15.09.93	Val Golding L PTS 6 Ashford
27.10.93	Darren McKenna W RSC 3 Stoke
01.12.93	Julius Francis L PTS 4 Bethnal Green
19.01.94	Dennis Bailey W RTD 2 Stoke
17.02.94	Dermot Gascoyne L RSC 1 Dagenham
09.04.94	Eddie Knight W RTD 5 Mansfield
11.05.94	John Rice W RSC 5 Sheffield
02.06.94	Devon Rhooms W RSC 2 Tooting
06.09.94	Mark Walker W RSC 5 Stoke
24.09.94	Dirk Wallyn L CO 3 Middlekerke, Belgium
26.10.94	Lee Archer W PTS 6 Stoke
09.12.94	Bruce Scott L CO 2 Bethnal Green
11.02.95	Rudiger May L PTS 6 Frankfurt, Germany
06.03.95	Simon McDougall W RSC 5 Mayfair
07.07.95	Nicky Piper L RTD 2 Cardiff
15.09.95	Steve Osborne W RSC 4 Mansfield
27.10.95	Nicky Wadman W RSC 1 Brighton
03.11.95	Monty Wright W RSC 4 Dudley
11.11.95	Denzil Browne W RSC 4 Halifax
30.01.96	Cesar Kazadi W RSC 3 Lille, France
11.05.96	Terry Dunstan L RSC 1 Bethnal Green *(British Cruiserweight Title Challenge)*

14.09.96	John Pierre W PTS 4 Sheffield
14.12.96	Nigel Rafferty W RTD 3 Sheffield
12.04.97	Nigel Rafferty W RSC 6 Sheffield
11.10.97	Kelly Oliver L RSC 8 Sheffield *(Vacant WBO Inter-Continental Cruiserweight Title)*
16.05.98	Jacob Mofokeng L RTD 4 Hammanskraal, South Africa
18.07.98	Kelly Oliver W RSC 2 Sheffield
23.01.99	Garry Delaney W PTS 12 Cheshunt *(Vacant WBO Inter-Continental Cruiserweight Title)*
15.05.99	William Barima W RTD 3 Sheffield
29.02.00	Tony Booth W RSC 2 Widnes
16.12.00	Bruce Scott L CO 6 Sheffield *(Vacant British Cruiserweight Title)*

Career: 32 contests, won 21, lost 11.

David Kehoe

Northampton. *Born* Northampton, 24
December, 1972
Lightweight. Ht. 5'10½"
Manager Self

06.02.96	Simon Frailing W CO 1 Basildon
20.04.96	Paul Salmon W PTS 6 Brentwood
12.11.96	Peter Nightingale L PTS 6 Dudley
28.04.97	Craig Kelley L DIS 3 Enfield
18.11.97	Peter Nightingale DREW 4 Mansfield
27.01.98	Paul Miles L PTS 4 Bethnal Green
11.03.98	Trevor Tacy W RTD 1 Bethnal Green
28.03.98	David Thompson W PTS 6 Crystal Palace
26.05.98	Dave Hinds W RSC 5 Mayfair
08.09.98	Marc Smith W PTS 6 Bethnal Green
12.01.99	Gary Flear L PTS 4 Bethnal Green
25.01.99	Roger Sampson L PTS 4 Glasgow
12.03.99	Jamie McKeever L RSC 2 Bethnal Green
02.07.99	Mark McGowan L RSC 3 Bristol *(Vacant British Masters Lightweight Title)*
13.09.99	Stephen Smith L DIS 2 Bethnal Green
05.10.99	John Humphrey L PTS 4 Bloomsbury
24.10.99	Young Muttley L RTD 1 Wolverhampton
02.12.99	Liam Maltby L PTS 4 Peterborough
19.02.00	Dariusz Snarski DREW 6 Prestwick
10.03.00	Ted Bami L PTS 4 Bethnal Green
17.04.00	Mark Hawthorne L PTS 4 Birmingham
25.07.00	P.J.Gallagher L PTS 6 Southwark
08.09.00	Dariusz Snarski W PTS 4 Hammersmith
27.11.00	Anthony Maynard L RSC 5 Birmingham

Career: 24 contests, won 7, drew 2, lost 15.

Barrie Kelley

Llanelli.*Born* Llanelli, 14 February, 1972
Lightweight. Former Welsh S.
Featherweight Champion. Ht. 5'6"
Manager Self

16.10.90	Ervine Blake W PTS 6 Evesham
21.11.90	Tony Falcone W PTS 6 Chippenham
29.11.90	John O'Meara W RSC 5 Bayswater
24.01.91	Martin Evans W PTS 6 Gorseinon
18.02.91	Tony Falcone L RSC 6 Mayfair
26.03.91	Dennis Adams W PTS 6 Bethnal Green
18.07.91	Robert Smyth DREW 6 Cardiff
16.09.91	Dominic McGuigan DREW 6 Mayfair
14.10.91	Michael Armstrong L CO 4 Manchester

20.11.91 Neil Haddock L PTS 6 Cardiff
03.02.92 Noel Carroll L PTS 8 Manchester
18.03.92 Mark Geraghty L PTS 8 Glasgow
05.04.92 Peter Judson L PTS 6 Bradford
30.09.92 Dean Bramhald W PTS 6 Solihull
28.10.92 Derek Amory W PTS 6 Cardiff
19.01.93 Edward Lloyd W PTS 10 Cardiff
(Vacant Welsh S. Featherweight Title)
10.11.93 J. T. Williams L RTD 3 Ystrad
(Welsh S. Featherweight Title Defence)
24.02.94 Peter Till L PTS 6 Walsall
19.11.94 Marcus McCrae W PTS 6 Cardiff
31.03.95 Mike Anthony Brown L RSC 2 Crystal
Palace
04.06.95 Paul Webster L RTD 1 Bethnal Green
10.11.95 Michael Hermon DREW 8 Bristol
12.01.96 Dennis Pedersen L RSC 4 Copenhagen,
Denmark
19.07.96 Tommy Janes L RSC 3 Ystrad
08.02.00 Steve Hanley W PTS 6 Wolverhampton
13.05.00 Franny Hogg L PTS 6 Barnsley
06.06.00 Steve Hanley L RSC 5 Brierley Hill
26.10.00 Woody Greenaway W PTS 6 Clydach
13.02.01 Tony Montana W PTS 6 Brierley Hill
13.03.01 Leo O'Reilly L RSC 5 Plymouth
16.06.01 Colin Dunne L CO 3 Dagenham
Career: 31 contests, won 12, drew 3, lost 16.

Damaen Kelly

Belfast. *Born* Belfast, 3 April, 1973
IBO Flyweight Champion. Former
Undefeated European Flyweight Champion.
Former Undefeated WBC International S.
Flyweight Champion. Former British &
Commonwealth Flyweight Champion.
Ht. 5'5"
Manager Self

27.09.97 Chris Thomas W RSC 1 Belfast
22.11.97 Bojidar Ivanov W CO 1 Manchester
20.12.97 Anthony Hanna W PTS 4 Belfast
14.02.98 Hristo Lessov W RSC 2 Southwark
14.03.98 Mark Reynolds W RSC 4 Bethnal
Green
02.05.98 Krasimir Tcholakov W RSC 3
Kensington
26.09.98 Mike Thomas W PTS 6 Uncasville,
USA
12.12.98 Alfonso Zvenyika W PTS 12 Chester
(Commonwealth Flyweight Title
Challenge)
13.03.99 Anthony Hanna W PTS 12 Manchester
(Vacant British Flyweight Title.
Commonwealth Flyweight Title
Defence)
22.05.99 Keith Knox L RTD 6 Belfast
(British & Commonwealth Flyweight
Title Defences)
16.10.99 Igor Gerasimov W RSC 4 Belfast
(Vacant WBC International
S. Flyweight Title)
12.02.00 Alexander Mahmutov W PTS 12
Sheffield
(European Flyweight Title Challenge)
12.06.00 Jose Antonio Lopez Bueno W PTS 12
Belfast
(European Flyweight Title Defence)
30.09.00 Zolile Mbitye W PTS 12 Peterborough
(IBO Flyweight Title Challenge)
17.02.01 Paulino Villabos W PTS 12 Bethnal
Green
(IBO Flyweight Title Defence)
Career: 15 contests, won 14, lost 1.

Colin Kenna

Dublin. *Born* Dublin, 28 July, 1976
Heavyweight. Ht. 6'1"
Manager J. Bishop

25.02.01 Slick Miller W RSC 3 Streatham
22.04.01 Eamonn Glennon W PTS 4 Streatham
Career: 2 contests, won 2.

Alan Kershaw

Leeds. *Born* Pontefract, 27 February, 1980
L. Welterweight. Ht. 5'9"
Manager M. Marsden

17.04.00 Craig Goodman W PTS 6 Bradford
13.05.00 Dave Hinds W PTS 4 Barnsley
25.06.00 Leo Turner W RSC 1 Wakefield

10.09.00 Marcus Portman L RSC 2 Walsall
20.10.00 Ray Wood W PTS 6 Manchester
30.11.00 Liam Maltby L PTS 6 Peterborough
05.02.01 Mally McIver L PTS 4 Hull
Career: 7 contests, won 4, lost 3.

Jawaid Khaliq (Akhtar)

Nottingham. *Born* Reading, 30 July, 1970
IBO Welterweight Champion. Former
Undefeated Commonwealth & Midlands
Area Welterweight Champion. Former
Undefeated Midlands Area & WBF
European L. Middleweight Champion.
Ht. 5'10½"
Manager T. Gilmour/C. Aston

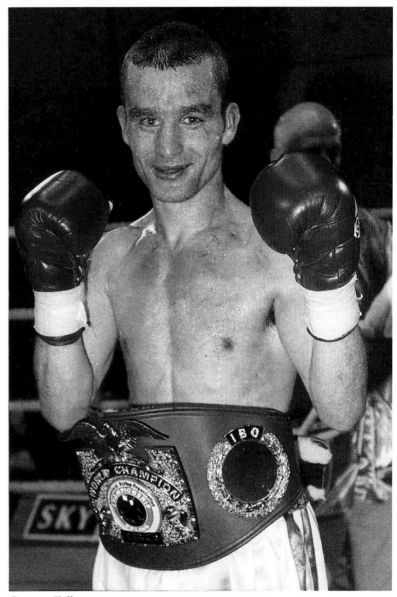

Damaen Kelly   Les Clark

107

18.08.97	Richard Inquieti W RSC 5 Nottingham
13.09.97	Martin Holgate W RSC 6 Millwall
13.12.97	Mark Ramsey DREW 4 Sheffield
07.02.98	Mehrdud Takaloo W RSC 4 Cheshunt
07.03.98	Koba Kulu W PTS 4 Reading
05.09.98	Harry Butler W PTS 4 Telford
03.12.98	Frederic Klose L PTS 8 Epernay, France
27.09.99	Lee Murtagh W RSC 5 Leeds
	(Vacant WBF European L. Middleweight Title)
14.12.99	Dirk Kaltenbach W CO 2 Telde, Gran Canaria
15.01.00	Lee Bird W RSC 4 Doncaster
27.02.00	Jason Collins W PTS 6 Leeds
21.05.00	Dennis Berry W RSC 6 Derby
	(Vacant Midlands Area L. Middleweight Title)
13.08.00	Ernie Smith W RSC 4 Nottingham

	(Vacant Midlands Area Welterweight Title)
28.10.00	Trevor Smith W RSC 1 Coventry
27.11.00	Sean Sullivan W PTS 12 Birmingham
	(Vacant Commonwealth Welterweight Title)
26.02.01	Howard Clarke W PTS 6 Nottingham
11.06.01	Willy Wise W PTS 12 Nottingham
	(IBO Welterweight Title Challenge)

Career: 17 contests, won 15, drew 1, lost 1.

Tasawar Khan

Bradford. *Born* Bradford, 10 June, 1980
S. Featherweight. Ht. 5'5"
Manager C. Ashton

10.06.01	Jason Edwards L PTS 6 Ellesmere Port

Career: 1 contest, lost 1.

John Killian

Finchley. *Born* South Africa, 24 August, 1976
L. Heavyweight. Ht. 6'0"
Manager J. Oyebola

16.06.01	Calvin Stonestreet W PTS 4 Wembley

Career: 1 contest, won 1.

Nathan King

Mountain Ash. *Born* Aberdare, 19 March, 1981
L. Heavyweight. Ht. 6'3"
Manager F. Warren/E. Calzaghe

27.01.01	Tony Oakey L PTS 6 Bethnal Green
28.04.01	Pinky Burton W PTS 4 Cardiff
09.06.01	Michael Pinnock W PTS 4 Bethnal Green

Career: 3 contests, won 2, lost 1.

Nathan King   Les Clark

David Kirk

Sutton in Ashfield. *Born* Mansfield, 5 October, 1974
L. Welterweight. Former Undefeated WBF European Welterweight Champion. Ht. 5'8"
Manager J. Ashton

01.11.96	Arv Mittoo W PTS 6 Mansfield
04.12.96	Stuart Rimmer W PTS 6 Stoke
20.02.97	Chris Price W PTS 6 Mansfield
16.03.97	Gary Hibbert L PTS 6 Shaw
25.03.97	Miguel Matthews W PTS 6 Wolverhampton
28.04.97	Mark Breslin L PTS 8 Glasgow
06.10.97	Christian Brady L PTS 6 Birmingham
30.10.97	Trevor Tacy L PTS 6 Newark
08.12.97	Nick Hall L PTS 6 Nottingham
12.01.98	Juha Temonen DREW 6 Helsinki, Finland
24.01.98	Jason Cook L RSC 3 Cardiff
24.02.98	Roy Rutherford L PTS 6 Edgbaston
11.03.98	Patrick Gallagher L PTS 6 Bethnal Green
27.04.98	Tommy Peacock L PTS 6 Manchester
08.05.98	Chris Barnett L PTS 6 Manchester

Jawaid Khaliq   Les Clark

23.05.98	Graham Earl L PTS 4 Bethnal Green
04.06.98	Mark Richards L PTS 6 Dudley
21.09.98	Steve McLevy L PTS 8 Glasgow
12.10.98	Malcolm Melvin L PTS 10 Birmingham
	(Midlands Area L. Welterweight Title Challenge)
31.10.98	Bernard Paul L PTS 6 Southend
28.11.98	Glenn McClarnon L PTS 4 Belfast
11.12.98	Charlie Kane L PTS 8 Prestwick
20.02.99	Dennis Berry L PTS 10 Thornaby
	(Vacant Continental European Welterweight Title)
09.05.99	Sammy Smith L PTS 6 Bracknell
20.05.99	Steve Brumant W PTS 4 Kensington
05.06.99	Neil Sinclair L PTS 8 Cardiff
11.09.99	Glenn McClarnon L PTS 6 Sheffield
20.10.99	Dave Gibson W PTS 6 Stoke
18.11.99	Adrian Chase W PTS 10 Mayfair
	(Vacant WBF European Welterweight Title)
26.11.99	Gerard Murphy L RTD 3 Hull
25.03.00	Jacek Bielski L PTS 6 Liverpool
29.04.00	Eamonn Magee L RSC 8 Wembley
13.08.00	Ram Singh W PTS 6 Newark
09.09.00	Mally McIver L PTS 6 Newark
23.09.00	Steve Murray L PTS 4 Bethnal Green
09.10.00	Steve Saville W PTS 8 Birmingham
19.11.00	Gavin Down L PTS 10 Chesterfield
	(Vacant British Masters L.Welterweight Title)
01.12.00	Alan Bosworth DREW 8 Peterborough
04.02.01	Mark Winters L PTS 6 Queensferry
28.02.01	Ossie Duran L PTS 8 Kensington
	(Vacant WBF European Welterweight Title)
10.03.01	Junior Witter L RSC 2 Bethnal Green
10.04.01	Colin Lynes L PTS 6 Wembley
20.04.01	Mark Winters L PTS 6 Dublin
16.06.01	Oscar Hall L PTS 6 Derby

Career: 44 contests, won 9, drew 2, lost 33.

Adrian Kirkbride

Carlisle. *Born* Penrith, 11 February, 1971
Middleweight. Ht. 5'10"
Manager P. McCausland

22.01.99	Shaun O'Neill W PTS 6 Carlisle
03.04.99	Lee Molloy L PTS 4 Carlisle
19.02.00	Piotr Bartnicki L RSC 1 Prestwick
06.06.00	Scott Millar L RSC 2 Motherwell
20.10.00	Balazs Szabo W PTS 6 Belfast
01.04.01	Gary Logan L RSC 1 Southwark

Career: 6 contests, won 2, lost 4.

Neil Kirkwood

Barnsley. *Born* Barnsley, 30 November, 1969
Central Area Heavyweight Champion.
Ht. 6'4"
Manager Self

17.03.94	Gary Williams W RSC 1 Lincoln
16.05.94	Joey Paladino W RSC 2 Cleethorpes
26.08.94	Shane Woollas W RSC 6 Barnsley
11.03.95	Carl Gaffney W RSC 2 Barnsley
	(Vacant Central Area Heavyweight Title)
24.10.95	Julius Francis L RSC 7 Southwark
08.10.96	Nikolai Valouev L RSC 2 Battersea
11.04.97	Johnny Davison W RSC 3 Barnsley
23.10.98	Lennox Williams W RSC 2 Wakefield
27.05.00	Albert Sosnowski L RSC 1 Mayfair
21.10.00	Mark Krence L PTS 6 Sheffield
23.11.00	Petr Horacek L RSC 2 Bayswater

Career: 11 contests, won 6, lost 5.

Eddie Knight

Ashford. *Born* Ashford, 4 October, 1966
Former Southern Area L. Heavyweight
Champion. Ht. 5'11"
Manager Self

05.10.92	Shaun McCrory L PTS 6 Bristol
29.10.92	Adrian Wright L PTS 6 Bayswater
25.11.92	Julian Johnson L RSC 2 Mayfair
15.09.93	Terry Duffus W PTS 6 Ashford
09.04.94	John Keeton L RTD 5 Mansfield
27.05.94	Lee Sara W CO 2 Ashford
09.07.94	Mark Delaney L CO 4 Earls Court
17.09.94	Mark Hale W PTS 6 Crawley
13.12.94	Tim Robinson W RTD 2 Potters Bar
09.05.95	Mark Delaney L RSC 2 Basildon
30.01.96	Graham Townsend W PTS 4 Barking
04.03.96	Marko Salminen W RSC 2 Helsinki, Finland
17.12.96	Monty Wright L RSC 5 Bethnal Green
	(Vacant Southern Area L. Heavyweight Title)
20.05.97	Martin Jolley W PTS 6 Gillingham
09.09.97	Graham Townsend W RSC 6 Bethnal Green
16.05.98	Paul Bowen L RSC 3 Bethnal Green
16.01.99	Monty Wright W RSC 2 Bethnal Green
	(Southern Area L. Heavyweight Title Challenge)
02.06.00	Martin Jolley W RSC 5 Ashford
14.10.00	Butch Lesley L RSC 6 Wembley
	(Southern Area L.Heavyweight Title Defence)

Career: 19 contests, won 10, lost 9.

Paul Knights

Redhill. *Born* Redhill, 5 February, 1971
Welterweight. Ht. 5'10"
Manager B. Hearn

26.11.91	Steve Hearn W RSC 4 Bethnal Green
19.02.92	Seth Jones W RSC 5 Muswell Hill
16.06.92	Seth Jones W PTS 6 Dagenham
10.11.92	Alex Moffatt W CO 3 Dagenham
30.01.93	Dave Lovell W RSC 6 Brentwood
20.04.93	Mark Allen W PTS 6 Brentwood
26.06.93	Phil Found W PTS 4 Earls Court
28.09.93	Pat Delargy W RSC 3 Bethnal Green
11.01.94	Brian Coleman W RSC 4 Bethnal Green
09.02.94	Mark Allen W RSC 2 Brentwood
19.03.94	Alan Peacock W PTS 6 Millwall
11.06.94	John O. Johnson L PTS 6 Bethnal Green
17.09.94	Dewi Roberts W PTS 6 Crawley
17.02.95	Norman Dhalie W RTD 5 Crawley
16.03.95	Brian Coleman W RSC 2 Basildon
09.05.95	Alan Peacock W PTS 6 Basildon
28.10.95	Tony Swift W PTS 6 Kensington
23.01.96	Karl Taylor DREW 6 Bethnal Green
08.03.97	Dave Brazil L RSC 2 Brentwood
22.04.97	Peter Nightingale W PTS 6 Bethnal Green
11.07.97	Paul Miles W PTS 6 Brighton
27.01.98	Adrian Chase L RSC 1 Bethnal Green
20.05.99	Matthew Barr W RSC 1 Barking
29.06.99	Dean Nicholas W RSC 2 Bethnal Green
01.04.00	Delroy Mellis L RSC 3 Bethnal Green
23.01.01	Brian Coleman W PTS 6 Crawley

Career: 26 contests, won 21, drew 1, lost 4.

Keith Knox

Bonnyrigg. *Born* Edinburgh, 20 June, 1967
Former British & Commonwealth
Flyweight Champion. Former Undefeated
Scottish Flyweight Champion. Ht. 5'3"
Manager T. Gilmour

04.03.94	Ian Bailie W CO 3 Irvine
28.03.94	Terry Gaskin W PTS 6 Musselburgh
20.09.94	Tiger Singh W PTS 6 Musselburgh
21.11.94	Neil Parry W PTS 6 Glasgow
16.01.95	Neil Parry W PTS 6 Musselburgh
20.02.95	Lyndon Kershaw DREW 6 Glasgow
05.04.95	Louis Veitch DREW 6 Irvine
18.09.95	Shaun Norman W PTS 8 Glasgow
20.11.95	Louis Veitch L RSC 6 Glasgow
	(Vacant Scottish Flyweight Title. Elim. British Flyweight Title)
21.03.96	Mickey Cantwell L PTS 12 Southwark
	(Vacant British Flyweight Title)
13.09.96	Jesper Jensen L PTS 12 Ringsted, Denmark
	(European Flyweight Title Challenge)
27.01.97	Ady Lewis L PTS 12 Glasgow
	(Vacant British Flyweight Title)
02.06.97	Anthony Hanna W PTS 6 Glasgow
25.10.97	Jason Thomas L PTS 8 Queensferry
13.02.98	Jason Whitaker W PTS 6 Barrhead
01.06.98	Alfonso Zvenyika L RSC 8 Glasgow
	(Commonwealth Flyweight Title Challenge)
22.03.99	Shaun Norman W PTS 8 Glasgow
22.05.99	Damaen Kelly W RTD 6 Belfast
	(British & Commonwealth Flyweight Title Challenges)
16.10.99	Jason Booth L RSC 10 Belfast
	(British & Commonwealth Title Defences)
20.03.00	Jamie Evans W PTS 6 Glasgow
05.06.00	Colin Moffett W RSC 3 Glasgow
02.12.00	Delroy Spencer L RSC 6 Bethnal Green
20.03.01	Jose Garcia L PTS 12 Glasgow
	(IBO L. Flyweight Title Challenge)

Career: 23 contests, won 13, drew 2, lost 8.

Mark Krence

Chesterfield. *Born* Chesterfield, 24 August, 1976
Heavyweight. Ht. 6'5"
Manager D. Hobson

09.04.00	Slick Miller W PTS 6 Alfreton
21.10.00	Neil Kirkwood W PTS 6 Sheffield
11.12.00	Tony Booth W PTS 6 Sheffield
20.01.01	Nigel Rafferty W PTS 4 Bethnal Green
24.03.01	Mark Williams W PTS 4 Sheffield

Career: 5 contests, won 5.

Koba Kulu (Tika)

Holloway. *Born* Zaire, 1 August, 1967
L. Middleweight. Ht. 5'11¼"
Manager Self

15.11.97	Mehrdud Takaloo L RSC 3 Bristol
07.02.98	Anas Oweida W RSC 3 Cheshunt
17.02.98	James Lowther L PTS 4 Leeds
07.03.98	Jawaid Khaliq L PTS 4 Reading
25.04.98	Michael Jones L RSC 3 Cardiff
21.11.98	Zoltan Sarossy W RSC 4 Southwark
19.12.98	Anthony Farnell L RTD 5 Liverpool
27.02.99	Anthony Farnell L RSC 1 Oldham
04.09.99	Nicky Thurbin L PTS 8 Bethnal Green
13.11.99	Brian Knudsen L PTS 6 Hull
27.05.00	Jamie Moore L RTD 3 Southwark
02.11.00	Chris Nembhard L PTS 6 Kensington

Career: 12 contests, won 2, lost 10.

Scott Lansdowne

Leicester. *Born* Leicester, 11 August, 1972
Heavyweight. WBF European S.
Cruiserweight Champion. Ht. 5'10"
Manager D. Hobson

15.12.98 Gary Williams W PTS 6 Sheffield
11.09.99 Luke Simpkin W PTS 4 Sheffield
09.12.99 Geoff Hunter W PTS 6 Sheffield
20.05.00 Gary Williams W RSC 1 Leicester
　　　　　(Vacant WBF European
　　　　　S. Cruiserweight Title)
21.10.00 Adam Cale W RSC 5 Sheffield
29.01.01 Nigel Rafferty W PTS 4 Peterborough
Career: 6 contests, won 6.

Liam Lathbury

Brighton. *Born* Bath, 10 February, 1981
S. Middleweight. Ht. 5'10"
Manager C. Sanigar

16.09.00 Gary Jones W RSC 5 Bethnal Green
09.12.00 Freddie Yemofio W PTS 4 Southwark
03.02.01 Rob Stevenson W PTS 6 Brighton
05.05.01 Harry Butler W PTS 6 Brighton
Career: 4 contests, won 4.

Liam Lathbury　　　　　Les Clark

Danny Lawson

Plymouth. *Born* Plymouth, 27 May, 1971
Featherweight. Ht. 5'5¾"
Manager Self

17.06.94 Danny Ruegg W PTS 6 Plymouth
07.10.94 Jobie Tyers L PTS 6 Taunton
07.02.95 Mark Reynolds L PTS 4 Ipswich
06.05.95 Tony Falcone L RSC 2 Shepton Mallet

20.03.96 Henry Jones L CO 1 Cardiff
20.03.97 Jason Booth L RSC 3 Newark
30.11.98 Mark Payne L RSC 1 Leicester
26.02.99 Frankie DeMilo L PTS 6 Longford
19.03.99 Willie Valentine L RSC 1 Weston
　　　　　super Mare
09.05.99 Tommy Craig L RSC 2 Bracknell
06.05.00 Shane Mallon DREW 6 Southwark
18.05.00 Rocky Dean L RSC 1 Bethnal Green
08.09.00 Simon Stowell L RSC 1 Bristol
22.10.00 Shane Mallon W PTS 4 Streatham
01.12.00 Daniel Ring L PTS 4 Peterborough
12.12.00 Andrew Greenaway L PTS 6 Clydach
02.01.01 Gareth Payne L RSC 1 Coventry
02.02.01 Jamie Evans L RSC 1 Portsmouth
13.03.01 Simon Stowell L RSC 2 Plymouth
Career: 19 contests, won 2, drew 1, lost 16.

Nigel Leake

Wakefield. *Born* Normanton, 13 June, 1969
S. Featherweight. Ht. 5'6"
Manager Self

31.01.97 Andy Ross W PTS 6 Pentre Halkyn
11.02.97 Charlie Rumbol W RSC 3 Bethnal
　　　　　Green
20.04.97 Garry Burrell W PTS 6 Leeds
11.09.97 Phillip Ndou L RSC 2 Widnes
23.10.97 Benny Jones W PTS 6 Mayfair
06.02.98 Lee Armstrong L PTS 6 Wakefield
21.04.98 Manuel Calvo L CO 4 Madrid, Spain
23.10.98 Lee Armstrong L RSC 3 Wakefield
　　　　　(Vacant Central Area S. Featherweight
　　　　　Title)
17.03.99 Dave Travers W PTS 6 Stoke
29.05.99 Michael Gomez L RSC 2 Halifax
　　　　　(Vacant IBF Inter-Continental
　　　　　Featherweight Title)
16.10.99 Marc Callaghan L PTS 4 Bethnal
　　　　　Green
27.11.99 Jamie McKeever L RSC 2 Liverpool
18.09.00 Barry Hawthorne L RSC 4 Glasgow
26.10.00 Nigel Senior L PTS 6 Stoke
Career: 14 contests, won 5, lost 9.

Kevin Lear

West Ham. *Born* Whitechapel, 3 May, 1977
Lightweight. Ht. 5'7¼"
Manager F. Maloney

13.09.99 Demir Nanev W RSC 4 Bethnal Green
15.11.99 Steve Hanley W RSC 1 Bethnal Green
19.02.00 Lee Williamson W PTS 4 Dagenham
13.03.00 Marco Fattore W PTS 4 Bethnal Green
13.04.00 Rakhim Mingaleev W PTS 4 Holborn
25.07.00 Dave Hinds W PTS 6 Southwark
13.11.00 Pete Buckley W PTS 6 Bethnal Green
10.03.01 Joel Viney W RSC 2 Bethnal Green
26.03.01 Dave Hinds W CO 1 Wembley
03.04.01 Steve Hanley W PTS 6 Bethnal Green
Career: 10 contests, won 10.

James Lee (Birchall)

Portsmouth. *Born* Portsmouth, 29
December, 1974
L. Middleweight. Ht. 5'11"
Manager N. Christian

03.11.00 Neil Bonner W PTS 4 Ebbw Vale
11.12.00 Dean Walker W PTS 6 Sheffield
02.02.01 Robert Weston L PTS 6 Portsmouth
16.03.01 Jed Tytler W RSC 3 Portsmouth
Career: 4 contests, won 3, lost 1.

James Lee　　　　　Les Clark

Nicky Leech

Nottingham. *Born* Nottingham, 6 June,
1981
Welterweight. Ht. 5'10"
Manager J. Gill

03.06.01 Richard Inquieti W PTS 6 Hanley
Career: 1 contest, won 1.

Matty Leonard

South Oxhey. *Born* Watford, 3 May, 1973
Lightweight. Ht. 5'6"
Manager C. Magri

30.10.99 Wayne Jones W RSC 3 Southwark
09.03.00 Dave Tatton DREW 6 Bethnal Green
01.07.00 Keith Jones L RSC 4 Southwark
Career: 3 contests, won 1, drew 1, lost 1.

(Herbert) Butch Lesley

Islington. *Born* Chelmsford, 21 April, 1973
Former Southern Area L. Heavyweight
Champion. Ht. 6'2½"
Manager A. Simms

02.09.95 Lester Jacobs L PTS 4 Wembley
16.10.95 David Larkin L RSC 4 Mayfair
23.01.96 Michael Pinnock W PTS 4 Bethnal
　　　　　Green
09.04.96 Jerry Mortimer W RSC 3 Stevenage
25.06.96 Graham Townsend L PTS 6 Stevenage
05.11.96 Sammy Storey L DIS 3 Belfast
08.03.97 Mark Delaney L PTS 6 Brentwood
11.11.97 Martin Jolley W PTS 6 Bethnal Green
10.01.98 Martin Jolley W PTS 4 Bethnal Green
30.03.98 Waldemar Barta W PTS 6 Tenerife
27.02.99 Dennis Doyley W RSC 5 Bethnal
　　　　　Green
12.12.99 Rob Stevenson W PTS 6 Chigwell
25.07.00 Dean Ashton W PTS 6 Southwark
14.10.00 Eddie Knight W RSC 6 Wembley
　　　　　(Southern Area L.Heavyweight Title
　　　　　Challenge)
02.12.00 Jason Barker W RSC 1 Chigwell
18.02.01 Paul Bonson W PTS 6 Southwark

26.03.01 Tony Oakey L PTS 10 Wembley
(Southern Area L. Heavyweight Title Defence)
16.06.01 Tony Booth W RSC 3 Dagenham
Career: 18 contests, won 12, lost 6.

Delroy Leslie

Carshalton. *Born* Jamaica, 22 February, 1970
Former Undefeated Southern Area Middleweight Champion. Former Undefeated Southern Area L. Middleweight Champion. Ht. 5'11½"
Manager B. Baker

29.04.93 Phil Found W PTS 6 Mayfair
14.06.93 Jason Barker W RTD 3 Bayswater
16.09.93 Jamie Davidson W PTS 6 Southwark
06.03.95 Shaun Cogan W RSC 1 Mayfair
20.04.95 Clayton Hollingsworth W PTS 6 Mayfair
23.06.95 Jonathan Thaxton L PTS 6 Bethnal Green
03.12.95 Adrian Chase W RSC 4 Southwark
02.04.96 Richie Edwards L RSC 3 Southwark
17.06.97 Ben Lockhart W CO 1 Nashville, USA
24.06.97 Julius Brown W CO 2 Nashville, USA
01.07.97 Booker T. Mulline W RSC 3 Nashville, USA
08.07.97 Dexter Phillips W RSC 3 Nashville, USA
24.07.97 Cassius Caldwell W CO 2 Cayce, USA
29.07.97 Mario Hereford W RSC 2 Nashville, USA
05.08.97 Charles Brown W RSC 1 Nashville, USA
12.08.97 William Lee W RSC 1 Nashville, USA
30.09.97 Don Greene W PTS 4 Nashville, USA
07.10.97 Reggie Strickland W PTS 4 Nashville, USA
14.10.97 Reggie Strickland W PTS 6 Nashville, USA
21.10.97 Tim Green W RSC 1 Nashville, USA
04.11.97 Jason Stewart W CO 1 Nashville, USA
25.11.97 Mario Hereford W RSC 3 Nashville, USA
14.05.98 Matthew Tait L PTS 6 Acton
10.09.98 Ojay Abrahams W PTS 10 Acton
(Vacant Southern Area L. Middleweight Title)
20.08.99 Ensley Bingham L RSC 9 Bloomsbury
(British L. Middleweight Title Challenge)
05.10.99 Matthew Barney W PTS 10 Bloomsbury
(Vacant Southern Area Middleweight Title)
10.03.00 Ruben Groenewald W PTS 12 Bethnal Green
(Interim WBF Middleweight Title)
08.09.00 Lester Jacobs L RSC 8 Hammersmith
(WBF Middleweight Title Defence)
08.12.00 Darren Ashton W RTD 3 Crystal Palace
19.05.01 Harry Butler W PTS 6 Wembley
Career: 30 contests, won 25, lost 5.

Ady Lewis

Bury. *Born* Bury, 31 May, 1975
Former British & Commonwealth Bantamweight Champion. Former Undefeated Commonwealth, British &

Central Area Flyweight Champion. Ht. 4'10½"
Manager J. Doughty/T. Gilmour

25.04.94 Darren Greaves W RSC 1 Bury
02.06.94 Dave Campbell W RSC 1 Middleton
22.09.94 Neil Parry W RSC 3 Bury
21.11.94 Daryl McKenzie W RSC 4 Glasgow
17.01.95 Yusuf Vorajee W RSC 2 Worcester
16.02.95 Chip O'Neill W RSC 1 Bury
06.03.95 Mark Cokely W RSC 5 Mayfair
09.05.95 Pete Buckley W PTS 4 Basildon
25.06.96 Graham McGrath W RSC 1 Stevenage
13.10.96 Gary Hickman W RSC 3 Shaw
01.12.96 Louis Veitch W PTS 10 Shaw
(Vacant Central Area Flyweight Title)
27.01.97 Keith Knox W PTS 12 Glasgow
(Vacant British Flyweight Title)
27.05.97 Mark Reynolds W PTS 12 Mayfair
(British Flyweight Title Defence)
11.09.97 Peter Culshaw W RSC 8 Widnes
(British Flyweight Title Defence. Commonwealth Flyweight Title Challenge)
22.11.97 David Guerault L RSC 4 Manchester
(European Flyweight Title Challenge)
08.04.98 Nicky Wilders W RSC 3 Liverpool
25.10.98 Ian Turner DREW 8 Shaw
22.01.99 Louis Veitch W RSC 2 Carlisle
22.06.99 Noel Wilders L RSC 6 Ipswich
(Final Elim. British Bantamweight Title)
04.12.99 Anthony Hanna W PTS 6 Manchester
01.04.00 Francis Ampofo W PTS 12 Bethnal Green
(Vacant British & Commonwealth Bantamweight Titles)
09.09.00 Tommy Waite L RSC 4 Manchester
(British & Commonwealth Bantamweight Title Defences)
26.02.01 Nicky Booth L RSC 7 Nottingham
(British & Commonwealth Bantamweight Title Challenges)
Career: 23 contests, won 18, drew 1, lost 4.

Lennox Lewis

Hadley Wood. *Born* London, 2 September, 1965
Former WBC, IBF & IBO Heavyweight Champion. Former Undefeated WBA, British, European & Commonwealth Heavyweight Champion. Ht. 6'4¾"
Manager Self

27.06.89 Al Malcolm W CO 2 Kensington
21.07.89 Bruce Johnson W RSC 2 Atlantic City, USA
25.09.89 Andrew Gerrard W RSC 4 Crystal Palace
10.10.89 Steve Garber W CO 1 Hull
05.11.89 Melvin Epps W DIS 2 Kensington
18.12.89 Greg Gorrell W RSC 5 Kitchener, Canada
31.01.90 Noel Quarless W RSC 2 Bethnal Green
22.03.90 Calvin Jones W CO 1 Gateshead
14.04.90 Mike Simwelu W CO 1 Kensington
09.05.90 Jorge Dascola W CO 1 Kensington
20.05.90 Dan Murphy W RSC 6 Sheffield
27.06.90 Ossie Ocasio W PTS 8 Kensington
11.07.90 Mike Acey W RSC 2 Mississauga, Canada
31.10.90 Jean Chanet W RSC 6 Crystal Palace
(European Heavyweight Title Challenge)

06.03.91 Gary Mason W RSC 7 Wembley
(British Heavyweight Title Challenge. European Heavyweight Title Defence)
12.07.91 Mike Weaver W CO 6 Lake Tahoe, USA
30.09.91 Glenn McCrory W CO 2 Kensington
(British & European Heavyweight Title Defences)
21.11.91 Tyrell Biggs W RSC 3 Atlanta, USA
01.02.92 Levi Billups W PTS 10 Las Vegas, USA
30.04.92 Derek Williams W RSC 3 Kensington
(British & European Heavyweight Title Defence. Commonwealth Heavyweight Title Challenge)
11.08.92 Mike Dixon W RSC 4 Atlantic City, USA
31.10.92 Razor Ruddock W RSC 2 Earls Court
(Final Elim. WBC Heavyweight Title & Commonwealth Heavyweight Title Defence)
08.05.93 Tony Tucker W PTS 12 Las Vegas, USA
(WBC Heavyweight Title Defence)
01.10.93 Frank Bruno W RSC 7 Cardiff
(WBC Heavyweight Title Defence)
06.05.94 Phil Jackson W RSC 8 Atlantic City, USA
(WBC Heavyweight Title Defence)
24.09.94 Oliver McCall L RSC 2 Wembley
(WBC Heavyweight Title Defence)
13.05.95 Lionel Butler W RSC 5 Sacramento, USA
(Elim. WBC Heavyweight Title)
02.07.95 Justin Fortune W RSC 4 Dublin
07.10.95 Tommy Morrison W RSC 6 Atlantic City, USA
10.05.96 Ray Mercer W PTS 10 New York City, USA
07.02.97 Oliver McCall W RSC 5 Las Vegas, USA
(Vacant WBC Heavyweight Title)
12.07.97 Henry Akinwande W DIS 5 Lake Tahoe, USA
(WBC Heavyweight Title Defence)
04.10.97 Andrew Golota W RSC 1 Atlantic City, USA
(WBC Heavyweight Title Defence)
28.03.98 Shannon Briggs W RSC 5 Atlantic City, USA
(WBC Heavyweight Title Defence)
26.09.98 Zeljko Mavrovic W PTS 12 Uncasville, USA
(WBC Heavyweight Title Defence)
13.03.99 Evander Holyfield DREW 12 New York City, USA
(WBC Heavyweight Title Defence. WBA & IBF Heavyweight Title Challenges)
13.11.99 Evander Holyfield W PTS 12 Las Vegas, USA
(WBC Heavyweight Title Defence. WBA & IBF Heavyweight Title Challenges)
29.04.00 Michael Grant W CO 2 New York City, USA
(WBC & IBF Heavyweight Title Defences)
15.07.00 Frans Botha W RSC 2 Millwall
(WBC, IBF & IBO Heavyweight Title Defences)
11.11.00 David Tua W PTS 12 Las Vegas, USA
(WBC, IBF & IBO Heavyweight Title Defences)

Lennox Lewis   Les Clark

22.04.01 Hasim Rahman L CO 5 Brakpan, South
Africa
*(WBC, WBA & IBO Heavyweight Title
Defences)*
Career: 41 contests, won 38, drew 1, lost 2.

Willie Limond

Glasgow. *Born* Glasgow, 2 February, 1979
S. Featherweight. Ht. 5'7"
Manager A. Morrison/F. Warren

12.11.99 Lennie Hodgkins W RTD 1 Glasgow
13.12.99 Steve Hanley W PTS 6 Glasgow
24.02.00 Nigel Senior W RSC 6 Glasgow
18.03.00 Phil Lashley W RSC 1 Glasgow
07.04.00 Jimmy Beech W RSC 2 Glasgow
26.05.00 Billy Smith W PTS 4 Glasgow
24.06.00 Haroon Din W PTS 4 Glasgow
10.11.00 Danny Connelly W PTS 6 Glasgow
17.12.00 Billy Smith W PTS 6 Glasgow
15.02.01 Marcus Portman W PTS 6 Glasgow
03.04.01 Trevor Smith W PTS 4 Bethnal Green
27.04.01 Choi Tseveenpurev W PTS 6 Glasgow
Career: 12 contests, won 12.

Neil Linford

Leicester. *Born* Leicester, 29 September,
1977
S. Middleweight. Ht. 5'10¾"
Manager K. Sanders

30.10.98 Israel Khumalo W RSC 2 Peterborough
30.11.98 David Baptiste W PTS 4 Peterborough
15.12.98 Johannes Ngiba W CO 2 Durban,
South Africa
16.01.99 Dean Powell W RSC 1 Bethnal Green
22.02.99 Leigh Wicks W PTS 4 Peterborough
24.04.99 Adrian Houldey W RSC 2
Peterborough
17.05.99 Jason Barker L RSC 3 Peterborough
15.07.99 Hussain Osman L RSC 5 Peterborough
07.02.00 Mark Dawson W PTS 4 Peterborough
04.03.00 Darren Ashton W PTS 6 Peterborough
25.05.00 Michael Pinnock W PTS 4
Peterborough
30.09.00 Matthew Barney W PTS 10
Peterborough
(Elim. British S. Middleweight Title)
30.11.00 Darren Ashton W PTS 4 Peterborough
29.01.01 Brian Magee L PTS 12 Peterborough
*(Vacant IBO Inter-Continental
S. Middleweight Title)*
23.06.01 Jon Penn W RSC 3 Peterborough
Career: 15 contests, won 12, lost 3.

Neil Linford   Les Clark

Earl Ling

Norwich. *Born* Kings Lynn, 9 March, 1972
L. Heavyweight. Ht. 5'10"
Manager Self

08.09.92 Eddie Collins W PTS 6 Norwich
11.05.93 Mark Hale L RSC 2 Norwich
12.12.94 Clinton Woods L RSC 5 Cleethorpes
04.12.95 Jeff Finlayson L PTS 6 Manchester
26.02.96 Peter Waudby L PTS 6 Hull
19.03.96 James Lowther L RSC 4 Leeds
16.05.98 Dean Ashton DREW 6 Chigwell
02.07.98 Dean Ashton L RSC 2 Ipswich
17.09.98 Jimmy Steel DREW 6 Brighton
19.01.99 Israel Khumalo L RSC 1 Ipswich
15.07.00 Mike Duffield W PTS 6 Norwich
04.11.00 Andrew Facey L PTS 6 Derby
16.06.01 Andrew Facey DREW 6 Derby
Career: 13 contests, won 2, drew 3, lost 8.

Wayne Llewelyn

Beckenham. *Born* Greenwich, 20 April,
1970
Heavyweight. Ht. 6'3½"
Manager Self

18.01.92 Chris Coughlan W RSC 3 Kensington
30.03.92 Steve Stewart W RSC 4 Eltham
23.04.92 Gary Charlton W RSC 6 Eltham
10.12.92 Gary McCrory W RSC 2 Glasgow
23.05.93 Cordwell Hylton W PTS 6 Brockley
01.12.93 Manny Burgo W PTS 6 Bethnal Green
14.04.94 Vance Idiens W RSC 1 Battersea
22.05.94 Cordwell Hylton W CO 2 Crystal Palace
03.05.95 Mitch Rose W PTS 4 New York City, USA
07.07.95 Vance Idiens W RSC 1 Cardiff
11.08.95 Carlos Monroe W RSC 3 Louisiana, USA
26.04.96 Steve Garber W CO 1 Cardiff
08.06.96 Dermot Gascoyne W RSC 4 Newcastle
22.03.97 Mike Sedillo W CO 2 Wythenshawe
20.09.97 Michael Murray W RTD 4 Aachen, Germany
21.03.98 Everton Davis W PTS 8 Bethnal Green
06.06.98 Pele Reid L CO 1 Liverpool
(Elim. British Heavyweight Title)
18.02.99 Derek Williams W RSC 3 Bossier City, USA
03.06.99 Frankie Swindell L CO 2 Mount Pleasant, USA
21.08.99 Terry Veners W RSC 3 Coachella, USA
28.11.99 Terry Veners W CO 2 Monterey, USA
10.03.00 William Barima W CO 1 Bethnal Green
19.03.00 Augustin Corpus L PTS 8 Tunica, USA
14.10.00 Michael Sprott W RSC 3 Wembley
08.12.00 Alex Vasiliev L RSC 1 Crystal Palace
01.04.01 Luke Simpkin W PTS 6 Southwark
Career: 26 contests, won 22, lost 4.

Paul Lloyd

Ellesmere Port. *Born* Bebington, 7 December, 1968
Former Undefeated British, Commonwealth & European Bantamweight Champion.
Former Undefeated Central Area S. Bantamweight Champion. Ht. 5'7"
Manager Self

25.09.92 Graham McGrath W RSC 3 Liverpool
23.10.92 Kid McAuley W PTS 4 Liverpool
20.11.92 Des Gargano W PTS 4 Liverpool
15.12.92 Glyn Shepherd W RSC 1 Liverpool
27.02.93 Miguel Matthews W PTS 6 Ellesmere Port
04.05.93 Andrew Bloomer W PTS 6 Liverpool
02.07.93 Ronnie Stephenson W RTD 1 Liverpool
30.10.93 Marty Chestnut W RSC 1 Chester
11.12.93 Gerald Shelton W RSC 3 Liverpool
25.02.94 Ady Benton W RSC 5 Chester
(Vacant Central Area S. Bantamweight Title)
06.05.94 Pete Buckley W RTD 4 Liverpool
26.09.94 Chris Clarkson L RSC 4 Liverpool
25.03.95 Richie Wenton L RSC 5 Chester
(British S. Bantamweight Title Challenge)
16.06.95 Garry Burrell W RSC 2 Liverpool
24.11.95 Michael Parris L RSC 4 Chester
03.02.96 Julian Gomez W CO 2 Liverpool
07.10.96 Nathan Sting W RSC 6 Lewisham
(Vacant Commonwealth Bantamweight Title)
18.02.97 Lybo Nkoko W CO 1 Cheshunt
(Commonwealth Bantamweight Title Defence)

16.04.97 Simphiwe Pamana W RSC 11 Bethnal Green
(Commonwealth Bantamweight Title Defence)
25.10.97 Francis Ampofo W PTS 12 Queensferry
(Commonwealth Bantamweight Title Defence. Vacant British Bantamweight Title)
23.03.98 Tim Austin L RSC 2 Hull
(IBF Bantamweight Title Challenge)
26.09.98 Drew Docherty W PTS 12 York
(British & Commonwealth Bantamweight Title Defences)
12.12.98 Luigi Mancini W RSC 12 Chester
(Vacant European Bantamweight Title)
03.04.99 Marco Antonio Barrera L RTD 1 Kensington
(WBO S. Bantamweight Title Challenge)
29.10.99 Johnny Bredahl L RSC 1 Copenhagen, Denmark
(European & IBC Bantamweight Title Challenges)
10.03.00 Foudil Madani W CO 1 Chigwell
15.07.00 Noel Wilders L PTS 12 Millwall
(IBO Bantamweight Title Challenge)
Career: 27 contests, won 20, lost 7.

Gary Lockett

Cwmbran. *Born* Pontypool, 25 November, 1976
L. Middleweight. Ht. 5'10"
Manager B. Hearn/B. Devine

06.09.96 Ernie Loveridge W PTS 4 Liverpool
26.10.96 Charlie Paine W RSC 4 Liverpool
24.10.98 Lee Bird W RSC 2 Liverpool
27.02.99 Carl Smith W RSC 2 Bethnal Green
15.05.99 Mike Whittaker W RSC 2 Blackpool
19.06.99 Kid Halls W CO 1 Dublin
09.03.00 Kevin Thompson W CO 2 Liverpool
04.11.00 David Baptiste W PTS 4 Bethnal Green
23.01.01 Abdul Mehdi W RSC 2 Crawley
03.03.01 Hussain Osman W CO 2 Wembley
07.04.01 Howard Clarke W RSC 2 Wembley
08.05.01 Mike Algoet W PTS 6 Barnsley
Career: 12 contests, won 12.

Gary Logan

Croydon. *Born* Lambeth, 10 October, 1968
Southern Area Middleweight Champion.
Former Undefeated Southern Area Welterweight Champion. Ht. 5'8¾"
Manager Self

05.10.88 Peppy Muire W RTD 3 Wembley
02.11.88 Tony Gibbs W PTS 6 Southwark
07.12.88 Pat Dunne W PTS 6 Piccadilly
12.01.89 Mike Russell W CO 1 Southwark
20.02.89 Dave Griffiths W RSC 5 Mayfair
29.03.89 Ronnie Campbell W PTS 6 Wembley
10.05.89 Tony Britland W CO 1 Kensington
07.06.89 Davey Hughes W CO 1 Wembley
24.08.89 Mike English W CO 2 Tampa, USA
04.10.89 Simon Eubank W PTS 6 Kensington
12.10.89 Jimmy Thornton W PTS 6 Southwark
08.11.89 Chris Blake L PTS 8 Wembley
10.01.90 Julian Eavis W PTS 8 Kensington
03.03.90 Anthony Joe Travis W CO 5 Wembley
09.05.90 Joseph Alexander W PTS 8 Wembley
13.09.90 Manuel Rojas W PTS 8 Watford

16.01.91 Julian Eavis W RSC 5 Kensington
18.02.91 Gordon Blair W CO 1 Mayfair
25.04.91 Trevor Ambrose W PTS 8 Mayfair
17.10.91 Des Robinson W PTS 8 Southwark
15.10.92 Mick Duncan W PTS 8 Lewisham
17.12.92 Roy Rowland W RSC 4 Wembley
(Vacant Southern Area Welterweight Title)
23.05.93 Glyn Rhodes W CO 3 Brockley
25.06.93 Gordon Blair W RSC 6 Battersea
14.08.93 Paul King W CO 2 Hammersmith
28.11.93 Paul King W CO 4 Southwark
11.12.93 Horace Fleary W PTS 8 Dusseldorf, Germany
09.02.94 Graham Cheney L RSC 10 Bethnal Green
(WBC International Welterweight Title Challenge)
29.09.94 Ojay Abrahams W PTS 10 Bethnal Green
(Southern Area Welterweight Title Defence)
25.10.94 Nick Hall DREW 8 Southwark
02.06.95 Del Bryan L RSC 11 Bethnal Green
(British Welterweight Title Challenge)
21.03.96 Paul Wesley W PTS 6 Southwark
13.04.96 Ensley Bingham L RSC 6 Wythenshawe
(British L. Middleweight Title Challenge)
01.04.01 Adrian Kirkbride W RSC 1 Southwark
03.06.01 Spencer Fearon W RSC 2 Southwark
(Vacant Southern Area Middleweight Title)
Career: 35 contests, won 30, drew 1, lost 4.

Jamie Logan

Nottingham. *Born* Lincoln, 9 April, 1975
Middleweight. Ht. 6'1"
Manager J. Gill

07.12.00 David Smales L PTS 6 Stoke
18.03.01 Gary Dixon L PTS 6 Shaw
01.04.01 Peter Jackson L PTS 6 Wolverhampton
20.05.01 Peter Jackson L PTS 6 Wolverhampton
03.06.01 Paul Martin L PTS 6 Hanley
Career: 5 contests, lost 5.

Paul Lomax

Sunderland. *Born* Sunderland, 11 May, 1974
S. Middleweight. Ht. 6'0½"
Manager T. Callighan

23.07.00 Reece McAllister L PTS 6 Hartlepool
10.06.01 Tony Byrne L PTS 6 Ellesmere Port
Career: 2 contests, lost 2.

Keith Long

Brixton. *Born* Greenwich, 30 July, 1968
Heavyweight. Ht. 5'11½"
Manager A. Gee

15.02.97 Steve Cranston W PTS 4 Tooting
04.02.99 Gordon Minors W PTS 6 Lewisham
24.04.99 Derek McCafferty L PTS 4 Peterborough
07.08.99 Israel Ajose DREW 6 Dagenham
29.11.99 Mark Potter W PTS 8 Wembley
13.04.00 Harry Senior W PTS 10 Holborn
18.11.00 Luke Simpkin W RSC 3 Dagenham
Career: 7 contests, won 5, drew 1, lost 1.

Andrew Lowe

Hackney. *Born* Hackney, 23 June, 1974
S. Middleweight. Ht. 5'10"
Manager T. Sims

19.05.01 Rob Stevenson W PTS 4 Wembley
16.06.01 William Webster W RSC 2 Dagenham
Career: 2 contests, won 2.

David Lowry

Belfast. *Born* Belfast, 1 March, 1975
Featherweight. Ht. 5'7"
Manager F. Maloney

13.03.99 Chris Lyons W PTS 4 Manchester
22.05.99 Wee Barry W RTD 1 Belfast
22.06.99 Carl Allen W PTS 4 Ipswich
16.10.99 Sean Grant W RSC 1 Belfast
10.12.99 Assen Vassilev L PTS 4 Nicosia, Cyprus
12.06.00 Gary Flear W PTS 4 Belfast
25.07.00 Anthony Hanna W PTS 4 Southwark
11.11.00 Gary Flear L PTS 4 Belfast
Career: 8 contests, won 6, lost 2.

David Lowry   Les Clark

James Lowther

Leeds. *Born* Leeds, 28 June, 1976
L. Middleweight. Former Undefeated IBO Inter-Continental Middleweight Champion. Ht. 5'11"
Manager T. O'Neill/T. Gilmour

12.01.95 Warren Stephens W CO 4 Leeds
25.03.95 Scott Doyle W PTS 6 Rothwell
19.05.95 Eddie Haley W RSC 5 Leeds
19.03.96 Earl Ling W RSC 4 Leeds
06.12.96 Martin Jolley W PTS 6 Leeds
07.03.97 Gordon Behan W PTS 6 Northampton
13.06.97 Raziq Ali W PTS 6 Leeds
17.02.98 Koba Kulu W PTS 4 Leeds
12.05.98 Jason Barker W PTS 4 Leeds
26.09.98 Harry Butler W RSC 6 York
21.11.98 Pedro Carragher W RSC 6 Leeds
03.12.98 Jim Webb L PTS 10 Mayfair

(Vacant All-Ireland L. Middleweight Title)
19.04.99 Stevie McCready L PTS 6 Glasgow
15.09.99 David Baptiste L RSC 3 Harrogate
27.03.00 Stevie McCready W RTD 11 Barnsley
(Vacant IBO Inter-Continental Middleweight Title)
25.09.00 Hussain Osman W PTS 8 Barnsley
24.02.01 Mehrdud Takaloo L PTS 12 Bethnal Green
(IBF Inter-Continental L.Middleweight Title Challenge)
Career: 17 contests, won 13, lost 4.

Colin Lynes

Hornchurch. *Born* Whitechapel, 26 November, 1977
L. Welterweight. Ht. 5'7½"
Manager Self

04.06.98 Les Frost W CO 1 Barking
23.07.98 Ram Singh W CO 1 Barking

22.10.98 Brian Coleman W RSC 2 Barking
31.10.98 Marc Smith W PTS 4 Basingstoke
10.12.98 Trevor Smith W RSC 1 Barking
25.02.99 Dennis Griffin W PTS 6 Kentish Town
20.05.99 Mark Haslam W PTS 4 Barking
18.05.00 Jason Vlasman W RSC 2 Bethnal Green
16.09.00 Karl Taylor W PTS 6 Bethnal Green
14.10.00 Brian Coleman W PTS 6 Wembley
09.12.00 Jimmy Phelan W PTS 6 Southwark
17.02.01 Mark Ramsey W PTS 6 Bethnal Green
10.04.01 David Kirk W PTS 6 Wembley
Career: 13 contests, won 13.

Nick Lyon

Boston. *Born* Boston, 23 March, 1981
L. Middleweight. Ht. 5'10"
Manager K. Sanders

23.06.01 Brendan Rollinson L RSC 4 Peterborough
Career: 1 contest, lost 1.

James Lowther   Les Clark

M

Matthew McAllister

Glasgow. *Born* Glasgow, 8 July, 1971
L. Heavyweight. Ht. 6'1¹/₂"
Manager A. Morrison

10.11.00 Shayne Webb W PTS 6 Glasgow
Career: 1 contest, won 1.

(Gary) Reece McAllister

Newton Aycliffe. *Born* Bishop Auckland,
30 March, 1970
S. Middleweight. Ht. 6'0¹/₂"
Manager T. Callighan

26.11.99 Ganny Dovidovas L RSC 1 Bayswater
26.02.00 Mike White L PTS 4 Carlisle
25.03.00 Albert Rybacki L RSC 2 Liverpool
23.07.00 Paul Lomax W PTS 6 Hartlepool
10.10.00 Craig Clayton W RSC 4 Brierley Hill
24.11.00 Paul Owen W PTS 6 Darlington
17.05.01 Andy Vickers W RSC 1 Leeds
21.06.01 Paul Owen DREW 6 Sheffield
Career: 8 contests, won 4, drew 1, lost 3.

Enzo Maccarinelli

Swansea. *Born* Swansea, 20 August, 1980
Cruiserweight. Ht. 6'4"
Manager D. Gardiner

02.10.99 Paul Bonson W PTS 4 Cardiff
11.12.99 Mark Williams W RSC 1 Merthyr
26.02.00 Nigel Rafferty W RSC 3 Swansea
12.05.00 Lee Swaby L CO 3 Swansea
11.12.00 Chris Woollas W PTS 4 Widnes
28.04.01 Darren Ashton W CO 1 Cardiff
Career: 6 contests, won 5, lost 1.

Kevin McCarthy

Milton Keynes. *Born* Bletchley, 10 March,
1972
Former Undefeated Southern Area
Welterweight Champion. Ht. 5'9¹/₂"
Manager D. Mancini

03.07.96 Paul Webb W RSC 2 Wembley
24.10.96 Peter Nightingale DREW 6 Wembley
20.11.96 Donovan Davey W PTS 6 Wembley
29.01.97 Craig Hartwell W RSC 1 Bethnal
Green
03.04.97 Brian Coleman W PTS 6 Wembley
30.04.97 Costas Katsantonis L RSC 6 Acton
11.11.97 Arv Mittoo W PTS 6 Bethnal Green
27.01.98 Brian Coleman W PTS 6 Streatham
23.02.98 Peter Nightingale W PTS 6 Windsor
16.04.98 Dean Bramhald W PTS 8 Mayfair
27.10.98 Paul Miles W RSC 2 Brentford
12.12.98 Harry Dhami L PTS 10 Southwark
*(Southern Area Welterweight Title
Challenge)*
16.02.99 Danny Bell W PTS 6 Brentford
08.05.99 Trevor Smith W RSC 1 Bethnal Green
27.05.00 Adrian Chase W RSC 4 Southwark
*(Vacant Southern Area Welterweight
Title)*
16.09.00 David Baptiste L RSC 6 Bethnal Green
Career: 16 contests, won 12, drew 1, lost 3.

Colin McCash

Accrington. *Born* Dundee, 29 October,
1977
L. Middleweight. Ht. 5'11"
Manager B. Myers

22.09.00 Mark Paxford DREW 6 Wrexham
21.10.00 Dean Walker DREW 6 Sheffield
05.12.00 Chris Steele W RSC 4 Nottingham
Career: 3 contests, won 1, drew 2.

Colin McCash   Les Clark

Glenn McClarnon

Lurgan. *Born* Carrickfergus, 1 July, 1974
L. Welterweight. Ht. 5'9"
Manager Self

20.12.97 Marc Smith W PTS 4 Belfast
21.02.98 Andrew Reed W CO 1 Belfast
28.04.98 Brian Robb W RSC 2 Belfast
18.09.98 Mark Ramsey W PTS 4 Belfast
28.11.98 David Kirk W PTS 4 Belfast
12.01.99 Ram Singh W RSC 1 Bethnal Green
25.01.99 Dean Nicholas W CO 1 Glasgow
12.03.99 Mark Ramsey W PTS 6 Bethnal Green
25.05.99 Steve Tuckett W PTS 6 Mayfair
11.09.99 David Kirk W PTS 6 Sheffield
27.11.99 Chris Barnett L PTS 12 Liverpool
*(Vacant IBO International L.
Welterweight Title)*
01.04.00 Bernard Paul W RTD 5 Bethnal Green
19.08.00 Brian Coleman W PTS 6 Brentwood
13.10.00 Allan Vester L PTS 12 Aarhus,
Denmark
*(IBF Inter-Continental L.Welterweight
Title Challenge)*
02.12.00 John Ameline L PTS 4 Bethnal Green
03.03.01 Peter Dunn W PTS 4 Wembley
28.04.01 Jacek Bielski L PTS 12 Wroclaw,
Poland
*(Vacant IBO Inter-Continental
Welterweight Title)*
Career: 17 contests, won 13, lost 4.

Ross McCord

Swansea. *Born* Swansea, 31 August, 1977
L. Welterweight. Ht. 5'10"
Manager Self

02.12.97 Harry Butler L RSC 3 Swansea
23.05.98 Sony Thind W RSC 1 Bethnal Green
25.11.98 Pedro Thompson W RSC 2 Clydach
07.12.98 Sammy Smith L RSC 5 Acton
20.02.99 Scott Garrett L RSC 2 Thornaby
23.04.99 Darren Underwood W RSC 1 Clydach
31.10.99 Arv Mittoo W PTS 6 Raynes Park
26.02.00 Woody Greenaway L PTS 4 Swansea
09.03.00 Karim Bouali L RSC 1 Bethnal Green
22.07.00 Iain Eldridge L RSC 2 Watford
12.12.00 Woody Greenaway L PTS 6 Clydach
Career: 11 contests, won 4, lost 7.

Robert McCracken

Birmingham. *Born* Birmingham, 31 May,
1968
Former Undefeated Commonwealth
Middleweight Champion. Former
Undefeated British L. Middleweight
Champion. Ht. 6'0"
Manager Self

24.01.91 Mick Mulcahy W RSC 1 Brierley Hill
13.02.91 Gary Barron W RTD 2 Wembley
06.03.91 Tony Britland W RSC 2 Wembley
12.04.91 Dave Andrews W RSC 4 Willenhall
08.05.91 Tony Gibbs W CO 1 Kensington
30.05.91 Paul Murray W RSC 2 Birmingham
04.07.91 Marty Duke W RSC 1 Alfreton
25.07.91 John Smith W RTD 1 Dudley
31.10.91 Newton Barnett W DIS 2 Oakengates
28.11.91 Michael Oliver W RSC 3 Liverpool
12.02.92 Paul Lynch W RSC 4 Wembley
01.10.92 Horace Fleary W PTS 8 Telford
02.11.92 Ensley Bingham W RSC 10
Wolverhampton
(Elim. British L. Middleweight Title)
20.01.93 Leigh Wicks W PTS 8 Wolverhampton
17.02.93 Ernie Loveridge W CO 4 Bethnal
Green
24.04.93 Martin Smith W RSC 10 Birmingham
*(Final Elim. British L. Middleweight
Title)*
29.06.93 Steve Langley W RSC 4 Edgbaston
01.12.93 Chris Peters W PTS 8 Kensington
23.02.94 Andy Till W PTS 12 Watford
*(British L. Middleweight Title
Challenge)*
10.09.94 Steve Foster W PTS 12 Birmingham
(British L. Middleweight Title Defence)
11.10.94 Dean Cooper W RSC 4 Bethnal Green
10.02.95 Paul Wesley W PTS 12 Birmingham
(British L. Middleweight Title Defence)
21.04.95 Sergio Medina W RSC 7 Dudley
01.09.95 Jorge Sclarandi W PTS 10
Wolverhampton
03.11.95 Fitzgerald Bruney W PTS 12 Dudley
*(Vacant Commonwealth Middleweight
Title)*
03.04.96 Paul Busby W RTD 7 Bethnal Green
*(Commonwealth Middleweight Title
Defence)*
15.05.96 Humberto Aranda W RSC 5 Cardiff
01.10.96 Fitzgerald Bruney W PTS 12
Birmingham
*(Commonwealth Middleweight Title
Defence)*
12.11.96 Glen Odem W PTS 10 Dudley

12.09.97	Joe Stevenson W CO 1 Pikesville, USA
27.02.98	Lonnie Beasley W PTS 10 Studio City, USA
31.10.98	Napoleon Pitt W RSC 6 Atlantic City, USA
06.03.99	Steve Fisher W RSC 10 Atlantic City, USA
29.04.00	Keith Holmes L RSC 11 Wembley *(WBC Middleweight Title Challenge)*
10.04.01	Howard Eastman L RSC 10 Wembley *(British & Commonwealth Middleweight Title Challenges. Vacant European Middleweight Title)*

Career: 35 contests, won 33, lost 2.

Spencer McCracken

Birmingham. *Born* Birmingham, 8 August, 1969
Welterweight. Ht. 5'9"
Manager Self

15.10.91	Stuart Dunn DREW 6 Dudley
09.12.91	Seth Jones W RSC 2 Brierley Hill
27.10.92	Dave Lovell W PTS 4 Cradley Heath
07.12.92	Mark Antony W CO 1 Birmingham
22.02.93	Rick North W PTS 8 Birmingham
16.03.93	Ricky Mabbett W PTS 6 Edgbaston
18.05.93	Tony Britland W CO 1 Edgbaston
06.12.93	Jimmy Thornton W PTS 6 Birmingham
19.01.94	Julian Eavis W PTS 8 Solihull
28.03.94	Marty Duke W RSC 2 Birmingham
23.05.94	Ojay Abrahams W PTS 6 Walsall
25.10.94	Julian Eavis W PTS 6 Edgbaston
11.05.95	Tony Foster W PTS 6 Dudley
05.06.95	Stefan Scriggins L PTS 8 Birmingham
01.10.96	Danny Quacoe W RTD 3 Birmingham
23.10.96	Shaun Stokes W PTS 8 Halifax
12.11.96	Ojay Abrahams W PTS 8 Dudley
28.04.97	Dennis Berry W RSC 10 Hull *(Final Elim. British Welterweight Title)*
27.03.98	Prince Kasi Kaihau W PTS 8 Telford
05.09.98	Paul Samuels L PTS 8 Telford
12.12.98	Peter Nightingale W PTS 8 Southwark
22.10.99	Peter Malinga W PTS 12 Coventry *(Vacant IBO Welterweight Title)*
17.04.00	Mark Ramsey W PTS 8 Birmingham
27.11.00	Harry Dhami L PTS 12 Birmingham *(British Welterweight Title Challenge)*

Career: 24 contests, won 19, drew 1, lost 4.

Geoff McCreesh

Bracknell. *Born* Stockton, 12 June, 1970
Former Undefeated British Welterweight
Champion. Former Undefeated Southern
Area L. Middleweight Champion. Ht. 5'10"
Manager Self

16.02.94	Tony Walton W PTS 6 Stevenage
12.03.94	Barry Thorogood W PTS 6 Cardiff
22.03.94	Mark Dawson W PTS 6 Bethnal Green
20.05.94	Robert Peel W RSC 2 Acton
02.07.94	Julian Eavis W PTS 4 Keynsham
18.11.94	Andrew Furlong W PTS 6 Bracknell
13.12.94	Ojay Abrahams W PTS 6 Potters Bar
20.01.95	Clay O'Shea W RSC 1 Bethnal Green *(Vacant Southern Area L. Middleweight Title)*
03.03.95	Dennis Berry W RTD 5 Bracknell
16.12.95	Michael Smyth L DIS 4 Cardiff
19.01.96	Steve Goodwin L DIS 5 Bracknell
02.03.96	Peter Varnavas W PTS 4 Newcastle
13.03.96	Kevin Thompson W PTS 6 Wembley

09.04.96	Vince Rose W RSC 4 Stevenage
10.05.96	George Wilson W PTS 6 Wembley
25.06.96	Wayne Shepherd W PTS 4 Stevenage
27.08.96	Jimmy Vincent W RSC 1 Windsor
28.09.96	George Wilson W PTS 4 Barking
05.11.96	Dingaan Thobela W CO 2 Hammanskraal, South Africa
19.01.97	Peter Malinga L RTD 5 Durban, South Africa
19.07.97	Kevin Lueshing W RSC 10 Wembley *(British Welterweight Title Challenge)*
13.09.97	Paul Ryan W RSC 2 Millwall *(British Welterweight Title Defence. Vacant WBO Inter-Continental Welterweight Title)*
29.11.97	Michele Piccirillo L RSC 9 Novara, Italy *(Vacant European Welterweight Title)*
14.07.98	Michael Smyth W CO 7 Reading *(British Welterweight Title Defence)*
31.10.98	Ross Hale W RSC 4 Basingstoke *(British Welterweight Title Defence)*
13.02.99	Paul Wesley W PTS 8 Newcastle
26.06.99	Ojay Abrahams W PTS 8 Millwall
27.11.99	Leigh Wicks W PTS 6 Lubeck, Germany
15.07.00	Adrian Stone L RSC 6 Millwall *(IBO L.Middleweight Title Challenge)*
26.04.01	Ossie Duran L PTS 6 Kensington

Career: 30 contests, won 23, lost 7.

John McDermott

Horndon. *Born* Basildon, 26 February, 1980
Heavyweight. Ht. 6'3"
Manager J. Branch

23.09.00	Slick Miller W RSC 1 Bethnal Green
21.10.00	Gary Williams W PTS 4 Wembley
13.11.00	Geoff Hunter W RSC 1 Bethnal Green
27.01.01	Eamonn Glennon W RSC 1 Bethnal Green
24.02.01	Alexei Osokin W PTS 4 Bethnal Green
26.03.01	Mal Rice W RSC 2 Wembley
09.06.01	Luke Simpkin W PTS 6 Bethnal Green

Career: 7 contests, won 7.

Thomas McDonagh   Harry Goodwin

Thomas McDonagh

Manchester. *Born* Manchester, 8 December, 1980
L. Middleweight. Ht. 6'0"
Manager F. Warren

09.10.99	Lee Molyneux W PTS 4 Manchester
06.11.99	Lee Molyneux W PTS 4 Widnes
11.12.99	Arv Mittoo W RSC 2 Liverpool
29.01.00	Emmanuel Marcos W PTS 4 Manchester
29.02.00	William Webster W RTD 2 Widnes
25.03.00	Lee Molyneux W PTS 6 Liverpool
16.05.00	Richie Murray W PTS 4 Warrington
29.05.00	David Baptiste W PTS 6 Manchester
04.09.00	Colin Vidler W PTS 6 Manchester
11.12.00	Richie Murray W PTS 6 Widnes
15.01.01	Kid Halls W RSC 4 Manchester
10.02.01	Harry Butler W PTS 6 Widnes
17.03.01	David Baptiste W PTS 4 Manchester

Career: 13 contests, won 13.

Errol McDonald

Nottingham. *Born* Nottingham, 11 March, 1964
S. Middleweight. Ht. 5'10"
Manager Self

21.10.85	Dave Heaver W CO 1 Mayfair
05.11.85	Robert Armstrong W RSC 4 Wembley
20.01.86	Lenny Gloster W PTS 8 Mayfair
17.02.86	Kid Milo DREW 6 Mayfair
27.02.86	Gary Flear W RSC 5 Bethnal Green
09.04.86	Lenny Gloster W PTS 6 Kensington
29.10.86	Gerry Beard W RSC 4 Piccadilly
19.01.87	Mark Simpson W CO 5 Mayfair
30.08.87	Jose Maria Castillo W RSC 3 Marbella, Spain
30.09.87	Roy Callaghan W RSC 4 Mayfair
18.11.87	Billy Cairns W RTD 3 Bethnal Green
03.02.88	Mike English W RSC 2 Wembley
29.03.88	Ramon Nunez W RSC 3 Wembley
21.04.88	Nick Meloscia W PTS 8 Bethnal Green
26.09.88	Jimmy Thornton W RTD 2 Piccadilly
05.10.88	Alfredo Reyes W CO 2 Wembley
30.11.88	Sammy Floyd W RSC 3 Southwark
18.01.89	Nick Meloscia W RSC 1 Kensington
19.12.89	Mick Mulcahy W RSC 3 Bethnal Green
27.01.90	Joe Hernandez W PTS 8 Sheffield
28.03.90	Robert Lewis W RSC 4 Bethnal Green
25.04.90	Mario Lopez W CO 1 Brighton
05.06.90	Steve Larrimore W RSC 9 Nottingham
18.11.90	Ray Taylor W RTD 3 Birmingham
23.02.91	Juan Rondon W RSC 7 Brighton
08.06.91	Patrizio Oliva L DIS 12 La Spezia, Italy *(European Welterweight Title Challenge)*
10.12.91	Jose Luis Saldivia W PTS 8 Sheffield
10.03.92	Robert Wright L CO 3 Bury
24.11.92	Gordon Blair W RSC 5 Doncaster
12.01.93	Orlando Otero W RSC 4 Aachen, Germany
16.02.93	Peter Till W PTS 8 Tooting
16.03.93	Michael Driscoll L PTS 10 Mayfair *(Elim. British L. Welterweight Title)*
25.10.93	Wayne Appleton L PTS 8 Glasgow
24.01.94	Ojay Abrahams L RSC 2 Glasgow
07.05.96	Nick Odore L RSC 4 Mayfair
21.11.98	Bobby Banghar W CO 6 Southwark
26.02.99	Andrew Flute L RSC 4 West Bromwich
29.04.99	Mark Baker L PTS 10 Bethnal Green

17.07.99 Neville Brown L RSC 3 Doncaster
06.05.00 Richie Woodhall L RTD 7 Frankfurt, Germany
12.08.00 Mario Veit L RSC 3 Wembley
Career: 41 contests, won 29, drew 1, lost 11.

Jason McElligott

Shepherds Bush. *Born* London, 3 June, 1971
Welterweight. Ht. 5'8"
Manager D. Currivan

02.12.97 Paul Salmon L PTS 6 Windsor
23.02.98 Ram Singh W PTS 6 Windsor
26.03.98 Mark Harrison W PTS 6 Acton
02.11.00 Dave Travers W PTS 4 Kensington
10.11.00 Darren Melville L RSC 2 Mayfair
01.04.01 Reggie Robshaw L PTS 4 Southwark
05.05.01 Gary Harrison L PTS 6 Brighton
Career: 7 contests, won 3, lost 4.

Conroy McIntosh

Wolverhampton. *Born* Wolverhampton, 5 December, 1973
L. Middleweight. Ht. 5'7"
Manager T. Marshall

31.01.01 Ross Murray W CO 1 Piccadilly
23.06.01 Francie Doherty L PTS 4 Peterborough
Career: 2 contests, won 1, lost 1.

Kevin McIntyre

Paisley. *Born* Paisley, 5 May, 1978
Welterweight. Ht. 5'10½"
Manager N. Sweeney/A. Morrison

13.11.98 Ray Wood W RSC 4 Glasgow
18.02.99 Gareth Dooley W RSC 3 Glasgow
21.05.99 Mohamed Helel W PTS 6 Glasgow
26.06.99 Karim Bouali L RTD 1 Glasgow
18.03.00 Chris Hall W RSC 3 Glasgow
07.04.00 Dave Travers W RSC 4 Glasgow
26.05.00 Tommy Peacock W RSC 5 Glasgow
24.06.00 Lee Williamson W PTS 4 Glasgow
02.10.00 Paul Denton W PTS 6 Glasgow
10.11.00 Mark Ramsey W RSC 4 Glasgow
17.12.00 Ernie Smith W PTS 6 Glasgow
15.02.01 John Humphrey L RSC 4 Glasgow
27.04.01 Michael Smyth W PTS 6 Glasgow
Career: 13 contests, won 11, lost 2.

(Malcolm) Mally McIver

Dewsbury. *Born* Dewsbury, 29 January, 1974
Lightweight. Ht. 5'9"
Manager Self

12.02.00 Arv Mittoo W PTS 4 Sheffield
27.05.00 Paul Philpott W PTS 4 Southwark
09.09.00 David Kirk W PTS 6 Newark
05.02.01 Alan Kershaw W PTS 4 Hull
24.03.01 Steve Hanley W PTS 4 Sheffield
02.06.01 Keith Jones W PTS 6 Wakefield
Career: 6 contests, won 6.

John Mackay (Mukaya)

Coulsden. *Born* Uganda, 20 October, 1981
Featherweight. Ht. 5'6"
Manager T. Bowers

15.06.01 Chris Emanuele L RSC 4 Millwall
Career: 1 contest, lost 1.

Jamie McKeever

Birkenhead. *Born* Birkenhead, 7 July, 1979
S. Featherweight. Ht. 5'6½"
Manager B. Hearn

12.03.98 Dave Hinds W PTS 4 Liverpool
08.04.98 Kid McAuley W RTD 1 Liverpool
06.06.98 Brian Coleman W PTS 4 Liverpool
21.07.98 Stuart Rimmer W PTS 4 Widnes
31.10.98 John T. Kelly L PTS 6 Southend
22.01.99 Garry Burrell W RSC 2 Carlisle
12.03.99 David Kehoe W RSC 2 Bethnal Green
28.05.99 Arv Mittoo W PTS 6 Liverpool
02.10.99 Lee Armstrong DREW 6 Cardiff
27.11.99 Nigel Leake W RSC 2 Liverpool
01.07.00 Gary Flear L PTS 4 Manchester
09.10.00 Marc Callaghan W PTS 6 Liverpool
20.03.01 Craig Docherty L RSC 3 Glasgow
Career: 13 contests, won 9, drew 1, lost 3.

Andy McLean

Newcastle. *Born* Durham, 13 January, 1976
Lightweight. Ht. 5'8"
Manager T. Callighan

17.03.01 Steve Hanley W PTS 4 Manchester
Career: 1 contest, won 1.

Ian McLeod

Kilmarnock. *Born* Edinburgh, 11 June, 1969
Former Undefeated Commonwealth & IBO Inter-Continental S. Featherweight Champion. Ht. 5'9"
Manager T. Gilmour

23.11.92 Robert Braddock DREW 6 Glasgow
29.03.93 Graham McGrath W PTS 6 Glasgow
21.02.94 Graham McGrath W CO 6 Glasgow
04.03.94 Chip O'Neill W RSC 2 Irvine
23.11.94 Chris Jickells W PTS 6 Irvine
05.04.95 Colin Innes W RSC 5 Irvine
22.01.96 Chris Jickells W PTS 8 Glasgow
23.09.96 Robert Braddock W RSC 3 Glasgow
28.02.97 Carl Allen W RTD 3 Kilmarnock
28.04.98 Patrick Gallagher W RSC 7 Belfast
  (Vacant IBO Inter-Continental S. Featherweight Title)
11.12.98 Lee Armstrong W RSC 8 Prestwick
  (IBO Inter-Continental S. Featherweight Title Defence)
19.02.00 Mick O'Malley W RSC 6 Prestwick
  (Commonwealth S. Featherweight Title Challenge)
01.07.00 Affif Djelti L PTS 12 Manchester
  (IBO S.Featherweight Title Challenge)
11.12.00 Michael Gomez L PTS 12 Widnes
  (British S. Featherweight Title Challenge)
Career: 14 contests, won 11, drew 1, lost 2.

Mark McManus (Quirey)

Basildon. *Born* Basildon, 16 April, 1974
Cruiserweight. Ht. 6'0½"
Manager F. Warren/F. Maloney

13.11.00 Jason Brewster W RTD 2 Bethnal Green
27.01.01 Kevin Barrett L RSC 1 Bethnal Green
Career: 2 contests, won 1, lost 1.

Mark McManus　　　　　Les Clark

Brian Magee

Belfast. *Born* Lisburn, 9 June, 1975
IBO Inter-Continental S. Middleweight Champion. Ht. 6'0"
Manager Self

13.03.99 Dean Ashton W RSC 2 Manchester
22.05.99 Richard Glaysher W RSC 1 Belfast
22.06.99 Chris Howarth W RSC 1 Ipswich
13.09.99 Dennis Doyley W RSC 3 Bethnal Green
16.10.99 Michael Pinnock W RSC 3 Belfast
12.02.00 Terry Morrill W RTD 4 Sheffield
21.02.00 Rob Stevenson W RSC 5 Southwark
20.03.00 Darren Ashton W RTD 5 Mansfield
15.04.00 Pedro Carragher W CO 2 Bethnal Green
12.06.00 Jason Barker W PTS 8 Belfast
11.11.00 Teimouraz Kikelidze W RSC 4 Belfast
29.01.01 Neil Linford W PTS 12 Peterborough
  (Vacant IBO Inter-Continental S. Middleweight Title)
Career: 12 contests, won 12.

Eamonn Magee

Belfast. *Born* Belfast, 13 July, 1971
Commonwealth L. Welterweight Champion. Ht. 5'9"
Manager M. O'Callaghan

25.11.95 Pete Roberts W CO 4 Dublin
09.03.96 Steve McGovern W PTS 4 Millstreet
28.05.96 John Stovin W RSC 2 Belfast
03.09.96 Kevin McKillan W RTD 4 Belfast
05.11.96 Shaun Stokes W RSC 2 Belfast
28.01.97 Karl Taylor W PTS 6 Belfast
03.03.97 Troy Townsend W RSC 1 Austin, USA
28.03.97 Teddy Reid L PTS 6 Boston, USA
29.04.97 Peter Nightingale W RTD 2 Belfast
02.06.97 Kevin McKillan W RSC 3 Belfast
  (Elim. All-Ireland L. Welterweight Title)
14.02.98 Dennis Griffin W RSC 2 Southwark
26.09.98 Allan Hall W RSC 7 York
30.11.98 Paul Burke L PTS 12 Manchester
  (Vacant Commonwealth L. Welterweight Title)

117

22.05.99 Alan Temple W CO 3 Belfast
10.07.99 Karl Taylor W RTD 3 Southwark
13.09.99 Paul Burke W RSC 6 Bethnal Green
(Commonwealth L. Welterweight Title Challenge)
16.10.99 Radoslav Gaidev W RSC 1 Belfast
04.03.00 Joseph Miyumo W RSC 1 Peterborough
(Commonwealth L. Welterweight Title Defence)
29.04.00 David Kirk W RSC 8 Wembley
16.09.00 Pavel Melnikov W PTS 8 Bethnal Green
11.11.00 Shea Neary W PTS 12 Belfast
(Commonwealth L. Welterweight Title Defence)
13.03.01 Alan Bosworth W RSC 5 Plymouth

12.05.01 Harrison Methula W RSC 7 Plymouth
(Commonwealth L. Welterweight Title Defence)

Career: 23 contests, won 21, lost 2.

(Jason) Jay Mahoney

Peterborough. *Born* Peterborough, 21 September, 1971
Welterweight. Ht 5'8"
Manager Self

05.12.94 Shaun O'Neill W PTS 6 Houghton le Spring
20.02.95 David Thompson W RSC 4 Manchester
08.03.95 Peter Hickenbottom W PTS 6 Solihull
03.04.95 Blue Butterworth W PTS 6 Manchester

02.10.95 Anthony Maynard L PTS 8 Birmingham
17.12.96 Roger Hunte W RSC 5 Bethnal Green
24.02.97 Chris Barnett W PTS 6 Manchester
02.01.01 Andrzej Butowicz L PTS 4 Coventry
20.01.01 Brett James L PTS 4 Bethnal Green
25.02.01 Gavin Down L RSC 1 Derby
23.06.01 Gary Greenwood W PTS 4 Peterborough

Career: 11 contests, won 7, lost 4.

(Jasim) Jaz Malik

Wandsworth. *Born* Cardiff, 4 April, 1973
L. Welterweight. Ht. 5'11½"
Manager G. Mason

05.03.00 Steve Sharples W RSC 1 Shaw
04.07.00 Dave Travers W PTS 6 Tooting
30.11.00 Jimmy Phelan L RSC 4 Bloomsbury
29.03.01 Darren Melville L RSC 1 Hammersmith

Career: 4 contests, won 2, lost 2.

Shane Mallon

Kingston. *Born* Chertsey, 26 June, 1974
Flyweight. Ht. 5'10"
Manager Self

05.11.96 Colin Moffett L RSC 2 Belfast
02.12.97 Nick Tooley L RSC 1 Windsor
26.02.98 Nicky Booth L RSC 4 Hull
23.04.98 Chris Hicks L PTS 6 Neath
31.10.99 Delroy Spencer L PTS 6 Raynes Park
14.11.99 Paddy Folan L PTS 6 Bradford
06.05.00 Danny Lawson DREW 6 Southwark
12.06.00 Oleg Kiryukin L RSC 2 Belfast
22.10.00 Danny Lawson L PTS 4 Streatham

Career: 9 contests, drew 1, lost 8.

Liam Maltby

Yaxley. *Born* Peterborough, 17 May, 1979
Lightweight. Ht. 5'9¼"
Manager K. Sanders

30.10.98 Dave Travers W PTS 4 Peterborough
30.11.98 Benny Jones L RSC 1 Peterborough
22.02.99 Ernie Smith L PTS 4 Peterborough
20.09.99 Dave Travers W PTS 4 Peterborough
02.12.99 David Kehoe W PTS 4 Peterborough
07.02.00 Dave Hinds W PTS 4 Peterborough
04.03.00 Lee Williamson W PTS 6 Peterborough
25.05.00 Steve Hanley W PTS 4 Peterborough
30.09.00 Marco Fattore W PTS 6 Peterborough
30.11.00 Alan Kershaw W PTS 6 Peterborough
29.01.01 Trevor Smith W PTS 6 Peterborough
26.03.01 Lee Williamson W PTS 6 Peterborough
23.06.01 Jimmy Phelan W RTD 3 Peterborough

Career: 13 contests, won 11, lost 2.

Andy Manning

Sheffield. *Born* Sheffield, 1 June, 1970
L. Heavyweight. Ht. 5'7½"
Manager Self

07.10.91 Mark Hale W PTS 6 Liverpool
04.11.91 Steve Thomas L PTS 6 Merthyr
02.12.91 Marc Rowley W PTS 6 Liverpool
03.03.92 Justin Clements DREW 6 Cradley Heath
18.03.92 Willie Quinn L PTS 6 Glasgow
29.04.92 Adrian Wright W PTS 6 Stoke
11.05.92 Julian Johnson W PTS 6 Llanelli
18.05.92 John Oxenham L PTS 6 Marton

Eamonn Magee   Les Clark

25.01.93	Joe McCluskey L PTS 6 Glasgow	
26.06.97	Paul Bonson W PTS 6 Sheffield	
26.11.97	Johnny Hooks W PTS 6 Sheffield	
08.12.97	Johnny Hooks W PTS 6 Nottingham	
20.09.98	Carl Nicholson W PTS 6 Sheffield	
13.05.00	Jimmy Steel W PTS 4 Barnsley	
25.06.00	Paul Bonson L PTS 10 Wakefield	

(Vacant Central Area L. Heavyweight Title)

25.07.00	Paul Bowen L PTS 4 Southwark	
20.01.01	Mark Baker L PTS 8 Bethnal Green	

Career: 17 contests, won 9, drew 1, lost 7.

Andy Manning   Les Clark

Abdul Mannon

Burnley. *Born* Bangladesh, India, 5 April, 1972
L. Welterweight. Ht. 5'3"
Manager B. Myers

08.03.94	Brian Eccles W RSC 2 Kettering	
17.05.94	Keith Jones W PTS 6 Kettering	
27.10.94	Marty Chestnut L DIS 2 Millwall	
24.01.95	Chris Lyons W PTS 6 Piccadilly	
08.06.95	Brian Carr L PTS 6 Glasgow	
17.06.95	Henry Jones L PTS 6 Cardiff	
14.10.95	Stephen Smith L RSC 3 Munich, Germany	
22.11.95	Des Gargano L PTS 6 Mayfair	
17.12.95	Brian Carr L PTS 8 Glasgow	
05.02.96	Benny May L RSC 4 Bexleyheath	
16.03.96	Mike Deveney L RSC 2 Glasgow	
27.03.01	Dave Travers L PTS 6 Brierley Hill	

Career: 12 contests, won 3, lost 9.

Emmanuel Marcos

Haringey. *Born* Luanda, 13 July, 1976
Welterweight. Ht. 5'4"
Manager Self

06.11.99	John Humphrey L PTS 4 Bethnal Green	
29.01.00	Thomas McDonagh L PTS 4 Manchester	
21.10.00	Isam Khalil L RSC 1 Wembley	

Career: 3 contests, lost 3.

(Patrick) Paddy Martin

Nuneaton. *Born* Birmingham, 6 April, 1974
Welterweight. Ht. 6'0"
Manager J. Griffin

20.05.00	Martin Scotland L RSC 5 Leicester	
09.10.00	Simon Sherrington L RSC 5 Birmingham	
03.12.00	Mark Paxford L RSC 3 Shaw	
18.03.01	Andy Abrol L RSC 3 Shaw	

Career: 4 contests, lost 4.

Paul Martin

Birmingham. *Born* Meriden, 24 April, 1973
Middleweight. Ht. 5'8"
Manager R. Gray/P. Cowdell

28.11.00	Martyn Bailey L PTS 6 Brierley Hill	
03.06.01	Jamie Logan W PTS 6 Hanley	

Career: 2 contests, won 1, lost 1.

Paul Maskell

Canning Town. *Born* Plaistow, 2 November, 1972
Cruiserweight. Ht. 6'3"
Manager M. Brennan

20.12.99	Rob Galloway W RSC 1 Bethnal Green	
05.02.00	Paul Bonson W PTS 4 Bethnal Green	
01.04.00	Nigel Rafferty W PTS 4 Bethnal Green	
29.09.00	Mark Williams L RSC 2 Bethnal Green	

Career: 4 contests, won 3, lost 1.

Paul Maskell   Les Clark

Alex Mason

Wolverhampton. *Born* Wolverhampton, 27 February, 1975
Former Undefeated Midlands Area S. Middleweight Champion. Ht. 5'11"
Manager Self

09.12.96	Carlton Williams L PTS 6 Leicester	
16.01.97	Lee Simpkin W PTS 6 Solihull	
29.01.97	Chris Pollock W RSC 5 Stoke	
07.03.97	Mark Sawyers W PTS 6 Weston super Mare	

20.03.97	Carlton Williams W PTS 6 Solihull	
15.04.97	Mike Thompson W RSC 2 Edgbaston	
23.08.97	Patrick Rubes L PTS 6 Playas las Americas, Tenerife	
08.10.97	Prince Kasi Kaihau DREW 6 Stoke	
11.11.97	Phil Epton W RSC 2 Edgbaston	
03.12.97	Paul Bonson DREW 6 Stoke	
15.01.98	Paul Bonson W PTS 6 Solihull	
24.02.98	Simon Andrews W PTS 6 Edgbaston	
26.03.98	Phil Ball W PTS 6 Solihull	
21.05.98	Peter Waudby DREW 8 Solihull	
24.09.98	Simon Andrews W PTS 8 Edgbaston	
13.10.98	Peter Waudby W PTS 8 Wolverhampton	
26.11.98	Phil Epton W PTS 6 Edgbaston	
11.02.99	Darren Ashton L PTS 10 Dudley	

(Vacant Midlands Area L. Heavyweight Title)

22.04.99	Dean Ashton W PTS 10 Dudley	

(Vacant Midlands Area S. Middleweight Title)

21.09.99	Kid Dongo L RSC 12 Santa de la Cruz, Tenerife	

(WBA Continental Euro-African L. Heavyweight Title Challenge)

24.02.00	Martin Jolley W PTS 10 Edgbaston	

(Midlands Area S. Middleweight Title Defence)

17.04.00	Clint Johnson W PTS 6 Birmingham	
24.11.00	Paul Bonson W PTS 6 Darlington	
09.12.00	David Starie L CO 3 Southwark	

(British S. Middleweight Title Challenge)

Career: 24 contests, won 16, drew 3, lost 5.

(Nicholas) Miguel Matthews

Ystalfera. *Born* Glanamman, 22 December, 1965
Featherweight. Ht. 5'7"
Manager Self

21.09.88	Terry Collins L PTS 6 Basildon	
28.09.88	Eugene Maloney DREW 6 Edmonton	
25.10.88	Hugh Ruse L PTS 6 Pontadawe	
15.11.88	Tommy Bernard W RSC 2 Chigwell	
14.12.88	Richie Wenton L CO 2 Kirkby	
14.02.89	Brian Robb W RSC 2 Wolverhampton	
06.03.89	Mickey Markie L PTS 8 Northampton	
21.03.89	Ronnie Stephenson DREW 6 Wolverhampton	
11.04.89	Hugh Ruse W PTS 6 Aberavon	
05.06.89	Lester James DREW 6 Birmingham	
12.06.89	Colin McMillan L RSC 3 Battersea	
06.09.89	Marcel Herbert L PTS 6 Aberavon	
20.09.89	Des Gargano L PTS 6 Stoke	
28.09.89	Steve Walker L PTS 6 Cardiff	
17.10.89	Alan Roberts W PTS 6 Cardiff	
24.10.89	Jimmy Clark L PTS 6 Watford	
06.11.89	Mickey Markie DREW 8 Northampton	
03.12.89	Johnny Bredahl L PTS 6 Copenhagen, Denmark	
19.02.90	Mickey Markie L PTS 8 Kettering	
27.02.90	Pete Buckley DREW 6 Evesham	
21.03.90	Rocky Lawlor L PTS 8 Solihull	
03.09.90	Derek Amory L PTS 6 Dudley	
01.10.90	Pete Buckley L PTS 8 Cleethorpes	
09.10.90	Pete Buckley W PTS 8 Wolverhampton	
29.10.90	Pete Buckley L PTS 6 Birmingham	
21.11.90	Jason Primera L PTS 8 Solihull	
12.12.90	Paul Harvey L PTS 6 Basildon	
19.12.90	Paul Forrest L PTS 6 Preston	
07.03.91	Bradley Stone L RSC 4 Basildon	
04.04.91	Mark Tierney L PTS 6 Watford	

16.04.91	Craig Dermody L PTS 6 Nottingham
25.04.91	Bradley Stone L PTS 6 Basildon
23.05.91	Jason Lepre L PTS 6 Southampton
31.05.91	Danny Connelly L PTS 8 Glasgow
13.06.91	Tony Silkstone L PTS 6 Hull
24.06.91	Jimmy Owens L PTS 6 Liverpool
09.09.91	Moussa Sangare L RSC 5 Forges les Eux, France
09.10.91	Mark Loftus DREW 6 Manchester
24.10.91	Kevin Middleton L PTS 6 Dunstable
31.10.91	Brian Robb DREW 6 Oakengates
11.11.91	Peter Judson L PTS 6 Stratford on Avon
21.11.91	Craig Dermody L PTS 6 Burton
28.11.91	Dave Hardie L PTS 6 Glasgow
11.12.91	Jimmy Clark L PTS 6 Basildon
08.01.92	Ceri Farrell W PTS 6 Burton
31.01.92	John Green DREW 6 Manchester
20.02.92	Edward Cook L PTS 6 Glasgow
27.02.92	Craig Dermody L PTS 6 Liverpool
25.03.92	John Armour L PTS 6 Dagenham
01.06.92	Danny Porter L PTS 6 Glasgow
07.07.92	Tony Falcone L PTS 6 Bristol
14.07.92	Prince Naseem Hamed L RSC 3 Mayfair
30.09.92	Jonjo Irwin L PTS 6 Solihull
17.10.92	Mark Bowers L PTS 6 Wembley
24.11.92	Kid McAuley L PTS 6 Doncaster
14.12.92	Barry Jones L PTS 6 Cardiff
30.01.93	Tim Yeates L PTS 6 Brentwood
27.02.93	Paul Lloyd L PTS 6 Ellesmere Port
18.03.93	Kevin Middleton L PTS 6 Lewisham
17.04.93	Fabian Zavattini L PTS 6 Lausanne, Switzerland
05.05.93	Conn McMullen DREW 6 Belfast
15.05.93	Dave McHale L RSC 4 Glasgow
10.07.93	Russell Rees L PTS 6 Cardiff
22.09.93	Marcus McCrae L PTS 6 Bethnal Green
06.10.93	Mark Geraghty L PTS 6 Glasgow
30.10.93	Gary Thornhill L PTS 6 Chester
22.11.93	Ian McGirr L PTS 6 Glasgow
29.11.93	Tim Yeates DREW 6 Ingatestone
18.12.93	John White L PTS 6 Manchester
14.01.94	Kevin Middleton L PTS 6 Bethnal Green
28.01.94	Frederic Perez L PTS 8 Sete, France
10.04.94	Mark Geraghty L PTS 8 Glasgow
25.04.94	Hugh Collins L PTS 8 Glasgow
22.05.94	Mike Anthony Brown W RSC 5 Crystal Palace
06.06.94	Russell Davison W PTS 6 Glasgow
21.07.94	Mike Anthony Brown L PTS 6 Battersea
20.09.94	Drew Docherty L PTS 8 Musselburgh
17.02.95	Michael Alldis L PTS 8 Crawley
06.03.95	Michael Armstrong L PTS 6 Mayfair
09.06.95	Moussa Sangare L CO 2 Grande Synthe, France
29.09.95	Paul Ingle L RSC 4 Bethnal Green
29.11.95	Chris Jickells W PTS 6 Solihull
06.12.95	Gary Marston L PTS 8 Stoke
18.12.95	Graham McGrath W PTS 8 Mayfair
24.01.96	Gary Marston W PTS 8 Stoke
13.02.96	Dean Amory L PTS 8 Wolverhampton
21.02.96	Terry Whittaker L PTS 6 Batley
06.03.96	Fred Reeve W PTS 6 Solihull
24.04.96	Gary Marston L PTS 8 Solihull
04.05.96	Richard Evatt L PTS 6 Dagenham
14.05.96	Patrick Mullings L PTS 6 Dagenham
25.06.96	Paul Griffin L PTS 6 Mansfield
03.09.96	Paul Ireland L PTS 6 Belfast
14.09.96	Dean Pithie L PTS 4 Sheffield
28.09.96	Frederic Perez L PTS 8 Barking

15.10.96	Elvis Parsley L PTS 8 Wolverhampton
09.11.96	Michael Brodie L PTS 6 Manchester
21.11.96	Carl Allen L PTS 8 Solihull
04.12.96	Elvis Parsley L PTS 6 Stoke
14.12.96	Paul Griffin L PTS 4 Sheffield
25.03.97	David Kirk L PTS 6 Wolverhampton
12.05.97	Kelton McKenzie L PTS 6 Leicester
21.05.97	Alex Moon DREW 4 Liverpool
26.09.97	Graham McGrath W PTS 6 Port Talbot
04.10.97	Scott Harrison W RSC 4 Muswell Hill
13.10.98	Chris Lyons W PTS 6 Wolverhampton
24.09.99	Chris Williams L PTS 10 Merthyr
	(Vacant Welsh S. Featherweight title)
27.10.99	Pete Buckley L PTS 8 Birmingham
14.12.99	Christophe du Busillet L PTS 6 Telde, Gran Canaria
11.12.00	Dave Hinds L PTS 6 Birmingham

Career: 110 contests, won 15, drew 11, lost 84.

Tommy Matthews

Bewdley. *Born* Solihull, 27 March, 1981
L. Heavyweight. Ht. 6'0"
Manager D. Gardiner

12.12.00	Mark Phillips L PTS 6 Clydach
29.01.01	Hughie Doherty L PTS 4 Peterborough
17.02.01	Allan Foster L PTS 4 Bethnal Green
28.02.01	Elvis Michailenko L PTS 4 Kensington
09.03.01	Elvis Michailenko L PTS 4 Millwall
18.03.01	Lee Woodruff L RSC 2 Shaw

Career: 6 contests, lost 6.

(Patrick) P.J. Maxwell (Drinkwater)

Sheffield. *Born* USA, 20 March, 1979
L. Middleweight. Ht. 5'8"
Manager F. Warren

17.03.98	Danny Thornton W PTS 6 Sheffield
12.08.00	Matthew Ashmole W RSC 3 Wembley
26.03.01	Jason Collins L PTS 4 Wembley

Career: 3 contests, won 2, lost 1.

P.J. Maxwell   Harry Goodwin

Anthony Maynard

Birmingham. *Born* Birmingham, 12
January, 1972
Midlands Area Lightweight Champion.
Ht. 5'8"
Manager Self

17.10.94	Malcolm Thomas W PTS 6 Birmingham
02.11.94	Dean Phillips W PTS 6 Birmingham
25.01.95	Neil Smith L PTS 6 Stoke
07.02.95	Anthony Campbell W PTS 8 Wolverhampton
08.03.95	Scott Walker W PTS 6 Solihull
28.03.95	Kid McAuley W PTS 8 Wolverhampton
11.05.95	Gary Hiscox W RSC 4 Dudley
06.06.95	Richard Swallow L RSC 2 Leicester
02.10.95	Jay Mahoney W PTS 8 Birmingham
26.10.95	Ray Newby W PTS 8 Birmingham
17.01.96	Tom Welsh W RSC 8 Solihull
06.03.96	G. G. Goddard W RSC 3 Solihull
20.03.97	Richard Swallow W PTS 6 Solihull
24.10.97	Brian Coleman W CO 1 Birmingham
27.03.98	Gary Flear W RSC 9 Telford
	(Vacant Midlands Area Lightweight Title)
30.05.98	Michael Ayers W PTS 8 Bristol
21.11.98	Stephen Smith L PTS 10 Southwark
27.11.00	David Kehoe W RSC 5 Birmingham
07.04.01	Alfred Kotey L RTD 6 Wembley
	(Vacant WBF Inter-Continental Lightweight Title)
11.06.01	Woody Greenaway W PTS 4 Nottingham

Career: 20 contests, won 16, lost 4.

Lee Meager

Salford. *Born* Salford, 18 January, 1978
S. Featherweight. Ht. 5'8"
Manager M. Roe

16.09.00	Pete Buckley W PTS 4 Bethnal Green
14.10.00	Chris Jickells W PTS 4 Wembley
18.11.00	Billy Smith W RSC 1 Dagenham
09.12.00	Jason Nesbitt W RSC 2 Southwark
05.02.01	Carl Allen DREW 6 Hull
13.03.01	Lennie Hodgkins W RSC 3 Plymouth
12.05.01	Jason White W PTS 4 Plymouth

Career: 7 contests, won 6, drew 1.

Lee Meager   Les Clark

Delroy Mellis

Brixton. *Born* Jamaica, 7 January, 1971
Southern Area L. Middleweight Champion.
Ht. 5'8"
Manager B. Baker

27.02.98	Pat Larner L PTS 4 Brighton	
16.04.98	Sonny Thind L RTD 5 Mayfair	
09.06.98	Darren Christie L PTS 4 Hull	
10.09.98	Paul Miles W RSC 3 Acton	
03.10.98	Wayne Asker L PTS 6 Crawley	
06.11.98	Darren Bruce L RTD 3 Mayfair	
21.01.99	Darren Christie L PTS 6 Piccadilly	
04.02.99	Sergei Dzindziruk L RSC 3 Lewisham	
24.03.99	Martyn Thomas W RSC 3 Bayswater	
20.05.99	Daniel James L PTS 4 Barking	
02.07.99	Jason Williams L PTS 6 Bristol	
30.09.99	Steve Brumant L PTS 6 Kensington	
16.10.99	Jacek Bielski L PTS 6 Bethnal Green	
18.11.99	Dennis Griffin W RSC 5 Mayfair	
29.11.99	George Scott L PTS 6 Wembley	
20.03.00	Lance Crosby L PTS 4 Mansfield	
01.04.00	Paul Knights W RSC 3 Bethnal Green	
15.05.00	Christian Brady W RSC 6 Birmingham	
01.07.00	Cham Joof DREW 6 Southwark	
22.07.00	Alan Gilbert W RSC 3 Watford	
	(Vacant Southern Area L.Middleweight Title)	
22.10.00	Allan Gray W RSC 6 Streatham	
	(Southern Area L.Middleweight Title Defence)	
23.01.01	Alan Gilbert W RSC 3 Crawley	
	(Southern Area L. Middleweight Title Defence)	
20.04.01	Chris Nembhard W RSC 8 Millwall	
	(Southern Area L. Middleweight Title Defence)	

Career: 23 contests, won 9, drew 1, lost 13.

Darren Melville

Canning Town. *Born* Tobago, 13
September, 1975
Lightweight. Ht. 5'8"
Manager T. Bowers

29.09.00	Lee Williamson W RSC 4 Bethnal Green	
10.11.00	Jason McElligott W RSC 2 Mayfair	
23.02.01	Keith Jones W PTS 4 Barking	
09.03.01	Billy Smith W PTS 4 Millwall	
29.03.01	Jaz Malik W RSC 1 Hammersmith	
20.04.01	Marcus Portman W RSC 3 Millwall	
15.06.01	Isaac Sebaduka W PTS 6 Millwall	

Career: 7 contests, won 7.

Malcolm Melvin

Birmingham. *Born* Birmingham, 5
February, 1967
Former Undefeated All-Ireland & Midlands
Area L. Welterweight Champion. Ht. 5'7"
Manager Self

28.11.85	Steve Foster DREW 6 Ilkeston	
04.12.85	Simon Collins L PTS 6 Stoke	
24.03.86	Rocky McGran L PTS 6 Mayfair	
10.04.86	Lincoln Pennant W PTS 6 Leicester	
21.04.86	Malcolm Davies W PTS 6 Birmingham	
07.05.86	Julian Monville W PTS 6 Solihull	
19.01.88	Antonio Fernandez L RSC 4 Kings Heath	
07.03.88	John Ellis L PTS 6 Piccadilly	
03.12.89	Dave Jenkins W PTS 6 Birmingham	
05.02.90	Trevor Meikle W PTS 6 Brierley Hill	

22.02.90	Chris Saunders L PTS 4 Hull	
19.03.90	Barry North W PTS 6 Brierley Hill	
30.04.90	Andy Kent W RSC 5 Brierley Hill	
04.06.90	Brendan Ryan L RSC 7 Edgbaston	
03.09.90	Dave Jenkins W PTS 8 Dudley	
13.11.90	Brendan Ryan W RSC 10 Edgbaston	
	(Vacant Midlands Area L. Welterweight Title)	
18.03.91	Carl Brasier W PTS 6 Piccadilly	
17.06.91	Dean Bramhald W PTS 6 Edgbaston	
21.05.92	Mark Kelly W PTS 8 Cradley Heath	
05.10.92	Ross Hale L PTS 10 Bristol	
	(Elim. British L. Welterweight Title)	
17.11.92	Tusikoleta Nkalankete DREW 8 Paris, France	
16.03.93	Shaun Cogan W PTS 10 Edgbaston	
	(Vacant All-Ireland L. Welterweight Title & Midlands Area L. Welterweight Title Defence)	
29.06.93	Mark Kelly W PTS 6 Edgbaston	
24.11.93	Alan Peacock W PTS 8 Solihull	
08.03.94	Julian Eavis W PTS 6 Edgbaston	
28.06.94	John Smith W PTS 6 Edgbaston	
18.02.95	Ross Hale L PTS 12 Shepton Mallet	
	(British & Commonwealth L. Welterweight Title Challenges)	
21.05.96	Karl Taylor W PTS 10 Edgbaston	
	(Midlands Area L. Welterweight Title Defence)	
03.06.96	Jamie Morris W RSC 2 Birmingham	
09.06.97	Jimmy Phelan W RSC 2 Birmingham	
30.09.97	Wayne Windle W PTS 6 Edgbaston	
24.02.98	Ray Newby W PTS 6 Edgbaston	
12.10.98	David Kirk W PTS 10 Birmingham	
	(Midlands Area L. Welterweight Title Defence)	
13.02.99	Junior Witter L RSC 2 Newcastle	
	(Vacant WBF L. Welterweight Title)	
06.12.99	Harry Butler W PTS 8 Birmingham	
13.03.00	Peter Nightingale W PTS 6 Birmingham	
14.10.00	Harry Dhami L PTS 12 Wembley	
	(British Welterweight Title Challenge)	

Career: 37 contests, won 25, drew 2, lost 10.

Ankar Miah   Les Clark

Ankar Miah

Covent Garden. *Born* Bangladesh, India, 11
September, 1975
Flyweight. Ht. 5'0"
Manager A. Urry

04.07.00	Delroy Spencer L RSC 3 Tooting	
16.03.01	Gwyn Evans L PTS 6 Portsmouth	

Career: 2 contests, lost 2.

(Elviss) Elvis Michailenko

Canning Town. *Born* Jormala, Latvia, 13
September, 1976
WBF European L. Heavyweight Champion.
Ht. 5'11½"
Manager A. Bowers

18.05.00	Adam Cale W PTS 4 Bethnal Green	
21.09.00	Shpetim Hoti W PTS 4 Bloomsbury	
09.10.00	Tony Dodson DREW 6 Liverpool	
02.11.00	Freddie Yemofio W PTS 6 Kensington	
28.02.01	Tommy Matthews W PTS 4 Kensington	
09.03.01	Tommy Matthews W PTS 4 Millwall	
20.04.01	Dean Ashton W RSC 4 Millwall	
16.06.01	Sven Hamer W RSC 6 Wembley	
	(Vacant WBF European L. Heavyweight Title)	

Career: 8 contests, won 7, drew 1.

Elvis Michailenko   Les Clark

Scott Millar

Ayr. *Born* Irvine, 30 November, 1976
Welterweight. Ht. 6'0"
Manager T. Gilmour

21.02.00	William Webster W PTS 6 Glasgow	
03.03.00	David Smales DREW 6 Irvine	
06.06.00	Adrian Kirkbride W RSC 2 Motherwell	
23.02.01	Robert Burton L CO 5 Irvine	

Career: 4 contests, won 2, drew 1, lost 1.

Joe Miller

Stirling. *Born* Stirling, 22 July, 1974
L. Middleweight. Ht. 5'10"
Manager T. Gilmour

20.03.00	Gavin Pearson W PTS 6 Glasgow	
18.09.00	Peter Dunn W PTS 6 Glasgow	

Career: 2 contests, won 2.

Scott Miller

Hull. *Born* Hull, 27 July, 1979
Lightweight. Ht. 5'5"
Manager F. Maloney

16.12.00 Jason White W PTS 4 Sheffield
10.02.01 Steve Hanley W RSC 3 Widnes
Career: 2 contests, won 2.

(Alvin) Slick Miller

Doncaster. *Born* Doncaster, 12 May, 1968
Heavyweight. Ht. 6'2"
Manager J. Rushton

28.04.94 Declan Faherty L RSC 2 Hull
06.10.94 Kent Davis L PTS 6 Hull
17.11.94 Graham Wassell L RSC 1 Sheffield
29.09.95 Mark Richardson L PTS 6 Hartlepool
13.01.96 Geoff Hunter DREW 6 Halifax
13.02.96 Danny Williams L RSC 1 Bethnal
         Green
15.03.96 Tony Booth L PTS 6 Hull
22.03.96 Tony Dowling L RSC 4 Mansfield
26.09.96 Steve Pettit L PTS 6 Walsall
22.11.96 Tony Booth L RSC 5 Hull
17.03.97 Michael Sprott L CO 1 Mayfair
25.04.97 Pele Lawrence L PTS 6 Mere
16.05.97 Edwin Cleary DREW 6 Hull
20.10.97 Neil Simpson L RTD 1 Leicester
16.04.98 Kevin Mitchell L RSC 2 Mayfair
08.06.98 Stevie Pettit W CO 1 Birmingham
30.11.98 Neil Simpson L CO 3 Leicester
23.01.99 Faisal Mohammed L RSC 2 Cheshunt
25.03.99 Nigel Rafferty L PTS 8 Edgbaston
17.04.99 Ahmet Oner L RSC 1 Dublin
24.10.99 Nigel Rafferty W RSC 4
         Wolverhampton
25.03.00 Brian Kilbride W RSC 1 Liverpool
09.04.00 Mark Krence L PTS 6 Alfreton
11.06.00 Glenn Williams L PTS 4 Salford
08.07.00 Tony Dowling W PTS 4 Widnes
23.09.00 John McDermott L RSC 1 Bethnal
         Green
03.02.01 Scott Baker W RSC 4 Brighton
18.02.01 Hughie Robertson W RSC 2 Southwark
25.02.01 Colin Kenna L RSC 3 Streatham
05.05.01 Danny Percival W CO 1 Edmonton
Career: 30 contests, won 6, drew 2, lost 22.

Gordon Minors

Chester. *Born* Enfield, 20 March, 1967
Heavyweight. Ht. 6'2"
Manager J. Davies

14.10.98 Shane MacLaren W RSC 1 Blackpool
29.10.98 Paul Fiske W RSC 3 Newcastle
12.12.98 Willie Clyde W RSC 1 Chester
21.01.99 Karl Andrews W PTS 1 Piccadilly
04.02.99 Keith Long L PTS 6 Lewisham
22.05.99 Danny Watts W CO 1 Belfast
30.09.00 Luke Simpkin DREW 4 Peterborough
23.11.00 Jacklord Jacobs L RSC 4 Bayswater
         *(Vacant British Masters Heavyweight
         Title)*
30.06.01 Tomasz Bonin L RSC 4 Tarnow,
         Poland
Career: 9 contests, won 5, drew 1, lost 3.

Ross Minter

Crawley. *Born* Crawley, 10 November, 1978
Welterweight. Ht. 5'7³/₄"
Manager F. Warren/F. Maloney

26.03.01 Brian Coleman W PTS 4 Wembley
05.05.01 Trevor Smith W RTD 3 Edmonton
Career: 2 contests, won 2.

Peter Mitchell

Southampton. *Born* Southampton, 26 May,
1967
S. Middleweight. Ht. 5'10½"
Manager Self

21.09.94 Paul Matthews W PTS 6 Cardiff
12.10.94 Andy Ewen L PTS 6 Sheffield
08.03.95 Paul Webb W RSC 1 Bloomsbury
19.04.95 Nicky Thurbin L PTS 6 Bethnal Green
02.06.95 Danny Ryan L PTS 6 Bethnal Green
13.11.95 Barrie Bessant W RSC 2 Barnstaple
04.12.95 Darren Sweeney L PTS 8 Birmingham
09.03.96 Jim Rock L PTS 6 Millstreet
03.06.96 Gordon Behan DREW 6 Birmingham
21.01.97 Darren Dorrington L RSC 5 Bristol
07.03.97 Peter Vosper W PTS 8 Weston super
         Mare
24.03.97 Darren Dorrington L RSC 7 Bristol
29.04.97 Danny Ryan DREW 6 Belfast
30.08.97 Steve Roberts L PTS 6 Cheshunt
27.02.98 Paul Carr W PTS 6 Brighton
17.09.98 Dean Ashton W PTS 6 Brighton
03.10.98 Jason Barker L RSC 2 Crawley
06.10.00 Scott Dann L RSC 3 Maidstone
01.12.00 Steven Bendall L PTS 8 Peterborough
Career: 19 contests, won 6, drew 2, lost 11.

(Arvill) Arv Mittoo

Birmingham. *Born* Birmingham, 8 July,
1971
Welterweight. Ht. 5'8"
Manager Self

31.01.96 Alan Bosworth L PTS 6 Stoke
13.02.96 Tommy Janes L PTS 6 Cardiff
21.02.96 Danny Lutaaya L PTS 6 Piccadilly
20.05.96 Terry Whittaker L CO 5 Cleethorpes
29.06.96 Craig Stanley L PTS 4 Erith
23.09.96 Thomas Bradley DREW 6 Cleethorpes
03.10.96 John T. Kelly L PTS 6 Sunderland
01.11.96 David Kirk L PTS 6 Mansfield
14.11.96 Thomas Bradley L RSC 4 Sheffield
22.05.97 Craig Stanley W RSC 3 Southwark
02.09.97 Trevor Tacy L PTS 6 Manchester
22.09.97 Steve Conway L PTS 6 Cleethorpes
09.10.97 Steve Conway L PTS 6 Leeds
23.10.97 Marco Fattore L PTS 6 Mayfair
11.11.97 Kevin McCarthy L PTS 6 Bethnal
         Green
03.12.97 Marc Smith W PTS 6 Stoke
31.01.98 Harry Andrews L PTS 4 Edmonton
06.03.98 Gavin McGill W PTS 6 Hull
18.03.98 Marc Smith W PTS 6 Stoke
26.03.98 Danny Lutaaya DREW 6 Piccadilly
11.04.98 Charlie Rumbol L PTS 4 Southwark
21.04.98 Adam Spelling W PTS 4 Edmonton
02.10.98 Sammy Smith L PTS 4 Cheshunt
16.10.98 Mark Haslam L PTS 6 Salford
25.11.98 Brian Coleman L PTS 6 Clydach
27.01.99 Ernie Smith DREW 6 Stoke
26.02.99 Mark Payne L PTS 4 Coventry
17.03.99 Marc Smith L PTS 6 Stoke
20.05.99 John Humphrey L PTS 6 Barking
28.05.99 Jamie McKeever L PTS 6 Liverpool
04.06.99 Oscar Hall L PTS 6 Hull
02.07.99 Wahid Fats L PTS 6 Manchester
21.07.99 Brian Gentry L RSC 4 Bloomsbury
20.10.99 Steve Saville L PTS 8 Stoke

31.10.99 Ross McCord L PTS 6 Raynes Park
15.11.99 Lee Sharp L PTS 6 Glasgow
22.11.99 Mohamed Helel L PTS 6 Piccadilly
29.11.99 Peter Swinney L PTS 4 Wembley
11.12.99 Thomas McDonagh L RSC 2 Liverpool
12.02.00 Mally McIver L PTS 4 Sheffield
10.03.00 Jason Hall W RSC 3 Bethnal Green
08.04.00 Junior Witter L PTS 4 Bethnal Green
17.04.00 Gavin Pearson L PTS 6 Glasgow
13.05.00 Chris Steele W RSC 3 Barnsley
21.05.00 Gavin Down L PTS 6 Derby
06.06.00 Casey Brooke W PTS 6 Brierley Hill
15.07.00 Steve Conway L PTS 6 Norwich
30.09.00 Mark Florian L PTS 4 Peterborough
07.10.00 Jesse James Daniel L PTS 4 Doncaster
16.11.00 Lance Crosby L RSC 3 Hull
28.01.01 Stuart Elwell L PTS 6 Wolverhampton
19.02.01 Lee Sharp L PTS 6 Glasgow
26.02.01 Gavin Wake L PTS 4 Nottingham
24.03.01 Richard Holden L PTS 6 Newark
01.04.01 Babatunde Ajayi L PTS 6 Southwark
20.04.01 Manzo Smith L PTS 4 Millwall
08.05.01 Robert Burton L PTS 4 Barnsley
04.06.01 Gary Porter L PTS 6 Glasgow
16.06.01 Gavin Down L PTS 6 Derby
Career: 59 contests, won 9, drew 3, lost 47.

Colin Moffett

Belfast. *Born* Belfast, 15 April, 1975
Flyweight. Ht. 5'6"
Manager B. Hearn

05.11.96 Shane Mallon W RSC 2 Belfast
28.01.97 Anthony Hanna W PTS 4 Belfast
29.04.97 Gary Hickman W PTS 4 Belfast
02.06.97 Jason Thomas L RSC 3 Belfast
20.12.97 Graham McGrath DREW 4 Belfast
18.09.98 Anthony Hanna DREW 4 Belfast
28.11.98 Shaun Norman W PTS 4 Belfast
31.07.99 Waj Khan W CO 1 Carlisle
16.10.99 Delroy Spencer L PTS 4 Bethnal Green
05.06.00 Keith Knox L RSC 3 Glasgow
02.12.00 Dale Robinson L PTS 4 Bethnal Green
Career: 11 contests, won 5, drew 2, lost 4.

Faisal Mohammed

Kilburn. *Born* Ghana, 16 March, 1974
Cruiserweight. Ht. 6'1¹/₂"
Manager Self

26.09.98 Mark Williams W RSC 2 Norwich
31.10.98 Adam Cale W RSC 2 Basingstoke
23.01.99 Slick Miller W RSC 2 Cheshunt
02.06.00 Nigel Rafferty W PTS 4 Ashford
18.11.00 Nigel Rafferty W RSC 3 Dagenham
20.01.01 Mark Williams W RSC 3 Bethnal
         Green
17.02.01 Darren Ashton W RSC 1 Bethnal
         Green
Career: 7 contests, won 7.

Lee Molloy

Liverpool. *Born* Liverpool, 20 July, 1974
Middleweight. Ht. 6'1¹/₄"
Manager B. Hearn

03.12.98 Wayne Shepherd W PTS 4 Mayfair
03.04.99 Adrian Kirkbride W PTS 4 Carlisle
28.05.99 Shaun O'Neill W PTS 4 Liverpool
27.11.99 Martyn Bailey W RSC 2 Liverpool
25.03.00 Danny Thornton L RSC 2 Liverpool
09.10.00 Martin Jolley W PTS 4 Liverpool
26.05.01 Hussain Osman L RSC 1 Bethnal Green
Career: 7 contests, won 5, lost 2.

Lee Molloy　　　　　Les Clark

Lee Molyneux

Liverpool. *Born* Liverpool, 19 April, 1970
Welterweight. Ht. 5'9¾"
Manager T. Miller

13.10.96	C. J. Jackson W PTS 6 Shaw
04.12.96	Gary Hiscox L PTS 6 Stoke
20.03.97	Junior Witter L RSC 6 Salford
03.05.97	Anthony Farnell L PTS 4 Manchester
08.10.97	Andy Peach W PTS 6 Stoke
11.11.97	Dean Bramhald DREW 6 Edgbaston
30.11.97	Dean Nicholas L PTS 6 Shaw
14.12.97	Frank O'Connor W RSC 3 Glasgow
03.02.98	Shaun O'Neill DREW 6 Yarm
12.03.98	Kevin McKillan L PTS 4 Liverpool
23.03.98	Jan Cree DREW 6 Glasgow
06.06.98	Nigel Bradley DREW 4 Liverpool
18.07.98	Anthony Farnell L CO 3 Sheffield
13.11.98	Scott Dixon L PTS 4 Brighton
01.12.98	John Green L RSC 1 Yarm
27.02.99	Oscar Hall L PTS 4 Oldham
27.03.99	Gavin Down L PTS 4 Derby
27.06.99	Gavin Down L PTS 6 Alfreton
04.09.99	Jyri Kjaell L PTS 6 Bethnal Green
09.10.99	Thomas McDonagh L PTS 4 Manchester
28.10.99	Shaun Horsfall L PTS 6 Burnley
06.11.99	Thomas McDonagh L PTS 4 Widnes
26.11.99	Marcus Walters L PTS 6 Bayswater
11.12.99	Michael Jennings L PTS 4 Liverpool
18.02.00	Peter Nightingale L PTS 6 West Bromwich
29.02.00	Michael Jennings L PTS 6 Widnes
25.03.00	Thomas McDonagh L PTS 6 Liverpool
14.04.00	Gary Reid L PTS 6 Manchester
18.05.00	John Humphrey L PTS 6 Bethnal Green
25.05.00	Brian Coleman W PTS 6 Peterborough
01.07.00	Marcus Walters L PTS 6 Southwark
13.08.00	Oscar Hall L PTS 6 Nottingham
16.09.00	Mickey Yikealo W RSC 2 Bethnal Green

Career: 33 contests, won 5, drew 4, lost 24.

(Elton) Tony Montana (Gashi)

Sheffield. *Born* Yugoslavia, 5 August, 1982
L. Welterweight. Ht. 5'8"
Manager B. Ingle

24.11.00	Dave Gibson W PTS 6 Hull
03.12.00	Gary Greenwood DREW 6 Shaw
31.01.01	Pete Buckley W PTS 6 Piccadilly
13.02.01	Barrie Kelley L PTS 6 Brierley Hill
06.03.01	Chris Price W PTS 6 Yarm
18.03.01	Ray Wood DREW 6 Shaw
26.03.01	Francis Barrett L PTS 4 Wembley
24.05.01	Ajose Olusegun L RSC 1 Kensington

Career: 8 contests, won 3, drew 2, lost 3.

Alex Moon　　　　　Les Clark

Alex Moon

Liverpool. *Born* Fazackerley, 17 November, 1971
Commonwealth S. Featherweight Champion. Former Undefeated WBU Inter-Continental Featherweight Champion. Ht. 5'7½"
Manager T. Gilmour

08.09.95	Marty Chestnut W RSC 3 Liverpool
24.11.95	G. G. Goddard L RTD 2 Chester
03.02.96	Chris Price W RSC 2 Liverpool
06.09.96	Jason Squire W PTS 4 Liverpool
26.10.96	Kelton McKenzie W RSC 3 Liverpool
03.12.96	Keith Jones W RTD 5 Liverpool
01.03.97	David Jeffrey W RSC 2 Liverpool
21.05.97	Miguel Matthews DREW 4 Liverpool
26.09.97	Bamana Dibateza W PTS 6 Liverpool
28.11.97	Elvis Parsley DREW 6 Bethnal Green
12.03.98	Deva Reymond W PTS 8 Liverpool
08.04.98	Stefy Bull W RSC 3 Liverpool
21.07.98	Georghe Parashiv W PTS 8 Widnes
24.10.98	Khayelethu Booi W PTS 12 Liverpool *(Vacant WBU Inter-Continental Featherweight Title)*
13.02.99	Jonjo Irwin L PTS 12 Newcastle *(British Featherweight Title Challenge)*
15.05.99	Jason Thomas W PTS 8 Blackpool
29.02.00	Craig Spacie L PTS 6 Widnes

25.03.00	Keith Jones W PTS 6 Liverpool
19.02.01	Anthony Hanna W PTS 6 Glasgow
20.03.01	Charles Shepherd W PTS 12 Glasgow *(Vacant Commonwealth S. Featherweight Title)*
24.04.01	Karim Nashar W PTS 12 Liverpool *(Commonwealth S. Featherweight Title Defence)*

Career: 21 contests, won 16, drew 2, lost 3.

Jamie Moore

Salford. *Born* Salford, 4 November, 1978
Welterweight. Ht. 5'8"
Manager S. Foster/S. Wood

09.10.99	Clive Johnson W RSC 3 Manchester
13.11.99	Peter Nightingale W PTS 4 Hull
19.12.99	Paul King W PTS 6 Salford
29.02.00	David Baptiste W RSC 3 Manchester
20.03.00	Harry Butler W RSC 2 Mansfield
14.04.00	Jimmy Steel W PTS 6 Manchester
27.05.00	Koba Kulu W RTD 3 Southwark
07.10.00	Leigh Wicks W PTS 4 Doncaster
12.11.00	Prince Kasi Kaihau W RSC 2 Manchester
25.11.00	Wayne Shepherd W RSC 3 Manchester
17.03.01	Richie Murray W RSC 1 Manchester
27.05.01	Paul Denton W RSC 3 Manchester

Career: 12 contests, won 12.

(Jason) J.J. Moore

Mansfield. *Born* Nottingham, 28 February, 1972
S. Featherweight. Ht. 5'6"
Manager J. Ashton

25.02.01	Craig Spacie L PTS 4 Derby
06.03.01	Craig Spacie L PTS 6 Yarm
24.03.01	Wayne Wheeler W RSC 4 Newark

Career: 3 contests, won 1, lost 2.

Tony Moran

Liverpool. *Born* Liverpool, 4 July, 1973
Heavyweight. Ht. 6'6"
Manager T. Miller

26.04.01	Shaun Bowes L PTS 6 Gateshead

Career: 1 contest, lost 1.

Leighton Morgan

Treharris. *Born* Caerphilly, 27 February, 1978
Cruiserweight. Ht. 6'2"
Manager T. Woodward

16.06.01	Rasmus Ojemaye W RSC 3 Wembley

Career: 1 contest, won 1.

Terry Morrill

Hull. *Born* Hull, 2 February, 1965
Cruiserweight. Former Central Area L. Middleweight Champion. Ht. 5'10¼"
Manager Self

10.12.88	Chris Richards W PTS 6 Crystal Palace
08.02.89	Newton Barnett W PTS 6 Kensington
28.03.89	Skip Jackson L RSC 5 Glasgow
27.06.89	Mark Howell W PTS 6 Kensington
10.10.89	Spencer Alton W PTS 6 Hull
15.11.89	Davey Hughes DREW 4 Lewisham
08.12.89	Tony Baker W PTS 6 Doncaster

22.02.90	Mark Holden W RSC 7 Hull
	(Central Area L. Middleweight Title
	Challenge)
10.04.90	Ernie Noble W RSC 7 Doncaster
20.05.90	Jason Rowe L CO 6 Sheffield
	(Central Area L. Middleweight Title
	Defence)
31.10.90	Shaun Cummins L RSC 1 Crystal
	Palace
14.03.91	Delroy Waul DREW 8 Middleton
28.05.91	Eamonn Loughran L CO 1 Cardiff
16.10.92	Shamus Casey W PTS 6 Hull
16.09.93	Des Robinson W PTS 8 Hull
12.11.93	Shamus Casey W PTS 6 Hull
09.05.96	Lee Simpkin W RSC 5 Hull
06.11.96	Roy Chipperfield W RSC 1 Hull
28.11.96	Jeff Finlayson W PTS 6 Hull
27.02.97	Prince Kasi Kaihau W PTS 6 Hull
21.11.97	Mark Dawson W PTS 6 Hull
28.03.98	Howard Eastman L RTD 4 Hull
09.06.98	Glenn Williams L PTS 4 Hull
30.09.99	Sven Hamer L PTS 6 Kensington
23.10.99	Danilo Haeussler L PTS 8 Telford
13.11.99	Jamie Warters L PTS 8 Hull
12.02.00	Brian Magee L RTD 4 Sheffield
25.07.00	Konstantin Schvets L PTS 6 Southwark
05.05.01	Peter Haymer L PTS 4 Edmonton
Career: 29 contests, won 15, drew 2, lost 12.

Sam Mottram

Alfreton. *Born* Mansfield, 16 August, 1982
L. Middleweight. Ht. 5'11"
Manager M. Shinfield

26.04.01	Chris Steele W PTS 6 Gateshead
10.05.01	Chris Steele W PTS 6 Sunderland
03.06.01	Tony Smith W PTS 6 Hanley
Career: 3 contests, won 3.

Matt Mowatt

Sheffield. *Born* Sheffield, 8 March, 1967
S. Middleweight. Ht. 5'10"
Manager Self

22.10.90	Adrian Din L PTS 6 Cleethorpes
29.10.90	Mike Phillips L PTS 6 Birmingham
27.11.90	Paul Walters L PTS 6 Stoke
11.12.90	Russell Washer L RSC 6 Evesham
23.01.91	Mike Phillips L RSC 6 Stoke
30.09.91	Joe Kilshaw DREW 6 Liverpool
21.10.91	Warren Stowe L RSC 3 Bury
20.11.91	Hugh Fury W PTS 6 Solihull
28.11.91	Rob Stevenson W PTS 6 Hull
09.12.91	Hugh Fury L RTD 5 Bradford
24.02.92	Willie Yeardsley L PTS 6 Bradford
17.03.98	Shamus Casey L PTS 6 Sheffield
30.04.98	Shane Thomas W PTS 6 Pentre Halkyn
14.06.98	Wayne Shepherd DREW 6 Shaw
20.09.98	Wayne Shepherd L PTS 6 Sheffield
25.04.99	Andy Vickers L PTS 6 Leeds
11.09.99	Chris Howarth W PTS 4 Sheffield
28.10.99	Wayne Shepherd L PTS 6 Burnley
10.12.99	Steve Ryan L PTS 6 Nicosia, Cyprus
27.02.00	Simon Andrews W PTS 6 Plymouth
27.03.00	Matt Scriven W PTS 4 Barnsley
09.04.00	Gary Beardsley L PTS 6 Alfreton
20.05.00	Ian Toby L PTS 6 Rotherham
19.11.00	Gary Beardsley L PTS 10 Chesterfield
	(Vacant British Masters Middleweight
	Title)
08.12.00	Albert Rybacki L PTS 4 Crystal Palace
22.02.01	Ian Toby L PTS 6 Sunderland

16.03.01	Matthew Barney L RSC 1 Portsmouth
	(British Masters S. Middleweight Title
	Challenge)
Career: 27 contests, won 6, drew 2, lost 19.

Tony Mulholland

Liverpool. *Born* Liverpool, 24 November, 1972
Featherweight. Ht. 5'6³/₄"
Manager Self

16.08.96	Graham McGrath W RSC 3 Liverpool
22.11.96	Keith Jones W PTS 4 Liverpool
04.04.97	Keith Jones W PTS 4 Liverpool
11.09.97	Chris Williams W PTS 4 Widnes
18.04.98	Pete Buckley W PTS 4 Manchester
06.06.98	Pete Buckley W PTS 6 Liverpool
19.12.98	Chris Williams DREW 4 Liverpool
04.09.99	Dean Murdoch W PTS 4 Bethnal Green
06.11.99	Dean Murdoch W RSC 6 Widnes
11.12.99	Gary Flear W PTS 4 Liverpool
29.02.00	Pete Buckley W PTS 4 Widnes
25.03.00	Steve Hanley W PTS 6 Liverpool
08.07.00	Lee Williamson W PTS 8 Widnes
10.02.01	Anthony Hanna W PTS 4 Widnes
Career: 14 contests, won 13, drew 1.

Patrick Mullings

Harrow. *Born* Harlesden, 19 October, 1970
S. Bantamweight. Former Commonwealth
Featherweight Champion. Former British &
IBO S. Bantamweight Champion. Former
Undefeated WBC International & IBO
Inter-Continental S. Bantamweight
Champion. Ht. 5'4½"
Manager F. Maloney

13.12.94	Graham McGrath W PTS 4 Ilford
23.01.95	Des Gargano W PTS 4 Bethnal Green
30.03.95	Graham McGrath W RSC 3 Bethnal
	Green
04.06.95	Des Gargano W PTS 6 Bethnal Green
21.09.95	Pete Buckley W PTS 6 Battersea
15.12.95	Pete Buckley W PTS 4 Bethnal Green
05.02.96	Pete Buckley W PTS 8 Bexleyheath
21.03.96	Danny Ruegg W RSC 3 Southwark
14.05.96	Miguel Matthews W PTS 6 Dagenham
11.12.96	Phil Lashley W RSC 3 Southwark
18.02.97	Spencer Oliver L RSC 10 Cheshunt
	(Vacant Southern Area
	S. Bantamweight Title)
20.05.97	Ricky Beard W RTD 3 Edmonton
12.07.97	Francky Leroy W RSC 1 Earls Court
	(Vacant WBC International
	S. Bantamweight Title)
06.12.97	Hiviva Hdrian W RSC 1 Wembley
	(WBC International S. Bantamweight
	Title Defence)
10.01.98	Euloge Sita Makinza W RTD 5 Bethnal
	Green
28.03.98	Martin Krastev W RSC 3 Hull
	(Vacant IBO S. Bantamweight Title)
02.05.98	Rakhim Mingaleev W PTS 8
	Kensington
08.08.98	Simon Ramoni L PTS 12 Scarborough
	(IBO S. Bantamweight Title Defence)
30.11.98	Marty Chestnut W RSC 2 Peterborough
06.02.99	Brian Carr W PTS 12 Halifax
	(Vacant British S. Bantamweight Title)
24.04.99	Drew Docherty L PTS 12 Peterborough
	(British S. Bantamweight Title
	Defence)

10.07.99	Maxim Pougatchev W RSC 4
	Southwark
01.10.99	Ravil Muhamadiarov W PTS 6 Bethnal
	Green
06.11.99	Michael Alldis L PTS 12 Bethnal
	Green
	(Vacant British S. Bantamweight Title)
29.11.99	Eric Odumasi W PTS 12 Wembley
	(Vacant Commonwealth Featherweight
	Title)
24.01.00	Scott Harrison L PTS 12 Glasgow
	(Commonwealth Featherweight Title
	Defence)
14.04.00	Vladimir Borov W RSC 12 Manchester
	(Vacant IBO Inter-Continental
	S. Bantamweight Title)
27.05.00	Simon Ramoni L RSC 8 Southwark
	(IBO S. Bantamweight Title Challenge)
07.04.01	Alexander Tiranov W RSC 3 Wembley
Career: 29 contests, won 23, lost 6.

Gerard Murphy

Uddingston. *Born* Glasgow, 5 October, 1977
Welterweight. Ht. 5'10"
Manager F. Warren/A. Morrison

13.06.97	Ivan Walker W PTS 6 Paisley
05.07.97	Paul Salmon W PTS 4 Glasgow
12.09.97	Scott Dixon L PTS 8 Glasgow
28.11.97	Stuart Rimmer W PTS 6 Hull
24.04.98	Dean Bramhald W RSC 2 Glasgow
27.11.98	Les Frost W PTS 6 Hull
07.12.98	Ray Newby W PTS 6 Nottingham
09.04.99	Ivan Walker W RSC 3 Glasgow
21.05.99	Prince Kasi Kaihau W PTS 6 Glasgow
26.11.99	David Kirk W RTD 3 Hull
18.03.00	Paul King W RSC 1 Glasgow
24.06.00	Steve Brumant W PTS 4 Glasgow
17.12.00	Prince Kasi Kaihau W PTS 6 Glasgow
Career: 13 contests, won 12, lost 1.

Lawrence Murphy

Uddingston. *Born* Bellshill, 9 February, 1976
Middleweight. Ht. 6'1"
Manager A. Morrison

15.05.98	Mark Owens W RSC 2 Edinburgh
17.09.98	Lee Bird W RSC 3 Glasgow
13.11.98	Ian Toby W PTS 6 Glasgow
18.02.99	Mike Duffield W RSC 2 Glasgow
26.06.99	Harry Butler W RSC 1 Glasgow
17.12.00	Michael Alexander W PTS 6 Glasgow
Career: 6 contests, won 6.

Michael Murray

Manchester. *Born* Preston, 3 September, 1964
Former Undefeated Central Area
Heavyweight Champion. Ht. 6'1"
Manager Self

23.02.88	Gypsy John Fury L PTS 6 Oldham
28.04.88	Ian Nelson W RSC 6 Manchester
17.11.88	Steve Garber W PTS 6 Stockport
07.02.89	Rocky Burton W PTS 6 Manchester
10.05.89	Barry Ellis W RSC 3 Solihull
08.09.89	Noel Quarless L PTS 8 Liverpool
17.10.89	John Westgarth W RTD 4 Oldham
06.02.90	Al Malcolm W RSC 5 Oldham

02.06.90 Gypsy John Fury L RTD 6 Manchester
30.04.91 Steve Garber W CO 1 Stockport
19.09.91 Carl Gaffney W RSC 8 Stockport
(Vacant Central Area Heavyweight Title)
22.10.91 Markus Bott W RSC 7 Hamburg, Germany
07.12.91 Steve Gee W RSC 7 Manchester
14.04.92 Clifton Mitchell L RSC 8 Mansfield
28.11.92 Ricky Sekorski W PTS 8 Manchester
27.02.93 Herbie Hide L RSC 5 Dagenham
(Vacant British Heavyweight Title)
30.09.94 Terry Dunstan L PTS 8 Bethnal Green
10.12.94 Scott Welch L PTS 8 Manchester
23.02.95 Derek Williams W PTS 8 Southwark
17.05.95 John Ruiz L RSC 4 Ipswich
14.10.95 Zeljko Mavrovic L RSC 4 Munich, Germany
14.11.95 Mike Holden W PTS 6 Bury
16.12.95 Keith Fletcher W DIS 3 Cardiff
05.02.96 Julius Francis W PTS 10 Bexleyheath
(Elim. British Heavyweight Title)
31.05.96 Mark Hulstrom L RSC 2 Copenhagen, Denmark
06.07.96 Herbie Hide L RSC 6 Manchester
09.11.96 Danny Williams L CO 1 Manchester
25.02.97 Pele Reid L RSC 1 Sheffield
19.07.97 Johnny Nelson L PTS 4 Wembley
20.09.97 Wayne Llewelyn L RTD 4 Aachen, Germany
14.03.98 Michael Sprott L PTS 6 Bethnal Green
11.04.98 Kevin McBride W RSC 3 Southwark
22.08.98 Timo Hoffman L PTS 8 Leipzig, Germany
30.01.99 Scott Welch L PTS 8 Bethnal Green
27.02.99 Matthew Ellis L PTS 8 Bethnal Green
05.06.99 Willi Fischer L PTS 8 Frankfurt, Germany
04.09.99 Rene Monse L PTS 6 Magdeburg, Germany
23.10.99 Rene Monse L PTS 6 Telford
18.12.99 Luan Krasniqi L PTS 8 Southwark
06.05.00 Danny Williams L RSC 6 Frankfurt, Germany
27.11.00 Albert Sosnowski L RSC 5 Birmingham
05.05.01 Mark Potter L PTS 8 Edmonton
Career: 42 contests, won 16, lost 26.

Oneal Murray

Balham. *Born* Jamaica, 8 March, 1973
Cruiserweight. Ht. 6'0"
Manager M. Hill

29.03.01 Oddy Papantoniou L PTS 4 Hammersmith
Career: 1 contest, lost 1.

Richie Murray

Liverpool. *Born* Liverpool, 1 April, 1970
L. Middleweight. Ht. 5'11"
Manager J. Ingle

13.12.99 Ernie Smith W RSC 5 Cleethorpes
16.05.00 Thomas McDonagh L PTS 4 Warrington
13.11.00 Mickey Yikealo W RSC 3 Bethnal Green
11.12.00 Thomas McDonagh L PTS 6 Widnes
17.03.01 Jamie Moore L RSC 1 Manchester
Career: 5 contests, won 2, lost 3.

Richie Murray　　　　　　　Les Clark

Ross Murray

Ashington. *Born* Ashington, 1 October, 1981
L. Middleweight. Ht. 5'8"
Manager G. McCrory

01.12.00 Damien Brown W CO 1 Peterborough
31.01.01 Conroy McIntosh L CO 1 Piccadilly
Career: 2 contests, won 1, lost 1.

Ross Murray　　　　　　　Les Clark

Steve Murray

Harlow. *Born* Harlow, 5 October, 1975
Former Undefeated IBF Inter-Continental Welterweight Champion. Ht. 5'6"
Manager F. Warren

10.10.98 Keith Jones W RSC 4 Bethnal Green
14.11.98 Dave Travers W RSC 2 Cheshunt
23.01.99 Marc Smith W RSC 1 Cheshunt
30.01.99 Dewi Roberts W RSC 1 Bethnal Green
03.04.99 Woody Greenaway W CO 2 Kensington
01.05.99 Keith Jones W RSC 6 Crystal Palace
26.06.99 Brian Coleman W PTS 6 Millwall
07.08.99 Pete Buckley W PTS 6 Dagenham
15.11.99 Karl Taylor W RSC 1 Bethnal Green
29.01.00 Keith Jones W PTS 4 Manchester
19.02.00 Juan Carlos Zummaraga W RSC 1 Dagenham
(Vacant IBF Inter-Continental Lightweight Title)
29.05.00 Wahid Fats W RSC 3 Manchester
24.06.00 Nono Junior W RSC 4 Glasgow
12.08.00 Alan Temple W RSC 2 Wembley
(IBF Inter-Continental Lightweight Title Defence. Elim. British Lightweight Title)
23.09.00 David Kirk W PTS 4 Bethnal Green
24.02.01 Serguei Starkov W PTS 8 Bethnal Green
05.05.01 Bobby Vanzie L RSC 7 Edmonton
(British Lightweight Title Challenge)
Career: 17 contests, won 16, lost 1.

Lee Murtagh

Leeds. *Born* Leeds, 30 September, 1973
L. Middleweight. Ht. 5'9¼"
Manager J. Doughty

12.06.95 Dave Curtis W PTS 6 Bradford
25.09.95 Roy Gbasai W PTS 6 Bradford
30.10.95 Cam Raeside L PTS 6 Bradford
11.12.95 Donovan Davey W PTS 6 Bradford
13.01.96 Peter Varnavas W PTS 6 Halifax
05.02.96 Shamus Casey W PTS 6 Bradford
20.05.96 Shaun O'Neill W PTS 6 Bradford
24.06.96 Michael Alexander W PTS 6 Bradford
28.10.96 Jimmy Vincent L RSC 2 Bradford
14.04.97 Lee Simpkin W PTS 6 Bradford
09.10.97 Brian Dunn W PTS 6 Leeds
05.03.98 Wayne Shepherd W PTS 6 Leeds
08.08.98 Alan Gilbert W PTS 4 Scarborough
13.03.99 Keith Palmer DREW 6 Manchester
27.09.99 Jawaid Khaliq L RSC 5 Leeds
(Vacant WBF European L. Middleweight Title)
27.02.00 Gareth Lovell W PTS 6 Leeds
24.09.00 Jon Foster W PTS 6 Shaw
03.12.00 Michael Alexander W PTS 6 Shaw
17.05.01 Ojay Abrahams L RSC 2 Leeds
(Vacant British Masters L. Middleweight Title)
Career: 19 contests, won 14, drew 1, lost 4.

(Lee) Young Muttley (Woodley)

Wednesbury. *Born* West Bromwich, 17 May, 1976
L. Welterweight. Ht. 5'8½"
Manager M. Shinfield

03.09.99 Dave Hinds W RSC 4 West Bromwich
24.10.99 David Kehoe W RTD 1 Wolverhampton
22.01.00 Wahid Fats L PTS 4 Birmingham
18.02.00 Stuart Rimmer W RSC 1 West Bromwich
27.11.00 Peter Dunn W RSC 3 Birmingham
Career: 5 contests, won 4, lost 1.

Ronnie Nailen

Glasgow. *Born* Belfast, 2 April, 1981
Welterweight. Ht. 5'10"
Manager J. Breen

24.05.01 David White W PTS 6 Glasgow
Career: 1 contest, won 1.

Ian Napa

Hackney. *Born* Zimbabwe, 14 March, 1978
Southern Area Flyweight Champion.
Ht. 5'1"
Manager F. Warren

06.06.98 Nick Tooley W PTS 6 Liverpool
14.07.98 Nicky Booth W PTS 6 Reading
10.10.98 Sean Green W PTS 6 Bethnal Green
30.01.99 Delroy Spencer W PTS 6 Bethnal Green
15.11.99 Mark Reynolds W PTS 10 Bethnal Green
(Southern Area Flyweight Title Challenge)
19.02.00 Anthony Hanna W PTS 6 Dagenham
08.04.00 Delroy Spencer W PTS 8 Bethnal Green
15.07.00 Jamie Evans W PTS 4 Millwall
13.11.00 Jason Booth L PTS 12 Bethnal Green
(British & Commonwealth Flyweight Title Challenges)
24.02.01 Oleg Kiryukhin W PTS 6 Bethnal Green
09.06.01 Peter Culshaw L RSC 8 Bethnal Green
(WBU Flyweight Title Challenge)
Career: 11 contests, won 9, lost 2.

(Jimmy) Shea Neary

Liverpool. *Born* Liverpool, 18 May, 1968
Former WBU L. Welterweight Champion.
Former Undefeated Central Area L.
Welterweight Champion. Ht. 5'7½"
Manager Self

03.09.92 Simon Ford W RSC 1 Liverpool
05.10.92 Shaun Armstrong W RSC 6 Liverpool
02.11.92 Jason Barker W RSC 3 Liverpool
01.12.92 Chris Saunders W PTS 6 Liverpool
22.02.93 Vaughan Carnegie W RSC 1 Liverpool
29.03.93 John Smith W PTS 6 Liverpool
06.09.93 Wayne Shepherd W RTD 2 Liverpool
25.10.93 Mark Antony W RSC 1 Liverpool
13.06.94 Mark Pearce W RSC 4 Liverpool
07.12.94 Tony Foster W RSC 2 Stoke
25.01.95 John Smith W RSC 5 Stoke
15.03.95 Tony Swift W RSC 3 Stoke
16.06.95 Hugh Forde W RTD 6 Liverpool
08.09.95 Nigel Bradley W RSC 2 Liverpool
(Vacant Central Area L. Welterweight Title)
24.11.95 Mark Richardson W CO 1 Chester
03.02.96 Terry Sutherland W CO 2 Liverpool
26.10.96 Darryl Tyson W PTS 12 Liverpool
(Vacant WBU L. Welterweight Title)
01.03.97 Jeremiah Malinga W RSC 3 Liverpool
(WBU L. Welterweight Title Defence)

12.03.98 Andy Holligan W RSC 6 Liverpool
(WBU L. Welterweight Title Defence)
21.07.98 Naas Scheepers W PTS 12 Widnes
(WBU L. Welterweight Title Defence)
24.10.98 Juan Carlos Villareal W PTS 12 Liverpool
(WBU L. Welterweight Title Defence)
19.06.99 Mike Griffith W RSC 4 Dublin
(WBU L. Welterweight Title Defence)
11.03.00 Mickey Ward L RSC 8 Kensington
(WBU L. Welterweight Title Defence)
25.07.00 Alan Bosworth W PTS 10 Southwark
11.11.00 Eamonn Magee L PTS 12 Belfast
(Commonwealth L.Welterweight Title Challenge)
Career: 25 contests, won 23, lost 2.

Dominic Negus

Havering. *Born* Bethnal Green, 28 July, 1970
Former Southern Area Cruiserweight Champion. Ht. 6'2"
Manager F. Maloney

03.09.96 Gareth Thomas W RSC 2 Bethnal Green
28.09.96 Patrick Lawrence W RSC 2 Barking
11.01.97 Naveed Anwar W RTD 2 Bethnal Green
04.03.97 Nigel Rafferty W PTS 4 Southwark
20.05.97 Nigel Rafferty W PTS 4 Edmonton
17.06.97 Chris Henry W RSC 10 Cheshunt
(Southern Area Cruiserweight Title Challenge)
02.09.97 Trevor Small DREW 8 Southwark
11.11.97 Constantin Ochrej W CO 6 Bethnal Green
21.04.98 Bruce Scott L RSC 9 Edmonton
(Southern Area Cruiserweight Title Defence)
22.10.98 Kevin Mitchell L RTD 5 Barking
18.02.99 Kevin Mitchell W PTS 10 Barking
(Vacant Southern Area Cruiserweight Title)
13.09.99 Chris Woollas W PTS 10 Bethnal Green
(Elim. British Cruiserweight Title)
08.09.00 Tony Booth L PTS 6 Bristol
06.10.00 Garry Delaney L PTS 10 Maidstone
(Southern Area Cruiserweight Title Challenge)
26.05.01 Paul Fiske W CO 1 Bethnal Green
Career: 15 contests, won 10, drew 1, lost 4.

Johnny Nelson

Sheffield. *Born* Sheffield, 4 January, 1967
WBO Cruiserweight Champion. Former
Undefeated British & European
Cruiserweight Champion. Former WBF
Heavyweight Champion. Former WBF
Cruiserweight Champion. Former
Undefeated Central Area Cruiserweight
Champion. Ht. 6'2"
Manager B. Ingle/F. Warren

18.03.86 Peter Brown L PTS 6 Hull
15.05.86 Tommy Taylor L PTS 6 Dudley
03.10.86 Magne Havnaa L PTS 4 Copenhagen, Denmark
20.11.86 Chris Little W PTS 6 Bredbury
19.01.87 Gypsy Carman W PTS 6 Mayfair
02.03.87 Doug Young W PTS 6 Huddersfield

10.03.87 Sean Daly W RSC 1 Manchester
28.04.87 Brian Schumacher L PTS 8 Halifax
03.06.87 Byron Pullen W RSC 3 Southwark
14.12.87 Jon McBean W RSC 6 Edgbaston
01.02.88 Dennis Bailey L PTS 8 Northampton
24.02.88 Cordwell Hylton W RSC 1 Sheffield
25.04.88 Kenny Jones W CO 1 Liverpool
04.05.88 Crawford Ashley W PTS 8 Solihull
06.06.88 Lennie Howard W CO 2 Mayfair
31.08.88 Andrew Gerrard W PTS 8 Stoke
26.10.88 Danny Lawford W RSC 2 Sheffield
(Vacant Central Area Cruiserweight Title)
04.04.89 Steve Mormino W RSC 2 Sheffield
21.05.89 Andy Straughn W CO 8 Finsbury Park
(British Cruiserweight Title Challenge)
02.10.89 Ian Bulloch W CO 2 Hanley
(British Cruiserweight Title Defence)
27.01.90 Carlos de Leon DREW 12 Sheffield
(WBC Cruiserweight Title Challenge)
14.02.90 Dino Homsey W RSC 7 Brentwood
28.03.90 Lou Gent W CO 4 Bethnal Green
(British Cruiserweight Title Defence)
27.06.90 Arthur Weathers W RSC 2 Kensington
05.09.90 Andre Smith W PTS 8 Brighton
14.12.90 Markus Bott W RSC 12 Karlsruhe, Germany
(Vacant European Cruiserweight Title)
12.03.91 Yves Monsieur W RTD 8 Mansfield
(European Cruiserweight Title Defence)
16.05.92 James Warring L PTS 12 Fredericksburg, USA
(IBF Cruiserweight Title Challenge)
15.08.92 Norbert Ekassi L RSC 3 Ajaccio, France
29.10.92 Corrie Sanders L PTS 10 Morula, South Africa
30.04.93 Dave Russell W RSC 11 Melbourne, Australia
(WBF Cruiserweight Title Challenge)
11.08.93 Tom Collins W RSC 1 Mansfield
(WBF Cruiserweight Title Defence)
01.10.93 Francis Wanyama L DIS 10 Waregem, Belgium
(WBF Cruiserweight Title Defence)
20.11.93 Jimmy Thunder W PTS 12 Auckland, New Zealand
(WBF Heavyweight Title Challenge)
05.04.94 Henry Akinwande L PTS 10 Bethnal Green
05.11.94 Nikolai Kulpin W PTS 12 Bangkok, Thailand
(WBF Heavyweight Title Defence)
22.08.95 Adilson Rodrigues L PTS 12 Sao Paulo, Brazil
(WBF Heavyweight Title Defence)
03.12.95 Adilson Rodrigues L PTS 12 Sao Paulo, Brazil
(WBF Heavyweight Title Challenge)
20.01.96 Tony Booth W RSC 2 Mansfield
14.12.96 Dennis Andries W RSC 7 Sheffield
(Vacant British Cruiserweight Title)
22.02.97 Patrice Aouissi W RSC 7 Berck sur Mer, France
(Vacant European Cruiserweight Title)
19.07.97 Michael Murray W PTS 4 Wembley
11.10.97 Dirk Wallyn W RSC 1 Sheffield
(European Cruiserweight Title Defence)
18.07.98 Peter Oboh W RTD 6 Sheffield
27.03.99 Carl Thompson W RSC 5 Derby
(WBO Cruiserweight Title Challenge)

15.05.99 Bruce Scott W PTS 12 Sheffield
(WBO Cruiserweight Title Defence)
07.08.99 Willard Lewis W RTD 4 Dagenham
(WBO Cruiserweight Title Defence)
18.09.99 Sione Asipeli W PTS 12 Las Vegas,
USA
(WBO Cruiserweight Title Defence)
06.11.99 Christophe Girard W CO 4 Widnes
(WBO Cruiserweight Title Defence)
08.04.00 Pietro Aurino W RTD 7 Bethnal Green
(WBO Cruiserweight Title Defence)
07.10.00 Adam Watt W RSC 5 Doncaster
(WBO Cruiserweight Title Defence)
27.01.01 George Arias W PTS 12 Bethnal Green
(WBO Cruiserweight Title Defence)
Career: 52 contests, won 39, drew 1, lost 12.

Chris Nembhard
Leytonstone. *Born* Jamaica, 26 December,
1976
L. Middleweight. Ht. 6'1"
Manager T. Bowers

29.09.00 Gary Ojuederie W RSC 1 Bethnal
Green
02.11.00 Koba Kulu W PTS 6 Kensington
10.11.00 William Webster W RSC 1 Mayfair
15.02.01 Keith Ellwood W RSC 2 Glasgow
23.02.01 David Baptiste W PTS 8 Barking
09.03.01 Rob Stevenson W RSC 2 Millwall
20.04.01 Delroy Mellis L RSC 8 Millwall
*(Southern Area L. Middleweight Title
Challenge)*
Career: 7 contests, won 6, lost 1.

Chris Nembhard   Les Clark

Jason Nesbitt
Birmingham. *Born* Birmingham, 15
December, 1973
Lightweight. Ht. 5'9"
Manager N. Nobbs

Johnny Nelson   Les Clark

127

06.11.00 Stephen Chinnock L PTS 6 Wolverhampton
09.12.00 Lee Meager L RSC 2 Southwark
29.01.01 Henry Castle L CO 6 Peterborough
27.03.01 Billy Smith W PTS 6 Brierley Hill
21.05.01 Sid Razak L PTS 6 Birmingham
04.06.01 Andrew Ferrans L RSC 2 Glasgow
Career: 6 contests, won 1, lost 5.

Jason Nesbitt   Les Clark

Eddie Nevins

Manchester. *Born* Manchester, 17 April, 1975
S. Featherweight. Ht. 5'6"
Manager S. Foster/S. Wood

17.10.98 Simon Chambers W RSC 4 Manchester
26.10.98 Dave Hinds W PTS 6 Manchester
30.11.98 Keith Jones W PTS 4 Manchester
13.03.99 Gary Jenkinson W PTS 4 Manchester
02.07.99 Ram Singh W CO 1 Manchester
06.11.99 Bradley Pryce L RSC 2 Widnes
21.05.00 Lennie Hodgkins W RSC 1 Shaw
12.08.00 Paul Halpin L PTS 6 Wembley
12.11.00 Mohamed Helel W PTS 4 Manchester
15.01.01 Pete Buckley W PTS 4 Manchester
10.02.01 Alex Arthur L RSC 1 Widnes
26.03.01 Henry Castle L RSC 2 Peterborough
Career: 12 contests, won 8, lost 4.

Dean Nicholas

South Shields. *Born* South Shields, 9 May, 1973
Welterweight. Ht. 5'9"
Manager T. Callighan

22.09.95 David Thompson W PTS 6 Hull
02.11.95 Paul Scott W PTS 6 Houghton le Spring
20.11.95 Shaun Gledhill W RSC 4 Glasgow
14.02.96 Shaun O'Neill W PTS 6 Sunderland
22.04.96 John Smith W PTS 6 Glasgow
09.05.96 John Docherty L PTS 6 Glasgow

23.09.96 Mark Breslin L PTS 8 Glasgow
01.12.96 C. J. Jackson DREW 6 Shaw
27.02.97 Keith Scott L PTS 6 Sunderland
09.10.97 Donovan Davey W PTS 6 Hull
27.10.97 Ray Newby L RSC 4 Nottingham
30.11.97 Lee Molyneux W PTS 6 Shaw
03.02.98 Leon Cessiron L RSC 4 Pont Audemer, France
07.04.98 Jose Etinoff L CO 1 Epernay, France
29.10.98 Richard Inquieti W RSC 1 Newcastle
25.01.99 Glenn McClarnon L CO 1 Glasgow
29.05.99 Peter Dunn W PTS 6 South Shields
29.06.99 Paul Knights L RSC 2 Bethnal Green
17.04.00 James Docherty L RSC 6 Glasgow
23.10.00 James Hare L RSC 1 Glasgow
24.11.00 Oscar Hall L PTS 6 Darlington
05.02.01 Danny Parkinson L PTS 6 Bradford
23.02.01 Richard Inquieti W PTS 6 Irvine
19.03.01 Darren Spencer L RSC 4 Glasgow
Career: 24 contests, won 10, drew 1, lost 13.

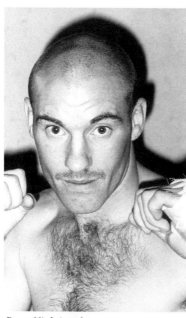

Peter Nightingale   Les Clark

Peter Nightingale

Tipton. *Born* Tipton, 20 January, 1969
L. Middleweight. Former Undefeated Midlands Area Welterweight Champion.
Ht. 5'10"
Manager Self

24.10.96 Kevin McCarthy DREW 6 Wembley
12.11.96 David Kehoe W PTS 6 Dudley
08.03.97 Georgie Smith L RSC 1 Brentwood
22.04.97 Paul Knights L PTS 6 Bethnal Green
29.04.97 Eamonn Magee L RTD 2 Belfast
09.09.97 Daniel James L PTS 6 Bethnal Green
18.11.97 David Kehoe DREW 4 Mansfield
06.12.97 Harry Andrews L PTS 4 Wembley
06.01.98 Terry Roberts L PTS 6 Brighton
27.01.98 Allan Gray L PTS 6 Streatham
23.02.98 Kevin McCarthy L PTS 6 Windsor
03.04.98 Brian Coleman W PTS 6 West Bromwich

21.04.98 Patrick Pasi W RSC 2 Edmonton
09.05.98 James Hare L PTS 4 Sheffield
04.06.98 Danny Bell W PTS 6 Dudley
03.10.98 Brian Coleman W PTS 6 West Bromwich
28.11.98 James Hare L PTS 6 Sheffield
12.12.98 Spencer McCracken L PTS 8 Southwark
26.02.99 Brian Coleman W PTS 6 West Bromwich
01.04.99 Danny Bell W PTS 10 Birmingham
          (*Vacant Midlands Area Welterweight Title*)
23.06.99 Lee Bird W PTS 6 West Bromwich
24.10.99 Brian Coleman W PTS 10 Wolverhampton
          (*Midlands Area Welterweight Title Defence*)
13.11.99 Jamie Moore L PTS 4 Hull
18.02.00 Lee Molyneux W PTS 6 West Bromwich
13.03.00 Malcolm Melvin L PTS 6 Birmingham
28.01.01 William Webster W PTS 6 Wolverhampton
16.03.01 Paul Dyer L PTS 6 Portsmouth
01.04.01 Nick Hall DREW 6 Wolverhampton
Career: 28 contests, won 11, drew 3, lost 14.

Robert Norton

Stourbridge. *Born* Dudley, 20 January, 1972
Former WBU Cruiserweight Champion.
Ht. 6'2"
Manager Self

30.09.93 Stuart Fleet W CO 2 Walsall
27.10.93 Kent Davis W PTS 6 West Bromwich
02.12.93 Eddie Pyatt W RSC 2 Walsall
26.01.94 Lennie Howard W PTS 6 Birmingham
17.05.94 Steve Osborne W PTS 6 Kettering
05.10.94 Chris Woollas DREW 6 Wolverhampton
30.11.94 L. A. Williams W RSC 2 Wolverhampton
10.02.95 Newby Stevens W RSC 3 Birmingham
22.02.95 Steve Osborne W PTS 6 Telford
21.04.95 Cordwell Hylton W PTS 6 Dudley
25.10.95 Nigel Rafferty W RSC 6 Telford
31.01.96 Gary Williams W RSC 2 Birmingham
25.04.96 Steve Osborne W RSC 5 Mayfair
01.10.96 Andrew Benson W RSC 6 Birmingham
12.11.96 Nigel Rafferty W PTS 8 Dudley
11.02.97 Touami Benhamed W RSC 5 Bethnal Green
16.04.97 Tony Booth W RSC 4 Bethnal Green
20.12.97 Darren Corbett L PTS 12 Belfast
          (*Commonwealth Cruiserweight Title Challenge*)
03.04.98 Adrian Nicolai W RSC 2 West Bromwich
03.10.98 Tim Brown W CO 3 West Bromwich
01.04.99 Jacob Mofokeng W PTS 12 Birmingham
          (*WBU Cruiserweight Title Challenge*)
24.09.99 Sebastiaan Rothmann L RSC 8 Merthyr
          (*WBU Cruiserweight Title Defence*)
30.09.00 Tony Booth W RSC 3 Peterborough
18.11.00 Darron Griffiths W PTS 10 Dagenham
          (*Elim. British Cruiserweight Title*)
05.02.01 Lee Swaby W PTS 8 Hull
Career: 25 contests, won 22, drew 1, lost 2.

Tony Oakey

Portsmouth. *Born* Portsmouth, 2 January, 1976
Commonwealth L. Heavyweight Champion. Former Undefeated Southern Area L. Heavyweight Champion. Ht. 5'8"
Manager F. Maloney

12.09.98	Smokey Enison W RSC 2 Bethnal Green
21.11.98	Zak Chelli W RSC 1 Southwark
16.01.99	Jimmy Steel W PTS 4 Bethnal Green
06.03.99	Mark Dawson W PTS 4 Southwark
10.07.99	Jimmy Steel W PTS 4 Southwark
01.10.99	Michael Pinnock W PTS 4 Bethnal Green
21.02.00	Darren Ashton W PTS 4 Southwark
13.03.00	Martin Jolley W PTS 6 Bethnal Green
21.10.00	Darren Ashton W PTS 4 Wembley
27.01.01	Nathan King W PTS 6 Bethnal Green
26.03.01	Butch Lesley W PTS 10 Wembley
	(Southern Area L. Heavyweight Title Challenge)
08.05.01	Hastings Rasani W RSC 10 Barnsley
	(Vacant Commonwealth L. Heavyweight Title)

Career: 12 contests, won 12.

Tony Oakey   Les Clark

Stephen Oates

Fulham. *Born* Leeds, 11 July, 1975
Bantamweight. Ht. 5'5½"
Manager F. Warren

29.11.97	Gary Hickman W PTS 4 Norwich
17.01.98	Chris Emanuele W RSC 4 Bristol
07.02.98	Stevie Quinn W PTS 4 Cheshunt
07.03.98	Marty Chestnut W PTS 6 Reading
16.05.98	Harry Woods W PTS 4 Bethnal Green
14.07.98	John Matthews L PTS 4 Reading
10.10.98	Graham McGrath W PTS 4 Bethnal Green
14.11.98	Chris Jickells W PTS 6 Cheshunt
13.02.99	Delroy Pryce L PTS 6 Newcastle
03.04.99	Ross Cassidy W RSC 1 Kensington
26.06.99	Harry Woods W PTS 6 Millwall
04.09.99	Danny Ruegg W PTS 6 Bethnal Green
15.11.99	Jason Thomas W PTS 6 Bethnal Green
19.02.00	Jason Thomas W PTS 6 Dagenham
21.10.00	Daniel Ring W RSC 1 Wembley
16.12.00	Chris Jickells W PTS 4 Sheffield
17.03.01	Chris Emanuele W PTS 8 Manchester
09.06.01	Nathan Sting L PTS 8 Bethnal Green

Career: 18 contests, won 15, lost 3.

Stephen Oates   Les Clark

Peter Oboh

Brockley. *Born* Nigeria, 6 September, 1968
L. Heavyweight. Ht. 6'2"
Manager D. Powell

12.05.93	Antonio Russo W RSC 5 Cassino, Italy
14.01.94	Ridha Soussi W PTS 6 Tagliacozzo, Italy
13.05.94	Antonio Pasqualino W RSC 2 Avellino, Italy
16.10.95	Tim Redman W RTD 2 Mayfair
09.07.96	Yuri Yelistratov W PTS 6 Bethnal Green
27.08.96	Joe Siluvangi L RSC 6 Windsor
03.12.96	Andy Lambert W CO 1 Liverpool
04.03.97	Garry Delaney L DIS 8 Southwark
01.11.97	Scott Welch L PTS 6 Glasgow
18.07.98	Johnny Nelson L RTD 6 Sheffield
26.09.98	Ole Klemetsen W CO 1 York
21.11.98	Terry Dunstan L PTS 8 Southwark
18.06.99	Thomas Hansvoll W RSC 2 Vejle, Denmark
21.07.99	Ray Kane W RSC 2 Bloomsbury
29.01.01	Chris Davies W RSC 8 Peterborough
	(Elim. Commonwealth L. Heavyweight Title)

Career: 15 contests, won 10, lost 5.

Valery Odin

London. *Born* Guadeloupe, 23 December, 1974
S. Middleweight. Ht. 6'2½"
Manager T. Bowers

15.06.01	Tom Cannon W PTS 4 Millwall

Career: 1 contest, won 1.

Cathal O'Grady

Kildare. *Born* Dublin, 6 March, 1977
Cruiserweight. Ht. 6'0"
Manager B. Peters

27.09.97	Richie Chapman W RSC 1 Belfast
08.11.97	Cliff Elden W RSC 1 Southwark
06.12.97	L. A. Williams W RSC 1 Wembley
20.12.97	Tim Redman W RSC 2 Belfast
31.01.98	Bruno Wuestenberghs W RSC 1 Edmonton
14.03.98	Tim Brown W PTS 6 Bethnal Green
02.05.98	Trevor Small W RSC 2 Kensington
19.09.98	Lee Swaby W RSC 1 Dublin
22.01.99	Nigel Rafferty W CO 2 Dublin
17.04.99	Kevin Mitchell W RSC 1 Dublin
15.05.99	Darron Griffiths L RSC 5 Blackpool
16.10.99	Tony Booth W CO 4 Belfast
18.12.99	Trevor Small W PTS 6 Southwark
29.04.00	Paul Bonson W PTS 4 Wembley
12.06.00	Chris Davies L RSC 1 Belfast
08.09.00	Casney Truesdale W RSC 3 New York City, USA
24.03.01	Jose Torres W RSC 3 Worcester, Mass, USA
20.04.01	Tony Dowling W RSC 1 Dublin

Career: 18 contests, won 16, lost 2.

Sunkanmi Ogunbiyi

London. *Born* Nigeria, 5 May, 1977
Flyweight. Ht. 5'5"
Manager J. Oyebola

24.05.01	Sergei Tasimov W PTS 4 Kensington
16.06.01	Delroy Spencer W PTS 4 Wembley

Career: 2 contests, won 2.

Rasmus Ojemaye

London. *Born* Nigeria, 28 May, 1969
Cruiserweight. Ht. 5'10"
Manager J. Oyebola

24.05.01	Collice Mutizwa W CO 2 Kensington
16.06.01	Leighton Morgan L RSC 3 Wembley

Career: 2 contests, won 1, lost 1.

Gary Ojuederie

Watford. *Born* Watford, 13 September, 1979
L. Middleweight. Ht. 6'0"
Manager B. Lawrence

29.09.00	Chris Nembhard L RSC 1 Bethnal Green

Career: 1 contest, lost 1.

Kelly Oliver

Lincoln. *Born* Lincoln, 11 November, 1973
Former Undefeated WBO Inter-Continental & British Masters Cruiserweight Champion. Ht. 6'3"
Manager C. Sanigar

20.01.96	Steve Osborne W RSC 4 Mansfield
16.03.96	Marvin O'Brien W RSC 2 Glasgow
13.04.96	Andrew Benson W PTS 4 Wythenshawe
06.07.96	John Pierre W PTS 4 Manchester
14.09.96	Tony Booth W RSC 2 Sheffield
30.11.96	Nigel Rafferty W PTS 6 Tylorstown
18.01.97	Tony Booth W RSC 4 Swadlincote
14.03.96	Chris Woollas W PTS 6 Reading
05.06.97	Darren Westover W RTD 1 Bristol
02.08.97	Chris Woollas W RSC 3 Barnsley
11.10.97	John Keeton W RSC 8 Sheffield
	(Vacant WBO Inter-Continental Cruiserweight Title)
15.11.97	Sergei Korolev W PTS 12 Bristol
	(WBO Inter-Continental Cruiserweight Title Defence)
21.03.98	Brian la Spada W RSC 6 Bethnal Green
	(WBO Inter-Continental Cruiserweight Title Defence)
18.04.98	Nigel Rafferty W RSC 4 Manchester
18.07.98	John Keeton L RSC 2 Sheffield
19.06.99	Chris P. Bacon W PTS 8 Dublin
03.12.99	John Wyborn W RSC 2 Peterborough
05.03.00	Lee Swaby W PTS 10 Peterborough
	(Vacant British Masters Cruiserweight Title)
17.05.00	John Kiser W PTS 10 New York City, USA
01.09.00	Sebastiaan Rothmann L RSC 10 Brakpan, South Africa
	(WBU Cruiserweight Title Challenge)

Career: 20 contests, won 18, lost 2.

Ajose Olusegun

London. *Born* Nigeria, 6 December, 1979
L. Welterweight. Ht. 5'9"
Manager J. Oyebola

24.05.01	Tony Montana W RSC 1 Kensington
21.06.01	Woody Greenaway W RSC 1 Earls Court

Career: 2 contests, won 2.

Leo O'Reilly　　　Les Clark

Leo O'Reilly

Bexleyheath. *Born* Gravesend, 4 October, 1979
L. Welterweight. Ht. 5'6"
Manager M. Roe

16.09.00	Dave Hinds W RSC 2 Bethnal Green
30.09.00	Stuart Rimmer W RSC 2 Peterborough
14.10.00	Marco Fattore W PTS 4 Wembley
18.11.00	Dave Travers W RSC 3 Dagenham
09.12.00	Pete Buckley W PTS 4 Southwark
05.02.01	Woody Greenaway W CO 1 Hull
13.03.01	Barrie Kelley W RSC 5 Plymouth
12.05.01	David White W PTS 4 Plymouth

Career: 8 contests, won 8.

(Muhammed) Huggy Osman

Bradford. *Born* Bradford, 7 December, 1971
Cruiserweight. Ht. 6'3"
Manager Self

18.10.99	Geoff Hunter W PTS 6 Bradford
14.11.99	Lennox Williams W PTS 6 Bradford
01.12.99	Steve Loftus W RSC 3 Stoke
06.03.00	Paul Fiske W PTS 6 Bradford
08.07.00	Dave Faulkner DREW 6 Rotherham
04.12.00	Brian Gascoigne W PTS 6 Bradford

Career: 6 contests, won 5, drew 1.

Huggy Osman　　　Les Clark

Hussain Osman

Camden Town. *Born* Syria, 25 July, 1973
Middleweight. Ht. 5'9½"
Manager I. Akay

09.05.99	Wayne Asker W PTS 4 Bracknell
20.05.99	Karim Bouali W PTS 4 Barking
15.07.99	Neil Linford W RSC 5 Peterborough
05.10.99	Ojay Abrahams W PTS 4 Bloomsbury
05.02.00	Joey Ainscough W PTS 4 Bethnal Green
01.04.00	George Foreman W PTS 4 Bethnal Green
22.05.00	Steve Timms W RSC 2 Coventry
25.09.00	James Lowther L PTS 8 Barnsley
03.03.01	Gary Lockett L CO 2 Wembley
26.05.01	Lee Molloy W RSC 1 Bethnal Green
04.06.01	Richard Williams L PTS 10 Hartlepool

Career: 11 contests, won 8, lost 3.

Paul Owen

Sheffield. *Born* Sheffield, 3 October, 1975
Middleweight. Ht. 5'10½"
Manager Self

05.05.00	Shane Thomas DREW 6 Pentre Halkyn
08.07.00	Chris Crook W RSC 1 Rotherham
05.10.00	Andy Vickers L PTS 6 Sunderland
24.11.00	Reece McAllister L PTS 6 Darlington
07.12.00	Ian Toby L RTD 5 Sunderland
05.02.01	Steve Timms L RSC 1 Bradford
10.05.01	Gary Dixon W RSC 3 Sunderland
21.06.01	Reece McAllister DREW 6 Sheffield

Career: 8 contests, won 2, drew 2, lost 4.

Paul Owen　　　Les Clark

(Tokunbo) Toks Owoh (Owomoyela)

Belsize Park. *Born* Newham, 21 July, 1972
S. Middleweight. Ht. 5'10½"
Manager F. Warren

24.10.95	Marvin O'Brien W RSC 2 Southwark
08.11.95	Dave Fulton W RSC 1 Bethnal Green
29.11.95	Nicky Wadman W PTS 6 Southwark
19.01.96	Ernie Loveridge W PTS 4 Bracknell
27.03.97	James Branch W RSC 1 Norwich
02.08.97	Peter Vosper W RSC 1 Barnsley
29.11.97	Sven Hamer W PTS 8 Norwich
27.03.98	Darren Ashton W RSC 2 Telford
25.04.98	Omar Sheika L RSC 4 Cardiff
26.09.98	Tony Booth W PTS 6 Norwich
30.01.99	Israel Khumalo W RSC 2 Bethnal Green
03.04.99	Paul Wesley W CO 5 Kensington
26.06.99	Peter Mason W RSC 1 Millwall
23.10.99	Eddie Haley W RSC 3 Telford
29.02.00	Konstantin Okhrej W RTD 4 Widnes
19.06.00	Tony Booth W RSC 3 Burton
23.09.00	Glencoffe Johnson L RSC 6 Bethnal Green
	(Vacant IBF Inter-Continental S.Middleweight Title)

Career: 17 contests, won 15, lost 2.

Alan Page

Manchester. *Born* Manchester, 17 April, 1976
Middleweight. Ht. 6'0"
Manager F. Maloney/S. Foster/S. Wood

01.07.00	William Webster W PTS 4 Manchester
09.09.00	Piotr Bartnicki W PTS 4 Manchester
12.11.00	Dean Ashton W RSC 2 Manchester

Career: 3 contests, won 3.

Alan Page   Les Clark

Keith Palmer

Sheffield. *Born* Sheffield, 20 April, 1970
Middleweight. Ht. 5'9"
Manager B. Ingle/F. Warren

12.11.97	Jeff Finlayson L PTS 6 Blackpool
02.12.97	Matthew Barr W RSC 4 Windsor
01.02.99	Wayne Appleton L PTS 4 Bradford
13.03.99	Lee Murtagh DREW 6 Manchester
02.11.00	Colin Vidler W PTS 6 Kensington
24.11.00	Andy Vickers L RSC 3 Darlington

Career: 6 contests, won 2, drew 1, lost 3.

(Odysseas) Oddy Papantoniou

Bristol. *Born* Bristol, 12 July, 1974
Cruiserweight. Ht. 5'10½"
Manager T. Woodward

29.03.01	Oneal Murray W PTS 4 Hammersmith
26.04.01	Calvin Stonestreet L PTS 6 Kensington
12.05.01	Gareth Hogg L RSC 2 Plymouth

Career: 3 contests, won 1, lost 2.

Danny Parkinson

Bradford. *Born* Bradford, 6 August, 1980
Welterweight. Ht. 5'11"
Manager Self

12.06.00	Ram Singh W RSC 3 Bradford
04.12.00	Ram Singh W PTS 6 Bradford
05.02.01	Dean Nicholas W PTS 6 Bradford
19.03.01	Lee Sharp L PTS 6 Glasgow

Career: 4 contests, won 3, lost 1.

Levi Pattison

Leeds. *Born* Kings Lynn, 10 September, 1975
Flyweight. Ht. 5'5½"
Manager M. Marsden

17.07.99	Graham McGrath W PTS 4 Doncaster
15.01.00	Sean Green L PTS 4 Doncaster
25.06.00	Paddy Folan W PTS 6 Wakefield
27.11.00	Chris Edwards L PTS 4 Birmingham
08.05.01	Delroy Spencer W PTS 4 Barnsley
17.05.01	Gary Ford W RSC 5 Leeds

Career: 6 contests, won 4, lost 2.

Mark Paxford

Wigan. *Born* Leigh, 18 February, 1979
L. Middleweight. Ht. 5'9¼"
Manager R. Jones

22.09.00	Colin McCash DREW 6 Wrexham
03.12.00	Paddy Martin W RSC 3 Shaw
04.02.01	Matt Scriven W PTS 6 Queensferry

Career: 3 contests, won 2, drew 1.

Gareth Payne

Coventry. *Born* Coventry, 14 April, 1973
S. Bantamweight. Ht. 5'3"
Manager J. Griffin/J. Harding

12.07.99	Lennie Hodgkins W PTS 4 Coventry
22.10.99	Danny Mulligan W RSC 2 Coventry
14.12.99	Paul Quarmby W PTS 4 Coventry
22.01.00	Sean Grant W RSC 1 Birmingham
22.05.00	Nicky Booth L PTS 4 Coventry
28.10.00	Chris Emanuele W CO 1 Coventry
02.01.01	Danny Lawson W RSC 1 Coventry

Career: 7 contests, won 6, lost 1.

Mark Payne

Coventry. *Born* Coventry, 29 March, 1976
Featherweight. Ht. 5'6"
Manager Self

11.05.98	Dave Travers W RTD 3 Leicester
24.09.98	David Jeffrey W RSC 2 Edgbaston
30.11.98	Danny Lawson W RSC 1 Leicester
11.12.98	Stevie Quinn W RSC 2 Cheshunt
26.02.99	Arv Mittoo W PTS 4 Coventry
12.07.99	John Barnes W PTS 4 Coventry
05.10.99	Isaac Sebaduka W PTS 6 Bloomsbury
14.12.99	Harry Woods W PTS 4 Coventry
10.03.00	Vlado Varhegyi W PTS 6 Bethnal Green
08.09.00	Vladimir Borov W PTS 6 Hammersmith
28.10.00	Rakhim Mingaleev W PTS 6 Coventry
02.01.01	Keith Jones W PTS 6 Coventry
19.05.01	Dazzo Williams L PTS 8 Wembley

Career: 13 contests, won 12, lost 1.

Tommy Peacock

Liverpool. *Born* Liverpool, 24 October, 1969
L. Welterweight. Ht. 5'9"
Manager S. Foster/S. Wood

22.11.96	Wayne Jones W RSC 4 Liverpool
04.04.97	Craig Kelley W PTS 6 Liverpool
13.08.97	John Bailey W PTS 6 Chester, USA
23.09.97	Lee Raheem W PTS 6 Ledyard, USA
17.11.97	Mark Haslam W DIS 5 Manchester
02.02.98	Anthony Campbell DREW 6 Manchester
27.04.98	David Kirk W PTS 6 Manchester
06.06.98	Marc Smith W RSC 4 Liverpool
21.06.98	Dean Bramhald W PTS 6 Liverpool
19.12.98	Darren Underwood W RSC 3 Liverpool
27.02.99	Richard Hatton L RSC 2 Oldham *(Vacant Central Area L. Welterweight Title)*
26.06.99	Mark Ramsey DREW 4 Millwall
06.11.99	Mohamed Helel W PTS 4 Widnes
01.02.00	Souleymane M'Baye L RTD 4 Paris, France
02.03.00	Karim Bouali L PTS 4 Birkenhead
26.05.00	Kevin McIntyre L RSC 5 Glasgow
23.01.01	Kevin Bennett L RSC 5 Crawley

Career: 17 contests, won 10, drew 2, lost 5.

Tommy Peacock   Les Clark

Gavin Pearson

Bradford. *Born* Bradford, 10 March, 1977
Welterweight. Ht. 5'10"
Manager Self

26.11.98	Bobby Lyndon W PTS 6 Bradford
07.12.98	Dale Lowe L PTS 6 Cleethorpes
21.02.99	Les Frost W PTS 6 Bradford
12.03.99	Piotr Banicki DREW 4 Bethnal Green
03.04.99	Piotr Banicki DREW 4 Carlisle
06.05.99	Paul Swindles W PTS 6 Sunderland
29.05.99	Craig Smith L RSC 1 South Shields
12.09.99	Mike Watson W PTS 6 Nottingham
14.11.99	Chris Steele W PTS 6 Bradford
26.11.99	Peter Dunn DREW 6 Wakefield

131

09.12.99	John Marsden W PTS 6 Sunderland
06.03.00	John Marsden W PTS 6 Bradford
20.03.00	Joe Miller L PTS 6 Glasgow
17.04.00	Arv Mittoo W PTS 6 Glasgow
15.05.00	John Marsden W CO 5 Bradford
25.06.00	Robbie Sivyer L PTS 6 Wakefield
04.12.00	Dave Hinds W PTS 6 Bradford
05.02.01	Robert Burton L RSC 3 Bradford
17.05.01	Peter Dunn W PTS 6 Leeds

Career: 19 contests, won 11, drew 3, lost 5.

Gavin Pearson   Les Clark

Jon Penn   Les Clark

Jon Penn

Hemsworth. *Born* Sheffield, 21 January, 1973
S. Middleweight. Ht. 5'8½"
Manager Self

09.10.97	Ian Toby W PTS 6 Hull
11.11.97	Clint Johnson L RSC 2 Leeds
15.12.97	Mike Duffield W RSC 2 Cleethorpes
26.02.98	Ian Toby DREW 6 Sunderland
05.04.98	Jimmy Steel W RSC 5 Shaw
21.05.98	Eddie Haley W RSC 2 Bradford
20.09.98	Jason Barker W PTS 6 Sheffield
28.11.98	Danny Ryan W RSC 4 Belfast
06.03.99	Howard Eastman L RSC 3 Southwark *(Vacant IBO Inter-Continental S. Middleweight Title)*
26.06.99	Mario Veit L RSC 3 Millwall
10.12.99	Milko Stoikov W CO 1 Warsaw, Poland
12.02.00	Jimmy Steel W PTS 6 Sheffield
21.10.00	Paul Bonson W PTS 6 Sheffield
26.03.01	Michael Bowen L RSC 5 Wembley
23.06.01	Neil Linford L RSC 3 Peterborough

Career: 15 contests, won 9, drew 1, lost 5.

Matthew Pepper

Scunthorpe. *Born* Scunthorpe, 23 April, 1979
L. Heavyweight. Ht. 6'0"
Manager T. Petersen

03.12.98	Martin Thompson L CO 4 Hull
30.04.99	Steve Timms L RSC 3 Scunthorpe
26.11.99	Jim Milner W RSC 5 Hull
15.01.00	Damon Hague L CO 1 Doncaster
09.04.00	Damon Hague L RSC 3 Alfreton
11.05.00	Ivan Botton L RSC 4 Newark
09.06.00	Andrew Facey L RSC 1 Hull
30.08.00	Mike Duffield L RSC 4 Scunthorpe
24.03.01	Mark Brookes L RSC 1 Sheffield

Career: 9 contests, won 1, lost 8.

Danny Percival

Southend. *Born* Southend, 3 May, 1973
Heavyweight. Ht. 6'0"
Manager F. Maloney

21.10.00	Chris Woollas W PTS 4 Wembley
13.11.00	Gary Williams W PTS 4 Bethnal Green
10.03.01	Eamonn Glennon W PTS 4 Bethnal Green
05.05.01	Slick Miller L CO 1 Edmonton

Career: 4 contests, won 3, lost 1.

Jimmy Phelan

Hull. *Born* London, 18 June, 1971
Lightweight. Former Central Area Lightweight Champion. Ht. 5'9"
Manager Self

23.11.93	T. J. Smith L PTS 6 Kettering
16.12.93	Paul Bowen W PTS 6 Walsall
10.02.94	Micky Hall L PTS 6 Hull
11.10.94	Colin Dunne L PTS 6 Bethnal Green
31.10.94	George Naylor L PTS 6 Liverpool
16.03.95	Bobby Guynan W RSC 5 Basildon
01.07.95	A. M. Milton W PTS 6 Kensington
22.09.95	Tony Foster W PTS 10 Hull *(Central Area Lightweight Title Challenge)*
08.12.95	Yifru Retta L RSC 5 Bethnal Green
15.03.96	Carl Tilley L PTS 6 Hull
27.09.96	Wayne Rigby L PTS 10 Hull *(Central Area Lightweight Title Defence)*
03.02.97	Kelton McKenzie L RSC 5 Leicester
14.03.97	Kid McAuley W PTS 6 Hull

04.04.97	Scott Dixon L PTS 6 Glasgow
03.05.97	Mark Winters L PTS 4 Manchester
09.06.97	Malcolm Melvin L RSC 2 Birmingham
19.09.97	Marc Smith W PTS 6 Hull
17.11.97	Craig Kelley W PTS 6 Manchester
24.01.98	Dean Phillips L PTS 6 Cardiff
23.03.98	Steve McLevy W RSC 8 Glasgow
18.09.98	Gary Hibbert L PTS 6 Manchester
26.09.98	Antonio Ramirez L PTS 6 Norwich
25.05.00	Pete Buckley DREW 6 Hull
16.11.00	Keith Jones DREW 6 Hull
30.11.00	Jaz Malik W RSC 4 Bloomsbury
09.12.00	Colin Lynes L PTS 6 Southwark
24.03.01	Roger Sampson L PTS 4 Sheffield
02.06.01	Steve Conway L PTS 4 Wakefield
23.06.01	Liam Maltby L RTD 3 Peterborough

Career: 29 contests, won 9, drew 2, lost 18.

Mark Phillips

St Clare's. *Born* Carmarthen, 28 April, 1975
S. Middleweight. Ht. 6'0"
Manager C. Sanigar

26.10.00	Shayne Webb W PTS 6 Clydach
12.12.00	Tommy Matthews W PTS 6 Clydach
13.03.01	William Webster W RTD 1 Plymouth

Career: 3 contests, won 3.

Paul Philpott

Southampton. *Born* Southampton, 31 May, 1973
L. Welterweight. Ht. 5'6"
Manager J. Bishop

27.05.00	Mally McIver L PTS 4 Southwark
22.10.00	Chill John L PTS 6 Streatham

Career: 2 contests, lost 2.

Esham Pickering

Newark. *Born* Newark, 7 August, 1976
British Masters Bantamweight Champion. Ht. 5'5"
Manager B. Ingle/F. Warren

23.09.96	Brendan Bryce W RSC 5 Cleethorpes
24.10.96	Kevin Sheil W PTS 6 Lincoln
22.11.96	Amjid Mahmood W RSC 2 Hull
09.12.96	Des Gargano W RTD 2 Chesterfield
16.12.96	Graham McGrath W PTS 6 Cleethorpes
20.03.97	Robert Braddock W RSC 6 Newark
12.04.97	Graham McGrath W PTS 4 Sheffield
26.04.97	Mike Deveney W PTS 4 Swadlincote
16.05.97	Chris Price W PTS 6 Hull
26.06.97	Graham McGrath W PTS 6 Salford
01.11.97	Mike Deveney W RSC 8 Glasgow *(Elim. British Featherweight Title)*
09.05.98	Jonjo Irwin L PTS 12 Sheffield *(Vacant British Featherweight Title)*
11.09.98	Louis Veitch W PTS 6 Newark
15.08.99	Chris Lyons W RSC 2 Derby
23.10.99	Ian Turner W PTS 6 Telford
20.11.99	Marc Smith W PTS 6 Grantham
19.02.00	Kevin Gerowski W PTS 10 Newark *(Vacant British Masters Bantamweight Title. Elim. British Bantamweight Title)*
13.08.00	Lee Williamson W PTS 6 Nottingham
16.12.00	Mauricio Martinez L RSC 1 Sheffield *(WBO Bantamweight Title Challenge)*

Career: 19 contests, won 17, lost 2.

Wayne Pinder

Manchester. *Born* Manchester, 15 April, 1978
Middleweight. Ht. 6'0"
Manager S. Foster/S. Wood

27.04.98 C. J. Jackson W PTS 6 Manchester
01.06.98 Carlton Williams W PTS 6 Manchester
26.10.98 Mark Owens DREW 6 Manchester
28.02.99 Lee Bird W RSC 5 Shaw
13.03.99 Paul O'Rourke W RSC 3 Manchester
02.05.99 Carl Smith W RSC 5 Shaw
02.07.99 Donovan Davey W PTS 6 Manchester
19.09.99 Paul King W PTS 6 Shaw
11.06.00 Colin Vidler W PTS 6 Salford
01.07.00 Gary Beardsley W PTS 4 Manchester
09.09.00 Ian Toby W PTS 4 Manchester
12.11.00 James Donoghue W PTS 6 Manchester
17.03.01 Leigh Wicks W PTS 4 Manchester
27.05.01 Dean Ashton W PTS 6 Manchester
Career: 14 contests, won 13, drew 1.

Michael Pinnock

Birmingham. *Born* Birmingham, 6 June, 1965
Cruiserweight. Ht. 6'0"
Manager Self

19.05.95 David Flowers L PTS 6 Leeds
13.06.95 Mark Snipe L PTS 6 Basildon
20.06.95 Darren Sweeney L PTS 8 Birmingham
06.09.95 Steve Loftus L PTS 6 Stoke
21.09.95 Luan Morena L PTS 4 Battersea
24.10.95 Graham Townsend L PTS 4 Southwark
17.11.95 Graham Townsend L PTS 4 Bethnal Green
03.12.95 Neville Smith L RSC 5 Southwark
23.01.96 Butch Lesley L PTS 4 Bethnal Green
05.03.96 Panayiotis Panayiotiou L PTS 4 Bethnal Green
16.03.96 Mark Hickey L PTS 6 Barnstaple
25.03.96 Lee Simpkin W PTS 6 Birmingham
03.04.96 Jason Hart L PTS 6 Bethnal Green
24.04.96 Gordon Behan L PTS 6 Solihull
03.05.96 David Larkin DREW 6 Sheffield
14.05.96 Mervyn Penniston L RSC 2 Dagenham
19.07.96 Chris Davies L PTS 6 Ystrad
29.07.96 Stuart Fleet L RSC 3 Skegness
04.10.96 Paul Bonson L PTS 6 Wakefield
28.10.96 Zak Goldman DREW 6 Leicester
14.11.96 Paul Bonson DREW 6 Sheffield
21.11.96 Darren Sweeney W RSC 5 Solihull
26.11.96 Mark Smallwood L PTS 6 Wolverhampton
03.02.97 Neil Simpson L PTS 6 Leicester
09.06.97 Mark Hobson L PTS 6 Bradford
05.07.97 Paschal Collins L PTS 6 Glasgow
02.09.97 Mike Gormley L PTS 6 Manchester
18.09.97 Martin Jolley DREW 6 Alfreton
04.10.97 Zoltan Sarossy L PTS 4 Muswell Hill
27.10.97 Johnny Hooks DREW 6 Nottingham
11.11.97 Graham Townsend L PTS 8 Bethnal Green
25.11.97 Barry Thorogood L PTS 8 Wolverhampton
15.12.97 Greg Scott-Briggs L PTS 6 Nottingham
02.02.98 Glenn Williams L CO 5 Manchester
30.04.98 Bobby Banghar L PTS 6 Purfleet
18.05.98 John O'Brien L PTS 6 Cleethorpes
22.10.98 Paul Carr L PTS 8 Barking
29.10.98 Paul Carr DREW 6 Bayswater
05.12.98 Dave Stenner W RSC 3 Bristol
03.04.99 Robert Zlotkowski L PTS 4 Carlisle
15.05.99 Damon Hague L PTS 4 Sheffield
05.06.99 Leif Keiski L PTS 6 Cardiff
02.07.99 Mike Gormley L RSC 6 Manchester
01.10.99 Tony Oakey L PTS 4 Bethnal Green
16.10.99 Brian Magee L RSC 3 Belfast
17.04.00 Gordon Behan L PTS 6 Birmingham
15.05.00 Tony Booth L PTS 6 Cleethorpes
25.05.00 Neil Linford L PTS 6 Peterborough
08.09.00 Steven Spartacus L PTS 4 Hammersmith
10.11.00 Tony Griffiths L PTS 4 Mayfair
01.12.00 Allan Foster L PTS 4 Peterborough
29.01.01 Ivan Botton W PTS 4 Peterborough
20.03.01 Joe Gillon L PTS 6 Glasgow
28.03.01 Darren Ashton DREW 6 Piccadilly
09.06.01 Nathan King L PTS 4 Bethnal Green
21.06.01 Paul Bonson L PTS 6 Sheffield
Career: 56 contests, won 4, drew 7, lost 45.

Dean Pithie

Coventry. *Born* Coventry, 18 January 1974
Former Undefeated WBC International S. Featherweight Champion. Former WBO Inter-Continental S. Featherweight Champion. Ht. 5'5"
Manager Self

17.02.95 Kid McAuley W RSC 3 Cumbernauld
13.04.95 Kid McAuley W RSC 1 Bloomsbury
01.07.95 Pete Buckley W PTS 4 Kensington
22.07.95 G. G. Goddard W PTS 4 Millwall
21.10.95 Anthony Campbell W PTS 4 Bethnal Green
10.11.95 Kelton McKenzie DREW 6 Derby
26.04.96 Kelton McKenzie W PTS 6 Cardiff
25.06.96 Lewis Reynolds W RSC 2 Mansfield
14.09.96 Miguel Matthews W PTS 4 Sheffield
14.12.96 Marty Chestnut W RSC 3 Sheffield
18.01.97 Harry Escott W RSC 4 Swadlincote
25.02.97 Pete Buckley W PTS 4 Sheffield
26.04.97 David Morris W PTS 8 Swadlincote
11.10.97 Stefy Bull W RSC 11 Sheffield
(*Vacant WBO Inter-Continental S. Featherweight Title*)
27.03.98 Paul Griffin W RSC 9 Telford
(*WBO Inter-Continental S. Featherweight Title Defence*)
06.06.98 Gary Thornhill L CO 8 Liverpool
(*WBO Inter-Continental S. Featherweight Title Defence*)
02.10.98 Keith Jones W PTS 8 Cheshunt
11.12.98 Kelton McKenzie W RSC 7 Cheshunt
(*Elim. British S. Featherweight Title*)
26.02.99 Andrew Matabola L RSC 8 Coventry
(*Vacant WBC International S. Featherweight Title*)
12.07.99 Andrew Matebola W RSC 2 Coventry
(*WBC International S. Featherweight Title Challenge*)
22.10.99 Frank Kiwanuka W RSC 2 Coventry
(*WBC International S. Featherweight Title Defence*)
14.12.99 Mzonke Fana W PTS 12 Coventry
(*WBC International S. Featherweight Title Defence*)
29.02.00 Michael Gomez L PTS 12 Widnes
(*British S. Featherweight Title Challenge*)
22.05.00 Wiseman Jim DREW 12 Coventry
(*Vacant WBF Inter-Continental S. Featherweight Title*)
28.10.00 Affif Djelti L CO 6 Coventry
(*IBO S.Featherweight Title Challenge*)
10.04.01 Keith Jones W PTS 4 Wembley
Career: 26 contests, won 20, drew 2, lost 4.

Gary Porter

Glasgow. *Born* Glasgow, 12 September, 1978
L. Middleweight. Ht. 5'9"
Manager B. Watt

04.06.01 Arv Mittoo W PTS 6 Glasgow
Career: 1 contest, won 1.

Marcus Portman

West Bromwich. *Born* West Bromwich, 26 September, 1980
L. Welterweight. Ht. 6'0"
Manager D. Bradley

18.02.00 Ray Wood W PTS 6 West Bromwich
28.03.00 Billy Smith W PTS 6 Wolverhampton
10.09.00 Alan Kershaw W RSC 2 Walsall
15.02.01 Willie Limond L PTS 6 Glasgow
01.04.01 Tony Smith W PTS 6 Wolverhampton
20.04.01 Darren Melville L RSC 3 Millwall
Career: 6 contests, won 4, lost 2.

Mark Potter Dave Rawlings

Mark Potter

Walthamstow. *Born* Rush Green, 27 February, 1975
Southern Area Heavyweight Champion. Ht. 6'1"
Manager Self

19.07.97 J. A. Bugner W PTS 6 Wembley
02.09.97 Rob Albon W RSC 1 Southwark
06.12.97 Johnny Davison W CO 1 Wembley
27.02.98 Lennox Williams W CO 1 Brighton
21.04.98 Geoff Hunter W RSC 1 Edmonton
23.05.98 Shane Woollas W PTS 4 Bethnal Green
12.09.98 Abdelrani Berbachi W RTD 4 Bethnal Green
22.09.98 Antoine Palatis L PTS 8 Pont Audemir, France
21.11.98 Ladislav Husarik W RSC 6 Southwark
08.05.99 Piotr Jurczyk W RSC 1 Bethnal Green
10.07.99 Stanislav Tomcatchov W RSC 3 Southwark

13.09.99 Derek McCafferty W PTS 6 Bethnal Green
29.11.99 Keith Long L PTS 8 Wembley
13.03.00 Danny Watts W RSC 6 Bethnal Green
(Vacant Southern Area Heavyweight Title)
27.05.00 Mal Rice W CO 1 Southwark
23.09.00 Luke Simpkin W PTS 6 Bethnal Green
21.10.00 Danny Williams L RSC 6 Wembley
(Commonwealth & WBO Inter-Continental Heavyweight Title Challenges. Vacant British Heavyweight Title)
05.05.01 Michael Murray W PTS 8 Edmonton
Career: 18 contests, won 15, lost 3.

Martin Power

Camden Town. *Born* London, 14 February, 1980
Bantamweight. Ht. 5'6"
Manager F. Maloney

09.06.01 Sean Grant W PTS 4 Bethnal Green
Career: 1 contest, won 1.

Chris Price

Sheffield. *Born* Rotherham, 4 March, 1977
Lightweight. Ht. 5'9"
Manager Self

06.09.95 Shaun Gledhill L PTS 6 Stoke
23.10.95 Jason Squire L PTS 6 Leicester
14.11.95 Colin Innes W PTS 6 Yarm
03.02.96 Alex Moon L RSC 2 Liverpool
20.03.96 Johnny Miller L PTS 6 Stoke
15.05.96 Tommy Janes L RSC 4 Cardiff
22.08.96 John Briffa L RSC 2 Salford
22.11.96 Kid McAuley DREW 6 Hull
09.12.96 Robbie Sivyer DREW 6 Chesterfield
17.12.96 Dean Bramhald L PTS 6 Doncaster
20.02.97 David Kirk L PTS 6 Mansfield
20.03.97 Peter Gabbitus L PTS 6 Doncaster
29.04.97 Shaun Gledhill L PTS 6 Manchester
16.05.97 Esham Pickering L PTS 6 Hull
22.05.97 Ervine Blake L PTS 6 Solihull
13.06.97 Scott Dixon L PTS 6 Paisley
09.10.97 Trevor Smith L PTS 6 Leeds
04.12.97 Carl Tilley L PTS 6 Doncaster
05.03.98 Kid McAuley W PTS 6 Leeds
16.03.98 Vic Broomhead L PTS 6 Nottingham
24.03.98 Dean Murdoch L PTS 6 Wolverhampton
03.04.98 Brian Robb L PTS 6 West Bromwich
28.04.98 John Paul Temple W PTS 6 Brentford
13.05.98 Tony Smith L PTS 6 Scunthorpe
05.06.98 Jim Betts L PTS 6 Hull
15.05.99 Oscar Hall L PTS 4 Sheffield
04.06.99 Mark Halstead DREW 6 Hull
20.11.99 Gavin McGill L PTS 4 Grantham
28.11.99 Roger Sampson L PTS 4 Chesterfield
19.02.00 Jim Betts L PTS 6 Newark
27.02.00 Steve Conway L RTD 3 Leeds
19.06.00 Jim Betts L PTS 4 Burton
19.11.00 Jesse James Daniel L PTS 4 Chesterfield
06.03.01 Tony Montana L PTS 6 Yarm
Career: 34 contests, won 3, drew 3, lost 28.

Sean Pritchard

Aberbargoed. *Born* Caerphilly, 19 April, 1975
S. Middleweight. Ht. 6'2"
Manager Self

19.09.98 John O'Brien L PTS 6 Dublin
31.10.98 Jason Ratcliff L RSC 4 Southend
19.03.99 John O'Brien W PTS 8 Weston super Mare
10.04.99 Donovan Smillie L RSC 1 Manchester
29.05.99 Darren Rhodes DREW 4 Halifax
24.09.99 Steven Bendall L PTS 6 Merthyr
02.10.99 Tony Dodson L RSC 3 Cardiff
08.09.00 Scott Dann L RSC 5 Bristol
Career: 8 contests, won 1, drew 1, lost 6.

Bradley Pryce (Price)

Newbridge. *Born* Newport, 15 March, 1981
WBO Inter-Continental Lightweight Champion. Ht. 5'11"
Manager E. Calzaghe

17.07.99 Dave Hinds W PTS 4 Doncaster
23.10.99 David Jeffrey W RSC 3 Telford
06.11.99 Eddie Nevins W RSC 2 Widnes
29.01.00 Pete Buckley W PTS 4 Manchester
29.02.00 Carl Allen W PTS 4 Widnes
16.05.00 Carl Allen W RSC 3 Warrington
15.07.00 Gary Flear W RSC 1 Millwall
07.10.00 Gary Reid W RSC 5 Doncaster
27.01.01 Joel Viney W RSC 3 Bethnal Green
17.03.01 Brian Coleman W PTS 4 Manchester
28.04.01 Jason Hall W PTS 12 Cardiff
(Vacant WBO Inter-Continental Lightweight Title)
Career: 11 contests, won 11.

Byron Pryce (Price)

Newbridge. *Born* Newport, 16 May, 1978
L. Welterweight. Ht. 6'0"
Manager Self

23.10.96 Fred Reeve W RSC 1 Halifax
21.06.97 Craig Kelley DREW 4 Cardiff
12.05.01 Wayne Wheeler W RSC 2 Plymouth
Career: 3 contests, won 2, drew 1.

Delroy Pryce (Price)

Newbridge. *Born* Newport, 25 May, 1979
Featherweight. Ht. 5'7"
Manager F. Warren/E. Calzaghe

21.06.97 John Farrell DREW 4 Cardiff
30.01.99 Graham McGrath W PTS 4 Bethnal Green
13.02.99 Stephen Oates W PTS 6 Newcastle
08.04.00 Pete Buckley W PTS 4 Bethnal Green
19.06.00 Pete Buckley W PTS 4 Burton
21.10.00 Chris Jickells W PTS 4 Wembley
27.01.01 Nedal Hussein L CO 3 Bethnal Green
Career: 7 contests, won 5, drew 1, lost 1.

Stevie Quinn

Newtownards. *Born* Newtonards, 14 November, 1969
S. Bantamweight. Ht. 5'7"
Manager O. McMahon

07.02.98 Stephen Oates L PTS 4 Cheshunt
28.04.98 Tommy Waite L RSC 3 Belfast
11.12.98 Mark Payne L RSC 2 Cheshunt
17.04.99 Chris Edwards W RSC 4 Dublin
22.05.99 Ross Cassidy W PTS 4 Belfast
16.10.99 Anthony Hanna L PTS 4 Belfast
19.02.00 Barry Hawthorne W RSC 5 Prestwick
12.06.00 Mickey Coveney L PTS 4 Belfast
20.10.00 Sean Grant W RSC 2 Belfast
11.11.00 Paul Weir W PTS 4 Belfast
27.01.01 Hussein Hussein L RTD 2 Bethnal Green
01.04.01 Richmond Asante W PTS 4 Southwark
28.04.01 Noel Wilders L RTD 6 Cardiff
Career: 13 contests, won 6, lost 7.

Delroy Pryce   Les Clark

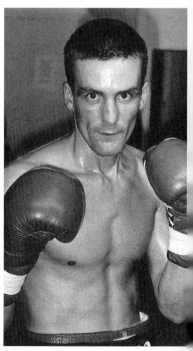

Stevie Quinn   Les Clark

R

Nigel Rafferty

Wolverhampton. *Born* Wolverhampton, 29
December, 1967
Heavyweight. Former Midlands Area
Cruiserweight Champion. Ht. 5'11"
Manager R. Gray

05.06.89	Carl Watson L PTS 6 Birmingham
28.06.89	Tony Hodge L PTS 6 Brentwood
06.07.89	Tony Hodge W PTS 6 Chigwell
04.09.89	Joe Frater L PTS 6 Grimsby
24.10.89	Paul Wesley W PTS 6 Wolverhampton
22.11.89	Paul Wesley W PTS 8 Stafford
28.11.89	Paul Wesley W PTS 6 Wolverhampton
04.12.89	Dean Murray W PTS 6 Grimsby
20.12.89	Paul Wright DREW 6 Kirkby
17.01.90	Gil Lewis L PTS 6 Stoke
31.01.90	Antoine Tarver L PTS 4 Bethnal Green
19.02.90	Paul Wesley W PTS 8 Birmingham
19.03.90	Terry Gilbey W PTS 6 Grimsby
01.05.90	Sean Heron L RSC 2 Oldham
13.09.90	Paul Murray W PTS 6 Watford
27.09.90	Paul Murray DREW 6 Birmingham
09.10.90	Paul Murray W PTS 6 Wolverhampton
24.10.90	Andrew Flute L CO 6 Dudley
27.11.90	Carlos Christie L PTS 8 Wolverhampton
06.12.90	Carlos Christie L PTS 6 Wolverhampton
28.01.91	Alan Richards DREW 8 Birmingham
04.03.91	Carlos Christie L PTS 8 Birmingham
26.03.91	Lee Prudden W PTS 6 Wolverhampton
13.05.91	Tony Behan W DIS 7 Birmingham
05.06.91	Lee Prudden L PTS 6 Wolverhampton
10.09.91	Paul Busby L RSC 2 Wolverhampton
20.11.91	Julian Johnson DREW 6 Cardiff
02.12.91	Kesem Clayton W PTS 8 Birmingham
21.01.92	Glenn Campbell L RSC 6 Stockport
30.03.92	Simon McDougall W PTS 8 Coventry
25.04.92	Sammy Storey L RSC 3 Belfast
16.06.92	Garry Delaney L CO 5 Dagenham
24.11.92	Graham Burton W PTS 8 Wolverhampton
02.12.92	John J. Cooke L PTS 6 Bardon
23.03.93	Stephen Wilson W RSC 3 Wolverhampton
14.04.93	Ole Klemetsen L RSC 2 Kensington
19.05.93	Zak Chelli L RSC 3 Leicester
22.09.93	Martin Jolley W PTS 6 Chesterfield
12.10.93	Carl Smallwood DREW 8 Wolverhampton
28.10.93	Lee Archer L PTS 8 Walsall
08.12.93	Darren Ashton L PTS 6 Stoke
26.01.94	Monty Wright L PTS 6 Birmingham
08.02.94	Greg Scott-Briggs W PTS 6 Wolverhampton
17.02.94	Glenn Campbell L RSC 7 Bury
18.04.94	Graham Burton W PTS 8 Walsall
23.05.94	Darren Ashton L PTS 6 Walsall
15.06.94	Darron Griffiths L RSC 4 Southwark
03.08.94	Leif Keiski L RSC 5 Bristol
20.10.94	John J. Cooke L RSC 7 Walsall
	(Midlands Area L. Heavyweight Title Challenge)
13.12.94	Paul Lawson L RSC 4 Ilford
20.03.95	John Foreman W PTS 10 Birmingham
	(Midlands Area Cruiserweight Title Challenge)
19.04.95	Bruce Scott L RSC 2 Bethnal Green
17.05.95	Ole Klemetsen L RSC 4 Ipswich
06.07.95	Tony Booth L RSC 7 Hull
26.08.95	Darren Corbett L PTS 6 Belfast
20.09.95	Darren Westover L PTS 6 Potters Bar
29.09.95	Paul Lawson L PTS 6 Bethnal Green
07.10.95	Darren Corbett L PTS 6 Belfast
25.10.95	Robert Norton L RSC 6 Telford
21.02.96	Martin Langtry L CO 4 Batley
	(Midlands Area Cruiserweight Title Defence)
20.05.96	Albert Call DREW 6 Cleethorpes
30.05.96	Tony Dowling L PTS 6 Lincoln
27.08.96	Chris Okoh L RSC 4 Windsor
26.09.96	Paul Wesley DREW 6 Walsall
09.10.96	Chris Woollas L PTS 6 Stoke
28.10.96	Neil Simpson L PTS 8 Leicester
12.11.96	Robert Norton L PTS 8 Dudley
30.11.96	Kelly Oliver L PTS 6 Tylorstown
14.12.96	John Keeton L RTD 3 Sheffield
28.01.97	Darren Corbett L PTS 10 Belfast
	(All-Ireland Cruiserweight Title Challenge)
04.03.97	Dominic Negus L PTS 4 Southwark
25.03.97	Tony Booth DREW 8 Wolverhampton
12.04.97	John Keeton L RSC 6 Sheffield
20.05.97	Dominic Negus L PTS 4 Edmonton
19.07.97	Terry Dunstan L RTD 4 Wembley
11.11.97	Stevie Pettit L PTS 10 Edgbaston
	(Vacant Midlands Area Cruiserweight Title)
21.11.97	Carl Heath L PTS 6 Hull
15.12.97	Tony Booth L PTS 6 Cleethorpes
24.02.98	Stevie Pettit W PTS 10 Edgbaston
	(Midlands Area Cruiserweight Title Challenge)
18.04.98	Kelly Oliver L RSC 4 Manchester
24.09.98	Stevie Pettit DREW 10 Edgbaston
	(Midlands Area Cruiserweight Title Defence)
29.10.98	Tony Booth L PTS 8 Bayswater
24.11.98	Tim Brown L PTS 8 Wolverhampton
12.12.98	Mike Holden L RTD 2 Chester
22.01.99	Cathal O'Grady L CO 2 Dublin
27.02.99	Rudiger May L PTS 8 Berlin, Germany
25.03.99	Slick Miller W PTS 8 Edgbaston
22.04.99	Kevin Burton W PTS 6 Dudley
27.05.99	Chris Woollas L PTS 10 Edgbaston
	(Midlands Area Cruiserweight Title Defence)
15.06.99	Alain Simon L RSC 6 Tenerife, Spain
12.09.99	Wayne Buck L PTS 6 Nottingham
24.10.99	Slick Miller L RSC 4 Wolverhampton
08.12.99	Adam Cale W PTS 6 Stoke
18.02.00	Jason Brewster W PTS 6 West Bromwich
26.02.00	Enzo Maccarinelli L RSC 3 Swansea
01.04.00	Paul Maskell L PTS 4 Bethnal Green
09.04.00	Brian Gascoigne L PTS 6 Alfreton
15.05.00	Dave Faulkner W PTS 6 Bradford
02.06.00	Faisal Mohammed L PTS 4 Ashford
06.11.00	Jason Brewster L PTS 8 Wolverhampton
18.11.00	Faisal Mohammed L RSC 3 Dagenham
20.01.01	Mark Krence L PTS 4 Bethnal Green
29.01.01	Scott Lansdowne L PTS 4 Peterborough
17.02.01	Cengiz Koc L PTS 4 Bethnal Green

Career: 104 contests, won 26, drew 9, lost 69.

Mark Ramsey

Birmingham. *Born* Birmingham, 24
January, 1968
Welterweight. Ht. 5'7½"
Manager Self

15.11.89	Mick O'Donnell W RSC 1 Lewisham
08.12.89	Dave Pierre L RSC 2 Doncaster
22.02.90	Karl Taylor W RSC 4 Hull
10.04.90	George Jones W RSC 6 Doncaster
20.05.90	Steve Pollard W PTS 6 Sheffield
18.10.90	Neil Haddock L RSC 5 Birmingham
30.05.91	Colin Sinnott W PTS 6 Birmingham
05.12.91	Carl Hook W RSC 5 Oakengates
27.01.93	Andrew Jervis W PTS 6 Stoke
12.02.93	Reymond Deva W PTS 6 Aubervilliers, France
04.03.93	Dave Pierre L PTS 8 Peterborough
01.05.93	Vyacheslav Ianowski L PTS 8 Berlin, Germany
02.07.93	Andreas Panayi DREW 6 Liverpool
05.08.93	Jean Chiarelli W RSC 4 Ascona, Italy
01.10.93	Freddy Demeulenaere W RSC 3 Waregem, Belgium
26.03.94	James Osunsedo W RSC 4 Dortmund, Germany
07.05.94	Andrei Sinepupov L PTS 12 Dnepropetrousk, Ukraine
	(Vacant WBO Penta-Continental Lightweight Title)
30.11.94	Mark Elliot W RSC 10 Wolverhampton
	(Elim. British L. Welterweight Title)
20.05.95	Ahmed Katejev L RTD 5 Hamburg, Germany
	(WBC International Welterweight Title Challenge)
15.09.95	Paul Dyer L PTS 6 Mansfield
23.10.95	Stefan Scriggins L PTS 8 Leicester
12.02.96	Alan McDowall L PTS 8 Glasgow
16.03.96	Alan McDowall L PTS 8 Glasgow
28.06.96	Poli Diaz W RSC 4 Madrid, Spain
12.11.96	Paul Samuels L RSC 4 Dudley
24.02.97	Bobby Vanzie DREW 8 Glasgow
25.03.97	Joshua Clottey L PTS 8 Lewisham
30.04.97	Anthony Campbell L PTS 6 Acton
20.05.97	Peter Richardson L PTS 8 Edmonton
09.08.97	George Scott L PTS 10 San Gennaro Vesuviano, Italy
27.10.97	Steve McLevy L PTS 6 Glasgow
13.12.97	Jawaid Khaliq DREW 4 Sheffield
07.02.98	Junior Witter DREW 6 Cheshunt
24.02.98	Bruno Wartelle L PTS 10 Porto, Portugal
28.03.98	Justin Juuko L PTS 8 Hull
30.05.98	Richard Hatton L PTS 6 Bristol
18.09.98	Glenn McClarnon L PTS 4 Belfast
23.11.98	Benny Jones W PTS 6 Piccadilly
05.12.98	Jason Williams L PTS 6 Bristol
22.01.99	Neil Sinclair L CO 3 Dublin
12.03.99	Glenn McClarnon L PTS 6 Bethnal Green
23.04.99	Dave Hinds W PTS 6 Clydach
15.05.99	Corey Johnson L PTS 8 Sheffield
07.06.99	Scott Dixon L PTS 8 Glasgow
26.06.99	Tommy Peacock DREW 4 Millwall
17.07.99	Richard Hatton L PTS 6 Doncaster
16.10.99	Bernard McComiskey L PTS 6 Belfast
21.02.00	Charlie Kane L PTS 6 Glasgow
11.03.00	Darren Bruce DREW 6 Kensington
17.04.00	Spencer McCracken L PTS 8 Birmingham
04.09.00	Michael Jennings L PTS 6 Manchester
16.09.00	Zoltan Sarossy W PTS 8 Bethnal Green
28.09.00	Ossie Duran L RSC 2 Kensington
03.11.00	Jason Williams W CO 6 Ebbw Vale
10.11.00	Kevin McIntyre L RSC 4 Glasgow
23.01.01	James Hare L PTS 6 Crawley
17.02.01	Colin Lynes L PTS 6 Bethnal Green
13.03.01	Pavel Melnikov L PTS 8 Plymouth

20.04.01 John Humphrey L PTS 10 Millwall
(Vacant British Masters Welterweight Title)
19.05.01 David Walker L PTS 4 Wembley
16.06.01 John Tiftik W PTS 6 Dagenham
Career: 61 contests, won 18, drew 6, lost 37.

(Shahid) Sid Razak

Birmingham. *Born* Birmingham, 9 March, 1973
Featherweight. Ht. 5'7"
Manager R. Gray/P. Cowdell

13.02.01 Neil Read W PTS 6 Brierley Hill
27.03.01 Tommy Thomas W RSC 2 Brierley Hill
21.05.01 Jason Nesbitt W PTS 6 Birmingham
Career: 3 contests, won 3.

Neil Read

Bilston. *Born* Wolverhampton, 9 February, 1972
Featherweight. Ht. 5'4"
Manager P. Bowen

08.02.00 Gary Groves W PTS 6 Wolverhampton
10.09.00 Stephen Chinnock L RSC 5 Walsall
30.11.00 Paddy Folan L PTS 6 Blackpool
13.02.01 Sid Razak L PTS 6 Brierley Hill
08.03.01 John-Paul Ryan W PTS 6 Stoke
Career: 5 contests, won 2, lost 3.

Gavin Rees

Newbridge. *Born* Newport, 10 May, 1980
WBO Inter-Continental Featherweight Champion. Ht. 5'7"
Manager F. Warren/E. Calzaghe

05.09.98 John Farrell W PTS 4 Telford
05.12.98 Ernie Smith W PTS 4 Bristol
27.03.99 Graham McGrath W RSC 2 Derby
05.06.99 Wayne Jones W RSC 2 Cardiff
11.12.99 Dave Hinds W RSC 2 Liverpool
19.02.00 Pete Buckley W PTS 4 Dagenham
29.05.00 Willie Valentine W RSC 3 Manchester
23.09.00 Pete Buckley W PTS 4 Bethnal Green
13.11.00 Steve Hanley W RSC 1 Bethnal Green
15.01.01 Chris Jickells W RSC 2 Manchester
28.04.01 Vladimir Borov W RSC 4 Cardiff
(Vacant WBO Inter-Continental Featherweight Title)
Career: 11 contests, won 11.

Russell Rees

Gilfach Goch. *Born* Pontypridd, 4 October, 1974
L. Middleweight. Ht. 5'7"
Manager D. Gardiner

19.01.93 Chip O'Neill W RSC 1 Cardiff
06.02.93 Eunan Devenney W RSC 3 Cardiff
30.03.93 Ian Reid W PTS 6 Cardiff
10.07.93 Miguel Matthews W PTS 6 Cardiff
29.01.94 Andrew Reed W PTS 6 Cardiff
03.11.00 Des Sowden W RSC 1 Ebbw Vale
Career: 6 contests, won 6.

Gary Reid

Wolverhampton. *Born* Jamaica, 20 November, 1972
L. Welterweight. Ht. 5'5½"
Manager S. Foster/S. Wood

09.12.98 Carl Tilley W CO 1 Stoke
11.02.99 Ted Bami L RSC 2 Dudley
23.03.99 Lee Williamson W PTS 6 Wolverhampton
07.10.99 Stuart Rimmer W RSC 2 Mere
19.12.99 Nono Junior L PTS 6 Salford
14.04.00 Lee Molyneux W PTS 6 Manchester
18.05.00 Sammy Smith W RSC 1 Bethnal Green
23.07.00 Kevin Bennett L RSC 4 Hartlepool
21.09.00 Karim Bouali L PTS 4 Bloomsbury
07.10.00 Bradley Pryce L RSC 5 Doncaster
Career: 10 contests, won 5, lost 5.

Robin Reid

Runcorn. Liverpool, 19 February, 1971
WBF S. Middleweight Champion. Former WBC S. Middleweight Champion. Ht. 5'9"
Manager Self

27.02.93 Mark Dawson W RSC 1 Dagenham
06.03.93 Julian Eavis W RSC 2 Glasgow
10.04.93 Andrew Furlong W PTS 6 Swansea
10.09.93 Juan Garcia W PTS 6 San Antonio, USA
09.10.93 Ernie Loveridge W PTS 4 Manchester
18.12.93 Danny Juma DREW 6 Manchester
09.04.94 Kesem Clayton W RSC 1 Mansfield
04.06.94 Andrew Furlong W RSC 2 Cardiff
17.08.94 Andrew Jervis W RSC 1 Sheffield
19.11.94 Chris Richards W RSC 3 Cardiff
04.02.95 Bruno Westenberghs W RSC 1 Cardiff
04.03.95 Marvin O'Brien W RSC 6 Livingston
06.05.95 Steve Goodwin W CO 1 Shepton Mallet
10.06.95 Martin Jolley W CO 1 Manchester
22.07.95 John Duckworth W PTS 8 Millwall
15.09.95 Trevor Ambrose W CO 5 Mansfield
10.11.95 Danny Juma W PTS 8 Derby

Gary Reid Les Clark

26.01.96 Stinger Mason W RSC 2 Brighton
16.03.96 Andrew Flute W RSC 7 Glasgow
26.04.96 Hunter Clay W RSC 1 Cardiff
08.06.96 Mark Dawson W RSC 5 Newcastle
31.08.96 Don Pendleton W RTD 4 Dublin
12.10.96 Vincenzo Nardiello W CO 7 Milan,
Italy
(WBC S. Middleweight Title Challenge)
08.02.97 Giovanni Pretorius W RSC 7 Millwall
(WBC S. Middleweight Title Defence)
03.05.97 Henry Wharton W PTS 12 Manchester
(WBC S. Middleweight Title Defence)
11.09.97 Hassine Cherifi W PTS 12 Widnes
(WBC S. Middleweight Title Defence)
19.12.97 Thulani Malinga L PTS 12 Millwall

(WBC S. Middleweight Title Defence)
18.04.98 Graham Townsend W RSC 6
Manchester
13.02.99 Joe Calzaghe L PTS 12 Newcastle
*(WBO S. Middleweight Title
Challenge)*
24.06.00 Silvio Branco L PTS 12 Glasgow
*(WBU S. Middleweight Title
Challenge)*
08.12.00 Mike Gormley W RSC 1 Crystal
Palace
(Vacant WBF S. Middleweight Title)
19.05.01 Roman Babaev W RSC 3 Wembley
(WBF S. Middleweight Title Defence)
Career: 32 contests, won 28, drew 1, lost 3.

Darren Rhodes

Leeds. *Born* Leeds, 16 September, 1975
Middleweight. Ht. 5'11"
Manager F. Warren

18.07.98 Andy Kemp W RSC 1 Sheffield
10.10.98 Perry Ayres W CO 2 Bethnal Green
27.02.99 Gareth Lovell W PTS 4 Oldham
01.05.99 Carlton Williams W RSC 4 Crystal
Palace
29.05.99 Sean Pritchard DREW 4 Halifax
09.10.99 Leigh Wicks W PTS 4 Manchester
11.12.99 Leigh Wicks W PTS 4 Liverpool
25.03.00 Leigh Wicks W PTS 4 Liverpool
29.05.00 Dean Ashton W RSC 3 Manchester
08.07.00 Jason Collins DREW 4 Widnes
04.09.00 Jason Collins L PTS 4 Manchester
11.12.00 Paul Wesley W PTS 4 Widnes
17.03.01 Andrew Facey W PTS 4 Manchester
Career: 13 contests, won 10, drew 2, lost 1.

Darren Rhodes   Harry Goodwin

Ryan Rhodes

Sheffield. *Born* Sheffield, 20 November,
1976
Former Undefeated WBO Inter-Continental
Middleweight Champion. Former
Undefeated British & IBF Inter-Continental
L. Middleweight Champion. Ht. 5'8½"
Manager B. Ingle/F. Warren

04.02.95 Lee Crocker W RSC 2 Cardiff
04.03.95 Shamus Casey W CO 1 Livingston
06.05.95 Chris Richards W PTS 6 Shepton
Mallet
15.09.95 John Rice W RSC 2 Mansfield
10.11.95 Mark Dawson W PTS 6 Derby
20.01.96 John Duckworth W RSC 2 Mansfield
26.01.96 Martin Jolley W CO 3 Brighton
11.05.96 Martin Jolley W RSC 2 Bethnal Green
25.06.96 Roy Chipperfield W RSC 1 Mansfield
14.09.96 Del Bryan W PTS 6 Sheffield
14.12.96 Paul Jones W RSC 8 Sheffield
(Vacant British L. Middleweight Title)
25.02.97 Peter Waudby W CO 1 Sheffield
(British L. Middleweight Title Defence)

Robin Reid   Les Clark

137

14.03.97   Del Bryan W RSC 7 Reading
           (British L. Middleweight Title Defence)
12.04.97   Lindon Scarlett W RSC 1 Sheffield
           *(Vacant IBF Inter-Continental
           L. Middleweight Title)*
02.08.97   Ed Griffin W RSC 2 Barnsley
           *(IBF Inter-Continental L. Middleweight
           Title Defence. Vacant WBO
           L. Middleweight Title)*
11.10.97   Yuri Epifantsev W RSC 2 Sheffield
           (Final Elim. WBO Middleweight Title)
13.12.97   Otis Grant L PTS 12 Sheffield
           (Vacant WBO Middleweight Title)
18.07.98   Lorant Szabo W RSC 8 Sheffield
           *(WBO Inter-Continental Middleweight
           Title Challenge)*
28.11.98   Fidel Avendano W RSC 1 Sheffield
           *(WBO Inter-Continental Middleweight
           Title Defence)*
27.03.99   Peter Mason W RSC 1 Derby
17.07.99   Jason Matthews L CO 2 Doncaster
           (Vacant WBO Middleweight Title)
15.01.00   Eddie Haley W RSC 5 Doncaster
16.05.00   Ojay Abrahams W PTS 6 Warrington
21.10.00   Michael Alexander W PTS 6 Wembley
16.12.00   Howard Clarke W PTS 6 Sheffield

Career: 25 contests, won 23, lost 2.

Mal Rice   Les Clark

Mal Rice

Flint. *Born* Mancot, 19 July, 1975
Heavyweight. Ht. 6'2"
Manager J. Davies

26.11.97   Gary Cavey W CO 2 Stoke
29.01.98   Lennox Williams W PTS 6 Pentre
           Halkyn
30.03.98   Bruno Foster L PTS 6 Bradford
30.04.98   Lennox Williams W PTS 6 Pentre
           Halkyn
21.06.98   Shane Woollas L PTS 6 Liverpool
18.02.00   Gary Williams L PTS 6 Pentre Halkyn
13.03.00   Patrick Halberg W RSC 2 Bethnal
           Green

05.05.00   Gary Williams L PTS 4 Pentre Halkyn
27.05.00   Mark Potter L CO 1 Southwark
26.03.01   John McDermott L RSC 2 Wembley

Career: 10 contests, won 4, lost 6.

Paul Richardson

Blackpool. *Born* Oxford, 17 October, 1972
Heavyweight. Ht. 5'10½"
Manager L. Veitch

09.06.00   Jason Brewster W PTS 6 Blackpool
30.11.00   Dave Faulkner W PTS 6 Blackpool
22.01.01   Paul Fiske W PTS 6 Glasgow
08.03.01   Dave Faulkner W RSC 2 Blackpool
01.04.01   Jason Brewster W RSC 4
           Wolverhampton

Career: 5 contests, won 5.

Peter Richardson

Middlesbrough. *Born* Middlesbrough, 24
June, 1970
Welterweight. Ht. 5'9¼"
Manager Self

23.02.95   John O. Johnson W RSC 5 Southwark
27.04.95   Carl Roberts W RSC 1 Bethnal Green
25.05.95   Everald Williams W RSC 6 Reading
02.07.95   John Smith W PTS 6 Dublin
29.09.95   Tony Foster W RSC 1 Bethnal Green
15.12.95   Karl Taylor W PTS 8 Bethnal Green
19.01.96   Steve Pollard W PTS 8 Bracknell
21.03.96   Adrian Chase W RSC 2 Southwark
14.05.96   Trevor Meikle W RSC 2 Dagenham
29.06.96   Kevin McKillan W CO 2 Erith
07.10.96   Rimvidas Billius L RSC 6 Lewisham
11.01.97   Rimvidas Billius W PTS 10 Bethnal
           Green
01.03.97   John Smith W RSC 5 Liverpool
20.05.97   Mark Ramsey W PTS 8 Edmonton
30.08.97   Michael Smyth L RSC 5 Cheshunt
           (Elim. British Welterweight Title)
14.02.98   Dennis Berry L RSC 3 Southwark
18.11.00   Costas Katsantonis W PTS 4
           Dagenham

Career: 17 contests, won 14, lost 3.

Wayne Rigby

Manchester. *Born* Manchester, 19 July,
1973
Former Undefeated IBO Inter-Continental
Lightweight Champion. Former British
Lightweight Champion. Former Undefeated
Central Area Lightweight Champion.
Ht. 5'6"
Manager Self

27.02.92   Lee Fox L PTS 6 Liverpool
08.06.92   Leo Turner W PTS 6 Bradford
02.07.92   Leo Turner W CO 5 Middleton
05.10.92   Colin Innes W PTS 6 Manchester
01.12.92   John T. Kelly L PTS 6 Hartlepool
02.06.94   Kid McAuley W PTS 6 Middleton
13.06.94   Chris Clarkson W PTS 6 Liverpool
22.09.94   Mark Hargreaves W PTS 6 Bury
06.03.95   Kelton McKenzie L PTS 8 Leicester
18.05.95   John T. Kelly W PTS 6 Middleton
05.06.95   Hugh Collins W RSC 4 Glasgow
17.01.96   Kid McAuley W PTS 6 Solihull
24.03.96   Steve Tuckett W PTS 6 Shaw
27.09.96   Jimmy Phelan W PTS 10 Hull
           *(Central Area Lightweight Title
           Challenge)*

07.03.97   Alan Bosworth W RSC 5 Northampton
10.01.98   Tanveer Ahmed W PTS 12 Bethnal
           Green
           (Vacant British Lightweight Title)
11.04.98   Matt Brown W RTD 8 Southwark
           (British Lightweight Title Defence)
17.10.98   Bobby Vanzie L RSC 10 Manchester
           (British Lightweight Title Defence)
31.07.99   Mark McGowan W RSC 4 Carlisle
11.09.99   Alan Temple L PTS 8 Sheffield
04.12.99   Mark Haslam W CO 3 Peterborough
27.05.00   Dariusz Snarski W RSC 8 Mayfair
           *(Vacant IBO Inter-Continental
           Lightweight Title)*
01.07.00   Michael Ayers L RSC 10 Manchester
           (IBO Lightweight Title Challenge)
03.03.01   Michael Ayers L PTS 12 Wembley
           (IBO Lightweight Title Challenge)

Career: 24 contests, won 17, lost 7.

Stuart Rimmer

St Helens. *Born* St Helens, 22 April, 1971
L. Welterweight. Ht. 5'6"
Manager Self

13.02.90   Dave Croft W PTS 6 Wolverhampton
07.03.90   Mark Antony L RSC 1 Doncaster
23.04.90   Dave Croft W CO 2 Birmingham
01.05.90   Neil Foran L RSC 2 Oldham
04.06.90   Frankie Foster L PTS 6 Glasgow
27.06.90   Bernard McComiskey L PTS 6
           Kensington
12.09.90   Steve Griffith W RSC 2 Bethnal Green
27.09.90   Andrew Morgan W PTS 6 Birmingham
09.10.90   Jim Lawler W CO 2 Wolverhampton
29.10.90   Tony Feliciello L RSC 5 Birmingham
27.11.90   Alan Peacock L RSC 4 Glasgow
12.02.91   Andrew Morgan L PTS 8
           Wolverhampton
24.04.91   Steve Winstanley L PTS 6 Preston
04.06.91   Michael Ayers L CO 1 Bethnal Green
10.09.91   Shaun Cooper L RSC 2
           Wolverhampton
27.03.96   Wayne Pardoe L RSC 3 Stoke
02.10.96   Vic Broomhead W CO 5 Stoke
29.11.96   Rocky Ferrari W RSC 5 Glasgow
04.12.96   David Kirk L PTS 6 Stoke
23.10.97   Bobby Vanzie L RTD 8 Mayfair
           *(Vacant Central Area Lightweight
           Title)*
28.11.97   Gerard Murphy L PTS 6 Hull
06.05.98   Brian Coleman W PTS 6 Blackpool
05.06.98   Terry Roberts L PTS 4 Southend
21.07.98   Jamie McKeever L PTS 4 Widnes
01.12.98   Andy Green L RTD 5 Yarm
15.05.99   Gary Ryder L RSC 1 Blackpool
07.10.99   Gary Reid L RSC 2 Mere
18.02.00   Young Muttley L RSC 1 West
           Bromwich
27.05.00   David Walker L RSC 2 Southwark
30.09.00   Leo O'Reilly L RSC 2 Peterborough

Career: 30 contests, won 8, lost 22.

Daniel Ring

Peterborough. *Born* Peterborough, 1
November, 1978
Bantamweight. Ht. 5'8"
Manager Self

26.11.98   Paddy Folan DREW 6 Bradford
15.12.98   Waj Khan L PTS 6 Sheffield
17.03.99   Frankie DeMilo L RSC 2 Kensington
17.05.99   Chris Emanuele DREW 6 Cleethorpes

15.08.99	Ross Cassidy L PTS 6 Derby
03.12.99	Chris Edwards W PTS 4 Peterborough
05.03.00	David Jeffrey L PTS 6 Peterborough
22.07.00	Jamie Yelland L PTS 4 Watford
21.10.00	Stephen Oates L RSC 1 Wembley
01.12.00	Danny Lawson W PTS 4 Peterborough
02.02.01	Gary Evans W RSC 4 Portsmouth
11.06.01	Jim Betts L PTS 6 Nottingham

Career: 12 contests, won 3, drew 2, lost 7.

Andy Roberts

Doncaster. *Born* Doncaster, 4 March, 1976
Flyweight. Former Undefeated Central
Area Bantamweight Champion. Former
Central Area Flyweight Champion. Ht. 5'3"
Manager Self

20.10.94	Robert Grubb DREW 6 Walsall
12.12.94	Jason Morris W PTS 6 Doncaster
09.02.95	Robert Grubb DREW 6 Doncaster
22.03.95	Michael Edwards L PTS 6 Stoke
06.04.95	Steve Williams L PTS 6 Sheffield
05.05.95	Jason Morris W PTS 6 Doncaster
22.06.95	Paul Quarmby L PTS 6 Houghton le Spring
30.06.95	Stefy Bull L PTS 4 Doncaster
17.10.95	Robert Grubb L PTS 6 Wolverhampton
08.11.95	Graham McGrath W PTS 6 Scunthorpe
28.11.95	Graham McGrath L PTS 6 Wolverhampton
26.01.96	Darren Greaves W RSC 5 Doncaster
29.03.96	Graham McGrath L PTS 6 Doncaster
20.05.96	Neil Parry L PTS 6 Bradford
24.06.96	Neil Parry L PTS 6 Bradford
12.09.96	Steve Williams L PTS 6 Doncaster
23.09.96	Willie Smith W RSC 4 Bradford
03.10.96	Chip O'Neill W PTS 6 Sunderland
17.12.96	Neil Parry DREW 6 Doncaster
20.03.97	Marcus Duncan W PTS 10 Doncaster *(Central Area Bantamweight Title Challenge)*
10.07.97	David Coldwell W RSC 3 Doncaster *(Vacant Central Area Flyweight Title)*
12.11.97	Louis Veitch L PTS 10 Blackpool *(Central Area Flyweight Title Defence)*
04.12.97	David Coldwell L PTS 6 Doncaster
19.03.98	Anthony Hanna W PTS 6 Doncaster
13.05.98	Graham McGrath DREW 6 Scunthorpe
18.09.98	Barry Waite L RSC 1 Belfast
18.03.99	Terry Gaskin L RSC 8 Doncaster
17.07.99	Chris Emanuele L PTS 4 Doncaster
15.01.00	Terry Gaskin L RSC 8 Doncaster *(Vacant Central Area Flyweight Title)*
21.05.00	Gary Ford DREW 6 Shaw
23.07.00	Mbwana Matumla L RSC 2 Dar es Salaam, Tanzania *(WBA Inter-Continental S.Flyweight Title Challenge)*
07.10.00	Chris Edwards L PTS 4 Doncaster

Career: 32 contests, won 9, drew 5, lost 18.

Steve Roberts

West Ham. *Born* Newham, 3 December,
1972
WBF L. Middleweight Champion. Former
Undefeated WBF S. Middleweight
Champion. Former Undefeated Southern
Area L. Middleweight Champion. Ht. 5'11"
Manager B. Hearn

Steve Roberts   Les Clark

139

16.03.95	Julian Eavis W PTS 6 Basildon
23.05.95	Andy Peach W RSC 3 Potters Bar
13.06.95	Robbie Dunn W RSC 3 Basildon
20.09.95	Jason Hart W RSC 5 Potters Bar
30.09.95	Dick Hanns-Kat W CO 1 Basildon
25.11.95	Ernie Loveridge W PTS 4 Dagenham
23.01.96	Andrew Jervis W PTS 6 Bethnal Green
20.04.96	Peter Vosper W PTS 6 Brentwood
04.05.96	George Richards W PTS 6 Dagenham
27.09.96	Rob Stevenson W PTS 6 Stevenage
27.11.96	Lindon Scarlett W PTS 6 Bethnal Green
08.03.97	Adan Lugo W CO 4 Brentwood
08.04.97	Gilbert Jackson W PTS 10 Bethnal Green
	(Vacant Southern Area L. Middleweight Title)
30.08.97	Peter Mitchell W PTS 6 Cheshunt
08.10.97	Darren Covill W PTS 6 Poplar
05.06.98	Danny Quacoe W RTD 4 Southend
20.12.99	Mike Whittaker W PTS 6 Bethnal Green
05.02.00	Danny Thornton W PTS 6 Bethnal Green
01.04.00	Chris Crook W RSC 3 Bethnal Green
16.06.00	Mike Algoet W PTS 12 Bloomsbury
	(Vacant WBF S. Middleweight Title)
19.08.00	Scott Dixon W RSC 9 Brentwood
	(Vacant WBF L.Middleweight Title)
02.12.00	Mohammed Hissani W RSC 7 Bethnal Green
	(WBF L. Middleweight Title Defence)
03.03.01	Sergio Acuna W RSC 1 Wembley
	(WBF L. Middleweight Title Defence)
07.04.01	Keith Mullings W RSC 2 Wembley
	(WBF L. Middleweight Title Defence)
26.05.01	William Gare W RSC 9 Bethnal Green
	(WBF L. Middleweight Title Defence)

Career: 25 contests, won 25.

Hughie Robertson

Millwall. *Born* Haverfordwest, 4 March, 1975
Heavyweight. Ht. 5'11½"
Manager F. Maloney

18.02.01 Slick Miller L RSC 2 Southwark
Career: 1 contest, lost 1.

Dale Robinson

Huddersfield. *Born* Huddersfield, 9 April, 1980
Central Area Flyweight Champion.
Ht. 5'4"
Manager T. Gilmour/C. Aston

25.09.00	John Barnes W PTS 4 Barnsley
28.10.00	Delroy Spencer W RSC 4 Coventry
02.12.00	Colin Moffett W PTS 4 Bethnal Green
26.02.01	Christophe Rodrigues W PTS 6 Nottingham
07.04.01	Andrei Kostin W PTS 6 Wembley
08.05.01	Terry Gaskin W RTD 3 Barnsley
	(Central Area Flyweight Title Challenge)

Career: 6 contests, won 6.

Dale Robinson Les Clark

Steve Robinson

Cardiff. *Born* Cardiff, 13 December, 1968
Former European & WBO Inter-Continental Featherweight Champion.
Former WBO Featherweight Champion.
Former Undefeated WBA Penta-Continental & Welsh Featherweight Champion. Ht. 5'8"
Manager B. Hearn

01.03.89	Alan Roberts W PTS 6 Cardiff
13.03.89	Terry Smith W RTD 4 Piccadilly
06.04.89	Nicky Lucas L PTS 8 Cardiff
04.05.89	John Devine W PTS 6 Mayfair
19.08.89	Marcel Herbert L PTS 6 Cardiff
13.11.89	Shane Silvester W RSC 2 Brierley Hill
10.07.90	Mark Bates L PTS 6 Canvey Island
12.09.90	Tim Driscoll L PTS 8 Bethnal Green
26.09.90	Russell Davison W PTS 8 Manchester
03.10.90	Drew Docherty L PTS 8 Solihull
22.10.90	Alan McKay L PTS 6 Mayfair
19.11.90	Neil Haddock W RSC 9 Cardiff
19.12.90	Brian Roche DREW 6 Preston
24.04.91	Russell Davison W RTD 6 Preston
28.05.91	Colin Lynch W RSC 6 Cardiff
18.07.91	Peter Harris W PTS 10 Cardiff
	(Welsh Featherweight Title Challenge)
31.01.92	Henry Armstrong L PTS 6 Manchester
11.05.92	Neil Haddock L PTS 10 Llanelli
	(Vacant Welsh S. Featherweight Title)
07.10.92	Edward Lloyd W RTD 8 Barry
30.10.92	Stephane Haccoun W PTS 8 Istres, France
01.12.92	Dennis Oakes W RTD 2 Liverpool
19.01.93	Paul Harvey W PTS 12 Cardiff
	(Vacant WBA Penta-Continental Featherweight Title)
13.02.93	Medhi Labdouni L PTS 8 Paris, France
17.04.93	John Davison W PTS 12 Washington
	(Vacant WBO Featherweight Title)
10.07.93	Sean Murphy W CO 9 Cardiff
	(WBO Featherweight Title Defence)
23.10.93	Colin McMillan W PTS 12 Cardiff
	(WBO Featherweight Title Defence)
12.03.94	Paul Hodkinson W CO 12 Cardiff
	(WBO Featherweight Title Defence)
04.06.94	Freddy Cruz W PTS 12 Cardiff
	(WBO Featherweight Title Defence)
01.10.94	Duke McKenzie W CO 9 Cardiff
	(WBO Featherweight Title Defence)
04.02.95	Domingo Damigella W PTS 12 Cardiff
	(WBO Featherweight Title Defence)
07.07.95	Pedro Ferradas W RSC 9 Cardiff
	(WBO Featherweight Title Defence)
30.09.95	Prince Naseem Hamed L RSC 8 Cardiff
	(WBO Featherweight Title Defence)
18.09.96	Kelton McKenzie W PTS 8 Tylorstown
03.02.97	Billy Hardy L PTS 12 Sunderland
	(European Featherweight Title Challenge)
08.03.97	Tomas Serrano W CO 1 Brentwood
	(Vacant WBO Inter-Continental Featherweight Title)
08.05.97	Julio Cesar Sanchez W CO 7 Mansfield
	(WBO Inter-Continental Featherweight Title Defence)
27.09.97	Andrew Matabola W CO 5 Belfast
	(WBO Inter-Continental Featherweight Title Defence)
18.11.97	Aldrich Johnson W RSC 7 Mansfield
	(WBO Inter-Continental Featherweight Title Defence)
25.04.98	Jean Dibateza W PTS 8 Cardiff
03.10.98	Welcome Ncita DREW 12 East London, South Africa
	(WBO Inter-Continental Featherweight Title Defence)
23.02.99	Santiago Rojas W PTS 8 Cardiff
30.04.99	Manuel Calvo W PTS 12 Leganes, Spain
	(Vacant European Featherweight Title)
12.07.99	Martin Krastev W RSC 1 Coventry
02.10.99	Claude Chinon W RSC 10 Cardiff
	(European Featherweight Title Defence)
04.12.99	Jonjo Irwin W PTS 12 Manchester
	(European Featherweight Title Defence)
11.03.00	Juan Carlos Ramirez L RSC 11 Kensington
	(WBO Inter-Continental Featherweight Title Defence)
23.06.00	Istvan Kovacs L PTS 12 Budapest, Hungary
	(European Featherweight Title Defence. WBC International Featherweight Title Challenge)
03.11.00	Cassius Baloyi L PTS 12 Ebbw Vale
	(WBU Featherweight Title Challenge)
25.05.01	Manuel Calvo L PTS 12 Leganes, Spain
	(Vacant European Featherweight Title)

Career: 49 contests, won 32, drew 2, lost 15.

George Robshaw

Leeds. *Born* Hull, 14 March, 1976
Middleweight. Ht. 6'0"
Manager F. Maloney

07.10.00 William Webster W PTS 4 Doncaster
Career: 1 contest, won 1.

Reggie Robshaw

Leeds. *Born* Wakefield, 10 June, 1977
L. Middleweight. Ht. 5'10"
Manager D. Powell

01.04.01 Jason McElligott W PTS 4 Southwark
Career: 1 contest, won 1.

Derek Roche

Leeds. *Born* New Ross, 19 July 1972
L. Middleweight. Former British
Welterweight Champion. Former
Undefeated Central Area Welterweight
Champion. Ht. 5'9"
Manager T. Gilmour

26.09.94 Michael Alexander W RSC 6 Bradford
05.12.94 Shamus Casey W PTS 6 Bradford
30.01.95 Carl Smith W RSC 3 Bradford
23.02.95 Charlie Paine W CO 1 Hull
25.03.95 Rob Stevenson W PTS 6 Rothwell
12.06.95 Paul King W PTS 6 Bradford
25.09.95 Hughie Davey W PTS 6 Bradford
11.11.95 Rick North W RSC 2 Halifax
11.12.95 Kevin McKenzie W RSC 3 Bradford
13.01.96 Shamus Casey W PTS 6 Halifax
07.03.96 Wayne Shepherd W RSC 3 Bradford
23.09.96 Trevor Meikle W PTS 10 Bradford
*(Central Area Welterweight Title
Challenge)*
23.10.96 Paul Miles W RSC 2 Halifax
09.12.96 Gary Beardsley W RSC 2 Bradford
17.02.97 Michael Alexander W DIS 4 Bradford
09.06.97 Chris Saunders W RSC 4 Bradford
*(Central Area Welterweight Title
Defence. Elim. British Welterweight
Title)*
13.11.97 Hughie Davey W RSC 3 Bradford
23.02.98 Darren McInulty W PTS 6 Glasgow
06.11.98 Del Bryan W RSC 10 Mayfair
*(Vacant IBO Inter-Continental
L. Middleweight Title)*
10.04.99 Charlie Kane W RSC 7 Manchester
(Vacant British Welterweight Title)
31.07.99 Georgie Smith W PTS 12 Carlisle
(British Welterweight Title Defence)
22.10.99 Scott Dixon W PTS 12 Coventry
(British Welterweight Title Defence)
27.03.00 Harry Dhami L PTS 12 Barnsley
(British Welterweight Title Defence)
25.09.00 Brian Coleman W PTS 6 Barnsley
11.11.00 Adrian Stone L RSC 2 Belfast
(IBO L.Middleweight Title Challenge)
08.05.01 Paul Denton W PTS 6 Barnsley
Career: 26 contests, won 24, lost 2.

Jim Rock

Dublin. *Born* Dublin, 12 March, 1972
Middleweight. All-Ireland S. Middleweight
& L. Middleweight Champion. Former
Undefeated WAA Inter-Continental S.
Middleweight Champion. WBF European
L. Middleweight Champion. Ht. 5'11"
Manager M. O'Callaghan

25.11.95 Craig Lynch W PTS 4 Dublin
09.03.96 Peter Mitchell W PTS 6 Millstreet
03.09.96 Rob Stevenson W PTS 6 Belfast
05.11.96 Danny Quacoe W RSC 4 Belfast
28.01.97 Roy Chipperfield W RTD 2 Belfast
12.04.97 George Richards W PTS 6 Sheffield
13.09.97 Robert Njie W CO 3 Millwall

18.04.98 Ensley Bingham L RSC 7 Manchester
19.09.98 Michael Monaghan W PTS 12 Dublin
*(Vacant WAA Inter-Continental
S. Middleweight Title)*
14.12.98 Perry Ayres W RTD 3 Cleethorpes
22.01.99 Jimmy Vincent W PTS 10 Dublin
20.02.99 Pedro Carragher W RSC 3 Thornaby
*(Vacant WBF European
L. Middleweight Title)*
17.04.99 Michael Alexander W RSC 1 Dublin
*(Vacant All-Ireland S. Middleweight
Title)*
19.06.99 Kevin Thompson W PTS 4 Dublin
15.04.00 Allan Gray W PTS 10 Bethnal Green
*(Vacant All-Ireland L. Middleweight
Title)*
12.06.00 Alan Gilbert W PTS 6 Belfast
20.10.00 Brooke Welby W RSC 3 Belfast
11.11.00 David Baptiste W PTS 4 Belfast
08.12.00 Tommy Attardo W PTS 8 Worcester,
Mass, USA
24.03.01 Hollister Elliott W CO 6 Worcester,
Mass, USA
20.04.01 Jason Collins W PTS 6 Dublin
Career: 21 contests, won 20, lost 1.

Brendan Rollinson

Hull. *Born* Hull, 8 January, 1974
L. Middleweight. Ht. 6'0"
Manager D. Smith

25.05.00 Pedro Thompson W RSC 2 Hull
25.07.00 Colin Vidler L PTS 4 Southwark
16.11.00 Matthew Ashmole W PTS 6 Hull
23.06.01 Nick Lyon W RSC 4 Peterborough
Career: 4 contests, won 3, lost 1.

James Rooney

Hartlepool. *Born* Hartlepool, 30 April, 1978
Lightweight. Ht. 5'10"
Manager M. Marsden

26.02.00 Marc Smith W PTS 4 Carlisle
27.03.00 Pete Buckley W PTS 4 Barnsley
13.05.00 Sebastian Hart W PTS 6 Barnsley
23.07.00 Duncan Armstrong W RSC 3
Hartlepool
01.10.00 Nigel Senior W PTS 6 Hartlepool
02.12.00 Gary Flear W PTS 4 Bethnal Green
11.02.01 Dave Hinds W PTS 6 Hartlepool
20.03.01 Lee Williamson W PTS 4 Glasgow
06.05.01 Lee Williamson W PTS 6 Hartlepool
04.06.01 Steve Hanley W PTS 4 Hartlepool
Career: 10 contests, won 10.

Jason Rowland

West Ham. *Born* London, 6 August, 1970
WBU L. Welterweight Champion. Former
Undefeated British L. Welterweight
Champion. Ht. 5'9¾"
Manager F. Warren

19.09.89 Terry Smith W RSC 1 Millwall
15.11.89 Mike Morrison W PTS 6 Reading
14.02.90 Eamonn Payne W PTS 6 Millwall
17.04.90 Dave Jenkins W CO 1 Millwall
22.05.90 Mike Morrison W PTS 6 St Albans
12.02.91 Vaughan Carnegie W PTS 6 Basildon
07.03.91 Vaughan Carnegie W CO 2 Basildon
11.12.91 Brian Cullen W RSC 4 Basildon
30.04.92 Steve Pollard W RSC 2 Kensington
17.12.92 Jimmy Vincent W PTS 6 Wembley
10.02.93 Seth Jones W RSC 2 Lewisham

18.03.93 John Smith W PTS 6 Lewisham
04.03.94 Dewi Roberts W RSC 1 Bethnal Green
26.04.94 Ray Hood W CO 1 Bethnal Green
12.09.94 Steve Burton W RSC 1 Mayfair
11.10.94 Phil Found W RSC 4 Bethnal Green
09.11.94 Floyd Churchill W RSC 2 Millwall
09.12.94 Richard Swallow W RSC 2 Bethnal
Green
03.03.95 Nigel Bradley W RSC 3 Bethnal Green
29.11.95 Bernard Paul L CO 1 Bethnal Green
*(Southern Area L. Welterweight Title
Challenge. Elim. British
L. Welterweight Title)*
27.03.97 Kevin McKillan W PTS 8 Norwich
13.09.97 Brian Coleman W PTS 8 Millwall
16.05.98 Mark Winters W PTS 12 Bethnal
Green
*(British L. Welterweight Title
Challenge)*
01.05.99 Alan Temple W PTS 6 Crystal Palace
15.11.99 Jonathan Thaxton W RSC 5 Bethnal
Green
(British L. Welterweight Title Defence)
21.10.00 Victor Baranov W PTS 12 Wembley
(Vacant WBU L.Welterweight Title)
Career: 26 contests, won 25, lost 1.

Roy Rutherford

Coventry. *Born* Coventry, 4 August, 1973
Featherweight. Ht. 5'6"
Manager Self

24.02.98 David Kirk W PTS 6 Edgbaston
26.03.98 Vic Broomhead W PTS 6 Solihull
23.04.98 Dave Hinds W RSC 5 Edgbaston
21.05.98 Carl Allen W PTS 6 Solihull
24.09.98 Dean Murdoch W RSC 3 Edgbaston
14.12.98 Keith Jones W PTS 6 Birmingham
08.03.99 Marc Smith W PTS 6 Birmingham
19.06.99 Marc Smith W RTD 2 Dublin
22.10.99 Woody Greenaway W PTS 4 Coventry
14.12.99 Keith Jones W PTS 4 Coventry
22.01.00 Chris Williams W PTS 8 Birmingham
22.05.00 Alexander Tiranov W PTS 6 Coventry
28.10.00 Richard Evatt L PTS 10 Coventry
07.04.01 Nikolai Eremeev DREW 4 Wembley
26.05.01 Marc Callaghan W RSC 3 Bethnal
Green
Career: 15 contests, won 13, drew 1, lost 1.

John-Paul Ryan

Northampton. *Born* Enfield, 1 April, 1971
Bantamweight. Ht. 5'5"
Manager J. Cox

07.12.00 Paddy Folan W PTS 6 Stoke
08.03.01 Neil Read L PTS 6 Stoke
Career: 2 contests, won 1, lost 1.

Gary Ryder

Liverpool. *Born* Fazackerley, 17 December,
1971
Welterweight. Ht. 5'7"
Manager T. Gilmour

03.02.96 Andy Davidson W RSC 1 Liverpool
05.03.99 Trevor Tacy W PTS 4 Liverpool
15.05.99 Stuart Rimmer W RSC 1 Blackpool
09.03.00 Benny Jones W PTS 4 Liverpool
19.02.01 Mohamed Helel W RSC 1 Glasgow
04.06.01 Kevin Bennett W RSC 6 Hartlepool
Career: 6 contests, won 6.

S

Roger Sampson

Sheffield. *Born* Sheffield, 3 July, 1972
Lightweight. Ht. 5'7¼"
Manager B. Ingle

26.06.97	Robbie Sivyer W PTS 6 Sheffield
06.10.97	Lee Armstrong W PTS 6 Bradford
09.02.98	Gary Jenkinson L PTS 6 Bradford
17.03.98	Gary Jenkinson W PTS 6 Sheffield
20.09.98	John T. Kelly W PTS 6 Sheffield
19.10.98	Bradley Welsh L PTS 8 Glasgow
03.12.98	Michael Ayers W PTS 6 Mayfair
25.01.99	David Kehoe W PTS 4 Glasgow
28.11.99	Chris Price W PTS 4 Chesterfield
24.03.01	Jimmy Phelan W PTS 4 Sheffield

Career: 10 contests, won 8, lost 2.

Jason Samuels

Cardiff. *Born* Newport, 11 December, 1973
L. Middleweight. Ht. 6'0"
Manager Self

02.07.99	Luke Clayfield W RSC 1 Bristol
10.10.00	Steve Brumant W PTS 6 Brierley Hill

Career: 2 contests, won 2.

Paul Samuels

Newport. *Born* Newport, 23 March, 1973
Welsh L. Middleweight Champion. Former
Undefeated IBF Inter-Continental L.
Middleweight Champion. Ht. 6'0"
Manager Self

11.11.95	Wayne Windle W RSC 2 Halifax
13.02.96	Jon Harrison W CO 1 Cardiff
05.03.96	Tom Welsh W RSC 3 Bethnal Green
13.03.96	Brian Coleman W PTS 6 Wembley
15.05.96	Gary Hiscox W RSC 3 Cardiff
12.11.96	Mark Ramsey W RSC 4 Dudley
21.06.97	Howard Clarke W PTS 8 Caridff
15.11.97	Justin Simmons W CO 1 Bristol
24.01.98	Prince Kasi Kaihau W CO 3 Cardiff
25.04.98	Del Bryan W PTS 8 Cardiff
05.09.98	Spencer McCracken W PTS 8 Telford
05.12.98	Craig Winter W CO 2 Bristol
	(Vacant Welsh L. Middleweight Title)
27.03.99	Pedro Carragher W RSC 2 Derby
05.06.99	Eric Holland W RSC 9 Cardiff
	(Vacant IBF Inter-Continental L. Middleweight Title)
23.10.99	Ojay Abrahams W PTS 8 Telford
19.02.00	Wayne Alexander L RSC 3 Dagenham
	(Vacant British L. Middleweight Title)
23.01.01	Rob Dellapenna DREW 4 Crawley

Career: 17 contests, won 15, drew 1, lost 1.

Stewart Sanderson

Glasgow. *Born* Bellshill, 21 November, 1981
Featherweight. Ht. 5'9"
Manager R. Bannon

24.05.01	Jason Thomas DREW 6 Glasgow

Career: 1 contest, drew 1.

Inderpaul Sandhu

Alfreton. *Born* Derby, 16 December, 1989
Lightweight. Ht. 5'11"
Manager M. Shinfield

26.02.01	Duncan Armstrong W PTS 4 Nottingham
11.06.01	Joel Viney W PTS 4 Nottingham

Career: 2 contests, won 2.

Steve Saville

Wolverhampton. *Born* Wolverhampton, 29
September, 1976
L. Welterweight. Ht. 5'4"
Manager Self

08.06.98	Simon Chambers W RSC 2 Birmingham
07.10.98	Dave Hinds W PTS 6 Stoke
26.11.98	Dave Hinds W PTS 6 Edgbaston
14.12.98	Woody Greenaway L PTS 6 Birmingham
27.01.99	Darren Woodley W PTS 6 Stoke
23.03.99	Benny Jones W PTS 6 Wolverhampton
14.06.99	Trevor Tacy L PTS 8 Birmingham
12.10.99	Gary Flear W RSC 6 Wolverhampton
20.10.99	Arv Mittoo W PTS 8 Stoke
08.02.00	Marc Smith W PTS 6 Wolverhampton
13.03.00	Dave Gibson W RSC 6 Birmingham
09.10.00	David Kirk L PTS 8 Birmingham
06.11.00	Woody Greenaway W CO 5 Wolverhampton
28.11.00	Danny Connelly W PTS 8 Brierley Hill
11.12.00	Keith Jones W PTS 8 Birmingham
01.04.01	Gavin Down L RSC 3 Alfreton
	(Vacant Midlands Area L. Welterweight Title)

Career: 16 contests, won 12, lost 4.

Steve Saville   *Les Clark*

Billy Schwer

Luton. *Born* Luton, 12 April, 1969
IBO L. Welterweight Champion. Former
Undefeated European Lightweight
Champion. Former Commonwealth
Lightweight Champion. Former Undefeated
British Lightweight Champion. Ht. 5'8½"
Manager Self

04.10.90	Pierre Conan W RSC 1 Bethnal Green
31.10.90	Mark Antony W RSC 2 Wembley
12.12.90	Sean Casey W RSC 1 Kensington
16.01.91	Dave Jenkins W PTS 6 Kensington
07.02.91	John Smith W RSC 2 Watford
06.03.91	Chubby Martin W RSC 3 Wembley
04.04.91	Andy Robins W RSC 2 Watford
17.04.91	Chris Saunders W RSC 1 Kensington
02.05.91	Karl Taylor W RSC 2 Northampton
30.06.91	Chris Saunders W RSC 3 Southwark
11.09.91	Tony Foster W PTS 8 Hammersmith
26.09.91	Felix Kelly W RSC 2 Dunstable
24.10.91	Patrick Kamy W CO 1 Dunstable
20.11.91	Marcel Herbert W PTS 8 Kensington
12.02.92	Tomas Quinones W CO 8 Wembley
25.03.92	Bobby Brewer W RSC 4 Kensington
03.09.92	Wayne Windle W CO 1 Dunstable
28.10.92	Carl Crook W RTD 9 Kensington
	(British & Commonwealth Lightweight Title Challenges)
17.12.92	Mauricio Aceves W RSC 3 Wembley
24.02.93	Paul Burke L RSC 7 Wembley
	(British & Commonwealth Lightweight Title Defences)
15.06.93	Farid Benredjeb W PTS 8 Hemel Hempstead
10.11.93	Paul Burke W PTS 12 Watford
	(British & Commonwealth Lightweight Title Challenges)
16.02.94	Sean Murphy W RSC 3 Stevenage
	(British & Commonwealth Lightweight Title Defences)
04.03.94	John Roby W RSC 2 Bethnal Green
22.03.94	Edgar Castro W CO 5 Bethnal Green
11.05.94	Howard Grant W RSC 9 Stevenage
	(Commonwealth Lightweight Title Defence)
09.11.94	Manuel Hernandez W CO 6 Millwall
28.01.95	Rafael Ruelas L RSC 8 Las Vegas, USA
	(IBF Lightweight Title Challenge)
12.05.95	Stephen Chungu W RSC 11 Bethnal Green
	(Commonwealth Lightweight Title Defence)
23.06.95	Bruno Rabanales W DIS 6 Bethnal Green
28.10.95	Ditau Molefyane W CO 8 Kensington
	(Commonwealth Lightweight Title Defence)
25.11.95	David Tetteh L RSC 12 Dagenham
	(Commonwealth Lightweight Title Defence)
15.03.96	Edward Lloyd W RTD 5 Dunstable
16.05.96	Gareth Jordan W RSC 3 Dunstable
24.10.96	Alan Temple W PTS 8 Wembley
20.11.96	Jean-Michel Moulun W RTD 7 Wembley
25.10.97	Oscar Garcia Cano W RSC 10 Zaragoza, Spain
	(European Lightweight Title Challenge)
14.03.98	Jean Gomis W PTS 10 Bethnal Green
12.09.98	Manuel Carlos Fernandes W RTD 7 Bethnal Green
	(European Lightweight Title Defence)
16.01.99	Zoltan Kalocsai W RSC 7 Bethnal Green
	(European Lightweight Title Defence)
08.05.99	Sandro Casamonica W RTD 8 Bethnal Green
	(European Lightweight Title Defence)
29.11.99	Steve Johnston L PTS 12 Wembley
	(WBC Lightweight Title Challenge)

14.10.00 Colin Dunne L PTS 12 Wembley
(WBU Lightweight Title Challenge)
07.04.01 Newton Villareal W PTS 12 Wembley
(IBO L. Welterweight Title Challenge)
Career: 44 contests, won 39, lost 5.

Bruce Scott

Hackney. *Born* Jamaica, 16 August, 1969
British & Commonwealth Cruiserweight
Champion. Former Undefeated Southern
Area Cruiserweight Champion. Ht. 5'9½"
Manager F. Warren

25.04.91 Mark Bowen L PTS 6 Mayfair
16.09.91 Randy B. Powell W RSC 5 Mayfair
21.11.91 Steve Osborne W PTS 6 Burton
27.04.92 John Kaighin W CO 4 Mayfair
07.09.92 Lee Prudden W PTS 6 Bethnal Green
03.12.92 Mark Pain W RSC 5 Lewisham
15.02.93 Paul McCarthy W PTS 6 Mayfair
22.04.93 Sean O'Phoenix W RSC 3 Mayfair
14.06.93 John Oxenham W RSC 1 Bayswater
04.10.93 Simon McDougall W PTS 6 Mayfair
16.12.93 Bobby Mack W RSC 4 Newport
05.04.94 Steve Osborne W RSC 5 Bethnal Green
17.10.94 Bobbi Joe Edwards W PTS 8 Mayfair
09.12.94 John Keeton W CO 2 Bethnal Green
19.04.95 Nigel Rafferty W RSC 2 Bethnal Green
19.05.95 Cordwell Hylton W RSC 1 Southwark
11.11.95 Tony Booth W RSC 3 Halifax
05.03.96 Nick Manners W RSC 5 Bethnal Green
13.07.96 Tony Booth W PTS 8 Bethnal Green

Bruce Scott   Les Clark

30.11.96 Nicky Piper L RSC 7 Tylorstown
*(Commonwealth L. Heavyweight Title
Challenge)*
15.05.97 Grant Briggs W RSC 2 Reading
04.10.97 Tony Booth L PTS 8 Muswell Hill
21.04.98 Dominic Negus W RSC 9 Edmonton
*(Southern Area Cruiserweight Title
Challenge)*
28.11.98 Darren Corbett W RSC 10 Belfast
*(Commonwealth Cruiserweight Title
Challenge. Vacant British
Cruiserweight Title)*
15.05.99 Johnny Nelson L PTS 12 Sheffield
(WBO Cruiserweight Title Challenge)
17.07.99 Juan Carlos Gomez L RSC 6
Dusseldorf, Germany
(WBC Cruiserweight Title Challenge)
08.04.00 Chris Woollas W RSC 2 Bethnal
Green
24.06.00 Adam Watt L RSC 4 Glasgow
*(Vacant Commonwealth Cruiserweight
Title)*
16.12.00 John Keeton W CO 6 Sheffield
(Vacant British Cruiserweight Title)
10.03.01 Garry Delaney W RTD 3 Bethnal
Green
*(British Cruiserweight Title Defence.
Vacant Commonwealth Cruiserweight
Title)*

Career: 30 contests, won 24, lost 6.

Greg Scott-Briggs

Chesterfield. *Born* Swaziland, 6 February,
1966
Cruiserweight. Ht. 6'1"
Manager J. Ashton

04.02.92 Mark McBiane W PTS 6 Alfreton
03.03.92 Tony Colclough W RSC 2 Cradley
Heath
30.03.92 Carl Smallwood L PTS 6 Coventry
27.04.92 Richard Atkinson L PTS 6 Bradford
28.05.92 Steve Walton W PTS 6 Gosforth
04.06.92 Joe Frater L PTS 6 Cleethorpes
30.09.92 Carl Smallwood L PTS 6 Solihull
17.03.93 Carl Smallwood L PTS 8 Stoke
26.04.93 Tony Colclough W RSC 4 Glasgow
08.06.93 Peter Flint W RSC 1 Derby
07.09.93 Steve Loftus W RSC 2 Stoke
22.09.93 Paul Hanlon W PTS 6 Chesterfield
04.11.93 Lee Archer L PTS 8 Stafford
24.11.93 Tony Colclough W PTS 6 Solihull
08.12.93 Lee Archer W RTD 6 Stoke
08.02.94 Nigel Rafferty L PTS 6
Wolverhampton
17.02.94 Lee Archer L PTS 8 Walsall
11.03.94 Monty Wright L CO 1 Bethnal Green
26.09.94 Dave Battey W RSC 4 Cleethorpes
11.10.94 Mark Smallwood L PTS 8
Wolverhampton
29.10.94 Mark Smallwood L PTS 6 Cannock
12.11.94 Thomas Hansvoll L PTS 4 Randers,
Denmark
30.11.94 Monty Wright L PTS 6
Wolverhampton
06.03.95 Neil Simpson L RTD 5 Leicester
15.09.95 David Flowers L PTS 6 Darlington
29.11.95 Neil Simpson L DIS 7 Solihull
*(Vacant Midlands Area L. Heavyweight
Title)*
20.03.96 Stinger Mason W PTS 6 Stoke
26.10.96 Danny Peters L PTS 6 Liverpool
13.06.97 Jamie Warters L RSC 5 Leeds

15.12.97 Michael Pinnock W PTS 6 Nottingham
11.05.98 Neil Simpson L PTS 6 Leicester
25.11.98 Sven Hamer L CO 2 Streatham
13.03.99 Ole Klemetsen L CO 4 Manchester
24.04.99 Monty Wright W RSC 3 Peterborough
20.05.99 Sven Hamer W RSC 5 Kensington
03.10.99 Carl Smallwood W PTS 6 Chesterfield
09.04.00 Tony Booth L PTS 10 Alfreton
*(Vacant British Masters
L. Heavyweight Title)*
15.07.00 Clinton Woods L RSC 3 Millwall
Career: 38 contests, won 15, lost 23.

Matt Scriven

Nottingham. *Born* Nottingham, 1
September, 1973
L. Middleweight. Ht. 5'10"
Manager M. Shinfield

26.11.97 Shamus Casey W PTS 6 Stoke
08.12.97 Shane Thomas W PTS 6 Bradford
20.03.98 C. J. Jackson L PTS 6 Ilkeston
15.05.98 Lee Bird W RSC 5 Nottingham
08.10.98 Stevie McCready L RTD 3 Sunderland
01.04.99 Adrian Houldey W PTS 6 Birmingham
25.04.99 Danny Thornton L RSC 4 Leeds
27.06.99 Shane Junior L RSC 2 Alfreton
11.09.99 David Arundel L RTD 1 Sheffield
20.03.00 James Docherty L PTS 8 Glasgow
27.03.00 Matt Mowatt L PTS 4 Barnsley
09.04.00 David Matthews W PTS 6 Alfreton
06.06.00 Jackie Townsley L RSC 3 Motherwell
04.11.00 Brett James L RTD 1 Bethnal Green
04.02.01 Mark Paxford L PTS 6 Queensferry
26.02.01 Pedro Thompson W RTD 1
Nottingham
12.03.01 Ernie Smith W PTS 6 Birmingham
20.03.01 James Docherty L RSC 1 Glasgow
21.05.01 Christian Brady L RSC 5 Birmingham
*(Vacant Midlands Area Welterweight
Title)*
Career: 18 contests, won 7, lost 11.

Isaac Sebaduka

Brixton. *Born* Uganda, 1 January, 1976
Lightweight. Ht. 5'5¾"
Manager A. Gee

12.07.97 Danny Adams DREW 4 Earls Court
27.10.97 Gary Flear L PTS 6 Nottingham
23.07.98 Chris Williams W RSC 5 Barking
05.10.99 Mark Payne L PTS 6 Bloomsbury
06.11.99 Keith Jones L PTS 4 Bethnal Green
13.03.00 David Jeffrey W RSC 1 Bethnal Green
17.04.00 Richard Evatt W RSC 2 Birmingham
01.07.00 Nikolai Melandovics L RSC 1
Southwark
*(Vacant WBF European Featherweight
Title)*
15.06.01 Darren Melville L PTS 6 Millwall
Career: 9 contests, won 3, drew 1, lost 5.

Harry Senior

Charlton. *Born* Lewisham, 26 November,
1969
Former Undefeated Southern Area
Heavyweight Champion. Ht. 6'2"
Manager B. Lawrence

19.07.96 Omar Gutierrez L PTS 4 Waukegan,
USA

01.04.97 Badara M'Baye L PTS 6 Marseilles,
France
02.09.97 Luan Krasniqi L PTS 4 Southwark
02.11.97 Frank Bohme W RSC 4 Halle,
Germany
06.01.98 Steve Jay W PTS 6 Brighton
14.03.98 Andy Lambert W CO 1 Bethnal Green
11.04.98 Craig Bowen-Price L PTS 6
Southwark
02.07.98 Marat Tekouev W RSC 4 Ipswich
12.09.98 Michael Sprott W RSC 6 Bethnal
Green
*(Vacant Southern Area Heavyweight
Title)*
02.10.98 Tim Knight W PTS 6 Warsaw, Poland
12.12.98 Matthew Ellis L PTS 8 Southwark
13.03.99 Craig Bowen-Price DREW 4
Manchester
08.05.99 Mike Holden W PTS 8 Bethnal Green
18.12.99 Danny Williams L PTS 12 Southwark
*(Vacant Commonwealth Heavyweight
Title)*
13.03.00 Alex Vasiliev L PTS 8 Bethnal Green
13.04.00 Keith Long L PTS 10 Holborn
13.07.00 Georgi Kandelaki L PTS 8 Bethnal
Green
Career: 17 contests, won 7, drew 1, lost 9.

Nigel Senior

Nottingham. *Born* Wallsend, 19 November,
1962
S. Featherweight. Ht. 5'5"
Manager J. Gill

03.10.85 Mark Needham W RSC 4 Nottingham
14.10.85 Anthony Brown L PTS 6 Leicester
21.10.85 Peter Bowen DREW 6 Nottingham
11.11.85 Sugar Gibiliru L RSC 5 Liverpool
24.03.86 Joe Donohoe L PTS 6 Mayfair
07.04.86 Billy Joe Dee W PTS 6 Nottingham
15.04.86 Ricky Andrews W PTS 6 Merton
23.04.86 Nigel Haddock L PTS 6 Stoke
19.05.86 Nigel Haddock DREW 6 Nottingham
09.06.86 Nigel Crook W PTS 6 Manchester
23.08.86 Tony Graham DREW 6 Manchester
04.09.86 Gary King W PTS 6 Merton
23.09.86 Carl Cleasby W PTS 6 Batley
20.10.86 Gary Maxwell L PTS 8 Nottingham
29.10.86 Nigel Haddock L PTS 6 Ebbw Vale
11.11.86 Darren Connellan L PTS 6 Batley
28.11.86 Ian Honeywood W RSC 5
Peterborough
16.12.86 Paul Timmons L PTS 6 Alfreton
27.01.87 Russell Davison DREW 8 Manchester
09.02.87 Joe Duffy W CO 3 Glasgow
16.02.87 Dean Bramhald W PTS 8 Glasgow
14.03.87 Floyd Havard L RSC 5 Southwark
13.04.87 John Bennie L PTS 6 Glasgow
01.05.87 Gary de Roux L PTS 8 Peterborough
04.06.87 John Feeney L PTS 8 Sunderland
28.09.87 George Jones L PTS 8 Birmingham
09.11.87 Rocky Lawlor L RSC 5 Birmingham
27.01.88 Ronnie Green L PTS 8 Stoke
24.02.88 John Bennie L PTS 6 Glasgow
08.03.88 Billy Joe Dee W PTS 6 Batley
23.03.88 Glyn Rhodes L PTS 8 Sheffield
30.03.88 Paul Gadney L PTS 6 Bethnal Green
17.04.88 Dave Kettlewell W PTS 6
Peterborough
25.04.88 Dean Bramhald L PTS 8 Nottingham
10.09.88 Herve Jacob L PTS 8 Grande-Synthe,
France

07.10.88 Daniel Londas L PTS 8 Bordeaux,
France
25.01.89 Henry Armstrong L PTS 8 Stoke
14.02.89 John Davison L RSC 8 Sunderland
20.03.89 Wayne Weekes L PTS 6 Nottingham
24.04.89 Ian Honeywood L PTS 4 Nottingham
10.05.89 Nigel Wenton L RSC 2 Kensington
19.04.90 Les Walsh L PTS 8 Oldham
30.04.90 Kruga Hydes W PTS 6 Nottingham
21.05.90 Peter Konyegwachie L RSC 7 Mayfair
07.09.90 Jimmy Owens L PTS 6 Liverpool
18.10.90 Frankie Foster L CO 2 Hartlepool
*(Vacant Northern Area
S. Featherweight Title)*
03.12.90 Mark Antony L PTS 8 Cleethorpes
10.12.90 Noel Carroll W PTS 6 Nottingham
06.03.91 Richard Joyce L PTS 8 Croydon
01.12.99 Chris Jickells L RSC 2 Stoke
24.02.00 Willie Limond L RSC 6 Glasgow
26.03.00 Steve Brook L PTS 6 Nottingham
17.04.00 Steve Brook L PTS 6 Bradford
11.05.00 John Barnes L PTS 6 Sunderland
20.05.00 Gary Wilson L PTS 6 Rotherham
06.06.00 Barry Hawthorne L PTS 6 Motherwell
10.09.00 Steve Gethin DREW 6 Walsall
22.09.00 Jason Edwards W PTS 6 Wrexham
01.10.00 James Rooney L PTS 6 Hartlepool
09.10.00 Ricky Eccleston L PTS 4 Liverpool
26.10.00 Nigel Leake W PTS 6 Stoke
04.11.00 Marc Callaghan L RSC 4 Bethnal
Green
07.12.00 Alex Stewart W PTS 8 Stoke
22.01.01 Craig Docherty L RSC 4 Glasgow
08.03.01 Jason White L PTS 8 Stoke
24.03.01 Carl Greaves L CO 6 Newark
*(Vacant Midlands Area
S. Featherweight Title)*
18.06.01 Dave Cotterill L PTS 6 Bradford
Career: 67 contests, won 16, drew 5, lost 46.

Nigel Senior   Les Clark

Lee Sharp

Edinburgh. *Born* Doncaster, 19 September, 1975
Welterweight. Ht. 6'0"
Manager T. Gilmour

15.11.99	Arv Mittoo W PTS 6 Glasgow	
21.02.00	Iain Eldridge W PTS 6 Glasgow	
20.03.00	Jason Vlasman L PTS 6 Glasgow	
19.02.01	Arv Mittoo W PTS 6 Glasgow	
19.03.01	Danny Parkinson W PTS 6 Glasgow	

Career: 5 contests, won 4, lost 1.

Steve Sharples

Bolton. *Born* Bolton, 21 May, 1971
S. Featherweight. Ht. 5'8"
Manager J. Doughty

05.03.00 Jaz Malik L RSC 1 Shaw
24.09.00 Lennie Hodgkins W PTS 6 Shaw
Career: 2 contests, won 1, lost 1.

Charles Shepherd

Carlisle. *Born* Burnley, 28 June, 1970
Former IBO S. Featherweight Champion.
Former Undefeated British, Commonwealth
& IBO Inter-Continental S. Featherweight
Champion. Ht. 5'4"
Manager J. Doughty/T. Gilmour

28.10.91	Chris Aston W PTS 6 Leicester
31.01.92	Alan McDowall L RSC 3 Glasgow
18.05.92	Mark Legg W PTS 6 Marton
25.09.92	George Naylor W RSC 4 Liverpool
22.10.92	Didier Hughes L PTS 4 Bethnal Green
13.02.93	Nigel Wenton W PTS 8 Manchester
23.05.93	Cham Joof W PTS 4 Brockley
21.10.93	Karl Taylor W RTD 5 Bayswater
09.02.94	Justin Juuko L RSC 5 Bethnal Green
21.04.94	Tony Foster L PTS 10 Hull
	(Vacant Central Area Lightweight Title)
29.09.94	Frankie Foster W RSC 3 Tynemouth
08.03.95	Bamana Dibateza W PTS 8 Solihull
26.04.95	Kelton McKenzie W RSC 7 Solihull
23.05.95	Michael Ayers L RSC 3 Potters Bar
	(British Lightweight Title Challenge)
14.11.95	John Stovin W RSC 4 Bury
22.04.96	Marc Smith W RSC 2 Crystal Palace
29.06.96	P. J. Gallagher L PTS 12 Erith
	(British S. Featherweight Title Challenge)
28.10.96	Harry Escott W PTS 8 Glasgow
22.09.97	Dave McHale W RSC 10 Glasgow
	(Vacant British S. Featherweight Title)
08.11.97	Matt Brown W PTS 12 Southwark
	(British S. Featherweight Title Defence)
02.05.98	Peter Judson W PTS 12 Kensington
	(British S. Featherweight Title Defence)
22.01.99	Trust Ndlovu W CO 6 Carlisle
	(Vacant Commonwealth S. Featherweight Title)
03.04.99	Smith Odoom W PTS 12 Carlisle
	(Commonwealth S. Featherweight Title Defence)
31.07.99	Tom Johnson W PTS 12 Carlisle
	(Vacant IBO S. Featherweight Title)
26.02.00	Affif Djelti L RSC 6 Carlisle
	(IBO S. Featherweight Title Defence)
05.06.00	Rakhim Mingaleev W PTS 12 Glasgow
	(Vacant IBO Inter-Continental S. Featherweight Title)
18.09.00	James Armah L RTD 9 Glasgow
	(Vacant Commonwealth S. Featherweight Title)
11.11.00	Tontcho Tontchev L PTS 12 Belfast
	(WBA International S. Featherweight Title Challenge)
20.03.01	Alex Moon L PTS 12 Glasgow
	(Vacant Commonwealth S. Featherweight Title)

Career: 29 contests, won 19, lost 10.

Wayne Shepherd

Carlisle. *Born* Whiston, 3 June, 1959
Middleweight. Ht. 5'6"
Manager Self

07.10.91	Benji Joseph W PTS 6 Bradford
28.10.91	Noel Henry W PTS 6 Leicester
16.12.91	Dave Maj DREW 6 Manchester
03.02.92	Dave Maj L PTS 6 Manchester
30.03.92	Hughie Davey L PTS 6 Bradford
18.05.92	Dave Whittle W PTS 6 Marton
14.10.92	Richard Swallow L PTS 6 Stoke
31.10.92	George Scott L RSC 6 Earls Court
13.02.93	Delroy Waul L RSC 5 Manchester
31.03.93	Derek Grainger L RSC 4 Barking
11.06.93	Hughie Davey L PTS 6 Gateshead
06.09.93	Shea Neary L RTD 2 Liverpool
26.01.94	James McGee W PTS 6 Stoke
28.02.94	Craig Winter L PTS 6 Manchester
02.03.95	Denny Johnson L PTS 6 Cramlington
06.04.95	Shaun Stokes L PTS 6 Sheffield
22.05.95	Peter Varnavas W PTS 6 Morecambe
01.06.95	Tommy Quinn L PTS 6 Musselburgh
29.07.95	Shaun O'Neill L PTS 4 Whitley Bay
07.10.95	Neil Sinclair L PTS 6 Belfast
30.10.95	John Stronach L PTS 6 Bradford
11.12.95	Shamus Casey L PTS 6 Morecambe
07.03.96	Derek Roche L RSC 3 Bradford
22.04.96	Gilbert Eastman L PTS 4 Crystal Palace
25.06.96	Geoff McCreesh L PTS 4 Stevenage
26.09.96	John Docherty L PTS 6 Glasgow
10.11.96	John Docherty L PTS 6 Glasgow
22.12.96	Chris Barnett L PTS 6 Salford
16.03.97	C. J. Jackson L PTS 6 Shaw
14.10.97	Joe Townsley L PTS 8 Kilmarnock
22.11.97	G. L. Booth L PTS 4 Manchester
05.03.98	Lee Murtagh L PTS 6 Leeds
20.03.98	Wayne Burchell L PTS 6 Leeds
28.04.98	Danny Ryan L DIS 4 Belfast
14.06.98	Matt Mowatt DREW 6 Shaw
20.09.98	Matt Mowatt W PTS 6 Sheffield
12.10.98	Danny Thornton L PTS 6 Bradford
03.12.98	Lee Molloy L PTS 4 Mayfair
22.01.99	Lee Bird W PTS 6 Carlisle
16.02.99	Paul O'Rourke L PTS 6 Leeds
07.08.99	Alan Gilbert DREW 8 Dagenham
	(Vacant British Masters L. Middleweight Title)
28.10.99	Matt Mowatt W PTS 6 Burnley
15.11.99	James Docherty L PTS 8 Glasgow
14.12.99	Joe Townsley L PTS 6 Coventry
26.02.00	Martin Thompson W PTS 4 Carlisle
05.03.00	Jason Collins L PTS 6 Shaw
21.05.00	Andy Vickers L PTS 6 Shaw
23.10.00	Jackie Townsley L PTS 4 Glasgow
25.11.00	Jamie Moore L RSC 3 Manchester
22.01.01	Joe Townsley L PTS 6 Glasgow
20.03.01	Scott Dixon L PTS 6 Glasgow
28.03.01	Andrew Buchanan L RSC 2 Piccadilly

Career: 52 contests, won 9, drew 3, lost 40.

Simon Sherrington

Birmingham. *Born* Birmingham, 14 July, 1971
L. Middleweight. Ht. 5'9½"
Manager P. Cowdell

09.10.00 Paddy Martin W RSC 5 Birmingham
28.11.00 Pedro Thompson W RSC 5 Brierley Hill
Career: 2 contests, won 2.

Luke Simpkin

Swadlincote. *Born* Derby, 5 May, 1979
Heavyweight. Ht. 6'2"
Manager Self

24.09.98	Simon Taylor W CO 3 Edgbaston
16.10.98	Chris P. Bacon L PTS 6 Salford
10.12.98	Jason Flisher W RSC 5 Barking
04.02.99	Danny Watts L CO 3 Lewisham
28.05.99	Tommy Bannister W RSC 4 Liverpool
07.09.99	Owen Beck L PTS 4 Dagenham
11.09.99	Scott Lansdowne L PTS 4 Sheffield
11.03.00	Albert Sosnowski L PTS 4 Kensington
27.03.00	Mark Hobson L PTS 4 Barnsley
29.04.00	Johan Thorbjoernsson L PTS 4 Wembley
23.09.00	Mark Potter L PTS 6 Bethnal Green
30.09.00	Gordon Minors DREW 4 Peterborough
18.11.00	Keith Long L RSC 3 Dagenham
03.02.01	Paul Buttery W RSC 1 Manchester
01.04.01	Wayne Llewelyn L PTS 6 Southwark
24.04.01	Darren Chubbs L PTS 4 Liverpool
06.05.01	Billy Bessey L PTS 6 Hartlepool
09.06.01	John McDermott L PTS 6 Bethnal Green

Career: 18 contests, won 4, drew 1, lost 13.

Neil Simpson

Coventry. *Born* London, 5 July, 1970
British L. Heavyweight Champion. Former
Undefeated Commonwealth L.
Heavyweight Champion. Former Midlands
Area L. Heavyweight Champion. Ht. 6'2"
Manager J. Griffin/J. Harding

04.10.94	Kenny Nevers W PTS 4 Mayfair
20.10.94	Johnny Hooks W RSC 2 Walsall
05.12.94	Chris Woollas L PTS 6 Cleethorpes
15.12.94	Paul Murray W PTS 6 Walsall
06.03.95	Greg Scott-Briggs W RTD 5 Leicester
17.03.95	Thomas Hansvold L PTS 4 Copenhagen, Denmark
26.04.95	Craig Joseph L PTS 6 Solihull
11.05.95	Andy McVeigh L CO 2 Dudley
24.06.95	Dave Owens W RSC 1 Cleethorpes
25.09.95	Tony Booth L PTS 6 Cleethorpes
11.10.95	Darren Ashton W RSC 3 Solihull
29.11.95	Greg Scott-Briggs W DIS 7 Solihull
	(Vacant Midlands Area L. Heavyweight Title)
19.02.96	Stephen Wilson L PTS 6 Glasgow
27.03.96	Tony Booth L PTS 6 Whitwick
26.04.96	Dean Francis L RSC 3 Cardiff
02.10.96	Chris Davies W PTS 6 Cardiff
28.10.96	Nigel Rafferty W PTS 8 Leicester
03.12.96	Danny Peters L PTS 6 Liverpool
03.02.97	Michael Pinnock W PTS 6 Leicester
25.04.97	Stuart Fleet L PTS 10 Cleethorpes
	(Midlands Area L. Heavyweight Title Defence)
20.10.97	Slick Miller W RTD 1 Leicester
15.12.97	Chris Woollas L PTS 6 Cleethorpes

11.05.98	Greg Scott-Briggs W PTS 6 Leicester
30.11.98	Slick Miller W CO 3 Leicester
26.02.99	Adam Cale W RSC 3 Coventry
12.07.99	Tony Booth W PTS 10 Coventry
	(Elim. British L. Heavyweight Title)
14.12.99	Darren Corbett L PTS 12 Coventry
	(Vacant IBO Inter-Continental
	L. Heavyweight Title)
22.05.00	Mark Baker W PTS 12 Coventry
	(Vacant British & Commonwealth
	L. Heavyweight Titles)
18.11.00	Mark Delaney W RSC 1 Dagenham
	(British L. Heavyweight Title Defence)

Neil Simpson   Les Clark

02.01.01	Hastings Rasani W CO 4 Coventry
	(Vacant Commonwealth
	L. Heavyweight Title)
06.04.01	Yawe Davis L RSC 3 Grosseto, Italy
	(Vacant European L. Heavyweight
	Title)

Career: 31 contests, won 19, lost 12.

Neil Sinclair

Belfast. *Born* Belfast, 23 February, 1974
Welterweight. Ht. 5'10½"
Manager J. Breen

14.04.95	Marty Duke W RSC 2 Belfast
27.05.95	Andrew Jervis L RSC 3 Belfast
17.07.95	Andy Peach W RSC 1 Mayfair
26.08.95	George Wilson W PTS 4 Belfast
07.10.95	Wayne Shepherd W PTS 6 Belfast
02.12.95	Brian Coleman W RTD 1 Belfast
13.04.96	Hughie Davey W PTS 6 Liverpool
28.05.96	Prince Kasi Kaihau W RSC 2 Belfast
03.09.96	Dennis Berry L PTS 6 Belfast
27.09.97	Trevor Meikle W RSC 5 Belfast
20.12.97	Chris Pollock W RTD 3 Belfast
21.02.98	Leigh Wicks W RSC 1 Belfast
19.09.98	Paul Denton W RSC 1 Dublin
07.12.98	Michael Smyth W CO 1 Acton
22.01.99	Mark Ramsey W CO 3 Dublin
05.06.99	David Kirk W PTS 8 Cardiff
16.10.99	Paul Dyer W RSC 8 Belfast
18.03.00	Dennis Berry W RSC 2 Glasgow
16.05.00	Paul Dyer W RSC 6 Warrington
24.06.00	Chris Henry W RSC 1 Glasgow
12.08.00	Adrian Chase W RSC 2 Wembley
16.12.00	Daniel Santos L CO 2 Sheffield
	(WBO Welterweight Title Challenge)
28.04.01	Zoltan Szilii W CO 2 Cardiff

Career: 23 contests, won 20, lost 3.

(Raminderbir) Ram Singh

Wisbech. *Born* Crewe, 13 August, 1969
Welterweight. Ht. 5'11"
Manager Self

06.06.94	Wahid Fats L RSC 3 Manchester
26.09.94	Robert Howard W PTS 6 Morecambe
17.11.94	Terry Whittaker L PTS 6 Sheffield
24.11.94	Paul Scott L PTS 6 Newcastle
05.12.94	Liam Dineen L PTS 6 Houghton le
	Spring
12.01.95	Steve Tuckett L RSC 6 Leeds
21.02.95	Glen Hopkins L RSC 1 Sunderland
03.04.95	Dave Madden L PTS 6 Northampton
27.04.95	Paul Hamilton W RSC 2 Hull
14.06.95	Terry Whittaker L PTS 6 Batley
28.09.95	John T. Kelly L PTS 6 Sunderland
05.10.95	Garry Burrell L PTS 8 Glasgow
29.01.96	Marco Fattore DREW 6 Piccadilly
21.02.96	Dave Fallon L PTS 6 Piccadilly
19.03.96	Andy Green L PTS 6 Leeds
01.04.96	Hurricane Hughes W PTS 6 Bradford
22.04.96	John T. Kelly L PTS 6 Manchester
09.05.96	Liam Dineen L PTS 6 Sunderland
30.05.96	Steve Conway L PTS 6 Lincoln
13.06.96	Thomas Bradley L RSC 1 Sheffield
24.02.97	Phil Molyneux L PTS 6 Manchester
11.11.97	Franny Hogg L PTS 6 Leeds
04.12.97	Pete Stanway W PTS 6 Hull
03.02.98	John T. Kelly L PTS 6 Yarm
13.02.98	Lee McBride W RSC 5 Barrhead
23.02.98	Jason McElligott L PTS 6 Windsor
20.03.98	Cam Raeside L RSC 4 Ilkeston
21.05.98	Jason Brattley L PTS 6 Bradford
23.07.98	Colin Lynes L CO 1 Barking
12.10.98	Gavin McGill L PTS 6 Nottingham
19.10.98	James Docherty L PTS 6 Glasgow
03.12.98	Peter Lennon W PTS 6 Hull
11.12.98	Jan Cree DREW 4 Prestwick
12.01.99	Glenn McClarnon L RSC 1 Bethnal
	Green
27.03.99	Gavin McGill L PTS 4 Derby
21.05.99	Mark Halstead DREW 6 Glasgow
02.07.99	Eddie Nevins L CO 1 Manchester
12.06.00	Danny Parkinson L RSC 3 Bradford
15.07.00	Dave Gibson L PTS 6 Norwich

13.08.00   David Kirk L PTS 6 Nottingham
30.08.00   Gavin Down L PTS 6 Scunthorpe
09.09.00   Lee Byrne L RSC 2 Manchester
26.10.00   Peter Dunn L PTS 6 Stoke
04.11.00   Oscar Hall L PTS 6 Derby
19.11.00   Richard Holden L PTS 6 Chesterfield
04.12.00   Danny Parkinson L PTS 6 Bradford
11.12.00   Oscar Hall L CO 4 Cleethorpes
25.02.01   Steve Conway L RSC 2 Derby
08.06.01   Brian Gifford W PTS 6 Hull
23.06.01   Brian Gifford DREW 4 Peterborough
Career: 50 contests, won 7, drew 4, lost 39.

(Sukhdarshan) Tiger Singh (Mahal)

Peterborough. *Born* India, 28 October, 1970
S. Bantamweight. Ht. 5'8"
Manager Self

10.12.92   Ian Baillie W PTS 6 Corby
11.05.93   Anthony Hanna L PTS 6 Norwich
06.10.93   Anthony Hanna L PTS 6 Solihull
28.10.93   Nick Tooley L PTS 6 Torquay
30.11.93   Vince Feeney L PTS 6 Leicester
02.03.94   Lyndon Kershaw L PTS 6 Solihull
09.05.94   Terry Gaskin W RSC 2 Bradford
20.09.94   Keith Knox L PTS 6 Musselburgh
28.11.94   Terry Gaskin W PTS 6 Manchester
08.03.95   Lyndon Kershaw L PTS 6 Solihull
26.04.95   Darren Noble W PTS 6 Solihull
14.09.95   Mark Reynolds L RSC 3 Battersea
08.12.95   Shaun Hall W PTS 6 Leeds
04.10.96   Noel Wilders L PTS 6 Wakefield
01.11.96   Steve Williams L PTS 6 Mansfield
30.10.98   Henry Jones L CO 4 Peterborough
08.07.00   Chris Emanuele L RSC 1 Rotherham
Career: 17 contests, won 5, lost 12.

David Smales

Birstall. *Born* Staincliffe, 21 May, 1977
L. Middleweight. Ht. 5'10"
Manager Self

05.06.98   Peter Lennon W CO 6 Hull
15.06.98   Lee Bird W RSC 1 Bradford
25.10.98   Mark Harrison L RSC 4 Shaw
26.11.98   Lee Williamson L PTS 6 Bradford
20.02.99   Paul Swindles L RSC 3 Bradford
14.06.99   Shaun O'Neill L PTS 6 Bradford
18.10.99   Craig Goodman W PTS 6 Glasgow
06.11.99   Piotr Bartnicki L PTS 6 Bethnal Green
01.12.99   Craig Goodman W PTS 6 Stoke
03.03.00   Scott Millar DREW 6 Irvine
28.03.00   Richard Inquieti L PTS 6 Hartlepool
15.05.00   Richard Holden DREW 6 Cleethorpes
22.09.00   Martyn Bailey L RSC 3 Wrexham
07.12.00   Jamie Logan W PTS 6 Stoke
08.04.01   Chris Steele W PTS 6 Wrexham
Career: 15 contests, won 6, drew 2, lost 7.

Donovan Smillie

Bradford. *Born* Bradford, 9 August, 1975
L. Middleweight. Ht. 5'10½"
Manager F. Maloney

10.04.99   Sean Pritchard W RSC 1 Manchester
02.05.99   Mark Dawson W PTS 6 Shaw
04.12.99   Mark Dawson W PTS 4 Manchester
14.04.00   Dennis Doyley W PTS 4 Manchester
25.11.00   Ojay Abrahams L RSC 2 Manchester
Career: 5 contests, won 4, lost 1.

Billy Smith

Stourport. *Born* Kidderminster, 10 June, 1978
Lightweight. Ht. 5'7"
Manager P. Cowdell/R. Gray

28.03.00   Marcus Portman L PTS 6 Wolverhampton
07.04.00   Barry Hughes L PTS 6 Glasgow
18.05.00   Manzo Smith L PTS 4 Bethnal Green
26.05.00   Willie Limond L PTS 4 Glasgow
07.07.00   Gareth Jordan L PTS 6 Chigwell
15.07.00   David Walker L RTD 2 Millwall
09.09.00   Ricky Eccleston L PTS 4 Manchester
24.09.00   Choi Tseenpurev L RTD 2 Shaw
18.11.00   Lee Meager L RSC 1 Dagenham
17.12.00   Willie Limond L PTS 6 Glasgow
03.02.01   Scott Spencer L PTS 6 Brighton
09.03.01   Darren Melville L PTS 4 Millwall
27.03.01   Jason Nesbitt L PTS 6 Brierley Hill
Career: 13 contests, lost 13.

Billy Smith   Les Clark

Danny Smith

Great Yarmouth. *Born* Great Yarmouth, 6 October, 1979
Middleweight. Ht. 6'0"
Manager S. Pollard

15.07.00   Gary Jones W RSC 1 Norwich
04.11.00   Rob Stevenson DREW 6 Derby
28.03.01   Simeon Cover W PTS 6 Piccadilly
08.06.01   Rob Stevenson W PTS 6 Hull
Career: 4 contests, won 3, drew 1.

Ernie Smith

Stourport. *Born* Kidderminster, 10 June, 1978
Welterweight. Ht. 5'8"
Manager Self

24.11.98   Woody Greenaway L PTS 6 Wolverhampton
05.12.98   Gavin Rees L PTS 4 Bristol
27.01.99   Arv Mittoo DREW 6 Stoke

11.02.99   Tony Smith W PTS 6 Dudley
22.02.99   Liam Maltby W PTS 4 Peterborough
08.03.99   Wayne Jones W PTS 6 Birmingham
18.03.99   Carl Greaves L PTS 6 Doncaster
25.03.99   Brian Coleman L PTS 6 Edgbaston
27.05.99   Brian Coleman W PTS 6 Edgbaston
14.06.99   Dave Gibson W PTS 6 Birmingham
22.06.99   Koba Gogoladze L RSC 1 Ipswich
03.10.99   Gavin Down L RSC 1 Chesterfield
30.11.99   Brian Coleman L PTS 8 Wolverhampton
13.12.99   Richie Murray L RSC 5 Cleethorpes
24.02.00   Brian Coleman L PTS 6 Edgbaston
02.03.00   Oscar Hall L PTS 6 Birkenhead
10.03.00   John Tiftik L PTS 4 Chigwell
18.03.00   Biagio Falcone L PTS 4 Glasgow
07.04.00   Barry Connell L PTS 6 Glasgow
06.05.00   Matthew Barr L PTS 4 Southwark
15.05.00   Harry Butler L PTS 6 Birmingham
26.05.00   Biagio Falcone L PTS 4 Glasgow
06.06.00   Chris Henry L PTS 8 Brierley Hill
08.07.00   Mehrdud Takaloo L RSC 4 Widnes
13.08.00   Jawaid Khaliq L RSC 4 Nottingham
          (*Vacant Midlands Area Welterweight Title*)
24.09.00   Shaun Horsfall L PTS 6 Shaw
09.10.00   Dave Gibson W PTS 6 Birmingham
22.10.00   Matthew Barr L PTS 6 Streatham
06.11.00   Stuart Elwell L PTS 6 Wolverhampton
25.11.00   Michael Jennings L PTS 4 Manchester
03.12.00   Shaun Horsfall L PTS 6 Shaw
17.12.00   Kevin McIntyre L PTS 6 Glasgow
20.01.01   David Walker L RTD 1 Bethnal Green
12.03.01   Matt Scriven L PTS 6 Birmingham
24.03.01   Bobby Banghar L PTS 4 Chigwell
12.05.01   Jon Harrison L PTS 4 Plymouth
21.05.01   Brian Coleman W PTS 6 Birmingham
03.06.01   Babatunde Ajayi L PTS 4 Southwark
16.06.01   Bobby Banghar L PTS 4 Dagenham
Career: 39 contests, won 7, drew 1, lost 31.

Manzo Smith   Les Clark

(Stephen) Manzo Smith

Canning Town. *Born* Enfield, 10 April, 1979
Welterweight. Ht. 5'11"
Manager A. Bowers

147

18.05.00	Billy Smith W PTS 4 Bethnal Green
30.05.00	Woody Greenaway W PTS 4 Kensington
29.09.00	Jon Honney W PTS 4 Bethnal Green
09.03.01	Dave Travers W PTS 4 Millwall
20.04.01	Arv Mittoo W PTS 4 Millwall

Career: 5 contests, won 5.

Stephen Smith

Kentish Town. *Born* Hammersmith, 18 July, 1973
IBC L. Welterweight Champion. Former Undefeated IBF Inter-Continental Lightweight Champion. Former Undefeated German International S. Featherweight Champion. Ht. 5'8"
Manager Self

17.09.94	Marty Chestnut W RSC 5 Leverkusen, Germany
08.10.94	Jason Lepre W RSC 1 Halle, Germany
11.02.95	Fred Reeve W CO 1 Frankfurt, Germany
25.03.95	Pascal Ragaut W PTS 6 Dusseldorf, Germany
27.05.95	Vladimir Komarov W RSC 5 Dortmund, Germany
09.09.95	Juan Leiva W RSC 6 Bielfield, Germany
14.10.95	Abdul Mannon W RSC 3 Munich, Germany
17.02.96	Kid McAuley W RSC 4 Dortmund, Germany
20.04.96	Senturk Ozdemir W PTS 10 Dusseldorf, Germany *(German International S. Featherweight Title Challenge)*
25.05.96	Chris Jickells W RSC 3 Leipzig, Germany
22.06.96	Brian Robb W RSC 4 Dortmund, Germany
31.08.96	Angel Vasilev W PTS 8 Palma de Mallorca
23.11.96	Manny Santiago W PTS 8 Munich, Germany
15.02.97	Ullises Chong W RSC 2 Vienna, Austria
13.04.97	Peter Feher W CO 1 Cologne, Germany
01.06.97	Emmanuel Burton W DIS 3 Riesa, Germany
05.10.97	Bruno Rabanales W RSC 7 Gera, Germany
08.11.97	Rudy Valentino W PTS 8 Southwark
11.04.98	Ervine Blake W RTD 4 Southwark
30.05.98	Ferenc Szakallas W RSC 3 Riesa, Germany
21.11.98	Anthony Maynard W PTS 10 Southwark
06.03.99	Gary Flear W RTD 7 Southwark *(Vacant IBF Inter-Continental Lightweight Title)*
08.05.99	Ivo Golakov W RSC 3 Bethnal Green *(IBF Inter-Continental Lightweight Title Defence)*
13.09.99	David Kehoe W DIS 2 Bethnal Green
21.02.00	Bobby Vanzie L RSC 9 Southwark *(British & Commonwealth Lightweight Title Challenges)*
27.05.00	Michael Davies W PTS 10 Southwark
13.07.00	Assen Vassilev W RSC 1 Bethnal Green
18.11.00	Leonti Voronchuk W PTS 6 Dagenham
10.04.01	Zoltan Kalocsai W PTS 12 Wembley *(Vacant IBC L. Welterweight Title)*

Career: 29 contests, won 28, lost 1.

Tony Smith

Sheffield. *Born* Sheffield, 15 August, 1967
L. Middleweight. Ht. 5'8"
Manager Self

12.03.97	Richard Inquieti L RSC 2 Stoke
25.04.97	Dean Bramhald L PTS 6 Cleethorpes
03.05.97	Anas Oweida L RSC 1 Manchester
09.06.97	Christian Brady L RSC 4 Birmingham
10.07.97	Mark Allen L PTS 6 Doncaster
08.10.97	Marc Smith L PTS 6 Stoke
20.11.97	Marc Smith W PTS 6 Solihull
04.12.97	Dean Bramhald L PTS 6 Doncaster
15.01.98	Marc Smith L PTS 6 Solihull
13.05.98	Chris Price W PTS 6 Scunthorpe
21.05.98	Marc Smith L PTS 6 Solihull
21.09.98	Dave Gibson L RSC 6 Cleethorpes
09.12.98	Sean O'Sullivan L PTS 6 Stoke
11.02.99	Ernie Smith L PTS 6 Dudley
18.03.99	Rene Grayel DREW 6 Doncaster
15.05.99	Michael Jennings L RSC 1 Blackpool
04.10.99	Barry Hughes L RSC 5 Glasgow
30.11.99	Craig Clayton L PTS 6 Wolverhampton
08.12.99	Craig Clayton L PTS 6 Stoke
21.05.00	Shaun Horsfall L RSC 4 Shaw
03.02.01	Danny Wray L RSC 1 Brighton
12.03.01	Casey Brooke W PTS 6 Birmingham
01.04.01	Marcus Portman L PTS 6 Wolverhampton
03.06.01	Sam Mottram L PTS 6 Hanley

Career: 24 contests, won 3, drew 1, lost 20.

Trevor Smith

Birmingham. *Born* Birmingham, 24 October, 1965
L. Welterweight. Ht. 5'8"
Manager Self

04.02.95	Steve Burton W RSC 6 Cardiff
04.03.95	Mark Winters L PTS 6 Livingston
05.05.95	Shaun Stokes DREW 6 Doncaster
02.09.95	Martin Holgate L RSC 2 Wembley
09.10.97	Chris Price W PTS 6 Leeds
11.11.97	Richard Inquieti W RSC 3 Edgbaston
08.12.97	Dave Gibson W PTS 6 Leicester
27.01.98	Benny Jones W PTS 4 Piccadilly
11.03.98	Terry Roberts L PTS 6 Bethnal Green
26.03.98	John Paul Temple W RSC 5 Piccadilly
09.05.98	Oscar Hall L PTS 4 Sheffield
26.05.98	Jason Cook W RSC 1 Mayfair
17.09.98	Tanveer Ahmed L PTS 6 Glasgow
17.10.98	Chris Barnett L PTS 4 Manchester
10.12.98	Colin Lynes L RSC 1 Barking
25.02.99	Sammy Smith L RSC 2 Kentish Town
08.05.99	Kevin McCarthy L RSC 1 Bethnal Green
25.05.00	Lance Crosby L PTS 6 Hull
09.09.00	Dave Gibson W PTS 6 Newark
23.09.00	Francis Barrett L RSC 1 Bethnal Green
28.10.00	Jawaid Khaliq L RSC 1 Coventry
29.01.01	Liam Maltby L PTS 6 Peterborough
17.02.01	Costas Katsantonis L RSC 3 Bethnal Green
03.04.01	Willie Limond L PTS 4 Bethnal Green
05.05.01	Ross Minter L RTD 3 Edmonton

Career: 25 contests, won 8, drew 1, lost 16.

Michael Smyth

Barry. *Born* Caerphilly, 22 February, 1970
Welsh Welterweight Champion. Ht. 5'9¾"
Manager Self

02.05.91	Carl Brasier W RSC 2 Kensington
28.05.91	Rick North W RSC 1 Cardiff
18.07.91	Mike Morrison W RSC 2 Cardiff
03.09.91	Julian Eavis W PTS 6 Cardiff
20.11.91	Mike Russell W RSC 3 Cardiff
17.12.91	Julian Eavis W PTS 6 Cardiff
19.05.92	Ojay Abrahams W PTS 6 Cardiff
07.10.92	David Lake W CO 2 Barry
14.11.92	Des Robinson W PTS 6 Cardiff
10.07.93	Ernie Loveridge W RSC 6 Cardiff
23.10.93	Chris Saunders W PTS 6 Cardiff
12.03.94	Gordon Blair W RSC 4 Cardiff
21.07.94	Maurice Forbes W RSC 3 Battersea
24.09.94	Mike DeMoss W RSC 1 Wembley
25.10.94	Scott Doyle W CO 1 Southwark
25.01.95	Rick North W DIS 4 Cardiff
17.06.95	Kevin Lueshing L RSC 3 Cardiff *(Final Elim. British Welterweight Title)*
20.09.95	Howard Clarke DREW 6 Ystrad
25.10.95	Nigel Bradley W RSC 4 Cardiff
16.12.95	Geoff McCreesh W DIS 4 Cardiff
25.05.96	Maxim Nesterenko L RSC 5 St Petersburg, Russia *(Vacant WBC International Welterweight Title)*
19.07.96	Alexei Perevozchikov W RSC 5 Ystrad
02.10.96	Andrew Murray L PTS 12 Cardiff *(Commonwealth Welterweight Title Challenge)*
26.02.97	Paul King W CO 1 Cardiff
30.08.97	Peter Richardson W RSC 5 Cheshunt *(Elim. British Welterweight Title)*
14.07.98	Geoff McCreesh L CO 7 Reading *(British Welterweight Title Challenge)*
07.12.98	Neil Sinclair L CO 1 Acton
24.09.99	Jason Williams W RSC 3 Merthyr *(Vacant Welsh Welterweight Title)*
05.02.00	Darren Bruce L CO 5 Bethnal Green *(IBO Inter-Continental Welterweight Title Challenge)*
27.04.01	Kevin McIntyre L PTS 6 Glasgow

Career: 30 contests, won 22, drew 1, lost 7.

Danny Southam

Barnsley. *Born* Barnsley, 6 April, 1978
Cruiserweight. Ht. 6'0"
Manager T. Schofield

26.11.96	Pat Durkin W PTS 6 Sheffield
17.03.97	Liam Richardson W RSC 5 Glasgow
11.04.97	Kevin Mitchell W RSC 3 Barnsley
15.05.97	Ian Henry DREW 6 Sunderland
11.11.97	Jamie Warters L PTS 6 Leeds
27.02.98	Mark Snipe L RSC 2 Brighton
26.11.98	Mark Hobson L RSC 5 Bradford
16.02.99	Clint Johnson W RSC 5 Leeds
02.07.99	Mark Levy L RTD 3 Manchester
20.03.00	Tony Dowling L PTS 4 Mansfield
25.06.00	Brian Gascoigne W RSC 4 Wakefield
09.09.00	Tony Dodson L RSC 2 Manchester

Career: 12 contests, won 5, drew 1, lost 6.

Des Sowden

Plymouth. *Born* Plymouth, 13 August, 1974
L. Middleweight. Ht. 5'6"
Manager Self

04.06.98	Adam Spelling L CO 3 Barking

26.09.98 Ted Bami L RSC 1 Southwark
25.11.98 Brian Gentry L RSC 6 Streatham
26.02.99 Alan Bosworth L PTS 6 Longford
17.03.99 Peter Dunn L PTS 6 Kensington
09.05.99 Wee Barry W DIS 2 Bracknell
26.06.99 Barry Hughes L CO 1 Glasgow
18.11.99 Iain Eldridge L RSC 4 Mayfair
27.02.00 Dean Murdoch L RSC 5 Plymouth
07.04.00 Steven Bendall L RSC 3 Bristol
03.11.00 Russell Rees L RSC 1 Ebbw Vale
Career: 11 contests, won 1, lost 10.

Craig Spacie

Chesterfield. *Born* Chesterfield, 13 March, 1976
Lightweight. Ht. 5'5½"
Manager J. Ashton

18.09.97 Robert Braddock W RSC 6 Alfreton
03.12.97 Dave Travers W RSC 3 Stoke
16.05.98 Michael Gomez L RSC 3 Bethnal Green
14.10.98 Chris Williams W PTS 6 Stoke
02.12.98 David Morris DREW 6 Stoke
17.03.99 Carl Allen L PTS 8 Stoke
03.10.99 Dean Murdoch W RSC 5 Chesterfield
28.11.99 Andy Green W PTS 6 Chesterfield
18.01.00 Marco Fattore W RTD 1 Mansfield
29.02.00 Alex Moon W PTS 6 Widnes
20.03.00 Chris Williams L PTS 6 Mansfield
11.05.00 Pete Buckley W PTS 4 Newark
25.02.01 J.J.Moore W PTS 4 Derby
06.03.01 J.J.Moore W PTS 6 Yarm
Career: 14 contests, won 10, drew 1, lost 3.

Steven Spartacus   Les Clark

Steven Spartacus (Smith)

Ipswich. *Born* Bury St Edmunds, 3 November, 1976
L. Heavyweight. Ht. 5'10½"
Manager T. Sims

08.09.00 Michael Pinnock W PTS 4 Hammersmith
30.09.00 Martin Jolley W PTS 6 Chigwell
24.03.01 Calvin Stonestreet W PTS 4 Chigwell
16.06.01 Kevin Burton W RSC 1 Dagenham
Career: 4 contests, won 4.

Darren Spencer

Liverpool. *Born* Liverpool, 1 September, 1975
Welterweight. Ht. 5'8"
Manager T. Gilmour

20.11.00 Richard Inquieti W RSC 1 Glasgow
03.02.01 Brian Coleman W PTS 6 Manchester
22.02.01 Peter Dunn L PTS 6 Sunderland
19.03.01 Dean Nicholas W RSC 4 Glasgow
Career: 4 contest, won 3, lost 1.

Darren Spencer   Les Clark

Delroy Spencer

Wolverhampton. *Born* Walsall, 25 July, 1968
Flyweight. Ht. 5'4"
Manager D. Poston

30.10.98 Gwyn Evans L PTS 4 Peterborough
21.11.98 Jamie Evans W PTS 4 Southwark
30.01.99 Ian Napa L PTS 6 Bethnal Green
26.02.99 Chris Edwards W PTS 6 West Bromwich
30.04.99 Nicky Booth L PTS 6 Scunthorpe
06.06.99 Nicky Booth L PTS 4 Nottingham
19.06.99 Willie Valentine L PTS 4 Dublin
16.10.99 Colin Moffett W PTS 4 Bethnal Green
31.10.99 Shane Mallon W PTS 6 Raynes Park
29.11.99 Lee Georgiou L PTS 4 Wembley
19.02.00 Steffen Norskov L PTS 4 Aalborg, Denmark
08.04.00 Ian Napa L PTS 8 Bethnal Green
15.04.00 Lee Georgiou L PTS 4 Bethnal Green
04.07.00 Ankar Miah W RSC 3 Tooting
13.07.00 Darren Hayde W PTS 4 Bethnal Green
30.09.00 Paul Weir L PTS 8 Chigwell
28.10.00 Dale Robinson L RSC 4 Coventry
02.12.00 Keith Knox W PTS 6 Bethnal Green
08.05.01 Levi Pattison L PTS 4 Barnsley
22.05.01 Mimoun Chent L DIS 5 Telde, Gran Canaria
16.06.01 Sunkanmi Ogunbiyi L PTS 4 Wembley
Career: 21 contests, won 7, lost 14.

Scott Spencer

Brighton. *Born* Bath, 22 October, 1975
Lightweight. Ht. 5'9¼"
Manager R. Davies

04.11.00 Dave Cotterill W PTS 4 Bethnal Green
03.02.01 Billy Smith W PTS 6 Brighton
Career: 2 contests, won 2.

Scott Spencer   Les Clark

Michael Sprott

Reading. *Born* Reading, 16 January, 1975
Heavyweight. Ht. 6'0¾"
Manager D. Powell

20.11.96 Geoff Hunter W RSC 1 Wembley
19.02.97 Johnny Davison W CO 2 Acton
17.03.97 Slick Miller W CO 1 Mayfair
16.04.97 Tim Redman W CO 2 Bethnal Green
20.05.97 Waldeck Fransas W PTS 6 Edmonton
02.09.97 Gary Williams W PTS 6 Southwark
08.11.97 Darren Fearn W PTS 6 Southwark
06.12.97 Nick Howard W RSC 1 Wembley
10.01.98 Johnny Davison W RSC 2 Bethnal Green
14.02.98 Ray Kane W RTD 1 Southwark
14.03.98 Michael Murray W PTS 6 Bethnal Green
12.09.98 Harry Senior L RSC 6 Bethnal Green *(Vacant Southern Area Heavyweight Title)*
16.01.99 Gary Williams W PTS 6 Bethnal Green
10.07.99 Chris Woollas W RTD 4 Southwark
18.01.00 Tony Booth W PTS 6 Mansfield
14.10.00 Wayne Llewelyn L RSC 3 Wembley
17.02.01 Timo Hoffmann W PTS 8 Bethnal Green
24.03.01 Timo Hoffmann L PTS 8 Magdeburg, Germany
Career: 18 contests, won 15, lost 3.

149

David Starie   Les Clark

David Starie

Bury St Edmunds. *Born* Bury St Edmunds,
11 June, 1974
British & Commonwealth S. Middleweight
Champion. Former Undefeated IBO Inter-
Continental S. Middleweight Champion.
Ht. 6'0"
Manager G. Holmes

24.09.94	Paul Murray W RSC 2 Wembley	
25.10.94	Dave Owens W PTS 6 Southwark	
07.02.95	Marvin O'Brien W PTS 6 Ipswich	
30.03.95	Mark Dawson W RSC 1 Bethnal Green	
17.05.95	Marvin O'Brien W RSC 5 Ipswich	
14.09.95	John Duckworth W PTS 6 Battersea	
20.10.95	Hunter Clay W PTS 8 Ipswich	
15.12.95	Carlos Christie W CO 4 Bethnal Green	
21.03.96	Paul Murray W RSC 1 Southwark	
14.05.96	Phil Ball W RSC 1 Dagenham	
09.07.96	John Duckworth W RSC 1 Bethnal Green	
03.09.96	Pascal Mercier W RSC 3 Bethnal Green	
26.11.96	Ray Webb W RSC 6 Bethnal Green	
08.04.97	Sammy Storey W RSC 7 Bethnal Green *(Vacant British S. Middleweight Title)*	
19.07.97	Dean Francis L RSC 6 Wembley *(British S. Middleweight Title Defence)*	
14.02.98	Enzo Giordano W RSC 4 Southwark	
28.03.98	Clinton Woods W PTS 12 Hull *(Commonwealth S. Middleweight Title Challenge)*	
02.07.98	Danny Juma W RSC 1 Ipswich	
21.11.98	Ali Forbes W CO 11 Southwark *(Commonwealth S. Middleweight Title Defence. Vacant British S. Middleweight Title)*	
19.01.99	Willie Quinn W RSC 3 Ipswich *(British & Commonwealth S. Middleweight Title Defences)*	
24.04.99	Zaourbek Hetagourov W RSC 1 Peterborough	

22.06.99	Mark Baker W PTS 12 Ipswich *(British & Commonwealth S. Middleweight Title Defences)*	
19.10.99	Teimouraz Kikelidze W PTS 12 Bethnal Green *(Vacant IBO Inter-Continental S. Middleweight Title)*	
29.01.00	Joe Calzaghe L PTS 12 Manchester *(WBO S. Middleweight Title Challenge)*	
18.11.00	Guy Waters W RSC 6 Dagenham *(Commonwealth S. Middleweight Title Defence)*	
09.12.00	Alex Mason W CO 3 Southwark *(British S. Middleweight Title Defence)*	
24.03.01	Andrew Flute W RTD 3 Sheffield	

Career: 27 contests, won 25, lost 2.

Jimmy Steel

Stoke. *Born* Stoke, 22 June, 1970
L. Heavyweight. Ht. 5'7"
Manager Self

25.04.96	Andy Gray W PTS 6 Mayfair	
13.10.96	Johnny Whiteside L RSC 2 Shaw	
11.01.97	Enzo Giordano L PTS 4 Bethnal Green	
04.04.97	Michael Thomas L PTS 6 Brighton	
19.09.97	Jason Ratcliff L PTS 6 Southend	
11.11.97	Enzo Giordano L RSC 1 Bethnal Green	
21.12.97	Mike Gormley L PTS 6 Salford	
06.02.98	Pedro Carragher L PTS 6 Wakefield	
17.02.98	Gary Savage W PTS 6 Leeds	
17.03.98	Jason Barker L PTS 6 Sheffield	
05.04.98	Jon Penn L RSC 5 Shaw	
01.06.98	Jeff Finlayson DREW 6 Manchester	
09.06.98	Zoltan Sarossy L RSC 1 Hull	
17.09.98	Earl Ling DREW 6 Brighton	
14.10.98	Jeff Finlayson DREW 6 Blackpool	
13.11.98	Tony Griffiths L PTS 4 Brighton	
27.11.98	Damon Hague DREW 6 Nottingham	
16.01.99	Tony Oakey L PTS 4 Bethnal Green	
26.02.99	Ganny Dovidavas L PTS 6 Bethnal Green	
06.05.99	Dave Johnson L PTS 6 Sunderland	
28.05.99	Robert Zlotkowski L PTS 6 Liverpool	
10.07.99	Tony Oakey L PTS 4 Southwark	
07.10.99	Mike White L PTS 6 Mere	
30.10.99	Mike White L PTS 4 Peterlee	
14.12.99	Jim Twite L PTS 4 Coventry	
12.02.00	Jon Penn L PTS 6 Sheffield	
29.02.00	Mike Gormley L RSC 3 Manchester	
14.04.00	Jamie Moore L PTS 6 Manchester	
13.05.00	Andy Manning L PTS 4 Barnsley	
27.05.00	Dean Doyle L PTS 4 Mayfair	
19.08.00	Tony Dodson L RSC 3 Brentwood	
11.12.00	Mark Brookes L PTS 6 Sheffield	

Career: 32 contests, won 2, drew 4, lost 26.

Chris Steele

Dodworth. *Born* Barnsley, 28 March, 1980
L. Middleweight. Ht. 6'0"
Manager T. Callighan

14.11.99	Gavin Pearson L PTS 6 Bradford	
02.03.00	Elias Boswell W RSC 4 Blackpool	
13.05.00	Arv Mittoo L RSC 3 Barnsley	
05.12.00	Colin McCash L RSC 4 Nottingham	
08.03.01	Andy Abrol L RSC 6 Blackpool	
08.04.01	David Smales L PTS 6 Wrexham	
26.04.01	Sam Mottram L PTS 6 Gateshead	
10.05.01	Sam Mottram L PTS 6 Sunderland	
11.06.01	Darrell Grafton L RSC 1 Nottingham	

Career: 9 contests, won 1, lost 8.

Chris Steele   Les Clark

Rob Stevenson

Hull. *Born* Hull, 16 March, 1971
Middleweight. Ht. 5'9"
Manager Self

28.11.91	Matt Mowatt L PTS 6 Hull	
26.03.92	Steve Scott W PTS 6 Hull	
04.04.92	Chris Mulcahy L PTS 8 Cleethorpes	
29.04.92	Alan Williams W PTS 6 Liverpool	
01.06.92	Chris Mulcahy L PTS 6 Manchester	
13.10.92	Dean Hiscox L PTS 6 Wolverhampton	
26.11.92	Steve Scott L PTS 6 Hull	
18.02.93	Warren Stephens W PTS 6 Hull	
25.02.93	Ron Hopley DREW 6 Bradford	
29.04.93	Billy McDougall DREW 6 Hull	
01.07.93	Ron Hopley W PTS 6 York	
02.12.93	Ian Noble W PTS 6 Hartlepool	
13.12.93	Prince Kasi Kaihau L RSC 5 Doncaster	
24.02.94	David Sumner W PTS 6 Hull	
24.02.95	Billy Collins L PTS 6 Irvine	
25.03.95	Derek Roche L PTS 6 Rothwell	
01.07.95	Paul Carr L PTS 6 Kensington	
22.09.95	Brian Dunn L PTS 6 Hull	
03.11.95	David Bain L PTS 6 Dudley	
25.11.95	Jim Webb L PTS 6 Dublin	
04.12.95	David Radford L CO 2 Manchester	
26.02.96	Shamus Casey W PTS 6 Hull	
09.05.96	Carlton Williams L PTS 6 Hull	
03.09.96	Jim Rock L PTS 6 Belfast	
27.09.96	Steve Roberts L PTS 6 Stevenage	
27.02.97	Roy Chipperfield W RSC 5 Hull	
20.03.97	Phil Epton L PTS 6 Doncaster	
01.05.97	Lee Simpkin W PTS 6 Hull	
20.05.97	Ahmet Dottuev L CO 1 Edmonton	
04.12.97	Gary Savage L PTS 6 Hull	
17.01.98	Darren Dorrington L RSC 3 Bristol	
06.03.98	Warren Bowers W PTS 6 Hull	
28.03.98	Jason Hart L PTS 6 Crystal Palace	
26.09.98	Spencer Fearon L CO 2 Norwich	
12.12.99	Butch Lesley L PTS 6 Chigwell	
21.02.00	Brian Magee L RSC 5 Southwark	
04.11.00	Danny Smith DREW 6 Derby	
24.11.00	Lee Bird W PTS 6 Hull	
11.12.00	Carl Wall L PTS 4 Widnes	
20.01.01	John Tiftik L PTS 4 Bethnal Green	
03.02.01	Liam Lathbury L PTS 6 Brighton	
25.02.01	Damon Hague L PTS 8 Derby	

09.03.01 Chris Nembhard L RSC 2 Millwall
19.05.01 Andrew Lowe L PTS 4 Wembley
08.06.01 Danny Smith L PTS 6 Hull
Career: 45 contests, won 11, drew 3, lost 31.

Alex Stewart (Psaltis)

Luton. *Born* Greece, 6 December, 1969
Featherweight. Ht. 5'7"
Manager J. Cox

22.07.00 Jezz D'Agostino W PTS 4 Watford
07.12.00 Nigel Senior L PTS 8 Stoke
Career: 2 contests, won 1, lost 1.

Dave Stewart

London. *Born* Irvine, 5 September, 1975
Lightweight. Ht. 6'0¼"
Manager A. Morrison

15.02.01 Danny Connelly W PTS 6 Glasgow
27.04.01 Woody Greenaway W PTS 6 Glasgow
Career: 2 contests, won 2.

Adrian Stone

Bristol. *Born* Bristol, 19 July, 1971
Welterweight. IBO L. Middleweight
Champion. Former Undefeated IBO Inter-
Continental Welterweight Champion.
Ht. 5'7"
Manager Self

06.02.93 Sean Daughtry W PTS 6 New York City, USA
16.04.93 James Crosby T. DRAW 2 Hamilton, USA
08.05.93 Rey Robinson W PTS 4 East Mahanoy, USA
28.05.93 Nate Reynolds W RSC 4 Hamilton, USA
10.07.93 George Mitchell W RSC 2 Bushill, USA
10.11.93 Ernest Stroman W PTS 4 Atlantic City, USA
23.01.94 Sylvie Furlong W CO 1 Boston, USA
20.02.94 Robert West W CO 2 Biloxi, USA
21.04.94 Victor Perez W PTS 8 Ledyard, USA
22.07.94 John Jester W CO 3 Robinsonville, USA
18.08.94 Wayne Richards W CO 5 Melville, USA
19.10.94 Curtis Peoples W RSC 7 Catskill, USA
14.12.94 Israel Figueroa W RSC 2 Boston, USA
17.02.95 Ross Thompson W DIS 7 Atlantic City, USA
07.04.95 James Hughes L RSC 10 Salem, USA
(USBA Welterweight Title Challenge)
21.07.95 John Duplessis W RSC 5 New Orleans, USA
10.11.95 Roger Turner W RSC 9 Atlantic City, USA
03.02.96 Darryl Lattimore W RSC 1 Liverpool
01.04.96 Mroslav Gregoriev W CO 1 Den Bosch, Holland
14.05.96 Skipper Kelp L PTS 10 Ledyard, USA
18.10.96 Gilberto Flores T. DRAW 5 New York City, USA
15.11.96 Otilio Villareal W PTS 10 Somerset, USA
12.12.96 Johar Lashlin W CO 2 Vancouver, Canada
(Vacant IBO Inter-Continental Welterweight Title)
27.03.97 John-John Pacquing W RSC 6 Edmonton, Canada

29.07.97 Greg Johnson W RSC 4 New York City, USA
12.12.97 Bobby Butters W RSC 2 Mason City, USA
25.04.98 Desi Ford W CO 4 Biloxi, USA
18.08.98 Vernon Forrest L RSC 11 Tunica, USA
(Vacant NABF Welterweight Title)
18.02.99 Darren Covill W RSC 2 Barking
28.08.99 Benji Singleton W RSC 3 Hamilton, USA
14.01.00 Michael Corleone W RSC 3 Long Island, USA
15.04.00 Michael Carruth W RTD 5 Bethnal Green
(Vacant IBO L. Middleweight Title)
15.07.00 Geoff McCreesh W RSC 6 Millwall
(IBO L.Middleweight Title Defence)
11.11.00 Derek Roche W RSC 2 Belfast
(IBO L. Middleweight Title Defence)
13.03.01 Joe Townsley W PTS 12 Plymouth
(IBO L. Middleweight Title Defence)
Career: 35 contests, won 30, drew 2, lost 3.

Calvin Stonestreet

Tunbridge Wells. *Born* Pembury, 8 June, 1974
L. Heavyweight. Ht. 5'11½"
Manager M. O'Callaghan

23.01.01 Paul Bonson L PTS 4 Crawley
24.03.01 Steven Spartacus L PTS 4 Chigwell
26.04.01 Oddy Papantoniou W PTS 6 Kensington
16.06.01 John Killian L PTS 4 Wembley
Career: 4 contests, won 1, lost 3.

Calvin Stonestreet   Les Clark

Simon Stowell

Bristol. *Born* Bristol, 12 May, 1971
S. Bantamweight. Ht. 5'7"
Manager C. Sanigar

08.09.00 Danny Lawson W RSC 1 Bristol
06.10.00 Jamie Yelland DREW 4 Maidstone
13.03.01 Danny Lawson W RSC 2 Plymouth
Career: 3 contests, won 2, drew 1.

Michelle Sutcliffe

Leeds. *Born* Leeds, 3 February, 1967
WBF & IFBA Flyweight Champion.
Former Undefeated WIBF International
Flyweight Champion. Ht. 5'4"
Manager Self

11.02.96 Regina Halmich L RSC 2 Germany
24.05.98 Para Draine L RSC 5 New Jersey, USA
28.06.98 Diane Berry W PTS 5 Warrington
12.02.99 Sengul Ozokcu L PTS 6 Denmark
27.09.99 Veerle Braspenningx W RSC 7 Leeds
(Vacant WIBF International Flyweight Title)
27.02.00 Francesca Lupo W PTS 10 Leeds
(Vacant WBF Flyweight Title)
15.05.00 Jan Wild W PTS 6 Cleethorpes
07.10.00 Regina Halmich L PTS 10 Berlin, Germany
(WIBF L.Flyweight Title Challenge)
19.11.00 Kim Messer L PTS 10 Seoul, South Korea
(IFBA L. Flyweight Title Challenge)
17.05.01 Marietta Ivanova W RSC 5 Leeds
(WBF Flyweight Title Defence. Vacant IFBA Flyweight Title)
Career: 10 contests, won 5, lost 5.

Lee Swaby

Lincoln. *Born* Lincoln, 14 May, 1976
Former Undefeated British Masters
Cruiserweight Champion. Ht. 6'2"
Manager Self

29.04.97 Naveed Anwar W PTS 6 Manchester
19.06.97 Liam Richardson W RSC 4 Scunthorpe
30.10.97 Phil Ball W RSC 3 Newark
17.11.97 L. A. Williams W PTS 6 Manchester
02.02.98 Tim Redman L PTS 6 Manchester
27.02.98 John Wilson W CO 3 Glasgow
07.03.98 Phill Day L PTS 4 Reading
08.05.98 Chris P. Bacon L RSC 3 Manchester
17.07.98 Chris P. Bacon L PTS 6 Mere
19.09.98 Cathal O'Grady L RSC 1 Dublin
20.12.98 Mark Levy L RTD 5 Salford
23.06.99 Lee Archer W PTS 6 West Bromwich
04.09.99 Garry Delaney L PTS 8 Bethnal Green
03.10.99 Brian Gascoigne DREW 6 Chesterfield
11.12.99 Owen Beck L PTS 4 Liverpool
05.03.00 Kelly Oliver L PTS 10 Peterborough
(Vacant British Masters Cruiserweight Title)
15.04.00 Mark Levy W PTS 4 Bethnal Green
12.05.00 Enzo Maccarinelli W CO 3 Swansea
26.05.00 Steffen Nielsen L PTS 4 Holbaek, Denmark
09.09.00 Tony Dowling W RSC 9 Newark
(Vacant British Masters Cruiserweight Title)
05.02.01 Robert Norton L PTS 8 Hull
24.03.01 Crawford Ashley L PTS 8 Sheffield
30.04.01 Eamonn Glennon W PTS 6 Glasgow
02.06.01 Denzil Browne DREW 8 Wakefield
Career: 24 contests, won 10, drew 2, lost 12.

Louis Swales

Hull. *Born* Guisborough, 27 July, 1979
S. Middleweight. Ht. 6'0½"
Manager F. Maloney

16.12.00 Jason Collins DREW 4 Sheffield
10.02.01 Andrew Facey L RSC 3 Widnes
Career: 2 contests, drew 1, lost 1.

T

Matthew Tait

Harrow. *Born* Hillingdon, 15 April, 1973
Middleweight. Ht. 5'10½"
Manager Self

17.12.96	Dean Powell W PTS 6 Bethnal Green
29.01.97	Paul Webb W RTD 1 Bethnal Green
11.02.97	Dean Powell W RSC 4 Bethnal Green
12.07.97	Lee Bird W PTS 6 Earls Court
09.09.97	Chris Pollock W RSC 5 Bethnal Green
28.11.97	Mark Sawyers W PTS 6 Bethnal Green
11.03.98	Vince Rose W PTS 6 Bethnal Green
28.04.98	Freddie Yemofio W PTS 6 Brentford
14.05.98	Delroy Leslie W PTS 6 Acton
17.02.01	William Webster W PTS 4 Bethnal Green
24.03.01	Andrew Facey L PTS 4 Chigwell

Career: 11 contests, won 10, lost 1.

Mehrdud Takaloo (Takalobigashi)

Margate. *Born* Iran, 23 September, 1975
IBF Inter-Continental L. Middleweight
Champion. Ht. 5'9"
Manager F. Warren

19.07.97	Harry Butler W RSC 1 Wembley
13.09.97	Michael Alexander W PTS 4 Millwall
15.11.97	Koba Kulu W RSC 3 Bristol
19.12.97	Mark Sawyers W PTS 4 Millwall
07.02.98	Jawaid Khaliq L RSC 4 Cheshunt
16.05.98	Anas Oweida W RSC 1 Bethnal Green
10.10.98	Michael Jones L PTS 6 Bethnal Green
30.01.99	Darren McInulty W RSC 5 Bethnal Green
03.04.99	Gareth Lovell W RSC 6 Kensington
26.06.99	Leigh Wicks W CO 3 Millwall
04.09.99	Carlton Williams W RSC 4 Bethnal Green
23.10.99	Prince Kasi Kaihau W RSC 3 Telford
29.01.00	Paul King W RSC 2 Manchester
08.04.00	Biagio Falcone W RTD 4 Bethnal Green
08.07.00	Ernie Smith W RSC 4 Widnes
12.08.00	Howard Clarke W PTS 12 Wembley *(Vacant IBF Inter-Continental L.Middleweight Title)*
13.11.00	Jason Collins W RSC 2 Bethnal Green
24.02.01	James Lowther W PTS 12 Bethnal Green *(IBF Inter-Continental L.Middleweight Title Defence)*

Career: 18 contests, won 16, lost 2.

Dave Tatton

Gillingham. *Born* Gillingham, 19
September, 1967
Lightweight. Ht. 5'8"
Manager D. Currivan

30.04.99	David Thompson W PTS 6 Purfleet
09.03.00	Matty Leonard DREW 6 Bethnal Green
12.05.00	Woody Greenaway W PTS 4 Swansea
11.06.00	Mark Haslam L PTS 4 Salford
22.07.00	Marco Fattore W RSC 2 Watford

Career: 5 contests, won 3, drew 1, lost 1.

Darren Taylor

Bramhall. *Born* Bracknell, 7 December,
1978
Flyweight. Ht. 5'3"
Manager J. Evans

23.11.00	Tommy Thomas W RSC 1 Bayswater
03.06.01	Chris Edwards DREW 6 Hanley

Career: 2 contests, won 1, drew 1.

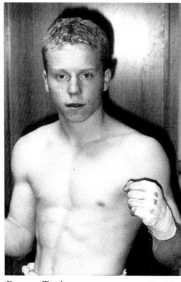

Darren Taylor   Les Clark

Karl Taylor

Birmingham. *Born* Birmingham, 5 January,
1966
L. Welterweight. Former Undefeated
Midlands Area Lightweight Champion.
Ht. 5'5"
Manager Self

18.03.87	Steve Brown W PTS 6 Stoke
06.04.87	Paul Taylor L PTS 6 Southampton
12.06.87	Mark Begley W RSC 1 Leamington
18.11.87	Colin Lynch W RSC 4 Solihull
29.02.88	Peter Bradley L PTS 8 Birmingham
04.10.89	Mark Antony W CO 2 Stafford
30.10.89	Tony Feliciello L PTS 8 Birmingham
06.12.89	John Davison L PTS 8 Leicester
23.12.89	Regilio Tuur L RTD 1 Hoogvliet, Holland
22.02.90	Mark Ramsey L RSC 4 Hull
29.10.90	Steve Walker DREW 6 Birmingham
10.12.90	Elvis Parsley L PTS 6 Birmingham
16.01.91	Wayne Windle W PTS 8 Stoke
02.05.91	Billy Schwer L RSC 2 Northampton
25.07.91	Peter Till L RSC 4 Dudley *(Midlands Area Lightweight Title Challenge)*
24.02.92	Charlie Kane L PTS 8 Glasgow
28.04.92	Richard Woolgar W PTS 6 Wolverhampton
29.05.92	Alan McDowall L PTS 6 Glasgow
25.07.92	Michael Armstrong L RSC 3 Manchester
02.11.92	Hugh Forde L PTS 6 Wolverhampton
23.11.92	Dave McHale L PTS 8 Glasgow
22.12.92	Patrick Gallagher L RSC 3 Mayfair

13.02.93	Craig Dermody L RSC 5 Manchester
31.03.93	Craig Dermody W PTS 6 Barking
07.06.93	Mark Geraghty W PTS 8 Glasgow
13.08.93	Giorgio Campanella L CO 6 Arezzo, Italy
05.10.93	Paul Harvey W PTS 6 Mayfair
21.10.93	Charles Shepherd L RTD 5 Bayswater
21.12.93	Patrick Gallagher L PTS 6 Mayfair
09.02.94	Alan Levene W RSC 2 Brentwood
01.03.94	Shaun Cogan L PTS 6 Dudley
15.03.94	Patrick Gallagher L PTS 6 Mayfair
18.04.94	Peter Till W PTS 10 Walsall *(Midlands Area Lightweight Title Challenge)*
24.05.94	Michael Ayers DREW 8 Sunderland
12.11.94	P. J. Gallagher L PTS 6 Dublin
29.11.94	Dingaan Thobela W PTS 8 Cannock
31.03.95	Michael Ayers L RSC 8 Crystal Palace *(British Lightweight Title Challenge)*
06.05.95	Cham Joof W PTS 8 Shepton Mallet
23.06.95	Poli Diaz L PTS 8 Madrid, Spain
02.09.95	Paul Ryan L RSC 3 Wembley
04.11.95	Carl Wright L PTS 6 Liverpool
15.12.95	Peter Richardson L PTS 8 Bethnal Green
23.01.96	Paul Knights DREW 6 Bethnal Green
05.03.96	Andy Holligan L PTS 6 Barrow
20.03.96	Mervyn Bennett W PTS 8 Cardiff
21.05.96	Malcolm Melvin L PTS 10 Edgbaston *(Midlands Area L. Welterweight Title Challenge)*
07.10.96	Joshua Clottey L RSC 2 Lewisham
20.12.96	Anatoly Alexandrov L RSC 7 Bilbao, Spain
28.01.97	Eamonn Magee L PTS 6 Belfast
28.02.97	Mark Breslin L RSC 6 Kilmarnock
30.08.97	Gilbert Eastman L PTS 4 Cheshunt
25.10.97	Tontcho Tontchev L PTS 4 Queensferry
22.11.97	Bobby Vanzie L PTS 6 Manchester
18.04.98	Richard Hatton L RSC 1 Manchester
18.07.98	James Hare L PTS 4 Sheffield
26.09.98	Oktay Urkal L PTS 8 Norwich
28.11.98	Junior Witter L PTS 4 Sheffield
06.03.99	George Scott L RSC 4 Southwark
15.05.99	Jon Thaxton L PTS 6 Sheffield
10.07.99	Eamonn Magee L RTD 3 Southwark
06.11.99	Alan Sebire W PTS 6 Widnes
15.11.99	Steve Murray L RSC 1 Bethnal Green
19.08.00	Iain Eldridge L PTS 4 Brentwood
04.09.00	Tomas Jansson L PTS 6 Manchester
16.09.00	Colin Lynes L PTS 6 Bethnal Green
09.12.00	David Walker L PTS 6 Southwark
10.02.01	Matthew Hatton L PTS 4 Widnes
10.03.01	Francis Barrett L RSC 3 Bethnal Green
10.04.01	Costas Katsantonis L PTS 4 Wembley
16.06.01	Brett James DREW 4 Wembley

Career: 70 contests, won 15, drew 4, lost 51.

Alan Temple

Hartlepool. *Born* Hartlepool, 21 October,
1972
Lightweight. Ht. 5'8"
Manager G. Robinson

29.09.94	Stevie Bolt W CO 2 Bethnal Green
22.11.94	Phil Found W PTS 6 Bristol
07.02.95	Brian Coleman W PTS 6 Ipswich
27.04.95	Everald Williams L PTS 6 Bethnal Green
29.09.95	Kevin McKillan W PTS 6 Hartlepool
23.11.95	Rudy Valentino L RSC 3 Marton
02.03.96	Tony Foster W PTS 6 Newcastle

08.06.96	Micky Hall W RSC 2 Newcastle	
20.09.96	Scott Dixon L PTS 4 Glasgow	
24.10.96	Billy Schwer L PTS 8 Wembley	
04.12.96	Harry Escott W PTS 8 Hartlepool	
12.02.97	Tanveer Ahmed L RSC 8 Glasgow	
	(Elim. British Lightweight Title)	
13.02.98	Bobby Vanzie L CO 8 Seaham	
	(Elim. British Lightweight Title)	
21.03.98	Michael Ayers L RSC 2 Bethnal Green	
31.10.98	Alan Bosworth W PTS 6 Basingstoke	
20.02.99	Ivan Walker W PTS 4 Thornaby	
05.03.99	David Burke L PTS 8 Liverpool	
01.05.99	Jason Rowland L PTS 6 Crystal Palace	
22.05.99	Eamonn Magee L CO 3 Belfast	
26.06.99	Steve McLevy W RSC 6 Glasgow	
11.09.99	Wayne Rigby W PTS 8 Sheffield	
02.11.99	Souleymane M'Baye L RTD 7 Ciudad Real, Spain	
12.08.00	Steve Murray L RSC 2 Wembley	
	(IBF Inter-Continental Lightweight Title Challenge. Elim. British Lightweight Title)	
26.03.01	Jonathan Thaxton L PTS 4 Wembley	
04.06.01	Gary Hibbert W PTS 6 Hartlepool	

Career: 25 contests, won 12, lost 13.

Jonathan Thaxton

Norwich. *Born* Norwich, 10 September, 1974
Former Southern Area, IBF & WBO Inter-Continental L. Welterweight Champion. Ht. 5'6"
Manager B. Ingle/F. Warren

09.12.92	Scott Smith W PTS 6 Stoke	
03.03.93	Dean Hiscox W PTS 6 Solihull	
17.03.93	John O. Johnson W PTS 6 Stoke	
23.06.93	Brian Coleman W PTS 8 Gorleston	
22.09.93	John Smith W PTS 6 Wembley	
07.12.93	Dean Hollington W RSC 3 Bethnal Green	
10.03.94	B. F. Williams W RSC 4 Watford	
	(Vacant Southern Area L. Welterweight Title)	
18.11.94	Keith Marner L PTS 10 Bracknell	
	(Southern Area L. Welterweight Title Defence)	
26.05.95	David Thompson W RSC 6 Norwich	
23.06.95	Delroy Leslie W PTS 6 Bethnal Green	
12.08.95	Rene Prins L PTS 8 Zaandam, Holland	
08.12.95	Colin Dunne L RSC 5 Bethnal Green	
	(Vacant Southern Area Lightweight Title)	
20.01.96	John O. Johnson W RSC 4 Mansfield	
13.02.96	Paul Ryan W RSC 1 Bethnal Green	
25.06.96	Mark Elliot W CO 5 Mansfield	
	(Vacant IBF Inter-Continental L. Welterweight Title)	
14.09.96	Bernard Paul W PTS 12 Sheffield	
	(Vacant WBO Inter-Continental L. Welterweight Title)	
27.03.97	Paul Burke W RSC 9 Norwich	
	(IBF & WBO Inter-Continental L. Welterweight Title Defences)	
28.06.97	Gagik Chachatrian W RSC 2 Norwich	
	(IBF & WBO Inter-Continental L. Welterweight Title Defences)	
29.11.97	Rimvidas Billius W PTS 12 Norwich	
	(IBF & WBO Inter-Continental L. Welterweight Title Defences)	
26.09.98	Emanuel Burton L RSC 7 Norwich	
	(IBF & WBO Inter-Continental L. Welterweight Title Defences)	

15.05.99	Karl Taylor W PTS 6 Sheffield	
07.08.99	Brian Coleman W PTS 6 Dagenham	
15.11.99	Jason Rowland L RSC 5 Bethnal Green	
	(British L. Welterweight Title Challenge)	
15.07.00	Kimoun Kouassi W RSC 3 Norwich	
21.10.00	Richard Hatton L PTS 12 Wembley	
	(Vacant British L.Welterweight Title)	
26.03.01	Alan Temple W PTS 4 Wembley	

Career: 26 contests, won 20, lost 6.

Jason Thomas

Merthyr Tydfill. *Born* Pontypridd, 7 October, 1976
Bantamweight. Ht. 5'6"
Manager Self

28.11.95	Henry Jones W PTS 4 Cardiff	
08.12.95	John Sillo L PTS 6 Liverpool	
13.01.96	Paul Griffin L RSC 2 Manchester	
02.10.96	Henry Jones L PTS 4 Cardiff	
23.10.96	Noel Wilders L PTS 6 Halifax	
27.11.96	Jason Booth L PTS 4 Swansea	
02.06.97	Colin Moffett W RSC 3 Belfast	
02.08.97	Peter Culshaw L PTS 8 Barnsley	
14.10.97	Graham McGrath W PTS 6 Wolverhampton	
25.10.97	Keith Knox W PTS 8 Queensferry	
04.12.97	Sean Green DREW 4 Doncaster	
13.02.98	Nick Tooley W PTS 6 Weston super Mare	
18.04.98	Hector Orozco DREW 4 Manchester	
14.05.98	John Matthews L PTS 6 Acton	
03.10.98	Michael Alldis L PTS 6 Crawley	
06.02.99	Noel Wilders L PTS 10 Halifax	
	(Elim. British Bantamweight Title)	
15.05.99	Alex Moon L PTS 8 Blackpool	
24.09.99	Frankie DeMilo W RSC 2 Merthyr	
15.11.99	Stephen Oates L PTS 6 Bethnal Green	
19.02.00	Stephen Oates L PTS 6 Dagenham	
29.03.00	Frankie DeMilo L RSC 8 Piccadilly	
	(Vacant British Masters S. Bantamweight Title)	
06.10.00	Takalani Ndlovu L RSC 2 Maidstone	
05.12.00	Kevin Gerowski L PTS 8 Nottingham	
24.05.01	Stewart Sanderson DREW 6 Glasgow	
08.06.01	Karim Quibir L CO 4 Orense, Spain	

Career: 25 contests, won 6, drew 3, lost 16.

(Michael) Tommy Thomas

Plymouth. *Born* Plymouth, 9 October, 1971
Featherweight. Ht. 5'6"
Manager N. Christian

Tommy Thomas   Les Clark

23.11.00 Darren Taylor L RSC 1 Bayswater
02.02.01 Gwyn Evans L RSC 4 Portsmouth
27.03.01 Sid Razak L RSC 2 Brierley Hill
Career: 3 contests, lost 3.

(Adrian) Carl Thompson

Manchester. *Born* Manchester, 26 May,
1964
IBO Cruiserweight Champion. Former

Carl Thompson   Les Clark

WBO Cruiserweight Champion. Former
Undefeated European, British & WBC
International Cruiserweight Champion.
Ht. 6'0"
Manager Self

06.06.88 Darren McKenna W RSC 2 Manchester
11.10.88 Paul Sheldon W PTS 6 Wolverhampton
13.02.89 Steve Osborne W PTS 6 Manchester
07.03.89 Sean O'Phoenix W RSC 4 Manchester

04.04.89 Keith Halliwell W RSC 1 Manchester
04.05.89 Tenko Ernie W CO 4 Mayfair
12.06.89 Steve Osborne W PTS 8 Manchester
11.07.89 Peter Brown W RSC 5 Batley
31.10.89 Crawford Ashley L RSC 6 Manchester
*(Vacant Central Area L. Heavyweight
Title)*
21.04.90 Francis Wanyama L PTS 6 St
Amandsberg, Belgium
07.03.91 Terry Dixon W PTS 8 Basildon
01.04.91 Yawe Davis L RSC 2 Monaco, Monte
Carlo
04.09.91 Nicky Piper W RSC 3 Bethnal Green
04.06.92 Steve Lewsam W RSC 8 Cleethorpes
(Vacant British Cruiserweight Title)
17.02.93 Arthur Weathers W CO 2 Bethnal
Green
*(Vacant WBC International
Cruiserweight Title)*
31.03.93 Steve Harvey W CO 1 Bethnal Green
25.07.93 Willie Jake W CO 3 Oldham
02.02.94 Massimiliano Duran W CO 8 Ferrara,
Italy
*(European Cruiserweight Title
Challenge)*
14.06.94 Akim Tafer W RSC 6 Epernay, France
*(European Cruiserweight Title
Defence)*
10.09.94 Dionisio Lazario W RSC 1
Birmingham
13.10.94 Tim Knight W RSC 5 Paris, France
10.06.95 Ralf Rocchigiani L RSC 11
Manchester
(Vacant WBO Cruiserweight Title)
13.04.96 Albert Call W RTD 4 Wythenshawe
09.11.96 Jason Nicholson W PTS 8 Manchester
26.04.97 Keith McMurray W RSC 4 Zurich,
Switzerland
04.10.97 Ralf Rocchigiani W PTS 12 Hannover,
Germany
(WBO Cruiserweight Title Challenge)
18.04.98 Chris Eubank W PTS 12 Manchester
(WBO Cruiserweight Title Defence)
18.07.98 Chris Eubank W RSC 9 Sheffield
(WBO Cruiserweight Title Defence)
27.03.99 Johnny Nelson L RSC 5 Derby
(WBO Cruiserweight Title Defence)
03.12.99 Terry Dunstan W CO 12 Peterborough
(Vacant British Cruiserweight Title)
13.05.00 Alain Simon W RSC 6 Barnsley
*(Vacant European Cruiserweight
Title)*
25.09.00 Alexei Illiin W RSC 2 Barnsley
*(European Cruiserweight Title
Defence)*
03.02.01 Uriah Grant W RSC 5 Manchester
(IBO Cruiserweight Title Challenge)
Career: 33 contests, won 28, lost 5.

(Patrick) Pedro Thompson

Birmingham. *Born* Birmingham, 27 July,
1962
L. Middleweight. Ht. 5'9½"
Manager Self

03.10.98 Joe Skeldon W RSC 5 West
Bromwich
25.11.98 Ross McCord L RSC 2 Clydach
22.04.99 Craig Clayton W PTS 6 Dudley
15.05.99 Reagan Denton L PTS 4 Sheffield
20.09.99 Sergei Dziniruk L RTD 2
Peterborough

02.12.99	Julian Kacanolli W PTS 6 Peterborough
12.12.99	Darren Boys L PTS 6 Chigwell
24.02.00	Martin Scotland W RSC 4 Edgbaston
23.03.00	Ojay Abrahams DREW 6 Bloomsbury
25.05.00	Brendan Rollinson L RSC 2 Hull
02.10.00	Keith Ellwood L RSC 3 Glasgow
28.11.00	Simon Sherrington L RSC 5 Brierley Hill
04.02.01	Martyn Bailey L PTS 6 Queensferry
26.02.01	Matt Scriven L RTD 1 Nottingham

Career: 14 contests, won 4, drew 1, lost 9.

Pedro Thompson   Les Clark

(Patrick) Wes Thompson

Leytonstone. *Born* Jamaica, 28 October, 1968
Heavyweight. Ht. 6'2"
Manager B. Baker

30.11.00 Adey Cook L RSC 4 Bloomsbury
Career: 1 contest, lost 1.

Gary Thornhill

Liverpool. *Born* Liverpool, 11 February, 1968
Former Undefeated British Featherweight Champion. Former Undefeated WBO Inter-Continental & Central Area S. Featherweight Champion. Ht. 5'6½"
Manager S. Vaughan

27.02.93	Brian Hickey W CO 4 Ellesmere Port
02.07.93	Dougie Fox W CO 1 Liverpool
30.10.93	Miguel Matthews W PTS 6 Chester
01.12.93	Wayne Windle W PTS 6 Stoke
25.02.94	Edward Lloyd DREW 6 Chester
06.05.94	Derek Amory W RSC 1 Liverpool
25.03.95	Craig Kelley W PTS 6 Chester
20.04.95	Michael Hermon W RSC 6 Liverpool
30.06.95	Chip O'Neill W RTD 3 Liverpool
04.11.95	Kid McAuley W PTS 6 Liverpool
08.12.95	Des Gargano W RTD 2 Liverpool
	(Vacant Central Area S. Featherweight Title)

13.04.96	Dominic McGuigan W RSC 3 Liverpool
25.06.96	Chris Jickells W PTS 6 Stevenage
11.12.96	Justin Juuko L RSC 8 Southwark
	(Commonwealth S. Featherweight Title Challenge)
13.12.97	Pete Buckley W PTS 6 Sheffield
06.06.98	Dean Pithie W CO 8 Liverpool
	(WBO Inter-Continental S. Featherweight Title Challenge)
19.12.98	Steve Conway W RSC 9 Liverpool
	(WBO Inter-Continental S. Featherweight Title Defence)
07.08.99	Chris Jickells W RSC 4 Dagenham
04.09.99	Michael Gomez L RSC 2 Bethnal Green
	(Vacant British S. Featherweight Title)
06.11.99	Marc Smith W PTS 6 Widnes
11.12.99	Pete Buckley W PTS 6 Liverpool
29.02.00	Benny Jones W PTS 6 Widnes
16.05.00	Richie Wenton W RTD 8 Warrington
	(Vacant British Featherweight Title)
09.06.01	Pete Buckley W PTS 4 Bethnal Green

Career: 24 contests, won 21, drew 1, lost 2.

Danny Thornton

Sheffield. *Born* Leeds, 20 July, 1978
Middleweight. Ht. 5'10"
Manager Self

06.10.97	Pedro Carragher L PTS 6 Bradford
13.11.97	Shaun O'Neill DREW 6 Bradford
08.12.97	Shaun O'Neill DREW 6 Bradford
09.02.98	Roy Chipperfield W RSC 4 Bradford
17.03.98	P. J. Maxwell L PTS 6 Sheffield
30.03.98	Mark Owens W PTS 6 Bradford
15.05.98	Danny Bell W PTS 6 Nottingham
15.06.98	Jimmy Hawk W PTS 6 Bradford
12.10.98	Wayne Shepherd W PTS 6 Bradford
21.02.99	Shaun O'Neill W RSC 5 Bradford
25.04.99	Matt Scriven W RSC 4 Leeds
14.06.99	Martin Thompson W PTS 6 Bradford
18.10.99	Paul Henry W PTS 4 Bradford
14.11.99	Dean Ashton W PTS 4 Bradford
06.12.99	Lee Blundell L PTS 6 Bradford
05.02.00	Steve Roberts L PTS 6 Bethnal Green
25.03.00	Lee Molloy W RSC 2 Liverpool
06.06.00	Joe Townsley L RSC 7 Motherwell
	(IBO Inter-Continental L. Middleweight Title Challenge)
30.11.00	Lee Blundell L RSC 8 Blackpool
	(Vacant Central Area L. Middleweight Title)
20.03.01	Ian Toby W PTS 8 Leeds

Career: 20 contests, won 12, drew 2, lost 6.

John Tiftik

St Pancras. *Born* London, 3 June, 1975
L. Middleweight. Ht. 5'7½"
Manager A. Simms

07.12.98	Mark Weller W CO 4 Acton
10.03.00	Ernie Smith W PTS 4 Chigwell
27.05.00	Colin Vidler W PTS 4 Southwark
07.07.00	Casey Brooke W RSC 2 Chigwell
30.09.00	Lee Bird W PTS 6 Chigwell
02.12.00	Brian Coleman W PTS 4 Chigwell
20.01.01	Rob Stevenson W PTS 4 Bethnal Green
16.06.01	Mark Ramsey L PTS 6 Dagenham

Career: 8 contests, won 7, lost 1.

Steve Timms

West Bromwich. *Born* West Bromwich, 10 December, 1974
Middleweight. Ht. 5'11"
Manager M. Shinfield

30.04.99	Matthew Pepper W RSC 3 Scunthorpe
02.07.99	Paul O'Rourke W RSC 2 Manchester
03.09.99	William Webster W RSC 4 West Bromwich
03.12.99	Allan Foster L RSC 4 Peterborough
22.01.00	Pedro Carragher DREW 4 Birmingham
02.03.00	Pedro Carragher W PTS 6 Blackpool
28.03.00	Andy Vickers W RSC 4 Hartlepool
22.05.00	Hussain Osman L RSC 2 Coventry
05.02.01	Paul Owen W RSC 1 Bradford
26.04.01	Andrew Buchanan L RSC 4 Gateshead

Career: 10 contests, won 6, drew 1, lost 3.

Ian Toby   Les Clark

Ian Toby

North Shields. *Born* North Shields, 18 May, 1972
S. Middleweight. Ht. 5'10½"
Manager T. Conroy

22.09.97	Mike Duffield W PTS 6 Cleethorpes
09.10.97	Jon Penn L PTS 6 Hull
21.10.97	Mike Duffield L PTS 6 Yarm
11.11.97	Gary Savage W PTS 6 Leeds
29.11.97	Paul Bowen L RSC 4 Norwich
09.02.98	Darren Rees W PTS 6 Bradford
26.02.98	Jon Penn DREW 6 Sunderland
23.04.98	Mike Whittaker W PTS 6 Newcastle
12.05.98	Wayne Burchell L PTS 6 Leeds
14.06.98	Mike Whittaker L PTS 6 Shaw
29.10.98	Eddie Haley L PTS 10 Newcastle
	(Vacant Northern Area Middleweight Title)
13.11.98	Lawrence Murphy L PTS 6 Glasgow

155

13.02.99	Eddie Haley L RSC 6 Newcastle	

(Northern Area Middleweight Title Challenge)

09.04.99	Biagio Falcone L RSC 3 Glasgow
10.06.99	Tony Rowbotham L PTS 4 Hartlepool
26.06.99	Biagio Falcone L PTS 4 Glasgow
15.08.99	Damon Hague L PTS 6 Derby
02.11.99	Javier Martinez W DIS 3 Ciudad Real, Spain
03.12.99	Steven Bendall L PTS 6 Peterborough
29.01.00	Anthony Farnell L RSC 3 Manchester
05.03.00	Lee Blundell L RTD 3 Shaw
11.05.00	Dean Ashton W PTS 6 Sunderland
20.05.00	Matt Mowatt W PTS 6 Rotherham
05.06.00	Albert Rybacki L PTS 4 Glasgow
09.09.00	Wayne Pinder L PTS 4 Manchester
01.10.00	Ian Cooper L RSC 4 Hartlepool
07.12.00	Paul Owen W RTD 5 Sunderland
11.02.01	Andy Vickers L PTS 6 Hartlepool
22.02.01	Matt Mowatt W PTS 6 Sunderland
20.03.01	Danny Thornton L PTS 8 Leeds
30.04.01	Biagio Falcone L RSC 2 Glasgow

Career: 31 contests, won 9, drew 1, lost 21.

Jackie Townsley

Motherwell. *Born* Bellshill, 9 February, 1973
Middleweight. Ht. 5'11¾"
Manager T. Gilmour

20.09.99	Shaun O'Neill W RSC 4 Glasgow
06.06.00	Matt Scriven W RSC 3 Motherwell
23.10.00	Wayne Shepherd W PTS 4 Glasgow

Career: 3 contests, won 3.

Joe Townsley

Cleland. *Born* Bellshill, 13 January, 1972
Former Undefeated IBO Inter-Continental
L. Middleweight Champion. Ht. 5'9¼"
Manager T. Gilmour

20.03.95	Hughie Davey L PTS 6 Glasgow
05.04.95	Brian Dunn W RSC 3 Irvine
18.11.95	Kevin Toomey W RSC 6 Glasgow
14.02.96	Shamus Casey W PTS 6 Sunderland
18.03.96	Robbie Bell W PTS 6 Glasgow
03.06.96	Shamus Casey W PTS 6 Glasgow
26.09.96	Prince Kasi Kaihau W PTS 8 Glasgow
10.11.96	Michael Alexander W PTS 8 Glasgow
14.03.97	Michael Alexander W PTS 6 Irvine
02.06.97	Hughie Davey W PTS 8 Glasgow
14.10.97	Wayne Shepherd W PTS 8 Kilmarnock
24.11.97	Tony Walton W PTS 6 Glasgow
23.03.98	Pedro Carragher W PTS 6 Glasgow
21.09.98	Pedro Carragher W PTS 6 Glasgow
11.12.98	Gary Savage W RSC 6 Prestwick
25.01.99	Jim Webb W PTS 12 Glasgow

(Vacant IBO Inter-Continental L. Middleweight Title)

20.09.99	Jon Foster W PTS 6 Glasgow
14.12.99	Wayne Shepherd W PTS 6 Coventry
19.02.00	Oscar Checa W RTD 4 Prestwick

(IBO Inter-Continental L. Middleweight Title Defence)

06.06.00	Danny Thornton W RSC 7 Motherwell

(IBO Inter-Continental L. Middleweight Title Defence)

22.01.01	Wayne Shepherd W PTS 6 Glasgow
13.03.01	Adrian Stone L PTS 12 Plymouth

(IBO L. Middleweight Title Challenge)

Career: 22 contests, won 20, lost 2.

Dave Travers

Rowley Regis. *Born* Smethwick, 21 September, 1971
L. Welterweight. Ht. 5'6"
Manager Self

14.10.97	Ian Turner DREW 6 Wolverhampton
20.11.97	Chris Lyons L PTS 6 Solihull
03.12.97	Craig Spacie L RSC 3 Stoke
10.02.98	Kid McAuley W PTS 6 Wolverhampton
18.03.98	Benny Jones L PTS 6 Stoke
11.05.98	Mark Payne L RTD 3 Leicester
11.09.98	Chris Emanuele W RSC 2 Newark
13.10.98	Chris Jickells L PTS 6 Wolverhampton
30.10.98	Liam Maltby L PTS 4 Peterborough
14.11.98	Steve Murray L RSC 2 Cheshunt
27.01.99	John Bermingham W PTS 6 Stoke
09.02.99	Chris Lyons L PTS 6 Wolverhampton
18.02.99	Gary Steadman L PTS 6 Barking
17.03.99	Nigel Leake L PTS 6 Stoke
17.05.99	Jim Betts L RTD 4 Cleethorpes
15.08.99	Gavin McGill L PTS 6 Derby
03.09.99	Jimmy Gould L PTS 6 West Bromwich
20.09.99	Liam Maltby L PTS 4 Peterborough
28.03.00	Duncan Armstrong L PTS 6 Wolverhampton
07.04.00	Kevin McIntyre L RSC 4 Glasgow
20.05.00	Haroon Din L PTS 6 Leicester
06.06.00	Lee Williamson L PTS 6 Brierley Hill
04.07.00	Jaz Malik L PTS 6 Tooting
13.07.00	Danny Hunt L PTS 4 Bethnal Green
12.08.00	Barry Hughes L PTS 4 Wembley
24.09.00	Lee Armstrong L PTS 6 Shaw
02.11.00	Jason McElligott L PTS 4 Kensington
18.11.00	Leo O'Reilly L RSC 3 Dagenham
03.02.01	Chill John L PTS 4 Brighton
13.02.01	Gary Greenwood L PTS 6 Brierley Hill
09.03.01	Manzo Smith L PTS 4 Millwall
27.03.01	Abdul Mannon W PTS 6 Brierley Hill

Career: 32 contests, won 4, drew 1, lost 27.

Choi Tseveenpurev

Oldham. *Born* Mongolia, 6 October, 1971
Featherweight. Ht. 5'5¾"
Manager J. Doughty

21.05.00	David Jeffrey W RSC 2 Shaw
24.09.00	Billy Smith W RTD 2 Shaw
03.12.00	Chris Williams W PTS 4 Shaw
27.04.01	Willie Limond L PTS 6 Glasgow

Career: 4 contests, won 3, lost 1.

Ian Turner

Tredegar. *Born* Abergavenny, 6 November, 1975
S. Bantamweight. Former Undefeated Welsh Bantamweight Champion. Ht. 5'8"
Manager D. Gardiner

29.05.96	Henry Jones W PTS 6 Ebbw Vale
19.07.96	Marty Chestnut W PTS 6 Ystrad
02.10.96	Kevin Sheil W PTS 6 Cardiff
14.10.97	Dave Travers DREW 6 Wolverhampton
02.12.97	Henry Jones W RSC 8 Swansea

(Vacant Welsh Bantamweight Title)

03.04.98	Matthew Harris W PTS 8 Ebbw Vale
25.10.98	Ady Lewis DREW 8 Shaw
23.02.99	David Morris L PTS 10 Cardiff

(Vacant Welsh Featherweight Title)

23.10.99	Esham Pickering L PTS 6 Telford
03.12.99	Frankie DeMilo L PTS 6 Peterborough
12.05.00	David Jeffrey W PTS 6 Swansea
26.05.00	Brian Carr L PTS 6 Glasgow
03.11.00	Frankie DeMilo L PTS 10 Ebbw Vale

(British Masters S. Bantamweight Title Challenge)

Career: 13 contests, won 6, drew 2, lost 5.

Leo Turner

Bradford. *Born* Bradford, 17 September, 1970
Lightweight. Ht. 5'9"
Manager J. Celebanski

08.06.92	Wayne Rigby L PTS 6 Bradford
02.07.92	Wayne Rigby L CO 5 Middleton
12.10.92	Micky Hall L RSC 5 Bradford
14.12.92	Fred Reeve W RSC 2 Bradford
25.01.93	Alan Graham L PTS 6 Bradford
08.11.93	Tim Hill L RTD 4 Bradford
07.02.94	Paul Goode W RSC 3 Bradford
03.03.94	Colin Innes DREW 6 Newcastle
21.04.94	Colin Innes L PTS 6 Gateshead
09.05.94	Ian Richardson DREW 6 Bradford
13.06.94	Colin Innes W PTS 6 Bradford
20.10.94	Carl Roberts W RSC 3 Middleton
24.11.94	Ian Richardson W RSC 6 Newcastle
30.01.95	Trevor George L PTS 6 Bradford
25.06.00	Alan Kershaw L RSC 1 Wakefield
26.10.00	Dave Cotterill W PTS 6 Stoke
13.11.00	Geir Inge Jorgensen L CO 3 Bethnal Green
09.04.01	Duncan Armstrong W PTS 6 Bradford

Career: 18 contests, won 7, drew 2, lost 9.

Leo Turner   Les Clark

(Jeremy) Jed Tytler

Hartlepool. *Born* Beverley, 8 September, 1972
L. Middleweight. Ht. 5'9¼"
Manager G. Robinson

16.03.01	James Lee L RSC 3 Portsmouth
24.05.01	Charden Ansoula L RSC 2 Kensington

Career: 2 contests, lost 2.

UV

Willie Valentine

Dublin. *Born* Dublin, 1 October, 1970
Featherweight. Ht. 5'3"
Manager D. Ingle

19.09.98	Sean Grant W PTS 4 Dublin
22.01.99	Graham McGrath W PTS 4 Dublin
19.03.99	Danny Lawson W RSC 1 Weston super Mare
17.04.99	Kevin Gerowski W PTS 6 Dublin
19.06.99	Delroy Spencer W PTS 4 Dublin
29.05.00	Gavin Rees L RSC 3 Manchester
12.05.01	Harry Woods L PTS 4 Plymouth

Career: 7 contests, won 5, lost 2.

Bobby Vanzie

Bradford. *Born* Bradford, 11 January, 1974
British Lightweight Champion. Former
Commonwealth Lightweight Champion.
Former Undefeated Central Area
Lightweight Champion. Ht. 5'5"
Manager J. Doughty/T. Gilmour

22.05.95	Alan Peacock W RSC 1 Morecambe
29.10.95	Steve Tuckett W RSC 2 Shaw
14.11.95	John Smith W PTS 6 Bury
07.03.96	John Smith W PTS 6 Bradford
02.06.96	Anthony Campbell W PTS 6 Shaw
28.10.96	Richard Swallow W PTS 6 Bradford
24.02.97	Mark Ramsey DREW 8 Glasgow
08.06.97	C. J. Jackson W RSC 3 Shaw
23.10.97	Stuart Rimmer W RTD 8 Mayfair *(Vacant Central Area Lightweight Title)*
22.11.97	Karl Taylor W PTS 6 Manchester
13.02.98	Alan Temple W CO 3 Seaham *(Elim. British Lightweight Title)*
01.06.98	Gary Flear W PTS 6 Manchester
17.10.98	Wayne Rigby W RSC 10 Manchester *(British Lightweight Title Challenge)*
01.04.99	Anthony Campbell W PTS 12 Birmingham *(British Lightweight Title Defence)*
28.05.99	Athanus Nzau W RSC 10 Liverpool *(Vacant Commonwealth Lightweight Title)*
13.09.99	Brian Coleman W PTS 6 Bethnal Green
04.12.99	Vincent Howard W PTS 12 Manchester *(Commonwealth Lightweight Title Defence)*
21.02.00	Stephen Smith W RSC 9 Southwark *(British & Commonwealth Lightweight Title Defences)*
17.04.00	Paul Kaoma W RSC 2 Birmingham *(Commonwealth Lightweight Title Defence)*
09.09.00	Joseph Charles W RSC 6 Manchester *(Commonwealth Lightweight Title Defence)*
09.10.00	Laatekwei Hammond W RSC 8 Liverpool *(Commonwealth Lightweight Title Defence)*
03.02.01	James Armah L PTS 12 Manchester *(Commonwealth Lightweight Title Defence)*

05.05.01	Steve Murray W RSC 7 Edmonton *(British Lightweight Title Defence)*

Career: 23 contests, won 21, drew 1, lost 1.

Andy Vickers

Darlington. *Born* Darlington, 18 June, 1976
Middleweight. Ht. 5'10¾"
Manager T. O'Neill

25.04.99	Matt Mowatt W PTS 6 Leeds
11.10.99	Peter McCormack W PTS 6 Birmingham
30.10.99	Rob Galloway W PTS 6 Peterlee
09.12.99	Martin Thompson W PTS 6 Sheffield
24.02.00	Chris Crook L PTS 6 Sunderland
28.03.00	Steve Timms L RSC 4 Hartlepool
21.05.00	Wayne Shepherd W PTS 6 Shaw
05.10.00	Paul Owen W PTS 6 Sunderland
24.11.00	Keith Palmer W RSC 3 Darlington
11.02.01	Ian Toby W PTS 6 Hartlepool
17.05.01	Reece McAllister L RSC 1 Leeds

Career: 11 contests, won 8, lost 3.

Colin Vidler

Isle of Sheppey. *Born* Maidstone, 20 May, 1970
Middleweight. Ht. 5'8"
Manager D. Currivan

15.11.99	Reagan Denton L PTS 4 Bethnal Green
20.01.00	Brett James L PTS 6 Piccadilly
24.02.00	Barry Connell L PTS 6 Glasgow
09.03.00	Dave Martin DREW 6 Bethnal Green
27.05.00	John Tiftik L PTS 4 Southwark
11.06.00	Wayne Pinder L PTS 6 Salford
04.07.00	Brett James L PTS 4 Tooting
25.07.00	Brendan Rollinson W PTS 4 Southwark
04.09.00	Thomas McDonagh L PTS 6 Manchester
06.10.00	Clive Johnson W PTS 6 Maidstone
02.11.00	Keith Palmer L PTS 6 Kensington
13.11.00	Sharam Foughami L PTS 4 Bethnal Green

Career: 12 contests, won 2, drew 1, lost 9.

Bobby Vanzie   Les Clark

Jimmy Vincent

Birmingham. *Born* Barnet, 5 June, 1969
L. Middleweight. Ht. 5'8"
Manager Self

19.10.87	Roy Williams W PTS 6 Birmingham
11.11.87	Mick Greenwood W PTS 6 Stafford
19.11.87	Darryl Pettit W RSC 6 Ilkeston
24.11.87	Roy Williams W PTS 6 Wolverhampton
14.02.88	Niel Leggett L PTS 6 Peterborough
29.02.88	Billy Cawley W CO 1 Birmingham
13.04.88	Dave Croft W PTS 6 Wolverhampton
16.05.88	Barry North W PTS 6 Wolverhampton
14.06.88	Dean Dickinson W PTS 6 Birmingham
20.09.88	Henry Armstrong L PTS 6 Stoke
10.10.88	Henry Armstrong L PTS 6 Manchester
17.10.88	Dean Dickinson W PTS 6 Birmingham
14.11.88	Peter Gabbitus L PTS 6 Stratford upon Avon
22.11.88	Barry North W RSC 4 Wolverhampton
12.12.88	Tony Feliciello L PTS 8 Birmingham
09.09.92	Mark Dawson L PTS 6 Stoke
23.09.92	Mark Epton W RSC 6 Leeds
17.12.92	Jason Rowland L PTS 6 Wembley
06.03.93	Mark Tibbs W PTS 6 Glasgow
27.08.96	Geoff McCreesh L RSC 1 Windsor
26.09.96	David Bain W RSC 3 Walsall
28.10.96	Lee Murtagh W RSC 2 Bradford
18.01.97	Tommy Quinn W RSC 1 Swadlincote
25.02.97	Kevin Adamson W PTS 6 Sheffield
25.03.97	Gary Jacobs L RSC 1 Lewisham
25.10.97	Ahmed Dottuev L PTS 6 Queensferry
29.01.98	Craig Winter L PTS 6 Pentre Halkyn
28.03.98	Zoltan Sarossy DREW 6 Hull
18.09.98	Danny Ryan L PTS 12 Belfast *(Vacant IBO Inter-Continental S. Middleweight Title)*
24.10.98	Darren Dorrington DREW 6 Bristol
25.11.98	Cornelius Carr L PTS 6 Streatham
05.12.98	Wayne Alexander L RSC 3 Bristol
22.01.99	Jim Rock L PTS 10 Dublin
29.04.99	Anthony McFadden L PTS 6 Bethnal Green
11.12.00	Harry Butler W PTS 6 Birmingham

Career: 35 contests, won 17, drew 2, lost 16.

Joel Viney

Blackpool. *Born* Manchester, 25 September, 1973
S. Featherweight. Ht. 5'7³/₄"
Manager L. Veitch

02.03.00	Duncan Armstrong W PTS 6 Blackpool
09.06.00	Gareth Wiltshaw W PTS 6 Blackpool
30.11.00	Dave Cotterill L RSC 1 Blackpool
27.01.01	Bradley Pryce L RSC 3 Bethnal Green
10.03.01	Kevin Lear L RSC 2 Bethnal Green
04.06.01	Barry Hawthorne L PTS 8 Glasgow
11.06.01	Inderpaul Sandhu L PTS 4 Nottingham

Career: 7 contests, won 2, lost 5.

Jason Vlasman

Liverpool. *Born* Liverpool, 23 April, 1971
L. Welterweight. Ht. 5'7¹/₂"
Manager T. Miller

01.12.99	Mohamed Helel W PTS 4 Yarm
13.12.99	Barry Hughes L RSC 2 Glasgow
20.03.00	Lee Sharp W PTS 6 Glasgow
18.05.00	Colin Lynes L RSC 2 Bethnal Green
14.10.00	David Walker L RSC 1 Wembley

Career: 5 contests, won 2, lost 3.

Joel Viney   Les Clark

Jason Vlasman   Les Clark

WXYZ

Tommy Waite
Belfast. *Born* Belfast, 11 March, 1972
All-Ireland Bantamweight Champion.
Former British & Commonwealth
Bantamweight Champion. Ht. 5'4"
Manager B. Hearn

28.05.96	Graham McGrath W PTS 4 Belfast
03.09.96	Danny Ruegg W RSC 4 Belfast
05.11.96	Graham McGrath W PTS 4 Belfast
28.01.97	Rowan Williams W PTS 4 Belfast
29.04.97	Henry Jones W PTS 4 Belfast
02.06.97	Louis Veitch W RSC 5 Belfast
27.09.97	Sean Green L RSC 3 Belfast
20.12.97	Vince Feeney W PTS 10 Belfast
	(Vacant All-Ireland Bantamweight Title)
28.04.98	Stevie Quinn W RSC 3 Belfast
29.06.99	Anthony Hanna W PTS 4 Bethnal Green
27.11.99	Kevin Gerowski L PTS 6 Liverpool
17.04.00	Chris Emanuele W PTS 6 Bradford
09.09.00	Ady Lewis W RSC 4 Manchester
	(British & Commonwealth Bantamweight Title Challenges)
09.10.00	Nicky Booth L PTS 12 Liverpool
	(British & Commonwealth Bantamweight Title Defences)

Career: 14 contests, won 11, lost 3.

Gavin Wake
Leeds. *Born* Leeds, 25 June, 1979
Welterweight. Ht. 5'11"
Manager M. Marsden

26.02.01	Arv Mittoo W PTS 4 Nottingham
09.04.01	Richard Inquieti W PTS 6 Bradford
08.05.01	Brian Coleman W PTS 4 Barnsley
21.06.01	Lee Williamson W PTS 6 Sheffield

Career: 4 contests, won 4.

David Walker
Sidcup. *Born* Bromley, 17 June, 1976
Welterweight. Ht. 5'10"
Manager Self

29.04.00	Dave Fallon W RSC 1 Wembley
27.05.00	Stuart Rimmer W RSC 2 Southwark
15.07.00	Billy Smith W RTD 2 Millwall
16.09.00	Keith Jones W PTS 6 Bethnal Green
14.10.00	Jason Vlasman W RSC 1 Wembley
18.11.00	Gary Flear W PTS 4 Dagenham
09.12.00	Karl Taylor W PTS 6 Southwark
20.01.01	Ernie Smith W RTD 1 Bethnal Green
17.02.01	Paul Denton W PTS 4 Bethnal Green
19.05.01	Mark Ramsey W PTS 4 Wembley

Career: 10 contests, won 10.

Dean Walker
Sheffield. *Born* Sheffield, 25 April, 1979
L. Middleweight. Ht. 5'11"
Manager D. Hobson

21.10.00	Colin McCash DREW 6 Sheffield
11.12.00	James Lee L PTS 6 Sheffield

Career: 2 contests, drew 1, lost 1.

Carl Wall
Liverpool. *Born* Liverpool, 29 July, 1976
L. Middleweight. Ht. 5'10¾"
Manager S. Vaughan

11.12.00	Rob Stevenson W PTS 4 Widnes
10.02.01	Brian Coleman W RSC 1 Widnes

Career: 2 contest, won 2.

Carl Wall   Les Clark

Marcus Walters
Kings Cross. *Born* Cardiff, 16 April, 1979
Welterweight. Ht. 5'7½"
Manager Self

30.09.99	Robert Mann W RSC 1 Kensington
26.11.99	Lee Molyneux W PTS 6 Bayswater
01.07.00	Lee Molyneux W PTS 6 Southwark

Career: 3 contests, won 3.

Jamie Warters
Leeds. *Born* York, 16 December, 1973
L. Heavyweight. Ht. 6'1"
Manager Self

15.09.95	Phil Reid W RSC 5 Darlington
07.12.95	Scott Beasley W PTS 6 Hull
19.03.96	Declan Faherty W PTS 6 Leeds
13.06.97	Greg Scott-Briggs W RSC 5 Leeds
11.11.97	Danny Southam W PTS 6 Leeds
17.02.98	P. R. Mason W CO 2 Leeds
12.05.98	Warren Stowe W PTS 6 Leeds
26.09.98	Tim Brown L RSC 4 York
15.07.99	Kevin Mitchell W CO 1 Peterborough
13.11.99	Terry Morrill W PTS 8 Hull
21.10.00	Jason Barker W PTS 4 Sheffield

Career: 11 contests, won 10, lost 1.

Martin Watson
Coatbridge. *Born* Bellshill, 12 May, 1981
Lightweight. Ht. 5'8"
Manager R. Bannon

24.05.01	Shaune Danskin W RSC 3 Glasgow

Career: 1 contest, won 1.

Shayne Webb
Bargoed. *Born* Merthyr Tydfil, 12 January, 1978
L. Heavyweight. Ht. 5'11"
Manager D. Gardiner

05.02.00	Dean Doyle L PTS 4 Bethnal Green
26.10.00	Mark Phillips L PTS 6 Clydach
10.11.00	Matthew McAllister L PTS 6 Glasgow

Career: 3 contests, lost 3.

William Webster
Birmingham. *Born* Birmingham, 14 March, 1970
Middleweight. Ht. 6'0"
Manager Self

05.06.99	Brian Knudsen L RSC 4 Cardiff
15.08.99	Edwin Cleary L PTS 6 Derby
03.09.99	Steve Timms L RSC 4 West Bromwich
12.11.99	Biagio Falcone L PTS 6 Glasgow
20.11.99	Gary Beardsley L PTS 6 Grantham
02.12.99	Wayne Elcock L PTS 6 Peterborough
13.12.99	Biagio Falcone L RSC 1 Glasgow
21.02.00	Scott Millar L PTS 6 Glasgow
29.02.00	Thomas McDonagh L RTD 2 Widnes
28.03.00	Peter McCormack L PTS 6 Wolverhampton
13.04.00	Steve Ryan L PTS 4 Holborn
15.05.00	Mike Duffield W PTS 6 Birmingham
29.05.00	Michael Jennings L PTS 6 Manchester
19.06.00	Damon Hague L PTS 4 Burton
01.07.00	Alan Page L PTS 4 Manchester
25.09.00	Reagan Denton L PTS 4 Barnsley
07.10.00	George Robshaw L PTS 4 Doncaster
10.11.00	Chris Nembhard L RSC 1 Mayfair
28.01.01	Peter Nightingale L PTS 6 Wolverhampton
17.02.01	Matthew Tait L PTS 4 Bethnal Green
25.02.01	Gary Beardsley L PTS 6 Derby
13.03.01	Mark Phillips L RTD 1 Plymouth
16.06.01	Andrew Lowe L RSC 2 Dagenham

Career: 23 contests, won 1, lost 22.

Paul Weir
Irvine. *Born* Glasgow, 16 September, 1967
Flyweight. Former WBO L. Flyweight Champion. Former Undefeated WBO M. Flyweight Champion. Ht. 5'3"
Manager Self

27.04.92	Eduardo Vallejo W CO 2 Glasgow
09.07.92	Louis Veitch W PTS 6 Glasgow
21.09.92	Neil Parry W RSC 4 Glasgow
23.11.92	Shaun Norman W PTS 8 Glasgow
06.03.93	Kevin Jenkins W PTS 8 Glasgow
15.05.93	Fernando Martinez W RSC 7 Glasgow
	(Vacant WBO M. Flyweight Title)
25.10.93	Lindi Memani W PTS 12 Glasgow
	(WBO M. Flyweight Title Defence)
02.02.94	Josue Camacho L PTS 12 Glasgow
	(WBO L. Flyweight Title Challenge)
23.11.94	Paul Oulden W PTS 12 Irvine
	(Vacant WBO L. Flyweight Title)
05.04.95	Ric Magramo W PTS 12 Irvine
	(WBO L. Flyweight Title Defence)
29.07.95	Jose Luis Velarde W PTS 10 Whitley Bay
18.11.95	Jacob Matlala L TD 5 Glasgow
	(WBO L. Flyweight Title Defence)
13.04.96	Jacob Matlala L RSC 10 Liverpool
	(WBO L. Flyweight Title Challenge)
03.06.96	Louis Veitch W CO 1 Glasgow

11.10.96 Lyndon Kershaw W PTS 6 Mayfair
28.02.97 Anthony Hanna W PTS 8 Kilmarnock
02.05.97 Jesper Jensen L RSC 8 Randers, Denmark
(European Flyweight Title Challenge)
26.01.98 Alfonso Zvenyika L RSC 11 Glasgow
(Vacant Commonwealth Flyweight Title)
30.09.00 Delroy Spencer W PTS 8 Chigwell
11.11.00 Stevie Quinn L PTS 4 Belfast
Career: 20 contests, won 14, lost 6.

Richie Wenton

Liverpool. *Born* Liverpool, 28 October, 1967
Featherweight. Former Undefeated British & WBO Inter-Continental S. Bantamweight Champion. Ht. 5'8"
Manager F. Warren

14.12.88 Miguel Matthews W CO 2 Kirkby
25.01.89 Sean Casey W PTS 4 Belfast
10.04.89 Stuart Carmichael W RSC 2 Mayfair
13.12.89 Joe Mullen W RSC 5 Kirkby
21.02.90 Ariel Cordova W PTS 6 Belfast
17.03.90 Mark Johnson W PTS 4 Belfast
28.03.90 Jose Luis Vasquez W PTS 6 Manchester
23.05.90 Graham O'Malley W PTS 6 Belfast
09.07.90 Eugene Pratt W CO 1 Miami Beach, USA
15.09.90 Graham O'Malley W PTS 6 Belfast
30.10.90 Alejandro Armenta W RSC 2 Belfast
12.02.91 Sean Casey W PTS 4 Belfast
31.03.92 Graham O'Malley W PTS 6 Stockport
25.07.92 Ramos Agare W RSC 3 Manchester
26.09.92 Floyd Churchill L RSC 2 Earls Court
28.04.93 Kelton McKenzie W PTS 8 Dublin
13.11.93 Des Gargano W PTS 8 Cullompton
26.04.94 Bradley Stone W RSC 10 Bethnal Green
(Vacant British S. Bantamweight Title)
01.10.94 Neil Swain L RTD 5 Cardiff
25.03.95 Paul Lloyd W RSC 5 Chester
(British S. Bantamweight Title Defence)
30.06.95 Mike Parris W PTS 12 Liverpool
(Vacant WBO Inter-Continental S. Bantamweight Title)
09.10.95 Vincenzo Belcastro L PTS 12 San Benedetto, Italy
(European S. Bantamweight Title Challenge)
06.02.96 Wilson Docherty W PTS 12 Basildon
(British S. Bantamweight Title Defence)
19.09.96 Efren Gonzalez W PTS 8 Manchester
12.07.97 Mauricio Bernal W RSC 2 Dusseldorf, Germany
31.10.98 Marco Antonio Barrera L RTD 3 Atlantic City, USA
(Vacant WBO S. Bantamweight Title)
29.05.99 Pete Buckley W PTS 6 Halifax
06.11.99 Graham McGrath W RTD 3 Widnes
16.05.00 Gary Thornhill W PTS 8 Warrington
(Vacant British Featherweight Title)
24.03.01 Scott Harrison L RSC 4 Sheffield
(Commonwealth Featherweight Title Challenge. Vacant British Featherweight Title)
Career: 30 contests, won 24, lost 6.

Richie Wenton　　　　　Les Clark

Paul Wesley

Birmingham. *Born* Birmingham, 2 May, 1962
S. Middleweight. Ht. 5'9"
Manager Self

20.02.87 B. K. Bennett L PTS 6 Maidenhead
18.03.87 Darryl Ritchie DREW 4 Stoke
08.04.87 Dean Murray W PTS 6 Evesham
29.04.87 John Wright W PTS 4 Loughborough
12.06.87 Leon Thomas W RSC 2 Leamington
16.11.87 Steve McCarthy L CO 8 Southampton
25.01.88 Paul Murray W PTS 8 Birmingham
29.02.88 Paul Murray DREW 8 Birmingham
15.03.88 Johnny Williamson W CO 2 Bournemouth
09.04.88 Joe McKenzie W RSC 6 Bristol
10.05.88 Tony Meszaros W PTS 8 Edgbaston
21.03.89 Carlton Warren L CO 2 Wandsworth
10.05.89 Rod Douglas L CO 1 Kensington
24.10.89 Nigel Rafferty L PTS 6 Wolverhampton
22.11.89 Nigel Rafferty L PTS 8 Stafford
28.11.89 Nigel Rafferty L PTS 6 Wolverhampton
05.12.89 Ian Strudwick L PTS 6 Catford
24.01.90 Rocky Feliciello W PTS 6 Solihull
19.02.90 Nigel Rafferty L PTS 8 Birmingham
22.03.90 John Ashton L PTS 10 Wolverhampton
(Midlands Area Middleweight Title Challenge)
17.04.90 Winston May DREW 8 Millwall
09.05.90 Alan Richards W PTS 8 Solihull
04.06.90 Julian Eavis W PTS 8 Birmingham
18.09.90 Shaun Cummins L RSC 1 Wolverhampton
17.10.90 Julian Eavis W PTS 6 Stoke
23.01.91 Wally Swift Jnr L PTS 10 Solihull
(Midlands Area L. Middleweight Title Challenge)
20.03.91 Horace Fleary L RSC 5 Solihull
16.05.91 Delroy Waul L RSC 7 Liverpool
04.07.91 Neville Brown W RSC 1 Alfreton
31.07.91 Francesco dell'Aquila L PTS 8 Casella, Italy

03.10.91 Neville Brown L PTS 8 Burton
29.10.91 Tony Collins DREW 8 Kensington
03.03.92 Antonio Fernandez L PTS 10 Cradley Heath
(Vacant Midlands Area Middleweight Title)
10.04.92 Jean-Charles Meuret L PTS 8 Geneva, Switzerland
03.06.92 Sumbu Kalambay L PTS 10 Salice Terme, Italy
29.10.92 Ian Strudwick W RSC 1 Bayswater
14.11.92 Paul Busby L PTS 8 Cardiff
24.11.92 Paul Jones W RSC 2 Doncaster
16.03.93 Chris Pyatt L PTS 10 Mayfair
04.06.93 Jacques le Blanc L PTS 10 Moncton, Canada
28.07.93 Antonio Fernandez L RSC 3 Brixton
(Midlands Area Middleweight Title Challenge)
09.10.93 Warren Stowe W PTS 10 Manchester
(Elim. British L. Middleweight Title)
09.02.94 Steve Collins L PTS 8 Brentwood
10.02.95 Robert McCracken L PTS 12 Birmingham
(British L. Middleweight Title Challenge)
24.02.95 Scott Doyle W PTS 8 Weston super Mare
18.03.95 Crisanto Espana L PTS 6 Millstreet
21.04.95 Gilbert Jackson L RSC 6 Dudley
(Elim. British L. Middleweight Title)
31.01.96 Howard Eastman L RSC 1 Birmingham
21.03.96 Gary Logan L PTS 6 Southwark
13.04.96 Harry Simon L RTD 4 Wythenshawe
26.09.96 Nigel Rafferty DREW 6 Walsall
19.10.96 Glenn Catley L RSC 7 Bristol
25.03.97 Chris Johnson L CO 2 Lewisham
07.02.98 Paul Carr L PTS 6 Cheshunt
07.03.98 Omar Sheika L RTD 4 Reading
23.09.98 Lester Jacobs L CO 4 Bloomsbury
13.02.99 Geoff McCreesh L PTS 8 Newcastle
03.04.99 Toks Owoh L CO 5 Kensington
23.03.00 Lester Jacobs L PTS 6 Bloomsbury
13.04.00 Sam Soliman L PTS 6 Holborn
19.08.00 Adrian Dodson L PTS 4 Brentwood
18.11.00 Paul Bowen L PTS 4 Dagenham
11.12.00 Darren Rhodes L PTS 4 Widnes
08.03.01 Lee Blundell L RSC 3 Blackpool
Career: 64 contests, won 16, drew 5, lost 43.

Robert Weston

Cardiff. *Born* Cardiff, 6 May, 1977
L. Middleweight. Ht. 5'10"
Manager T. Russell

02.02.01 James Lee W PTS 6 Portsmouth
Career: 1 contest, won 1.

Wayne Wheeler

Plymouth. *Born* Plymouth, 24 February, 1970
Lightweight. Ht. 5'8"
Manager N. Christian

24.03.01 J.J.Moore L RSC 4 Newark
12.05.01 Byron Pryce L RSC 2 Plymouth
Career: 2 contests, lost 2.

David White

Cardiff. *Born* Cardiff, 18 April, 1975
Welterweight. Ht. 5'9"
Manager D. Gardiner

23.09.00 Matthew Hatton L PTS 4 Bethnal
Green
25.11.00 Matthew Hatton L PTS 4 Manchester
28.01.01 Jimmy Gould L PTS 6 Wolverhampton
05.02.01 Lance Crosby DREW 4 Hull
24.02.01 Francis Barrett L PTS 4 Bethnal Green
28.04.01 Ahmet Kaddour L PTS 4 Cardiff
12.05.01 Leo O'Reilly L PTS 4 Plymouth
24.05.01 Ronnie Nailen L PTS 6 Glasgow
Career: 8 contests, drew 1, lost 7.

David White Les Clark

Jason White

Cardiff. *Born* Cardiff, 18 November, 1978
S. Featherweight. Ht. 5'6"
Manager D. Gardiner

27.11.00 Stephen Chinnock L PTS 4
Birmingham
16.12.00 Scott Miller L PTS 4 Sheffield
08.03.01 Nigel Senior W PTS 8 Stoke
12.05.01 Lee Meager L PTS 4 Plymouth
Career: 4 contests, won 1, lost 3.

Jason White Les Clark

Mike White

Salford. *Born* North Shields, 14 December,
1973
S,. Middleweight. Ht. 5'11"
Manager T. Conroy

17.07.98 Mike Duffield L PTS 6 Mere
18.09.98 Shamus Casey W PTS 6 Manchester
29.10.98 Clint Johnson W PTS 6 Newcastle
20.12.98 Rob Galloway W PTS 6 Salford
06.02.99 Juan Nelongo L PTS 6 Tenerife, Spain
25.02.99 Shamus Casey W RSC 1 Sunderland
29.05.99 Chris Crook W PTS 6 South Shields
07.10.99 Jimmy Steel W PTS 6 Mere
30.10.99 Jimmy Steel W PTS 4 Peterlee
27.11.99 Robert Zlotkowski L PTS 6 Liverpool
26.02.00 Reece McAllister W PTS 4 Carlisle
05.10.00 Chris Crook W RSC 4 Sunderland
11.02.01 Ian Cooper L RSC 9 Hartlepool
(*Vacant Northern Area
S. Middleweight Title*)
26.04.01 Paul Bonson W PTS 6 Gateshead
Career: 14 contests, won 10, lost 4.

Lee Whitehead

Manchester. *Born* Barton, 16 July, 1965
Cruiserweight. Ht. 5'10¾"
Manager S. Foster/S. Wood

09.10.95 Roy Chipperfield W RSC 2 Manchester
04.12.95 Phil Ball W PTS 6 Manchester
13.01.96 Elwen Brooks W PTS 6 Manchester
26.02.96 Kevin Burton W PTS 6 Manchester
13.04.96 Mark Snipe L PTS 4 Wythenshawe
02.06.96 Andy Fletcher W RSC 2 Shaw
22.08.96 Peter Mason W PTS 6 Salford
19.09.96 Brian Galloway W PTS 4 Manchester
22.12.96 Martin Jolley DREW 6 Salford
18.01.97 Mark Dawson W PTS 6 Manchester
26.06.97 Martin Jolley W PTS 6 Salford
19.09.97 Carl Nicholson L PTS 6 Salford
22.11.97 Kevin Burton DREW 4 Manchester
21.12.97 Mark Dawson L RSC 4 Salford
23.02.98 Peter Federenko L PTS 6 Salford
27.05.01 Darren Ashton L RSC 2 Manchester
Career: 16 contests, won 9, drew 2, lost 5.

Leigh Wicks

Brighton. *Born* Worthing, 29 July, 1965
S. Middleweight. Ht. 5'6¼"
Manager Self

29.04.87 Fidel Castro W PTS 6 Hastings
26.09.87 Jason Rowe W PTS 6 Hastings
18.11.87 Lou Ayres W PTS 6 Holborn
26.01.88 Theo Marius L PTS 8 Hove
15.02.88 Shamus Casey W PTS 6 Copthorne
26.04.88 Franki Moro DREW 8 Hove
04.05.88 Tony Britton W PTS 8 Wembley
18.05.88 Mark Howell W RSC 8 Portsmouth
25.05.88 Newton Barnett DREW 8 Hastings
22.11.88 Roy Callaghan L PTS 8 Basildon
16.03.89 Tony Britland W PTS 8 Southwark
12.10.89 Tony Gibbs W CO 2 Southwark
08.02.90 Ernie Noble W PTS 8 Southwark
26.04.90 Julian Eavis DREW 8 Mayfair
06.11.90 Gordon Blair W PTS 8 Mayfair
10.01.91 Barry Messam W PTS 6 Wandsworth
14.02.91 Kevin Thompson W PTS 8
Southampton
21.10.91 Tony Britland W RSC 3 Mayfair
20.02.92 Mick Duncan L PTS 8 Glasgow

30.04.92 Darren Morris DREW 6 Mayfair
19.10.92 Bozon Haule W PTS 8 Mayfair
20.01.93 Robert McCracken L PTS 8
Wolverhampton
17.02.93 Kevin Lueshing L PTS 6 Bethnal
Green
22.04.93 Warren Stowe L PTS 6 Bury
27.10.95 Danny Quacoe W RSC 4 Brighton
18.11.95 Gary Jacobs L RTD 3 Glasgow
26.01.96 Wayne Appleton L PTS 6 Brighton
05.03.96 Kevin Thompson L PTS 6 Bethnal
Green
24.03.97 Ross Hale L PTS 6 Bristol
08.04.97 Ahmet Dottuev L RSC 1 Bethnal
Green
29.05.97 Nicky Thurbin L PTS 8 Mayfair
11.07.97 Darren Covill L RSC 2 Brighton
27.11.97 Lester Jacobs L PTS 6 Bloomsbury
06.12.97 Rhoshi Wells L PTS 4 Wembley
21.02.98 Neil Sinclair L RSC 1 Belfast
24.03.98 Ojay Abrahams L PTS 6 Bethnal Green
05.06.98 Darren Bruce L PTS 6 Southend
25.11.98 Darren Covill W PTS 4 Streatham
22.02.99 Neil Linford L PTS 4 Peterborough
26.06.99 Mehrdud Takaloo L CO 3 Millwall
09.10.99 Darren Rhodes L PTS 4 Manchester
27.11.99 Geoff McCreesh L PTS 6 Lubeck,
Germany
11.12.99 Darren Rhodes L PTS 4 Liverpool
21.02.00 Sergei Dzinziruk L RSC 2 Southwark
25.03.00 Darren Rhodes L PTS 4 Liverpool
08.04.00 Spencer Fearon L PTS 4 Bethnal Green
02.06.00 Allan Foster L PTS 4 Ashford
24.06.00 Scott Dixon L PTS 4 Glasgow
01.07.00 Karim Hussine L PTS 6 Southwark
30.09.00 Bobby Banghar L PTS 4 Peterborough
07.10.00 Jamie Moore L PTS 4 Doncaster
11.11.00 Brian Knudsen L RSC 5 Belfast
17.03.01 Wayne Pinder L PTS 4 Manchester
29.03.01 Lester Jacobs L PTS 6 Hammersmith
05.05.01 Ty Browne L PTS 6 Brighton
08.06.01 Jason Collins L PTS 4 Hull
Career: 56 contests, won 16, drew 4, lost 36.

Leigh Wicks Les Clark

Jan Wild (Cooper)

Stockton. *Born* Stockton, 6 June, 1964
Bantamweight. Ht. 5'4½"
Manager T. Miller

01.12.99	Audrey Guthrie W PTS 4 Yarm
15.05.00	Michelle Sutcliffe L PTS 6 Cleethorpes
01.07.00	Cathy Brown L PTS 6 Southwark
	(Vacant WBF Pan-European Flyweight Title)

Career: 3 contests, won 1, lost 2.

Noel Wilders

Castleford. *Born* Castleford, 4 January, 1975
IBO Bantamweight Champion. Former Undefeated British & Central Area Bantamweight Champion. Ht. 5'5"
Manager T. Callighan

16.03.96	Neil Parry W RTD 4 Sheffield
04.06.96	Graham McGrath W PTS 6 York
04.10.96	Tiger Singh W PTS 6 Wakefield
23.10.96	Jason Thomas W PTS 6 Halifax
12.03.97	John Matthews W PTS 6 Stoke
20.04.97	Shaun Anderson W PTS 6 Leeds
13.11.97	Anthony Hanna W PTS 6 Bradford
06.02.98	Marcus Duncan W RSC 6 Wakefield
	(Vacant Central Area Bantamweight Title)
21.05.98	Matthew Harris W PTS 6 Bradford
18.07.98	Sean Grant W RSC 4 Sheffield
23.10.98	Fondil Madani W DIS 7 Wakefield
28.11.98	Ross Cassidy W PTS 8 Sheffield
06.02.99	Jason Thomas W PTS 10 Halifax
	(Elim. British Bantamweight Title)
24.04.99	Anthony Hanna W PTS 6 Peterborough
22.06.99	Ady Lewis W RSC 6 Ipswich
	(Final Elim. British Bantamweight Title)
30.10.99	Francis Ampofo W PTS 12 Peterlee
	(Vacant British Bantamweight Title)
18.01.00	Steve Williams W RTD 11 Mansfield
	(British Bantamweight Title Defence)
20.03.00	Kamel Guerfi W PTS 12 Mansfield
	(Vacant IBO Bantamweight Title)
15.07.00	Paul Lloyd W PTS 12 Millwall
	(IBO Bantamweight Title Defence)
28.04.01	Stevie Quinn W RTD 6 Cardiff

Career: 20 contests, won 20.

Chris Williams

Merthyr. *Born* Merthyr, 25 December, 1977
Welsh S. Featherweight Champion.
Ht. 5'6½"
Manager Self

26.02.97	John Matthews L RSC 1 Cardiff
03.05.97	Michael Gomez W PTS 4 Manchester
11.09.97	Tony Mulholland L PTS 4 Widnes
27.10.97	Ronnie McPhee L PTS 4 Musselburgh
08.12.97	Graham McGrath W PTS 6 Birmingham
13.02.98	David Jeffrey W RSC 3 Weston super Mare
03.04.98	Greg Upton W RSC 5 Ebbw Vale
04.06.98	Brian Robb W RSC 4 Dudley
23.07.98	Isaac Sebaduka L RSC 5 Barking
14.10.98	Craig Spacie L PTS 6 Stoke
19.12.98	Tony Mulholland DREW 4 Liverpool
05.06.99	Barry Jones L PTS 6 Cardiff
19.06.99	David Burke L RTD 1 Dublin
24.09.99	Miguel Matthews W PTS 10 Merthyr
	(Vacant Welsh S. Featherweight Title)
11.12.99	Marc Smith W PTS 4 Merthyr
22.01.00	Roy Rutherford L PTS 8 Birmingham
20.03.00	Craig Spacie W PTS 6 Mansfield
03.12.00	Choi Tseveenpurev L PTS 4 Shaw

Career: 18 contests, won 8, drew 1, lost 9.

Danny Williams

Brixton. *Born* London, 13 July, 1973
British, Commonwealth & WBO Inter-Continental Heavyweight Champion. Ht. 6'3"
Manager F. Warren

21.10.95	Vance Idiens W CO 2 Bethnal Green
09.12.95	Joey Paladino W RSC 1 Bethnal Green
13.02.96	Slick Miller W RSC 1 Bethnal Green
09.03.96	James Wilder W PTS 4 Millstreet
13.07.96	John Pierre W PTS 4 Bethnal Green
31.08.96	Andy Lambert W RSC 2 Dublin
09.11.96	Michael Murray W CO 1 Manchester
08.02.97	Shane Woollas W RSC 2 Millwall
03.05.97	Albert Call W RSC 4 Manchester
19.07.97	R. F. McKenzie W RSC 2 Wembley
15.11.97	Bruce Douglas W RSC 2 Bristol
19.12.97	Derek Amos W RSC 4 New York City, USA
21.02.98	Shane Woollas W RSC 2 Belfast
16.05.98	Antonio Diaz W CO 3 Bethnal Green
10.10.98	Antoine Palatis W PTS 12 Bethnal Green
	(Vacant WBO Inter-Continental Heavyweight Title)
03.04.99	Julius Francis L PTS 12 Kensington
	(British & Commonwealth Heavyweight Title Challenges)
02.10.99	Ferenc Deak W RTD 1 Namur, Belgium
18.12.99	Harry Senior W PTS 12 Southwark
	(Vacant Commonwealth Heavyweight Title)
19.02.00	Anton Nel W CO 5 Dagenham
06.05.00	Michael Murray W RSC 6 Frankfurt, Germany
24.06.00	Craig Bowen-Price W CO 1 Glasgow
23.09.00	Quinn Navarre W RSC 6 Bethnal Green
21.10.00	Mark Potter W RSC 6 Wembley
	(Commonwealth & WBO Inter-Continental Heavyweight Title Defences. Vacant British Heavyweight Title)
09.06.01	Kali Meehan W RSC 1 Bethnal Green
	(Commonwealth Heavyweight Title Defence)

Career: 24 contests, won 23, lost 1.

Noel Wilders   Les Clark   *Danny Williams*   Les Clark

(Wayne) Darren Williams

Swansea. *Born* Swansea, 17 July, 1975
L. Middleweight. Ht. 5'8"
Manager Self

21.06.97 John Smith W PTS 4 Cardiff
26.09.97 Harry Butler W PTS 6 Port Talbot
02.12.97 Steve Tuckett L PTS 6 Swansea
24.01.98 Paul Salmon W PTS 4 Cardiff
23.04.98 Danny Quacoe W PTS 8 Neath
05.09.98 Anthony Farnell L RTD 4 Telford
12.12.00 Gareth Jones DREW 6 Clydach
20.04.01 Richard Inquieti W PTS 6 Dublin
Career: 8 contests, won 5, drew 1, lost 2.

(Darren) Dazzo Williams

Hereford. *Born* Lambeth, 19 March, 1974
Featherweight. Ht. 5'8"
Manager D. Gardiner

24.02.01 Mickey Coveney W CO 1 Bethnal
Green
19.05.01 Mark Payne W PTS 8 Wembley
Career: 2 contests, won 2.

Gary Williams

Nottingham. *Born* Nottingham, 25
September, 1965
Heavyweight, Ht. 5'11½"
Manager Self

27.04.92 Damien Caesar L RSC 4 Mayfair
07.09.92 J. A. Bugner L PTS 4 Bethnal Green
06.10.92 Scott Welch L PTS 4 Antwerp,
Belgium
01.12.92 Kenny Sandison W PTS 6 Liverpool
27.01.93 Kenny Sandison DREW 6 Stoke
13.02.93 Kevin McBride L PTS 4 Manchester
01.03.93 Ashley Naylor DREW 6 Bradford
29.03.93 Kevin Cullinane W RSC 2 Liverpool
26.04.93 Ashley Naylor W PTS 6 Bradford
10.08.93 Peter Smith L RSC 4 Marula, South
Africa
08.12.93 Graham Arnold L PTS 6 Hull
02.02.94 Vincenzo Cantatore L CO 2 Ferrara,
Italy
17.03.94 Neil Kirkwood L RSC 1 Lincoln
10.09.94 Clayton Brown L PTS 4 Birmingham
04.10.94 Mike Holden L RSC 4 Mayfair
13.12.94 Damien Caesar L RSC 2 Ilford
18.03.95 Darren Corbett DREW 4 Millstreet
06.05.95 Clayton Brown L PTS 4 Shepton
Mallet
10.06.95 Joey Paladino L PTS 6 Manchester
15.09.95 Adrian Kneeshaw W RSC 6 Mansfield
11.10.95 Shane Woollas L PTS 6 Solihull
03.11.95 Tony Henry W PTS 6 Dudley
24.11.95 Pele Reid L RSC 1 Manchester
12.01.96 John Pettersson DREW 4 Copenhagen,
Denmark
31.01.96 Robert Norton L RSC 2 Birmingham
21.03.96 Mika Kihlstrom L PTS 4 Southwark
02.04.96 Doug Liggion L PTS 4 Southwark
22.04.96 Shane Woollas L PTS 10 Cleethorpes
(*Vacant Midlands Area Heavyweight
Title*)
27.05.96 Jukka Jarvinen L PTS 6 Helsinki,
Finland
09.07.96 Sugar Raj Kumar Sangwan L PTS 4
Bethnal Green
08.10.96 Owen Bartley L PTS 4 Battersea
26.11.96 Israel Ajose L CO 2 Bethnal Green
18.01.97 Craig Bowen-Price L CO 1 Manchester

28.04.97 Jarrod Corrigan W RSC 4 Hull
02.09.97 Michael Sprott L PTS 6 Southwark
06.10.97 Johnny Davison W PTS 8 Piccadilly
15.12.97 Shane Woollas L RSC 8 Cleethorpes
(*Midlands Area Heavyweight Title
Challenge*)
15.12.98 Scott Lansdowne L PTS 6 Sheffield
16.01.99 Michael Sprott L PTS 6 Bethnal Green
04.02.99 Rimas Priczmantas L PTS 4 Lewisham
22.02.99 Derek McCafferty L CO 1
Peterborough
27.04.99 Tommy Bannister L PTS 4 Bethnal
Green
28.05.99 Albert Sosnowski L RSC 4 Liverpool
26.06.99 Patrick Halberg L PTS 4 Millwall
17.07.99 Roman Bugaj L RSC 4 Gdansk, Poland
07.10.99 Paul Fiske W PTS 6 Sunderland
27.11.99 Tommy Bannister W PTS 4 Liverpool
09.12.99 Paul Fiske W PTS 6 Sunderland
29.01.00 Petr Horacek L PTS 4 Manchester
18.02.00 Mal Rice W PTS 6 Pentre Halkyn
05.05.00 Mal Rice W PTS 4 Pentre Halkyn
20.05.00 Scott Lansdowne L RSC 1 Leicester
(*Vacant WBF European
S. Cruiserweight Title*)
21.10.00 John McDermott L PTS 4 Wembley
13.11.00 Danny Percival L PTS 4 Bethnal Green
04.06.01 Billy Bessey L PTS 4 Hartlepool
Career: 55 contests, won 12, drew 4, lost 39.

Glenn Williams

Manchester. *Born* Manchester, 31 July,
1969
Former Undefeated Central Area L.
Heavyweight Champion. Ht. 6'3"
Manager S. Foster

27.11.97 Mark Hilding W RSC 4 Bloomsbury
02.02.98 Michael Pinnock W CO 5 Manchester
27.04.98 Peter Mason W RSC 3 Manchester
09.06.98 Terry Morrill W PTS 4 Hull
18.09.98 Mike Gormley L RSC 2 Manchester
(*Vacant Central Area S. Middleweight
Title*)
30.11.98 P. R. Mason W CO 2 Manchester
20.12.98 Paul Bonson W PTS 6 Salford
13.03.99 Darren Ashton W PTS 4 Manchester
03.04.99 Michael Bowen L RSC 8 Kensington
09.10.99 Darren Ashton W PTS 6 Manchester
04.12.99 Paul Bonson W PTS 4 Manchester
11.06.00 Slick Miller W PTS 4 Salford
12.11.00 Paul Bonson W PTS 10 Manchester
(*Central Area L. Heavyweight Title
Challenge*)
Career: 13 contests, won 10, lost 3.

(Leon) Jason Williams

Swansea. *Born* Swansea, 11 July, 1974
Welterweight. Ht. 5'11"
Manager C. Sanigar

19.04.97 Jon Harrison L PTS 6 Plymouth
21.06.97 Dewi Roberts W RSC 1 Cardiff
26.09.97 Darren Covill W PTS 6 Port Talbot
15.11.97 Peter Federenko W PTS 4 Bristol
24.01.98 Danny Quacoe W PTS 4 Cardiff
23.02.98 Adrian Chase W PTS 6 Windsor
30.03.98 Rob Pitters W RSC 3 Tenerife
30.05.98 Prince Kasi Kaihau W CO 2 Bristol
14.07.98 Jon Harrison W RTD 2 Reading
05.12.98 Mark Ramsey W PTS 6 Bristol
23.04.99 Harry Butler W RSC 7 Clydach
05.06.99 Paul Miles W RSC 2 Cardiff

02.07.99 Delroy Mellis W PTS 6 Bristol
24.09.99 Michael Smyth L RSC 3 Merthyr
(*Vacant Welsh Welterweight Title*)
07.04.00 David Baptiste W PTS 6 Bristol
08.09.00 Karim Bouali L RSC 5 Bristol
03.11.00 Mark Ramsey L CO 6 Ebbw Vale
Career: 17 contests, won 13, lost 4.

Mark Williams

Birmingham. *Born* Birmingham, 16
September, 1969
Cruiserweight. Ht. 6'1"
Manager Self

18.09.98 Mark Levy L PTS 6 Manchester
26.09.98 Faisal Mohammed L RSC 2 Norwich
10.12.98 Anthony Wright W PTS 6 Barking
19.01.99 Cliff Elden W PTS 6 Ipswich
24.03.99 Kenny Gayle DREW 6 Bayswater
29.04.99 Frode Stenasham L RSC 4 Bethnal
Green
23.06.99 Jason Brewster DREW 6 West
Bromwich
11.12.99 Enzo Maccarinelli L RSC 1 Merthyr
20.03.00 Michael Thompson L PTS 4 Mansfield
04.07.00 Kenny Gayle L PTS 4 Tooting
29.09.00 Paul Maskell W RSC 2 Bethnal Green
20.01.01 Faisal Mohammed L RSC 3 Bethnal
Green
24.03.01 Mark Krence L PTS 4 Sheffield
21.06.01 Ali Forbes L PTS 4 Earls Court
Career: 14 contests, won 3, drew 2, lost 9.

Richard Williams   Les Clark

Richard Williams

Stockwell. *Born* London, 9 May, 1971
Commonwealth L. Middleweight
Champion. Ht. 5'9½"
Manager B. Hearn

08.03.97 Marty Duke W RSC 3 Brentwood

163

30.06.97 Danny Quacoe W PTS 4 Bethnal Green
02.09.97 Michael Alexander L PTS 4 Southwark
16.10.99 Pedro Carragher W RSC 2 Bethnal
Green
06.11.99 Lee Bird W RSC 4 Bethnal Green
20.12.99 Harry Butler W RSC 1 Bethnal Green
17.04.00 Kevin Thompson W CO 1 Birmingham
16.06.00 Piotr Bartnicki W RSC 3 Bloomsbury
08.09.00 Dean Ashton W RSC 1 Hammersmith
04.11.00 Howard Clarke W CO 4 Bethnal Green
02.12.00 Aziz Daari W RSC 2 Bethnal Green
23.01.01 Tony Badea W RSC 3 Crawley
(Commonwealth L. Middleweight Title
Challenge)
04.06.01 Hussain Osman W PTS 10 Hartlepool
Career: 13 contests, won 12, lost 1.

Lee Williamson

Worcester. *Born* Worcester, 3 February,
1974
Welterweight. Ht. 5'9"
Manager Self

26.10.98 Trevor Tacy L PTS 6 Manchester
26.11.98 David Smales W PTS 6 Bradford
16.01.99 Graham Earl L RSC 4 Bethnal Green
23.03.99 Gary Reid L PTS 6 Wolverhampton
22.04.99 Brian Gifford W PTS 6 Dudley
15.05.99 James Hare L RSC 2 Sheffield
11.10.99 Carl Allen W PTS 6 Birmingham
28.10.99 Mark Hargreaves L PTS 6 Burnley
30.11.99 Marc Smith W PTS 6 Wolverhampton
11.12.99 Brian Carr DREW 6 Liverpool
24.01.00 Craig Docherty L PTS 6 Glasgow
08.02.00 Carl Allen L PTS 8 Wolverhampton
19.02.00 Kevin Lear L PTS 4 Dagenham
04.03.00 Liam Maltby L PTS 6 Peterborough
28.03.00 Carl Allen L PTS 8 Wolverhampton
06.06.00 Dave Travers W PTS 6 Brierley Hill
24.06.00 Kevin McIntyre L PTS 4 Glasgow
08.07.00 Tony Mulholland L PTS 8 Widnes
13.08.00 Esham Pickering L PTS 6 Nottingham
29.09.00 Darren Melville L RSC 4 Bethnal
Green
21.10.00 Graham Earl L RSC 3 Wembley
24.11.00 Pete Buckley W PTS 6 Hull
09.12.00 Terry Butwell L PTS 4 Southwark
27.01.01 Danny Hunt W RSC 2 Bethnal Green
10.02.01 Geir Inge Jorgensen L RSC 3 Widnes
20.03.01 James Rooney L PTS 4 Glasgow
26.03.01 Liam Maltby L PTS 6 Peterborough
03.04.01 Danny Hunt L PTS 4 Bethnal Green
06.05.01 James Rooney L PTS 6 Hartlepool
21.06.01 Gavin Wake L PTS 6 Sheffield
Career: 30 contests, won 7, drew 1, lost 22.

Gareth Wiltshaw

Stoke. *Born* Stoke, 22 August, 1980
Featherweight. Ht. 5'7"
Manager W. Swift

17.04.00 John Meade W PTS 6 Bradford
09.06.00 Joel Viney L PTS 6 Blackpool
08.07.00 Kevin England DREW 6 Rotherham
20.11.00 Al Garrett L PTS 6 Glasgow
30.11.00 Mickey Coveney L PTS 4
Peterborough
18.02.01 Richmond Asante L PTS 4 Southwark
08.04.01 Jason Edwards L PTS 6 Wrexham
20.05.01 Stephen Chinnock L PTS 6
Wolverhampton
03.06.01 Mickey Coveney L PTS 4 Southwark
Career: 9 contests, won 1, drew 1, lost 7.

Gareth Wiltshaw   Les Clark

Juliette Winter

Derby. *Born* Whitehaven, 21 February,
1973
Bantamweight. Ht. 5'6"
Manager C. Mitchell

16.06.01 Sara Hall L RTD 4 Derby
Career: 1 contest, lost 1.

Mark Winters

Belfast. *Born* Antrim, 29 December, 1971
Former British L. Welterweight Champion.
Ht. 5'8"
Manager Self

04.03.95 Trevor Smith W PTS 6 Livingston
10.06.95 Mark McGowan W PTS 6 Manchester
09.09.95 Anthony Campbell W PTS 4 Cork
25.11.95 John O. Johnson W RSC 2 Dublin
13.01.96 Rick North W PTS 4 Manchester
09.03.96 Danny Quacoe W RSC 2 Millstreet
08.06.96 Brian Coleman W PTS 4 Newcastle
31.08.96 John Smith W PTS 4 Dublin
30.11.96 Paul Dyer W PTS 6 Tylorstown
14.03.97 Paul Denton W PTS 8 Reading
03.05.97 Jimmy Phelan W PTS 4 Manchester
11.10.97 Carl Wright W PTS 12 Sheffield
(Vacant British L. Welterweight Title)
21.02.98 Bernard Paul W PTS 12 Belfast
(British L. Welterweight Title Defence)
16.05.98 Jason Rowland L PTS 12 Bethnal
Green
(British L. Welterweight Title Defence)
05.09.98 Junior Witter L PTS 8 Telford
23.10.99 James Hare DREW 6 Telford
11.12.99 Richard Hatton L RSC 4 Liverpool
(WBO Inter-Continental
L. Welterweight Title Challenge)
04.02.01 David Kirk W PTS 6 Queensferry
20.04.01 David Kirk W PTS 6 Dublin
Career: 19 contests, won 15, drew 1, lost 3.

Junior Witter

Bradford. *Born* Bradford, 10 March, 1974
Former Undefeated WBF L. Welterweight
Champion. Ht. 5'7"
Manager B. Ingle

18.01.97 Cam Raeside DREW 6 Swadlincote
04.03.97 John Green W PTS 6 Yarm
20.03.97 Lee Molyneux W RSC 6 Salford
25.04.97 Trevor Meikle W PTS 6 Mere
15.05.97 Andreas Panayi W RSC 5 Reading
02.08.97 Brian Coleman W PTS 4 Barnsley
04.10.97 Michael Alexander W PTS 4
Hannover, Germany
07.02.98 Mark Ramsey DREW 6 Cheshunt
05.03.98 Brian Coleman W PTS 6 Leeds
18.04.98 Jan Bergman W PTS 6 Manchester
05.09.98 Mark Winters W PTS 8 Telford
28.11.98 Karl Taylor W PTS 4 Sheffield
13.02.99 Malcolm Melvin W RSC 2 Newcastle
(Vacant WBF L. Welterweight Title)
17.07.99 Isaac Cruz W PTS 8 Doncaster
06.11.99 Harry Butler W PTS 6 Widnes
21.03.00 Mrhai Iourgh W RSC 1 Telde, Gran
Canaria
08.04.00 Arv Mittoo W PTS 4 Bethnal Green
24.06.00 Zab Judah L PTS 12 Glasgow
(IBF L. Welterweight Title Challenge)
20.10.00 Steve Conway W RTD 4 Belfast
25.11.00 Chris Henry W RSC 3 Manchester
10.03.01 David Kirk W RSC 2 Bethnal Green
22.05.01 Fabrice Faradji W RSC 1 Telde, Gran
Canaria
Career: 22 contests, won 19, drew 2, lost 1.

Ray Wood (Shearwood)

Liverpool. *Born* Liverpool, 3 May, 1971
L. Welterweight. Ht. 5'6½"
Manager S. Foster/S. Wood

13.11.98 Kevin McIntyre L RSC 4 Glasgow
05.03.99 Brian Gifford W CO 2 Liverpool
15.05.99 Peter Dunn DREW 4 Blackpool
18.02.00 Marcus Portman L PTS 6 West
Bromwich
09.03.00 Gary Greenwood L PTS 4 Liverpool
20.10.00 Alan Kershaw L PTS 6 Manchester
12.11.00 Dave Gibson W PTS 6 Manchester
18.03.01 Tony Montana DREW 6 Shaw
Career: 8 contests, won 2, drew 2, lost 4.

Richie Woodhall

Telford. *Born* Birmingham, 17 April, 1968
Former WBC S. Middleweight Champion.
Former Undefeated European &
Commonwealth Middleweight Champion.
Ht. 6'2"
Manager F. Warren

18.10.90 Kevin Hayde W RSC 3 Birmingham
30.11.90 Robbie Harron W RSC 2 Birmingham
16.01.91 Chris Haydon W RSC 3 Kensington
21.02.91 Shamus Casey W RSC 3 Walsall
30.05.91 Marty Duke W RSC 4 Birmingham
29.08.91 Nigel Moore W RSC 1 Oakengates
31.10.91 Colin Pitters W PTS 8 Oakengates
04.02.92 Graham Burton W RSC 2 Alfreton
26.03.92 Vito Gaudiosi W CO 1 Telford
(Vacant Commonwealth Middleweight
Title)
01.10.92 John Ashton W PTS 12 Telford
(Commonwealth Middleweight Title
Defence)

04.12.92	Horace Fleary W PTS 8 Telford
16.03.93	Carlo Colarusso W PTS 8 Wolverhampton
24.04.93	Royan Hammond W PTS 10 Birmingham
27.10.93	Garry Meekison W PTS 12 West Bromwich
	(Commonwealth Middleweight Title Defence)
01.03.94	Heath Todd W RSC 7 Dudley
16.03.94	Greg Lonon W RSC 6 Birmingham
05.10.94	Jacques le Blanc W PTS 12 Wolverhampton
	(Commonwealth Middleweight Title Defence)
30.11.94	Art Serwano W RSC 11 Wolverhampton
	(Commonwealth Middleweight Title Defence)
22.02.95	Silvio Branco W RSC 9 Telford
	(Vacant European Middleweight Title)
25.10.95	Zdravko Kostic W PTS 12 Telford
	(European Middleweight Title Defence)
31.01.96	Derek Wormald W RSC 10 Birmingham
	(European Middleweight Title Defence)
19.10.96	Keith Holmes L RSC 12 Upper Marlboro, USA
	(WBC Middleweight Title Challenge)
11.09.97	Bernice Barber W RSC 3 Widnes
27.03.98	Thulani Malinga W PTS 12 Telford
	(WBC S. Middleweight Title Challenge)
05.09.98	Glenn Catley W PTS 12 Telford
	(WBC S. Middleweight Title Defence)
13.02.99	Vincenzo Nardiello W RSC 6 Newcastle
	(WBC S. Middleweight Title Defence)
23.10.99	Markus Beyer L PTS 12 Telford
	(WBC S. Middleweight Title Defence)
06.05.00	Errol McDonald W RTD 7 Frankfurt, Germany
16.12.00	Joe Calzaghe L RSC 10 Sheffield
	(WBO S. Middleweight Title Challenge)

Career: 29 contests, won 26, lost 3.

Richie Woodhall   Les Clark

Lee Woodruff

Lancaster. *Born* Lancaster, 27 February, 1980
L. Heavyweight. Ht. 5'11"
Manager B. Myers

18.03.01	Tommy Matthews W RSC 2 Shaw
26.04.01	Paul Buchanan L PTS 6 Gateshead

Career: 2 contests, won 1, lost 1.

Clinton Woods

Sheffield. *Born* Sheffield, 1 May, 1972
WBC International L. Heavyweight
Champion. Former Undefeated British,
European & Commonwealth L.
Heavyweight Champion. Former
Commonwealth S. Middleweight
Champion. Former Undefeated Central
Area S. Middleweight Champion. Ht. 6'2"
Manager Self

17.11.94	Dave Proctor W PTS 6 Sheffield
12.12.94	Earl Ling W RSC 5 Cleethorpes
23.02.95	Paul Clarkson W RSC 1 Hull
06.04.95	Japhet Hans W RSC 3 Sheffield
16.05.95	Kevin Burton W PTS 6 Cleethorpes
14.06.95	Kevin Burton W RSC 6 Batley
21.09.95	Paul Murray W PTS 6 Sheffield
20.10.95	Phil Ball W RSC 4 Mansfield
22.11.95	Andy Ewen W RSC 3 Sheffield
05.02.96	Chris Walker W RSC 6 Bradford
16.03.96	John Duckworth W PTS 8 Sheffield
13.06.96	Ernie Loveridge W PTS 6 Sheffield
14.11.96	Craig Joseph W PTS 10 Sheffield
	(Vacant Central Area S. Middleweight Title)
20.02.97	Rocky Shelly W RSC 2 Mansfield
10.04.97	Darren Littlewood W RSC 6 Sheffield
	(Central Area S. Middleweight Title Defence)
26.06.97	Darren Ashton W PTS 6 Sheffield
25.10.97	Danny Juma W PTS 8 Queensferry
26.11.97	Jeff Finlayson W PTS 8 Sheffield
06.12.97	Mark Baker W PTS 12 Wembley
	(Vacant Commonwealth S. Middleweight Title)
28.03.98	David Starie L PTS 12 Hull
	(Commonwealth S. Middleweight Title Defence)
18.06.98	Peter Mason W RTD 4 Sheffield
30.11.98	Mark Smallwood W RSC 7 Manchester
13.03.99	Crawford Ashley W RSC 8 Manchester
	(British, Commonwealth & European L. Heavyweight Title Challenges)
10.07.99	Sam Leuii W RSC 6 Southwark
	(Commonwealth L. Heavyweight Title Defence)
11.09.99	Lenox Lewis W RSC 10 Sheffield
	(Commonwealth L. Heavyweight Title Defence)
10.12.99	Terry Ford W RTD 4 Warsaw, Poland
12.02.00	Juan Nelongo W PTS 12 Sheffield
	(European L. Heavyweight Title Defence)
29.04.00	Ole Klemetsen W RSC 9 Wembley
	(European L. Heavyweight Title Defence)
15.07.00	Greg Scott-Briggs W RSC 3 Millwall
24.03.01	Ali Forbes W RTD 10 Sheffield
	(Vacant WBC International L. Heavyweight Title)

Career: 30 contests, won 29, lost 1.

Harry Woods

Bargoed. *Born* Caerphilly, 13 February, 1975
Bantamweight. Ht. 5'4"
Manager D. Gardiner

07.07.95	Henry Jones W PTS 4 Cardiff
29.09.95	Dave Martin DREW 4 Bloomsbury
25.10.95	Mark Hughes DREW 8 Cardiff
28.11.95	Chris Thomas W RSC 1 Cardiff
20.12.95	Dave Martin W CO 2 Usk
20.03.96	Anthony Hanna W PTS 6 Cardiff
29.05.96	Shaun Norman W RSC 5 Ebbw Vale
18.09.96	Louis Veitch L DIS 4 Tylorstown
02.10.96	Jose Ramon Bartolme W RSC 3 Cardiff
06.11.96	Rowan Williams W PTS 6 Tylorstown
27.11.96	Matthew Harris W PTS 8 Swansea
28.12.96	Alex Baba L PTS 12 Accra, Ghana
	(WBC International Flyweight Title Challenge)
26.02.97	Jose Antonio Lopez L RSC 5 Cardiff
03.04.98	Des Gargano L RSC 6 Ebbw Vale
16.05.98	Stephen Oates L PTS 4 Bethnal Green
04.06.99	Dmitri Kirilov L PTS 6 Malaga, Spain
26.06.99	Stephen Oates L PTS 6 Millwall
12.11.99	Brian Carr L PTS 6 Glasgow
14.12.99	Mark Payne L PTS 4 Coventry
08.09.00	Frankie DeMilo L RTD 6 Bristol
	(British Masters S. Bantamweight Title Challenge)
12.05.01	Willie Valentine W PTS 4 Plymouth

Career: 21 contests, won 10, drew 2, lost 9.

Chris Woollas

Epworth. *Born* Scunthorpe, 22 November, 1973
Heavyweight. Midlands Area Cruiserweight
Champion. Ht. 5'11"
Manager Self

17.08.94	Darren Littlewood W RSC 4 Sheffield
05.10.94	Robert Norton DREW 6 Wolverhampton
05.12.94	Neil Simpson W PTS 6 Cleethorpes
10.02.95	Monty Wright L RSC 4 Birmingham
30.06.95	Kenny Nevers L RSC 2 Doncaster
25.09.95	Cliff Elden DREW 6 Cleethorpes
08.11.95	Stevie Pettit W PTS 6 Walsall
17.11.95	Markku Salminen L PTS 6 Helsinki, Finland
11.12.95	Cliff Elden DREW 6 Cleethorpes
15.02.96	Pele Lawrence W RSC 6 Sheffield
29.02.96	John Pierre DREW 6 Scunthorpe
16.03.96	David Jules W PTS 6 Sheffield
22.04.96	Jacklord Jacobs DREW 4 Crystal Palace
30.05.96	Martin Langtry L RSC 6 Lincoln
	(Midlands Area Cruiserweight Title Challenge)
03.09.96	Darren Corbett L RSC 7 Belfast
02.10.96	Rocky Shelly W RSC 6 Stoke
09.10.96	Nigel Rafferty W PTS 6 Stoke
28.10.96	Colin Brown L PTS 8 Glasgow
10.11.96	Michael Gale DREW 6 Glasgow
25.11.96	Albert Call L PTS 6 Cleethorpes
17.12.96	Darren Corbett L RSC 1 Doncaster
16.01.97	Mark Smallwood L PTS 8 Solihull
31.01.97	Tim Redman L PTS 6 Pentre Halkyn
14.03.97	Kelly Oliver L PTS 6 Reading
24.03.97	Mikael Lindblad L RSC 7 Helsinki, Finland
19.06.97	Ian Henry W PTS 6 Scunthorpe

02.08.97 Kelly Oliver L RSC 3 Barnsley
15.12.97 Neil Simpson W PTS 6 Cleethorpes
26.01.98 Colin Brown W PTS 6 Glasgow
26.03.98 Cliff Elden L PTS 4 Scunthorpe
06.05.98 Simon McDougall W PTS 6 Blackpool
21.07.98 Matthew Ellis L RSC 5 Widnes
11.09.98 Lennox Williams W PTS 6 Cleethorpes
12.03.99 Albert Sosnowski L PTS 4 Bethnal Green
27.05.99 Nigel Rafferty W PTS 10 Edgbaston
(Midlands Area Cruiserweight Title Challenge)
10.07.99 Michael Sprott L RTD 4 Southwark
13.09.99 Dominic Negus L PTS 10 Bethnal Green
(Elim. British Cruiserweight Title)
09.10.99 Chris P. Bacon L PTS 4 Manchester
30.10.99 Terry Dunstan L RSC 1 Southwark
08.04.00 Bruce Scott L RSC 2 Bethnal Green
13.07.00 Firat Aslan L RSC 2 Bethnal Green
08.09.00 Petr Horacek L PTS 4 Hammersmith
21.10.00 Danny Percival L PTS 4 Wembley
18.11.00 Matthew Ellis L PTS 4 Dagenham
11.12.00 Enzo Maccarinelli L PTS 4 Widnes
Career: 45 contests, won 13, drew 6, lost 26.

Chris Woollas   Les Clark

Shane Woollas
Epworth. *Born* Scunthorpe, 28 July, 1972
Midlands Area Heavyweight Champion.
Ht. 6'2"
Manager Self

26.08.94 Neil Kirkwood L RSC 6 Barnsley
28.07.95 Rob Albon W RTD 4 Epworth
11.10.95 Gary Williams W PTS 6 Solihull
08.11.95 David Jules W PTS 6 Scunthorpe
26.01.96 Nigel Williams W RSC 2 Doncaster
31.01.96 David Jules L PTS 6 Stoke
22.04.96 Gary Williams W PTS 10 Cleethorpes
(Vacant Midlands Area Heavyweight Title)
29.07.96 David Jules L PTS 6 Skegness
31.08.96 Willi Fischer L CO 2 Palma de Mallorca

08.10.96 Mika Kihlstrom L PTS 4 Battersea
06.11.96 Kevin McBride L RSC 2 Hull
08.02.97 Danny Williams L RSC 2 Millwall
19.06.97 Lennox Williams W PTS 6 Scunthorpe
15.12.97 Gary Williams W RSC 8 Cleethorpes
(Midlands Area Heavyweight Title Defence)
11.01.98 Fred Westgeest L PTS 6 Riesa, Germany
21.02.98 Danny Williams L RSC 2 Belfast
23.05.98 Mark Potter L PTS 4 Bethnal Green
21.06.98 Mal Rice W PTS 6 Liverpool
02.07.98 Georgi Kandelaki L RSC 4 Ipswich
11.09.98 Bruno Foster W PTS 6 Cleethorpes
26.09.98 Luan Krasniqi L RSC 3 York
30.11.98 Craig Bowen-Price L RSC 2 Manchester
30.04.99 Brian Gascoigne DREW 6 Scunthorpe
30.10.99 Gavin McGhin L CO 4 Peterlee
12.02.00 Patrick Halberg L PTS 6 Sheffield
05.02.01 Crawford Ashley L RSC 4 Hull
10.04.01 Petr Horacek DREW 4 Wembley
16.06.01 Eric Butterbean Esch L RSC 1 Wembley
Career: 28 contests, won 9, drew 2, lost 17.

Danny Wray
Shoreham. *Born* Camberwell, 5 July, 1980
L. Middleweight. Ht. 5'9¹/₄"
Manager R. Davies

03.02.01 Tony Smith W RSC 1 Brighton
05.05.01 Freddie Yemofio W PTS 6 Brighton
Career: 2 contests, won 2.

Nigel Wright
Hartlepool. *Born* Bishop Auckland, 22 June, 1979
L. Welterweight. Ht. 5'9"
Manager G. Robinson

10.02.01 Keith Jones W PTS 4 Widnes
Career: 1 contest, won 1.

Jamie Yelland   Les Clark

Jamie Yelland
Watford. *Born* London, 5 March, 1975
S. Bantamweight. Ht. 5'5"
Manager J. Evans

11.03.00 Chris Emanuele W PTS 4 Kensington
22.07.00 Daniel Ring W PTS 4 Watford
06.10.00 Simon Stowell DREW 4 Maidstone
31.10.00 John Barnes W PTS 6 Hammersmith
07.04.01 John Barnes W PTS 4 Wembley
Career: 5 contests, won 4, drew 1.

Freddie Yemofio
Hayes. *Born* London, 15 July, 1969
S. Middleweight. Ht. 5'10"
Manager Self

31.08.93 Lee Sara L PTS 6 Croydon
30.09.93 Martin Rosamond L PTS 6 Hayes
20.05.94 Lee Blundell L RSC 6 Acton
30.09.94 Jason Hart L PTS 6 Bethnal Green
26.05.95 Robert Harper W PTS 6 Norwich
28.04.98 Matthew Tait L PTS 6 Brentford
14.05.98 Matt Galer L RSC 4 Acton
07.12.98 Matthew Barney L PTS 4 Acton
12.08.00 Spencer Fearon L RSC 4 Wembley
02.11.00 Elvis Michailenko L PTS 6 Kensington
09.12.00 Liam Lathbury L PTS 4 Southwark
29.01.01 Francie Doherty L RSC 4 Peterborough
05.05.01 Danny Wray L PTS 6 Brighton
12.05.01 Simon Andrews L PTS 4 Plymouth
Career: 14 contests, won 1, lost 13.

Steve Yorath
Cardiff. *Born* Cardiff, 8 August, 1965
Cruiserweight. Ht. 6'2"
Manager Self

21.11.85 Dai Davies L RSC 5 Blaenavon
13.03.86 John Ashton L CO 3 Alfreton
08.05.90 Rob Albon L PTS 6 Brentford
06.07.90 Phil Soundy L CO 3 Brentwood
17.09.90 Chris Coughlan W PTS 6 Cardiff
24.09.90 John Williams L PTS 6 Mayfair
03.10.90 Phil Soundy L PTS 6 Basildon
19.10.90 Neils H. Madsen L PTS 6 Skive, Denmark
15.04.91 Tony Colclough W PTS 6 Wolverhampton
24.04.91 Phil Soundy W PTS 6 Basildon
28.05.91 R. F. McKenzie W PTS 6 Cardiff
27.06.91 Denzil Browne L PTS 6 Leeds
21.01.92 Graham Arnold W PTS 6 Norwich
31.03.92 Graham Arnold L PTS 6 Norwich
18.05.92 Marco van Spaendonck L PTS 4 Valkenswaard, Holland
23.09.92 Denzil Browne L PTS 8 Leeds
25.11.92 Terry Dunstan L PTS 8 Mayfair
24.02.93 Derek Angol L RSC 5 Wembley
03.04.93 Biko Botowamungu L RSC 5 Vienna, Austria
10.07.93 Chris Okoh L PTS 6 Cardiff
31.08.93 Devon Rhooms L PTS 6 Croydon
04.10.93 Terry Dixon L RSC 4 Mayfair
09.04.94 Dermot Gascoyne L CO 3 Mansfield
27.08.94 Kent Davis W PTS 6 Cardiff
08.09.94 Sean Heron L PTS 6 Glasgow
18.11.94 John Wilson L PTS 6 Glasgow
27.11.94 Owen Bartley DREW 6 Southwark
25.01.95 Kent Davis L PTS 6 Cardiff
05.05.01 Auckland Aumatangi L PTS 6 Perth, Australia
18.06.01 Abel Lelan L PTS 6 Sidney, Australia
Career: 30 contests, won 6, drew 1, lost 23.

British Area Title Bouts During 2000-2001

Central Area

Titleholders at 30 June 2001

Fly: Dale Robinson. **Bantam:** *vacant.* **S. Bantam:** *vacant.* **Feather:** *vacant.* **S. Feather:** Lee Armstrong. **Light:** Gary Hibbert. **L. Welter:** *vacant.* **Welter:** *vacant.* **L. Middle:** Lee Blundell. **Middle:** *vacant.* **S. Middle:** *vacant.* **L. Heavy:** *vacant.* **Cruiser:** Denzil Browne. **Heavy:** Neil Kirkwood.

12 November 2000	Paul Bonson L PTS 10 Glenn Williams, Manchester (L. Heavyweight Title Defence)
30 November 2000	Lee Blundell W RSC 8 Danny Thornton, Blackpool (Vacant L. Middleweight Title)
5 February 2001	Denzil Browne W RSC 5 Tony Booth, Hull (Vacant Cruiserweight Title)
8 May 2001	Terry Gaskin L RTD 3 Dale Robinson, Barnsley (Flyweight Title Defence)

Between 1 July 2000 and 30 June 2001, Glenn Williams (L. Heavy) retired and Mike Gormley (S. Middle) forfeited his title following his losing contest against Robin Reid at the championship weight.

Midlands Area

Titleholders at 30 June 2001

Fly: Anthony Hanna. **Bantam:** Steve Williams. **S. Bantam:** Carl Allen. **Feather:** *vacant.* **S. Feather:** Carl Greaves. **Light:** Anthony Maynard. **L. Welter:** Gavin Down. **Welter:** Christian Brady. **L. Middle:** *vacant.* **Middle:** Gordon Behan. **S. Middle:** *vacant.* **L. Heavy:** Darren Ashton. **Cruiser:** Chris Woollas. **Heavy:** Shane Woollas.

13 August 2000	Jawaid Khaliq W RSC 4 Ernie Smith, Nottingham (Vacant Welterweight Title)
24 March 2001	Carl Greaves W CO 6 Nigel Senior, Newark (Vacant S. Featherweight Title)
1 April 2001	Gavin Down W RSC 3 Steve Saville, Alfreton (Vacant L. Welterweight Title)
21 May 2001	Christian Brady W RSC 5 Matt Scriven, Birmingham (Vacant Welterweight Title)

Between 1 July 2000 and 30 June 2001, Malcolm Melvin (L. Welter) and Jawaid Khaliq (Welter and L. Middle) relinquished their titles, while Alex Mason (S. Middle) retired.

Northern Area

Titleholders at 30 June 2001

Fly: *vacant.* **Bantam:** *vacant.* **S. Bantam:** *vacant.* **Feather:** *vacant.* **S. Feather:** *vacant.* **Light:** *vacant.* **L. Welter:** *vacant.* **Welter:** *vacant.* **L. Middle:** *vacant.* **Middle:** Eddie Haley. **S. Middle:** Ian Cooper. **L. Heavy:** *vacant.* **Cruiser:** *vacant.* **Heavy:** *vacant.*

| 11 February 2001 | Ian Cooper W RSC 9 Mike White, Hartlepool (Vacant S. Middleweight Title) |

Between 1 July 2000 and 30 June 2001, John T. Kelly (Light) and Paul King (Welter) retired.

Terry Gaskin (left) put his Central Area flyweight title on the line against Dale Robinson and lost

Les Clark

Northern Ireland Area

Titleholders at 30 June 2001 - None

Scottish Area

Titleholders at 30 June 2001

Fly: *vacant.* **Bantam:** Shaun Anderson. **S. Bantam:** *vacant.* **Feather:** Brian Carr. **S. Feather:** *vacant.* **Light:** *vacant.* **L. Welter:** *vacant.* **Welter:** *vacant.* **L. Middle:** *vacant.* **Middle:** John Docherty. **S. Middle:** Jason Barker. **L. Heavy:** *vacant.* **Cruiser:** *vacant.* **Heavy:** *vacant.*

2 October 2000	Jason Barker W PTS 10 Biagio Falcone, Glasgow (Vacant S. Middleweight Title)

Between 1 July 2000 and 30 June 2001, Willie Quinn (S. Middle) retired.

Southern Area

Titleholders at 30 June 2001

Fly: Ian Napa. **Bantam:** *vacant.* **S. Bantam:** *vacant.* **Feather:** *vacant.* **S. Feather:** *vacant.* **Light:** Graham Earl. **L. Welter:** Daniel James. **Welter:** Paul Dyer. **L. Middle:** Delroy Mellis. **Middle:** Gary Logan. **S. Middle:** Matthew Barney. **L. Heavy:** *vacant.* **Cruiser:** Garry Delaney. **Heavy:** Mark Potter.

2 July 2000	Delroy Mellis W RSC 3 Alan Gilbert, Watford (Vacant L. Middleweight Title)
6 October 2000	Dominic Negus L PTS 10 Garry Delaney, Maidstone (Cruiserweight Title Defence)
14 October 2000	Eddie Knight L RSC 6 Butch Lesley, Wembley (L. Heavyweight Title Defence)
22 October 2000	Delroy Mellis W RSC 6 Allan Gray, Streatham (L. Middleweight Title Defence)
23 January 2001	Delroy Mellis W RSC 3 Alan Gilbert, Crawley (L. Middleweight Title Defence)
2 February 2001	Paul Dyer W PTS 10 David Baptiste, Portsmouth (Vacant Welterweight Title)
10 March 2001	Graham Earl W RSC 8 Brian Gentry, Bethnal Green (Vacant Lightweight Title)
26 March 2001	Butch Lesley L PTS 10 Tony Oakey, Wembley (L. Heavyweight Title Defence)
20 April 2001	Delroy Mellis W RSC 8 Chris Nembhard, Millwall (L. Middleweight Title Defence)
3 June 2001	Gary Logan W RSC 2 Spencer Fearon, Southwark (Vacant Middleweight Title)

Between 1 July 2000 and 30 June 2001, Kevin McCarthy (Welter) and Matt Brown (S. Feather) retired, while Paul Halpin (Feather), Delroy Leslie (Middle) and Tony Oakey (L. Heavy) relinquished their titles.

Welsh Area

Titleholders at 30 June 2001

Fly: *vacant.* **Bantam:** *vacant.* **S. Bantam:** *vacant.* **Feather:** *vacant.* **S. Feather:** Chris Williams. **Light:** *vacant.* **L. Welter:** Jason Cook. **Welter:** Michael Smyth. **L. Middle:** Paul Samuels. **Middle:** *vacant.* **S. Middle:** *vacant.* **L. Heavy:** *vacant.* **Cruiser:** Darron Griffiths. **Heavy:** *vacant.*

Between 1 July 2000 and 30 June 2001, Ian Turner (Bantam) relinquished his title, while David Morris (Feather) retired.

Western Area

Titleholders at 30 June 2001

Fly: *vacant.* **Bantam:** *vacant.* **S. Bantam:** Frankie DeMilo. **Feather:** *vacant.* **S. Feather:** *vacant.* **Light:** *vacant.* **L. Welter:** *vacant.* **Welter:** *vacant.* **L. Middle:** *vacant.* **Middle:** *vacant.* **S. Middle:** Darren Dorrington. **L. Heavy:** *vacant.* **Cruiser:** *vacant.* **Heavy:** *vacant.*

Between 1 July 2000 and 30 June 2001, Greg Upton (S. Feather) retired.

Luton's Graham Earl (left) pictured on his way to winning the vacant Southern Area lightweight title against Brian Gentry last March

Les Clar

British Title Bouts During 2000-2001

All of last season's title bouts are shown in date order within their weight divisions and give the contestants' respective weights, along with the scorecard if going to a decision. Every contest is summarised briefly and all referees are named.

Flyweight

13 November 2000   Jason Booth 8.0 (England) W PTS 12 Ian Napa 7.12$^{1}/_{4}$ (England), York Hall, Bethnal Green, London. Referee: Dave Parris 118-112. Although outreached and lacking in power, Napa gave it his best shot and threw a greater amount of punches than the champion but failed to make a dent. Booth worked well to both head and body, showing a good defence, and was well worth his victory. This fight also involved Booth's Commonwealth title.

Bantamweight

9 September 2000   Ady Lewis 8.4$^{3}/_{4}$ (England) L RSC 4 Tommy Waite 8.6 (Ireland), Bowler's Arena, Manchester. Lewis was extremely unfortunate to lose both his British and Commonwealth titles after a clash of heads opened up a nasty cut on his right eyelid and the referee, Mark Green, stopped the fight at 2.08 of the fourth round without giving the corner a chance to get to work on it during the interval. The lighter punching Waite had been down in the second, was beginning to be worked over when the finish came, and had looked to be on his way to defeat.

9 October 2000   Tommy Waite 8.5$^{3}/_{4}$ (Ireland) L PTS 12 Nicky Booth 8.5$^{1}/_{2}$ (England), Everton Park Leisure Centre, Liverpool. On his victory, Booth joined his brother Jason as a British and Commonwealth champion and the pair became the only brothers, other than George and John Feeney, to hold British titles simultaneously. He also became the youngest British champion at the weight since 1923. Taking the fight at three days notice, replacing Sandile Sobandla of South Africa, the 20-year-old youngster proved more than a match for the champion, cutting his right eye in the third and, in the main, outboxing his rival from the centre of the ring to well merit Paul Thomas' 117-114 points verdict.

26 February 2001   Nicky Booth 8.5$^{3}/_{4}$ (England) W RSC 7 Ady Lewis 8.5 (England), Harvey Hadden Leisure Centre, Nottingham. Given an opportunity to regain the British and Commonwealth titles, Lewis made it extremely tough for the youngster as the fight swung one way then the other, but ultimately found the champion too good and too big for him in what was a great contest. In the seventh round, Booth was badly hurt by a body punch, but instead of looking to hold on he gradually fought his way back to put Lewis down and, on rising at nine, referee Richie Davies halted the action at 2.35 with the latter in no position to defend himself.

S. Bantamweight

4 November 2000   Michael Alldis 8.10 (England) W RSC 6 Drew Docherty 8.9$^{3}/_{4}$ (Scotland), York Hall, Bethnal Green, London. In control virtually throughout, Alldis was just too powerful for the former undefeated champion, whose chances of regaining the title were not helped when he picked up a cut over the left eye in the second following a head clash. The finish came in the sixth round when Docherty was caught by a cracking right hand to the jaw and, on rising at the count of six, he was lurching about on unsteady legs when rescued by Mickey Vann at 1.29 on the clock.

Featherweight

24 March 2001   Scott Harrison 9.0 (Scotland) W RSC 4 Richie Wenton 8.13 (England), Ponds Forge International Leisure Centre, Sheffield. Primarily a contest to decide the British title after Gary Thornhill forfeited in September, having failed the drug test following his championship fight against Richie Wenton, it also involved Harrison's Commonwealth crown. After sizing his opponent up for a couple of rounds, it was soon clear that Harrison was going to do a job on the former British super-bantamweight champion, who was rescued by Dave Parris, when not fighting back, with just three seconds of the fourth round remaining.

S. Featherweight

8 July 2000   Michael Gomez 9.2$^{1}/_{2}$ (England) W CO 2 Carl Greaves 9.3$^{1}/_{4}$ (England), Kingsway Leisure Centre, Widnes. This was a big step up in class for the challenger, and it soon showed. Following a feeling out first round, Gomez soon went to work in the second and immediately prior to the bell a heavy left hook to Greaves' head sent him crashing on to his back where he was counted out by John Keane at 3.09.

11 December 2000   Michael Gomez 9.2$^{1}/_{2}$ (England) W PTS 12 Ian McLeod 9.3$^{1}/_{2}$ (Scotland), Kingsway Leisure Centre, Widnes. In winning the Lonsdale Belt outright, Gomez achieved a major ambition and, at the same time, established himself as the best super-feather in the country. In McLeod, the champion faced a gritty opponent who would not surrender and although Gomez fully merited Richie Davies' 118-110 decision, his body punching badly slowing the tough Scot down, it was never easy, with both men cut over their left eyes at the finish.

Lightweight

5 May 2001   Bobby Vanzie 9.8$^{1}/_{2}$ (England) W RSC 7 Steve Murray 9.8$^{3}/_{4}$ (England), Lee Valley Leisure Centre, Edmonton, London. Down twice in the first round and looking unlikely to survive, the champion came back strongly to win the next few rounds, despite having a point deducted for too much holding and losing the sixth. However, in the seventh, there was a dramatic change in events. A left-right to the jaw dumped Murray, badly shaken, to the floor and, although he got up at three, he was soon under the cosh, which led to the referee, Paul Thomas, jumping in at 0.53 to save him from further punishment.

L. Welterweight

21 October 2000   Richard Hatton 9.13$^{1}/_{2}$ (England) W PTS 12 Jonathan Thaxton 9.13 (England), The Conference Centre, Wembley. Referee: Paul Thomas 117-113. In what was a contest for the vacant title, made after Jason Rowland handed in his belt earlier in the month to go for the WBU championship, Hatton overcame a badly cut left eye to punch out a solid points victory over Thaxton, who proved just what a tough character he was when continually fighting back against all the odds. Although Thaxton was cut under both eyes, he made light of his problems, and there was always a chance that he could pull off a shock win if Hatton's injuries worsened. Hatton relinquished the title on winning the WBU championship on 26 March 2001.

Welterweight

14 October 2000 Harry Dhami 10.6 (England) W PTS 12 Malcom Melvin 10.7 (England), The Conference Centre, Wembley. Despite John Keane's wide 118-110 points margin, in what was a difficult fight to score Dhami was never able to raise his game and the trade paper, *Boxing News*, saw it much closer with the result hinging on the last round. Regardless of that, it was a pretty uninspiring fight, especially as it involved the title, and Dhami, for one, would have been glad it was all over, while Melvin would wonder how different the result might have been if he'd had more than three days to prepare.

27 November 2000 Harry Dhami 10.6¾ (England) W PTS 12 Spencer McCracken 10.6¼ (England), Aston Villa Leisure Centre, Birmingham. Referee: John Keane 118-111. This was a different Harry Dhami to the man who fought Malcolm Melvin and, this time, John Keane's scoreline of 118-111 fully reflected the champion's superiority, despite him being cut over the left eye in the sixth. It was Dhami's left jab which stopped tough guy McCracken from getting to close quarters, where he could have worked the body, which was probably the deciding factor. However, that aside, the challenger, who was coming back from a broken right hand, was just unable to turn things around.

L. Middleweight

Wayne Alexander failed to defend during the period.

Middleweight

10 April 2001 Howard Eastman 11.5 (England) W RSC 10 Robert McCracken 11.5¾ (England), The Conference Centre, Wembley, England. Judges: Larry O'Connell, Terry O'Connor, John Keane. In winning a Lonsdale Belt outright and, at the same time, successfully defending the Commonwealth title, while also fighting for the vacant European crown, Eastman comprehensively beat his toughest challenger, who was rescued by Dave Parris at 1.54 of the tenth round, having taken a count of four. This was the fight that Eastman needed to prove he was world class and that he most certainly did. After taking control in the seventh, both outworking and outpunching McCracken, he went up a gear and it was a terrific right uppercut that did all the damage and brought the fight to its conclusion.

S. Middleweight

9 December 2000 David Starie 11.13¼ (England) W CO 3 Alex Mason 11.13¾ (England), Elephant & Castle Leisure Centre, Southwark, London. Handed an unexpected championship opportunity, Mason failed to raise his game and was well beaten, being counted out by Marcus McDonnell at 1.47 of the third round on one knee following a left-right combination. It had been a big step up in class and the

challenger had neither the guile or skill required which would have enabled him to get his power punches off from close range.

L. Heavyweight

18 November 2000 Neil Simpson 12.6¾ (England) W RSC 1 Mark Delaney 12.5½ (England), Goresbrook Leisure Centre, Dagenham. This was undoubtedly Simpson's best-ever performance. Fighting in front of a home crowd, the experienced Delaney was expected to do well but was caught cold as a right to the jaw paved the way for a non-stop body attack which sent him down for a mandatory eight count after less than 30 seconds. With the challenger allowed to continue, Simpson then kept up a relentless two-handed attack until the referee, Roy Francis, stepped to rescue Delaney at 0.60, thus posting one of the quickest wins in the championship record books.

Cruiserweight

16 December 2000 Bruce Scott 13.6 (England) W CO 6 John Keeton 13.7½ (England), The Arena, Sheffield. Contested for the vacant title after Carl Thompson relinquished in August to concentrate on his European championship, the under pressure Scott came roaring back to put a second notch on the Lonsdale Belt when knocking out hard-man Keeton with a right uppercut followed by a left hook, Terry O'Connor completing the count at 2.08 of the sixth. The new champion had been under fire almost non-stop since the start in a pier-six brawl, but had somehow come back to cut Keeton over the left eye and find the finishing punches in what was to be the final round

10 March 2001 Bruce Scott 13.5¾ (England) W RTD 3 Garry Delaney 13.8 (England), York Hall, Bethnal Green, London. Although there had been no knockdowns as such, Delaney had been under heavy pressure throughout from an avenging Scott (who had lost to Delaney at amateur level several years earlier) and was forced to call it a day while on his stool at the end of the third round after his left eye closed shut, the referee, Terry O'Connor, accepting the retirement. With his victory, Scott won the Lonsdale Belt outright.

Heavyweight

21 October 2000 Danny Williams 18.1 (England) W RSC 6 Mark Potter 16.10 (England), The Conference Centre, Wembley. Booked to defend against Williams, Mike Holden, who was unavailable due to a virus infection, relinquished the title immediately prior to the fight on the grounds that he would get first crack at the winner of Williams, who defended his Commonwealth crown, and late substitute, Potter. In one of the most dramatic and exciting championship fights of recent years, Williams somehow conjured up a victory after partially dislocating his shoulder in the third round and fighting on until it came out completely in the sixth. By then, Potter had been floored three times, once from a low blow which cost Williams two points. When the arm finally came out of its socket all looked lost for Williams, until a tremendous left uppercut put Potter down for a nine count. On rising, Potter was then floored by a terrific left hook and after getting up again, this time at the count of eight, John Coyle brought the contest to a halt at 2.41 of the round, leaving a pained but exuberant Williams to celebrate.

Lord Lonsdale Challenge Belts: Outright Winners

Outright Winners of the National Sporting Club's Challenge Belt, 1909-1935 (21)

Under pressure from other promoters with bigger venues, and in an effort to sustain their monopoly – having controlled championship fights in Britain up until that point in time – the National Sporting Club launched the belt in 1909. They did so on the proviso that there should be eight weight divisions – fly, bantam, feather, light, welter, middle, light-heavy, and heavy – and that to win a belt outright a champion must score three title-match victories at the same weight, but not necessarily consecutively. Worth a substantial amount of money, and carrying a £1 a week pension from the age of 50, the President of the NSC, Lord Lonsdale, donated the first of 22 belts struck. Known as the Lonsdale Belt, despite the inscription reading: 'The National Sporting Club's Challenge Belt', the first man to put a notch on a belt was Freddie Welsh, who outpointed Johnny Summers for the lightweight title on 8 November 1909, while Jim Driscoll became the first man to win one outright. The record time for winning the belt is held by Jim Higgins (279 days).

FLYWEIGHT	Jimmy Wilde; Jackie Brown
BANTAMWEIGHT	Digger Stanley; Joe Fox; Jim Higgins; Johnny Brown; Dick Corbett; Johnny King
FEATHERWEIGHT	Jim Driscoll; Tancy Lee; Johnny Cuthbert; Nel Tarleton
LIGHTWEIGHT	Freddie Welsh
WELTERWEIGHT	Johnny Basham; Jack Hood
MIDDLEWEIGHT	Pat O'Keefe; Len Harvey; Jock McAvoy
L. HEAVYWEIGHT	Dick Smith
HEAVYWEIGHT	Bombardier Billy Wells; Jack Petersen

Note: Both Dick Corbett and Johnny King – with one notch apiece on the 'special' British Empire Lonsdale Belt that was struck in 1933 and later presented to the winner of the Tommy Farr v Joe Louis fight – were allowed to keep their Lonsdale Belts with just two notches secured; Freddie Welsh, also with two notches, was awarded a belt due to his inability to defend because of the First World War; the first bantam belt came back into circulation and was awarded to Johnny Brown; Al Foreman, with just one notch on the second lightweight belt, took it back to Canada with him without the consent of the BBBoC; while the second light-heavy belt was awarded to Jack Smith of Worcester for winning a novices heavyweight competition. Having emigrated to New Zealand, Smith later presented the visiting Her Majesty The Queen with the belt and it now hangs in the BBBoC's offices.

Outright Winners of the BBBoC Lord Lonsdale Challenge Belt, 1936-2001 (106)

Re-introduced by the British Boxing Board of Control as the Lord Lonsdale Challenge Belt, but of less intrinsic value – Benny Lynch's eight-round win over Pat Palmer (16 September 1936 at Shawfield Park, Glasgow) got the new version underway – Eric Boon became the first man to win one outright, in 1939, following victories over Dave Crowley (2) and Arthur Danahar. Since those early days, six further weight divisions have been added and, following on from Henry Cooper's feat of winning three Lonsdale Belts outright, on 10 June 1981 the BBBoC's rules and regulations were amended to read that no boxer shall receive more than one belt as his own property, in any one weight division. From 1 September 1999, any boxer putting a notch on a Lonsdale Belt for the first time will require three more notches at the same weight before he can call the belt his own. However, men who already have a notch on the Lonsdale Belt prior to 1 September 1999 can contest it under the former ruling of three winning championship contests at the same weight. Incidentally, the fastest of the modern belt winners is Ryan Rhodes (90 days), while Chris and Kevin Finnegan are the only brothers to have each won a belt outright.

FLYWEIGHT	Jackie Paterson; Terry Allen; Walter McGowan; John McCluskey; Hugh Russell; Charlie Magri; Pat Clinton; Robbie Regan; Francis Ampofo; Ady Lewis
BANTAMWEIGHT	Johnny King; Peter Keenan (2); Freddie Gilroy; Alan Rudkin; Johnny Owen; Billy Hardy; Drew Docherty
S. BANTAMWEIGHT	Richie Wenton; Michael Brodie
FEATHERWEIGHT	Nel Tarleton; Ronnie Clayton (2); Charlie Hill; Howard Winstone (2); Evan Armstrong; Pat Cowdell; Robert Dickie; Paul Hodkinson; Colin McMillan; Sean Murphy; Jonjo Irwin

S. FEATHERWEIGHT	Jimmy Anderson; John Doherty; Floyd Havard; Charles Shepherd; Michael Gomez
LIGHTWEIGHT	Eric Boon; Billy Thompson; Joe Lucy; Dave Charnley; Maurice Cullen; Ken Buchanan; Jim Watt; George Feeney; Tony Willis; Carl Crook; Billy Schwer; Michael Ayers; Bobby Vanzie
L. WELTERWEIGHT	Joey Singleton; Colin Power; Clinton McKenzie; Lloyd Christie; Andy Holligan; Ross Hale
WELTERWEIGHT	Ernie Roderick; Wally Thom; Brian Curvis (2); Ralph Charles; Colin Jones; Lloyd Honeyghan; Kirkland Laing; Del Bryan; Geoff McCreesh; Derek Roche
L. MIDDLEWEIGHT	Maurice Hope; Jimmy Batten; Pat Thomas; Prince Rodney; Andy Till; Robert McCracken; Ryan Rhodes; Ensley Bingham
MIDDLEWEIGHT	Pat McAteer; Terry Downes; Johnny Pritchett; Bunny Sterling; Alan Minter; Kevin Finnegan; Roy Gumbs; Tony Sibson; Herol Graham; Neville Brown; Howard Eastman
S. MIDDLEWEIGHT	Sammy Storey; David Starie
L. HEAVYWEIGHT	Randy Turpin; Chic Calderwood; Chris Finnegan; Bunny Johnson; Tom Collins; Dennis Andries; Tony Wilson; Crawford Ashley
CRUISERWEIGHT	Johnny Nelson; Terry Dunstan; Bruce Scott
HEAVYWEIGHT	Henry Cooper (3); Horace Notice; Lennox Lewis; Julius Francis

Note: Walter McGowan and Charlie Magri, with one notch apiece, kept their belts under the three years/no available challengers' ruling, while Johnny King, with two notches, was awarded the belt on the grounds that the Second World War stopped him from making further defences. Incidentally, King and Nel Tarleton are the only men to have won both the NSC and BBBoC belts outright.

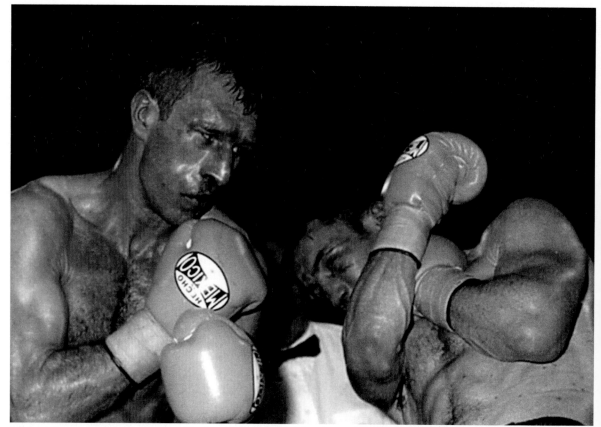

Michael Gomez (right) won the super-featherweight belt outright when outscoring Ian McLeod last December   Les Clark

172

British Champions Since Gloves, 1878-2001

The listings below show the tenure of all British champions at each weight since gloves (two ounces or more) were introduced to British rings under Queensberry Rules. Although Charley Davis (147 lbs) had beaten Ted Napper (140 lbs) with gloves in 1873, we start with Denny Harrington, who defeated George Rooke for both the English and world middleweight titles in London on 12 March 1878. We also make a point of ignoring competition winners, apart from Anthony Diamond who beat Dido Plumb for the middles title over 12 rounds, basically because full championship conditions or finish fights of three-minute rounds were not applied. Another point worth bearing in mind, is that prior to the 1880s there were only three weights – heavy, middle and light. Anything above 154 lbs, the middleweight limit, was classified a heavyweight contest, whereas below, say 133 lbs, was considered to be a lightweight bout. Therefore, to put things into current perspective, in many cases we have had to ascertain the actual poundage of fighters concerned and relate them to the modern weight classes. Another point worth remembering is that men born outside Britain who won international titles in this country, are not recorded for fear of added confusion and, although many of the champions or claimants listed before 1909 were no more than English titleholders, having fought for the 'championship of England', for our purposes they carry the 'British' label.

Prior to 1909, the year that the Lord Lonsdale Challenge Belt was introduced and weight classes subsequently standardised, poundages within divisions could vary quite substantially, thus enabling men fighting at different weights to claim the same 'title' at the same time. A brief history of the weight fluctuations between 1891 and 1909, shows:

Bantamweight   With the coming of gloves, the division did not really take off until Nunc Wallace established himself at 112 lbs on beating (small) Bill Goode after nine rounds in London on 12 March 1889. Later, with Wallace fighting above the weight, Billy Plimmer was generally recognised as the country's leading eight stoner, following victories over Charles Mansford and Jem Stevens, and became accepted as world champion when George Dixon, the number one in America's eyes, gradually increased his weight. In 1895, Pedlar Palmer took the British title at 112 lbs, but by 1900 he had developed into a 114 pounder. Between 1902 and 1904, Joe Bowker defended regularly at 116 lbs and in 1909 the NSC standardised the weight at 118 lbs, even though the USA continued for a short while to accept only 116 lbs.

Featherweight   Between 1886 and 1895, one of the most prestigious championship belts in this country was fought for at 126 lbs and, although George Dixon was recognised in the USA as world featherweight champion – gradually moving from 114 to 122 lbs – no major international contests took place in Britain during the above period at his weight. It was only in 1895, when Fred Johnson took the British title at 120 lbs, losing it to Ben Jordan two years later, that we came into line with the USA. Ben Jordan became an outstanding champion who, between 1898 and 1899, was seen by the NSC as world champion at 120 lbs. However, first Harry Greenfield, then Jabez White and Will Curley, continued to claim the 126 lbs version of the British title and it was only in 1900, when Jack Roberts beat Curley, that the weight limit was finally standardised at nine stone.

Lightweight   Outstanding champions often carried their weights as they grew in size. A perfect example of this was Dick Burge, the British lightweight champion from 1891-1901, who gradually increased from 134 to 144 lbs, while still maintaining his right to the title. It was not until 1902 that Jabez White brought the division into line with the USA. Later, both White, and then Goldswain, carried their weight up to 140 lbs and it was left to Johnny Summers to set the current limit of 135 lbs.

Welterweight   The presence of Dick Burge fighting from 134 to 144 lbs plus up until 1900, explains quite adequately why the welterweight division, although very popular in the USA, did not take off in this country until 1902. The championship was contested between 142 and 146 lbs in those days and was not really supported by the NSC, but by 1909 with their backing it finally became established at 147 lbs.

On 8 September 1970, Bunny Sterling became the first immigrant to win a British title under the ten-year residential ruling, while earlier, on 28 June 1948, Dick Turpin won the British middleweight title and, in doing so, became the first coloured fighter to win the title, thus breaking down the so-called 'colour bar'.

Note that the Lonsdale Belt notches (title bout wins) relate to NSC, 1909-1935, and BBBoC, 1936-2001.

Champions in **bold** are accorded national recognition.

*Undefeated champions (Does not include men who forfeited titles).

Title Holder	Lonsdale Belt Notches	Tenure	Title Holder	Lonsdale Belt Notches	Tenure	Title Holder	Lonsdale Belt Notches	Tenure
Flyweight (112 lbs)			**Percy Jones**	1	1914	**Joe Symonds**	1	1915-1916
Sid Smith		1911	Joe Symonds		1914	**Jimmy Wilde***	3	1916-1923
Sid Smith	1	1911-1913	**Tancy Lee**	1	1914-1915	**Elky Clark***	2	1924-1927
Bill Ladbury		1913-1914	Jimmy Wilde		1914-1915	**Johnny Hill***	1	1927-1929

173

Title Holder	Lonsdale Belt Notches	Tenure
Jackie Brown		1929-1930
Bert Kirby	1	1930-1931
Jackie Brown	3	1931-1935
Benny Lynch*	2	1935-1938
Jackie Paterson	4	1939-1948
Rinty Monaghan*	1	1948-1950
Terry Allen	1	1951-1952
Teddy Gardner*	1	1952
Terry Allen*	2	1952-1954
Dai Dower*	1	1955-1957
Frankie Jones	2	1957-1960
Johnny Caldwell*	1	1960-1961
Jackie Brown	1	1962-1963
Walter McGowan*	1	1963-1966
John McCluskey*	3	1967-1977
Charlie Magri*	1	1977-1981
Kelvin Smart	1	1982-1984
Hugh Russell*	3	1984-1985
Duke McKenzie*	2	1985-1986
Dave Boy McAuley*	1	1986-1988
Pat Clinton*	3	1988-1991
Robbie Regan	1	1991
Francis Ampofo	1	1991
Robbie Regan*	2	1991-1992
Francis Ampofo	3	1992-1996
Mickey Cantwell*	1	1996-1997
Ady Lewis*	3	1997-1998
Damaen Kelly	1	1999
Keith Knox	1	1999
Jason Booth	2	1999-

Bantamweight (118 lbs)

Title Holder	Lonsdale Belt Notches	Tenure
Nunc Wallace*		1889-1891
Billy Plimmer		1891-1895
Tom Gardner		1892
Willie Smith		1892-1896
Nunc Wallace		1893-1895
George Corfield		1893-1896
Pedlar Palmer		1895-1900
Billy Plimmer		1896-1898
Harry Ware		1899-1900
Harry Ware		1900-1902
Andrew Tokell		1901-1902
Jim Williams		1902
Andrew Tokell		1902
Harry Ware		1902
Joe Bowker		1902-1910
Owen Moran		1905-1907
Digger Stanley		1906-1910
Digger Stanley	2	1910-1913
Bill Beynon	1	1913
Digger Stanley	1	1913-1914
Curley Walker*	1	1914-1915
Joe Fox*	3	1915-1917
Tommy Noble	1	1918-1919
Walter Ross*	1	1919-1920
Jim Higgins	3	1920-1922
Tommy Harrison		1922-1923
Bugler Harry Lake	1	1923
Johnny Brown	3	1923-1928
Alf Pattenden	2	1928-1929
Johnny Brown		1928
Teddy Baldock		1928-1929
Teddy Baldock*	1	1929-1931
Dick Corbett	1	1931-1932
Johnny King	1	1932-1934
Dick Corbett*	1	1934
Johnny King	1+2	1935-1947

Title Holder	Lonsdale Belt Notches	Tenure
Jackie Paterson	2	1947-1949
Stan Rowan*	1	1949
Danny O'Sullivan	1	1949-1951
Peter Keenan	3	1951-1953
John Kelly	1	1953-1954
Peter Keenan	3	1954-1959
Freddie Gilroy*	4	1959-1963
Johnny Caldwell	1	1964-1965
Alan Rudkin	1	1965-1966
Walter McGowan	1	1966-1968
Alan Rudkin*	4	1968-1972
Johnny Clark*	1	1973-1974
Dave Needham	1	1974-1975
Paddy Maguire	1	1975-1977
Johnny Owen*	4	1977-1980
John Feeney	1	1981-1983
Hugh Russell	1	1983
Davy Larmour	1	1983
John Feeney	1	1983-1985
Ray Gilbody	2	1985-1987
Billy Hardy*	5	1987-1991
Joe Kelly	1	1992
Drew Docherty	4	1992-1997
Paul Lloyd	2	1997-1999
Noel Wilders*	2	1999-2000
Ady Lewis	1	2000
Tommy Waite	1	2000
Nicky Booth	2	2000-

S. Bantamweight (122 lbs)

Title Holder	Lonsdale Belt Notches	Tenure
Richie Wenton*	3	1994-1996
Michael Brodie*	3	1997-1999
Patrick Mullings	1	1999
Drew Docherty*	1	1999
Michael Alldis	3	1999-

Featherweight (126 lbs)

Title Holder	Lonsdale Belt Notches	Tenure
Bill Baxter		1884-1891
Harry Overton		1890-1891
Billy Reader		1891-1892
Fred Johnson		1891-1895
Harry Spurden		1892-1895
Jack Fitzpatrick		1895-1897
Fred Johnson		1895-1897
Harry Greenfield		1896-1899
Ben Jordan*		1897-1900
Jabez White		1899-1900
Will Curley		1900-1901
Jack Roberts		1901-1902
Will Curley		1902-1903
Ben Jordan*		1902-1905
Joe Bowker		1905
Johnny Summers		1906
Joe Bowker		1905-1906
Jim Driscoll		1906-1907
Spike Robson		1906-1907
Jim Driscoll*	3	1907-1913
Spike Robson		1907-1910
Ted Kid Lewis*	1	1913-1914
Llew Edwards*	1	1915-1917
Charlie Hardcastle	1	1917
Tancy Lee*	3	1917-1919
Mike Honeyman	2	1920-1921
Joe Fox*	1	1921-1922
George McKenzie	2	1924-1925
Johnny Curley	2	1925-1927
Johnny Cuthbert	1	1927-1928
Harry Corbett	1	1928-1929
Johnny Cuthbert	2	1929-1931
Nel Tarleton	1	1931-1932
Seaman Tommy Watson	2	1932-1934

Two of Britain's favourite featherweight champions, Sammy McCarthy (left) and Terry Spinks

Title Holder	Lonsdale Belt Notches	Tenure
Nel Tarleton	2	1934-1936
Johnny McGrory	1	1936-1938
Jim Spider Kelly	1	1938-1939
Johnny Cusick	1	1939-1940
Nel Tarleton*	3	1940-1947
Ronnie Clayton	6	1947-1954
Sammy McCarthy	1	1954-1955
Billy Spider Kelly	1	1955-1956
Charlie Hill	3	1956-1959
Bobby Neill	1	1959-1960
Terry Spinks	2	1960-1961
Howard Winstone*	7	1961-1969
Jimmy Revie	2	1969-1971
Evan Armstrong	2	1971-1972
Tommy Glencross	1	1972-1973
Evan Armstrong*	2	1973-1975
Vernon Sollas	1	1975-1977
Alan Richardson	2	1977-1978
Dave Needham	2	1978-1979
Pat Cowdell*	3	1979-1982
Steve Sims*	1	1982-1983
Barry McGuigan*	2	1983-1986
Robert Dickie	3	1986-1988
Peter Harris	1	1988
Paul Hodkinson*	3	1988-1990
Sean Murphy	2	1990-1991
Gary de Roux	1	1991
Colin McMillan*	3	1991-1992
John Davison*	1	1992-1993
Sean Murphy	1	1993
Duke McKenzie*	1	1993-1994
Billy Hardy*	1	1994
Michael Deveney	1	1995
Jonjo Irwin	2	1995-1996
Colin McMillan	1	1996-1997
Paul Ingle*	3	1997-1998
Jonjo Irwin*	2	1998-1999
Gary Thornhill	1	2000
Scott Harrison	1	2001-

S. Featherweight (130 lbs)

Title Holder	Lonsdale Belt Notches	Tenure
Jimmy Anderson*	3	1968-1970
John Doherty	1	1986
Pat Cowdell	1	1986
Najib Daho	1	1986-1987
Pat Cowdell	1	1987-1988
Floyd Havard	1	1988-1989
John Doherty	1	1989-1990
Joey Jacobs	1	1990
Hugh Forde	1	1990
Kevin Pritchard	1	1990-1991
Robert Dickie	1	1991
Sugar Gibiliru	1	1991
John Doherty	1	1991-1992
Michael Armstrong	1	1992
Neil Haddock	2	1992-1994
Floyd Havard*	3	1994-1995
P. J. Gallagher	2	1996-1997
Charles Shepherd	3	1997-1999
Michael Gomez	4	1999-

Lightweight (135 lbs)

Title Holder	Lonsdale Belt Notches	Tenure
Dick Burge		1891-1897
Harry Nickless		1891-1894
Tom Causer		1894-1897
Tom Causer		1897
Dick Burge*		1897-1901
Jabez White		1902-1906
Jack Goldswain		1906-1908
Johnny Summers		1908-1909
Freddie Welsh	1	1909-1911
Matt Wells	1	1911-1912
Freddie Welsh*	1	1912-1919
Bob Marriott*	1	1919-1920
Ernie Rice	1	1921-1922
Seaman Nobby Hall		1922-1923
Harry Mason		1923-1924
Ernie Izzard	2	1924-1925
Harry Mason		1924-1925
Harry Mason*	1	1925-1928
Sam Steward		1928-1929
Fred Webster		1929-1930
Al Foreman*	1	1930-1932
Johnny Cuthbert		1932-1934
Harry Mizler		1934
Jackie Kid Berg		1934-1936
Jimmy Walsh	1	1936-1938
Dave Crowley	1	1938
Eric Boon	3	1938-1944
Ronnie James*	1	1944-1947
Billy Thompson	3	1947-1951
Tommy McGovern	1	1951-1952
Frank Johnson	1	1952-1953
Joe Lucy	1	1953-1955
Frank Johnson	1	1955-1956
Joe Lucy	2	1956-1957
Dave Charnley*	3	1957-1965
Maurice Cullen	4	1965-1968
Ken Buchanan	2	1968-1971
Willie Reilly*	1	1972
Jim Watt	1	1972-1973
Ken Buchanan*	1	1973-1974
Jim Watt*	2	1975-1977
Charlie Nash*	1	1978-1979
Ray Cattouse	2	1980-1982
George Feeney*	3	1982-1985
Tony Willis	3	1985-1987
Alex Dickson	1	1987-1988
Steve Boyle	2	1988-1990
Carl Crook	5	1990-1992
Billy Schwer	1	1992-1993
Paul Burke	1	1993
Billy Schwer*	2	1993-1995
Michael Ayers*	5	1995-1997
Wayne Rigby	2	1998
Bobby Vanzie	4	1998-

L. Welterweight (140 lbs)

Title Holder	Lonsdale Belt Notches	Tenure
Des Rea	1	1968-1969
Vic Andreetti*	2	1969-1970
Des Morrison	1	1973-1974
Pat McCormack	1	1974
Joey Singleton	3	1974-1976
Dave Boy Green*	1	1976-1977
Colin Power*	2	1977-1978
Clinton McKenzie	1	1978-1979
Colin Power	1	1979
Clinton McKenzie	5	1979-1984
Terry Marsh*	1	1984-1986
Tony Laing*	1	1986
Tony McKenzie	2	1986-1987
Lloyd Christie	3	1987-1989
Clinton McKenzie*	1	1989
Pat Barrett*	2	1989-1990
Tony Ekubia	1	1990-1991
Andy Holligan	3	1991-1994
Ross Hale	4	1994-1995
Paul Ryan	1	1995-1996
Andy Holligan*	1	1996-1997
Mark Winters	2	1997-1998
Jason Rowland*	2	1998-2000
Richard Hatton*	1	2000-2001

Welterweight (147 lbs)

Title Holder	Lonsdale Belt Notches	Tenure
Charlie Allum		1903-1904
Charlie Knock		1904-1906
Curly Watson		1906-1910
Young Joseph		1908-1910
Young Joseph	1	1910-1911
Arthur Evernden		1911-1912
Johnny Summers		1912
Johnny Summers	2	1912-1914
Tom McCormick		1914
Matt Wells		1914
Johnny Basham	3	1914-1920
Matt Wells		1914-1919
Ted Kid Lewis		1920-1924
Tommy Milligan*		1924-1925
Hamilton Johnny Brown		1925
Harry Mason		1925-1926
Jack Hood*	3	1926-1934
Harry Mason		1934
Pat Butler*		1934-1936
Dave McCleave		1936
Jake Kilrain	1	1936-1939
Ernie Roderick	5	1939-1948
Henry Hall	1	1948-1949
Eddie Thomas	2	1949-1951
Wally Thom	1	1951-1952
Cliff Curvis*	1	1952-1953
Wally Thom	2	1953-1956
Peter Waterman*	2	1956-1958
Tommy Molloy	2	1958-1960
Wally Swift	1	1960
Brian Curvis*	7	1960-1966
Johnny Cooke	2	1967-1968
Ralph Charles*	3	1968-1972
Bobby Arthur	1	1972-1973
John H. Stracey*	1	1973-1975
Pat Thomas	2	1975-1976
Henry Rhiney	2	1976-1979
Kirkland Laing	1	1979-1980
Colin Jones*	3	1980-1982
Lloyd Honeyghan*	2	1983-1985
Kostas Petrou	1	1985
Sylvester Mittee	1	1985
Lloyd Honeyghan*	1	1985-1986
Kirkland Laing	4	1987-1991
Del Bryan	2	1991-1992
Gary Jacobs*	2	1992-1993
Del Bryan	4	1993-1995
Chris Saunders	1	1995-1996
Kevin Lueshing	1	1996-1997
Geoff McCreesh*	4	1997-1999
Derek Roche	3	1999-2000
Harry Dhami	3	2000-

L. Middleweight (154 lbs)

Title Holder	Lonsdale Belt Notches	Tenure
Larry Paul	2	1973-1974
Maurice Hope*	3	1974-1977
Jimmy Batten	3	1977-1979
Pat Thomas	3	1979-1981
Herol Graham*	2	1981-1983
Prince Rodney*	1	1983-1984
Jimmy Cable	2	1984-1985
Prince Rodney	2	1985-1986
Chris Pyatt*	1	1986
Lloyd Hibbert*	1	1987
Gary Cooper	1	1988
Gary Stretch	2	1988-1990

Title Holder	Lonsdale Belt Notches	Tenure
Wally Swift Jnr	2	1991-1992
Andy Till	3	1992-1994
Robert McCracken*	3	1994-1995
Ensley Bingham*	2	1996
Ryan Rhodes*	3	1996-1997
Ensley Bingham	3	1997-1999
Wayne Alexander	1	2000-

Middleweight (160 lbs)

Title Holder	Lonsdale Belt Notches	Tenure
Denny Harrington		1876-1880
William Sheriff*		1880-1883
Bill Goode		1887-1890
Toff Wall*		1890
Ted Pritchard		1890-1895
Ted White		1893-1895
Ted White*		1895-1896
Anthony Diamond*		1898
Dick Burge*		1898-1900
Jack Palmer		1902-1903
Charlie Allum		1905-1906
Pat O'Keefe		1906
Tom Thomas	1	1906-1910
Jim Sullivan	1	1910-1912
Jack Harrison*	1	1912-1913
Pat O'Keefe	2	1914-1916
Bandsman Jack Blake	1	1916-1918
Pat O'Keefe*	1	1918-1919
Ted Kid Lewis		1920-1921
Tom Gummer	1	1920-1921
Gus Platts		1921
Johnny Basham		1921
Ted Kid Lewis	2	1921-1923
Johnny Basham		1921
Roland Todd		1923-1925
Roland Todd		1925-1927
Tommy Milligan	1	1926-1928
Frank Moody		1927-1928
Alex Ireland		1928-1929
Len Harvey	5	1929-1933
Jock McAvoy	3+2	1933-1944
Ernie Roderick	1	1945-1946
Vince Hawkins	1	1946-1948
Dick Turpin	2	1948-1950
Albert Finch	1	1950
Randy Turpin*	1	1950-1954
Johnny Sullivan	1	1954-1955
Pat McAteer*	3	1955-1958
Terry Downes	1	1958-1959
John Cowboy McCormack	1	1959
Terry Downes	2	1959-1962
George Aldridge	1	1962-1963
Mick Leahy	1	1963-1964
Wally Swift	1	1964-1965
Johnny Pritchett*	4	1965-1969
Les McAteer	1	1969-1970
Mark Rowe	1	1970
Bunny Sterling	4	1970-1974
Kevin Finnegan*	1	1974
Bunny Sterling*	1	1975
Alan Minter	3	1975-1977
Kevin Finnegan	1	1977
Alan Minter*	1	1977-1978
Tony Sibson	1	1979
Kevin Finnegan*	1	1979-1980
Roy Gumbs	3	1981-1983
Mark Kaylor	1	1983-1984
Tony Sibson*	1	1984
Herol Graham*	1	1985-1986
Brian Anderson	1	1986-1987
Tony Sibson*	1	1987-1988
Herol Graham	4	1988-1992
Frank Grant	2	1992-1993
Neville Brown	6	1993-1998
Glenn Catley*	1	1998
Howard Eastman	3	1998-

S. Middleweight (168 lbs)

Title Holder	Lonsdale Belt Notches	Tenure
Sammy Storey	2	1989-1990
James Cook*	1	1990-1991
Fidel Castro	2	1991-1992
Henry Wharton*	1	1992-1993
James Cook	1	1993-1994
Cornelius Carr*	1	1994
Ali Forbes	1	1995
Sammy Storey*	1	1995
Joe Calzaghe*	2	1995-1997
David Starie	1	1997
Dean Francis*	2	1997-1998
David Starie	4	1998-

L. Heavyweight (175lbs)

Title Holder	Lonsdale Belt Notches	Tenure
Dennis Haugh		1913-1914
Dick Smith	2	1914-1916
Harry Reeve*	1	1916-1917
Dick Smith	1	1918-1919
Boy McCormick*	1	1919-1921
Jack Bloomfield*	1	1922-1924
Tom Berry	1	1925-1927
Gipsy Daniels*	1	1927
Frank Moody	1	1927-1929
Harry Crossley	1	1929-1932
Jack Petersen*	1	1932
Len Harvey*	1	1933-1934
Eddie Phillips		1935-1937
Jock McAvoy	1	1937-1938
Len Harvey	2	1938-1942
Freddie Mills*	1	1942-1950
Don Cockell	2	1950-1952
Randy Turpin*	1	1952
Dennis Powell	1	1953
Alex Buxton	2	1953-1955
Randy Turpin*	1	1955
Ron Barton*	1	1956
Randy Turpin*	2	1956-1958
Chic Calderwood	3	1960-1963
Chic Calderwood*	1	1964-1966
Young John McCormack	2	1967-1969
Eddie Avoth	2	1969-1971
Chris Finnegan	2	1971-1973
John Conteh*	2	1973-1974
Johnny Frankham	1	1975
Chris Finnegan*	1	1975-1976
Tim Wood	1	1976-1977
Bunny Johnson*	3	1977-1981
Tom Collins	3	1982-1984
Dennis Andries*	5	1984-1986
Tom Collins*	1	1987
Tony Wilson	3	1987-1989
Tom Collins*	1	1989-1990
Steve McCarthy	1	1990-1991
Crawford Ashley*	3	1991-1992
Maurice Core*	2	1992-1994
Crawford Ashley	3	1994-1999
Clinton Woods*	1	1999-2000
Neil Simpson	2	2000-

Cruiserweight (190 lbs)

Title Holder	Lonsdale Belt Notches	Tenure
Sam Reeson*	1	1985-1986
Andy Straughn	1	1986-1987
Roy Smith	1	1987
Tee Jay	1	1987-1988
Glenn McCrory*	2	1988
Andy Straughn	1	1988-1989
Johnny Nelson*	3	1989-1991
Derek Angol*	2	1991-1992
Carl Thompson*	1	1992-1994
Dennis Andries	1	1995
Terry Dunstan*	3	1995-1996
Johnny Nelson*	1	1996-1998
Bruce Scott	1	1998-1999
Carl Thompson*	1	1999-2000
Bruce Scott	2	2000-

Heavyweight (190 lbs +)

Title Holder	Lonsdale Belt Notches	Tenure
Tom Allen*		1878-1882
Charlie Mitchell*		1882-1894
Jem Smith		1889-1891
Ted Pritchard		1891-1895
Jem Smith		1895-1896
George Chrisp		1901
Jack Scales		1901-1902
Jack Palmer		1903-1906
Gunner Moir		1906-1909
Iron Hague		1909-1910
P.O. Curran		1910-1911
Iron Hague		1910-1911
Bombardier Billy Wells	3	1911-1919
Joe Beckett		1919
Frank Goddard		1919
Joe Beckett*	1	1919-1923
Frank Goddard		1923-1926
Phil Scott*		1926-1931
Reggie Meen		1931-1932
Jack Petersen	3	1932-1933
Len Harvey		1933-1934
Jack Petersen		1934-1936
Ben Foord		1936-1937
Tommy Farr*	1	1937-1938
Len Harvey*	1	1938-1942
Jack London	1	1944-1945
Bruce Woodcock	2	1945-1950
Jack Gardner	1	1950-1952
Johnny Williams	1	1952-1953
Don Cockell*	1	1953-1956
Joe Erskine	2	1956-1958
Brian London	1	1958-1959
Henry Cooper*	9	1959-1969
Jack Bodell	1	1969-1970
Henry Cooper	1	1970-1971
Joe Bugner	1	1971
Jack Bodell	1	1971-1972
Danny McAlinden	1	1972-1975
Bunny Johnson	1	1975
Richard Dunn	2	1975-1976
Joe Bugner*	1	1976-1977
John L. Gardner*	2	1978-1980
Gordon Ferris	1	1981
Neville Meade	1	1981-1983
David Pearce*	1	1983-1985
Hughroy Currie	1	1985-1986
Horace Notice*	4	1986-1988
Gary Mason	2	1989-1991
Lennox Lewis*	3	1991-1993
Herbie Hide*	1	1993-1994
James Oyebola	1	1994-1995
Scott Welch*	1	1995-1996
Julius Francis	4	1997-2000
Mike Holden*	1	2000
Danny Williams	1	2000-

Retired or Inactive Post-War British Champions: Career Summary

Includes all British champions, along with British boxers who have won major international titles since 1945, who had retired by July 2000 or have been inactive since that date. The section does not include champions still active (for their records see under Active British-Based Boxers), while undefeated champions are those who relinquished their titles, not forfeited them.

George Aldridge British Middleweight Champion, 1962-1963. *Born* 01.02.36. *From* Market Harborough. *Pro Career* 1956-1963 (52 contests, won 36, drew 2, lost 14).

Terry Allen British Flyweight Champion, 1951-1952. Undefeated British Flyweight Champion, 1952-1954. European and World Flyweight Champion, 1950. *From* Islington. Birthname - Edward Govier. *Deceased* 1987. *Pro Career* 1942-1954 (74 contests, won 60, drew 1, lost 13).

Brian Anderson British Middleweight Champion, 1986-1987. *Born* 09.07.61. *From* Sheffield. *Pro Career* 1980-1987 (39 contests, won 27, drew 3, lost 9).

Jimmy Anderson Undefeated British S. Featherweight Champion, 1968-1970. *Born* 01.10.42. *From* Waltham Cross. *Pro Career* 1964-1971 (37 contests, won 27, drew 1, lost 9).

Vic Andreetti Undefeated British L. Welterweight Champion, 1969-1970. *Born* 29.01.42. *From* Hoxton. *Pro Career* 1961-1969 (67 contests, won 51, drew 3, lost 13).

Dennis Andries Undefeated British L. Heavyweight Champion, 1984-86. World L. Heavyweight Champion (WBC version), 1986-1987, 1989, and 1990-1991. British Cruiserweight Champion, 1995. *Born* Guyana 05.11.53. *From* Hackney. *Pro Career* 1978-1996 (65 contests, won 49, drew 2, lost 14).

Derek Angol Undefeated British Cruiserweight Champion, 1991-1992. Undefeated Commonwealth Cruiserweight Champion, 1989-1993. *Born* 28.11.64. *From* Camberwell. *Pro Career* 1986-1996 (31 contests, won 28, lost 3).

Evan Armstrong British Featherweight Champion, 1971-1972. Undefeated British Featherweight Champion, 1973-1975. Commonwealth Featherweight Champion, 1974. *Born* 15.02.43. *From* Ayr. *Pro Career* 1963-1974 (54 contests, won 39, drew 1, lost 14).

Michael Armstrong British S. Featherweight Champion, 1992. *Born* 18.12.68. *From* Moston. Birthname - Morris. *Pro Career* 1987-1994 (26 contests, won 18, drew 1, lost 7).

Bobby Arthur British Welterweight Champion, 1972-1973. *Born* 25.07.47. *From* Coventry. *Pro Career* 1967-1976 (41 contests, won 26, lost 15).

Eddie Avoth British L. Heavyweight Champion, 1969-1971. Commonwealth L. Heavyweight Champion, 1970-1971. *Born* 02.05.45. *From* Cardiff. *Pro Career* 1963-1972 (53 contests, won 44, lost 9).

Pat Barrett Undefeated British L. Welterweight Champion, 1989-1990. European L. Welterweight Champion, 1990-1992. *Born* 22.07.67. *From* Manchester. *Pro Career* 1987-1994 (42 contests, won 37, drew 1, lost 4).

Ron Barton Undefeated British L. Heavyweight Champion, 1956. *Born* 25.02.33. *From* West Ham. *Pro Career* 1954-1961 (31 contests, won 26, lost 5).

Jimmy Batten British L. Middleweight Champion, 1977-1979. *Born* 07.11.55. *From* Millwall. *Pro Career* 1974-1983 (49 contests, won 40, lost 9).

Nigel Benn Commonwealth Middleweight Champion, 1988-1989. World Middleweight Champion (WBO version), 1990. World S. Middleweight Champion (WBC version), 1992-1996. *Born* 22.01.64. *From* Ilford. *Pro Career* 1987-1996 (48 contests, won 42, drew 1, lost 5).

Ensley Bingham Undefeated British L. Middleweight Champion, 1996. British L. Middleweight Champion, 1997-1999. *Born* 27.05.63. *From* Manchester. *Pro Career* 1986-1999 (28 contests, won 20, lost 8).

Jack Bodell British Heavyweight Champion, 1969-1970 and 1971-1972. Commonwealth Heavyweight Champion, 1971-1972. European Heavyweight Champion, 1971. *Born* 11.08.40. *From* Swadlincote. *Pro Career* 1962-1972 (71 contests, won 58, lost 13).

Steve Boyle British Lightweight Champion, 1988-1990. *Born* 28.11.62. *From* Glasgow. *Pro Career* 1983-1993 (33 contests, won 25, drew 2, lost 6).

Cornelius Boza-Edwards Undefeated European S. Featherweight Champion, 1982. World S. Featherweight Champion, 1981 (WBC version). *Born* Uganda, 27.05.56. *From* London. *Pro Career* 1976-1987 (53 contests, won 45, drew 1, lost 7).

Jim Brady British Empire Bantamweight Championship Claimant, 1941-1945. *From* Dundee. *Deceased* 1980. *Pro Career* 1932-1947 (169 contests, won 104, drew 15, lost 50).

Jackie Brown British and British Empire Flyweight Champion, 1962-1963. *Born* 02.03.35. *From* Edinburgh. *Pro Career* 1958-1966 (44 contests, won 32, drew 1, lost 10, no contest 1).

Neville Brown British Middleweight Champion, 1993-1998. *Born* 26.02.66. *From* Burton. *Pro Career* 1989-2000 (40 contests, won 32, lost 8).

Frank Bruno Undefeated European Heavyweight Champion, 1985-1986. World Heavyweight Champion (WBC version), 1995-96. *Born* 16.11.61. *From* Wandsworth. *Pro Career* 1982-1996 (45 contests, won 40, lost 5).

Del Bryan British Welterweight Champion, 1991-1992 and 1993-1995. *Born* 16.04.1967. *From* Birmingham. *Pro Career* 1986-1998 (52 contests, won 32, drew 1, lost 19).

Ken Buchanan Undefeated British Lightweight Champion, 1968-1971, and 1973-1974. Undefeated European Lightweight Champion, 1974-1975. World Lightweight Champion, 1970-1971. World Lightweight Champion, (WBA version), 1971-1972. *Born* 28.06.45. *From* Edinburgh. *Pro Career* 1965-1982 (69 contests, won 61, lost 8).

Joe Bugner British, Commonwealth and European Heavyweight Champion, 1971. Undefeated European Heavyweight Champion, 1972-1975. European Heavyweight Champion, 1976-1977. Undefeated British and Commonwealth Heavyweight Champion, 1976-1977. *Born* Hungary, 13.03.50. *From* Bedford. *Pro Career* 1967-1999 (83 contests, won 69, drew 1, lost 13).

Paul Burke British and Commonwealth Lightweight Champion, 1993. Commonwealth L. Welterweight Champion, 1997 and 1998-1999. *Born* 25.07.66. *From* Preston. *Pro Career* 1987-1999 (43 contests, won 28, drew 2, lost 13).

Alex Buxton British L. Heavyweight Champion, 1953-1955. *Born* 10.05.25. *From* Watford. *Pro Career* 1942-1963 (125 contests, won 78, drew 4, lost 43).

Jimmy Cable British L. Middleweight Champion, 1984-1985. European L. Middleweight Champion, 1984. *Born* 07.09.57. *From* Crawley. *Pro Career* 1980-1988 (41 contests, won 30, drew 2, lost 9).

Chic Calderwood British and British Empire L. Heavyweight Champion, 1960-1963. Undefeated British L. Heavyweight Champion, 1964-1966. *Born* 09.01.37. *From* Craigneuk. Birthname - Charles Calderwood. *Deceased* 1966. *Pro Career* 1957-1966 (55 contests, won 44, drew 1, lost 9, no contest 1).

Johnny Caldwell Undefeated British Flyweight Champion, 1960-1961. British and British Empire Bantamweight Champion, 1964-1965. World Bantamweight Champion (EBU version), 1961-1962. *Born* 07.05.38. *From* Belfast. *Pro Career* 1958-1965 (35 contests, won 29, drew 1, lost 5).

Mickey Cantwell Undefeated British Flyweight Champion, 1996-1997. *Born* 23.11.64. *From* Eltham. *Pro Career* 1991-2000 (21 contests, won 14, drew 1, lost 6).

Fidel Castro British S. Middleweight Champion, 1991-1992. *Born* 17.04.63. *From* Nottingham. Birthname - Smith. *Pro Career* 1987-1995 (30 contests, won 22, lost 8).

Ray Cattouse British Lightweight Champion, 1980-1982. *Born* 24.07.52. *From* Balham. *Pro Career* 1975-1983 (31 contests, won 26, drew 3, lost 2).

Ralph Charles Undefeated British and British Empire/Commonwealth Welterweight Champion, 1968-1972. European Welterweight Champion, 1970-1971. *Born* 05.02.43. *From* West Ham. *Pro Career* 1963-1972 (43 contests, won 39, lost 4).

Dave Charnley Undefeated British Lightweight Champion, 1957-1965. British Empire Lightweight Champion, 1959-1962. European Lightweight Champion, 1960-1963. *Born* 10.10.35. *From* Dartford. *Pro Career* 1954-1964 (61 contests, won 48, drew 1, lost 12).

Lloyd Christie British L. Welterweight Champion, 1987-1989. *Born* 28.02.62. *From* Wolverhampton. *Pro Career* 1981-1989 (46 contests, won 24, drew 1, lost 21).

Johnny Clark Undefeated British and European Bantamweight Champion, 1973-1974. *Born* 10.09.47. *From* Walworth. *Pro Career* 1966-1974 (43 contests, won 39, drew 1, lost 3).

Ronnie Clayton British Featherweight Champion, 1947-1954. British Empire Featherweight Championship Claimant, 1947-1951. European Featherweight Champion, 1947-1948. *Born* 09.02.23. *From* Blackpool. *Deceased* 1999. *Pro Career* 1941-1954 (113 contests, won 79, drew 8, lost 26).

Pat Clinton Undefeated British Flyweight Champion, 1988-1991. Undefeated European Flyweight Champion, 1990-1991. World Flyweight Champion (WBO version), 1992-1993. *Born* 04.04.64. *From* Croy. *Pro Career* 1985-1991 (23 contests, won 20, lost 3).

Ray Close Undefeated European S. Middleweight Champion, 1993. *Born* 20.01.69. *From* Belfast. *Pro Career* 1988-1997 (29 contests, won 25, drew 1, lost 3).

Don Cockell British L. Heavyweight Champion, 1950-1952. Undefeated European L. Heavyweight Champion, 1951-1952. Undefeated British Heavyweight Champion, 1953-1956. British Empire Heavyweight Championship Claimant, 1953-1954. Undefeated British Empire Heavyweight Champion, 1954-1956. *Born* 22.09.28. *From* Battersea. *Deceased* 1983. *Pro Career* 1946-1956 (80 contests, won 65, drew 1, lost 14).

Steve Collins Undefeated World Middleweight Champion (WBO version), 1994-1995. Undefeated World S. Middleweight Champion (WBO version), 1995-1997. *Born* 21.07.64. *From* Dublin. *Pro Career* 1986-1997 (39 contests, won 36, lost 3).

Tom Collins British L. Heavyweight Champion, 1982-1984. Undefeated British L. Heavyweight Champion, 1987 and 1989-1990. European L. Heavyweight Champion, 1987-1988 and 1990-1991. *Born* Curacao, 01.07.55. *From* Leeds. *Pro Career* 1977-1993 (50 contests, won 26, drew 2, lost 22).

John Conteh Undefeated British, Commonwealth and European L. Heavyweight Champion, 1973-1974. World L. Heavyweight Champion (WBC version), 1974-1977. *Born* 27.05.51. *From* Liverpool. *Pro Career* 1971-1980 (39 contests, won 34, drew 1, lost 4).

James Cook Undefeated British S. Middleweight Champion, 1990-1991. British S. Middleweight Champion, 1993-1994. European S. Middleweight Champion, 1991-1992. *Born* Jamaica, 17.05.59. *From* Peckham. *Pro Career* 1982-1994 (35 contests, won 25, lost 10).

Johnny Cooke British and British Empire Welterweight Champion, 1967-1968. *Born* 17.12.34. *From* Bootle. *Pro Career* 1960-1971 (93 contests, won 52, drew 7, lost 34).

Gary Cooper British L. Middleweight Champion, 1988. *Born* 31.05.57. *From* Lymington. *Pro Career* 1978-1989 (27 contests, won 16, drew 2, lost 9).

Henry Cooper Undefeated British Heavyweight Champion, 1959-1969. British Heavyweight Champion, 1970-1971. British Empire/Commonwealth Heavyweight Champion, 1959-1971. Undefeated European Heavyweight Champion, 1964 and 1968-1969. European Heavyweight Champion, 1970-1971. *Born* 03.05.34. *From* Bellingham. *Pro Career* 1954-1971 (55 contests, won 40, drew 1, lost 14).

Maurice Core Undefeated British L. Heavyweight Champion, 1992-1994. *Born* 22.06.65. *From* Manchester. Birthname - Maurice Coore. *Pro Career* 1990-1996 (18 contests, won 15, drew 1, lost 2).

Pat Cowdell Undefeated British Featherweight Champion, 1979-1982. Undefeated European Featherweight Champion, 1982-1983. British S. Featherweight Champion, 1986 and 1987-1988. European S. Featherweight Champion, 1984-1985. *Born* 18.08.53. *From* Warley. *Pro Career* 1977-1988 (42 contests, won 36, lost 6).

Carl Crook British and Commonwealth Lightweight Champion, 1990-1992. *Born* 10.11.63. *From* Chorley. *Pro Career* 1985-1993 (31 contests, won 26, drew 1, lost 4).

Maurice Cullen British Lightweight Champion, 1965-1968. *Born* 30.12.37. *From* Shotton. *Pro Career* 1959-1970 (55 contests, won 45, drew 2, lost 8).

Hughroy Currie British Heavyweight Champion, 1985-1986. *Born* Jamaica, 09.02.59. *From* Catford. *Pro Career* 1981-1989 (29 contests, won 17, drew 1, lost 11).

Brian Curvis Undefeated British and British Empire Welterweight Champion, 1960-1966. *Born* 14.08.37. *From* Swansea. Birthname - Brian Nancurvis. *Pro Career* 1959-1966 (41 contests, won 37, lost 4).

Cliff Curvis Undefeated British Welterweight Champion, 1952-1953. British Empire Welterweight Championship Claimant, 1952. *Born* 02.11.27. *From* Swansea. Birthname - Cliff Nancurvis. *Pro Career* 1944-1953 (55 contests, won 42, drew 1, lost 12).

Najib Daho British S. Featherweight Champion, 1986-1987. Commonwealth Lightweight Champion, 1989-1990. *Born* Morocco, 13.01.59. *From* Manchester. *Deceased* 1993. *Pro Career* 1977-1991 (60 contests, won 34, drew 1, lost 25).

John Davison Undefeated British Featherweight Champion, 1992-1993. *Born* 30.09.58. *From* Newcastle. *Pro Career* 1988-1993 (20 contests, won 15, lost 5).

Gary DeRoux British Featherweight Champion, 1991. *Born* 04.11.62. *From* Peterborough. *Pro Career* 1986-1993 (22 contests, won 13, drew 1, lost 8).

Mike Deveney British Featherweight Champion, 1995. *Born* 14.12.65. *From* Paisley. *Pro Career* 1991-1998 (42 contests, won 22, drew 1, lost 19).

Robert Dickie British Featherweight Champion, 1986-1988. British S. Featherweight Champion, 1991. *Born* 23.06.64. *From* Swansea. *Pro Career* 1983-1993 (28 contests, won 22, drew 2, lost 4).

Alex Dickson British Lightweight Champion, 1987-1988. *Born* 01.10.62. *From* Larkhall. *Pro Career* 1985-1989 (22 contests, won 18, drew 1, lost 3).

John Doherty British S. Featherweight Champion, 1986, 1989-1990, and 1991-1992. *Born* 17.07.62. *From* Bradford. *Pro Career* 1982-1992 (39 contests, won 28, drew 3, lost 8).

Pat Doherty Commonwealth Lightweight Champion, 1989. *Born* 12.04.62. *From* Croydon. *Pro Career* 1981-1989 (32 contests, won 18, drew 3, lost 11).

Dai Dower Undefeated British Flyweight Champion, 1955-1957. Undefeated British Empire Flyweight Champion, 1954-1957. European Flyweight Champion, 1955. *Born* 26.06.33. *From* Abercynon. *Pro Career* 1953-1958 (37 contests, won 34, lost 3).

Terry Downes British Middleweight Champion, 1958-1959 and 1959-1962. World Middleweight Champion (NY/EBU version), 1961-1962. *Born* 09.05.36. *From* Paddington. *Pro Career* 1957-1964 (44 contests, won 35, lost 9).

Richard Dunn British and Commonwealth Heavyweight Champion, 1975-1976. European Heavyweight Champion, 1976. *Born* 19.01.45. *From* Bradford. *Pro Career* 1969-1977 (45 contests, won 33, lost 12).

Terry Dunstan Undefeated British Cruiserweight Champion, 1995-1996. Undefeated European Cruiserweight Champion, 1998. *Born* 21.10.68. *From* Vauxhall. *Pro Career* 1992-1999 (21 contests, won 19, lost 2).

Tony Ekubia British L. Welterweight Champion, 1990-1991. Commonwealth L. Welterweight Champion, 1989-1991. *Born* Nigeria, 06.03.60. *From* Manchester. *Pro Career* 1986-1993 (25 contests, won 21, lost 4).

Joe Erskine British Heavyweight Champion, 1956-1958. British Empire Heavyweight Champion, 1957-1958. *Born* 26.01.34. *From* Cardiff. *Deceased* 1990. *Pro Career* 1954-1964 (54 contests, won 45, drew 1, lost 8).

Chris Eubank Undefeated WBO Middleweight Champion, 1990-1991. WBO S. Middleweight Title, 1991-1995. *Born* 08.08.1966. *From* Brighton. *Pro Career* 1985-1998 (52 contests, won 45, drew 2, lost 5).

George Feeney Undefeated British Lightweight Champion, 1982-1985. *Born* 09.02.57. *From* West Hartlepool. *Pro Career* 1977-1984 (29 contests, won 19, lost 10).

John Feeney British Bantamweight Champion, 1981-1983 and 1983-1985. *Born* 15.05.58. *From* West Hartlepool. *Pro Career* 1977-1987 (48 contests, won 35, lost 13).

Gordon Ferris British Heavyweight Champion, 1981. *Born* 21.11.52. *From* Enniskillen. *Pro Career* 1977-1982 (26 contests, won 20, lost 6).

Darren Fifield Commonwealth Flyweight Champion, 1993-1994. *Born* 09.10.69. *From* Henley. *Pro Career* 1992-1996 (13 contests, won 7, drew 2, lost 4).

Albert Finch British Middleweight Champion, 1950. *Born* 16.05.26. *From* Croydon. *Pro Career* 1945-1958 (103 contests, won 72, drew 9, lost 21, no contest 1).

Chris Finnegan British L. Heavyweight Champion, 1971-1973. Undefeated British L. Heavyweight Champion, 1975-1976. Commonwealth L. Heavyweight Champion, 1971-1973. European L. Heavyweight Champion, 1972. *Born* 05.06.44. *From* Iver. *Pro Career* 1968-1975 (37 contests, won 29, drew 1, lost 7).

Kevin Finnegan British Middleweight Champion, 1977. Undefeated British Middleweight Champion, 1974 and 1979-1980. European Middleweight Champion, 1974-1975 and 1980. *Born* 18.04.48. *From* Iver. *Pro Career* 1970-1980 (47 contests, won 35, drew 1, lost 11).

Hugh Forde British S. Featherweight Champion, 1990. Commonwealth S. Featherweight Champion, 1991. *Born* 07.05.64. *From* Birmingham. *Pro Career* 1986-1995 (31 contests, won 24, lost 7).

Steve Foster Commonwealth L. Middleweight Champion, 1996-1997. *Born* 28.12.60. *From* Salford. *Pro Career* 1981-1999 (39 contests, won 20, drew 2, lost 17).

Dean Francis Undefeated British and European S. Middleweight

Champion, 1997-1998. *Born* 23.01.1974. *From* Basingstoke. *Pro Career* 1994-1998 (23 contests, won 21, lost 2).

Johnny Frankham British L. Heavyweight Champion, 1975. *Born* 06.06.48. *From* Reading. *Pro Career* 1970-1976 (40 contests, won 28, drew 1, lost 11).

Jack Gardner British Heavyweight Champion, 1950-1952. British Empire Heavyweight Championship Claimant, 1950-1952. European Heavyweight Champion, 1951. *Born* 06.11.26. *From* Market Harborough. *Deceased* 1978. *Pro Career* 1948-1956 (34 contests, won 28, lost 6).

John L. Gardner Undefeated British Heavyweight Champion, 1978-1980. Undefeated Commonwealth Heavyweight Champion, 1978-1981. Undefeated European Heavyweight Champion, 1980-1981. *Born* 19.03.53. *From* Hackney. *Pro Career* 1973-1983 (39 contests, won 35, lost 4).

Teddy Gardner Undefeated British and European Flyweight Champion, 1952. British Empire Flyweight Championship Claimant, 1952. *Born* 27.01.22. *From* West Hartlepool. *Deceased* 1977. *Pro Career* 1938-1952 (66 contests, won 55, drew 3, lost 8).

Sugar Gibiliru British S. Featherweight Champion, 1991. *Born* 13.07.66. *From* Liverpool. *Pro Career* 1984-1995 (55 contests, won 16, drew 7, lost 32).

Ray Gilbody British Bantamweight Champion, 1985-1987. *Born* 21.03.60. *From* Warrington. *Pro Career* 1983-1987 (16 contests, won 11, drew 1, lost 4).

Freddie Gilroy Undefeated British and British Empire Bantamweight Champion, 1959-1963. European Bantamweight Champion, 1959-1960. *Born* 07.03.36. *From* Belfast. *Pro Career* 1957-1962 (31 contests, won 28, lost 3).

Tommy Glencross British Featherweight Champion, 1972-1973. *Born* 31.07.47. *From* Glasgow. *Pro Career* 1967-1978 (48 contests, won 31, drew 1, lost 16).

Herol Graham Undefeated British L. Middleweight Champion, 1981-1983. Undefeated Commonwealth L. Middleweight Champion, 1981-1984. Undefeated European L. Middleweight Champion, 1983-1984. Undefeated British Middleweight Champion, 1985-1986. British Middleweight Champion, 1988-1992. European Middleweight Champion, 1986-1987. *Born* 13.09.59. *From* Sheffield. *Pro Career* 1978-1998 (54 contests, won 48, lost 6).

Frank Grant British Middleweight Champion, 1992-1993. *Born* 22.05.65. *From* Bradford. *Pro Career* 1986-1993 (26 contests, won 22, lost 4).

Dave Boy Green Undefeated British and European L. Welterweight Champion, 1976-1977. European Welterweight Champion, 1979. *Born* 02.06.53. *From* Chatteris. *Pro Career* 1974-1981 (41 contests, won 37, lost 4).

Roy Gumbs British Middleweight Champion, 1981-1983. Commonwealth Middleweight Champion, 1983. *Born* St Kitts, 05.09.54. *From* Tottenham. *Pro Career* 1976-1985 (40 contests, won 26, drew 3, lost 11).

Neil Haddock British S. Featherweight Champion, 1992-1994. *Born* 22.06.64. *From* Llanelli. *Pro Career* 1987-1994 (26 contests, won 14, drew 1, lost 11).

Ross Hale British and Commonwealth L. Welterweight Champion, 1994-1995. *Born* 28.02.1967. *From* Bristol. *Pro Career* 1989-1998 (33 contests, won 29, lost 4).

Henry Hall British Welterweight Champion, 1948-1949. *Born* 06.09.22. *From* Sheffield. *Deceased* 1979. *Pro Career* 1945-1952 (66 contests, won 43, drew 3, lost 20).

Billy Hardy Undefeated British Bantamweight Champion, 1987-1991. Undefeated British Featherweight Champion, 1994. Undefeated Commonwealth Featherweight Champion, 1992-1996. European Featherweight Champion, 1995-1998. *Born* 05.09.1964. *From* Sunderland. *Pro Career* 1983-1998 (48 contests, won 37, drew 2, lost 9).

Paul Harvey Commonwealth S. Featherweight Champion, 1991-1992. *Born* 10.11.64. *From* Ilford. *Pro Career* 1989-1994 (22 contests, won 16, drew 1, lost 5).

Floyd Havard British S. Featherweight Champion, 1988-1989. Undefeated British S. Featherweight Champion, 1994-1995. *Born* 16.10.65. *From* Swansea. *Pro Career* 1985-1996 (36 contests, won 34, lost 2).

Vince Hawkins British Middleweight Champion, 1946-1948. *Born* 15.04.23. *From* Eastleigh. *Pro Career* 1940-1950 (86 contests, won 75, drew 1, lost 10).

Lloyd Hibbert Undefeated British L. Middleweight Champion, 1987. Commonwealth L. Middleweight Champion, 1987. *Born* 29.06.59. *From* Birmingham. *Pro Career* 1979-1987 (23 contests, won 19, lost 4).

Herbie Hide Undefeated British Heavyweight Champion, 1993-1994. WBO

Heavyweight Champion, 1997-1999. *Born* 27.08.1971. *From* Norwich. *Pro Career* 1989-1999 (33 contests, won 31, lost 2).

Charlie Hill British Featherweight Champion, 1956-1959. *Born* 20.06.30. *From* Cambuslang. *Pro Career* 1953-1959 (36 contests, won 31, lost 5).

Paul Hodkinson Undefeated British Featherweight Champion, 1988-1990. Undefeated European Featherweight Champion, 1989-1991. World Featherweight Champion, 1991-1993 (WBC version). *Born* 14.09.65. *From* Liverpool. *Pro Career* 1986-1994 (26 contests, won 22, drew 1, lost 3).

Andy Holligan British and Commonwealth L. Welterweight Champion, 1991-1994 and 1996-1997. *Born* 06.06.67. *From* Liverpool. *Pro Career* 1987-1998 (30 contests, won 27, lost 3).

Lloyd Honeyghan Undefeated British Welterweight Champion, 1983-1985 and 1985-1986. Undefeated Commonwealth & European Champion, 1985-1986. World Welterweight Champion, 1986. World Welterweight Champion (WBC version), 1986-1987 and 1988-1989. World Welterweight Champion (IBF version), 1986-1987. Commonwealth L. Middleweight Champion, 1993-1994. *Born* 22.04.60, Jamaica. *From* Bermondsey. *Pro Career* 1980-1995 (48 contests, won 43, lost 5).

Maurice Hope Undefeated British L. Middleweight Champion, 1974-1977. Undefeated Commonwealth L. Middleweight Champion, 1976-1979. Undefeated European L. Middleweight Champion, 1976-1978. World L. Middleweight Champion (WBC version), 1979-1981. *Born* Antigua, 06.12.51. *From* Hackney. *Pro Career* 1973-1982 (35 contests, won 30, drew 1, lost 4).

Mickey Hughes Commonwealth L. Middleweight Champion, 1992-1993. *Born* 13.06.62. *From* St Pancras. *Pro Career* 1985-1993 (31 contests, won 24, lost 7).

Mo Hussein Commonwealth Lightweight Champion, 1987-1989. *Born* 17.11.62. *From* West Ham. *Pro Career* 1982-1989 (27 contests, won 23, lost 4).

Jonjo Irwin British Featherweight Champion, 1995-1996. Undefeated British Featherweight Champion, 1998-1999. Commonwealth Featherweight Champion, 1996-1997. *Born* 31.05.69. *From* Doncaster. *Pro Career* 1992-1999 (24 contests, won 19, lost 5).

Gary Jacobs Undefeated British Welterweight Champion, 1992-1993. Commonwealth Welterweight Champion, 1988-1989. European Welterweight Champion, 1993-1994. *Born* 10.12.65. *From* Glasgow. *Pro Career* 1985-1997 (53 contests, won 45, lost 8).

Joey Jacobs British S. Featherweight Champion, 1990. *Born* 01.10.60. *From* Manchester. *Pro Career* 1986-1991 (15 contests, won 10, lost 5).

Ronnie James Undefeated British Lightweight Champion, 1944-1947. *Born* 08.10.17. *From* Swansea. *Deceased* 1977. *Pro Career* 1933-1947 (119 contests, won 98, drew 5, lost 16).

Tee Jay British Cruiserweight Champion, 1987-1988. *Born* Ghana, 21.01.62. Birthname - Taju Akay. *From* Notting Hill. *Pro Career* 1985-1991 (19 contests, won 14, drew 1, lost 4).

Bunny Johnson British and Commonwealth Heavyweight Champion, 1975. Undefeated British L. Heavyweight Champion, 1977-1981. *Born* Jamaica, 10.05.47. *From* Birmingham. Birthname - Fitzroy Johnson. *Pro Career* 1968-1981 (73 contests, won 55, drew 1, lost 17).

Frank Johnson British Lightweight Champion, 1952-1953 and 1955-1956. British Empire Lightweight Championship Claimant, 1953. *Born* 27.11.28. *From* Manchester. Birthname - Frank Williamson. *Deceased* 1970. *Pro Career* 1946-1957 (58 contests, won 47, lost 11).

Barry Jones Undefeated WBO S. Featherweight Champion, 1997-1998. *Born* 03.05.74. *From* Cardiff. *Pro Career* 1992-2000 (20 contests, won 18, drew 1, lost 1).

Colin Jones Undefeated British Welterweight Champion, 1980-1982. Undefeated Commonwealth Welterweight Champion, 1981-1984. Undefeated European Welterweight Champion, 1982-1983. *Born* 21.03.59. *From* Gorseinon. *Pro Career* 1977-1985 (30 contests, won 26, drew 1, lost 3).

Frankie Jones British Flyweight Champion, 1957-1960. British Empire Flyweight Champion, 1957. *Born* 12.02.33. *From* Plean. *Deceased* 1991. *Pro Career* 1955-1960 (25 contests, won 17, lost 8).

Peter Kane Undefeated World Flyweight Champion, 1938-1939. European Bantamweight Champion, 1947-1948. *Born* 28.04.18. *From* Golborne. Birthname - Peter Cain. *Deceased* 1991. *Pro Career* 1934-1948 (102 contests, won 92, drew 2, lost 7, no contest 1).

Mark Kaylor British and Commonwealth Middleweight Champion, 1983-1984. *Born* 11.05.61. *From* West Ham. *Pro Career* 1980-1991 (48 contests, won 40, drew 1, lost 7).

Peter Keenan British Bantamweight Champion, 1951-1953 and 1954-1959. British Empire Bantamweight Champion, 1955-1959. European

Bantamweight Champion, 1951-1952 and 1953. *Born* 08.08.28. *From* Glasgow. *Deceased* 2000. *Pro Career* 1948-1959 (66 contests, won 54, drew 1, lost 11).

Billy Spider Kelly British Featherweight Champion, 1955-1956. British Empire Featherweight Championship Claimant, 1954. British Empire Featherweight Champion, 1954-1955. *Born* 21.04.32. *From* Londonderry. *Pro Career* 1950-1962 (83 contests, won 56, drew 4, lost 23).

Joe Kelly British Bantamweight Champion, 1992. *Born* 18.05.64. *From* Glasgow. *Pro Career* 1985-1992 (27 contests, won 18, drew 2, lost 7).

John Kelly British and European Bantamweight Champion, 1953-1954. *Born* 17.01.32. *From* Belfast. *Pro Career* 1951-1957 (28 contests, won 24, lost 4).

Johnny King British Bantamweight Champion, 1932-1934 and 1935-1947. British Empire Bantamweight Championship Claimant, 1932-1934. *Born* 08.01.12. *From* Manchester. *Deceased* 1963. *Pro Career* 1926-1947 (222 contests, won 158, drew 15, lost 48, no contest 1).

Kirkland Laing British Welterweight Champion, 1987-1991. European Welterweight Champion, 1990. *Born* 20.06.54, Jamaica. *From* Nottingham. *Pro Career* 1975-1994 (56 contests, won 43, drew 1, lost 12).

Tony Laing Undefeated British L. Welterweight Champion, 1986. Commonwealth L. Welterweight Champion, 1987-1988. *Born* 22.09.57. *From* Nottingham. *Pro Career* 1977-1988 (18 contests, won 13, drew 1, lost 4).

Davy Larmour British Bantamweight Champion, 1983. *Born* 02.04.52. *From* Belfast. *Pro Career* 1977-1983 (18 contests, won 11, lost 7).

Mick Leahy British Middleweight Champion, 1963-1964. *Born* Cork, 12.03.35. *From* Coventry. *Pro Career* 1956-1965 (72 contests, won 46, drew 7, lost 19).

Stewart Lithgo Commonwealth Cruiserweight Champion, 1984. *Born* 02.06.57. *From* West Hartlepool. *Pro Career* 1977-1987 (30 contests, won 16, drew 2, lost 12).

Brian London British and British Empire Heavyweight Champion, 1958-1959. *Born* 19.06.34. *From* Blackpool. Birthname - Brian Harper. *Pro Career* 1955-1970 (58 contests, won 37, drew 1, lost 20).

Jack London British Heavyweight Champion, 1944-1945. British Empire Heavyweight Championship Claimant, 1944-1945. *Born* 23.06.13. *From* West Hartlepool. Birthname - Jack Harper. *Deceased* 1964. *Pro Career* 1931-1949 (141 contests, won 95, drew 5, lost 39, no contests 2).

Eamonn Loughran Undefeated Commonwealth Welterweight Champion, 1992-1993. WBO Welterweight Champion, 1993-1996. *Born* 05.06.70. *Fron* Ballymena. *Pro Career* 1987-1996 (30 contests, won 26, drew 1, lost 2, no contest 1).

Joe Lucy British Lightweight Champion, 1953-1955 and 1956-1957. *Born* 09.02.30. *From* Mile End. *Deceased* 1991. *Pro Career* 1950-1957 (37 contests, won 27, lost 10).

Kevin Lueshing British Welterweight Champion, 1996-1997. *Born* 17.04.1968. *From* Beckenham. *Pro Career* 1991-1999 (25 contests, won 21, lost 4).

Danny McAlinden British and Commonwealth Heavyweight Champion, 1972-1975. *Born* Newry, 01.06.47. *From* Coventry. *Pro Career* 1969-1981 (45 contests, won 31, drew 2, lost 12).

Les McAteer British and British Empire Middleweight Champion, 1969-1970. *Born* 19.08.45. *From* Birkenhead. *Pro Career* 1965-1979 (39 contests, won 27, drew 2, lost 10).

Pat McAteer Undefeated British Middleweight Champion, 1955-1958. British Empire Middleweight Champion, 1955-1958. *Born* 17.03.32. *From* Birkenhead. *Pro Career* 1952-1958 (57 contests, won 49, drew 2, lost 6).

Dave McAuley Undefeated British Flyweight Champion, 1986-1988. World Flyweight Champion (IBF version), 1989-1992. *Born* 15.06.61. *From* Larne. *Pro Career* 1983-1992 (23 contests, won 18, drew 2, lost 3).

Sammy McCarthy British Featherweight Champion, 1954-1955. *Born* 05.11.31. *From* Stepney. *Pro Career* 1951-1957 (53 contests, won 44, drew 1, lost 8).

Steve McCarthy British L. Heavyweight Champion, 1990-1991. *Born* 30.07.62. *From* Southampton. *Pro Career* 1987-1994 (17 contests, won 12, drew 1, lost 4).

John McCluskey Undefeated British Flyweight Champion, 1967-1977. Commonwealth Flyweight Champion, 1970-1971. *Born* 23.01.44. *From* Hamilton. *Pro Career* 1965-1975 (38 contests, won 23, lost 15).

John Cowboy McCormack British Middleweight Champion, 1959. European Middleweight Champion, 1961-1962. *Born* 09.01.35. *From* Maryhill. *Pro Career* 1957-1966 (45 contests, won 38, lost 7).

Young John McCormack British L. Heavyweight Champion, 1967-1969. *Born* Dublin, 11.12.44. *From* Brixton. *Pro Career* 1963-1970 (42 contests, won 33, drew 1, lost 8).

Pat McCormack British L. Welterweight Champion, 1974. *Born* Dublin, 28.04.46. *From* Brixton. *Pro Career* 1968-1975 (49 contests, won 30, drew 1, lost 18).

Glenn McCrory Undefeated British Cruiserweight Champion, 1988. Undefeated Commonwealth Cruiserweight Champion, 1987-1989. World Cruiserweight Champion (IBF version), 1989-1990. *Born* 23.09.64. *From* Annfield Plain. *Pro Career* 1984-1993 (39 contests, won 30, drew 1, lost 8).

Jim McDonnell Undefeated European Featherweight Champion, 1985-1987. *Born* 12.09.60. *From* Camden Town. *Pro Career* 1983-1998 (30 contests, won 26, lost 4).

Tommy McGovern British Lightweight Champion, 1951-1952. *Born* 05.02.24. *From* Bermondsey. *Deceased* 1989. *Pro Career* 1947-1953 (66 contests, won 45, drew 4, lost 17).

Walter McGowan Undefeated British Flyweight Champion, 1963-1966. Undefeated British Empire Flyweight Champion, 1963-1969. World Flyweight Champion (WBC version), 1966. British and British Empire Bantamweight Champion, 1966-1968. *Born* 13.10.42. *From* Hamilton. *Pro Career* 1961-1969 (40 contests, won 32, drew 1, lost 7).

Barry McGuigan Undefeated British Featherweight Champion, 1983-1986. Undefeated European Featherweight Champion, 1983-1985. World Featherweight Champion (WBA version), 1985-1986. *Born* 28.02.61. *From* Clones. *Pro Career* 1981-1989 (35 contests, won 32, lost 3).

Clinton McKenzie British L. Welterweight Champion, 1978-1979 and 1979-1984. Undefeated British L. Welterweight Champion, 1989. European L. Welterweight Champion, 1981-1982. *Born* 15.09.55. *From* Croydon. *Pro Career* 1976-1989 (50 contests, won 36, lost 14).

Duke McKenzie Undefeated British Flyweight Champion, 1985-1986. Undefeated European Flyweight Champion, 1986-1988. World Flyweight Champion (IBF version), 1988-1989. World Bantamweight Champion (WBO version), 1991-1992. World S. Bantamweight Champion (WBO version), 1992-1993. Undefeated British S. Featherweight Champion, 1993-1994. *Born* 05.05.63. *From* Croydon. *Pro Career* 1982-1998 (46 contests, won 39, lost 7).

Tony McKenzie British L. Welterweight Champion, 1986-1987. *Born* 04.03.63. *From* Leicester. *Pro Career* 1983-1993 (34 contests, won 26, drew 1, lost 7).

Colin McMillan Undefeated British Featherweight Champion, 1991-1992. British Featherweight Champion, 1996-1997. Undefeated Commonwealth Featherweight Champion, 1992. World Featherweight Champion (WBO version), 1992. *Born* 12.02.66. *From* Barking. *Pro Career* 1988-1997 (35 contests, won 31, lost 4).

Noel Magee Commonwealth L. Heavyweight Champion, 1995. *Born* 16.12.65. *From* Belfast. *Pro Career* 1985-1997 (37 contests, won 27, drew 2, lost 8).

Charlie Magri Undefeated British Flyweight Champion, 1977-1981. Undefeated European Flyweight Champion, 1979-1983 and 1984-1985. European Flyweight Champion, 1985-1986. World Flyweight Champion (WBC version), 1983. *Born* Tunisia, 20.07.56. *From* Stepney. *Pro Career* 1977-1986 (35 contests, won 30, lost 5).

Paddy Maguire British Bantamweight Champion, 1975-1977. *Born* 26.09.48. *From* Belfast. *Pro Career* 1969-1977 (35 contests, won 26, drew 1, lost 8).

Terry Marsh Undefeated British L. Welterweight Champion, 1984-1986. European L. Welterweight Champion, 1985-1986. Undefeated World L. Welterweight Champion (IBF version), 1987. *Born* 07.02.58. *From* Basildon. *Pro Career* 1981-1987 (27 contests, won 26, drew 1).

Gary Mason British Heavyweight Champion, 1989-1991. *Born* Jamaica, 15.12.62. *From* Wandsworth. *Pro Career* 1984-1991 (36 contests, won 35, lost 1).

Jason Matthews Undefeated Commonwealth Middleweight Champion, 1999. WBO Middleweight Champion, 1999. *Born* 20.07.70. *From* Hackney. *Pro Career* 1995-1999 (23 contests, won 21, lost 2).

Neville Meade British Heavyweight Champion, 1981-1983. *Born* Jamaica, 12.09.48. *From* Swansea. *Pro Career* 1974-1983 (34 contests, won 20, drew 1, lost 13).

Freddie Mills Undefeated British L. Heavyweight Champion, 1942-1950. British Empire L. Heavyweight Championship Claimant, 1942-1950.

Undefeated European L. Heavyweight Champion, 1947-1950. World L. Heavyweight Champion (GB version), 1942-1946. World L. Heavyweight Champion, 1948-1950. *Born* 26.06.19. *From* Bournemouth. *Deceased* 1965. *Pro Career* 1936-1950 (101 contests, won 77, drew 6, lost 18).

Alan Minter British Middleweight Champion, 1975-1977. Undefeated British Middleweight Champion, 1977-1978. European Middleweight Champion, 1977. Undefeated European Middleweight Champion, 1978-1979. World Middleweight Champion, 1980. *Born* 17.08.51. *From* Crawley. *Pro Career* 1972-1981 (49 contests, won 39, lost 9, no contest 1).

Sylvester Mittee British Welterweight Champion, 1985. Commonwealth Welterweight Champion, 1984-1985. *Born* St Lucia, 29.10.56. *From* Bethnal Green. *Pro Career* 1977-1988 (33 contests, won 28, lost 5).

Tommy Molloy British Welterweight Champion, 1958-1960. *Born* 02.02.34. *From* Birkenhead. *Pro Career* 1955-1963 (43 contests, won 34, drew 2, lost 6, no contest 1).

Rinty Monaghan Undefeated British and World Flyweight Champion, 1948-1950. British Empire Flyweight Championship Claimant, 1948-1950. Undefeated European Flyweight Champion, 1949-1950. World Flyweight Champion (NBA version), 1947-1948. *Born* 21.08.20. *From* Belfast. Birthname - John Monaghan. *Deceased* 1984. *Pro Career* 1934-1949 (66 contests, won 51, drew 6, lost 9).

Des Morrison British L. Welterweight Champion, 1973-1974. *Born* Jamaica, 01.02.50. *From* Bedford. *Pro Career* 1970-1982 (50 contests, won 36, drew 2, lost 12).

Sean Murphy British Featherweight Champion, 1990-1991 and 1993. *Born* 01.12.64. *From* St Albans. *Pro Career* 1986-1994 (27 contests, won 22, lost 5).

Charlie Nash Undefeated British Lightweight Champion, 1978-1979. Undefeated European Lightweight Champion, 1979-1980. European Lightweight Champion, 1980-1981. *Born* 10.05.51. *From* Derry. *Pro Career* 1975-1983 (30 contests, won 25, lost 5).

Dave Needham British Bantamweight Champion, 1974-1975. British Featherweight Champion, 1978-1979. *Born* 15.08.51. *From* Nottingham. *Pro Career* 1971-1980 (39 contests, won 30, drew 1, lost 8).

Bobby Neill British Featherweight Champion, 1959-1960. *Born* 10.10.33. *From* Edinburgh. *Pro Career* 1955-1960 (35 contests, won 28, lost 7).

Horace Notice Undefeated British and Commonwealth Heavyweight Champion, 1986-1988. *Born* 07.08.57. *From* Birmingham. *Pro Career* 1983-1988 (16 contests, won 16).

John O'Brien British Empire Featherweight Champion, 1967. *Born* 20.02.37. *From* Glasgow. *Deceased* 1979. *Pro Career* 1956-1971 (47 contests, won 30, lost 17).

Chris Okoh Commonwealth Cruiserweight Champion, 1995-1997. *Born* 18.04.69. *From* Croydon. *Pro Career* 1993-1999 (16 contests, won 14, lost 2).

Spencer Oliver European S. Bantamweight Champion, 1997-1998. *Born* 27.03.75. *From* Barnet. *Pro Career* 1995-1998 (15 contests, won 14, lost 1).

Danny O'Sullivan British Bantamweight Champion, 1949-1951. *Born* 06.01.23. *From* Finsbury Park. *Deceased* 1990. *Pro Career* 1947-1951 (43 contests, won 33, drew 1, lost 9).

Johnny Owen Undefeated British Bantamweight Champion, 1977-1980. Undefeated Commonwealth Bantamweight Champion, 1978-1980. Undefeated European Bantamweight Champion, 1980. *Born* 07.01.56. *From* Merthyr. *Deceased* 1980. *Pro Career* 1976-1980 (28 contests, won 25, drew 1, lost 2).

James Oyebola British Heavyweight Champion, 1994-1995. *Born* Nigeria 10.06.61. *From* Paddington. *Pro Career* 1987-1996 (23 contests, won 18, drew 1, lost 4).

Jackie Paterson British Flyweight Champion, 1939-1948. British Empire Flyweight Championship Claimant, 1940-1948. World Flyweight Champion, 1943-1947. World Flyweight Champion (GB/NY version), 1947-1948. British Bantamweight Champion, 1947-1949. British Empire Bantamweight Championship Claimant, 1945-1949. European Bantamweight Champion, 1946. *Born* 05.09.20. *From* Springfield. *Deceased* 1966. *Pro Career* 1938-1950 (92 contests, won 64, drew 3, lost 25).

Bernard Paul Commonwealth L. Welterweight Champion, 1997-1999. *Born* 22.20.65. *From* Tottenham. *Pro Career* 1991-2000 (35 contests, won 21, drew 4, lost 10).

Larry Paul British L. Middleweight Champion, 1973-1974. *Born* 19.04.52. *From* Wolverhampton. *Pro Career* 1973-1978 (40 contests, won 30, drew 1, lost 9).

David Pearce Undefeated British Heavyweight Champion, 1983-1985.

Born 08.05.59. *From* Newport. *Deceased* 2000. *Pro Career* 1978-1984 (21 contests, won 17, drew 1, lost 3).

Kostas Petrou British Welterweight Champion, 1985. *Born* 17.04.59. *From* Birmingham. *Pro Career* 1981-1988 (37 contests, won 30, lost 7).

Tiger Al Phillips European Featherweight Champion, 1947. British Empire Featherweight Championship Claimant, 1947. *Born* 25.01.20. *From* Aldgate. *Deceased* 1999. *Pro Career* 1938-1951 (89 contests, won 72, drew 3, lost 14).

Nicky Piper Undefeated Commonwealth L. Heavyweight Champion, 1995-1997. *Born* 05.05.66. *From* Cardiff. *Pro Career* 1989-1997 (33 contests, won 26, drew 2, lost 5).

Dennis Powell British L. Heavyweight Champion, 1953. *Born* 12.12.24. *From* Four Crosses. *Deceased* 1993. *Pro Career* 1947-1954 (68 contests, won 42, drew 4, lost 22).

Colin Power Undefeated British L. Welterweight Champion, 1977-1978. British L. Welterweight Champion, 1979. European L. Welterweight Champion, 1978. *Born* 02.02.56. *From* Paddington. *Pro Career* 1975-1983 (34 contests, won 28, drew 1, lost 5).

Kevin Pritchard British S. Featherweight Champion, 1990-1991. *Born* 26.09.61. *From* Liverpool. *Pro Career* 1981-1991 (48 contests, won 23, drew 3, lost 22).

Johnny Pritchett Undefeated British Middleweight Champion, 1965-1969. Undefeated British Empire Middleweight Champion, 1967-1969. *Born* 15.02.43. *From* Bingham. *Pro Career* 1963-1969 (34 contests, won 32, drew 1, lost 1).

Chris Pyatt Undefeated British L. Middleweight Champion, 1986. European L. Middleweight Champion, 1986-1987. Undefeated Commonwealth L. Middleweight Champion, 1991-1992. Commonwealth L. Middleweight Champion, 1995-1996. World Middleweight Champion (WBO version), 1993-1994. *Born* 03.07.63. *From* Leicester. *Pro Career* 1983-1997 (51 contests, won 46, lost 5).

Des Rea British L. Welterweight Champion, 1968-1969. *Born* 09.01.44. *From* Belfast. *Pro Career* 1964-1974 (69 contests, won 28, drew 5, lost 36).

Mark Reefer Undefeated Commonwealth S. Featherweight Champion, 1989-1990. *Born* 16.03.64. Birthname - Mark Thompson. *From* Dagenham. *Pro Career* 1983-1992 (32 contests, won 23, drew 1, lost 8).

Sam Reeson Undefeated British Cruiserweight Champion, 1985-1986. Undefeated European Cruiserweight Champion, 1987-1988. *Born* 05.01.63. *From* Battersea. *Pro Career* 1983-1989 (26 contests, won 24, lost 2).

Robbie Regan Undefeated World Bantamweight Champion (WBO version), 1996-1997. British Flyweight Champion, 1991. Undefeated British Flyweight Champion, 1991-1992. Undefeated European Flyweight Champion, 1992-1993 and 1994-1995. *Born* 30.08.68. *From* Cefn Forest. *Pro Career* 1989-1996 (22 contests, won 17, drew 3, lost 2).

Willie Reilly Undefeated British Lightweight Champion, 1972. *Born* 25.03.47. *From* Glasgow. *Pro Career* 1968-1972 (23 contests, won 13, drew 3, lost 7).

Jimmy Revie British Featherweight Champion, 1969-1971. *Born* 08.07.47. *From* Stockwell. *Pro Career* 1966-1976 (48 contests, won 38, drew 1, lost 9).

Henry Rhiney British Welterweight Champion, 1976-1979. European Welterweight Champion, 1978-1979. *Born* Jamaica, 28.11.51. *From* Luton. *Pro Career* 1973-1980 (57 contests, won 32, drew 6, lost 19).

Alan Richardson British Featherweight Champion, 1977-1978. *Born* 04.11.48. *From* Fitzwilliam. *Pro Career* 1971-1978 (27 contests, won 17, drew 1, lost 9).

Dick Richardson European Heavyweight Champion, 1960-1962. *Born* 01.06.34. *From* Newport. *Deceased* 1999. *Pro Career* 1954-1963 (47 contests, won 31, drew 2, lost 14).

Ernie Roderick British Welterweight Champion, 1939-1948. European Welterweight Champion, 1946-1947. British Middleweight Champion, 1945-1946. *Born* 25.01.14. *From* Liverpool. *Deceased* 1986. *Pro Career* 1931-1950 (142 contests, won 114, drew 4, lost 24).

Prince Rodney Undefeated British L. Middleweight Champion, 1983-1984. British L. Middleweight Champion, 1985-1986. *Born* 31.10.58. *From* Huddersfield. *Pro Career* 1977-1990 (41 contests, won 31, drew 1, lost 9).

Stan Rowan Undefeated British Bantamweight Champion, 1949. British Empire Bantamweight Championship Claimant, 1949. *Born* 06.09.24. *From* Liverpool. *Deceased* 1997. *Pro Career* 1942-1953 (67 contests, won 46, drew 5, lost 16).

Mark Rowe British and Commonwealth Middleweight Champion, 1970.

Born 12.07.47. *Born* 12.07.47. *From* Camberwell. *Pro Career* 1966-1973 (47 contests, won 38, drew 1, lost 8).

Alan Rudkin British Bantamweight Champion, 1965-1966. Undefeated British Bantamweight Champion, 1968-1972. British Empire Bantamweight Champion, 1965-1966 and 1968-1969. European Bantamweight Champion, 1971. Undefeated Commonwealth Bantamweight Champion, 1970-1972. *Born* 18.11.41. *From* Liverpool. *Pro Career* 1962-1972 (50 contests, won 42, lost 8).

Hugh Russell Undefeated British Flyweight Champion, 1984-1985. British Bantamweight Champion, 1983. *Born* 15.12.59. *From* Belfast. *Pro Career* 1981-1985 (19 contests, won 17, lost 2).

Paul Ryan British and Commonwealth L. Welterweight Champion, 1995-1996. *Born* 02.02.65. *From* Hackney. *Pro Career* 1991-1997 (28 contests, won 25, lost 3).

Chris Saunders British Welterweight Champion, 1995-1996. *Born* 15.08.1969. *From* Barnsley. *Pro Career* 1990-1999 (38 contests, won 16, drew 1, lost 21).

Tony Sibson British Middleweight Champion, 1979. Undefeated British Middleweight Champion, 1984 and 1987-1988. Undefeated Commonwealth Middleweight Champion, 1980-1983 and 1984-1988. Undefeated European Middleweight Champion, 1980-1982. European Middleweight Champion, 1984-1985. *Born* 09.04.58. *From* Leicester. *Pro Career* 1976-1988 (63 contests, won 55, drew 1, lost 7).

Steve Sims Undefeated British Featherweight Champion, 1982-1983. *Born* 10.10.58. *From* Newport. *Pro Career* 1977-1987 (29 contests, won 14, drew 1, lost 14).

Joey Singleton British L. Welterweight Champion, 1974-1976. *Born* 06.06.51. *From* Kirkby. *Pro Career* 1973-1982 (40 contests, won 27, drew 2, lost 11).

Kelvin Smart British Flyweight Champion, 1982-1984. *Born* 18.12.60. *From* Caerphilly. *Pro Career* 1979-1987 (29 contests, won 17, drew 2, lost 10).

Roy Smith British Cruiserweight Champion, 1987. *Born* 31.08.61. *From* Nottingham. *Pro Career* 1985-1991 (26 contests, won 18, lost 8).

Vernon Sollas British Featherweight Champion, 1975-1977. *Born* 14.08.54. *From* Edinburgh. *Pro Career* 1973-1977 (33 contests, won 25, drew 1, lost 7).

Terry Spinks British Featherweight Champion, 1960-1961. *Born* 28.02.38. *From* Canning Town. *Pro Career* 1957-1962 (49 contests, won 41, drew 1, lost 7).

Bunny Sterling British Middleweight Champion, 1970-1974. Undefeated British Middleweight Champion, 1975. Commonwealth Middleweight Champion, 1970-1972. European Middleweight Champion, 1976. *Born* Jamaica, 04.04.48. *From* Finsbury Park. *Pro Career* 1966-1977 (57 contests, won 35, drew 4, lost 18).

John H. Stracey Undefeated British Welterweight Champion, 1973-1975. Undefeated European Welterweight Champion, 1974-1975. World Welterweight Champion (WBC version), 1975-1976. *Born* 22.09.50. *From* Bethnal Green. *Pro Career* 1969-1978 (51 contests, won 45, drew 1, lost 5).

Andy Straughn British Cruiserweight Champion, 1986-1987 and 1988-1989. *Born* Barbados, 25.12.59. *From* Hitchin. *Pro Career* 1982-1990 (27 contests, won 18, drew 2, lost 7).

Gary Stretch British L. Middleweight Champion, 1988-1990. *Born* 04.11.65. *From* St Helens. *Pro Career* 1985-1993 (25 contests, won 23, lost 2).

Johnny Sullivan British Empire Middleweight Championship Claimant, 1954. British and British Empire Middleweight Champion, 1954-1955. *Born* 19.12.32. *From* Preston. Birthname - John Hallmark. *Pro Career* 1948-1960 (97 contests, won 68, drew 3, lost 26).

Wally Swift British Welterweight Champion, 1960. British Middleweight Champion, 1964-1965. *Born* 10.08.36. *From* Nottingham. *Pro Career* 1957-1969 (88 contests, won 68, drew 3, lost 17).

Wally Swift Jnr British L. Middleweight Champion, 1991-1992. *Born* 17.02.66. *From* Birmingham. *Pro Career* 1985-1994 (38 contests, won 26, drew 1, lost 11).

Nel Tarleton British Featherweight Champion, 1931-1932 and 1934-1936. Undefeated British Featherweight Champion, 1940-1947. Undefeated British Empire Featherweight Championship Claimant, 1940-1947. *Born* 14.01.06. *From* Liverpool. *Deceased* 1956. *Pro Career* 1926-1945 (144 contests, won 116, drew 8, lost 20).

Wally Thom British Welterweight Champion, 1951-1952 and 1953-1956. British Empire Welterweight Championship Claimant, 1951-1952. European Welterweight Champion, 1954-1955. *Born* 14.06.26. *From* Birkenhead. *Deceased* 1980. *Pro Career* 1949-1956 (54 contests, won 42, drew 1, lost 11).

Eddie Thomas British Welterweight Champion, 1949-1951. European Welterweight Champion, 1951. British Empire Welterweight Championship Claimant, 1951. *Born* 27.07.26. *From* Merthyr. *Deceased* 1997. *Pro Career* 1946-1954 (48 contests, won 40, drew 2, lost 6).

Pat Thomas British Welterweight Champion, 1975-1976. British L. Middleweight Champion, 1979-1981. *Born* St Kitts, 05.05.50. *From* Cardiff. *Pro Career* 1970-1984 (57 contests, won 35, drew 3, lost 18, no contest 1).

Billy Thompson British Lightweight Champion, 1947-1951. European Lightweight Champion, 1948-1949. *Born* 20.12.25. *From* Hickleton Main. *Pro Career* 1945-1953 (63 contests, won 46, drew 4, lost 13).

Andy Till British L. Middleweight Champion, 1992-1994. *Born* 22.08.63. *From* Northolt. *Pro Career* 1986-1995 (24 contests, won 19, lost 5).

Dick Turpin British Middleweight Champion, 1948-1950. British Empire Middleweight Championship Claimant, 1948-1949. *Born* 26.11.20. *From* Leamington Spa. *Deceased* 1990. *Pro Career* 1937-1950 (103 contests, won 76, drew 6, lost 20, no contest 1).

Randy Turpin Undefeated British Middleweight Champion, 1950-1954. British Empire Middleweight Championship Claimant, 1952-1954. European Middleweight Champion, 1951-1954. World Middleweight Champion, 1951. World Middleweight Champion (EBU version), 1953. Undefeated British L. Heavyweight Champion, 1952, 1955, and 1956-1958. British Empire L. Heavyweight Championship Claimant, 1952-1954. Undefeated British Empire L. Heavyweight Champion, 1954-1955. *Born* 07.06.28. *From* Leamington Spa. *Deceased* 1966. *Pro Career* 1946-1958 (73 contests, won 64, drew 1, lost 8).

Keith Wallace Undefeated Commonwealth Flyweight Champion, 1983-1984. *Born* 29.03.61. *From* Liverpool. *Deceased* 2000. *Pro Career* 1982-1990 (25 contests, won 20, lost 5).

Peter Waterman Undefeated British Welterweight Champion, 1956-1958. Undefeated European Welterweight Champion, 1958. *Born* 08.12.34. *From* Clapham. *Deceased* 1986. *Pro Career* 1952-1958 (46 contests, won 41, drew 2, lost 3).

Michael Watson Undefeated Commonwealth Middleweight Champion, 1989-1991. *Born* 15.03.65. *From* Islington. *Pro Career* 1984-1991 (30 contests, won 25, drew 1, lost 4).

Jim Watt British Lightweight Champion, 1972-1973. Undefeated British Lightweight Champion, 1975-1977. Undefeated European Lightweight Champion, 1977-1979. World Lightweight Champion (WBC version), 1979-1981. *Born* 18.07.48. *From* Glasgow. *Pro Career* 1968-1981 (46 contests, won 38, lost 8).

Scott Welch Undefeated British Heavyweight Champion, 1995-1996. Commonwealth Heavyweight Champion, 1995-1997. *Born* 21.04.1968. *From* Shoreham. *Pro Career* 1992-1999 (26 contests, won 22, lost 4).

Henry Wharton Undefeated British S. Middleweight Champion, 1992-1993. Undefeated Commonwealth Champion, 1991-1997. Undefeated European S. Middleweight Champion, 1995-1996. *Born* 23.11.1967. *From* York. *Pro Career* 1989-1998 (31 contests, won 27, drew 1, lost 3).

Derek Williams Commonwealth Heavyweight Champion, 1988-1992. European Heavyweight Champion, 1989-1992. *Born* 11.03.65. *From* Peckham. *Pro Career* 1984-1999 (35 contests, won 22, lost 13).

Johnny Williams British Heavyweight Champion, 1952-1953. British Empire Heavyweight Championship Claimant, 1952-1953. *Born* 25.12.26. *From* Rugby. *Pro Career* 1946-1956 (75 contests, won 60, drew 4, lost 11).

Tony Willis British Lightweight Champion, 1985-1987. *Born* 17.06.60. *From* Liverpool. *Pro Career* 1981-1989 (29 contests, won 25, lost 4).

Nick Wilshire Commonwealth L. Middleweight Champion, 1985-1987. *Born* 03.11.61. *From* Bristol. *Pro Career* 1981-1987 (40 contests, won 36, lost 4).

Tony Wilson British L. Heavyweight Champion, 1987-1989. *Born* 25.04.64. *From* Wolverhampton. *Pro Career* 1985-1993 (29 contests, won 20, drew 1, lost 8).

Howard Winstone Undefeated British Featherweight Champion, 1961-1969. European Featherweight Champion, 1963-1967. World Featherweight Champion (WBC version), 1968. *Born* 15.04.39. *From* Merthyr. *Deceased* 2000. *Pro Career* 1959-1968 (67 contests, won 61, lost 6).

Tim Wood British L. Heavyweight Champion, 1976-1977. *Born* 10.08.51. *From* Leicester. *Pro Career* 1972-1979 (31 contests, won 19, drew 1, lost 11).

Bruce Woodcock British Heavyweight Champion, 1945-1950. British Empire Heavyweight Championship Claimant, 1945-1950. European Heavyweight Champion, 1946-1949. *Born* 18.01.21. *From* Doncaster. *Deceased* 1997. *Pro Career* 1942-1950 (39 contests, won 35, lost 4).

Commonwealth Title Bouts During 2000-2001

All of last season's title bouts are shown in date order within their weight divisions and give the contestants' respective weights, along with the scorecard if going to a decision. Every contest involving a British fighter is summarised briefly and all British officials are named.

Flyweight

13 November 2000 Jason Booth 8.0 (England) W PTS 12 Ian Napa 7.12$^{1}/_{4}$ (England), York Hall, Bethnal Green, London, England. Referee: Dave Parris 118-112. For a summary, see under British Title Bouts During 2000-2001.

26 February 2001 Jason Booth 8.0 (England) W CO 2 Nokuthula Tshabangu 7.13$^{3}/_{4}$ (Zimbabwe), Harvey Hadden Leisure Centre, Nottingham, England. Whilst the challenger was inept to say the least, and the first round was a getting to know you round, Booth quickly got down to business in the second, putting his rival down for six with a left hook. On getting up, Tshabangu was soon on the floor again from a cluster of blows and was counted out by Larry O'Connell at 2.52 of the session.

Bantamweight

9 September 2000 Ady Lewis 8.4$^{3}/_{4}$ (England) L RSC 4 Tommy Waite 8.6 (Ireland), Bowler's Arena, Manchester, England. Referee: Mark Green. For a summary, see under British Title Bouts During 2000-2001.

9 October 2000 Tommy Waite 8.5$^{3}/_{4}$ (Ireland) L PTS 12 Nicky Booth 8.5$^{1}/_{2}$ (England), Everton Park Leisure Centre, Liverpool, England. Referee: Paul Thomas 117-114. For a summary, see under British Title Bouts During 2000-2001.

26 February 2001 Nicky Booth 8.5$^{3}/_{4}$ (England) W RSC 7 Ady Lewis 8.5 (England), Harvey Hadden Leisure Centre, Nottingham, England. Referee: Richie Davies. For a summary, see under British Title Bouts During 2000-2001.

S. Bantamweight

Nedal Hussein (Australia) failed to make a defence during the period and relinquished the title on winning the WBU championship on 29 June 2001.

Featherweight

11 November 2000 Scott Harrison 9.0 (Scotland) W RSC 12 Eric Odumasi 8.13 (Ghana), Waterfront Hotel, Belfast, Ireland. Standing his ground, and boxing with economy and precision, Harrison once again showed what a promising fighter he is. Despite the challenger setting a blistering pace, the Scot was always in control, cutting Odumasi on the left eye in the fifth and generally allowing him to attack before running out of steam. Finally, a left hook brought Odumasi to his knees in the 12th round and, on rising at the count of eight, Richie Davies waved it off with 2.29 of the fight remaining.

24 March 2001 Scott Harrison 9.0 (Scotland) W RSC 4 Richie Wenton 8.13 (England), Ponds Forge International Leisure Centre, Sheffield, England. Referee: Dave Parris. For a summary, see under British Title Bouts During 2000-2001.

S. Featherweight

18 September 2000 James Armah 9.4 (Ghana) W RTD 9 Charles Shepherd 9.2$^{3}/_{4}$ (England), Forte Posthouse Hotel, Glasgow, Scotland. Billed for the vacant title after Ian McLeod (Scotland) gave up his belt in June 2000 in order to prepare for an IBO championship challenge, Armah was just too good for his tough opponent in a head-on clash of aggression. Unfortunately, for Shepherd's supporters he neither had the power or the guile to turn the fight around and when his right eye was badly cut in the eighth the writing was on the wall. Having bravely battled through the ninth round, his offending eye almost closed, his manger, Jack Doughty, called the referee, Roy Francis, over and the contest was at an end. Armah relinquished the title on winning the Commonwealth lightweight crown on 3 February 2001.

20 March 2001 Alex Moon 9.3$^{3}/_{4}$ (England) W PTS 12 Charles Shepherd 9.3$^{1}/_{4}$ (England), Bellahouston Leisure Centre, Glasgow, Scotland. In a battle of give and take, Moon just about prevailed to land John Keane's 115-114 decision. It was probably Shepherd's last chance and he gave it everything, especially after being cut over the right eye in the seventh round following a clash of heads. However, despite often being under the cosh, Moon was never out of the fight and stood his ground to become the new champion.

Lightweight

9 September 2000 Bobby Vanzie 9.7$^{3}/_{4}$ (England) W RSC 6 Joseph Charles 9.9 (Trinidad), Bowler's Arena, Manchester, England. Knocked down three times, Charles was no match for the champion and was considered by the referee, Ian John-Lewis, to be in no position to defend himself, the contest being halted at 2.10 of the sixth round.

9 October 2000 Bobby Vanzie 9.8$^{1}/_{2}$ (England) W RSC 8 Laatekwei Hammond 9.9 (Ghana), Everton Park Leisure Centre, Liverpool, England. In a scrambling, untidy affair, with Vanzie boxing way below his best, the challenger, cut on the left eye in the fourth, twice got lucky to floor his man without ever looking likely to stop him. Finally, Vanzie imposed himself on his opponent in the eighth when landing with a right-hand counter that put Hammond down for eight. On rising, the Ghanaian was deemed by the referee, John Keane, to be unable to defend himself and the action was stopped at 0.23 of the round.

3 February 2001 Bobby Vanzie 9.9 (England) L PTS 12 James Armah 9.9 (Ghana), Bowler's Arena, Manchester, England. Well conditioned and coming forward continuously, the 'Bukom Fire' could not be subdued and just about deserved to lift the title, 115-114 on Mickey Vann's scorecard, despite the lack of quality. For his part, Vanzie tried to kid his rival into giving him breathing space, but the Ghanaian would not be denied and never gave the champion room to move, let alone get get his punches off.

L. Welterweight

11 November 2000 Eamonn Magee 10.0 (Ireland) W PTS 12 Shea Neary 10.0 (England), Waterfront Hotel, Belfast, Ireland. Many were stunned when Roy Francis, the referee, decided that Magee had successfully defended his title with a scorecard reading 116-114 and vented their feelings loudly. In what had been a tactical affair rather than the expected punch up, Neary boxed extremely well and surprised the champion by his defence, while the latter never really got into his stride and only came alive in short bursts. A rematch would seem to be obvious.

12 May 2001   Eamonn Magee 9.13½ (Ireland) W RSC 7 Harrison Methula 9.13¼ (South Africa), The Pavilions, Plymouth, England. Despite having marked height and reach advantage, the challenger was prepared to come forward throwing punches, some connecting, many not, a tactic that seemed to hold Magee up for some time. However, once the Irishman got his punches off the end was in sight and a southpaw left to the head in round seven saw Methula come apart. Stumbling across the ring from the effects of the punch, the South African dropped down to take the mandatory eight count and, on rising, John Coyle stopped the contest at 0.32.

Welterweight

27 November 2000   Jawaid Khaliq 10.7 (England) W PTS 12 Sean Sullivan 10.6 (New Zealand), Aston Villa Leisure Centre, Birmingham, England. Referee: Larry O'Connell. Contested for the vacant title after Scott Dixon moved up a weight division in August 2000, Khaliq, never having gone beyond six rounds, took control early on and dictated most of the action. However, the hard man from Auckland, not a fighter who buckles easily, continued to chug away at close quarters whenever he could before losing by a wide 119-110. Khaliq vacated the championship on winning the IBO title on 11 June 2001.

L. Middleweight

23 January 2001   Tony Badea 10.11½ (Canada) L RSC 3 Richard Williams 10.13¼ (England), The Leisure Centre, Crawley, England. For a man who had yet to travel beyond four rounds, Williams arrived on the title scene with a bang, being almost punch perfect in his dismantling of the champion. Try as he could to get going, Badea was stopped in his tracks by a whole range of punches and it was no surprise when he hit the deck in round three. Although Badea got up there was no stopping Williams, who finished his rival off with a terrific right uppercut which dropped him to his knees and ended the contest at 0.47 on the clock, Richie Davies calling a halt.

Middleweight

16 September 2000   Sam Soliman 11.5¾ (Australia) L PTS 12 Howard Eastman 11.4½ (England), York Hall, Bethnal Green, London, England. This was not an easy fight for the unbeaten Eastman, who found it difficult to deal with such an awkward customer and failed to cut the ring down, often being one dimensional. Although Soliman was cut over the right eye in the eighth, Eastman continued to labour and Larry O'Connell's 117-113 score in his favour did little to please the fans who expected more.

10 April 2001   Howard Eastman 11.5 (England) W RSC 10 Robert McCracken 11.5¾ (England), The Conference Centre, Wembley, England. Referee: Dave Parris. Judges: Larry O'Connell, Terry O'Connor, John Keane. Billed for the vacant European title, but also involving the British and Commonwealth championships. For a summary, see under British Title Bouts During 2000-2001.

S. Middleweight

18 November 2000   David Starie 11.13½ (England) W RSC 6 Guy Waters 11.13¾ (Australia), Goresbrook Leisure Centre, Dagenham, England. This was more like it for Starie as he quickly got down to work, outboxing his experienced challenger and setting him up for what was to come. It was in round six that the champion really got his big punches off the ground and series of heavy blows saw Waters up against the ropes and not defending himself when the referee, Mickey Vann, stepped in at the 2.14 mark to bring the contest to a conclusion.

L. Heavyweight

2 January 2001   Neil Simpson 12.6 (England) W CO 4 Hastings Rasani 12.3¾ (Zimbabwe), The Skydome, Coventry, England. Matched for the vacant title after Clinton Woods (England) had decided to hand back his belt in March 2000 to pursue a WBC championship fight, the pair served up a real ding dong with enough excitement to last a dozen or so rounds not just four. Floored four times in a hectic opening six minutes, Simpson somehow weathered the storm and came roaring back to outbox his heavy-hitting opponent in the third and take him apart in the fourth. Knocked down twice in the same corner, Rasani was counted out by the third man, Paul Thomas, three seconds after the bell rang to end round four. The unfortunate Simpson eventually forfeited the title on 6 April 2001 when losing to the Ugandan-born Yawe Davis in a European championship fight.

8 May 2001   Tony Oakey 12.5 (England) W RSC 10 Hastings Rasani 12.1½ (Zimbabwe), The Metrodome, Barnsley, England. Despite being badly outreached, Oakey made light of it to make the body his target and to rough up Rasani in doing so. Both men landed and took solid punches, but as time dragged on it was Oakey's deliveries that were having more effect and two heavy left hooks eventually put the Zimbabwean down in the tenth. Although Rasani rose at eight, there would be no respite and with Oakey incessantly raining in punch after punch, the referee, Mark Green, jumped in to the rescue at 1.57 on the clock.

Cruiserweight

10 March 2001   Bruce Scott 13.5¾ (England) W RTD 3 Garry Delaney 13.8 (England), York Hall, Bethnal Green, London, England. Referee: Terry O'Connor. This one was billed for the vacant title when it appeared that the champion, Adam Watt (Australia), had all but retired. For a summary, see under British Title Bouts During 2000-2001.

Heavyweight

21 October 2000   Danny Williams 18.1 (England) W RSC 6 Mark Potter 16.10 (England), The Conference Centre, Wembley, England. Referee: John Coyle. For a summary, see under British Title Bouts During 2000-2001.

9 June 2001   Danny Williams 17.11½ (England) W RSC 1 Kali Meehan 16.11 (New Zealand), York Hall, Bethnal Green, London, England. Despite the unbeaten New Zealander arriving in this country with a good reputation it counted for nothing as Williams took just 32 seconds to retain the title, Meehan being rescued by Terry O'Connor following two heavy knockdowns from right handers. The result also produced the quickest ever Commonwealth title victory, thus eclipsing Derek Williams' 55-second job on Hughroy Currie in 1989.

Commonwealth Champions, 1887-2001

Since the 1997 edition, Harold Alderman's magnificent research into Imperial British Empire title fights has introduced many more claimants/champions than were shown previously. Prior to 12 October 1954, the date that the British Commonwealth and Empire Boxing Championships Committee was formed, there was no official body as such and the Australian and British promoters virtually ran the show, with other members of the British Empire mainly out in the cold. We have also listed Canadian representatives, despite championship boxing in that country being contested over ten or 12 rounds at most, but they are not accorded the same kind of recognition that their British and Australian counterparts are. On 8 September 1970, Bunny Sterling became the first immigrant to win a British title under the ten-year residential ruling and from that date on champions are recorded by domicile rather than by birthplace. Reconstituted as the British Commonwealth Boxing Championships Committee on 22 November 1972, and with a current membership that includes Australia, Bahama, Ghana, Guyana, Jamaica, Kenya, New Zealand, Nigeria, South Africa, Tanzania, Trinidad and Tobago, Zambia, and Zimbabwe, in 1989 the "British" tag was dropped.

COMMONWEALTH COUNTRY CODE
A = Australia; BAH = Bahamas; BAR = Barbados; BER = Bermuda; C = Canada; E = England; F = Fiji; GH = Ghana; GU = Guyana; I = Ireland; J = Jamaica; K = Kenya; N = Nigeria; NZ = New Zealand; NI = Northern Ireland; PNG = Papua New Guinea; SA = South Africa; SAM = Samoa; S = Scotland; T = Tonga; TR = Trinidad; U = Uganda; W = Wales; ZA = Zambia; ZI = Zimbabwe.

Champions in **bold** denote those recognised by the British Commonwealth and Empire Boxing Championships Committee (1954 to date) and, prior to that, those with the best claims

*Undefeated champions (Does not include men who forfeited titles)

Title Holder	Birthplace/ Domicile	Tenure	Title Holder	Birthplace/ Domicile	Tenure	Title Holder	Birthplace/ Domicile	Tenure
Flyweight (112 lbs)			**Jim Higgins**	S	1920-1922	Johnny Gaudes	C	1937-1939
Elky Clark*	S	1924-1927	**Tommy Harrison**	E	1922-1923	Lefty Gwynn	C	1939
Harry Hill	E	1929	**Bugler Harry Lake**	E	1923	Baby Yack	C	1939-1940
Frenchy Belanger	C	1929	**Johnny Brown**	E	1923-1928	**Jim Brady**	S	1941-1945
Vic White	A	1929-1930	Billy McAllister	A	1928-1930	**Jackie Paterson**	S	1945-1949
Teddy Green	A	1930-1931	**Teddy Baldock***	E	1928-1930	**Stan Rowan**	E	1949
Jackie Paterson	S	1940-1948	Johnny Peters	E	1930	**Vic Toweel**	SA	1949-1952
Rinty Monaghan*	NI	1948-1950	**Dick Corbett**	E	1930-1932	**Jimmy Carruthers***	A	1952-1954
Teddy Gardner	E	1952	**Johnny King**	E	1932-1934	Peter Keenan	S	1955-1959
Jake Tuli	SA	1952-1954	**Dick Corbett**	E	1934	**Freddie Gilroy***	NI	1959-1963
Dai Dower*	W	1954-1957	Frankie Martin	C	1935-1937	**Johnny Caldwell**	NI	1964-1965
Frankie Jones	S	1957	Baby Yack	C	1937	**Alan Rudkin**	E	1965-1966
Dennis Adams*	SA	1957-1962						
Jackie Brown	S	1962-1963						
Walter McGowan*	S	1963-1969						
John McCluskey	S	1970-1971						
Henry Nissen	A	1971-1974						
Big Jim West*	A	1974-1975						
Patrick Mambwe	ZA	1976-1979						
Ray Amoo	N	1980						
Steve Muchoki	K	1980-1983						
Keith Wallace*	E	1983-1984						
Richard Clarke	J	1986-1987						
Nana Yaw Konadu*	GH	1987-1989						
Alfred Kotey*	GH	1989-1993						
Francis Ampofo*	E	1993						
Daren Fifield	E	1993-1994						
Francis Ampofo	E	1994-1995						
Danny Ward	SA	1995-1996						
Peter Culshaw	E	1996-1997						
Ady Lewis*	E	1997-1998						
Alfonso Zvenyika	ZI	1998						
Damaen Kelly	NI	1998-1999						
Keith Knox	S	1999						
Jason Booth	E	1999-						
Bantamweight (118 lbs)								
Digger Stanley	E	1904-1905						
Owen Moran	E	1905						
Ted Green	A	1905-1911						
Charlie Simpson*	A	1911-1912						

Nicky Booth (right) seen making a successful defence of the Commonwealth bantam title against Ady Lewis

Les Clark

Title Holder	Birthplace/ Domicile	Tenure
Walter McGowan	S	1966-1968
Alan Rudkin	E	1968-1969
Lionel Rose*	A	1969
Alan Rudkin*	E	1970-1972
Paul Ferreri	A	1972-1977
Sulley Shittu	GH	1977-1978
Johnny Owen*	W	1978-1980
Paul Ferreri	A	1981-1986
Ray Minus*	BAH	1986-1991
John Armour*	E	1992-1996
Paul Lloyd*	E	1996-2000
Ady Lewis	E	2000
Tommy Waite	NI	2000
Nicky Booth	E	2000-

S. Bantamweight (122 lbs)

Title Holder	Birthplace/ Domicile	Tenure
Neil Swain	W	1995
Neil Swain	W	1996-1997
Michael Brodie	E	1997-1999
Nedal Hussein*	A	2000-2001

Featherweight (126 lbs)

Title Holder	Birthplace/ Domicile	Tenure
Jim Driscoll*	W	1908-1913
Llew Edwards	W	1915-1916
Charlie Simpson*	A	1916
Tommy Noble	E	1919-1921
Bert Spargo	A	1921-1922
Bert McCarthy	A	1922
Bert Spargo	A	1922-1923

Title Holder	Birthplace/ Domicile	Tenure
Billy Grime	A	1923
Ernie Baxter	A	1923
Leo Kid Roy	C	1923
Bert Ristuccia	A	1923-1924
Barney Wilshur	C	1923
Benny Gould	C	1923-1924
Billy Grime	A	1924
Leo Kid Roy	C	1924-1932
Johnny McGrory	S	1936-1938
Jim Spider Kelly	NI	1938-1939
Johnny Cusick	E	1939-1940
Nel Tarleton	E	1940-1947
Tiger Al Phillips	E	1947
Ronnie Clayton	E	1947-1951
Roy Ankrah	GH	1951-1954
Billy Spider Kelly	NI	1954-1955
Hogan Kid Bassey*	N	1955-1957
Percy Lewis	TR	1957-1960
Floyd Robertson	GH	1960-1967
John O'Brien	S	1967
Johnny Famechon*	A	1967-1969
Toro George	NZ	1970-1972
Bobby Dunne	A	1972-1974
Evan Armstrong	S	1974
David Kotey*	GH	1974-1975
Eddie Ndukwu	N	1977-1980
Pat Ford*	GU	1980-1981
Azumah Nelson*	GH	1981-1985
Tyrone Downes	BAR	1986-1988
Thunder Aryeh	GH	1988-1989
Oblitey Commey	GH	1989-1990
Modest Napunyi	K	1990-1991
Barrington Francis*	C	1991
Colin McMillan*	E	1992
Billy Hardy*	E	1992-1996
Jonjo Irwin	E	1996-1997
Paul Ingle*	E	1997-1999
Patrick Mullings	E	1999-2000
Scott Harrison	S	2000-

S. Featherweight (130 lbs)

Title Holder	Birthplace/ Domicile	Tenure
Billy Moeller	A	1975-1977
Johnny Aba*	PNG	1977-1982
Langton Tinago	ZI	1983-1984
John Sichula	ZA	1984
Lester Ellis*	A	1984-1985
John Sichula	ZA	1985-1986
Sam Akromah	GH	1986-1987
John Sichula	ZA	1987-1989
Mark Reefer*	E	1989-1990
Thunder Aryeh	GH	1990-1991
Hugh Forde	E	1991
Paul Harvey	E	1991-1992
Tony Pep	C	1992-1995
Justin Juuko*	U	1995-1998
Charles Shepherd*	E	1999
Mick O'Malley	A	1999-2000
Ian McLeod*	S	2000
James Armah*	GH	2000-2001
Alex Moon	E	2001-

Lightweight (135 lbs)

Title Holder	Birthplace/ Domicile	Tenure
Jim Burge	A	1890
George Dawson*	A	1890
Harry Nickless	E	1892-1894
Arthur Valentine	E	1894-1895
Dick Burge*	E	1894-1895
Jim Murphy*	NZ	1894-1897
Eddie Connolly*	C	1896-1897
Jack Goldswain	E	1906-1908
Jack McGowan	A	1909
Hughie Mehegan	A	1909-1910

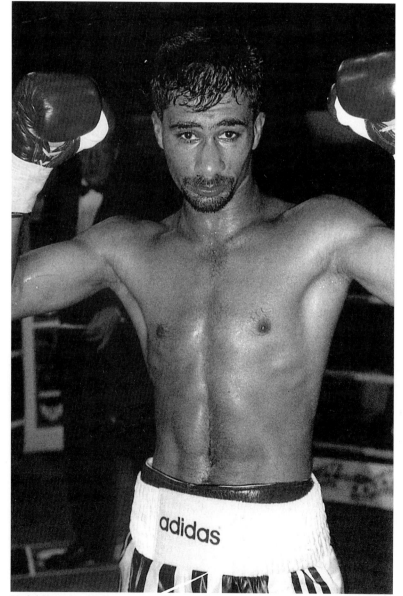

Nedal Hussein, the Commonwealth super-bantam champion Les Clark

Title Holder	Birthplace/ Domicile	Tenure
Johnny Summers*	E	1910
Hughie Mehegan	A	1911
Freddie Welsh*	W	1912-1914
Ernie Izzard	E	1928
Tommy Fairhall	A	1928-1930
Al Foreman	E	1930-1933
Jimmy Kelso	A	1933
Al Foreman*	E	1933-1934
Laurie Stevens*	SA	1936-1937
Dave Crowley	E	1938
Eric Boon	E	1938-1944
Ronnie James*	W	1944-1947
Arthur King	C	1948-1951
Frank Johnson	E	1953
Pat Ford	A	1953-1954
Ivor Germain	BAR	1954
Pat Ford	A	1954-1955
Johnny van Rensburg	SA	1955-1956
Willie Toweel	SA	1956-1959
Dave Charnley	E	1959-1962
Bunny Grant	J	1962-1967
Manny Santos*	NZ	1967
Love Allotey	GH	1967-1968
Percy Hayles	J	1968-1975
Jonathan Dele	N	1975-1977
Lennox Blackmore	GU	1977-1978
Hogan Jimoh	N	1978-1980
Langton Tinago	ZI	1980-1981
Barry Michael	A	1981-1982
Claude Noel	T	1982-1984
Graeme Brooke	A	1984-1985
Barry Michael*	A	1985-1986
Langton Tinago	ZI	1986-1987
Mo Hussein	E	1987-1989
Pat Doherty	E	1989
Najib Daho	E	1989-1990
Carl Crook	E	1990-1992
Billy Schwer	E	1992-1993
Paul Burke	E	1993
Billy Schwer	E	1993-1995
David Tetteh	GH	1995-1997
Billy Irwin	C	1997
David Tetteh	GH	1997-1999
Bobby Vanzie	E	1999-2001
James Armah	GH	2001-

L. Welterweight (140 lbs)

Title Holder	Birthplace/ Domicile	Tenure
Joe Tetteh	GH	1972-1973
Hector Thompson	A	1973-1977
Baby Cassius Austin	A	1977-1978
Jeff Malcolm	A	1978-1979
Obisia Nwankpa	N	1979-1983
Billy Famous	N	1983-1986
Tony Laing	E	1987-1988
Lester Ellis	A	1988-1989
Steve Larrimore	BAH	1989
Tony Ekubia	E	1989-1991
Andy Holligan	E	1991-1994
Ross Hale	E	1994-1995
Paul Ryan	E	1995-1996
Andy Holligan	E	1996-1997
Bernard Paul	E	1997-1999
Eamonn Magee	NI	1999-
Paul Burke	E	1997
Felix Bwalya*	ZA	1997
Paul Burke	E	1998-1999
Eamonn Magee	NI	1999-

Welterweight (147 lbs)

Title Holder	Birthplace/ Domicile	Tenure
Tom Williams	A	1892-1895
Dick Burge	E	1895-1897
Eddie Connelly*	C	1903-1905

Title Holder	Birthplace/ Domicile	Tenure
Joe White*	C	1907-1909
Johnny Summers	E	1912-1914
Tom McCormick	I	1914
Matt Wells	E	1914-1919
Fred Kay	A	1915
Tommy Uren	A	1915-1916
Fritz Holland	A	1916
Tommy Uren	A	1916-1919
Fred Kay	A	1919-1920
Johnny Basham	W	1919-1920
Bermondsey Billy Wells	E	1922
Ted Kid Lewis	E	1920-1924
Tommy Milligan*	S	1924-1925
Jack Carroll	A	1928
Charlie Purdie	A	1928-1929
Wally Hancock	A	1929-1930
Tommy Fairhall*	A	1930
Jack Carroll	A	1934-1938
Eddie Thomas	W	1951
Wally Thom	E	1951-1952
Cliff Curvis	W	1952
Gerald Dreyer	SA	1952-1954
Barry Brown	NZ	1954
George Barnes	A	1954-1956
Darby Brown	A	1956
George Barnes	A	1956-1958
Johnny van Rensburg	SA	1958
George Barnes	A	1958-1960
Brian Curvis*	W	1960-1966
Johnny Cooke	E	1967-1968
Ralph Charles*	E	1968-1972
Clyde Gray	C	1973-1979
Chris Clarke	C	1979
Clyde Gray*	C	1979-1980
Colin Jones*	W	1981-1984
Sylvester Mittee	E	1984-1985
Lloyd Honeyghan*	E	1985-1986
Brian Janssen	A	1987
Wilf Gentzen	A	1987-1988
Gary Jacobs	S	1988-1989
Donovan Boucher	C	1989-1992
Eamonn Loughran*	NI	1992-1993
Andrew Murray*	GU	1993-1997
Kofi Jantuah*	GH	1997-2000
Scott Dixon*	S	2000
Jawaid Khaliq*	E	2000-2001

L. Middleweight (154 lbs)

Title Holder	Birthplace/ Domicile	Tenure
Charkey Ramon*	A	1972-1975
Maurice Hope*	E	1976-1979
Kenny Bristol	GU	1979-1981
Herol Graham*	E	1981-1984
Ken Salisbury	A	1984-1985
Nick Wilshire	E	1985-1987
Lloyd Hibbert	E	1987
Troy Waters*	A	1987-1991
Chris Pyatt*	E	1991-1992
Mickey Hughes	E	1992-1993
Lloyd Honeyghan	E	1993-1994
Leo Young	A	1994-1995
Kevin Kelly	A	1995
Chris Pyatt	E	1995-1996
Steve Foster	E	1996-1997
Kevin Kelly	A	1997-1999
Tony Badea	C	1999-2001
Richard Williams	E	2001-

Middleweight (160 lbs)

Title Holder	Birthplace/ Domicile	Tenure
Chesterfield Goode	E	1887-1890
Toff Wall	E	1890-1891
Jim Hall	A	1892-1893
Bill Heffernan	NZ	1894-1896

Title Holder	Birthplace/ Domicile	Tenure
Bill Doherty	A	1896-1897
Billy Edwards	A	1897-1898
Dido Plumb*	E	1898-1901
Tom Duggan	A	1901-1903
Jack Palmer*	E	1902-1904
Jewey Cooke	E	1903-1904
Tom Dingey	C	1904-1905
Jack Lalor	SA	1905
Ted Nelson	A	1905
Tom Dingey	C	1905
Sam Langford*	C	1907-1911
Ed Williams	A	1908-1910
Arthur Cripps	A	1910
Dave Smith	A	1910-1911
Jerry Jerome	A	1913
Arthur Evernden	E	1913-1914
Mick King	A	1914-1915
Les Darcy*	A	1915-1917
Ted Kid Lewis	E	1922-1923
Roland Todd	E	1923-1926
Len Johnson	E	1926-1928
Tommy Milligan	S	1926-1928
Alex Ireland	S	1928-1929
Len Harvey	E	1929-1933
Del Fontaine	C	1931
Ted Moore	E	1931
Jock McAvoy	E	1933-1939
Ron Richards*	A	1940
Ron Richards*	A	1941-1942
Bos Murphy	NZ	1948
Dick Turpin	E	1948-1949
Dave Sands*	A	1949-1952
Randy Turpin	E	1952-1954
Al Bourke	A	1952-1954
Johnny Sullivan	E	1954-1955
Pat McAteer	E	1955-1958
Dick Tiger	N	1958-1960
Wilf Greaves	C	1960
Dick Tiger*	N	1960-1962
Gomeo Brennan	BAH	1963-1964
Tuna Scanlon*	NZ	1964
Gomeo Brennan	BAH	1964-1966
Blair Richardson*	C	1966-1967
Milo Calhoun	J	1967
Johnny Pritchett*	E	1967-1969
Les McAteer	E	1969-1970
Mark Rowe	E	1970
Bunny Sterling	E	1970-1972
Tony Mundine*	A	1972-1975
Monty Betham	NZ	1975-1978
Al Korovou	A	1978
Ayub Kalule	U	1978-1980
Tony Sibson*	E	1980-1983
Roy Gumbs	E	1983
Mark Kaylor	E	1983-1984
Tony Sibson*	E	1984-1988
Nigel Benn	E	1988-1989
Michael Watson*	E	1989-1991
Richie Woodhall	E	1992-1995
Robert McCracken	E	1995-1997
Johnson Tshuma	SA	1997-1998
Paul Jones	E	1998-1999
Jason Matthews*	E	1999
Alain Bonnamie*	C	1999-2000
Sam Soliman	A	2000
Howard Eastman	GU	2000-

S. Middleweight (168 lbs)

Title Holder	Birthplace/ Domicile	Tenure
Rod Carr	A	1989-1990
Lou Cafaro	A	1990-1991
Henry Wharton*	E	1991-1997

Title Holder	Birthplace/ Domicile	Tenure
Clinton Woods	E	1997-1998
David Starie	E	1998-
L. Heavyweight (175 lbs)		
Dave Smith*	A	1911-1915
Jack Bloomfield*	E	1923-1924
Tom Berry	E	1927
Gipsy Daniels*	W	1927
Len Harvey	E	1939-1942
Freddie Mills*	E	1942-1950
Randy Turpin*	E	1952-1955
Gordon Wallace	C	1956-1957
Yvon Durelle*	C	1957-1959
Chic Calderwood	S	1960-1963
Bob Dunlop*	A	1968-1970
Eddie Avoth	W	1970-1971
Chris Finnegan	E	1971-1973
John Conteh*	E	1973-1974
Steve Aczel	A	1975
Tony Mundine	A	1975-1978
Gary Summerhays	C	1978-1979
Lottie Mwale	ZA	1979-1985
Leslie Stewart*	TR	1985-1987
Willie Featherstone	C	1987-1989
Guy Waters*	A	1989-1993
Brent Kosolofski	C	1993-1994
Garry Delaney	E	1994-1995
Noel Magee	I	1995
Nicky Piper*	W	1995-1997
Crawford Ashley	E	1998-1999
Clinton Woods*	E	1999-2000

Title Holder	Birthplace/ Domicile	Tenure
Neil Simpson	E	2001
Tony Oakey	E	2001-
Cruiserweight (190 lbs)		
Stewart Lithgo	E	1984
Chisanda Mutti	ZA	1984-1987
Glenn McCrory*	E	1987-1989
Apollo Sweet	A	1989
Derek Angol*	E	1989-1993
Francis Wanyama	U	1994-1995
Chris Okoh	E	1995-1997
Darren Corbett	NI	1997-1998
Bruce Scott	E	1998-1999
Adam Watt*	A	2000-2001
Bruce Scott	E	2001-
Heavyweight (190 lbs +)		
Peter Jackson*	A	1889-1901
Dan Creedon	NZ	1896-1903
Billy McColl	A	1902-1905
Tim Murphy	A	1905-1906
Bill Squires	A	1906-1909
Bill Lang	A	1909-1910
Tommy Burns*	C	1910-1911
P.O. Curran	I	1911
Dan Flynn	I	1911
Bombardier Billy Wells	E	1911-1919
Bill Lang	A	1911-1913
Dave Smith	A	1913-1917
Joe Beckett*	E	1919-1923
Phil Scott	E	1926-1931

Title Holder	Birthplace/ Domicile	Tenure
Larry Gains	C	1931-1934
Len Harvey	E	1934
Jack Petersen	W	1934-1936
Ben Foord	SA	1936-1937
Tommy Farr	W	1937
Len Harvey*	E	1939-1942
Jack London	E	1944-1945
Bruce Woodcock	E	1945-1950
Jack Gardner	E	1950-1952
Johnny Williams	W	1952-1953
Don Cockell	E	1953-1956
Joe Bygraves	J	1956-1957
Joe Erskine	W	1957-1958
Brian London	E	1958-1959
Henry Cooper	E	1959-1971
Joe Bugner	E	1971
Jack Bodell	E	1971-1972
Danny McAlinden	NI	1972-1975
Bunny Johnson	E	1975
Richard Dunn	E	1975-1976
Joe Bugner*	E	1976-1977
John L. Gardner*	E	1978-1981
Trevor Berbick	C	1981-1986
Horace Notice*	E	1986-1988
Derek Williams	E	1988-1992
Lennox Lewis*	E	1992-1993
Henry Akinwande	E	1993-1995
Scott Welch	E	1995-1997
Julius Francis*	E	1997-1999
Danny Williams	E	1999-

England's Howard Eastman (left) won the Commonwealth middles title on beating Sam Soliman last September   Les Clark

European Title Bouts During 2000-2001

All of last season's title bouts are shown in date order within their weight division and give the boxers' respective weights, along with the scorecard if going to a decision. There is also a short summary of any bout that involved a British contestant, and British officials are listed where applicable.

Flyweight

9 December 2000   Alexander Mahmutov 7.13 (Russia) W PTS 12 David Guerault 7.12$^1/_2$ (France), Villeurbanne, France. Scorecards: 115-114, 116-114, 116-113. Contested for the vacant title after Damaen Kelly (Ireland) relinquished the belt in September 2000 to concentrate on an IBO world title challenge.

23 March 2001   Alexander Mahmutov 7.11$^3/_4$ (Russia) W PTS 12 Jose Lopez Bueno 7.12$^1/_2$ (Spain), Zaragoza, Spain. Scorecards: 115-114, 117-112, 117-112.

30 June 2001   Alexander Mahmutov 7.12$^1/_2$ (Russia) W PTS 12 Jason Booth 7.13 (England), Madrid, Spain. Scorecards: 118-112, 116-114, 116-114. This was a contest that Booth should have won handily, but inexperience let him down. Still, he looked to have won it, and with Mahmutov cut over both eyes if he had stuck to his boxing instead of getting involved at close quarters the decision would surely have been his.

Bantamweight

6 October 2000   Luigi Castiglione 8.6 (Italy) W PTS 12 Jesper Jensen 8.5$^1/_4$ (Denmark), Naestved, Denmark. Scorecards: 116-112, 116-113, 111-117. Referee: Larry O'Connell. The title had become vacant after Johnny Bredahl (Denmark) relinquished on 2 June 2000, due to him being unable to prepare in time for a 17 June defence.

12 March 2001   Luigi Castiglione 8.4$^3/_4$ (Italy) L PTS 12 Fabien Guillerme 8.6 (France), Paris, France. Scorecards: Mickey Vann 116-113, 114-116, 114-115.

12 June 2001   Fabien Guillerme 8.6 (France) L PTS 12 Alex Yagupov 8.6 (Russia), Nice, France. Scorecards: 113-114, 112-116, 113-114. Referee: Mickey Vann.

S. Bantamweight

1 July 2000   Michael Brodie 8.9 (England) W CO 4 Mustapha Hame 8.9 (France), Bowler's Arena, Manchester, England. Knocked down in the first round by an overhand southpaw left, the champion came roaring back with a mixture of body attacks and straight punches. The end came 1.08 into the fourth when Hame failed to beat the count following a left hook to the ribs, having been down the previous round after taking a body shot that was deemed to have been low. Brodie relinquished the title in September 2000 in order to prepare for a challenge on the WBC title.

30 November 2000   Vladislav Antonov 8.4 (Russia) W PTS 12 Sergei Devakov 8.2 (Ukraine), Elancourt, France. Scorecards: 116-112, 117-112, 116-113.

6 March 2001   Vladislav Antonov 8.9$^1/_2$ (Russia) L RSC

7 Salim Medjkoune 8.9 (France), Clermont Ferrand, France.

Featherweight

25 May 2001   Manuel Calvo 8.13$^1/_4$ (Spain) W PTS 12 Steve Robinson 8.13$^1/_4$ (Wales), Leganes, Spain. Scorecards: 116-113, 116-114, 115-115. Billed for the vacant title following the Hungarian, Istvan Kovacs' decision to give up his belt after he had won the WBO crown on 27 January 2001, Calvo just about deserved the verdict with his better work. Having learned from their first fight, the Spaniard never allowed Robinson to work the body for any period of time and used his left hand to distance himself from his opponent, despite carrying a cut left eye from the fifth round on.

S. Featherweight

1 September 2000   Boris Sinitsin 9.3 (Russia) L PTS 12 Dennis Holbaek Pedersen 9.4 (Denmark), Kolding,

Michael Brodie, England's former undefeated EBU super-bantamweight champion   Les Clark

Denmark. Scorecards: Roy Francis 114-116, 114-116, 113-117. Pedersen relinquished the title in November 2000, due to increased weight.

20 January 2001   Tontcho Tontchev 9.3³/₄ (Bulgaria) W RTD 1 Anatoly Alexandrov 9.3³/₄ (Russia), York Hall, Bethnal Green, London, England. Referee: John Coyle. Judge: Terry O'Connor. Tontchev vacated in June to pursue a world title shot.

Lightweight

16 September 2000   Julien Lorcy 9.6¹/₂ (France) W RSC 3 Gianni Gelli 9.7 (Italy), Chateaureoux, France. Referee: John Coyle. Lorcy relinquished the title in January 2001 to concentrate on a crack at the WBA crown.

26 May 2001   Stefano Zoff 9.6¹/₄ (Italy) W RSC 10 Djamel Lifa 9.7¹/₄ (France), Trieste, Italy. Judge: Richie Davies.

L. Welterweight

7 October 2000   Oktay Urkal 10.0 (Germany) W PTS 12 Gabriel Mapouka 9.13 (France), Berlin, Germany. Scorecards: 118-112, 116-114, 113-116. Urkal relinquished the title in May 2001 to concentrate on a WBA/WBC championship fight against Kostya Tszyu, scheduled for June.

23 June 2001   Gianluca Branco 9.13¹/₂ (Italy) W PTS 12 Gabriel Mapouka 9.12¹/₂ (France), Massy, France. Scorecards: Dave Parris 115-114, 116-113, 114-114. Referee: Richie Davies.

Welterweight

1 July 2000   Alessandro Duran 10.5¹/₂ (Italy) W PTS 12 Jose Ramon Escriche 10.6 (Spain), Ferrara, Italy. Scorecards: Terry O'Connor 118-110, 118-111, 118-111.

3 November 2000   Alessandro Duran 10.6 (Italy) L PTS 12 Thomas Damgaard 10.6³/₄ (Denmark), Copenhagen, Denmark. Scorecards: John Keane 115-114, 113-116, 114-115. Damgaard was stripped of the title in February 2001 for refusing to give Duran a rematch.

4 May 2001   Alessandro Duran 10.6¹/₂ (Italy) W RSC 9 Maxim Nesterenko 10.6 (Russia), Bologna, Italy.

L. Middleweight

29 January 2001   Mamadou Thiam 10.12¹/₂ (France) W RSC 8 Paolo Pizzamiglio 10.12¹/₂ (Italy), Paris, France. With Roman Karmazin (Russia) having relinquished on 26 September 2000 to concentrate on a WBC title challenge, this was for the vacant title.

14 May 2001   Mamadou Thiam 10.13¹/₂ (France) W RSC 9 Michael Rask 10.13¹/₄ (Denmark), Paris, France. Judge: John Coyle.

Middleweight

12 August 2000   Erland Betare 11.6 (Italy) W PTS 12 Davide Ciarlante 11.6 (Italy), St Martin, French Antilles.

Scorecards: Paul Thomas 117-113, 116-112, 116-112. Betare, rated number one by the WBC, vacated the title in December 2000 to concentrate on a world title challenge.

10 April 2001   Howard Eastman 11.5 (England) W RSC 10 Robert McCracken 11.5³/₄ (England), The Conference Centre, Wembley, England. Referee: Dave Parris. Judges: Larry O'Connell, Terry O'Connor, John Keane. Billed for the vacant European title, but also involving the British and Commonwealth championships. For a summary, see under British Title Bouts During 2000-2001.

S. Middleweight

16 September 2000   Andrei Shkalikov 11.13 (Russia) W RSC 8 Frederik Alvarez 11.13¹/₄ (Denmark), Chateauroux, France. Judge: John Coyle. Billed for the vacant title after Bruno Girard (France) handed his belt back in October 1999 in order to challenge for the WBA championship. Judge: John Coyle.

27 January 2001   Andrei Shkalikov 11.13¹/₂ (Russia) L PTS 12 Danilo Haeussler 11.13¹/₂ (Germany), Riesa, Germany. Scorecards: 113-116, 114-115, 115-113. Referee: Larry O'Connell.

L. Heavyweight

6 April 2001   Yawe Davis 12.6³/₄ (Italy) W RSC 3 Neil Simpson 12.3¹/₂ (England), Grosseto, Italy. In a fight for the vacant title, Clinton Woods having relinquished his crown in October 2000 in order to pursue a world title shot, Simpson was ultimately not strong enough for the veteran, Davis. As game as ever, especially after being weakened by unnecessary weight problems, the Englishman was knocked to the floor with two minutes of the third underway and, on rising, the referee stopped the fight due to a badly-cut right eye.

Cruiserweight

25 September 2000   Carl Thompson 13.8 (England) W RSC 2 Alexei Iliin 13.7¹/₂ (Russia), The Metrodome, Barnsley, England. Outscored during the opening round, Thompson merely bided his time before catching up with the Russian in the second. A terrific left hook, followed by a further salvo of punches, put Iliin down and, on rising at the count of nine, he was deemed to be in no position to defend himself. Thompson relinquished the title on winning the IBO championship on 3 February 2001.

21 April 2001   Alexander Gurov 13.7¹/₄ (Ukraine) W RSC 8 Torsten May 13.7 (Germany), Erfort, Germany.

Heavyweight

25 November 2000   Vitali Klitschko 18.1 (Ukraine) W PTS 12 Timo Hoffmann 17.10¹/₂ (Germany), Hanover, Germany. Scorecards: 120-108, 120-108, 119-109. Referee: Richie Davies. Contested for the vacant title following Vladimir Klitschko's decision to relinquish in July 2000, in order to challenge for the WBO crown.

European Champions, 1909-2001

Prior to 1946, the championship was contested under the auspices of the International Boxing Union, re-named that year as the European Boxing Union (EBU). The IBU had come into being when Victor Breyer, a Paris-based journalist and boxing referee who later edited the Annuaire du Ring (first edition in 1910), warmed to the idea of an organisation that controlled boxing right across Europe, regarding rules and championship fights between the champions of the respective countries. He first came to London at the end of 1909 to discuss the subject with the NSC, but went away disappointed. However, at a meeting between officials from Switzerland and France in March 1912, the IBU was initially formed and, by June of that year, had published their first ratings. By April 1914, Belgium had also joined the organisation, although it would not be until the war was over that the IBU really took off. Many of the early champions shown on the listings were the result of promoters, especially the NSC, billing their own championship fights. Although the (French dominated) IBU recognised certain champions, prior to being re-formed in May 1920, they did not find their administrative 'feet' fully until other countries such as Italy (1922), Holland (1923), and Spain (1924), produced challengers for titles. Later in the 1920s, Germany (1926), Denmark (1928), Portugal (1929) and Romania (1929) also joined the fold. Unfortunately, for Britain, its representatives (Although the BBBoC, as we know it today, was formed in 1929, an earlier attempt to form a Board of Control had been initiated in April 1918 by the NSC and it was that body who were involved here) failed to reach agreement on the three judges' ruling, following several meetings with the IBU early in 1920 and, apart from Elky Clark (fly), Ernie Rice and Alf Howard (light), and Jack Hood (welter), who conformed to that stipulation, fighters from these shores would not be officially recognised as champions until the EBU was formed in 1946. This led to British fighters claiming the title after beating IBU titleholders, or their successors, under championship conditions in this country. The only men who did not come into this category were Kid Nicholson (bantam), and Ted Kid Lewis and Tommy Milligan (welter), who defeated men not recognised by the IBU. For the record, the first men recognised and authorised, respectively, as being champions of their weight classes by the IBU were: Sid Smith and Michel Montreuil (fly), Charles Ledoux (bantam), Jim Driscoll and Louis de Ponthieu (feather), Freddie Welsh and Georges Papin (light), Georges Carpentier and Albert Badoud (welter), Georges Carpentier and Ercole Balzac (middle), Georges Carpentier and Battling Siki (light-heavy and heavy).

EUROPEAN COUNTRY CODE
AU = Austria; BEL = Belgium; BUL = Bulgaria; CRO = Croatia; CZ = Czechoslovakia; DEN = Denmark; E = England; FIN = Finland; FR = France; GER = Germany; GRE = Greece; HOL = Holland; HUN = Hungary; ITA = Italy; KAZ = Kazakhstan; LUX = Luxembourg; NI = Northern Ireland; NOR = Norway; POR = Portugal; ROM = Romania; RUS = Russia; S = Scotland; SP = Spain; SWE = Sweden; SWI = Switzerland; TU = Turkey; UK = Ukraine; W = Wales; YUG = Yugoslavia.

Champions in **bold** denote those recognised by the IBU/EBU

*Undefeated champions (Does not include men who may have forfeited titles)

Title Holder	Birthplace/ Domicile	Tenure	Title Holder	Birthplace/ Domicile	Tenure	Title Holder	Birthplace/ Domicile	Tenure
Flyweight (112 lbs)			Teddy Gardner*	E	1952	Damaen Kelly*	NI	2000
Sid Smith	E	1913	Louis Skena*	FR	1953-1954	**Alexander Mahmutov**	RUS	2000-
Bill Ladbury	E	1913-1914	**Nazzareno Giannelli**	ITA	1954-1955			
Percy Jones	W	1914	**Dai Dower**	W	1955	**Bantamweight (118 lbs)**		
Joe Symonds	E	1914	**Young Martin**	SP	1955-1959	Joe Bowker	E	1910
Tancy Lee	S	1914-1916	**Risto Luukkonen**	FIN	1959-1961	Digger Stanley	E	1910-1912
Jimmy Wilde	W	1914-1915	**Salvatore Burruni***	ITA	1961-1965	**Charles Ledoux**	FR	1912-1921
Jimmy Wilde*	W	1916-1923	**Rene Libeer**	FR	1965-1966	Bill Beynon	W	1913
Michel Montreuil	BEL	1923-1925	**Fernando Atzori**	ITA	1967-1972	Tommy Harrison	E	1921-1922
Elky Clark*	S	1925-1927	**Fritz Chervet**	SWI	1972-1973	**Charles Ledoux**	FR	1922-1923
Victor Ferrand	SP	1927	**Fernando Atzori**	ITA	1973	Bugler Harry Lake	E	1923
Emile Pladner	FR	1928-1929	**Fritz Chervet***	SWI	1973-1974	Johnny Brown	E	1923-1928
Johnny Hill	S	1928-1929	**Franco Udella**	ITA	1974-1979	**Henry Scillie***	BEL	1925-1928
Eugene Huat	FR	1929	**Charlie Magri***	E	1979-1983	Kid Nicholson	E	1928
Emile Degand	BEL	1929-1930	**Antoine Montero**	FR	1983-1984	Teddy Baldock	E	1928-1931
Kid Oliva	FR	1930	**Charlie Magri***	E	1984-1985	**Domenico Bernasconi**	ITA	1929
Lucien Popescu	ROM	1930-1931	**Franco Cherchi**	ITA	1985	**Carlos Flix**	SP	1929-1931
Jackie Brown	E	1931-1935	**Charlie Magri**	E	1985-1986	**Lucien Popescu**	ROM	1931-1932
Praxile Gyde	FR	1932-1935	**Duke McKenzie***	E	1986-1988	**Domenico Bernasconi**	ITA	1932
Benny Lynch	S	1935-1938	**Eyup Can***	TU	1989-1990	**Nicholas Biquet**	BEL	1932-1935
Kid David*	BEL	1935-1936	**Pat Clinton***	S	1990-1991	**Maurice Dubois**	SWI	1935-1936
Ernst Weiss	AU	1936	**Salvatore Fanni**	ITA	1991-1992	**Joseph Decico**	FR	1936
Valentin Angelmann*	FR	1936-1938	**Robbie Regan***	W	1992-1993	**Aurel Toma**	ROM	1936-1937
Enrico Urbinati*	ITA	1938-1943	**Luigi Camputaro**	ITA	1993-1994	**Nicholas Biquet**	BEL	1937-1938
Raoul Degryse	BEL	1946-1947	**Robbie Regan***	W	1994-1995	**Aurel Toma**	ROM	1938-1939
Maurice Sandeyron	FR	1947-1949	**Luigi Camputaro***	ITA	1995-1996	**Ernst Weiss**	AU	1939
Rinty Monaghan*	NI	1949-1950	**Jesper Jensen**	DEN	1996-1997	**Gino Cattaneo**	ITA	1939-1941
Terry Allen	E	1950	**David Guerault***	FR	1997-1999	**Gino Bondavilli***	ITA	1941-1943
Jean Sneyers*	BEL	1950-1951	**Alexander Mahmutov**	RUS	1999-2000	**Jackie Paterson**	S	1946

Title Holder	Birthplace/Domicile	Tenure
Theo Medina	FR	1946-1947
Peter Kane	E	1947-1948
Guido Ferracin	ITA	1948-1949
Luis Romero	SP	1949-1951
Peter Keenan	S	1951-1952
Jean Sneyers*	BEL	1952-1953
Peter Keenan	S	1953
John Kelly	NI	1953-1954
Robert Cohen*	FR	1954-1955
Mario D'Agata	ITA	1955-1958
Piero Rollo	ITA	1958-1959
Freddie Gilroy	NI	1959-1960
Pierre Cossemyns	BEL	1961-1962
Piero Rollo	ITA	1962
Alphonse Halimi	FR	1962
Piero Rollo	ITA	1962-1963
Mimoun Ben Ali	SP	1963
Risto Luukkonen	FIN	1963-1964
Mimoun Ben Ali	SP	1965
Tommaso Galli	ITA	1965-1966
Mimoun Ben Ali	SP	1966-1968
Salvatore Burruni*	ITA	1968-1969
Franco Zurlo	ITA	1969-1971
Alan Rudkin	E	1971
Agustin Senin*	SP	1971-1973
Johnny Clark*	E	1973-1974
Bob Allotey	SP	1974-1975
Daniel Trioulaire	FR	1975-1976
Salvatore Fabrizio	ITA	1976-1977
Franco Zurlo	ITA	1977-1978
Juan Francisco Rodriguez	SP	1978-1980
Johnny Owen*	W	1980
Valerio Nati	ITA	1980-1982
Giuseppe Fossati	ITA	1982-1983
Walter Giorgetti	ITA	1983-1984
Ciro de Leva*	ITA	1984-1986
Antoine Montero	FR	1986-1987
Louis Gomis*	FR	1987-1988
Fabrice Benichou	FR	1988
Vincenzo Belcastro*	ITA	1988-1990
Thierry Jacob*	FR	1990-1992
Johnny Bredahl*	DEN	1992
Vincenzo Belcastro	ITA	1993-1994
Prince Naseem Hamed*	E	1994-1995
John Armour*	E	1995-1996
Johnny Bredahl	DEN	1996-1998
Paul Lloyd*	E	1998-1999
Johnny Bredahl*	DEN	1999-2000
Luigi Castiglione	ITA	2000-2001
Fabien Guillerme	FR	2001
Alex Yagupov	RUS	2001-

S. Bantamweight (122 lbs)

Title Holder	Birthplace/Domicile	Tenure
Vincenzo Belcastro	ITA	1995-1996
Salim Medjkoune	FR	1996
Martin Krastev	BUL	1996-1997
Spencer Oliver	E	1997-1998
Sergei Devakov	UK	1998-1999
Michael Brodie*	E	1999-2000
Vladislav Antonov	RUS	2000-2001
Salim Medjkoune	FR	2001-

Featherweight (126 lbs)

Title Holder	Birthplace/Domicile	Tenure
Young Joey Smith	E	1911
Jean Poesy	FR	1911-1912
Jim Driscoll*	W	1912-1913
Ted Kid Lewis*	E	1913-1914
Louis de Ponthieu*	FR	1919-1920
Arthur Wyns	BEL	1920-1922
Billy Matthews	E	1922
Eugene Criqui*	FR	1922-1923
Edouard Mascart	FR	1923-1924
Charles Ledoux	FR	1924
Henri Hebrans	BEL	1924-1925
Antonio Ruiz	SP	1925-1928
Luigi Quadrini	ITA	1928-1929
Knud Larsen	DEN	1929
Jose Girones	SP	1929-1934
Maurice Holtzer*	FR	1935-1938
Phil Dolhem	BEL	1938-1939
Lucien Popescu	ROM	1939-1941
Ernst Weiss	AU	1941
Gino Bondavilli	ITA	1941-1945
Ermanno Bonetti*	ITA	1945-1946
Tiger Al Phillips	E	1947
Ronnie Clayton	E	1947-1948
Ray Famechon	FR	1948-1953
Jean Sneyers	BEL	1953-1954
Ray Famechon	FR	1954-1955
Fred Galiana*	SP	1955-1956
Cherif Hamia	FR	1957-1958
Sergio Caprari	ITA	1958-1959
Gracieux Lamperti	FR	1959-1962
Alberto Serti	ITA	1962-1963
Howard Winstone	W	1963-1967
Jose Legra*	SP	1967-1968
Manuel Calvo	SP	1968-1969
Tommaso Galli	ITA	1969-1970
Jose Legra*	SP	1970-1972
Gitano Jiminez	SP	1973-1975
Elio Cotena	ITA	1975-1976
Nino Jimenez	SP	1976-1977
Manuel Masso	SP	1977
Roberto Castanon*	SP	1977-1981
Salvatore Melluzzo	ITA	1981-1982
Pat Cowdell*	E	1982-1983
Loris Stecca*	ITA	1983
Barry McGuigan*	NI	1983-1985
Jim McDonnell*	E	1985-1987
Valerio Nati*	ITA	1987
Jean-Marc Renard*	BEL	1988-1989
Paul Hodkinson*	E	1989-1991
Fabrice Benichou	FR	1991-1992
Maurizio Stecca	ITA	1992-1993
Herve Jacob	FR	1993
Maurizio Stecca	ITA	1993
Stephane Haccoun	FR	1993-1994
Stefano Zoff	ITA	1994
Medhi Labdouni	FR	1994-1995
Billy Hardy	E	1995-1998
Paul Ingle*	E	1998-1999
Steve Robinson	W	1999-2000
Istvan Kovacs*	HUN	2000-2001
Manuel Calvo	SP	2001-

S. Featherweight (130 lbs)

Title Holder	Birthplace/Domicile	Tenure
Tommaso Galli	ITA	1971-1972
Domenico Chiloiro	ITA	1972
Lothar Abend	GER	1972-1974
Sven-Erik Paulsen*	NOR	1974-1976
Roland Cazeaux	FR	1976
Natale Vezzoli	ITA	1976-1979
Carlos Hernandez	SP	1979
Rodolfo Sanchez	SP	1979
Carlos Hernandez	SP	1979-1982
Cornelius Boza-Edwards*	E	1982
Roberto Castanon	SP	1982-1983
Alfredo Raininger	ITA	1983-1984
Jean-Marc Renard	BEL	1984
Pat Cowdell	E	1984-1985
Jean-Marc Renard*	BEL	1986-1987
Salvatore Curcetti	ITA	1987-1988
Piero Morello	ITA	1988
Lars Lund Jensen	DEN	1988
Racheed Lawal	DEN	1988-1989
Daniel Londas*	FR	1989-1991
Jimmy Bredahl*	DEN	1992
Regilio Tuur	HOL	1992-1993
Jacobin Yoma	FR	1993-1995
Anatoly Alexandrov*	KAZ	1995-1996
Julian Lorcy*	FR	1996
Djamel Lifa	FR	1997-1998
Anatoly Alexandrov*	RUS	1998
Dennis Holbaek Pedersen	DEN	1999-2000
Boris Sinitsin	RUS	2000
Dennis Holbaek Pedersen*	DEN	2000
Tontcho Tontchev*	BUL	2001

Lightweight (135 lbs)

Title Holder	Birthplace/Domicile	Tenure
Freddie Welsh	W	1909-1911
Matt Wells	E	1911-1912
Freddie Welsh*	W	1912-1914
Georges Papin	FR	1920-1921
Ernie Rice	E	1921-1922
Seaman Nobby Hall	E	1922-1923
Harry Mason	E	1923-1926
Fred Bretonnel	FR	1924
Lucien Vinez	FR	1924-1927
Luis Rayo*	SP	1927-1928
Aime Raphael	FR	1928-1929
Francois Sybille	BEL	1929-1930
Alf Howard	E	1930
Harry Corbett	E	1930-1931
Francois Sybille	BEL	1930-1931
Bep van Klaveren	HOL	1931-1932
Cleto Locatelli	ITA	1932
Francois Sybille	BEL	1932-1933
Cleto Locatelli*	ITA	1933
Francois Sybille	BEL	1934
Carlo Orlandi*	ITA	1934-1935
Enrico Venturi*	ITA	1935-1936
Vittorio Tamagnini	ITA	1936-1937
Maurice Arnault	FR	1937
Gustave Humery	FR	1937-1938
Aldo Spoldi*	ITA	1938-1939
Karl Blaho	AU	1940-1941
Bruno Bisterzo	ITA	1941
Ascenzo Botta	ITA	1941
Bruno Bisterzo	ITA	1941-1942
Ascenzo Botta	ITA	1942
Roberto Proietti	ITA	1942-1943
Bruno Bisterzo	ITA	1943-1946
Roberto Proietti*	ITA	1946
Emile Dicristo	FR	1946-1947
Kid Dussart	BEL	1947
Roberto Proietti	ITA	1947-1948
Billy Thompson	E	1948-1949
Kid Dussart	BEL	1949
Roberto Proietti*	ITA	1949-1950
Pierre Montane	FR	1951
Elis Ask	FIN	1951-1952
Jorgen Johansen	DEN	1952-1954
Duilio Loi*	ITA	1954-1959
Mario Vecchiatto	ITA	1959-1960
Dave Charnley	E	1960-1963
Conny Rudhof*	GER	1963-1964
Willi Quatuor*	GER	1964-1965
Franco Brondi	ITA	1965
Maurice Tavant	FR	1965-1966
Borge Krogh	DEN	1966-1967
Pedro Carrasco*	SP	1967-1969

Title Holder	Birthplace/Domicile	Tenure
Miguel Velazquez	SP	1970-1971
Antonio Puddu	ITA	1971-1974
Ken Buchanan*	S	1974-1975
Fernand Roelandts	BEL	1976
Perico Fernandez*	SP	1976-1977
Jim Watt*	S	1977-1979
Charlie Nash*	NI	1979-1980
Francisco Leon	SP	1980
Charlie Nash	NI	1980-1981
Joey Gibilisco	ITA	1981-1983
Lucio Cusma	ITA	1983-1984
Rene Weller	GER	1984-1986
Gert Bo Jacobsen	DEN	1986-1988
Rene Weller*	GER	1988
Policarpo Diaz*	SP	1988-1990
Antonio Renzo	ITA	1991-1992
Jean-Baptiste Mendy*	FR	1992-1994
Racheed Lawal	DEN	1994
Jean-Baptiste Mendy*	FR	1994-1995
Angel Mona	FR	1995-1997
Manuel Carlos Fernandes	FR	1997
Oscar Garcia Cano	SP	1997
Billy Schwer*	E	1997-1999
Oscar Garcia Cano	SP	1999-2000
Lucien Lorcy*	FR	2000-2001
Stefano Zoff	ITA	2001-

L. Welterweight (140 lbs)

Title Holder	Birthplace/Domicile	Tenure
Olli Maki	FIN	1964-1965
Juan Sombrita-Albornoz	SP	1965
Willi Quatuor*	GER	1965-1966
Conny Rudhof	GER	1967
Johann Orsolics	AU	1967-1968
Bruno Arcari*	ITA	1968-1970
Rene Roque	FR	1970-1971
Pedro Carrasco*	SP	1971-1972
Roger Zami	FR	1972
Cemal Kamaci	TU	1972-1973
Toni Ortiz	SP	1973-1974
Perico Fernandez*	SP	1974
Jose Ramon Gomez-Fouz	SP	1975
Cemal Kamaci*	TU	1975-1976
Dave Boy Green*	E	1976-1977
Primo Bandini	ITA	1977
Jean-Baptiste Piedvache	FR	1977-1978
Colin Power	E	1978
Fernando Sanchez	SP	1978-1979
Jose Luis Heredia	SP	1979
Jo Kimpuani	FR	1979-1980
Giuseppe Martinese	ITA	1980
Antonio Guinaldo	SP	1980-1981
Clinton McKenzie	E	1981-1982
Robert Gambini	FR	1982-1983
Patrizio Oliva*	ITA	1983-1985
Terry Marsh	E	1985-1986
Tusikoleta Nkalankete	FR	1987-1989
Efren Calamati	ITA	1989-1990
Pat Barrett	E	1990-1992
Valery Kayumba	ITA	1992-1993
Christian Merle	FR	1993-1994
Valery Kayumba	FR	1994
Khalid Rahilou*	FR	1994-1996
Soren Sondergaard*	DEN	1996-1998
Thomas Damgaard*	DEN	1998-2000
Oktay Urkal*	GER	2000-2001
Gianluca Branco	ITA	2001-

Welterweight (147 lbs)

Title Holder	Birthplace/Domicile	Tenure
Young Joseph	E	1910-1911
Georges Carpentier*	FR	1911-1912
Albert Badoud*	SWI	1915-1921
Johnny Basham	W	1919-1920
Ted Kid Lewis	E	1920-1924
Piet Hobin	BEL	1921-1925
Billy Mack	E	1923
Tommy Milligan	S	1924-1925
Mario Bosisio*	ITA	1925-1928
Leo Darton	BEL	1928
Alf Genon	BEL	1928-1929
Gustave Roth	BEL	1929-1932
Adrien Aneet	BEL	1932-1933
Jack Hood*	E	1933
Gustav Eder	GER	1934-1936
Felix Wouters	BEL	1936-1938
Saverio Turiello	ITA	1938-1939
Marcel Cerdan*	FR	1939-1942
Ernie Roderick	E	1946-1947
Robert Villemain*	FR	1947-1948
Livio Minelli	ITA	1949-1950
Michele Palermo	ITA	1950-1951
Eddie Thomas	W	1951
Charles Humez*	FR	1951-1952
Gilbert Lavoine	FR	1953-1954
Wally Thom	E	1954-1955
Idrissa Dione	FR	1955-1956
Emilio Marconi	ITA	1956-1958
Peter Waterman*	E	1958
Emilio Marconi	ITA	1958-1959
Duilio Loi*	ITA	1959-1963
Fortunato Manca*	ITA	1964-1965
Jean Josselin	FR	1966-1967
Carmelo Bossi	ITA	1967-1968
Fighting Mack	HOL	1968-1969
Silvano Bertini	ITA	1969
Jean Josselin	FR	1969
Johann Orsolics	AU	1969-1970
Ralph Charles	E	1970-1971
Roger Menetrey	FR	1971-1974
John H. Stracey*	E	1974-1975
Marco Scano	ITA	1976-1977
Jorgen Hansen	DEN	1977
Jorg Eipel	GER	1977
Alain Marion	FR	1977-1978
Jorgen Hansen	DEN	1978
Josef Pachler	AU	1978
Henry Rhiney	E	1978-1979
Dave Boy Green	E	1979
Jorgen Hansen*	DEN	1979-1981
Hans-Henrik Palm	DEN	1982
Colin Jones*	W	1982-1983
Gilles Elbilia	FR	1983-1984
Gianfranco Rosi	ITA	1984-1985
Lloyd Honeyghan*	E	1985-1986
Jose Varela	GER	1986-1987
Alfonso Redondo	SP	1987
Mauro Martelli*	SWI	1987-1988
Nino la Rocca	ITA	1989
Antoine Fernandez	FR	1989-1990
Kirkland Laing	E	1990
Patrizio Oliva*	ITA	1990-1992
Ludovic Proto	FR	1992-1993
Gary Jacobs*	S	1993-1994
Jose Luis Navarro	SP	1994-1995
Valery Kayumba	FR	1995
Patrick Charpentier*	FR	1995-1996
Andrei Pestriaev*	RUS	1997
Michele Piccirillo*	ITA	1997-1998
Maxim Nesterenko	RUS	1998-1999
Alessandro Duran	ITA	1999
Andrei Pestriaev	RUS	1999-2000
Alessandro Duran	ITA	2000
Thomas Damgaard	DEN	2000-2001
Alessandro Duran	ITA	2001-

L. Middleweight (154 lbs)

Title Holder	Birthplace/Domicile	Tenure
Bruno Visintin	ITA	1964-1966
Bo Hogberg	SWE	1966
Yolande Leveque	FR	1966
Sandro Mazzinghi*	ITA	1966-1968
Remo Golfarini	ITA	1968-1969
Gerhard Piaskowy	GER	1969-1970
Jose Hernandez	SP	1970-1972
Juan Carlos Duran	ITA	1972-1973
Jacques Kechichian	FR	1973-1974
Jose Duran	SP	1974-1975
Eckhard Dagge	GER	1975-1976
Vito Antuofermo	ITA	1976
Maurice Hope*	E	1976-1978
Gilbert Cohen	FR	1978-1979
Marijan Benes	YUG	1979-1981
Louis Acaries	FR	1981
Luigi Minchillo*	ITA	1981-1983
Herol Graham*	E	1983-1984
Jimmy Cable	E	1984
Georg Steinherr	GER	1984-1985
Said Skouma*	FR	1985-1986
Chris Pyatt	E	1986-1987
Gianfranco Rosi*	ITA	1987
Rene Jacquot*	FR	1988-1989
Edip Secovic	AU	1989
Giuseppe Leto	ITA	1989
Gilbert Dele*	FR	1989-1990
Said Skouma	FR	1991
Mourad Louati	HOL	1991
Jean-Claude Fontana	FR	1991-1992
Laurent Boudouani	FR	1992-1993
Bernard Razzano	FR	1993-1994
Javier Castillejos	SP	1994-1995
Laurent Boudouani*	FR	1995-1996
Faouzi Hattab	FR	1996
Davide Ciarlante*	ITA	1996-1997
Javier Castillejo*	SP	1998
Mamadou Thiam*	FR	1998-2000
Roman Karmazin*	RUS	2000
Mamadou Thiam	FR	2001-

Middleweight (160 lbs)

Title Holder	Birthplace/Domicile	Tenure
Georges Carpentier*	FR	1912-1918
Ercole Balzac	FR	1920-1921
Gus Platts	E	1921
Willem Westbroek	HOL	1921
Johnny Basham	W	1921
Ted Kid Lewis	E	1921-1923
Roland Todd	E	1923-1924
Ted Kid Lewis	E	1924-1925
Bruno Frattini	ITA	1924-1925
Tommy Milligan	S	1925-1928
Rene Devos	BEL	1926-1927
Barthelemy Molina	FR	1928
Alex Ireland	S	1928-1929
Mario Bosisio	ITA	1928
Leone Jacovacci	ITA	1928-1929
Len Johnson	E	1928-1929
Marcel Thil	FR	1929-1930
Mario Bosisio	ITA	1930-1931
Poldi Steinbach	AU	1931
Hein Domgoergen	GER	1931-1932
Ignacio Ara	SP	1932-1933
Gustave Roth	BEL	1933-1934
Marcel Thil*	FR	1934-1938
Edouard Tenet	FR	1938
Bep van Klaveren	HOL	1938
Anton Christoforidis	GRE	1938-1939

EUROPEAN CHAMPIONS, 1909-2001

Title Holder	Birthplace/Domicile	Tenure
Edouard Tenet	FR	1939
Josef Besselmann*	GER	1942-1943
Marcel Cerdan	FR	1947-1948
Cyrille Delannoit	BEL	1948
Marcel Cerdan	FR	1948
Cyrille Delannoit	BEL	1948-1949
Tiberio Mitri*	ITA	1949-1950
Randy Turpin	E	1951-1954
Tiberio Mitri	ITA	1954
Charles Humez	FR	1954-1958
Gustav Scholz*	GER	1958-1961
John Cowboy McCormack	S	1961-1962
Chris Christensen	DEN	1962
Laszlo Papp*	HUN	1962-1965
Nino Benvenuti*	ITA	1965-1967
Juan Carlos Duran	ITA	1967-1969
Tom Bogs	DEN	1969-1970
Juan Carlos Duran	ITA	1970-1971
Jean-Claude Bouttier	FR	1971-1972
Tom Bogs*	DEN	1973
Elio Calcabrini	ITA	1973-1974
Jean-Claude Bouttier	FR	1974
Kevin Finnegan	E	1974-1975
Gratien Tonna*	FR	1975
Bunny Sterling	E	1976
Angelo Jacopucci	ITA	1976
Germano Valsecchi	ITA	1976-1977
Alan Minter	E	1977
Gratien Tonna	FR	1977-1978
Alan Minter*	E	1978-1979
Kevin Finnegan	E	1980
Matteo Salvemini	ITA	1980
Tony Sibson*	E	1980-1982
Louis Acaries	FR	1982-1984
Tony Sibson	E	1984-1985
Ayub Kalule	DEN	1985-1986
Herol Graham	E	1986-1987
Sumbu Kalambay*	ITA	1987
Pierre Joly	FR	1987-1988
Christophe Tiozzo*	FR	1988-1989
Francesco dell' Aquila	ITA	1989-1990
Sumbu Kalambay*	ITA	1990-1993
Agostino Cardamone*	ITA	1993-1994
Richie Woodhall*	E	1995-1996
Alexandre Zaitsev	RUS	1996
Hassine Cherifi*	FR	1996-1998
Agostino Cardamone*	ITA	1998
Erland Betare*	FR	1999-2000
Howard Eastman	E	2001-

S. Middleweight (168 lbs)

Title Holder	Birthplace/Domicile	Tenure
Mauro Galvano*	ITA	1990-1991
James Cook	E	1991-1992
Franck Nicotra*	FR	1992
Vincenzo Nardiello	ITA	1992-1993
Ray Close*	NI	1993
Vinzenzo Nardiello	ITA	1993-1994
Frederic Seillier*	FR	1994-1995
Henry Wharton*	E	1995-1996
Frederic Seillier*	FR	1996
Andrei Shkalikov*	RUS	1997
Dean Francis*	E	1997-1998
Bruno Girard*	FR	1999
Andrei Shkalikov	RUS	2000-2001
Danilo Haeussler	GER	2001-

L. Heavyweight (175 lbs)

Title Holder	Birthplace/Domicile	Tenure
Georges Carpentier	FR	1913-1922
Battling Siki	FR	1922-1923

Title Holder	Birthplace/Domicile	Tenure
Emile Morelle	FR	1923
Raymond Bonnel	FR	1923-1924
Louis Clement	SWI	1924-1926
Herman van T'Hof	HOL	1926
Fernand Delarge	BEL	1926-1927
Max Schmeling*	GER	1927-1928
Michele Bonaglia*	ITA	1929-1930
Ernst Pistulla*	GER	1931-1932
Adolf Heuser	GER	1932
John Andersson	SWE	1933
Martinez de Alfara	SP	1934
Marcel Thil	FR	1934-1935
Merlo Preciso	ITA	1935
Hein Lazek	AU	1935-1936
Gustave Roth	BEL	1936-1938
Adolf Heuser*	GER	1938-1939
Luigi Musina*	ITA	1942-1943
Freddie Mills*	E	1947-1950
Albert Yvel	FR	1950-1951
Don Cockell*	E	1951-1952
Conny Rux*	GER	1952
Jacques Hairabedian	FR	1953-1954
Gerhard Hecht	GER	1954-1955
Willi Hoepner	GER	1955
Gerhard Hecht	GER	1955-1957
Artemio Calzavara	ITA	1957-1958
Willi Hoepner	GER	1958
Erich Schoeppner	GER	1958-1962
Giulio Rinaldi	ITA	1962-1964
Gustav Scholz*	GER	1964-1965
Giulio Rinaldi	ITA	1965-1966
Piero del Papa	ITA	1966-1967
Lothar Stengel	GER	1967-1968
Tom Bogs*	DEN	1968-1969
Yvan Prebeg	YUG	1969-1970
Piero del Papa	ITA	1970-1971
Conny Velensek	GER	1971-1972
Chris Finnegan	E	1972
Rudiger Schmidtke	GER	1972-1973
John Conteh*	E	1973-1974
Domenico Adinolfi	ITA	1974-1976
Mate Parlov*	YUG	1976-1977
Aldo Traversaro	ITA	1977-1979
Rudi Koopmans	HOL	1979-1984
Richard Caramonolis	FR	1984
Alex Blanchard	HOL	1984-1987
Tom Collins	E	1987-1988
Pedro van Raamsdonk	HOL	1988
Jan Lefeber	HOL	1988-1989
Eric Nicoletta	FR	1989-1990
Tom Collins	E	1990-1991
Graciano Rocchigiani*	GER	1991-1992
Eddie Smulders	HOL	1993-1994
Fabrice Tiozzo*	FR	1994-1995
Eddy Smulders	HOL	1995-1996
Crawford Ashley	E	1997
Ole Klemetsen*	NOR	1997-1998
Crawford Ashley	E	1998-1999
Clinton Woods*	E	1999-2000
Yawe Davis	ITA	2001-

Cruiserweight (190 lbs)

Title Holder	Birthplace/Domicile	Tenure
Sam Reeson*	E	1987-1988
Angelo Rottoli	ITA	1989
Anaclet Wamba*	FR	1989-1990
Johnny Nelson*	E	1990-1992
Akim Tafer*	FR	1992-1993
Massimiliano Duran	ITA	1993-1994
Carl Thompson	E	1994
Alexander Gurov	UK	1995
Patrice Aouissi	FR	1995

Title Holder	Birthplace/Domicile	Tenure
Alexander Gurov*	UK	1995-1996
Akim Tafer*	FR	1996-1997
Johnny Nelson	E	1997-1998
Terry Dunstan*	E	1998
Alexei Iliin	RUS	1999
Torsten May*	GER	1999-2000
Carl Thompson*	E	2000-2001
Alexander Gurov	UK	2001-

Heavyweight (190 lbs +)

Title Holder	Birthplace/Domicile	Tenure
Georges Carpentier	FR	1913-1922
Battling Siki	FR	1922-1923
Erminio Spalla	ITA	1923-1926
Paolino Uzcudun	SP	1926-1928
Harry Persson	SWE	1926
Pierre Charles	BEL	1929-1931
Hein Muller	GER	1931-1932
Pierre Charles	BEL	1932-1933
Paolino Uzcudun	SP	1933
Primo Carnera	ITA	1933-1935
Pierre Charles	BEL	1935-1937
Arno Kolbin	GER	1937-1938
Hein Lazek	AU	1938-1939
Adolf Heuser	GER	1939
Max Schmeling*	GER	1939-1941
Olle Tandberg	SWE	1943
Karel Sys*	BEL	1943-1946
Bruce Woodcock	E	1946-1949
Joe Weidin	AU	1950-1951
Jack Gardner	E	1951
Hein Ten Hoff	GER	1951-1952
Karel Sys	BEL	1952
Heinz Neuhaus	GER	1952-1955
Franco Cavicchi	ITA	1955-1956
Ingemar Johansson*	SWE	1956-1959
Dick Richardson	W	1960-1962
Ingemar Johansson*	SWE	1962-1963
Henry Cooper*	E	1964
Karl Mildenberger	GER	1964-1968
Henry Cooper*	E	1968-1969
Peter Weiland	GER	1969-1970
Jose Urtain	SP	1970
Henry Cooper	E	1970-1971
Joe Bugner	E	1971
Jack Bodell	E	1971
Jose Urtain	SP	1971-1972
Jurgen Blin	GER	1972
Joe Bugner*	E	1972-1975
Richard Dunn	E	1976
Joe Bugner	E	1976-1977
Jean-Pierre Coopman	BEL	1977
Lucien Rodriguez	FR	1977
Alfredo Evangelista	SP	1977-1979
Lorenzo Zanon*	SP	1979-1980
John L. Gardner*	E	1980-1981
Lucien Rodriguez	FR	1981-1984
Steffen Tangstad	NOR	1984-1985
Anders Eklund	SWE	1985
Frank Bruno	E	1985-1986
Steffen Tangstad	NOR	1986
Alfredo Evangelista	SP	1987
Anders Eklund	SWE	1987
Francesco Damiani	ITA	1987-1989
Derek Williams	E	1989-1990
Jean Chanet	FR	1990
Lennox Lewis*	E	1990-1992
Henry Akinwande*	E	1993-1995
Zeljko Mavrovic*	CRO	1995-1998
Vitali Klitschko*	UK	1998-1999
Vladimir Klitschko*	UK	1999-2000
Vitali Klitschko	UK	2000-

A-Z of Current World Champions

by Eric Armit

Shows the record since 1 July 2000, plus career summary and pen portrait, of all men holding IBF, WBA, WBC and WBO titles as at 30 June 2001. The author has also produced the same data for those who first won titles between 1 July 2000 and 30 June 2001, but were no longer champions at the end of the period in question. Incidentally, the place name given is the respective boxer's domicile and may not necessarily be his birthplace, while all nicknames are shown where applicable in brackets. Not included are British fighters – Joe Calzaghe (WBO super-middleweight champion) and Johnny Nelson (WBO cruiserweight champion). Their full records can be found among the Active British-Based Boxers: Career Records' section.

Clarence (Bad To The Bones) Adams

Henderson, USA. *Born* 6 July, 1974
WBA S. Bantamweight Champion

Major Amateur Honours: No major honours, but claims 168 wins in 172 fights and 47 titles
Turned Pro: April 1990
Significant Results: Gabriel Bernal W PTS 8, Javier Diaz W PTS 12, Orlando Canizales L RTD 11, Frank Toledo L RSC 4, Kevin Kelley DREW 12, Edwin Santana DREW 12, Aristead Clayton W PTS 10, Nestor Garza W PTS 12
Type/Style: Sharp and classy with good movement, but not a big puncher and prone to injury
Points of Interest: 5'5" tall. Started boxing at just five years of age and his achievements were featured in a TV programme when he was nine. Originally managed by his father, his career was interrupted when he suffered a broken jaw in losing to Orlando Canizales. He also dislocated his shoulder in two other losses. His brother Fred was also a pro. Was unbeaten in his first 27 fights and has 19 wins inside the distance. Has made two defences of his WBA title since winning it from Nestor Garza in March 2000. His bad luck continued as he broke his right hand again in beating Garza, and yet again in stopping Fernandez

05.08.00	Andres Fernandez W RSC 6 Madison *(WBA S. Bantamweight Title Defence)*
23.03.01	Ivan Alvarez W PTS 12 Owensboro *(WBA S. Bantamweight Title Defence)*
Career: 47 contests, won 41, drew 3, lost 3.	

Jose Antonio (Jaguar) Aguirre

Cardenas, Mexico. *Born* 5 July, 1975
WBC M. Flyweight Champion

Major Amateur Honours: His amateur record shows 15 wins in 18 fights and he was the Mexican Golden Gloves champion in 1995
Turned Pro: February 1995
Significant Results: Cruz Zamora L PTS 10, Paulino Villalobos W PTS 10, Gustavo Andrade W CO 1, Rafael Orozco W KO 2, Wandee Singwangcha W PTS 12
Type/Style: A switch hitter and a good technician with a strong body attack, he also has a solid chin
Points of Interest: 5'4" tall. Is the first world champion from Tabasco State and originally studied to be a Doctor. Won the WBC title in February 2000 and has made three defences. Unbeaten in his last 14 fights, he has 15 wins inside the distance

07.07.00	Jose Luis Zepeda W CO 5 Villahermosa *(WBC M. Flyweight Title Defence)*
21.10.00	Erdene Chuluun W RSC 4 Mexico City *(WBC M. Flyweight Title Defence)*
02.02.01	Manny Melchor W PTS 12 Tijuana *(WBC M. Flyweight Title Defence)*

Pedro (Rockero) Alcazar

Panama City, Panama. *Born* 16 September, 1975
WBO S. Flyweight Champion

Major Amateur Honours: None known
Turned Pro: September 1995
Significant Results: Edgar Monserrat L PTS 10, Leon Salazar W RSC 7, Marcos Sanchez W PTS 12
Type/Style: A classy, speedy boxer with good movement a fair punch and a good chin
Points of Interest: Moved down from super-bantamweight to win the WBO super-flyweight title. Gets his nickname from his love of rock and roll and has 13 wins inside the distance

31.08.00	Jose Estrada DREW 10 San Jose
28.10.00	Jose Morales W RSC 3 Panama City
02.02.01	Sergio Perez W PTS 12 Panama City
27.04.01	Alex Saavedra W RSC 3 Panama City
16.06.01	Adonis Rivas W PTS 12 Panama City *(WBO S. Flyweight Title Challenge)*
Career: 24 contests, won 22, drew 1, lost 1.	

Rosendo (Buffalo) Alvarez

Managua, Nicaragua. *Born* 6 May, 1970
WBA L. Flyweight Champion. Former WBA M. Flyweight Champion

Major Amateur Honours: Competed in the 1991 Pan American Games and claims 66 wins in 78 fights
Turned Pro: December 1992
Significant Results: Jose Bonilla W PTS 12, Chana Porpaoin W PTS 12, Kermin Guardia W CO 3, Jose Bonilla W CO 11, Eric Chavez W PTS 12, Songkram Porpaoin W RSC 11, Ricardo Lopez T DRAW 7, Ricardo Lopez L PTS 12
Type/Style: A fine boxer who is both skilful and fast and a good in-fighter, he also has a fair punch
Points of Interest: 5'5" tall. Has 18 wins inside the distance under his belt and has beaten both of the Porpaoin twins. Made five defences of his WBA mini-flyweight title before losing it when he failed to make the weight for his second fight with Ricardo Lopez. Is another fighter who has had problems with drink and drugs

12.08.00	Beibis Mendoza L DIS 7 Las Vegas *(Vacant WBA L. Flyweight Title)*
08.12.00	Cipriano Landa W RSC 2 Managua
03.03.01	Beibis Mendoza W PTS 12 Las Vegas *(WBA L. Flyweight Title Challenge)*
Career: 32 contests, won 29, drew 1, lost 2.	

Tim (Cincinnati Kid) Austin
Cincinnati, USA. *Born* 14 April, 1971
IBF Bantamweight Champion

Major Amateur Honours: Was the 1986 US Junior champion, the National Golden Gloves champion in 1990 and 1991 and the Unites States Champion in 1991. Won a bronze medal in the 1992 Olympics and won and lost against Istvan Kovacs. Claims 113 wins in 122 fights
Turned Pro: April 1993
Significant Results: Javier Diaz T. Draw 1, Mbulelo Botile W RSC 8, Paul Lloyd W RSC 2, Adrian Kaspari W RSC 1, Sergio Aguila W CO 1, Bernardo Mendoza W RSC 1
Type/Style: Is a southpaw with a long reach and a knockout punch in each hand
Points of Interest: 5'6" tall. Was inactive for 17 months with a broken jaw before winning the IBF title from Mbulelo Botile in July 1997 and has made only seven defences in four years. Has 21 wins inside the distance, with 11 coming in the first round

11.08.00	Arthur Johnson W PTS 12 Las Vegas *(IBF Bantamweight Title Defence)*
03.03.01	Jesus Perez W RSC 6 Las Vegas *(IBF Bantamweight Title Defence)*
16.06.01	Steve Dotse W RSC 6 Cincinnati *(IBF Bantamweight Title Defence)*
Career: 24 contests, won 23, drew 1.	

Paulie Ayala
Fort Worth, USA. *Born* 22 April, 1970
WBA Bantamweight Champion

Major Amateur Honours: The US Junior champion in 1986, he won a silver medal in the 1992 United States Championships and was runner up in the 1992 Olympic trials to Sergio Reyes. Claims 360 wins in 384 fights
Turned Pro: November 1992
Significant Results: Mario Diaz W PTS 12, Ivan Alvarez W PTS 12, Cuauhtemoc Gomez W PTS 12, Joichiro Tatsuyoshi L TD 7, Johnny Tapia W PTS 12
Type/Style: Clever southpaw. Although a good tactical fighter he is also able to rough it up with the best. Is not a big puncher
Points of Interest: 5'5" tall. Lost to Joichiro Tatsuyoshi in a challenge for the WBC title in 1998 and has 12 wins

inside the distance. Johnny Tapia was unbeaten in 48 fights before Paulie defeated him to win the WBA title in June 1999. Has made three title defences

07.10.00	Johnny Tapia W PTS 12 Las Vegas
30.03.01	Hugo Dianzo W PTS 12 Fort Worth *(WBA Bantamweight Title Defence)*
Career: 32 contests, won 31, lost 1.	

Marco Antonio Barrera

Marco Antonio (Baby Faced Assassin) Barrera
Mexico City, Mexico. *Born* 17 January, 1974
Former Undefeated WBO S. Bantamweight Champion. Former Undefeated Mexican S. Flyweight Champion

Major Amateur Honours: None known, but claims only four losses in 60 fights
Turned Pro: November 1989
Significant Results: Carlos Salazar W PTS 10, Frankie Toledo W RSC 2, Kennedy McKinney W CO 12, Jesse Benavides W CO 3, Junior Jones L DIS 5 and L PTS 12, Richie Wenton W RTD 3, Paul Lloyd W RTD 1
Type/Style: A compact box-fighter with a hard punch in both hands, but is a bit mechanical
Points of Interest: 5'7" tall. Attended the University of Mexico. A natural southpaw who fights right handed, despite losing a hotly disputed decision to Erik Morales in a match for both the WBC and WBO super-bantamweight titles, the WBO reinstated him as

champion. Took part in 18 WBO super-bantamweight title fights before relinquishing the title to move up to featherweight. Has 38 wins inside the distance

09.09.00	Jose Luis Valbuena W PTS 12 New Orleans *(WBO S. Bantamweight Title Defence)*
01.12.00	Jesus Salud W RTD 6 Las Vegas *(WBO S. Bantamweight Title Defence)*
07.04.01	Naseem Hamed W PTS 12 Las Vegas
Career: 56 contests, won 52, lost 3, no contest 1.	

Mbulelo Botile
East London, South Africa. *Born* 23 July, 1972
Former IBF Featherweight Champion. Former IBF Bantamweight Champion. Former Undefeated South African Bantamweight Champion

Major Amateur Honours: South African champion and claims 80 wins in 85 fights
Turned Pro: July 1989
Significant Results: Harold Mestre W CO 2, Sammy Stewart W PTS 12, Ancee Gedeon W CO 11, Aristead Clayton W PTS 12, Tim Austin L RSC 8, Hector Lizarraga W PTS 10
Type/Style: Is a fine boxer and a good counter puncher
Points of Interest: 5'6" tall. Started boxing at the age of ten and won the IBF bantamweight title in April 1995, making six defences before losing the title to Tim Austin in July 1997. A stable-mate of Vuyani Bungu, he turned professional at 17 and has 16 wins inside the distance

16.12.00	Paul Ingle W RSC 12 Sheffield *(IBF Featherweight Title Challenge)*
06.04.01	Frankie Toledo L PTS 12 Las Vegas *(IBF Featherweight Title Defence)*
Career: 29 contests, won 27, lost 2.	

Joel (Cepillo) Casamayor
Guantanamo, Cuba. *Born* 12 July, 1971
WBA S. Featherweight Champion

Major Amateur Honours: The World Junior champion in 1989, a gold medallist in the 1992 Olympics, he won silver medals in the 1993 World Championships, the 1994 World Cup

and the Goodwill Games. Claims just 30 losses in over 400 fights
Turned Pro: September 1996
Significant Results: Julio Gervacio W RSC 2, Jose Luis Noyola W PTS 12, Antonio Hernandez W PTS 12, David Santos W PTS 12, Jong-Kwon Baek W RSC 2
Type/Style: A tall southpaw, he is a classy, slick and clever boxer who lacks a heavy punch
Points of Interest: 6'2" tall. Started boxing at the age of eight. Defected from Cuba in 1996 and was with Main Events before being dropped by them for allegedly drinking and not training hard enough. Won the WBA interim title in June 1999 by beating Antonio Hernandez and gained full recognition with his win over Jong-Kwon Baek in May last year. Has 15 wins inside the distance and has made three title defences

22.07.00	Bernard Harris W PTS 10 Miami	
16.09.00	Radford Beasley W RSC 5 Las Vegas *(WBA S. Featherweight Title Defence)*	
06.01.01	Roberto Garcia W RSC 9 Las Vegas *(WBA S. Featherweight Title Defence)*	
05.05.01	Edwin Santana W PTS 12 Philadelphia *(WBA S. Featherweight Title Defence)*	

Career: 25 contests, won 25.

Jose Luis Castillo

Empalme, Mexico. *Born* 14 December, 1973
WBC Lightweight Champion. Former Undefeated Mexican Featherweight and S. Featherweight Champion

Major Amateur Honours: None, but claims 30 wins in 33 fights
Turned Pro: May 1990
Significant Results: Cesar Soto L RSC 2, Javier Jauregui L RSC 10 (twice), Rafael Olivera W RSC 7, Hector Marquez W RSC 10, Javier Alvarez L RSC 11, Sandro Marcos W RSC 6, Jorge Paez W RSC 5, Steve Johnston W PTS 12
Type/Style: A tight, compact boxer and sharp puncher who likes to work inside, he has a good chin but is prone to cuts
Points of Interest: 5'9" tall. His father

was also a pro and fought for the Mexican lightweight title. Jose Luis turned pro at the age of just 16 and was a former sparring partner to Julio Cesar Chavez. Has 39 wins inside the distance and three of his four losses have been due to cuts. Won the WBC title by beating Steve Johnston in June last year and has made three defences

15.09.00	Steve Johnston DREW 12 Denver *(WBC Lightweight Title Defence)*	
20.01.01	Cesar Bazan W RSC 6 Las Vegas *(WBC Lightweight Title Defence)*	
16.06.01	Sung-Ho Yuh W RSC 1 Hermosillo *(WBC Lightweight Title Defence)*	

Career: 48 contests, won 43, drew 1, lost 4.

Jose Luis Castillo

Julio Pablo Chacon

Las Heras, Argentina. *Born* 22 May, 1975
WBO Featherweight Champion

Major Amateur Honours: Won a bronze medal in the 1996 Olympic Games, a gold medal in the 1995 Pan-American Games and competed in the 1994 World Cup and 1993 Pan-American Games. Claims 53 wins in 62 fights
Turned Pro: October 1996
Significant Results: Ever Beleno W DIS 3, Mauricio Julio W CO 4, Wilson Palacio W RSC 8, Freddie Norwood L PTS 12
Type/Style: Is a good stylish boxer with speed and accuracy
Points of Interest: 5'4" tall. Won his first 33 fights, has 29 wins inside the distance and is trained by Amilcar

Brusa who looked after Carlos Monzon. Lost to Freddie Norwood in a challenge for the WBA title in May 2000. His father was also a boxer

09.09.00	Claudio Martinet L PTS 10 Corrientes	
28.10.00	Justo Martinez W PTS 12 Mendoza	
16.12.00	Sergio Liendo W RTD 3 Buenos Aires	
24.02.01	Claudio Martinet W CO 5 Necochea	
16.06.01	Istvan Kovacs W RSC 6 Budapest *(WBO Featherweight Title Challenge)*	

Career: 42 contests, won 40, lost 2.

Yo-Sam Choi

South Korea. *Born* 1 March, 1972
WBC L. Flyweight Champion. Former South Korean L. Flyweight Champion

Major Amateur Honours: None known
Turned Pro: July 1993
Significant Results: San-Gik Yang L PTS 12, Kenzo Ando W PTS 10, Jun Arlos W PTS 12, Saman Sorjaturong W PTS 12
Type/Style: Is a short, slick, busy two-handed puncher with a rough, tough approach. Is also a good body puncher
Points of Interest: Managed by a lady and sponsored by a Korean Corporation, he has 12 wins by knockout or stoppage. Has only fought outside Korea once. Won the title from Saman Sorjaturong in October 1999 and has made only one defence due to the economic situation in South Korea

30.01.01	Saman Sorjaturong W KO 7 Seoul *(WBC L. Flyweight Title Defence)*	

Career: 24 contests, won 23, lost 1.

DeMarcus (Chop Chop) Corley

Washington, USA. *Born* 3 June, 1974
WBO L. Welterweight Champion

Major Amateur Honours: National Golden Gloves champion 1995
Turned Pro: May 1996
Significant Results: Dillon Carew T DRAW 3, Daniel Lujan L PTS 10, Ener Julio W PTS 12
Type/Style: Is a flashy, quick-punching southpaw
Points of Interest: Only received the chance to win the WBO title when the champion, and former victim, Ener Julio, was shown to have cataracts in both eyes five days before the fight. Colourful, and known to wear red

tights and yellow boots into the ring, he has 16 wins inside the distance

05.04.01	Dillon Carew W PTS 10 Washington
30.06.01	Felix Flores W RSC 1 Las Vegas *(Vacant WBO L. Welterweight Title)*
Career: 27 contests, won 25, drew 1, lost 1.	

Oscar de la Hoya

Montebello, USA. *Born* 4 February, 1973
WBC L. Middleweight Champion. Former WBC Welterweight Champion. Former Undefeated WBC L.Welterweight, IBF and WBO Lightweight and WBO S. Featherweight Champion

Major Amateur Honours: Was the gold medal winner in the 1992 Olympics, the United States champion in 1990 and 1991 and the National Golden Gloves champion in 1989
Turned Pro: November 1992
Significant Results: Genaro Hernandez W RSC 6, Jesse Leija W RSC 2, Julio Cesar Chavez W RSC 4 and W RTD 8, Miguel Gonzalez W PTS 12, Pernell Whitaker W PTS 12, Hector Camacho W PTS 12, Ike Quartey W PTS 12, Oba Carr W RSC 11, Felix Trinidad L PTS 12, Derrell Coley W RSC 7, Shane Mosley L PTS 12
Type/Style: Is a smooth, classy boxer, who is a fast and accurate puncher
Points of Interest: 5'11" tall. Having beaten 14 world or former world champions, he has 28 wins inside the distance and has won six versions of world titles in five divisions. Boxing since the age of six, Oscar lost the WBC title to Felix Trinidad but defeated Derrell Coley in an eliminator and was declared WBC champion again when Trinidad moved up, only to lose the title to Shane Mosley in June 2000

24.03.01	Arturo Gatti W RSC 5 Las Vegas
23.06.01	Javier Castillejo W PTS 12 Las Vegas *(WBC L. Middleweight Title Challenge)*
Career: 36 contests, won 34, lost 2.	

Nelson Dieppa

Vieques, Puerto Rico. *Born* 25 February, 1971
WBO L.Flyweight Champion

Major Amateur Honours: Won a bronze medal in the 1991 World Championships and a bronze medal in the 1991 Pan-American Games. Also competed in the 1992 Olympic Games
Turned Pro: February 1993
Significant Results: Pablo Tiznado W CO 6, Carlos Murillo L PTS 10, Ramon Hurtado W CO 3
Type/Style: Is a clever, slick boxer and solid right-hand puncher
Points of Interest: Trained by Felix Trinidad (senior) and has 11 wins inside the distance. His first crack at the title saw the winner, Will Grigsby, fail a drugs test and stripped of the title

22.07.00	Will Grigsby L PTS 12 Miami *(Vacant WBO L. Flyweight Title)*
28.11.00	Julio Coronel W PTS 10 Las Vegas
14.04.01	Andy Tabanas W RSC 11 New York City *(Vacant WBO L. Flyweight Title)*
Career: 21 contests, won 18, drew 1, lost 2.	

Steve (Flat Tax) Forbes

Portland, USA. *Born* 26 February, 1977
IBF S. Featherweight Champion

Major Amateur Honours: A five-time Washington and Oregon champion, he competed in the 1994 National Golden Gloves finals. Claims 57 wins in 67 fights
Turned Pro: December 1996
Significant Results: Alejandro Gonzalez L PTS 12, Ernest Zepeda W PTS 10
Type/Style: Stylish and a quick counter puncher with excellent jab, he also has a solid punch
Points of Interest: Trained by Floyd Mayweather (senior), he started boxing at the age of ten. Has only five wins inside the distance

18.08.00	Moises Pedroza W PTS 10 Concho
16.09.00	David Santos W PTS 12 Detroit
03.12.00	John Brown W RSC 8 Miami *(Vacant IBF S. Featherweight Title)*
Career: 20 contests, won 19, lost 1.	

Vernon (The Viper) Forrest

Augusta, USA. *Born* 21 February, 1971
IBF Welterweight Champion

Major Amateur Honours: A silver medallist in the 1991 World Championships and a competitor in the 1992

Olympics, he won a gold medal in the 1992 World Championships
Turned Pro: November 1992
Significant Results: Adrian Stone W RSC 11, Steve Martinez W RSC 1, Santiago Samaniego W CO 7, Vince Phillips W PTS 12
Type/Style: Tall and quick, he has a long reach and a strong jab
Points of Interest: 6'0" tall. Attending college under a boxing scholarship, he lost to Kostya Tszyu in the 1991 World Championships, but beat Shane Mosley and Steve Johnston in the Olympic trials. With 25 stoppages or knockouts, his first fight for the vacant IBF title was declared a no contest when Raul Frank was cut

26.08 00	Raul Frank NC 3 Las Vegas *(Vacant IBF Welterweight title)*
12.05.01	Raul Frank W PTS 12 New York City *(Vacant IBF Welterweight title)*
Career: 33 contests, won 32, no contest 1.	

Vernon Forrest

Acelino (Popo) Freitas

Salvador de Bahia, Brazil. *Born* 21 September, 1975
WBO S. Featherweight Champion. Former Undefeated Brazilian Lightweight Champion

Major Amateur Honours: Won a silver medal in the 1995 Pan-American Games. Claims 72 wins in 74 fights and won 14 Brazilian titles

Turned Pro: July 1995
Significant Results: Anatoly Alexandrov W CO 1, Claudio Martinet W CO 3, Barry Jones W RSC 8, Javier Jauregui W RSC 1, Lemuel Nelson W RSC 2
Type/Style: Strong and aggressive, he has fast hands, is a quick starter, and packs a crushing punch in his right hand, but gets careless
Points of Interest: 5'7" tall. Brother Luiz Carlos is also a pro and a double Brazilian champion. Has won all of his 29 fights inside the distance, 22 within the first three rounds, and has 12 first-round finishes. 'Popo' has made six defences since winning the title from Anatoly Alexandrov in August 1999, but is having difficulty with the weight

23.09.00	Carlos Rios W RSC 9 Rama *(WBO S. Featherweight Title Defence)*
16.12.00	Daniel Alicea W RSC 1 Sheffield
27.01.01	Orlando Soto W RSC 1 Brasilia *(WBO S. Featherweight Title Defence)*
Career: 29 contests, won 29.	

Derrick (Smoke) Gainer

Pensacola, USA. *Born* 22 August, 1972
WBA Featherweight Champion

Major Amateur Honours: None, but had around 30 bouts
Turned Pro: July 1990
Significant Results: Harold Warren W PTS 12 (twice), Kevin Kelley L CO 8, Donovan Carey W RSC 6, Diego Corrales L RSC 3
Type/Style: Has an upright southpaw style and is a good boxer, although his chin is not too sound
Points of Interest: 5'9" tall with a 72" reach. Was managed by Roy Jones, but broke with him a few months back. Initially a flyweight when he turned pro, he lost in a challenge for the IBF title to Diego Corrales. His fight with Freddie Norwood went ahead for the vacant WBA title, despite the latter being stripped for failing to make the weight. Has 24 wins inside the distance

09.09.00	Freddie Norwood W RSC 11 New Orleans *(Vacant WBA Featherweight Title)*
24.02.01	Victor Polo W PTS 12 Tampa *(WBA Featherweight Title Defence)*
17.05.01	Cedric Mingo W RSC 2 Biloxi
Career: 43 contest, won 38, lost 5.	

Jomo Gamboa

Cebu City, Philippines. Born 25 April, 1973
Former WBA M. Flyweight Champion. Former Undefeated Philippines M. Flyweight Champion

Major Amateur Honours: None
Turned Pro: March 1993
Significant Results: Saman Sorjaturong L RSC 7, Carlos Murillo W RSC 1, Pichitnoi Sitbangprachan L PTS 12, Saturo Abe W CO 6, Noel Arambulet L PTS 12
Type/Style: Is a tough and aggressive little pressure fighter
Points of Interest: Unsuccessful in shots at WBC and WBA light-flyweight titles, and losing to Noel Arambulet in a previous fight for the WBA title, all of his world title fights have taken place outside of the Philippines. Joma, who now has 21 wins inside the distance, won the title when Arambulet failed to make the weight

20.08.00	Noel Arambulet W PTS 12 Tokyo *(Vacant WBA M. Flyweight Title)*
06.12.00	Keitaro Hoshino L PTS 12 Yokohama *(WBA M. Flyweight Title Defence)*
05.05.01	Pigmy Muangchaiya W RSC 5 Quezon City
Career: 37 contests, won 30, drew 1, lost 6.	

Silvio (Torito) Gamez

Parmana, Venezuela. *Born* 8 August, 1963
Former WBA S. Flyweight Champion. Former WBA L. Flyweight Champion. Former WBA Flyweight Champion. Former Undefeated WBA M. Flyweight Champion. Former Undefeated Latin American Flyweight Champion. Former Undefeated Venezuelan L. Flyweight Champion

Major Amateur Honours: Won 70 of 76 fights
Turned Pro: April 1985
Significant Results: Bong-Jun Kim W PTS 12, Myung-Woo Yuh L PTS 12 (twice), Shiro Yahiro W RSC 9, Pichitnoi Sithbangprachan W RSC 6, Saen Sorploenchit L PTS 12, Hugo Soto W RSC 3, Sornpichai Pisnurachan L CO 8
Type/Style: A busy little fighter, he has fast hands and is a good combination puncher
Points of Interest: 5'0" tall. Is the only

Venezuelan to win world titles at four weights, despite losing three consecutive challenges for WBA titles. Also won the WBA interim super-flyweight title. Announced his retirement after losing to Celes Kobayashi

09.10.00	Hideki Todaka W RSC 7 Nagoya *(WBA S. Flyweight Title Challenge)*
11.03.01	Celes Kobayashi L RSC 10 Yokohama *(WBA S. Flyweight Title Defence)*
Career: 42 contests, won 33, drew 1, lost 8.	

Juan Carlos (The Black Panther) Gomez

Havana, Cuba. *Born* 27 July, 1973
WBC Cruiserweight Champion

Major Amateur Honours: World Junior champion in 1990. Claims to have lost only twice, to Antoine Tarver and Sven Ottke, in 160 fights
Turned Pro: May 1995
Significant Results: Brian la Spada W RSC 11, Marcelo Dominguez W PTS 12 (twice), Guy Waters W RSC 6, Alexei Iliin W RSC 2, Imamu Mayfield W CO 3
Type/Style: Southpaw. Has a flashy, hands-down style with fast fists
Points of Interest: 6'4" tall with an 80" reach. Having defected whilst on tour with the Cuban team in 1994, he is now based in Germany. Defected again, this time from his German management in March 2001, but returned to the fold a few months later. Has made nine title defences and has 27 wins by kayo or stoppage

16.12.00	Jorge Castro W RSC 10 Essen *(WBC Cruiserweight Title Defence)*
Career: 32 contests, won 32.	

Artur (Atuiz) Grigorian

Tashkent, Uzbekistan. *Born* 20 October, 1967
WBO Lightweight Champion

Major Amateur Honours: A gold medal winner in the 1990 Goodwill Games, he won a silver medal in the 1991 World Championships and competed in the 1992 Olympics and the 1993 World Championships. Also won a gold medal in the Chemical Cup in 1994 and claims 361 wins in 384 fights
Turned Pro: April 1994

Significant Results: Antonio Rivera W CO 12, David Armstrong W PTS 12, Marco Rudolph W RSC 6, Oscar Garcia Cano W PTS 12, Michael Clark CO 5, Wilson Galli W RSC 10, Sandro Casamonica W RSC 9

Type/Style: Is a stylish box-fighting southpaw

Points of Interest: 5'9" tall with a 69" reach. A former WBO interim champion who was awarded the full title without fighting for it, he has 21 wins inside the distance. The WBO champion since 1996, with 14 title defences to his credit, he once beat Shane Mosley as an amateur

25.11.00	Antonio Pitalua W PTS 12 Hanover *(WBO Lightweight Title Defence)*
24.02.01	Jose Angel Perez W RSC 6 Hamburg *(WBO Lightweight Title Defence)*
16.06.01	Aldo Rios W PTS 12 Budapest *(WBO Lightweight Title Defence)*
Career: 33 contests, won 33.	

Will (Steel) Grigsby

St Paul, USA. *Born* 19 March,1970
Former Undefeated WBO L. Flyweight Champion. Former IBF L. Flyweight Champion

Major Amateur Honours: Olympic trialist for the US team in 1988 and a quarter finalist in the 1988 National Golden Gloves tournament
Turned Pro: November 1988
Significant Results: Michael Carbajal L PTS 4, Jesus Lopez W PTS 12, Ratanapol Sowvoraphin W PTS 12, Carmelo Caceres W PTS 12, Ricardo Lopez L PTS 12
Type/Style: Has fast footwork and quick hands, but is not a puncher
Points of Interest: 5'4" tall. Lost in his second paid fight to Michael Carbajal and was inactive from 1989 to 1994. Lost his IBF title to Ricardo Lopez in his second defence and was stripped of the WBO title for failing a drugs test. Raises pit bull terriers as a hobby

| 22.07.00 | Nelson Dieppa W PTS 12 Miami *(Vacant WBO L. Flyweight Title)* |
| **Career:** 18 contests, won 15, drew 1, lost 2. | |

Kermin Guardia

Turbo, Colombia. *Born* 17 January, 1970
WBO M. Flyweight Champion.

Former Undefeated Colombian M. Flyweight Champion

Major Amateur Honours: None known
Turned Pro: June 1991
Significant Results: Marcelino Bolivar W PTS 12, Ricardo Lopez L PTS 12, Rosendo Alvarez L CO 3, Eric Jamili W RSC 5 and W PTS 12, Luis Lazarate W PTS 12
Type/Style: Southpaw. Is an intelligent, stylish little boxer with an excellent jab and hard punch, especially with the right hook
Points of Interest: Won his first 21 contests, but lost in challenges for the WBC and WBA titles before winning the WBO title in May 1998. Has made only three defences of the WBO title in three years and was inactive last year. Has 20 wins inside the distance

| 06.04.01 | Juan Alfonso Keb Baas W PTS 12 Merida *(WBO M. Flyweight Title Defence)* |
| **Career:** 36 contests, won 33, lost 2, no decision 1. | |

Takanori Hatakeyama

Aomori, Japan. *Born* 28 July, 1975
WBA Lightweight Champion. Former WBA S. Featherweight Champion. Former Undefeated Japanese S. Featherweight Champion

Major Amateur Honours: None known
Turned Pro: June 1993
Significant Results: Yong-Soo Choi DREW 12 and W PTS 12, Koji Arasawa W RSC 9, Saul Duran DREW 12, Lakva Sim L RSC 5, Gilberto Serrano W RSC 8
Type/Style: Although a busy, hard puncher with good movement, his defence is a bit weak
Points of Interest: 5'8" tall. Was the Japanese novice champion in 1994. Made two defences of the WBA super-featherweight title, but retired to try acting after losing the title to Lakva Sim in June 1999. Has made two title defences since winning the WBA title from Gilberto Serrano in June 1999 and has 19 wins by kayo or stoppage. Is coached by Rudy Hernandez, the brother of the former WBC super-featherweight champion, Genaro Hernandez

11.10.00	Hiroyuki Sakamoto W RTD 10 Yokohama *(WBA Lightweight Title Defence)*
17.02.01	Rick Roberts Yoshimura DREW 12 Tokyo *(WBA Lightweight Title Defence)*
Career: 28 contests, won 24, drew 3, lost 1.	

Virgil Hill

Williston, USA. *Born* 18 January, 1964
WBA Cruiserweight Champion. Former WBA and IBF L. Heavyweight Champion

Major Amateur Honours: Was a silver medallist in the 1982 United States Championships, won a bronze medal in the 1983 World Cup and was the National Golden Gloves champion in 1984. Won a silver medal in the 1984 Olympic Games
Turned Pro: November 1984
Significant Results: Leslie Stewart W CO 3, Bobby Czyz W PTS 12, James Kinchen W RSC 1, Thomas Hearns L PTS 12, Frank Tate W PTS 12, Fabrice Tiozzo W PTS 12, Crawford Ashley W PTS 12, Louis del Valle W PTS 12, Henry Maske W PTS 12, Dariusz Michalczewski L PTS 12, Roy Jones L CO 4
Type/Style: A stand-up boxer with an effective, rather than exciting style, he is also a strong jabber and good puncher with both hands
Points of Interest: 6'1" tall. Had two reigns as the WBA light-heavyweight champion and took part in 24 world title bouts in that division. Overcame drugs and alcohol problems to return to the top with his shock stoppage of Tiozzo and has 22 wins inside the distance

| 09.12.00 | Fabrice Tiozzo W RSC 1 Villeurbanne *(WBA Cruiserweight Title Challenge)* |

Dave Hilton

Montreal, Canada. *Born* 9 December, 1963
Former Undefeated WBC S. Middleweight Champion. Former Undefeated Canadian Welterweight and Middleweight Champion

Major Amateur Honours: None but

claims only three losses in 105 fights
Turned Pro: February 1981
Significant Results: Steve Little WPTS 10, Alan Bonnamie L PTS 10, Stephane Ouellet W RSC 12, W CO 3 and L PTS 10
Type/Style: 5'9" tall. Is a tough and aggressive battler
Points of Interest: Dad was a pro, his brother, Matthew, was an IBF light-middleweight champion and another brother, Alex, is also a pro. David turned pro at the age of 17 and has 26 wins inside the distance. Had already spent time in jail from a previous conviction before being found guilty of sex offences and having his WBC title taken away

08.09.00	Stephane Ouellet L PTS 10 Montreal	
15.12.00	Dingaan Thobela W PTS 12 Montreal *(WBC S. Middleweight Title Challenge)*	
Career: 44 contests, won 39, drew 3, lost 2.		

Evander (The Real Deal) Holyfield

Atmore, USA. *Born* 19 October, 1962
Former WBC, IBF and WBA Heavyweight Champion. Former Undefeated WBC, IBF and WBA Cruiserweight Champion

Major Amateur Honours: A bronze medallist at the 1984 Olympic Games, he was the National Golden Gloves champion in 1984 and won a silver medal in the 1983 Pan-American Games
Turned Pro: November 1984
Significant Results: George Foreman W PTS 12, Riddick Bowe L RSC 8, L PTS 12 and W PTS 12, Michael Moorer L PTS 12, Mike Tyson W RSC 11 and W DIS 3, Lennox Lewis DREW 12 and L PTS 12
Type/Style: Is a tough and aggressive battler who appeared to get better with age
Points of Interest: 6'2" tall Has taken part in 21 world title fights, and has scored 24 wins by stoppage or kayo. His career was almost finished by a heart problem diagnosis.

12.08.00	John Ruiz W PTS 12 Las Vegas *(Vacant WBA Heavyweight Title)*	
03.03.01	John Ruiz L PTS 12 Las Vegas *(WBA Heavyweight Title Defence)*	
Career: 43 contests, won 37, drew 1, lost 5.		

Bernard (The Executioner) Hopkins

Philadelphia, USA. *Born* 15 January, 1965
WBC and IBF Middleweight Champion

Major Amateur Honours: None, but claims 95 wins in 99 fights
Turned Pro: October 1988
Significant Results: Roy Jones L PTS 12, Lupe Aquino W PTS 12, Segundo Mercado DREW 12 and W PTS 12, Robert Allen NC 4 and W RSC 7, Antwun Echols W PTS 12, Syd Vanderpool W PTS 12
Type/Style: Is a strong if mechanical boxer and a powerful puncher with fast hands
Points of Interest: 6'0" tall with a 71" reach. The nephew of former pro, Art McCloud, after spending five years in jail he lost his first paid fight. Entering the ring wearing an executioners mask and a cape, Bernard has 28 wins inside the distance. Having lost to Roy Jones in his first attempt to win the IBF title and drawn with Segundo Mercado for the vacant title before beating Mercado in a return in April 1995, he has now made 13 title defences. Injured his ankle against Robert Allen when he was pushed out of the ring and the bout was declared a no contest

01.12.00	Antwun Echols W RSC 10 Las Vegas *(IBF Middleweight Title Defence)*	
14.04.01	Keith Holmes W PTS 12 New York City *(IBF Middleweight Title Defence. WBC Middleweight Title Challenge)*	
Career: 43 contests, won 39, drew 1, lost 2, no contests 1.		

Keitaro Hoshino

Kanagawa, Japan. *Born* 14 August, 1969
Former WBA M. Flyweight Champion. Former Undefeated Japanese M. Flyweight Champion

Major Amateur Honours: None, but claims 30 wins and seven losses
Turned Pro: November 1988
Significant Results: Ernesto Rubillar W PTS 10 (twice), Satoshi Yoshida W PTS 10, Makoto Suzuki W RSC 9
Type/Style: Is a typical two-fisted, aggressive battler, but is not a hard puncher
Points of Interest: Lost his first paid contest and suffered three defeats in

four fights in 1993. Inactive throughout 1999, he was the oldest Japanese to win a world title at his first attempt. Managed by the former WBA flyweight champion, Susumu Hanagata, Keitaro has made five defences of his Japanese title and has only five quick wins

06.12.00	Jomo Gamboa W PTS 12 Yokohama *(WBA M. Flyweight Title Challenge)*	
16.04.01	Chana Porpaoin L PTS 12 Yokohama *(WBA M. Flyweight Title Defence)*	
Career: 28 contests, won 21, lost 7.		

Vassily (Tiger) Jirov

Alma Aty, Kazakhstan. *Born* 4 April, 1974
IBF Cruiserweight Champion

Major Amateur Honours: Won a gold medal in the 1996 Olympic Games, where he was also voted the outstanding boxer of the tournament. A bronze medal winner in the 1993 and 1995 World Championships, a gold medallist in the 1992 European Junior Championships, and a bronze medallist in the 1994 Asian Games, he also competed in the 1994 World Cup
Turned Pro: January 1997
Significant Results: Arthur Williams W RSC 7, Dale Brown W CO 10, Saul Montana W RSC 9
Type/Style: Carrying a high guard, he is a busy southpaw with a solid chin and is also a powerful body puncher
Points of Interest: 6'1" tall. Starting boxing at the age of 14, and also known as Valeryvich Zhirov, he has only fought once in his home country as a professional. With 26 wins inside the distance, Vassily has made four defences of the IBF title he won in 1999 when beating Arthur Williams

29.07.00	Earl Butler W RSC 2 Phoenix	
06.02.01	Alex Gonzalez W CO 1 Almaty *(IBF Cruiserweight Title Defence)*	
24.03.01	Terry McGroom W CO 1 Las Vegas *(IBF Cruiserweight Title Defence)*	
Career: 28 contests, won 28.		

Roy Jones

Pensacola, USA. *Born* 16 January, 1969
WBC, WBA and IBF L. Heavyweight

Champion. Former Undefeated IBF Middleweight and S. Middleweight Champion

Major Amateur Honours: Was a silver medallist in the 1988 Olympics and the National Golden Gloves champion in 1986 and 1987
Turned Pro: May 1989
Significant Results: Bernard Hopkins W PTS 12, James Toney W PTS 12, Mike McCallum W PTS 12, Montell Griffin L DIS 9 and W RSC 1, Virgil Hill W CO 4, Louis del Valle W PTS 12, Reggie Johnson W PTS 12, David Telesco W PTS 12, Richard Hall W RSC 11
Type/Style: A brilliant boxer with fast, skilful, lightning reflexes, he also has a kayo punch in either hand
Points of Interest: 5'11" tall. Originally trained and managed by his father, Roy, he also plays basketball to a high standard and has appeared in films. With 36 wins inside the distance, Roy was only a welterweight when he won the Golden Gloves and has now made eight defences of his IBF super-middleweight title. Lost his WBC title to Montell Griffin in March 1997, but won it back just four months later

09.09.00	Eric Harding W RTD 10 New Orleans *(WBC,WBA and IBF L. Heavyweight Title Defences)*
24.02.01	Derrick Harmon W RTD 10 Tampa *(WBC, WBA and IBF L. Heavyweight Title Defences*

Career: 45 contests, won 44, lost 1.

Willie Jorrin

Sacramento, USA. *Born* 21 November, 1969
WBC S. Bantamweight Champion

Major Amateur Honours: The USA Junior champion in 1984 and an amateur International, he competed in the 1992 Olympic trials. Claims a 158-18 record
Turned Pro: February 1993
Significant Results: Antonio Ramirez W PTS 10, George Parra W RSC 7, Aristead Clayton W PTS 12, Marcos Badillo W PTS 10
Type/Style: Is a nimble, clever, busy little fighter with fast hands and a quick in-and-out style. Not a big puncher though
Points of Interest: 5'5" tall. Originally

trained by his Father, Willie has eight brothers and two sisters. His record shows 12 wins inside the distance

09.09.00	Michael Brodie W PTS 12 Manchester *(Vacant WBC S. Bantamweight Title)*
19.01.01	Oscar Larios W PTS 12 Sacramento *(WBC S. Bantamweight Title Defence)*

Career: 28 contests, won 28.

Willie Jorrin   Les Clark

Zab Judah

New York, USA. *Born* 27 October, 1977
IBF L. Welterweight Champion

Major Amateur Honours: As the three-times New York Golden Gloves champion and a bronze medal winner in the 1995 National Golden Gloves, he was a reserve for the United States team at the 1996 Olympic Games. Claims 110 wins in 115 fights
Turned Pro: September 1996
Significant Results: Mickey Ward W PTS 12, Darryl Tyson W RSC 11, Wilfredo Negron W RSC 4, Jan Bergman W CO 4, Junior Witter W PTS 12
Type/Style: A stylish, classy, very fast and flashy southpaw with tremendous talent, but is brash and arrogant
Points of Interest: 5'7" tall. Dad, Yoel, was a former world kick-boxing champion and trained Zab at the

Judah Brothers Gym from the age of six. Earlier known as 'Pernell Whitaker Jr' because of the time he spent sparring with the former world champion, Zab has two brothers who also won New York Golden Gloves titles. Won the IBF interim title in January 1999 by beating Wilfredo Negron and the vacant title by beating Jan Bergman in February last year. Has made five defences and has 21 wins inside the distance

05.08.00	Terron Millett W RSC 4 Uncasville *(IBF L.Welterweight Title Defence)*
20.10.00	Hector Quiroz W RSC 8 Auburn Hills *(IBF L.Welterweight Title Defence)*
13.01.01	Reggie Green W RSC 10 Uncasville *(IBF L.Welterweight Title Defence)*
23.06.01	Allan Vester W RSC 3 Uncasville *(IBF L. Welterweight Title Defence)*

Career: 28 contests, won 27, no contest 1.

Zab Judah

Ener Julio

El Reton, Colombia. *Born* 14 October, 1973
Former Undefeated WBO L.Welterweight Champion

Major Amateur Honours: None known
Turned Pro: June 1994
Significant Results: Hector Lopez L PTS 10, Newton Villarreal W PTS 8, David Ojeda W RSC 11, DeMarcus Corley L PTS 12, Jose Zuniga W PTS 12
Type/Style: Although an aggressive

and hard puncher, his defence is not too sound, but he has a good chin
Points of Interest: Only fighting outside Colombia on three occasions, he has 16 wins by knockout or stoppage and has never been stopped. Had just two fights in the last 21 months and then had to give up his title due to having cataracts in both eyes

22.07.00	Randall Bailey W PTS 12 Miami *(WBO L. Welterweight Title Challenge)*

Vladimir (The Steel Hammer) Klitschko

Kiev, Ukraine. *Born* 25 March, 1976
WBO Heavyweight Champion. Former Undefeated European Heavyweight Champion

Major Amateur Honours: His list of honours include a gold medal in the 1993 European Junior Championships, a silver medal in the 1994 World Junior Championships, a silver medal in the 1994 World Military Championships, a gold medal in the 1995 World Military Championships, a silver medal in the 1996 European Championships and a gold medal in the 1996 Olympics
Turned Pro: November 1996
Significant Results: Ross Puritty L RSC 11, Axel Schulz W RSC 8, Paea Wolfgramm W CO 1, David Bostice W RSC 2
Type/Style: Despite having a mechanical jab and cross approach, his reach and punching power is hard to combat. However, there is some question over his stamina
Points of Interest: 6'7" tall. Originally wanting to be a doctor, his father is a general in the Ukrainian army, Vladimir started boxing at the age of 14, losing his first amateur fight. Has 33 wins inside the distance, of which 25 have come in the first three rounds. He made only one defence of his European title after winning it when beating Axel Schulz in September 1999. His brother, Vitali, was also the WBO heavyweight champion

14.10.00	Chris Byrd W PTS 12 Cologne *(WBO Heavyweight Title Challenge)*
24.03.01	Derrick Jefferson W RSC 2 Munich *(WBO Heavyweight Title Defence)*
Career: 37 contests, won 36, lost 1.	

Celes Kobayashi

Kanagawa, Japan. *Born* 27 February, 1973
WBA S. Flyweight Champion. Former Undefeated Japanese Flyweight Champion

Major Amateur Honours: None known
Turned Pro: April 1992
Significant Results: Cris Saguid W RSC 9, Nolito Cabato L PTS 10 and W PTS 10, Katsuhiro Akita W PTS 10
Type/Style: An aggressive southpaw with a tight, high guard, he is game and durable and has good stamina
Points of Interest: After losing two of his first three fights, it took him three attempts to win the Japanese flyweight crown, after which he then made two defences of the title. Has 14 wins inside the distance

20.08.00	Malcolm Tunacao DREW 12 Tokyo *(WBC Flyweight Title Challenge)*
11.03.01	Silvio Gamez W RSC 10 Yokohama *(WBA S. Flyweight Title Challenge)*
Career: 30 contests, won 23, drew 3, lost 4.	

Istvan (Koko) Kovacs

Budapest, Hungary. *Born* 17 August, 1970
Former WBO Featherweight Champion. Former Undefeated European Featherweight Champion

Major Amateur Honours: A gold medallist in the European Junior Championships in 1988, he also won gold medals at the 1991 and 1996 European Championships, the 1991 and 1997 World Championships and the 1996 Olympic Games. Other successes include a bronze in the 1993 European Championships, a bronze at the 1992 Olympic Games and a further bronze in the 1994 World Cup
Turned Pro: December 1997
Significant Results: Vincenzo Belcastro W PTS 8, Nabaloum Dramane W PTS 12, Steve Robinson W PTS 12
Type/Style: Clever and stylish, but not a hard puncher, he has an excellent fighting brain and a good defence
Points of Interest: 5'8" tall with a 66" reach. Started boxing in 1985 and had almost 300 amateur fights after being inspired to take up boxing by the achievements of the great Lazlo Papp. Has ten wins inside the distance

14.10.00	Agustin Lorenzo W RSC 1 Cologne
27.01.01	Antonio Diaz W RSC 12 Munich *(Vacant WBO Featherweight Title)*
16.06.01	Julio Pablo Chacon L RSC 6 Budapest *(WBO Featherweight Title Defence)*
Career: 20 contests, won 20, lost 1.	

Armand Krajnc

Landskrona, Sweden. *Born* Slovenia, 7 August, 1973
WBO Middleweight Champion

Major Amateur Honours: None known, but claims 63 wins in 70 fights
Turned Pro: October 1996
Significant Results: Bahri Ahmeti W PTS 10, Jason Matthews W RSC 8, Jonathan Corn W CO 2
Type/Style: Neat and organised, he is a competent boxer with a good jab and a strong right-hand punch
Points of Interest: 6'0" tall with a 75" reach. Brought up in Sweden, but based in Germany as there is no professional boxing in Sweden, Armand originally worked as a toolmaker. After coming in as a late substitute to beat Jason Matthews and win the vacant WBO title in November 1999, he has made two defences and has 18 wins inside the distance

07.10.00	Bert Schenk W RSC 6 Berlin *(WBO Middleweight Title Defence)*
Career: 24 contests, won 24.	

Andrew (Six Heads) Lewis

Georgetown, Guyana. *Born* 14 December, 1970
WBA Welterweight Champion

Major Amateur Honours: Competed in the 1992 Olympics and claims 45 wins in 48 fights
Turned Pro: February 1993
Significant Results: Han Kim T DRAW 2, Rafael Williams W RSC 2, Teddy Reid W PTS 12
Type/Style: Is a flashy, quick, pressure fighting southpaw who can also switch to orthodox
Points of Interest: 5'8" tall. Following his father, who was a pro, Andrew started boxing at the age of five and has 19 wins by stoppage or kayo as a paid fighter. His nickname comes from a beaten opponent saying he saw six heads after Lewis knocked him down. Changes trainers regularly

17.11.00	Sebastian Valdez W RSC 2 Reno
17.02.01	James Page W RSC 7 Las Vegas
	(Vacant WBA Welterweight Title)
28.04.01	Larry Marks W PTS 12 New York City
	(WBA Welterweight Title Defence)

Career: 22 contests, won 20, drew 1.

Roberto (Mako) Leyva

Puerto Penasco, Mexico. *Born* 27 October, 1979
IBF M. Flyweight Champion

Major Amateur Honours: None known
Turned Pro: February 1998
Significant Results: None
Type/Style: An aggressive pressure fighter, he is a southpaw with a hard left-hand punch
Points of Interest: Dad was a fisherman but died when Roberto was very young. With 17 wins inside the distance, his title-winning effort was his first fight outside Mexico. Earlier in his career he won a WBC Youth title

04.08.00	Roberto Gomez W PTS 10 Ensenada
03.11.00	Luis Valdez W RSC 4 Ensenada
04.12.00	Victor Burgos W RSC 8 Tijuana
23.03.01	Martin Armenta W RSC 4 Tijuana
29.04.01	Daniel Reyes W PTS 12 New York City
	(Vacant IBF M. Flyweight Title)

Career: 19 contests, won 19.

Ricardo (Finito) Lopez

Cuernavaca, Mexico. *Born* 25 July, 1967
IBF L. Flyweight Champion. Former Undefeated WBC, WBA and WBO M. Flyweight Champion

Major Amateur Honours: Mexican Golden Gloves champion in 1984. Lost only one of 41 fights
Turned Pro: January 1985
Significant Results: Saman Sorjaturong W RSC 2, Rocky Lim W CO 2, Ala Villamor W CO 8, Alex Sanchez W RSC 5, Rosendo Alvarez T DRAW 7 and W PTS 12, Will Grigsby W PTS 12
Type/Style: Is a dazzling craftsman and a fast, accurate puncher
Points of Interest: 5'5" tall. Has fought in 25 world title fights, winning 24 and fighting a technical draw with Rosendo Alvarez in the other. Beat Alex Sanchez for the WBO title, but was stripped of

the title seven months later without defending. Won the WBA title with a victory over Alvarez in November 1998, even though both fighters were over the weight limit, before winning the IBF light-flyweight title when decisioning Will Grigsby in October 1999. Is considered to be one of the modern greats

| 02.12.00 | Ratanapol Sowvoraphin W RSC 3 Las Vegas |
| | *(IBF L. Flyweight Title Defence)* |

Career: 50 contests, won 49, drew 1.

Ricardo Lopez

Felix Machado

Bolivar, Venezuela. *Born* 22 August, 1972
IBF S. Flyweight Champion. Former Undefeated Venezuelan Bantamweight Champion

Major Amateur Honours: Won a silver medal in the 1989 World Junior Championships
Turned Pro: April 1993
Significant Results: Edicson Torres W PTS 10, Fernando Blanco W PTS 12, Adonis Cruz L DIS 8, Daorung Chuwatana L PTS 12, Julio Gamboa DREW 12
Type/Style: A tall, methodical southpaw who has a good chin but is not a big puncher
Points of Interest: Lost to Daorung Chuwatana in a challenge for the WBA bantamweight title in 1997 and

drew with Julio Gamboa for the vacant IBF title in May last year. Has 11 wins inside the distance since losing his first pro fight

22.07.00	Julio Gamboa W PTS 12 Miami
	(Vacant IBF S. Flyweight Title)
16.12.00	William de Souza W RSC 3 Maracay
	(IBF S. Flyweight Title Defence)
16.06.01	Mauricio Pastrana W PTS 12 Cincinnati
	(IBF S. Flyweight Title Defence)

Career: 25 contests, won 21, drew 1, lost 3.

Mauricio Martinez   Les Clark

Mauricio Martinez

Colon, Panama. *Born* 20 May, 1975
WBO Bantamweight Champion. Former Undefeated Panamanian Bantamweight Champion

Major Amateur Honours: As the Panamanian Golden Gloves champion, he competed in the 1995 Pan-American Games
Turned Pro: July 1995
Significant Results: Freddie Norwood L RSC 2, Hector Acero Sanchez L PTS 8 (twice), Marcos Badillo W RSC 10, Jorge Reyes W CO 4
Type/Style: Is a neat boxer with an awkward southpaw style and a hard right-hand punch, although his defence is not too sound

Points of Interest: Was on the floor three times against Lester Fuentes when winning the title and has 14 wins by stoppage or kayo. Works part time

| 04.09.00 | Lester Fuentes W RSC 5 Manchester *(Vacant WBO Bantamweight Title)* |
| 16.12.00 | Esham Pickering W RSC 1 Sheffield *(WBO Bantamweight Title Defence)* |

Career: 23 contests, won 19, drew 1, lost 3.

Floyd (Little Stone) Mayweather

Grand Rapids, USA. *Born* 24 February, 1977
WBC S. Featherweight Champion

Major Amateur Honours: The national Golden Gloves champion in 1993, 1994 and 1996, his first national title was at 106lbs. Was the United States champion in 1995 and won a bronze medal in the 1996 Olympics. Winning 84 of 90 fights, he also competed in the 1995 World Championships
Turned Pro: October 1996
Significant Results: Genaro Hernandez W RTD 8, Angel Manfredy W RSC 2, Carlos Rios W PTS 12, Justin Juuko W RSC 9, Carlos Gerena W RTD 7, Gregorio Vargas W PTS 12
Type/Style: Talented and flashy with fast hands, he has great reflexes and a hard punch
Points of Interest: 5'8" tall. His father, Lloyd, was a good professional and his uncle, Roger, was the WBA super-featherweight and WBC light-welterweight champion. Has made seven title defences and his record shows 19 wins inside the distance

21.10.00	Emanuel Burton W RSC 9 Detroit
20.01.01	Diego Corrales W RSC 10 Las Vegas *(WBC S. Featherweight Title Defence)*
26.05.01	Carlos Hernandez W PTS 12 Grand Rapids *(WBS S. Featherweight Title Defence)*

Career: 26 contests, won 26.

Beibis Mendoza

Rio Cedro, Colombia. *Born* 20 June, 1975
Former WBA L. Flyweight Champion. Former Undefeated Colombian L. Flyweight Champion

Major Amateur Honours: Competed in the 1996 Olympic Games

Turned Pro: November 1996
Significant Results: Fidel Julio W CO 2, Luis Doria W RSC 8, Rafael Orozco W CO 2
Type/Style: Stylish and quick handed, he is a good boxer with a kayo punch
Points of Interest: 5'3" tall. Has 23 wins inside the distance, with 17 coming in the first three rounds

| 12.08.00 | Rosendo Alvarez W DIS 7 Las Vegas *(Vacant WBA L. Flyweight Title)* |
| 03.03.01 | Rosendo Alvarez L PTS 12 Las Vegas *(WBA L. Flyweight Title Defence)* |

Career: 29 contests, won 28, lost 1.

Dariusz Michalczewski

Hamburg, Germany. *Born* Gdansk, Poland, 5 May, 1968
WBO L. Heavyweight Champion. Former Undefeated WBA and IBF L. Heavyweight Champion. Former Undefeated WBO Cruiserweight Champion

Major Amateur Honours: Won a bronze medal in the 1986 European Junior Championships, a silver medal in the 1989 European Championships, and a gold medal in the 1991 European Championships
Turned Pro: September 1991
Significant Results: Leonzer Barber W PTS 12, Nestor Giovannini W CO 10, Graciano Rocchigiani W DIS 7 and W RTD 9, Virgil Hill W PTS 12, Nicky Piper W RTD 7, Mark Prince W RSC 8, Drake Thadzi W RSC 9, Montell Griffin W RSC 4
Type/Style: Is a hard-punching and aggressive pressure fighter, who is strong with a solid jab but lacks a sound defence
Points of Interest: Won championships for both Poland and Germany as an amateur and had 34 wins inside the distance. Won WBA and IBF titles by beating Virgil Hill in June 1997, but relinquished both in the same month that he won them. Has made 19 defences of his WBO title

| 16.12.00 | Ka-Dy King W RSC 7 Essen *(WBO L. Heavyweight Title Defence)* |
| 05.05.01 | Alejandro Lakatus W CO 9 Braunschweig *(WBO L. Heavyweight Title Defence)* |

Career: 44 contests, won 44.

Byron (The Hammer from Bama) Mitchell

Jasper, USA. *Born* 31 October, 1973
WBA S. Middleweight Champion

Major Amateur Honours: Won a bronze medal in the 1994 United States Championships, a bronze medal in the 1995 PAL Championships and competed in the 1996 Olympic trials. Also won amateur international honours
Turned Pro: June 1996
Significant Results: Adam Garland W RSC 1, Frank Liles W RSC 11, Bruno Girard DREW 12 and L PTS 12
Type/Style: Is a stiff, upright boxer with only moderate skills, but is a hard puncher, particularly with the left hook
Points of Interest: 6'0" tall. Having studied sports medicine, he first won the WBA title by beating Frank Liles in June 1999, but lost it to Bruno Girard in April last year. Has 17 wins inside the distance

16.09.00	Vince Durham W PTS 10 Ozark
03.02.01	Anton Robinson W PTS 10 Las Vegas
03.03.01	Manuel Siaca W RSC 12 Las Vegas *(Vacant WBA S. Middleweight Title)*

Career: 25 contests, won 23, drew 1, lost 1.

Fernando Montiel

Fernando (Cochulito) Montiel

Los Mochis, Mexico. *Born* 1 March, 1979
WBO Flyweight Champion

Major Amateur Honours: Claims 33 wins in 36 fights and was a local

205

Golden Gloves champion
Turned Pro: December 1966
Significant Results: Paulino Villalobos DREW 10 and W PTS 10, Sergio Millan W PTS 10, Cruz Carbajal W RSC 4
Type/Style: Is a clever and stylish boxer with a good uppercut
Points of Interest: 5'4" tall. The youngest of a fighting family, his father and four brothers were all boxers. Won his first 11 bouts inside the distance and has 17 wins by knockout or stoppage. Trained by a Japanese conditioner, he is based in Mexico

15.12.00	Isidro Garcia W RSC 7 Ciudud Obregon *(WBO Flyweight Title Challenge)*
24.03.01	Zoltan Lunka W RSC 7 Munich *(WBO Flyweight Title Defence)*
25.05.01	Juan Domingo Cordoba W CO 1 Acapulco *(WBO Flyweight Title Defence)*
Career: 23 contests, won 22, drew 1.	

Erik (The Terrible) Morales

Tijuana, Mexico. *Born* 1 September, 1976
WBC Featherweight Champion. Former Undefeated WBC S. Bantamweight Champion. Former Undefeated WBO S. Bantamweight Champion. Former Undefeated Mexican S. Bantamweight Champion

Major Amateur Honours: None, but claims 108 wins in 114 fights
Turned Pro: March 1993
Significant Results: Daniel Zaragoza W CO 11, Jose Luis Bueno W CO 2, Hector Acero Sanchez W PTS 12, Junior Jones W RSC 4, Angel Chacon W RSC 2, Juan Carlos Ramirez W RSC 9, Reynante Jamili W RSC 6, Wayne McCullough W PTS 12, Marco Antonio Barrera W PTS 12
Type/Style: Is a cool, upright, pressure fighter who can bang hard with both hands
Points of Interest: 5'8" tall. His dad fought Orlando Canizalez as a pro and his brother, Diego, is a former WBO super-flyweight champion. Having turned pro at the age of 16, he has 29 wins inside the distance and made nine defences of his WBC super-bantamweight title before relinquishing it last year. After he beat Marco Antonio

Barrera for the WBO title on a hotly disputed decision, he again relinquished.

02.09.00	Kevin Kelley W RSC 7 El Paso
09.12.00	Rodney Jones W CO 1 Tijuana
17.02.01	Gustavo Espadas W PTS 12 Las Vegas *(WBC Featherweight Title Challenge)*
Career: 40 contests, won 40.	

Erik Morales

Eric (Little Hands of Stone) Morel

Madison, USA. *Born* Puerto Rico, 1 October, 1975
WBA Flyweight Champion

Major Amateur Honours: His honours included a silver medal in the 1992 World Junior Championships for Puerto Rico, a silver medal in the 1993 National Golden Gloves, a gold medal in the 1994 National Golden Gloves, and a silver medal in the 1994 and 1996 United States Championships. In between, he was the USA Junior champion in 1993. Competed in the 1995 Pan-American Games and the 1996 Olympic Games
Turned Pro: October 1996
Significant Results: Rodolfo Blanco W PTS 12, Ysaias Zamudio W RSC 7, Miguel Granados W PTS 12
Type/Style: Has a string bean, slick upright southpaw style, with a sharp jab
Points of Interest: 5'3" tall. Started boxing in 1983 in Puerto Rico and works part time at the Holiday Inn.

With 17 wins inside the distance under his belt, he moved down from super-flyweight to win the WBA flyweight title

05.08.00	Sornpichai Pisanurachan W PTS 12 Madison *(WBA Flyweight Title Challenge)*
07.10.00	Alberto Ontiveros W PTS 12 Las Vegas *(WBA Flyweight Title Defence)*
15.12.00	Gilberto Keb-Baas W PTS 12 Madison *(WBA Flyweight Title Defence)*
08.06.01	Jose de Jesus W RTD 8 Baraboo *(WBA Flyweight Title Defence)*
Career: 30 contests, won 30.	

Shane (Sugar) Mosley

Lynwood, USA. *Born* 7 September, 1971
WBC Welterweight Champion. Former Undefeated IBF Lightweight Champion

Major Amateur Honours: Was the 1989, 1990 and 1992 United States champion. Won a silver medal in the 1989 World Junior Championships, but lost in the finals of the US Olympic trials to Vernon Forrest
Turned Pro: February 1993
Significant Results: Phillip Holiday W PTS 12, Juan Molina W RSC 8, James Leija W RTD 9, Golden Johnson W CO 7, John Brown W RSC 8, Oscar de la Hoya W PTS 12
Type/Style: A slick and smooth, fast-handed stylist with quick reflexes and good mobility, he can also punch with power
Points of Interest: 5'9" tall with a 74" reach. Started boxing at eight years of age and is trained by his father. He also beat Oscar de la Hoya as an amateur. With 34 wins inside the distance, and eight defences of the IBF lightweight title behind him, he relinquished the belt and moved up. Has made two defences of his WBC title since winning it from de la Hoya in June 2000. Owns a day-care centre with his dad

04.11.00	Antonio Diaz W RSC 6 New York City *(WBC Welterweight Title Defence)*
10.03.01	Shannan Taylor W RTD 5 Las Vegas *(WBC Welterweight Title Defence)*
Career: 37 contests, won 37.	

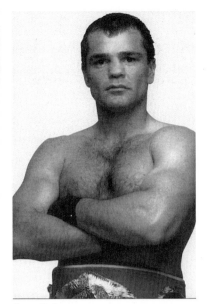

Sven Ottke

Sven Ottke

Berlin, Germany. *Born* 3 June, 1967
IBF S. Middleweight Champion.
Former Undefeated German L.
Heavyweight Champion

Major Amateur Honours: Was a
quarter-finalist in the 1988 Olympic
Games. Won a bronze medal in the
1989 World Championships, gold
medals in the 1991 and 1996 European
Championships, a bronze medal in the
1993 European Championships, and a
silver medal in the 1994 World Cup.
Competed in the 1992 and 1996
Olympics
Turned Pro: March 1997
Significant Results: Charles Brewer W
PTS 12, Giovanni Nardiello W CO 3,
Thomas Tate W TD 11, Glencoffe
Johnson W PTS 12, Lloyd Bryan W
PTS 12
Type/Style: Good tactically, and a
clever southpaw with an awkward
style, he is a slow starter and not a
hard puncher
Points of Interest: 5'11" tall. Did not
turn professional until he was 29, due
to a long spell as a world-class
amateur. Has only stopped or knocked
out four opponents. After beating
Chris Byrd, Jason Matthews, Juan
Carlos Gomez and Michael Moorer
while an amateur, Sven has now
defended his IBF title nine times since

winning it from Charles Brewer in
October 1998

02.09.00	Charles Brewer W PTS 12 Magdeburg *(IBF S. Middleweight Title Defence)*
16.12.00	Silvio Branco W PTS 12 Karlsruhe *(IBF S. Middleweight Title Defence)*
24.03.01	James Crawford WRSC 8 Magdeburg *(IBF S. Middleweight Title Defence)*
09.06.01	Ali Ennebati W RSC 11 Nuremberg *(IBF S. Middleweight Title Defence)*

Career: 23 contests, won 23.

Irene (Mambaco) Pacheco

San Juan de Uraba, Colombia. *Born* 26
March, 1971
IBF Flyweight Champion

Major Amateur Honours: None known
Turned Pro: November 1993
Significant Results: Luis Cox W RSC
9, Ferid Ben Jeddu W RSC 4, Pedro
Pena W CO 11
Type/Style: A clever boxer who is
mainly southpaw but can switch, he is
also a good body puncher
Points of Interest: 5'6" tall. Never
fighting for any other major title
before becoming IBF champion, he
has stopped or knocked out 13 of his
last 14 opponents and has only been
taken the distance six times. Fighting
outside Colombia just twice, Irene has
made three title defences since
winning the vacant IBF title by beating
Luis Cox in April 1999

10.11.00	Masibulele Makepula W PTS 12 Las Vegas *(IBF Flyweight Title Defence)*

Career: 26 contests, won 26.

Manny Pacquiao

Bukidnon, Philippines. *Born* 12
December, 1976
IBF S. Bantamweight Champion.
Former WBC Flyweight Champion

Major Amateur Honours: None, but
started at 13 and won 60 of 64 fights
Turned Pro: January 1995
Significant Results: Chockchai
Chokwiwat W CO 5, Melvin
Magramo W PTS 10, Chatchai
Sasakul W CO 8, Gabriel Mira W CO
4, Medgoen Singsurat L CO 3,
Reynante Jamili W RSC 2, Arnulfo
Barotillo W CO 4
Type/Style: A stocky, aggressive and

hard-punching southpaw, his defence
is not too hot
Points of Interest: Turned pro at the
age of 18. Having won the WBC
flyweight title by knocking out
Chatchai Sasakul in December 1998,
making one defence before losing it to
Medgoen Singsurat in September
1999, he promptly moved straight up
to super-bantamweight. Following his
brother, Bobby, who was also a
professional fighter, he has 24 wins
inside the distance

14.10.00	Nedal Hussein W RSC 10 Antipolo
24.02.01	Tetsurora Senrima W RSC 5 Antipolo
28.04.01	Wetyhya Sakmuangkiang W CO 6 Kidapawan
23.06.01	Lehlohonolo Ledwaba W RSC 6 Las Vegas *(IBF S. Bantamweight Title Challenge)*

Chana Porpaoin

Petchabon Province, Thailand. *Born*
25 March, 1966
WBA M. Flyweight Champion.
Former Undefeated Thai M. Flyweight
Champion

Major Amateur Honours: None
Turned Pro: May 1988
Significant Results: Phalan
Lukmingkwan W PTS 8, Manny
Melchor W PTS 10, Hideyuki Ohashi
W PTS 12, Carlos Murillo W PTS 12
(twice), Rosendo Alvarez L PTS 12
Type/Style: Is a slick, quick and busy
little boxer with a good chin
Points of Interest: Despite never
boxing as an amateur, coming straight
from kick boxing, he was unbeaten in
his first 35 fights. He won the WBA
title in February 1993 by beating
Hideyuki Ohashi in Tokyo and made
nine defences, but had only one fight
each year during 1996, 1997 and 1998.
Has stopped 16 opponents, his two
draws both being technical draws.
Twin brother, Songkram, once held
the WBA mini-flyweight interim title

01.09.00	Tiger Kiakniwat W CO 4 Bangkok
19.10.00	Ernesto Rubillar T DRAW 8 Ratchaburi
24.01.01	Diny Kirimaseh W PTS 6 Bangkok
16.04.01	Keitaro Hoshino W PTS 12 Yokohama *(WBA M. Flyweight Title Challenge)*

Career: 47 contests, won 44, drew 2, lost 1.

Hasim Rahman

Baltimore, USA. *Born* 7 November, 1972
WBC & IBF Heavyweight Champion

Major Amateur Honours: Competed in the 1994 United States Championships
Turned Pro: December 1994
Significant Results: Trevor Berbick W PTS 10, Jesse Ferguson W PTS 12, David Tua L RSC 10, Oleg Maskaev L CO 8, Corrie Sanders W RSC 7
Type/Style: Solid with limited skills, he is an explosive right-hand puncher
Points of Interest: 6'2" tall. Has had to overcome a career-threatening spine injury and needed 500 stitches to head and face after a car accident. Still carries five bullets from a shooting in his body and has been arrested about a dozen times. A shock winner over Lennox Lewis, he has 29 wins inside the distance

04.08.00	Frankie Swindell W RTD 7 Las Vegas
22.04.01	Lennox Lewis W CO 5 Brakpan *(WBC and IBF Heavyweight Title Challenges)*
Career: 37 contests, won 35, lost 2.	

John (The Quite Man) Ruiz

Chelsea, USA. *Born* 4 January, 1972
WBA Heavyweight Champion

Major Amateur Honours: Competed in the World Championships in 1991 and won a gold medal in the 1991 Olympic Festival, before losing in the 1992 Olympic trials
Turned Pro: August 1992
Significant Results: Sergei Kobozev L PTS 10, Julius Francis W CO 4, Danell Nicholson L PTS 12, Boris Powell W PTS 10, David Tua L RSC 1, Tony Tucker W RSC 11, Jerry Ballard W RSC 4
Type/Style: Strong with an upright style, he has a solid jab
Points of Interest: 6'2" tall. Named after John Kennedy, he is the first boxer of Puerto Rican origins to win the heavyweight title. Although plagued by hand problems, John has 27 wins inside the distance

12.08.00	Evander Holyfield L PTS 12 Las Vegas *(Vacant WBA Heavyweight Title)*
03.03.01	Evander Holyfield W PTS 12 Las Vegas *(WBA Heavyweight Title Challenge)*
Career: 41 contests, won 37, lost 4.	

Veeraphol (Death Mask) Sahaprom

Nakhon Ratchaseema, Thailand. *Born* 16 November, 1968
WBC Bantamweight Champion.
Former WBA Bantamweight Champion

Major Amateur Honours: None
Turned Pro: December 1994
Significant Results: Daourang Chuwatana W PTS 12, Nana Yaw Konadu L RSC 2, Rolando Pascua W PTS 10, Joichiro Tatsuyoshi W CO 6, Adan Vargas W PTS 12
Type/Style: Is a flat-footed, classy stalker with a high, tight guard, who is a big right-hand puncher
Points of Interest: 5'4" tall. Came out of kick boxing into professional boxing, winning the WBC International title in his first fight, and the WBA title in his fourth. His real name is Veeraphol Sumranklang, but he now fights as Veeraphol Sahaprom. Holding the WBA title for only four months, he has made six defences of his WBC title. Getting his nickname from his stony expression when fighting, he has won 22 bouts inside the distance

16.08.00	Jaime Barcelona W RSC 8 Bangkok
05.12.00	Oscar Arciniega W RSC 5 Bangkok *(WBC Bantamweight Title Defence)*
30.01.01	Hasan Ambon W PTS 10 Bangkok
12.03.01	Roberto Lopez W RTD 6 Paris
14.05.01	Ricardo Barajas W RSC 3 Paris *(WBC Bantamweight Title Defence)*
Career: 33 contests, won 32, lost 1.	

Agapito (Cyclone) Sanchez

La Victoria, Dominican Republic.
Born 14 February, 1970
WBO S. Bantamweight Champion.
Former Undefeated Dominican S. Flyweight Champion

Major Amateur Honours: None known
Turned Pro: November 1989
Significant Results: Max Gomez W PTS 12, Marco Antonio Barrera L PTS 12, Javier Marquez L PTS 12, Cesar Soto L RSC 2, Freddie Norwood L PTS 12, Javier Jauregui W PTS 10, Gustavo Espadas L PTS 10, Oscar Larios W RSC 5, Gerard Martinez W RSC 11
Type/Style: Tough, slick and quick with a good jab, his body punches have a habit of straying low
Points of Interest: Failed in a previous shot at the WBO title when outpointed by Marco Antonio Barrera in 1995. Has 20 wins inside the distance

19.08.00	Juan Carlos Ramirez W PTS 10 Mashantucket
23.06.01	Jorge Monsalvo W RSC 7 Las Vegas *(Vacant WBO S. Bantamweight Title)*
Career: 41 contests, won 33, drew 1, lost 7.	

Daniel Santos

San Juan, Puerto Rico. *Born* 10 October, 1975
WBO Welterweight Champion

Major Amateur Honours: Won a bronze medal in the 1992 World Junior Championships, a silver medal in the 1995 Pan-American Games and a bronze medal in the 1996 Olympic Games. Competed in the 1993 and 1995 World Championships and in the 1994 Goodwill Games
Turned Pro: September 1996
Significant Results: Luis Verdugo T DRAW 1, William Ruiz W RSC 3, Ray Lovato W RSC 2, Kofi Jantuah L RSC 5, Ahmed Kotiev L PTS 12 and W CO 5
Type/Style: A fast, clever and flashy southpaw who is a heavy left-handed puncher, he has a questionable chin and is suspect on stamina
Points of Interest: 6'0" tall. Having lost to David Reid in the Pan-American Games, he was unbeaten in his first 21 pro fights, losing a disputed decision to Ahmed Kotiev in his first challenge for the WBO title, before the WBO ordered a rematch, which Santos won in May 2000. Has 19 wins inside the distance

29.07.00	Giovanni Parisi W RSC 4 Reggio Calabria *(WBO Welterweight Title Defence)*
16.12.00	Neil Sinclair W CO 2 Sheffield *(WBO Welterweight Title Defence)*
Career: 27 contests, won 24, drew 1, lost 2.	

Harry (Exterminator) Simon

Walvis Bay, Namibia. *Born* 21 October, 1972
WBO L. Middleweight Champion

Major Amateur Honours: Competed in the 1992 Olympic Games but lost in the first series. An African champion and three times South African champion, he claims just two losses in 273 fights
Turned Pro: January 1994
Significant Results: Del Bryan W RSC 6, Ronald Wright W PTS 12, Kevin Lueshing W RSC 3

Type/Style: Strong and powerful, and a charismatic boxer with a sound defence, he has a good chin and plenty of stamina

Points of Interest: Real name Harry Saayman. Having started boxing in 1980 before working in a diamond mine, Harry is the first ever world boxing champion from Namibia. Trained by Brian Mitchell, the former WBA champion, he has 17 wins inside the distance, but has made only four WBO title defences in three years

23.09.00	Rodney Jones W PTS 12 Rama *(WBO L. Middleweight Title Defence)*
10.02.01	Wayne Alexander W RSC 5 Widnes *(WBO L. Middleweight Title Defence)*
Career: 21 contests, won 21.	

Paul (The New Pittsburgh Kid) Spadafora

Pittsburgh, USA. *Born* 5 September, 1975
IBF Lightweight Champion

Major Amateur Honours: Claiming 65 wins in 70 fights, he was twice a State champion and competed in two United States Championships, but failed to win a medal
Turned Pro: October 1995
Significant Results: Troy Fletcher W PTS 8, Sam Girard W PTS 10, Israel Cardona W PTS 12, Renato Cornett W RSC 11, Victoriano Sosa W PTS 12
Type/Style: A clever southpaw, he has fast hands, an excellent jab, and good footwork, but is not a puncher
Points of Interest: 5'9" tall. A distant cousin to former world light-heavyweight champion, Joey Maxim, his grandfather and brother both being boxers, Paul has had a stormy life with his father dying of a drug overdose and him being shot in the leg by a policeman. Is a natural right hander who fights left handed only because he copied his brother. Having stopped or knocked out 15 opponents, Paul has made five defences since winning the vacant IBF title with the win over Israel Cardona in August 1999

09.09.00	Rodney Jones W RSC 3 Chester
16.12.00	Billy Irwin W PTS 12 Pittsburg *(IBF Lightweight Title Defence)*
08.05.01	Joel Perez W PTS 12 Pittsburg *(IBF Lightweight Title Defence)*
Career: 33 contests, won 33.	

Dingaan (The Rose of Soweto) Thobela

Soweto, South Africa. *Born* 24 September, 1966
Former WBC S. Middleweight Champion. Former WBA Lightweight Champion. Former Undefeated WBO Lightweight Champion. Former Undefeated South African S. Featherweight and S. Middleweight Champion

Major Amateur Honours: A South African champion, he claims only three losses in 83 fights
Turned Pro: June 1986
Significant Results: Daniel Londas W PTS 12, Mauricio Aceves W RSC 8 and W PTS 12, Antonio Rivera W PTS 12, Tony Lopez L PTS 12 and W PTS 12, Orzubek Nazarov L PTS 12 (twice), Karl Taylor L PTS 8, Geoff McCreesh L CO 2, Cornelius Carr L PTS 12, Soon Botes W PTS 12
Type/Style: Charismatic and naturally talented, but lacking in dedication, he has a good defence and is a fine counter puncher
Points of Interest: 5'7". As the first South African to win national titles in such a wide range as super-featherweight to super-middleweight, Dingaan originally wanted to be a teacher but took up boxing instead. Has 26 wins inside the distance and has taken part in nine world title bouts

01.09.00	Glenn Catley W CO 12 Brakpan *(WBC S. Middleweight Title Challenge)*
15.12.00	Dave Hilton L PTS 12 Montreal *(WBC S. Middleweight Title Defence)*
Career: 50 contests, won 40, drew 2, lost 8.	

Harry Simon   Les Clark

Masamori Tokuyama

North Korea. *Born* Tokyo, Japan, 17 September, 1974
WBC S. Flyweight Champion

Major Amateur Honours: None, his record being just 12 wins in 17 fights
Turned Pro: September 1994
Significant Results: Manny Melchor L PTS 10, Nolito Cabato DREW 10 and L TD 7, Hiroki Ioka W RSC 5, Pone Saengmorakot W PTS 12
Type/Style: Tall and upright with a sharp jab and fast hands, he has no punch
Points of Interest: 5'8" tall. Real name is Chang-Soo Hong and he is the first North Korean to win a world title, his title defence against In-Joo Cho being the first time that a North Korean and a South Korean have fought each other for a world title in Korea. His father was a karate teacher

27.08.00	In-Joo Cho W PTS 12 Osaka
	(WBC S. Flyweight Title Challenge)
12.12.00	Akihiko Nago W PTS 12 Osaka
	(WBC S. Flyweight Title Defence)
20.05.01	In-Joo Cho W CO 5 Seoul
	(WBC S. Flyweight Title Defence)

Frankie (The Shark) Toledo

Newark, USA. *Born* 12 April, 1970
IBF Featherweight Champion

Major Amateur Honours: Competed in the 1988 National Golden Gloves
Turned Pro: December 1989
Significant Results: Clarence Adams W RSC 4, Hector Acero W PTS 10, Marco Antonio Barrera L RSC 2, Max Gomez W PTS 12, Cassius Baloyi L PTS 12, Orlando Canizales W PTS 10, Manuel Medina L PTS 10
Type/Style: Is a clever but light-punching southpaw
Points of Interest: From a fighting family, his brother David is also a pro, his loss to Marco Antonio Barrera in 1995 was for the WBO super-bantamweight title. Has 15 wins inside the distance

04.11.00	John Roby W PTS 6 Marshalltown
06.04.01	Mbulelo Botile W PTS 12 Las Vegas
	(IBF Featherweight Title Challenge)
Career:	46 contests, won 40, drew 1, lost 5.

Felix (Tito) Trinidad

Cupoy Alto, Puerto Rico. *Born* 10 January, 1973

WBA Middleweight Champion. Former Undefeated WBA and IBF L. Middleweight Champion. Former Undefeated WBC and IBF Welterweight Champion

Major Amateur Honours: A Puerto Rican amateur champion at five weights, he won 51 of 57 fights
Turned Pro: March 1990
Significant Results: Maurice Blocker W CO 2, Hector Camacho W PTS 12, Yori 'Boy' Campas W RSC 4, Oba Carr W RSC 8, Kevin Lueshing W RSC 3, Pernell Whitaker W PTS 12, Oscar de la Hoya W PTS 12, David Reid W PTS 12
Type/Style: Although a good boxer, his real strength being his explosive punching power, he is also a great finisher when he has a man hurt
Points of Interest: 5'10" tall. Has taken part in 20 world title fights at three weights and won them all, 16 inside the distance. Started boxing when he was 12 years old and is managed by his dad, who was also a pro, and earlier on in his career won the Puerto Rican featherweight title

22.07.00	Mamadou Thiam W RSC 3 Miami
	(WBA L. Middleweight Title Defence)
02.12.00	Fernando Vargas W RSF 12 Las Vegas
	(WBA L. Middleweight Title Defence and IBF L. Middleweight Title Challenge)
12.05.01	William Joppy W RSC 5 New York City
	(WBA Middleweight Title Challenge)
Career:	37 contests, won 37.

Kostya Tszyu

Australia. *Born* Serov, Russia, 19 September, 1969
WBC and WBA L.Welterweight Champion. Former IBF L.Welterweight Champion

Major Amateur Honours: Was the European Junior champion in 1986, won a World Junior Championship silver medal in 1987, the European Games' gold medal in 1989 and 1991, a bronze medal in the 1989 World Championships, and was the gold medal winner in the 1991 World Championships
Turned Pro: March 1992
Significant Results: Jake Rodriguez W RSC 6, Roger Mayweather W PTS 12, Hugo Pineda W RSC 11, Jan Bergman W CO 6, Vince Phillips L RSC 10,

Rafael Ruelas W RSC 8, Diosbelys Hurtado W RSC 5, Miguel Gonzalez W RSC 10
Type/Style: An aggressive two-fisted fighter, he is a dangerous puncher with both hands
Points of Interest: 5'7" tall. Born in Russia but now based in Australia, Kostya (real christian name is Konstantin) has 22 wins inside the distance and made six defences of the IBF title before being stopped by Vince Phillips in May 1997. Won the vacant WBC title by halting Miguel Gonzalez in August 1999 and has made five defences. Wears his hair in a ponytail

29.07.00	Julio Cesar Chavez W RSC 6 Phoenix
	(WBC L. Welterweight Title Defence)
03.02.01	Sharmba Mitchell W RTD 7 Las Vegas
	(WBC L. Welterweight Title Defence. WBA L. Welterweight Title Challenge)
23.06.01	Oktay Urkal W PTS 12 Uncasville
	(WBC & WBA L. Welterweight Title Defences)
Career:	29 contests, won 27, drew 1, lost 1.

Pongsaklek Wonjongkam

Nakhornatchaseema, Thailand. *Born* 11 August, 1977
WBC Flyweight Champion

Major Amateur Honours: None
Turned Pro: December 1994
Significant Results: Randy Mangubat W CO 3, Mzukisi Sikali W RSC 1, Juanito Rubillar W PTS 10
Type/Style: A tough, aggressive pressure fighter, he is a southpaw with a wicked right hook
Points of Interest: 5'1" tall. His last loss was in December 1995 and he is unbeaten in his last 34 bouts, with 22 wins inside the distance to his name. Has also boxed under the names of Nakornthong Parkview and Sithkanongsak

01.07.00	Ramil Anito W PTS 10 Nakonpatom
25.08.00	Junior Milla W RSC 3 Sakonnakow
22.09.00	Nat Barcelona W RSC 6 Bangkok
29.12.00	Ramil Anito W RSC 5 Kong Island
02.03.01	Malcolm Tunacao W RSC 1 Pichit Province
	(WBC Flyweight Title Challenge)
08.05.01	Alavin Felisada W PTS 10 Udonthani
Career:	42 contests, won 40, lost 2.

World Title Bouts During 2000-2001

by Bob Yalen

All of last season's title bouts for the IBF, WBA, WBC and WBO are shown in date order within their weight division and give the boxers' respective weights, along with the scorecard if going to a decision. There is also a short summary of every bout that involved a British contestant, and British officials, where applicable, are listed. Yet again there were no WORLD TITLE FIGHTS as such – even if you allow for Roy Jones (L. Heavy) who held three of the major four titles – just a proliferation of champions recognised by the above four commissions and spread over 17 weight divisions. Until there is a mood to legislate boxing from just one world body, or at least separate bodies who will work together, then the days of one champion per weight division are doomed.

M. Flyweight

IBF

29 April 2001   Roberto Leyva 7.6$\frac{1}{2}$ (Mexico) W PTS 12 Daniel Reyes 7.6$\frac{1}{4}$ (Colombia), New York City, USA. Scorecards: 114-113, 115-112, 115-112. Contested for the vacant title after Zolani Petelo (South Africa) relinquished the belt in December 2000 due to weight-making problems.

WBA

20 August 2000   Noel Arambulet 7.8$\frac{1}{2}$ (Venezuela) L PTS 12 Jomo Gamboa 7.7 (Philippines), Tokyo, Japan. Scorecards: 114-116, 115-116, 116-114. Arambulet forfeited his title on the scales and Gamboa was awarded the title on the decision.

6 December 2000   Jomo Gamboa 7.6$\frac{3}{4}$ (Philippines) L PTS 12 Keitaro Hoshino 7.7 (Japan), Yokohama, Japan. Scorecards: 112-117, 113-115, 113-115.

16 April 2001   Keitaro Hoshino 7.7 (Japan) L PTS 12 Chana Porpaoin 7.7 (Thailand), Yokohama, Japan. Scorecards: 113-115, 113-115, 118-110.

WBC

7 July 2000   Jose Antonio Aguirre 7.5$\frac{1}{2}$ (Mexico) W CO 5 Jose Luis Zepeda 7.5$\frac{3}{4}$ (Mexico), Villahermosa, Mexico.

21 October 2000   Jose Antonio Aguirre 7.6 (Mexico) W RSC 4 Erdene Chuluun 7.7 (Mongolia), Mexico City, Mexico.

2 February 2001   Jose Antonio Aguirre 7.7 (Mexico) W PTS 12 Manny Melchor 7.7 (Philippines), Tijuana, Mexico. Scorecards: 120-108, 120-107, 118-110.

WBO

6 April 2001   Kermin Guardia 7.7 (Colombia) W PTS 12 Juan Alfonso Keb-Baas 7.7 (Mexico), Merida, Mexico. Scorecards: 115-112, 115-112, 115-111.

L. Flyweight

IBF

2 December 2000   Ricardo Lopez 7.9$\frac{1}{2}$ (Mexico) W RSC 3 Ratanapol Sowvoraphin 7.9$\frac{1}{2}$ (Thailand), Las Vegas, USA.

WBA

12 August 2000   Beibis Mendoza 7.9$\frac{1}{2}$ (Colombia) W DIS 7 Rosendo Alvarez 7.10 (Nicaragua), Las Vegas, USA. Billed for the vacant title after Pichitnoi Chor-Siriwat (Thailand) was stripped of the belt in July 2000 for failing to meet Alvarez within the given time.

3 March 2001   Beibis Mendoza 7.9 (Colombia) L PTS 12 Rosendo Alvarez 7.10 (Nicaragua), Las Vegas, USA. Scorecards: 112-115, 113-114, 14-113.

WBC

30 January 2001   Yo-Sam Choi 7.9$\frac{3}{4}$ (South Korea) W CO 7 Saman Sorjaturong 7.8$\frac{1}{4}$ (Thailand), Seoul, South Korea.

WBO

22 July 2000   Will Grigsby 7.9$\frac{1}{2}$ (USA) W PTS 12 Nelson Dieppa 7.10 (Puerto Rico), Miami, USA. Scorecards: 116-112, 115-113, 115-113. A vacant title fight after Masibulele Makepula (South Africa) relinquished the championship in March 2000 in favour of maintaining his WBU belt. Grigsby forfeited the championship belt in October 2000 after testing positive following his title win.

3 February 2001   Andy Tabanas 7.10 (Philippines) DREW 12 Fahlan Sakkriren 7.9$\frac{1}{2}$ (Thailand), Las Vegas, USA. Scorecards: 114-114, 116-112, 113-115. Following the decision, the title continued to remain vacant.

14 April 2001   Nelson Dieppa 7.9 (Puerto Rico) W RSC 11 Andy Tabanas 7.9$\frac{1}{2}$ (Philippines), New York City, USA.

Flyweight

IBF

10 November 2000   Irene Pacheco 7.13 (Colombia) W PTS 12 Masibulele Makepula 7.13 (South Africa), Las Vegas, USA. Scorecards: 118-110, 117-111, 114-114.

WBA

5 August 2000   Sornpichai Pisanurachan 7.13$\frac{3}{4}$ (Thailand) L PTS 12 Eric Morel 7.13 (USA), Madison, Wisconsin, USA. Scorecards: 107-120, 109-118, 109-117.

7 October 2000   Eric Morel 8.0 (USA) W PTS 12 Alberto Ontiveros 8.0 (Mexico), Las Vegas, USA. Scorecards: 120-107, 120-107, 120-108.

15 December 2000   Eric Morel 8.0 (USA) W PTS 12 Gilberto Keb-Baas 8.0 (Mexico), Madison, Wisconsin, USA. Scorecards: 116-111, 117-109, 117-109.

8 June 2001   Eric Morel 8.0 (USA) W RTD 8 Jose de Jesus 7.13 (Venezuela), Baraboo, Wisconsin, USA.

WBC

20 August 2000   Malcolm Tunacao 7.13$\frac{1}{2}$ (Philippines) DREW 12 Celes Kobayashi 7.13$\frac{1}{2}$ (Japan), Tokyo, Japan. Scorecards: 115-113, 112-115, 113-113.

2 March 2001 Malcolm Tunacao 8.0 (Philippines) L RSC 1 Pongsaklek Wonjongkam 8.0 (Thailand), Pichit Province, Thailand.

WBO

12 August 2000 Isidro Garcia 7.13³/₄ (Mexico) W RSC 6 Jose Rafael Sosa 7.13³/₄ (Argentine), Cordoba, Argentine.

15 December 2000 Isidro Garcia 7.13³/₄ (Mexico) L RSC 7 Fernando Montiel 8.0 (Mexico), Ciudud Obregon, Mexico.

24 March 2001 Fernando Montiel 7.13¹/₂ (Mexico) W RSC 7 Zoltan Lunka 7.13¹/₂ (Romania), Munich, Germany.

25 May 2001 Fernando Montiel 8.0 (Mexico) W CO 1 Juan Domingo Cordoba 8.0 (Argentine), Acapulco, Mexico.

S. Flyweight

IBF

22 July 2000 Felix Machado 8.3 (Venezuela) W PTS 12 Julio Gamboa 8.3 (Nicaragua), Miami, USA. Scorecards: 120-108, 119-109, 119-109. Again billed for the vacant title, which was first vacated in February 2000 after Mark Johnson was sent to prison, this was the second time the pair tried to settle the championship.

16 December 2000 Felix Machado 8.3 (Venezuela) W RSC 3 William de Souza 8.1¹/₂ (Panama), Maracay, Venezuela.

16 June 2001 Felix Machado 8.3 (Venezuela) W PTS 12 Mauricio Pastrana 8.1³/₄ (Colombia), Cincinnati, USA. Scorecards: 118-110, 116-112, 117-111.

WBA

9 October 2000 Hideki Todaka 8.3 (Japan) L RSC 7 Silvio Gamez 8.2³/₄ (Venezuela), Nagoya, Japan.

11 March 2001 Silvio Gamez 8.1³/₄ (Venezuela) L RSC 10 Celes Kobayashi 8.3 (Japan), Yokohama, Japan.

WBC

27 August 2000 In-Joo Cho 8.3 (South Korea) L PTS 12 Masamori Tokuyama 8.2³/₄ (Japan), Osaka, Japan. Scorecards: 107-119, 109-117, 110-116.

12 December 2000 Masamori Tokuyama 8.3 (Japan) W PTS 12 Akihiko Nago 8.2³/₄ (Japan), Osaka, Japan. Scorecards: 118-108, 117-109, 117-109.

20 May 2001 Masamori Tokuyama 8.2³/₄ (Japan) W CO 5 In-Joo Cho 8.3 (South Korea), Seoul, South Korea.

WBO

2 September 2000 Adonis Rivas 8.3 (Nicaragua) W PTS 12 Joel Luna Zarate 8.2 (Mexico), Managua, Nicaragua. Scorecards: 116-112, 115-113, 118-112.

16 June 2001 Adonis Rivas 8.2¹/₄ (Nicaragua) L PTS 12 Pedro Alcazar 8.2³/₄ (Panama), Panama City, Panama. Scorecards: 112-116, 112-116, 116-114.

Bantamweight

IBF

11 August 2000 Tim Austin 8.5³/₄ (USA) W PTS 12 Arthur Johnson 8.5 (USA), Las Vegas, USA. Scorecards: 120-108, 120-108, 120-108.

3 March 2001 Tim Austin 8.5 (USA) W RSC 6 Jesus Perez 8.5 (Colombia), Las Vegas, USA.

16 June 2001 Tim Austin 8.6 (USA) W RSC 6 Steve Dotse 8.6 (Ghana), Cincinnati, USA.

WBA

30 March 2001 Paulie Ayala 8.6 (USA) W PTS 12 Hugo Dianzo 8.6 (Mexico), Fort Worth, USA. Scorecards: 115-113, 115-113, 115-112. Earlier, on 16 December 2000, Eidy Moya (Venezuela) outscored Saohin Srithai Condo (Thailand) over 12 rounds in Maracay, Venezuela to land the vacant interim title.

WBC

5 December 2000 Veeraphol Sahaprom 8.6 (Thailand) W RSC 5 Oscar Arciniega 8.4³/₄ (Mexico), Bangkok, Thailand.

14 May 2001 Veeraphol Sahaprom 8.5¹/₂ (Thailand) W RSC 3 Ricardo Barajas 8.5³/₄ (Mexico), Paris, France. Judge: John Keane.

WBO

4 September 2000 Mauricio Martinez 8.5¹/₄ (Panama) W RSC 5 Lester Fuentes 8.4³/₄ (Nicaragua), Wythenshawe Forum, Manchester, England. Referee: Mickey Vann. Judges: Dave Parris, Paul Thomas, John Coyle. Contested for the vacant title after Johnny Tapia handed his belt back in August 2000 due to weight-making difficulties.

16 December 2000 Mauricio Martinez 8.5¹/₂ (Panama) W RSC 1 Esham Pickering 8.5³/₄ (England), The Arena, Sheffield, England. Judge: Paul Thomas. Unfortunately, the English challenger was found wanting and was saved from further punishment after 1.12 of the first round when the referee called it off. Pickering had been put down twice and on the second occasion the third man did not even bother to take up the count.

S. Bantamweight

IBF

6 October 2000 Lehlohonolo Ledwaba 8.9¹/₂ (South Africa) W CO 8 Eduardo Alvarez 8.9¹/₄ (Argentine), The Leisure Centre, Maidstone, England. Referee: Roy Francis. Judge: Dave Parris.

17 February 2001 Lehlohonolo Ledwaba 8.8³/₄ (South Africa) W RSC 9 Arnel Barotillo 8.9³/₄ (Philippines), Brakpan, South Africa. Judge: Roy Francis.

22 April 2001 Lehlohonolo Ledwaba 8.9³/₄ (South Africa) W PTS 12 Carlos Contreras 8.9 (Mexico), Brakpan, South Africa. Scorecards: Roy Francis 117-112, 118-110, 116-112.

23 June 2001 Lehlohonolo Ledwaba 8.10 (South Africa) L RSC 6 Manny Pacquiao 8.9 (Philippines), Las Vegas, USA.

WBA

5 August 2000 Clarence Adams 8.10 (USA) W RSC 6 Andres Fernandez 8.9³/₄ (USA), Madison, Wisconsin, USA. On 23 November 2000 in Nagoya, Japan, Yober Ortega (Venezuela) stopped Kozo Ishii (Japan) in the 11th round to win the vacant interim title.

23 March 2001 Clarence Adams 8.10 (USA) W PTS 12 Ivan Alvarez 8.10 (Colombia), Owensboro, Kentucky, USA. Scorecards: 115-112, 116-111, 115-112.

WBC

9 September 2000 Willie Jorrin 8.9³/₄ (USA) W PTS 12 Michael Brodie 8.10 (England), Bowler's Arena, Manchester, England. Referee: Richie Davies. Scorecards: 115-112, 116-112, 114-114. Billed for the vacant title following Erik Morales (USA) decision to give up his belt in September 2000 to fight in a higher weight division, Brodie looked to have well won but was forced to accept the fact that at least two of the judges somehow got it wrong, which also cost him his unbeaten record. Apart from a knockdown in the tenth round the better boxing came from Brodie, while the American threw less punches and was mainly ineffective.

19 January 2001 Willie Jorrin 8.10 (USA) W PTS 12 Oscar Larios 8.10 (Mexico), Sacramento, USA. Scorecards: 115-113, 115-113, 115-113.

WBO

9 September 2000 Marco Antonio Barrera 8.8¹/₂ (Mexico) W PTS 12 Jose Luis Valbuena 8.8¹/₂ (Venezuela), New Orleans, USA. Scorecards: 115-113, 117-111, 116-112.

1 December 2000 Marco Antonio Barrera 8.10 (Mexico) W RTD 6 Jesus Salud 8.10 (USA), Las Vegas, USA.

Barrera vacated the title in May 2001, following his win over Prince Naseem Hamed, in order to compete as a featherweight, despite refusing to accept the IBO version that was at stake in his fight with the latter.

23 June 2001 Agapito Sanchez 8.10 (Dominican Republic) W RSC 7 Jorge Monsalvo 8.9 (Colombia), Las Vegas, USA.

Featherweight
IBF

16 December 2000 Paul Ingle 8.13¹/₄ (England) L RSC 12 Mbulelo Botile 8.12¹/₂ (South Africa), The Arena, Sheffield, England. Referee: Judge: Roy Francis. Right from the start of this tragic fight, Ingle looked to be subdued and was never his normal, confident self. The South African, showing economy and landing with quality punches, always looked in control and opened cuts over both of Ingle's eyes, but the champion looked to last the distance despite taking a count in the 11th. However, Botile had other ideas and went straight on the attack, landing a heavy left hook which put Ingle down, and prompted the referee, Dave Parris, to call a halt at 0.20 of the final round. The rest is history, with Ingle rushed to hospital where he had a blood clot removed, and continuing to recover during the ensuing months. Boxing fans everywhere wish him well.

Michael Brodie (right) storms into Willie Jorrin during their contest for the vacant WBC super-bantamweight title, won by Jorrin

Les Clark

6 April 2001   Mbulelo Botile 8.13³/₄ (South Africa) L PTS 12 Frankie Toledo 9.0 (USA), Las Vegas, USA. Scorecards: 110-118, 111-117, 109-119.

WBA

9 September 2000   Freddie Norwood 9.1³/₄ (USA) L RSC 11 Derrick Gainer 8.13³/₄ (USA), New Orleans, USA. Following his victory, Gainer was named as the champion after Norwood technically lost his title on the scales.

24 February 2001   Derrick Gainer 8.13¹/₂ (USA) W PTS 12 Victor Polo 8.13³/₄ (Colombia), Tampa, USA. Scorecards: 115-112, 118-109, 113-114.

WBC

17 February 2001   Gustavo Espadas 8.12¹/₂ (Mexico) L PTS 12 Erik Morales 8.13 (Mexico), Las Vegas, USA. Scorecards: 113-115, 112-116, 112-116. Earlier, on 2 September 2000 in El Paso, USA, Morales stopped Kevin Kelley (USA) inside seven rounds to win the vacant interim title.

WBO

19 August 2000   Prince Naseem Hamed 9.0 (England) W RSC 4 Augie Sanchez 9.0 (USA), Mashantucket, Connecticut, USA. Yet again, the Prince went close to the wire, being often embarrassed by an average challenger before blasting him out chillingly in the fourth round. Having been chopped down earlier himself, despite the lack of a count, the champion finally got his punches together in the fourth and a cracking left, followed by a right-left-right sent Sanchez into dreamland and forced the referee to dispense with the count at 2.34 of the round. Hamed relinquished the title in October 2000 rather than fight Istvan Kovacs instead of a more marketable opponent.

27 January 2001   Istvan Kovacs 9.0 (Hungary) W RSC 12 Antonio Diaz 8.13¹/₂ (USA), Munich, Germany.

16 June 2001   Istvan Kovacs 9.0 (Hungary) L RSC 6 Julio Pablo Chacon 8.13 (Argentine), Budapest, Hungary.

S. Featherweight

IBF

2 September 2000   Diego Corrales 9.3³/₄ (USA) W RSC 3 Angel Manfredy 9.4 (USA), El Paso, USA. Corrales' management team relinquished the title on his behalf in October 2000 so that he could challenge for Floyd Mayweather's WBC crown

3 December 2000   Steve Forbes 9.4 (USA) W RSC 8 John Brown 9.4 (USA), Miami, USA.

WBA

16 September 2000   Joel Casamayor 9.4 (Cuba) W RSC 5 Radford Beasley 9.3¹/₂ (USA), Las Vegas, USA.

6 January 2001   Joel Casamayor 9.4 (Cuba) W RSC 9 Roberto Garcia 9.3¹/₂ (USA), Las Vegas, USA.

5 May 2001   Joel Casamayor 9.3 (Cuba) W PTS 12 Edwin Santana 9.2 (Dominican Republic), Philadelphia, Mississippi, USA. Scorecards: 120-107, 120-107, 119-108.

WBC

20 January 2001   Floyd Mayweather 9.4 (USA) W RSC 10 Diego Corrales 9.4 (USA), Las Vegas, USA. Judge: John Keane.

26 May 2001   Floyd Mayweather 9.4 (USA) W PTS 12 Carlos Hernandez 9.2¹/₂ (USA), Grand Rapids, USA. Scorecards: 116-111, 117-109, 119-109.

WBO

23 September 2000   Acelino Freitas 9.4 (Brazil) W RSC 9 Carlos Rios 9.3¹/₂ (Argentine), Rama, Ontario, Canada.

27 January 2001   Acelino Freitas 9.4 (Brazil) W RSC 1 Orlando Soto 9.3³/₄ (Panama), Brasilia, Brazil.

Lightweight

IBF

16 December 2000   Paul Spadafora 9.9 (USA) W PTS 12 Billy Irwin 9.8¹/₂ (Canada), Pittsburgh, USA. Scorecards: 116-111, 117-110, 118-109.

8 May 2001   Paul Spadafora 9.9 (USA) W PTS 12 Joel Perez 9.9 (USA), Pittsburgh, USA. Scorecards: 119-108, 120-107, 119-108.

WBA

11 October 2000   Takanori Hatakeyama 9.9 (Japan) W RTD 10 Hiroyuki Sakamoto 9.9 (Japan), Yokohama, Japan.

17 February 2001   Takanori Hatakeyama 9.9 (Japan) DREW 12 Rick Roberts Yoshimura 9.9 (Japan), Tokyo, Japan. Scorecards: 112-115, 116-111, 114-114.

WBC

15 September 2000   Jose Luis Castillo 9.8 (Mexico) DREW 12 Steve Johnston 9.9 (USA), Denver, USA. Scorecards: John Keane 114-114, 114-114, 114-115.

20 January 2000   Jose Luis Castillo 9.9 (Mexico) W RSC 6 Cesar Bazan 9.8¹/₂ (Mexico), Las Vegas, USA.

16 June 2001   Jose Luis Castillo 9.8¹/₂ (Mexico) W RSC 1 Sung-Ho Yuh 9.7 (South Korea), Hermosillo, Mexico.

WBO

25 November 2000   Artur Grigorian 9.8³/₄ (Uzbekistan) W PTS 12 Antonio Pitalua 9.8 (Colombia), Hanover, Germany. Scorecards: 114-112, 116-111, 115-112.

24 February 2001   Artur Grigorian 9.9 (Uzbekistan) W RSC 6 Jose Angel Perez 9.9 (Spain), Hamburg, Germany

16 June 2001   Artur Grigorian 9.9 (Uzbekistan) W PTS 12 Aldo Rios 9.7¹/₂ (Argentine), Budapest, Hungary. Scorecards: 117-110, 117-110, 116-111.

L. Welterweight

IBF

5 August 2000   Zab Judah 9.12 (USA) W RSC 4 Terron Millett 9.13¹/₂ (USA), Uncasville, Connecticut, USA.

20 October 2000   Zab Judah 9.13¹/₄ (USA) W RSC 8 Hector Quiroz 10.0 (Mexico), Auburn Hills, Michigan, USA.

13 January 2001   Zab Judah 9.12¹/₄ (USA) W RSC 10 Reggie Green 9.13 (USA), Uncasville, Connecticut, USA.

23 June 2001   Zab Judah 9.12¹/₂ (USA) W RSC 3 Allan Vester 9.12 (Denmark), Uncasville, Connecticut, USA.

WBA

16 September 2000   Sharmba Mitchell 9.13 (USA) W PTS 12 Felix Flores 9.13¹/₂ (Puerto Rico), Las Vegas, USA. Scorecards: 116-111, 116-111, 116-113.

3 February 2001   Sharmba Mitchell 9.13 (USA) L RTD 7 Kostya Tszyu 10.0 (Russia), Las Vegas, USA.

23 June 2001   Kostya Tszyu 9.13½ (Russia) W PTS 12 Oktay Urkal 9.12½ (Germany), Uncasville, Connecticut, USA. Scorecards: Terry O'Connor 116-113, 116-112, 115-113.

WBC

29 July 2000   Kostya Tszyu 9.13½ (Russia) W RSC 6 Julio Cesar Chavez 10.0 (Mexico), Phoenix, Arizona, USA.

3 February 2001   Kostya Tszyu 9.12½ (Russia) W RTD 7 Sharmba Mitchell 9.13 (USA), Las Vegas, USA.

23 June 2001   Kostya Tszyu 9.13½ (Russia) W PTS 12 Oktay Urkal 9.12½ (Germany), Uncasville, Connecticut, USA. Scorecards: Terry O'Connor 116-113, 116-112, 115-113.

WBO

22 July 2000   Randall Bailey 9.13 (USA) L PTS 12 Ener Julio 9.13¾ (Colombia), Miami, USA. Scorecards: 111-113, 111-114, 115-111. Julio forfeited the title in June 2001 when it was discovered that he had cataracts in both eyes prior to a defence against Felix Flores.

30 June 2001   DeMarcus Corley 10.0 (USA) W RSC 1 Felix Flores 10.0 (Puerto Rico), Las Vegas, USA.

Welterweight

IBF

26 August 2000   Raul Frank 10.7 (USA) NC 3 Vernon Forrest 10.6½ (USA), Las Vegas, USA. Contested for the vacant title after Felix Trinidad (Puerto Rico) moved up to light-middleweight in March 2000, the title remained open on the result of this one.

12 May 2001   Vernon Forrest 10.5½ (USA) W PTS 12 Raul Frank 10.7 (USA), New York City, USA. Scorecards: 120-108, 118-110, 118-110.

WBA

17 February 2001   Andrew Lewis 10.7 (Guyana) W RSC 7 James Page 10.6 (USA), Las Vegas, USA. With Page stripped of the championship in September 2000 for failing to fulfil a mandatory defence against Lewis because of contractual problems, this was a vacant title fight.

28 April 2001   Andrew Lewis 10.6½ (Guyana) W PTS 12 Larry Marks 10.4¼ (USA), New York City, USA. Scorecards: 119-109, 120-108, 119-109.

WBC

4 November 2000   Shane Mosley 10.6½ (USA) W RSC 6 Antonio Diaz 10.6½ (USA), New York City, USA.

10 March 2001   Shane Mosley 10.7 (USA) W RTD 5 Shannan Taylor 10.7 (Australia), Las Vegas, USA. Judge: Larry O'Connell.

WBO

29 July 2000   Daniel Santos 10.6½ (Dominican Republic) W RSC 4 Giovanni Parisi 10.5¾ (Italy), Reggio Calabria, Italy.

16 December 2000   Daniel Santos 10.7 (Dominican Republic) W CO 2 Neil Sinclair 10.6 (Ireland), The Arena,

Sheffield, England. Referee: John Coyle. Judge: Mickey Vann. Sent down early on in the fight, Sinclair soon recovered and gained hope that he could win inside the distance when a heavy right put the southpaw champion on the canvas for a count of seven immediately prior to the bell to end the first round. However, despite looking wary of the challenger's power, Santos bided his time and, in beating his man to the punch, dropped him with a solid left for the full count at 2.25 of the second.

L. Middleweight

IBF

26 August 2000   Fernando Vargas 10.13 (USA) W RSC 4 Ross Thompson 10.13½ (USA), Las Vegas, USA.

2 December 2000   Fernando Vargas 11.0 (USA) L RSC 12 Felix Trinidad 11.0 (Puerto Rico), Las Vegas, USA. Trinidad relinquished the title in May 2001 in order to take part in the middleweight unification programme.

WBA

22 July 2000   Felix Trinidad 11.0 (Puerto Rico) W RSC 3 Mamadou Thiam 10.12½ (France), Miami, USA.

2 December 2000   Felix Trinidad 11.0 (Puerto Rico) W RSC 12 Fernando Vargas 11.0 (USA), Las Vegas, USA. Trinidad relinquished the title, along with his IBF crown, in May 2001.

WBC

21 July 2000   Javier Castillejo 10.13¾ (Spain) W PTS 12 Tony Marshall 11.0 (USA), Leganes, Spain. Scorecards: 116-114, 117-112, 118-110.

21 October 2000   Javier Castillejo 11.0 (Spain) W RSC 4 Javier Martinez 10.12¾ (Spain), Mexico City, Mexico.

23 June 2001   Javier Castillejo 11.0 (Spain) L PTS 12 Oscar de la Hoya 11.0 (USA), Las Vegas, USA. 108-119, 108-119, 108-119.

WBO

23 September 2000   Harry Simon 11.0 (Namibia) W PTS 12 Rodney Jones 10.13½ (USA), Rama, Ontario, Canada. Scorecards: 117-111, 117-111, 114-114.

10 February 2001   Harry Simon 10.12¼ (Namibia) W RSC 5 Wayne Alexander 11.0 (England), Kingsway Leisure Centre, Widnes, England. Judge: Dave Parris. Taking the fight at 24 hours notice after Robert Allen pulled out following an argument over the weigh-in procedure, Alexander gave it his best shot but was beaten by an accomplished champion. Despite being hit with the best single shot of the fight, in the second round, Simon remained on his feet and when the challenger's hands began to let him down he took total control. Down in the final minute of the fifth, on rising Alexander was subjected to a battering and, when unable to fight back, was rescued by the referee, Paul Thomas, at 2.43 of the round.

Middleweight

IBF

1 December 2000   Bernard Hopkins 11.4½ (USA) W RSC 10 Antwun Echols 11.6 (USA), Las Vegas, USA.

14 April 2001 Bernard Hopkins 11.5 (USA) W PTS 12 Keith Holmes 11.3½ (USA), New York City, USA. Scorecards: 119-108, 118-109, 117-110.

WBA

16 September 2000 William Joppy 11.6 (USA) W PTS 12 Hassine Cherifi 11.5 (France), Las Vegas, USA. Scorecards: 119-106, 118-107, 118-107.

2 December 2000 William Joppy 11.5½ (USA) W RSC 4 Jonathan Reid 11.6 (USA), Las Vegas, USA.

12 May 2001 William Joppy 11.4¾ (USA) L RSC 5 Felix Trinidad 11.5½ (Puerto Rico), New York City, USA.

WBC

14 April 2001 Keith Holmes 11.3½ (USA) L PTS 12 Bernard Hopkins 11.5 (USA), New York City, USA. Scorecards: 108-119, 109-118, 110-117.

WBO

7 October 2000 Armand Krajnc 11.5 (Slovenia) W RSC 6 Bert Schenk 11.5½ (Germany), Berlin, Germany.

S. Middleweight

IBF

2 September 2000 Sven Ottke 11.13½ (Germany) W PTS 12 Charles Brewer 11.13 (USA), Magdeburg, Germany. Scorecards: 116-111, 116-112, 113-116.

16 December 2000 Sven Ottke 11.11 (Germany) W PTS 12 Silvio Branco 11.13¾ (Italy), Karlsruhe, Germany. Scorecards: 117-111, 117-111, 116-112.

24 March 2001 Sven Ottke 11.13¾ (Germany) W RSC 8 James Crawford 11.13¼ (USA), Magdeburg, Germany.

9 June 2001 Sven Ottke 11.12½ (Germany) W RSC 11 Ali Ennebati 11.11½ (Algeria), Nuremberg, Germany.

WBA

16 September 2000 Bruno Girard 11.13½ (France) W PTS 12 Manuel Siaca 11.13½ (Puerto Rico), Chateauroux, France. Referee: John Coyle. Scorecards: 117-111, 116-113, 113-117. Girard forfeited the title in February 2001 when refusing a rematch against Siaca due to contractual problems.

3 March 2001 Byron Mitchell 12.0 (USA) W RSC 12 Manuel Siaca 12.0 (Puerto Rico), Las Vegas, USA.

WBC

1 September 2000 Glenn Catley 11.13¼ (England) L CO 12 Dingaan Thobela 11.13 (South Africa), Brakpan, South Africa. Having gone to the wire in his last couple of fights, this time Catley was on the receiving end of a result that created much controversy. Although it later transpired that Catley would have lost on the scorecards at the final bell, he was counted out with just seven seconds left on the clock, having been smashed down with a flurry of punches and failing to make it up in time. In the aftermath, Catley claimed that he had never been hit so hard before, thus provoking the argument that Thobela's bandages had been

Britain's Wayne Alexander (right) did remarkably well against the WBO light-middles champion, Harry Simon, after taking the fight as a substitute

Les Clark

tampered with. Following an inquiry, despite no concrete evidence of wrong doing, the WBC ordered the winner of Thobela v Dave Hilton to meet the winner of Eric Lucas v Catley.

15 December 2000   Dingaan Thobela 11.12¹/₂ (South Africa) L PTS 12 Dave Hilton 11.6¹/₂ (Canada), Montreal, Canada. Scorecards: 115-113, 113-115, 111-117. Hilton forfeited the title in April 2001 when he was jailed for sex crimes.

WBO

12 August 2000   Joe Calzaghe 12.0 (Wales) W RSC 5 Omar Sheika 11.13 (USA), Conference Centre, Wembley, England. Judge: Mickey Vann. In what was undoubtedly Calzaghe's best performance for some time, not only did his hands stand up but his confidence flooded back as he handled the American challenger, who came to fight, with ease. Cut at the end of the fourth over the left eye, with the other eye being cut early in the fifth and taking a steady stream of punches, the referee came to Sheika's rescue and stopped the action in the champion's favour at 2.08 of the round.

16 December 2000   Joe Calzaghe 11.13³/₄ (Wales) W RSC 10 Richie Woodhall 11.13¹/₂ (England), The Arena, Sheffield, England. Referee: Roy Francis. Judges: Dave Parris, John Coyle. Following on from the Paul Ingle tragedy was not easy for either man, but both gave it their best shot with the champion proving just too strong and powerful for his rival. Although Woodhall was still in the fight up to the ninth round, his punches had no effect on Calzaghe and when he was put down at the end of the round the finish was in sight. The champion came roaring out for the tenth and, on not fighting back, Woodhall was rescued by Roy Francis at 0.28 of the round.

28 April 2001   Joe Calzaghe 11.13³/₄ (Wales) W RSC 1 Mario Veit 11.13 (Germany), The International Arena, Cardiff, Wales. Judge: Roy Francis. This was Calzaghe at his best, firing on all cylinders and giving Veit no chance to settle, while finishing him off at 1.52 of the first round when the referee rescued the unbeaten German from further punishment. Veit had never shown and following two knockdowns and an incessant barrage of blows, the third man had no option but to stop what had quickly become an uneven contest.

L. Heavyweight
IBF

9 September 2000   Roy Jones 12.5¹/₂ (USA) W RTD 10 Eric Harding 12.5³/₄ (USA), New Orleans, USA.

24 February 2001   Roy Jones 12.6 (USA) W RTD 10 Derrick Harmon 12.7 (USA), Tampa, USA.

WBA

9 September 2000   Roy Jones 12.5¹/₂ (USA) W RTD 10 Eric Harding 12.5³/₄ (USA), New Orleans, USA.

24 February 2001   Roy Jones 12.6 (USA) W RTD 10 Derrick Harmon 12.7 (USA), Tampa, USA.

WBC

9 September 2000   Roy Jones 12.5¹/₂ (USA) W RTD 10 Eric Harding 12.5³/₄ (USA), New Orleans, USA.

24 February 2001   Roy Jones 12.6 (USA) W RTD 10 Derrick Harmon 12.7 (USA), Tampa, USA.

WBO

16 December 2000   Dariusz Michalczewski 12.7 (Poland) W RSC 7 Ka-Dy King 12.7 (USA), Essen, Germany.

5 May 2001   Dariusz Michalczewski 12.7 (Poland) W CO 9 Alejandro Lakatus 12.6¹/₂ (Spain), Braunschweig, Germany.

Cruiserweight
IBF

6 February 2001   Vassily Jirov 13.6 (Kazakhstan) W CO 1 Alex Gonzales 13.7³/₄ (Puerto Rico), Almaty, Kazakhstan. Judge: Ian John-Lewis.

24 March 2001   Vassily Jirov 13.8 (Kazakhstan) W CO 1 Terry McGroom 13.8 (USA), Las Vegas, USA.

WBA

9 December 2000   Fabrice Tiozzo 13.8 (France) L RSC 1 Virgil Hill 13.8 (USA), Villeurbanne, France.

WBC

16 December 2000   Juan Carlos Gomez 13.7 (Cuba) W RSC 10 Jorge Castro 13.1 (Argentine), Essen, Germany. Referee: Larry O'Connell.

WBO

7 October 2000   Johnny Nelson 13.7¹/₄ (England) W RSC 5 Adam Watt 13.7³/₄ (Australia), The Dome, Doncaster, England. Despite not much going on during the first four sessions, Nelson stepped up a few gears in the fifth, his speed being a decisive weapon against an inexperienced challenger. After getting up from a right-hand counter, Watt walked straight into a cracking left-right which put him down motionless and led the referee, Dave Parris, to dispense with count at 2.12 of the round.

27 January 2001   Johnny Nelson 13.7³/₄ (England) W PTS 12 George Arias 13.7¹/₄ (Brazil), York Hall, Bethnal Green, London, England. Scorecards: Roy Francis 120-110, 119-110, 120-108. Disappointingly, for the fans, Nelson appeared to let this one go the distance when it appeared that he was the Brazilian's master throughout. To Arias' credit he was durable and did not come to lay down, but he was neither of the champion's class nor could he ever have been confident of landing a punch that would make the scoring irrelevant, the result being almost predictable.

Heavyweight
IBF

15 July 2000   Lennox Lewis 17.12 (England) W RSC 2 Frans Botha 16.12 (South Africa), London Arena, Millwall, London, England. Judge: Roy Francis. This was Lennox Lewis at his best, intent on destroying the opposition and ultimately doing so. There was no doubting that Botha came to fight, but the champion's power was too much for him and following a first round where he got a good look at his opponent Lewis completed the job at 2.39 of the second. The finish was punch perfect. A right, a short left uppercut, followed by another right, lifted the South

African off his feet and sent him crashing through the ropes on to the ring apron where he was rescued by the referee, Larry O'Connell.

11 November 2000 Lennox Lewis 17.11 (England) W PTS 12 David Tua 17.7 (New Zealand), Las Vegas, USA. Scorecards: 117-111, 119-109, 118-110. Despite Tua being expected to make things difficult for Lewis, the occasions were few and far between as he slumped to a lopsided points defeat. While many thought the champion should finish his rival early, he took no chances and almost appeared casual at times as yet another opponent was eliminated.

22 April 2001 Lennox Lewis 18.1½ (England) L CO 5 Hasim Rahman 17.0 (USA), Brakpan, South Africa. Judge: Dave Parris. Looking overconfident and casual beyond belief, especially when fighting at altitude, Lewis was taken out by the 20-1 underdog at 2.32 of the fifth round in one of the biggest upsets of all time. While Lewis played to the gallery, Rahman, a man trailing on points, cut up and ready to be taken, suddenly unleashed a bombshell right hander which caught the champion flush as he was backing away. With Lewis contracted for a return he will start favourite again if he can get better prepared.

WBA

12 August 2000 Evander Holyfield 16.0 (USA) W PTS 12 John Ruiz 15.11 (USA), Las Vegas, USA. Scorecards: 116-112, 114-113, 114-113. Following on from Lennox Lewis forfeiting the title in April 2000 for meeting the WBC's choice, Michael Grant, rather than Ruiz, the WBA's first choice challenger, this contest decided the vacant title.

3 March 2001 Evander Holyfield 15.7 (USA) L PTS 12 John Ruiz 16.3 (USA), Las Vegas, USA. Scorecards: 110-116, 111-115, 111-114.

WBC

15 July 2000 Lennox Lewis 17.12 (England) W RSC 2 Frans Botha 16.12 (South Africa), London Arena, Millwall, London, England. Referee: Larry O'Connell. Judge: Roy Francis.

11 November 2000 Lennox Lewis 17.11 (England) W PTS 12 David Tua 17.7 (New Zealand), Las Vegas, USA. Scorecards: 117-111, 119-109, 118-110.

22 April 2001 Lennox Lewis 18.1½ (England) L CO 5 Hasim Rahman 17.0 (USA), Brakpan, South Africa. Judge: Dave Parris.

WBO

14 October 2000 Chris Byrd 15.3½ (USA) L PTS 12 Vladimir Klitschko 17.0 (Ukraine), Cologne, Germany. Scorecards: 106-120, 108-118, 107-119.

24 March 2001 Vladimir Klitschko 17.8 (Ukraine) W RSC 2 Derrick Jefferson 18.8 (USA), Munich, Germany.

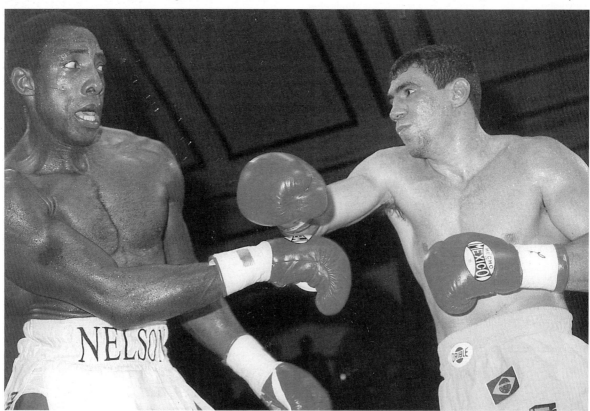

Johnny Nelson (left), Britain's WBO cruiserweight champion, made an easy defence against the Brazilian, George Arias

Les Clark

Early Gloved Championship Boxing: The True Facts (Part 4)

by Harold Alderman

Following on from last year's exploration of how the weight classes came into being in the early days of gloved boxing, this time round we examine 126 to 138lbs. Recognising that many fights listed by weight division prior to the advent of the named weight divisions and weight limits announced by the National Sporting Club in 1909 did not add up, I started my research in the early 1960s. Using world-wide newspaper reports, which included a thorough examination of the *Sporting Life*, *Mirror of Life*, *Sportsman*, and *Police Gazette*, etc, it did not take long to discover that the vast majority of fights, certainly in this country, were made at every two pounds, plus or minus two pounds. This is how it was as boxing transferred from the bare-knuckle days to gloves, passing through phases of driving gloves, kid gloves, and two-ounce gloves to what we have today. This section also includes much of Barry Hugman's research within the American newspaper libraries.

126lbs to 128lbs (9st to 9st 2lbs)

1872

16 April   Bat Mullins w pts 5 Jack Ward (Greenwich), Prince of Wales Grounds, Bow, London. The final of a 128lbs championship cup. The tournament started on 1 April and saw Mullins beat James Skipper and Jim Bibby, while Ward defeated Obe Atterbury and Bill Crane. Interestingly, in the space of eight days, Mullins won open to the world competitions at 133lbs, 154lbs and all weights above.

30 November   Bat Mullins challenged the world at 128lbs with knuckles, Billy Edwards (Birmingham born, but residing in New York) preferred – *Bells Life*.

1877

18 August   Bat Mullins, the winner of the 'Bow' cup stated in *Bells Life* that he was unable to find opponents for a gloved fight.

1 September   Hugh Burns challenges Mullins for the cup, although it was felt at the time that the latter would find it difficult to make the weight.

1878

6 April   Billy McLeod (Ancoats) challenges all England at 128lbs, MoQ Rules, £25 a side, Samuel 'Pat' Perry (Birmingham) preferred – *Sporting Life*. He then challenged James Wright (Gorton) on 2 June and again on 29 June.

20 September   Billy McLeod w co 6 James Wright, Manchester private show. Although not billed for the title, it was contested under MoQ Rules with gloves for a £50 cup and the winner claimed the championship at 128lbs.

19 October   James Wright challenges Billy McLeod to a return under MoQ Rules at 126lbs, give or take two pounds – *Sporting Life*.

25 November   Billy McLeod stated in the *Sporting Life* that he would now be boxing at 136lbs. In later years, McLeod joined the Salvation Army and in 1905 a book on his life, written by The Reverend Albert Dearden, was published, but was anti–boxing and gave little detail on McLeod's boxing career as it was.

1881

30 April   Jem Carney (Birmingham), just back from the USA, challenges the world at 128lbs, £50 or £100 a side, but was really only interested in bare-knuckle fighting. Earlier, in the year, Gerald Griffin and Ned Condon had won competitions at the weight, but failed to take their claims any further.

1882

7 September   Joe Thornley (Hanley) challenges the world – *Sporting Life*. A day later, Young Gibson (Bilston) accepted the challenge and also challenged the world. However, his side stake was considered too small for championship status.

1884

5 September   'Young' Jacob Hyams challenges all England at the weight for £50 or £100 – *Sporting Life*.

1886

3 March   Harry Gilmore (Toronto) w rtd 9 'California' Jack Dempsey, Norris, Michigan, USA. Billed for the world 128lbs title, with Gilmore weighing 127lbs and Dempsey (not to be confused with The Nonpareil) scaling 126lbs, various papers also reported the men's weights as 130lbs and 132lbs, respectively.

1887

16 June   Sam Blakelock w pts 12 Reuben Baxter (Shoreditch), Lambeth School of Arms, Paradise Street, London. Made at 128lbs. Although no billing was given, Blakelock would claim the English title on the result.

Jem Carney

24 August Sam Blakelock w pts 12 Reuben Baxter, Lambeth School of Arms, Paradise Street, London. Latterly considered to have been a defence of Blakelock's title claim.

9 September Blakelock, now called the English champion, left for the USA but returned on 23 October, having been unable to get bouts and with Ike O'Neill refusing to meet him.

1888

5 June Bill 'Tricky' Hook (Spitalfields) w co 25 Bill 'Dido' Hopwood (Bermondsey), private London show restricted to 40 people. Billed for the English 128lbs title, Hook (128) fainted following his win. Hopwood weighed 126½lbs.

1890

6 November Enoch Thomas (Birmingham) challenges all 126 and 128lbs men to settle the championships – *Sporting Life*.

3 December Jack Edwards (Poplar) challenges all between 126 and 130lbs, Harry Overton (Birmingham) and Bill Reader preferred. In the same issue of the *Sporting Life*, Reader challenged Austin Gibbons (USA, born in Liverpool) for the world 128lbs title.

6 December Bill Reader challenges Harry Overton at 128lbs ringside – *Sporting Life*.

1892

9 November Harry Greenfield (Camden Town) challenges Arthur Callan (Wood Green) at 128lbs, £50 a side and the best purse to decide the championship – *Sporting Life*.

23 November Will Newell challenges all England – *Sporting Life*.

1893

28 January Harry Spurden (Battersea) challenges Arthur Valentine (Lambeth) at 128lbs and 6pm weigh in – *Sporting Life*.

22 March Harry Greenfield challenges Darkey Barton (Battersea) at the weight – *Sporting Life*. In the same edition of the paper, Bill Day (Hackney) challenged all England, Darkey Barton preferred.

1894

19 March Bill Corbett (Lambeth) drew 12 Jack Fitzgibbons (St George's), Greyhound Hotel Assembly Rooms, Newmarket. A private show with no championship billing as such, but both men were looking to claim the title. On 16 April, at the Raglan Music Hall in Union Street, The Borough, London witnessed one of the 'greatest' last rounds ever seen when Corbett was outscored over 12 rounds at 128lbs by Tom Ashwick (Southwark).

21 April Tom Causer (Bermondsey) w pts 4 Jack Loader (Barnsbury), St Andrew's Hall, Newman Street, off Oxford Street, London. The final of Frank Hindes' championship competition. In previous rounds, Causer had eliminated Charlie Tilley and Tom Ireland.

25 May Harry Spurden w rtd 22 Darkey Barton, Bollingbroke Club, Northcote Road, Clapham, London. A finish fight at catchweights, with both men over 126lbs, involving £50 a side and a £100 purse, saw Spurden extend his 126lbs title claim.

10 September Jack Fitzgibbons w pts 6 Bill Corbett, Goodwin Gym, Kingsland Road, Shoreditch, London. Just a normal six rounder, later gossip gave it championship status at 128lbs.

31 October Bill Corbett w co 15 Johnny Ryan (St Helens), Percy Cottage, Newcastle. Billed for the English 128lbs championship, the monetary reward of a £50 purse was not large enough for general consent to be given.

17 November Charlie Tilley (Somers Town) w pts 4 Ted Gamble (St James'), Central Hall, Holborn, London. With Harry Greenfield eliminated by Gamble earlier, this was the final of a Frank Hindes' championship competition.

1896

22 January Jim Curran (Rotherham) challenges Jack Fitzpatrick, the former English 126lbs champion, at 128lbs.

29 February Tom Causer challenges all up to £500 a side and an NSC purse to settle the world title – *Sporting Life*.

9 September Alf Garrett and Jack Williamson challenge all England, and are accepted by Harry Brown (Liverpool, but born in Jamaica) to box at the NSC – *Sporting Life*.

1897

3 February Harry Greenfield challenges the world up to £500 a side – *Sporting Life*

17 February Ben Clark (Bow) challenges the world, £50 a side and an NSC purse, no one barred – *Sporting Life*.

26 April Ted Marlow (Stratford) w co 2 Ben Clark, NSC, King Street, Covent Garden, London. Made at 128lbs, £50 a side and a £100 purse, but with no title billing, Marlow still claimed the English title on his victory.

26 April George Dixon (Canada) w pts 20 Johnny Griffin (USA), New York City, USA. Billed for the world 128lbs title.

9 August Billy O'Donnell (Memphis, USA) w pts 20 Hugh Fitzsimmons (Greenport, New York, USA), Brooklyn, USA. Billed at 128lbs for the American title, O'Donnell was deserving of the recognition following wins over Jack Delaney (w co 19 in New York City, USA on 27 February, 1897), Joe Bernstein (w pts 20 in New York City, USA on 15 May, 1897) and a 20–round draw against Eddie Curry at Staten Island, New York, USA on 25 July, 1897.

14 September Billy O'Donnell drew 20 Eddie Curry, Staten Island, New York, USA. Although no weights were reported it was thought to involve O'Donnell's American title claim at the weight.

4 October Harry Greenfield challenges Jack Fitzpatrick and Harry Spurden to decide the English title at £200 a side – *Sporting Life*. On 7 October, Fitzpatrick accepted.

15 October Joe Bernstein w pts 20 Billy O'Donnell, Brooklyn, New York, USA. Not billed for the American title but thought to involve O'Donnell's claim.

1 December Tommy White (Chicago, USA) challenges all at the weight – *Sporting Life*. In the same paper, on 24 December, Harry Greenfield challenged the world.

1898

24 August Jim Barry (St James') challenges all England over 20 rounds, Jack Fairclough (St Helens) preferred – *Sporting Life*.

20 December Harry Greenfield again challenges the world, this time up to £500 a side – *Sporting Life*.

1899

25 March Denny Gallagher (USA, born England), having recently arrived in the country from the USA, challenges all England – *Sporting Life*.

11 August George Dixon drew 25 Eddie Santry (Chicago, USA), New York City, USA. Billed for the title at 127lbs.

15 August Jack Goldswain (Bermondsey) challenges the world at 128lbs, for an NSC purse – *Sporting Life*. However, by December he was boxing at 134lbs.

24 August Tom Ireland (Mile End) challenges the world between 126 and 130lbs – *Sporting Life*. A day later, he is accepted by Harry Greenfield.

9 September Jack Dixon (Nova Scotia), a Canadian negro, challenges the world over 15 or 20 rounds – *Sporting Life*.

20 November Jabez White (Birmingham) w co 8 Harry Greenfield, NSC, King Street, Covent Garden, London. Billed for the English title over 15 rounds, £150 a side and a £150 purse, White was generally recognised as champion.

1900

17 January Jabez White, the English champion, challenges the world, £500 a side and best purse, Eddie Santry preferred at 128lbs, or Will Curley (Newcastle) at 127lbs – *Sporting Life*. Nine days later, Curley accepted at 128lbs.

5 February Jabez White challenges Harry Ware (Mile End) – *Sporting Life*.

22 February Jabez White protested at Tommy Hogan (Pittsburgh, USA) v Bill Chester (Mile End) being billed for the world title when he is the recognised English champion at the weight, while Chester is recognised at 130lbs.

26 February Tommy Hogan w co 8 Bill Chester, NSC, King Street, Covent Garden, London. Contested over 15 rounds and billed for the world 128lbs title.

20 March Jack Roberts (Drury Lane) challenges all England, £50 or £100 a side, which is repeated the next day – *Sporting Life*.

12 April Will Curley w co 1 Jabez White, Ginnett's Circus, Newcastle. Originally billed for the 126lbs English title, it was changed to 127lbs as White was unable to make the original weight.

7 May Ted Marlow w rsc 3 Jack Wood (Bermondsey), NSC, King Street, Covent Garden, London. Billed for the vacant title after Jabez White was no longer able to make the weight, Marlow (9st 1¾lbs) defeated Wood (127¾), who also struggled to get down to 128lbs.

2 June George Cunningham w pts 15 Bill Chester, Wonderland, Whitechapel Road, London. Reported in the *MoL* as being for the 128lbs English gold and silver championship belt, £100 a side and £100 purse, two–minute rounds ruled it out of having full recognition. Later, the *Sportsman* stated that the bout was set at 130lbs, while the *Sporting Life* failed to even report it.

12 June   Terry McGovern (USA) w co 3 Tommy White, New York City, USA. Stated in the *MoL* and *Sportsman* to have been made at 128lbs with White, ½lb over the weight paying forfeit, some American newspapers reported it to have been made at 122lbs and that both men were over the limit.

16 July   Terry McGovern w rtd 3 Frank Erne (USA), New York City, USA. Although a handicap match, with Erne agreeing not to exceed 128lbs, McGovern was seen in some American eyes as the greatest fighter ever, having won four world titles at different weights.

9 November   Tommy Hogan, who still claims to be the 128lbs champion despite losing to Ben Jordan at 124lbs, challenges all England – *Sporting Life*.

1901

21 February   Bob Russell (Limehouse) challenges Bert Adams (Spitalfields), the recent winner of an English championship belt competition, to decide the English title at the NSC over 15 rounds – *Sporting Life*.

12 August   A match made between Will Curley and Kid Broad (USA, born Liskeard) to decide the world 128lbs title at the NSC has fallen through – *Sporting Life*.

1902

3 February   Will Curley w co 3 Jack Roberts, Ginnett's Circus, Newcastle. Billed for the English 128lbs title, £300 a side and a £500 purse, Roberts continued to claim the English 126lbs title as Curley was unable to make 126lbs for the above fight.

7 May   Harry Lyons (Chicago, USA), who claims to be the American champion at the weight, challenges Jack Roberts, Will Curley and Ben Jordan to decide the world title at 128lbs – *Sporting Life*.

17 May   Jack Roberts challenges the American, Tommy Hogan, who claims that he has never been beaten at the weight and is still the world champion – *Sporting Life*. However, on 22 September, it was reported that Hogan had died suddenly after contracting typhoid fever.

27 May   Sid Scales (St Luke's) challenges all men inside 128lbs, Will Curley preferred, to decide the championship – *Sporting Life*.

31 October   Jack Roberts' challenge to all at the weight has been accepted by Joe Bernstein – *Sporting Life*.

22 December   Will Curley w co 8 George Proctor (Southwark), Ginnett's Circus, Newcastle. Although billed for the English title, the fight was not taken too seriously as the £100 purse was not seen as a championship purse.

1903

2 February   Will Curley should be seen as the English 128lbs champion reported the *Sporting Life*.

21 March   Nat Smith (Paddington) w co 20 Jack Dixon, Ginnett's Circus, Newcastle. Made at 127lbs, Smith, the ABA featherweight champion in 1897, failed to make his claim at the weight stick.

30 March   Dick Lee (Kentish Town) w rtd 9 Jack Roberts, Wonderland, Whitechapel Road, London. Contested over 15 three–minute rounds, with Will Curley retired, Lee's claim at the weight was fairly strong.

31 March   Young Corbett (USA) w co 11 Terry McGovern, San Francisco, USA. Given American world featherweight title billing at 127lbs with both men unable to get inside 126lbs.

16 April   Dick Lee challenges all England, £50 a side and the best purse – *Sporting Life*.

26 May   Dick Lee challenges the world, Kid Broad preferred – *Sporting Life*.

1904

15 December   Alf Reed (Canning Town), who had recently won an English championship belt, challenges all England – *Sporting Life*.

1905

6 March   Young Joseph (Aldgate) w pts 10 Dick Lee, Wonderland, Whitechapel Road, London. With Joseph putting out one of the favourites, 'Seaman' Hayes (Hoxton), in an earlier round, this was the final of an English championship belt competition, contested over three–minute rounds. Three days later, Lee challenged Joseph to a return, £50 or a £100 a side and an NSC purse.

9 August   Dick Lee challenges all England, £50 or £100 a side, which is repeated throughout the year – *Sporting Life*.

11 September   Dick Lee challenges Abe Attell, America's 122lbs champion, who is visiting England, to a match at 128lbs to decide the world title – *Sporting Life*.

9 November   'Seaman' Arthur Hayes challenges all England over 20 rounds, Dick Lee preferred – *Sporting Life*.

1906

31 January   'Seaman' Arthur Hayes claims the English title as he believes that Young Joseph can no longer make the weight – *Sporting Life*. However, on 17 February, the paper reports Joseph as the English 128lbs champion.

19 February   'Seaman' Arthur Hayes w pts 15 Dick Lee, NSC, King Street, Covent Garden, London. Made at 128lbs, despite the lack of title billing Hayes (127) was considered to be the English champion at the weight following his win over Lee (128).

19 March   Johnny Summers (Canning Town) w pts 20 'Seaman' Arthur Hayes, NSC, King Street, Covent Garden, London. Advertised for the English 128lbs title, Summers scaled 127¾lbs to Hayes' 128. Despite the result, Hayes was still listed in the *Sporting Life* as being the English champion in May.

1907

28 January   'Seaman' Arthur Hayes w pts 15 Boss Edwards (Marylebone), NSC, King Street, Covent Garden, London. Despite there being no title billing, Hayes (127) was still recognised as champion by many following his victory over Edwards (127).

25 March   Tommy Burns (Widnes) w pts 15 'Seaman' Arthur Hayes, NSC, King Street, Covent Garden, London. Made at 128lbs, despite a lack of billing Burns could consider himself to have a claim to the English title following his win.

15 July   'Seaman' Arthur Hayes w rtd 4 Kid Davis (Guernsey, late USA), St Julian's Hall, Guernsey, Channel Islands. Billed as being the first ever English title fight held on the island, with two–minute rounds in play, small purses, and Davis born in Nigeria, it wasn't considered as such throughout the rest of the country.

1908

15 January   In the *Sporting Life* list of English champions, Boss Edwards is regarded as holding the 128lbs title.

11 February   On this date, the NSC introduced the eight named weight divisions, thus ending English champions at every two pounds.

128lbs to 130lbs (9st 2lbs to 9st 4lbs)

1872

21 January   Bat Mullins challenges Ted Napper to meet at the Bells' Life offices on 2 February to agree a contest at 130lbs. However, Mullins and his backers failed to keep the appointment.

28 December   James 'Punch' Dowsett nd 4 Bill Green, The Griffin, Shoreditch, London. Initially articled for three rounds for a silver cup presented by J.Hamblin, on there being no conclusion the judges decided there would have to be a rematch.

1876

4 January   James 'Punch' Dowsett w pts 4 Bill Green, The Griffin, Shoreditch, London. At the end of three rounds, which appeared to have gone Green's way, the referee ordered another round, which went Dowsett's way.

1877

8 September   Jemmy Highland (Birmingham) challenges Hugh Burns, £50 a side – *Bells Life*.

1878

9 March   Billy Nable (The Borough) accepted Clack Sullivan's challenge under MoQ Rules.

1880

29 March   Harry Mead (St Luke's) w pts 3 Jack Watts (Clerkenwell), Central Baths, St John Street, St Luke's, London. The final of a silver cup competition.

30 March   Harry Mead w pts 3 'Young' Harry Solomons, The Five Inkhorns, Shoreditch, London. Although called a 9 stone competition, Mead scaled 128lbs to Solomons' 129. Meads eliminated Bob Laxton in an earlier round.

4 August   Jemmy Highland challenges the world, £50 or £100 a side, which is repeated on 25 and 28 August – *Sporting Life*.

10 November   Jackie Moore (Glasgow) challenges all England, £25 to £50 a side – *Sporting Life*.

1882

3 April   Harry Mead w pts 4 Billy Green, King's Road Baths, Chelsea, London. Final of a 130lbs competition.

14 August   Harry Mead w pts 3 J. Brock, West End School of Arms, Newman Street, off Oxford Street, Westminster, London. The final of a Bob Habbijams' ten guinea cup competition.

1883

13 January   Young Nolan (New York, USA), now in England, challenges the world, £50 to £100 a side – *Sporting Life*.

1884

5 September   'Young' Jacob Hyams challenges all England for a prize value of up to £100, which is accepted by Jim Kendrick (Lambeth) three days later – *Sporting Life*

30 October   Jim Kendrick drew 17 'Young' Jacob Hyams. Considered to be for the 130lbs lightweight title and contested near London.

11 December   Sam Baxter (Shoreditch) w pts 3 Mark Dooley, The Bell, Red Lion Market, London. The final of 'Uncle Joes' 130lbs competition. Earlier, Baxter eliminated George Crawley and Bob Laxton, while Dooley beat Charley Cheese and Redmond Condon.

1885

28 May   Edward Brome (Battersea) challenges all England at 130lbs – *Sporting Life*.

1886

2 February   Sam Baxter w co 2 Harry Mead, West End School of Arms, Newman Street, off Oxford Street, Westminster, London. The final of Bob Habbijams' championship belt competition, it was also reported as a 132lbs competition.

27 February   Jack McAuliffe (USA) w co 17 Jack Hopper (New York, USA), New York City, USA. Contested in the East New York Ballroom for the American and world 130lbs title, using kid gloves and under MoQ Rules, McAuliffe weighed 130lbs to Hopper's 128.

12 August   Sam Baxter should be recognised as the world 130lbs champion – *Sporting Life*.

3 December   Sam Baxter w pts 3 Charlie Mitchell (Bethnal Green), West School of Arms, Newman Street, off Oxford Street, Westminster, London. Having won Bob Habbijams' belt for the second time, it became Baxter's property. On 21 December, the *Sporting Life* again supported Baxter's claim to the world title, a statement that was supported editorially by the *Sportsman*.

1887

14 November   Bill Whatley (Walworth) w pts 3 Patsy Carrick, School of Arms, Paradise Street, Lambeth, London. The final of an English silver championship belt competition.

1889

9 March   Bill Whatley challenges George Wilson (Leicester) to a return at 130lbs, having been beaten by the latter at catchweights – *Sporting Life*. Wilson later replied that he couldn't make anything below 137lbs.

14 December   Harry Denny (Shoreditch) w pts 4 Bill Whatley, Saddlers Wells Theatre, St John Street, Clerkenwell, London. Following wins over Stanton Abbott and Tom Euston, Denny reached the final of a 130lb championship competition which had started out involving the 132lbs class. Whatley defeated Bill Baxter and Harry Southgate.

18 December   Austin Gibbons (USA, born Liverpool) w co 24 Mike Cushing (New Jersey, USA), Hoboken, New Jersey, USA. Billed for the American and world 130lbs title, having been articled for 126lbs, Gibbons claimed the title following his victory.

1890

24 January   'Iron Bark' Jim Burge (Australia) w rtd 22 Sam Baxter, Sydney, Australia. Billed for world and Imperial Empire 130lbs title, Baxter (130) was considered unbeatable at the weight in England and when news came though that Burge (128½) had won many bets were taken on the decision being wrongly decided.

20 May   Bill Reader (Fulham) accepted Jem Carney's challenge to the world at 130lbs, £500 a side and under MoQ Rules with gloves.

31 May   Jem Carney (Birmingham) stated categorically that his challenge to the world was with knuckles and under London Rules – *Sporting Life*. The same edition of the paper claimed that Bill Whatley should still be recognised as the champion.

29 November   Austin Gibbons challenges Bill Reader and Harry Overton (Birmingham) to settle the world 130lbs championship, $2,000 a side – *Sporting Life*.

1891

10 April   Bill Whatley, the English 130lb champion, challenges Austin Gibbons, £100 a side, but just 30 days later admits that he cannot make the weight anymore – *Sporting Life*.

30 May   George Johnson (Hackney w rtd 1 Harry Mead, Her Majesty's Theatre, Haymarket, London. The final of Frank Hindes' 130lbs championship competition.

1892

6 April   Bill Reader, who calls himself the English champion, has a claim that cannot be substantiated as all his contests have been at 126lbs, reported the *Sporting Life*.

19 September   Billy Graham (Liverpool) challenges all England and is accepted by Maurice Phillips (Mile End) two days later – *Sporting Life*.

10 October   At the weigh in for the world title fight between Stanton Abbott (Westminster) v Austin Gibbons, due to be held at the NSC that day, Gibbons suddenly insisted on being allowed to scale 132lbs as he was unable to make 130lbs anymore and the fight was cancelled.

9 November   Young Griffo (Sydney, Australia) drew 25 Martin Denny (Melbourne, Australia), Sydney, Australia. With Griffo unable to make 126lbs anymore, this was billed for the world 130lbs title.

21 November   Arthur Valentine (Lambeth) w rtd 9 Maurice Phillips, NSC, King Street, Covent Garden, London. Billed for the English title, although not recognised as such throughout much of the country, Valentine weighed 129½lbs to Phillips' 128¾.

30 November   Stanton Abbott claims to be both the 130 and 132lb English champion – *Sporting Life*. The same day, Jim Hill challenged Arthur Valentine, £25 a side and best purse.

20 December   Young Griffo w pts 12 Jerry Marshall (New York), Sydney, Australia. Billed for the world 130lbs title.

1893

10 January   Maurice Phillips challenges Arthur Valentine to a return championship match – *Sporting Life*. Other challenges in the same paper follow thick and fast, including Phillips to Arthur Callan (Wood Green) and Valentine to Bill Corbett (Lambeth).

28 February   Young Griffo w dis 4 Jerry Marshall, Sydney, Australia. Billed for the 130lbs world title.

12 June   Arthur Valentine challenges all England at the weight – *Sportsman*

27 June   Martin Denny, who claims the world title, arrives in England and challenges all, Arthur Valentine preferred – *Sporting Life*. The same day, in the same edition, Valentine challenges Denny, £200 a side and an NSC purse.

28 June   Tom Ireland (Mile End) w pts 4 Ted Ware (Mile End), The Hope, Banner Street, St Luke's, London. The final of an all–England competition.

7 July   John 'Ponk' Andrews (Bethnal Green) challenges Tom Ireland – *Sporting Life*.

30 October   Martin Denny w pts 20 Joe Lambert (Soho), NSC, King Street, Covent Garden, London. Despite a lack of billing, Denny, who weighed 128½lbs, put his claim on the line with Lambert scaling 127½.

18 November   Jim Dawson, the Army champion, challenges all England at the weight for an NSC purse – *Sporting Life*.

27 November   Tom Woolley (Walsall) challenges all England – *Sporting Life*.

13 December   Arthur Valentine should be considered the English champion – *Sporting Life*.

26 December   Tom Ireland w pts 20 Darkey Barton (Battersea), Harewood Street Gym, Leeds. Made at 130lbs, there was no title billing as such, but Ireland's claim at the weight was almost certainly on the line.

1894

4 June   Martin Denny w pts 20 Bill Eyles (Islington), NSC, King Street, Covent Garden, London. Involving Denny's world title claim, Eyles weighed 127½lbs to Denny's 129½.

15 December   Jack Fitzgibbons (St George's) w pts 4 Charlie Tilley (Somers Town), Central Hall, Holborn, London. The final of Frank Hindes' championship competition and Richard K. Fox Police Gazette gold medal. In later years, it was said to have been for the Police Gazette championship belt.

1895

2 February   Ted Ware (Mile End) w pts 4 Steve Smith (West Green), Central Hall, Holborn, London. The final of Frank Hindes' all–England championship final.

16 February   Jack Fitzgibbons w co 1 Tom Ireland, Central Hall, Holborn, London. The final of another all–England championship competition.

21 April   Billy Ross (Manchester) claims to be the holder of the 130lbs world championship belt. However, there was much doubting his claim and and accuracy of his so-called record and he was never given much credit. Ross died in April, 1948, his age given as either 77 or 80.

15 October   Eddie Connolly (Canada, born New York) w co 3 Frank Gerrard (USA), Cleveland, USA. With both men inside 130lbs, Connolly claimed the American version of the title at the weight. However, unable to make that weight easily again, the winner moved up a class.

27 November   Jerry Donoghue (Mile End) w pts 4 Joe Anderson (Spitalfields), Excelsior Baths, Mansford Street, Bethnal Green, London. The final of a silver belt championship competition.

1896

7 March   Harry Brown (Liverpool, born Jamaica) challenges all England at the weight – *Mirror of Life*. As he was unable to fight for a British title, he later changed his challenge to incorporate the world.

9 November   Harry Greenfield (Camden Town) w rsc 9 James Curran (Rotherham), Excelsior School of Arms, Sheffield. Often reported as having English championship billing, it was a tremendous fight for £100 a side and a £100 purse.

1897

20 October   Harry Greenfield, the rightful English 130lbs champion, challenges Tom Causer at the weight – *Sporting Life*. Greenfield, who had just received a forfeit from Jack Fitzpatrick over a proposed 128lbs contest, went on to challenge the world at 126lbs.

10 November   Charley Miner (New York, USA), currently in England, challenges the world at the weight – *Sporting Life*. Strangely, Miner made his British debut at 126lbs on 21 December.

1898

21 February   Spike Sullivan w rtd 15 Harry Greenfield, NSC, King Street, Covent Garden, London. Billed for the world 130lbs title, but actually articled at 131lbs, Sullivan scaled 130lbs to Greenfield's 128.

31 March   George Dixon (USA, born Canada) drew 20 Tommy White (Chicago, USA), Syracuse, USA. Billed for the American and world 130lbs title.

7 May   Jack Rose (Lambeth) challenges all England at the weight, £200 a side and an NSC purse, and on 28 December in the same issue of the *Sporting Life* is called the English champion.

1899

18 February   Jim Barry (St James') challenges all England, £50 a side and an NSC purse, Ted Ware preferred – *Sporting Life*.

27 February   Jack Roberts (Drury Lane) w pts 20 Frank Guest (Plymouth), NSC, King Street, Covent Garden, London. Although there was no billing as such, it was made at 130lbs, £50 a side and a £100 purse, and was certainly under championship conditions.

24 April   Ted Marlow (Stratford) w pts 20 Jim Barry, NSC, King Street, Covent Garden, London. Billed for the English title, Marlow weighed 129lbs and Barry 129½lbs.

24 August   Tom Ireland challenges the world between 126 and 130lbs and is accepted by Harry Greenfield. Ireland was being called the English 134lbs champion and ex-English 128lbs champion – *Sporting Life*.

15 September   Jack Dixon (Nova Scotia, Canada) challenges the world, 15 or 20 rounds and an NSC purse – *Sporting Life*.

2 October   Bill Chester (Mile End) w co 1 Ted Marlow, NSC, King Street, Covent Garden, London. Billed for the English title, £100 a side and £100 purse, both men scaled 129lbs.

2 October   Louden Campbell (Pittsburgh, USA) w pts 20 Joe Handler (New York, born Russia), New York City, USA. Although there was no billing as such, this was accepted as an American title claim at the weight.

24 October   Bill Chester challenges the world, £200 up to £500 a side, Jack Roberts preferred – *Sporting Life*. Later in the year, he posted a £25 deposit with the paper, who reported that Jack Goldswain (Bermondsey) was the preferred choice.

23 October   Jack Goldswain w co 7 Jack Roberts, NSC, King Street, Covent Garden, London. Although there was no billing denoting an English title fight, with £100 a side and a £100 purse, Goldswain (129½) was accepted as being the champion following his victory over Roberts (127¼), especially as many supporters felt that Bill Chester was merely a competition boxer with a big punch who occasionally got lucky.

11 December   Tom Ireland w rtd 5 Jack Roberts, NSC, King Street, Covent Garden, London. Stated to be made at 128lbs, with both men coming in at 129lbs, by his win Ireland continued to claim the English 130lbs title.

1900

17 March   Harry Greenfield challenges all England at the weight – *Sporting Life*.

1 May   Bill Chester still has a right to the English title – *Sporting Life*. Chester was supposed to have been outpointed by George Cunningham (Bethnal Green) over 15 two–minute rounds at Wonderland in Whitechapel Road on 2 June, a fight that was reported in the *Mirror of Life*, but neither the *Sporting Life* or *Sportsman* carried a report and the result has to be treated as suspect.

9 November   Tommy Hogan (New York, USA), the world 128lbs champion, challenges all England at 130lbs, £200 up to £500 a side – *Sporting Life*

1901

31 August   Bill Wood (Clapton) w dis 4 Bob Russell (Limehouse), Wonderland, Whitechapel Road, London. As the final of an English championship competition, the fact that it was contested over six two–minute rounds gave it very little credibility.

15 November   Jack Fairclough (St Helens) challenges all England, for £50 up to £100 a side and an NSC purse, Harry Chamberlain preferred – *Sporting Life*.

20 December   Fred McKenzie (Homerton), back from his successful tour of America, challenges all England – *Sporting Life*.

1902

2 January   Bill Chester stated in the *Sporting Life* that he should be considered for 130lbs title action as that was his best weight.

16 January   Martin Duffy (Chicago, USA) was listed by the *Sporting Life* as being the American 130lbs champion. Six days later, he outpointed Artie Simms (Akron, Ohio) in Detroit over 15 rounds, although the weights were not declared and no title billing given.

25 February   Bill Chester challenges all of America, no one barred – *Sporting Life*.

24 May   Bob Russell challenges all England, £50 or £100 a side and an NSC purse – *Sporting Life*.

12 July   Bob Russell w pts 6 Harry Chamberlain (Bow), Wonderland, Whitechapel Road, London. The final of a six two–minute rounds championship belt competition, in previous rounds Russell eliminated Harry Fowler and Nat Smith, while Chamberlain beat Bill Corbett and Jack Goldswain.

13 August   Bob Russell, whose 130lbs championship belt is on display in the Coopers Arms, Limehouse, is now fighting in the 132lbs class according to the *Sporting Life*.

16 October   Young Corbett (Denver, USA) w rtd 7 Joe Bernstein (New York, USA), Baltimore, USA. Contested at catchweights, Corbett scaling 130lbs to Bernstein's 124½, some reports gave it 130lb world title billing.

8 November   Will Curley (Newcastle) w pts 15 Billy Barrett (Brooklyn, USA), Ginnett's Circus, Newcastle. With Curley weighing 128½lbs to Barrett's 130 the contest was given some world title billing, although not shown as such in the *Mirror of Life*, but the winner never pursued the championship and retired a few fights later.

24 November   Jack Goldswain challenges all England and is accepted by George Winters (Rotherhithe) a day later, while also that week Harry Mansfield's challenge to all England is accepted by George Franklin (Bristol) – *Sporting Life*.

26 November   Kid Lewis (USA) challenges all England at the weight – *Sporting Life*.

26 December   Dick Lee (Kentish Town) w pts 20 Billy Barrett, The Gymnastic Club, Dale Street, Liverpool. Although there was no title billing, Lee, the ex ABA featherweight champion, had a fair claim to the English title following the result. However, other contests in Liverpool against Harry Mansfield (w pts 20 on 29 January, 1903), Billy Barrett (drew 20 on 28 May) and Billy Barrett (w pts 20 on 29 October, 1903), despite being good results carried no real weight as they were all contested over two–minute rounds.

1903

14 January   Young Corbett w rsc 18 Austin Rice (New York, USA), Hot Springs, USA. Billed for the world 130lbs title, with individual weights lacking.

26 February   Young Corbett drew 20 Eddie Hanlon (San Francisco, USA), San Francisco, USA. Billed for the world 130lbs title with both men inside the weight. Other fights thought to involve Corbett at 130lbs which can not be substantiated were against Jack O'Keefe (w co 3 in St Louis on 19 May) and Hugh Murphy (w co 6 on 25 June and w co 11 on 27 October, both in Boston).

30 June Eddie Hanlon drew 20 Benny Yanger (New York, USA), San Francisco, USA. Billed for the legitimate world 130lbs title according to the *San Francisco Chronicle*.

29 September Eddie Hanlon w pts 20 Benny Yanger, San Francisco, USA. Another match which was billed for the legitimate world 130lbs title.

26 November Jim Walker, the champion of South Africa, challenges all England, £500 a side – *Sporting Life*.

29 December Young Corbett w rsc 16 Eddie Hanlon, San Francisco, USA. Billed for the world 129lbs title in a match articled at 127lbs, give or take two pounds, Corbett scaled 129lbs to Hanlon's 128.

1904

29 February Young Corbett w rsc 11 Dave Sullivan (Boston, USA), San Francisco, USA. Billed for the world 130lbs title.

9 March Dick Lee is claiming to be the English champion at the weight in the *Mirror of Life*.

25 March Jimmy Britt (San Francisco, USA) w pts 20 Young Corbett, San Francisco. Billed for the world 130lbs title, Britt was also the claimant of the 'white' 133lbs championship and moved on immediately.

12 November Bob Russell is still billing himself as the English champion at the weight – *Mirror of Life*.

29 November Battling Nelson w rtd 10 Young Corbett, San Francisco, USA. Billed for the world 130lbs title, in his very next fight Nelson contested the vacant world lightweight title when outpointed by Jimmy Britt over 20 rounds in San Francisco, USA on 20 December.

1905

7 January Sam Harper (St James') w pts 6 Joe Fletcher (Camberwell), Corn Exchange, Ashford, Kent. The final of an all–England competition.

26 February Joe Fletcher w pts 10 Boss Edwards (Marylebone), Royal Horticultural Hall, St Vincent Square, Westminster, London. Despite the lack of title billing, Fletcher claimed to be the English champion at the weight on the result.

12 December Charlie Lampey (Canning Town) challenges all England – *Sporting Life*.

1907

19 January Jim Lloyd (Newcastle) challenges all England – *Sporting Life*.

5 December Jim Lloyd w pts 20 Tommy Burns (Widnes), The Gymnastic Club, Christian Street, Liverpool. Although not a billed title bout, after beating Burns (127½) Lloyd (129½) was claiming the championship, a claim that was disputed by Boss Edwards who, in 5 January, 1908 edition of the *Sporting Life*, was calling himself the champion.

1908

11 May 'Seaman' Arthur Hayes (Hoxton) w pts 15 Jim Lloyd, NSC, King Street, Covent Garden, London. Made at 130lbs, Lloyd's claim disintegrated on the result, while Hayes was only interested in the featherweight title.

29 August Although Jim Lloyd continued to challenge all England at the weight, possibly on the strength of his 20-round points win over Darky Haley (Leytonstone) at The Christian Street Gymnastic Club in Liverpool on 13 August, he was not considered top drawer in persisting to take contests of two–minute rounds.

1909

16 January Charlie Lampey is calling himself the English champion in the *Sporting Life*, which is repeated in the 6th February edition.

11 February Following the introduction of the eight named weight divisions on this date, interest in the 130lbs class waned. Although Boss Edwards was advertising himself as the English champion at the poundage towards the end of the year, the weight class effectively became part of the lightweight division, certainly as far as Britain was concerned.

1917

15 March Arthur O'Leary (Providence, USA) w pts 15 Jimmy Kane (USA), Providence, USA. Not given much credence, that appears to be it until Johnny Dundee re–introduced the weight division in New York City at the end of 1921.

130lbs to 132lbs (9st 4lbs to 9st 6lbs)

1872

10 February Ted Napper (Shoreditch) challenges the world, up to £100 a side, having been challenged at 130lbs by Bat Mullins, who failed to show – *Bells Life*.

1873

11 January Ted Napper challenges the world to a 'spar' for points or endurance and is accepted a week later by Bat Mullins, who put down a £5 deposit – *Bells Life*. On 15 March, Mullins challenged Napper to cover his deposit. The death of Napper was reported on 22 October 1879 and he was buried in Manor Park Cemetry (grave number 533).

1 February Bat Mullins, calling himself the lightweight champion, challenges the world with gloves – *Bells Life*.

1874

27 April Billy McLeod (Manchester) drew 33 Tom Scattergood (Salford), Cloak Street, Hulme, Manchester. Scheduled to be fought to a finish for a 30 guinee purse, the fight was broken up by the police who failed to prove that it was anything other than a sparring match as the men were wearing gloves. McLeod weighed 131½lbs to Scattergood's 126½lbs.

1878

18 September Soldier Robinson (Clerkenwell) w rtd 16 Tom Stockley, Jack Baldock's East London Gym, Dean Street, Shadwell, London. A finish fight with gloves at 132lbs, it had no title billing as such but Robinson was seen as a claimant

1879

4 June Jimmy Highland (Birmingham) challenges all England, £100 a side – *Sporting Life*.

20 September Samuel 'Pat' Perry (Birmingham) challenges all England, Jimmy Highland preferred – *Sporting Life*. This challenge was repeated in 18 November edition of *Bells Life*.

17 December Samuel 'Pat' Perry, despite being mainly a bare–knuckle fighter, is also billing himself as the champion glove fighter at the weight – *Sportsman*.

1881

30 August Tom Noble (Bermondsey) w co 26 Curley Creamer (Manchester). The venue was about 20 miles from London and restricted to 22 people. Contested as a finish fight at 132lbs, Noble weighed 132lbs to Creamer's 130. Despite there being no title billing, Noble would claim to be the English champion at the weight.

20 October Ned Condon w pts 3 Jim Cheese, The Griffin, Shoreditch, London. The final of a 132lbs competition.

1884

27 January Harry Mead (Clerkenwell) w rtd 2 J.Sullivan, The Spread Eagle, Kingsland Road, Shoreditch, London. The final of an all–England professional competition, in an earlier round Mead had eliminated Bob Laxton.

1885

12 January Jim Kendrick (Lambeth) w pts 3 Harry Bartlett (Somers Town), West End School of Arms, Newman Street, off Oxford Street, Westminster, London. The final of an all–England competition.

15 January Arthur Cooper (Clerkenwell) w pts 3 Bill Cheese (Hoxton), The Blue Anchor, Church Lane, Shoreditch, London. The final of an all–England competition, in an earlier round Jim Kendrick was eliminated by Cheese.

13 April Tom Sterck (Holborn) w rtd 2 Jack Tierney (Bloomsbury), The Lamb and Flag, Rose Street, Covent Garden, London. The final of an all–England competition.

12 May Dick Burge (Cheltenham) challenges the world to a finish with gloves, up to £50 a side, and is accepted by Tom Sterck nine days later – *Sporting Life*.

31 August Jack Hall (late of England) w co 3 (4 also given) 'Young' George Powell, Sydney, Australia. Billed for the Australian 132lbs lightweight title under MoQ Rules with gloves, Hall challenged the world on the result.

16 September Dick Burge again challenges the world with gloves, up to £50 a side, Anthony Diamond (Birmingham) preferred – *Sporting Life*.

1886

2 February Sam Baxter (Shoreditch) w co 2 Harry Mead, West End School of Arms, Newman Street, off Oxford Street, Westminster, London. The final of Bob Habbijams' championship belt competition.

3 December Sam Baxter w pts 3 Charlie Mitchell (Bethnal Green), West End School of Arms, Newman Street, off Oxford Street, Westminster, London. The final of Bob Habbijams' championship belt competition.

1887

30 August Sam Baxter should be recognised as the English champion – *Sportsman*. This was repeated in the 30 November and 17 December editions of the paper. The *Sporting Life* ran the same story the following year in their 14 January, 15 March and 18 August editions.

1888

14 April Sam Baxter w pts 4 Harry Mead, Royal Horticultural Hall, Islington High Street, London. The final of Ben Hyams' English championship competition.

30 November Tom Euston is billed as the English champion – *Sportsman*.

8 December Harry Denny (Sheffield) w pts 4 Bill Whatley (Walworth), Royal Aquarium Theatre, Westminster, London. The final of Frank Hindes' English championship competition. In previous rounds, Denny eliminated Stanton Abbott and Tommy Walker, while Whatley defeated 'Black' Jack Stevens and George Wilson.

15 December Sam Baxter w pts 3 George Wilson (Leicester), Her Majesty's Theatre, Haymarket, London. The final of the Pelican Club's world and English championship competition. In previous rounds, Baxter beat 'Black' Jack Stevens and Bill 'Dido' Hopwood, while Wilson eliminated Stanton Abbott and Tom Euston.

1889

12 January Sam Baxter is referred to as the world champion, which was repeated in the 14 and 29 January editions – *Sporting Life*.

15 April Tom Euston w pts 3 Patsy Griffiths, Pelican Club, Soho, London. The final of a championship competition decided on the referee's casting vote.

27 July Sam Baxter is the undisputed champion at the weight – *Sporting Life*.

1890

6 January Dave Burke challenges all England over 12 rounds, £50 a side and best purse, Bill Reader (Fulham) and Sam Blakelock preferred – *Sporting Life*.

6 August Bill Whatley challenges all England – *Sporting Life*.

7 November Austin Gibbons (USA, born Liverpool) w co 19 Mike Cushing (New Jersey), Oakland Beach, Rhode Island, USA. Billed for the world 132lbs title to a finish.

1891

10 April Bill Whatley, the English champion, challenges all England, up to £120 a side – *Sportsman*. This was repeated in 28th April edition.

25 May Harry Overton (Birmingham) w co 7 Bill Whatley, NSC, King Street, Covent Garden, London. Although not billed as such, this fight was recognised as involving the English title at the weight.

22 August Harry Overton should be recognised as the English champion – *Sporting Life*. This was repeated in the 19th and 29th December editions.

23 November Harry Overton w co 4 Bill Reader, NSC, King Street, Covent Garden, London. Billed for the English title, with both men inside 132lbs, despite being articled at 132lbs, give or take two pounds. On the result, Overton challenged Jack McAuliffe at 134lbs.

1892

29 February Stanton Abbott w co 12 Harry Overton, NSC, King Street, Covent Garden, London. Billed for the English title, Abbott weighed 130½lbs to Overton's 131½lbs.

12 March Wag Andrews (Shoreditch) w rtd 5 Frank Young (Stepney), The Goodwin Gym, Kingsland Road, Shoreditch, London. The final of Ben Hyams' all–England championship competition over seven rounds.

31 May Stanton Abbott is the English champion at the weight – *Sporting Life*. The paper repeated the statement in the 30th November and 5th December editions.

1893

23 January Stanton Abbott w rtd 18 Sam Baxter, NSC, King Street, Covent Garden, London. Although not reported as an English 132lbs title fight in all papers, it was generally recognised as such.

25 January Stanton Abbott challenged the world, Jack McAuliffe preferred – *Sporting Life*. Abbott arrived in New York, USA On 17 March and never returned to Britain.

31 January Arthur Valentine (Lambeth) challenges Harry Overton, £200 a side – *Sporting Life*.

4 May Darkey Barton (Battersea) challenges all England and is accepted by Bill Whatley and Ginger Stevens a day later – *Sporting Life*.

8 May Arthur Valentine w co 14 Harry Overton, NSC, King Street, Covent Garden, London. With Abbott in America, this was recognised as being for the English title. Valentine weighed 131lbs to Overton's 132.

1894

8 January Stanton Abbott w rtd 15 Jack Falvey (USA), Providence, Rhode Island, USA. With the weights set at 132lbs or under, this belonged to Abbott's world title claim at the weight.

26 February Bill Eyles (Islington) w pts 4 Arthur Callan (Wood Green), NSC, King Street, Covent Garden, London. The final of an all–England competition.

21 April Stanton Abbott, having taken out American Citizenship papers, is still claiming to be the English 132lbs champion – *Mirror of Life*. The paper pointed out that Valentine should be recognised as being in the 134lbs class as he could no longer make the weight.

12 May Arthur Callan challenges all England – *Sporting Life*.

19 July Stanton Abbott w rsc 5 Johnny Young (USA), Alexandria, Maryland, USA. Thought to have involved Abbott's 132lb title claim – Young was claiming the American 130lbs title – The former fought in the 134lbs class from hereon.

14 August Johnny Boyle (Glasgow) claims to be the true English champion at the weight after his propsed contest against Arthur Valentine fell though, due to the latter failing to make the weight – *Mirror of Life*.

17 September Jim Murphy (New Zealand) w dis 24 'Iron Bark' Jim Burge (Australia), Couper's Circus, Johannesburg, South Africa. Made at 132lbs, with both men inside, and a finish fight, this should be seen as involving Burge's claim at the weight. Murphy, the brother of the famed 'Torpedo', lost when Burge's second rushed into the ring claiming that Murphy was repeatedly hitting Burge, who was decked three times in the 24th round, while he was on the floor.

10 November Maurice 'Dummy' Winters (Australia) w pts 3 Jewey Cooke (Bloomsbury), Eden Theatre, Long Acre, London. The final of an open competition.

1895

19 July Arthur Callan challenges the world, Young Griffo (Australia), George 'Kid' Lavigne (USA) and Tom Lynch (Ireland) preferred – *Sporting Life*.

1896

9 January Eddie Connolly Canada) w rtd 3 Jimmy Dime (USA), Cleveland, Ohio, USA. Billed for the American and world 132lbs title.

1897

8 January Tom Causer (Bermondsey) challenges the world, £200 a side and an NSC purse – *Sporting Life*. The challenge is repeated in the 30th January and 9th March issues.

30 April George 'Kid' Lavigne (Saginaw, Michigan) w rtd 11 Eddie Connolly, New York City, USA. Billed for the American 132lbs title, both men were on the weight.

1898

7 January Spike Sullivan (Boston, USA) challenges the world – *Sporting Life*.

21 February Spike Sullivan w rtd 15 Harry Greenfield (Camden Town), NSC, King Street, Covent Garden, London. An international match made at 131lbs, Sullivan weighed in at 130lbs and Greenfield scaled 131.

28 December Jack Rose (Lambeth) is claiming to be the English champion – *Sporting Life*.

1899

1 November Bill Wood (Clapton) challenges all England for an NSC purse – *Sporting Life*.

20 November Tom Dixon (Newcastle) w co 4 Harry Lane (Poplar), Standard Theatre, Gateshead. Although billed for the English title, it was not recognised as such, the monetry returns not being high enough for championship participation.

1900

6 January Tom Dixon is stated to be the English champion – *Mirror of Life*.

27 January Harry Tongue (Birmingham) challenges Tom Dixon to decide the championship over 15 or 20 rounds, up to £100 a side and best purse – *Sporting Life*.

30 January Jack Rose challenges all England – *Sporting Life*.

10 March Jack Goldswain (Bermondsey) challenges all, up to £100 a side and best purse, Harry Tongue preferred – *Sporting Life*. This was repeated in the 14th March edition, while challenging Tom Ireland and Ted Marlow.

12 March	George Cunningham (Bethnal Green) w pts 6 Bill Nolan (Drury Lane), Wonderland, Whitechapel Road, London. The final of an English championship competition of six two–minute rounds, in previous rounds Cunningham beat Dick Dean and Harry Spurden, while Nolan eliminated Bill Corbett and Tom Ireland.
16 April	Dave Wallace (Holloway) w co 6 Harry Tongue, The Manchester Gymnastic Club. With both men inside 132lbs, Tongue lost his claim to the title despite a lack of billing.
5 July	Jabez White (Birmingham) challenges the world at 132lbs – *Sporting Life*. This is repeated in the 17th August and 21st December editions as 130 to 132lbs.
1 August	Tom Ireland and Jack Goldswain are both claiming the English title – *Mirror of Life*.
2 August	Tom Ireland w rtd 2 Jack Goldswain, Wonderland, Whitechapel Road, London. Billed for the English title using four–ounce gloves, £100 a side and a £100 purse, Ireland scaled 131½lbs, while Goldswain was spot on the mark.
7 August	Bill Chester (Mile End) challenges Tom Ireland for the English title, £100 a side – *Sporting Life*.
11 August	Jabez White challenges Tom Ireland, up to £500 a side and best purse – *Sporting Life*.
6 December	George Cunningham w pts 6 Bill Nolan, Wonderland, Whitechapel Road, London. The final of an English championship competition.
13 December	Jabez White challenges the world, Bill Chester preferred – *Sporting Life*.

1901

21 January	Tom Ireland challenges the world – *Sporting Life*.
7 February	Harry Greenfield challenges all England – *Sporting Life*.
21 February	George Cunningham challenges all England – *Sporting Life*.
4 March	Bill Chester w co 1 Bill Wood, NSC, King Street, Covent Garden, London. Billed for the English title , £100 a side and £100 purse, and scheduled for 15 rounds, Wood was knocked out inside two minutes.
18 March	Bill Chester v Jabez White is made for June and involves the English title – *Sporting Life*. Unfortunately, it was cancelled in May.
28 March	Artie Simms (USA) challenges all England – *Sporting Life*.
6 August	Jabez White is calling himself the English champion at the weight – *Mirror of Life*. In quick succession, Harry Greenfield (28 September), Harry Chamberlain (25 October) and Charley Evans (29 October) are all claiming to be the English champion at the weight. However, it seems more likely that Evans was claiming the 132 to 134lbs title.

1902

9 January	Jack Goldswain challenges all England – *Sporting Life*.
18 February	Harry Greenfield challenges all England at the weight – *Sporting Life*.
20 March	Jabez White challenges all England over 20 rounds of three–minutes duration, up to £200 a side and best purse – *Sporting Life*.
24 April	Peter Brown (Woolwich) w pts 3 Tom Ireland, New Adelphi, Maiden Lane, The Strand, London. The final of a championship competition. In previous rounds, Brown beat Harry Greenfield and Bill Nolan, while Ireland defeated Harry Benson and 'Corporal' Jack Saunders.
28 April	Bob Russell (Limehouse) w pts 10 George Cunningham, NSC, King Street, Covent Garden, London. Not a billed title bout and not over the championship distance, but Russell was claiming the title on the result.
21 July	Harry Mansfield (Bristol) w pts 15 Ivor Thomas (Ynshir), The Ivor Arms, Pontypridd. Billed for the English title, but contested over two–minute rounds, the winner was not generally recognised as having a sound claim.
29 July	An advertised English title bout between Bill Chester and Bob Russell, scheduled for 25 August, was altered to ten two–minute rounds at 134lbs – *Sporting Life*.
17 September	Bob Russell has accepted Jabez White's challenge of £100 a side and best purse – *Sporting Life*.
5 November	Harry Mansfield w co 8 Dave Wallace (Islington), Harry Thomas' Booth, Normandy Street, Cardiff. Billed for the English title, and scheduled for 15 two–minute rounds, both the monetary reward and two–minute rounds meant that it was not taken too seriously elsewhere.
8 December	Bob Russell challenges all England – *Sporting Life*.
10 December	Harry Greenfield is the next man to issue a challenge to all of England's 132lb men – *Sporting Life*.

1903

3 June	Bob Russell challenges all England, £100 a side and best purse – *Sporting Life*. However, Russell set sail for South Africa on 31 July and was not involved in the weight class again.

1905

18 January	Walter Thomas (Birmingham) challenges all England – *Sporting Life*.
10 August	Joe Fletcher (Camberwell) challenges all England, Young Joseph (Aldgate) preferred – *Sporting Life*.
9 November	Joe Fletcher challenges Dick Lee (Kentish Town), up to £100 a side and NSC purse, over 15 or 20 rounds to decide the English championship – *Sporting Life*.
23 November	Joe Fletcher dnc 6 Tom Hall (Lambeth), The Lecture Hall, Deptford High Street, London. Billed for the English title, and scheduled for 15 two–minute rounds, the fight was declared a no contest after the referee decided that there was no chance of a fair fight. Three days later, Fletcher again challenged all England, up to £200 a side, through the medium of the *Sporting Life*.

1906

17 January	Joe Fletcher is the champion of England, a statement that is repeated in the 20th January and 10th February editions of the *Sporting Life*.

1907

28 September	Dick Lee challenges all England over 15 or 20 Rounds, Jim Holland (Widnes), Freddie Welsh (Pontypridd), 'Seaman' Arthur Hayes (Hoxton) and Charlie Lampey (Canning Town) preferred – *Mirror of Life*.

1908

16 March	'Seaman' Arthur Hayes w rsc 8 Boss Edwards (Marylebone), NSC, King Street, Covent Garden, London. Although there was no title billing attached, by beating Edwards (131) in a 15 three–minute rounder, Hayes (129½) had every right to claim the 132lbs title.
25 November	Dick Lee w pts 20 'Seaman' Arthur Hayes, NSC, King Street, Covent Garden, London. Following his victory over Hayes (128), despite there being no title billing Lee (131½) was now claiming the English 132lbs title.

1909

11 February	Following the introduction of the eight named weight divisions by the NSC on this date, the weight class effectively faded away.

132lbs to 134lbs (9st 6lbs to 9st 8lbs)
1871

6 November	Bat Mullins (Covent Garden) w pts 3 E.Whyman, The Jolly Butchers, Camden Town, London. The final of a silver cup for men under 135lbs, open to the world. Five days later, at the same venue, the pair met again, this time with Mullins winning a 154lbs trophy.

1872

6 February	Bat Mullins w pts 3 Denny Harrington, The Spencers Arms, Dudley Street, Soho, London. The final of an all–England 134lbs championship competition for Jimmy Shaw's silver cup. Earlier, Mullins eliminated Ted Napper.

1873

11 January	Ted Napper will 'spar' with any man wearing gloves, up to £100, for points or endurance – *Bells Life*.

1874

28 July	'Young' Bill Kennedy (Somers Town) w pts 3 Young Donnelly (Islington), Hall of Science, Old Street, St Luke's, London. The final of one open competition.
8 September	'Young' Bill Kennedy w pts Young Purvey, Hall of Science, Old Street, St Luke's, London. The final of another open competition.
23 September	J. Flaherty nd 4 Young Harker, The Little Bell, Whitecross Street, off Old Street, St Luke's, London. The final of an open competition. With both men deserving of victory, they each received a silver cup.

1875

16 February	James 'Punch' Dowsett (Hackney) w pts 3 Jim Laxton (St Luke's), Hall of Science, Old Street, St Luke's, London. The final of a 135lbs competition.

1876

11 January	Jim Laxton w dis 3 George 'Punch' Callow, The Griffin

Shoreditch High Street, London. The final of a 135lbs open competition.

1885

22 June Young Mitchell (San Francisco, USA) w co 35 Jack Keenan, San Francisco, USA. Contested with large gloves, and under MoQ Rules, Mitchell (134), who outweighed his opponent by eight pounds, won a fight that was given Pacific Coast, American and world title billing.

1887

15 January Jack McAuliffe (USA, born Cork, Ireland) w rtd 28 Harry Gilmore (Toronto, Canada), Lawrence, Mass, USA. A finish fight for the American and world 133lbs title saw McAuliffe (132¾) beat Gilmore (128½) to win the Ed Holske international challenge belt. Wearing skin–tight gloves, $2,500 a side and and a $5,000 purse, it was contested under MoQ Rules.

13 May Ed Holske awarded his international 133lbs challenge belt to Jem Carney (Birmingham) after the latter had gone to America to make a match with McAuliffe, which he was unable to do. On receiving the belt, which weighed six pounds and was valued at £250, Carney said he would defend against anyone at the weight.

16 November Jem Carney drew 74 Jack McAuliffe, Revere, USA. Held in a stable attached to the Atlantic Hotel on westerly Rhode Island, and six miles from Boston, the fight was contested in skin–tight gloves and governed by MoQ Rules. Following the fight, Carney (128), who had McAuliffe (130½) down and out at the time of the stoppage (due to the ring being broken into by McAuliffe's supporters) had a clear claim to the title. The fight had lasted for four hours, 56 minutes and the referee suggested a postponement of up to a week for the bout to be resumed. However, while Carney was in good condition, a couple of days later McAuliffe was under medical care and in no contion to fight on, leaving the Englishman robbed of the decision.

10 December Still under the doctor from injuries received on 16 November, McAuliffe blatantly refused Carney a return fight – *Sportsman*.

23 December Mike Daly (Bangor, Maine, USA) is now claiming the 133lbs title, Jem Carney having retired. Carney formally forfeited the title to Daly, whom he had boxed a three–round exhibition with in Boston on 19 December and the latter challenged all at the weight, Jack McAuliffe preferred.

1888

11 January 'Young' Jacob Hyams (London) challenges Mike Daly or Jack McAuliffe to decide the world title. Hyams knocked out Jack Jones (Lambeth) in 25 rounds on 27 February in a London private show, but no weights were declared.

10 October Jack McAuliffe w co 11 Billy Dacey (USA), Dover, New Jersey, USA. Billed for the world title and contested in skin–tight gloves under MoQ Rules, McAullife weighed 131½lbs to Dacey's 130.

1889

13 February Jack McAuliffe drew 64 Billy Myer USA), North Judson, USA. Contested in skin–tight gloves under MoQ Rules, with both men inside 133lbs, Myer laid claim to the championship following the result. The fight was brought to an end by the referee, who felt that a clear result wouldn't have been forthcoming.

23 February Sam Baxter (Shoreditch) w rtd 2 Dave Galvin (Kentish Town), Royal Aquarium Theatre, Westminster, London. The final of Frank Hindes' 134lbs world championship competition.

25 February Alf Suffolk (Vauxhall) w co 1 Fred Mansford, Pelican Club, Piccadilly, London. The final of a 134lbs competition, which despite not carrying championship billing was recognised as such.

16 March Harry Denny (Shoreditch) w pts 4 Alf Suffolk, Royal Agricultural Hall, Islington High Street, London. The final of Charley White's 134lbs championship competition, in earlier rounds Denny beat Dave Galvin and Andy Cannon, while Suffolk eliminated Charley Lloyd and Jim Jefford.

19 March Jim Carroll (London) w co 16 Sam Blakelock (Battersea, London), San Francisco, USA. Made at 133lbs with small gloves, Carroll weighed 131¾lbs to Blakelock's 132½. Billed for the world 133lbs title, Blakelock was badly weakened in having to shed weight from 153lbs just ten days earlier.

16 April Alf Suffolk w pts 3 William 'Dido' Hopwood (Bethnal Green), The Circus, Talbot Street, Nottingham. The final of an English championship belt competition.

5 December The *Sportsman* stated that Jack McAuliffe had forfeited his claim to the American and world titles by his failure to get down to 133lbs.

1890

11 March Sam Blakelock w dis 7 Dave Burke (Bethnal Green), The Social Club, Kennington, London. Billed for the English 134lbs title and a £100 purse.

17 March Jack McAuliffe admitted that he couldn't make 133lbs for a prospective defence against Jimmy Carroll on 21 March and, while the fight went ahead at 137lbs, he forfeited the 133lbs title to the Englishman.

22 May Andy Bowen (USA) w co 43 Billy Myer, New Orleans, USA. In suffering his first defeat, in a finish fight billed for the 133lbs lightweight title, using five–ounce gloves, Myer (133½) lost his championship claim to Bowen (130¾).

17 June A return match made on this date for the English 133lbs title, give or take a pound, between Sam Blakelock and Dave Burke later fell through.

16 September Jimmy Carroll w co 21 Andy Bowen, New Orleans, USA. Although billed for the world 135lbs title, both Carroll (133½) and Bowen (130½) were inside 134lbs (see under 135lbs also).

16 October Jim Verrall (Peckham) w co 6 Alf Suffolk, School of Arms, Paradise Street, Lambeth, London. Billed for the English 134lbs title, £50 a side and purse.

1891

26 January Jim Verrall w co 18 Sam Blakelock, Ormonde Club, Walworth Road, London. Although not reported as such, this fight was considered to be for the English 134lbs title, but due to its brutality it effectively finished both men.

7 April Joe Fielden (Manchester), currently in the USA, challenges the world, up to $5,000 a side, Jack McAuliffe, Billy Myer, or Jack Carroll preferred – *Sportsman*.

19 May Andy Bowen w dis 24 Billy Myer, New Orleans, USA. Billed for the American and world 134lbs title.

25 May Dick Burge (Newcastle) w dis 11 Jem Carney, Hop & Malt Exchange, The Borough, London. Billed for Carney's version of the world 133lbs title, using two–ounce gloves, Burge (133) beat the 34–year–Brummie, who had only ever boxed with gloves on three occasions and had been considered retired. The bout itself was farcical, with Carney (132½), who fought a bare–knuckle sort of fight, being disqualified for throwing his man.

16 June Austin Gibbons (USA, born Liverpool) w co 4 Jim Verrall, Pelican Club, Soho, London. Billed for the world 134lbs title, Gibbons weighed 133½lbs to Verrall's 134.

2 December Harry Overton (Birmingham), a claimant to the English title, challenges Jack McAuliffe to decide the world title and Stanton Abbott to decide the English championship – *Sporting Life*.

1892

20 January Austin Gibbons challenges Jem Carney or Dick Burge to a fight that would produce a world champion at 134lbs, up to £500 a side and best purse – *Sporting Life*.

26 March Jim Verrall is still claiming the English 134lbs title, despite his loss to Austin Gibbons – *Sporting Life*.

8 October Harry Overton challenges Jim Verrall, £100 a side and best purse, to decide the English title – *Sporting Life*.

12 October Stanton Abbott challenges all America, Andy Bowen preferred, at any weight between 128 and 134lbs – *Sporting Life*. Seven days later, Austin Gibbons stated that he couldn't get below 134lbs anymore and challenged Abbott above 136lbs, but was turned down.

8 November Dick Burge should be seen as the English 134lbs champion – *Sporting Life*.

22 December The Crescent Club in New Orleans offered a $20,000 purse for a Jack McAuliffe v Dick Burge world title fight.

1893

25 January Stanton Abbott, who is claiming the English 132lbs title, challenges Jack McAuliffe or anyone else in the USA for the world 133lbs title – *Sporting Life*. On 28 February, McAuliffe accepted Abbott's challenge.

2 February Stanton Abbott has a better claim to the English 133lbs title than Dick Burge, who has failed to box under 140lbs for the last two years, reported the *Sportsman*.

27 March George Dawson (Australia) challenges Jack McAuliffe for the world 133lbs title, $5,000 a side – *Sporting Life*.

8 May Arthur Valentine (Lambeth) w co 4 Harry Overton, NSC, King Street, Covent Garden, London. Despite not being billed for the 134lbs title, with both men inside the weight in

	a fight scheduled for 20 rounds, the result gave Valentine a legitimate claim to the English championship.
2 August	Maurice 'Dummy' Winters (Australia) challenges all England at 133lbs – *Sporting Life*. On 16 October at the NSC, Winters was retired in the seventh round of a 20 rounder by William Eyles (Islington).
30 August	Arthur Valentine should be recognised as the English 134lbs champion stated the *Sporting Life*.

1894

15 February	Walter Butler (Paddington) w rsc 1 Jack Harland (Marylebone), NSC, King Street, Covent Garden, London. Despite there being no title billing attached to this match at 134lbs, on his victory Butler claimed the English title.
9 April	Walter Eyles w co 14 Walter Butler, NSC, King Street, Covent Garden, London. In a match made at 134lbs, following his win over Butler (133), Eyles took over the former's English title claim.
21 April	Harry Webster (Kings Cross) w pts 4 Ginger Stewart (Battersea), St Andrew's Hall, Newman Street, off Oxford Street, Westminster, London. The final of Frank Hindes' English 134lbs championship competition.
20 July	Joe Walcott (USA, born Barbados) challenges any man in the world at 133lbs, Arthur Valentine, Austin Gibbons, Stanton Abbott and Horace Leeds (Atlantic City, USA) preferred – *Sporting Life*. In the same issue, Leeds challenged Jack McAuliffe to decide the world 133lbs title, to which the latter insisted on the weight being set at 135lbs. Leeds then stated that if McAuliffe refused to meet him at 133lbs, he would claim the title.
21 August	Walter Eyles challenges all England, Arthur Valentine preferred – *Sporting Life*.
21 August	Jack Everhardt (New Orleans, USA) w co 25 Stanton Abbott, New Orleans, USA. Billed for the world 133lbs title, Everhardt scaled 132¹/₂lbs to Abbott's 132.
5 October	Arthur Valentine, the English 134lbs champion, challenges the world at 133lbs, give or take two pounds – *Sporting Life*.
20 October	Walter Eyles w pts 4 Harry Webster, Central Hall, Holborn, London. The final of Frank Hindes' English championship competition.
7 November	Walter Eyles challenges all England at 134lbs – *Sporting Life*.
1 December	Pat Daly (Ireland) accepts Arthur Valentine's challenge at 134lbs and, at the same time, challenges the world at the weight – *Sporting Life*.

1895

4 March	Arthur Valentine, the English 134lbs champion, is on his way to America where he hopes to fight George 'Kid' Lavigne to settle the world title at the weight.
4 April	Walter Eyles challenges all England at 134lbs – *Sporting Life*.
6 April	Arthur Locke (Camberwell) w pts 4 Walter Eyles, Central Hall, Holborn, London. The final of Frank Hindes' all–England 134lbs competition.
10 May	Arthur Valentine again challenges the world – *Sporting Life*. Unfortunately, Valentine's title aspiration were dealt a bad blow by the American, Billy Ernst, who stopped him inside five rounds on 12 October at Long Island, New York, USA. Although no weights were disclosed, Ernst later said that because of his win he would be claiming the English 134lbs title, which was pure nonsense.
13 May	Tom Ireland (Mile End) w pts 3 Alf Bannister (St Luke's), NSC, King Street, Covent Garden, London. The final of an all–England competition, in earlier rounds Ireland beat Harry Webster and Pat Daly, while Bannister eliminated Alf Greenbank and Owen Sweeney.
26 August	George 'Kid' Lavigne w co 5 Jimmy Handler (USA), Maspeth, New York, USA. Made at 133lbs, it involved the American title at the weight.
September	Arthur Locke w pts 3 Tom Ireland, The Greyhound, Newmarket. The final of an English 134lbs championship tournament.
12 October	George 'Kid' Lavigne drew 20 Young Griffo (Australia), Maspeth, New York, USA. Although there was no mention of the title in the New York Herald, with both men inside 133lbs Lavigne's claim at the weight would have been at stake.
24 October	Jack Everhardt drew 20 Owen Ziegler, New Orleans, USA. With both men inside 133lbs, Everhardt's title claim at the weight was at stake.
2 December	George 'Kid' Lavigne w pts 15 Joe Walcott, Maspeth, New

	York, USA. Billed for the American 133lbs title, with both men weighing 131¹/₂lbs, according to the articles of agreement Walcott had to kayo Lavigne if he wanted to win the championship.
16 December	Following a newspaper victory in a six–round no–decision bout against Stanton Abbott, the winner, Billy Ernst, stated that as he had beaten Arthur Valentine at 134lbs and Abbott at 133lbs he would claim the English lightweight title.
30 December	Jack Daly drew 37 Stanton Abbott, Providence, Rhode Island, USA. With Daly introduced as the American 134lbs champion and Abbott as the English 132lbs titleholder, which he wasn't, the fight proved nothing, especially with no weights given or, indeed, stipulated.

1896

13 January	Tom Ireland w pts Ted Ware (Mile End), NSC, King Street, Covent Garden, London. The final of an all–England 134lbs competition, in previous rounds Ireland eliminated Archie Phillips and Harry Webster and Ware put out Jim Thompson and Jack Fitzgibbons.
3 February	Arthur Callan (Wood Green) w pts 20 Arthur Locke, NSC, King Street, Covent Garden, London. Callan stated that this was a defence of his English 134lbs title claim, despite a lack of billing.
10 February	Arthur Valentine, although currently boxing at 140lbs, is reported as still being the English 134lbs champion, a statement which is repeated in the 12th and 26th February and 14th March editions of the *Sporting Life*. His challenge was accepted by Pat Daly (London, born Ireland) on 22 February.
22 May	Pat Daly w pts 12 Arthur Valentine, The Social Club, Kennington, London. In later years, Daly claimed that this was for the English title, Valentine weighing 133¹/₂lbs and Daly 133 and being scheduled for 20 rounds. His story was that, with Valentine on the floor in the 12th round, the latter's seconds invaded the ring and the referee, T.Hulls, shouted Daly is the winner and left the building. Daly formally claimed the title on 26 June.
29 May	Pat Daly challenges all England at 134lbs – *Sporting Life*.
26 June	Pat Daly challenges the world at 134lbs over 20 rounds, £200 a side, Young Griffo preferred – *Sporting Life*.
6 August	Arthur Callan, who is the English 134lbs champion, challenges the world at the weight, Harry Greenfield preferred – *Sporting Life*. Greenfield, who up to that time had been boxing in the 130lbs class, accepted the challenge on 11 August.
11 August	Pat Daly stated that he couldn't see what right Arthur Callan had to the English 134lbs title and he was happy to give Callan a return with the English championship on the line.
2 October	Harry Webster w pts 8 George Baxter (Shoreditch), The New Adelphi, Maiden Lane, The Strand, London. The final of an English championship competition.
6 October	Pat Daly challenges George 'Kid' Lavigne or anyone else in the world for the 133 to 135lbs title – *Sporting Life*.
12 October	Tom Ireland w pts 3 Ted Ware, Excelsior Baths, Mansford Street, Bethnal Green, London. The final of an all–England competition, in previous rounds Ireland beat Arthur Phillips and Harry Wilson, while Ware defeated Jack Philo and Arthur Wilkinson.
24 November	Eddie Connolly (Canada) w co 5 Tom Causer (Bermondsey), The Olympic Club, Barwick Street, Birmingham. Initially billed for the 130lbs title, but with Causer unable to make the weight due to catching a chill the fight went on at 134lbs. Still given world title involvement in some quarters, Connolly scaling 132¹/₂lbs and Causer 132 according to the *Sporting Life*, while the *Mirror of Life* gave both men to be 133¹/₂lbs.
1 December	Arthur Valentine, now over his illness, challenges all at 134lbs, Pat Daly preferred – *Sporting Life*. Valentine was found dying in the street on 2 December 1901, aged 28, never having really recovered his full health.
30 December	Tom Causer w rtd 5 Maurice Greenfield (Birmingham), The Olympic Club, Barwick Street, Birmingham. The final of a 134lbs English championship competition for Thomas Dewar's silver cup, Causer beat Walter Eyles and Tom Ireland in earlier rounds, while Greenfield, the son of the late Alf Greenfield, defeated Arthur Locke and Tom Spring.

1897

8 February	George 'Kid' Lavigne w pts 25 Kid McPartland (New York, USA), New York City, USA. Billed for the American and world 133 lb titles, Lavigne weighed 131¹/₂lbs to McPartland's 133.

14 April Although Arthur Locke is reported as being the English 134lbs champion in the *Sporting Life*, he had surely lost any claim he might have had when beaten by Arthur Callan on 3 February 1896.

24 April Joe Anderson w pts 6 Tom Ireland, Excelsior Baths, Mansford Street, Bethnal Green, London. The final of Harry Wright's English 134lbs silver belt championship competition.

31 May Johnny Hughes (Islington) w co 10 Jim Curran (Rotherham), NSC, King Street, Covent Garden, London. Despite there being no title billing in this one, a 20 rounder at 133lbs, and with Hughes, a booth fighter, making his debut in a genuine match, the winner was eventually credited as being the English champion following the result.

7 October Arthur Callan challenges the world at 134lbs – *Sporting Life*.

20 October Tom Causer challenges all England at 134lbs, up to £500 a side, and puts down a £50 deposit to bind the American, Spike Sullivan, to a match for the world 134lbs title – *Sporting Life*.

19 November Walter Eyles challenges the world, up to £100 a side, Jewey Cooke preferred – *Sporting Life*.

24 November Jack Daly w co 19 Billy Ernst, Williamsburg, New York, USA. Scheduled for 20 rounds and billed for the world 133lbs title.

8 December Tom Causer is calling himself the English 134lbs champion, which is repeated in the 11th, 22nd and 27th editions of the *Sporting Life*.

11 December Spike Sullivan challenges the world at 133lbs – *Sporting Life*. On the same day, a £50 deposit was placed binding Sullivan to a match at 138lbs, £200 a side and an NSC purse, by Johnny Hughes, who is claiming the English championship at 134lbs.

1898

5 January Tom Causer challenges the world at 134lbs, up to £500 a side – *Sporting Life*.

7 January Arthur Callan challenges all England over 20 rounds at 134lbs – *Sporting Life*.

1 February Tom Causer, once and for all, challenges Spike Sullivan for the world 134lbs title, up to £500 a side, having had a £50 deposit at the offices of the *Sporting Life* since October 1897 to bind a match with the American – *Sporting Life*.

23 February Spike Sullivan challenges the world between 132 and 135lbs, £500 a side, Tom Causer preferred – *Sporting Life*.

10 March Tom Causer w pts 12 Arthur Locke, Norfolk Road Drill Hall, Sheffield. This was the final of an English 134lbs championship belt competition which started in Birmingham at the Olympic Club before being moved to Sheffield after the promoters did a runner with the takings. Initially, there had been a entry list of eight, but on the night there were just two men left, hence £50 a side and a £50 purse. Causer announced his retirement from competitive boxing on 12 December.

12 March Johnny Hughes is still claiming to be the English 134lbs champion – *Sporting Life*.

16 March Walter Eyles challenges the world at 134lbs – *Sporting Life*.

6 April Spike Sullivan is claiming the world 133lbs championship – *Mirror of Life*.

28 September George 'Kid' Lavigne drew 25 Frank Erne (USA, born Zurich, Switzerland), New York City, USA. Billed for the American/world 133lbs title, the pre–fight agreement stated that if the bout went the distance then a draw would be announced, regardless of points scored.

2 December Joe Anderson is still claiming to be the English 134lbs champion, having won a championship belt competition in April 1897. However, any claim he may have had was surely washed away when he was knocked out in the second round by Billy Gordon, a Boston–American negro, on 5 December 1898. Although only an eight rounder, it puts Anderson's claim in perspective.

28 December Arthur Locke claims the English title seeing that Tom Causer has retired – *Sporting Life*.

1899

2 January Ted Ware challenges the world, up to £100 a side, and left a £25 deposit with the *Sporting Life* to bind a match. Two days later, Arthur Callan challenged the world.

6 March Tom Ireland w pts 6 'Young' George Cunningham (Bethnal Green), Wonderland, Whitechapel Road, London. The final of an English 134lbs championship belt competition, in previous rounds Ireland beat Charlie Tilley and Alf Bannister, while Cunningham, the son of an old timer of the

3 July same name, deposed of Ted Ware and Bill Percy. The belt was then placed on display at The Essex Arms, Stratford. Billed for the world 133lbs title, Kid Lavigne and Frank Erne met at 135lbs instead.

15 August Harry Walsh (Montreal), the Canadian 134lbs champion, challenges all at the weight, although Jim Popp (Toronto) is considered the best Canadian in the weight class – *Sporting Life*. Interestingly, Popp was knocked out in the sixth round by Spike Sullivan in Buffalo on 20 December 1899. No weights were given.

25 August Alf Bannister challenges all England over 20 rounds – *Sporting Life*.

22 November Jack Goldswain (Bermondsey) challenges Tom Dixon (Newcastle) to settle the English title, up to a £100 a side and an NSC purse – *Sporting Life*.

4 December Frank Erne w rsc 25 Jack O'Brien (USA), New York City, USA. Reportedly a 133lbs defence of the title that Erne had won at 135lbs.

12 December Jack Goldswain challenges all England at 134lbs, £200 a side and an NSC purse – *Sporting Life*.

1900

9 February Joe Gans (Baltimore, USA) w co 14 Spike Sullivan, New York City, USA. Billed as an eliminator for the world 133lbs title, the winner to meet Frank Erne, Gans was undoubtedly the coloured champion at the weight at this moment in time.

12 February Jabez White (Birmingham) challenges Jim Curran at 134lbs over 20 rounds, £500 a side and best purse, but the latter stated he couldn't make that weight anymore – *Sporting Life*.

14 March Charlie Tilley (Somers Town) challenges Tom Ireland at 134lbs, up to £100 a side and an NSC purse, to settle the title – *Sporting Life*. In the same edition, Jack Wood challenged all England.

21 March Tom Ireland w co 11 Harry Greenfield (Camden Town), The New Goodwin Club, Kingsland Road, Shoreditch, London. In a match made at 134lbs, despite a lack of title billing this was a defence of Ireland's claim at the weight.

23 March Frank Erne w rtd 12 Joe Gans, New York City, USA. Billed for the world 133lbs title, Erne weighing 131lbs to Gans' 133, Erne clinched his victory when Gans was so badly cut he had to retire from the fight.

26 April Tom Ireland w co 8 Harry Greenfield, Wonderland, Whitechapel Road, London. Made at 134lbs, and thought to have been scheduled for 20 two–minute rounds, despite no title billing it would appear that Ireland's claim was again on the line in this one.

21 July Jim Barry (St James') challenges all England at 134lbs, up to £50 a side and an NSC purse – *Sporting Life*.

2 August Tom Ireland w rtd 7 Jack Goldswain, Wonderland, Whitechapel Road, London. Billed for the English 134lbs title (despite being reported as 132lbs), and scheduled for 15 three–minute rounds, Goldswain retired with a badly damaged hand.

29 September Jabez White challenges all England at 134lbs – *Sporting Life*.

1 October Tom Dixon w rsc 7 Jim Barry, NSC, King Street, Covent Garden, London. No title billing given in this, a match made at 134lbs, but following his win Dixon claimed the English title at the weight.

10 October Walter Eyles is still claiming to be the English 134lbs champion – *Mirror of Life*.

31 October Ted Fitzgerald, the champion of Australia, challenges all England, up to £200 a side, Jabez White preferred – *Sporting Life*. White echoed a day later.

19 November Tom Dixon w co 16 Ernie Veitch (St George's), Standard Theatre, Gateshead. Made at 133lbs, despite the lack of championship conditions Dixon's claim to the English title was obviously at stake.

21 November Jack Goldswain again challenges all England over 15 or 20 rounds, George Cunningham preferred – *Sporting Life*.

24 December Jabez White challenges Spike Sullivan at 134lbs, up to £200 a side and an NSC purse – *Sporting Life*.

31 December Tom Ireland challenges all England, up to £100 a side and an NSC purse – *Sporting Life*. Ireland had been retired with a damaged hand in the tenth round of a catchweight bout against Harry Greenfield on 24 October 1900 (New Goodwin Club, Kingsland Road, Shoreditch, London) but was still seen by many as the true English champion.

1901

1 January Jabez White challenges any 134lbs man in the world, Jack O'Brien (USA, born Nova Scotia) preferred, up to £200 a side and an NSC purse – *Sporting Life*. This was repeated in the 15th and 28th January editions of the paper.

23 February	Ted Ware w pts 7 (extra round) 'Corporal' Billy Fairclough (St Helens), Wonderland, Whitechapel Road, London. The final of Joe Smith's 134lbs English gold and silver belt competition, in the earlier rounds Ware eliminated Harry Benson and Tom Ireland, while Fairclough beat Bill Ward and Peter Brown (Woolwich). The final itself should have been won by Fairclough, who appeared to win every round reported the *Sporting Life*.
8 March	Ted Ware, whose championship belt is on display at The Railway Tavern, East India Dock Road, challenges Jim Barry, up to £100 a side and an NSC purse. However, Barry cannot make the weight anymore – *Sporting Life*.
4 April	Tom Dixon challenges all England at 134lbs, up to £50 a side, Tom Ireland preferred – *Sporting Life*. A day later, the challenge is accepted by Alf Bannister and then Harry Greenfield.
10 April	Artie Simms (Chicago, USA) challenges the world at 133lbs, up to £500 a side, Jabez White preferred – *Sporting Life*. In the same edition of the paper, somewhat surprisingly, he also challenged the world at 126lbs.
15 April	Walter Eyles challenges all England at 134lbs and is followed by Alf Bannister two days later – *Sporting Life*.
27 April	Tom Dixon challenges all England at 134lbs, Jack Goldswain, Harry Greenfield and Tom Ireland preferred – *Sporting Life*.
11 May	Tom Ireland, the English 134lbs champion, challenges all England at the weight, up to £500 a side, Jabez White and Bill Chester (Mile End) preferred – *Sporting Life*.
29 May	Kid Parker, the champion of the American west who is currently in England, challenges all England at 133 or 135lbs – *Sporting Life*. However, he returned home on 12 June before a match could be made.
3 August	Bill Nolan (Drury Lane) w pts 6 Ted Ware, Wonderland, Whitechapel Road, London. The final of an English gold and silver championship belt competition, in previous rounds Nolan beat Harry Greenfield and Bill Wood and Ware defeated Jim Maloney (Hackney) and Jack Goldswain.
26 September	Harry Greenfield challenges all England, Bill Chester and Tom Ireland preferred – *Sporting Life*. Two days later, Greenfield is reported as the English 134lbs champion in the same paper.
21 October	Bob Russell (Limehouse) w pts 10 Bill Wood (Clapton), NSC, King Street, Covent Garden, London. An English 134lbs championship belt competition.
24 October	Bill Chester (Mile End) is the English 134lbs champion – *Sporting Life*.
28 October	George Cunningham w pts 10 Harry Greenfield, NSC, King Street, Covent Garden, London. Made at 134lbs, although not over the championship distance Greenfield's claim would have been at stake.
5 November	Jim Roberts (Brynmawr, late South Africa) w rtd 12 Alf Bannister, The New Adelphi, Maiden Lane, The Strand, London. Made at 134lbs, Roberts claimed to be the South African champion, a claim that failed to stand up when challenged.
25 November	Ernie Veitch w pts 6 Bill Corbett (Lambeth), Wonderland, Whitechapel Road, London. The final of an all-England championship competition, in previous rounds Veitch beat Harry Fowler and Charlie Tilley, while Corbett deposed of Bill Eyles and Harry Benson.

1902

1 February	Jack Goldswain challenges Harry Greenfield to decide the English 134lbs title – *Sporting Life*.
8 February	Ernie Veitch w co 1 Joe Scott (Stoke Newington), Wonderland, Whitechapel Road, London. The final of an English 134lbs championship competition, to get to the final Veitch defeated Harry Benson and Peter Brown (Woolwich), while Scott eliminated Tom Dyer and Jack Goldswain.
25 April	Bill Chester challenges all England at 134lbs, £100 a side, Jabez White preferred – *Sporting Life*.
26 April	Jabez White w rsc 5 Bill Chester, NSC, King Street, Covent Garden, London. Although the *Sporting Life* and *Mirror of Life* gave the contest title billing at 134lbs, despite both men claiming the English championship at the weight it was really a ten rounder. However, on the result White's claim was immeasurably strengthened and three days later it was reported in the *Sporting Life* that he was the English champion.
12 May	Jabez White challenges the world at 132lbs (almost certainly should have read 134lbs), £200 a side, Spike Sullivan and Bill Chester preferred – *Sporting Life*.

21 June	Jabez White w pts 15 Spike Sullivan, NSC, King Street, Covent Garden, London. Billed for the world 134lbs title, both men came in spot on the weight.
21 August	Jabez White, the world 134lbs champion, challenges the world at the weight, Jack Golswain or Harry Greenfield preferred – *Sporting Life*.
16 September	Jabez White challenges the winner of the Terry McGovern v Young Corbett bout in the USA – *Sporting Life*.
1 October	Jabez White accepts the challenges of Bob Russell and Will Curley (Newcastle) – *Sporting Life*.
22 October	Jabez White, the holder of the world 134lbs title, challenges the world at the weight and is prepared to meet Young Corbett at 133lbs – *Sporting Life*.
17 November	Bill Chester sees himself as the English 134lbs champion in the absence of Jabez White, the world champion at the weight – *Sporting Life*.
10 December	Harry Greenfield challenges all England at 134lbs – *Sporting Life*.

1903

31 January	Jack Goldswain, the ex–English champion at 130 and 132lbs, challenges Jabez White at 134lbs with five–ounce gloves and an NSC purse – *Sporting Life*.
9 March	Jack O'Keefe (USA) w dis 6 Jimmy Britt (USA), Portland, USA. Billed for the world 'white' American title, with both inside the weight, Britt was mysteriously disqualified after having O'Keefe down several times and all but done for. Justice was served when, following the fight, it was discovered that the referee was part of a syndicate that had bet heavily against Britt. On that information coming to light, Britt retained public supprt.
11 March	Joe Gans w co 11 Steve Crosby (USA), Hot Springs, USA. The Philadelphia Item reported this one as another successful defence of the lightweight title for Gans, at 134lbs.
28 April	Jimmy Britt w pts 20 Willie Fitzgerald (Brooklyn, USA, born Waterford, Ireland), San Francisco, USA. Billed for the American 'white' 133lbs lightweight title, both men made the weight.
18 May	Harry Mansfield (Bristol) drew 15 Jack Goldswain, The Hamilton Rooms, Park Street, Bristol. This one was given English title status at 134lbs despite being contested over two–minute rounds.
13 June	Jimmy Britt drew 20 Jack O'Keefe, Butte, USA. Advertised for the 133lbs 'white' lightweight title, following the fight Britt demanded that Joe Gans prove his ability to make the same weight.
10 November	Jimmy Britt w rsc 20 Charley Seiger (Hoboken, New Jersey, USA), San Francisco, USA. Billed for the 'white' 133lbs lightweight title.
15 November	Jabez White, the world 134lbs champion, is presented with a championship belt valued at 100 guineas at a special ceremony held in Birmingham.
20 November	Jimmy Britt w pts 25 Martin Canole (Fall River, Mass, USA), Colma, USA. Billed for the 'white' 133lbs lightweight title.

1904

8 July	Jabez White should be seen by all as the world 134lbs champion as he will defend against any reasonable challenger – *Sporting Life*.
25 October	Bob Russell, who is being billed as the English 134lbs champion while in the USA, challenges Jabez White and Joe Gans at the weight – *Sporting Life*.
31 October	Joe Gans w dis 5 Jimmy Britt, San Francisco, USA. For over two years Britt had disputed the title, firstly drawing the 'colour bar' and later claiming that Gans was incapable of making 133lbs. However, while Gans proved he could make the weight for this one it obviously left him weakened, something that was painfully exploited by Britt. The only thing that saved Gans was Britt's impetuosity. Having downed the coloured man twice in the fourth round, Britt was excused hitting him after the bell because of the din but there was no excuse in the fifth and he was finally disqualified after hitting his rival who was in the act of rising from another knockdown. Britt continued to claim the title on the grounds that the action of the referee was unwarranted and that, in the eyes of most Californians, he was still the champion.
9 December	Jack Nelson (Newcastle), who had been boxing in the 140lbs class, challenges Bob Russell to a bout that will decide the English 134lbs title over 20 three–minute rounds – *Sporting Life*.

20 December Jimmy Britt w pts 20 Battling Nelson, San Francisco, USA. Although George Siler, the famous referee, writing in the *Chicago Tribune* reported that Joe Gans should still be considered the champion, this was billed for the 133lbs title.

21 December Now that Joe Gans cannot get below 135lbs any longer, Jimmy Britt (133) and Jabez White (134) should be seen as world champions at those weights – *Sporting Life*.

1905

27 January Bob Russell challenges the world at 134lbs – *Sporting Life*.

29 March Bob Russell claims to be the current 134lbs world champion – *Sporting Life*.

1 May Joe Fletcher (Camberwell) drew 20 Young Joseph (Aldgate), NSC, King Street, Covent Garden, London. Despite a lack of title billing, both Fletcher (133) and Joseph (134) claimed the English 134lbs title on the result.

5 May Jimmy Britt w co 20 Jabez White, San Francisco, USA. Billed for the world 133lbs title, with both men inside, Britt strengthened his right to the title following his win over the English champion with just 20 seconds of the bout remaining.

6 May Fred Buckland, the South African 134lbs champion who was born in Northamptonshire, England, challenges Britt for the 133lbs 'white' title – *Sporting Life*.

30 May Freddie Welsh, who has done the majority of his boxing in the USA despite being born in Pontypridd, Wales, challenges all England at 133lbs – *Sporting Life*.

20 July Bob Russell stated in the *Sporting Life* that as he couldn't get championship bouts at 134lbs he was retiring.

21 July Jimmy Britt w pts 20 Kid Sullivan (USA), San Francisco, USA. Billed for the 133lbs world title, both men were inside the weight.

9 September Battling Nelson w co 18 Jimmy Britt, San Francisco, USA. Although scheduled for 45 rounds and billed for the 133lbs championship, with both men inside, George Siler, writing in the *Chicago Tribune*, was not slow to extol the virtues of Joe Gans as the real champion.

1906

8 January Jabez White, who still claimed the English 134lbs title, weighed in over 136lbs for a proposed English title bout against Bob Russell on this date.

16 April Joe Fletcher challenges Jabez White to decide the English 134lbs title, up to £100 a side – *Sporting Life*.

3 September Joe Gans w dis 42 Battling Nelson, Goldfield, Nevada, USA. In a finish fight that introduced Tex Rickard as a boxing promoter, Gans once again achieved general recognition as champion. However, it was a big price to pay. Forced to make 133lbs ringside, he made it but finally ruined his health beyond repair as the tuberculosis that would eventually ravage his body and kill him (Gans died on 10 August 1910) set in.

18 September Joe Fletcher challenges all England at 134lbs – *Sporting Life*. Fletcher repeated the challenge on 3 October, with Bob Russell preferred. However, in the same issue Russell was calling himself the English 140lbs champion, which effectively ruled him out.

26 October Young Joseph challenges Joe Fletcher to decide the English 134lbs title, up to £100 a side and an NSC purse – *Sporting Life*.

19 December Young Joseph challenges the world, up to £100 a side, Alf Reed (Canning Town), who had twice outpointed him earlier in the year, preferred – *Sporting Life*.

26 December Jabez White challenges Jack Goldswain to decide the English 133lbs title. Strangely, by this time neither man could make the required weight – *Mirror of Life*.

1907

1 January Joe Gans w co 8 Kid Herman (USA), Tonopah, Nevada, USA. Billed for the world 133lbs title, both men were inside the weight.

12 January Battling Nelson, on holiday in England, is offered £250 to fight Jabez White, which was politely declined as being unacceptable – *Sporting Life*.

14 January Joe Fletcher w rsc 13 Jack Turner (Glasgow), NSC, King Street, Covent Garden, London. Billed for the English 134lbs title, Fletcher scaling 132½lbs to Turner's 131, and scheduled for 15 rounds duration.

25 January Joe Fletcher challenges Battling Nelson, £200 a side and best purse, but Nelson will fight nobody for less than a £1,500 purse – *Sporting Life*.

4 February Joe Fletcher challenges the world at 133lbs – *Sporting Life*.

31 July Jimmy Britt w pts 20 Battling Nelson, San Francisco, USA.

Billed for the 'white' 133lbs title, Britt regained the championship on the result.

15 August Freddie Welsh w pts 15 Dick Lee (Kentish Town), Welsh National Athletic Club, Merthyr. With both men inside 134lbs, Welsh later claimed that he won the English title on the result, but with two-minute rounds in play his claim wouldn't have carried much weight outside Wales.

9 September Joe Gans w rtd 6 Jimmy Britt, San Francisco, USA. Billed for the 133lbs world title, both men scaled 132lbs.

12 October Freddie Welsh, now claiming the English title at the weight, challenges all England at 133lbs, up to £1,000 a side – *Mirror of Life*. In response to that, on 9 November, in the same paper, Joe Fletcher reiterates that he is the English champion, which is followed two weeks later by a similar statement from Jabez White, who had effectively retired.

1908

13 January Jack Ward (Gloucester) w co 2 Alf Reed, NSC, King Street, Covent Garden, London. Although not a billed title bout, and not contested over the championship distance, the *Gloucester Citizen* reported that Ward won the English 134lbs title in this fight. Three days later, Ward challenged Joe Fletcher to a bout for the English title.

3 March Jimmy Britt nd–drew 10 Battling Nelson, Los Angeles, USA. Made at 133lbs, and with both men inside, Britt's 'white' title was at stake in this one.

30 March Joe Fletcher w co 7 Jack Ward, NSC, King Street, Covent Garden, London. Although billed for the English 135lbs title, Fletcher, who weighed 133¼lbs to to Ward's 133½ legitimately had a claim on both titles. The following day, Ward was still calling himself the English 134lbs champion.

14 May Joe Gans w rsc 11 Rudy Unholz (USA), San Francisco, USA. Made for the world title at 133lbs, Gans scaled 133lbs and Unholz 132¾.

4 July Battling Nelson w co 17 Joe Gans, San Francisco, USA. Billed for the world 133lbs title, both men made the weight according to the reports.

9 September Battling Nelson w co 21 Joe Gans, San Francisco, USA. Despite a lack of billing, Nelson (131¼) successfully defended the world 133lbs title with his defeat of Gans (133).

12 October Dick Lee challenges both Jack Ward and Joe Fletcher to defend their English title claims against him, up to £100 a side – *Mirror of Life*. On 5 December the challenge is repeated, but to Ward alone.

2 November Jimmy Britt w pts 12 Johnny Summers (Canning Town), Wonderland, Whitechapel Road, London. Contested at catchweights with no weights announced, Summers was billed as being the 134lbs English champion.

14 November Dick Lee drew 10 Jack Ward, Welsh National SC, Castle Street, Merthyr. Made at 133lbs, but with no title billing and not over a championship distance the result decided nothing anyway.

1909

23 January Freddie Welsh challenges the world at 133lbs, Jimmy Britt and Johnny Summers preferred – *Mirror of Life*.

11 February With the announcement by the NSC of the eight named weight divisions being introduced, the lightweight division, certainly involving British (English) titles, was set at 135lbs for all future championship matches.

22 February Johnny Summers w pts 20 Jimmy Britt, NSC, King Street, Covent Garden, London. Made at catchweights, which Britt had insisted on, Summers had obviously wanted the contest to be set at 133lbs in order to take over the American's 'white' title claim. However, by his victory Summers spelt the end of Britt's title ambitions.

29 May Battling Nelson w co 23 Dick Hyland (USA), San Francisco, USA. Billed for the world 133lbs championship.

22 June Battling Nelson w co 5 Jack Clifford (USA), Oklahoma City, USA. Billed for the world 133lbs title, Clifford was not really championship calibre, being not much better than a sparring partner.

13 July Battling Nelson nd–l pts 10 Ad Wolgast (USA), Los Angeles, USA. Made at 133lbs for the world title, albeit being a no–decision bout, both men safely made the weight according to the *Los Angeles Times*.

1910

22 February Ad Wolgast w rsc 40 Battling Nelson, Richmond, California, USA. Scheduled for 45 rounds of world championship boxing at 133lbs, Wolgast weighed 132¼lbs to Nelson's 133.

30 May Freddie Welsh drew 20 Packey McFarland (USA), NSC, King Street, Covent Garden, London. Although not billed as such it was seen as a 133lbs title fight by the newspapers, which was surprising with Ad Wolgast being generally recognised as the champion at that weight. Also surprising was the fact that the match was made at 133lbs (the American limit) and not 135lbs as stipulated for British championship matches.

10 June   Ad Wolgast nd–l pts 10 Jack Redmond (USA), Milwaukee, USA. With both men inside 130lbs, the Los Angeles Times reported that the champion snapped a bone in his left forearm early on but was forced to carry on in order to safeguard his title.

29 September   Ad Wolgast nd–w pts 10 Tommy McFarland (USA), Fond du Lac, USA. The *Daily Commonwealth* newspaper reported that McFarland's attempt to wrest the 133lbs title from Wolgast was a vain one from start to finish.

1911

3 March   Ad Wolgast nd–l pts 10 Knockout Brown (USA), New York City, USA. A return match at 133lbs less than a month after their six–round no–decision affair in Philadelphia, Brown yet again had the better of things.

17 March   Ad Wolgast w rsc 4 George Memsic (USA), Los Angeles, USA. The *Los Angeles Daily Times* gave this as a title defence at 133lbs, with Wolgast weighing 129$^{1}/_{2}$lbs to Memsic's 132$^{1}/_{2}$.

31 March   Ad Wolgast w rtd 5 Antonio LaGrave (USA), San Francisco, USA. Knowing that LaGrave was walking about at 140lbs two weeks prior to their championship contest, Wolgast insisted on a ringside weigh–in. While Wolgast was obviously comfortable at 131lbs, LaGrave, who barely made the required 133lbs, was drained at the weight and slumped to a quick defeat.

27 May   Ad Wolgast w rtd 16 Frankie Burns (USA), San Francisco, USA. Billed for the world 133lbs title.

4 July   Ad Wolgast w co 13 Owen Moran (Birmingham, England), San Francisco, USA. Both men were announced as being inside the required 133lbs, with Moran scaling 130 the day prior to the fight.

1912

4 July   Ad Wolgast w co 13 Joe Rivers (USA), Los Angeles, USA. An amazing world 133lbs title fight shrouded in controversy, saw both men knocked down simultaneously before the referee lifted Wolgast (130) up and supported him, while counting Rivers (133) out.

4 November   Ad Wolgast nd–drew 10 Joe Mandot (USA), New Orleans, USA. According to the *New Orleans Daily Picayune*, with both men inside 133lbs Mandot was bidding to win the title. On the day, the challenger scaled 130lbs.

28 November Willie Ritchie (USA) w dis 16 Ad Wolgast, San Francisco, USA. Billed for the world 133lbs championship, the title changed hands on the result.

1913

4 July   Willie Ritchie w co 11 Joe Rivers, San Francisco, USA. Ritchie, who was already struggling to make the recognised American lightweight limit of 133lbs, arbitrarily raised the poundage to 134lbs for this one, with both men inside.

10 November Willie Ritchie, who was still having difficulty in making the required 133lbs American limit for his no–decision title defence against Leach Cross, once again raised the limit to 135lbs, which then fell into line with Britain.

134lbs to 136lbs (9st 8lbs to 9st 10lbs)

1873

11 January   Ted Napper (Shoreditch) will 'spar' with gloves against any man in the world between 132 to 136lbs, up to £100 a side, either for points or endurance – *Bells Life*.

1880

24 May   Charlie Norton w rtd 8 Alf Heath, Baltimore, USA. Contested between Englishmen on American soil, and recognised as the first lightweight championship fight with gloves to a finish under MoQ Rules, Norton (134) beat Heath (135) using hard gloves. It was stated to be only the third fight of Norton's career and his debut in the USA.

19 June   John Boylan (Dublin) challenges any 136lbs man in the world, £25 a side upwards – *Bells Life*.

1881

23 July   Samuel 'Pat' Perry claims to be the world 136lbs champion – *Sportsman* (20th August edition of the *Sporting Life* gives him as the 134lbs champion). However, Perry is known as a bare–knuckle fighter and not much, if anything at all, is known about his ability with gloves.

1885

23 May   Anthony Diamond (Birmingham), the ex-amateur champion, challenges all England at 136lbs, MoQ Rules, £100 a side, and up to ten rounds – *Sporting Life*.

1886

29 October   Jack McAuliffe (USA, born Cork, Ireland) w co 21 Bill Frazier (Boston, USA). Made at 135lbs, McAuliffe scaling 138$^{1}/_{2}$lbs to Frazier's 129$^{1}/_{2}$, it was contested under MoQ Rules in skin–tight gloves and McAuliffe was forced to pay forfeit. Strangely, the New York Herald reported the weights as 133$^{1}/_{2}$ and 130$^{1}/_{2}$lbs respectively. However, for their return match on 15 December, Frazier pulled out after McAuliffe weighed in at 132lbs, and this time it was his turn to pay forfeit.

1887

28 March   Jimmy Mitchell (Philadelphia, USA) drew 16 Paddy Smith (Brooklyn, USA), Philadelphia, USA. Billed for the American 136lbs title and the Police Gazette championship belt.

17 June   Jem Carney (Birmingham) w rtd 11 Jimmy Mitchell, Long Island Sound, USA. Billed for the world 136lbs title (despite it being advertised as 133lbs, the weight that Carney was meant to meet Jack McAuliffe, who pulled out) after Mitchell substituted for McAuliffe, both men scaled 136lbs exactly in what was a MoQ Rules finish fight contested in light tan gloves of the thinnest kind.

19 October   Billy Myer (USA) w co 5 Harry Gilmore (Canada), St Croix, Wisconsin, USA. Billed for the American and North–West American titles, it was contested in skin–tight gloves under MoQ Rules. Myer weighed 135lbs and Gilmour came in at 134$^{1}/_{2}$.

10 December Jem Carney, the holder of the 134 and 136lb world championships, announced his retirement and forfeited his titles to Mike Daly, the New England champion, who had earlier challenged him to a title bout.

12 December Dick Burge (Newcastle) challenges all England at 136lbs and two days later is accepted by Sam Baxter (Shoreditch) – *Sportsman*.

1888

5 January   Sam Baxter, the world 132lbs champion, is happy to meet Dick Burge – *Sportsman*.

19 January   Billy Myer w co 1 Harry Gilmore, North Judson, USA. Contested in skin–tight gloves to a finish and under MoQ Rules, Myers scaled 135lbs to Gilmore's 132.

1 February   Mike Daly drew 15 Jimmy Carroll (London), Boston, USA. With Daly billed as the 135lbs champion of America and weighing 133lbs to Carroll's 133$^{3}/_{4}$, his title claim was at risk despite decisions not being given in Boston at the time. MoQ Rules applied and two–ounce gloves were used. However, on 5 December 1889, Daly's claim was deemed to be worthless by the *New York Herald* when he received by far the worst of another 15–round draw in Boston, against Jack McAuliffe, albeit weighing 138lbs to his opponent's 141. That apart, Daly is not seen as having any further major fights until 1893 when defeated by Austin Gibbons.

18 July   Ben Seth (Lambeth) challenges the world at 136lbs – *Sportsman*.

19 July   Ben Seth w rtd 7 Bill Cheese (Hoxton), School of Arms, Paradise Street, Lambeth, London. Cut from endurance to 12 rounds because James Clarke's silver championship belt was unavailable, Seth still claimed the English title at 136lbs on his victory.

20 August   Ben Seth drew 8 George Wilson (Leicester), Rutland Hall Rink, Leicester. Billed for the English 136lbs title, but not over a championship distance, the decision was met by uproar. On 31 August, Seth emigrated to Australia.

4 September   George Holden (Manchester) challenges all England, up to £50 a side – *Sportsman*.

13 September Billy Myer w pts 20 Danny Needham (St Paul, USA), Minneapolis, USA. Contested in skin–tight gloves under MoQ Rules, Myer weighed 133$^{1}/_{4}$lbs and Needham 134$^{1}/_{2}$.

1889

23 January   Dick Burge, who had fought a six–round no–decision bout against Anthony Diamond on 21 January, challenges Diamond at 136lbs, give or take two pounds, up to £100 a side – *Sporting Life*.

2 June   'Iron Bark' Jim Burge (Australia) drew 39 George Dawson (Australia), Sydney, Australia. Billed for the Australian 136lbs title, Dawson, the challenger, broke his right hand during the fight.

11 June   Dick Burge challenges Sam Baxter over 20 rounds at 136lbs, up to £200 a side – *Sporting Life*.

16 July   Tom Tully, the English coloured lightweight champion, challenges the world, no one barred – *Sporting Life*.

1890

21 March   Jack McAuliffe w co 47 Jimmy Carroll, San Francisco, USA. With McAuliffe unable to make the articled 133lbs, a few days before the fight it was announced that he had surrendered that title to Carroll and that the contest would go on at a higher weight. According to the *San Francisco Chronicle*, McAuliffe scaled 134¹/₂lbs to Carroll's 135¹/₂ with five–ounce gloves in use.

16 September Jimmy Carroll w co 21 Andy Bowen (USA), New Orleans, USA. Billed for the American 135lbs lightweight title, Carroll weighed 133¹/₂ to Bowen's 130¹/₂. Following a 43rd round kayo at the hands of Billy Myer in New Orleans on 22 December 1891, Carroll's claim appears to expire, even though the match was made at 140lbs.

1891

11 September Jack McAuliffe w rsc 6 Austin Gibbons (USA, born Liverpool), Hoboken, New Jersey, USA. Made at 135lbs, and contested in four–ounce gloves, McAuliffe was spot on the weight while Gibbons scaled 130¹/₂lbs.

12 September Joe Wilson (Leicester) w co 14 Alf Suffolk (Lambeth), Pelican Club, Gerrard Street, Soho, London. Billed for the English 136lbs title, with both men on the weight.

28 November Joe Wilson challenges Jem Carney to decide the world title with two–ounce gloves, up to £500 a side – *Sporting Life*. A few days later, Wilson stated that he wasn't disputing Carney's claim to the bare–knuckle title as he didn't want to break the law.

1892

6 January   George Sullivan challenges Joe Wilson for the English 136lbs title and, on 28 January, Frank Howson (Sheffield), despite being an 140lbs man, challenged Wilson at 136lbs.

2 February   George Sullivan challenges all England over 20 rounds for an NSC purse, no one barred – *Sporting Life*.

28 March   Sam Baxter w rtd 20 Joe Wilson, NSC, King Street, Covent Garden, London. Billed for the English 136lbs title, £100 a side and a £200 purse, Baxter weighed 130¹/₂lbs to Wilson's 134¹/₂.

29 March   Stanton Abbott (Westminster), the English 132lbs champion, challenges Sam Baxter at either 132, 134 or 136lbs.

7 May   Andy Cannon (St Luke's) challenges all England – *Sporting Life*.

1893

12 December Joe Wilson challenges all England at 136lbs – *Sporting Life*.

1894

2 February   Owen Sweeney (Fulham) w rtd 1 Pat Kennedy (Hoxton), Central Hall, Holborn, London. The final of an all–England competition, in previous rounds Sweeney beat Dick Gorman and Jack Donoghue, while Kennedy deposed of Connie Collins and Frank Young.

23 February   'Iron Bark' Jim Burge is still the Australian 136lbs lightweight champion according to the *Sporting Life*.

5 March   Ted Cain (Birmingham) challenges all England at 136lbs – *Sporting Life*.

19 March   Arthur Valentine (Lambeth) w pts 20 'Iron Bark' Jim Burge, Raglan Music Hall, Union Street, The Borough, London. Made at 135lbs, despite a lack of Imperial British Empire title billing Valentine was the English title at the weight.

25 September Jack Everhardt (USA) drew 25 Stanton Abbott, New Orleans, USA. Billed for the world 135lbs title, Abbot had become an American citizen in April 1894.

1 November   Harry Webster (Kentish Town) challenges all England in four–ounce gloves at 136lbs, up to £50 a side – *Sporting Life*.

2 November   Arthur Valentine challenges all England at 136lbs, but only in excess of £200 a side – *Sporting Life*.

17 November Jim Thompson (Catford) w rtd 3 George Sullivan, Central Hall, Holborn, London. The final of Frank Hindes' English championship competition.

14 December George 'Kid' Lavigne (Saginaw, Michigan, USA) w co 18 Andy Bowen, New Orleans, USA. Billed for the 135lbs championship of America, with Lavigne on the weight, unfortunately, Bowen (133) never regained conciousness and was pronounced dead during the early hours of the following morning.

1895

19 April   Billy Hill w dis 12 Young Starlight, Boston, USA. Billed for the coloured world 136lbs title.

1896

31 March   Jack Everhardt w co 15 Horace Leeds (USA), New York City, USA. Made at 135lbs, Everhardt extended his claim at the weight. The end of the fight came when Leeds, a former top–class amateur, was knocked out, remaining unconscious for 50 minutes.

1 June   On this day at the NSC, London, George 'Kid' Lavigne defeated Dick Burge in a 138lbs world title fight. However, with neither man weighing above 136lbs, Lavigne (134) extended his American claim at 135lbs to that of world.

10 July   Jack Everhardt drew 20 Young Griffo (Australia), New York City, USA. With both men inside 135lbs, it was another defence of Everhardt's claim at the weight. However, following a further defeat at the hands of George 'Kid' Lavigne in his next fight, despite it being at 138lbs again, he finally forfeited any recognition he had at 135lbs.

6 October   Pat Daly (Westminster) challenges George 'Kid' Lavigne at 135lbs for the world title – *Sporting Life*.

9 November   Billy Hill w co 14 Arthur Callan (Wood Green), NSC, King Street, Covent Garden, London. In some quarters given world title billing at 136lbs, Hill claimed to be the world coloured champion at the weight, while Callan was claiming the English title.

1897

25 January   Pat Daly w pts 15 Billy Hill, NSC, King Street, Covent Garden, London. Billed for the world 136lbs title claimed by Hill (134), £100 a side and a £100 purse, according to the *Mirror of Life* Daley weighed 133¹/₂lbs, while the *Sporting Life* gave both men at 135lbs.

29 October   George 'Kid' Lavigne w rtd 12 Joe Walcott (USA, born Barbados), San Francisco, USA. In a return match, this time at 135lbs, Walcott, who was billed as the world welterweight champion, struggled to make the weight and, although inside on the night, weakened himself considerably. Following his victory, Lavigne had a fair claim to the welter title as well as holding on to his lightweight laurels.

29 November Spike Sullivan (USA, born Ireland) w pts 20 Jim Curran (Rotherham), NSC, King Street, Covent Garden, London. Made at 135lbs, although there was no title billing attached Sullivan (135) would have had a genuine claim at the weight on beating Curran (134¹/₂). Curran challenged Sullivan to a return at 137lbs in the aftermath only to be told that the American, who could easily make the 130lbs limit, refused to box over 135lbs.

1898

23 February   Spike Sullivan challenges the world at 135lbs, up to £500 a side, Tom Causer (Bermondsey) preferred – *Sporting Life*.

14 March   Johnny Hughes (Canning Town), calling himself the English 136lbs champion, challenges all – *Sporting Life*. On 25 April, at the NSC, London, Hughes (135³/₄) outpointed Jim Curran (136) over 20 rounds in a fight billed for the English 138lbs title, thus backing up his claim of being able to get inside 136lbs.

17 May   Arthur Callan w dis 7 Joe Francis (Bath), Brock Street Hall, Bath. Made at 136lbs, while there was no championship billing attached (monetary rewards hardly being substantial) Callan held his claim at the weight. On 17 April 1900, Callan again beat Francis at 136lbs, this time in Manchester, but his claim by then was not existent.

5 July   Walter Eyles (Islington) challenges all over 20 rounds, up to £100 a side – *Sporting Life*.

3 October   Arthur Locke (Camberwell) w pts 20 Walter Eyles, The Glengall Club, Old Kent Road, Bermondsey, London. Not given title billing, despite both men claiming the title, in a match made at 136lbs Locke weighed 135lbs to Eyles' 134. Locke announced his retirement on 11 January 1899, his hands being unable to stand up to another battle in the ring.

3 December   Jim Curran challenges the world from 135 to 140lbs, Bobby Dobbs (Kentucky, USA), Tom Causer and Johnny Hughes preferred – *Sporting Life*. This was repeated on 24 December.

23 December Tom Causer challenges Bobby Dobbs at 136lbs, up to £500 a side – *Sporting Life*.

1899

24 April   Walter Eyles w pts 20 Joe Francis, Brock Street Hall, Bath. Made at 136lbs, this was a defence of Eyles' claim despite the lack of billing.

3 July   Frank Erne (USA) w pts 20 (25 in *Sporting Life*) George 'Kid' Lavigne, Although reported by the *New York Herald* and *Chicago Tribune* to be made at 133lbs, the *Buffalo*

Courier stated that the scales were set at 135lbs with both men inside.

1900

22 February	Jabez White (Birmingham) challenges Jim Curran at 136lbs, up to £200 a side – *Sporting Life*. Strangely, in the same issue, White, calling himself the English 128lbs champion, announced his retirement from boxing.
11 December	Harry Greenfield (Camden Town) drew 15 Tom Ireland (Mile End), West End School of Arms, Newman Street, off Oxford Street, Westminster, London. Not given title billing, but with both men inside 136lbs, Greenfield weighing 135½lbs to Ireland's 135, it would have carried a claim if there had been a clear winner.

1901

23 March	Tim McGrath challenges all England at 136lbs – *Sporting Life*.
27 April	Tom Dixon (Newcastle) challenges Tom Ireland, who is claiming the English title, at 136lbs – *Sporting Life*.
6 August	Charlie Knock (Stratford) challenges all England at 136lbs – *Sporting Life*.
30 October	Bill Chester (Mile End), the claimant of the English title at 134lbs, challenges all England at 138lbs, up to £100 a side – *Sporting Life*.
10 December	Pat Daly challenges all at 136lbs to decide the lightweight title at the weight, although it was doubtful whether Daly could make it at the time – *Sporting Life*.
21 December	Pat Daly, the English 140lbs champion, accepts the challenge of Bill Chester to decide the 136lbs championship, up to £200 a side and an NSC purse. However, a fight against Chester was put on hold when the NSC received an offer from the world champion, Frank Erne, to defend his title against Daly, an offer that was duly accepted. Unfortunately, on 3 January 1902 the *Sporting Life* reported that Erne v Daly was off due to the latter being unable to get down to 136lbs.
31 December	Bill Chester again challenges all England at 136lbs – *Sporting Life*.

1902

1 January	Jim Maloney (Hackney), late of the USA, stated that he had never claimed the English 136lbs title but would be happy to meet Bill Chester, who also claimed that he had never sought the title at 136lbs as his best weight was still 130lbs – *Sporting Life*.
4 January	Bill Chester said that his final offer to Jim Maloney was 15 or 20 rounds at 136lbs, £100 a side and best purse, which was accepted the very next day – *Sporting Life*.
6 January	Tom Ireland challenges Jim Maloney at 136lbs over 20 rounds, £50 a side and best purse – *Sporting Life*.
10 January	Artie Simms (Akron, Ohio, USA) challenges Pat Daly at 136lbs, give or take nil, £100 a side, and placed a £25 deposit with the *Sporting Life* to secure the match.
7 May	Joe Gans (Baltimore, USA) challenges all England and is accepted by Jim Maloney, who also challenges all England at 136lbs – *Sporting Life*.
12 May	Joe Gans w co 1 Frank Erne, Fort Erie, USA. Billed for the world lightweight title at 135lbs, Gans scaled 133¼lbs and Erne 132½.
14 May	Jack Nelson (Newcastle) w dis 3 Jim Maloney, Ginnett's Circus, Newcastle. Billed for the English 136lbs title, and deservedly so, most of the national press disputed the billing. Years later, in the *South Wales Gazette* on 31 March 1937, it was stated that Frank Guest from Gloucester had won the English 136lbs title from Nelson. However, no such match can be traced.
27 June	Joe Gans w rtd 3 George 'Elbows' McFadden (USA), San Francisco, USA. Although stated by some sources to be a world title fight at 133lbs, Gans defended at 135 with McFadden weighing in at 131lbs the day before.
24 July	Joe Gans w co 15 Rufe Turner (USA), Oakland, USA. Billed for the world 135lbs title, Turner was half a pound over the weight with Gans said to be spot on.
25 July	Joe Gans challenges all England between 136 and 138lbs, up to £200 a side – *Sporting Life*.
9 October	Bill Chester w dis 13 Jim Maloney, London National Athletic Club, Marylebone Road, London. Billed for the English 136lbs title over 20 rounds, it was not generally recognised as such due to the fact that it was contested over two–minute rounds.
13 October	Joe Gans w co 5 Kid McPartland (USA), Fort Erie, USA. The *Buffalo Courier* reported this to be a world title bout

with the scales set at 135lbs and neither man tipping the beam.

26 November	Jimmy Britt w co 7 Frank Erne, San Francisco, USA. Made at 135lbs ringside, Britt claimed the 'white' title on the grounds that he would not be challenging Joe Gans, preferring to draw the colour bar instead. Having knocked out the former champion, Kid Lavigne, inside eight rounds on 25 May 1902 at the same venue, this was Britt's fourth professional start.
11 December	Spike Sullivan w co 14 Bill Chester, London National Athletic Club, Marylebone Road, London. Billed for the world 136lbs title, with both men inside, it was scheduled for 15 rounds,

1903

1 January	Joe Gans w dis 11 Gus Gardner (USA), New Britain, Connecticut, USA. Billed for the title at 136lbs, a weight that Gans was more comfortable with at this stage of his career, both men were inside.
25 February	William 'Spike' Robson (USA, born Cork) is claiming to be the world 136lbs champion – *Sporting Life*.
29 May	Joe Gans w co 10 Willie Fitzgerald (USA), San Francisco, USA. Billed for world title at 135lbs.
9 June	Bobby Thompson, the Canadian lightweight champion, challenges the world at 135lbs – *Sporting Life*.
28 August	Jack Goldswain challenges all England at the weight – *Sporting Life*.

1904

21 January	Joe Gans w pts 10 Willie Fitzgerald, Detroit, USA. Another billed world title defence for Joe Gans at 135lbs.

1905

11 March	Bob Russell (Limehouse), listed as the English 136lbs lightweight champion, challenges the world, up to £100 a side and an NSC purse, Joe Fletcher (Camberwell) preferred – *Sporting Life*.
28 October	Jabez White challenges the world at the weight, no one barred, £200 a side and best purse, Battling Nelson (USA), Fred Buckland (South Africa) and Bob Russell preferred – *Sporting Life*.

1906

8 January	Jabez White w pts 15 Bob Russell, Warwickshire Horse Repository, Birmingham. Billed for the English 136lbs title, the fight went ahead despite White being five ounces over the weight and having to pay forfeit. Following the fight, White claimed the English title at the weight.
15 February	Jabez White refused a fight with Joe Gans, due to him upholding the colour bar, but would meet Battling Nelson, Young Corbett (USA) or Jimmy Britt – *Sporting Life*.
27 June	Bill Wood (Clapton) challenges all England – *Sporting Life*.
23 July	Joe Gans w pts 20 Dave Holly (Philadelphia, USA), Seattle, USA. Billed for the 135lbs world title, Gans scaled 133½lbs with Holly also safely inside the limit.

1907

2 January	Charley Hickman (Manchester) challenges all England at 136lbs, up to £100 a side – *Sporting Life*. The challenge was repeated in the 19th January edition of the *Mirror of Life*.
3 August	Billy Stewart (Wallsend) w pts 20 Jack Nelson, Ginnett's Circus, Newcastle. Despite the lack of title billing, Nelson's weakened claim to the English 136lbs title was at stake in this one.
15 August	Young Joseph (Aldgate) challenges Peter Brown (Woolwich), up to £200 a side, presumably to contest the English 136lbs title – *Sporting Life*.
19 August	Johnny Summers (Canning Town) challenges all England, up to £500 a side and an NSC purse – *Sporting Life*. Two days later his challenge is accepted by Freddie Welsh (Pontypridd).
22 August	Joe Fletcher challenges all England, up to £100 a side, Freddie Welsh preferred, and is accepted by Young Joseph two days later – *Sporting Life*.
27 September	Joe Gans w pts 20 George Memsic (USA), Los Angeles, USA. Billed for the 135lbs world championship, both men made the weight.

1908

11 January	Joe Fletcher, who claims the English 136lbs lightweight title, challenges all England, up to £100 a side – *Sporting Life*.
14 March	Jack Ward (Gloucester), the English lightweight champion, challenges the world at 135lbs, up to £200 a side – *Mirror of Life*.
30 March	Joe Fletcher w co 7 Jack Ward, NSC, King Street, Covent

Garden, London.Billed for the English 135lbs title, Fletcher scaled 133¾lbs and Ward 133½.

10 April Dick Lee (Kentish Town) is reported by the *Sporting Life* as being the English 136lbs champion.

13 May Bill Wood challenges all England at the weight, Jack Ward preferred – *Sporting Life*.

8 August Jack Ward challenges all England, up to £200 a side and best purse – *Sporting Life*.

1909

11 February With the introduction of the eight named weight classes specified by the NSC, the *Mirror of Life* reported that Dick Lee should be recognised as being the British (English) champion at 135lbs.

20 July Joe Fletcher stated that he is the rightful holder of the British 135lbs title, having won it when defeating Jack Ward, and would gladly defend it against Freddie Welsh over 20 rounds. However, when they did meet, on 6 September 1909, it was made at 140lbs and Fletcher was knocked out in the 12th round.

23 August Freddie Welsh w rtd 12 Henri Piet (France), The Pavilion, Mountain Ash. Billed for the European 135lbs title.

8 November Freddie Welsh w pts 20 Johnny Summers, NSC, King Street, Covent Garden, London. Billed for the British and European 135lb titles.

1911

27 February Matt Wells w pts 20 Freddie Welsh, NSC, King Street, Covent Garden, London. Billed for the British and European 135lb titles.

1912

26 April Packy McFarland (USA) nd–w pts 10 Matt Wells, New York City, USA. Billed for the world 135lb title, with both men inside the weight, according to the *New York Times* McFarland won the 'press decision' handily. However, without an inside the distance result, a claim would fall on deaf ears.

11 November Freddie Welsh w pts 20 Matt Wells, NSC, King Street, Covent Garden, London. Billed for the British and European 135lb titles.

6 December Freddie Welsh w pts 20 Hughie Mehegan (Australia), NSC, King Street, Covent Garden, London. Billed for the vacant British Imperial Empire and world titles, Welsh had originally signed to fight Ad Wolgast for the world title but the latter pulled out with appendicitis. When fit again, and with the Welshman back in England, Wolgast defended at 133lbs against Willie Ritchie instead.

1913

10 February Freddie Welsh w rtd 3 Paul Brevieres (France), Cardiff. Billed for the European 135lb title.

3 March Freddie Welsh w rsc 10 Raymond Vittet, Drill Hall, Sheffield. Billed for the European 135lb title.

10 November Willie Ritchie (USA) nd–w pts 10 Leach Cross (USA), New York City, USA. In this fight, Ritchie, the 133/134lbs champion, raised the American version of the world title up by one pound to 135lbs, which then fell into line with Britain and the rest of the world where it remains to this day.

136lbs to 138lbs (9st 10lbs to 9st 12lbs)

1884

6 March Nonpareil Jack Dempsey (USA, born Ireland) w rtd 9 Billy Dacey (USA), New York City, USA. Contested in fencing gloves under MoQ Rules to a finish on the Long Island shoreline, Dempsey, weighing 138lbs, won when Dacey (136) was retired by his corner at the end of round nine.

30 July Nonpareil Jack Dempsey w rtd 22 George Fulljames (Canada, born London), New York City, USA. Billed as a lightweight title fight despite the reported differences in the weights – Dempsey was reported as being 137lbs by the *New York World*, as 140 in the *Ring Record Book* and as 145 in the *Chicago Tribune*, while Fulljames was reported as 126, 156 and 124lbs, respectively. Contested under London Prize Ring Rules in hard kid gloves at Seguins Point, Princes Bay, Dempsey forced a retirement after 41 minutes and 37 seconds of fighting.

1888

5 May Johnny Robinson (South Shields) challenges the world at 138lbs, up to £500 a side, Dick Burge (Newcastle) preferred – *Sportsman*.

5 November Johnny Robinson drew 12 Dick Burge, St George's Drill Hall, Newcastle. Billed for the English 138lbs title, Robinson

weighing 136½lbs to Burge's 138, the distance was cut from 20 rounds on the insistence of the local authorities.

10 November Ben Seth (Lambeth) w co 2 Jack Hall (Melbourne, born London), Melbourne, Australia. Given Australian title billing at 138lbs, while no weight was given for Hall, Seth was reported to scale 137lbs.

1890

11 December Joe Wilson (Leicester) challenges all England at 138lbs – *Sporting Life*.

1892

5 September Jack McAuliffe (USA, born Cork, Ireland) w co 15 Billy Myer (Streator, Illinois, USA), New Orleans, USA. Made at 138lbs, with McAuliffe scaling 137¾lbs to Myer's 137½, it was contested in four-ounce gloves.

2 December Austin Gibbons (USA, born Liverpool) challenges William Robinson, known as 'Cock Robin', at 138lbs, but will not fight him at 142lbs – *Sportsman*.

1893

24 January Dick Burge has just returned from America, having failed to make a match with Jack McAuliffe, who said that he was not prepared to meet the Englishman at 138lbs because his best weight was 133lbs. This was strange, as McAuliffe had weighed 138lbs for his last fight.

15 July Dick Burge challenges Jack McAuliffe to a contest that would settle the 138lbs world title, especially now that neither he nor McAuliffe get get below 136lbs any more – *Sporting Life*.

1894

12 May Martin Denny, the Australian 137lbs lightweight champion, challenges all at the weight – *Sporting Life*.

19 June Billy Myer challenges all England at 137lbs, Harry Nickless, Arthur Valentine and Johnny Boyle (Glasgow) preferred – *Sporting Life*.

11 July Joe Walcott (USA, born Barbados) challenges all England between 136 and 140lbs, up to £500 a side – *Sportsman*.

19 November Jack McAuliffe nc 3 Owen Ziegler (USA), New York City, USA. In a match made at 138lbs, the fight was called off after McAuliffe broke his left hand in the second round. With McAuliffe still recognised as the lightweight champion according to the *New York Herald*, he announced his retirement from the ring the following month.

1895

30 May George 'Kid' Lavigne (Saginaw, Michigan, USA) w pts 20 Jack Everhardt (New Orleans, USA), New York City, USA. Billed for the American 138lbs title, Everhardt, who was claiming the 135lbs American title, was unable to stop Lavigne's charge to the world title.

1896

1 June George 'Kid' Lavigne w rsc 17 Dick Burge, NSC, King Street, London. Billed for the 138lbs world title, it was thought that Burge would have difficulty in getting below 140lbs. In the event, he came in considerably weakened at 136lbs, while the American weighed a comfortable 134lbs, giving him a strong claim to the 135lbs title as well.

13 July Arthur Callan (Wood Green) w rsc 10 Alf Bannister (Camden Town), The Goodwin Gym, Kingsland Road, Shoreditch, London. Despite there being no English championship billing attached, following his defeat of Bannister (137) at 138lbs Callan (136) would have had a fair claim to the title.

27 October George 'Kid' Lavigne w co 24 Jack Everhardt, New York City, USA. Billed for the world 138lbs title, it was reckoned to be one of the greatest fight ever witnessed at that time.

7 December Harry Webster (Kings Cross) w pts 20 Owen Sweeney (Fulham), NSC, King Street, Covent Garden, London. Made at 138lbs, with Webster weighing 134lbs to Sweeney's 132, the former's title claim at the weight emanated from this contest.

17 December Alf Bannister challenges all England at 138lbs – *Sporting Life*.

1898

7 January Spike Sullivan (USA, born Ireland) challenges both Johnny Hughes (Canning Town) and Tom Causer (Bermondsey) at 138lbs, up to £200 a side – *Sporting Life*.

17 March George 'Kid' Lavigne drew 20 'Wilmington' Jack Daly (USA), Cleveland, Ohio, USA. Billed for the world 137lbs lightweight title, Daly looked to have won clearly.

25 April Johnny Hughes w pts 20 Jim Curran (Rotherham), NSC, King Street, Covent Garden, London. Billed for the English

138lbs title, Hughes (135³/₄), who was announced as the champion, was out of action for a year after catching rheumatic fever. Curran weighed 136lbs.

23 May Harry Webster w dis 5 Jack Cullen (Melbourne, Australia), NSC, King Street, Covent Garden, London. Although there was no title billing, Cullen was reported as the Australian champion at the weight, while Webster, who had a claim to the English title, came in at 138lbs.

25 June Jack Daly, through his manager, is claiming the world 137lbs title by default, due to the failure of George 'Kid' Lavigne to sign for a return bout – *Sporting Life*.

29 August Kid McPartland (New York, USA) w pts 25 Jack Daly, New York City, USA. Made at 138lbs, Daly, whose 137lbs claim was on the line, looked to have won.

21 October Jim Curran, now in America, challenges the world between 138 and 140lbs – *Sporting Life*.

2 December Bobby Dobbs (Kentucky, USA) challenges Harry Webster at 138lbs, up to £200 a side and an NSC purse – *Sporting Life*.

20 December Bobby Dobbs challenges the world between 136 and 140lbs – *Sporting Life*.

24 December Jim Curran, now back from the States, challenges the world between 137 and 140lbs, up to £500 a side, Bobby Dobbs, Tom Causer or Johnny Hughes preferred – *Sporting Life*.

1899

24 March Kid McPartland drew 25 Eddie Connolly (Canada, born USA), Made at 138lbs, this was a defence of McPartland's title claim at the weight.

10 April Jewey Cooke challenges all England at 138lbs, up to £200 a side, and put down a £50 deposit with the *Sporting Life* to secure a match.

13 September Johnny Hughes challenges the world at 138lbs, up to £200 a side and an NSC purse – *Sporting Life*.

27 October Alf Bannister challenges all England at 138lbs and is accepted by Charley Esmond, £100 a side and best purse – *Sporting Life*.

1900

17 September Johnny Hughes challenges the world at 138lbs, no one barred – *Sporting Life*. Two days later, his challenge is accepted by Patsy Sweeney (New York, USA, born Ireland) at £100 a side, and also by George 'Elbows' McFadden – *Sporting Life*.

3 October Patsy Sweeney repeated his acceptance of Johnny Hughes' challenge – *Sporting Life*.

1901

18 March Pat Daly challenges Harry Webster or any man in the world of 138lbs, up to £500 a side – *Sporting Life*.

4 September Pat Daly challenges all England at 138lbs, up to £200 a side, Charlie Knock preferred – *Sporting Life*.

9 September Charlie Knock w co 3 Tom Dixon (Newcastle), Standard Theatre, Gateshead. No title billing as such, but Knock (138) claimed the English title on the strength of his win over Dixon (138).

30 October Bill Chester challenges all England between 134 and 140lbs – *Sporting Life*.

31 October Pat Daly challenges all England between 138 and 144lbs, up to £200 a side – *Sporting Life*.

1902

16 January Pat Daly challenges the world at 138lbs, up to £100 a side, and put down a £10 deposit with the *Sporting Life* to secure a match.

15 March Jim Maloney (Hackney) challenges all England over 20 rounds at 138lbs, up to £100 a side and best purse, Johnny Hughes, Pat Daly, Jim Curran and Tom Woodley (Fulham) preferred – *Sporting Life*.

2 May Joe Gans, the world champion between 135 and 138lbs, challenges all England, up to £200 a side, Pat Daly, Jabez White and Johnny Hughes preferred – *Sporting Life*. This was accepted in the 1st May issue by Jim Maloney who, at the same time, accepted the challenge to all England by Herman Miller (Baltimore, USA).

24 June Frank Erne (USA) w co 7 Jim Maloney, NSC, King Street, Covent Garden, London. Following his defeat at the hands of Joe Gans at 135lbs, Erne laid claim to the 'white' lightweight title. Billed for the world 138lbs title, Erne (136¹/₂) defeated Maloney (138), who substituted for Pat Daly.

1 September Jim Maloney states that he has accepted repeated challenges from Spike Sullivan and Pat Daly, but both men keep ignoring him. On 3 September, in the *Sporting Life*, both Bill Chester and Sullivan said that they would be happy to meet

Maloney at 136lbs, but efforts to make the match with Sullivan came to an end when the American fell off a bike and injured himself.

5 September Jim Maloney turned up at the offices of the *Sporting Life* to make a match with Pat Daly, but the latter failed to show and Maloney had the right to claim by forfeit any titles that Daly held or claimed to hold – *Sporting Life*.

14 September On this day a proposed Jim Maloney v Bill Chester fell through when Maloney's backer failed to put down his first deposit – *Sporting Life*.

17 September Joe Gans w co 5 Gus Gardner (USA), Baltimore, USA. Billed for the 138lbs world title over 20 rounds, Gardner was little more than Gans' sparring partner.

14 November Joe Gans w co 14 Charley Seiger (USA), Baltimore, USA. Billed for the 138lbs world title.

1903

3 March Jim Maloney challenges all England at 138lbs, which is repeated on 8 May – *Sporting Life*.

20 April Jabez White w pts 15 Spike Sullivan, NSC, King Street, Covent Garden, USA. Billed for the world 137lbs title, White weighed 136lbs to Sullivan's 137.

4 July Joe Gans w co 5 Buddy King (USA), Butte, USA. Billed for the world 138lbs title, it also involved the coloured title at the weight.

28 August Jack Goldswain (Bermondsey) challenges all England at 138lbs – *Sporting Life*.

8 September Tom Edmunds (Birmingham) challenges all England – *Sporting Life*. The challenge is repeated on 9 November.

30 October Jack Nelson (Newcastle) challenges all England, up to £100 a side – *Sporting Life*.

1904

6 January Joe Gans challenges Jabez White for the world's undisputed 138lbs title over 15 or 20 rounds, up to £200 a side – *Sporting Life*. This was turned down by White who said that he would never fight a coloured man.

13 March Pat Daly challenges all England at 138lbs over 15 or 20 rounds, Jabez White preferred – *Sporting Life*.

28 March Joe Gans w pts 10 Gus Gardner, Saginaw, Michigan, USA. Billed for the 138lbs title.

21 April Joe Gans w pts 15 Sam Bolen (USA), Baltimore, USA. Although not clearly defined, this was thought to be a defence of Gans' 138lbs title.

3 December Jack Nelson w pts 20 Harry Greenfield (Camden Town), Ginnett's Circus, Newcastle. Billed for the English 138lbs title, £50 a side and a £100 purse.

1905

17 February Tom Edmunds challenges all England at 138lbs, which is repeated in the 30th March edition of the *Sporting Life*.

28 October Jabez White challenges the world at 138lbs, £200 a side and best purse, Battling Nelson (USA), Fred Buckland (South Africa) and Bob Russell (Limehouse) preferred – *Sporting Life*.

4 November Bill Wood (Clapton) challenges all England at 138lbs – *Sporting Life*.

1906

9 January Jim Hook (Billingsgate) challenges all England at 138lbs over 15 or 20 rounds, with Tom Edmunds, Jack Meekins (Woolwich), Bill Chester (Mile End) and Jack Nelson preferred – *Sporting Life*.

26 January Bobby Dobbs, the 144lbs world champion, challenges Jabez White at 138lbs, to which White replied that he had never met a coloured man and never would – *Sporting Life*.

23 February Tom Edmunds challenges Jabez White, the English 136lbs champion, to decide the English title at 138lbs – *Sporting Life*.

1 September Charley Hickman (Manchester) challenges all England at 138lbs, up to £50 a side – *Sporting Life*.

1907

17 April Joe Fletcher (Camberwell) challenges Freddie Welsh (Pontypridd) over 15 or 20 rounds, £100 a side and an NSC purse, to decide the English title at 137lbs. On 22 April, Welsh accepted the challenge only if Fletcher would raise the stakes to £200 a side – *Sporting Life*.

27 November Joe Fletcher is claiming to be the 138lbs champion of England – *Sporting Life*.

1909

11 February With the advent of the eight named weight classes on this day, the 138lbs class faded away overnight.

World Champions Since Gloves, 1889-2001

Since I began to carry out extensive research into world championship boxing from the very beginnings of gloved action, I discovered much that needed to be amended regarding the historical listings as we know them, especially prior to the 1920s. Although yet to finalise my researches, despite making considerable changes, the listings are the most comprehensive ever published. Bearing all that in mind, and using a wide range of American newspapers, the aim has been to discover just who had claims, valid or otherwise. Studying the records of all the recognised champions, supplied by Professor Luckett Davis and his team, fights against all opposition have been analysed to produce the ultimate data. Because there were no boxing commissions as such in America prior to the 1920s, the yardstick used to determine valid claims were victories over the leading fighters of the day and recognition given within the newspapers. Only where that criteria has been met have I adjusted previous information.

Championship Status Code:

AU = Austria; AUST = Australia; CALIF = California; CAN = Canada; CLE = Cleveland Boxing Commission; EBU = European Boxing Union; FL = Florida; FR = France; GB = Great Britain; GEO = Georgia; H = Hawaii; IBF = International Boxing Federation; IBU = International Boxing Union; ILL = Illinois; LOUIS = Louisiana; MARY = Maryland; MASS = Massachusetts; MICH = Michigan; NBA = National Boxing Association; NC = North Carolina; NY = New York; PEN = Pennsylvania; SA = South Africa; TBC = Territorial Boxing Commission; USA = United States; WBA = World Boxing Association; WBC = World Boxing Council; WBO = World Boxing Organisation.

Champions in **bold** are accorded universal recognition.

*Undefeated champions (Only relates to universally recognised champions prior to 1962 and thereafter WBA/WBC/IBF/WBO champions. Does not include men who forfeited titles).

Title Holder	Birthplace	Tenure	Status	Title Holder	Birthplace	Tenure	Status
M. Flyweight (105 lbs)				Yoko Gushiken	Japan	1976-1981	WBA
Kyung-Yung Lee*	S Korea	1987	IBF	Freddie Castillo	Mexico	1978	WBC
Hiroki Ioka	Japan	1987-1988	WBC	Sor Vorasingh	Thailand	1978	WBC
Silvio Gamez*	Venezuela	1988-1989	WBA	Sun-Jun Kim	S Korea	1978-1980	WBC
Samuth Sithnaruepol	Thailand	1988-1989	IBF	Shigeo Nakajima	Japan	1980	WBC
Napa Kiatwanchai	Thailand	1988-1989	WBC	Hilario Zapata	Panama	1980-1982	WBC
Bong-Jun Kim	S Korea	1989-1991	WBA	Pedro Flores	Mexico	1981	WBA
Nico Thomas	Indonesia	1989	IBF	Hwan-Jin Kim	S Korea	1981	WBA
Rafael Torres	Dom Republic	1989-1992	WBO	Katsuo Tokashiki	Japan	1981-1983	WBA
Eric Chavez	Philippines	1989-1990	IBF	Amado Ursua	Mexico	1982	WBC
Jum-Hwan Choi	S Korea	1989-1990	WBC	Tadashi Tomori	Japan	1982	WBC
Hideyuki Ohashi	Japan	1990	WBC	Hilario Zapata	Panama	1982-1983	WBC
Fahlan Lukmingkwan	Thailand	1990-1992	IBF	Jung-Koo Chang*	S Korea	1983-1988	WBC
Ricardo Lopez*	Mexico	1990-1997	WBC	Lupe Madera	Mexico	1983-1984	WBA
Hi-Yon Choi	S Korea	1991-1992	WBA	Dodie Penalosa	Philippines	1983-1986	IBF
Manny Melchor	Philippines	1992	IBF	Francisco Quiroz	Dom Republic	1984-1985	WBA
Hideyuki Ohashi	Japan	1992-1993	WBA	Joey Olivo	USA	1985	WBA
Ratanapol Sowvoraphin	Thailand	1992-1996	IBF	Myung-Woo Yuh	S Korea	1985-1991	WBA
Chana Porpaoin	Thailand	1993-1995	WBA	Jum-Hwan Choi	S Korea	1986-1988	IBF
Paul Weir*	Scotland	1993-1994	WBO	Tacy Macalos	Philippines	1988-1989	IBF
Alex Sanchez	Puerto Rico	1993-1997	WBO	German Torres	Mexico	1988-1989	WBC
Rosendo Alvarez	Nicaragua	1995-1996	WBA	Yul-Woo Lee	S Korea	1989	WBC
Ratanapol Sowvoraphin	Thailand	1996-1997	IBF	Muangchai Kitikasem	Thailand	1989-1990	IBF
Ricardo Lopez*	Mexico	1997-1998	WBC/WBO	Jose de Jesus	Puerto Rico	1989-1992	WBO
Zolani Petelo*	S Africa	1997-2000	IBF	Humberto Gonzalez	Mexico	1989-1990	WBC
Ricardo Lopez*	Mexico	1998	WBC	Michael Carbajal*	USA	1990-1993	IBF
Eric Jamili	Philippines	1998	WBO	Rolando Pascua	Philippines	1990-1991	WBC
Kermin Guardia	Colombia	1998-	WBO	Melchor Cob Castro	Mexico	1991	WBC
Ricardo Lopez*	Mexico	1998-1999	WBA/WBC	Humberto Gonzalez	Mexico	1991-1993	WBC
Wandee Chor Chareon	Thailand	1999-2000	WBC	Hiroki Ioka	Japan	1991-1992	WBA
Noel Arambulet	Venezuela	1999-2000	WBA	Josue Camacho	Puerto Rico	1992-1994	WBO
Jose Antonio Aguirre	Mexico	2000-	WBC	Myung-Woo Yuh*	S Korea	1992-1993	WBA
Jomo Gamboa	Philippines	2000	WBA	Michael Carbajal	USA	1993-1994	IBF/WBC
Keitaro Hoshino	Japan	2000-2001	WBA	Silvio Gamez	Venezuela	1993-1995	WBA
Chana Porpaoin	Thailand	2001-	WBA	Humberto Gonzalez	Mexico	1994-1995	WBC/IBF
Roberto Levya	Mexico	2001-	IBF	Michael Carbajal*	USA	1994	WBO
				Paul Weir	Scotland	1994-1995	WBO
L. Flyweight (108 lbs)				Hi-Yong Choi	S Korea	1995-1996	WBA
Franco Udella	Italy	1975	WBC	Saman Sorjaturong*	Thailand	1995	WBC/IBF
Jaime Rios	Panama	1975-1976	WBA	Jacob Matlala*	South Africa	1995-1997	WBO
Luis Estaba	Venezuela	1975-1978	WBC	Saman Sorjaturong	Thailand	1995-1999	WBC
Juan Guzman	Dom Republic	1976	WBA	Carlos Murillo	Panama	1996	WBA

Title Holder	Birthplace	Tenure	Status
Michael Carbajal	USA	1996-1997	IBF
Keiji Yamaguchi	Japan	1996	WBA
Pichitnoi Chor Siriwat	Thailand	1996-2000	WBA
Mauricio Pastrana	Colombia	1997-1998	IBF
Jesus Chong	Mexico	1997	WBO
Melchor Cob Castro	Mexico	1997-1998	WBO
Mauricio Pastrana	Colombia	1997-1998	IBF
Juan Domingo Cordoba	Argentina	1998	WBO
Jorge Arce	Mexico	1998-1999	WBO
Will Grigsby	USA	1998-1999	IBF
Michael Carbajal*	USA	1999-2000	WBO
Ricardo Lopez	Mexico	1999-	IBF
Yo-Sam Choi	S Korea	1999-	WBC
Masibuleke Makepula*	S Africa	2000	WBO
Will Grigsby	USA	2000	WBO
Beibis Mendoza	Colombia	2000-2001	WBA
Rosendo Alvarez	Nicaragua	2001-	WBA
Nelson Dieppa	Puerto Rico	2001-	WBO

Flyweight (112 lbs)

Title Holder	Birthplace	Tenure	Status
Johnny Coulon	Canada	1910	USA
Sid Smith	England	1911-1913	GB
Sid Smith	England	1913	GB/IBU
Bill Ladbury	England	1913-1914	GB/IBU
Percy Jones	Wales	1914	GB/IBU
Tancy Lee	Scotland	1915	GB/IBU
Joe Symonds	England	1915-1916	GB/IBU
Jimmy Wilde	Wales	1916	GB/IBU
Jimmy Wilde	Wales	1916-1923	
Pancho Villa*	Philippines	1923-1925	
Fidel la Barba	USA	1925-1927	NBA/CALIF
Fidel la Barba*	USA	1927	
Johnny McCoy	USA	1927-1928	CALIF
Izzy Schwartz	USA	1927-1929	NY
Frenchy Belanger	Canada	1927-1928	NBA
Newsboy Brown	Russia	1928	CALIF
Frankie Genaro	USA	1928-1929	NBA
Emile Pladner	France	1929	NBA/IBU
Frankie Genaro	USA	1929-1931	NBA/IBU
Midget Wolgast	USA	1930-1935	NY
Young Perez	Tunisia	1931-1932	NBA/IBU
Jackie Brown	England	1932-1935	NBA/IBU
Jackie Brown	England	1935	GB/NBA
Benny Lynch	Scotland	1935-1937	GB/NBA
Small Montana	Philippines	1935-1937	NY/CALIF
Valentin Angelmann	France	1936-1938	IBU
Peter Kane*	England	1938-1939	NBA/NY/GB/IBU
Little Dado	Philippines	1938-1939	CALIF
Little Dado	Philippines	1939-1943	NBA/CALIF
Jackie Paterson	Scotland	1943-1947	
Jackie Paterson	Scotland	1947-1948	GB/NY
Rinty Monaghan	Ireland	1947-1948	NBA
Rinty Monaghan*	Ireland	1948-1950	
Terry Allen	England	1950	
Dado Marino	Hawaii	1950-1952	
Yoshio Shirai	Japan	1952-1954	
Pascual Perez	Argentina	1954-1960	
Pone Kingpetch	Thailand	1960-1962	
Fighting Harada	Japan	1962-1963	
Pone Kingpetch	Thailand	1963	
Hiroyuki Ebihara	Japan	1963-1964	
Pone Kingpetch	Thailand	1964-1965	
Salvatore Burruni	Italy	1965	
Salvatore Burruni	Italy	1965-1966	WBC
Horacio Accavallo*	Argentina	1966-1968	WBA
Walter McGowan	Scotland	1966	WBC
Chartchai Chionoi	Thailand	1966-1969	WBC
Efren Torres	Mexico	1969-1970	WBC
Hiroyuki Ebihara	Japan	1969	WBA
Bernabe Villacampo	Philippines	1969-1970	WBA
Chartchai Chionoi	Thailand	1970	WBC
Berkrerk Chartvanchai	Thailand	1970	WBA
Masao Ohba*	Japan	1970-1973	WBA
Erbito Salavarria	Philippines	1970-1971	WBC

Title Holder	Birthplace	Tenure	Status
Betulio Gonzalez	Venezuela	1971-1972	WBC
Venice Borkorsor*	Thailand	1972-1973	WBC
Chartchai Chionoi	Thailand	1973-1974	WBA
Betulio Gonzalez	Venezuela	1973-1974	WBC
Shoji Oguma	Japan	1974-1975	WBC
Susumu Hanagata	Japan	1974-1975	WBA
Miguel Canto	Mexico	1975-1979	WBC
Erbito Salavarria	Philippines	1975-1976	WBA
Alfonso Lopez	Panama	1976	WBA
Guty Espadas	Mexico	1976-1978	WBA
Betulio Gonzalez	Venezuela	1978-1979	WBA
Chan-Hee Park	S Korea	1979-1980	WBC
Luis Ibarra	Panama	1979-1980	WBA
Tae-Shik Kim	S Korea	1980	WBA
Shoji Oguma	Japan	1980-1981	WBC
Peter Mathebula	S Africa	1980-1981	WBA
Santos Laciar	Argentina	1981	WBA
Antonio Avelar	Mexico	1981-1982	WBC
Luis Ibarra	Panama	1981	WBA
Juan Herrera	Mexico	1981-1982	WBA
Prudencio Cardona	Colombia	1982	WBC
Santos Laciar*	Argentina	1982-1985	WBA
Freddie Castillo	Mexico	1982	WBC
Eleonicio Mercedes	Dom Republic	1982-1983	WBC
Charlie Magri	Tunisia	1983	WBC
Frank Cedeno	Philippines	1983-1984	WBC
Soon-Chun Kwon	S Korea	1983-1985	IBF
Koji Kobayashi	Japan	1984	WBC
Gabriel Bernal	Mexico	1984	WBC
Sot Chitalada	Thailand	1984-1988	WBC
Hilario Zapata	Panama	1985-1987	WBA
Chong-Kwan Chung	S Korea	1985-1986	IBF
Bi-Won Chung	S Korea	1986	IBF
Hi-Sup Shin	S Korea	1986-1987	IBF
Fidel Bassa	Colombia	1987-1989	WBA
Dodie Penalosa	Philippines	1987	IBF
Chang-Ho Choi	S Korea	1987-1988	IBF
Rolando Bohol	Philippines	1988	IBF
Yong-Kang Kim	S Korea	1988-1989	WBC
Duke McKenzie	England	1988-1989	IBF
Elvis Alvarez*	Colombia	1989	WBO
Sot Chitalada	Thailand	1989-1991	WBC
Dave McAuley	Ireland	1989-1992	IBF
Jesus Rojas	Venezuela	1989-1900	WBA
Yukihito Tamakuma	Japan	1990-1991	WBA
Isidro Perez	Mexico	1990-1992	WBO
Yul-Woo Lee	S Korea	1990	WBA
Muangchai Kitikasem	Thailand	1991-1992	WBC
Elvis Alvarez	Colombia	1991	WBA
Yong-Kang Kim	S Korea	1991-1992	WBA
Pat Clinton	Scotland	1992-1993	WBO
Rodolfo Blanco	Colombia	1992	IBF
Yuri Arbachakov	Russia	1992-1997	WBC
Aquiles Guzman	Venezuela	1992	WBA
Pichit Sitbangprachan*	Thailand	1992-1994	IBF
David Griman	Venezuela	1992-1994	WBA
Jacob Matlala	S Africa	1993-1995	WBO
Saen Sorploenchit	Thailand	1994-1996	WBA
Alberto Jimenez	Mexico	1995-1996	WBO
Francisco Tejedor	Colombia	1995	IBF
Danny Romero*	USA	1995-1996	IBF
Mark Johnson*	USA	1996-1998	IBF
Jose Bonilla	Venezuela	1996-1998	WBA
Carlos Salazar	Argentina	1996-1998	WBO
Chatchai Sasakul	Thailand	1997-1998	WBC
Hugo Soto	Argentina	1998-1999	WBA
Ruben Sanchez	Mexico	1998-1999	WBO
Manny Pacquiao	Philippines	1998-1999	WBC
Silvio Gamez	Venezuela	1999	WBA
Irene Pacheco	Colombia	1999-	IBF
Jose Antonio Lopez	Spain	1999	WBO
Sornpichai Pisanurachan	Thailand	1999-2000	WBA
Medgoen Singsurat	Thailand	1999-2000	WBC
Isidro Garcia	Mexico	1999-2000	WBO

Title Holder	Birthplace	Tenure	Status
Malcolm Tunacao	Philippines	2000-2001	WBC
Eric Morel	USA	2000-	WBA
Fernando Montiel	Mexico	2000-	WBO
Pongsaklek Wonjongkam	Thailand	2001-	WBC

S. Flyweight (115 lbs)

Title Holder	Birthplace	Tenure	Status
Rafael Orono	Venezuela	1980-1981	WBC
Chul-Ho Kim	S Korea	1981-1982	WBC
Gustavo Ballas	Argentina	1981	WBA
Rafael Pedroza	Panama	1981-1982	WBA
Jiro Watanabe	Japan	1982-1984	WBA
Rafael Orono	Venezuela	1982-1983	WBC
Payao Poontarat	Thailand	1983-1984	WBC
Joo-Do Chun	S Korea	1983-1985	IBF
Jiro Watanabe	Japan	1984-1986	WBC
Kaosai Galaxy*	Thailand	1984-1992	WBA
Elly Pical	Indonesia	1985-1986	IBF
Cesar Polanco	Dom Republic	1986	IBF
Gilberto Roman	Mexico	1986-1987	WBC
Elly Pical	Indonesia	1986-1987	IBF
Santos Laciar	Argentina	1987	WBC
Tae-Il Chang	S Korea	1987	IBF
Jesus Rojas	Colombia	1987-1988	WBC
Elly Pical	Indonesia	1987-1989	IBF
Gilberto Roman	Mexico	1988-1989	WBC
Jose Ruiz	Puerto Rico	1989-1992	WBO
Juan Polo Perez	Colombia	1989-1990	IBF
Nana Yaw Konadu	Ghana	1989-1990	WBC
Sung-Il Moon	S Korea	1990-1993	WBC
Robert Quiroga	USA	1990-1993	IBF
Jose Quirino	Mexico	1992	WBO
Katsuya Onizuka	Japan	1992-1994	WBA
Johnny Bredahl	Denmark	1992-1994	WBO
Julio Cesar Borboa	Mexico	1993-1994	IBF
Jose Luis Bueno	Mexico	1993-1994	WBC
Hiroshi Kawashima	Japan	1994-1997	WBC
Harold Grey	Colombia	1994-1995	IBF
Hyung-Chul Lee	S Korea	1994-1995	WBA
Johnny Tapia*	USA	1994-1997	WBO
Alimi Goitia	Venezuela	1995-1996	WBA
Carlos Salazar	Argentina	1995-1996	IBF
Harold Grey	Colombia	1996	IBF
Yokthai Sith-Oar	Thailand	1996-1997	WBA
Danny Romero	USA	1996-1997	IBF
Gerry Penalosa	Philippines	1997-1998	WBC
Johnny Tapia*	USA	1997-1998	IBF/WBO
Satoshi Iida	Japan	1997-1998	WBA
In-Joo Cho	S Korea	1998-2000	WBC
Victor Godoi	Argentina	1998-1999	WBO
Jesus Rojas	Venezuela	1998-1999	WBA
Mark Johnson	USA	1999-2000	IBF
Diego Morales	Mexico	1999	WBO
Hideki Todaka	Japan	1999-2000	WBA
Adonis Rivas	Nicaragua	1999-2001	WBO
Felix Machado	Venezuela	2000-	IBF
Masamori Tokuyama	Japan	2000-	WBC
Silvio Gamez	Venezuela	2000-2001	WBA
Celes Kobayashi	Japan	2001-	WBA
Pedro Alcazar	Panama	2001-	WBO

Bantamweight (118 lbs)

Title Holder	Birthplace	Tenure	Status
Tommy Kelly	USA	1889	
George Dixon	Canada	1889-1890	
Chappie Moran	England	1889-1890	
Tommy Kelly	USA	1890-1892	
Billy Plimmer	England	1892-1895	
Pedlar Palmer	England	1895-1899	
Terry McGovern	USA	1899	USA
Pedlar Palmer	England	1899-1900	GB
Terry McGovern*	USA	1899-1900	
Clarence Forbes	USA	1900	
Johnny Reagan	USA	1900-1902	
Harry Ware	England	1900-1902	GB
Harry Harris	USA	1901	

Title Holder	Birthplace	Tenure	Status
Harry Forbes	USA	1901-1902	
Kid McFadden	USA	1901	
Dan Dougherty	USA	1901	
Andrew Tokell	England	1902	GB
Harry Ware	England	1902	GB
Harry Forbes	USA	1902-1903	USA
Joe Bowker	England	1902-1904	GB
Frankie Neil	USA	1903-1904	USA
Joe Bowker*	England	1904-1905	
Frankie Neil	USA	1905	USA
Digger Stanley	England	1905-1907	
Owen Moran	England	1905-1907	
Jimmy Walsh	USA	1905-1908	USA
Owen Moran	England	1907	GB
Monte Attell	USA	1908-1910	
Jimmy Walsh	USA	1908-1911	
Digger Stanley	England	1909-1912	GB
Frankie Conley	Italy	1910-1911	
Johnny Coulon	Canada	1910-1911	
Monte Attell	USA	1910-1911	
Johnny Coulon	Canada	1911-1913	USA
Charles Ledoux	France	1912-1913	GB/IBU
Eddie Campi	USA	1913-1914	
Johnny Coulon	Canada	1913-1914	
Kid Williams	Denmark	1913-1914	
Kid Williams	Denmark	1914-1915	
Kid Williams	Denmark	1915-1917	
Johnny Ertle	USA	1915-1918	
Pete Herman	USA	1917-1919	
Pal Moore	USA	1918-1919	
Pete Herman	USA	1919-1920	
Joe Lynch	USA	1920-1921	
Pete Herman	USA	1921	
Johnny Buff	USA	1921-1922	
Joe Lynch	USA	1922-1923	
Joe Lynch	USA	1923-1924	NBA
Joe Burman	England	1923	NY
Abe Goldstein	USA	1923-1924	NY
Joe Lynch	USA	1924	
Abe Goldstein	USA	1924	
Eddie Martin	USA	1924-1925	
Charley Rosenberg	USA	1925-1926	
Charley Rosenberg	USA	1926-1927	NY
Bud Taylor*	USA	1926-1928	NBA
Bushy Graham*	Italy	1928-1929	NY
Al Brown	Panama	1929-1931	
Al Brown	Panama	1931	NY/IBU
Pete Sanstol	Norway	1931	CAN
Al Brown	Panama	1931-1933	
Al Brown	Panama	1933-1934	NY/NBA/IBU
Speedy Dado	Philippines	1933	CALIF
Baby Casanova	Mexico	1933-1934	CALIF
Sixto Escobar	Puerto Rico	1934	CAN
Sixto Escobar	Puerto Rico	1934-1935	NBA
Al Brown	Panama	1934-1935	NY/IBU
Lou Salica	USA	1935	CALIF
Baltazar Sangchilli	Spain	1935-1938	IBU
Lou Salica	USA	1935	NBA/NY
Sixto Escobar	Puerto Rico	1935-1937	NBA/NY
Harry Jeffra	USA	1937-1938	NY/NBA
Sixto Escobar	Puerto Rico	1938	NY/NBA
Al Brown	Panama	1938	IBU
Sixto Escobar	Puerto Rico	1938-1939	
George Pace	USA	1939-1940	NBA
Lou Salica	USA	1939	CALIF
Tony Olivera	USA	1939-1940	CALIF
Little Dado	Philippines	1940-1941	CALIF
Lou Salica	USA	1940-1942	NY/NBA
Lou Salica	USA	1941	
Kenny Lindsay	Canada	1941	CAN
Lou Salica	USA	1941-1942	
Lou Salica	USA	1942	NY
David Kui Kong Young	Hawaii	1942-1943	H
Manuel Ortiz	USA	1942-1943	NBA

Title Holder	Birthplace	Tenure	Status
Manuel Ortiz	USA	1943-1945	NY/NBA
Kui Kong Young	Hawaii	1943	TBC
Rush Dalma	Philippines	1943-1945	TBC
Manuel Ortiz	USA	1945-1947	
Harold Dade	USA	1947	
Manuel Ortiz	USA	1947-1950	
Vic Toweel	S Africa	1950-1952	
Jimmy Carruthers*	Australia	1952-1954	
Robert Cohen	Algeria	1954	
Robert Cohen	Algeria	1954-1956	NY/EBU
Raton Macias	Mexico	1955-1957	NBA
Mario D'Agata	Italy	1956-1957	NY/EBU
Alphonse Halimi	Algeria	1957	NY/EBU
Alphonse Halimi	Algeria	1957-1959	
Joe Becerra*	Mexico	1959-1960	
Alphonse Halimi	Algeria	1960-1961	EBU
Eder Jofre	Brazil	1960-1962	NBA
Johnny Caldwell	Ireland	1961-1962	EBU
Eder Jofre	Brazil	1962-1965	
Fighting Harada	Japan	1965-1968	
Lionel Rose	Australia	1968-1969	
Ruben Olivares	Mexico	1969-1970	
Chuchu Castillo	Mexico	1970-1971	
Ruben Olivares	Mexico	1971-1972	
Rafael Herrera	Mexico	1972	
Enrique Pinder	Panama	1972	
Enrique Pinder	Panama	1972-1973	WBC
Romeo Anaya	Mexico	1973	WBA
Rafael Herrera	Mexico	1973-1974	WBC
Arnold Taylor	S Africa	1973-1974	WBA
Soo-Hwan Hong	S Korea	1974-1975	WBA
Rodolfo Martinez	Mexico	1974-1976	WBC
Alfonso Zamora	Mexico	1975-1977	WBA
Carlos Zarate	Mexico	1976-1979	WBC
Jorge Lujan	Panama	1977-1980	WBA
Lupe Pintor*	Mexico	1979-1983	WBC
Julian Solis	Puerto Rico	1980	WBA
Jeff Chandler	USA	1980-1984	WBA
Albert Davila	USA	1983-1985	WBC
Richard Sandoval	USA	1984-1986	WBA
Satoshi Shingaki	Japan	1984-1985	IBF
Jeff Fenech*	Australia	1985-1987	IBF
Daniel Zaragoza	Mexico	1985	WBC
Miguel Lora	Colombia	1985-1988	WBC
Gaby Canizales	USA	1986	WBA
Bernardo Pinango*	Venezuela	1986-1987	WBA
Takuya Muguruma	Japan	1987	WBA
Kelvin Seabrooks	USA	1987-1988	IBF
Chang-Yung Park	S Korea	1987	WBA
Wilfredo Vasquez	Puerto Rico	1987-1988	WBA
Kaokor Galaxy	Thailand	1988	WBA
Orlando Canizales*	USA	1988-1994	IBF
Sung-Il Moon	S Korea	1988-1989	WBA
Raul Perez	Mexico	1988-1991	WBC
Israel Contrerras*	Venezuela	1989-1991	WBO
Kaokor Galaxy	Thailand	1989	WBA
Luisito Espinosa	Philippines	1989-1991	WBA
Greg Richardson	USA	1991	WBC
Gaby Canizales	USA	1991	WBO
Duke McKenzie	England	1991-1992	WBO
Joichiro Tatsuyushi*	Japan	1991-1992	WBC
Israel Contrerras	Venezuela	1991-1992	WBA
Eddie Cook	USA	1992	WBA
Victor Rabanales	Mexico	1992-1993	WBC
Rafael del Valle	Puerto Rico	1992-1994	WBO
Jorge Elicier Julio	Colombia	1992-1993	WBA
Il-Jung Byun	S Korea	1993	WBC
Junior Jones	USA	1993-1994	WBA
Yasuei Yakushiji	Japan	1993-1995	WBC
John Michael Johnson	USA	1994	WBA
Daorung Chuwatana	Thailand	1994-1995	WBA
Alfred Kotey	Ghana	1994-1995	WBO
Harold Mestre	Colombia	1995	IBF

Title Holder	Birthplace	Tenure	Status
Mbulelo Botile	S Africa	1995-1997	IBF
Wayne McCullough	Ireland	1995-1997	WBC
Veeraphol Sahaprom	Thailand	1995-1996	WBA
Daniel Jimenez	Puerto Rico	1995-1996	WBO
Nana Yaw Konadu	Ghana	1996	WBA
Robbie Regan*	Wales	1996-1998	WBO
Daorung Chuwatana	Thailand	1996-1997	WBA
Sirimongkol Singmanassak	Thailand	1997	WBC
Nana Yaw Konadu	Ghana	1997-1998	WBA
Tim Austin	USA	1997-	IBF
Joichiro Tatsuyoshi	Japan	1997-1998	WBC
Jorge Elicier Julio	Colombia	1998-2000	WBO
Johnny Tapia	USA	1998-1999	WBA
Veeraphol Sahaprom	Thailand	1998-	WBC
Paulie Ayala	USA	1999-	WBA
Johnny Tapia*	USA	2000	WBO
Mauricio Martinez	Panama	2000-	WBO

S. Bantamweight (122 lbs)

Title Holder	Birthplace	Tenure	Status
Rigoberto Riasco	Panama	1976	WBC
Royal Kobayashi	Japan	1976	WBC
Dong-Kyun Yum	S Korea	1976-1977	WBC
Wilfredo Gomez*	Puerto Rico	1977-1983	WBC
Soo-Hwan Hong	S Korea	1977-1978	WBA
Ricardo Cardona	Colombia	1978-1980	WBA
Leo Randolph	USA	1980	WBA
Sergio Palma	Argentina	1980-1982	WBA
Leonardo Cruz	Dom Republic	1982-1984	WBA
Jaime Garza	USA	1983-1984	WBC
Bobby Berna	Philippines	1983-1984	IBF
Loris Stecca	Italy	1984	WBA
Seung-In Suh	S Korea	1984-1985	IBF
Victor Callejas	Puerto Rico	1984-1986	WBA
Juan Meza	Mexico	1984-1985	WBC
Ji-Won Kim*	S Korea	1985-1986	IBF
Lupe Pintor	Mexico	1985-1986	WBC
Samart Payakarun	Thailand	1986-1987	WBC
Louie Espinosa	USA	1987	WBA
Seung-Hoon Lee*	S Korea	1987-1988	IBF
Jeff Fenech*	Australia	1987-1988	WBC
Julio Gervacio	Dom Republic	1987-1988	WBA
Bernardo Pinango	Venezuela	1988	WBA
Daniel Zaragoza	Mexico	1988-1990	WBC
Jose Sanabria	Venezuela	1988-1989	IBF
Juan J. Estrada	Mexico	1988-1989	WBA
Fabrice Benichou	Spain	1989-1990	IBF
Kenny Mitchell	USA	1989	WBO
Valerio Nati	Italy	1989-1990	WBO
Jesus Salud	USA	1989-1990	WBA
Welcome Ncita	S Africa	1990-1992	IBF
Paul Banke	USA	1990	WBC
Orlando Fernandez	Puerto Rico	1990-1991	WBO
Luis Mendoza	Colombia	1990-1991	WBA
Pedro Decima	Argentina	1990-1991	WBC
Kiyoshi Hatanaka	Japan	1991	WBC
Jesse Benavides	USA	1991-1992	WBO
Daniel Zaragoza	Mexico	1991-1992	WBC
Raul Perez	Mexico	1991-1992	WBA
Thierry Jacob	France	1992	WBC
Wilfredo Vasquez	Puerto Rico	1992-1995	WBA
Tracy Harris Patterson	USA	1992-1994	WBC
Duke McKenzie	England	1992-1993	WBO
Kennedy McKinney	USA	1992-1994	IBF
Daniel Jimenez	Puerto Rico	1993-1995	WBO
Vuyani Bungu *	S Africa	1994-1999	IBF
Hector Acero-Sanchez	Dom Republic	1994-1995	WBC
Marco Antonio Barrera	Mexico	1995-1996	WBO
Antonio Cermeno *	Venezuela	1995-1997	WBA
Daniel Zaragoza	Mexico	1995-1997	WBC
Junior Jones	USA	1996-1997	WBO
Erik Morales*	USA	1997-2000	WBC
Kennedy McKinney*	USA	1997-1998	WBO
Enrique Sanchez	Mexico	1998	WBA

Title Holder	Birthplace	Tenure	Status
Marco Antonio Barrera	Mexico	1998-2000	WBO
Nestor Garza	Mexico	1998-2000	WBA
Lehlohonola Ledwaba	S Africa	1999-2001	IBF
Erik Morales	USA	2000	WBC/WBO
Erik Morales*	USA	2000	WBC
Marco Antonio Barrera*	Mexico	2000-2001	WBO
Clarence Adams	USA	2000-	WBA
Willie Jorrin	USA	2000-	WBC
Manny Pacquiao	Philippines	2001-	IBF
Agapito Sanchez	Dom Republic	2001-	WBO

Featherweight (126 lbs)

Title Holder	Birthplace	Tenure	Status
Ike Weir	Ireland	1889-1890	
Billy Murphy	New Zealand	1890-1893	
George Dixon	Canada	1890-1893	
Young Griffo	Australia	1890-1893	
Johnny Griffin	USA	1891-1893	
Solly Smith	USA	1893	
George Dixon	Canada	1893-1896	
Solly Smith	USA	1896-1898	
Frank Erne	USA	1896-1897	
George Dixon	Canada	1896-1900	
Harry Greenfield	England	1897-1899	
Ben Jordan	England	1897-1899	
Will Curley	England	1897-1899	
Dave Sullivan	Ireland	1898	
Ben Jordan	England	1899-1905	GB
Eddie Santry	USA	1899-1900	
Terry McGovern	USA	1900	
Terry McGovern	USA	1900-1901	USA
Young Corbett II	USA	1901-1903	USA
Eddie Hanlon	USA	1903	
Young Corbett II	USA	1903-1904	
Abe Attell	USA	1903-1904	
Abe Attell	USA	1904-1911	USA
Joe Bowker	England	1905-1907	GB
Jim Driscoll	Wales	1907-1912	GB
Abe Attell	USA	1911-1912	
Joe Coster	USA	1911	
Joe Rivers	Mexico	1911	
Johnny Kilbane	USA	1911-1912	
Jim Driscoll*	Wales	1912-1913	GB/IBU
Johnny Kilbane	USA	1912-1922	USA
Johnny Kilbane	USA	1922-1923	NBA
Johnny Dundee	Italy	1922-1923	NY
Eugene Criqui	France	1923	
Johnny Dundee*	Italy	1923-1924	
Kid Kaplan	Russia	1925	NY
Kid Kaplan*	Russia	1925-1926	
Honeyboy Finnegan	USA	1926-1927	MASS
Benny Bass	Russia	1927-1928	NBA
Tony Canzoneri	USA	1927-1928	NY
Tony Canzoneri	USA	1928	
Andre Routis	France	1928-1929	
Bat Battalino	USA	1929-1932	
Bat Battalino	USA	1932	NBA
Tommy Paul	USA	1932-1933	NBA
Kid Chocolate*	Cuba	1932-1934	NY
Baby Arizmendi	Mexico	1932-1933	CALIF
Freddie Miller	USA	1933-1936	NBA
Baby Arizmendi	Mexico	1934-1935	NY
Baby Arizmendi	Mexico	1935-1936	NY/MEX
Baby Arizmendi	Mexico	1936	MEX
Petey Sarron	USA	1936-1937	NBA
Henry Armstrong	USA	1936-1937	CALIF/MEX
Mike Belloise	USA	1936	NY
Maurice Holtzer	France	1937-1938	IBU
Henry Armstrong*	USA	1937-1938	NBA/NY
Leo Rodak	USA	1938	MARY
Joey Archibald	USA	1938-1939	NY
Leo Rodak	USA	1938-1939	NBA
Joey Archibald	USA	1939-1940	
Joey Archibald	USA	1940	NY

Title Holder	Birthplace	Tenure	Status
Petey Scalzo	USA	1940-1941	NBA
Jimmy Perrin	USA	1940	LOUIS
Harry Jeffra	USA	1940-1941	NY/MARY
Joey Archibald	USA	1941	NY/MARY
Richie Lemos	USA	1941	NBA
Chalky Wright	Mexico	1941-1942	NY/MARY
Jackie Wilson	USA	1941-1943	NBA
Willie Pep	USA	1942-1946	NY
Jackie Callura	Canada	1943	NBA
Phil Terranova	USA	1943-1944	NBA
Sal Bartolo	USA	1944-1946	NBA
Willie Pep	USA	1946-1948	
Sandy Saddler	USA	1948-1949	
Willie Pep	USA	1949-1950	
Sandy Saddler*	USA	1950-1957	
Hogan Kid Bassey	Nigeria	1957-1959	
Davey Moore	USA	1959-1963	
Sugar Ramos	Cuba	1963-1964	
Vicente Saldivar*	Mexico	1964-1967	
Raul Rojas	USA	1967	CALIF
Howard Winstone	Wales	1968	WBC
Raul Rojas	USA	1968	WBA
Johnny Famechon	France	1968-1969	AUST
Jose Legra	Cuba	1968-1969	WBC
Shozo Saijyo	Japan	1968-1971	WBA
Johnny Famechon	France	1969-1970	WBC
Vicente Saldivar	Mexico	1970	WBC

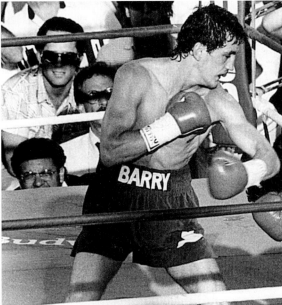

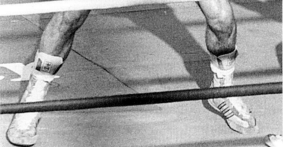

Barry McGuigan, Britain's WBA world featherweight champion, 1985-1986

Title Holder	Birthplace	Tenure	Status
Kuniaki Shibata	Japan	1970-1972	WBC
Antonio Gomez	Venezuela	1971-1972	WBA
Clemente Sanchez	Mexico	1972	WBC
Ernesto Marcel*	Panama	1972-1974	WBA
Jose Legra	Cuba	1972-1973	WBC
Eder Jofre	Brazil	1973-1974	WBC
Ruben Olivares	Mexico	1974	WBA
Bobby Chacon	USA	1974-1975	WBC
Alexis Arguello*	Nicaragua	1974-1977	WBA
Ruben Olivares	Mexico	1975	WBC
David Kotey	Ghana	1975-1976	WBC
Danny Lopez	USA	1976-1980	WBC
Rafael Ortega	Panama	1977	WBA
Cecilio Lastra	Spain	1977-1978	WBA
Eusebio Pedroza	Panama	1978-1985	WBA
Salvador Sanchez*	Mexico	1980-1982	WBC
Juan Laporte	Puerto Rico	1982-1984	WBC
Min-Keun Oh	S Korea	1984-1985	IBF
Wilfredo Gomez	Puerto Rico	1984	WBC
Azumah Nelson*	Ghana	1984-1988	WBC
Barry McGuigan	Ireland	1985-1986	WBA
Ki-Yung Chung	S Korea	1985-1986	IBF
Steve Cruz	USA	1986-1987	WBA
Antonio Rivera	Puerto Rico	1986-1988	IBF
Antonio Esparragoza	Venezuela	1987-1991	WBA
Calvin Grove	USA	1988	IBF
Jeff Fenech*	Australia	1988-1989	WBC
Jorge Paez*	Mexico	1988-1990	IBF
Maurizio Stecca	Italy	1989	WBO
Louie Espinosa	USA	1989-1990	WBO
Jorge Paez*	Mexico	1990-1991	IBF/WBO
Marcos Villasana	Mexico	1990-1991	WBC
Kyun-Yung Park	S Korea	1991-1993	WBA
Troy Dorsey	USA	1991	IBF
Maurizio Stecca	Italy	1991-1992	WBO
Manuel Medina	Mexico	1991-1993	IBF
Paul Hodkinson	England	1991-1993	WBC
Colin McMillan	England	1992	WBO
Ruben Palacio	Colombia	1992-1993	WBO
Tom Johnson	USA	1993-1997	IBF
Steve Robinson	Wales	1993-1995	WBO
Gregorio Vargas	Mexico	1993	WBC
Kevin Kelley	USA	1993-1995	WBC
Eloy Rojas	Venezuela	1993-1996	WBA
Alejandro Gonzalez	Mexico	1995	WBC
Manuel Medina	Mexico	1995	WBC
Prince Naseem Hamed*	England	1995-1997	WBO
Luisito Espinosa	Philippines	1995-1999	WBA
Wilfredo Vasquez	Puerto Rico	1996-1998	WBA
Prince Naseem Hamed *	England	1997	WBO/IBF
Prince Naseem Hamed*	England	1997-1999	WBO
Hector Lizarraga	Mexico	1997-1998	IBF
Freddie Norwood	USA	1998	WBA
Manuel Medina	Mexico	1998-1999	IBF
Antonio Cermeno	Venezuela	1998-1999	WBA
Cesar Soto	Mexico	1999	WBC
Freddie Norwood	USA	1999-2000	WBA
Prince Naseem Hamed	England	1999-2000	WBC/WBO
Paul Ingle	England	1999-2000	IBF
Prince Naseem Hamed*	England	2000	WBO
Gustavo Espadas	Mexico	2000-2001	WBC
Derrick Gainer	USA	2000-	WBA
Mbulelo Botile	S Africa	2000-2001	IBF
Istvan Kovacs	Hungary	2001	WBO
Erik Morales	USA	2001-	WBC
Frankie Toledo	USA	2001-	IBF
Julio Pablo Chacon	Argentina	2001-	WBO

S. Featherweight (130 lbs)

Title Holder	Birthplace	Tenure	Status
Johnny Dundee	Italy	1921-1923	NY
Jack Bernstein	USA	1923	NY
Jack Bernstein	USA	1923	NBA/NY
Johnny Dundee	Italy	1923-1924	NBA/NY
Kid Sullivan	USA	1924-1925	NBA/NY
Mike Ballerino	USA	1925	NBA/NY
Tod Morgan	USA	1925-1929	NBA/NY
Benny Bass	Russia	1929-1930	NBA/NY
Benny Bass	Russia	1930-1931	NBA
Kid Chocolate	Cuba	1931-1933	NBA
Frankie Klick	USA	1933-1934	NBA
Sandy Saddler	USA	1949-1950	NBA
Sandy Saddler	USA	1950-1951	CLE
Harold Gomes	USA	1959-1960	NBA
Flash Elorde	Philippines	1960-1962	NBA
Flash Elorde	Philippines	1962-1967	WBA
Raul Rojas	USA	1967	CALIF
Yoshiaki Numata	Japan	1967	WBA
Hiroshi Kobayashi	Japan	1967-1971	WBA
Rene Barrientos	Philippines	1969-1970	WBC
Yoshiaki Numata	Japan	1970-1971	WBC
Alfredo Marcano	Venezuela	1971-1972	WBA
Ricardo Arredondo	Mexico	1971-1974	WBC
Ben Villaflor	Philippines	1972-1973	WBA
Kuniaki Shibata	Japan	1973	WBA
Ben Villaflor	Philippines	1973-1976	WBA
Kuniaki Shibata	Japan	1974-1975	WBC
Alfredo Escalera	Puerto Rico	1975-1978	WBC
Sam Serrano	Puerto Rico	1976-1980	WBA
Alexis Arguello*	Nicaragua	1978-1980	WBC
Yasutsune Uehara	Japan	1980-1981	WBA
Rafael Limon	Mexico	1980-1981	WBC
Cornelius Boza-Edwards	Uganda	1981	WBC
Sam Serrano	Puerto Rico	1981-1983	WBA
Rolando Navarrete	Philippines	1981-1982	WBC
Rafael Limon	Mexico	1982	WBC
Bobby Chacon	USA	1982-1983	WBC
Roger Mayweather	USA	1983-1984	WBA
Hector Camacho*	Puerto Rico	1983-1984	WBC
Rocky Lockridge	USA	1984-1985	WBA
Hwan-Kil Yuh	S Korea	1984-1985	IBF
Julio Cesar Chavez*	Mexico	1984-1987	WBC
Lester Ellis	England	1985	IBF
Wilfredo Gomez	Puerto Rico	1985-1986	WBA
Barry Michael	England	1985-1987	IBF
Alfredo Layne	Panama	1986	WBA
Brian Mitchell*	S Africa	1986-1991	WBA
Rocky Lockridge	USA	1987-1988	IBF
Azumah Nelson	Ghana	1988-1994	WBC
Tony Lopez	USA	1988-1989	IBF
Juan Molina*	Puerto Rico	1989	WBO
Juan Molina	Puerto Rico	1989-1990	IBF
Kamel Bou Ali	Tunisia	1989-1992	WBO
Tony Lopez	USA	1990-1991	IBF
Joey Gamache*	USA	1991	WBA
Brian Mitchell*	S Africa	1991-1992	IBF
Genaro Hernandez	USA	1991-1995	WBA
Juan Molina*	Puerto Rico	1992-1995	IBF
Daniel Londas	France	1992	WBO
Jimmy Bredahl	Denmark	1992-1994	WBO
Oscar de la Hoya*	USA	1994	WBO
James Leija	USA	1994	WBC
Gabriel Ruelas	USA	1994-1995	WBC
Regilio Tuur*	Surinam	1994-1997	WBO
Eddie Hopson	USA	1995	IBF
Tracy Harris Patterson	USA	1995	IBF
Yong-Soo Choi	S Korea	1995-1998	WBA
Arturo Gatti*	Canada	1995-1997	IBF
Azumah Nelson	Ghana	1996-1997	WBC
Genaro Hernandez	USA	1997-1998	WBC
Barry Jones*	Wales	1997-1998	WBO
Roberto Garcia	USA	1998-1999	IBF
Anatoly Alexandrov	Kazakhstan	1998-1999	WBO
Takenori Hatakeyama	Japan	1998-1999	WBA
Floyd Mayweather	USA	1998-	WBC
Lakva Sim	Mongolia	1999	WBA
Acelino Freitas	Brazil	1999-	WBO

Title Holder	Birthplace	Tenure	Status
Diego Corrales*	USA	1999-2000	IBF
Jong-Kwon Baek	S Korea	1999-2000	WBA
Joel Casamayor	Cuba	2000-	WBA
Steve Forbes	USA	2000-	IBF

Lightweight (135 lbs)

Title Holder	Birthplace	Tenure	Status
Jack McAuliffe	Ireland	1889-1894	USA
Jem Carney	England	1889-1891	
Jimmy Carroll	England	1889-1891	
Dick Burge	England	1891-1896	GB
George Lavigne	USA	1894-1896	USA
George Lavigne	USA	1896	
George Lavigne	USA	1896-1897	
Eddie Connolly	Canada	1896-1897	
George Lavigne	USA	1897-1899	
Frank Erne	Switzerland	1899-1902	
Joe Gans	USA	1902	
Joe Gans	USA	1902-1906	
Jabez White	England	1902-1905	GB
Jimmy Britt	USA	1902-1905	
Battling Nelson	Denmark	1905-1907	
Joe Gans	USA	1906-1908	
Battling Nelson	Denmark	1908-1910	
Ad Wolgast	USA	1910-1912	
Willie Ritchie	USA	1912	
Freddie Welsh	Wales	1912-1914	GB
Willie Ritchie	USA	1912-1914	USA
Freddie Welsh	Wales	1914-1917	
Benny Leonard*	USA	1917-1925	
Jimmy Goodrich	USA	1925	NY
Rocky Kansas	USA	1925-1926	
Sammy Mandell	USA	1926-1930	
Al Singer	USA	1930	
Tony Canzoneri	USA	1930-1933	
Barney Ross*	USA	1933-1935	
Tony Canzoneri	USA	1935-1936	
Lou Ambers	USA	1936-1938	
Henry Armstrong	USA	1938-1939	
Lou Ambers	USA	1939-1940	
Sammy Angott	USA	1940-1941	NBA
Lew Jenkins	USA	1940-1941	NY
Sammy Angott*	USA	1941-1942	
Beau Jack	USA	1942-1943	NY
Slugger White	USA	1943	MARY
Bob Montgomery	USA	1943	NY
Sammy Angott	USA	1943-1944	NBA
Beau Jack	USA	1943-1944	NY
Bob Montgomery	USA	1944-1947	NY
Juan Zurita	Mexico	1944-1945	NBA
Ike Williams	USA	1945-1947	NBA
Ike Williams	USA	1947-1951	
Jimmy Carter	USA	1951-1952	
Lauro Salas	Mexico	1952	
Jimmy Carter	USA	1952-1954	
Paddy de Marco	USA	1954	
Jimmy Carter	USA	1954-1955	
Wallace Bud Smith	USA	1955-1956	
Joe Brown	USA	1956-1962	
Carlos Ortiz	Puerto Rico	1962-1963	
Carlos Ortiz*	Puerto Rico	1963-1964	WBA/WBC
Kenny Lane	USA	1963-1964	MICH
Carlos Ortiz	Puerto Rico	1964-1965	
Ismael Laguna	Panama	1965	
Carlos Ortiz	Puerto Rico	1965-1966	
Carlos Ortiz*	Puerto Rico	1966-1967	WBA
Carlos Ortiz	Puerto Rico	1967-1968	
Carlos Teo Cruz	Dom Republic	1968-1969	
Mando Ramos	USA	1969-1970	
Ismael Laguna	Panama	1970	
Ismael Laguna	Panama	1970	WBA
Ken Buchanan*	Scotland	1970-1971	WBA
Ken Buchanan	Scotland	1971	
Ken Buchanan	Scotland	1971-1972	WBA
Pedro Carrasco	Spain	1971-1972	WBC
Mando Ramos	USA	1972	WBC
Roberto Duran*	Panama	1972-1978	WBA
Chango Carmona	Mexico	1972	WBC
Rodolfo Gonzalez	Mexico	1972-1974	WBC
Guts Ishimatsu	Japan	1974-1976	WBC
Esteban de Jesus	Puerto Rico	1976-1978	WBC
Roberto Duran*	Panama	1978-1979	
Jim Watt	Scotland	1979-1981	WBC
Ernesto Espana	Venezuela	1979-1980	WBA
Hilmer Kenty	USA	1980-1981	WBA
Sean O'Grady	USA	1981	WBA
Alexis Arguello*	Nicaragua	1981-1983	WBC
Claude Noel	Trinidad	1981	WBA
Arturo Frias	USA	1981-1982	WBA
Ray Mancini	USA	1982-1984	WBA
Edwin Rosario	Puerto Rico	1983-1984	WBC
Charlie Choo Choo Brown	USA	1984	IBF
Harry Arroyo	USA	1984-1985	IBF
Livingstone Bramble	USA	1984-1986	WBA
Jose Luis Ramirez	Mexico	1984-1985	WBC
Jimmy Paul	USA	1985-1986	IBF
Hector Camacho*	Puerto Rico	1985-1987	WBC
Edwin Rosario	Puerto Rico	1986-1987	WBA
Greg Haugen	USA	1986-1987	IBF
Vinny Pazienza	USA	1987-1988	IBF
Jose Luis Ramirez	Mexico	1987-1988	WBC
Julio Cesar Chavez*	Mexico	1987-1988	WBA
Greg Haugen	USA	1988-1989	IBF
Julio Cesar Chavez*	Mexico	1988-1989	WBA/WBC
Mauricio Aceves	Mexico	1989-1990	WBO
Pernell Whitaker*	USA	1989	IBF
Edwin Rosario	Puerto Rico	1989-1990	WBA
Pernell Whitaker*	USA	1989-1990	IBF/WBC
Juan Nazario	Puerto Rico	1990	WBA
Pernell Whitaker*	USA	1990-1992	IBF/WBC/WBA
Dingaan Thobela*	S Africa	1990-1992	WBO
Joey Gamache	USA	1992	WBA
Miguel Gonzalez*	Mexico	1992-1996	WBC
Giovanni Parisi*	Italy	1992-1994	WBO
Tony Lopez	USA	1992-1993	WBA
Fred Pendleton	USA	1993-1994	IBF
Dingaan Thobela	S Africa	1993	WBA
Orzubek Nazarov	Kyrghzstan	1993-1998	WBA
Rafael Ruelas	USA	1994-1995	IBF
Oscar de la Hoya*	USA	1994-1995	WBO
Oscar de la Hoya*	USA	1995	WBO/IBF
Oscar de la Hoya*	USA	1995-1996	WBO
Phillip Holiday	S Africa	1995-1997	IBF
Jean-Baptiste Mendy	France	1996-1997	WBC
Artur Grigorian	Uzbekistan	1996-	WBO
Steve Johnston	USA	1997-1998	WBC
Shane Mosley*	USA	1997-1999	IBF
Jean-Baptiste Mendy	France	1998-1999	WBA
Cesar Bazan	Mexico	1998-1999	WBC
Steve Johnston	USA	1999-2000	WBC
Julien Lorcy	France	1999	WBA
Stefano Zoff	Italy	1999	WBA
Paul Spadafora	USA	1999-	IBF
Gilberto Serrano	Venezuela	1999-2000	WBA
Takanori Hatakeyama	Japan	2000-	WBA
Jose Luis Castillo	Mexico	2000-	WBC

L. Welterweight (140 lbs)

Title Holder	Birthplace	Tenure	Status
Pinkey Mitchell	USA	1922-1926	NBA
Mushy Callahan	USA	1926-1927	NBA
Mushy Callahan	USA	1927-1930	NBA/NY
Mushy Callahan	USA	1930	NBA
Jackie Kid Berg	England	1930-1931	NBA
Tony Canzoneri	USA	1931-1932	NBA
Johnny Jadick	USA	1932	NBA
Johnny Jadick	USA	1932-1933	PEN
Battling Shaw	Mexico	1933	LOUIS

WORLD CHAMPIONS SINCE GLOVES, 1889-2001

Title Holder	Birthplace	Tenure	Status
Tony Canzoneri	USA	1933	LOUIS
Barney Ross*	USA	1933-1935	ILL
Maxie Berger	Canada	1939	CAN
Harry Weekly	USA	1941-1942	LOUIS
Tippy Larkin	USA	1946-1947	NY/NBA
Carlos Ortiz	Puerto Rico	1959-1960	NBA
Duilio Loi	Italy	1960-1962	NBA
Duilio Loi	Italy	1962	WBA
Eddie Perkins	USA	1962	WBA
Duilio Loi*	Italy	1962-1963	WBA
Roberto Cruz	Philippines	1963	WBA
Eddie Perkins	USA	1963-1965	WBA
Carlos Hernandez	Venezuela	1965-1966	WBA
Sandro Lopopolo	Italy	1966-1967	WBA
Paul Fujii	Hawaii	1967-1968	WBA
Nicolino Loche	Argentina	1968-1972	WBA
Pedro Adigue	Philippines	1968-1970	WBC
Bruno Arcari*	Italy	1970-1974	WBC
Alfonso Frazer	Panama	1972	WBA
Antonio Cervantes	Colombia	1972-1976	WBA
Perico Fernandez	Spain	1974-1975	WBC
Saensak Muangsurin	Thailand	1975-1976	WBC
Wilfred Benitez	USA	1976	WBA
Miguel Velasquez	Spain	1976	WBC
Saensak Muangsurin	Thailand	1976-1978	WBC
Antonio Cervantes	Colombia	1977-1980	WBA
Wilfred Benitez*	USA	1977-1978	NY
Sang-Hyun Kim	S Korea	1978-1980	WBC
Saoul Mamby	USA	1980-1982	WBC
Aaron Pryor*	USA	1980-1984	WBA
Leroy Haley	USA	1982-1983	WBC
Bruce Curry	USA	1983-1984	WBC
Johnny Bumphus	USA	1984	WBA
Bill Costello	USA	1984-1985	WBC
Gene Hatcher	USA	1984-1985	WBA
Aaron Pryor	USA	1984-1985	IBF
Ubaldo Sacco	Argentina	1985-1986	WBA
Lonnie Smith	USA	1985-1986	WBC
Patrizio Oliva	Italy	1986-1987	WBA
Gary Hinton	USA	1986	IBF
Rene Arredondo	Mexico	1986	WBC
Tsuyoshi Hamada	Japan	1986-1987	WBC
Joe Manley	USA	1986-1987	IBF
Terry Marsh*	England	1987	IBF
Juan M. Coggi	Argentina	1987-1990	WBA
Rene Arredondo	Mexico	1987	WBC
Roger Mayweather	USA	1987-1989	WBC
James McGirt	USA	1988	IBF
Meldrick Taylor	USA	1988-1990	IBF
Hector Camacho	Puerto Rico	1989-1991	WBO
Julio Cesar Chavez*	Mexico	1989-1990	WBC
Julio Cesar Chavez*	Mexico	1990-1991	IBF/WBC
Loreto Garza	USA	1990-1991	WBA
Greg Haugen	USA	1991	WBO
Hector Camacho	Puerto Rico	1991-1992	WBO
Edwin Rosario	Puerto Rico	1991-1992	WBA
Julio Cesar Chavez	Mexico	1991-1994	WBC
Rafael Pineda	Colombia	1991-1992	IBF
Akinobu Hiranaka	Japan	1992	WBA
Carlos Gonzalez	Mexico	1992-1993	WBO
Pernell Whitaker*	USA	1992-1993	IBF
Morris East	Philippines	1992-1993	WBA
Juan M. Coggi	Argentina	1993-1994	WBA
Charles Murray	USA	1993-1994	IBF
Zack Padilla*	USA	1993-1994	WBO
Frankie Randall	USA	1994	WBC
Jake Rodriguez	USA	1994-1995	IBF
Julio Cesar Chavez	Mexico	1994-1996	WBC
Frankie Randall	USA	1994-1996	WBA
Konstantin Tszyu	Russia	1995-1997	IBF
Sammy Fuentes	Puerto Rico	1995-1996	WBO
Juan M. Coggi	Argentina	1996	WBA
Giovanni Parisi	Italy	1996-1998	WBO

Title Holder	Birthplace	Tenure	Status
Oscar de la Hoya*	USA	1996-1997	WBC
Frankie Randall	USA	1996-1997	WBA
Khalid Rahilou	France	1997-1998	WBA
Vince Phillips	USA	1997-1999	IBF
Carlos Gonzalez	Mexico	1998-1999	WBO
Sharmba Mitchell	USA	1998-2001	WBA
Terron Millett	USA	1999	IBF
Randall Bailey	USA	1999-2000	WBO
Kostya Tszyu	Russia	1999-2001	WBC
Zab Judah	USA	2000-	IBF
Ener Julio	Colombia	2000-2001	WBO
Kostya Tszyu	Russia	2001-	WBA/WBC
DeMarcus Corley	USA	2001-	WBO

Welterweight (147 lbs)

Title Holder	Birthplace	Tenure	Status
Paddy Duffy	USA	1889-1890	
Tommy Ryan	USA	1891-1894	
Mysterious Billy Smith	USA	1892-1894	
Tommy Ryan	USA	1894-1897	USA
Tommy Ryan	USA	1897-1899	
Dick Burge	GB	1897	
George Green	USA	1897	
Tom Causer	GB	1897	
Joe Walcott	Barbados	1897	
George Lavigne	USA	1897-1899	
Dick Burge	GB	1897-1898	
Mysterious Billy Smith	USA	1898-1900	
Bobby Dobbs	USA	1898-1902	
Rube Ferns	USA	1900	
Matty Matthews	USA	1900	
Eddie Connolly	Canada	1900	
Matty Matthews	USA	1900-1901	
Rube Ferns	USA	1901	
Joe Walcott	Barbados	1901-1906	
Eddie Connolly	Canada	1902-1903	GB
Matty Matthews	USA	1902-1903	
Rube Ferns	USA	1903	
Martin Duffy	USA	1903-1904	
Honey Mellody	USA	1904	
Jack Clancy	USA	1904-1905	GB
Dixie Kid	USA	1904-1905	
Buddy Ryan	USA	1904-1905	
Sam Langford	Canada	1904-1905	
George Petersen	USA	1905	
Jimmy Gardner	USA	1905	
Mike Twin Sullivan	USA	1905-1906	
Joe Gans	USA	1906	
Joe Walcott	Barbados	1906	USA
Honey Mellody	USA	1906	USA
Honey Mellody	USA	1906-1907	
Joe Thomas	USA	1906-1907	
Mike Twin Sullivan	USA	1907-1911	
Jimmy Gardner	USA	1907-1908	
Frank Mantell	USA	1907-1908	
Harry Lewis	USA	1908-1910	
Jack Blackburn	USA	1908	
Jimmy Gardner	USA	1908-1909	
Willie Lewis	USA	1909-1910	
Harry Lewis	USA	1910-1911	GB/FR
Jimmy Clabby	USA	1910-1911	
Dixie Kid	USA	1911-1912	GB/FR
Ray Bronson	USA	1911-1914	
Marcel Thomas	France	1912-1913	FR
Wildcat Ferns	USA	1912-1913	
Spike Kelly	USA	1913-1914	
Mike Glover	USA	1913-1915	
Mike Gibbons	USA	1913-1914	
Waldemar Holberg	Denmark	1914	
Tom McCormick	Ireland	1914	
Matt Wells	England	1914-1915	AUSTR
Kid Graves	USA	1914-1917	
Jack Britton	USA	1915	
Ted Kid Lewis	England	1915-1916	

244

Title Holder	Birthplace	Tenure	Status
Jack Britton	USA	1916-1917	
Ted Kid Lewis	England	1917	
Ted Kid Lewis	England	1917-1919	
Jack Britton	USA	1919-1922	
Mickey Walker	USA	1922-1923	
Mickey Walker	USA	1923-1924	NBA
Dave Shade	USA	1923	NY
Jimmy Jones	USA	1923	NY/MASS
Mickey Walker	USA	1924-1926	
Pete Latzo	USA	1926-1927	
Joe Dundee	Italy	1927-1928	
Joe Dundee	Italy	1928-1929	NY
Jackie Fields	USA	1929	NBA
Jackie Fields	USA	1929-1930	
Young Jack Thompson	USA	1930	
Tommy Freeman	USA	1930-1931	
Young Jack Thompson	USA	1930	
Lou Brouillard	Canada	1931-1932	
Jackie Fields	USA	1932-1933	
Young Corbett III	Italy	1933	
Jimmy McLarnin	Ireland	1933-1934	
Barney Ross	USA	1934	
Jimmy McLarnin	Ireland	1934-1935	
Barney Ross	USA	1935-1938	
Barney Ross	USA	1938	NY/NBA
Felix Wouters	Belgium	1938	IBU
Henry Armstrong	USA	1938-1940	
Fritzie Zivic	USA	1940	
Fritzie Zivic	USA	1940-1941	NY/NBA
Izzy Jannazzo	USA	1940-1942	MARY
Red Cochrane	USA	1941-1942	NY/NBA
Red Cochrane	USA	1942-1946	
Marty Servo	USA	1946	
Sugar Ray Robinson*	USA	1946-1951	
Johnny Bratton	USA	1951	NBA
Kid Gavilan	Cuba	1951-1952	NBA/NY
Kid Gavilan	Cuba	1952-1954	

Title Holder	Birthplace	Tenure	Status
Johnny Saxton	USA	1954-1955	
Tony de Marco	USA	1955	
Carmen Basilio	USA	1955-1956	
Johnny Saxton	USA	1956	
Carmen Basilio*	USA	1956-1957	
Virgil Akins	USA	1957-1958	MASS
Virgil Akins	USA	1958	
Don Jordan	Dom Republic	1958-1960	
Benny Kid Paret	Cuba	1960-1961	
Emile Griffith	Virgin Islands	1961	
Benny Kid Paret	Cuba	1961-1962	
Emile Griffith	Virgin Islands	1962-1963	
Luis Rodriguez	Cuba	1963	
Emile Griffith*	Virgin Islands	1963-1966	
Willie Ludick	S Africa	1966-1968	SA
Curtis Cokes*	USA	1966	WBA
Curtis Cokes*	USA	1966-1967	WBA/WBC
Charley Shipes	USA	1966-1967	CALIF
Curtis Cokes	USA	1968-1969	
Jose Napoles	Cuba	1969-1970	
Billy Backus	USA	1970-1971	
Jose Napoles	Cuba	1971-1972	
Jose Napoles*	Cuba	1972-1974	WBA/WBC
Hedgemon Lewis	USA	1972-1974	NY
Jose Napoles	Cuba	1974-1975	
Jose Napoles	Cuba	1975	WBC
Angel Espada	Puerto Rico	1975-1976	WBA
John H. Stracey	England	1975-1976	WBC
Carlos Palomino	Mexico	1976-1979	WBC
Pipino Cuevas	Mexico	1976-1980	WBA
Wilfred Benitez	USA	1979	WBC
Sugar Ray Leonard	USA	1979-1980	WBC
Roberto Duran	Panama	1980	WBC
Thomas Hearns	USA	1980-1981	WBA
Sugar Ray Leonard	USA	1980-1981	WBC
Sugar Ray Leonard*	USA	1981-1982	
Don Curry*	USA	1983-1984	WBA
Milton McCrory	USA	1983-1985	WBC
Don Curry*	USA	1984-1985	WBA/IBF
Don Curry	USA	1985-1986	
Lloyd Honeyghan	Jamaica	1986	
Lloyd Honeyghan	Jamaica	1986-1987	WBC/IBF
Mark Breland	USA	1987	WBA
Marlon Starling	USA	1987-1988	WBA
Jorge Vaca	Mexico	1987-1988	WBC
Lloyd Honeyghan	Jamaica	1988-1989	WBC
Simon Brown*	Jamaica	1988-1991	IBF
Tomas Molinares	Colombia	1988-1989	WBA
Mark Breland	USA	1989-1990	WBA
Marlon Starling	USA	1989-1990	WBC
Genaro Leon*	Mexico	1989	WBO
Manning Galloway	USA	1989-1993	WBO
Aaron Davis	USA	1990-1991	WBA
Maurice Blocker	USA	1990-1991	WBC
Meldrick Taylor	USA	1991-1992	WBA
Simon Brown*	Jamaica	1991	WBC/IBF
Simon Brown	Jamaica	1991	WBC
Maurice Blocker	USA	1991-1993	IBF
James McGirt	USA	1991-1993	WBC
Crisanto Espana	Venezuela	1992-1994	WBA
Gert Bo Jacobsen*	Denmark	1993	WBO
Pernell Whitaker	USA	1993-1997	WBC
Felix Trinidad*	Puerto Rico	1993-2000	IBF
Eamonn Loughran	Ireland	1993-1996	WBO
Ike Quartey	Ghana	1994-1998	WBA
Jose Luis Lopez	Mexico	1996-1997	WBO
Michael Loewe*	Romania	1997-1998	WBO
Oscar de la Hoya	USA	1997-1999	WBC
Ahmed Kotiev	Russia	1998-2000	WBO
James Page	USA	1998-2000	WBA
Oscar de la Hoya	USA	2000	WBC
Daniel Santos	Puerto Rico	2000-	WBO
Shane Mosley	USA	2000-	WBC

Kid Gavilan, king of the welters, 1951-1954

245

Title Holder	Birthplace	Tenure	Status
Andrew Lewis	Guyana	2001-	WBA
Vernon Forrest	USA	2001-	IBF
L. Middleweight (154 lbs)			
Emile Griffith*	USA	1962-1963	AU
Denny Moyer	USA	1962-1963	WBA
Ralph Dupas	USA	1963	WBA
Sandro Mazzinghi	Italy	1963-1965	WBA
Nino Benvenuti	Italy	1965-1966	WBA
Ki-Soo Kim	S Korea	1966-1968	WBA
Sandro Mazzinghi	Italy	1968-1969	WBA
Freddie Little	USA	1969-1970	WBA
Carmelo Bossi	Italy	1970-1971	WBA
Koichi Wajima	Japan	1971-1974	WBA
Oscar Albarado	USA	1974-1975	WBA
Koichi Wajima	Japan	1975	WBA
Miguel de Oliveira	Brazil	1975	WBC
Jae-Do Yuh	S Korea	1975-1976	WBA
Elisha Obed	Bahamas	1975-1976	WBC
Koichi Wajima	Japan	1976	WBA
Jose Duran	Spain	1976	WBA
Eckhard Dagge	Germany	1976-1977	WBC
Miguel Castellini	Argentina	1976-1977	WBA
Eddie Gazo	Nicaragua	1977-1978	WBA
Rocky Mattioli	Italy	1977-1979	WBC
Masashi Kudo	Japan	1978-1979	WBA
Maurice Hope	Antigua	1979-1981	WBC
Ayub Kalule	Uganda	1979-1981	WBA
Wilfred Benitez	USA	1981-1982	WBC
Sugar Ray Leonard*	USA	1981	WBA
Tadashi Mihara	Japan	1981-1982	WBA
Davey Moore	USA	1982-1983	WBA
Thomas Hearns*	USA	1982-1986	WBC
Roberto Duran*	Panama	1983-1984	WBA
Mark Medal	USA	1984	IBF
Mike McCallum*	Jamaica	1984-1987	WBA
Carlos Santos	Puerto Rico	1984-1986	IBF
Buster Drayton	USA	1986-1987	IBF
Duane Thomas	USA	1986-1987	WBC
Matthew Hilton	Canada	1987-1988	IBF
Lupe Aquino	Mexico	1987	WBC
Gianfranco Rosi	Italy	1987-1988	WBC
Julian Jackson*	Virgin Islands	1987-1990	WBA
Don Curry	USA	1988-1989	WBC
Robert Hines	USA	1988-1989	IBF
John David Jackson*	USA	1988-1993	WBO
Darrin van Horn	USA	1989	IBF
Rene Jacqot	France	1989	WBC
John Mugabi	Uganda	1989-1990	WBC
Gianfranco Rosi	Italy	1989-1994	IBF
Terry Norris	USA	1990-1993	WBC
Gilbert Dele	France	1991	WBA
Vinny Pazienza*	USA	1991-1992	WBA
Julio Cesar Vasquez	Argentina	1992-1995	WBA
Verno Phillips	USA	1993-1995	WBO
Simon Brown	USA	1993-1994	WBC
Terry Norris	USA	1994	WBC
Vince Pettway	USA	1994-1995	IBF
Luis Santana	Dom Republic	1994-1995	WBC
Pernell Whitaker*	USA	1995	WBA
Gianfranco Rosi	Italy	1995	WBO
Carl Daniels	USA	1995	WBA
Verno Phillips	USA	1995	WBO
Paul Vaden	USA	1995	IBF
Terry Norris*	USA	1995	WBC
Paul Jones	England	1995-1996	WBO
Terry Norris	USA	1995-1997	IBF/WBC
Julio Cesar Vasquez	Argentina	1995-1996	WBA
Bronco McKart	USA	1996	WBO
Ronald Wright	USA	1996-1998	WBO
Laurent Boudouani	France	1996-1999	WBA
Terry Norris	USA	1997	WBC
Raul Marquez	USA	1997	IBF

Title Holder	Birthplace	Tenure	Status
Luis Campas	Mexico	1997-1998	IBF
Keith Mullings	USA	1997-1999	WBC
Harry Simon	Namibia	1998-	WBO
Fernando Vargas	USA	1998-2000	IBF
Javier Castillejo	Spain	1999-2001	WBC
David Reid	USA	1999-2000	WBA
Felix Trinidad	Puerto Rico	2000	WBA
Felix Trinidad*	Puerto Rico	2000-2001	IBF/WBA
Oscar de la Hoya	USA	2001-	WBC
Middleweight (160 lbs)			
Nonpareil Jack Dempsey	Ireland	1889-1891	USA
Bob Fitzsimmons	England	1891-1893	USA
Jim Hall	Australia	1892-1893	GB
Bob Fitzsimmons	England	1893-1894	
Bob Fitzsimmons	England	1894-1899	
Frank Craig	USA	1894-1895	GB
Dan Creedon	New Zealand	1895-1897	GB
Tommy Ryan	USA	1895-1896	
Kid McCoy	USA	1896-1898	
Tommy Ryan	USA	1898-1905	
Charley McKeever	USA	1900-1902	
George Gardner	USA	1901-1902	
Jack O'Brien	USA	1901-1905	
George Green	USA	1901-1902	
Jack Palmer	England	1902-1903	GB
Hugo Kelly	USA	1905-1908	
Jack Twin Sullivan	USA	1905-1908	
Sam Langford	Canada	1907-1911	
Billy Papke	USA	1908	
Stanley Ketchel	USA	1908	
Billy Papke	USA	1908	
Stanley Ketchel	USA	1908-1910	
Billy Papke	USA	1910-1913	
Stanley Ketchel*	USA	1910	
Hugo Kelly	USA	1910-1912	
Cyclone Johnny Thompson	USA	1911-1912	
Harry Lewis	USA	1911	
Leo Houck	USA	1911-1912	
Georges Carpentier	France	1911-1912	
Jack Dillon	USA	1912	
Frank Mantell	USA	1912-1913	
Frank Klaus	USA	1912-1913	
Georges Carpentier	France	1912	IBU
Jack Dillon	USA	1912-1915	
Eddie McGoorty	USA	1912-1913	
Frank Klaus	USA	1913	IBU
Jimmy Clabby	USA	1913-1914	
George Chip	USA	1913-1914	
Joe Borrell	USA	1913-1914	
Jeff Smith	USA	1913-1914	
Eddie McGoorty	USA	1914	AUSTR
Jeff Smith	USA	1914	AUSTR
Al McCoy	USA	1914-1917	
Jimmy Clabby	USA	1914-1915	
Mick King	Australia	1914	AUSTR
Jeff Smith	USA	1914-1915	AUSTR
Young Ahearn	England	1915-1916	
Les Darcy*	Australia	1915-1917	AUSTR
Mike Gibbons	USA	1916-1917	
Mike O'Dowd	USA	1917-1920	
Johnny Wilson	USA	1920-1921	
Johnny Wilson	USA	1921-1922	NBA/NY
Bryan Downey	USA	1921-1922	OHIO
Johnny Wilson	USA	1922-1923	NBA
Dave Rosenberg	USA	1922	NY
Jock Malone	USA	1922-1923	OHIO
Mike O'Dowd	USA	1922-1923	NY
Johnny Wilson	USA	1923	
Harry Greb	USA	1923-1926	
Tiger Flowers	USA	1926	
Mickey Walker	USA	1926-1931	
Gorilla Jones	USA	1932	NBA

Title Holder	Birthplace	Tenure	Status	Title Holder	Birthplace	Tenure	Status
Marcel Thil	France	1932-1933	NBA/IBU	**Marcel Cerdan**	Algeria	1948-1949	
Marcel Thil	France	1933-1937	IBU	**Jake la Motta**	USA	1949-1950	
Ben Jeby	USA	1933	NY	Jake la Motta	USA	1950-1951	NY/NBA
Lou Brouillard	Canada	1933	NY	Sugar Ray Robinson	USA	1950-1951	PEN
Lou Brouillard	Canada	1933	NY/NBA	**Sugar Ray Robinson**	USA	1951	
Vearl Whitehead	USA	1933	CALIF	**Randy Turpin**	England	1951	
Teddy Yarosz	USA	1933-1934	PEN	**Sugar Ray Robinson***	USA	1951-1952	
Vince Dundee	USA	1933-1934	NY/NBA	Randy Turpin	England	1953	GB/EBU
Teddy Yarosz	USA	1934-1935	NY/NBA	**Carl Bobo Olson**	Hawaii	1953-1955	
Babe Risko	USA	1935-1936	NY/NBA	**Sugar Ray Robinson**	USA	1955-1957	
Freddie Steele	USA	1936-1938	NY/NBA	**Gene Fullmer**	USA	1957	
Fred Apostoli	USA	1937-1938	IBU	**Sugar Ray Robinson**	USA	1957	
Edouard Tenet	France	1938	IBU	**Carmen Basilio**	USA	1957-1958	
Young Corbett III	Italy	1938	CALIF	**Sugar Ray Robinson**	USA	1958-1959	
Freddie Steele	USA	1938	NBA	Sugar Ray Robinson	USA	1959-1960	NY/EBU
Al Hostak	USA	1938	NBA	Gene Fullmer	USA	1959-1962	NBA
Solly Krieger	USA	1938-1939	NBA	Paul Pender	USA	1960-1961	NY/EBU
Fred Apostoli	USA	1938-1939	NY	Terry Downes	England	1961-1962	NY/EBU
Al Hostak	USA	1939-1940	NBA	Paul Pender	USA	1962	NY/EBU
Ceferino Garcia	Philippines	1939-1940	NY	Dick Tiger	Nigeria	1962-1963	NBA
Ken Overlin	USA	1940-1941	NY	**Dick Tiger**	Nigeria	1963	
Tony Zale	USA	1940-1941	NBA	**Joey Giardello**	USA	1963-1965	
Billy Soose	USA	1941	NY	**Dick Tiger**	Nigeria	1965-1966	
Tony Zale	USA	1941-1947		**Emile Griffith**	Virgin Islands	1966-1967	
Rocky Graziano	USA	1947-1948		**Nino Benvenuti**	Italy	1967	
Tony Zale	USA	1948		**Emile Griffith**	Virgin Islands	1967-1968	

Terry Downes (left), a future world middleweight champion, is seen here on his way to a 13th-round stoppage win over Phil Edwards on 30 September 1958. With his victory came the British title

Title Holder	Birthplace	Tenure	Status
Nino Benvenuti	Italy	1968-1970	
Carlos Monzon	Argentina	1970-1974	
Carlos Monzon*	Argentina	1974-1976	WBA
Rodrigo Valdez	Colombia	1974-1976	WBC
Carlos Monzon*	Argentina	1976-1977	
Rodrigo Valdez	Colombia	1977-1978	
Hugo Corro	Argentina	1978-1979	
Vito Antuofermo	Italy	1979-1980	
Alan Minter	England	1980	
Marvin Hagler	USA	1980-1987	
Marvin Hagler	USA	1987	WBC/IBF
Sugar Ray Leonard	USA	1987	WBC
Frank Tate	USA	1987-1988	IBF
Sumbu Kalambay	Zaire	1987-1989	WBA
Thomas Hearns	USA	1987-1988	WBC
Iran Barkley	USA	1988-1989	WBC
Michael Nunn	USA	1988-1991	IBF
Roberto Duran	Panama	1989-1990	WBC
Doug de Witt	USA	1989-1990	WBO
Mike McCallum	Jamaica	1989-1991	WBA
Nigel Benn	England	1990	WBO
Chris Eubank*	England	1990-1991	WBO
Julian Jackson	Virgin Islands	1990-1993	WBC
James Toney*	USA	1991-1993	IBF
Gerald McClellan*	USA	1991-1993	WBO
Reggie Johnson	USA	1992-1993	WBA
Gerald McClellan*	USA	1993-1995	WBC
Chris Pyatt	England	1993-1994	WBO
Roy Jones*	USA	1993-1994	IBF
John David Jackson	USA	1993-1994	WBA
Steve Collins*	Ireland	1994-1995	WBO
Jorge Castro	Argentina	1994	WBA
Julian Jackson	Virgin Islands	1995	WBC
Bernard Hopkins	USA	1995-2001	IBF
Lonnie Bradley*	USA	1995-1998	WBO
Quincy Taylor	USA	1995-1996	WBC
Shinji Takehara	Japan	1995-1996	WBA
Keith Holmes	USA	1996-1998	WBC
William Joppy	USA	1996-1997	WBA
Julio Cesar Green	Dom Republic	1997-1998	WBA
William Joppy	USA	1998-2001	WBA
Hassine Cherifi	France	1998-1999	WBC
Otis Grant*	Canada	1998	WBO
Bert Schenk	Germany	1999	WBO
Keith Holmes	USA	1999-2001	WBC
Jason Matthews	England	1999	WBO
Armand Krajnc	Slovenia	1999-	WBO
Bernard Hopkins	USA	2001-	WBC/IBF
Felix Trinidad	Puerto Rico	2001-	WBA

S. Middleweight (168 lbs)

Title Holder	Birthplace	Tenure	Status
Murray Sutherland	Scotland	1984	IBF
Chong-Pal Park*	S Korea	1984-1987	IBF
Chong-Pal Park	S Korea	1987-1988	WBA
Graciano Rocchigiani*	Germany	1988-1989	IBF
Fully Obelmejias	Venezuela	1988-1989	WBA
Sugar Ray Leonard*	USA	1988-1990	WBC
Thomas Hearns*	USA	1988-1991	WBO
In-Chul Baek	S Korea	1989-1990	WBA
Lindell Holmes	USA	1990-1991	IBF
Christophe Tiozzo	France	1990-1991	WBA
Mauro Galvano	Italy	1990-1992	WBC
Victor Cordoba	Panama	1991-1992	WBA
Darrin van Horn	USA	1991-1992	IBF
Chris Eubank	England	1991-1995	WBO
Iran Barkley	USA	1992-1993	IBF
Michael Nunn	USA	1992-1994	WBA
Nigel Benn	England	1992-1996	WBC
James Toney	USA	1993-1994	IBF
Steve Little	USA	1994	WBA
Frank Liles	USA	1994-1999	WBA
Roy Jones*	USA	1994-1997	IBF
Steve Collins*	Ireland	1995-1997	WBO

Title Holder	Birthplace	Tenure	Status
Thulani Malinga	S Africa	1996	WBC
Vincenzo Nardiello	Italy	1996	WBC
Robin Reid	England	1996-1997	WBC
Charles Brewer	USA	1997-1998	IBF
Joe Calzaghe	Wales	1997-	WBO
Thulani Malinga	S Africa	1997-1998	WBC
Richie Woodhall	England	1998-1999	WBC
Sven Ottke	Germany	1998-	IBF
Byron Mitchell	USA	1999-2000	WBA
Markus Beyer	Germany	1999-2000	WBC
Bruno Girard	France	2000-2001	WBA
Glenn Catley	England	2000	WBC
Dingaan Thobela	S Africa	2000	WBC
Dave Hilton	Canada	2000-2001	WBC
Byron Mitchell	USA	2001-	WBA

L. Heavyweight (175 lbs)

Title Holder	Birthplace	Tenure	Status
Jack Root	Austria	1903	
George Gardner	Ireland	1903	
George Gardner	Ireland	1903	USA
Bob Fitzsimmons	England	1903-1905	USA
Jack O'Brien	USA	1905-1911	
Sam Langford	Canada	1911-1913	
Georges Carpentier	France	1913-1920	IBU
Jack Dillon	USA	1914-1916	USA
Battling Levinsky	USA	1916-1920	USA
Georges Carpentier	France	1920-1922	
Battling Siki	Senegal	1922-1923	
Mike McTigue	Ireland	1923-1925	
Paul Berlenbach	USA	1925-1926	
Jack Delaney*	Canada	1926-1927	
Jimmy Slattery	USA	1927	NBA
Tommy Loughran	USA	1927	NY
Tommy Loughran*	USA	1927-1929	
Jimmy Slattery	USA	1930	NY
Maxie Rosenbloom	USA	1930-1931	
Maxie Rosenbloom	USA	1931-1933	NY
George Nichols	USA	1932	NBA
Bob Godwin	USA	1933	NBA
Maxie Rosenbloom	USA	1933-1934	
Maxie Rosenbloom	USA	1934	NY
Joe Knight	USA	1934-1935	FL/NC/GEO
Bob Olin	USA	1934-1935	NY
Al McCoy	Canada	1935	CAN
Bob Olin	USA	1935	NY/NBA
John Henry Lewis	USA	1935-1938	NY/NBA
Gustav Roth	Belgium	1936-1938	IBU
Ad Heuser	Germany	1938	IBU
John Henry Lewis	USA	1938	
John Henry Lewis	USA	1938-1939	NBA
Melio Bettina	USA	1939	NY
Len Harvey	England	1939-1942	GB
Billy Conn	USA	1939-1940	NY/NBA
Anton Christoforidis	Greece	1941	NBA
Gus Lesnevich	USA	1941	NBA
Gus Lesnevich	USA	1941-1946	NY/NBA
Freddie Mills	England	1942-1946	GB
Gus Lesnevich	USA	1946-1948	
Freddie Mills	England	1948-1950	
Joey Maxim	USA	1950-1952	
Archie Moore	USA	1952-1960	
Archie Moore	USA	1960-1962	NY/EBU
Harold Johnson	USA	1961-1962	NBA
Harold Johnson	USA	1962-1963	
Willie Pastrano	USA	1963	
Willie Pastrano*	USA	1963-1964	WBA/WBC
Eddie Cotton	USA	1963-1964	MICH
Willie Pastrano	USA	1964-1965	
Jose Torres	Puerto Rico	1965-1966	
Dick Tiger	Nigeria	1966-1968	
Bob Foster	USA	1968-1970	
Bob Foster*	USA	1970-1972	WBC
Vicente Rondon	Venezuela	1971-1972	WBA

Bob Foster*	USA	1972-1974	
John Conteh	England	1974-1977	WBC
Victor Galindez	Argentina	1974-1978	WBA
Miguel Cuello	Argentina	1977-1978	WBC
Mate Parlov	Yugoslavia	1978	WBC
Mike Rossman	USA	1978-1979	WBA
Marvin Johnson	USA	1978-1979	WBC
Victor Galindez	Argentina	1979	WBA
Matt Saad Muhammad	USA	1979-1981	WBC
Marvin Johnson	USA	1979-1980	WBA
Mustafa Muhammad	USA	1980-1981	WBA
Michael Spinks*	USA	1981-1983	WBA
Dwight Muhammad Qawi	USA	1981-1983	WBC
Michael Spinks*	USA	1983-1985	
J. B. Williamson	USA	1985-1986	WBC
Slobodan Kacar	Yugoslavia	1985-1986	IBF
Marvin Johnson	USA	1986-1987	WBA
Dennis Andries	Guyana	1986-1987	WBC
Bobby Czyz	USA	1986-1987	IBF
Thomas Hearns*	USA	1987	WBC
Leslie Stewart	Trinidad	1987	WBA
Virgil Hill	USA	1987-1991	WBA
Charles Williams	USA	1987-1993	IBF
Don Lalonde	Canada	1987-1988	WBC
Sugar Ray Leonard*	USA	1988	WBC
Michael Moorer*	USA	1988-1991	WBO
Dennis Andries	Guyana	1989	WBC
Jeff Harding	Australia	1989-1990	WBC
Dennis Andries	Guyana	1990-1991	WBC
Leonzer Barber	USA	1991-1994	WBO
Thomas Hearns	USA	1991-1992	WBA
Jeff Harding	Australia	1991-1994	WBC
Iran Barkley*	USA	1992	WBA
Virgil Hill*	USA	1992-1996	WBA
Henry Maske	Germany	1993-1996	IBF
Mike McCallum	Jamaica	1994-1995	WBC
Dariusz Michalczewski*	Poland	1994-1997	WBO
Fabrice Tiozzo	France	1995-1997	WBC
Virgil Hill	USA	1996-1997	IBF/WBA
Roy Jones	USA	1997	WBC
Montell Griffin	USA	1997	WBC
Dariusz Michalczewski*	Poland	1997	WBO/IBF/WBA
Dariusz Michalczewski	Poland	1997-	WBO
William Guthrie	USA	1997-1998	IBF
Roy Jones*	USA	1997-1998	WBC
Lou del Valle	USA	1997-1998	WBA
Reggie Johnson	USA	1998-1999	IBF
Roy Jones*	USA	1998-1999	WBC/WBA
Roy Jones	USA	1999-	WBC/WBA/IBF

Cruiserweight (190 lbs)

Marvin Camel	USA	1979-1980	WBC
Carlos de Leon	Puerto Rico	1980-1982	WBC
Ossie Ocasio	Puerto Rico	1982-1984	WBA
S. T. Gordon	USA	1982-1983	WBC
Marvin Camel	USA	1983-1984	IBF
Carlos de Leon	Puerto Rico	1983-1985	WBC
Lee Roy Murphy	USA	1984-1986	IBF
Piet Crous	S Africa	1984-1985	WBA
Alfonso Ratliff	USA	1985	WBC
Dwight Muhammad Qawi	USA	1985-1986	WBA
Bernard Benton	USA	1985-1986	WBC
Carlos de Leon	Puerto Rico	1986-1988	WBC
Evander Holyfield*	USA	1986-1987	WBA
Rickey Parkey	USA	1986-1987	IBF
Evander Holyfield*	USA	1987-1988	WBA/IBF
Evander Holyfield*	USA	1988	
Taoufik Belbouli*	France	1989	WBA
Carlos de Leon	Puerto Rico	1989-1990	WBC
Glenn McCrory	England	1989-1990	IBF
Robert Daniels	USA	1989-1991	WBA
Boone Pultz	USA	1989-1990	WBO
Jeff Lampkin*	USA	1990-1991	IBF
Magne Havnaa*	Norway	1990-1992	WBO
Masimilliano Duran	Italy	1990-1991	WBC
Bobby Czyz	USA	1991-1993	WBA

Anaclet Wamba	Congo	1991-1995	WBC
James Warring	USA	1991-1992	IBF
Tyrone Booze	USA	1992-1993	WBO
Al Cole*	USA	1992-1996	IBF
Marcus Bott	Germany	1993	WBO
Nestor Giovannini	Argentina	1993-1994	WBO
Orlin Norris	USA	1993-1995	WBA
Dariusz Michalczewski*	Poland	1994-1995	WBO
Ralf Rocchigiani	Germany	1995-1997	WBO
Nate Miller	USA	1995-1997	WBA
Marcelo Dominguez	Argentina	1995-1998	WBC
Adolpho Washington	USA	1996-1997	IBF
Uriah Grant	USA	1997	IBF
Carl Thompson	England	1997-1999	WBO
Imamu Mayfield	USA	1997-1998	IBF
Fabrice Tiozzo	France	1997-2000	WBA
Juan Carlos Gomez	Cuba	1998-	WBC
Arthur Williams	USA	1998-1999	IBF
Johnny Nelson	England	1999-	WBO
Vassily Jirov	Kazakhstan	1999-	IBF
Virgil Hill	USA	2000-	WBA

Heavyweight (190 lbs+)

John L. Sullivan	USA	1889-1892	USA
Peter Jackson	Australia	1889-1892	
Frank Slavin	Australia	1890-1892	GB/AUST
Peter Jackson	Australia	1892-1893	GB/AUST
James J. Corbett	USA	1892-1894	USA
James J. Corbett	USA	1894-1895	
James J. Corbett	USA	1895-1897	
Peter Maher	Ireland	1895-1896	
Bob Fitzsimmons	England	1896-1897	
Bob Fitzsimmons	England	1897-1899	
James J. Jeffries	USA	1899-1902	
James J. Jeffries	USA	1902-1905	
Denver Ed Martin	USA	1902-1903	
Jack Johnson	USA	1902-1908	
Bob Fitzsimmons	England	1905	
Marvin Hart	USA	1905-1906	
Jack O'Brien	USA	1905-1906	
Tommy Burns	Canada	1906-1908	
Jack Johnson	USA	1908-1909	
Jack Johnson	USA	1909-1915	
Sam Langford	USA	1909-1911	
Sam McVey	USA	1911-1912	
Sam Langford	USA	1912-1914	
Luther McCarty	USA	1913	
Arthur Pelkey	Canada	1913-1914	
Gunboat Smith	USA	1914	
Harry Wills	USA	1914	
Georges Carpentier	France	1914	
Sam Langford	USA	1914-1915	
Jess Willard	USA	1915-1919	
Joe Jeannette	USA	1915	
Sam McVey	USA	1915	
Harry Wills	USA	1915-1916	
Sam Langford	USA	1916-1917	
Bill Tate	USA	1917	
Sam Langford	USA	1917-1918	
Harry Wills	USA	1918-1926	
Jack Dempsey	USA	1919-1926	
Gene Tunney*	USA	1926-1928	
Max Schmeling	Germany	1930-1932	
Jack Sharkey	USA	1932-1933	
Primo Carnera	Italy	1933-1934	
Max Baer	USA	1934-1935	
James J. Braddock	USA	1935	
James J. Braddock	USA	1935-1936	NY/NBA
George Godfrey	USA	1935-1936	IBU
James J. Braddock	USA	1936-1937	
Joe Louis*	USA	1937-1949	
Ezzard Charles	USA	1949-1950	NBA
Lee Savold	USA	1950-1951	GB/EBU
Ezzard Charles	USA	1950-1951	NY/NBA
Joe Louis	USA	1951	GB/EBU
Jersey Joe Walcott	USA	1951	NY/NBA

WORLD CHAMPIONS SINCE GLOVES, 1889-2001

Jersey Joe Walcott	USA	1951-1952	
Rocky Marciano*	USA	1952-1956	
Floyd Patterson	USA	1956-1959	
Ingemar Johansson	Sweden	1959-1960	
Floyd Patterson	USA	1960-1962	
Sonny Liston	USA	1962-1964	
Muhammad Ali	USA	1964	
Muhammad Ali*	USA	1964-1967	WBC
Ernie Terrell	USA	1965-1967	WBA
Muhammad Ali	USA	1967	
Joe Frazier*	USA	1968-1970	WBC
Jimmy Ellis	USA	1968-1970	WBA
Joe Frazier	USA	1970-1973	
George Foreman	USA	1973-1974	
Muhammad Ali	USA	1974-1978	
Leon Spinks	USA	1978	
Leon Spinks	USA	1978	WBA
Larry Holmes*	USA	1978-1983	WBC
Muhammad Ali*	USA	1978-1979	WBA
John Tate	USA	1979-1980	WBA
Mike Weaver	USA	1980-1982	WBA
Michael Dokes	USA	1982-1983	WBA
Gerrie Coetzee	S Africa	1983-1984	WBA
Larry Holmes	USA	1983-1985	IBF
Tim Witherspoon	USA	1984	WBC
Pinklon Thomas	USA	1984-1986	WBC
Greg Page	USA	1984-1985	WBA
Tony Tubbs	USA	1985-1986	WBA
Michael Spinks	USA	1985-1987	IBF
Tim Witherspoon	USA	1986	WBA
Trevor Berbick	Jamaica	1986	WBC
Mike Tyson*	USA	1986-1987	WBC
James Smith	USA	1986-1987	WBA
Mike Tyson*	USA	1987	WBA/WBC
Tony Tucker	USA	1987	IBF
Mike Tyson	USA	1987-1989	
Mike Tyson	USA	1989-1990	IBF/WBA/WBC
Francesco Damiani	Italy	1989-1991	WBO
James Douglas	USA	1990	IBF/WBA/WBC
Evander Holyfield	USA	1990-1992	IBF/WBA/WBC
Ray Mercer	USA	1991-1992	WBO
Michael Moorer*	USA	1992-1993	WBO
Riddick Bowe	USA	1992	IBF/WBA/WBC
Riddick Bowe	USA	1992-1993	IBF/WBA
Lennox Lewis	England	1992-1994	WBC
Tommy Morrison	USA	1993	WBO
Michael Bentt	England	1993-1994	WBO
Evander Holyfield	USA	1993-1994	WBA/IBF
Herbie Hide	England	1994-1995	WBO
Michael Moorer	USA	1994	WBA/IBF
Oliver McCall	USA	1994-1995	WBC
George Foreman	USA	1994-1995	WBA/IBF
Riddick Bowe*	USA	1995-1996	WBO
George Foreman*	USA	1995	IBF
Bruce Seldon	USA	1995-1996	WBA
Frank Bruno	England	1995-1996	WBC
Frans Botha	S Africa	1995-1996	IBF
Mike Tyson	USA	1996	WBC
Michael Moorer	USA	1996-1997	IBF
Henry Akinwande*	England	1996-1997	WBO
Mike Tyson	USA	1996	WBA
Evander Holyfield*	USA	1996-1997	WBA
Lennox Lewis*	England	1997-1999	WBC
Herbie Hide	England	1997-1999	WBO
Evander Holyfield	USA	1997-1999	IBF/WBA
Vitali Klitschko	Ukraine	1999-2000	WBO
Lennox Lewis	England	1999-2000	IBF/WBA/WBC
Chris Byrd	USA	2000	WBO
Lennox Lewis	England	2000-2001	IBF/WBC
Evander Holyfield	USA	2000-2001	WBA
Vladimir Klitschko	Ukraine	2000-	WBO
John Ruiz	USA	2001-	WBA
Hasim Rahman	USA	2001-	WBA/IBF

Joe Frazier, the heavyweight champion between 1968 and 1973

Harry Goodwin

A youthful looking Muhammad Ali, the legendary heavyweight champion

Derek Rowe

250

PRO-AM BOXING EQUIPMENT

32 ST HELENS ROAD, PRESCOT, MERSEYSIDE, L34 6HS, U.K.

TEL: 0151 426 0888 FAX: 0151 426 7299

**FULL RANGE OF PAFFEN SPORTS
PRO & AMATEUR EQUIPMENT**

**EVERYTHING EVERLAST
MAKES - WE SELL
GLOVES, HEADGEAR, SHORTS,
BOOTS, PUNCHBAGS, SPEEDBAGS**

**FULL RANGE OF ADIDAS
BOXING BOOTS & CLOTHING IN STOCK**

FULL RANGE OF TWINS GLOVES

251

THE HOME OF SPORT AND FRIENDSHIP
PEACOCK GYMNASIUM
EUROPE'S PREMIER BOXING GYM

AM & PRO BOXING
FULLY EQUIPPED GYM
KICKBOXING
KHAI-BO
KARATE
AEROBICS
TRAINING CIRCUITS
ULTIMATE FIGHT
TEAM
SUNBEDS/SAUNA

WITH OVER 6000 MEMBERS ALREADY, WE WELCOME NEW MEMBERS DAILY TO COME ALONG AND ENJOY OUR FACILITIES AND FRIENDLY ATMOSPHERE.

OPENING TIMES: MON-FRIDAY 9.30AM TO 9.00PM
SATURDAY   10.00AM TO 4.00PM
SUNDAY   10.00AM TO 1.00PM

MEMBERSHIP: ADULTS: £10 PER YEAR PLUS £3.00 PER SESSION
NON MEMBERS: £5.00
UNDER 16S: £5.00 PER YEAR + 50P PER SESSION

PEACOCK A.B.C.
AFFILIATED TO THE ABA, LONDON ABA, LY, NABC

PATRONS	PRESIDENT	CHAIRMAN
TONY BANKS MP	A. BOWERS	W. COX
F. BRUNO ESQ	VICE PRESIDENTS	VICE CHAIRMAN
B. MURRAY ESQ	M. BOWERS	B. BOWERS
J. FITZPATRICK MP	R.C. HILDER	
GEORGE WALKER		
BILLY WALKER		

APPEAL STEWARDS	ADMINISTRATIVE STEWARDS	
P. HUGHMAN QC	MR J. BULL	MRS J. BULL
F. CUTTS LB HONS	J. TURNER	P. BOWERS
P. BLACK QC	J. HALL	

GENERAL SECRETARY	TREASURER	ASS. TREASERER	MEDICAL OFFICER	M.E. ASSISTANT
D. TRIPHOOK	P. KINGSLEY	P. LYONS F.C.A.	DR DUBAL	J. RINGWOOD

JNR. SQ. COMP.SEC.	RECORDER	HEAD COACH	COACHES
T. SMITH	M. ALLAG	G. BOWERS	F. RUSSELL, ANDRE OLLEY, ROY ANDRE, JOHN VAUGHAN

THE RECENTLY FORMED PEACOCK A.B.C. WELCOMES PROSPECTIVE BOXERS TO JOIN THEIR RANKS FOR THE FORTHCOMING SEASON 2001/2002

PEACOCK HOUSE CAXTON ST NORTH CANNING TOWN LONDON E16 1JL
TEL: (020) 7511 3799/(020) 7476 8427   FAX: (020) 7476 8359
EMAIL: **peacockgym@aol.com**

252

Highlights From the 2000-2001 Amateur Season

by Chris Kempson

Without doubt, Audley Harrison made this a memorable season for amateur boxing in these islands with his gold medal super-heavyweight triumph at the Sydney 2000 Olympic Games, having become the first Englishman to win an Olympic gold medal since Chris Finnegan's middleweight triumph in Mexico City in 1968. The giant Repton southpaw boxed four times for his gold medal triumph, but could have fallen at the first hurdle when trailing on points to Alexei Lezin before pulling a left hook out of the bag to stop the Russian in the last round. Oleksei Mazikin from the Ukraine was comfortably outscored 19-9 in the quarter-final and the Italian, Paolo Vidoz, was summarily dismissed 32-16 in the semi-final (the 15-point rule erroneously not being enforced). On 1 October in the last contest of the tournament, Audley thumped Mukhtarkhan Dildabekov from Kazakhstan 30-16 in the final to eventually stand on the Olympic rostrum with the gold medal round his neck. The MBE was later bestowed on him, along with various other accolades and trophies.

The popular Harrison made his professional debut in May and looks set to earn a fortune in the paid ranks. His then Repton club mate, Courtney Fry, lost in the first series at light-heavyweight to Ghana's Charles Adamu, while a similar fate befell Ireland's Michael Roche in the light-middleweight division when he succumbed to Turkey's Firat Karagollu.

The Odyssey Arena in Belfast staged the World Senior Championships (3-10 June), the first time they had been brought to these shores, and proved to be England's best ever, having never won a medal at this event before. Heavyweight David Haye, now with east London's Broad Street, struck silver, middleweight Carl Froch (Phoenix, Nottingham) secured bronze, while Irish welterweight, James Moore (Arklow, Wicklow), also claimed bronze. Indeed, the Irish may have hoped for a larger medal tally, having got a record six boxers through to the quarter finals, but it was not to be.

Haye won three times to set up a final clash with Cuba's Odlanier Solis Fonte and almost stopped his rival in the opening round before being eventually outgunned and stopped in the third round. It was an outstanding performance by Haye, which augurs well for his future. Carl Froch showed fine form, also winning three times, to reach the semi-finals where he was outscored 28-16 by the Russian southpaw, Andrei Gogolev, the eventual gold medallist. Ireland's James Moore boxed and won four bouts to reach the semi-finals, where he met America's Anthony Thompson, who triumphed 36-24 over the Irishman. The championships drew good crowds and can be considered to have been a major success for the Irish hosts.

All in all it was a very successful season for both England's junior and senior internationalists who went on the road to various tournaments around the globe. In July (6-8), England captured two golds and two silvers in the annual International Junior Olympic tournament in the

United States at Northern Michigan University in Marquette. Darlington's Martin Stead and Derry Matthews, of Liverpool's Salisbury Club, both struck gold, while Wednesbury's Mohammed Shazad and Peterborough's Fred Holmes each took silver.

England scooped three bronze medals at the 30th Golden Jubilee edition of a multi-nations held in the southern Hungarian town of Szeged from 20-23 July. Shannon's ABA bantamweight champion, Steve Foster, tall Broad Street southpaw welterweight, Michael Lomax, and Stephen Birch (St Helen's Town), at light-middleweight, were the successful trio.

All seven of England's entrants in the under-19 multi-nations event held in Eger, Hungary from 16-21 August, came home with a medal. Golds went to Terry Fletcher of Karmand and Matt Macklin (Small Heath Police), silver to Liverpool's Mark Moran (Golden Gloves) and Zavdhul Zaman of Middlesbrough, with Wigan's Craig Lyon, Matthew Marsh (West Ham) and Femi Fehintola of Karmand each capturing bronze.

The prestigious Felix Stamm multi-nations tournament in Warsaw, Poland, from 25-28 October, saw glorious successes for five of our top senior talent. Hollington's light-fly, Darren Langley, and Repton's light-welter, Danny Happe, were the gold medallists; Stephen Birch (St Helens Town) took silver at light-middle; while Liverpool's Stephen Burke (Salisbury) at lightweight and Nottingham Phoenix middleweight, Carl Froch, won bronze.

The World Junior Championships were held in Budapest, Hungary from 4-12 November and only Ireland's Coleman Barrett (Olympic, Galway) came home with a medal, a commendable bronze, in the heavyweight division.

All five members of England's team won a medal at the junior multi-nations tournament in Salonica, Greece from 22-27 November. Zavdhul Zaman (Middlesbrough) struck gold, and there were silvers for Femi Fehintola (Karmand) and Daniel Teasdale (Grimethorpe and Cudworth), with bronze for Scott McDonald (Fitzroy Lodge) and Paul Smith (Rotunda).

England picked up three gold, one silver and three bronze medals at the Copenhagen Box Cup from 23-26 November. The golds went to Danny Happe (Repton) at light-welter, Carl Froch (Phoenix, Nottingham) at middleweight and David Haye (Fitzroy Lodge) at heavyweight, with the Fisher light-middleweight, Matthew Thirwall, grabbing silver. Bronze medals were collected by Steven Bell (Nichols Police) at featherweight, Michael Lomax (Broad Street) at welterweight and David Dolan (Plains Farm) at heavyweight.

England netted six medals at the Arena Cup in Pula, Croatia (2-5 May). Flyweight Darren Langley (Hollington), bantamweight Mark Moran (Golden Gloves, Liverpool) and heavyweight David Haye (Fitzroy Lodge) won gold, while featherweight David Mulholland (Salisbury, Liverpool), light-welterweight Gavin Smith (Karmand) and super-heavyweight Matthew Grainger (Woking) picked up bronze.

Nick McDonald (Vauxhall Motors) won silver at the annual junior multi-nations in Alghero, Sardinia (28 May - 3 June), with David Pendleton (East Durham Academy) and David Price (Long Lane) each earning bronze. However, the Scottish light-middleweight, Brian Peacock, was the star of this tournament, winning three times to land a wonderful gold medal. Ireland won silver through lightweight Roy Sheahan and bronze came via Paul Hyland at light-flyweight, and at flyweight via Lee Thomas.

England had some fine success at the 22nd annual Acropolis Cup multi-nations in Athens from 14-17 June. the Dolan brothers, James and David from Plains Farm, scooped silver as did Small Heath's Matthew Macklin. Bronze medals were secured at bantamweight by Mark Moran and at featherweight by William Corcoran.

The first Anglo-Gaelic Championships were held in Swansea, on 26-27 June, at the Baglan Social Club. These championships, like their predecessor event, the Gaelic Games, were dominated by Ireland who, in winning the President's Trophy, won nine of the 15 golds. Wales won three golds, Scotland landed two and England took the other.

On the international front there was an early 4-2 defeat for England on 1 July against France, with one draw, at La Teste de Buch, near Bordeaux. England schoolboys ventured to Russia, boxing two matches; first in Vladimir on 24 July, winning 7-6, and then losing 6-5 in Gyskrystaini on 28 July, making it 12 bouts each overall. Ireland forced two fine draws 6-6 and 3-3 against the United States in October in Mashantucket, Connecticut and Denver, Colorado, respectively.

England triumphed 5-2 over the United States on 20 November in the annual HABAD charity clash at the Park Lane Hilton, winning the last four bouts to seal their victory.

Scotland's youngsters were victorious over their English under-19 counterparts at the Royal Lancaster Hotel in London on 5 February, when winning 4-2, while Ireland were beaten 5-4 by the USA in Dublin on 27 April and then again by the same score in Waterford on 29 April.

England schoolboys beat South Africa 8-3 at the Flamingo Rooms in Keresforth Hall, Barnsley on 2 April and then by 6-3 at the Britannia Hotel in London's Docklands on 6 April, to take the series 14-6. Also, on 6 April, Young Ireland edged out Young Italy 6-5 at the National Stadium in Dublin.

England enjoyed a successful trip to Canada, winning both their matches, the first by 7-3 at Regina in Saskatchewan (4 May) and the second by 4-3 at Moose Jaw (7 May) in the same province.

The first Four Nations tournament between England, Scotland, Ireland and Wales took place in the magnificent St George's Hall in Liverpool (12-13 April), England finishing top with four golds, six silver and two bronze, Ireland coming in second on 4-4-4, Scotland third on 2-2-3 and Wales fourth on 2-0-3.

Salisbury's Stephen Burke (left) won the 2001 ABA lightweight title, his second, when outpointing Tristan Davies (Donnington ex-Servicemen)

Les Clark

England schoolboys continued their fine recent run of success with a tight 8-7 victory over Ireland in Dungarvon on 13 May.

England beat France 4-2 in a junior international match at Saint-Sebastian-sur-Loire on 16 June.

The finals of the senior ABA Championship were staged once again at the Barnsley Metrodome (30 March) – with Fisher's Matthew Thirwall, the star of the show, destroying Stephen Birch (St Helens Town) inside two rounds to claim his first ABA title. There were five other new champions: Craig Lyon (Wigan), son of eight-time ABA champion John (who trains him), Matthew Marsh (West Ham), Gavin Smith (Karmand), Matthew Macklin (Small Heath) and Matthew Grainger (Woking). Steve Foster (Shannon) and the Dolan brothers, James and David (Plains Farm), each won for the second time in a row, while Courtney Fry now with Salisbury, Liverpool captured his third title with as many clubs (Islington and Repton being the other two). There were victories for Steven Bell (Nichols Police), Stephen Burke (Salisbury, Liverpool) and Carl Froch (Phoenix, Nottingham), who were previous titleholders.

The Irish Senior Championship finals, held as usual at the National Stadium in Dublin (23 February), saw eight-time champion Neil Gough (St Paul's, Waterford) defeated in the welterweight final by James Moore (Arklow, Wicklow), who was also named the tournament's "Best Boxer". Moore had lost to Gough in last year's final. Defending champions, Liam Cunningham (Saints, Belfast),

Damien McKenna (Holy Family, Drogheda), Michael Roche (Sunnyside, Cork), Alan and Stephen Reynolds (St Joseph's Sligo) and John Kinsella (Crumlin, Dublin) retained their titles. John Paul Kinsella (St Fergal's, Wicklow), John Paul Campbell (St Patrick's, South Meath), Noel Monteith (Dockers, Belfast), Michael Kelly (Dealgan, Louth) and Kenneth Egan (Neilstown, Dublin) bagged the other crowns.

In Scotland, the ABS senior finals were staged at the Monklands Time Capsule, Coatbridge on 2 March. The Inverness stylist, Scott McKay, retained his flyweight title with a masterly display of the noble art, while club mate Sandy Robb captured Scotland's first-ever cruiserweight title. The Inverness hat-trick was brought about by heavyweight, Andy Young. Forgewood's Tony McPake won again this year, as did Ian Mullarvie (Phoenix, Glasgow), while other title claimants were Nick Bonini (Hawick), John Davidson (Bannockburn), Mark Hastie (Forgewood), top prospect Kevin Anderson (Denbeath), Colin McNeil (Fauldhouse), Jamie Coyle (Bannockburn), Steve McGuire (Glenrothes) and Lee Ramsey (Kingdom).

The Welsh held their senior championships as usual at the Afan Lido, Port Talbot, on 23 March. Five reigning champions reclaimed their titles as follows: Darren Edwards (Cwmavon Hornets), Shaun Bowers (Rhondda), Ceri Hall (Penyrheol), Stuart Phillips (Cwmavon Hornets) and Kevin Evans (Carmarthen), who took his fifth successive heavyweight crown. Other title-holders were Ryan Power (Torfaen Warriors), James Mwasigallah

Matthew Macklin, from the Small Heath club, won the 2001 ABA welterweight title when beating Penhill's Justin Turley (left), a three-time loser

Les Clark

(Splott Adventure), Jamie Evans (Army), Robert Davies (Cwmavon Hornets), Francisco Borg (Prince of Wales), Michael Allen (Palace, North Wales) and Scott Gammer (Pembroke), who won his fourth title in three different weight divisions.

The National Novice Finals were staged at the Leisure Centre in Knottingly on 16 December.

The finals of the NACYP Championships also took place in December. The Class A finals were held at the Leisure Centre in Peterlee on 15 December, the Class B finals took place in the Marriott Hotel, Bristol on 11 December and the Class C finals at the London Hilton Hotel on 4 December.

The Junior ABA Class 5 finals went to the National Sports Centre gymnasium at Crystal Palace on 21 April, while the Junior ABA Class 6 finals were held at the Winter Gardens in Margate, also on 21 April.

The 35th and last Stable Lads Championships were held at the London Hilton on 6 November. However, because nowadays over half the racing workforce is female, the relatively few number of lads left is sadly not enough to continue boxing.

Radical changes were made to the ABA Senior Championships. The eight regional champions took part in the open draw and boxed off the national quarter-finals and semis on consecutive days in March.

Annual four nations tournaments involving England, Scotland, Wales and Ireland were instituted in four different age groups – schools, cadet, junior and senior. And, it was thrilling to see BBC television providing coverage of the ABA quarter-finals, semis and finals, the four nations senior tournament and the World Senior Championships, being a much needed boost for amateur boxing.

The National Schoolboy Championship debacle at the Broadway Theatre in Barking, eventually led to the curtailment of the evening programme on 9 March and the postponement of 10 March session. Some of the remaining bouts were rearranged for 28 April at the Barnsley Metrodome, while others took place at different venues. This kind of fiasco must never happen again and an inquiry is looking into the cause of the crowd problems at Barking.

On 12 April, English amateur boxing received a handsome £13.8m of "World Class Performance Funding" from Sport England. The money will be used for preparation and competition at international level up until the 2008 Olympic Games and there will be three categories of funding – Potential, Performance and Elite – over the four international age groups. The legendary American professional trainer, Emanuel Steward from Detroit, poured money and resources into north London's St Pancras ABC, which was re-named St Pancras Kronk, while in east London, the Peacock Gymnasium sponsored various domestic championship and international events before opening their own Peacock ABC in their Canning Town headquarters in April.

It has been a privilege to write about this wonderfully successful amateur season and, while the legacy of Audley Harrison is an awesome act to follow, our emerging junior talent, together with our established senior talent, must aim to follow in his footsteps. On a personal note, it is a joy to be back once again with the *British Boxing Yearbook* team.

Craig Lyon (left), the son of the record-breaking John, and England's light-fly entrant in the World Junior Championships, is shown stopping the Army's Stefan Symes to win the 2001 ABA title

Les Clark

ABA National Championships, 2000-2001

Combined Services

RAF, RN & Army Championships   RAF Uxbridge - 24 & 25 January
L. Fly: *final:* S. Symes (Army) wo. **Fly:** *final:* D. Barriball (Army) wo. **Bantam:** *final:* P. Murray (Army) wo. **Feather:** no entries. **Light:** *final:* K. Davie (RN) w pts S. Richards (Army). **L. Welter:** *semi-finals:* J. Cronin (Army) wo, J. Cusick (RN) w rsc 4 S. O'Donnell (RAF); *final:* J. Cusick w pts J. Cronin. **Welter:** *final:* S. Briggs (Army) w rsc 3 G. Alderson (RN). **L. Middle:** *final:* M. McMahon (Army) wo. **Middle:** *final:* D. Frost (Army) wo. **L. Heavy:** *final:* L. Spare (Army) wo. **Cruiser:** *semi-finals:* V. Jones (Army) wo, T. Hindley (RN) w co 2 I. Aldridge (RAF); *final:* T. Hindley w pts V. Jones. **Heavy:** *semi-finals:* N. Siggs (RAF) wo, M. O'Connell (RN) w pts N. Okoth (Army); *final:* N. Siggs w dis 4 M. O'Connell. **S. Heavy:** no entries.

Eastern Counties v Home Counties

Essex Division   Civic Centre, Grays - 2 February
L. Fly: no entries. **Fly:** no entries. **Bantam:** no entries. **Feather:** *semi-finals:* B. Morgan (Stanford le Hope) wo, L. Otte (Castle) w rsc 2 D. Morgan (Canvey); *final:* L. Otte w co 3 B. Morgan. **Light:** *final:* J. Martin (Stanford le Hope) wo. **L. Welter:** *final:* R. Brown (Chalvedon) wo. **Welter:** no entries. **L. Middle:** *final:* J. Gunn (Stanford le Hope) wo. **Middle:** *final:* J. Cullinane (Southend) w pts H. Seaman (Castle). **L. Heavy:** *final:* H. Mahdavian (Brook) w rsc 3 M. Brown (Chalvedon). **Cruiser:** no entries. **Heavy:** *final:* S. St John (Berry Boys) wo. **S. Heavy:** no entries.

Mid-Anglia Division
L. Fly: no entries. **Fly:** no entries. **Bantam:** no entries. **Feather:** no entries. **Light:** no entries. **L. Welter:** no entries. **Welter:** *final:* B. Hudson (Cambridge Police) wo. **L. Middle:** no entries. **Middle:** no entries. **L. Heavy:** no entries. **Cruiser:** no entries. **Heavy:** no entries. **S. Heavy:** no entries.

Norfolk Division   Kingfisher ABC, Great Yarmouth - 13 January
L. Fly: no entries. **Fly:** no entries. **Bantam:** no entries. **Feather:** no entries. **Light:** *final:* F. Crosswell (Kingfisher) wo. **L. Welter:** no entries. **Welter:** no entries. **L. Middle:** *final:* B. Parr (Kingfisher) wo. **Middle:** no entries. **L. Heavy:** no entries. **Cruiser:** no entries. **Heavy:** no entries. **S. Heavy:** no entries.

Suffolk Division   Kingfisher ABC, Great Yarmouth - 13 January
L. Fly: no entries. **Fly:** no entries. **Bantam:** no entries. **Feather:** no entries. **Light:** no entries. **L. Welter:** *final:* K. Jackson (New Astley) wo. **Welter:** *final:* C. Nunn (New Astley) wo. **L. Middle:** no entries. **Middle:** *final:* A. Sims (Triple A) wo. **L. Heavy:** no entries. **Cruiser:** no entries. **Heavy:** *final:* S. Potter (Hurstlea & Kerridge) wo. **S. Heavy:** *final:* K. Fajimolu (Hurstlea & Kerridge) wo.

Eastern Counties   Sports Centre, Beccles - 17 February
L. Fly: no entries. **Fly:** no entries. **Bantam:** no entries. **Feather:** *final:* L. Otte (Castle) wo. **Light:** *final:* F. Crosswell (Kingfisher) w rsc 4 J. Martin (Stanford le Hope). **L. Welter:** *final:* K. Jackson (New Astley) w pts R. Brown (Chalvedon). **Welter:** B. Hudson (Cambridge Police) w pts C. Nunn (New Astley). **L. Middle:** *final:* J. Gunn (Stanford le Hope) w pts B. Parr (Kingfisher). **Middle:** *final:* J. Cullinane (Southend) w pts A. Sims (Triple A). **L. Heavy:** *final:* H. Mahdavian (Brook) wo. **Cruiser:** no entries. **Heavy:** *final:* S. St John (Berry Boys) w pts S. Potter (Hurstlea & Kerridge). **S. Heavy:** *final:* K. Fajimolu (Hurstlea & Kerridge) wo.

Home Counties   Leisure Centre, Berinsfield - 24 February
L. Fly: no entries. **Fly:** no entries. **Bantam:** no entries. **Feather:** no entries. **Light:** *final:* H. Rahman (Callowland) wo. **L. Welter:** *final:* N. Ward (Mo's) w rsc 3 I. Reading (Hitchin). **Welter:** *final:* J. Akram (Slough) w co 1 J. Grant (Berinsfield). **L. Middle:** *final:* E. Matthews (Callowland) w pts C. Marks (Farley). **Middle:** *final:* C. Woods (Wolvercote) wo. **L. Heavy:** *final:* S. Price (Pinewood Starr) w pts S. Lawler (Luton Shamrock). **Cruiser:** no entries. **Heavy:** no entries. **S. Heavy:** *final:* M. Legg (Callowland) w pts S. Dunn (Callowland).

Eastern Counties v Home Counties   Football Ground, Thame - 3 March
L. Fly: no entries. **Fly:** no entries. **Bantam:** no entries. **Feather:** L. Otte (Castle) wo. **Light:** F. Crosswell (Kingfisher) w pts H. Rahman (Callowland). **L. Welter:** K. Jackson (New Astley) w co 1 H. Rahman (Callowland). **Welter:** B. Hudson (Cambridge Police) w pts J.Akram (Slough). **L. Middle:** E. Matthews (Callowland) w co 1 J. Gunn (Stanford le Hope). **Middle:** J. Cullinane (Southend) w pts C. Woods (Wolvercote). **L. Heavy:** S. Price (Pinewood Starr) w co 1 H. Mahdavian (Brook). **Cruiser:** no entries. **Heavy:** S. St John (Berry Boys) wo. **S. Heavy:** M. Legg (Callowland) w co 2 K. Fajimolu (Hurstlea & Kerridge).

London

North-East Division   York Hall, Bethnal Green - 8 February
L. Fly: no entries. **Fly:** *final:* M. Marsh (West Ham) w rsc 3 T. Joyett (Repton). **Bantam:** *final:* M. Gadaffi (Repton) w rtd 3 T. Gurunaidu (Fairbairn House). **Feather:** *final:* R. Sictorness (Repton) wo. **Light:** *semi-finals:* P. Gurunaidu (Fairbairn House) wo, D. Barker (Repton) w pts M. Burke (Broad Street); *final:* D. Barker w rtd 3 P. Gurunaidu. **L. Welter:** *final:* D. Happe (Repton) wo. **Welter:** *final:* T. Cesay (Repton) w dis 4 M. Lomax (Broad Street). **L. Middle:** *final:* D. Cadman (Repton) w rsc 4 P. Masterson (Alma). **Middle:** *semi-finals:* D. Robinson (Repton) wo, D. Verdi (Repton) w pts J. Reilly (Broad Street); *final:* D. Robinson wo D. Verdi. **L. Heavy:** *semi-finals:* A. Boyd (Broad Street) wo, A. Southwick (Dagenham) w pts A. Lowe (Repton); *final:* A. Southwick w rsc 3 A. Boyd. **Cruiser:** *semi-finals:* A. Stables (Repton) wo, P. Souter (Broad Street) w pts M. Lee (Repton); *final:* P. Souter w pts A. Stables. **Heavy:** *final:* J. Zikic (Repton) wo. **S. Heavy:** *final:* R. McCallum (Broad Street) w pts A. Edwards (Repton).

North-West Division   Irish Centre, Camden Town - 5 February
L. Fly: no entries. **Fly:** no entries. **Bantam:** *final:* M. Power (St

Pancras) wo. **Feather:** *final:* W. Corcoran (Stowe) w pts R. Walstad (St Pancras). **Light:** *final:* F. Ryan (St Pancras) w pts K. Elias (Dale Youth). **L. Welter:** *semi-finals:* I. Neha (Hanwell) w pts J. Barrett (Trojan Police), J. O'Donnell (Stowe) w pts A. Theophane (All Stars); *final:* J. O'Donnell w pts I. Neha. **Welter:** *final:* J. Morrison (All Stars) w pts A. Neunie (Trojan Police). **L. Middle:** no entries. **Middle:** *semi-finals:* J. Barrett (Trojan Police) wo, C. Campbell (Trojan Police) w rsc 2 G. Synetos (St Pancras); *final:* C. Campbell w pts J. Barrett. **L. Heavy:** *semi-finals:* G. Ugbiro (Trojan Police) wo, R. Faustino (All Stars) w pts T. Simao (All Stars); *final:* R. Faustino w pts G. Ugbiro. **Cruiser:** *semi-finals:* E. Sitta (All Stars) wo, A. Aliy (Haringey Police) w rsc 1 C. Barrett (Trojan Police); *final:* A. Aliy w rsc 1 E. Sitta. **Heavy:** *final:* D. Brighton (Hayes) w pts A. Al Fady (All Stars). **S. Heavy:** *final:* P. Danquah (All Stars) w pts P. Pierson (Trojan Police).

South-East Division   National Sports Centre, Crystal Palace - 1 February & Earlsfield ABC Gym, Wandsworth - 9 February
L. Fly: *final:* D. Langley (Hollington) w pts S. McDonald (Fitzroy Lodge). **Fly:** *final:* S. Langley (Hollington) wo. **Bantam:** no entries. **Feather:** *final:* D. Lawrence (Danson Youth) w pts D. Twumasi (Fitzroy Lodge). **Light:** *final:* D. Pereira (Fitzroy Lodge) wo. **L. Welter:** *final:* G. Woolcombe (Marvels Lane) wo. **Welter:** *semi-finals:* A. Small (Fitzroy Lodge) w co 1 E. Mbwakongo (Fisher), M. Reigate (Fitzroy Lodge) w pts M. Barber (Fisher); *final:* M. Reigate w rsc 1 A. Small. **L. Middle:** *quarter-finals:* S. Webb (Bromley & Downham) wo, B. Aird (Fisher) wo, J. Hudson (Fitzroy Lodge) wo, M. Thirwall (Fisher) w rsc 3 G. Nenowhe (Eltham); *semi-finals:* S. Webb w pts B. Aird, M. Thirwall w rsc 3 J. Hudson; *final:* M. Thirwall w pts S. Webb. **Middle:** *final:* S. Tobin (Fitzroy Lodge) wo. **L. Heavy:** *final:* S. Johnson (Miguel's) w pts A. Coates (New Addington). **Cruiser:** *final:* J. Sawicki (Eltham) wo. **Heavy:** *final:* I. Lewison (Miguel's) wo. **S. Heavy:** *final:* S. Dumetz (Miguel's) wo.

South-West Division   Earlsfield ABC Gym, Wandsworth - 9 February
L. Fly: no entries. **Fly:** no entries. **Bantam:** no entries. **Feather:** no entries. **Light:** no entries. **L. Welter:** *final:* Lenny Daws (Rosehill) w pts G. Lowndes (Kingston). **Welter:** *final:* Luke Daws (Rosehill) w pts A. Freeman (Kingston). **L. Middle:** *final:* H. Komakech (Kingston) wo. **Middle:** no entries. **L. Heavy:** no entries. **Cruiser:** no entries. **Heavy:** no entries. **S. Heavy:** *final:* E. Gandi (Battersea) wo.

London Semi-Finals & Finals   York Hall, Bethnal Green - 22 February & 1 March
L. Fly: *final:* D. Langley (Hollington) wo. **Fly:** *final:* M. Marsh (West Ham) w dis 3 S. Langley (Hollington). **Bantam:** *final:* M. Power (St Pancras) w pts M. Gadaffi (Repton). **Feather:** D. Lawrence (Danson Youth) withdrew; *final:* W. Corcoran (Stowe) w pts R. Sictorness (Repton). **Light:** *semi-finals:* F. Ryan (St Pancras) wo, D. Barker (Repton) w pts D. Pereira (Fitzroy Lodge); *final:* D. Barker w pts F. Ryan. **L. Welter:** *semi-finals:* Lennie Daws (Rosehill) w rsc 1 G. Woolcombe (Marvels Lane), D. Happe (Repton) w rsc 4 J. O'Donnell (Stowe); *final:* D. Happe w pts Lennie Daws. **Welter:** *semi-finals:* T. Cesay (Repton) w pts M. Reigate (Fitzroy Lodge), Luke Daws (Rosehill) w pts J. Morrison (All Stars); *final:* T. Cesay w pts Luke Daws. **L. Middle:** *semi-finals:* D. Cadman (Repton) wo, M. Thirwall (Fisher) w rsc 2 H. Komakech (Kingston); *final:* M. Thirwall w co 3 D. Cadman. **Middle:** *semi-finals:* D. Robinson (Repton) wo, C. Campbell (Trojan Police) w rsc 3 S. Tobin (Fitzroy Lodge); *final:* D. Robinson w pts C. Campbell. **L. Heavy:** *semi-finals:* S. Johnson

(Miguel's) wo, A. Southwick (Dagenham) w pts R. Faustino (All Stars); *final:* A. Southwick w rsc 4 S. Johnson. **Cruiser:** *semi-finals:* A. Aliy (Haringey Police) wo, P. Souter (Broad Street) w pts J. Sawicki (Eltham); *final:* P. Souter w pts A. Aliy. **Heavy:** D. Brighton (Hayes) withdrew; *final:* J. Zikic (Repton) w pts I. Lewison (Miguel's). **S. Heavy:** *semi-finals:* R. McCallum (Broad Street) w pts P. Pierson (Trojan Police) - replaced P. Danqhah (All Stars), E. Gandi (Battersea) w rsc 1 S. Dumetz (Miguel's); *final:* R. McCallum w rsc 2 E. Gandi.

Midland Counties

Northern Zone   Festival Hall Leisure Centre, Kirkby in Ashfield - 16 February, Belvedere Club, Burton on Trent - 22 February & Swallows Hotel, Solihull - 23 February
L. Fly: no entries. **Fly:** *final:* J. Mulhern (Triumph) wo. **Bantam:** no entries. **Feather:** *final:* D. Walton (Willenhall) w pts M. Mayes (Braunstone). **Light:** *semi-finals:* C. Johnson (Chesterfield Ath) wo, M. Teague (Grimsby SoB) w pts R. Cartlidge (St George's); *final:* M. Teague and C. Johnson both disqualified in 1st round. **L. Welter:** *semi-finals:* C. Smith (Kingsthorpe) w rsc 2 S. Haywood (Chadd), P. McKervey (Bulkington) w pts D. Benson (Grimsby); *final:* C. Smith w pts P. McKervey. **Welter:** *final:* J. Flinn (Coventry Boys) w rsc 4 D. Jenkinson (Terry Allen SoB). **L. Middle:** *final:* M. Concepcion (Belgrave) w pts N. Lyons (Boston Gemini). **Middle:** *final:* C. Froch (Phoenix) w pts R. Mazurek (Leamington). **L. Heavy:** no entries. **Cruiser:** *final:* I. Johnson (Derby Trinity) w pts P. Beardsmore (South Normanton). **Heavy:** no entries. **S. Heavy:** *final:* J. Callum (Coventry Boys) wo.

Southern Zone   Saddler's Club, Walsall - 8 February & Gala Baths, West Bromwich - 16 February
L. Fly: no entries. **Fly:** *final:* A. Odud (Birmingham City) w pts B. Lewis (Heath Town). **Bantam:** *final:* S. Walton (Donnington Ex-Servicemen) wo. **Feather:** *final:* R. Wyatt (Lye) w pts N. Marston Shrewsbury Severnside). **Light:** *final:* T. Davies (Donnington Ex-Servicemen) w pts S. Lawton Queensberry). **L. Welter:** *final:* C. Brumant (Birmingham Irish) wo. **Welter:** *semi-finals:* T. Adams (Birmingham Irish) wo, M. Macklin (Small Heath) w pts J. Scanlon (Birmingham City); *final:* M. Macklin w rsc 3 T. Adams. **L. Middle:** *semi-finals:* C. Hubbard (Queensberry) w co 4 L. Hallett (Wednesbury), M. Fowles (Birmingham City); *final:* C. Hubbard w pts M. Fowles. **Middle:** *semi-finals:* H. Jamil (Birmingham City) w rtd 2 J. Brannigan (Small Heath), K. Blower (Heath Town) w pts A. Alexander (Birmingham City); *final:* H. Jamil w pts K. Blower. **L. Heavy:** *final:* S. Jones (Rugeley Police) wo. **Cruiser:** *final:* K. Hitchens (Birmingham City) w pts R. Doran (Shrewsbury Severnside). **Heavy:** *final:* D. Smith (Donnington Ex-Servicemen) wo. **S. Heavy:** no entries.

Midland Counties Finals   Sports & Social Club, Barras Heath - 10 March
L. Fly: no entries. **Fly:** J. Mulhern (Triumph) w pts A. Odud (Birmingham City). **Bantam:** S. Walton (Donnington Ex-Servicemen) wo. **Feather:** D. Walton (Willenhall) w pts R. Wyatt (Lye). **Light:** T. Davies (Donnington Ex-Servicemen) w pts R. Cartlidge (St George's) - Cartlidge was called up when both boxers in the Northern Zone final were disqualified. **L. Welter:** C. Smith (Kingsthorpe) w pts C. Brumant (Birmingham Irish). **Welter:** M. Macklin (Small Heath) w rsc 4 J. Flinn (Coventry Boys). **L. Middle:** M. Concepcion (Belgrave) w rtd 1 C. Hubbard (Queensberry). **Middle:** C. Froch (Phoenix) w pts H. Jamil

(Birmingham City). **L. Heavy:** S. Jones (Rugeley Police) wo. **Cruiser:** K. Hitchens (Birmingham City) w rsc 4 I. Johnson (Derby Trinity). **Heavy:** D. Smith (Donnington Ex-Servicemen) wo. **S. Heavy:** J. Callum (Coventry Boys) wo.

North-East Counties

Tyne, Tees & Wear Division   High Pit, Cramlington - 15 & 21 February
L. Fly: no entries. **Fly:** no entries. **Bantam:** *final:* L. Harvey (Empire SoB) wo. **Feather:** *semi-finals:* J. Sayer (Benton) wo, R. Boyle (Birtley) w pts I. Ward (Darlington); *final:* R. Boyle w rsc 1 J. Sayer. **Light:** *final:* G. Gibson (Aycliffe) wo. **L. Welter:** *final:* G. Harmison (Newbiggin) wo. **Welter:** *final:* M. McLean (Birtley) w pts A. Close (Hartlepool Catholic). **L. Middle:** *quarter-finals:* H. Greenwell (Sunderland) wo, D. Temperley (Birtley) wo, D. Moyer (Felling) wo, G. Wharton (Shildon) w pts F. Jones (Albert Hill); *semi-finals:* H. Greenwell w pts D. Temperley, G. Wharton w pts F. Jones; *final:* H. Greenwell w pts G. Wharton. **Middle:** *semi-finals:* S. Ward (Sunderland) wo, S. McCrone (Spennymoor) w pts D. Spensley (Ormesby); *final:* S. McCrone w pts S. Ward. **L. Heavy:** *final:* T. Marsden (Birtley) w pts D. Hinds (Bishop Auckland). **Cruiser:** *final:* J. Dolan (Plains Farm) w pts D. McFarlane (Birtley). **Heavy:** *final:* D. Dolan (Plains Farm) w rsc 2 D. Waite (Bishop Auckland). **S. Heavy:** *final:* J. Robinson (Plains Farm) w co 1 R. Brown (Blaydon).

Yorkshire & Humberside Division   Wellington Street Theatre, Barnsley - 20 February
L. Fly: no entries. **Fly:** R. Nelson (Karmand) wo. **Bantam:** J. Hussain (Bradford Police) w rsc 2 J. Dyer (Burmantofts & Hunslet). **Feather:** C. Hooper (Scarborough) wo. **Light:** T. Fletcher (Karmand) wo. **L.Welter:** G. Smith (Karmand) wo. **Welter:** P. Rushton (Hoyle Mill) w pts G. Wake (Burmantofts & Hunslet). **L. Middle:** no entries. **Middle:** W. Weaver (Handsworth) w pts S. McDonald (St Paul's). **L. Heavy:** A. Khan (Unity) w pts D. Cockburn (Doncaster Plant). **Cruiser:** no entries. **Heavy:** no entries. **S. Heavy:** no entries.

North-East Counties Finals   Manor Club, Sheffield - 1 March
L. Fly: no entries. **Fly:** R. Nelson (Karmand) wo. **Bantam:** J. Hussain (Bradford Police) w pts L. Harvey (Empire SoB). **Feather:** R. Boyle (Birtley) w pts C. Hooper (Scarborough). **Light:** T. Fletcher (Karmand) w co 2 G. Gibson (Aycliffe). **L. Welter:** G. Smith (Karmand) wo G. Harmison (Newbiggin). **Welter:** M. McLean (Birtley) w pts P. Rushton (Hoyle Mill). **L. Middle:** H. Greenwell (Sunderland) wo. **Middle:** S. McCrone (Spennymoor) w rsc 3 W. Weaver (Handsworth). **L. Heavy:** T. Marsden (Birtley) w pts A. Khan (Unity). **Cruiser:** J. Dolan (Plains Farm) wo. **Heavy:** D. Dolan (Plains Farm) wo. **S. Heavy:** J. Robinson (Plains Farm) wo.

North-West Counties

East Lancs & Cheshire Division   Town Hall, Stockport - 15 February & Leisure Centre, Horwich - 25 February
L. Fly: no entries. **Fly:** *final:* O. Trainor (Shannon) wo. **Bantam:** *final:* S. Foster (Shannon) wo. **Feather:** *final:* S. Bell (Nichols Police) wo. **Light:** *final:* J. Gaskell (Nichols Police) w pts D. Boone (Centurians). **L. Welter:** *final:* J. Thomas (Blackpool &

Fylde) wo. **Welter:** *final:* S. Jackson (Mottram & Hattersley) wo. **L. Middle:** *final:* J. Aikenhead (Sale West) w rsc 3 B. Alston (Paramount). **Middle:** *quarter-finals:* J. McKinley (Viking) wo, T. Fend (Nichols Police) wo, J. Hamilton (Blackburn) wo, A. Delaney (Blackpool & Fylde) w pts N. Travis (Ardwick Lads); *semi-finals:* J. McKinley w pts T. Fend, A. Delaney w rsc 3 J. Hamilton; *final:* A. Delaney w rsc 1 J. McKinley. **L. Heavy:** *final:* M. Nilsen (Sale West) w pts T. Green (Bredbury & Stockport). **Cruiser:** *final:* Vince Docherty (Lancs Constabulary) wo. **Heavy:** no entries. **S. Heavy:** no entries.

West-Lancs & Cheshire Division   Everton Park Sports Centre, Liverpool - 12, 16 & 23 February
L. Fly: *final:* C. Lyon (Wigan) w pts G. Jones (Rotunda). **Fly:** no entries. **Bantam:** *final:* G. Davies (St Helens Town) wo. **Feather:** *final:* D. Mulholland (Salisbury) wo. **Light:** *final:* S. Burke (Salisbury) w pts L. Jennings (Tower Hill). **L. Welter:** *quarter-finals:* P. Grice (Knowsley Vale) wo, I. Clyde (Crewe) wo, S. Matthews (Stanley) w rsc 4 E. Roberts (Golden Gloves), R. Shearer (Runcorn) w pts A. Pinkham (Golden Star); *semi-finals:* P. Grice w pts I. Clyde, S. Matthews w pts R. Shearer; *final:* S. Matthews w pts P. Grice. **Welter:** *semi-finals:* A. McGuire (Kirkdale) w pts M. Murphy (Wigan), J. Stanley (Kirkby) w pts L. Andrews (Salisbury); *final:* A. McGuire w pts J. Stanley. **L. Middle:** *semi-finals:* S. Birch (St Helens Town) wo, L. Kempster (Halewood) w pts R. Turner (Golden Gloves); *final:* S. Birch w rsc 3 L. Kempster. **Middle:** *semi-finals:* W. Fleming (West Wirral) wo, N. Perkins (Kirkdale) w rsc 3 S. Gidman (Crewe); *final:* N. Perkins w pts W. Fleming. **L. Heavy:** J. Ainscough (Kirkdale) wo, C. Fry (Salisbury) w rsc 4 M. Brett (West Wirral); *final:* C. Fry w pts J. Ainscough. **Cruiser:** *final:* M. Carroll (Golden Gloves) w pts M. Stafford (Kirkby). **Heavy:** *final:* G. Turner (Golden Gloves) wo. **S. Heavy:** *final:* B. Maguire (Long Lane) wo.

North-West Counties Finals   Everton Park Sports Centre, Liverpool - 2 March
L. Fly: C. Lyon (Wigan) wo. **Fly:** O. Trainor (Shannon) wo. **Bantam:** S. Foster (Shannon) w pts G. Davies (St Helens Town). **Feather:** S. Bell (Nichols Police) w pts D. Mulholland (Salisbury). **Light:** S. Burke (Salisbury) w pts J. Gaskell (Nichols Police). **L. Welter:** S. Matthews (Stanley) w pts J. Thomas (Blackpool & Fylde). **Welter:** A. McGuire (Kirkdale) w pts S. Jackson (Mottram & Hattersley). **L. Middle:** S. Birch (St Helens Town) wo J. Aikenhead (Sale West). **Middle:** N. Perkins (Kirkdale) w pts A. Delaney (Blackpool & Fylde). **L. Heavy:** C. Fry (Salisbury) w pts M. Nilsen (Sale West). **Cruiser:** M. Carroll (Golden Gloves) w co 1 V. Docherty (Lancs Constabulary). **Heavy:** G. Turner (Golden Gloves) wo. B.Maguire (Long Lane) wo.

Southern Counties

Northgate Community Centre, Canterbury - 10 February & Leas Cliff Hall, Folkestone - 23 February
L. Fly: no entry. **Fly:** *final:* D. Bennett (St Mary's) wo. **Bantam:** *final:* J. Convey (St Mary's) w pts G. Mitchell (Basingstoke). **Feather:** *final:* H. Miah (Crawley) wo. **Light:** *semi-finals:* J. Alldis (Crawley) wo, W. Dunkley (Swanley) w pts S. Dhariwal (Gravesham); *final:* J. Alldis w pts W. Dunkley. **L. Welter:** *quarter-finals:* W. Sommerville (Portsmouth University) wo, A. Martin (Foley) wo, J. Berry (Sandwich) w rtd 2 S. Calvert (Leigh Park), L. Cook (Foley) w pts J. Howett (Fareham); *semi-finals:* J.

Berry w pts W. Sommerville; A. Martin w pts L. Cook; *final:* A. Martin w pts J. Berry. **Welter:** *semi-finals:* C. Nachford (Seaham) wo, J. Morris (Newport) w pts S. Collingwood (Canterbury); *final:* J. Morris w rsc 3 C. Nachman. **L. Middle:** *quarter-finals:* B. Halford (Shepway) wo, V. Walford (Ramsgate) wo, S. Smith (Sandwich) wo, M.Rennie (Grange) w rsc 4 C.Skinner (Snodland); *semi-finals:* M. Rennie w rsc 3 B. Halford, V. Walford w rsc 4 S. Smith; *final:* M. Rennie w rsc 2 V. Walford. **Middle:** *quarter-finals:* D. Wakefield (Dorking) wo, J. Cole (Newport) w co 1 M. Welch (Swanley), David Taylor (Foley) w pts Daniel Taylor (Foley), G. Smith (Shepway) w pts A. Ewence (Woking); *semi-finals:* David Taylor w co 1 G. Smith, D. Wakefield w pts J. Cole; *final:* David Taylor w pts D. Wakefield. **L. Heavy:** *semi-finals:* R. Walls (Sporting Ring) wo, T. Maxwell (Shepway) w rsc 1 D. Bowers (Fareham); *final:* R. Walls w pts T. Maxwell. **Cruiser:** *final:* C. Cameron (McKenzie's) wo. **Heavy:** *final:* T. Eastwood (Foley) wo. **S. Heavy:** *final:* M. Grainger (Woking) wo.

Western Counties

Northern Division   Badger Hill Pub, Frome - 10 February
L. Fly: no entries. **Fly:** no entries. **Bantam:** no entries. **Feather:** no entries. **Light:** *final:* R. Scutt (Sydenham) w pts W. Sweeney (Frome). **L. Welter:** *final:* J. Hicks (Yeovil & Reckleford) w pts J. Bickham (Taunton). **Welter:** *final:* J. Turley (Penhill RBL) wo. **L. Middle:** *final:* S. Mullins (Penhill RBL) w rsc 4 N. Wyatt (Bronx). **Middle:** *final:* D. Guthrie (Yeovil & Reckleford) w pts A. Derrick (Taunton). **L. Heavy:** *final:* P. Smyth (Empire) wo. **Cruiser:** *final:* G. Lee (Empire) wo. **Heavy:** P. Lewis (Taunton) w pts D. Beatty (Frome). **S. Heavy:** *final:* B. Harding (Penhill RBL) wo.

Southern Division   British Legion Club, Barnstaple - 3 February
L. Fly: no entries. **Fly:** no entries. **Bantam:** no entries. **Feather:** no entries. **Light:** *final:* M. Stuckey (Torbay) w pts M. Marshall (Paignton). **L. Welter:** *final:* C. Price (Exeter) w pts J. van Emmenis (Bideford). **Welter:** *final:* B. Patrick (Devonport) wo. **L. Middle:** *final:* P. Brown (Phoenix) w pts C. Drake (Mayflower). **Middle:** *final:* M. Plunkett (Poole) wo. **L. Heavy:** *final:* B. White (Apollo) w pts B. Wickendon (Launceston). **Cruiser:** no entries. **Heavy:** no entries. **S. Heavy:** *final:* N. Kendall (Apollo) w pts M. Elkins (Barnstaple).

Western Counties Finals   Pavilion Theatre, Exmouth - 23 February
L. Fly: no entries. **Fly:** no entries. **Bantam:** no entries. **Feather:** no entries. **Light:** M. Stuckey (Torbay) w pts R. Scutt (Sydenham). **L. Welter:** J. Hicks (Yeovil & Reckleford) w pts C. Price (Exeter). **Welter:** J. Turley (Penhill RBL) w rtd 2 B. Patrick (Devonport). **L. Middle:** S. Mullins (Penhill RBL) w pts P. Brown (Phoenix). **Middle:** D. Guthrie (Yeovil & Reckleford) w rsc 1 M. Plunkett (Poole). **L. Heavy:** P. Smyth (Empire) w rsc 3 B. White (Apollo). **Cruiser:** G. Lee (Empire) wo. **Heavy:** P. Lewis (Taunton) wo. **S. Heavy:** N. Kendall (Apollo) w pts B. Harding (Penhill RBL).

English ABA Semi-Finals & Finals

Everton Park Sports Centre, Liverpool - 16 & 17 March & The Metrodome, Barnsley - 30 March

L. Fly: *semi-finals:* S. Symes (Army) wo, C. Lyon (Wigan) w pts D. Langley (Hollington); *final:* C. Lyon w rsc 2 S. Symes. **Fly:** *quarter-finals:* O. Trainor (Shannon's) wo, D. Barriball (Army) wo, M. Marsh (West Ham) w pts J. Mulhern (Triumph), R. Nelson (Karmand) w pts D. Bennett (St Mary's); *semi-finals:* M. Marsh w pts R. Nelson, O. Trainor w pts D. Barriball; *final:* M. Marsh w pts O. Trainor. **Bantam:** *quarter-finals:* S. Foster (Shannon's) wo, J. Hussain (Bradford Police) wo, M. Power (St Pancras) w rsc 3 J. Convey (St Mary's), S. Walton (Donnington Ex-Servicemen) w pts P. Murray (Army); *semi-finals:* S. Foster w rsc 3 J. Hussain, M. Power w rsc 3 S. Walton; *final:* S. Foster w pts M. Power. **Feather:** *quarter-finals:* L. Otte (Castle) wo, D. Walton (Willenhall) wo, R. Boyle (Birtley) w pts H. Miah (Crawley), S. Bell (Nichols Police) w pts W. Corcoran (Stowe); *semi-finals:* S. Bell w pts R. Boyle, L. Otte w pts D. Walton; *final:* S. Bell w pts L. Otte. **Light:** *quarter-finals:* K. Davie (RN) w pts J. Alldis (Crawley), S. Burke (Salisbury) w pts F. Crosswell (Kingfisher), T. Davies (Donnington Ex-Servicemen) w rsc 4 M. Stuckey (Torbay), D. Barker (Repton) w pts T. Fletcher (Karmand); *semi-finals:* S. Burke w pts K. Davie, T. Davies w pts D. Barker; *final:* S. Burke w pts T. Davies. **L. Welter:** *quarter-finals:* S. Matthews (Stanley) w pts D. Happe (Repton), J. Cusick (RN) w rsc 1 J. Hicks (Yeovil & Reckleford), G. Smith (Karmand) w pts A. Martin (Foley), C. Smith (Kingsthorpe) w pts K. Jackson (New Astley); *semi-finals:* S. Matthews w pts J. Cusick, G. Smith w pts C. Smith; *final:* G. Smith w pts S. Matthews. **Welter:** *quarter-finals:* M. McLean (Birtley) w pts J. Morris (Newport), J. Turley (Penhill RBL) w pts A. Maguire (Kirkdale), S. Briggs (Army) w pts B. Hudson (Cambridge Police), M. Macklin (Small Heath) w pts T. Cesay (Repton); *semi-finals:* J. Turley w pts M. McLean, M. Macklin w rsc 2 S. Briggs; *final:* M. Macklin w pts J. Turley. **L. Middle:** *quarter-finals:* M. McMahon (Army) w co 2 H. Greenwell (Sunderland), M. Thirwall (Fisher) w co 2 M. Rennie (Grange), S. Birch (St Helens Town) w rsc 3 E. Matthews (Callowland), M. Concepcion (Belgrave) w pts S. Mullins (Penhill RBL); *semi-finals:* M. Thirwall w co 2 M. McMahon, S. Birch w pts M. Concepcion; *final:* M. Thirwall w rsc 2 S. Birch. **Middle:** *quarter-finals:* C. Froch (Phoenix) w rsc 2 D. Guthrie (Yeovil & Reckleford), D. Robinson (Repton) w pts S. McCrone (Spennymoor), D. Frost (Army) w rsc 2 J. Cullinane (Southend) N. Perkins (Kirkdale) w rsc 4 D. Taylor (Foley); *semi-finals:* C. Froch w rsc 4 D. Robinson, D. Frost wo N. Perkins; *final:* C. Froch w pts D. Frost. **L. Heavy:** *quarter-finals:* A. Southwick (Dagenham) w pts L. Spare (Army), C. Fry (Salisbury) w rsc 4 R. Walls (Sporting Ring), P. Smyth (Empire) w rsc 2 S. Jones (Rugeley), S. Price (Pinewood Starr) w pts T. Marsden (Birtley); *semi-finals:* C. Fry w rsc 4 A. Southwick, S. Price w dis 3 P. Smyth; *final:* C. Fry w pts S. Price. **Cruiser:** K. Hitchens (Birmingham City) wo, J. Dolan (Plains Farm) w rsc 3 T. Hindley (RN), P. Souter (Broad Street) w pts S. Cameron (McKenzie's) M. Carroll (Golden Gloves) w co 2 G. Lee (Empire); *semi-finals* J. Dolan w rsc 4 K. Hitchens, P. Souter w pts M. Carroll; *final:* J. Dolan w pts P. Souter. **Heavy:** *quarter-finals:* D. Dolan (Plains Farm) wo, T. Eastwood (Foley) w rsc 1 D. Smith (Donnington Ex Servicemen), G. Turner (Golden Gloves) w pts J. Zikic (Repton) P. Lewis (Taunton) w pts N. Siggs (RAF); *semi-finals:* D. Dolan w rsc 3 T. Eastwood, G. Turner w pts P. Lewis; *final:* D. Dolan w pts P. Lewis - replaced G. Turner. **S. Heavy:** *quarter-finals:* J. Callum (Coventry Boys) wo J. Robinson (Plains Farm), N. Kendall (Apollo) w pts B. Maguire (Long Lane), M. Legg (Callowland) w pts R. McCallum (Broad Street), M. Grainger (Woking) wo S. St John (Berry Boys); *semi-finals:* M. Legg w rsc 3 N. Kendall, M. Grainger w dis 3 J. Callum; *final:* M. Grainger w pts M. Legg.

Irish Championships, 2000-2001

Senior Tournament

The National Stadium, Dublin - 9, 10, 16, 17 & 23 February
L. Fly: *semi-finals:* J. P. Kinsella (St Fergal's, Wicklow) wo, P. Baker (Pegasus, Down) w rsc 3 J. Moore (St Francis, Limerick); *final:* J. P. Kinsella w pts P. Baker. **Fly:** *final:* L. Cunningham (Saints, Belfast) w pts D. Campbell (Glin, Dublin). **Bantam:** *semi-finals:* D. McKenna (Holy Family, Drogheda) wo, H. Cunningham (Saints, Belfast) w pts S. McAnee (Ring, Derry); *final:* D. McKenna w pts H. Cunningham. **Feather:** *semi-finals:* J. P. Campbell (St Patrick's, South Meath, Meath) wo, K. O'Hara (Immaculata, Belfast) w rsc 2 J. Simpson (Saviour's/Crystal, Waterford); *final:* J. P. Campbell w pts K. O'Hara. **Light:** *quarter-finals:* E. McEneaney (Dealgan, Louth) wo, T. Carlyle (Sacred Heart, Dublin) wo, K. Hogg (Larne, Antrim) w pts D. Hamill (All Saints, Belfast), N. Monteith (Dockers, Belfast) w rtd 4 H. Joyce (St Michael's, Athy); *semi-finals:* E. McEneaney w pts K. Hogg, N. Monteith w pts T. Carlyle; *final:* N. Monteith w pts E. McEneaney. **L. Welter:** *quarter-finals:* M. Wickham (St Patrick's, Wexford) w pts F. Turner (St Ibar's Wexford), M. Kelly (Dealgan, Louth) w pts S. McCann (Holy Family, Belfast), A. Carlyle (Sacred Heart, Dublin) w pts P. Jennings (Quarryvale, Dublin), P. McCloskey (St Canice's, Belfast) w pts T. Hamill (All Saints, Belfast); *semi-finals:* M. Kelly w pts M. Wickham, P. McCloskey w pts A. Carlyle; *final:* M. Kelly w pts P. McCloskey. **Welter:** *prelims:* N. Gough (St Paul's, Waterford) wo, D. Conlon (Crumlin, Dublin) wo, A. Gibson (Larne, Antrim) wo, G. McClure (Abbey, Down) wo, J. Moore (Arklow, Wicklow) wo, R. Murray (St Matthew's, Dublin) wo, G. McAuley (Star, Belfast) wo, P. Walsh (St Colman's, Cork) w pts A. Tierney (St Anthony's, Galway); *quarter finals:* N. Gough w pts D. Conlon, A. Gibson w pts G. McClure, J. Moore w pts R. Murray, G. McAuley w pts P. Walsh; *semi-finals:* N. Gough w rsc 2 A. Gibson, J. Moore w pts G. McAuley; *final:* J. Moore w pts N. Gough. **L. Middle:** *semi-finals:* M. Roche (Sunnyside, Cork) wo, J. Duddy (Ring, Derry) w rsc 3 D. Campbell (Drimnagh, Dublin); *final:* M. Roche w pts J. Duddy. **Middle:** *prelims:* K. Egan (Neilstown, Dublin) wo, K. Walsh (St Colman's, Cork) wo, M. McAllister (Belfast) wo, J. Waldron (Midfield, Mayo) wo, C. Carmichael (Holy Trinity, Belfast) wo, L. Senior (Crumlin, Dublin) wo, S. Keeler (St Saviour's, Dublin) wo, M. Lee (CIE, Dublin) w pts I. Timms (Quarryvale, Dublin); *quarter-finals:* K. Egan w pts K. Walsh, M. McAllister w pts J. Waldron, C. Carmichael w pts L. Senior, S. Keeler wo M. Lee; *semi-finals:* K. Egan w pts M. McAllister, C. Carmichael w pts S. Keeler; *final:* K. Egan w pts C. Carmichael. **L. Heavy:** *semi-finals:* A. Reynolds (St Joseph's, Sligo) w rsc 3 S. Lawlor (Grangecon, Kildare), J. Kelly (Manorhamilton, Leitrim) w pts T. Donnelly (Mark Heagney, Tyrone); *final:* A. Reynolds w co 2 J. Kelly. **Heavy:** *semi-finals:* S. Reynolds (St Joseph's, Sligo) wo, G. Dargan (CIE, Dublin) w pts S. Walsh (Drimnagh, Dublin); *final:* S. Reynolds w rsc 3 G. Dargan. **S. Heavy:** *semi-finals:* J. Kinsella (Crumlin, Dublin) w rsc 4 E. Falvey (St Colman's, Cork), J. Kiely (Corpus Christi, Limerick) w pts T. Black (Mark Heagney, Tyrone); *final:* J. Kinsella w rsc 2 J. Kiely.

Intermediate Finals

The National Stadium, Dublin - 1 December
L. Fly: P. Baker (Pegasus, Down) w rsc 2 M. Regan (Claremorris, Mayo). **Fly:** P. Carey (Sacred Heart, Belfast) w pts R. Simpson (Saviour's/Crystal, Waterford). **Bantam:** P. Lambe (Holy Trinity, Belfast) w pts D. Tuohy (Moate, Westmeath). **Feather:** S. Ormond (Quarryvale, Dublin) w pts F. McClurkin (St Agnes, Belfast). **Light:** K. Hogg (Larne, Antrim) w pts J. Dowling (Paulstown, Kilkenny). **L. Welter:** F. Turner (St Ibar's, Wexford) w pts D. Cullen (Edenderry, Offaly). **Welter:** M. Hoey (Ennis, Clare) w pts A. O'Neill (Crumlin, Dublin). **L. Middle:** D. Sutherland (St Saviour's, Dublin) w pts E. Colgan (Avona, Dublin). **Middle:** K. Egan (Nielstown, Dublin) w pts T. Moran (St Agnes, Westport, Mayo). **L. Heavy:** B. Ferry (Dunfanaghy, Donegal) w rsc 4 J. Waldron (Midfield, Mayo). **Heavy:** P. Sharkey (Crumlin, Dublin) w pts G. Smith (Cabra, Dublin). **S. Heavy:** G. O'Brien (Ballyduff, Kerry) w pts D. Oliver (Sandy Row, Belfast).

Junior Finals

The National Stadium, Dublin - 18 May
L. Fly: Paul Hyland (Golden Cobra, Dublin) w pts M. Magee (Dunfanaghy, Donegal). **Fly:** T. Lee (Oughterard, Galway) w rsc 3 C. Nash (St Joseph's, Derry). **Bantam:** Patrick Hyland (Golden Cobra, Dublin) w pts M. McKeown (St Patrick's, Newry). **Feather:** S. Ormond (Quarryvale, Dublin) w pts P. Roche (Avona, Dublin). **Light:** R. Sheehan (St Michael's, Athy, Kildare) w pts A. Magee (Dunfanaghy, Donegal). **L. Welter:** C. McAuley (Dungloe, Donegal) w pts A. Foley (St Michael's, Athy, Kildare). **Welter:** D. Barrett (Olympic, Galway) w pts D. Bergin (Loughglynn, Roscommon). **L. Middle:** A. O'Malley (Eagle, Westport, Mayo) w pts A. Leigh (St Francis, Limerick). **Middle:** M. Sweeney (Monivea, Mayo) w pts B. Fitzpatrick (West Finglas, Dublin). **L. Heavy:** R. O'Neill (Paulstown, Kilkenny) w pts S. Campbell (Bishop Kelly's, Omagh, Tyrone). **Heavy:** A. Hanley (Loughglynn, Roscommon) w pts S. Curran (Enniskillen, Fermanagh). **S. Heavy:** C. O'Donnell (Rosmuc, Galway) wo.

Scottish and Welsh Senior Championships, 2000-2001

Scotland ABA

The Time Capsule, Coatbridge - 10 February & 2 March, Tree Tops Hotel, Aberdeen - 15 February & Pettcur Bay Leisure Centre, Kinghorn - 23 February

L. Fly: *semi-finals:* N. Bonini (Hawick) wo, J. McPherson (Cleland) w pts S. Moles (Broadwood); *final:* N. Bonini w pts J. McPherson. **Fly:** *final:* S. McKay (Inverness) w rsc 3 D. Forsyth (Lanark Welfare). **Bantam:** *semi-finals:* J. Davidson (Bannockburn) w pts S. McLaughlin (St Francis'), S. Bartlett (Inverness) w pts M. Tod (Kingdom); *final:* J. Davidson w rsc 4 S. Bartlett. **Feather:** *prelims:* M. Hastie (Forgewood) wo, J. Marr (Bonnyrigg) wo, J. Simpson (Port Glasgow) wo, R. McNicol (Phoenix) wo, K. Dunne (Clydebank) wo, K. Florence (Kincorth) wo, S. Young (Lothian) w pts R. Park (Blantyre), F. Rafiq (Dennistoun) w pts M. Murray (Inverness); *quarter-finals:* M. Hastie w pts J. Marr, J. Simpson w pts R. McNicol, K. Dunne w rsc 3 K. Florence, F. Rafiq w pts S. Young; *semi-finals:* M. Hastie w pts J. Simpson, F. Rafiq w pts K. Dunne; *final:* M. Hastie w pts F. Rafiq. **Light:** *prelims:* J. McKeown (Barrhead) wo, G. McMillan (Blantyre) wo, G. McArthur (Clydebank) wo, J. Price (Peterhead) wo, P. King (Newarthill) wo, T. Graham (Auchengeich) wo, C. Bain (Hawick) wo, T. McPake (Forgewood) w pts R. Burns (Barn); *quarter-finals:* J. McKeown w pts G. McMillan, G. McArthur w pts J. Price, P. King w pts T. Graham, T. McPake w pts C. Bain; *semi-finals:* T. McPake w pts P. King, J. McKeown w pts G. McArthur; *final:* T. McPake w pts J. McKeown. **L. Welter:** *prelims:* B. Morrison (Forgewood) wo, M. Bett (Lanark Welfare) wo, S. McShane (Dennistoun) wo, K. Nowbaveh (Sparta) wo, K. Anderson (Denbeath) wo, C. Black (Barn) wo, L. McAllister (Granite City) wo, F. Kerr (Bannockburn) w co 4 M. McDonagh (Barn); *quarter-finals:* B. Morrison w pts M. Bett, S. McShane w rsc 1 K. Nowbaveh, K. Anderson w pts C. Black, F. Kerr w dis 3 L. McAllister; *semi-finals:* B. Morrison w rsc 3 S. McShane, K. Anderson w rsc 3 F. Kerr; *final:* K. Anderson w pts B. Morrison. **Welter:** *quarter-finals:* C. McNeil (Fauldhouse) wo, M. O'Neill (Sparta) wo, G. Young (Portobello) w rsc 3 M. Equi (Glasgow Noble Art), J. Murphy (Barn) w pts M. Reid (Insch); *semi-finals:* G. Young w pts J. Murphy, C. McNeil wo M. O'Neill; *final:* C. McNeil w pts G. Young. **L. Middle:** *quarter-finals:* C. McEwan (Clovenstone) wo, R. Hall (Elgin) wo, J. Coyle (Bannockburn) w pts B. Peacock (Barrhead), C. Dickson (Glasgow Noble Art) w pts I. Donnelly (Broadwood); *semi-finals:* C. McEwan w rsc 3 R. Hall, J. Coyle w rsc 4 C. Dickson; *final:* J. Coyle w pts C. McEwan. **Middle:** *prelims:* S. McGuire (Glenrothes) wo, D. Hill (Dennistoun) wo, D. Feeney (Phoenix) wo, S. Forsyth (Sparta) wo, R. Kerr (Bannockburn) wo, A. McLennan (Inverness) wo, B. Stewart (Inverness) wo, B. Singleton (Hawick) w pts A. Will (Insch); *quarter-finals:* S. McGuire w pts D. Hill, D. Feeney w rsc 2 S. Forsyth, R. Kerr w rsc 2 A. McLennan, B. Stewart w rtd 3 B. Singleton; *semi-finals:* R. Kerr w rsc 2 B. Stewart, S. McGuire w rsc 2 D. Feeney; *final:* S. McGuire w pts R. Kerr. **L. Heavy:** *quarter-finals:* L. Ramsay (Kingdom) wo, W. Graham (Newarthill) wo, B. Chakal (Leith Victoria) w rsc 3 W. McLung (Lawthorn), W. Clark (Glenrothes) w pts M. Loughlin (Leith Victoria); *semi-finals:* L. Ramsay wo W. Graham, W. Clark w pts B. Chakal; *final:* L. Ramsay w pts W. Clark. **Cruiser:** *semi-finals:* S. Robb (Inverness) w pts B. McFadden (Bannockburn), R. Parvez (Dennistoun) w pts A. Fleming (Livingston); *final:* S. Robb w R. Parvez. **Heavy:** *semi-finals:* H. McBean (Nomads) wo, A. Young (Inverness) w rsc 1 C. McFadden (Bannockburn); *final:* A. Young w pts H. McBean. **S. Heavy:** *semi-finals:* I. Millarvie (Phoenix) wo, J. Perry (Bathgate) w pts T. Cook (Glenrothes); *final:* I. Millarvie w co 1 J. Perry.

Wales ABA

The Afan Lido Sports Centre, Port Talbot - 17 February & 23 March, Dockers' Club, Swansea - 7 March & Ely British Legion Club, Cardiff - 8 March

L. Fly: *final:* R. Power (Torfaen Warriors) wo. **Fly:** *final:* J. Mwasigallah (Splott Adventure) w pts M. White (St Clare's). **Bantam:** *semi-final:* D. Edwards (Cwmavon Hornets) w rsc 4 H. Janes (Highfields), D. Davies (Merthyr) w pts L. Burgess (Porthcawl & Pyle); *final:* D. Edwards w pts D. Davies. **Feather:** *semi-finals:* J. Evans (Army) wo, D. Rees (Premier) w co 2 R. Bumford (Carmarthen); *final:* J. Evans w pts D. Rees. **Light:** *quarter-finals:* S. Bowers (Rhondda) wo, G. Perkins (Premier) wo, J. Bevan (Pembroke) wo, N. Burchett (Army) w rsc 1 S. Holmes (Llandarcy); *semi-finals:* S. Bowers w rsc 4 N. Burchett, G. Perkins w pts J. Bevan; *final:* S. Bowers w pts G. Perkins. **L. Welter:** *quarter-finals:* M. Collins (St Clare's) wo, C. Hall (Penyrheol) w pts B. Edmonds (Torfaen Warriors), L. Owen (Portmead & Blaenymaes) w pts S. Gilbert (Llandarcy), D. Bushbye (Army) w pts J. Cody (Jim Driscoll's); *semi-finals:* C. Hall w pts M. Collins, D. Bushbye w pts S. Gilbert; *final:* C. Hall w co 1 D. Bushbye. **Welter:** *quarter-finals:* G. Pritchard (Llangefni) w rsc 3 C. Morris (Llansamlet), P. Nicholls (Merthyr Ex-Servicemen) w pts S. Miller (Cardigan), S. Phillips (Cwmavon Hornets) w dis 3 J. Beaumont (Llandarcy), H. Evans (Carmarthen) w pts V. Bryan (Splott Adventure); *semi-finals:* G. Pritchard w rsc 3 P. Nicholls, S. Phillips w rsc 2 H. Evans; *final:* S. Phillips w G. Pritchard. **L. Middle:** *quarter-finals:* G. Husband (Jim Driscoll's) wo, R. Davies (Cwmavon Hornets) w dis 3 J. Hull (Highfields), A. Evans (Merthyr Ex-Servicemen) w pts A. Davies (Cardigan), A. James (Carmarthen) L. Mayer (Jim Driscoll's) *semi-finals:* R. Davies w pts G. Husband, A. Evans w rsc 3 A. James; *final:* R. Davies w pts A. Evans. **Middle:** *prelims:* K. Thomas (Pontypridd) wo, G. Powell (St Joseph's) wo, A. Jones (Aberystwyth) wo, N. Addis (Kyber Colts) wo, B. Hayward (Newbridge) wo, C. Chadwick (Llay) wo, S. Pepperall (Vale) w pts R. Allan (Palace), F. Borg (Prince of Wales) w pts P. Banman (Pembroke); *quarter-finals:* K. Thomas w pts G. Powell, F. Borg w pts S. Pepperall, A. Jones w pts N. Addis, B. Hayward w rsc 1 C. Chadwick; *semi-finals:* F. Borg w pts B. Hayward, K. Thomas w pts A. Jones; *final:* F. Borg w pts K. Thomas. **L. Heavy:** *semi-finals:* J. Walters (Prince of Wales) wo, M. Allen (Palace) w pts E. Davies (Aberaman); *final:* M. Allen w pts J. Walters. **Heavy:** *final:* K. Evans (Carmarthen) w rtd 1 D. Mais (Splott Adventure). **S. Heavy:** *semi-finals:* S. Gammer (Pembroke) w rsc 1 S. Whit (Kyber Colts), L. Ali (Splott Adventure) w rsc 4 A. Thoma (Merthyr Ex-Servicemen); *final:* S. Gammer w co 2 L. Ali.

Four Nations Tournament, 2001

St George's Hall, Liverpool - 12 & 13 April

L. Fly: *semi-finals:* N. Bonini (S) w rsc 2 R. Power (W), D. Langley (E) - replaced C. Lyon - w pts J. P. Kinsella (I); *final:* D. Langley w pts N. Bonini. *3rd place:* J. P. Kinsella w rsc 1 R. Power. **Fly:** *semi-finals:* M. Marsh (E) w pts J. Mwasigallah (W), L. Cunningham (I) w rsc S. McKay (S); *final:* M. Marsh w pts L. Cunningham. *3rd place:* J. Mwasigallah wo S. McKay. **Bantam:** *semi-finals:* D. Edwards (W) w pts S. Foster (E), D. McKenna (I) w pts J. Davidson (S); *final:* D. Edwards w pts D. McKenna. *3rd place:* S. Foster w pts J. Davidson. **Feather:** *semi-finals:* J. P. Campbell (I) w pts J. Evans (W), S. Bell (E) w pts M. Hastie (S); *final:* S. Bell w pts J. P. Campbell. *3rd place:* M. Hastie w pts J. Evans. **Light:** *semi-finals:* T. McPake (S) w pts S. Burke (E), N. Monteith (I) w pts S. Bowers (W); *final:* N. Monteith w pts T. McPake. *3rd place:* S. Burke w pts S. Bowers. **L. Welter:** *semi-finals:* K. Anderson (S) w pts C. Hall (W), G. Smith (E) w pts M. Kelly (I); *final:* K. Anderson w pts G. Smith. *3rd place:* M. Kelly w pts G. Smith. **Welter:** *semi-finals:* T. Cesay (E) - replaced M. Macklin - w pts G. Young (S) - replaced C. McNeil, J. Moore (I) w rsc 3 S. Phillips (W); *final:* J. Moore w pts T. Cesay. *3rd place:* G. Young w rsc 3 S. Phillips. **L. Middle:** *semi-finals:* M. Concepcion (E) - replaced M. Thirwall - w pts R. Davies (W), C. McEwan (S) - replaced J. Coyle - w pts M. Roche (I); *final:* C. McEwan w pts M. Concepcion. *3rd place:* M. Roche w pts R. Davies. **Middle:** *semi-finals:* K. Egan (I) w pts S. McGuire (S), D. Frost (E) - replaced C. Froch - w pts F. Borg (W); *final:* K. Egan w pts D. Frost. *3rd place:* S. McGuire w rsc 2 F. Borg. **L. Heavy:** *semi-finals:* C. Fry (E) w rsc 3 L. Ramsay (S), A. Reynolds (I) w rsc 3 M. Allen (W); *final:* C. Fry w pts A. Reynolds. *3rd place:* M. Allen wo S. Ramsay. **Heavy:** *semi-finals:* D. Dolan (E) w pts K. Evans (W), S. Reynolds (I) w rsc 3 A. Young (S); *final:* S. Reynolds w pts D. Dolan. *3rd place:* K. Evans w pts A. Young. **S. Heavy:** *semi-finals:* M. Grainger (E) wo I. Millarvie (S), S. Gammer (W) w pts J. Kinsella (I); *final:* S. Gammer w pts M. Grainger. *3rd place:* M. Grainger.

Code: E = England, I = Ireland, S = Scotland, W = Wales

Steve Foster, the 2001 ABA bantamweight champion

Les Clark

Carl Froch (right) beat the Army's Dean Frost to win the 2001 ABA middleweight title

Les Clark

British and Irish International Matches, and Championships, 2000-2001

Does not include multi-nation tournaments, despite them being recognised as international appearances, merely because space will not allow. The newly established Four-Nations Tournament is reported elsewhere in the amateur section and we apologise if any international matches have been missed, but we have covered all we were made aware of.

Internationals

England (2) v France (4), 1 draw   Bordeaux, France - 1 July
(English names first): **L. Fly:** G. Jones l pts B. Asloum. **Fly:** S. Doherty l pts G. Fresnois. **Bantam:** M. Power w pts M. Tridi. **Light:** S. Burke w pts M. Boulahras. **Welter:** M. Lomax l pts W. Blain. **L.Middle:** S. Birch l pts H. Bayram. **Heavy:** D. Dolan drew G. Procope. Note: Doherty represented England at U19 level.

Ireland (6) v USA (6)   Mashantucket, Connecticut - 17 October
(Irish names first): **L. Fly:** J. P. Kinsella w pts B. Martinez. **Fly:** D. Campbell l pts R. Jefferson. **Bantam:** D. McKenna l pts A. Garcia. **L. Welter:** A. Carlyle w pts P. Malignaggi, M. Kelly w pts J. Beeman, M. Wickham w pts E. Johnson. **Welter:** N. Gough l pts W. Wright, J. Moore l pts A. Thompson. **L. Middle:** J. Duddy l pts S. Powell. **Middle:** K. Walsh w pts E. Kelly. **L. Heavy:** A. Reynolds w pts D. Abron. **Heavy:** S. Reynolds l pts D. Vargas.

Ireland (3) v USA (3)   Denver, Colorado - 21 October
(Irish names first): **Bantam:** D. McKenna w pts C. Bowman. **L. Welter:** M. Wickham l pts C. Bernard. **Welter:** N. Gough l pts J. Webb, J. Moore w pts J. Parrison. **L. Middle:** J. Duddy l pts R. Cisneros. **Middle:** K. Walsh w pts T. Stepp.

England (5) v USA (2)   Hilton Hotel, Park Lane, London - 20 November
(English names first): **Fly:** D. Matthews w pts H. Villareal. **Bantam:** R. Boyle l rsc 4 C. Bowman, M. Power l pts M. Oliver. **Feather:** S. Bell w pts A. Pabon. S. Burke w pts P. Malignaggi. **L. Middle:** S. Briggs w pts W. Webb. **Heavy:** D. Haye w co 1 A. Reed. Note: Matthews and Boyle represented England at U19 level.

Young England (2) v Young Scotland (4)   Royal Lancaster Hotel, London - 5 February
(English names first): **L. Fly:** J. Fowl l pts U. Hussain. **Fly:** N. McDonald w pts J. Clair. **L. Welter:** A. Woodward w pts R. Burns, G. Woolcombe l pts K. Anderson. **Welter:** C. Pratt l pts G. Young. **L. Middle:** M. Marshall l pts B. Peacock.

Young Ireland (6) v Young Italy (5)   National Stadium, Dublin - 6 April
(Irish names first): **Bantam:** Patrick Hyland w pts F. Pizzo, T. Lee w pts V. Maria. **Feather:** P. Hendricks l pts G. Valentino. **Light:** M. Ryan l pts M. di Rocco, J. Clancy l pts C. Cirrillo. **L. Welter:** D. Bergin w pts C. Spinelli, A. Foley l pts C. Quero. **Welter:** G. McAuley w pts R. di Lillo. **Middle:** K. Egan w pts A. di Luisa. **L. Heavy:** A. Hanley l pts C. Russo, D. O'Toole w rsc 1 L. Emiliano.

Ireland (4) v USA (5)   National Stadium, Dublin - 27 April
(Irish names first): **L. Fly:** J. P. Kinsella l pts R. Siler. **Fly:** L. Cunningham l pts R. Martinez. **Bantam:** D. McKenna w pts J.

Vasquez. **Feather:** J. P. Campbell w pts A. Dirrell. **Welter:** J. Moore w pts B. Bush. **L. Middle:** M. Roche w pts J. Townsend. **Middle:** J. Duddy l pts A. Ward. **Heavy:** S. Reynolds l pts R. Booker. **S. Heavy:** E. Falvey l rsc 3 J. Estrada.

Ireland (4) v USA (5)   Woodlands Hotel, Waterford - 29 April
(Irish names first): **L. Fly:** P. Baker l pts R. Siler. **Fly:** D. Campbell l pts R. Martinez. **Bantam:** S. McAnee l pts J. Vasquez. **Feather:** S. Ormond l pts A. Dirrell. **Light:** H. Joyce w pts V. Kimbrough. **Welter:** N. Gough w pts B. Bush. **Middle:** R. Fox l pts A. Ward. **L. Heavy:** C. Barrett w pts D. Abron. **Heavy:** S. Reynolds w pts R. Booker.

England (7) v Canada (3)   Regina, Saskatchewan, Canada - 4 May
(English names first): **L. Fly:** C. Lyon l pts S. Gauthier. **Bantam:** S. Foster l pts B. Gaudet. **Feather:** S. Bell w pts B. Laham. **Light:** S. Burke w pts A. Hortie-Decarie. **L. Welter:** S. Matthews w pts R. Romero. **Welter:** T. Cesay w pts R. Savage. **L. Middle:** M. Thirwall l pts M. Walchiuk. **Middle:** C. Froch w pts D. Orr. **L. Heavy:** C. Fry w pts M. Storey. **Heavy:** D. Dolan w rsc 4 R. Henney.

England (4) v Canada (3)   Moose Jaw, Saskatchewan, Canada - 7 May
Bantam: S. Foster l pts A. Kooner. **Feather:** S. Bell w pts B. Laham. **Light:** S. Burke l pts A. Hortie-Decare. **L. Welter:** S. Matthews l pts R. Romero. **Welter:** T. Cesay w pts R. Savage. **Middle:** C. Froch w pts D. Orr. **L. Heavy:** J. Dolan w rsc 4 M. Storey.

Championships

Olympic Games   Sydney, Australia - 16 September to 1 October
L. Middle: M. Roche (Ireland) l pts F. Karagollu (Turkey). **L. Heavy:** C. Fry (England) l pts C. Adamu (Ghana). **S. Heavy:** A. Harrison (England) w rsc 4 A. Lezin (Russia), w pts O. Mazikin (Ukraine), w pts P. Vidoz (Italy), w pts M. Dildabekov (Kazakhstan).

World Junior Championships   Budapest, Hungary - 4 to 12 November
L. Fly: C. Lyon (England) l pts S. Salimov (Bulgaria). **Fly:** M. Marsh (England) l pts E. Soltani (Algeria). **Bantam:** M. Lindsay (Ireland) l pts Y. Sang-Young (Korea). M. Moran (England) w pts J. Koivula (Finland), withdrew following an injury. **Light:** J. Dowling (Ireland) l pts M. San Juan (Cuba). T. Fletcher (England) w pts R. Kuvadov (Turkmenistan), w rtd 3 I. Szili (Hungary), l rsc 3 K. Allakhverdin (Russia). **L. Welter:** C. O'Conaire (Ireland) l pts B. Kalinovic (Sweden). L. Beavis (England) w pts S. Brekalo

(Croatia), l rsc 2 P. Macias (Cuba). **Welter:** G. McAuley (Ireland) l pts D. Junak (Poland). M. Macklin (England) w rsc 3 J. Acs (Hungary). **L. Middle:** M. Mullaney (Ireland) l pts A. Laver (Kazakhstan). **Middle:** K. Egan (Ireland) l pts S. Grothe (Germany). **L. Heavy:** B. Ferry (Ireland) l pts L. Zigmund (Poland). **Heavy:** C. Barrett (Ireland) w pts A. Zolotenko (Estonia), l pts R. Greenberg (Israel).

World Senior Championships   Odyssey Arena, Belfast, Ireland - 3 to 10 June

L. Fly: J. P. Kinsella (Ireland) w pts S. Salimov (Bulgaria), l pts M. Velicu (Romania). **Fly:** L. Cunningham (Ireland) l rsc 1 V. Sydorenko (Ukraine). **Bantam:** D. Edwards (Wales) l rsc 1 J. Kane (Australia). D. McKenna (Ireland) w pts X. Zhao Rong (China), w pts G. Farkas (Hungary), l rsc 3 A. Agaguloglu (Turkey). S. Foster (England) w pts A. Isayev (Belarus), w rsc 3 A. Kooner (Canada), l pts S. Rotas (Dominican Republic). **Feather:** S. Bell (England) l rsc 3 R. Palyani (Turkey). J. P. Campbell (Ireland) w pts R. Pavlenkov (Estonia), l rsc 3 R. Palyani (Turkey). **Light:** N. Monteith (Ireland) l pts V. Kolesnyk (Ukraine). S. Burke (England) w pts L. Liang (China), l rsc 3 V. Biciulaitis (Lithuania). **L. Welter:** K. Anderson (Scotland) l pts S. Bykovski (Belarus). D. Happe (England) w pts A. Ahraoui (Germany), M.

Kelly (Ireland) w pts M. Allalou Algeria), w pts D. Happe (England), l pts W. Blain (France). **Welter:** C. McNeil (Scotland) w rsc 3 T. Cesay (England), w pts A. Ter Meliksetian (Brazil), l pts S. Husanov (Uzbekistan). J. Moore (Ireland) w pts A. Sotniks (Latvia), w pts D. Jasevicius (Lithuania), w pts L. Bundu (Italy), w pts F. Karagollu (Turkey), l pts A. Thompson (USA). **L. Middle:** M. Roche (Ireland) l pts A. Kavtaradze (Georgia). M. Thirwall (England) l pts D. Austin Echemendia (Cuba). J. Coyle (Scotland) l pts S. Kryschikhin (Belarus). **Middle:** S. McGuire (Scotland) l pts I. Szucs (Hungary). K. Egan (Ireland) w pts Y. El Awad (Denmark), w pts M. Krepstul (Lithuania), l pts Y. Despaigne Herrera (Cuba). C. Froch (England) w pts V. Alekperov (Azerbaijan), w pts A. Giannoulas (Greece), w pts L. Kutil (Czechoslovakia), l pts A. Gogolev (Russia). **L. Heavy:** A. Reynolds (Ireland) w rsc 3 V. Subacius (Lithuania), w pts T. Yildirim (Turkey), l rsc 2 J. Dovi (France). C. Fry (England) w pts D. Venter (South Africa), l pts C. Rasco (Romania). **Heavy:** S. Reynolds (Ireland) l rsc 2 S. Ibragimov (Russia). K. Evans (Wales) w pts E. Garai (Hungary), w pts S. Aslanidis (Greece), l rsc 3 O. Solis Fonte (Cuba). D. Haye (England) w rsc 3 P. Mesters (Holland), w pts S. Koeber (Germany), w pts V. Uzelkov (Ukraine), l rsc 3 O. Solis Fonte (Cuba). **S. Heavy:** E. Falvey (Ireland) l rsc 2 A. Povetkine (Russia).

Having defeated Martin Power (left) in the ABA bantam final, Steve Foster has now followed his fellow English International representative into the pro ranks

Les Clark

British Junior Championship Finals, 2000-2001

National Association of Clubs for Young People (NACYP)

Leisure Centre, Peterlee - 15 December

Class A: 42kg: S. Leonard (Darlington) w pts M. Graydon (Broad Plain). 45kg: S.Smith (Rotunda) w pts D. Roberts (Premier). 48kg: M. Robinson (Tower Hill) w pts J. Jacobs (Danson Youth). 51kg: D. Toman (Sacred Heart) w pts J. O'Connell (Dale Youth). 54kg: R. Godding (Chorley) w pts D. Smith (Dagenham). 57kg: B. Rose (Blackpool & Fylde) w pts M. Corcoran (Stowe). 60kg: S. Kennedy (Sunderland) w pts M. Jacobs (Harwich). 63.5kg: D. Anderson (Doncaster) w pts B. Frankland (Westree). 67kg: D. Booth (Joyce SoB) w pts J. Dennard (Chalvedon). 71kg: T. Jeffries (Sunderland) w pts M. Stokes (Trojan Police).

Marriott Hotel, Bristol - 11 December

Class B: 45kg: J. Fowl (Haileybury) w pts M. Hudson (Grainger Park). 48kg: N. McDonald (Vauxhall) w pts A. Bibby (Sandy). 51kg: M. Edmonds (Torfaen Warriors) w pts D. Broadhurst (Birmingham Irish). 54kg: J. Algar-Crees (Prince of Wales) w pts S. Flynn (Meadowbank). 57kg: J. Baker (Repton) w pts S. Jennings (Tower Hill). 60kg: J. McNally (Rotunda) w pts F. Smith (Foley). 63.5kg: L. Calvert (Finchley) w pts J. Wright (Shildon). 67kg: M. Nevin (Repton) w pts G. Symonds (Joyce SoB). 71kg: L. Siner (Salisbury) w pts S. Hunt (Repton). 75kg: R. Ainsworth (Scarborough) w rsc 2 M. Mitchell (Belhus Park).

Hilton Hotel, Mayfair, London - 4 December

Class C: 48kg: D. Swanson (Tower Hill) w rsc 2 R. Power (Torfaen Warriors). 51kg: K. Foley (St Joseph's) w rsc 4 N. Bonini (Hawick). 54kg: C. Male (Pleck) w pts A. Gardner (Medway GG) . 57kg: J. Fletcher (Karmand) w pts M. Corcoran (Trojan Police). 60kg: D. Barker (Repton) w pts D. Lambert (Karmand). 63.5kg: K. Anderson (Denbeath) w co 3 W. Killick (Marvels Lane). 67kg: T. Doherty (Pontypool & Panteg) w pts G. Young (Portobello). 71kg: M. Rennie (Grange) w co 2 A. Ainger (Handsworth). 75kg: G. Barr (Birtley) w rsc1 R. Pavelin (Gator). 81kg: J. Haye (Fitzroy Lodge) w dis 4 R. Parvez (Dennistoun).

Schools

Broadway Theatre, Barking - 9 March, Garrington's Sports & Social Club, Bromsgrove - 18 March, Keresforth Hall, Barnsley - 2 April & The Metrodome, Barnsley - 28 April

Class 1: 32kg: D. Curran (Grainger Park) w pts L. Langley (West Ham). 34kg: J. Saunders (Belhus Park) w pts E. Draper (Rawthorpe). 36kg: J. Bowman (Northside) w pts L. Turner (Alma). 39kg: D. Watson (Shildon) w pts P. Stokes (Trojan Police). 42kg: D. Lee (Birtley Police) wo P.C. Stokes (Trojan Police). 45kg: A. Sexton (Finchley) w pts A. Fletcher (Shildon). 48kg: Chris Riley (Wellington) w pts D. Kent (Golden Ring). 51kg: T. Jacobs (Harwich) w pts K. Dignam (Hartlepool). 54kg: J. Lee (Stevenage) w rsc 3 J. Thompson (Old Robin Hood). 57kg: G. Groves (Dale Youth) w pts J. Wale (Mexborough).

Class 2: 36kg: J. Radford (Newham) w pts J. Ogden (Batley & Dewsbury). 39kg: C. Smith (Onslow Lions) w pts J. Muldoon (Empire SoB). 42kg: P. Edwards (Salisbury) w pts S. Corcoran (Stowe). 45kg: R. Lee (Pleck) w pts S. McDonagh (Stowe). 48kg: A. Khan (Bury) w pts W. Page (West Ham). 51kg: K. Armstrong (Craghead) w pts J. Creamer (Portsmouth). 54kg: N. Ripley (Eltham) w pts M. Fielding (Stockbridge). 57kg: T. McDonagh (South Norwood & Victory) w pts D. Simms (St Helens). 60kg: T. Saunders (Cheshunt) w pts A. Knox (Bedlington). 63kg: J. O'Connor (Harlow) w pts J. Bolton (Bridlington). 66kg: M. Singh (St Theresa's) w pts S. Cadder (Walcot).

Class 3: 39kg: L. Mulholland (St Paul's) w pts M. O'Donnell (Dale Youth). 42kg: M. Grimes (Golden Gloves) w pts T. Mills (St Mary's). 45kg: L. Allon (St Paul's) w pts M. Graydon (Broad Plain). 48kg: B. Saunders (Spennymoor) w pts J. Cox (Walcot). 51kg: N. Ballan (Spennymoor) w pts J. O'Donnell (Dale Youth). 54kg: R. Mitchell (New Astley) w pts M. Bromby (St Paul's). 57kg: I. Aslam (Birmingham) w pts P. Saunders (Belhus Park). 60kg: J. Carney (Salisbury) w pts W. Marshall (Devonport Police). 63kg: G. Skehill (St George's) w dis 2 M. Jones (Atherstone). 66kg: T. Hill (Golden Ring) w pts M. Henderson (Empire SoB). 69kg: V. Collingwood (St Paul's) w pts J. Degale (Dale Youth).

Class 4: 42kg: S. Leonard (Darlington) w pts D. Foreman (Dagenham). 45kg: S. Smith (Rotunda) w rsc 1 M. Hassell (Medway GG). 48kg: A. Brennan (Triumph) w pts M. McDonagh (Hollington). 51kg: K. Mitchell (Dagenham) w rsc 2 C. Foreman (Bracebridge). 54kg: J. Richardson (Golden Ring) w pts J. Murray (Shannon). 57kg: B. Rose (Blackpool & Fylde) w pts P. Doherty (Cambridge). 60kg: W. Hibbert (Chalvedon) w pts J. McNally (Rotunda). 63.5kg: T. Coward (Wombwell & Dearne) w rsc 2 M. Nevin (Repton). 67kg: J. Smyth (Finchley) w pts D. Booth (Joyce SoB). 71kg: L. Siner (Salisbury) w pts B. Barrett (Trojan Police). 75kg: L. Dawson (Hartlepool Catholic) w pts J. Smith (Pinewood Starr).

ABA Youth

National Sports Centre, Crystal Palace - 21 April

Class 5 (born 1984): 45kg: M. Sedgewick (Wigan) w pts M. Hudson (Grainger Park). 48kg: C. Brahmbhatt (Danson Youth) w pts H. Trutzenbach (Kingfisher). 51kg: N. McDonald (Vauxhall) w pts K. Mitchell (Dagenham). 54kg: D. Herdman (Stevenage) w pts A. Railton (Shildon). 57kg: S. Jennings (Tower Hill) w pts P. Doherty (Cambridge). 60kg: J. McNally (Rotunda) w pts N. Weise (Eltham). 63.5kg: J. Spence (Kingsthorpe) w pts A. Quigley (Tower Hill). 67kg: D. O'Rourke (Rotunda) w pts G. Symonds (Hard & Fast). 71kg: R. Ashworth (Scarborough) w pts L. Siner (Salisbury) - contested at Bescott Stadium, Walsall on 24 May. 75kg: L. Jenman (Southwick) w pts L. Dawson (Hartlepool Catholic). 81kg: J. Boyd (Donnington Ex-Servicemen) w pts G. Daly (Southend). 86kg: S. Barnes (Terry Allen Unique) w pts M. Grainger (Boarshaw).

Class 6 (born 1983): 48kg: M. Stead (Darlington) w pts S. Ungi (Golden Gloves). 51kg: L. Haskins (Empire SoB) w dis 3 D. Matthews (Salisbury). 54kg: J. Kays (Ashton Albion) w pts A. Gardner (St Mary's). 57kg: A. Morris (West Wythenshawe) w pts M. Loppas (Gator). 60kg: J. Watson (Higherside) v J. Fletcher (Karmand) - failed to take place. 63.5kg: A. Woodward (Watchet) w pts S. Mullin (Golden Gloves). 67kg: J. Heggarty (St Mary's) w pts M. Old (Bury St Edmunds). 71kg: A. Ainger (Handsworth) w pts A. Woolf (Five Star). 75kg: P. Trott (Altrincham) v M. McDonagh (Finchley) - failed to take place. 81kg: D. Pendleton (East Durham Academy) w pts J. Haye (Fitzroy Lodge). 86kg: K. Armstrong (Craghead) w pts S. Doherty (Cambridge) contested at The Metrodome, Barnsley on 28 April. 91kg: D. Price (Long Lane) w pts R. Holmes (Slough). 91+kg: L. Hawkins (Pinewood Starr) wo.

ABA Champions, 1881-2001

L. Flyweight
1971 M. Abrams
1972 M. Abrams
1973 M. Abrams
1974 C. Magri
1975 M. Lawless
1976 P. Fletcher
1977 P. Fletcher
1978 J. Dawson
1979 J. Dawson
1980 T. Barker
1981 J. Lyon
1982 J. Lyon
1983 J. Lyon
1984 J. Lyon
1985 M. Epton
1986 M. Epton
1987 M. Epton
1988 M. Cantwell
1989 M. Cantwell
1990 N. Tooley
1991 P. Culshaw
1992 D. Fifield
1993 M. Hughes
1994 G. Jones
1995 D. Fox
1996 R. Mercer
1997 I. Napa
1998 J. Evans
1999 G. Jones
2000 J. Mulherne
2001 C. Lyon

Flyweight
1920 H. Groves
1921 W. Cuthbertson
1922 E. Warwick
1923 L. Tarrant
1924 E. Warwick
1925 E. Warwick
1926 J. Hill
1927 J. Roland
1928 C. Taylor
1929 T. Pardoe
1930 T. Pardoe
1931 T. Pardoe
1932 T. Pardoe
1933 T. Pardoe
1934 P. Palmer
1935 G. Fayaud
1936 G. Fayaud
1937 P. O'Donaghue
1938 A. Russell
1939 D. McKay
1944 J. Clinton
1945 J. Bryce
1946 R. Gallacher
1947 J. Clinton
1948 H. Carpenter
1949 H. Riley
1950 A. Jones
1951 G. John
1952 D. Dower
1953 R. Currie
1954 R. Currie
1955 D. Lloyd
1956 T. Spinks
1957 R. Davies
1958 J. Brown
1959 M. Gushlow
1960 D. Lee

1961 W. McGowan
1962 M. Pye
1963 M. Laud
1964 J. McCluskey
1965 J. McCluskey
1966 P. Maguire

1967 S. Curtis
1968 J. McGonigle
1969 D. Needham
1970 D. Needham
1971 P. Wakefield
1972 M. O'Sullivan

1973 R. Hilton
1974 M. O'Sullivan
1975 C. Magri
1976 C. Magri
1977 C. Magri
1978 G. Nickels

1979 R. Gilbody
1980 K. Wallace
1981 K. Wallace
1982 J. Kelly
1983 S. Nolan
1984 P. Clinton

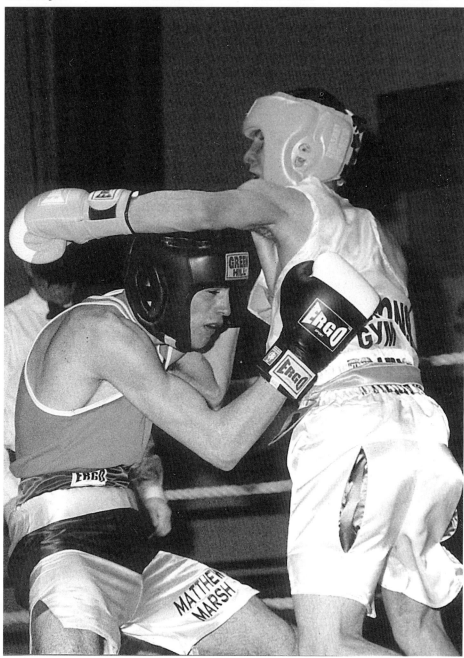

West Ham's Matthew Marsh (left) outscored Owen Trainor from Shannon's Gym to land the 2001 ABA flyweight crown

Les Clark

267

1985 P. Clinton	1946 C. Squire	1896 R. Gunn	1977 P. Cowdell	1931 D. McCleave
1986 J. Lyon	1947 D. O'Sullivan	1897 N. Smith	1978 M. O'Brien	1932 F. Meachem
1987 J. Lyon	1948 T. Profitt	1898 P. Lunn	1979 P. Hanlon	1933 H. Mizler
1988 J. Lyon	1949 T. Miller	1899 J. Scholes	1980 M. Hanif	1934 J. Rolland
1989 J. Lyon	1950 K. Lawrence	1900 R. Lee	1981 P. Hanlon	1935 F. Frost
1990 J. Armour	1951 T. Nicholls	1901 C. Clarke	1982 H. Henry	1936 F. Simpson
1991 P. Ingle	1952 T. Nicholls	1902 C. Clarke	1983 P. Bradley	1937 A. Danahar
1992 K. Knox	1953 J. Smillie	1903 J. Godfrey	1984 K. Taylor	1938 T. McGrath
1993 P. Ingle	1954 J. Smillie	1904 C. Morris	1985 F. Havard	1939 H. Groves
1994 D. Costello	1955 G. Dormer	1905 H. Holmes	1986 P. Hodkinson	1944 W. Thompson
1995 D. Costello	1956 O. Reilly	1906 A. Miner	1987 P. English	1945 J. Williamson
1996 D. Costello	1957 J. Morrissey	1907 C. Morris	1988 D. Anderson	1946 E. Thomas
1997 M. Hunter	1958 H. Winstone	1908 T. Ringer	1989 P. Richardson	1947 C. Morrissey
1998 J. Hegney	1959 D. Weller	1909 A. Lambert	1990 B. Carr	1948 R. Cooper
1999 D. Robinson	1960 F. Taylor	1910 C. Houghton	1991 J. Irwin	1949 A. Smith
2000 D. Robinson	1961 P. Benneyworth	1911 H. Bowers	1992 A. Temple	1950 R. Latham
2001 M. Marsh	1962 P. Benneyworth	1912 G. Baker	1993 J. Cook	1951 R. Hinson
	1963 B. Packer	1913 G. Baker	1994 D. Pithie	1952 F. Reardon
Bantamweight	1964 B. Packer	1914 G. Baker	1995 D. Burrows	1953 D. Hinson
1884 A. Woodward	1965 R. Mallon	1919 G. Baker	1996 T. Mulholland	1954 G. Whelan
1885 A. Woodward	1966 J. Clark	1920 J. Fleming	1997 S. Bell	1955 S. Coffey
1886 T. Isley	1967 M. Carter	1921 G. Baker	1998 D. Williams	1956 R. McTaggart
1887 T. Isley	1968 M. Carter	1922 E. Swash	1999 S. Miller	1957 J. Kidd
1888 H. Oakman	1969 M. Piner	1923 E. Swash	2000 H. Castle	1958 R. McTaggart
1889 H. Brown	1970 A. Oxley	1924 A. Beavis	2001 S. Bell	1959 P. Warwick
1890 J. Rowe	1971 G. Turpin	1925 A. Beavis		1960 R. McTaggart
1891 E. Moore	1972 G. Turpin	1926 R. Minshull	**Lightweight**	1961 P. Warwick
1892 F. Godbold	1973 P. Cowdell	1927 F. Webster	1881 F. Hobday	1962 B. Whelan
1893 E. Watson	1974 S. Ogilvie	1928 F. Meachem	1882 A. Bettinson	1963 B. O'Sullivan
1894 P. Jones	1975 S. Ogilvie	1929 F. Meachem	1883 A. Diamond	1964 J. Dunne
1895 P. Jones	1976 J. Bambrick	1930 J. Duffield	1884 A. Diamond	1965 A. White
1896 P. Jones	1977 J. Turner	1931 B. Caplan	1885 A. Diamond	1966 J. Head
1897 C. Lamb	1978 J. Turner	1932 H. Mizler	1886 G. Roberts	1967 T. Waller
1898 F. Herring	1979 R. Ashton	1933 J. Walters	1887 J. Hair	1968 J. Watt
1899 A. Avent	1980 R. Gilbody	1934 J. Treadaway	1888 A. Newton	1969 H. Hayes
1900 J. Freeman	1981 P. Jones	1935 E. Ryan	1889 W. Neale	1970 N. Cole
1901 W. Morgan	1982 R. Gilbody	1936 J. Treadaway	1890 A. Newton	1971 J. Singleton
1902 A. Miner	1983 J. Hyland	1937 A. Harper	1891 E. Dettmer	1972 N. Cole
1903 H. Perry	1984 J. Hyland	1938 C. Gallie	1892 E. Dettmer	1973 T. Dunn
1904 H. Perry	1985 S. Murphy	1939 C. Gallie	1893 W. Campbell	1974 J. Lynch
1905 W. Webb	1986 S. Murphy	1944 D. Sullivan	1894 W. Campbell	1975 P. Cowdell
1906 T. Ringer	1987 J. Sillitoe	1945 J. Carter	1895 A. Randall	1976 S. Mittee
1907 E. Adams	1988 K. Howlett	1946 P. Brander	1896 A. Vanderhout	1977 G. Gilbody
1908 H. Thomas	1989 K. Howlett	1947 S. Evans	1897 A. Vanderhout	1978 T. Marsh
1909 J. Condon	1990 P. Lloyd	1948 P. Brander	1898 H. Marks	1979 G. Gilbody
1910 W. Webb	1991 D. Hardie	1949 H. Gilliland	1899 H. Brewer	1980 G. Gilbody
1911 W. Allen	1992 P. Mullings	1950 P. Brander	1900 G. Humphries	1981 G. Gilbody
1912 W. Allen	1993 R. Evatt	1951 J. Travers	1901 A. Warner	1982 J. McDonnell
1913 A. Wye	1994 S. Oliver	1952 P. Lewis	1902 A. Warner	1983 K. Willis
1914 W. Allen	1995 N. Wilders	1953 P. Lewis	1903 H. Fergus	1984 A. Dickson
1919 W. Allen	1996 L. Eedle	1954 D. Charnley	1904 M. Wells	1985 E. McAuley
1920 G. McKenzie	1997 S. Oates	1955 T. Nicholls	1905 M. Wells	1986 J. Jacobs
1921 L. Tarrant	1998 L. Pattison	1956 T. Nicholls	1906 M. Wells	1987 M. Ayers
1922 W. Boulding	1999 M. Hunter	1957 M. Collins	1907 M. Wells	1988 C. Kane
1923 A. Smith	2000 S. Foster	1958 M. Collins	1908 H. Holmes	1989 M. Ramsey
1924 L. Tarrant	2001 S. Foster	1959 G. Judge	1909 F. Grace	1990 P. Gallagher
1925 A. Goom		1960 P. Lundgren	1910 T. Tees	1991 P. Ramsey
1926 F. Webster	**Featherweight**	1961 P. Cheevers	1911 A. Spenceley	1992 D. Amory
1927 E. Warwick	1881 T. Hill	1962 B. Wilson	1912 R. Marriott	1993 B. Welsh
1928 J. Garland	1882 T. Hill	1963 A. Riley	1913 R. Grace	1994 A. Green
1929 F. Bennett	1883 T. Hill	1964 R. Smith	1914 R. Marriott	1995 R. Rutherford
1930 H. Mizler	1884 E. Hutchings	1965 K. Buchanan	1919 F. Grace	1996 K. Wing
1931 F. Bennett	1885 J. Pennell	1966 H. Baxter	1920 F. Grace	1997 M. Hawthorne
1932 J. Treadaway	1886 T. McNeil	1967 K. Cooper	1921 G. Shorter	1998 A. McLean
1933 G. Johnston	1887 J. Pennell	1968 J. Cheshire	1922 G. Renouf	1999 S. Burke
1934 A. Barnes	1888 J. Taylor	1969 A. Richardson	1923 G. Shorter	2000 A. McLean
1935 L. Case	1889 G. Belsey	1970 D. Polak	1924 W. White	2001 S. Burke
1936 A. Barnes	1890 G. Belsey	1971 T. Wright	1925 E. Viney	
1937 A. Barnes	1891 F. Curtis	1972 K. Laing	1926 T. Slater	**L. Welterweight**
1938 J. Pottinger	1892 F. Curtis	1973 J. Lynch	1927 W. Hunt	1951 W. Connor
1939 R. Watson	1893 T. Davidson	1974 G. Gilbody	1928 F. Webster	1952 P. Waterman
1944 R. Bissell	1894 R. Gunn	1975 R. Beaumont	1929 W. Hunt	1953 D. Hughes
1945 P. Brander	1895 R. Gunn	1976 P. Cowdell	1930 J. Waples	1954 G. Martin

1955 F. McQuillan
1956 D. Stone
1957 D. Stone
1958 R. Kane
1959 R. Kane
1960 R. Day
1961 B. Brazier
1962 B. Brazier
1963 R. McTaggart
1964 R. Taylor
1965 R. McTaggart
1966 W. Hiatt
1967 B. Hudspeth
1968 E. Cole
1969 J. Stracey
1970 D. Davies
1971 M. Kingwell
1972 T. Waller
1973 N. Cole
1974 P. Kelly
1975 J. Zeraschi
1976 C. McKenzie
1977 J. Douglas
1978 D. Williams
1979 E. Copeland
1980 A. Willis
1981 A. Willis
1982 A. Adams
1983 D. Dent
1984 D. Griffiths
1985 I. Mustafa
1986 J. Alsop
1987 A. Holligan
1988 A. Hall
1989 A. Hall
1990 J. Pender
1991 J. Matthews
1992 D. McCarrick
1993 P. Richardson
1994 A. Temple
1995 A. Vaughan
1996 C. Wall
1997 R. Hatton
1998 N. Wright
1999 D. Happe
2000 N. Wright
2001 G. Smith

Welterweight
1920 F. Whitbread
1921 A. Ireland
1922 E. White
1923 P. Green
1924 P. O'Hanrahan
1925 P. O'Hanrahan
1926 B. Marshall
1927 H. Dunn
1928 H. Bone
1929 T. Wigmore
1930 F. Brooman
1931 J. Barry
1932 D. McCleave
1933 P. Peters
1934 D. McCleave
1935 D. Lynch
1936 W. Pack
1937 D. Lynch
1938 C. Webster
1939 R. Thomas
1944 H. Hall
1945 R. Turpin
1946 J. Ryan
1947 J. Ryan

1948 M. Shacklady
1949 A. Buxton
1950 T. Ratcliffe
1951 J. Maloney
1952 J. Maloney
1953 L. Morgan
1954 N. Gargano
1955 N. Gargano
1956 N. Gargano
1957 R. Warnes
1958 B. Nancurvis
1959 J. McGrail
1960 C. Humphries
1961 A. Lewis
1962 J. Pritchett
1963 J. Pritchett
1964 M. Varley
1965 P. Henderson
1966 P. Cragg
1967 D. Cranswick
1968 A. Tottoh
1969 T. Henderson
1970 T. Waller
1971 D. Davies
1972 T. Francis
1973 T. Waller
1974 T. Waller
1975 W. Bennett
1976 C. Jones
1977 C. Jones
1978 E. Byrne
1979 J. Frost
1980 T. Marsh
1981 T. Marsh
1982 C. Pyatt
1983 R. McKenley
1984 M. Hughes
1985 E. McDonald
1986 D. Dyer
1987 M. Elliot
1988 M. McCreath
1989 M. Elliot
1990 A. Carew
1991 J. Calzaghe
1992 M. Santini
1993 C. Bessey
1994 K. Short
1995 M. Hall
1996 J. Khaliq
1997 F. Barrett
1998 D. Walker
1999 A. Cesay
2000 F. Doherty
2001 M. Macklin

L. Middleweight
1951 A. Lay
1952 B. Foster
1953 B. Wells
1954 B. Wells
1955 B. Foster
1956 J. McCormack
1957 J. Cunningham
1958 S. Pearson
1959 S. Pearson
1960 W. Fisher
1961 J. Gamble
1962 J. Lloyd
1963 A. Wyper
1964 W. Robinson
1965 P. Dwyer
1966 T. Imrie
1967 A. Edwards

1968 E. Blake
1969 T. Imrie
1970 D. Simmonds
1971 A. Edwards
1972 L. Paul
1973 R. Maxwell
1974 R. Maxwell
1975 A. Harrison
1976 W. Lauder
1977 C. Malarkey
1978 E. Henderson
1979 D. Brewster
1980 J. Price
1981 E. Christie
1982 D. Milligan
1983 R. Douglas
1984 R. Douglas
1985 R. Douglas
1986 T. Velinor
1987 N. Brown
1988 W. Ellis
1989 N. Brown
1990 T. Taylor
1991 T. Taylor
1992 J. Calzaghe
1993 D. Starie
1994 W. Alexander
1995 C. Bessey
1996 S. Dann
1997 C. Bessey
1998 C. Bessey
1999 C. Bessey
2000 C. Bessey
2001 M. Thirwall

Middleweight
1881 T. Bellhouse
1882 A. H. Curnick
1883 A. J. Curnick
1884 W. Brown
1885 M. Salmon
1886 W. King
1887 R. Hair
1888 R. Hair
1889 G. Sykes
1890 J. Hoare
1891 J. Steers
1892 J. Steers
1893 J. Steers
1894 W. Sykes
1895 G. Townsend
1896 W. Ross
1897 W. Dees
1898 G. Townsend
1899 R. Warnes
1900 E. Mann
1901 R. Warnes
1902 E. Mann
1903 R. Warnes
1904 E. Mann
1905 J. Douglas
1906 A. Murdock
1907 R. Warnes
1908 W. Child
1909 W. Child
1910 R. Warnes
1911 W. Child
1912 E. Chandler
1913 W. Bradley
1914 H. Brown
1919 H. Mallin
1920 H. Mallin
1921 H. Mallin

1922 H. Mallin
1923 H. Mallin
1924 J. Elliot
1925 J. Elliot
1926 F. P. Crawley
1927 F. P. Crawley
1928 F. Mallin
1929 F. Mallin
1930 F. Mallin
1931 F. Mallin
1932 F. Mallin
1933 A. Shawyer
1934 J. Magill
1935 J. Magill
1936 A. Harrington
1937 M. Dennis
1938 H. Tiller
1939 H. Davies
1944 J. Hockley
1945 R. Parker
1946 R. Turpin
1947 R. Agland
1948 J. Wright
1949 S. Lewis
1950 P. Longo
1951 E. Ludlam
1952 T. Gooding
1953 R. Barton
1954 K. Phillips
1955 F. Hope
1956 R. Redrup
1957 P. Burke
1958 P. Hill
1959 F. Elderfield
1960 R. Addison
1961 J. Caiger
1962 A. Matthews
1963 A. Matthews
1964 W. Stack
1965 W. Robinson
1966 C. Finnegan
1967 A. Ball
1968 P. McCann
1969 D. Wallington
1970 J. Conteh
1971 A. Minter
1972 F. Lucas
1973 F. Lucas
1974 D. Odwell
1975 D. Odwell
1976 E. Burke
1977 R. Davies
1978 H. Graham
1979 N. Wilshire
1980 M. Kaylor
1981 B. Schumacher
1982 J. Price
1983 T. Forbes
1984 B. Schumacher
1985 D. Cronin
1986 N. Benn
1987 R. Douglas
1988 M. Edwards
1989 S. Johnson
1990 S. Wilson
1991 M. Edwards
1992 L. Woolcock
1993 J. Calzaghe
1994 D. Starie
1995 J. Matthews
1996 J. Pearce
1997 I. Cooper
1998 J. Pearce

1999 C. Froch
2000 S. Swales
2001 C. Froch

L. Heavyweight
1920 H. Franks
1921 L. Collett
1922 H. Mitchell
1923 H. Mitchell
1924 H. Mitchell
1925 H. Mitchell
1926 D. McCorkindale
1927 A. Jackson
1928 A. Jackson
1929 J. Goyder
1930 J. Murphy
1931 J. Petersen
1932 J. Goyder
1933 G. Brennan
1934 G. Brennan
1935 R. Hearns
1936 J. Magill
1937 J. Wilby
1938 A. S. Brown
1939 B. Woodcock
1944 E. Shackleton
1945 A. Watson
1946 J. Taylor
1947 A. Watson
1948 D. Scott
1949 *Declared no contest*
1950 P. Messervy
1951 G. Walker
1952 H. Cooper
1953 H. Cooper
1954 A. Madigan
1955 D. Rent
1956 D. Mooney
1957 T. Green
1958 J. Leeming
1959 J. Ould
1960 J. Ould
1961 J. Bodell
1962 J. Hendrickson
1963 P. Murphy
1964 J. Fisher
1965 E. Whistler
1966 R. Tighe
1967 M. Smith
1968 R. Brittle
1969 J. Frankham
1970 J. Rafferty
1971 J. Conteh
1972 W. Knight
1973 W. Knight
1974 W. Knight
1975 M. Heath
1976 G. Evans
1977 C. Lawson
1978 V. Smith
1979 A. Straughn
1980 A. Straughn
1981 A. Straughn
1982 G. Crawford
1983 A. Wilson
1984 A. Wilson
1985 J. Beckles
1986 J. Moran
1987 J. Beckles
1988 H. Lawson
1989 N. Piper
1990 J. McCluskey
1991 A. Todd

1992 K. Oliver	1894 H. King	1929 P. Floyd	1964 C. Woodhouse	1994 S. Burford
1993 K. Oliver	1895 W. E. Johnstone	1930 V. Stuart	1965 W. Wells	1995 M. Ellis
1994 K. Oliver	1896 W. E. Johnstone	1931 M. Flanagan	1966 A. Brogan	1996 T. Oakey
1995 K. Oliver	1897 G. Townsend	1932 V. Stuart	1967 P. Boddington	1997 B. Stevens
1996 C. Fry	1898 G. Townsend	1933 C. O'Grady	1968 W. Wells	1998 N. Hosking
1997 P. Rogers	1899 F. Parks	1934 P. Floyd	1969 A. Burton	1999 S. St John
1998 C. Fry	1900 W. Dees	1935 P. Floyd	1970 J. Gilmour	2000 D. Dolan
1999 J. Ainscough	1901 F. Parks	1936 V. Stuart	1971 L. Stevens	2001 D. Dolan
2000 P. Haymer	1902 F. Parks	1937 V. Stuart	1972 T. Wood	
2001 C. Fry	1903 F. Dickson	1938 G. Preston	1973 G. McEwan	**S. Heavyweight**
	1904 A. Horner	1939 A. Porter	1974 N. Meade	1982 A. Elliott
Cruiserweight	1905 F. Parks	1944 M. Hart	1975 G. McEwan	1983 K. Ferdinand
1998 T. Oakey	1906 F. Parks	1945 D. Scott	1976 J. Rafferty	1984 R. Wells
1999 M. Krence	1907 H. Brewer	1946 P. Floyd	1977 G. Adair	1985 G. Williamson
2000 J. Dolan	1908 S. Evans	1947 G. Scriven	1978 J. Awome	1986 J. Oyebola
2001 J. Dolan	1909 C. Brown	1948 J. Gardner	1979 A. Palmer	1987 J. Oyebola
	1910 F. Storbeck	1949 A. Worrall	1980 F. Bruno	1988 K. McCormack
Heavyweight	1911 W. Hazell	1950 P. Toch	1981 A. Elliott	1989 P. Passley
1881 R. Frost-Smith	1912 R. Smith	1951 A. Halsey	1982 H. Hylton	1990 K. McCormack
1882 H. Dearsley	1913 R. Smith	1952 E. Hearn	1983 H. Notice	1991 K. McCormack
1883 H. Dearsley	1914 E. Chandler	1953 J. Erskine	1984 D. Young	1992 M. Hopper
1884 H. Dearsley	1919 H. Brown	1954 B. Harper	1985 H. Hylton	1993 M. McKenzie
1885 W. West	1920 R. Rawson	1955 D. Rowe	1986 E. Cardouza	1994 D. Watts
1886 A. Diamond	1921 R. Rawson	1956 D. Rent	1987 J. Moran	1995 R. Allen
1887 E. White	1922 T. Evans	1957 D. Thomas	1988 H. Akinwande	1996 D. Watts
1888 W. King	1923 E. Eagan	1958 D. Thomas	1989 H. Akinwande	1997 A. Harrison
1889 A. Bowman	1924 A. Clifton	1959 D. Thomas	1990 K. Inglis	1998 A. Harrison
1890 J. Steers	1925 D. Lister	1960 L. Hobbs	1991 P. Lawson	1999 W. Bessey
1891 V. Barker	1926 T. Petersen	1961 W. Walker	1992 S. Welch	2000 J. McDermott
1892 J. Steers	1927 C. Capper	1962 R. Dryden	1993 P. Lawson	2001 M. Grainger
1893 J. Steers	1928 J. L. Driscoll	1963 R. Sanders		

David Dolan (Plains Farm) knocked out Taunton's Patrik Lewis (right) to win the 2001 ABA heavyweight title for the second year running

Les Clark

International Amateur Champions, 1904-2001

Shows all Olympic, World, European & Commonwealth champions since 1904. British silver and bronze medal winners are shown throughout, where applicable.

Country Code

ALG = Algeria; ARG = Argentina; ARM = Armenia; AUS = Australia; AUT = Austria; AZE = Azerbaijan; BEL = Belgium; BUL = Bulgaria; CAN = Canada; CEY = Ceylon (now Sri Lanka); CI = Channel Islands; CUB = Cuba; DEN = Denmark; DOM = Dominican Republic; ENG = England; ESP = Spain; EST = Estonia; FIJ = Fiji Islands; FIN = Finland; FRA = France; GBR = United Kingdom; GDR = German Democratic Republic; GEO = Georgia; GER = Germany (but West Germany only from 1968-1990); GHA = Ghana; GUY = Guyana; HOL = Netherlands; HUN = Hungary; IRL = Ireland; ITA = Italy; JAM = Jamaica; JPN = Japan; KAZ = Kazakhstan; KEN = Kenya; LIT = Lithuania; MAS = Malaysia; MEX = Mexico; MRI = Mauritius; NKO = North Korea; NIG = Nigeria; NIR = Northern Ireland; NOR = Norway; NZL = New Zealand; POL = Poland; PUR = Puerto Rico; ROM = Romania; RUS = Russia; SAF = South Africa; SCO = Scotland; SKO = South Korea; SR = Southern Rhodesia; STV = St Vincent; SWE = Sweden; TCH = Czechoslovakia; THA = Thailand; TUR = Turkey; UGA = Uganda; UKR = Ukraine; URS = USSR; USA = United States of America; UZB = Uzbekistan; VEN = Venezuela; WAL = Wales; YUG = Yugoslavia; ZAM = Zambia.

Olympic Champions, 1904-2000

St Louis, USA - 1904
Fly: G. Finnegan (USA). **Bantam:** O. Kirk (USA). **Feather:** O. Kirk (USA). **Light:** H. Spangler (USA). **Welter:** A. Young (USA). **Middle:** C. May (USA). **Heavy:** S. Berger (USA).

London, England - 1908
Bantam: H. Thomas (GBR). **Feather:** R. Gunn (GBR). **Light:** F. Grace (GBR). **Middle:** J.W.H.T. Douglas (GBR). **Heavy:** A. Oldman (GBR).
Silver medals: J. Condon (GBR), C. Morris (GBR), F. Spiller (GBR), S. Evans (GBR).
Bronze medals: W. Webb (GBR), H. Rodding (GBR), T. Ringer (GBR), H. Johnson (GBR), R. Warnes (GBR), W. Philo (GBR), F. Parks (GBR).

Antwerp, Belgium - 1920
Fly: F. Genaro (USA). **Bantam:** C. Walker (SAF). **Feather:** R. Fritsch (FRA). **Light:** S. Mossberg (USA). **Welter:** T. Schneider (CAN). **Middle:** H. Mallin (GBR). **L. Heavy:** E. Eagan (USA). **Heavy:** R. Rawson (GBR).
Silver medal: A. Ireland (GBR).
Bronze medals: W. Cuthbertson (GBR), G. McKenzie (GBR), H. Franks (GBR).

Paris, France - 1924
Fly: F. la Barba (USA). **Bantam:** W. Smith (SAF). **Feather:** J. Fields (USA). **Light:** H. Nielson (DEN). **Welter:** J. Delarge (BEL). **Middle:** H. Mallin (GBR). **L. Heavy:** H. Mitchell (GBR). **Heavy:** O. von Porat (NOR).
Silver medals: J. McKenzie (GBR), J. Elliot (GBR).

Amsterdam, Holland - 1928
Fly: A. Kocsis (HUN). **Bantam:** V. Tamagnini (ITA). **Feather:** B. van Klaveren (HOL). **Light:** C. Orlando (ITA). **Welter:** E. Morgan (NZL). **Middle:** P. Toscani (ITA). **L. Heavy:** V. Avendano (ARG). **Heavy:** A. Rodriguez Jurado (ARG).

Los Angeles, USA - 1932
Fly: I. Enekes (HUN). **Bantam:** H. Gwynne (CAN). **Feather:** C. Robledo (ARG). **Light:** L. Stevens (SAF). **Welter:** E. Flynn (USA). **Middle:** C. Barth (USA). **L. Heavy:** D. Carstens (SAF). **Heavy:** A. Lovell (ARG).

Berlin, West Germany - 1936
Fly: W. Kaiser (GER). **Bantam:** U. Sergo (ITA). **Feather:** O. Casanova (ARG). **Light:** I. Harangi (HUN). **Welter:** S. Suvio (FIN). **Middle:** J. Despeaux (FRA). **L. Heavy:** R. Michelot (FRA). **Heavy:** H. Runge (GER).

London, England - 1948
Fly: P. Perez (ARG). **Bantam:** T. Csik (HUN). **Feather:** E. Formenti (ITA). **Light:** G. Dreyer (SAF). **Welter:** J. Torma (TCH). **Middle:** L. Papp (HUN). **L. Heavy:** G. Hunter (SAF). **Heavy:** R. Iglesas (ARG).
Silver medals: J. Wright (GBR), D. Scott (GBR).

Helsinki, Finland - 1952
Fly: N. Brooks (USA). **Bantam:** P. Hamalainen (FIN). **Feather:** J. Zachara (TCH). **Light:** A. Bolognesi (ITA). **L. Welter:** C. Adkins (USA). **Welter:** Z. Chychla (POL). **L. Middle:** L. Papp (HUN). **Middle:** F. Patterson (USA). **L. Heavy:** N. Lee (USA). **Heavy:** E. Sanders (USA).
Silver medal: J. McNally (IRL).

Melbourne, Australia - 1956
Fly: T. Spinks (GBR). **Bantam:** W. Behrendt (GER). **Feather:** V. Safronov (URS). **Light:** R. McTaggart (GBR). **L. Welter:** V. Jengibarian (URS). **Welter:** N. Linca (ROM). **L. Middle:** L. Papp (HUN). **Middle:** G. Schatkov (URS). **L. Heavy:** J. Boyd (USA). **Heavy:** P. Rademacher (USA).
Silver medals: T. Nicholls (GBR), F. Tiedt (IRL).
Bronze medals: J. Caldwell (IRL), F. Gilroy (IRL), A. Bryne (IRL), N. Gargano (GBR), J. McCormack (GBR).

Rome, Italy - 1960
Fly: G. Torok (HUN). **Bantam:** O. Grigoryev (URS). **Feather:** F. Musso (ITA). **Light:** K. Pazdzior (POL). **L. Welter:** B. Nemecek (TCH). **Welter:** N. Benvenuti (ITA). **L. Middle:** W. McClure (USA). **Middle:** E. Crook (USA). **L. Heavy:** C. Clay (USA). **Heavy:** F. de Piccoli (ITA).
Bronze medals: R. McTaggart (GBR), J. Lloyd (GBR), W. Fisher (GBR).

Tokyo, Japan - 1964
Fly: F. Atzori (ITA). **Bantam:** T. Sakurai (JPN). **Feather:** S. Stepashkin (URS). **Light:** J. Grudzien (POL). **L. Welter:** J. Kulej (POL). **Welter:** M. Kasprzyk (POL). **L. Middle:** B. Lagutin (URS). **Middle:** V. Popenchenko (URS). **L. Heavy:** C. Pinto (ITA). **Heavy:** J. Frazier (USA).
Bronze medal: J. McCourt (IRL).

Mexico City, Mexico - 1968
L. Fly: F. Rodriguez (VEN). **Fly:** R. Delgado (MEX). **Bantam:** V. Sokolov (URS). **Feather:** A. Roldan (MEX). **Light:** R. Harris (USA). **L. Welter:** J. Kulej (POL). **Welter:** M. Wolke (GDR). **L. Middle:** B. Lagutin (URS). **Middle:** C. Finnegan (GBR). **L. Heavy:** D. Poznyak (URS). **Heavy:** G. Foreman (USA).

Munich, West Germany - 1972
L. Fly: G. Gedo (HUN). **Fly:** G. Kostadinov (BUL). **Bantam:** O. Martinez (CUB). **Feather:** B. Kusnetsov (URS). **Light:** J. Szczepanski (POL). **L. Welter:** R. Seales (USA). **Welter:** E. Correa (CUB). **L. Middle:** D. Kottysch (GER). **Middle:** V. Lemeschev (URS). **L. Heavy:** M. Parlov (YUG). **Heavy:** T. Stevenson (CUB).
Bronze medals: R. Evans (GBR), G. Turpin (GBR), A. Minter (GBR).

Montreal, Canada - 1976
L. Fly: J. Hernandez (CUB). **Fly:** L. Randolph (USA). **Bantam:** Y-J. Gu (NKO). **Feather:** A. Herrera (CUB). **Light:** H. Davis (USA). **L. Welter:** R. Leonard (USA). **Welter:** J. Bachfield (GDR). **L. Middle:** J. Rybicki (POL). **Middle:** M. Spinks (USA). **L. Heavy:** L. Spinks (USA). **Heavy:** T. Stevenson (CUB).
Bronze medal: P. Cowdell (GBR).

Moscow, USSR - 1980
L. Fly: S. Sabirov (URS). **Fly:** P. Lessov (BUL). **Bantam:** J. Hernandez (CUB). **Feather:** R. Fink (GDR). **Light:** A. Herrera (CUB). **L. Welter:** P. Oliva (ITA). **Welter:** A. Aldama (CUB). **L. Middle:** A. Martinez (CUB). **Middle:** J. Gomez (CUB). **L. Heavy:** S. Kacar (YUG). **Heavy:** T. Stevenson (CUB).
Bronze medals: H. Russell (IRL), A. Willis (GBR).

Los Angeles, USA - 1984
L. Fly: P. Gonzalez (USA). **Fly:** S. McCrory (USA). **Bantam:** M. Stecca (ITA). **Feather:** M. Taylor (USA). **Light:** P. Whitaker (USA). **L. Welter:** J. Page (USA). **Welter:** M. Breland (USA). **L. Middle:** F. Tate (USA).

Middle: J-S. Shin (SKO). **L. Heavy:** A. Josipovic (YUG). **Heavy:** H. Tillman (USA). **S. Heavy:** T. Biggs (USA).
Bronze medal: B. Wells (GBR).

Seoul, South Korea - 1988
L. Fly: I. Mustafov (BUL). **Fly:** H-S. Kim (SKO). **Bantam:** K. McKinney (USA). **Feather:** G. Parisi (ITA). **Light:** A. Zuelow (GDR). **L. Welter:** V. Yanovsky (URS). **Welter:** R. Wangila (KEN). **L. Middle:** S-H. Park (SKO). **Middle:** H. Maske (GDR). **L. Heavy:** A. Maynard (USA). **Heavy:** R. Mercer (USA). **S. Heavy:** L. Lewis (CAN).
Bronze medal: R. Woodhall (GBR).

Barcelona, Spain - 1992
L. Fly: R. Marcelo (CUB). **Fly:** C-C. Su (NKO). **Bantam:** J. Casamayor (CUB). **Feather:** A. Tews (GER). **Light:** O. de la Hoya (USA). **L. Welter:** H. Vinent (CUB). **Welter:** M. Carruth (IRL). **L. Middle:** J. Lemus (CUB). **Middle:** A. Hernandez (CUB). **L. Heavy:** T. May (GER). **Heavy:** F. Savon (CUB). **S. Heavy:** R. Balado (CUB).
Silver medal: W. McCullough (IRL).
Bronze medal: R. Reid (GBR).

Atlanta, USA - 1996
L. Fly: D. Petrov (BUL). **Fly:** M. Romero (CUB). **Bantam:** I. Kovaks (HUN). **Feather:** S. Kamsing (THA). **Light:** H. Soltani (ALG). **L. Welter:** H. Vinent (CUB). **Welter:** O. Saitov (RUS). **L. Middle:** D. Reid (USA). **Middle:** A. Hernandez (CUB). **L. Heavy:** V. Jirov (KAZ). **Heavy:** F. Savon (CUB). **S. Heavy:** Vladimir Klitschko (UKR).

Sydney, Australia - 2000
L. Fly: B. Aslom (FRA). **Fly:** W. Ponlid (THA). **Bantam:** G. Rigondeaux Ortiz (CUB). **Feather:** B. Sattarkhanov (KAZ). **Light:** M. Kindelan (CUB). **L. Welter:** M. Abdullaev (UZB). **Welter:** O. Saitov (RUS). **L. Middle:** Y. Ibraimov (KAZ). **Middle:** J. Gutierrez Espinosa (CUB). **L. Heavy:** A. Lebziak (RUS). **Heavy:** F. Savon (CUB). **S. Heavy:** A. Harrison (ENG).

World Champions, 1974-2001

Havana, Cuba - 1974
L. Fly: J. Hernandez (CUB). **Fly:** D. Rodriguez (CUB). **Bantam:** W. Gomez (PUR). **Feather:** H. Davis (USA). **Light:** V. Solomin (URS). **L. Welter:** A. Kalule (UGA). **Welter:** E. Correa (CUB). **L. Middle:** R. Garbey (CUB). **Middle:** R. Riskiev (URS). **L. Heavy:** M. Parlov (YUG). **Heavy:** T. Stevenson (CUB).

Belgrade, Yugoslavia - 1978
L. Fly: S. Muchoki (KEN). **Fly:** H. Strednicki (POL). **Bantam:** A. Horta (CUB). **Feather:** A. Herrera (CUB). **Light:** D. Andeh (NIG). **L. Welter:** V. Lvov (URS). **Welter:** V. Rachkov (URS). **L. Middle:** V. Savchenko (URS). **Middle:** J. Gomez (CUB). **L. Heavy:** S. Soria (CUB). **Heavy:** T. Stevenson (CUB).

Munich, West Germany - 1982
L. Fly: I. Mustafov (BUL). **Fly:** Y. Alexandrov (URS). **Bantam:** F. Favors (USA). **Feather:** A. Horta (CUB). **Light:** A. Herrera (CUB). **L. Welter:** C. Garcia (CUB). **Welter:** M. Breland (USA). **L. Middle:** A. Koshkin (URS). **Middle:** B. Comas (CUB). **L. Heavy:** P. Romero (CUB). **Heavy:** A. Jagubkin (URS). **S. Heavy:** T. Biggs (USA).
Bronze medal: T. Corr (IRL).

Reno, USA - 1986
L. Fly: J. Odelin (CUB). **Fly:** P. Reyes (CUB). **Bantam:** S-I. Moon (SKO). **Feather:** K. Banks (USA). **Light:** A. Horta (CUB). **L. Welter:** V. Shishov (URS). **Welter:** K. Gould (USA). **L. Middle:** A. Espinosa (CUB). **Middle:** D. Allen (USA). **L. Heavy:** P. Romero (CUB). **Heavy:** F. Savon (CUB). **S. Heavy:** T. Stevenson (CUB).

Moscow, USSR - 1989
L. Fly: E. Griffin (USA). **Fly:** Y. Arbachakov (URS). **Bantam:** E. Carrion (CUB). **Feather:** A. Khamatov (URS). **Light:** J. Gonzalez (CUB). **L. Welter:** I. Ruzinkov (URS). **Welter:** F. Vastag (Rom). **L. Middle:** I. Akopokhian (URS). **Middle:** A. Kurniavka (URS). **L. Heavy:** H. Maske (GDR). **Heavy:** F. Savon (CUB). **S. Heavy:** R. Balado (CUB).
Bronze medal: M. Carruth (IRL).

Sydney, Australia - 1991
L. Fly: E. Griffin (USA). **Fly:** I. Kovacs (HUN). **Bantam:** S. Todorov (BUL). **Feather:** K. Kirkorov (BUL). **Light:** M. Rudolph (GER). **L. Welter:** K. Tsziu (URS). **Welter:** J. Hernandez (CUB). **L. Middle:** J. Lemus (CUB). **Middle:** T. Russo (ITA). **L. Heavy:** T. May (GER). **Heavy:** F. Savon (CUB). **S. Heavy:** R. Balado (CUB).

Tampere, Finland - 1993
L. Fly: N. Munchian (ARM). **Fly:** W. Font (CUB). **Bantam:** A. Christov (BUL). **Feather:** S. Todorov (BUL). **Light:** D. Austin (CUB). **L. Welter:** H. Vinent (CUB). **Welter:** J. Hernandez (CUB). **L. Middle:** F. Vastag (ROM). **Middle:** A. Hernandez (CUB). **L. Heavy:** R. Garbey (CUB). **Heavy:** F. Savon (CUB). **S. Heavy:** R. Balado (CUB).
Bronze medal: D. Kelly (IRL).

Berlin, Germany - 1995
L. Fly: D. Petrov (BUL). **Fly:** Z. Lunka (GER). **Bantam:** R. Malachbekov (RUS). **Feather:** S. Todorov (BUL). **Light:** L. Doroftel (ROM). **L. Welter:** H. Vinent (CUB). **Welter:** J. Hernandez (CUB). **L. Middle:** F. Vastag (ROM). **Middle:** A. Hernandez (CUB). **L. Heavy:** A. Tarver (USA). **Heavy:** F. Savon (CUB). **S. Heavy:** A. Lezin (RUS).

Budapest, Hungary - 1997
L. Fly: M. Romero (CUB). **Fly:** M. Mantilla (CUB). **Bantam:** R Malakhbekov (RUS). **Feather:** I. Kovacs (HUN). **Light:** A. Maletin (RUS). **L. Welter:** D. Simion (ROM). **Welter:** O. Saitov (RUS). **L. Middle:** A. Duvergel (CUB). **Middle:** Z. Erdei (HUN). **L. Heavy:** A. Lebsiak (RUS). **Heavy:** F. Savon (CUB). **S. Heavy:** G. Kandelaki (GEO).
Bronze medal: S. Kirk (IRL).

Houston, USA - 1999
L. Fly: B. Viloria (USA). **Fly:** B. Jumadilov (KAZ). **Bantam:** R. Crinu (ROM). **Feather:** R. Juarez (USA). **Light:** M. Kindelan (CUB). **L. Welter:** M. Abdullaev (UZB). **Welter:** J. Hernandez (CUB). **L. Middle:** M. Simion (ROM). **Middle:** U. Haydarov (UZB). **L. Heavy:** M. Simms (USA). **Heavy:** M. Bennett (USA). **S. Heavy:** S. Samilsan (TUR).
Bronze medal: K. Evans (WAL).

Belfast, Northern Ireland - 2001
L. Fly: Y. Bartelemi Varela (CUB). **Fly:** J. Thomas (FRA). **Bantam:** G. Rigondeaux Ortiz (CUB). **Feather:** R. Palyani (TUR). **Light:** M. Kindelan Mesa (CUB). **L. Welter:** D. Luna Martinez (CUB). **Welter:** L. Aragon Armenteros (CUB). **L. Middle:** D. Austin Echemendia (CUB). **Middle:** A. Gogolev (RUS). **L. Heavy:** E. Makarenko (RUS). **Heavy:** O. Solis Fonte (CUB). **S. Heavy:** R. Chagaev (UZB).
Silver medal: D. Haye (ENG).
Bronze medals: J. Moore (IRL), C. Froch (ENG).

World Junior Champions, 1979-2000

Yokohama, Japan - 1979
L. Fly: R. Shannon (USA). **Fly:** P. Lessov (BUL). **Bantam:** P-K. Choi (SKO). **Feather:** Y. Gladychev (URS). **Light:** R. Blake (USA). **L. Welter:** I. Akopokhian (URS). **Welter:** M. McCrory (USA). **L. Middle:** A. Mayes (USA). **Middle:** A. Milov (URS). **L. Heavy:** A. Lebedev (URS). **Heavy:** M. Frazier (USA).
Silver medals: N. Wilshire (ENG), D. Cross (ENG).
Bronze medal: I. Scott (SCO).

Santa Domingo, Dominican Republic - 1983
L. Fly: M. Herrera (DOM). **Fly:** J. Gonzalez (DOM). **Bantam:** J. Molina (PUR). **Feather:** A. Miesses (DOM). **Light:** A. Beltre (DOM). **L. Welter:** A. Espinoza (CUB). **Welter:** M. Watkins (USA). **L. Middle:** U. Castillo (CUB). **Middle:** R. Batista (CUB). **L. Heavy:** O. Pought (USA). **Heavy:** A. Williams (USA). **S. Heavy:** L. Lewis (CAN).

Bucharest, Romania - 1985
L. Fly: R-S. Hwang (SKO). **Fly:** T. Marcelica (ROM). **Bantam:** R. Diaz (CUB). **Feather:** D. Maeran (ROM). **Light:** J. Teiche (GDR). **L. Welter:** W. Saeger (GDR). **Welter:** A. Stoianov (BUL). **L. Middle:** M. Franek (TCH). **Middle:** O. Zahalotskih (URS). **L. Heavy:** B. Riddick (USA). **Heavy:** F. Savon (CUB). **S. Heavy:** A. Prianichnikov (URS).

Havana, Cuba - 1987
L. Fly: E. Paisan (CUB). **Fly:** C. Daniels (USA). **Bantam:** A. Moya (CUB). **Feather:** G. Iliyasov (URS). **Light:** J. Hernandez (CUB). **L. Welter:** L. Mihai (ROM). **Welter:** F. Vastag (ROM). **L. Middle:** A. Lobsyak (URS). **Middle:** W. Martinez (CUB). **L. Heavy:** D. Yeliseyev (URS). **Heavy:** R. Balado (CUB). **S. Heavy:** L. Martinez (CUB).
Silver medal: E. Loughran (IRL).
Bronze medal: D. Galvin (IRL).

San Juan, Puerto Rico - 1989
L. Fly: D. Petrov (BUL). **Fly:** N. Monchai (FRA). **Bantam:** J. Casamayor (CUB). **Feather:** C. Febres (PUR). **Light:** A. Acevedo (PUR). **L. Welter:** E. Berger (GDR). **Welter:** A. Hernandez (CUB). **L. Middle:** L. Bedey

(CUB). **Middle:** R. Garbey (CUB). **L. Heavy:** R. Alvarez (CUB). **Heavy:** K. Johnson (CAN). **S. Heavy:** A. Burdiantz (URS).
Silver medals: E. Magee (IRL), R. Reid (ENG), S. Wilson (SCO).

Lima, Peru - 1990
L. Fly: D. Alicea (PUR). **Fly:** K. Pielert (GDR). **Bantam:** K. Baravi (URS). **Feather:** A. Vaughan (ENG). **Light:** J. Mendez (CUB). **L. Welter:** H. Vinent (CUB). **Welter:** A. Hernandez (CUB). **L. Middle:** A. Kakauridze (URS). **Middle:** J. Gomez (CUB). **L. Heavy:** B. Torsten (GDR). **Heavy:** I. Andreev (URS). **S. Heavy:** J. Quesada (CUB).
Bronze medal: P. Ingle (ENG).

Montreal, Canada - 1992
L. Fly: W. Font (CUB). **Fly:** J. Oragon (CUB). **Bantam:** N. Machado (CUB). **Feather:** M. Stewart (CAN). **Light:** D. Austin (CUB). **L. Welter:** O. Saitov (RUS). **Welter:** L. Brors (GER). **L. Middle:** J. Acosta (CUB). **Middle:** I. Arsangaliev (RUS). **L. Heavy:** S. Samilsan (TUR). **Heavy:** G. Kandeliaki (GEO). **S. Heavy:** M. Porchnev (RUS).
Bronze medal: N. Sinclair (IRL).

Istanbul, Turkey - 1994
L. Fly: J. Turunen (FIN). **Fly:** A. Jimenez (CUB). **Bantam:** J. Despaigne (CUB). **Feather:** D. Simion (ROM). **Light:** L. Diogenes (CUB). **L. Welter:** V. Romero (CUB). **Welter:** E. Aslan (TUR). **L. Middle:** G. Ledsvanys (CUB). **Middle:** M. Genc (TUR). **L. Heavy:** P. Aurino (ITA). **Heavy:** M. Lopez (CUB). **S. Heavy:** P. Carrion (CUB).

Havana, Cuba - 1996
L. Fly: L. Hernandez (CUB). **Fly:** L. Cabrera (CUB). **Bantam:** P. Miradal (CUB). **Feather:** E. Rodriguez (CUB). **Light:** R. Vaillan (CUB). **L. Welter:** T. Mergadze (RUS). **Welter:** J. Brahmer (GER). **L. Middle:** L. Mezquia (CUB). **Middle:** V. Pletniov (RUS). **L. Heavy:** O. Simon (CUB). **Heavy:** A. Yatsenko (UKR). **S. Heavy:** S. Fabre (CUB).
Bronze medal: R. Hatton (ENG).

Buenos Aires, Argentina - 1998
L. Fly: S. Tanasie (ROM). **Fly:** S. Yeledov (KAZ). **Bantam:** S. Suleymanov (UKR). **Feather:** I. Perez (ARG). **Light:** A. Solopov (RUS). **L. Welter:** Y. Tomashov (UKR). **Welter:** K. Oustarkhanov (RUS). **L. Middle:** S. Kostenko (UKR). **Middle:** M. Kempe (GER). **L. Heavy:** Y. Yohanson Martinez (CUB). **Heavy:** O. Solis Fonte (CUB). **S. Heavy:** B. Ohanyan (ARM).
Silver medal: H. Cunningham (IRL).
Bronze medal: D. Campbell (IRL).

Budapest, Hungary - 2000
L. Fly: Y. Leon Alarcon (CUB). **Fly:** O. Franco Vaszquez (CUB). **Bantam:** V. Tajbert (GER). **Feather:** G. Kate (HUN). **Light:** F. Adzsanalov (AZE). **L. Welter:** G. Galovkin (KAZ). **Welter:** S. Ustunel (TUR). **L. Middle:** D. Chernysh (RUS). **Middle:** F. Sullivan Barrera (CUB). **L. Heavy:** A. Shekmourov (RUS). **Heavy:** D., Medzhydov (UKR). **S. Heavy:** A. Dmitrienko (RUS).
Bronze medal: C. Barrett (IRL).

European Champions, 1924-2000

Paris, France - 1924
Fly: J. McKenzie (GBR). **Bantam:** J. Ces (FRA). **Feather:** R. de Vergnie (BEL). **Light:** N. Nielsen (DEN). **Welter:** J. Delarge (BEL). **Middle:** H. Mallin (GBR). **L. Heavy:** H. Mitchell (GBR). **Heavy:** O. von Porat (NOR).

Stockholm, Sweden - 1925
Fly: E. Pladner (FRA). **Bantam:** A. Rule (GBR). **Feather:** P. Andren (SWE). **Light:** S. Johanssen (SWE). **Welter:** H. Nielsen (DEN). **Middle:** F. Crawley (GBR). **L. Heavy:** T. Petersen (DEN). **Heavy:** B. Persson (SWE).
Silver medals: J. James (GBR), E. Viney (GBR), D. Lister (GBR).

Berlin, Germany - 1927
Fly: L. Boman (SWE). **Bantam:** K. Dalchow (GER). **Feather:** F. Dubbers (GER). **Light:** H. Domgoergen (GER). **Welter:** R. Caneva (ITA). **Middle:** J. Christensen (NOR). **L. Heavy:** H. Muller (GER). **Heavy:** N. Ramm (SWE).

Amsterdam, Holland - 1928
Fly: A. Kocsis (HUN). **Bantam:** V. Tamagnini (ITA). **Feather:** B. van Klaveren (HOL). **Light:** C. Orlandi (ITA). **Welter:** R. Galataud (FRA). **Middle:** P. Toscani (ITA). **L. Heavy:** E. Pistulla (GER). **Heavy:** N. Ramm (SWE).

Budapest, Hungary - 1930
Fly: I. Enekes (HUN). **Bantam:** J. Szeles (HUN). **Feather:** G. Szabo (HUN). **Light:** M. Bianchini (ITA). **Welter:** J. Besselmann (GER). **Middle:** C. Meroni (ITA). **L. Heavy:** T. Petersen (DEN). **Heavy:** J. Michaelson (DEN).

Los Angeles, USA - 1932
Fly: I. Enekes (HUN). **Bantam:** H. Ziglarski (GER). **Feather:** J. Schleinkofer (GER). **Light:** T. Ahlqvist (SWE). **Welter:** E. Campe (GER). **Middle:** R. Michelot (FRA). **L. Heavy:** G. Rossi (ITA). **Heavy:** L. Rovati (ITA).

Budapest, Hungary - 1934
Fly: P. Palmer (GBR). **Bantam:** I. Enekes (HUN). **Feather:** O. Kaestner (GER). **Light:** E. Facchini (ITA). **Welter:** D. McCleave (GBR). **Middle:** S. Szigetti (HUN). **L. Heavy:** P. Zehetmayer (AUT). **Heavy:** G. Baerlund (FIN).
Bronze medal: P. Floyd (GBR).

Milan, Italy - 1937
Fly: I. Enekes (HUN). **Bantam:** U. Sergo (ITA). **Feather:** A. Polus (POL). **Light:** H. Nuremberg (GER). **Welter:** M. Murach (GER). **Middle:** H. Chmielewski (POL). **L. Heavy:** S. Szigetti (HUN). **Heavy:** O. Tandberg (SWE).

Dublin, Eire - 1939
Fly: J. Ingle (IRL). **Bantam:** U. Sergo (ITA). **Feather:** P. Dowdall (IRL). **Light:** H. Nuremberg (GER). **Welter:** A. Kolczyski (POL). **Middle:** A. Raadik (EST). **L. Heavy:** L. Musina (ITA). **Heavy:** O. Tandberg (SWE).
Bronze medal: C. Evenden (IRL).

Dublin, Eire - 1947
Fly: L. Martinez (ESP). **Bantam:** L. Bogacs (HUN). **Feather:** K. Kreuger (SWE). **Light:** J. Vissers (BEL). **Welter:** J. Ryan (ENG). **Middle:** A. Escudie (FRA). **L. Heavy:** H. Quentemeyer (HOL). **Heavy:** G. O'Colmain (IRL).
Silver medals: J. Clinton (SCO), P. Maguire (IRL), W. Thom (ENG), G. Scriven (ENG).
Bronze medals: J. Dwyer (SCO), A. Sanderson (ENG), W. Frith (SCO), E. Cantwell (IRL), K. Wyatt (ENG).

Oslo, Norway - 1949
Fly: J. Kasperczak (POL). **Bantam:** G. Zuddas (ITA). **Feather:** J. Bataille (FRA). **Light:** M. McCullagh (IRL). **Welter:** J. Torma (TCH). **Middle:** L. Papp (HUN). **L. Heavy:** G. di Segni (ITA). **Heavy:** L. Bene (HUN).
Bronze medal: D. Connell (IRL).

Milan, Italy - 1951
Fly: A. Pozzali (ITA). **Bantam:** V. Dall'Osso (ITA). **Feather:** J. Ventaja (FRA). **Light:** B. Visintin (ITA). **L. Welter:** H. Schelling (GER). **Welter:** Z. Chychla (POL). **L. Middle:** L. Papp (HUN). **Middle:** S. Sjolin (SWE). **L. Heavy:** M. Limage (BEL). **Heavy:** G. di Segni (ITA).
Silver medal: J. Kelly (IRL).
Bronze medals: D. Connell (IRL), T. Milligan (IRL), A. Lay (ENG).

Warsaw, Poland - 1953
Fly: H. Kukier (POL). **Bantam:** Z. Stefaniuk (POL). **Feather:** J. Kruza (POL). **Light:** V. Jengibarian (URS). **L. Welter:** L. Drogosz (POL). **Welter:** Z. Chychla (POL). **L. Middle:** B. Wells (ENG). **Middle:** D. Wemhoner (GER). **L. Heavy:** U. Nietchke (GER). **Heavy:** A. Schotzikas (URS).
Silver medal: T. Milligan (IRL).
Bronze medals: J. McNally (IRL), R. Barton (ENG).

Berlin, West Germany - 1955
Fly: E. Basel (GER). **Bantam:** Z. Stefaniuk (POL). **Feather:** T. Nicholls (ENG). **Light:** H. Kurschat (GER). **L. Welter:** L. Drogosz (POL). **Welter:** N. Gargano (ENG). **L. Middle:** Z. Pietrzykowski (POL). **Middle:** G. Schatkov (URS). **L. Heavy:** E. Schoeppner (GER). **Heavy:** A. Schotzikas (URS).

Prague, Czechoslovakia - 1957
Fly: M. Homberg (GER). **Bantam:** O. Grigoryev (URS). **Feather:** D. Venilov (BUL). **Light:** K. Pazdzior (POL). **L. Welter:** V. Jengibarian (URS). **Welter:** M. Graus (URS). **L. Middle:** N. Benvenuti (ITA). **Middle:** Z. Pietrzykowski (POL). **L. Heavy:** G. Negrea (ROM). **Heavy:** A. Abramov (URS).
Bronze medals: R. Davies (WAL), J. Morrissey (SCO), J. Kidd (SCO), F. Teidt (IRL).

Lucerne, Switzerland - 1959
Fly: M. Homberg (GER). **Bantam:** H. Rascher (GER). **Feather:** J. Adamski (POL). **Light:** O. Maki (FIN). **L. Welter:** V. Jengibarian (URS). **Welter:** L. Drogosz (POL). **L. Middle:** N. Benvenuti (ITA). **Middle:** G. Schatkov (URS). **L. Heavy:** Z. Pietrzykowski (POL). **Heavy:** A. Abramov (URS).
Silver medal: D. Thomas (ENG).
Bronze medals: A. McClean (IRL), H. Perry (IRL), C. McCoy (IRL), H. Scott (ENG).

Belgrade, Yugoslavia - 1961
Fly: P. Vacca (ITA). **Bantam:** S. Sivko (URS). **Feather:** F. Taylor (ENG). **Light:** R. McTaggart (SCO). **L. Welter:** A. Tamulis (URS). **Welter:** R. Tamulis (URS). **L. Middle:** B. Lagutin (URS). **Middle:** T. Walasek (POL). **L. Heavy:** G. Saraudi (ITA). **Heavy:** A. Abramov (URS).
Bronze medals: P. Warwick (ENG), I. McKenzie (SCO), J. Bodell (ENG).

Moscow, USSR - 1963
Fly: V. Bystrov (URS). **Bantam:** O. Grigoryev (URS). **Feather:** S. Stepashkin (URS). **Light:** J. Kajdi (HUN). **L. Welter:** J. Kulej (POL). **Welter:** R. Tamulis (URS). **L. Middle:** B. Lagutin (URS). **Middle:** V. Popenchenko (URS). **L. Heavy:** Z. Pietrzykowski (POL). **Heavy:** J. Nemec (TCH).
Silver medal: A. Wyper (SCO).

Berlin, East Germany - 1965
Fly: H. Freisdadt (GER). **Bantam:** O. Grigoryev (URS). **Feather:** S. Stepashkin (URS). **Light:** V. Barranikov (URS). **L. Welter:** J. Kulej (POL). **Welter:** R. Tamulis (URS). **L. Middle:** V. Ageyev (URS). **Middle:** V. Popenchenko (URS). **L. Heavy:** D. Poznyak (URS). **Heavy:** A. Isosimov (URS).
Silver medal: B. Robinson (ENG).
Bronze medals: J. McCluskey (SCO), K. Buchanan (SCO), J. McCourt (IRL).

Rome, Italy - 1967
Fly: H. Skrzyczak (POL). **Bantam:** N. Giju (ROM). **Feather:** R. Petek (POL). **Light:** J. Grudzien (POL). **L. Welter:** V. Frolov (URS). **Welter:** B. Nemecek (TCH). **L. Middle:** V. Ageyev (URS). **Middle:** M. Casati (ITA). **L. Heavy:** D. Poznyak (URS). **Heavy:** M. Baruzzi (ITA).
Silver medal: P. Boddington (ENG).

Bucharest, Romania - 1969
L. Fly: G. Gedo (HUN). **Fly:** C. Ciuca (ROM). **Bantam:** A. Dumitrescu (ROM). **Feather:** L. Orban (HUN). **Light:** S. Cutov (ROM). **L. Welter:** V. Frolov (URS). **Welter:** G. Meier (GER). **L. Middle:** V. Tregubov (URS). **Middle:** V. Tarasenkov (URS). **L. Heavy:** D. Poznyak (URS). **Heavy:** I. Alexe (ROM).
Bronze medals: M. Dowling (IRL), M. Piner (ENG), A. Richardson (ENG), T. Imrie (SCO).

Madrid, Spain - 1971
L. Fly: G. Gedo (HUN). **Fly:** J. Rodriguez (ESP). **Bantam:** T. Badar (HUN). **Feather:** R. Tomczyk (POL). **Light:** J. Szczepanski (POL). **L. Welter:** U. Beyer (GDR). **Welter:** J. Kajdi (HUN). **L. Middle:** V. Tregubov (URS). **Middle:** J. Juotsiavitchus (URS). **L. Heavy:** M. Parlov (YUG). **Heavy:** V. Tchernishev (URS).
Bronze medals: N. McLaughlin (IRL), M. Dowling (IRL), B. McCarthy (IRL), M. Kingwell (ENG), L. Stevens (ENG).

Belgrade, Yugoslavia - 1973
L. Fly: V. Zasypko (URS). **Fly:** C. Gruescu (ROM). **Bantam:** A. Cosentino (FRA). **Feather:** S. Forster (GDR). **Light:** S. Cutov (ROM). **L. Welter:** M. Benes (YUG). **Welter:** S. Csjef (HUN). **L. Middle:** A. Klimanov (URS). **Middle:** V. Lemechev (URS). **L. Heavy:** M. Parlov (YUG). **Heavy:** V. Ulyanich (URS).
Bronze medal: J. Bambrick (SCO).

Katowice, Poland - 1975
L. Fly: A. Tkachenko (URS). **Fly:** V. Zasypko (URS). **Bantam:** V. Rybakov (URS). **Feather:** T. Badari (HUN). **Light:** S. Cutov (ROM). **L. Welter:** V. Limasov (URS). **Welter:** K. Marjaama (FIN). **L. Middle:** W. Rudnowski (POL). **Middle:** V. Lemechev (URS). **L. Heavy:** A. Klimanov (URS). **Heavy:** A. Biegalski (POL).
Bronze medals: C. Magri (ENG), P. Cowdell (ENG), G. McEwan (ENG).

Halle, East Germany - 1977
L. Fly: H. Srednicki (POL). **Fly:** L. Blazynski (POL). **Bantam:** S. Forster (GDR). **Feather:** R. Nowakowski (GDR). **Light:** A. Rusevski (YUG). **L. Welter:** B. Gajda (POL). **Welter:** V. Limasov (URS). **L. Middle:** V. Saychenko (URS). **Middle:** I. Shaposhnikov (URS). **L. Heavy:** D.

Kvachadze (URS). **Heavy:** E. Gorstkov (URS).
Bronze medal: P. Sutcliffe (IRL).

Cologne, West Germany - 1979
L. Fly: S. Sabirov (URS). **Fly:** H. Strednicki (POL). **Bantam:** N. Khrapzov (URS). **Feather:** V. Rybakov (URS). **Light.** V. Demianenko (URS). **L. Welter:** S. Konakbaev (URS). **Welter:** E. Muller (GER). **L. Middle:** M. Perunovic (YUG). **Middle:** T. Uusiverta (FIN). **L. Heavy:** A. Nikolyan (URS). **Heavy:** E. Gorstkov (URS). **S. Heavy:** P. Hussing (GER).
Bronze medal: P. Sutcliffe (IRL).

Tampere, Finland - 1981
L. Fly: I. Mustafov (BUL). **Fly:** P. Lessov (BUL). **Bantam:** V. Miroschnichenko (URS). **Feather:** R. Nowakowski (GDR). **Light:** V. Rybakov (URS). **L. Welter:** V. Shisov (URS). **Welter:** S. Konakvbaev (URS). **L. Middle:** A. Koshkin (URS). **Middle:** J. Torbek (URS). **L. Heavy:** A Krupin (URS). **Heavy:** A. Jagupkin (URS). **S. Heavy:** F. Damiani (ITA).
Bronze medal: G. Hawkins (IRL).

Varna, Bulgaria - 1983
L. Fly: I. Mustafov (BUL). **Fly:** P. Lessov (BUL). **Bantam:** Y. Alexandrov (URS). **Feather:** S. Nurkazov (URS). **Light:** E. Chuprenski (BUL). **L. Welter:** V. Shishov (URS). **Welter:** P. Galkin (URS). **L. Middle:** V. Laptev (URS). **Middle:** V. Melnik (URS). **L. Heavy:** V. Kokhanovski (URS). **Heavy:** A. Jagubkin (URS). **S. Heavy:** F. Damiani (ITA).
Bronze medal: K. Joyce (IRL).

Budapest, Hungary - 1985
L. Fly: R. Breitbarth (GDR). **Fly:** D. Berg (GDR). **Bantam:** L. Simic (YUG). **Feather:** S. Khachatrian (URS). **Light:** E. Chuprenski (BUL). **L. Welter:** S. Mehnert (GDR). **Welter:** I. Akopokhian (URS). **L. Middle:** M. Timm (GDR). **Middle:** H. Maske (GDR). **L. Heavy:** N. Shanavasov (URS). **Heavy:** A. Jagubkin (URS). **S. Heavy:** F. Somodi (HUN).
Bronze medals: S. Casey (IRL), J. Beckles (ENG).

Turin, Italy - 1987
L. Fly: N. Munchyan (URS). **Fly:** A. Tews (GDR). **Bantam:** A. Hristov (BUL). **Feather:** M. Kazaryan (URS). **Light:** O. Nazarov (URS). **L. Welter:** B. Abadjier (BUL). **Welter:** V. Shishov (URS). **L. Middle:** E. Richter (GDR). **Middle:** H. Maske (GDR). **L. Heavy:** Y. Vaulin (URS). **Heavy:** A. Vanderlijde (HOL). **S. Heavy:** U. Kaden (GDR).
Bronze medal: N. Brown (ENG).

Athens, Greece - 1989
L. Fly: I. Mustafov (BUL). **Fly:** Y. Arbachakov (URS). **Bantam:** S. Todorov (BUL). **Feather:** K. Kirkorov (BUL). **Light:** K. Tsziu (URS). **L. Welter:** I. Ruznikov (URS). **Welter:** S. Mehnert (GDR). **L. Middle:** I. Akopokhian (URS). **Middle:** H. Maske (GDR). **L. Heavy:** S. Lange (GDR). **Heavy:** A. Vanderlijde (HOL). **S. Heavy:** U. Kaden (GDR).
Bronze Medal: D. Anderson (SCO).

Gothenburg, Sweden - 1991
L. Fly: I. Marinov (BUL). **Fly:** I. Kovacs (HUN). **Bantam:** S. Todorov (BUL). **Feather:** P. Griffin (IRL). **Light:** V. Nistor (ROM). **L. Welter:** K. Tsziu (URS). **Welter:** R. Welin (SWE). **L. Middle:** I. Akopokhian (URS). **Middle:** S. Otke (GER). **L. Heavy:** D. Michalczewski (GER). **Heavy:** A. Vanderlijde (HOL). **S. Heavy:** E. Beloussov (URS).
Bronze medals: P. Weir (SCO), A. Vaughan (ENG).

Bursa, Turkey - 1993
L. Fly: D. Petrov (BUL). **Fly:** R. Husseinov (AZE). **Bantam:** R. Malakhbetov (RUS). **Feather:** S. Todorov (BUL). **Light:** J. Bielski (POL). **L. Welter:** N. Suleymanoglu (TUR). **Welter:** V. Karpaclauskas (LIT). **L. Middle:** F. Vastag (ROM). **Middle:** D. Eigenbrodt (GER). **L. Heavy:** I. Kshinin (RUS). **Heavy:** G. Kandelaki (GEO). **S. Heavy:** S. Rusinov (BUL).
Bronze medals: P. Griffin (IRL), D. Williams (ENG), K. McCormack (WAL).

Vejle, Denmark - 1996
L. Fly: D. Petrov (BUL). **Fly:** A. Pakeev (RUS). **Bantam:** I. Kovacs (HUN). **Feather:** R. Paliani (RUS). **Light:** L. Doroftei (ROM). **L. Welter:** O. Urkal (GER). **Welter:** H. Al (DEN). **L. Middle:** F. Vastag (ROM). **Middle:** S. Ottke (GER). **L. Heavy:** P. Aurino (ITA). **Heavy:** L. Krasniqi (GER). **S. Heavy:** A. Lezin (RUS).
Bronze medals: S. Harrison (SCO), D. Burke (ENG), D. Kelly (IRL).

Minsk, Belarus - 1998
L. Fly: S. Kazakov (RUS). **Fly:** V. Sidorenko (UKR). **Bantam:** S. Danilchenko (UKR). **Feather:** R. Paliani (TUR). **Light:** K. Huste (GER). **L. Welter:** D. Simion (ROM). **Welter:** O. Saitov (RUS). **L. Middle:** F. Esther

(FRA). **Middle:** Z. Erdei (HUN). **L. Heavy:** A. Lebsiak (RUS). **Heavy:** G. Fragomeni (ITA). **S. Heavy:** A. Lezin (RUS).
Silver Medals: B. Magee (IRL), C. Fry (ENG).
Bronze medal: C. Bessey (ENG).

Tampere, Finland - 2000

L. Fly: Valeri Sidorenko (UKR). **Fly:** Vladimir Sidorenko (UKR). **Bantam:** A. Agagueloglu (TUR). **Feather:** R. Paliani (TUR). **Light:** A. Maletin (RUS). **L. Welter:** A. Leonev (RUS). **Welter:** B. Ueluesoy (TUR). **L. Middle:** A. Catic (GER). **Middle:** Z. Erdei (HUN). **L. Heavy:** A. Lebsiak (RUS). **Heavy:** J. Chanet (FRA). **S. Heavy:** A. Lezin (RUS).

Note: Gold medals were awarded to the Europeans who went the furthest in the Olympic Games of 1924, 1928 & 1932.

European Junior Champions, 1970-1999

Miskolc, Hungary - 1970

L. Fly: Gluck (HUN). **Fly:** Z. Kismeneth (HUN). **Bantam:** A. Levitschev (URS). **Feather:** Andrianov (URS). **Light:** L. Juhasz (HUN). **L. Welter:** K. Nemec (HUN). **Welter:** Davidov (URS). **L. Middle:** A. Lemeschev (URS). **Middle:** N. Anfimov (URS). **L. Heavy:** O. Sasche (GDR). **Heavy:** J. Reder (HUN).
Bronze medals: D. Needham (ENG), R. Barlow (ENG), L. Stevens (ENG).

Bucharest, Romania - 1972

L. Fly: A. Turei (ROM). **Fly:** Condurat (ROM). **Bantam:** V. Solomin (URS). **Feather:** V. Lvov (URS). **Light:** S. Cutov (ROM). **L. Welter:** K. Pierwieniecki (POL). **Welter:** Zorov (URS). **L. Middle:** Babescu (ROM). **Middle:** V. Lemeschev (URS). **L. Heavy:** Mirounik (URS). **Heavy:** Subutin (URS).
Bronze medals: J. Gale (ENG), R. Maxwell (ENG), D. Odwell (ENG).

Kiev, Russia - 1974

L. Fly: A. Tkachenko (URS). **Fly:** V. Rybakov (URS). **Bantam:** C. Andreikovski (BUL). **Feather:** V. Sorokin (URS). **Light:** V. Limasov (URS). **L. Welter:** N. Sigov (URS). **Welter:** M. Bychkov (URS). **L. Middle:** V. Danshin (URS). **Middle:** D. Jende (GDR). **L. Heavy:** K. Dafinoiu (ROM). **Heavy:** K. Mashev (BUL).
Silver medal: C. Magri (ENG).
Bronze medals: G. Gilbody (ENG), K. Laing (ENG).

Izmir, Turkey - 1976

L. Fly: C. Seican (ROM). **Fly:** G. Khratsov (URS). **Bantam:** M. Navros (URS). **Feather:** V. Demoianeko (URS). **Light:** M. Puzovic (YUG). **L. Welter:** V. Zverev (URS). **Welter:** K. Ozoglouz (TUR). **L. Middle:** W. Lauder (SCO). **Middle:** H. Lenhart (GER). **L. Heavy:** I. Yantchauskas (URS). **Heavy:** B. Enjenyan (URS).
Silver medal: J. Decker (ENG).
Bronze medals: I. McLeod (SCO), N. Croombes (ENG).

Dublin, Ireland - 1978

L. Fly: R. Marx (GDR). **Fly:** D. Radu (ROM). **Bantam:** S. Khatchatrian (URS). **Feather:** H. Loukmanov (URS). **Light:** P. Oliva (ITA). **L. Welter:** V. Laptiev (URS). **Welter:** R. Filimanov (URS). **L. Middle:** A. Beliave (URS). **Middle:** G. Zinkovitch (URS). **L. Heavy:** I. Jolta (ROM). **Heavy:** P. Stoimenov (BUL).
Silver medals: M. Holmes (IRL), P. Hanlon (ENG), M. Courtney (ENG).
Bronze medals: T. Thompson (IRL), J. Turner (ENG), M. Bennett (WAL), J. McAllister (SCO), C. Devine (ENG).

Rimini, Italy - 1980

L. Fly: A. Mikoulin (URS). **Fly:** J. Varadi (HUN). **Bantam:** F. Rauschning (GDR). **Feather:** J. Gladychev (URS). **Light:** V. Shishov (URS). **L. Welter:** R. Lomski (BUL). **Welter:** T. Holonics (GDR). **L. Middle:** N. Wilshire (ENG). **Middle:** S. Laptiev (URS). **L. Heavy:** V. Dolgoun (URS). **Heavy:** V. Tioumentsev (URS). **S. Heavy:** S. Kormihtsine (URS).
Bronze medals: N. Potter (ENG), B. McGuigan (IRL), M. Brereton (IRL), D. Cross (ENG).

Schwerin, East Germany - 1982

L. Fly: R. Kabirov (URS). **Fly:** I. Filchev (BUL). **Bantam:** M. Stecca (ITA). **Feather:** B. Blagoev (BUL). **Light:** E. Chakimov (URS). **L. Welter:** S. Mehnert (GDR). **Welter:** T. Schmitz (GDR). **L. Middle:** B. Shararov (URS). **Middle:** E. Christie (ENG). **L. Heavy:** Y. Waulin (URS). **Heavy:** A. Popov (URS). **S. Heavy:** V. Aldoshin (URS).
Silver medal: D. Kenny (ENG).
Bronze medal: O. Jones (ENG).

Tampere, Finland - 1984

L. Fly: R. Breitbart (GDR). **Fly:** D. Berg (GDR). **Bantam:** K. Khdrian (URS). **Feather:** O. Nazarov (URS). **Light:** C. Furnikov (BUL). **L. Welter:** W. Schmidt (GDR). **Welter:** K. Doinov (BUL). **L. Middle:** O. Volkov (URS). **Middle:** R. Ryll (GDR). **L. Heavy:** G. Peskov (URS). **Heavy:** R. Draskovic (YUG). **S. Heavy:** L. Kamenov (BUL).
Bronze medals: J. Lowey (IRL), F. Harding (ENG), N. Moore (ENG).

Copenhagen, Denmark - 1986

L. Fly: S. Todorov (BUL). **Fly:** S. Galotian (URS). **Bantam:** D. Drumm (GDR). **Feather:** K. Tsziu (URS). **Light:** G. Akopkhian (URS). **L. Welter:** F. Vastag (ROM). **Welter:** S. Karavayev (URS). **L. Middle:** E. Elibaev (URS). **Middle:** A. Kurnabka (URS). **L. Heavy:** A. Schultz (GDR). **Heavy:** A. Golota (POL). **S. Heavy:** A. Prianichnikov (URS).

Gdansk, Poland - 1988

L. Fly: I. Kovacs (HUN). **Fly:** M. Beyer (GDR). **Bantam:** M. Aitzanov (URS). **Feather:** M. Rudolph (GDR). **Light:** M. Shaburov (URS). **L. Welter:** G. Campanella (ITA). **Welter:** D. Konsun (URS). **L. Middle:** K. Kiselev (URS). **Middle:** A. Rudenko (URS). **L. Heavy:** O. Velikanov (URS). **Heavy:** A. Ter-Okopian (URS). **S. Heavy:** E. Belusov (URS).
Bronze medals: P. Ramsey (ENG), M. Smyth (WAL).

Usti Nad Labem, Czechoslovakia - 1990

L. Fly: Z. Paliani (URS). **Fly:** K. Pielert (GDR). **Bantam:** K. Baravi (URS). **Feather:** P. Gvasalia (URS). **Light:** J. Hildenbrandt (GDR). **L. Welter:** N. Smanov (URS). **Welter:** A. Preda (ROM). **L. Middle:** A. Kakauridze (URS). **Middle:** J. Schwank (GDR). **L. Heavy:** Iljin (URS). **Heavy:** I. Andrejev (URS). **S. Heavy:** W. Fischer (GDR).
Silver medal: A. Todd (ENG).
Bronze medal: P. Craig (ENG).

Edinburgh, Scotland - 1992

L. Fly: M. Ismailov (URS). **Fly:** F. Brennfuhrer (GER). **Bantam:** S. Kuchler (GER). **Feather:** M. Silantiev (URS). **Light:** S. Shcherbakov (URS). **L. Welter:** O. Saitov (URS). **Welter:** H. Kurlumaz (TUR). **L. Middle:** Z. Erdie (HUN). **Middle:** V. Zhirov (URS). **L. Heavy:** D. Gorbachev (URS). **Heavy:** L. Achkasov (URS). **S. Heavy:** A. Mamedov (URS).
Silver medals: M. Hall (ENG), B. Jones (WAL).
Bronze medals: F. Slane (IRL), G. Stephens (IRL), C. Davies (WAL).

Salonika, Greece - 1993

L. Fly: O. Kiroukhine (UKR). **Fly:** R. Husseinov (AZE). **Bantam:** M. Kulbe (GER). **Feather:** E. Zakharov (RUS). **Light:** O. Sergeev (RUS). **L. Welter:** A. Selihanov (RUS). **Welter:** O. Kudinov (UKR). **L. Middle:** E. Makarenko (RUS). **Middle:** D. Droukovski (RUS). **L. Heavy:** A. Voida (RUS). **Heavy:** Vladimir Klitschko (UKR). **S. Heavy:** A. Moiseev (RUS).
Bronze medal: D. Costello (ENG).

Sifok, Hungary - 1995

L. Fly: D. Gaissine (RUS). **Fly:** A. Kotelnik (UKR). **Bantam:** A. Loutsenko (UKR). **Feather:** S. Harrison (SCO). **Light:** D. Simon (ROM). **L. Welter:** B. Ulusoy (TUR). **Welter:** O. Bouts (UKR). **L. Middle:** O. Bukalo (UKR). **Middle:** V. Plettnev (RUS). **L. Heavy:** A. Derevtsov (RUS). **Heavy:** C. O'Grady (RUS). **S. Heavy:** D. Savvine (RUS).
Silver medal: G. Murphy (SCO).
Bronze medal: N. Linford (ENG).

Birmingham, England - 1997

L. Fly: G. Balakshine (RUS). **Fly:** K. Dzhamoloudinov (RUS). **Bantam:** A. Shaiduline (RUS). **Feather:** D. Marciukaitis (LIT). **Light:** D. Baranov (RUS). **L. Welter:** A. Mishine (RUS). **Welter:** D. Yuldashev (UKR). **L. Middle:** A. Catic (GER). **Middle:** D. Lebedev (RUS). **L. Heavy:** V. Uzelkov (UKR). **Heavy:** S. Koeber (GER). **S. Heavy:** D. Pirozhenko (RUS).
Silver medal: S. Miller (ENG).
Bronze medals: S. Burke (ENG), M. Dean (ENG), P. Pierson (ENG), M. Lee (IRE).

Rijeka, Croatia - 1999

L. Fly: K. Kibalyuk (UKR). **Fly:** A. Bakhtin (RUS). **Bantam:** V. Simion (ROM). **Feather:** Kiutkhukow (BUL). **Light:** Pontilov (RUS). **L. Welter:** G. Ajetovic (YUG). **Welter:** S. Nouaouria (FRA). **L. Middle:** S. Kazantsev (RUS). **Middle:** D. Tsariouk (RUS). **L. Heavy:** Alexeev (RUS). **Heavy:** Alborov (RUS). **S. Heavy:** Soukhoverkov (RUS).
Bronze medal: S. Birch (ENG).

Note: The age limit for the championships were reduced from 21 to 19 in 1976.

Commonwealth Champions, 1930-1998

Hamilton, Canada - 1930
Fly: W. Smith (SAF). **Bantam:** H. Mizler (ENG). **Feather:** F. Meacham (ENG). **Light:** J. Rolland (SCO). **Welter:** L. Hall (SAF). **Middle:** F. Mallin (ENG). **L. Heavy:** J. Goyder (ENG). **Heavy:** V. Stuart (ENG).
Silver medals: T. Pardoe (ENG), T. Holt (SCO).
Bronze medals: A. Lyons (SCO), A. Love (ENG), F. Breeman (ENG).

Wembley, England - 1934
Fly: P. Palmer (ENG). **Bantam:** F. Ryan (ENG). **Feather:** C. Cattarall (SAF). **Light:** L. Cook (AUS). **Welter:** D. McCleave (ENG). **Middle:** A. Shawyer (ENG). **L. Heavy:** G. Brennan (ENG). **Heavy:** P. Floyd (ENG).
Silver medals: A. Barnes (WAL), J. Jones (WAL), F. Taylor (WAL), J. Holton (SCO).
Bronze medals: J. Pottinger (WAL), T. Wells (SCO), H. Moy (ENG), W. Duncan (NIR), J. Magill (NIR), Lord D. Douglas-Hamilton (SCO).

Melbourne, Australia - 1938
Fly: J. Joubert (SAF). **Bantam:** W. Butler (ENG). **Feather:** A. Henricus (CEY). **Light:** H. Groves (ENG). **Welter:** W. Smith (AUS). **Middle:** D. Reardon (WAL). **L. Heavy:** N. Wolmarans (SAF). **Heavy:** T. Osborne (CAN).
Silver medals: J. Watson (SCO), M. Dennis (ENG).
Bronze medals: H. Cameron (SCO), J. Wilby (ENG).

Auckland, New Zealand - 1950
Fly: H. Riley (SCO). **Bantam:** J. van Rensburg (SAF). **Feather:** H. Gilliland (SCO). **Light:** R. Latham (ENG). **Welter:** T. Ratcliffe (ENG). **Middle:** T. van Schalkwyk (SAF). **L. Heavy:** D. Scott (ENG). **Heavy:** F. Creagh (NZL).
Bronze medal: P. Brander (ENG).

Vancouver, Canada - 1954
Fly: R. Currie (SCO). **Bantam:** J. Smillie (SCO). **Feather:** L. Leisching (SAF). **Light:** P. van Staden (SR). **L. Welter:** M. Bergin (CAN). **Welter:** N. Gargano (ENG). **L. Middle:** W. Greaves (CAN). **Middle:** J. van de Kolff (SAF). **L. Heavy:** P. van Vuuren (SAF). **Heavy:** B. Harper (ENG).
Silver medals: M. Collins (WAL), F. McQuillan (SCO).
Bronze medals: D. Charnley (ENG), B. Wells (ENG).

Cardiff, Wales - 1958
Fly: J. Brown (SCO). **Bantam:** H. Winstone (WAL). **Feather:** W. Taylor (AUS). **Light:** R. McTaggart (SCO). **L. Welter:** H. Loubscher (SAF). **Welter:** J. Greyling (SAF). **L. Middle:** G. Webster (SAF). **Middle:** T. Milligan (NIR). **L. Heavy:** A. Madigan (AUS). **Heavy:** D. Bekker (SAF).
Silver medals: T. Bache (ENG), M. Collins (WAL), J. Jordan (NIR), R. Kane (SCO), S. Pearson (ENG), A. Higgins (WAL), D. Thomas (ENG).
Bronze medals: P. Lavery (NIR), D. Braithwaite (WAL), R. Hanna (NIR), A. Owen (SCO), J. McClory (NIR), J. Cooke (ENG), J. Jacobs (ENG), B. Nancurvis (ENG), R. Scott (SCO), W. Brown (WAL), J. Caiger (ENG), W. Bannon (SCO), R. Pleace (WAL).

Perth, Australia - 1962
Fly: R. Mallon (SCO). **Bantam:** J. Dynevor (AUS). **Feather:** J. McDermott (SCO). **Light:** E. Blay (GHA). **L. Welter:** C. Quartey (GHA). **Welter:** W. Coe (NZL). **L. Middle:** H. Mann (CAN). **Middle:** M. Calhoun (JAM). **L. Heavy:** A. Madigan (AUS). **Heavy:** G. Oywello (UGA).
Silver medals: R. McTaggart (SCO), J. Pritchett (ENG).
Bronze medals: M. Pye (ENG), P. Benneyworth (ENG), B. Whelan (ENG), B. Brazier (ENG), C. Rice (NIR), T. Menzies (SCO), H. Christie (NIR), A. Turmel (CI).

Kingston, Jamaica - 1966
Fly: S. Shittu (GHA). **Bantam:** E. Ndukwu (NIG). **Feather:** P. Waruinge (KEN). **Light:** A. Andeh (NIG). **L. Welter:** J. McCourt (NIR). **Welter:** E. Blay (GHA). **L. Middle:** M. Rowe (ENG). **Middle:** J. Darkey (GHA). **L. Heavy:** R. Tighe (ENG). **Heavy:** W. Kini (NZL).
Silver medals: P. Maguire (NIR), R. Thurston (ENG), R. Arthur (ENG), T. Imrie (SCO).
Bronze medals: S. Lockhart (NIR), A. Peace (SCO), F. Young (NIR), J. Turpin (ENG), D. McAlinden (NIR).

Edinburgh, Scotland - 1970
L. Fly: J. Odwori (UGA). **Fly:** D. Needham (ENG). **Bantam:** S. Shittu (GHA). **Feather:** P. Waruinge (KEN). **Light:** A. Adeyemi (NIG). **L. Welter:** M. Muruli (UGA). **Welter:** E. Ankudey (GHA). **L. Middle:** T. Imrie (SCO). **Middle:** J. Conteh (ENG). **L. Heavy:** F. Ayinla (NIG). **Heavy:** B. Masanda (UGA).

Silver medals: T. Davies (WAL), J. Gillan (SCO), D. Davies (WAL), J. McKinty (NIR).
Bronze medals: M. Abrams (ENG), A. McHugh (SCO), D. Larmour (NIR), S. Oglivie (SCO), A. Richardson (ENG), T. Joyce (SCO), P. Doherty (NIR), J. Rafferty (SCO), L. Stevens (ENG).

Christchurch, New Zealand - 1974
L. Fly: S. Muchoki (KEN). **Fly:** D. Larmour (NIR). **Bantam:** P. Cowdell (ENG). **Feather:** E. Ndukwu (NIG). **Light:** A. Kalule (UGA). **L. Welter:** O. Nwankpa (NIG). **Welter:** M. Muruli (UGA). **L. Middle:** L. Mwale (ZAM). **Middle:** F. Lucas (STV). **L. Heavy:** W. Knight (ENG). **Heavy:** N. Meade (ENG).
Silver medals: E. McKenzie (WAL), A. Harrison (SCO).
Bronze medals: J. Bambrick (SCO), J. Douglas (SCO), J. Rodgers (NIR), S. Cooney (SCO), R. Davies (ENG), C. Speare (ENG), G. Ferris (NIR).

Edmonton, Canada - 1978
L. Fly: S. Muchoki (KEN). **Fly:** M. Irungu (KEN). **Bantam:** B. McGuigan (NIR). **Feather:** A. Nelson (GHA). **Light:** A. Kalule (UGA). **L. Welter:** W. Braithwaite (GUY). **Welter:** M. McCallum (JAM). **L. Middle:** K. Perlette (CAN). **Middle:** P. McElwaine (AUS). **L. Heavy:** R. Fortin (CAN). **Heavy:** J. Awome (ENG).
Silver medals: J. Douglas (SCO), K. Beattie (NIR), D. Parkes (ENG), V. Smith (ENG).
Bronze medals: H. Russell (NIR), M. O'Brien (ENG), J. McAllister (SCO), T. Feal (WAL).

Brisbane, Australia - 1982
L. Fly: A. Wachire (KEN). **Fly:** M. Mutua (KEN). **Bantam:** J. Orewa (NIR). **Feather:** P. Konyegwachie (NIG). **Light:** H. Khalili (KEN). **L. Welter:** C. Ossai (NIG). **Welter:** C. Pyatt (ENG). **L. Middle:** S. O'Sullivan (CAN). **Middle:** J. Price (ENG). **L. Heavy:** F. Sani (FIJ). **Heavy:** W. de Wit (CAN).
Silver medals: J. Lyon (ENG), J. Kelly (SCO), R. Webb (NIR), P. Hanlon (ENG), J. McDonnell (ENG), N. Croombes (ENG), H. Hylton (ENG).
Bronze medals: R. Gilbody (ENG), C. McIntosh (ENG), R. Corr (NIR).

Edinburgh, Scotland - 1986
L. Fly: S. Olson (CAN). **Fly:** J. Lyon (ENG). **Bantam:** S. Murphy (ENG). **Feather:** B. Downey (CAN). **Light:** A. Dar (CAN). **L. Welter:** H. Grant (CAN). **Welter:** D. Dyer (SAF). **L. Middle:** D. Sherry (CAN). **Middle:** R. Douglas (ENG). **L. Heavy:** J. Moran (ENG). **Heavy:** J. Peau (NZL). **S. Heavy:** L. Lewis (CAN).
Silver medals: M. Epton (ENG), R. Nash (NIR), P. English (ENG), N. Haddock (WAL), J. McAlister (SCO), H. Lawson (SCO), D. Young (SCO), A. Evans (WAL).
Bronze medals: W. Docherty (SCO), J. Todd (NIR), K. Webber (WAL), G. Brooks (SCO), J. Wallace (SCO), C. Carleton (NIR), J. Jacobs (ENG), B. Lowe (NIR), D. Denny (NIR), G. Thomas (WAL), A. Mullen (SCO), G. Ferrie (SCO), P. Tinney (NIR), B. Pullen (WAL), E. Cardouza (ENG), J. Oyebola (ENG), J. Sillitoe (CI).

Auckland, New Zealand - 1990
L. Fly: J. Juuko (UGA). **Fly:** W. McCullough (NIR). **Bantam:** S. Mohammed (NIG). **Feather:** J. Irwin (ENG). **Light:** G. Nyakana (UGA). **L. Welter:** C. Kane (SCO). **Welter:** D. Defiagbon (NIG). **L. Middle:** R. Woodhall (ENG). **Middle:** C. Johnson (CAN). **L. Heavy:** J. Akhasamba (KEN). **Heavy:** G. Onyango (KEN). **S. Heavy:** M. Kenny (NZL).
Bronze medals: D. Anderson (SCO), M. Edwards (ENG), P. Douglas (NIR).

Victoria, Canada - 1994
L. Fly: H. Ramadhani (KEN). **Fly:** P. Shepherd (SCO). **Bantam:** R. Peden (AUS). **Feather:** C. Patton (CAN). **Light:** M. Strange (CAN). **L. Welter:** P. Richardson (ENG). **Welter:** N. Sinclair (NIR). **L. Middle:** J. Webb (NIR). **Middle:** R. Donaldson (CAN). **L. Heavy:** D. Brown (CAN). **Heavy:** O. Ahmed (KEN). **S. Heavy:** D. Dokiwari (NIG).
Silver medals: S. Oliver (ENG), J. Cook (WAL), M. Renaghan (NIR), M. Winters (NIR), J. Wilson (SCO).
Bronze medals: D. Costello (ENG), J. Townsley (SCO), D. Williams (ENG).

Kuala Lumpar, Malaysia - 1998
L. Fly: S. Biki (MAS). **Fly:** R. Sunee (MRI). **Bantam:** M. Yomba (TAN). **Feather:** A. Arthur (SCO). **Light:** R. Narh (GHA). **L. Welter:** M. Strange (CAN). **Welter:** J. Molitor (CAN). **L. Middle:** C. Bessey (ENG). **Middle:** J. Pearce (ENG). **L. Heavy:** C. Fry (ENG). **Heavy:** M. Simmons (CAN). **S. Heavy:** A. Harrison (ENG).
Silver medal: L. Cunningham (NIR).
Bronze medals: G. Jones (ENG), A. McLean (ENG), C. McNeil (SCO), J. Townsley (SCO), B. Magee (NIR), K. Evans (WAL).

The Triple Hitters' Boxing Quiz (Part 6)

Compiled by Ralph Oates

QUESTIONS

1. On 2 September 1908, Tommy Burns, in defence of his world heavyweight title, knocked out the challenger, Bill Lang, in round six. In which country did this contest take place?
   A. Canada.   B. America.   C. Australia.

2. On 18 June 1923, Pancho Villa won the world flyweight title when he knocked out the holder, Jimmy Wilde. In which round?
   A. Six.   B. Seven.   C. Eight.

3. Which former world middleweight champion was nicknamed 'The Georgia Deacon'?
   A. Tiger Flowers.   B. Mickey Walker.
   C. Harry Greb.

4. On 13 March 1944, Bruce Woodcock defeated Ken Shaw, who retired. Which was the round in question?
   A. Four.   B. Five.   C. Six.

5. On 15 April 1959, Howard Winstone outpointed Tommy Williams over six rounds. In which part of South Wales did this contest take place?
   A. Swansea.   B. Cardiff.   C. Porthcawl.

6. In which year did the former world middleweight champion, Carlos Monzon, make his professional debut?
   A. 1962.   B. 1963.   C. 1964.

7. In which round did Billy Walker stop Johnny Prescott in a bout which took place on 10 September 1963?
   A. Eight.   B. Nine.   C. Ten.

8. On 21 January 1969, Johnny Famechon won the WBC world featherweight title when he outpointed the holder, Jose Legra, over 15 rounds in a contest which took place in England. Who was the referee of this encounter?
   A. Harry Gibbs.   B. George Smith.
   C. Roland Dakin.

9. In which year was the former WBC world, British and European lightweight champion, Jim Watt, born?
   A. 1948.   B. 1949.   C. 1950.

10. John H. Stracey and Marshall Butler met in an eight-round contest at the Royal Albert Hall on 25 April 1972. What was the result?
    A. Points win for Stracey.   B. A draw.
    C. Points win for Butler.

11. In a defence of his European lightweight title, which took place on 25 July 1975, Ken Buchanan stopped Giancarlo Usai in round 12. In which country did this contest take place?
    A. Denmark.   B. Italy.   C. Spain.

12. Which boxer did not box in the southpaw stance?
    A. Chris Finnegan.   B. Alan Minter.
    C. Billy Walker.

13. Over how many rounds did Duke McKenzie outpoint David Capo in Atlantic City, USA on 15 January 1984?
    A. Four.   B. Six.   C. Eight.

14. Which British boxer knocked out Yawe Davis in three rounds on 19 April 1986, in a contest which took place in San Remo, Italy?
    A. Dennis Andries.   B. Tom Collins.
    C. Andy Straughn.

15. During his career, which opponent did Charlie Magri, the former WBC world, European and British flyweight champion, not meet in the professional ranks?
    A. Kelvin Smart.   B. Dave Smith.
    C. Bryn Griffiths.

16. Which boxer fought in the southpaw stance?
    A. Richard Dunn.   B. John McCluskey.
    C. John H. Stracey.

17. How many professional contests did the former European and British welterweight champion, Henry Rhiney, have during his career?
    A. 55.   B. 56.   C. 57.

18. In which round did Lennox Lewis knock out Jorge Dascola on 9 May 1990?
    A. One.   B. Two.   C. Three.

19. Johnny Nelson retained his European cruiserweight title on 12 March 1991 when Yves Monsieur retired. In which round did Nelson win?
A. Six.   B. Seven.   C. Eight.

20. David Tua knocked out Cecil Coffee in the first round on 9 December 1994. In which country did this contest take place?
A. America.   B. New Zealand.   C. Australia.

21. On 16 March 1996, Prince Naseem Hamed retained his WBO world featherweight title when he stopped Said Lawal in the first round. At this stage, how many first-round victories had Hamed achieved?
A. One.   B. Two.   C. Three.

22. Which one of the following did not hold the Commonwealth middleweight title during their respective professional careers?
A. Mark Rowe.   B. Bunny Sterling.
C. Alan Minter.

23. Joe Calzaghe captured the vacant WBO world super-middleweight championship on 11 October 1997 when he outpointed Chris Eubank over 12 rounds. Prior to going into this contest, Calzaghe was undefeated in how many bouts?
A. 22.   B. 23.   C. 24.

24. On 6 December 1997, Keith Mullings won the WBC world light-middleweight title when he stopped Terry Norris in round nine. In his previous contest, which took place on 13 September 1997, Mullings failed to capture the IBF version of the title when defending champion Raul Marquez defeated him. By which method did Norris lose?
A. Four-round stoppage.   B. Six-round knockout.
C. 12-round points decision.

25. Which promoter is associated with the World Sports Organisation?
A. Jonathan Feld.   B. Frank Maloney.
C. Graham Moughton.

26. Lennox Lewis retained his WBC world heavyweight title on 28 March 1998 when he stopped Shannon Briggs in round five. In which part of America did this contest take place?
A. New York.   B. Atlantic City.   C. Las Vegas.

27. On 28 March 1998, David Starie captured the Commonwealth super-middleweight title when he outpointed Clinton Woods, the holder, over 12

rounds. Who was the referee for this contest?
A. John Keane.   B. Roy Francis.   C. Dave Parris.

28. Howard Eastman won the vacant British middle-weight title on 30 November 1998 when he stopped Steve Foster in round seven. At this stage of his career, Eastman was undefeated in how many professional contests?
A. 17.   B. 18.   C. 19.

29. On 13 February 1999, Richard Evatt lost his IBO Inter-Continental featherweight title when he was outpointed over 12 rounds by Smith Odoom. In which country did this bout take place?
A. South Africa.   B. Poland.   C. France.

30. In which round did Michael Brodie stop Salim Medjkoune in defence of his European super-bantamweight title on 13 March 1999?
A. Nine.   B. Ten.   C. 11.

31. Over how many rounds did Jane Couch outpoint Neike Noller on 1 April 1999?
A. Six.   B. Eight.   C. Ten.

32. Who was the first boxer to defeat Michael Gomez in the professional ranks?
A. Chris Williams.   B. Danny Ruegg.
C. Greg Upton.

33. Which boxer was born on 13 March 1968?
A. Wayne Llewelyn.   B. Mike Holden.
C. Julius Francis.

34. Keith Knox won the British and Commonwealth flyweight titles on 22 May 1999 when the defending champion, Damaen Kelly, retired. Which was the round in question?
A. Four.   B. Five.   C. Six.

35. Lester Jacobs stopped David Baptiste in two rounds on 21 July 1999. At this stage of his career, Jacobs was undefeated in how many professional bouts?
A. 21.   B. 22.   C. 23.

36. Michelle Sutcliffe won the vacant WIBF International flyweight title on 27 September 1999, when she stopped Veerle Braspenningx in seven rounds. In which part of the country did this contest place?
A. London.   B. Manchester.   C. Leeds.

37. On 2 October 1999, Danny Williams defeated Ferenc

Deak, who retired in the first round. In which country did this contest take place?

A. France.   B. Belgium.   C. Holland.

38. In a world featherweight unification contest which took place in Detroit on 22 October 1999, the WBO holder, Prince Naseem Hamed, outpointed the WBC's Cesar Soto over 12 rounds. At this stage of his career, Hamed was undefeated in how many professional contests?

A. 32.   B. 33.   C. 34.

39. On 5 February 2000, Cathy Brown stopped Veerle Braspenningsx in round six. In which country did this contest take place?

A. England.   B. France.   C. Belgium.

40. On 21 February 2000, Bobby Vanzie retained his British and Commonwealth lightweight titles when stopping Stephen Smith in round nine. Who was the referee for this contest?

A. Terry O'Connor.   B. Roy Francis.
C. Mickey Vann.

41. Steve Robinson lost his WBO Inter-Continental featherweight title on 11 March 2000 when Juan Carlos Ramirez stopped him. In which round was he defeated?

A. 10.   B. 11.   C. 12.

42. On 18 March 2000, Floyd Mayweather retained his WBC world super-featherweight title when he outpointed Gregorio Vargas over 12 rounds. In which part of America did this contest take place?

A. Las Vegas.   B. New York.   C. Los Angeles.

43. Which lady is not a promoter?

A. Alma Ingle.   B. Tania Follett.
C. Katherine Morrison.

44. Over how many rounds did Ryan Rhodes outpoint Ojay Abrahams on 16 May 2000?

A. Six.   B. Eight.   C. Ten.

45. How many professional contests did the former European and British light-welterweight champion, Colin Power, have during his career?

A. 32.   B. 33.   V. 34.

46. On 18 May 2000, Colin Lynes stopped Jason Vlasman in round two. At this stage of his career, Lynes was undefeated in eight professional bouts. How many had he won inside the distance?

A. Four.   B. Five.   C. Six.

47. Mark Potter knocked out Mal Rice in round one on 27 May 2000. How many first-round victories had Mark achieved in the professional ranks at that time?

A. Four.   B. Five.   C. Six.

48. Adam Watt won the Commonwealth cruiserweight title on 24 June 2000 when he stopped Bruce Scott in round four. Who was the referee for this contest?

A. Terry O'Connor.   B. John Keane.
C. Dave Parris.

49. In defence of his IBO Inter-Continental featherweight title on 15 July 2000, Scott Harrison outpointed Tom Johnson over 12 rounds. Which version of the world featherweight title did Johnson formerly hold?

A. WBA.   B. WBC.   C. IBF.

50. Joe Calzaghe retained his WBO world super-middle-weight championship on 12 August 2000 when he stopped Omar Sheika. In which round did Calzaghe win?

A. Four.   B. Five.   C. Six.

ANSWERS

1. Australia. 2. Seven. 3. Tiger Flowers. 4. Five. 5. Cardiff. 6. 1963. 7. Ten. 8. George Smith. 9. 1948. 10. Points win for Butler. 11. Italy. 12. Billy Walker. 13. Four. 14. Tom Collins. 15. Kelvin Smart. 16. Richard Dunn. 17. 57. 18. One. 19. Eight. 20. New Zealand. 21. Two. 22. Alan Minter. 23. 22. 24. 12-round points decision. 25. Jonathan Feld. 26. Atlantic City. 27. John Keane. 28. 19. 29. Poland. 30. Nine. 31. Eight. 32. Greg Upton. 33. Mike Holden. 34. Six. 35. 21. 36. Leeds. 37. Belgium. 38. 33. 39. Belgium. 40. Terry O'Connor. 41. 11. 42. Las Vegas. 43. Tania Follett. 44. Six. 45. 34. 46. Five. 47. Six. 48. John Keane. 49. IBF. 50. Five.

LONDON
FOR ALL YOUR
BOXING
ESSENTIALS

LONSDALE SPORTS EQUIPMENT LTD.,
47 Beak Street, London W1F 9SE

Telephone 020 7437 1526

Fax 020 7734 2094

Larry O' Connell

(Class 'A' Star Referee)

Wishes

The British Boxing

Board of Control Yearbook

every success

O'CONNELL & YARDLEY

L. D. O'CONNELL F.I.P.G.
TERENCE A. YARDLEY
K. O'CONNELL

ENGRAVERS

5 Mill Street, London W1S 2AY
Telephone: 0207-499 6414 Fax: 0207-495 3963
email: oconnell.yardley@virgin.net

Fattorini

made the Lonsdale Belt shown here:
we also designed and made the
Commonwealth Championship Belt.

Whenever new medals, badges or special trophies are being considered,
we are glad to supply designs and estimates, without obligation

Thomas Fattorini Ltd
Regent Street Works, Birmingham B1 3HQ
telephone 0121-236 1307 **fax** 0121 200 1568
Email: sales@fattorini.co.uk www.fattorini.co.uk

Fattorini
Artists-craftsmen since 1827

Directory of Ex-Boxers' Associations

by Ron Olver

BOURNEMOUTH Founded 1980. Dai Dower (P); Percy Singer (T); Ken Wells (VC); Peter Fay (C & S), 24 Monkswell Green, Purewell, Christchurch, Dorset BH23 1MN.

CORK Founded 1973. HQ: Glen Boxing Club, Blackpool, Cork. William O'Leary (P & C); John Martin (S); Phil Murray (VC); John Donovan (T).

CORNWALL Founded 1989. HQ: Truro City Football Club. Len Magee (P); Stan Cullis (C); Jimmy Miller (T); John Sandow (VC); Bill Matthews (S), 33 Victoria Road, St Austell, Cornwall PL25 4QF.

CROYDON Founded 1982. HQ: Ivy House Club, Campbell Road, West Croydon. Tom Powell, BEM (P); Derek O'Dell (C); Bill Flemington (VC & T); Richard Evans (PRO); Gilbert Allnutt (S), 37 Braemar Avenue, Thornton Heath, Croydon CR9 7RJ.

EASTERN AREA Founded 1973. HQ: Norfolk Dumpling, Cattle Market, Hall Road, Norwich. Brian Fitzmaurice (P); Ron Springall (C); Clive Campling (VC).

HULL & EAST YORKSHIRE Founded 1996. HQ: The Rising Sun Hotel, Hull. Don Harrison (C); Stan Gossip (VC); Bert Smith (T); Micky Brooks (S); Geoff Rymer (PRO).

IPSWICH Founded 1970. HQ: Loco Club, Ipswich. Alby Kingham (P); Vic Thurlow (C & T); Michael Thurlow (S), 147 Clapgate Lane, Ipswich IP3 0RF.

IRISH Founded 1973. HQ: National Boxing Stadium, South Circular Road, Dublin. Richard O'Reilly, (S), 111 Downpatrick Road, Crumlin.

KENT & SUSSEX Founded 1997. HQ: RAFA Club, Chatham. Mick Smith (P & C); Ray Lambert (PRO); Paul Nihill, MBE (S & T), 5 Acre Close, Rochester, Kent ME1 2RE.

LEEDS Founded 1952. HQ: North Leeds WMC, Burmantofts, Lincoln Green, Leeds 9. Alan Richardson (P); Greg Steene (HP); Kevin Cunningham (C & S); Alan Alster (T); Frank Johnson (PRO), Franwyn, 7 Allenby Drive, Leeds.

LEICESTER Founded 1972. HQ: Belgrave WMC, Checketts Road, Leicester. Mick Greaves (P & C); Mrs Rita Jones (T); Norman Jones (S), 60 Dumbleton Avenue, Leicester LE3 2EG.

LONDON Founded 1971. HQ; St Pancras Social Club, Argyle Square, London. Stephen Powell (P); Micky O'Sullivan (C); Andy Williamson (VC); Ron Olver (PRO); Ray Caulfield (T); Mrs Mary Powell (S), 36 St Peters Street, Islington, London N1 8JT.

MANCHESTER Founded 1968. HQ: LMR Club, Whitworth Street West, Manchester. Tommy Proffitt (P); Jack Edwards (C); Kenny Baker (T); Jimmy Lewis (VC); Eddie Copeland (S), 9 Lakeside, Hadfield, Glossop, Derby SK13 1HW.

MERSEYSIDE (Liverpool) Founded 1973. HQ: Transport Drivers Club, Hockenhall Alley, Liverpool. Johnny Cooke (P); Terry Riley (C); Jim Boyd (VC); Jim Jenkinson (T); Sandy Manuel (S), 26 Cantsfield Street, Wavertree, Liverpool L7 4JZ.

NORTHAMPTON DISTRICT Founded 2001. Jeff Tite (P); Sam Monks (C); Joe Grundler (T); Sid Green (S), 8 Friars Close, Delapre, Northampton NN4 8PU.

NORTHAMPTONSHIRE Founded 1981. HQ: Cue Club, Bridge Street, Northampton. Dick Rogers (P); Gil Wilson (C); Peter Cripps (T); Pam Monaghan (S), 6 Derwent Close, Kings Heath, Northampton.

NORTHERN FEDERATION Founded 1974. Several member EBAs. Annual Gala. Eddie Monahan (S), 16 Braemar Avenue, Marshside, Southport.

NORTHERN IRELAND Founded 1970. HQ: Ulster Sports Club, Belfast. Terry McHale (P); Sean McCafferty (C); Sammy Thompson (T); Freddie Gilroy (PRO); Al Gibson (S), 900 Crumlin Road, Belfast.

NORTH STAFFS & SOUTH CHESHIRE Founded 1969. HQ: The Saggar Makers Bottom Knocker, Market Place, Burslem, Stoke on Trent. Tut Whalley (P); Roy Simms (VC); Les Dean (S); John Greatbach (T); Billy Tudor (C & PRO), 133 Sprinkbank Road, Chell Heath, Stoke on Trent, Staffs ST6 6HW.

NORWICH HQ: West End Retreat, Brown Street, Norwich. Les King (P); John Pipe (C); Jack Wakefield (T); Dick Sadd (S), 76 Orchard Street, Norwich.

NOTTINGHAM Founded 1979. HQ: The Earl Howe, Carlton Road, Sneinton, Nottingham. Frank Parkes (P); Len Chorley (C); Terry Bradley (VC); Diane Rooksby (T); John Kinsella (PRO); Graham Rooksby (S), 42 Spinney Road, Keyworth, Notts NG12 5LN.

PLYMOUTH Founded 1982. HQ: Exmouth Road Social Club, Stoke, Plymouth. Tom Pryce-Davies (C); Doug Halliday (VC & S); Arthur Willis (T); Buck Taylor (P & PRO), 15 Greenbank Avenue, St Judes, Plymouth PL4 9BT.

PRESTON Founded 1973. HQ: Barney's Piano Bar, Church Street, Preston. John Allen (P & C); Peter Osborne (S), 39 Prospect Place, Ashton, Preston PR2 1DL.

ST HELENS Founded 1983. HQ: Travellers Rest Hotel, Crab Street, St Helens. Johnny Molloy (P); Ray Britch (C); Jimmy O'Keefe (VC); Tommy McNamara (T); Paul Britch (S), 16 Oxley Street, Sutton, St Helens WA9 3PE

SCOTTISH Founded 1997. HQ: Iron Horse Public House, West Nile Street, Glasgow. Walter McGowan, MBE (P); Andy Grant (C); Charlie Sexton (VC); Frank O'Donnell (LP); Peter Baines (T); Liam McColgan (S), 25 Dalton Avenue, Linnvale, Clydebank G81 2SH.

SLOUGH Founded 1973. HQ: Faraday Hall Ex-Servicemens' Club, Slough. Max Quartermain (P); Pete Davis (C); Gordon Jones (T); Ernie Watkins (S), 5 Sunbury Road, Eton, Windsor.

SQUARE RING Founded 1978. HQ: Snooty Fox Hotel, St Marychurch. George Pook (P); Johnny Mudge (S); Jim Banks (T); Paul King (C), 10 Pine Court Apartments, Middle Warberry Road, Torquay.

SUNDERLAND Founded 1959. HQ: Hendon Gardens, Sunderland. Jack Wilson (P); Terry Lynn (C); Joe Riley (PRO); Wilf Lawrence (T); Les Simm (S), 21 Orchard Street, Pallion, Sunderland SR4 6QL.

SWANSEA & SOUTH WEST WALES Founded 1983. HQ: Villiers Arms, Neath Road, Hafod, Swansea. Cliff Curvis (P); Gordon Pape (C); Ernie Wallis (T); Len Smith (S), Cockett Inn, Cockett, Swansea SA2 0GB.

TRAMORE Founded 1981. HQ: Robinson Bar, Main Street, Tramore, Co Waterford. T. Flynn (P); C. O'Reilly (C); L. O'Brien (VC); W. Hutchinson (T); Peter Graham (S), 3 Riverstown, Tramore.

TYNESIDE Founded 1970. HQ: Pelaw Social Club, Heworth, Pelaw. Billy Charlton (P); Maxie Walsh (C); Gordon Smith (VC); Malcolm Dinning (T); Alan Gordon (S), 16 Dove Court, Birtley, Chester le Street, Durham PH3 1HB.

WELSH Founded 1976. HQ: Rhydyfelin Labour Club, Pontypridd. Robbie Regan (P); Ken Shannon (C); Ron Bruzas (T); Don James (S), 28 Woodfield Road, Talbot Green, Pontyclun, Mid-Glamorgan. Patron - Lord Brooks.

The above information is set at the time of going to press and no responsibility can be taken for any changes in officers or addresses of HQs that may happen between then and publication or changes that have not been notified to me.

ABBREVIATIONS

P - President. HP - Honorary President. LP - Life President. AP - Acting President. C - Chairman. VC - Vice Chairman. T - Treasurer. S - Secretary. PRO - Public Relations Officer and/or Press Officer.

Ron Olver (left) accepting the BBBoC 'Special Award' from the Yearbook editor, Barry J. Hugman

Les Clark

Obituaries

by Ron Olver

It is impossible to list everyone, but I have again done my best to include final tributes for as many of the well-known boxers and other familiar names within the sport who have passed away since the 2001 Yearbook was published. We honour them and will remember them.

AGRAMONTE Omelio *From* New York. *Died* 26 August 2000, aged 77. Born in Cuba, there is no record of his early pro fights prior to him coming to the USA at the end of World War 11, but he soon settled in, operating between the States and South America, and fought many of the top heavyweights of the day. Among the men he beat were Ted Lowry, Ansel Adams, Joe Lindsay, Bill Gilliam, John Holman, Abel Cestac, Red Applegate, Jimmy Walls and two Germans in Wilson Kohlbrecher and Richard Vogt. The men who defeated him read like a who's who of boxing and included Jimmy Bivins, Pat Comiskey, Lee Oma, 'Jersey' Joe Walcott, Elkins Brothers, Joe Louis (twice), Bob Baker (twice), Clarence Henry (twice), Britain's Johnny Williams, Bob Dunlap and Cleveland Williams, prior to him being defeated by Nino Valdes for the Cuban title (1953) and retiring. A year earlier, there was a lot of adverse publicity for the sport when Agramonte met Marvin Mercer in a boxer v wrestler contest of five minute-rounds and lost.

BAGWELL Hal *From* Gloucester. *Died* 9 May 2001, aged 82. Was erroneously in the *Guiness Book of Records*, which stated that he was reputedly undefeated in 183 consecutive fights between 10 August 1938 and 29 November 1948. Ten years at an average of 18 fights per year, including the war years, it couldn't have happened, and didn't, as Hal himself admitted in later years. Not under Board of Control jurisdiction, but Hal did have loads of fights on the booths. One authentic record set up by Hal was in remaining unbeaten for ten years and three months. The late Vic Hardwicke, ace compiler of records, traced 71 bouts in a career of 63 wins, three draws and five losses, Hal having started boxing in his teens in order to bring some money into the family. He was managed by a neighbour, Billy West. There were no shortage of fights, some licensed, some unlicensed, and, in the '30s, Captain Prince-Cox, who was promoting in Bristol, turned his attention to Gloucester where he was impressed with Hal. He started by matching him with the former British flyweight champion, Bert Kirby. Hal won. Then he was matched with the bantamweight champion, Johnny King, and was kayoed. In World War II, he went to France with the British Expeditionary Force and was at Dunkirk, and later involved in the D-Day landing. His ship, the Derrycunny, was sunk with the loss of 300 lives. Hal jumped into the water and was saved, being picked up by a small ship. Resuming boxing in 1946, he won the South Central lightweight title by beating Harry Legge (1947). In November of that year, Hal boxed in London for the first and only time when, as a substitute, he beat Cliff Anderson on a disqualification at the Royal Albert Hall. Promoter Jack Solomons offered him a series of fights, culminating in a British title fight within three months, but he had to live in London. Hal turned down this offer, not wishing to leave his home, family and his manager, Billy Wagner. After losing his Area title to Maurice Mancini on a narrow verdict (1949), he decided to retire.

BAND Sid *From* Worcester. *Died* 23 June 2000, aged 71. One of a family of eight, Sid joined a gym at the age of nine, winning the England and Wales Boys' Club bantam title. Joined the Army as an engineer and was posted to the Middle East where he won the 'Army In Egypt' featherweight title and United Services title (1947). Turned pro (1950). Boxed Mickey O'Sullivan in consecutive fights (1951), both ending in draws. Beat Johnny Brown, Arthur Shenton, Frank Argyle, Tommy Dunn and Alf Clarke. He later turned to coaching local amateurs and among his successes were Micky Baker and the two-times ABA champion, Alan Edwards.

Sid Band

BARNES Ray *From* Detroit, Michigan, USA. *Died* December 2000, aged 70. Starting out as a pro middleweight in 1946, he fought several big names in a career that saw him world rated before he retired in 1955. In Britain he is mainly remembered for an indifferent display against Yolande Pompey, which was blamed on his inactivity, this being his first fight after leaving the US Army. His first real setback had come when he was stopped by the Cocoa Kid in 1947, but he put that behind him when defeating good men such as Burl Charity, Tommy Yarosz, Jimmy Welch, Anton Raadik, Billy Brown, Chuck Hunter, Terry Moore and George Sherman. He also went ten rounds with 'Sugar' Ray Robinson, the world welterweight champion at the time, in 1950. More of a boxer than a fighter, he left the ring with a 42-fight record, showing 37 wins, one draw, and just four losses, and later became a top-class trainer.

Ray Barnes (left) in action against 'Sugar' Ray Robinson

BASSO Nat *From* London. *Died* 24 January 2001, aged 84. The son of Russian immigrants, Nat moved to Manchester in 1928. A leading MC for many years, he was also a trainer, manager, matchmaker, promoter and agent. His interest in boxing started when, as a youngster, he was taken to watch the boxing at London's Premierland. Chairman of the Central Area Council for 40 years, retiring four years ago at the age of 77, he became the oldest manager to produce his first national champion when Carl Thompson won the vacant British cruiserweight title (1992). During World War II he was a machine-gunner in the 2nd Battalion, Manchester Regiment. One of British boxing's most colourful characters, he was still working as an MC right up to the end.

BIANCARDI Giovanni *From* Italy. *Died* 24 June 2001, aged 62. Won the Italian amateur title in 1962, turning pro the same year. Was beaten by Vittorio Saraudi (1968) for the Italian light-heavyweight title, but the following year defeated Guerrino Scattolin for the vacant crown. He eventually lost the title to Gianfranco Macchia (1970) and announced his retirement after being stopped by Lothar Stengel.

BOYD Johnny *From* Peterborough. *Died* 28 March 2001, aged 78. Managed by Jimmy Munro, and travelling on the booths with the Weeklys and Sam Minto, the first bouts that can be traced for Johnny are in 1943. More of a boxer than a fighter, he certainly mixed in good company, beating among others, Paddy Roche, Des Jones (2), Bert Sanders, Ron Cooper, Red Pullen, Jack Lewis (3), Jackie Hughes, Johnny Blake (2), Ted Barter, Dick Turpin, George Howard, Freddie Price, Bob Cleaver and George Dilkes, all top middleweights of the day. He also outpointed two future British champions in Alex Buxton (1943) and Dick Turpin (1946). On the debit side, he was beaten by Tommy Jones (3), Bert Hyland (2), George Dilkes, Ginger Sadd, Dick Turpin (2), Bob Cleaver, Alby Hollister (2), Leon Fouquet, Jimmy Davis, Sammy Sullivan, Joe Rood and Dick Langley, the last four mentioned fights, all in 1949, being his last before retiring with a record showing 57 contests, of which he won 34, drew two and lost 20. There was also one no contest against Tommy Godfrey.

BRUNT Jimmy *From* Welling, Kent. *Died* 28 February 2001, aged 82. Joined the Royal Marines (1936) and boxed a lot as a pro during World War II, when he was frequently billed as Marine Jimmy Brunt, taking Jack Kid Berg to a points verdict (1945). Brother Jerry was a former fighter and became Jimmy's first trainer. After the war he settled in Australia, where he married Patricia Shields (1946), staying in the Marines until 1949. Became good friends with Dave Sands and was one of the pallbearers at Dave's funeral. Always involved in boxing, as well as being a fighter he became a trainer, referee and promoter. Trained local youths at the Police Citizens Boys' Club, and also at his own gym. Was a 50-year-old member of the RSI and Bowling Clubs and was also a member of the '39ers', the Royal Marines Association and Veteran Boxers' Association. His hobbies included fishing and entertaining.

BUSSO Johnny *From* Poughkeepsie, New York, USA. *Died* November 2000, aged 65. Starting out as a pro in 1952, Johnny, a lightweight, made a steady start before moving into world class in 1958 with wins over Larry Boardman, Lahouari Godih, Carlos Ortis and Joe Brown. Despite losing to Paolo Rosi and Carlos Ortiz in the same year, these solid victories earned him a world title shot against Joe Brown, which he lost on points over 15 rounds in Houston on 11 February, 1958. From hereon, however, it was all downhill, with defeats at the hands of Kenny Lane, Battling Torres, Lenny Matthews and Joey Donovan encouraging him to call it a day in 1961, leaving a record of 36 wins, 12 defeats and one draw from 49 contests.

Other men he beat worthy of mention included Rocky Randell, Dennis Pat Brady, Orlando Zulueta, Tommy Salem, Larry Boardman, again, and Gale Kerwin, while he was also defeated by Tommy Marciano, Gene Poirer, Bobby Courchesne and Ralph Dupas.

BUTLER Pat *From* Rothley, Leicestershire. *Died* 7 March 2001, aged 87. Pat was Britain's oldest surviving ex-champion, having turned pro in 1932. Managed by Leon Aldwick, he moved to the George Biddles stable later that year, winning the British welterweight title by beating Harry Mason (1934). Joined the RAF (1940) in World War II as a PTI and later became a trainer of parachutists, making more than 200 jumps. Was a pro for five years, embracing 116 fights, and averaging 23 per year, a remarkable record. His best performance was in beating Ernie Roderick (1934), who would go on to win British titles at welter and middleweight. Moved to Rhodesia (1951) as a PTI with the Rhodesian Air Force and took up farming there (1953). Later on, he went to Cape Town (1964), working at a golf club before returning to Rhodesia (1966) to run the Rocky Valley Boarding Kennels in Gwelo. Returned to Britain (1981) because of the unstable conditions in Zimbabwe, settling in Melton Mowbray. Joined Leicester EBA (1970s), while still in Gwelo, and became president (1992), only relinquishing the presidency when he became too ill to attend meetings (2000).

CARPENTER Henry *From* Peckham, London. *Died* 20 March 2001. Started with Peckham BC before joining Bradfield and won the ABA flyweight title in 1948. Selected for the Olympic Games that year, he turned pro immediately afterwards. During World War II his house was bombed, being a direct hit. His father and sister were killed, but although his mother survived she had to have a leg amputated. Fortunately, Henry and a mate were at the local cinema at the time, but this tragedy prevented him from joining the Forces, having favoured the Royal Navy. Was a leading contender for the British flyweight title as a pro and beat Billy Hazelgrove, Mickey Jones, Paddy Hardy, Jimmy Pearce, George Sutton, Glyn David, Joe Cairney, Kella Persson and Dennis Sale among others, before retiring in 1953 after being outpointed by Dai Dower. Also met men of the calibre of Joe Murphy, Teddy Gardner, Nazzareno Gianelli, Vic Herman and Terry Allen, the world flyweight champion.

CARRASCO Pedro *From* Spain. *Died* 28 January 2001, aged 57. Born in Brazil, Pedro turned pro in Italy (1962) before moving to Spain. Losing just one of his first 106 fights, on points against Aldo Pravisani (1964), he subsequently beat Pravisani twice. Won the European lightweight title when beating Borge Krogh, retaining it five times, he relinquished it to concentrate on a world title shot (1969). He then won the European light-welter title by beating Rene Roque (1971), before dropping down to lightweight to tackle Mando Ramos for the vacant WBC crown later that year. Carrasco was decked four times before Ramos was disqualified at the end of round 11 for

hitting low and on top of the head. In subsequent bouts, Ramos twice beat Carrasco on points. Retired in 1972.

COSGROVE Sammy *From* Belfast. *Died* July 2001, aged 67. A former chairman of the Northern Ireland EBA and Steward of the British Boxing Board of Control, Sammy turned to the paid ring in 1954 and had nine contests before retiring in 1957. Despite his success rate not being high, the quality of opposition included the likes of Jackie Willis, Billy Skelly, Matt Fulton, Percy James, Alf Cottam and Gordon Blakey.

DAVIS Terry *From* Barking, London. *Died* June 2001, aged 75. As the trainer of Barking BC, Terry guided, among others, European Junior bronze medallist, Orrie Jones (1982), Paul Harvey, and professional champion, Colin McMillan. Was a regular at local amateur tournaments for over 30 years.

DELVIN Ivan *From* Lambeth, London. *Died* October 2000, aged 80. Having become the secretary of Sussex EBA when Ernie Woodman passed on, Ivan worked hard to keep the EBA together. Was an expert in vintage cars, and when he joined the RAF extended his expertise to the areas of war planes and military history. Was also into boxing, weight-lifting and music. He became a talented jazz musician and was all set to tour the Far East with the RAF band, only for the tour to be cancelled, much to his disappointment. Also completed his Open University studies in history.

DOWNES Johnny *From* Hull. *Died* October 2000, aged 85. Twice met Bruce Woodcock, before his career was ended with the outbreak of World War II. Serving in the East Yorkshire Regiment prior to being transferred to the Parachute Regiment, he was awarded several medals. After the war, Johnny worked at Priestman's for 30 years as a blacksmith and was a regular at the Hull & District Sporting Club Dinners over ten years.

DURKIN Johnny *From* Leeds. *Died* 5 November 2000, aged 83. Christened 'Martin', when he turned pro his manager Mike Sunderland suggested he should take the ring name of 'Johnny'. Turning pro in 1931, it was estimated that he had 92 bouts altogether, winning 77, drawing four and losing 11. In the '30s, he was billed as one of the best featherweights in Britain, eventually being managed by Foster Thompson, the Leeds' promoter. After retiring, Johnny became the PTI and boxing instructor at Leeds University and was a stalwart in the Leeds EBA, becoming their president.

ELLIOT Johnny *From* Telford. *Died* 31 May 2001, aged 44. Turned pro in 1983 and won 11, drew two and lost 18. Was beaten by Willie Wright for the Midlands Area middleweight title (1985), but beat Blaine Logsden, who went on to fight for the vacant British light-heavyweight title (1987), and drew with John Ashton (1987). He also met Michael Watson (1985). Retiring after losing to Rod

Douglas (October 1987), his father Johnny, who boxed under the name of Johnny Kingston-Elliot, was a top-class amateur, and brother Mark was also a leading amateur who turned pro.

FAUX Betty *From* Liverpool. *Died* 21 April 2001, aged 68. Confined to a wheelchair, Betty and husband Jim started the Left Hook Club, which held no regular meetings, but which they formed specifically with the aim of holding functions to raise money in order to help former fighters in need. She was formerly a fully qualified boxing trainer and worked closely with the Merseyside EBA. Several years ago she organised a Tribute Night to Alan Rudkin, and had the brilliant idea of tracing and inviting the members of the Great Britain team that beat the United States ten-nil in 1961, a team of which Alan was a member. Most of that team accepted the invitation, which made it a wonderful night for everyone involved. Betty knew everyone and everyone knew her and respected her. She was a gracious lady, who, in spite of her own handicap, made helping others her main aim in life.

FEMIA Johnny *From* Louisiana, USA. *Died* 27 June 2001, aged 45, following a boating accident in which he was drowned. A world-class referee, his last assignment was officiating at the Robert Allen - Robert Muhammad fight on 20 June.

FERRER Seraphin *From* France. *Died* 20 February 2001, aged 69. Boxed in the 1952 Olympics, but was defeated in the first series by a Russian. He turned pro (1953) and in only his 14th bout won the French lightweight title by beating Auguste Caulet. In 1955, he stopped the former world champion, Paddy DeMarco, was himself stopped by Percy Bassett and then outpointed by Duilio Loi in a European title fight. Relinquished the French title without defending it (1956), continuing as a welterweight, he retired in 1958. Other good men that he met and beat included Jo Janssens, Louis van Hoeck, Johnny Butterworth, Hoacine Khalfi, Gunter Hase and Emilio Marconi.

FORTE Tommy *From* Philadelphia, USA. *Died* 15 January 2001, aged 82. In a pro career of 60 fights, with 44 wins (22 inside schedule), 13 losses, two draws and one no contest between 1936 and 1947, Tommy proved himself to be one of the finest bantams around, being beaten only by the best at his peak. He had two title shots, both against Lou Salica, and both going the distance, before calling it a day. Good men that he beat along the way included Henry Hook, Pablo Dano, Lou Transparenti, Joey Archibald and Spider Armstrong, while he lost to Al Brown (twice), Small Montana and Harry Jeffra before his career came to an end following a first-round kayo at the hands of Willie Weasel.

FUTTER Richard *From* Norwich. *Died* January 2001, aged 76. A leading boxing writer who contributed to Boxing News for many years, Richard was a fine athlete as a youngster – sprinting, swimming and playing soccer and boxing for Norwich Lads club as a junior. He was also a great fan of Norwich FC and carried the players' bags from the station to the ground. When he left school he worked in the boot and shoe industry, but achieved his first ambition by working as a free-lance journalist, covering Norwich speedway meetings. Joined the Navy at the age of 18, serving on minesweepers, and his medals included the Africa and Atlantic Stars. After World War II he worked as an apprentice with a printing and bookbinding firm until the late '50s, when he became a master bookbinder before being made a full partner. Continuing to write on boxing and soccer for the *Eastern Daily Press* and the *Evening News*, after his retirement from bookbinding he took up photography, providing photos for *Boxing News* and the local press. Enjoyed his involvement with the Norwich EBA over the years.

GABRIEL Ray *From* Wales. *Died* October 2000. A former Welsh amateur flyweight champion (1956), Ray later became vice-chairman of the Welsh EBA and travelled all over the country for the EBA cause. He will be sorely missed.

HAZELL Gordon *From* Bristol. *Died* 2 February 2001, aged 72. At the age of 11, Gordon won a Western Counties Schoolboy title and from 1944 to 1946 he won Western Counties titles from feather to welter. He then won the RAF middleweight title (1947) and retained it in 1948. His ambition was to be selected for the Olympic Games, but after being beaten by Ron Bebbington in the semi-finals of the ISBA Championships he turned pro under Nat Seller (1949). At that time, he was a packer in a tobacco factory but gave up the job to concentrate on his boxing (1952). Among his better performances was a win over Johnny Sullivan in a non-title fight, losing to him on two subsequent occasions, while his best performance was in beating the European champion, Tiberio Mitri, in a non-title fight. This was Mitri's first fight since disposing of Randolph Turpin in one round to win the title. After retiring, Gordon was employed at Clifton College to run their sport, and he started a boxing team that won the British Colleges Championships half a dozen times. Later, the headmaster and governors of Clifton College (rated sixth-best college in England) engaged him as a governor and selector of the students' selection committee. After retiring from Clifton, Gordon played for the Long Ashton Golf Club team. His parents both died in the early '50s and he never married, living with his married sister whose cooking was so important to him that he even took her to Glasgow when he boxed Willie Armstrong, in order for her to prepare a steak for him. Other good men he met and beat included Michael Stack, Bos Murphy, Ken Rowlands, Jeff Tite, Jacques Royer-Crecy, Richard Armah and Widmer Milandri. On the debit side, he could never get the better of the excellent American, Bobby Dawson, who beat him three times in 1953.

HERNANDEZ Gabriel *From* Dominica. *Died* 25 June

2001, committing suicide, aged 27. Outpointed by Sven Ottke for the IBF super-middleweight title (1999), his pro record consisted of 22 bouts of which he won 20 and lost two. Having boxed in the Olympic Games (1996), being beaten in his first contest, he settled with his family in Westchester, New York.

HOCKLEY Jimmy *From* Covent Garden, London. *Died* March 2001, aged 75. As an amateur, Jimmy won British Schools, ABA Junior and London Feds titles and was a founder-member of the Langham BC. Among his amateur victims were Albert Finch, Bob Foster, Eddie Quill and Arthur Danahar. Having won the ABA middleweight title (1944), he immediately turned pro and was soon meeting future champions such as Albert Finch and Vince Hawkins. He also met top-class men such as Mart Hart, Ron Grogan, Alby Hollister, 'Battling' Charlie Parkin, Al Allotey, Bob Cleaver, Harry Watson, Gene Fowler and George Howard. Unfortunate to suffer with eye problems throughout his career, a severe handicap, he sparred with Gus Lesnevich when the latter came to Britain to meet Freddie Mills for the world light-heavyweight title.

HYLTON Cordwell *From* Walsall. *Died* 8 January 2001, aged 42. Born in Jamaica, Cordwell came to Britain when he was six years old, eventually taking up judo and kung fu, qualifying as a chef, and getting a job as a cook at Walsall Hospital. After participating in 42 amateur bouts, he turned pro in 1980. Retiring in 1995, with a record of 73 contests, winning 27, losing 43 and drawing two, with one no contest, and twice being the Midlands Area cruiser-weight champion, he took up kick-boxing.

Cordwell Hylton (left) versus Wayne Llewelyn   Les Clark

JACKSON Bobby *From* Hull. *Died* October 2000, aged 79. Boxing before and after World War II, among his opponents were Jacky Ryder, George Frost, Billy Beech, Young Tyler and Les Tilsy. In 1947 he met Jack Woods at Hull, and the following July he promoted a bill at 'The Big Top', Hull, with the proceeds going to Lloyds Hospital, Bridlington. Then, in November, he promoted at the Grand Pavilion, Bridlington. Had a distinguished Army career. Being a Territorial, he was called up for service immediately in September 1939, serving with the 7th Green Howards in England, the Middle East and India. In 1943, having left Syria, he was captured and became a prisoner of war. However, on the way to Germany he forced open the door of the truck and jumped out. In doing so he sprained his ankle, but managed to move into the hills where he spent five months with the partisans and with the help of a guide he managed to reach Allied Forces near Caoli in March 1944. His awards included the 1939-45 Star, Africa Star, Defence Medal, War Medal and the Efficiency Medal (Territorial).

JACKSON Gordon *From* Leicester. *Died* November 2000. A former steward of the British Boxing Board of Control and inspector at many Midlands promotions, along with Johnny Griffin he was associated with several promotions at Loughborough Town Hall. He was also a prominent member of Leicester EBA.

JAMIESON Jack *From* Manchester. *Died* June 2001. A former trainer, Jack become life president of Manchester EBA. He was also a founder-member of the Northern Federation, whose Gala he attended every year.

JONES Harry *From* Hoxton, London. *Died* 12 October, 2000, aged 97. Was a pro in the '20s and '30s and, although his record is not available, it is understood he also boxed in the '40s, having several fights in Germany, once beating their champion. Was a popular member of LEBA, and attended as often as he could until two years ago when he was no longer able to make the journey. Loved to talk boxing and did his best to continue his exercises right up to the end. One lovely story concerns Harry in his boxing days. While walking along the street, a car pulled up and the driver, whom Harry knew, asked him if he fancied a substitute job that night. Where was the fight? Southend. Whom was he fighting? Not known. So off Harry went and found out his opponent was a heavyweight. Needless to say, Harry was stopped. "Who was your opponent?" he was asked. "I still don't know", he replied. "For all I know it could have been Primo Carnera".

JONES Jacky *From* Bolton. *Died* 15 August 2001, aged 76. In the Royal Navy between 1939 and 1945, Jackie launched his pro boxing career towards the end of the war, having had around 200 amateur contests, and by 1948 was meeting many of the leading middleweights prior to retiring in 1951. Although losing a fair few fights, Jacky never ducked anyone over here and was only beaten by men of good quality, such as Jimmy Bray, George Dilkes, Ginger Sadd, Joe Rood, Dave Goodwin, Johnny Nuttall and George Casson. He even took on Randy Turpin and Dave Sands within the space of three months in 1949, and despite being stopped was able to hold his head up. On the credit side, he defeated Ted Dexter, Johnny McGowan, Jackie Wilson (twice), Tommy Whelan, Arthur Raybould and Sammy Wilde before he bowed out when beaten by the rising youngster, Billy Ellaway, at Liverpool Stadium on 29 March 1951. For the past 45 years he had been living in

Crouch End, London, while working as a hod carrier on building sites, and more recently had been a porter in Friern Barnet Hospital.

KIHLSTROM Mika *From* Helsinki, Finland. *Died* October 2000, in a fire started at a gym, aged 31. Began in his home country in 1995 with wins over Jean Collin and Sean Daly. He then came to England and beat David Jules, Darren Fearn, Gary Williams, Doug Liggion, Owen Bartley, Shane Woollas and Rob Albon before Mike Holden stopped him on a cut-eye decision. Having left this country, he won the Finnish heavyweight title in September 1998 when stopping Tony Halme in five rounds, then decisioned the German, Hermann Bendl (1999), for the vacant WBB title, before losing his Finnish title when Halme knocked him out inside four rounds on 17 April 2000. His last fight saw him lose on points to Jari Markkanen, leaving him with 11 wins and three defeats from 14 contests.

KIRTLAND Ted *From* London. *Died* 17 December 2000, aged 87. Boxing under the name of Young Kirtland, he was said to have had 52 pro fights. In later years he ran a betting shop in Bethnal Green Road, London and was one of the original members of LEBA. Was awarded the MBE for services to charity.

KRAY Charlie *From* Bethnal Green. *Died* 4 April 2000, aged 73. As the elder brother of the notorious Kray twins, Ronnie and Reg, Charlie boxed as a pro welterweight in the late '40s through to 11 December 1951 when, appearing on an Albert Hall bill with both of his brothers, he was knocked out in the third round by the rising Lew Lazar, the younger brother of the well-known Harry. Having won a welterweight competition at Watford in 1949, beating Johnny Fraser, George Smith and Les Wood, other men that he met included Tommy Hinson, also one of three boxing brothers, Tommy Slade, Jim Blackburn, Vic Price and Jack Allen.

KRAY Reg *From* Bethnal Green. *Died* 1 October 2000, aged 67. Having boxed for Repton BC and the Robert Browning BC, at the age of 17 both the Kray twins made their professional debuts at the Mile End Arena on 31 July 1951, Reg getting his short career off to a flying start when beating Bobby Manito on points. A lightweight, always within a pound or two of Ron's weight, Reg had recorded seven contests and was still undefeated by the end of 1951, after beating Johnny Starr, George Goodsell, Bill Sliney (twice), who beat Ron, Bobby Woods and Bobby Manito again. Being called up for military service brought both his and Ron's short boxing careers to an end and spelled the beginning of their new, well documented careers outside the ring, which ended in life imprisonment. Both boys had started to box when they were ten and actually boxed each other on a number of occasions, which was stopped once their mother found out.

The Kray Twins, Ron and Reg

Don Linton

LINTON Don *From* Canterbury. *Died* 11 September 2000, aged 71. As an amateur between 1945 and 1949, Don had 43 bouts before making his pro debut (1950) under manager, Jack Jordan. Had only nine bouts, beating Al Vizor, Billy Scott, Tommy Willoughby and Johnny Godfrey, before retiring in 1951. Was a keep-fit fanatic, and also kept dogs.

LUFTSPRING Sammy *From* Toronto, Canada. *Died* November 2000, aged 85. One of nine children, Sammy was selected for the 1936 Olympics, but because of his Jewish background he bowed to the wishes of his parents not to compete because of the Nazis in Germany, the venue being Berlin. Having won the Canadian pro welterweight title, he was world rated (1940) and was in line for a title fight with the champion, Henry Armstrong. However, in a warm-up bout with Steve Belloise he was caught by a thumb in his left eye and that was the end of his career. He then became a referee with great success, officiating in over 2,000 bouts. After opening the Mercury Club in Tonge and Dundee Streets, which was a popular night spot, he eventually moved to Victoria Street and was visited by all-time greats like Joe Louis and Sugar Ray Robinson. Was inducted into Canada's Hall Of Fame (1985).

McCULLAGH Maxie *From* Mulligar, Ireland. *Died* May 2001, aged 79. Won five Leinster Juvenile titles before joining the Irish Army (1940), winning the Army title every year until he left (1946). Won National senior titles (1947 and 1949) and represented Ireland in the Olympics (1948), but lost in the quarter-finals on a disputed verdict. He then won the European Championship title (1949), becoming the first Irishman to pick up the honour outside his own country. Representing Ireland in 31 internationals (1946-52), he twice beat Eddie Thomas, who went on to become the British, British Empire and European professional champion. Having had around 500 amateur fights, he retired to coach the youngsters at his old Dublin club, Corinthians.

MAIER Dave *From* Milwaukee, Wisconsin, USA. *Died* 17 May 2000, aged 91. Turning pro in 1929, having missed representing America in the 1928 Olympic Games due to injury, Dave quickly moved through the light-heavyweight ranks, beating Jack Barry, Tiger Thomas, Lou Scozza, George Nichols and Maxie Rosenbloom, while suffering defeats at the hands of King Levinsky and Tommy Loughran. When the NBA stripped Rosenbloom for not making a defence of his world light-heavyweight title for six months on 6 June 1931, 44 men applied to contest a series of elimination bouts, Dave being among them. Advancing to the final after beating Abie Bain, Mike Mandell and Johnny Freeman, he was outpointed by Nichols on 18 March 1932 for the NBA version of the world title. He was then beaten inside six rounds by Billy Jones before taking a break and coming back in April 1934 to kayo Lee Savold in one round. There were to be just seven more fights, including losses to the hard-punching Sammy Slaughter and Larry Udell, which he later reversed,

prior to ending his career with a win over Henry Firpo (1935). After leaving the ring, he joined the Merchant Marine in 1936, took part in the invasion of Sicily (1943) and tried various jobs before retiring in 1972.

Dave Maier

Jackie Marshall

MARSHALL Jackie *From* Glasgow. *Died* 10 November 2000, aged 72. Wanted to box at the age of ten, but was told he was too young. However, when he was old enough he joined the Grove BC, won the Scottish Western District featherweight title (1945) and then the Scottish ABA title

(1946). Officials wanted him to wait until after the 1948 Olympics to box for pay, but after 84 amateur bouts he decided to turn pro (1946). Unfortunately, he was plagued by knuckle injuries and, despite an unsuccessful operation, the problem remained throughout his career. Beat top men like Vic Manini, Johnny Smith, Bert Hornby, Cliff Anderson, Mickey O'Neill, Ernie Vickers, Peter Fallon, Rees Moore and Johnny Flannigan, in a Scottish lightweight title eliminator. When he was 23 he went to the hospital for what he thought was to be a normal check-up, only to be advised to stop boxing. All set to challenge Willie Whyte for the Scottish title, he couldn't ignore the medical advice and retired with a record of 49 bouts, 38 wins, two draws and nine losses. He later became the treasurer of the Scottish EBA and coached in the Strathclyde Youth Association. Away from the boxing ring, his forte was ballroom-dancing, at which he won many honours.

MAXIM Joey *From* Cleveland, Ohio, USA. *Died* 2 June 2001, aged 79. Real name Guiseppe Antonio Berardinelli. A pro from 1941 to 1958, and managed by Jack Kearns, in World War II he was a PTI in US Army Air Force. Won the vacant American light-heavyweight title by beating Gus Lesnevich (1949) before winning the world title, beating Freddie Mills (1950). Was beaten by Ezzard Charles for the world heavyweight title (1951), but in the same year he

Joey Maxim

retained the world light-heavyweight crown when beating Irish Bob Murphy. He then retained the world light-heavyweight title again by beating Sugar Ray Robinson (1952), before losing his title to Archie Moore (1952). He also lost in return title fights with Moore (1953 and 1954). After that he concentrated on the heavyweight division, beating Floyd Patterson (1954), but losing twice to Eddie Machen (1957) prior to finishing his career in Europe (1958) after losing to Heinz Neuhaus, Mino Bozzano and Ulli Ritter. From 1955 to 1958, Joey won only one of nine contests, every one going the full distance. In other contests, he beat Jersey Joe Walcott, who subsequently beat him twice, and Bob Satterfield and Jimmy Bivins, thus avenging a previous defeat, while in five fights with Ezzard Charles he lost every one, all on points. He was also outpointed by world champions, Carl 'Bobo' Olson and Willie Pastrano. In fact, in 115 bouts, Joey lost only one inside the distance – to Curtis Sheppard. Joey had already beaten Sheppard, and three weeks after being stopped he won the rubber match by outpointing him. After retiring, Joey drove a taxi in Florida, later moving to Las Vegas, where appeared at various places, making personal appearances, meeting people, shaking hands, having photos taken and signing autographs, especially at the Marina Hotel. Stayed in Vegas for 20 years before coming back to Cleveland. His mother Henrietta survives him at the age of 97.

MEDEL Joe Real name Jose Navarro. *From* Mexico. *Died* February 2001, aged 62. A pro from 1955 to 1967, Joe won the Mexican bantam title by beating Jose Lopez (1959) and retained it against Eloy Sanchez (1960), Ignacio Pina (1961), Edmundo Esparza, Manny Barrios twice (1963), before losing it to Chucho Castillo (1967). Twice fighting for the world title, losing to Eder Jofre (1962) and to Fighting Harada (1967), top men in his record whom he beat included Mario de Leon, Danny Kid, Herman Marques, Mitsunori Seki, Sadao Yaoita, Walter McGowan, Jesus Pimental, Rudy Corona and Evan Armstrong. He also reversed the loss to Fighting Harada before quitting the ring.

MELO Eddie *From* Montreal, Canada. *Died* 6 April 2001, aged 40. Shot dead outside a sports bar in Mississauga, Ontario, he was the former Canadian middleweight and light-heavyweight contender. Lost to Vinnie Curto and Gary Summerhays, but beat Frank Bullard, Mark Johnson and reversed the Summerhays' defeat.

MESSERVY Peter *From* London (Born Northfields, nr Birmingham). *Died* February 2001, aged 80. One of the most interesting men who ever won an ABA title, Peter joined the Royal Navy as a 15-year-old boy, serving on HMS Royal Sovereign and HMS Resource in the Med and Atlantic during World War 11, and eventually rose to the status of Commander. He first came to prominence, boxing wise, after winning the Combined Services title in 1948 at the age of 27 and the following year he cemented those efforts by reaching the ABA light-heavyweight final.

Unfortunately, both he and his opponent, Sam Knowles, were thrown out of the ring in a double disqualification, the first time that had ever happened in an ABA Championships final. However, in 1950, Peter made amends by winning the title when outpointing Albert Gall and immediately retired with honour restored, having also represented England against Scotland. A hero in and out of the ring, in 1959, as a Royal Navy diver, he was awarded the George Medal after removing several live torpedoes from a Japanese submarine in the Singapore Straits.

MILLS Lennie *From* London. *Died* 12 May 2001. Boxing for Lynn BC, having been beaten by Dave Charley in the SE Divs final (1954), he was a runner up in the 1955 London championships at featherweight, losing to the ever-green Freddie Woodman. He retained the SE London title (1956), represented London ABA versus Berlin and the Army (1955-56), and in 254 bouts, he won 227 and lost 27. His father Ernie was also a boxer and member of the London Ex-Boxers' Association, and Lennie followed in his footsteps, becoming a committee-man, then vice-president.

MITRI Tiberio *From* Italy. *Died* 12 February 2001, after being hit by a train, aged 74. Unbeaten in his first 50 fights before losing to Jake LaMotta for the world middleweight title (1950), he had already won the European crown by

Tiberio Mitri (left), despite going 15 rounds he was unable to win the world middleweight title from Jake 'The Raging Bull' LaMotta in 1950

beating Cyrille Delannoit (1949). He then successfully defended it against Jean Stock, relinquished it, won it back by stopping Randolph Turpin in round one, before finally losing it to Charles Humez (1954). After retiring he became an actor, making several films in Italy and in Hollywood, working with Charlton Heston in *Ben Hur* and with David Niven in *The Best Of Enemies*. His last film was *Pugili* (1995), where he played an old fighter. He married three times, was reported to be a heavy drinker and a drug addict, and was reduced to begging in restaurants and bars. It was also reported that he suffered from Alzheimer's and Parkinson's Diseases, a sad and tragic end for a great fighter, with the amazing record of having lost only six fights in the whole of his illustrious career. Whilst he was twice unable to get the better of Charles Humez, men he did beat included Giovanni Manca, Laurent Dauthille (2), Dick Turpin, Kid Marcel (2), Dick Wagner, Claude Milazzo, Les Allen, Jimmy Lyggett (2), Baby Day, Pat McAteer and Jean Ruellet.

MYERS Joe *From* Oldham. *Died* August 2001, aged 90. Joe boxed from 1925 to 1935 at fly, bantam and featherweight, recording 88 wins, 15 draws and 39 defeats in 142 contests, according to a record put together by the late Vic Hardwicke. Among the better men he met were Jean Locatelli, Martin Gallagher, Minty Rose, Syd Williams, Len Wickwar, Archie Woodbine, George Marsden, whom he beat twice, Benny Thackaray, Joe Horridge, Bill Cakewell, Kid Socks and Johnny King, the former British and Empire bantamweight champion who beat him twice, in 1932 and 1933. In an attempt to win the vacant Northern Area flyweight title, he was outpointed over 15 rounds by Fred Bebbington in Liverpool on 25 July 1931.

NOTO Frederic *From* France. *Died* 18 February 2001, being shot at his home in Ajaccio, Corsica, aged 27. Started boxing in Toulon, later moving to Ajaccio (1995), he was beaten by Stephane Jacob for the French welterweight title (1998), before winning the French light-welterweight title by beating Nordine Mouchi (2000). Having boxed in Britain, being the first man to defeat Darren Bruce (1999), he was due to defend the French title against Souleymane Mbaye.

O'BRIEN Danny *From* Kilburn, London. *Died* 10 July 2001 on his 62nd birthday. Went to Salisbury Road School, for many years he was an altar boy at the Sacred Heart Church. As a schoolboy, representing Middlesex at soccer and cricket, Danny started boxing at St Marylebone BC under the blind trainer, Andy Newton. He later moved to Rotax BC and was the national schoolboy and youth champion, before becoming the Army and ISBA title-holder and reaching the semi-finals of the ABA Championships. Boxing for London ABA and England, whom he represented in the European Championships (1959), he joined the 11th Hussars and was posted to Northern Ireland. After Irish officials questioned Danny, who told them his father was born in Kerry and his mother in Wexford, he was invited to box for Ireland, also winning the Ulster and All-Ireland titles, and representing Ireland in the 1960 Olympics. Danny then turned pro with Sam Burns and was trained by Tommy Ryder and Danny Vary. His best wins were over Floyd Robertson in a non-title fight, and against Freddie King in a 'nobbins' fight at Shoreditch, before he retired with weight problems and became a taxi driver. In August 2000 he was given the shattering news that he had only around three months to live. That he survived as long as he did was a tribute to his spirit and the support of his family and friends.

O'KEEFE Tommy *From* Ashington. *Died* August 2001, aged 85. One of six boxing brothers, while working at Ellington Colliery he turned pro at 16 and won the Pitman's lightweight title (1934). In World War II, Tommy served in the 7th Battalion, Royal Northumberland Fusiliers, later also serving with the Duke of Wellington Regiment in Korea (1953). Although he had only two fingers and a thumb on his right hand it didn't stop him taking part in 120 bouts.

PALMER Jim *From* Consett. *Died* September 2000, aged 85. During the '30s, Jim had 231 pro bouts. One of seven children, when he started boxing he used to cycle from Consett to Newcastle to train at Joe Shepherd's gym, then cycle home again. Boxed Ginger Roberts four times, their final meeting being at Newcastle Town Moor during Race Week. Boxing in the booths, fighting ten rounds with the African Kid in one booth, eight rounds with Phil Milligan and four with Ginger in another booth, Jim received £2.50 for the three bouts before cycling home. In 1937 he went to Belfast on a day's notice to tackle 'Spider' Jim Kelly and, although not receiving the verdict, cut Kelly's eye in round seven, before decking him twice in the final round. He was the uncle of Glenn McCrory.

PASI Patrick *From* Walthamstow. *Died* 21 August 2001, ambushed and shot, aged 29. Known as Patrick Pasi, his real surname being Pasipanodua, he turned pro in August 1997 and had three fights as a light-middleweight, beating Harry Butler and losing to Tony Walton and Peter Nightingale before quitting in April 1998. Managed by Charlie Smith and trained by Alan Mortlock, he had no amateur experience but was a martials arts expert who was said to have met and beaten Shaolin monks in China.

PEARCE Billy *From* London. *Died* March 2001. A pro in the 1940s, and managed by Jack Burns, he also boxed on the booths. After retiring, Billy held a manager's licence, looking after Sammy McSpadden among others. For many years a member of LEBA, he had a variety of businesses, including a betting shop, a hotel, and a hairdressing salon, before becoming a taxi-driver. He also wrote articles for the cabbies' magazine and other periodicals.

PERUGINO Prisco *From* Italy. *Died* 21 January 2001, aged 28. Committing sucide by throwing himself in front of a train at Santa Maria Capua Vetere, Prisco was the

national and WBU Inter-Continental super-featherweight champion and had a record showing 21 fights, 19 wins (seven inside schedule) and two losses.

POPAL Ahmed *From* Australia. *Died* 9 April 2001, aged 30. Three days earlier he was meeting the Australian super-flyweight champion, Tony Pappa, for the vacant Victoria State bantamweight title. In round six they overbalanced and tumbled to the canvas, Popal cracking his head when landing, and he died without recovering consciousness. Turning pro in June 1999, he had lost both of his pro fights and had been inactive for nearly 15 months.

REA Dom *From* Coatbridge. *Died* 24 June 2001, aged 88. Originally billed as Young Rea until his 33rd bout, his real surname being 'Bovo', Dom had 110 bouts between 1931 and 1944, winning 46, drawing 11 and losing 53. Was introduced to boxing by his cousin, Tony Rea, who boxed professionally as Bert Gilroy, at the age of 15, and initially boxed as an amateur before graduating to the booths at the Coatbridge Fountain a year later. Recommended to the promoter, Pat McGreechan, by Tony, he turned pro and became a busy lightweight, taking part in 30 bouts in 1932, and fought mainly around the Glasgow area, meeting Mick Kenny, Peter and Al Veitch, Pat Logue, Jim McKenzie, Bob Fitzsimmons (not the legend), Jackie Quinn, Joe Connolly, Chick Harkins, Billy Stevens, Jim Cowie, Frank Markey and Sandy McKenzie, among others. During World War II, Dom, who was a skilled turner, worked for Henderson Engineering and carried on with the job until he was 66, a year past normal retirement.

REID Chris *From* Brooklyn, USA. *Died* June 2001, aged 38. Turned pro after losing in the semi-finals of the Olympic trials (1984) and was managed by Mickey Duff. Beaten by Graciano Rocchigiani for the IBF super middleweight title (1988), he was unbeaten in his first 19 bouts before losing to Fully Obel (1987). Boxed in Belfast on four occasions, beating Chris Coady, Paul Newman, Cordwell Hylton and Hugh Johnson, before retiring at 25. He later became a trainer, working with the British boxer, John Durkin, in Tinton Falls, New Jersey, where he established the Long Branch Boxing Club.

RINALDO Marco *From* Italy. *Died* 20 May 2001 in a car crash, aged 42. A pro from 1983 to 1992, Marco made three unsuccessful challenges for the Italian light-heavyweight title, losing to Noe Cruciani (1986) and Andrea Magi (1991 and 1992), finishing with 17 wins (ten inside schedule), seven defeats and a draw.

ROLLO Piero *From* Italy. *Died* February 2001, aged 73. The Italian amateur flyweight champion in 1947, Piero turned pro in 1950 and won the Italian bantamweight title (1955) and European title by beating Mario D'Agata (1958). Retained the European title twice before losing it to Freddie Gilroy (1959), but won it back by beating Pierre Cossemyns (1962), having lost to Cossemys in a title fight five months earlier. He again lost the title, this time to

Alphonse Halimi, but won it back by beating Halimi four months later (1962), before finally losing it to Ben Ali (1963). He had only three fights after that, retiring in 1964 with a record of 81 bouts, 61 wins, 13 defeats and seven draws. Apart from those already mentioned, other top-class men that he defeated included Tino Cardinale, Aldo Pravisani, David Gogotya, Roberto Spina, Dante Bini, Robert Tartari, Jimmy Carson, Tanny Campo, Jose Luis Martinez, Eugene le Cozannet, Kimpo Amarfio, Federico Scarponi, Dennis Adyei, Alex Ambrose, Mario Sitri, Billy Rafferty, Jackie Brown and Brian Cartwright.

SANDERS Ric *From* Leicester. *Died* 26 March 2001, aged 75. Having started boxing in the booths, as a pro he was a busy fighter and in 1946 had 36 bouts, followed by another 22 in 1947. Ric won the North Midlands Area welterweight title by beating Ken Page (1949) and before the end of that year had beaten Jim Wellard, Ron Price, Billy Biddles, Mick McGhee, Alf Danahar, Henry Hall, Les Vaughan and Bob Burniston – an impressive list. After that he lost a few and decided to retire. A natural composer of poems, the best of which was his *Elegy For The Darling Bairns Of The Dunblane Massacre*, he was also a fine entertainer, good pianist, raconteur, singer (especially of Irish songs), writer of scripts for sketches and sleight-of-hand merchant.

SATTARKHANOV Bekzat *From* Kazakhstan. *Died* 31 December 2000, in a car crash, aged 20. The Olympic gold medallist (featherweight) in 2000, after outpointing the American, Ricardo Juarez, in the final, an official protest was lodged at the way the Russian referee, Stanislav Kirsanov, allowed Sattarkkhanov to hold constantly in the final round. Although the AIBA suspended the referee for four years, the result stood. Earlier, Sattarkhanov had won the bantamweight silver medal at the World Junior Championships (1998), but was beaten in the first series of the French Multi-Nations at featherweight (1999).

SCOTLAND Beethavean *From* Maryland, USA. *Died* 2 July 2001, aged 26. Having taken the fight at short notice, Beethavean died from injuries sustained against George Khalid in New York in June, it being ruled an accidental death. He left a respectable record of 20 wins and seven losses, with one draw, from 28 fights.

SEWELL Danny *From* Tottenham, London. *Died* May 2001, aged 70. Weighed 11st 7lb when he was 14 and a year later well over 12st 10lb, making it difficult to get him fights. After World War II won the Great Britain Schoolboys heavyweight title and after only 20 amateur bouts top manager, Ted Broadribb, asked if he could sign Danny as a pro. This occurred the following year when Danny was 16. He was one of Freddie Mills' sparring-partners for the latter's world title fight with Gus Lesnevich, which Freddie won, and won his pro debut by knocking out Frank Farmer in 60 seconds (1946), having sold £200 worth of tickets. After winning three more bouts, the last against previously unbeaten Derek Alexander, Danny broke a bone in his right hand and had to wait

several months before having the plaster removed. All set to box an exhibition with Freddie Mills at Chelmsford (1947), Danny appeared to have a heavy cold, before collapsing and being taken to the Prince of Wales Hospital, Tottenham in a coma. Having recovered and improved prior to a relapse, he was then told that he had polio and that he would never walk again. This he would not accept. The American manager, Bill Daly, and his heavyweight, Lee Savold, took an interest in Danny and raised nearly £4,000 from a 'Benefit Night' to enable the youngster to go to America with the chance of a cure. The treatment was successful and in 1949 Danny returned to Britain completely cured. Told that he could fight again, he started by stopping Ben Bowden (1949) and continued by beating Les Pam, prior to being called up for National Service and spending two years as a PTI in the RAF. Following that, he spent two years as a gym instructor on the Cunard Queens, before taking over a pub called 'The Hope' in Bethnal Green (1953). Three years later, he went into the club business in London and in Paris, also branching out as an impresario, putting on concerts for the Infantile Paralysis Fellowship. He also supported the National Polio Vaccination Committee. His brother George had become an actor and Danny followed in his footsteps, starting as a stunt man and film extra (1957). The following year he had a good part in *One More River*, with Laurence Olivier (later Sir Laurence) and then played the major role of Bill Sikes in *Oliver* at the New Theatre, going with it to Broadway (1962). Settling in America with his wife Donna, Danny won the Actor of the Year award for his performance in Harold Pinter's *The Homecoming*. Whatever it was, Danny never gave up.

Danny Sewell

SHARP Tommy *From* Derby. *Died* March 2001. A professional boxer from 1932 to 1950, despite several long periods of inactivity and World War 11 Tommy took part in 37 recorded contests as a flyweight, winning 12, losing 19 and drawing six, meeting men such as Jeff Oscroft, Eddie Davies, Ronnie Jones, Owen Johnson, Gus Harris, Art Dykes and Glyn Evans, his last contest. Interestingly, he met the Wilkinson brothers on several occasions and, while he could never find a way past Maurice, he had a victory over Noel. After retiring, he remained in boxing, firstly as a manager, and then as the founder-member of Nottingham EBA, being a regular right up until his death. He was about to be made president, which was going to be a surprise, but, sadly, he passed away before he received the good news.

SHAW Sammy *From* Hull. *Died* June 2001, aged 81. A pro from 1933 to 1949, with a record of 49 wins, 17 losses, with one no contest and eight draws from 75 bouts, he met Harry Kid Silver four times, winning two and drawing two, (1937 and 1938), boxed a creditable draw with Frank Parkes and twice beat Jacky Ryan. Had 11 bouts in 1939, but only a few until 1948, when he resumed on a regular basis. In 1949, Sammy beat Peter Guichan, Al Young, Ronnie Taylor, Chris Kelly, Joe Carter and Kid Tanner, with losses against Morty Kelleher and Jackie Turpin (twice). His win over Tanner was his last bout (August 1949). Was a founder-member of the Hull & East Yorkshire EBA.

SICILIANO Al *From* Las Vegas, USA. *Died* January 2001, aged 70. Having won a Golden Gloves title in Washington (1951), he joined the Marines and then the LAPD, before moving to Vegas (1966). An inspector for 12 years, and a judge for eight years, his last official appearance as a judge was the previous month at the Marco Antonio Barrera v Jesus Salud WBO super-bantamweight title fight.

SILLETT Alan *From* Action, London. *Died* March 2001, aged 68. Boxing for CAV BC, Alan was a finalist in the ABA Youth Championships, before reaching the semi-finals of the ABA Championships (1952) as a bantamweight, and getting to the final of the ABA featherweight title (1953). He also represented the ABA and England on ten occasions when boxing for CAV and the Army. Turning pro in November 1954, he got off the mark with a 47-second win over George Dougan before being put down five times and stopped by Eddie McCormick a few weeks later. However, he was beginning to suffer from knuckle injuries and, although going through 1955 undefeated in eight contests with wins over George Connors, Jackie Tiller, Cliff Giles, Dave Robins, Ernie Savoury, Colin Barber and Jimmy Carson, and one draw, he was knocked out by George Dormer early in 1956. Despite coming back with two wins and a draw with Terry Toole, he was stopped by John Smillie and retired to continue his work as a mechanic.

SMART Tony *From* St Helens. *Died* 27 September 2000, aged 70. The trainer at St Helens BC, not to be confused with St Helens Town, he started the club around 30 years ago in his garden shed, when it was the St Helens Star BC. Later it became Greenall St Helens, and then just St Helens. His first champion was his son Tony, who won the Junior ABA Class 'B' 54kg title (1970). Between 1977 and 1989 the club produced several champions, including George Gilbody, Ray Gilbody, Keith Wallace and John Lyon. Norman Minteith, who has run the club for the past four years, said that they intended to change the name of the club to 'Mr Smart's ABC' to honour his memory. Norman took over when Tony became unwell.

SMITH George *From* Leith, Scotland. *Died* November 2001, aged 89. George's interest in boxing started in 1924, when employed by the Leith pawnbroker turned international impresario, Nat Dresner, to sell programmes for the Ted 'Kid' Lewis versus Tommy Milligan title fight at Edinburgh's Annandale Street Arena. Joining Leith Victoria BC, run by champion Tancy Lee, he won three consecutive Scottish vests in Norway and won national titles at fly and bantam. However, on failing to win a place in Scotland's Empire Games team in Canada (1930), he decided to become a referee and judge. During World War II, George served in the RAF, coaching a top team in Palestine, before resuming boxing activities in Scotland (1945) and becoming a pro referee (1950). Promoted to Star Class (1964), he refereed the return bout between Henry Cooper and Muhammad Ali at Highbury, home of Arsenal FC (1966).

SMITH Les *From* Yorkshire. *Died* September 2000, in his late 80s. Having settled in Bournemouth, and becoming secretary of the Bournemouth EBA, as a committee-member he was responsible for the rebirth of the EBA. A member of the famous Halle Orchestra under Sir John Barbaroli in the percussion section, Les was a brilliant pianist who continued to entertain at various EBA functions.

SOTO Sergio Ariel *From* Argentina. *Died* 18 October 2000, aged 26. Knocked out while sparring on 10 May, he continued after a short break but passed out, had convulsions, and was taken to Ramos Mejia Hospital. Having undergone an operation to remove a blood clot from the brain, and survived an infection of the lung to actually breathe without assistance in early June, he sadly took a turn for the worse and died suddenly. Did not win one of his seven pro fights, which included one draw.

SRISOMVONGSE Sahasombhop *From* Thailand. *Died* 26 December 2000, aged 62. A top promoter and also president of the Asian Boxing Council in south-east Asia, which is affiliated with the World Boxing Council, he was general sports manager of Channel 7 TV in Thailand. Helped produce many WBC champions and organised three great Conventions of the WBC in his home country (1985, 1991 and 1995).

TAKECHI Seiji *From* Japan. *Died* 10 August 2001, when committing suicide by hanging himself near the Kompire Shrine, Tokyo, aged 24. In July 2000, he won the OPBF light-middleweight title in controversial circumstances when the champion, Kookayul Song, who was ahead on points, sustained an eye injury at the end of round ten. The Korean referee declared a stoppage win for Song, but the verdict was reversed and awarded to Takechi on a technical decision. A rematch was ordered last November, which ended in a technical draw when Takechi floored Song in the opening round but then sustained a cut eye and could not continue. Last May they met for the third time, with Takechi winning a unanimous verdict. It was to be his last fight, having won ten of his 15 bouts, with two draws.

TANNER Allan *From* British Guiana. *Died* 13 September 2001, aged 78. The brother of Richie 'Kid' Tanner and Young Jack Johnson, Allan arrived in Liverpool, England during the summer of 1949 and immediately got down to work, beating good men such as Stan Gossip, Laurie Buxton, Jimmy Toweel and Jim Findlay, before taking in seven losses on the trot against Jo Vissers, Francis Bonnardel, Roger Baour, Frank Parkes, Johnny Malloy, Peter Fallon and Duilio Loi, all top fighters. From then on, however, although he lost a fair few fights, other vicims included Harry Hughes, Vince Marshall, Tommy McGovern, Gordon Goodman, Billy Dixon, Mickey O'Neill, Tony Lombard, Freddie Smith, Tommy McMenemy, Ellis Ask, Jan Nicolaas, Ron Cooper, Maurice Maury, Owen Trainor, Mickey Flanagan, Billy Shaw, Johnny Mahlangu, Werner Handke, Dai Davies, Stan Skinkiss, Cyril Evans, Al Sharpe and Emrys Jones before he called it a day in 1955. He also met Joe Lucy, Jorgen Johansen, Johnny Butterworth, Gerry Hassett, Lahouari Godih, Jimmy O'Connell, Sammy Bonnici and Piet van Klaveren. Prior to coming to Britain his earlier career is very sketchy, but Harold Alderman has been able to trace quite a few fights for him back to 1941, when boxing as either 'Young' or 'Sonny' Tanner he earned a reputation beating men of the class of Stinging Ant, Young Joe Louis, Kid Bururu, Luis Managas, Jose Alberto Dias and Young Finnegan, while losing on points to Ivor 'Kid' Germain (1946) and being stopped by Sandy Saddler (1948) and Young Finnegan (1949). Although both his brothers were champions of British Guiana, Allan appears not to have been, his bout against Freddo Simmons (1947) for the vacant British Guianan lightweight title ending with a no-contest decision in the fifth round.

TAYLOR Ollie *From* Brisbane, Australia. *Died* 31 December 2001. Prior to turning pro in 1961, Ollie, the elder brother of Wally, won a silver medal at the 1958 Empire Games, losing to Howard Winstone in the final of the bantamweight class, and took bronze in the 1960 Olympic Games. In a career between 1961 and 1964 there were only 14 bouts recorded, of which he won 11, lost two, against Bob Allotey and Johnny Famechon, and drew one with Les Dunn, his most notable victories coming against Bobby Sinn (2), Leo Espinosa, Danny Valdez, Gene Aragon, Ignacio Pina and Primo Zamparini, thus avenging his Olympic Games' semi-final defeat.

TERRANOVA Phil *From* New York City, USA. *Died* 16 March 2000, aged 80. A pro from 1941 to 1949, he won the NBA version of the world featherweight title when defeating Jackie Callura (1943) and successfully defended it against the same man in the same year before losing his claim to Sal Bartolo (1944). Phil then made two more attempts to land the title, losing to Bartolo for the NBA version in 1944 and to the magical Willie Pep for the undisputed crown (1945). He never quite reached those heights again but still posed a threat to any aspiring young contender. Among those he defeated were Aaron Seltzer, Johnny Dell, Lulu Constantino, Chico Morales, Cabey Lewis, Maxie Shapiro, Charley Riley, Jimmy McAllister, Sandy Saddler, the future featherweight champion, Willie Roache (twice), Humberto Zavala, Britain's Tommy McGovern and Buddy Hayes. He also met Chalky Wright, Maurice 'Lefty' LaChance, Harry Jeffra, Bernard Docusen, Arthur King, Spider Armstrong and Eddie Compo, before leaving the ring with 67 wins, 11 draws and 21 defeats from 99 contests.

THOMAS Phil *From* Middlesbrough. *Died* 4 August 2001, aged 93. A long-time official in the north east, the Phil Thomas School of Boxing in Middlesbrough, which produced Peter Richardson, among others, was named after him.

TOMASELLO Bobby *From* Massachusetts, USA. *Died* 25 October 2000, aged 24. Died five days after collapsing in the dressing-room following his televised draw against Steve Dotse. A super-featherweight who was showing great promise, he was hitherto undefeated in 15 bouts, including one draw.

TOOHIG Johnny *From* Croydon. *Died* September 2000, aged 83. Started in the '30s and retired in 1947, having recorded 89 bouts, of which he lost only 17. Managed by the late Alf Bliss, among his victims were Jack Watkins (twice), Ginger McDermott, Johnny Sage, Red McDonald, Mick O'Brien, Jimmy Bitmead, Les Haycox and George Fordham. His best performance was in drawing with Tommy Barnham (1938).

WELCH Coley *From* Portland, Maine, USA. *Died* 4 December 2000, aged 81. One of the many excellent coloured fighters operating first as a welter and then in the middleweight class in the States between 1937 and 1949, Coley's final record read 99 wins, five draws, 22 losses, only four inside schedule, in 126 contests. While losing to men such as Ernie Vigh (twice), Georgie Abrams, Tony Martin (twice), Jake LaMotta, George Kochan, Walter 'Popeye' Woods, Steve Belloise and Joe Blackwood, opponents he beat were of the calibre of Tony Fisher, Ted Lowry, Ernie Vigh, Tony Cisco, Jose Basora (twice), Izzy Jannazzo, Ralph Zannelli, Johnny Finazzo (twice) and Sonny Horne. Having been discharged from the US

Coastguard in 1943, and billed as the New England middleweight champion, he beat Joe 'Boyo' Mallon, an Englishman serving in the British Navy at the time. His final contest before calling it a day, on 5 April 1949, was a ten-round points defeat at the hands of Jose Contreras.

WELLARD Jim *From* Northampton. *Died* July 2001, aged 79. Never an amateur, Jim turned pro in 1937 and throughout his career suffered from damaged hands, because of his terrific power of punch. Among those he stopped were Harry Lazar, Harry Davis, Ric Sanders, Bob Cleaver, Stan Hawthorne, Teddy Lee and Reg Hoblyn. He also met champions Alex Buxton, Dick Turpin, Ernie Roderick and Harry Mizler. Retiring in 1951, in Liverpool he was known as Jim 'Hithard', despite his real surname being 'Woolard'. During World War II he was a Corporal PTI in the Royal Welsh Fusiliers. In later years, Jim was a 'regular' at meetings, reunions, and outings of the Northampton EBA.

WILKIE Bill *From* Tyneside. *Died* 2 March 2001, aged 55. Despite never entering the ring, Bill was a minefield of boxing information and his love of the sport, coupled with his admiration for fighting men, eventually saw him become secretary of the Newcastle EBA in April 1985. He also edited the newsletter. A pleasant man, who worked in the local shipyards with Swan Hunter, he was well liked and will be sorely missed.

WILSON Neville *From* Wolverhampton. *Died* December 2000, of natural causes, aged 40. The brother of the better-known Tony, the former British light-heavyweight champion, Neville was an honest, willing pro who campaigned between 1980 and 1982, retiring with eight wins, two draws and 11 defeats. Starting in September 1980 as a welter, some of the better men he met included Winston Burnett, Jimmy Cable, Cliff Curtis, Dudley McKenzie, Gary Buckle, Martin Patrick, a former ABA finalist, and Alan Hardiman.

WINSTONE Howard *From* Merthyr Tydfil, Wales. *Died* 30 September 2000, aged 61. As an amateur, Howard won the ABA bantamweight title and the Empire Games gold medal (1958) before turning pro in 1959 with manager, Eddie Thomas. Won the British featherweight title by beating Terry Spinks (1961), and defended it against Derry Treanor, Harry Carroll (1962) and Johnny Morrissey (1963). Won the European crown when beating Alberto Serti (1963) and successfully defended his British and European titles against Billy Calvert and John O'Brien (1963), and just the European crown against Yves Desmarets (1965). Beaten by Vicente Saldivar for the world title (1965), Howard retained his European crown against Andrea Silanos and Jan de Keers (1966), and his British and European titles against Lennie Williams (1966). Despite losing both world title fights against Vicente Saldivar (1967), he won the vacant world crown when beating Mitsunori Seki (1968), before losing it six months later to Jose Legra (1968). He then retired, having won 61

and lost six of 67 contests, a great record which would surely have been even better if he hadn't lost the tips of three fingers on his right hand in a factory accident when a teenager. However, he compensated this loss by developing a wonderful left-hand lead. In 2001, a memorial statue was erected in Merthyr, the money coming from an 'Appeal Fund' and resulting in donations from all over the world. At the time of his death, Howard was president of the Welsh Ex-Boxers' Association.

Howard Winstone

WRIGHT Johnny *From* Potters Bar. *Died* 12 July 2001, aged 72. An amateur with the Polytechnic BC and the Royal Navy, Johnny somewhat surprisingly turned pro in November 1951 - scoring a third-round kayo win over Frank Priest - almost three years after his memorable fight against the now-legendary Hungarian, Laszlo Papp, when taking the Olympic Games' silver medal at Wembley. Prior to that, he had an excellent junior record, winning an ABA youth title in 1944 and three Sea Cadet championships before winning the senior ABA crown in 1948 and covering himself in glory at the Olympics. While knocking up further wins as a professional over men like Bobby Fish, Sammy Milsom, Jeff Tite, George Roe and Jimmy Redgewell, and drawing with Eddie Phillips, while reversing a stoppage defeat by Michael Stack, a points defeat inflicted by Doncaster's Rocco King early in 1953 saw him walk away from the sport, his heart not really in it anymore. Was licensee of the 'Fallow Buck' in Clay Hill from 1961 to 1985 and in later years he lived in Dorset.

YOUNG Dick *From* California, USA. *Died* 15 March 2001, aged 85. Refereed his first contest in 1941 and his last in 1985. Was also a judge. Known as 'Kid Clorox', because he was considered to be super clean, among the many top bouts he refereed was the second one between Muhammad Ali and Ken Norton.

A Boxing Quiz With a Few Below the Belt (Part 6)

Compiled by Les Clark

QUESTIONS

1. Who did Dennis Andries beat at the Scottish Exhibition Centre in 1995 to win the vacant British cruiserweight title?

2. Who was Zack Padilla's last opponent?

3. On 23 July 1994 in Bismark, USA three world titles took place on the same bill. Can you name the three winners?

4. Who did James Oyebola defeat to win the British heavyweight title?

5. Who was Felix Trinidad's opponent when he won the IBF welterweight title?

6. When Ross Hale successfully defended his British light-welterweight title to win a Lonsdale Belt outright who was the referee?

7. Who took the WBO bantamweight title from Duke McKenzie and lost it two years later when defending it at York Hall, Bethnal Green?

8. Neville Brown successfully defended his British middleweight title against which Welshman?

9. Who did Oscar de la Hoya defeat to win the WBO light-welterweight title?

10. Which of the Ruelas brothers was the first to win a world title?

11. When Bruce Seldon won the WBA heavyweight title who did he defeat?

12. Against whom did Glenn McCrory challenge for the IBF cruiserweight title in July 1993?

13. Eduardo Nazario twice fought for the world super-flyweight title in 1993. Whom did he challenge?

14. Alexis Arguello took the WBC lightweight title from Jim Watt. Who was his first defence against?

15. Who did Cristanto Espana defeat in Manchester for the WBA welterweight title in October 1993?

16. How many times did former European and Commonwealth heavyweight champion, Henry Akinwande, fight for the British title?

17. Apart from winning the world heavyweight title, what did Jack Sharkey and Jersey Joe Walcott have in common?

18. Who did Nigel Benn defeat to win the Commonwealth middleweight title?

19. How many Olympic boxing gold medals did Cuba win in the Sydney Olympics?

20. Can you name two boxers who have each held the European lightweight title on four different occasions?

21. Did Herbie Hide ever fight for the British heavyweight title?

22. Dennis Andries fought the former British light-heavyweight champion, Tom Collins, on five occasions. What was the overall result?

23. Who did Lloyd Honeygan defeat to win the British welterweight title?

24. Duke McKenzie won the British flyweight title when facing only his fifth British opponent. True or False?

25. Audley Harrison won gold at the Sydney Olympics. What were the winning scores?

26. Can you name this boxer who was unbeaten as an amateur and successfully defended his WBC lightweight title against Freddy Roach, Cornelius Boza-Edwards, and Edwin Rosario before winning titles at higher weights?

27. Name the boxer who won bronze in the 1988 Olympics and went on to win the WBA bantamweight crown?

28. Can you name the British boxer who held the European light-middleweight title after Herol Graham, but before Chris Pyatt?

29. How many world title bouts has Iran Barkley participated in?

30. Who did Eusebio Pedroza face in his first challenge for a world title?

31. Bruno Arcari defeated Pedro Adigue for the light-welterweight title in February 1970 and relinquished in 1974. How many defences did he make?

32. Who did Jimmy Batten defeat to win the British light-middleweight title?

33. Who won the first world heavyweight title fight scheduled over 12 rounds?

34. Joe Bugner had his first 18 pro fights in London. Where did he have his 19th fight and against whom?

35. Who was the first black African to win an Olympic boxing gold medal?

36. Who is the only boxer to win a points decision over Joe Louis?

37. Pat Cowdell won the European featherweight title from Salvatore Melluzzo. Against whom did he make his first defence?

38. Can you name a former Welsh champion who fought Azumah Nelson?

39. How many times did Willie Pastrano box in a British ring?

40. George Feeney fought three boxers who won world titles. Can you name them?

41. Referee Harry Gibbs once made a double disqualification. Can you name the boxers involved?

42. Where was the venue for the first live televised British title bout and who were the contestants?

43. How many bouts did Najib Daho have before challenging Pat Cowdell for the British super-featherweight belt?

44. In what year did James 'The Heat' Kinchen win a ten-round points verdict over Buster Drayton at York Hall, Bethnal Green?

45. How many European title bouts did Tony Sibson lose?

46. Who won the most European title bouts – Dick Richardson, Karl Mildenburger or Ingemar Johansson?

47. What was the birthname of former British and British Empire middleweight champion, Johnny Sullivan?

48. Can you name the former European light-heavyweight champion who made the most successful defences?

49. George Walker made an unsuccessful challenge for the British light-heavyweight belt. Who defeated him?

50. Can you name the two boxers who contested the first British cruiserweight title bout?

ANSWERS

1: Denzil Browne. 2: Zack beat Juan Laporte for the WBO light-welterweight belt but retired shortly after due to suffering an aneurysm whilst sparring in the gym. 3: Al Cole beat Nate Miller, Mike McCallum beat Jeff Harding and Virgil Hill beat Frank Tate. 4: Clifton Mitchell. 5: Yori 'Boy' Campas. 6: Mickey Vann. 7: Rafael del Valle. 8: Carlo Colarusso. 9: Jorge Paez. 10: Rafael in February 1994. Gabriel won his in September 1994. 11: Tony Tucker. 12: Al Cole. 13: Johnny Bredahl. 14: Ray Mancini. 15: Donovan Boucher. 16: Henry never fought for the British title. 17: They both died in 1994. 18: Abdul Amora Sanda. 19: Four. 20: Francois Sybille and Roberto Proietti. 21: Yes, he beat Michael Murray for the vacant title. 22: Dennis won four and lost one. 23: Cliff Gilpin. 24: False. It was only his fourth British opponent and was against Danny Flynn for the vacant title. 25: 30 points to 16 points. 26: Hector Camacho. 27: Jorge Julio. 28: Jimmy Cable. 29: Nine, losing six of them. 30: Alfonso Zamora, who kayoed him in the second round. 31: Nine. 32: Albert Hillman. 33: Larry Holmes. 34: Mose Harrell in Manchester. 35: Robert Wangila. 36: Ezzard Charles. 37: Sepp Iten. 38: Don George. 39: He fought in Britain on seven occasions. 40: Cornelius Boza-Edwards, Ken Buchanan and Ray Mancini. 41: Alan Minter and Ray Magdziarz. 42: Palace Lido, Isle of Man. 43: 48. 44: They fought on 14 April 1985. 45: Tony never lost a European title fight. Prince Rodney v Mick Courtney. 46: Richardson four, Mildenburger seven, Johansson four. 47: John Hallmark. 48: Rudi Koopmans made ten successful defences. 49: Dennis Powell. 50: Sam Reeson and Stewart Lithgo.

Leading BBBoC License Holders: Names and Addresses

Licensed Promoters

John Ashton
1 Charters Close
Kirkby in Ashfield
Nottinghamshire
NG17 8PF
0162 372 1278

Jack Bishop
76 Gordon Road
Fareham
Hants PO16 7SS
0132 928 4708

David Bradley
Aston Hall, Aston Lane
Claverley
Nr Wolverhampton
WV5 7DZ
0174 671 0287

Pat Brogan
112 Crewe Road
Haslington
Crewe, Cheshire
0127 087 4825

Tony Burns
67 Peel Place
Clayhill Avenue
Ilford, Essex IG5 0PT
0208 551 3791

Trevor Callighan
40 Prescott Street
Halifax
West Yorkshire
HX1 2QW
0142 232 2592

Roy Cameron
43 Beaulieu Close
Colindale
London NW9 6SB
0208 205 2949

David Casey
424 Barking Road
London E13 8HJ
0207 377 6333

Eva Christian
80 Alma Road
Plymouth
Devon PL3 4HU
0175 225 2753

Annette Conroy
144 High Street East
Sunderland
Tyne and Wear
SR1 2BL
0191 567 6871

Pat Cowdell
129a Moat Road
Oldbury, Warley
West Midlands
0121 552 8082

Denis Cross
6 Partington Street
Newton Heath
Manchester M40 2AQ
0161 205 6651

David Currivan
15 Northolt Avenue
South Ruislip
Middlesex HA4 6SS
0208 841 9933

Michael Dalton
16 Edward Street
Grimsby
South Humberside
0147 231 0288

Ronnie Davies
3 Vallensdean Cottages
Hangleton Lane
Portslade, Sussex
0127 341 6497

Evans-Waterman Promotions
88 Windsor Road
Bray
Berkshire SL6 2DJ
0162 862 3640

Norman Fawcett
4 Wydsail Place
Gosforth
Newcastle upon Tyne
NE3 4QP
0191 213 1294

Joe Frater
The Cottage
Main Road
Grainthorpe
Louth,
Lincolnshire
0147 234 3194

Dave Garside
33 Lowthian Road
Hartlepool
Cleveland
TS26 8AL
0142 929 1611

Jimmy Gill
45 Blandford Road
Chilwell
Nottingham
NG9 4GY
0115 913 5482

Golden Fists Promotions
Robin Welch
119 High Road,
Loughton
Essex IG10 4LT
0208 502 1415

Ron Gray
Ingrams Oak
19 Hatherton Road
Cannock
Staffordshire
0154 350 2279

Johnny Griffin
0116 2262 9287
07989 215287

GSC Promotions
Ian Mcleod
c/o Glasgow Moat House
Congress Road
Glasgow G3 8QT
0141 222 2577

Jess Harding
54 Heath Drive
Potters Bar
Hertfordshire EN6 1EJ
0170 764 2982

Dennis Hobson
Unit 1, Industrial Estate
Century Street
Sheffield S9 5DX
0124 643 1116

Harry Holland
12 Kendall Close
Feltham, Middlesex
0208 867 0435

Lloyd Honeyghan
PO Box 17216
London SE17 1ZU
0795 640 5007

Hull & District Sporting Club
Mick Toomey
25 Purton Grove
Bransholme
Hull HU7 4QD
0148 282 4476

Alma Ingle
26 Newman Road
Wincobank
Sheffield S9 1LP
0114 281 1277

Lester Jacobs
2 Radnor Road
Peckham
London SE15 6UR
0207 639 4734

Lion Promotions
Lennox Lewis & Adrian
Ogun, Suite 201
Gainsborough House
81 Oxford Street
London W1D 2EU
0207 903 5074

Malcolm McKillop
14 Springfield Road
Mangotsfield
Bristol
0117 957 3567

Owen McMahon
3 Atlantic Avenue
Belfast
BT15 2HN
0123 274 3535

Gary Mason
18 Camberwell
Church Street
London
SE5 8QU
0795 858 6147

Matchroom
Barry Hearn
10 Western Road
Romford
Essex
RM1 3JT
0170 878 2200

Midland Sporting Club
John Mills
24 Perton Road
Wolverhampton
WV6 8DN
0121 505 2141

Alex Morrison
197 Swanston Street
Laird Business Park
Dalmarnock
Glasgow
G40 4HW
0141 554 7777

Katherine Morrison
197 Swanston Street
Laird Business Park
Dalmarnock
Glasgow
G40 4HW
0141 554 7777

Graham Moughton
1 Hedgemans Way
Dagenham
Essex RM9 6DB
0208 517 4070

Munro & Hyland
The Morton Suite
The Moat House Hotel
1 Paradise Street
Liverpool L1 8JD
0151 708 8331

William Murray
39 Garnerville Road
Belfast BT4 2QQ
0289 076 3282

National SC (Charity)
Cafe Royal
68 Regents Street
London W1R 6EL

Noble Art Promotions
Greg Steene/Bruce Baker
The Garden Flat
38 Lupus Street, Pimlico
London SW1V 3EB
0207 592 0102

North Staffs Sporting Club
J Baddeley
29 Redwood Avenue
Stone
Staffordshire
ST15 0DB
0178 220 2242

On Top Promotions
Ian Smith
13 Henderson Close
Upton
Merseyside L49 4Q1H
0151 677 6407

Panix Promotions
Panos Eliades
6 Bloomsbury Square
London WC1A 2LP
0207 242 2358

Parks Promotions
Wibsey Park Avenue
Wibsey
Bradford BD6 3QA
0127 469 1333

Peacock Promotions
Anthony Bowers
Peacock Gym
Caxton Street North
Canning Town
London E16 1JR
0207 511 3799

Steve Pollard
899 Beverley High Road
Hull HU6 9NJ
0148 280 3455

Prince Promotions
John Sheppard
Prince House
172 Psalter Lane
Sheffield
South Yorkshire
SI1 8UR
0114 220 3000

Joe Pyle
36 Manship Road
Mitcham
Surrey CR4 2AZ
0208 395 6907

R & R Events
Ricky Manners
Mabgate Mills
Mill 6, Unit B
Macauley Street
Mabgate
Leeds LS9 7DZ
0113 243 6017

Glyn Rhodes
70 Oldfield Road
Stannington
Sheffield S6
0114 233 1687

Ringside Sporting Promotions
Ensley Bingham &
Martin Matthews
13 Osborne Road
Altrincham
Cheshire WA15 8EU
0161 929 8088

Gus Robinson, MBE
Stranton House
Westview Road
Hartlepool
TS24 0BB
0142 923 4221

Christine Rushton
20 Alverley Lane
Balby
Doncaster
Yorkshire DN4 9AS
0130 231 0919

St Andrews Sporting Club
Tommy Gilmour
Posthouse Glasgow City
Bothwell Street
Glasgow G2 7EN
0141 248 5461

Kevin Sanders
135 Coneygree Road
Peterborough
Cambridgeshire
PE1 8LQ
0173 355 5916

Chris Sanigar
Bristol Boxing Gym
40 Thomas Street
St Agnes
Bristol
Avon BS2 9LL
0117 949 6699

Mike Shinfield
126 Birchwood Lane
Somercotes
Derbyshire
DE55 4NF
0177 360 3124

Showsport International
Paul Hennessey
9 Warple Road
Quinton
Birmingham B32 1RL
0121 242 1356

John Spensley
Inn of the Park
339 Linthorpe Road
Middlesborough
Cleveland TS5 6AD

Sporting Club of Wales
Paul Boyce
Brynamlwg
2 Pant Howell Ddu
Ynysmerdy
Briton Ferry
Neath SA11 2TU
0163 982 0322

Sports Network
Frank Warren
Centurion House
Bircherley Green
Hertford
Hertfordshire
SG14 1AP
0199 250 5550

Sportsman Promotions
Frank Quinlan
Hollinthorpe Low Farm
Swillington Lane
Leeds
Yorkshire LS26 8BZ
0113 287 0167

Norrie Sweeney
3 Saucehill Terrace
Paisley
Scotland PA2 6SY
0141 580 0269

Tara Promotions
Jack Doughty
Lane End Cottage
Golden Street
Off Buckstone Road
Shaw, Oldham OL1 8LY
01706 845753

TKO Promotions
Eugene Maloney
TKO Gym
1 Dellow Street
London E1 0BP
0207 265 9955

Jack Trickett
Acton Court Hotel
187 Buxton Road
Stockport
Cheshire
0161 483 6172

Michael Ulyatt
28 Blackthorn Lane
Willerby
Hull
0148 265 7200

Stephen Vaughan
72 East Damswood
Road, Speke
Liverpool L24 7RJ

Louis Veitch
35 Clinton Avenue
Blackpool FY1 4AE
0125 329 3083

Viking International Promotions
Stephen Mark Wood
Unit 12
Enterprise Park
Oldham Road
Manchester M40 3AL
0161 683 5693

Keith Walker
Wayside Bungalow
Selby Road
Eggborough DN14 0LN
0197 766 2616

Dave Woollas
Tudor Lodge
Bellshaw Lane
Belton
Nr Doncaster
Yorkshire DN9 1PF
0142 787 4266

World Sports Organisation
Unit 5, Ella Mews
Cressy Road
London NW3 2NH
0207 284 2133

Yorkshire Executive Sporting Club
John Celebanski
87 Crowtree Lane
Allerton
Bradford B8 0AN
0127 482 4015

Licensed Managers

Sam Adair
Ashfield Cottage
Barnstaple
Devon
EX31 4DB
0123 747 4989

Isola Akay
129 Portnall Road
Paddington
London
W9 3BN
0208 960 7724

Kofi Asante
102 Old Hospital Close
St James Drive
Balham
London
SW12 8SS
0208 672 0475

John Ashton
1 Charters Close
Kirkby in Ashfield
Nottinghamshire
NG17 8PF
0162 372 1278

Chris Aston
23 Juniper Grove Mews
Netherton
Huddersfield
West Yorkshire
HD4 7WG
0148 432 9616

Bruce Baker
PO Box 25188
London SW1V 3WL
0207 592 0102

Robert Bannan
1c Thornton Street
Townhead, Coatbridge
North Lanarkshire
ML5 2NZ
0123 660 6736

John Baxter
53 Battenburg Road
Leicester LE3 5HB
0116 243 2325

Tony Behan
Flat 6, 29 Roundlea Rd
Northfield
Birmingham B31 1DA
0771 002 2862

Sam Betts
The Railway Hotel
115 Station Road
Kirkham
Lancashire
PR4 2HD
0177 268 7973

Jack Bishop
76 Gordon Road
Fareham
Hants
PO16 7SS
0132 928 4708

Tony Borg
39 Clarence Street
Newport
Gwent
Wales
0163 378 2824

Peter Bowen
50 Newman Avenue
Lanesfield
Wolverhampton
West Midlands
WV4 6BZ
0190 282 8159

Jackie Bowers
36 Drew Road
Silvertown
London E16
0207 476 5530

Tony Bowers
3 The Green Walk
Chingford
London E4
0208 523 8113

David Bradley
The Dovecote
Aston Hall
Claverley
WV5 7DZ
0174 671 0287

John Branch
44 Hill Way
Holly Lodge Estate
London NE6 4EP

John Breen
Cedar Lodge
589 Antrim Road
Belfast BT15
0123 277 0238

Mike Brennan
2 Canon Avenue
Chadwell Heath
Romford, Essex
0208 599 4588

Michael Brooks
490 Hessle Road
Hull HU6 5AA
0148 227 1163

Steve Butler
107 Cambridge Street
Normanton
West Yorkshire
WF6 1ES
0192 489 1097

Trevor Callighan
40 Prescott Street
Halifax, West Yorkshire
HX1 2QW
0142 232 2592

Enzo Calzaghe
51 Caerbryn
Pentwynmawr
Newbridge, Gwent
South Wales
0149 524 8988

Ernie Cashmore
4 Beech Court
Birmingham
B43 6AB
0121 357 5841

John Celebanski
87 Crowtree Lane
Allerton
Bradford 8 0AN
01274 824015/542903

Nigel Christian
80 Alma Road
Plymouth
Devon
PL3 4HU
0175 225 2753

William Connelly
72 Clincart Road
Mount Florida
Glasgow G42
0141 632 5818

Tommy Conroy
144 High Street East
Sunderland
Tyne and Wear
0191 567 6871

Pat Cowdell
129a Moat Road
Oldbury
Warley
West Midlands
B68 8EE
0121 552 8082

John Cox
11 Fulford Drive
Links View
Northampton
NN2 7NX
0160 471 2107

Dave Currivan
15 Northolt Avenue
South Ruislip
Middlesex
0208 841 9933

David Davies
10 Bryngelli
Carmel
Llanelli
Dyfed SA14 7EL
0126 984 3204

Glyn Davies
63 Parc Brynmawr
Felinfoel
Llanelli
Dyfed SA15 4PG
0155 475 6282

John Davies
Unit 14, Rectors Yard
Rectors Lane
Penre Sandycroft
Deeside
Flintshire CH5 2DH
0124 453 8984

Ronnie Davies
3 Vallensdean Cottages
Hangleton Lane
Portslade
Sussex
0127 341 6497

Peter Defreitas
6 Stroud Close
Chadwell Heath
Romford
Essex
RM6 4AD
0183 678 1700

Brendan Devine
80 Fallbrook Drive
West Derby
Liverpool
L12 5NA
0151 263 1179

John Donnelly
15 Birkdale Avenue
St Annes on Sea
Lancashire
0125 371 2612

Jack Doughty
Lane End Cottage
Golden Street
Off Buckstones Road
Shaw
Oldham
OL2 8LY
01706 845753

Phil Duckworth
The Hampton Hotel
Longclose Lane
Richmond Hill
Leeds LS9 8NP

Mickey Duff
c/o Mrs E Allen
16 Herga Court
Harrow on the Hill
Middlesex
HA1 3RS
0208 423 6763

Paul Dykes
First Floor Gym
Swift House
Bryan Street
Hanley
Stoke on Trent
Staffordshire
0783 177 7310

Gwyn Evans
1 Merchistoun Road
Horndean
Portsmouth
Hants
PO8 9LS
0239 259 4504

Jim Evans
88 Windsor Road
Maidenhead
Berkshire SL6 2DJ
0162 823 640

Norman Fawcett
4 Wydsail Place
Gosforth
Newcastle upon Tyne
NE3 4QP
0191 213 1294

Stuart Fleet
269 St Nicholas Drive
Grimsby
Lincolnshire
0147 228 0181

Colin Flute
84 Summerhill Road
Coseley
West Midlands
WV14 8RE
0190 240 2699

Tania Follett
123 Calfridus Way
Bracknell
Berkshire
RG12 3HD
0134 445 5547

Steve Foster
62 Overdale
Swinton
Salford M27 5WZ
0161 794 1723

George Francis
11 Hillway
Holly Lodge Estate
London N6
0208 348 2898

Dai Gardiner
13 Hengoed Hall Drive
Cefn Hengoed
Mid Glamorgan
CF8 7JW
0163 328 4810

Dave Garside
33 Lowthian Road
Hartlepool
Cleveland
TS26 8AL
0142 929 1611

Anthony Gee
56 Bloombury Street
London
WC1B 3QT
0207 746 9100

Jimmy Gill
45 Blandford Road
Chilwell
Nottingham
NG9 4GY
0115 913 5482

Tommy Gilmour
St Andrews Sporting
Club
Posthouse Glasgow City
Bothwell Street
Glasgow G2 7EN
0141 248 5461

Mike Goodall
Gibbs Lane
Offenham
Evesham
Worcestershire
0138 644 2118

Billy Graham
116 Stockport Road
Mossley
Ashton under Lyme
Manchester
0145 783 5100

Lee Graham
28 Smeaton Court
50 Rockingham Street
London SE1 6PF

Ron Gray
Ingrams Oak
19 Hatherton Road
Cannock
Staffordshire
0154 350 2279

Johnny Griffin
0116 262 9287
07989 215287

Carl Gunns
Flat 2
Heathcliffe
469 Loughborough
Road
Birstall
Leicester
0116 267 1494

Christopher Hall
3 Dewhurst Road
Cheshunt
Hertford
EN8 9PG

Jess Harding
54 Heath Drive
Potters Bar
Hertfordshire
EN6 1EJ
0170 764 2982

Billy Hardy
23 Pembrey Court
Sothall
Sheffield
Yorkshire
S20 2GY
0114 247 7318

Tony Harris
152 Gainsford Crescent
Bestwood Estate
Nottingham
NG5 5HT
0115 913 6564

Kevin Hayde
162 Western Avenue
North
Cardiff
Wales
0122 222 7606

Pat Healy
1 Cranley Buildings
Brookes Market
Holborn
London EC1
0207 242 8121

Barry Hearn
Matchroom
10 Western Road
Romford
Essex RM1 3JT
0170 878 2200

Mick Hill
35 Shenstone House
Aldrington Road
Streatham
London SW16
0208 769 2218

Dennis Hobson
Dennis Hobson
Promotions
c/o Unit 1
Industrial Estate
Century Street
Sheffield S9 5DX
0124 625 2429

Harry Holland
12 Kendall Close
Feltham
Middlesex
0208 737 4886

Gordon Holmes
15 Robert Andrew
Close
Morley St Botolph
Wymondham
Norfolk
NR18 9AA
0195 360 7887

Lloyd Honeyghan
PO Box 17216
London SE17 1ZU

Geoff Hunter
6 Hawkshead Way
Winsford
Cheshire
CW7 2SZ
0160 686 2162

John Hyland
The Morton Suite
The Moat House Hotel
1 Paradise Street
Liverpool L1 8JD
0151 708 8331

Brendan Ingle MBE
26 Newman Road
Wincobank
Sheffield S9 1LP
0114 281 1277

Dominic Ingle
26 Newman Road
Sheffield S9 1LP
0114 281 1277

John Ingle
20 Rockmount Road
Wincobank
Sheffield S9
0114 261 7934

Richard Jones
1 Churchfields
Croft
Warrington
Cheshire
WA3 7JR
0192 576 5167

Jason King
27 Roman Road
Ingatestone
Essex
CM4 9AA
0127 735 3341

Brian Lawrence
50 Willow Vale
London W12
0208 723 0182

Buddy Lee
The Walnuts
Roman Bank
Leverington
Wisbech
Cambridgeshire
PE13 5AR
0194 558 3266

Pat Lynch
Gotherington
68 Kelsey Lane
Balsall Common
Near Coventry
West Midlands
CV7 7GL
0167 633374

Paul McCausland
20 Invernook Drive
Belfast
Northern Ireland
BT4 1RW
0123 220 2355

Gary McCrory
Croftside
Low Enterprise Park
Greencroft
Stanley
Co Durham
DH9 8NN
0120 723 7117

Jim McDonnell
2 Meadway
Hillside Avenue
Woodford Green
Essex
IG8 7RF
07860 770006

John McIntyre
941 Aikenhead Road
Glasgow
G44 4QE
0141 632 9114

Ian McLeod
14 Stewarton Crescent
Kilmarnock
Scotland
0141 222 2577

Owen McMahon
3 Atlantic Avenue
Belfast BT15
0289 074 3535

Colin McMillan
60 Billet Road
Chadwell Heath
Romford
Essex
RM6 5SU
0208 597 4464

Charlie Magri
48 Tavistock Gardens
Seven Kings
Ilford IG3 1BE
0207 739 9035 (shop)

Frank Maloney
Sports Network
Centurion House
Bircherley Green
Hertfordshire
SG14 1AP
0199 250 5550

Dennie Mancini
16 Rosedew Road
Off Fulham Palace Road
London W6 9ET
0207 437 1526

Ricky Manners
Mabgate Mills
Mill 6, Unit B
Macauley Street
Mabgate
Leeds LS9 7DZ
0113 243 6017

Michael Marsden
1 North View
Roydes Lane
Rothwell
Leeds
LS26 0BQ
0192 482 6499

Terry Marsh
141 Great Gregorie
Basildon
Essex

Tony Marshall
29 Seagull Bay Drive
Coseley
West Midlands
WV14 8AL
0121 520 3212

Gary Mason
18 Camberwell Church
Street
Camberwell Green
London SE5
0795 858 6147

Arthur Melrose
33 Easterhill Street
Glasgow G32 8LN
0141 778 4127

Tommy Miller
128 Clapton Mount
King Cross Road
Halifax
West Yorkshire
0142 236 1147

Clifton Mitchell
The Penine Hotel
Derby
Derbyshire DE1
0133 229 5380

Alex Morrison
197 Swanston Street
Laird Business Park
Dalmarnock
Glasgow G40 4HW
0141 554 7777

James Murray
87 Spean Street
Glasgow G44 4DS
0141 637 7926

Bert Myers
The Lodge
Lower House Lane
Burnley
Lancashire
0128 277 9300

Paul Newman
12 Edgehill Way
Portslade
Brighton
BN41 2PU
0127 341 9777

Norman Nobbs
364 Kings Road
Kingstanding
Birmingham
B44 0UG
0121 355 5341

Mark O'Callaghan
1 Keel Gardens
Southborough
Tunbridge Wells
Kent TN4 0JQ
0189 268 9979

Terry O'Neill
48 Kirkfield View
Colton Village
Leeds LS15 9DX
0113 225 6140

James Oyebola
194 Portnall Road
London W9
0208 930 9685

George Patrick
11 Daarle Avenue
Canvey Island
Essex SS8 9EN

Terry Petersen
21 Lynwood Crescent
Pontefract
West Yorkshire
WF8 3QT
0197 770 3512

Des Piercy
190 Harrington Road
South Norwood
London
SE25 4NE
0208 656 3290

Steve Pollard
899 Beverley High
Road
Hull
HU6 9NJ
0148 280 9455

David Poston
2 Whitegate Road
Daisy Bank
Bliston
West Midlands
WV14 8UY
0190 249 3040

Dean Powell
103 Rodney Road
Walworth
London SE17
0207 903 5074

Michael Quinn
64 Warren Road
Wanstead
London
E11 2NA

Howard Rainey
9 Castlebeck Drive
Sheffield S2 1NP
0114 264 4106

Glyn Rhodes
70 Oldfield Road
Stannington
Sheffield S6
0114 233 1687

Gus Robinson, MBE
Stranton House
Westview Road
Hartlepool
TS24 0BB
0142 923 4221

Mark Roe
48 Westbrooke Road
Sidcup
Kent
DA15 7PH
0208 309 9396

Ronnie Rush
4 Marcross Road
Ely
Cardiff
South Glamorgan
CF5 4RP
0122 259 3902

John Rushton
20 Alverley Lane
Balby
Doncaster
DN4 9AS
0130 231 0919

Kevin Russell
2 Spion Kop Road
Ynystawe
Swansea SA6 5AN
0179 284 6641

Joe Ryan
22B Adeyfield House
Cranwood Street
City Road
London EC1V 9NX
0207 686 1948

Kevin Sanders
135 Coneygree Road
Peterborough
Cambridgeshire
PE1 8LQ
0173 355 5916

Chris Sanigar
Bristol Boxing Gym
40 Thomas Street
St Agnes
Bristol BS2 9LL
0117 949 6699

Trevor Schofield
234 Doncaster Road
Barnsley
South Yorkshire
S70 1UQ
0122 629 7376

Mike Shinfield
126 Birchwood Lane
Somercotes
Derbyshire DE55 4NE
0177 360 3124

Tony Sims
205 Collier Row Lane
Romford
Essex RM5 3JA
0170 874 9940

Len Slater
78 Sutcliffe Avenue
Nunsthorpe
Grimsby
Lincolnshire
0147 287 9862

Charles Smith
209 Billet Road
Walthamstow
London
E17 5HG
0208 527 5557

Darkie Smith
21 Northumberland
House
Gaisford Street
London NW5 2EA
0207 916 1784

Les Southey
Oakhouse
Park Way
Hillingdon
Middlesex
0189 525 4719

Gerry Storey
41 Willowbank Gardens
Belfast
Northern Ireland
BT15 5AJ
0123 275 3819

Danny Sullivan
29 Mount Gould
Avenue, Mount Gould
Plymouth
Devon PL4 9HA
0175 266 0752

Norrie Sweeney
3 Saucehill Terrace
Paisley
Scotland PA2 6SY
0141 580 0269

Wally Swift
12 Garden Close
Knowle
Solihull
West Midlands B93 92F
0156 477 5140

Glenroy Taylor
95 Devon Close
Perivale
Middlesex
UB6 7DW

Jimmy Tibbs
44 Gyllyngdune
Gardens
Seven Kings
Essex
0208 599 0693

Terry Toole
6 Churchwell Close
Chipping Onger
Essex
CM5 9BH
0127 736 2372

Mick Toomey
25 Purton Grove
Bransholme
Hull
HU7 4QD
0148 282 4476

Jack Trickett
Acton Court Hotel
187 Buxton Road
Stockport
Cheshire
0161 483 6172

Danny Urry
Morland
Hurstfield Road
West Moseley
Surrey
KT8 1QU
0208 979 7947

Vernon Vanriel
56 Roseberry Avenue
London
N17 9SA

Stephen Vaughan
c/o Lee Maloney
72 East Damswood
Road
Speke
Liverpool L24

Louis Veitch
35 Clinton Avenue
Blackpool
FY1 4AE
0125 329 3083

Keith Walker
Meadow Croft
High Eggborough
Leeds
LS15 9DX

Frank Warren
Centurion House
Bircherley Green
Hertford
Hertfordshire
SG14 1AP
0199 250 5550

Robert Watt
32 Dowanhill Street
Glasgow G11
0141 334 7465

Jack Weaver
301 Coventry Road
Hinckley
Leicestershire
LE10 0NE
0145 561 9066

Malcolm Webb
51 Bedwellty Road
Aberbargoed
Bargoed
Mid Glamorgan
Wales CF81 9AX
0144 387 9118

Derek Williams
65 Virginia Road
Surrey
CR7 8EN
0208 458 0511

Derek Williams
17 Kings Street
Lostwithiel
Cornwall
PL22 0AQ

John Williams
3a Langham Road
Tottenham
London
N15 3QX

Alan Wilton
The Bridge
42 Derryboy Road
Crossgar
BT30 9LH

Stephen Wood
29 Mesne Lea Road
Worsley
Manchester
M28 7EU
0161 790 2579

Tex Woodward
Spaniorum Farm
Compton Greenfield
Bristol
BS12 3RX
0145 463 2448

Licensed Matchmakers

Neil Bowers
59 Carson Road
Canning Town
London E16 4BD
0207 473 5631

Ernie Fossey
26 Bell Lane
Brookmans Park
Hatfield, Hertfordshire
0170 765 6545

Steve Foster
62 Overdale
Swinton
Salford M27 5WZ
0161 794 1723

Dave Garside
33 Lowthian Road
Hartlepool
Cleveland TS26 8AL
0142 929 1611

John Gaynor
7 Westhorne Fold
Counthill Drive
Brooklands Road
Crumpsall
Manchester M8 4JN
0161 740 6993

Tommy Gilmour
Posthouse Glasgow City
Bothwell Street
Glasgow G2 7EN
0141 248 5461

Ron Gray
Ingrams Oak
19 Hatherton Road
Cannock
Staffordshire
0154 350 2279

John Ingle
20 Rockmount Road
Wincobank
Sheffield S9 1LP
0114 261 7934

Terry Johnson
1 Launceston Road
Park Hall
Walsall WS5 3ED
0192 262 6209

Graham Lockwood
106 Burnside Avenue
Skipton
N. Yorkshire
BD23 2DB
0175 679 2726

Charlie Magri
48 Tavistock Gardens
Seven Kings
Ilford
Essex
IG3 9BE
0207 739 9035

Dennie Mancini
16 Rosedew Road
Off Fulham Palace
Road
Hammersmith
London
W6 9ET
0207 437 1526

Tommy Miller
128 Clapton Mount
King Cross Road
Halifax
West Yorkshire
0142 236 1147

Ken Morton
3 St Quentin Mount
Sheffield
S17 4PQ
0114 262 1829

Stewart Nubley
94 Richmond Road
Kirkby in Ashfield
Nottinghamshire
NG17 7PW
0162 343 2357

Dean Powell
Lion Promotions
Suite 201
Gainsborough House
81 Oxford Street
London
W1D 2EU
0207 903 5074

Richard Poxon
148 Cliffefield Road
Sheffield
S8 9BS
0114 225 7856

John Rushton
20 Alverley Lane
Balby
Doncaster
South Yorkshire
0130 231 0919

Chris Sanigar
Bristol Boxing Gym
40 Thomas Street
St Agnes
Bristol BS2 9LL
0117 949 6699

Mike Shinfield
126 Birchwood Lane
Somercotes
Derbyshire
DE55 4NE
0177 360 3124

Len Slater
78 Sutcliffe Avenue
Nunsthorpe
Grimsby
Lincolnshire

Terry Toole
6 Churchwell Close
Chipping Onger
Essex CM5 9BH
0127 736 2372

Ian Watson
2 Jed Moor
Hepburn Village
Tyne & Wear
NE31 1ET

Licensed BBBoC Referees, Timekeepers, Ringwhips and Inspectors

Licensed Referees

Class 'B'

Billy Aird	Southern Area
Dean Bramhald	Midland Area
Mark Curry	Northern Area
Kenneth Curtis	Southern Area
Seamus Dunne	Southern Area
Paul Graham	Scottish Area
Christopher Kelly	Central Area
David Morgan	Welsh Area
Roy Snipe	Central Area
Andrew Wright	Northern Area

Class 'A'

Ivor Bassett	Welsh Area
Terence Cole	Northern Area
Lee Cook	Midlands Area
Philip Edwards	Central Area
Roddy Evans	Welsh Area
Howard Foster	Central Area
Keith Garner	Central Area
Anthony Green	Central Area
Michael Heatherwick	Welsh Area
Jeff Hinds	Southern Area
Al Hutcheon	Scottish Area
David Irving	Northern Ireland
John Irving	Northern Ireland
Wynford Jones	Welsh Area
Phil Kane	Central Area
Victor Loughin	Scottish Area
Grant Wallis	Western Area

Class 'A' Star

John Coyle	Midlands Area
Richard Davies	Southern Area
Mark Green	Southern Area

Mickey Vann, Class 'A' Star referee

Les Clark

John Keane	Midlands Area
Ian John-Lewis	Southern Area
Marcus McDonnell	Southern Area
Larry O'Connell	Southern Area
Terry O'Connor	Midlands Area
Dave Parris	Southern Area
Paul Thomas	Midlands Area
Mickey Vann	Central Area

Licensed Timekeepers

Roy Bicknell	Midlands Area
Roger Bowden	Western Area
Arnold Bryson	Northern Area
Neil Burder	Welsh Area
Ivor Campbell	Welsh Area
Richard Clark	Central Area
Anthony Dunkerley	Midlands Area
Dale Elliot	Northern Ireland
Robert Edgeworth	Southern Area
Harry Foxall	Midlands Area
Eric Gilmour	Scottish Area
Gary Grennan	Central Area
Brian Heath	Midlands Area
Greg Hue	Southern Area
Jon Lee	Western Area
Michael McCann	Southern Area
Peter McCann	Southern Area
Norman Maddox	Midlands Area
Gordon Pape	Welsh Area
Barry Pinder	Central Area
Raymond Rice	Southern Area
Colin Roberts	Central Area
James Russell	Scottish Area
Kevin Walters	Northern Area
Paul Webster	Central Area
Nick White	Southern Area

Licensed Ringwhips

Lester Arthur	Western Area
Albert Brewer	Southern Area
Michael Burke	Scottish Area
Steve Butler	Central Area
John Davis	Southern Area
Ernie Draper	Southern Area
Mike Goodall	Midlands Area
Simon Goodall	Midlands Area
Lee Gostolo	Central Area
Denzil Lewis	Western Area
Stuart Lithgo	Northern Area
Tommy Miller (Jnr)	Central Area
Kenneth Morton	Central Area
Tommy Rice	Southern Area
Sandy Risley	Southern Area
Ed Robinson	Southern Area
Trevor Russell	Welsh Area
Lee Taylor	Southern Area
James Wallace	Scottish Area

Inspectors

Herold Adams	Southern Area
Alan Alster	Central Area
William Ball	Southern Area
Richard Barber	Southern Area
Michael Barnett	Central Area
Don Bartlett	Midlands Area
Graham Bingham	Midlands Area
Fred Breyer	Southern Area
David Brown	Western Area
Walter Campbell	Northern Ireland
Ray Chichester	Welsh Area
Geoff Collier	Midlands Area
Michael Collier	Southern Area
Sammy Cosgrove	Northern Ireland
Constantin Cotzias	Southern Area
Julian Courtney	Welsh Area
Kevin Crawford	Central Area
John Crowe	Midlands Area
Jaswinder Dhaliwal	Midlands Area
Kevin Fulthorpe	Welsh Area
Bob Galloway	Southern Area
Paul Gooding	Northern Area
John Hall	Central Area
Eddie Higgins	Scottish Area
Michael Hills	Northern Area
Alan Honnibal	Western Area
David Hughes	Welsh Area
Francis Keenan	Northern Ireland
James Kirkwood	Scottish Area
Fred Little	Western Area
Bob Lonkhurst	Southern Area
Pat Magee	Northern Ireland
Paul McAllister	Northern Ireland
Sam McAughtry	Northern Ireland
Dave McAuley	Northern Ireland
Billy McCrory	Northern Ireland
Gerry McGinley	Scottish Area
Paul McKeown	Northern Ireland
Scott Morrison	Scottish Area
David Ogilvie	Northern Area
Dave Porter	Southern Area
Fred Potter	Northern Area
Les Potts	Midlands Area
Chris Rattenbury	Western Area
Bob Rice	Midlands Area
Geoffrey Rogers	Southern Area
Hugh Russell	Northern Ireland
J. Shea Jnr	Scottish Area
Neil Sinclair	Southern Area
Bert Smith	Central Area
John Toner	Northern Ireland
Nigel Underwood	Midlands Area
David Venn	Northern Area
Phil Waites	Midlands Area
Ernie Wallis	Welsh Area
Bob Williams	Southern Area
Geoff Williams	Midlands Area
Trevor Williams	Midlands Area
Paul Woollard	Scottish Area

LION PROMOTIONS & GOLDEN FISTS

THE PROMOTORS OF CHAMPIONS

Congratulate the British Boxing Board of Control Yearbook 2002

Lion Promotions
Gainsborough House
81 Oxford Street
London W1D 2EU
Tel: +44(0) 207 903 5074
Fax: +44(0) 207 903 5075
email: mediamachine1@hotmail.com

Golden Fists
119 High Road
Loughton
Essex IG10 4LT
Tel: +44(0) 208 502 1415
Fax: +44(0) 208 502 1419
email: davelewis@goldenfists.freeserve.co.uk

THE BRITISH MASTERS CHAMPIONSHIPS

Run by

PROFESSIONAL BOXING PROMOTERS ASSOCIATION

UNDER BBB OF C RULES

PRESENTS

THE BRITISH MASTERS CHAMPIONS

HEAVY:	JACKLORD JACOBS
CRUISER:	GARRY DELANEY
SUPER-MIDDLE:	MATTHEW BARNEY
MIDDLE:	GARY BEARDSLEY
LIGHT-MIDDLE:	OJAY ABRAHAMS
WELTER:	JOHN HUMPHREY
LIGHT-WELTER:	GAVIN DOWN
SUPER-FEATHER:	CARL GREAVES
SUPER-BANTAM:	FRANKIE DEMILO
BANTAM:	ESHAM PICKERING
FLY:	JIM BETTS

Vacant: Light-Heavy, Light, Feather

**THE PBPA
PO BOX 25188
LONDON
SW1V 3WL
TEL/FAX: 0207 592 0102**

Chairman: Bruce Baker
General Secretary: Greg Steene

MEMBERSHIP OPEN TO ALL SMALL HALL PROMOTERS

Glyn Rhodes
Sheffield Boxing Centre

Sponsored by Otter communications
Old Burton St School, Burton Street
Hillsborough, Sheffield 6
Location of the full Monty
Tel: 01142321332

Boxing services
Boxing equipment
Dietary advice
Sports massage
Sports psychology
Fitness training
Event management

**Celebrity sporting
evenings at the
Grosevnor House**

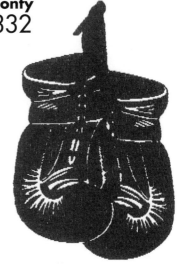

Sheffield Boxing Centre
amateur boxing club
matchmaker
Harry Cliffe

Glyn Rhodes Promotions
Tel: 0114 2331687 Fax: 0114 2326513 Mobile: 07747 070783
General manager: Lee Gostolo
Tel: 0114 2314483 Mobile: 07957 322284
Pro trainers: Matt Mowatt, Andy Manning, Steve Farnsworth
Amateur trainers: Frank Middleton, Phil Wood

JOHNNY GRIFFIN
BOXING PROMOTIONS & MANAGEMENT
Licensed by BBB of C

Congratulations to Barry J. Hugman on the publication of the British Boxing Yearbook 2002. It is greatly valued and appreciated. Keep up the good work. Wishing you continued success.

Also Directing:

Neil Simpson*   Light-Heavyweight Champion of Great Britain

Shaun Cummins   Former British & European Middleweight Title Challenger

Darron Griffiths*   Reigning Welsh Cruiserweight Champion

*Co-Manager

Members of the Professional Boxing Promoters' Association

For our services please telephone Johnny Griffin Leicester (0116) 2629287. Mobile 07989 215287

Other boxers available at all weights.

Dave Currivan
Boxing Promotions & Management
Licensed with B.B.B.C.
Member of P.B.P.A.

BOXERS LIST

Nono Junior	Lightweight
Jason McElligott	L. Welterweight
Ilias Miah	Lightweight
Freddie Yemofio	Middleweight

Always interested in good youngsters who are prepared to work hard

15 Northolt Avenue, South Ruislip, Middlesex HA4 6SS

Tel/Fax: 0208 841 9933
Mobile: 07889 034778

Gym: Dickie Gunn Gym (Rear of Hayes Sports Stadium) TRAINER: Anthony Campbell

---

MUNRO & HYLAND BROS.
INTERNATIONAL BOXING PROMOTERS AND MANAGERS
LIVERPOOL, ENGLAND

THE MOAT HOUSE HOTEL
1 PARADISE STREET
LIVERPOOL L1 8JD

TELEPHONE: 0151 708 8331
FAX: 0151 708 6701

DEAN POWELL

Professional Boxing Manager, Matchmaker, Trainer & International Agent

Licensed by the B.B.B. of C.

International Mobile
+44 (0) 7956 905741

Home Telephone
+44 (0) 20 7701 3843

Office
The Sport Entertainment & Media Group plc
Suite 302 Gainsborough House, 81 Oxford Street
London W1D 3EU

Tel: +44 (0) 20 7903 5282 / 5058   Fax: +44 (0) 20 7903 5357

JUNCTION 5

PRO GYM

TRAINER
RICKY ENGLISH
Licensed by the British Board of Control

BOXERS

Matt Legg	Heavyweight	Milton Keynes
Roland Yakubovski	Heavyweight	Watford
Kenny Gayle	Cruiserweight	Harrow
Ganny Dovidovas	Super-Middleweight	Watford
Michael Allanyne	Light-Middleweight	Watford
Rimas Kozanis	Lightweight	Watford
Marco Fattore	Lightweight	Watford
Matty Leonard	Super-Featherweight	South Oxhey

Junction 5, Lincolnsfield Centre,
Bushey Hall Drive, Bushey, Watford
Tel: 01923 224822 or Mobile: 07752 273077

JOHN ASHTON
PROMOTIONS

LIST 2000/2001 SEASON

Steve Williams	Bantamweight Midlands Champion	Mansfield
Carl Greaves	Super-Featherweight British Masters Champion	Newark
Craig Spacie	Super-Featherweight	Chesterfield
J. J. Moore	Super-Featherweight	Mansfield
Dave Kirk	Light-Welterweight WBF Inter-Continental Champion	Mansfield
Gary Beardsley	Middleweight British Masters Champion	Belper
Matt Galer	Middleweight	Burton
Greg Scott-Briggs	Light-Heavyweight	Chesterfield
Tony Dowling	Cruiserweight	Lincoln
Scott Lansdowne	Super-Cruiserweight WBF European Champion	Leicester
Sara Hall	Bantamweight	Chesterfield

* *

1 Charters Close, Kirkby in Ashfield, Nottinghamshire NG17 8PF
Tel: 01623 721278 Fax: 01623 721278 Mobile: 07885 463676
Email: john.ashton@ntlworld.com

GRAHAM MOUGHTON
BOXING MANAGEMENT
PROMOTIONS

*Would like to wish
BARRY HUGMAN
Every success with
his book*

*Training
COLIN LYNES
HORNCHURCH*

*1 Hedgemans Way
Dagenham
Essex RM9 6DB*

*Tel: 020 8517 4070
           020 8252 9238
Mobile: 07970 273721*

TREVOR CALLIGHAN

Promoter/Manager Licensed by British Boxing Board of Control

PROMOTIONS IN ASSOCIATION WITH JIMMY MOORE
40 PRESCOTT STREET, HALIFAX, WEST YORKSHIRE HX1 2QW
Tel: 01422 322592   Fax: 01422 351153

BOXERS:

Paul Harkness (South Shields)   Dean Nicholas (South Shields)
Michael Thompson (Ferryhill)   Duncan Armstrong (South Shields)
Reece McAllister (Newton Aycliffe)   Andy McLean (Newcastle)
Paul Lomax (Sunderland)   Sean Grant (Newton Aycliffe)
Chris Steele (Barnsley)   Noel Wilders (Castleford)

Trainers: Mick McVeigh, Michael Marsden

Viking International Promotions Ltd.

TAKING BOXING FORWARD

C/o Unit 12, Enterprise Park, Reliance Street, off Oldham Road, Manchester M40 3AL
Telephone: 0161-683 5693 Fax: 0161-683 5695

Promoter: Stephen Wood
Matchmaker: Steve Foster

Managers: Steve Foster/StephenWood
Trainers: Joe Gallagher/Oliver Harrison

Current List of V.I.P. Boxers
Lee Whitehead - Cruiserweight
Mike Gormley - Super-Middleweight
Wayne Pinder - Middleweight
Alan Page - Middleweight
Jamie Moore - Light-Middleweight
John Marshall - Light-Welterweight
Tommy Peacock - Light-Welterweight
Mark Haslam - Light-Welterweight
Ray Wood - Lightweight
Gary Reid - Super Featherweight
Eddie Nevins - Featherweight
Steve Foster Jnr - Bantamweight
Anthony Hughes - Bantamweight
Darren Cleary - Flyweight

NB All Above Fighters Are Managed By Ourselves, Other Boxers Are Available Through Our Associate Connections

Regular Promotions / Good Management / Top-Class Training
Any unattached boxer should contact us direct to discuss their future

Fully Licensed by the British Boxing Board of Control

KEVIN SANDERS
TRAINER OF CHAMPIONS
LICENSED MANAGER, PROMOTER AND TRAINER

INTERESTED IN TURNING PROFESSIONAL?

ALL ENQUIRIES:
01733 555916 - OFFICE
01733 561989 - FAX
07976 391718 - MOBILE

website: www.kspromotions.co.uk   email: kevin@kspromotions.co.uk

REGULAR PROMOTER OF SHOWS IN EAST ANGLIA

East Anglia's Finest Stable includes:
Heavyweight Derek McCafferty, Super-Middleweights Hughie Doherty and Neil Linford,
Light-Middleweight Nick Lyon, Welterweight Francie Doherty (ABA Champion 2000),
Lightweight Liam Maltby, Featherweight Henry Castle (ABA Champion 2000)

Michael Marsden
BOXING MANAGER/TRAINER
(Licensed by the British Boxing Board of Control)

Bodymania Fitness Centre, Marsh Street Car Park, Rothwell, Leeds LS26 0AG
Tel: 0113 2822210   Mobile: 07771 792250

Managed Boxers:

James Rooney	*Super-Featherweight*	*Hartlepool*
Kevin Bennett	*Light-Welterweight*	*Hartlepool*
Levi Patterson	*Flyweight*	*Leeds*
Paul Bonson	*Cruiserweight*	*Featherstone*
Peter Dunn	*Welterweight*	*Pontefract*
Jim Betts	*Bantamweight*	*Scunthorpe*
Darren Rhodes	*Middleweight*	*Leeds*
Andrew Close	*Light-Welterweight*	*Hartlepool*
Jon Penn	*Super-Middleweight*	*Hemsworth*
Gavin Wake	*Welterweight*	*Leeds*

Current Trainer of:
Noel Wilders Former Undefeated IBO & British Bantamweight Champion 21-0

email: www.mickmarsden@bodymania.fsnet.co.uk

THE CITY OF HULL'S PREMIER PROFESSIONAL BOXING PROMOTERS

B.B.B. of C. LTD Licensed 1991
Established 10 years

Headquarters & Gym
Ritz Bar Holderness Road Hull

CHAMPION CHARITY FUNDRAISERS

HONORARY PATRON: **SIR HENRY COOPER** (KSG, OBE)
HONORARY VICE PRESIDENT: **BARRY McGUIGAN** (MBE)
CHAIRMAN: **BRIAN LUEN**

HONORARY SECRETARY: MICK TOOMEY

TEL: 01482 824476

JOIN THE PROFESSIONALS
SHANNON'S GYM
FIGHTING FIT

Shannon's Gym
Crossley House
755 Ashton Old Road
Openshaw
Manchester M11 2HB
Telephone: (Gym) 0161-231-0572

Trainer
Bobby Shannon

Seconds
Nigel Hardman
Robert Shannon Jnr

TBS PROMOTIONS LTD
63 QUEENS ROAD
BUCKHURST HILL
ESSEX IG9 5BU

Office: 020 8504 9777   Gym: 07776 204028
Fax: 020 8505 2627   E-Mail: tburnsltd@aol.com

Promoter: Tony Burns Jnr   Manager: Tony Sims
Trainer: Danny Tovey   Trainer: Terry Steward

Current Boxers:

Barry Hughes	Lightweight	10 - 1
Butch Lesley	Light-Heavyweight	12 - 6
Andrew Lowe	Super-Middleweight	2 - 0
Steve Spartacus	Light-Heavyweight	4 - 0
John Tiftik	Welterweight	7 - 1
Paul Weir	Light-Flyweight	14 - 6

Licensed by The British Boxing Board of Control

SHOWSPORT
BOXING

PROMOTIONS
MANAGEMENT
TRAINING
TEL: 0870 442 8986

Tel: 0121 2421356
Fax: 0121 2421355

Email: paul.hennessy5@virgin.net

Dennis' Hobson
Promotions

*Professional Boxing Promotions
and Management
73 Darnall Road   Don Valley
Sheffield S95 A5*

Tel/Fax: 0114 243 5583
Email: dvsa@allwaysinternet.co.uk
Dennis Hobson: 07836 252 429

WINNING COMBINATION

Tel: (0191) 567 6871
Fax: (0191) 565 2581
Mobile: (07850) 434457

Tommy Conroy - Manager and Trainer
Annette Conroy - First North-East Lady Promoter
Matchmaker: Ken Morton
Trainers: Charlie Armstrong and Paul Fiske

144 High Street East,
Sunderland,
Tyne & Wear,
SR1 2BL, England.

Sunderland-Based Stable

Mike White Super-Middleweight (North Shields)
Ryan Kerr Light-Middleweight (Sunderland, via Bannockburn)
Danny Moir Light-Middleweight (Gateshead)
John Barnes Super-Bantamweight (Sunderland)

NORTH EAST EXECUTIVE SPORTING CLUB dates for 2002
Thursday 21 February
Thursday 9 May
Thursday 3 October
Thursday 5 December

Joe  Pyle

Boxing Promotions & Management
Wishes the British Boxing Yearbook Every Success

Promoted Fighters
Isaac Sebaduka S. Featherweight
Pele Reid Former WBO Inter-Continental Heavyweight Champion
Maurice Forbes L. Middleweight
Floyd Havard Former British S. Featherweight Champion
Oneal 'Big Reds' Murray Cruiserweight
Ossie Duran WBF European Welterweight Champion

TELEPHONE: 07974 505720
FAX: 0208 646 7793

website: www.joepyle.com   email: joepyle@boxing.fsbusiness.co.uk

CHRIS SANIGAR
Boxing Management Training
BRISTOL BOXING GYM, 40 THOMAS STREET
ST AGNES, BRISTOL BS2 9LL
TEL: 0117 949 6699 FAX: 0117 904 9373 Mobile: 07831 359978
csanigar@aol.com   www.bristolboxing.com

DAI GARDINER BOXING STABLE
TEL/FAX: 01443 812971 • MOBILE: 077111 52306

STEVE ROBINSON	Featherweight
MICHAEL SMYTH	Welterweight
JON HONEY	Welterweight
DAZZA WILLIAMS	S. Bantamweight
IAN TURNER	S. Bantamweight
JOHN MATTHEWS	L. Heavyweight
JASON THOMAS	Bantamweight
WOODY GREENAWAY	Lightweight
JASON SAMUELS	Middleweight
CHRIS DAVIES	L. Heavyweight
HARRY BUTLER	Middleweight
ENZO MACCARINELLI	Cruiserweight
KEITH JONES	Lightweight
DAVID WHITE	L. Welterweight
JASON WHITE	S. Featherweight
ANDREW GREENAWAY	Bantamweight

TRAINERS - PAT CHIDGEY, GARY THOMAS, ALLWYN JONES
GYMS - MERTHYR, GELLIGAER

PEACOCK PROMOTIONS

PROMOTER/MANAGER: TONY BOWERS
AGENT: ROY HILDER
TRAINERS: MARTIN BOWERS/JACKIE BOWERS
TRAINERS: DAVE ARMSTRONG/JOHN BOSCOE/JOHN HUMPHREY SNR
SECRETARY: SHELLEY PORTER

*WE ARE VERY PROUD TO BOTH PROMOTE AND MANAGE
THE FOLLOWING LIST OF PROFESSIONAL BOXERS:*

Boxer	Division	Title	Record
GARRY DELANEY (30)	CRUISER	BRITISH MASTERS CHAMPION	29-5-1
SCOTT DIXON (24)	LIGHT-MIDDLE	WBU INTER-CONTINENTAL CHAMPION	24-5-1
KARIM BOUALI (26)	LIGHT-WELTER	WBU INTER-CONTINENTAL CHAMPION	8-2-1
ELVIS MICHAILENKO (25)	LIGHT-HEAVY	WBF EUROPEAN CHAMPION	8-0-1
DANIEL JAMES (24)	LIGHT-WELTER	SOUTHERN AREA CHAMPION	12-1-0
JOHN 'BOY' HUMPHREY (20)	WELTER	BRITISH MASTERS CHAMPION	9-1-0
STEPHEN OATES (23)	SUPER-BANTAM		16-3-0
ALI FORBES (39)	LIGHT-HEAVY		13-7-1
CHRIS NEMBHARD (22)	MIDDLE		7-2-1
DARREN MELVILLE (25)	LIGHT		8-1-0
ROCKY DEAN (23)	BANTAM		4-1-0
MANZO SMITH (23)	WELTER		6-0-0
TONY GRIFFITHS (31)	SUPER-MIDDLE/LIGHT-HEAVY		5-4-0
GANNY DOVIDOVAS (27)	SUPER-MIDDLE		5-2-1
VALERY ODIN (26)	SUPER-MIDDLE		2-0-0
JOHN MACKAY (19)	FEATHER		1-1-0
ERIC TEYMOUR (20)	MIDDLE		2-0-0
THOMAS DA SILVA (23)	LIGHT-MIDDLE		1-0-0

**READY, WILLING AND ABLE
ANYTIME, ANYPLACE, ANYWHERE**

Boxers' Record Index

Advertisers

A LEGENDARY NAME IN THE FIGHT GAME

the **legend** lives on with
sport art
RELIVE FOREVER THE GREATEST MOMENTS IN RING HISTORY

Superb Limited Edition Art Prints and Originals from the U.K.'s renowned fight artists **DOREEN & BRIAN MEADOWS**

RECOGNISED WORLD WIDE FOR THEIR BOXING STUDIES. MANY WORLD CHAMPIONS PAST & PRESENT ARE PROUD OWNERS OF THEIR WORK

"Doreen & Brian wish Barry Hugman & The British Boxing Yearbook every success"

'PRIVATE COMMISIONS UNDERTAKEN'

For the finest selection of boxing art available
*Visit our web site at **www.sportartboxing.co.uk***
*or email us at **sales@sportartboxing.co.uk***

or alternatively send £1 for a brochure to:
4 BALMORAL DRIVE, HINDLEY, NR WIGAN, LANCS. WN2 3HS ENGLAND

TEL: +44 (0) 1942 258572 - 24 Hours FAX: +44 (0) 1942 253747

A LEGENDARY NAME IN THE FIGHT GAME